New Perspectives on

MICROSOFT® WORD 2000

Comprehensive

BEVERLY B. ZIMMERMAN
Brigham Young University

S. SCOTT ZIMMERMAN
Brigham Young University

ANN SHAFFER

APPROVED COURSEWARE

EXPERT

Thomson Learning™

ONE MAIN STREET, CAMBRIDGE, MA 02142

Australia • Canada • Denmark • Japan • Mexico • New Zealand • Philippines
Puerto Rico • Singapore • South Africa • Spain • United Kingdom • United States

New Perspectives on Microsoft® Word 2000 —Comprehensive is published by Course Technology.

Senior Editor	**Donna Gridley**
Senior Product Manager	**Rachel A. Crapser**
Product Manager	**Catherine V. Donaldson**
Acquisitions Editor	**Christine Guivernau**
Associate Product Manager	**Karen Shortill**
Editorial Assistant	**Melissa Dezotell**
Developmental Editor	**Ann Shaffer**
Production Editor	**Daphne Barbas**
Text Designer	**Meral Dabcovich**
Cover Art Designer	**Douglas Goodman**

For more information contact:

Course Technology
One Main Street
Cambridge, MA 02142
Or find us on the World Wide Web at: http://www.course.com

Trademarks

Course Technology and the Open Book logo are registered trademarks and CourseKits is a trademark of Course Technology. Custom Edition is a registered trademark of Thomson Learning.

The Thomson Learning logo is a registered trademark used herein under license.

Some of the product names and company names used in this book have been used for identification purposes only and may be trademarks or registered trademarks of their respective manufacturers and sellers.

Microsoft and the Office logo are either registered trademarks or trademarks of Microsoft Corporation in the United States and/or other countries. Course Technology is an independent entity from the Microsoft Corporation, and is not affiliated with Microsoft in any manner. This text may be used in assisting students to prepare for a Microsoft Office User Specialist Exam for Microsoft Word. Neither Microsoft Corporation, its designated review company, nor Course Technology warrants that use of this text will ensure passing the relevant exam.

Use of the Microsoft Office User Specialist Approved Courseware Logo on this product signifies that it has ben independently reviewed and approved in complying with the following standards: Acceptable coverage of all content related to the Microsoft Office Exam entitled *"Microsoft Word 2000"*; and sufficient performance-based exercises that relate closely to all required content, based on sampling of text.

Disclaimer

Course Technology reserves the right to revise this publication and make changes from time to time in its content without notice.

ISBN 0-7600-6995-6

Printed in the United States of America

2 3 4 5 6 7 8 9 10 BM 05 04 03 02 01

PREFACE

The New Perspectives Series

About New Perspectives

Course Technology's **New Perspectives Series** is an integrated system of instruction that combines text and technology products to teach computer concepts, the Internet, and microcomputer applications. Users consistently praise this series for innovative pedagogy, use of interactive technology, creativity, accuracy, and supportive and engaging style.

How is the New Perspectives Series different from other series?

The **New Perspectives Series** distinguishes itself by **innovative technology**, from the renowned Course Labs to the state-of-the-art multimedia that is integrated with our Concepts texts. Other distinguishing features include **sound instructional design, proven pedagogy,** and **consistent quality**. Each tutorial has students learn features in the context of solving a realistic case problem rather than simply learning a laundry list of features. With the **New Perspectives Series,** instructors report that students have a complete, integrative learning experience that stays with them. They credit this high retention and competency to the fact that this series incorporates critical thinking and problem-solving with computer skills mastery. In addition, we work hard to ensure accuracy by using a multi-step quality assurance process during all stages of development. Instructors focus on teaching and students spend more time learning.

Choose the coverage that's right for you

New Perspectives applications books are available in the following categories:

Brief

2-4 tutorials

Brief: approximately 150 pages long, two to four "Level I" tutorials, teaches basic application skills.

Introductory

6 or 7 tutorials, or Brief + 2 or 3 more tutorials

Introductory: approximately 300 pages long, four to seven tutorials, goes beyond the basic skills. These books often build out of the Brief book, adding two or three additional "Level II" tutorials.

Comprehensive

Introductory + 4 or 5 more tutorials. Includes Brief Windows tutorials and Additional Cases

Comprehensive: approximately 600 pages long, eight to twelve tutorials, all tutorials included in the Introductory text plus higher-level "Level III" topics. Also includes two Windows tutorials and three or four fully developed Additional Cases.The book you are holding is a Comprehensive book.

Advanced

Quick Review of basics + in-depth, high-level coverage

Advanced: approximately 600 pages long, covers topics similar to those in the Comprehensive books, but offer the highest-level coverage in the series. Advanced books assume students already know the basics, and therefore go into more depth at a more accelerated rate than the Comprehensive titles. Advanced books are ideal for a second, more technical course.

Office

Quick Review of basics + in-depth, high-level coverage

Office: approximately 800 pages long, covers all components of the Office suite as well as integrates the individual software packages with one another and the Internet.

Custom Editions

Choose from any of the above to build your own Custom Editions or CourseKits

Custom Books The New Perspectives Series offers you two ways to customize a New Perspectives text to fit your course exactly: *CourseKits*™ are two or more texts shrink-wrapped together, and offer significant price discounts. *Custom Editions*® offer you flexibility in designing your concepts, Internet, and applications courses. You can build your own book by ordering a combination of topics bound together to cover only the subjects you want. There is no minimum order, and books are spiral bound. Contact your Course Technology sales representative for more information.

What course is this book appropriate for?

New Perspectives on Microsoft® Word 2000—Comprehensive can be used in any course in which you want students to learn all the most important topics of Word 2000, including creating styles, outlines, tables, and tables of contents, creating form letters and mailing labels, integrating Word with other programs and with the World Wide Web, customizing toolbars and templates, recording macros, creating on-screen forms, managing long documents with master documents, faxing and routing documents, and drawing watermarks and 3-D objects. It is particularly recommended for a full-semester course on Microsoft Word 2000. This book assumes that students have learned basic Windows navigation and file management skills from Course Technology's *New Perspectives on Microsoft Windows 95—Brief*, or the equivalent book for Windows 98 or NT.

What is the Microsoft Office User Specialist Program?

The Microsoft Office User Specialist Program provides an industry-recognized standard for measuring an individual's mastery of an Office application. Passing one or more MOUS Program certification exams helps your students demonstrate their proficiency to prospective employers and gives them a competitive edge in the job marketplace. Course Technology offers a growing number of Microsoft-approved products that cover all of the required objectives for the MOUS Program exams. For a complete listing of Course Technology titles that you can use to help your students get certified, visit our Web sit at **www.course.com.**

New Perspectives on Microsoft Word 2000—Comprehensive has been approved by Microsoft as courseware for the Microsoft Office User Specialist (MOUS) Program. After completing the tutorials and exercises in this book, students may be prepared to take the MOUS expert exam for Microsoft Word 2000. For more information about certification, please visit the MOUS program site at **www.mous.net.**

Proven Pedagogy

CASE

Tutorial Case Each tutorial begins with a problem presented in a case that is meaningful to students. The case turns the task of learning how to use an application into a problem-solving process.

45-minute Sessions. Each tutorial is divided into sessions that can be completed in about 45 minutes to an hour. Sessions allow instructors to more accurately allocate time in their syllabus, and students to better manage their own study time.

1.
2.
3.

Step-by-Step Methodology We make sure students can differentiate between what they are to *do* and what they are to *read.* Through numbered steps – clearly identified by a gray shaded background – students are constantly guided in solving the case problem. In addition, the numerous screen shots with callouts direct students' attention to what they should look at on the screen.

TROUBLE?

TROUBLE? Paragraphs These paragraphs anticipate the mistakes or problems that students may have and help them continue with the tutorial.

Tutorial Tips Page This page, following the Table of Contents, offers students suggestions on how to effectively plan their study and lab time, what to do when they make a mistake, and how to use the Reference Windows, MOUS grids, Quick Checks, and other features of the New Perspectives Series.

Read

"Read This Before You Begin" Page Located opposite the first tutorial's opening page for each level of the text, the Read This Before You Begin Page helps introduce technology into the classroom. Technical considerations and assumptions about software are listed to save time and eliminate unnecessary aggravation. Notes about the Student Disks help instructors and students get the right files in the right places, so students get started on the right foot.

QUICK CHECK

Quick Check Questions Each session concludes with meaningful, conceptual Quick Check questions that test students' understanding of what they learned in the session. Answers to the Quick Check questions are provided at the end of each tutorial.

Reference Windows Reference Windows are succinct summaries of the most important tasks covered in a tutorial and they preview actions students will perform in the steps to follow.

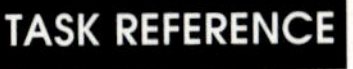

Task Reference Located as a table at the end of the book, the Task Reference contains a summary of how to perform common tasks using the most efficient method, as well as references to pages where the task is discussed in more detail.

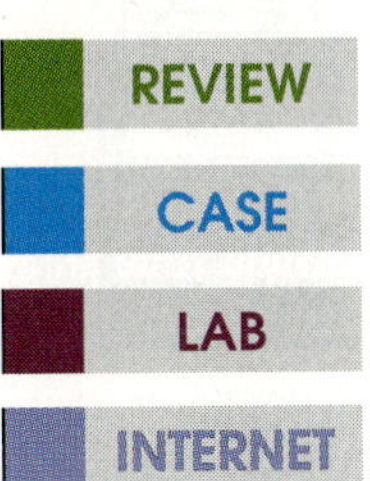

Explore

End-of-Tutorial Review Assignments, Case Problems, Internet Assignments, and Lab Assignments Review Assignments provide students with additional hands-on practice of the skills they learned in the tutorial using the same case presented in the tutorial. These Assignments are followed by three to four Case Problems that have approximately the same scope as the tutorial case but use a different scenario. In addition, some of the Review Assignments or Case Problems may include Exploration Exercises that challenge students, encourage them to explore the capabilities of the program they are using, and/or further extend their knowledge. Finally, if a Course Lab accompanies a tutorial, Lab Assignments are included after the Case Problems.

File Finder Chart This chart, located in the back of the book, visually explains how students should set up their Data Disks, what files should go in what folders, and what they'll be saving the files as in the course of their work.

Certification Skill Activity

MOUS Certification Chart In the back of the book, you'll find a chart that lists all the skills for the Microsoft Office User Specialist Expert Exam on Word 2000. With page numbers referencing where these skills are covered in this text and where students get hands-on practice in completing the skills, the chart can be used as an excellent study guide in preparing for the Word Expert MOUS exam.

The Instructor's Resource Kit for this title contains:

- Electronic Instructor's Manual
- Data Files
- Solution Files
- Course Labs
- Course Test Manager Testbank
- Course Test Manager Engine
- Figure files

These teaching tools come on CD-ROM. If you don't have access CD-ROM drive, contact your Course Technology customer service representative for more information.

The New Perspectives Supplements Package

Electronic Instructor's Manual Our Instructor's Manuals include tutorial overviews and outlines, technical notes, lecture notes, solutions, and Extra Case Problems. Many instructors use the Extra Case Problems for performance-based exams or extra credit projects. The Instructor's Manual is available as an electronic file, which you can get from the Instructor Resource Kit (IRK) CD-ROM or download it from **www.course.com.**

Data Files Data Files contain all of the data that students will use to complete the tutorials, Review Assignments, and Case Problems. A Readme file includes instructions for using the files. See the "Read This Before You Begin" page/pages for more information on Student Files.

Solution Files Solution Files contain every file students are asked to create or modify in the tutorials, Tutorial Assignments, Case Problems, and Extra Case Problems. A Help file on the Instructor's Resource Kit includes information for using the Solution files.

Course Labs: Concepts Come to Life These highly interactive computer-based learning activities bring concepts to life with illustrations, animations, digital images, and simulations. The Labs guide students step-by-step, present them with Quick Check questions, let them explore on their own, test their comprehension, and provide printed feedback. Lab icons at the beginning of the tutorial and in the tutorial margins indicate when a topic has a corresponding Lab. Lab Assignments are included at the end of each relevant tutorial. The Labs available with this book and the tutorials in which they appear are:

Tutorial 1
Windows 98

Tutorial 1
Windows 98

Tutorial 2
Windows 98

Tutorial 1
Word 2000

Tutorial 7
Word 2000

Figure Files Many figures in the text are provided on the IRK CD-ROM to help illustrate key topics or concepts. Instructors can create traditional overhead transparencies by printing the figure files. Or they can create electronic slide shows by using the figures in a presentation program such as PowerPoint.

Course Test Manager: Testing and Practice at the Computer or on Paper Course Test Manager is cutting-edge, Windows-based testing software that helps instructors design and administer practice tests and actual examinations. Course Test Manager can automatically grade the tests students take at the computer and can generate statistical information on individual as well as group performance.

Online Companions: Dedicated to Keeping You and Your Students Up-To-Date Visit our faculty sites and student sites on the World Wide Web at **www.course.com**. Here instructors can browse this text's password-protected Faculty Online Companion to obtain an online Instructor's Manual, Solution Files, Data Files, and more. Students can also access this text's Student Online Companion, which contains Student files and all the links that the students will need to complete their tutorial assignments.

More innovative technology

Course CBT

Enhance your students' Office 2000 classroom learning experience with self-paced computer-based training on CD-ROM. Course CBT engages students with interactive multimedia and hands-on simulations that reinforce and complement the concepts and skills covered in the textbook. All the content is aligned with the MOUS (Microsoft Office User Specialist) program, making it a great preparation tool for the certification exams. Course CBT also includes extensive pre- and post-assessments that test students' mastery of skills. These pre- and post-assessments automatically generate a "custom learning path" through the course that highlights only the topics students need help with.

Course Assessment

How well do your students *really* know Microsoft Office? Course Assessment is a performance-based testing program that measures students' proficiency in Microsoft Office 2000. Previously known as SAM, Course Assessment is available for Office 2000 in either a live or simulated environment. You can use Course Assessment to place students into or out of courses, monitor their performance throughout a course, and help prepare them for the MOUS certification exams.

WebCT

WebCT is a tool used to create Web-based educational environments and also uses WWW browsers as the interface for the course-building environment. The site is hosted on your school campus, allowing complete control over the information. WebCT has its own internal communication system, offering internal e-mail, a Bulletin Board, and a Chat room.

Course Technology offers pre-existing supplemental information to help in your WebCT class creation, such as a suggested Syllabus, Lecture Notes, Figures in the Book/Course Presenter, Student Downloads, and Test Banks in which you can schedule an exam, create reports, and more.

Acknowledgments

Sincere thanks to the reviewers for their excellent feedback: Janet Sheppard, Collin County Community College; Mary Dobranski, College of St. Mary; Tony Gabriel, Computer Learning Center. Thanks also go out to John Bosco, Quality Assurance Project Leader, and Nicole Ashton, John Freitas, Alex White, and Jeff Schwartz, QA testers, for verifying the technical accuracy of every step.

Many thanks to all the smart, friendly, helpful folks at Course Technology, including Melissa Dezotell, for managing the review process so smoothly, Karen Shortill, for her expertise on the supplements, and Catherine Donaldson, for all her contributions. In particular, thanks to Rachel Crapser, senior product manager, for steering us through the rough waters of the Office 2000 beta with so much professionalism and good cheer. Thanks to Robin Romer and Ann Shaffer, development editors, for their encouraging phone calls and expert editing. Thank you to Daphne Barbas, production editor, for magically transforming the manuscript into a published book.

Ann Shaffer, Beverly B. Zimmerman, & S. Scott Zimmerman

I also owe a great debt to Beverly and Scott Zimmerman, writers and teachers extraordinaire, for giving me the opportunity to be a part of their team. And special thanks to Lois Sachtjen, for being such a kind and helpful friend.

Ann Shaffer

BRIEF CONTENTS

BRIEF CONTENTS

Reference Window List

Tutorial Tips

These tutorials will help you learn about Microsoft Word 2000. The tutorials are designed to be worked through at a computer. Each tutorial is divided into sessions. Watch for the session headings, such as Session 1.1 and Session 1.2. Each session is designed to be completed in about 45 minutes, but take as much time as you need. It's also a good idea to take a break between sessions.

To use the tutorials effectively you, read the following questions and answers before you begin.

Where do I start?

Each tutorial begins with a case, which sets the scene for the tutorial and gives you background information to help you understand what you will be doing. Read the case before you go to the lab. In the lab, begin with the first session of a tutorial.

How do I know what to do on the computer?

Each session contains steps that you will perform on the computer to learn how to use Microsoft Word 2000. Read the text that introduces each series of steps. The steps you need to do at a computer are numbered and are set against a shaded background. Read each step carefully and completely before you try it.

How do I know if I did the step correctly?

As you work, compare your computer screen with the corresponding figure in the tutorial. Don't worry if your screen display is somewhat different from the figure. The important parts of the screen display are labeled in each figure. Check to make sure these parts are on your screen.

What if I make a mistake?

Don't worry about making mistakes—they are part of the learning process. Paragraphs labeled "TROUBLE?" identify common problems and explain how to get back on track. Follow the steps in a TROUBLE? paragraph only if you are having the problem described. If you run into other problems:

- Carefully consider the current state of your system, the position of the pointer, and any messages on the screen.
- Complete the sentence, "Now I want to…" Be specific, because identifying your goal will help you rethink the steps you need to take to reach that goal.
- If you are working on a particular piece of software, consult the Help system.
- If the suggestions above don't solve your problem, consult your technical support person for assistance.

How do I use the Reference Windows?

Reference Windows summarize the procedures you will learn in the tutorial steps. Do not complete the actions in the Reference Windows when you are working through the tutorial. Instead, refer to the Reference Windows while you are working on the assignments at the end of the tutorial.

How can I test my understanding of the material I learned in the tutorial?

At the end of each session, you can answer the Quick Check questions. The answers for the Quick Checks are at the end of that tutorial.

After you have completed the entire tutorial, you should complete the Review Assignments and Case Problems. They are carefully structured so that you will review what you have learned and then apply your knowledge to new situations.

What if I can't remember how to do something?

You should refer to the Task Reference at the end of the book; it summarizes how to accomplish tasks using the most efficient method.

Before you begin the tutorials, you should know the basics about your computer's operating system. You should also know how to use the menus, dialog boxes, Help system, and My Computer.

How can I prepare for MOUS Certification?

The Microsoft Office User Specialist (MOUS) logo on the cover of this book indicates that Microsoft has approved it as a study guide for Word 2000 MOUS Expert exam. At the back of this text, you'll see a chart that outlines the specific Microsoft certification skills for Excel 2000 that are covered in the tutorials. You'll need to learn these skills if you're interested in taking a MOUS exam. If you decide to take a MOUS exam, or if you just want to study a specific skill, this chart will give you an easy reference to the page number on which the skill is covered. To learn more about the MOUS certification program refer to the preface in the front of the book or go to http://www.mous.net.

Now that you've read the Tutorial Tips, you are ready to begin.

New Perspectives on

MICROSOFT® WINDOWS® 98

Read This Before You Begin

To the Student

Make Student Disk Program

To complete the Level I tutorials, Tutorial Assignments, and Projects, you need 2 Student Disks. Your instructor will either provide you with Student Disks or ask you to make your own.

If you are making your own Student Disks you will need 2 blank, formatted high-density disks and access to the Make Student Disk program. If you wish to install the Make Student Disk program to your home computer, you can obtain it from your instructor or from the Web. To download the Make Student Disk program from the Web, go to www.course.com, click Data Disks, and follow the instructions on the screen.

To install the Make Student Disk program, select and click the file you just downloaded from www.course.com, 5446-0.exe. Follow the on-screen instructions to complete the installation. If you have any trouble installing or obtaining the Make Student Disk program, ask your instructor or technical support person for assistance.

Once you have obtained and installed the Make Student Disk program, you can use it to create your student disks according to the steps in the tutorials.

Course Labs

The Level I tutorials in this book feature 3 interactive Course Labs to help you understand selected computer concepts. There are Lab Assignments at the end of Tutorials 1 and 2 that relate to these Labs. To start a Lab, click the **Start** button on the Windows 98 Taskbar, point to **Programs**, point to **Course Labs**, point to **New Perspectives Course Labs**, and click the name of the Lab you want to use.

Using Your Own Computer

If you are going to work through this book using your own computer, you need:

Computer System Microsoft Windows 98 must be installed on a local hard drive or on a network drive.

Student Disks You will not be able to complete the tutorials or exercises in this book using your own computer until you have your Student Disks. See "Make Student Disk Program" above for details on obtaining your student disks.

Course Labs See your instructor or technical support person to obtain the Course Lab software for use on your own computer.

Visit Our World Wide Web Site

Additional materials designed especially for you are available on the World Wide Web. Go to http://www.course.com.

To the Instructor

The Make Student Disk Program and Course Labs for this title are available on the Instructor's Resource Kit for this title. Follow the instructions in the Help file on the CD-ROM to install the programs to your network or standalone computer. For information on using the Make Student Disk Program or the Course Labs, see the "To the Student" section above. Students will be switching the default installation settings to Web style in Tutorial 2. You are granted a license to copy the Student Files and Course Labs to any computer or computer network used by students who have purchased this book.

OBJECTIVES

In this tutorial you will:

- Start and shut down Windows 98
- Identify the objects on the Windows 98 desktop
- Practice mouse functions
- Run software programs and switch between them
- Identify and use the controls in a window
- Use Windows 98 controls such as menus, toolbars, list boxes, scroll bars, option buttons, tabs, and check boxes
- Explore the Windows 98 Help system

LABS

EXPLORING THE BASICS

Investigating the Windows 98 Operating System

CASE

Your First Day on the Computer

You walk into the computer lab and sit down at a desk. There's a computer in front of you, and you find yourself staring dubiously at the screen. Where to start? As if in answer to your question, your friend Steve Laslow appears.

"You start with the operating system," says Steve. Noticing your puzzled look, Steve explains that the **operating system** is software that helps the computer carry out operating tasks such as displaying information on the computer screen and saving data on your disks. Your computer uses the **Microsoft Windows 98** operating system—Windows 98, for short.

Steve tells you that Windows 98 has a "gooey" or **graphical user interface (GUI)**, which uses pictures of familiar objects, such as file folders and documents, to represent a desktop on your screen. Microsoft Windows 98 gets its name from the rectangular work areas, called "windows," that appear on your screen.

Steve explains that much of the software available for Windows 98 has a standard graphical user interface. This means that once you have learned how to use one Windows software package, such as word-processing software, you are well on your way to understanding how to use other Windows software. Windows 98 lets you use more than one software package at a time, so you can easily switch between your word-processing software and your appointment book software, for example. Finally, Windows 98 makes it very easy to access the **Internet**, the worldwide collection of computers connected to one another to enable communication. All in all, Windows 98 makes your computer an effective and easy-to-use productivity tool.

Steve recommends that you get started right away by using some tutorials that will teach you the skills essential for using Microsoft Windows 98. He hands you a book and assures you that everything on your computer system is set up and ready to go.

SESSION 1.1

In this session, in addition to learning basic Windows terminology, you will learn how to use a pointing device, how to start and stop a program, and how to use more than one program at a time.

Starting Windows 98

Using a Keyboard

Windows 98 automatically starts when you turn on the computer. Depending on the way your computer is set up, you might be asked to enter your username and password.

To start Windows 98:

1. Turn on your computer.

TROUBLE? If prompted to do so, type your assigned username and press the Tab key. Then type your password and press the Enter key to continue.

TROUBLE? If this is the first time you have started your computer with Windows 98, messages might appear on your screen informing you that Windows is setting up components of your computer. If the Welcome to Windows 98 box appears, press and hold down the Alt key on your keyboard and then, while you hold down the Alt key, press the F4 key. The box closes.

After a moment, Windows 98 starts.

The Windows 98 Desktop

In Windows terminology, the area displayed on your screen represents a **desktop**—a workspace for projects and the tools needed to manipulate those projects. When you first start a computer, it uses **default** settings, those preset by the operating system. The default desktop, for example, has a plain teal background. However, Microsoft designed Windows 98 so that you can easily change the appearance of the desktop. You can, for example, add color, patterns, images, and text to the desktop background.

Many institutions design customized desktops for their computers. Figure 1-1 shows the default Windows 98 desktop and two other examples of desktops, one designed for a business, North Pole Novelties, and one designed for a school, the University of Colorado. Although your desktop might not look exactly like any of the examples in Figure 1-1, you should be able to locate objects on your screen similar to those in Figure 1-1. Look at your screen display and locate the objects labeled in Figure 1-1. The objects on your screen might appear larger or smaller than those in Figure 1-1, depending on your monitor's settings.

Figure 1-1 **THE WINDOWS 98 DESKTOP**

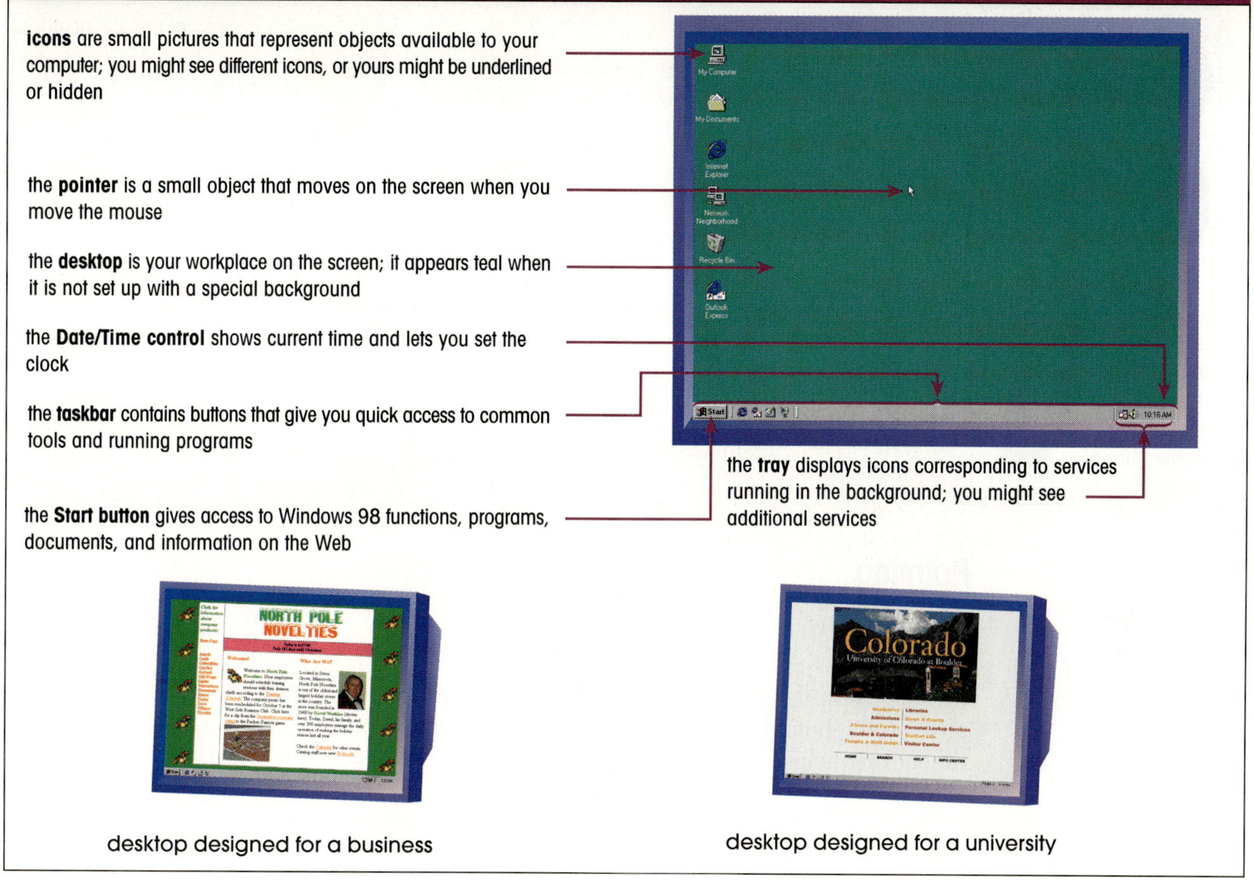

icons are small pictures that represent objects available to your computer; you might see different icons, or yours might be underlined or hidden

the **pointer** is a small object that moves on the screen when you move the mouse

the **desktop** is your workplace on the screen; it appears teal when it is not set up with a special background

the **Date/Time control** shows current time and lets you set the clock

the **taskbar** contains buttons that give you quick access to common tools and running programs

the **Start button** gives access to Windows 98 functions, programs, documents, and information on the Web

the **tray** displays icons corresponding to services running in the background; you might see additional services

desktop designed for a business

desktop designed for a university

If the screen goes blank or starts to display a moving design, press any key to restore the Windows 98 desktop.

Using a Pointing Device

A **pointing device** helps you interact with objects on the screen. Pointing devices come in many shapes and sizes; some are designed to ensure that your hand won't suffer fatigue while using them. Some are directly attached to your computer via a cable, whereas others function like a TV remote control and allow you to access your computer without being right next to it. Figure 1-2 shows examples of common pointing devices.

The most common pointing device is called a **mouse**, so this book uses that term. If you are using a different pointing device, such as a trackball, substitute that device whenever you see the term "mouse." In Windows 98 you need to know how to use the mouse to manipulate the objects on the screen. In this session you will learn about pointing and clicking. In Session 1.2 you will learn how to use the mouse to drag objects.

You can also interact with objects by using the keyboard; however, the mouse is more convenient for most tasks, so the tutorials in this book assume you are using one.

Figure 1-2 POINTING DEVICES

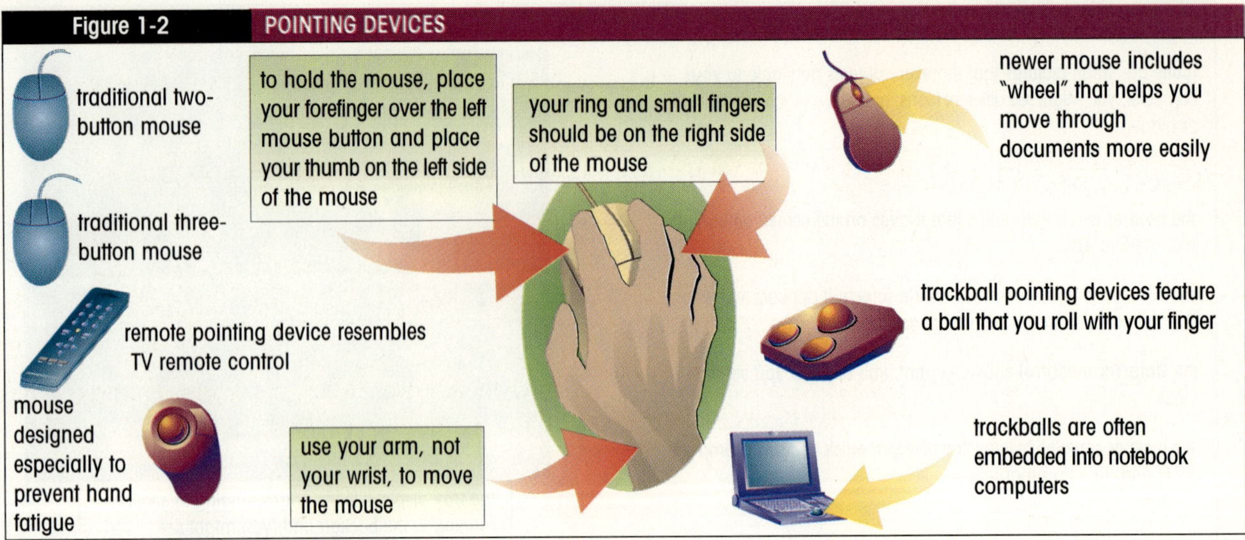

Pointing

You use a pointing device to move the pointer, in order to manipulate objects on the desktop. The pointer is usually shaped like an arrow, although it can change shape depending on where it is on the screen. How skilled you are in using a mouse depends on your ability to position the pointer. Most computer users place the mouse on a **mouse pad**, a flat piece of rubber that helps the mouse move smoothly. As you move the mouse on the mouse pad, the pointer on the screen moves in a corresponding direction.

You begin most Windows operations by positioning the pointer over a specific part of the screen. This is called **pointing**.

To move the pointer:

1. Position your right index finger over the left mouse button, as shown in Figure 1-2. Lightly grasp the sides of the mouse with your thumb and little fingers.

   TROUBLE? If you want to use the mouse with your left hand, ask your instructor or technical support person to help you use the Control Panel to swap the functions of the left and right mouse buttons. Be sure to find out how to change back to the right-handed mouse setting, so that you can reset the mouse each time you are finished in the lab.

2. Place the mouse on the mouse pad and then move the mouse. Watch the movement of the pointer.

   TROUBLE? If you run out of room to move your mouse, lift the mouse and place it in the middle of the mouse pad. Notice that the pointer does not move when the mouse is not in contact with the mouse pad.

When you position the mouse pointer over certain objects, such as the objects on the taskbar, a "tip" appears. These "tips" are called **ToolTips**, and they tell you the purpose or function of an object.

To view ToolTips:

1. Use the mouse to point to the **Start** button. After a few seconds, you see the tip "Click here to begin," as shown in Figure 1-3.

Figure 1-3 VIEWING TOOLTIPS

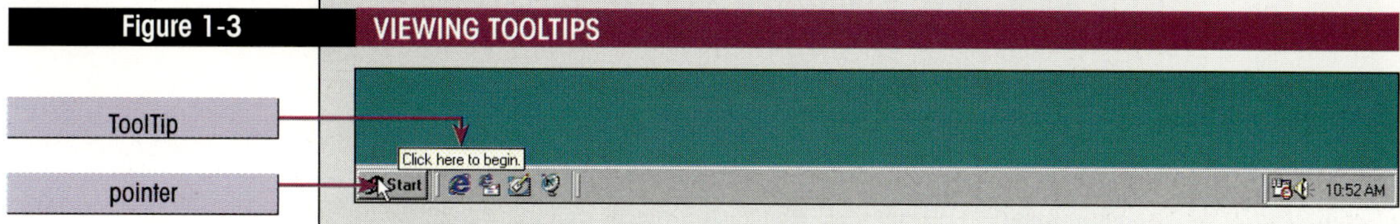

2. Point to the time on the right end of the taskbar. Notice that today's date (or the date to which your computer's time clock is set) appears.

Clicking

Clicking is when you press a mouse button and immediately release it. Clicking sends a signal to your computer that you want to perform an action on the object you click. In Windows 98 you can click using both the left and right mouse buttons, but most actions are performed using the left mouse button. If you are told to click an object, click it with the left mouse button, unless instructed otherwise.

When you click the Start button, the Start menu appears. A **menu** is a list of options that helps you work with software. The **Start menu** provides you with access to programs, documents, and much more. Try clicking the Start button to open the Start menu.

To open the Start menu:

1. Point to the **Start** button.

2. Click the left mouse button. An arrow ▶ following an option on the Start menu indicates that you can view additional choices by navigating a **submenu**, a menu extending from the main menu. See Figure 1-4.

Figure 1-4 START MENU

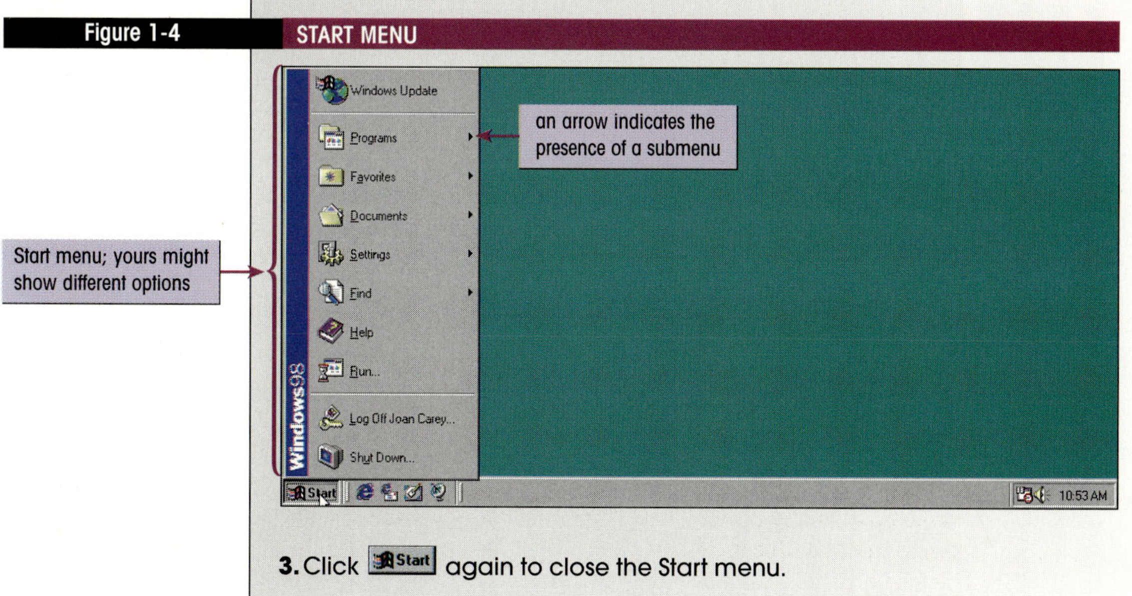

3. Click Start again to close the Start menu.

Next you'll learn how to open a submenu by selecting it.

Selecting

In Windows 98, pointing and clicking are often used to **select** an object, in other words, to choose it as the object you want to work with. Windows 98 shows you which object is selected by highlighting it, usually by changing the object's color, putting a box around it, or making the object appear to be pushed in, as shown in Figure 1-5.

Figure 1-5 SELECTED OBJECTS

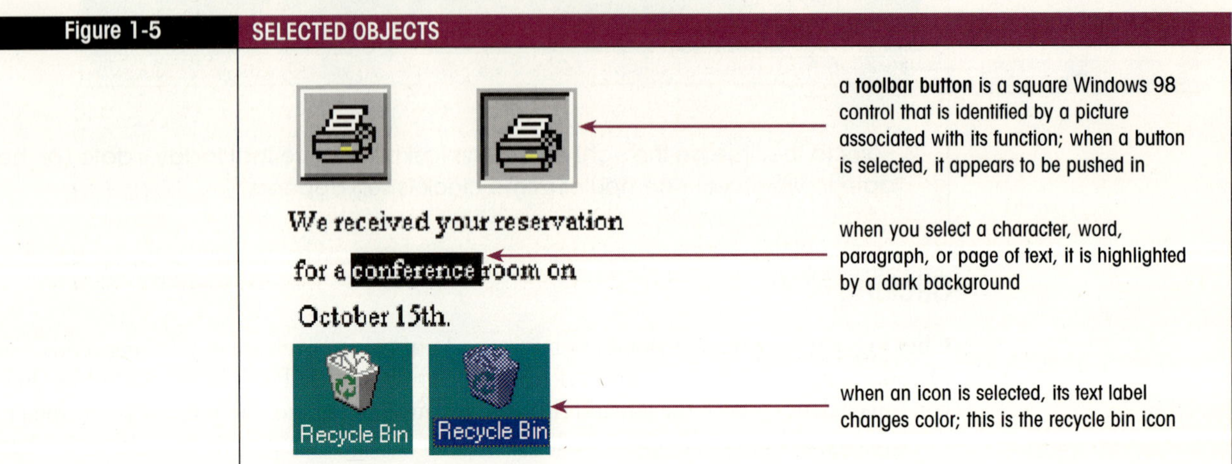

In Windows 98, depending on your computer's settings, some objects are selected when you simply point to them, others when you click them. Practice selecting the Programs option on the Start menu to open the Programs submenu.

To select an option on a menu:

1. Click the **Start** button and notice how it appears to be pushed in, indicating it is selected.
2. Point to the **Programs** option. After a short pause, the Programs submenu opens, and the Programs option is highlighted to indicate it is selected. See Figure 1-6.

   TROUBLE? If a submenu other than the Programs menu opens, you selected the wrong option. Move the mouse so that the pointer points to Programs.

   TROUBLE? If the Programs option doesn't appear, your Start menu might have too many options to fit on the screen. If that is the case, a small arrow appears at the top or bottom of the Start menu. Click first the top and then the bottom arrow to view additional Start menu options until you locate the Programs menu option, and then point to it.

Figure 1-6 PROGRAMS SUBMENU

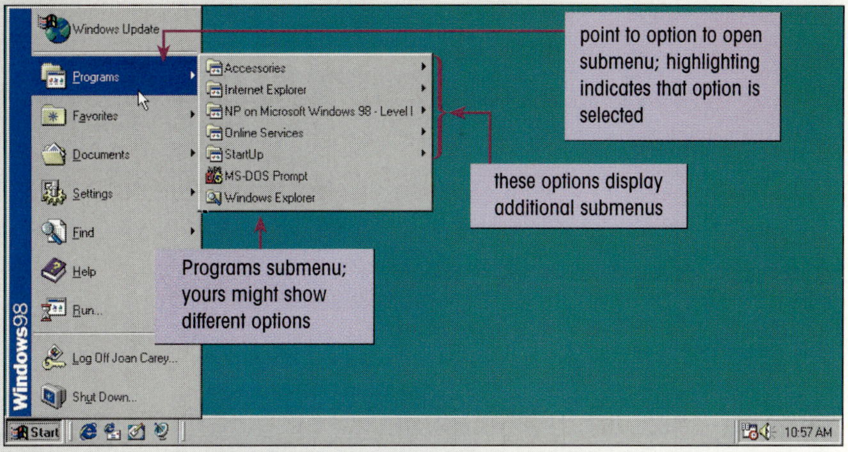

3. Now close the Start menu by clicking Start again.

You return to the desktop.

Right-Clicking

Pointing devices were originally designed with a single button, so the term "clicking" had only one meaning: you pressed that button. Innovations in technology, however, led to the addition of a second and even a third button (and more recently, options such as a wheel) that expanded the pointing device's capability. More recent software—especially that designed for Windows 98—takes advantage of additional buttons, especially the right button. However, the term "clicking" continues to refer to the left button; clicking an object with the *right* button is called **right-clicking**.

In Windows 98, right-clicking both selects an object and opens its **shortcut menu**, a list of options directly related to the object you right-clicked. You can right-click practically any object—the Start button, a desktop icon, the taskbar, and even the desktop itself—to view options associated with that object. For example, the first desktop shown in Figure 1-7 illustrates what happens when you click the Start button with the left mouse button to open the Start menu. Clicking the Start button with the right button, however, opens the Start button's shortcut menu, as shown in the second desktop.

Figure 1-7 CLICKING WITH THE LEFT AND RIGHT MOUSE BUTTONS

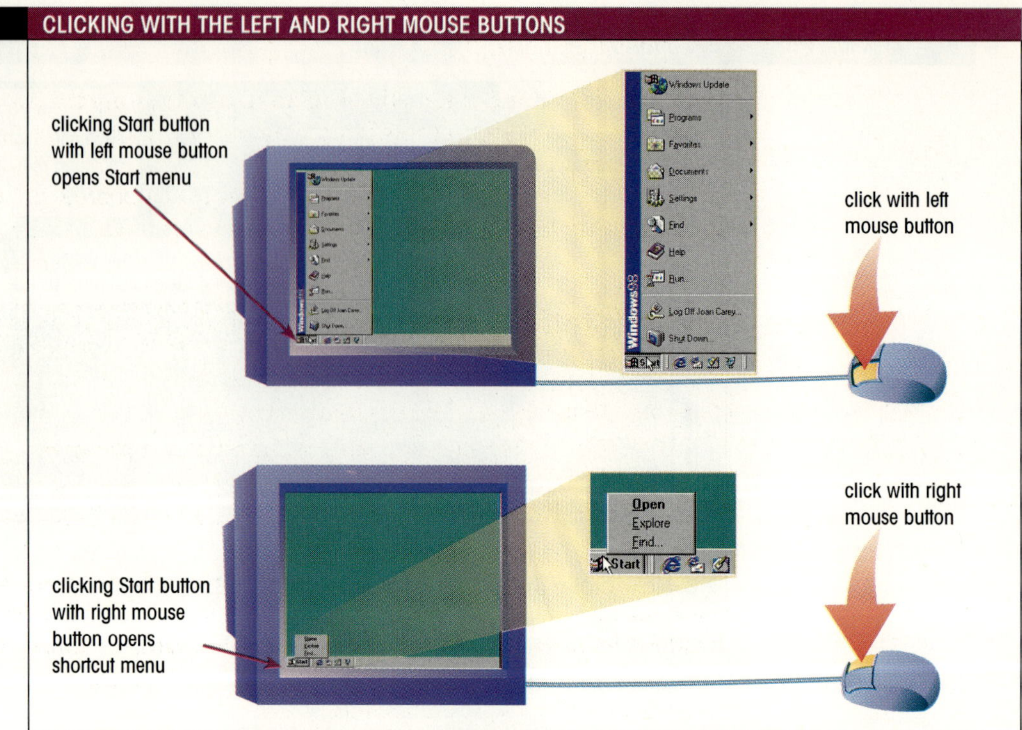

Try using right-clicking to open the shortcut menu for the Start button.

To right-click an object:

1. Position the pointer over the Start button.
2. Right-click the **Start** button. The shortcut menu that opens offers a list of options available to the Start button.

   TROUBLE? If you are using a trackball or a mouse with three buttons or a wheel, make sure you click the button on the far right, not the one in the middle.

   TROUBLE? If your menu looks slightly different from the one in Figure 1-8, don't worry. Computers with different software often have different options.

Figure 1-8 START BUTTON SHORTCUT MENU

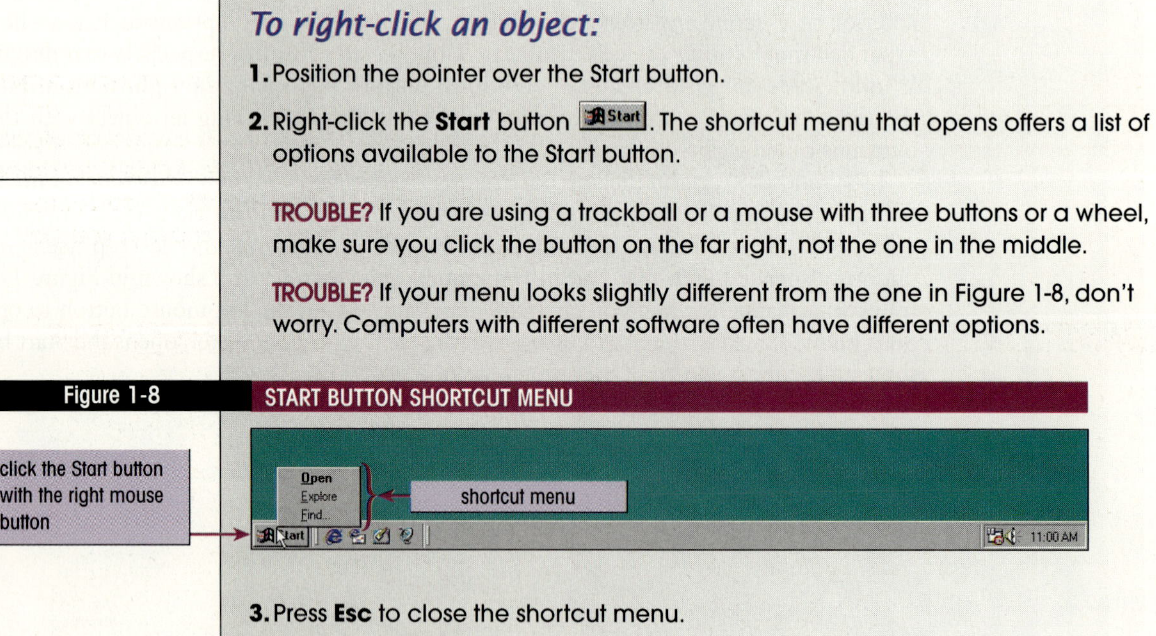

3. Press **Esc** to close the shortcut menu.

You again return to the desktop.

Starting and Closing a Program

The software you use is sometimes referred to as a **program** or an **application**. To use a program, such as a word-processing program, you must first start it. With Windows 98 you start a program by clicking the Start button.

The Reference Window below explains how to start a program. Don't do the steps in the Reference Window now; they are for your later reference.

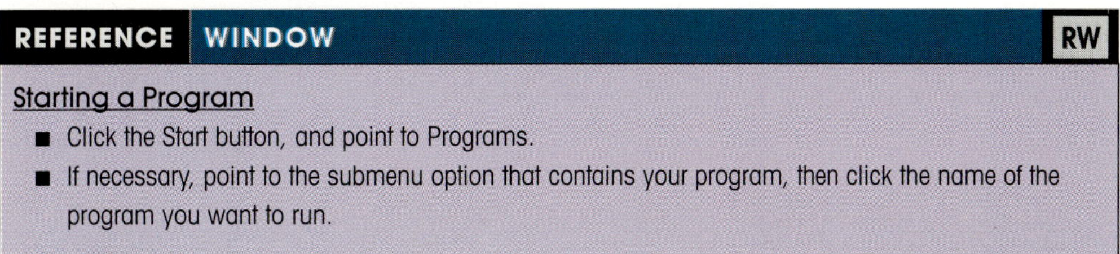

REFERENCE WINDOW RW

Starting a Program

- Click the Start button, and point to Programs.
- If necessary, point to the submenu option that contains your program, then click the name of the program you want to run.

Windows 98 includes an easy-to-use word-processing program called WordPad. Suppose you want to start the WordPad program and use it to write a letter or report. You open Windows 98 programs from the Start menu. Programs are usually located on the Programs submenu or on one of its submenus. To start WordPad, for example, you navigate the Programs and Accessories submenus.

To start the WordPad program from the Start menu:

1. Click the **Start** button to open the Start menu.
2. Point to **Programs**. The Programs submenu appears.
3. Point to **Accessories**. Another submenu appears. Figure 1-9 shows the open menus.

TROUBLE? If a different menu opens, you might have moved the mouse diagonally so that a different submenu opened. Move the pointer to the right across the Programs option, and then move it up or down to point to Accessories. Once you're more comfortable moving the mouse, you'll find that you can eliminate this problem by moving the mouse quickly.

Figure 1-9 START MENU

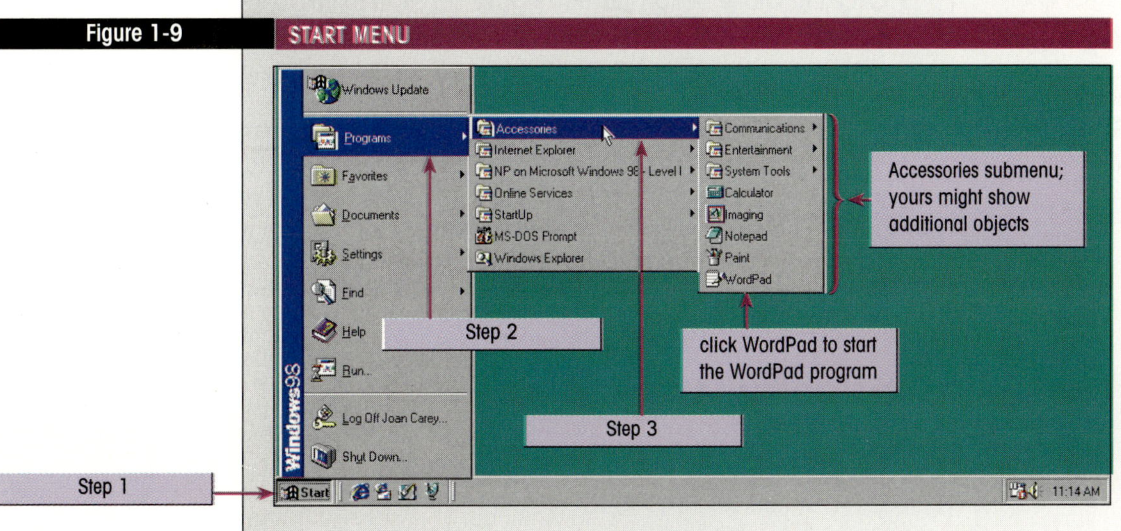

4. Click **WordPad**. The WordPad program opens, as shown in Figure 1-10. If the WordPad window does not fill the entire screen, don't worry. You will learn how to manipulate windows in Session 1.2.

Figure 1-10 THE WORDPAD PROGRAM

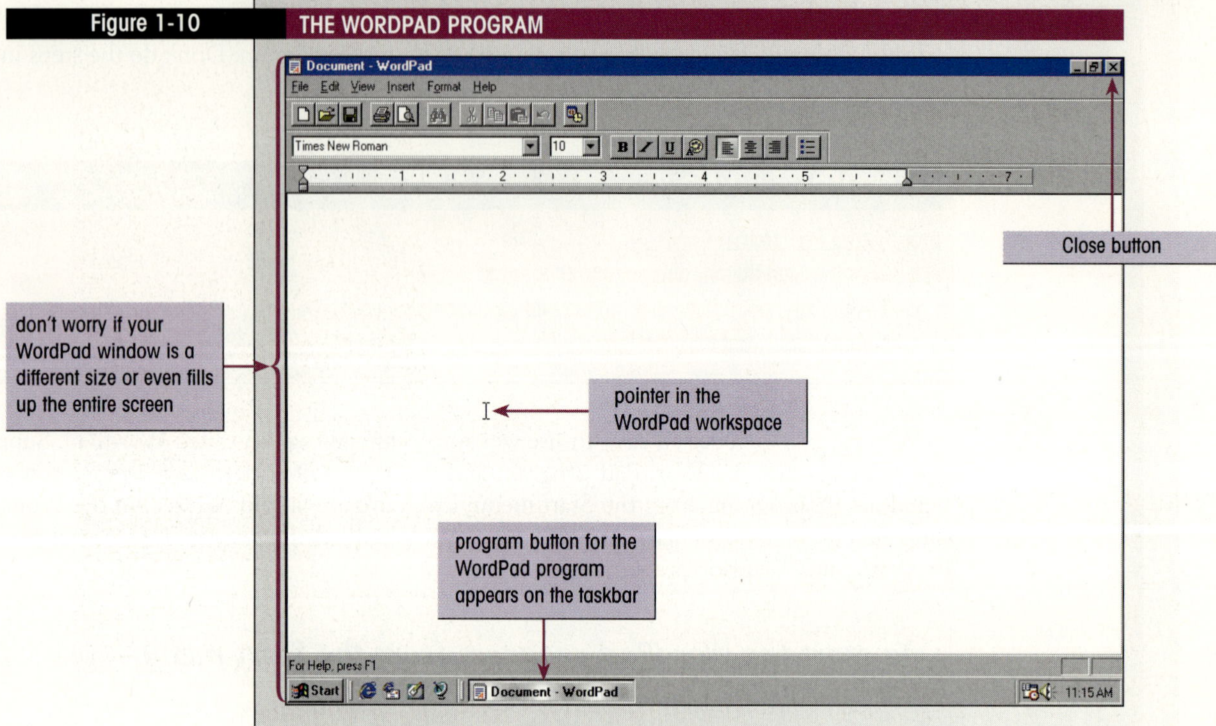

When a program is started, it is said to be **running**. A program button appears on the taskbar. **Program buttons** give you access to the programs running on the desktop.

When you are finished using a program, the easiest way to close it is to click the Close button ☒.

To exit the WordPad program:

1. Click the **Close** button ☒. See Figure 1-10. You return to the Windows 98 desktop.

Running Multiple Programs

One of the most useful features of Windows 98 is its ability to run multiple programs at the same time. This feature, known as **multitasking**, allows you to work on more than one project at a time and to switch quickly between projects. For example, you can start WordPad and leave it running while you then start the Paint program.

To run WordPad and Paint at the same time:

1. Start WordPad, then click the **Start** button Start again.
2. Point to **Programs**, then point to **Accessories**.

3. Click **Paint**. The Paint program appears, as shown in Figure 1-11. Now two programs are running at the same time.

Figure 1-11 THE PAINT PROGRAM

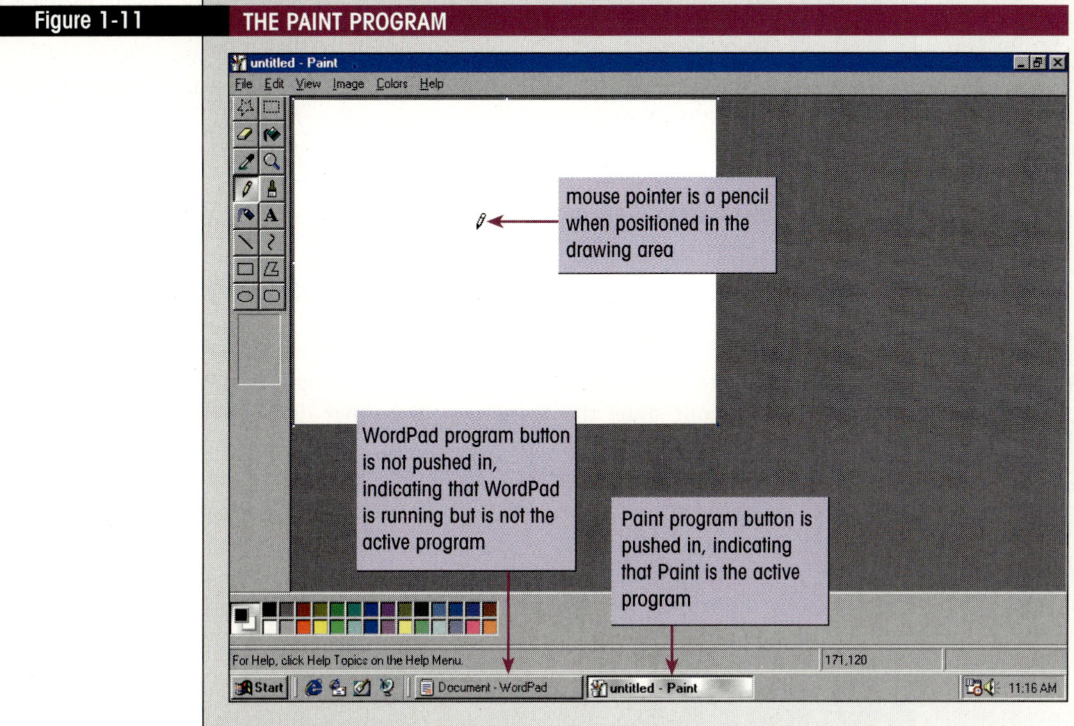

TROUBLE? If the Paint program does not fill the entire screen, don't worry. You will learn how to manipulate windows in Session 1.2.

What happened to WordPad? The WordPad program button is still on the taskbar, so even if you can't see it, WordPad is still running. You can imagine that it is stacked behind the Paint program, as shown in Figure 1-12.

Figure 1-12 PROJECTS STACKED ON A DESK

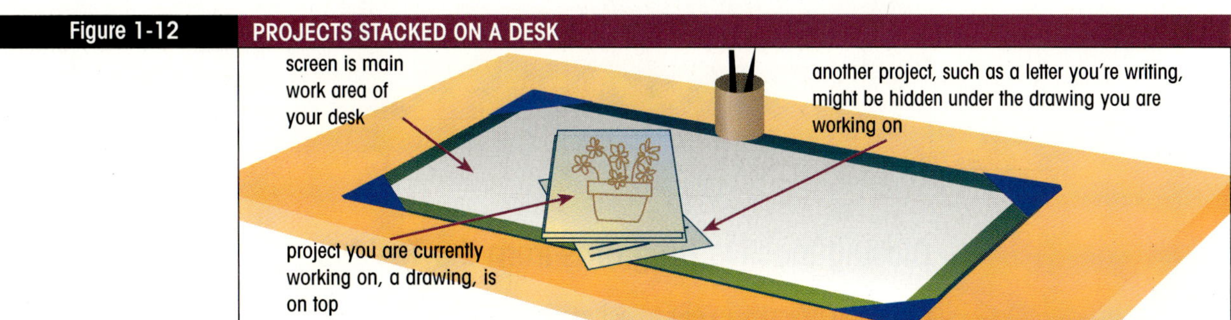

Switching Between Programs

Although Windows 98 allows you to run more than one program, only one program at a time is active. The **active** program is the program with which you are currently working. The easiest way to switch between programs is to use the buttons on the taskbar.

To switch between WordPad and Paint:

1. Click the button labeled **Document - WordPad** on the taskbar. The Document - WordPad button now looks as if it has been pushed in, to indicate that it is the active program, and WordPad moves to the front.
2. Next, click the button labeled **untitled - Paint** on the taskbar to switch to the Paint program.

The Paint program is again the active program.

Accessing the Desktop from the Quick Launch Toolbar

The Windows 98 taskbar, as you've seen, displays buttons for programs currently running. It also can contain **toolbars**, sets of buttons that give single-click access to programs or documents. In its default state, the Windows 98 taskbar displays the **Quick Launch toolbar**, which gives quick access to Web programs and to the desktop. Your taskbar might contain additional toolbars, or none at all.

When you are running more than one program but you want to return to the desktop, perhaps to use one of the desktop icons such as My Computer, you can do so by using one of the Quick Launch toolbar buttons. Clicking the Show Desktop button returns you to the desktop. The open programs are not closed; they are simply inactive.

To return to the desktop:

1. Click the **Show Desktop** button on the Quick Launch toolbar. The desktop appears, and both the Paint and WordPad programs are temporarily inactive. See Figure 1-13.

   TROUBLE? If the Quick Launch toolbar doesn't appear on your taskbar, right-click the taskbar, point to Toolbars, and then click Quick Launch and try Step 1 again.

Figure 1-13 ACCESSING THE DESKTOP

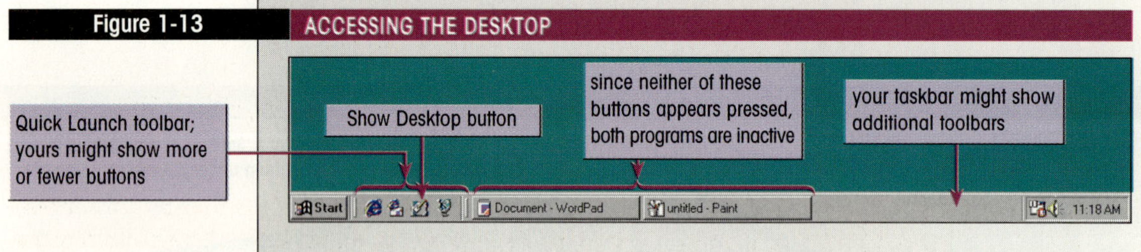

Closing Inactive Programs from the Taskbar

It is good practice to close each program when you are finished using it. Each program uses computer resources, such as memory, so Windows 98 works more efficiently when only the programs you need are open. You've already seen how to close an open program using the Close button. You can also close a program, whether active or inactive, by using the shortcut menu associated with the program button on the taskbar.

To close WordPad and Paint using the program button shortcut menus:

1. Right-click the **untitled - Paint** button on the taskbar. To right-click something, remember that you click it with the right mouse button. The shortcut menu for that program button opens. See Figure 1-14.

Figure 1-14 PROGRAM BUTTON SHORTCUT MENU

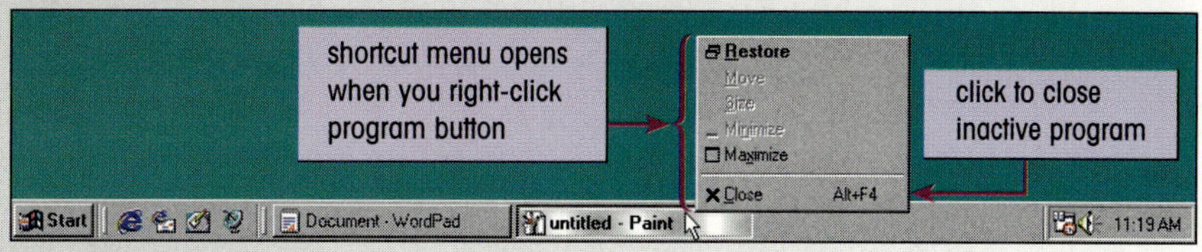

2. Click **Close**. The button labeled "untitled - Paint" disappears from the taskbar, and the Paint program closes.
3. Right-click the **Document - WordPad** button on the taskbar, and then click **Close**. The WordPad button disappears from the taskbar.

Shutting Down Windows 98

It is very important to shut down Windows 98 before you turn off the computer. If you turn off your computer without correctly shutting down, you might lose data and damage your files.

You should typically use the "Shut down" option when you want to turn off your computer. However, your school might prefer that you select the Log Off option on the Start menu. This option logs you out of Windows 98, leaves the computer turned on, and allows another user to log on without restarting the computer. Check with your instructor or technical support person for the preferred method at your school's computer lab.

To shut down Windows 98:

1. Click the **Start** button [Start] on the taskbar to display the Start menu.
2. Click the **Shut Down** menu option. A box titled "Shut Down Windows" opens.

   TROUBLE? If you can't see the Shut Down menu option, your Start menu has more options than your screen can display. A small arrow appears at the bottom of the Start menu. Click this button until the Shut Down menu option appears, and then click Shut Down.

   TROUBLE? If you are supposed to log off rather than shut down, click the Log Off option instead and follow your school's logoff procedure.

3. Make sure the **Shut down** option is preceded by a small black bullet. See Figure 1-15.

   TROUBLE? If your Shut down option is not preceded by a small black bullet, point to the circle preceding the Shut down option and click it. A small black bullet appears in the circle, indicating that Windows 98 will perform the Shut down option. Your Shut Down Windows dialog box might show additional options, such as Stand by.

Figure 1-15 SHUTTING DOWN

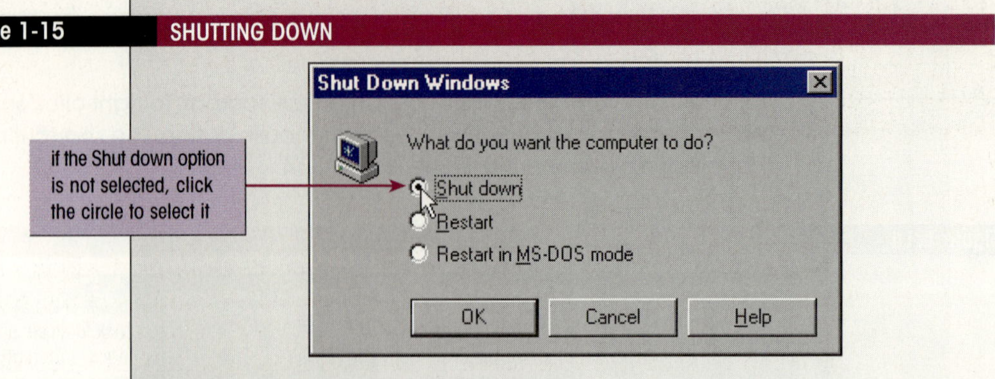

4. Click the **OK** button.

5. Click the **Yes** button if you are asked if you are sure you want to shut down.

6. Wait until you see a message indicating it is safe to turn off your computer. If your lab staff has requested you to switch off your computer after shutting down, do so now. Otherwise leave the computer running. Some computers turn themselves off automatically.

QUICK CHECK

1. What is the purpose of the taskbar?

2. The ______________ feature of Windows 98 allows you to run more than one program at a time.

3. The ______________ is a list of options that provides you with access to programs, documents, submenus, and more.

4. What should you do if you are trying to move the pointer to the left edge of your screen, but your mouse bumps into the keyboard?

5. Even if you can't see an open program on your desktop, the program might be running. How can you tell if a program is running?

6. Why is it good practice to close each program when you are finished using it?

7. Why should you shut down Windows 98 before you turn off your computer?

SESSION 1.2

In this session you will learn how to use many of the Windows 98 controls to manipulate windows and programs. You will also learn how to change the size and shape of a window; how to move a window; and how to use menus, dialog boxes, tabs, buttons, and lists to specify how you want a program to carry out a task.

Anatomy of a Window

When you run a program in Windows 98, it appears in a window. A **window** is a rectangular area of the screen that contains a program or data. Windows, spelled with an uppercase "W," is the name of the Microsoft operating system. The word "window" with a lowercase "w" refers to one of the rectangular areas on the screen. A window also contains controls for manipulating the window and for using the program. Figure 1-16 describes the controls you are likely to see in most windows.

Figure 1-16 WINDOW CONTROLS

CONTROL	DESCRIPTION
Menu bar	Contains the titles of menus, such as File, Edit, and Help
Pointer	Lets you manipulate window objects
Program button	Appears on the taskbar to indicate that a program is running on the desktop; appears pressed when program is active and not pressed when program is inactive
Sizing buttons	Let you enlarge, shrink, or close a window
Status bar	Provides you with messages relevant to the task you are performing
Title bar	Contains the window title and basic window control buttons
Toolbar	Contains buttons that provide you with shortcuts to common menu commands
Window title	Identifies the program and document contained in the window
Workspace	Part of the window you use to enter your work—to enter text, draw pictures, set up calculations, and so on

WordPad is a good example of a typical window, so try starting WordPad and identifying these controls in the WordPad window.

To look at window controls:

1. Make sure Windows 98 is running and you are at the Windows 98 desktop.
2. Start WordPad.

   TROUBLE? To start WordPad, click the Start button, point to Programs, point to Accessories, and then click WordPad.

3. On your screen, identify the controls labeled in Figure 1-17. Don't worry if your window fills the entire screen or is a different size. You'll learn to change window size shortly.

Figure 1-17 WORDPAD WINDOW CONTROLS

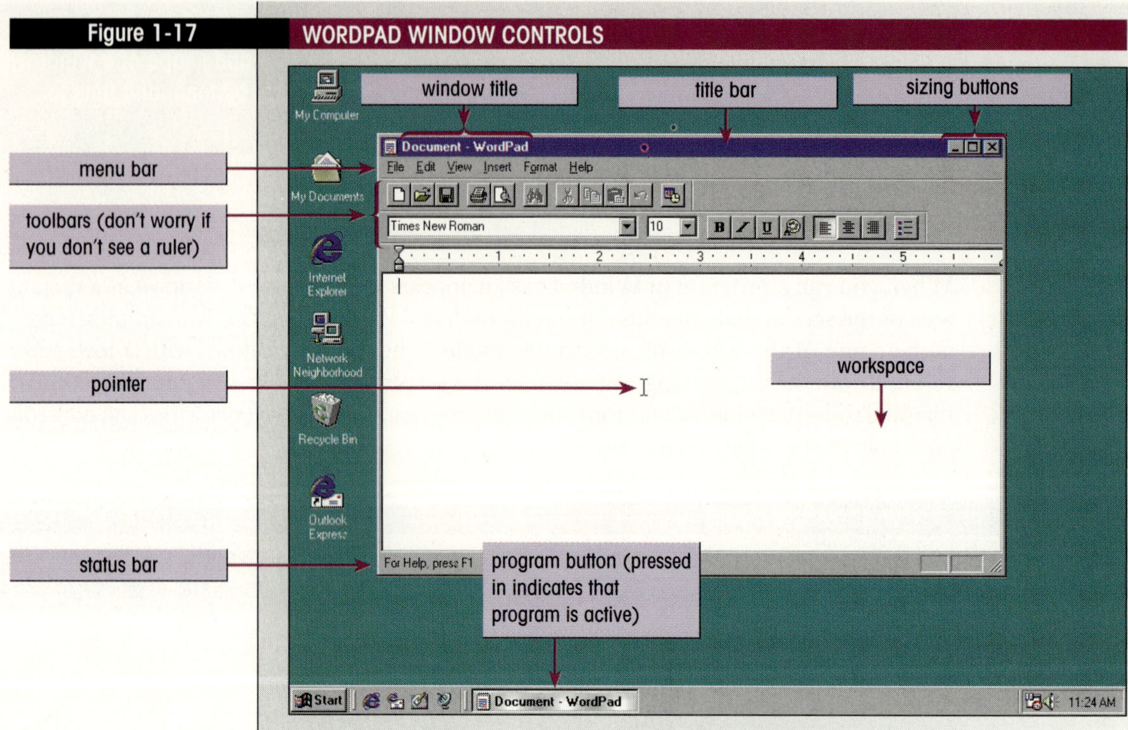

Manipulating a Window

There are three buttons located on the right side of the title bar. You are already familiar with the Close button. The Minimize button hides the window so that only its program button is visible on the taskbar. The other button either maximizes the window or restores it to a predefined size. Figure 1-18 shows how these buttons work.

Minimizing a Window

The Minimize button hides a window so that only the button on the taskbar remains visible. You can use the Minimize button when you want to temporarily hide a window but keep the program running.

To minimize the WordPad window:

1. Click the **Minimize** button. The WordPad window shrinks so that only the Document - WordPad button on the taskbar is visible.

   TROUBLE? If you accidentally clicked the Close button and closed the window, use the Start button to start WordPad again.

Figure 1-18 WINDOW BUTTONS

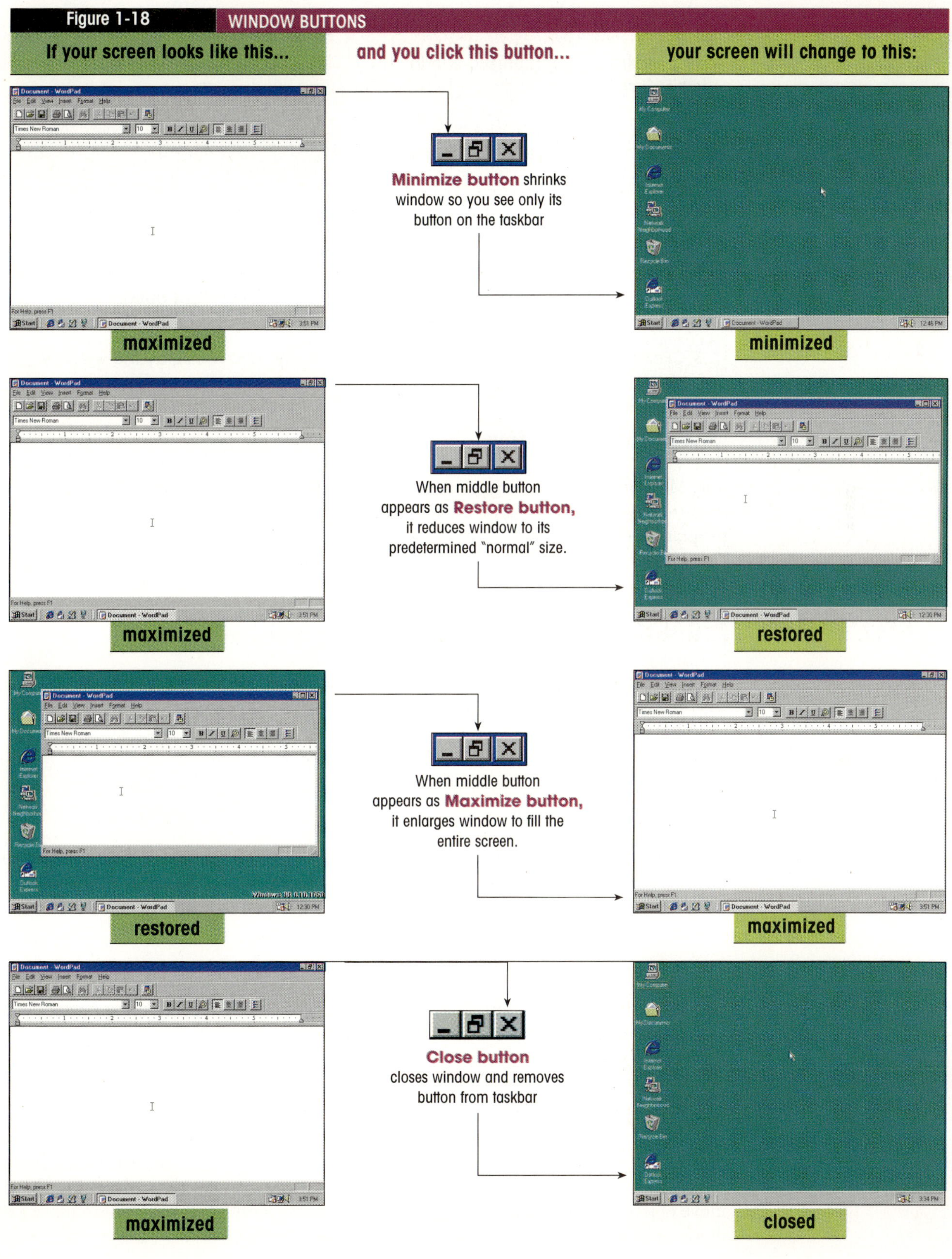

Redisplaying a Window

You can redisplay a minimized window by clicking the program's button on the taskbar. When you redisplay a window, it becomes the active window.

To redisplay the WordPad window:

1. Click the **Document - WordPad** button on the taskbar. The WordPad window is restored to its previous size. The Document - WordPad button looks pushed in as a visual clue that WordPad is now the active window.
2. The taskbar button provides another means of switching a window between its minimized and active state: click the **Document - WordPad** button on the taskbar again to minimize the window.
3. Click the **Document - WordPad** button once more to redisplay the window.

Maximizing a Window

The Maximize button enlarges a window so that it fills the entire screen. You will probably do most of your work using maximized windows because they allow you to see more of your program and data.

To maximize the WordPad window:

1. Click the **Maximize** button on the WordPad title bar.

   TROUBLE? If the window is already maximized, it will fill the entire screen, and the Maximize button won't appear. Instead, you'll see the Restore button. Skip Step 1.

Restoring a Window

The Restore button reduces the window so it is smaller than the entire screen. This is useful if you want to see more than one window at a time. Also, because of its smaller size, you can drag the window to another location on the screen or change its dimensions.

To restore a window:

1. Click the **Restore** button on the WordPad title bar. Notice that once a window is restored, changes to the Maximize button.

Moving a Window

You can use the mouse to move a window to a new position on the screen. When you hold down the mouse button while moving the mouse, you are said to be **dragging**. You can move objects on the screen by dragging them to a new location. If you want to move a window, you drag its title bar. You cannot move a maximized window.

To drag the WordPad window to a new location:

1. Position the mouse pointer on the WordPad window title bar.
2. While you hold down the left mouse button, move the mouse to drag the window. A rectangle representing the window moves as you move the mouse.
3. Position the rectangle anywhere on the screen, then release the left mouse button. The WordPad window appears in the new location.
4. Now drag the WordPad window to the upper-left corner of the screen.

Changing the Size of a Window

You can also use the mouse to change the size of a window. Notice the sizing handle at the lower-right corner of the window. The **sizing handle** provides a visible control for changing the size of a window.

To change the size of the WordPad window:

1. Position the pointer over the sizing handle . The pointer changes to a diagonal arrow ↘.
2. While holding down the mouse button, drag the sizing handle down and to the right.
3. Release the mouse button. Now the window is larger.
4. Practice using the sizing handle to make the WordPad window larger or smaller, and then maximize the WordPad window.

You can also drag the window borders left, right, up, or down to change a window's size.

Using Program Menus

Most Windows programs use menus to provide an easy way for you to select program commands. The menu bar is typically located at the top of the program window and shows the titles of menus such as File, Edit, and Help.

Windows menus are relatively standardized—most Windows programs include similar menu options. It's easy to learn new programs, because you can make a pretty good guess about which menu contains the command you want.

Selecting Commands from a Menu

When you click any menu title, choices for that menu appear below the menu bar. These choices are referred to as **menu options** or **commands**. To select a menu option, you click it. For example, the File menu is a standard feature in most Windows programs and contains the options typically related to working with a file: creating, opening, saving, and printing a file or document.

To select the Print Preview menu option from the File menu:

1. Click **File** in the WordPad menu bar to display the File menu. See Figure 1-19.

   TROUBLE? If you open a menu but decide not to select any of the menu options, you can close the menu by clicking its title again.

Figure 1-19 FILE MENU

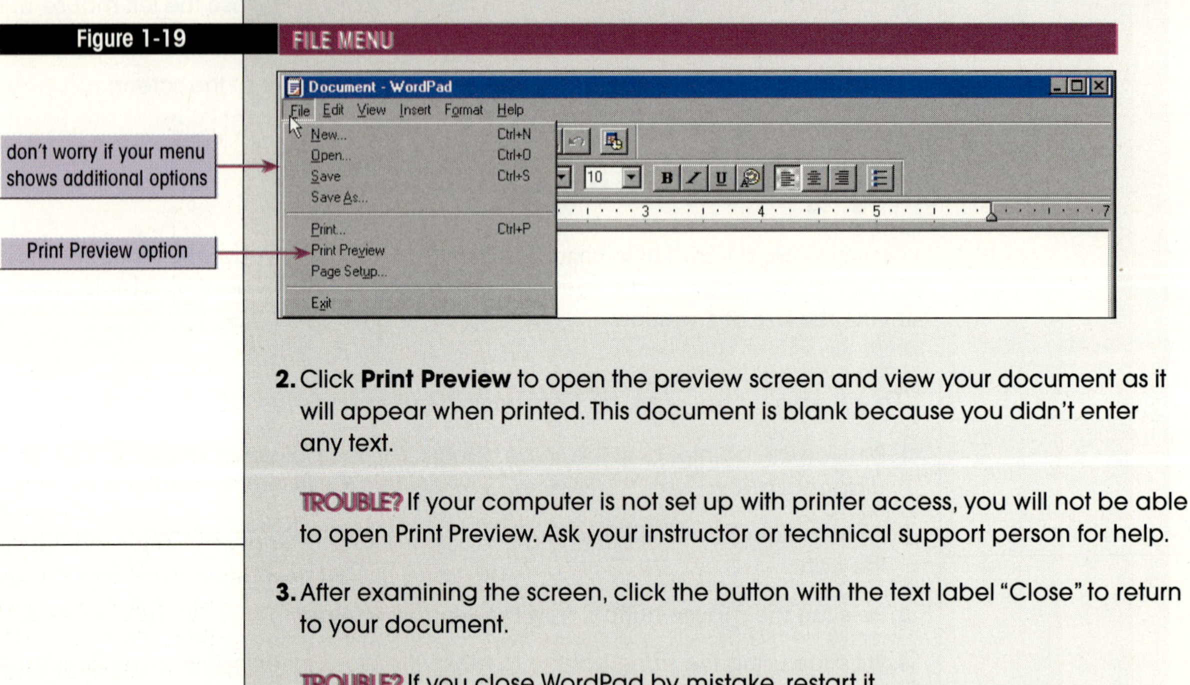

2. Click **Print Preview** to open the preview screen and view your document as it will appear when printed. This document is blank because you didn't enter any text.

   TROUBLE? If your computer is not set up with printer access, you will not be able to open Print Preview. Ask your instructor or technical support person for help.

3. After examining the screen, click the button with the text label "Close" to return to your document.

   TROUBLE? If you close WordPad by mistake, restart it.

Not all menu options immediately carry out an action—some show submenus or ask you for more information about what you want to do. The menu gives you hints about what to expect when you select an option. These hints are sometimes referred to as **menu conventions**. Figure 1-20 describes the Windows 98 menu conventions.

Figure 1-20 MENU CONVENTIONS

CONVENTION	DESCRIPTION
Check mark	Indicates a toggle, or "on-off" switch (like a light switch) that is either checked (turned on) or not checked (turned off)
Ellipsis	Three dots that indicate you must make additional selections after you select that option. Options without dots do not require additional choices—they take effect as soon as you click them. If an option is followed by an ellipsis, a dialog box opens that allows you to enter specifications for how you want a task carried out
Triangular arrow	Indicates presence of a submenu. When you point at a menu option that has a triangular arrow, a submenu automatically appears
Grayed-out option	Option that is not available. For example, a graphics program might display the Text Toolbar option in gray if there is no text in the graphic to work with
Keyboard shortcut	A key or combination of keys that you can press to activate the menu option without actually opening the menu

Figure 1-21 shows examples of these menu conventions.

Figure 1-21 EXAMPLES OF MENU CONVENTIONS

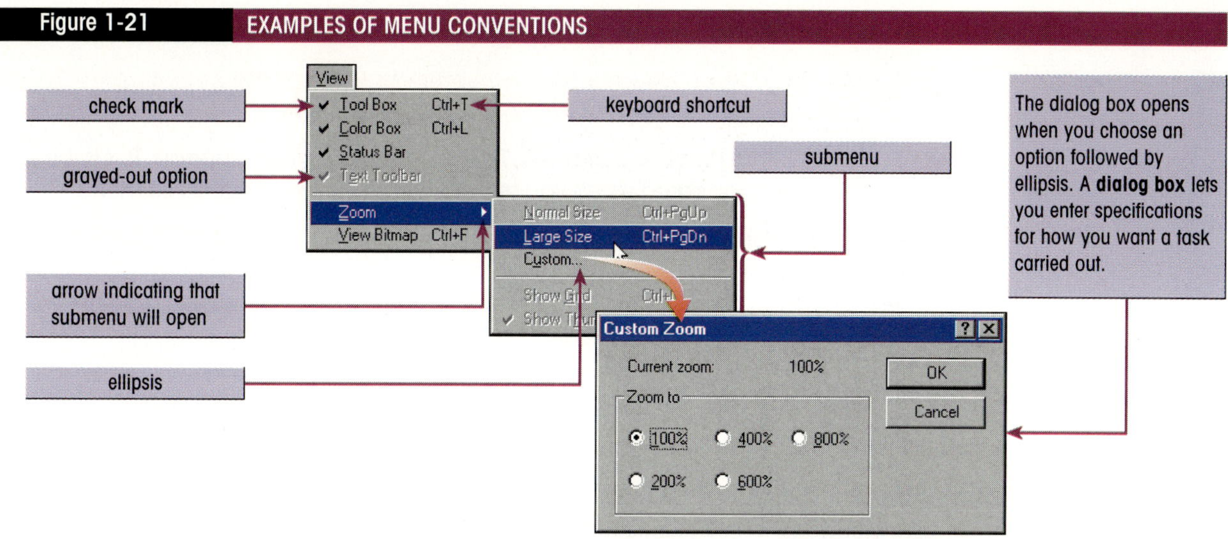

Using Toolbars

A toolbar, as you've seen, contains buttons that provide quick access to important commands. Although you can usually perform all program commands using menus, the toolbar provides convenient one-click access to frequently used commands. For most Windows 98 functions, there is usually more than one way to accomplish a task. To simplify your introduction to Windows 98 in this tutorial, we will usually show you only one method for performing a task. As you become more accomplished at using Windows 98, you can explore alternate methods.

In Session 1.1 you learned that Windows 98 programs include ToolTips, which indicate the purpose and function of a tool. Now is a good time to explore the WordPad toolbar buttons by looking at their ToolTips.

To find out a toolbar button's function:

1. Position the pointer over any button on the toolbar, such as the Print Preview button. After a short pause, the name of the button appears in a box near the button, and a description of the button appears in the status bar just above the Start button. See Figure 1-22.

Figure 1-22 TOOLBAR BUTTON AIDS

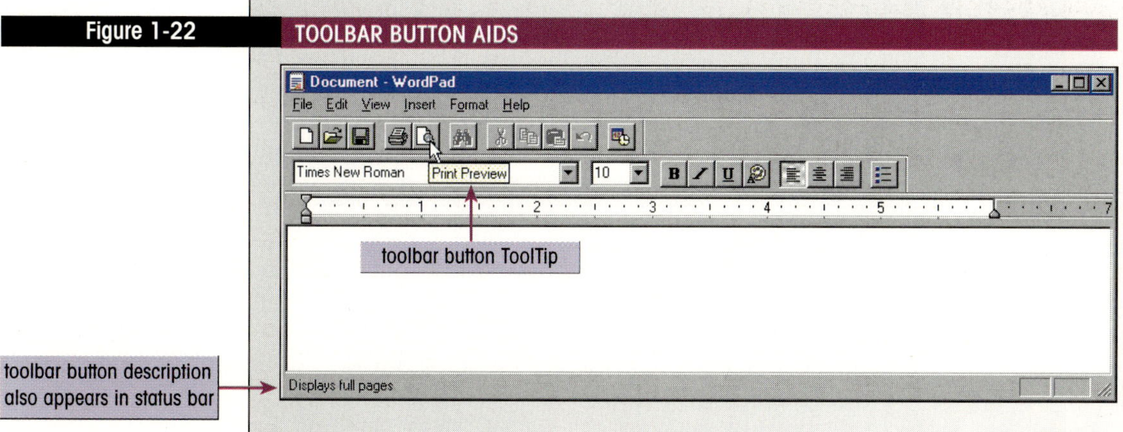

2. Move the pointer to each button on the toolbar to see its name and purpose.

You select a toolbar button by clicking it.

To select the Print Preview toolbar button:

1. Click the **Print Preview** button. The Print Preview screen appears. This is the same screen that appeared when you selected Print Preview from the File menu.
2. After examining the screen, click the button with the text label "Close" to return to your document.

Using List Boxes and Scroll Bars

As you might guess from the name, a **list box** displays a list of choices. In WordPad, date and time formats are shown in the Date/Time list box. List box controls usually include arrow buttons, a scroll bar, and a scroll box, as shown in Figure 1-23.

To use the Date/Time list box:

1. Click the **Date/Time** button to display the Date and Time dialog box. See Figure 1-23.

Figure 1-23 LIST BOX

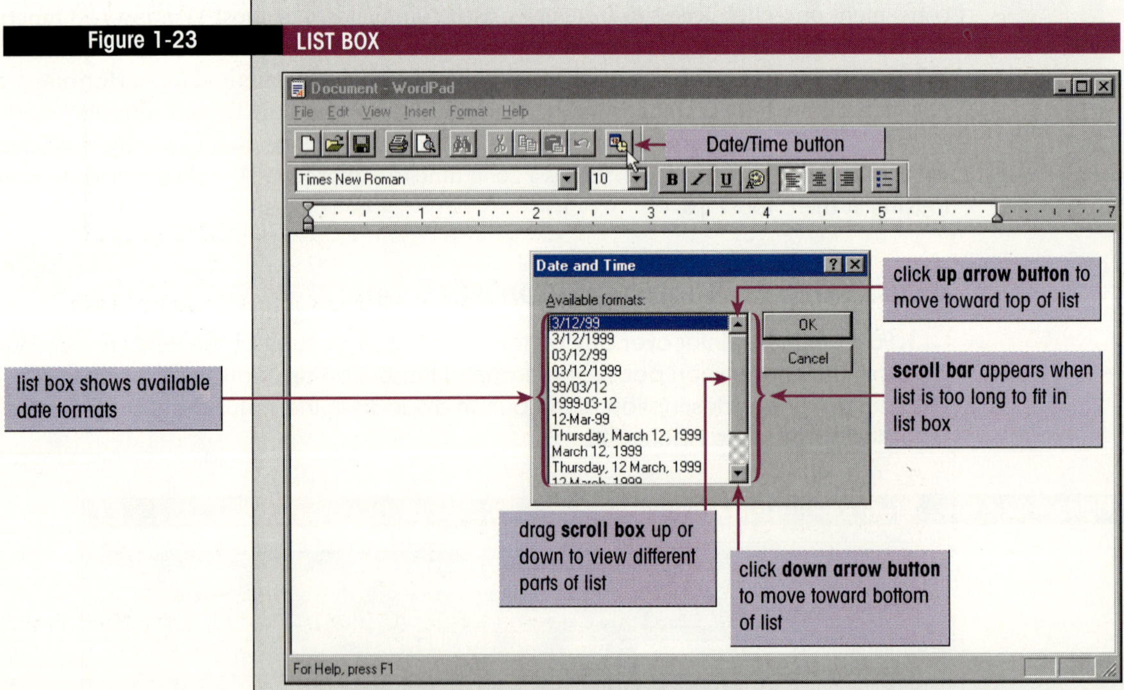

2. To scroll down the list, click the **down arrow** button. See Figure 1-23.
3. Find the scroll box on your screen. See Figure 1-23.
4. Drag the **scroll box** to the top of the scroll bar. Notice how the list scrolls back to the beginning.

TROUBLE? You learned how to drag when you learned to move a window. To drag the scroll box up, point to the scroll box, press and hold down the mouse button, and then move the mouse up.

5. Find a date format similar to "March 12, 1999." Click that date format to select it.

6. Click the **OK** button to close the Date and Time dialog box. This inserts the current date in your document.

You can access some list boxes directly from the toolbar. When a list box is on the toolbar, only the current option appears in the list box. A **list arrow** appears on the right of the box that you can click to view additional options.

To use the Font Size list box:

1. Click the **list arrow** shown in Figure 1-24.

Figure 1-24 FONT SIZE LIST ARROW

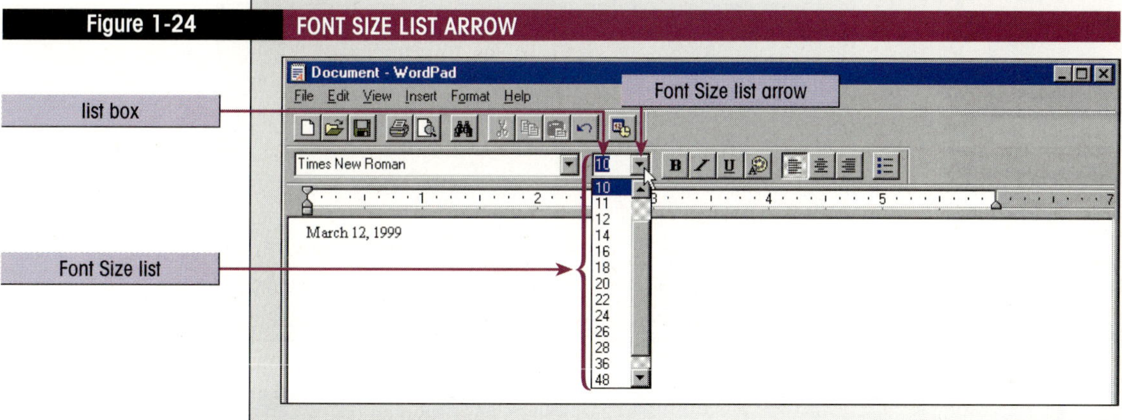

2. Click **18**. The list disappears, and the font size you selected appears in the list box.

3. Type a few characters to test the new font size.

4. Click the **Font Size** list arrow again.

5. Click **12**.

6. Type a few characters to test this type size.

7. Click the **Close** button to close WordPad.

8. When you see the message "Save changes to Document?" click the **No** button.

Using Dialog Box Controls

Recall that when you select a menu option or button followed by an ellipsis, a dialog box opens that allows you to provide more information about how a program should carry out a task. Some dialog boxes group different kinds of information into bordered rectangular areas called **panes**. Within these panes, you will usually find tabs, option buttons, check boxes, and other controls that the program uses to collect information about how you want it to perform a task. Figure 1-25 describes common dialog box controls.

Figure 1-25 DIALOG BOX CONTROLS

CONTROL	DESCRIPTION
Tabs	Modeled after the tabs on file folders, tab controls are often used as containers for other Windows 98 controls such as list boxes, radio buttons, and check boxes. Click the appropriate tab to view different pages of information or choices.
Option buttons	Also called **radio buttons**, option buttons allow you to select a single option from among one or more options.
Check boxes	Click a check box to select or deselect it; when it is selected, a check mark appears, indicating that the option is turned on; when deselected, the check box is blank and the option is off. When check boxes appear in groups, you can select or deselect as many as you want; they are not mutually exclusive, as option buttons are.
Spin boxes	Allow you to scroll easily through a set of numbers to choose the setting you want
Text boxes	Boxes into which you type additional information

Figure 1-26 displays examples of these controls.

Figure 1-26 EXAMPLES OF DIALOG BOX CONTROLS

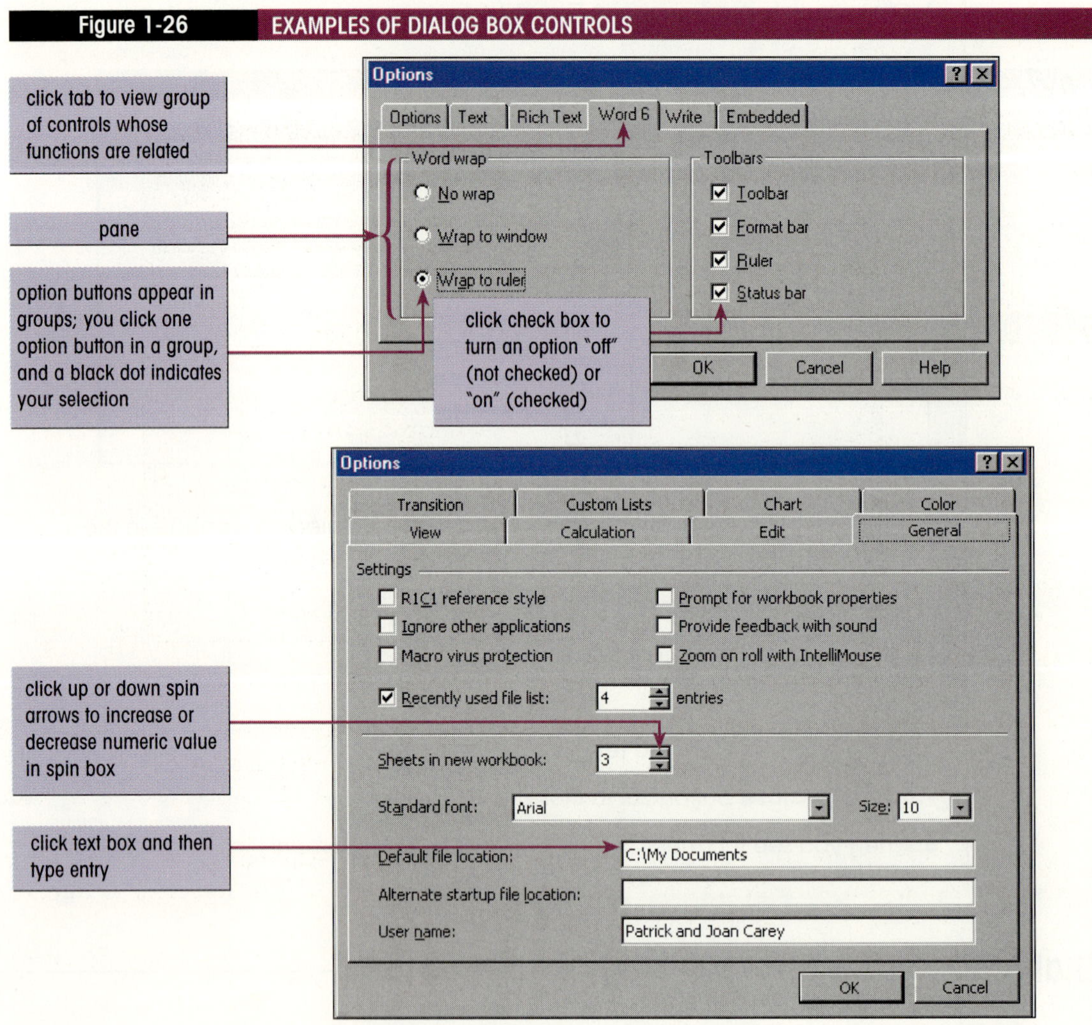

Using Help

Windows 98 **Help** provides on-screen information about the program you are using. Help for the Windows 98 operating system is available by clicking the Start button on the taskbar, then selecting Help from the Start menu. If you want Help for a program, such as WordPad, you must first start the program, then click Help on the menu bar.

When you start Help, a Windows Help window opens, which gives you access to help files stored on your computer as well as help information stored on Microsoft's Web site. If you are not connected to the Web, you only have access to the help files stored on your computer.

To start Windows 98 Help:

1. Click the **Start** button.
2. Click **Help**. The Windows Help window opens to the Contents tab. See Figure 1-27.

TROUBLE? If the Contents tab is not in front, click the Contents tab to view Help contents.

Figure 1-27 WINDOWS HELP WINDOW

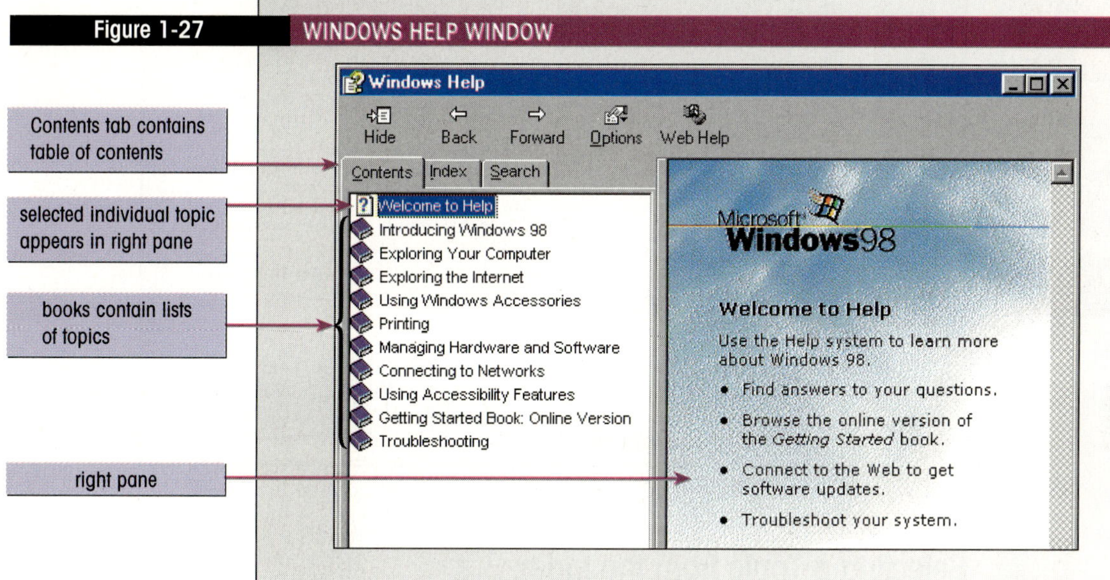

Help uses tabs for the three sections of Help: Contents, Index, and Search. The **Contents tab** groups Help topics into a series of books. You select a book by clicking it. The book opens, and a list of related topics appears from which you can choose. Individual topics are designated with the icon.

The **Index tab** displays an alphabetical list of all the Help topics from which you can choose. The **Search tab** allows you to search the entire set of Help topics for all topics that contain a word or words you specify.

Viewing Topics from the Contents Tab

You've already opened two of the Windows accessories, Paint and WordPad. Suppose you're wondering about the other accessory programs. You can use the Contents tab to find more information on a specific topic.

To use the Contents tab:

1. Click the **Using Windows Accessories** book icon. A list of topics and related books appears below the book title. You decide to explore entertainment accessories.
2. Click the **Entertainment** book icon.
3. Click the **CD Player** topic icon. Information about the CD Player accessory appears in the right pane, explaining how you can use the CD-ROM drive (if you have one) on your computer to play your favorite music CDs. See Figure 1-28.

Figure 1-28 LOCATING INFORMATION ABOUT CD PLAYER ACCESSORY

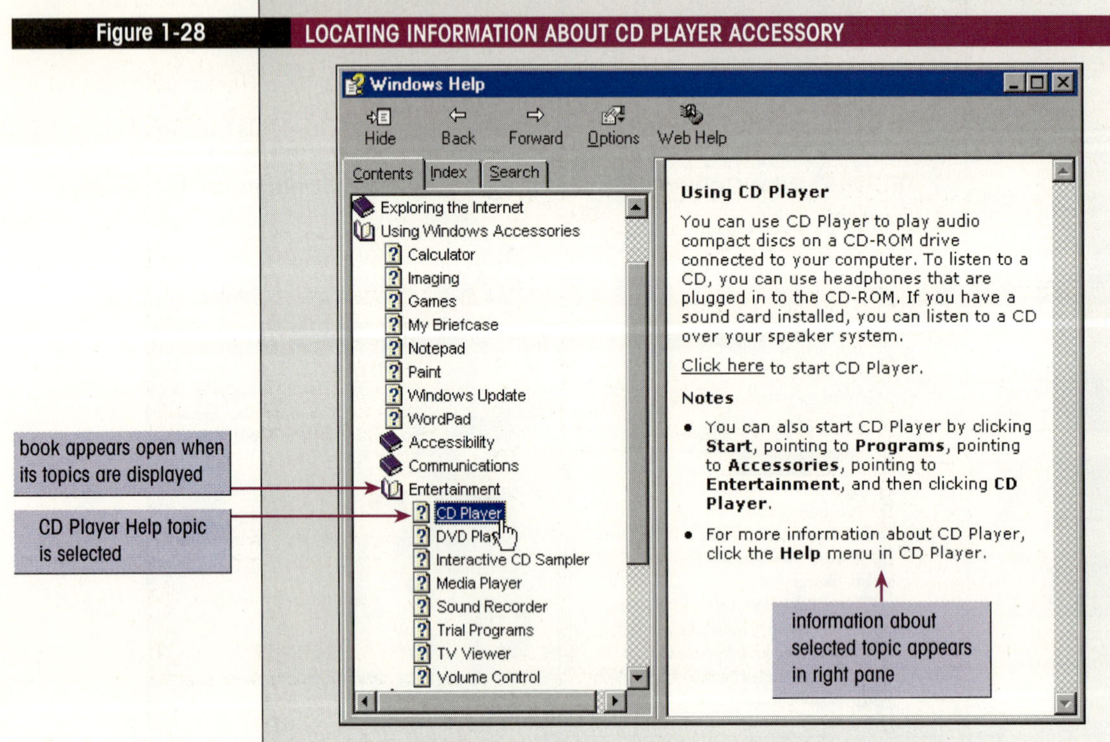

Selecting a Topic from the Index

The Index tab allows you to jump to a Help topic by selecting a topic from an indexed list. For example, you can use the Index tab to learn how to arrange the open windows on your desktop.

To find a Help topic using the Index tab:

1. Click the **Index** tab. A long list of indexed Help topics appears.

   TROUBLE? If this is the first time you've used Help on your computer, Windows 98 needs to set up the Index. This takes just a few moments. Wait until you see the list of index entries in the left pane, and then proceed to Step 2.

2. Drag the scroll box down to view additional topics.
3. You can quickly jump to any part of the list by typing the first few characters of a word or phrase in the box above the Index list. Click the box and then type **desktop** to display topics related to the Windows 98 desktop.

4. Click the topic **arranging windows on** and then click the **Display** button. When there is just one topic, it appears immediately in the right pane; otherwise, the Topics Found window opens, listing all topics indexed under the entry you're interested in. In this case, there are two choices.

5. Click **To minimize all open windows**, and then click the **Display** button. The information you requested appears in the right pane. See Figure 1-29. Notice in this topic that there is an underlined word: taskbar. You can click underlined words to view definitions or additional information.

Figure 1-29 USING THE INDEX TO LOCATE INFORMATION

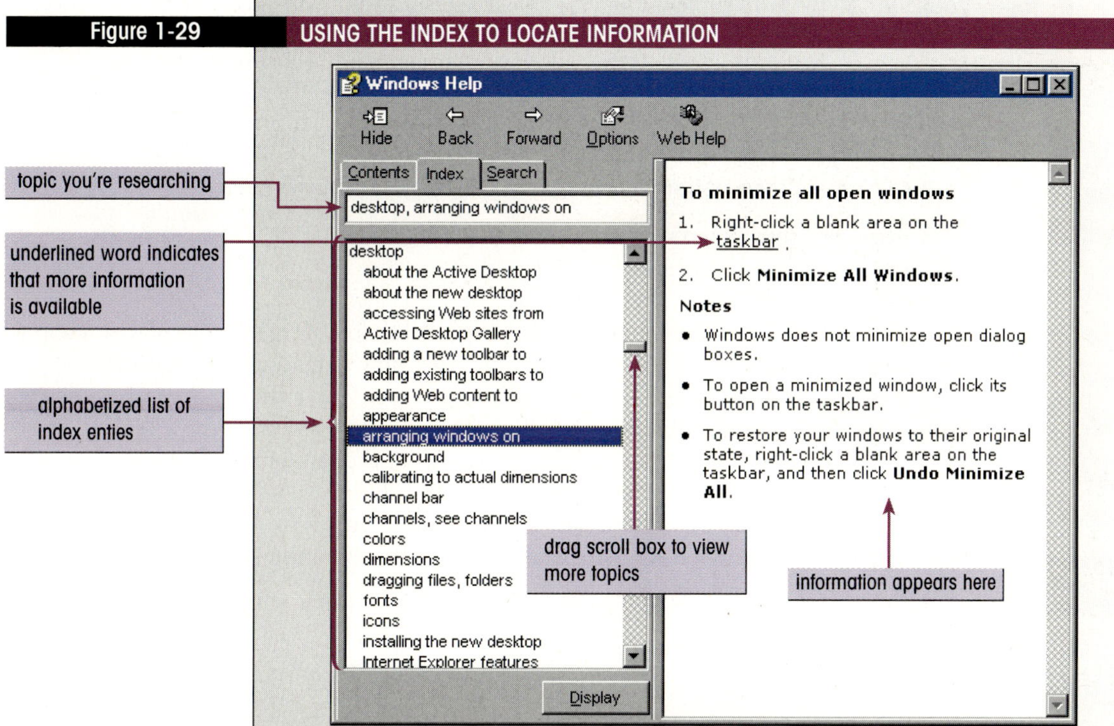

6. Click **taskbar**. A small box appears that defines the term "taskbar." See Figure 1-30.

Figure 1-30 VIEWING ADDITIONAL INFORMATION

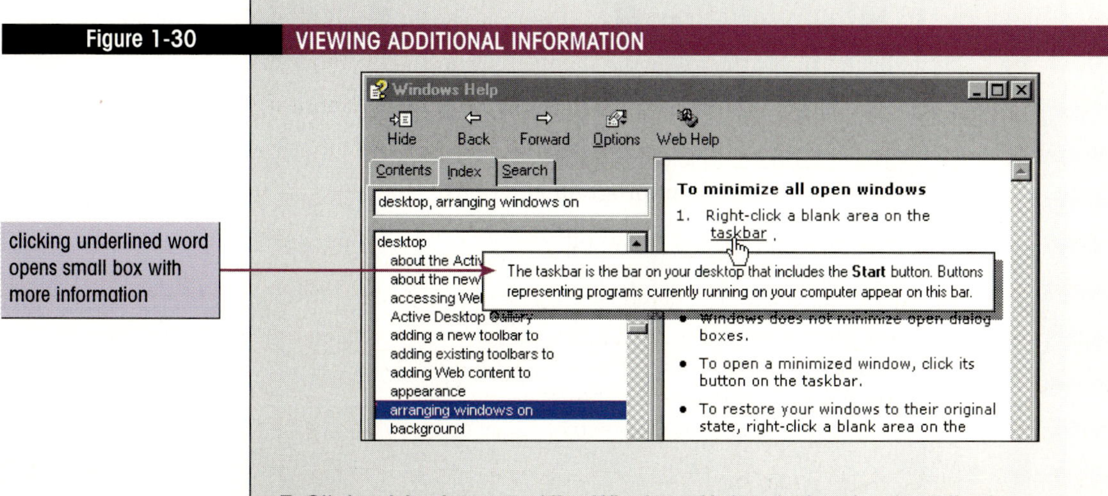

7. Click a blank area of the Windows Help window to close the box.

The third tab, the Search tab, works similarly to the Index tab, except that you type a word, and then the Help system searches for topics containing that word. You'll get a chance to experiment with the Search tab in the Tutorial Assignments.

Returning to a Previous Help Topic

You've looked at a few topics now. Suppose you want to return to the one you just saw. The Help window includes a toolbar of buttons that help you navigate the Help system. One of these buttons is the **Back** button, which returns you to topics you've already viewed. Try returning to the help topic on playing music CDs on your CD-ROM drive.

To return to a help topic:

1. Click the **Back** button. The Using CD Player topic appears.
2. Click the **Close** button ☒ to close the Windows Help window.
3. Log off or shut down Windows 98, depending on your lab's requirements.

Now that you know how Windows 98 Help works, don't forget to use it! Use Help when you need to perform a new task or when you forget how to complete a procedure.

You've finished the tutorial, and as you shut down Windows 98, Steve Laslow returns from class. You take a moment to tell him all you've learned: you know how to start and close programs and how to use multiple programs at the same time. You have learned how to work with windows and the controls they employ. Finally, you've learned how to get help when you need it. Steve congratulates you and comments that you are well on your way to mastering the fundamentals of using the Windows 98 operating system.

QUICK CHECK

1. What is the difference between the title bar and a toolbar?
2. Provide the name and purpose of each button:

   a. [minimize button] b. [maximize button] c. [restore button] d. ☒

3. Explain each of the following menu conventions:

   a. Ellipsis... b. Grayed-out c. ▸ d. ✔

4. A(n) ____________ consists of a group of buttons, each of which provides one-click access to important program functions.
5. What is the purpose of the scrollbar?
6. Option buttons allow you to select ____________ option(s) at a time.
7. It is a good idea to use ____________ when you need to learn how to perform new tasks.

TUTORIAL ASSIGNMENT

1. **Running Two Programs and Switching Between Them** In this tutorial you learned how to run more than one program at a time, using WordPad and Paint. You can run other programs at the same time, too. Complete the following steps and write out your answers to questions b through f:
   a. Start the computer. Enter your username and password if prompted to do so.
   b. Click the Start button. How many menu options are on the Start menu?
   c. Run the Calculator program located on the Accessories menu. How many program buttons are now on the taskbar (don't count toolbar buttons or items in the tray)?
   d. Run the Paint program and maximize the Paint window. How many programs are running now?
   e. Switch to Calculator. What are two visual clues that tell you that Calculator is the active program?
   f. Multiply 576 by 1457 using the Calculator accessory. What is the result?
   g. Close Calculator, then close Paint.

Explore

2. **WordPad Help** In Tutorial 1 you learned how to use Windows 98 Help. Just about every Windows 98 program has a help feature. Many computer users can learn to use a program just by using Help. To use Help, you start the program, then click the Help menu at the top of the screen. Try using WordPad Help:
   a. Start WordPad.
   b. Click Help on the WordPad menu bar, and then click Help Topics.
   c. Using WordPad Help, write out your answers to questions 1 through 4.
      1. How do you create a bulleted list?
      2. How do you set the margins in a document?
      3. How do you undo a mistake?
      4. How do you change the font style of a block of text?
   d. Close WordPad.

Explore

3. **The Search Tab** In addition to the Contents and Index tabs you worked with in this tutorial, Windows 98 Help also includes a Search tab. You may have heard that Windows 98 makes it possible to view television programs on your computer. You could browse through the Contents tab, although you might not know where to look to find information about television. You could also use the Index tab to search through the indexed entry. Or you could use the Search tab to find all Help topics that mention television.
   a. Start Windows 98 Help and use the Index tab to find information about television. How many topics are listed? What is their primary subject matter?
   b. Now use the Search tab to find information about television. Type "television" into the box on the Search tab, and then click the List Topics button.
   c. Write a paragraph comparing the two lists of topics. You don't have to view them all, but in your paragraph, indicate which tab seems to yield more information, and why. Close Help.

4. **Discover Windows 98** Windows 98 includes an online tour that helps you discover more about your computer and the Windows 98 operating system. You can use this tour to review what you learned in this tutorial and to pick up some new tips for using Windows 98. Complete the following steps and write out your answers to questions d–j.
   a. Click the Start button, point to Programs, point to Accessories, point to System Tools, and then click Welcome to Windows. If an error message appears at any point or if you can't locate this menu option, Welcome to Windows is probably not loaded on your computer. You will not be able to complete this assignment unless you have the Windows 98 CD. Check with your instructor.
   b. Click Discover Windows 98.
   c. Click Computer Essentials and follow the instructions on the screen to step through the tour.
   d. What is the "brain" of your computer, according to the tour information?
   e. What two devices do you use to communicate with your computer?

f. What is the purpose of the ESC key?
g. What is double-clicking?
h. What is the purpose of the top section of the Start menu?
i. What is another term for "submenu"?
j. What function key opens the Help feature in most software?

PROJECTS

1. There are many types of pointing devices on the market today. Go to the library and research the types of devices that are available. Consider what devices are appropriate for these situations: desktop or laptop computers, connected or remote devices, and ergonomic or standard designs (look up the word "ergonomic").

   Use up-to-date computer books, trade computer magazines such as *PC Computing* and *PC Magazine*, or the Internet (if you know how) to locate information. Your instructor might suggest specific resources you can use. Write a one-page report describing the types of devices available, the differing needs of users, special features that make pointing devices more useful, price comparisons, and finally, an indication of what you would choose if you needed to buy a pointing device.

2. Using the resources available to you, either through your library or the Internet (if you know how), locate information about the release of Windows 98. Computing trade magazines are an excellent source of information about software. Read several articles about Windows 98 and then write a one-page essay that discusses the features that seem most important to the people who have evaluated the software. If you find reviews of the software, mention the features that reviewers had the strongest reaction to, pro or con.

3. **Upgrading** is the process of placing a more recent version of a product onto your computer. When Windows 98 first came out, people had to decide whether or not they wanted to upgrade their computers to Windows 98. Interview several people you know (at least three) who are well-informed Windows computer users. Ask them whether they are using Windows 98 or an older version of Windows. If they are using an older version, ask why they have chosen not to upgrade. If they are using Windows 98, ask them why they chose to upgrade. Ask such questions as:

   a. What features convinced you to upgrade or made you decide to wait?
   b. What role did the price of the upgrade play?
   c. Would you have had (or did you have) to purchase new hardware to make the upgrade? How did this affect your decision?
   d. If you did upgrade, are you happy with that decision? If you didn't, do you intend to upgrade in the near future? Why, or why not?

   Write a single-page essay summarizing what you learned from these interviews about making the decision to upgrade.

4. Choose a topic you'd like to research using the Windows 98 online Help system. Look for information on your topic using all three tabs: the Contents tab, the Index tab, and the Search tab. Once you've found all the information you can, compare the three methods (Contents, Index, Search) of looking for information. Write a paragraph that discusses which tab proved the most useful. Did you reach the same information topics using all three methods? In a second paragraph, summarize what you learned about your topic. Finally, in a third paragraph, indicate under what circumstances you'd use which tab.

LAB ASSIGNMENTS

Using a Keyboard To become an effective computer user, you must be familiar with your primary input device—the keyboard. See the Read This Before You Begin page for information on installing and starting the lab.

1. The Steps for the Using a Keyboard Lab provide you with a structured introduction to the keyboard layout and the function of special computer keys. Click the Steps button and begin the Steps. As you work through the Steps, answer all of the Quick Check questions that appear. When you complete the Steps, you will see a Summary Report that summarizes your performance on the Quick Checks. Follow the directions on the screen to print the Summary Report.

2. In Explore, start the typing tutor. You can develop your typing skills using the typing tutor in Explore. Take the typing test and print out your results.

3. In Explore, try to improve your typing speed by 10 words per minute. For example, if you currently type 20 words per minute, your goal will be 30 words per minute. Practice each typing lesson until you see a message that indicates that you can proceed to the next lesson. Create a Practice Record, as shown here, to keep track of how much you practice. When you have reached your goal, print out the results of a typing test to verify your results.

   Practice Record

   Name:

   Section:

Start Date:	Start Typing Speed:	wpm
End Date:	End Typing Speed:	wpm
Lesson #:	Date Practiced/Time Practiced	

Using a Mouse A mouse is a standard input device on most of today's computers. You need to know how to use a mouse to manipulate graphical user interfaces and to use the rest of the Labs. See the Read This Before You Begin page for information on installing and starting the lab.

1. The Steps for the Using a Mouse Lab show you how to click, double-click, and drag objects using the mouse. Click the Steps button and begin the Steps. As you work through the Steps, answer all of the Quick Check questions that appear. When you complete the Steps, you will see a Summary Report that summarizes your performance on the Quick Checks. Follow the directions on the screen to print the Summary Report.

2. In Explore, create a poster, to demonstrate your ability to use a mouse and to control a Windows program. To create a poster for an upcoming sports event, select a graphic, type the caption for the poster, then select a font, font styles, and a border. Print your completed poster.

QUICK CHECK ANSWERS

Session 1.1

1. The taskbar contains buttons that give you access to tools and programs.
2. multitasking
3. Start menu
4. Lift the mouse up and move it to the right.
5. Its button appears on the taskbar.
6. To conserve computer resources such as memory.
7. To ensure you don't lose data and damage your files.

Session 1.2

1. The title bar identifies the window and contains window controls; toolbars contain buttons that provide you with shortcuts to common menu commands.
2. a. Minimize button shrinks window so you see button on taskbar
   b. Maximize button enlarges window to fill entire screen
   c. Restore button reduces window to predetermined size
   d. Close button closes window and removes button from taskbar
3. a. ellipsis indicates a dialog box will open
   b. grayed-out indicates option is not currently available
   c. arrow indicates a submenu will open
   d. check mark indicates a toggle option
4. toolbar
5. Scrollbars appear when the contents of a box or window are too long to fit; you drag the scroll box to view different parts of the contents.
6. one
7. online Help

OBJECTIVES

In this tutorial you will:

- Format a disk
- Enter, select, insert, and delete text
- Create and save a file
- Open, edit, and print a file
- Switch to Web style
- Create a Student Disk
- View the list of files on your disk and change view options
- Move, copy, delete, and rename a file
- Navigate Explorer windows
- Make a copy of your Student Disk

LABS

WORKING WITH FILES

Creating, Saving, and Managing Files

CASE

Distance Education

You recently purchased a computer in order to gain new skills and stay competitive in the job market. Your friend Shannon suggests that you broaden your horizons by enrolling in a few distance education courses. **Distance education**, Shannon explains, is formalized learning that typically takes place using a computer, replacing normal classroom interaction with modern communications technology. Many distance education courses take advantage of the **Internet**, a vast structure of millions of computers located all over the world that are connected together so that they are able to share information. The **World Wide Web**, usually called the **Web**, is a popular service on the Internet that makes information readily accesssible. Educators can make their course material available on the Web.

Windows 98 makes it possible for your computer to display content in a way that is similar to the way it appears on the Web, and Shannon is eager to show you how. She suggests, however, that first you should get more comfortable with your computer—especially using programs and files. Shannon points out that most of the software installed on your computer was created especially for the Windows 98 operating system. This software is referred to as **Windows 98 applications** or **Windows 98 programs**. You can use software designed for older operating systems, but Windows 98 applications take better advantage of the features of the Windows 98 operating system.

You typically use Windows 98 applications to create files. A **file**, often referred to as a **document**, is a collection of data that has a name and is stored in a computer. Once you create a file, you can open it, edit its contents, print it, and save it again—usually using the same application program you used to create it.

Shannon suggests that you become familiar with how to perform these tasks in Windows 98 applications. Then she'll show you how to set up your computer so it incorporates the look and feel of the Web. Finally, you'll spend time learning how to organize your files.

SESSION 2.1

In Session 2.1 you will learn how to format a disk so it can store files. You will create, save, open, and print a file. You will find out how the insertion point differs from the mouse pointer, and you will learn the basic skills for Windows 98 text entry, such as inserting, deleting, and selecting. *For the steps of this tutorial you will need two blank 3½-inch disks.*

Formatting a Disk

Before you can save files on a disk, the disk must be formatted. When the computer **formats** a disk, the magnetic particles on the disk surface are arranged so data can be stored on the disk. Today, many disks are sold preformatted and can be used right out of the box. However, if you purchase an unformatted disk, or if you have an old disk you want to completely erase and reuse, you can format the disk using the Windows 98 Format command. This command is available through the **My Computer window**, a window that gives you access to the objects on your computer. You open My Computer by using its icon on the desktop. You'll learn more about the My Computer window later in this tutorial.

The following steps tell you how to format a 3½-inch high-density disk using drive A. Your instructor will tell you how to revise the instructions given in these steps if the procedure is different for your lab equipment.

Make sure you are using a blank disk before you perform these steps.

To format a disk:

1. Start Windows 98, if necessary.
2. Write your name on the label of a 3½-inch disk and insert your disk in drive A. See Figure 2-1.

Figure 2-1 INSERTING A DISK INTO A DISK DRIVE

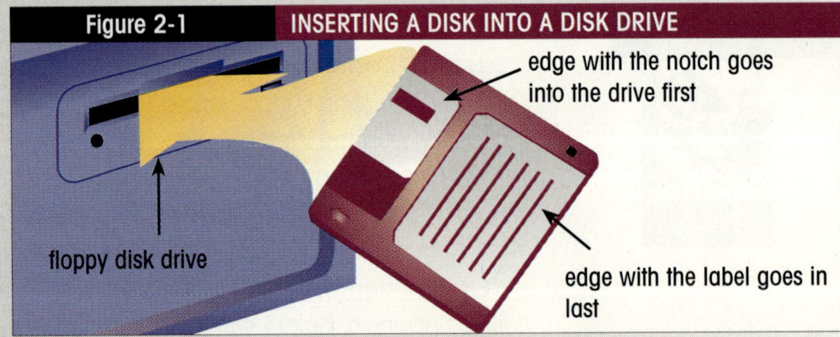

TROUBLE? If your disk does not fit in drive A, put it in drive B and substitute drive B for drive A in all of the steps for the rest of the tutorial.

3. Click the **My Computer** icon on the desktop. The icon is selected. Figure 2-2 shows the location of this icon on your desktop.

TROUBLE? If the My Computer window opens, skip Step 4. Your computer is using different settings, which you'll learn to change in Session 2.2.

4. Press **Enter** to open the My Computer window. See Figure 2-2 (don't worry if your window opens maximized).

TROUBLE? If you see a list instead of icons like those in Figure 2-2, click View, then click Large Icons. Don't worry if your toolbars don't exactly match those in Figure 2-2.

TROUBLE? If you see additional information or a graphic image on the left side of the My Computer window, Web view is enabled on your computer. Don't worry. You will learn how to enable and disable Web view in Session 2.2.

Figure 2-2 MY COMPUTER WINDOW

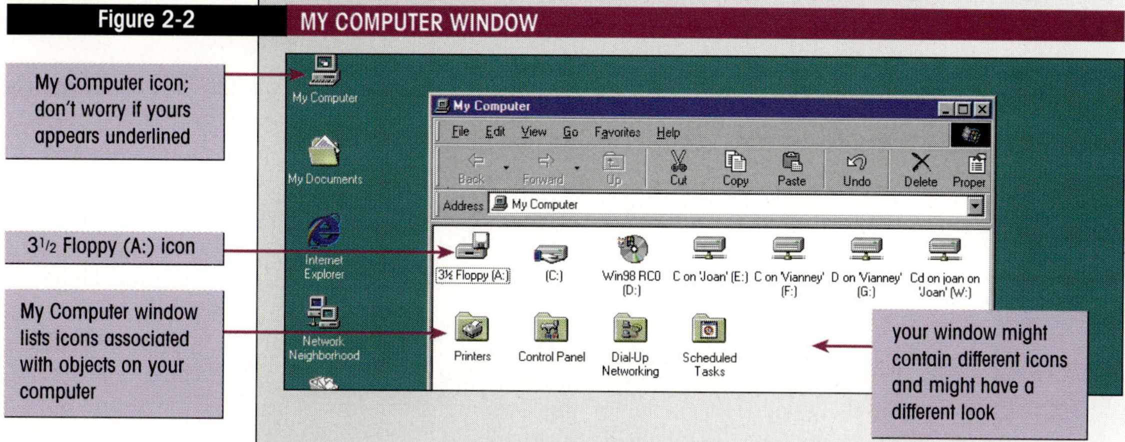

5. Right-click the **3½ Floppy (A:)** icon to open its shortcut menu.

6. Click **Format** on the shortcut menu. The Format dialog box opens.

7. Click the **Full** option button to perform a full format. Make sure the other dialog box settings on your screen match those in Figure 2-3.

Figure 2-3 FORMAT DIALOG BOX

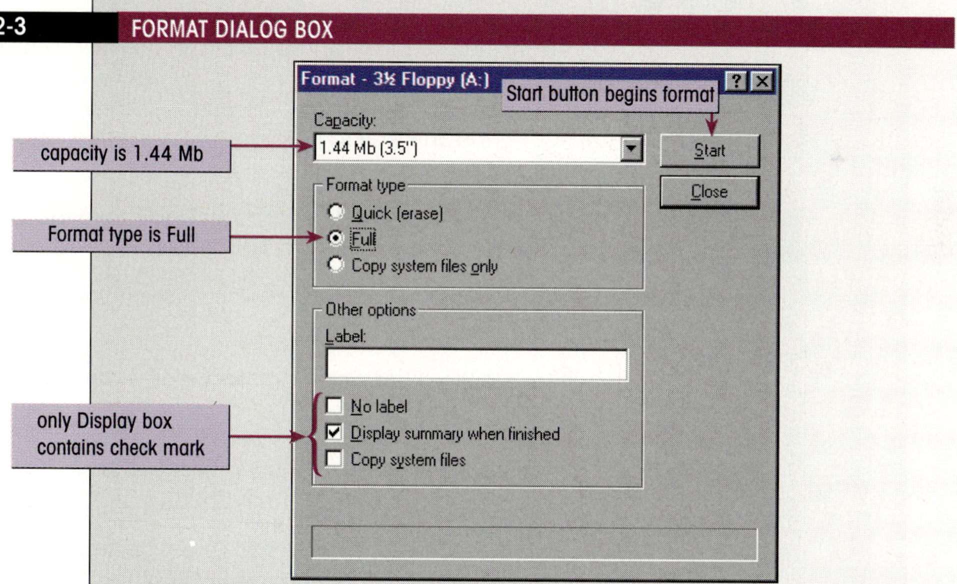

8. On the right side of the dialog box is a Start button. Click this **Start** button to begin formatting the disk. A series of blue boxes at the bottom of the Format window shows you how the format is progressing. When the format is complete, the Format Results dialog box appears.

9. Click the **Close** button, and then close any open windows on the desktop.

TROUBLE? To close the windows, click each Close button ☒.

Working with Text

To accomplish many computing tasks, you need to type text in documents and text boxes. Windows 98 facilitates basic text entry by providing a text-entry area, by showing you where your text will appear on the screen, by helping you move around on the screen, and by providing insert and delete functions.

When you type sentences of text, do not press the Enter key when you reach the right margin of the page. Most software contains a feature called **word wrap**, which automatically continues your text on the next line. Therefore, you should press Enter only when you have completed a paragraph.

If you type the wrong character, press the Backspace key to back up and delete the character. You can also use the Delete key. What's the difference between the Backspace and the Delete keys? The Backspace key deletes the character to the left, while the Delete key deletes the character to the right.

Now you will type some text using WordPad, to practice what you've learned about text entry. When you first start WordPad, notice the flashing vertical bar, called the **insertion point**, in the upper-left corner of the document window. The insertion point indicates where the characters you type will appear.

To type text in WordPad:

1. Start WordPad and locate the insertion point.

   TROUBLE? If the WordPad window does not fill the screen, click the Maximize button ☐.

   TROUBLE? If you can't find the insertion point, click in the WordPad workspace area.

2. Type your name, using the Shift key to type uppercase letters and using the Spacebar to type spaces, just as on a typewriter.
3. Press the **Enter** key to end the current paragraph and move the insertion point down to the next line.
4. As you type the following sentences, watch what happens when the insertion point reaches the right edge of the page:

   This is a sample typed in WordPad. See what happens when the insertion point reaches the right edge of the page.

   TROUBLE? If you make a mistake, delete the incorrect character(s) by pressing the Backspace key on your keyboard. Then type the correct character(s).

   TROUBLE? If your text doesn't wrap, your screen might be set up to display more information than the screen used for the figures in this tutorial. Type the sentences again until text wraps automatically.

The Insertion Point Versus the Pointer

The insertion point is not the same as the mouse pointer. When the mouse pointer is in the text-entry area, it is called the **I-beam pointer** and looks like I. Figure 2-4 explains the difference between the insertion point and the I-beam pointer.

Figure 2-4 THE INSERTION POINT VS. THE POINTER

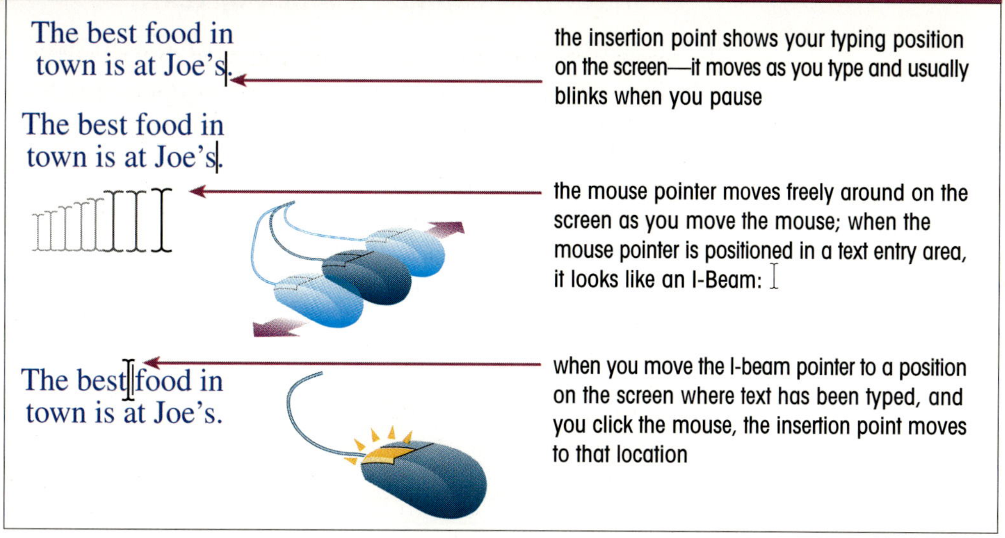

The best food in town is at Joe's.

the insertion point shows your typing position on the screen—it moves as you type and usually blinks when you pause

The best food in town is at Joe's.

the mouse pointer moves freely around on the screen as you move the mouse; when the mouse pointer is positioned in a text entry area, it looks like an I-Beam: I

The best food in town is at Joe's.

when you move the I-beam pointer to a position on the screen where text has been typed, and you click the mouse, the insertion point moves to that location

To enter text, you move the I-beam pointer to the location where you want to type, and then click. The insertion point jumps to the location you clicked and, depending on the program you are using, may blink to indicate the program is ready for you to type. When you enter text, the insertion point moves as you type.

To move the insertion point:

1. Check the locations of the insertion point and the I-beam pointer. The insertion point should be at the end of the sentence you typed in the last set of steps.

   TROUBLE? If you don't see the I-beam pointer, move your mouse until you see it.

2. Use the mouse to move the I-beam pointer to the word "sample," then click the mouse button. The insertion point jumps to the location of the I-beam pointer.
3. Move the I-beam pointer to a blank area near the bottom of the workspace, and click. Notice the insertion point does not jump to the location of the I-beam pointer. Instead the insertion point jumps to the end of the last sentence. The insertion point can move only within existing text. It cannot be moved out of the existing text area.

Selecting Text

Many text operations are performed on a **block** of text, which is one or more consecutive characters, words, sentences, or paragraphs. Once you select a block of text, you can delete it, move it, replace it, underline it, and so on. As you select a block of text, the computer highlights it. If you want to remove the highlighting, just click in the margin of your document.

If you want to delete the phrase "See what happens" in the text you just typed and replace it with the phrase "You can watch word wrap in action," you do not have to delete the first phrase one character at a time. Instead, you can highlight the entire phrase and then type the replacement phrase.

To select and replace a block of text:

1. Move the I-beam pointer just to the left of the word "See."
2. While holding down the mouse button, drag the I-beam pointer over the text to the end of the word "happens." The phrase "See what happens" should now be highlighted. See Figure 2-5.

   TROUBLE? If the space to the right of the word "happens" is also selected, don't worry. Your computer is set up to select spaces in addition to words. After completing Step 4, simply press the Spacebar to type an extra space if required.

Figure 2-5 HIGHLIGHTING TEXT

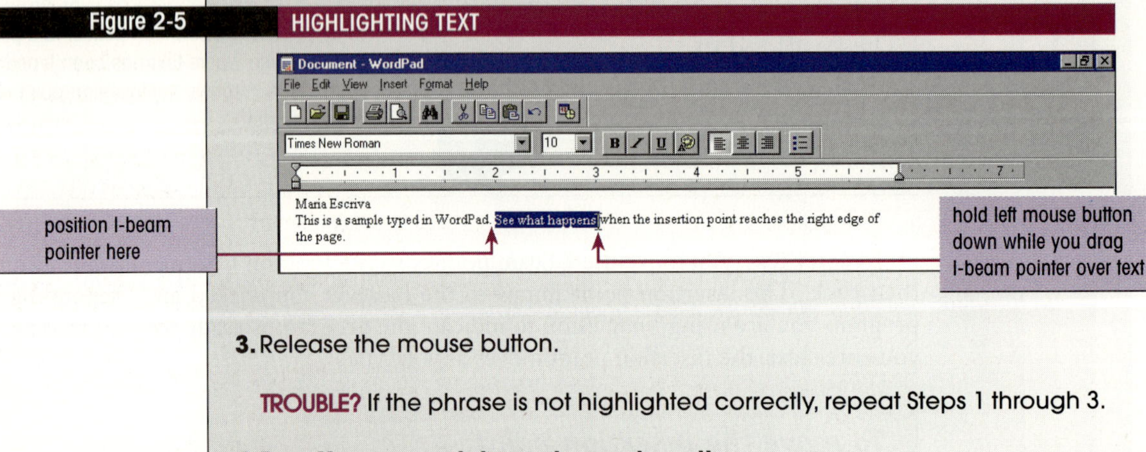

3. Release the mouse button.

   TROUBLE? If the phrase is not highlighted correctly, repeat Steps 1 through 3.

4. Type **You can watch word wrap in action**

The text you typed replaces the highlighted text. Notice you did not need to delete the highlighted text before you typed the replacement text.

Inserting a Character

Windows 98 programs usually operate in **insert mode**—when you type a new character, all characters to the right of the insertion point are pushed over to make room.

Suppose you want to insert the word "sentence" before the word "typed" in your practice sentences.

To insert text:

1. Move the I-beam pointer just before the word "typed," then click to position the insertion point.
2. Type **sentence**
3. Press the **Spacebar**.

Notice how the letters in the first line are pushed to the right to make room for the new characters. When a word gets pushed past the right margin, the **word-wrap** feature moves it down to the beginning of the next line.

Saving a File

As you type text, it is held temporarily in the computer's memory. For permanent storage, you need to save your work on a disk. In the computer lab, you will probably save your work on a floppy disk in drive A.

When you save a file, you must give it a name. Windows 98 allows you to use up to 255 characters in a filename, although usually the operating system requires some of those characters for designating file location and file type. So, while it is unlikely you would need that many characters, you should be aware that the full 255 characters might not always be available. You may use spaces and certain punctuation symbols in your filenames. You cannot use the symbols \ / ? : * " < > | in a filename, but other symbols such as & ; - and $ are allowed. Furthermore, filenames for files used by older Windows 3.1 or DOS applications (pre-1995 operating systems) must be eight characters or less. Thus when you save a file with a long filename in Windows 98, Windows 98 also creates an eight-character filename that can be used by older applications. The eight-character filename is created from the first six nonspace characters in the long filename, with the addition of a tilde (~) and a number. For example, the filename Car Sales for 1999 would be converted to Carsal~1.

Most filenames have an extension. An **extension** is a suffix, usually of three characters, separated from the filename by a period. In the filename Car Sales for 1999.doc, a period separates the filename from the file extension. The file extension "doc" helps categorize the file by type or by the software that created it. Files created with Microsoft Word software have a .doc extension, such as Resume.doc (pronounced "Resume dot doc"). In general you will not add an extension to your filenames, because the application software automatically does this for you.

Windows 98 keeps track of file extensions, but does not always display them. The steps in these tutorials refer to files using the filename, but not its extension. So if you see the filename Practice Text in the steps, but "Practice Text.doc" on your screen, don't worry—these refer to the same file. Also don't worry if you don't use consistent lowercase and uppercase letters when saving files. Usually the operating system doesn't distinguish between them. Be aware, however, that some programs are "case-sensitive"—they check for case in filenames.

Now you can save the document you typed.

To save a document:

1. Click the **Save** button on the toolbar. Figure 2-6 shows the location of this button and the Save As dialog box that appears after you click it.

Figure 2-6 SAVING A FILE

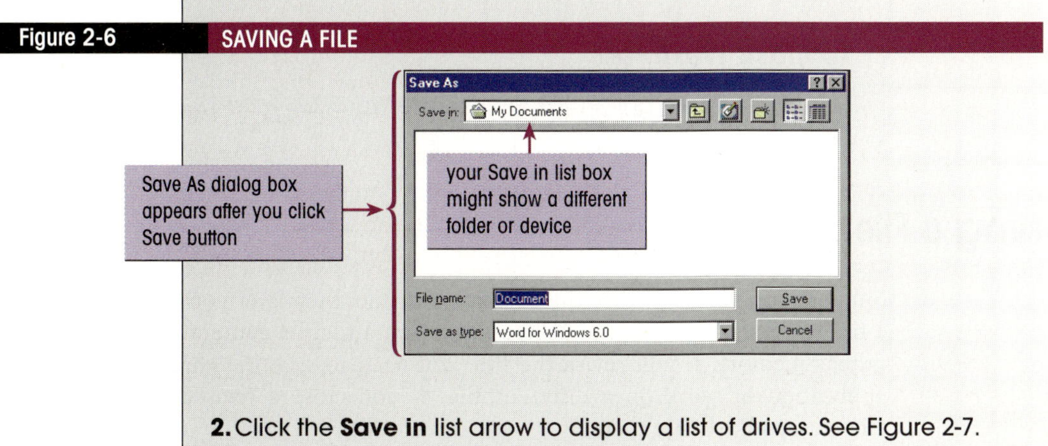

2. Click the **Save in** list arrow to display a list of drives. See Figure 2-7.

Figure 2-7 SELECTING THE DRIVE

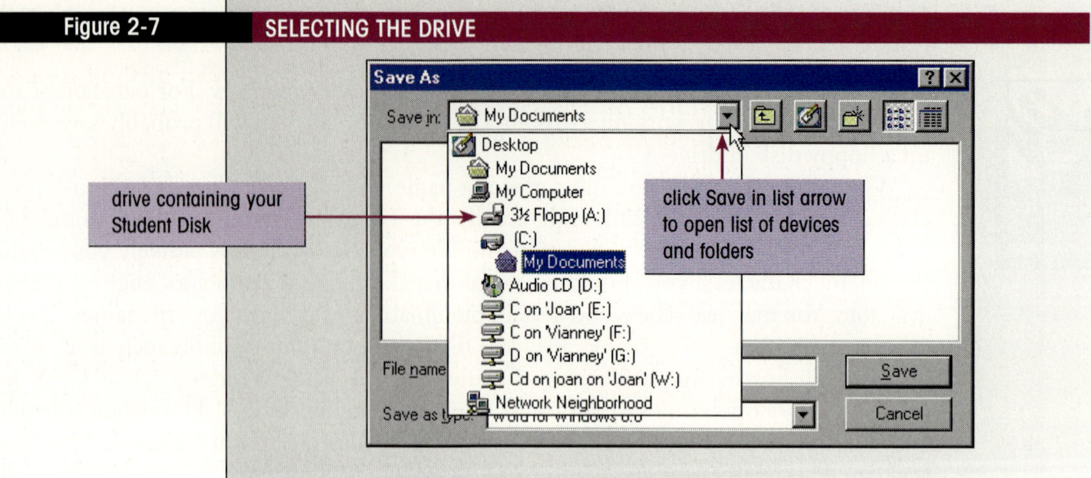

3. Click **3½ Floppy (A:)**, and select the text in the File name box.

   TROUBLE? To select the text, move the I-beam pointer to the beginning of the word "Document." While you hold down the mouse button, drag the I-beam pointer to the end of the word.

4. Type **Practice Text** in the File name box.

5. Click the **Save** button in the lower-right corner of the dialog box. Your file is saved on your Student Disk, and the document title, "Practice Text," appears on the WordPad title bar.

What if you try to close WordPad before you save your file? Windows 98 will display a message—"Save changes to Document?" If you answer "Yes," Windows will display the Save As dialog box so you can give the document a name. If you answer "No," Windows 98 will close WordPad without saving the document. Any changes you made to the document would be lost, so when you are asked if you want to save a file, answer Yes, unless you are absolutely sure you don't need to keep the work you just did.

After you save a file, you can work on another document or close WordPad. Since you have already saved your Practice Text document, you'll continue this tutorial by closing WordPad.

To close WordPad:

1. Click the **Close** button ☒ to close the WordPad window.

Opening a File

Suppose you save and close the Practice Text file, then later you want to revise it. To revise a file you must first open it. When you **open** a file, its contents are copied into the computer's memory. If you revise the file, you need to save the changes before you close the application or work on a different file. If you close a revised file without saving your changes, you will lose them.

Typically, you use one of two methods to open a file. You could select the file from the Documents list or the My Computer window, or you could start an application program and then use the Open button to open the file. Each method has advantages and disadvantages.

The first method for opening the Practice Text file simply requires you to select the file from the Documents list or from the My Computer window. With this method the document, not the application program, is central to the task; hence, this method is sometimes referred to as **document-centric**. You only need to remember the name of your document or file—you do not need to remember which application you used to create the document.

The Documents list contains the names of the last 15 documents used. You access this list from the Start menu. When you have your own computer, the Documents list is very handy. In a computer lab, however, the files other students use quickly replace yours on the list.

If your file is not in the Documents list, you can open the file by selecting it from the My Computer window. Windows 98 starts an application program you can use to revise the file, then automatically opens the file. The advantage of this method is its simplicity. The disadvantage is Windows 98 might not start the application you expect. For example, when you select Practice Text, you might expect Windows 98 to start WordPad because you used WordPad to create it. Depending on the software installed on your computer system, however, Windows 98 might start the Microsoft Word application instead. Usually this is not a problem. Although the application might not be the one you expect, you can still use it to revise your file.

To open the Practice Text file by selecting it from My Computer:

1. From the desktop, open the **My Computer** window.
2. Click the **3½ Floppy (A:)** icon in the My Computer window.

   TROUBLE? If the 3½ Floppy (A:) window opens, skip Step 3.

3. Press **Enter**. The 3½ Floppy (A:) window opens.
4. Click the **Practice Text** file icon.

   TROUBLE? If the Practice Text document appears in a word-processing window, skip Step 5.

5. Press **Enter**. Windows 98 starts an application program, then automatically opens the Practice Text file. You could make revisions to the document at this point, but instead, you'll close all the windows on your desktop so you can try the other method for opening files.

   TROUBLE? If Windows 98 starts Microsoft Word or another word-processing program instead of WordPad, don't worry. You can use Microsoft Word to revise the Practice Text document.

6. Close all open windows on the desktop.

The second method for opening the Practice Text file requires you to open WordPad, then use the Open button to select the Practice Text file. The advantage of this method is you can specify the application program you want to use—WordPad, in this case. This method, however, involves more steps than the method you tried previously.

To start WordPad and open the Practice Text file using the Open button:

1. Start WordPad and maximize the WordPad window.
2. Click the **Open** button on the toolbar.

3. Click the **Look in** list arrow to display a list of drives.
4. Click **3½ Floppy (A:)** from the list.
5. Click **Practice Text** to make sure it is highlighted. See Figure 2-8.

Figure 2-8 SELECTING THE FILE

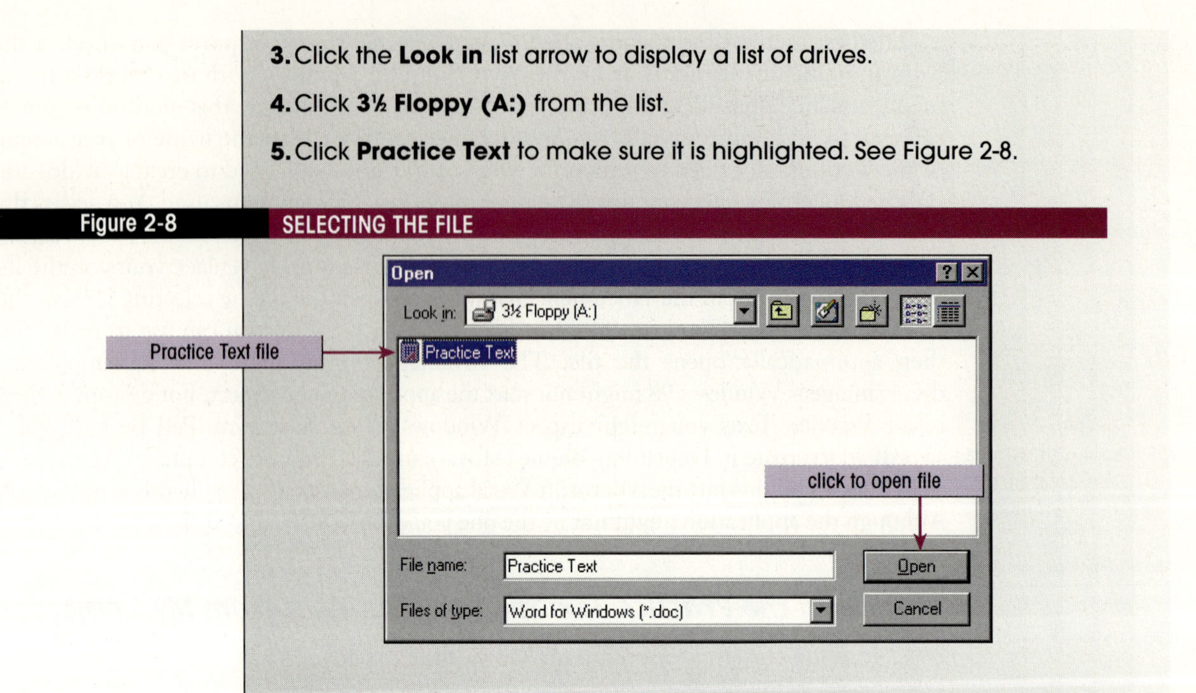

6. Click the **Open** button in the lower-right corner of the dialog box. Your document should appear in the WordPad work area.

Printing a File

Now that the Practice Text file is open, you can print it. It is a good idea to use Print Preview before you send your document to the printer. **Print Preview** shows on the screen exactly how your document will appear on paper. You can check your page layout so you don't waste paper printing a document that is not quite the way you want it. Your instructor might supply you with additional instructions for printing in your school's computer lab.

To preview, then print, the Practice Text file:

1. Click the **Print Preview** button on the toolbar.

   TROUBLE? If an error message appears, printing capabilities might not be set up on your computer. Ask your instructor or lab assistant for help, or skip this set of steps.

2. Look at your print preview. Before you print the document and use paper, you should make sure the font, margins, and other document features look the way you want them to.

   TROUBLE? If you can't read the document text on screen, click the Zoom In button.

3. Click the **Print** button. A Print dialog box appears. Study Figure 2-9 to familiarize yourself with the controls in the Print dialog box.

Figure 2-9 PRINTING A FILE

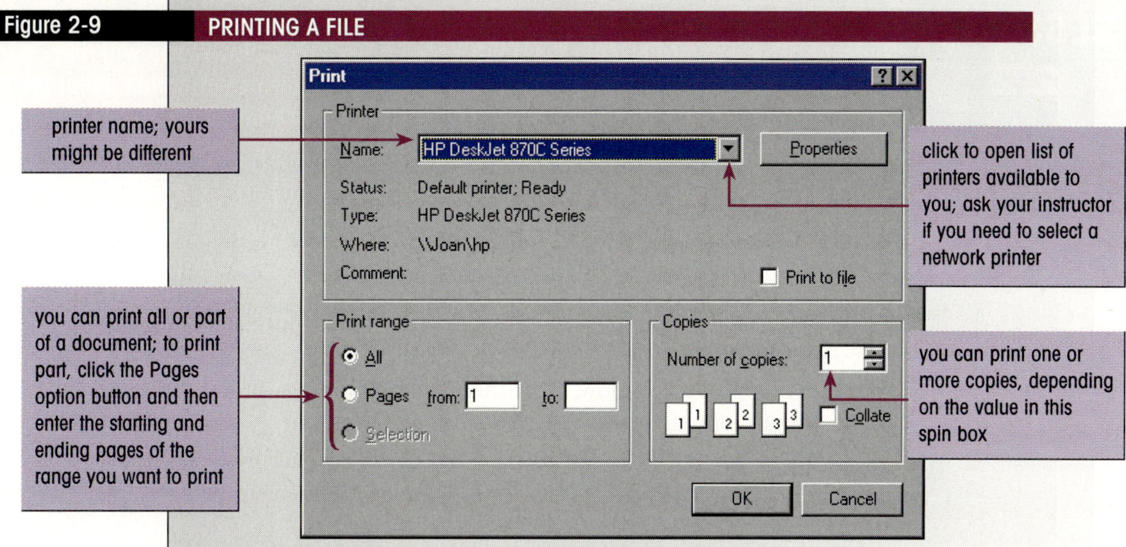

4. Make sure your screen shows the Print range set to "All" and the number of copies set to "1."
5. Click the **OK** button to print your document.

   TROUBLE? If your document does not print, make sure the printer has paper and the printer online light is on. If your document still doesn't print, ask your instructor or lab assistant for help.

6. Close WordPad.

   TROUBLE? If you see the message "Save changes to Document?" click the No button.

You've now learned how to create, save, open, and print word-processed files—essential skills for students in distance education courses that rely on word-processed reports transmitted across the Internet. Shannon assures you that the techniques you've just learned apply to most Windows 98 programs.

QUICK CHECK

1. A(n) ______________ is a collection of data that has a name and is stored on a disk or other storage medium.
2. ______________ erases all the data on a disk and arranges the magnetic particles on the disk surface so the disk can store data.
3. True or False: When you move the mouse pointer over a text entry area, the pointer shape changes to an I-bar.
4. What shows you where each character you type will appear?
5. ______________ automatically moves text down to the beginning of the next line when you reach the right margin.
6. How do you select a block of text?
7. In the filename New Equipment.doc, doc is a(n) ______________.

SESSION 2.2

In this session you will learn how to change settings in the My Computer window to control its appearance and the appearance of desktop objects. You will then learn how to use My Computer to manage the files on your disk; view information about the files on your disk; organize the files into folders; and move, delete, copy, and rename files. ***For this session you will use a second blank 3½-inch disk.***

Changing Desktop Style Settings

Shannon tells you that in Windows 98 you work with files by manipulating icons that represent them. These icons appear in many places: the desktop, the My Computer windows, the 3½ Floppy (A:) window, and other similar windows. The techniques you use to manipulate these icons depend on whether your computer is using Classic-style or Web-style settings or a customized hybrid. **Classic style** allows you to use the same techniques in Windows 98 that are used in Windows 95, the previous version of the Windows operating system. **Web style**, on the other hand, allows you to access files on your computer's hard drives just as you access files on the Web. In Classic style, to select an item you click it, and to open an item you click it and then press Enter. In Web style, to select an item you point to it, and to open an item you click it.

Thus, if you wanted to open your Practice Text document from the My Computer window, in Classic style you would click its icon and press Enter, but in Web style you would simply click its icon.

Switching to Web Style

By default, Windows 98 starts using a combination of Classic and Web style settings, but it uses Classic click settings. Your computer might have been set differently. If you have your own computer, you can choose which style you want to use. If you want to minimize the number of mouse actions for a given task, or if you want to explore your computer in the same way you explore the Web, you'll probably want to use Web style. On the other hand, if you are used to Classic style settings, you might want to continue using them. Shannon suggests that you use Web style because you'll be able to use the same techniques on the Web, and you'll be more at ease with your distance learning courses. The next set of steps shows you how to switch to Web style, and the rest of the tutorial assumes that you're using Web-style settings.

To switch styles:

1. Click the **Start** button Start and then point to **Settings**.
2. Click **Folder Options**. The Folder Options dialog box opens.

   TROUBLE? If you can't open the Folder Options dialog box, or you can't make any changes to it, you probably don't have permission to change these settings. If your computer is set to use Classic style and you can't change this setting, you will notice a few differences in subsequent steps in this tutorial. The TROUBLE? paragraphs will help to ensure that you learn the proper techniques for the settings you are using.

3. On the General tab, click the **Web style** option button. See Figure 2-10.

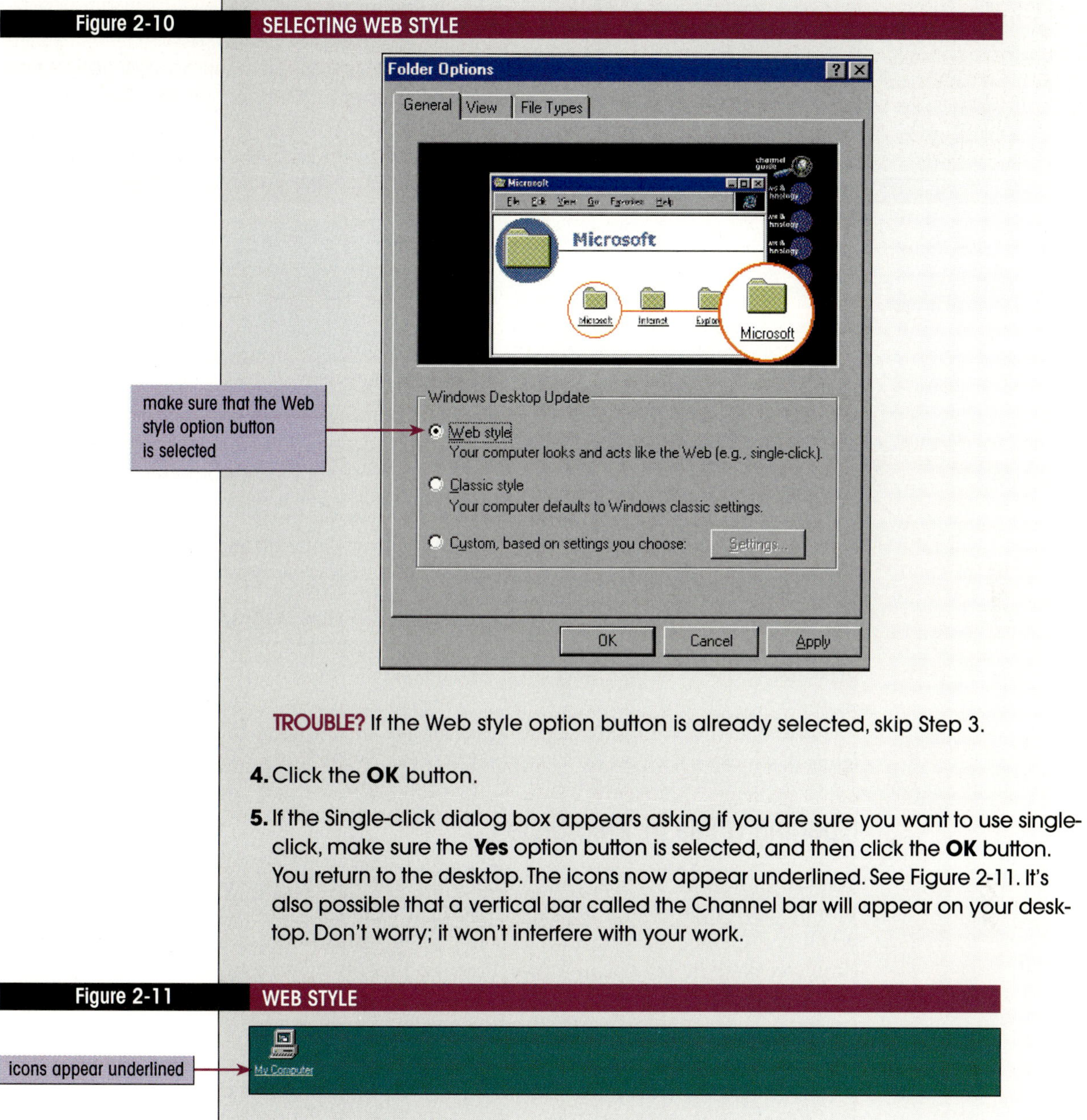

Figure 2-10 SELECTING WEB STYLE

TROUBLE? If the Web style option button is already selected, skip Step 3.

4. Click the **OK** button.

5. If the Single-click dialog box appears asking if you are sure you want to use single-click, make sure the **Yes** option button is selected, and then click the **OK** button. You return to the desktop. The icons now appear underlined. See Figure 2-11. It's also possible that a vertical bar called the Channel bar will appear on your desktop. Don't worry; it won't interfere with your work.

Figure 2-11 WEB STYLE

You are now using Web-style settings.

Selecting an Icon in Web Style

In Web style, you select an icon representing a device, folder, or file by pointing to the icon long enough for it to become highlighted. This technique is sometimes called **hovering**. The pointer changes from ↖ to ☝ when you point to the icon. Try selecting the My Computer icon in Web style.

To select the My Computer icon in Web style:

1. Position the pointer over the My Computer icon on the desktop and notice how the pointer changes from ↖ to ☝ and the color of the text label changes to show it is selected. See Figure 2-12.

Figure 2-12 SELECTING AN ICON IN WEB STYLE

pointer when you point at icon in Web style

TROUBLE? If the My Computer icon is not selected when you point to it, you might not be holding the mouse steadily. You need to steadily "hover" the pointer over the object long enough for the object to become highlighted. Simply passing the mouse over an object will not select it.

TROUBLE? If in Web style you click the My Computer icon instead of simply pointing at it, the My Computer window will open. Close the window and repeat Step 1.

TROUBLE? If you were unable to switch to Web style because you didn't have permission, you'll need to click the My Computer icon to select it.

Note that the Web style selection technique only applies to icons on the desktop and icons in windows such as My Computer.

Opening a File in Web Style

You saw in Session 2.1 that you can open the Practice Text document directly from the 3½ Floppy (A:) window. The steps in Session 2.1 assumed you were using Classic style. Now you'll try opening the Practice Text document using Web style. You open an object by simply clicking it. Try opening your Practice Text file in Web style.

To open the Practice Text file in Web style:

1. Click the **My Computer** icon. The My Computer window opens.

   TROUBLE? If you were unable to switch to Web style, you'll need to press Enter after Steps 1, 2, and 3.

2. Click the **3½ Floppy (A:)** icon. The 3½ Floppy (A:) window opens.
3. Click the **Practice Text** icon. Your word-processing software starts and the Practice Text file opens.
4. Close all open windows.

Now that you've practiced working with icons in Web style, you'll learn other tasks you can perform with these icons to manage your files.

Creating Your Student Disk

For the rest of this session, you must create a Student Disk that contains some practice files. *You can use the disk you formatted in the previous session.*

If you are using your own computer, the NP on Microsoft Windows 98 menu selection will not be available. Before you proceed, you must go to your school's computer lab and find a computer that has the NP on Microsoft Windows 98 program installed. If you cannot get the files from the lab, ask your instructor or lab assistant for help. Once you have made your own Student Disk, you can use it to complete this tutorial on any computer you choose.

To add the practice files to your Student Disk:

1. Write "Disk 1 - Windows 98 Tutorial 2 Student Disk" on the label of your formatted disk (the same disk you used to save your Practice Text file).
2. Place the disk in drive A.
3. Click the **Start** button Start.
4. Point to **Programs**.
5. Point to **NP on Microsoft Windows 98 - Level I**.

   TROUBLE? If NP on Microsoft Windows 98 - Level I is not listed ask your instructor or lab assistant for help.

6. Click **Disk 1 (Tutorial 2)**. A message box opens, asking you to place your disk in drive A.
7. Click the **OK** button. Wait while the program copies the practice files to your formatted disk. When all the files have been copied, the program closes.

Your Student Disk now contains practice files you will use throughout the rest of this tutorial.

My Computer

The My Computer icon, as you have seen, represents your computer, its storage devices, printers, and other objects. The My Computer icon opens into the My Computer window, which contains an icon for each of the storage devices on your computer. On most computer systems, the My Computer window also contains the Control Panel and Printers folders, which help you add printers, control peripheral devices, and customize your Windows 98 work environment. Depending on the services your computer is running, you might see additional folders such as Dial-Up Networking (for some Internet connections) or Scheduled Tasks (for scheduling programs provided with Windows 98) that help you keep your computer running smoothly). Figure 2-13 shows how the My Computer window relates to your computer's hardware.

Figure 2-13 RELATIONSHIP BETWEEN COMPUTER AND MY COMPUTER WINDOW

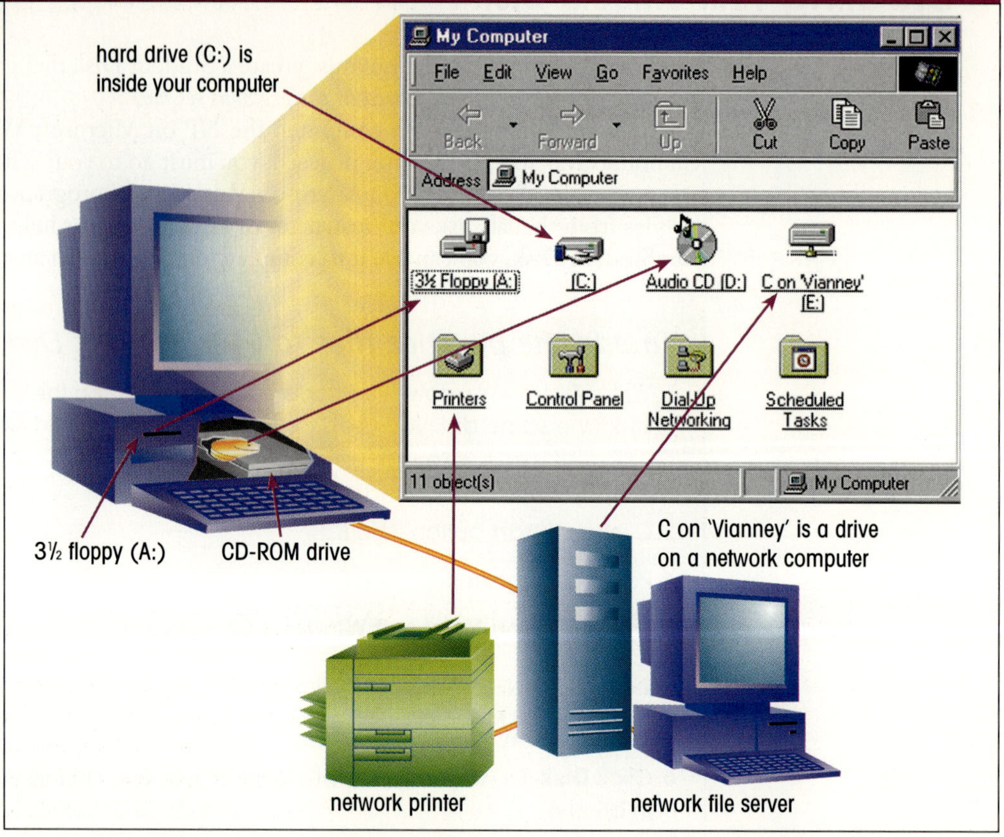

The first floppy drive on a computer is designated as drive A (if you add a second drive it is usually designated as drive B), and the first hard drive is designated drive C (if you add additional hard drives they are usually designated D, E, and so on).

You can use the My Computer window to keep track of where your files are stored and to organize your files. In this section of the tutorial you will move and delete files on your Student Disk in drive A. If you use your own computer at home or work, you will probably store your files on drive C instead of drive A. However, in a school lab environment you usually don't know which computer you will use, so you need to carry your files with you on a floppy disk that you use in drive A. In this session, therefore, you will learn how to work with the files on drive A. Most of what you learn will also work on your home or work computer when you use drive C (or other drives).

Now you'll open the My Computer window.

To open the My Computer window and explore the contents of your Student Disk:

1. Open the My Computer window.

2. Click the **3½ Floppy (A:)** icon. A window appears showing the contents of drive A; maximize this window if necessary. See Figure 2-14.

   TROUBLE? If you are using Classic style, click Settings, click the 3½ Floppy (A:) icon and then press Enter. Your window might look different from Figure 2-14; for example, you might see only files, and not the additional information on the left side of the window.

TROUBLE? If you see a list of filenames instead of icons, click View, then click Large Icons.

Figure 2-14 CONTENTS OF STUDENT DISK

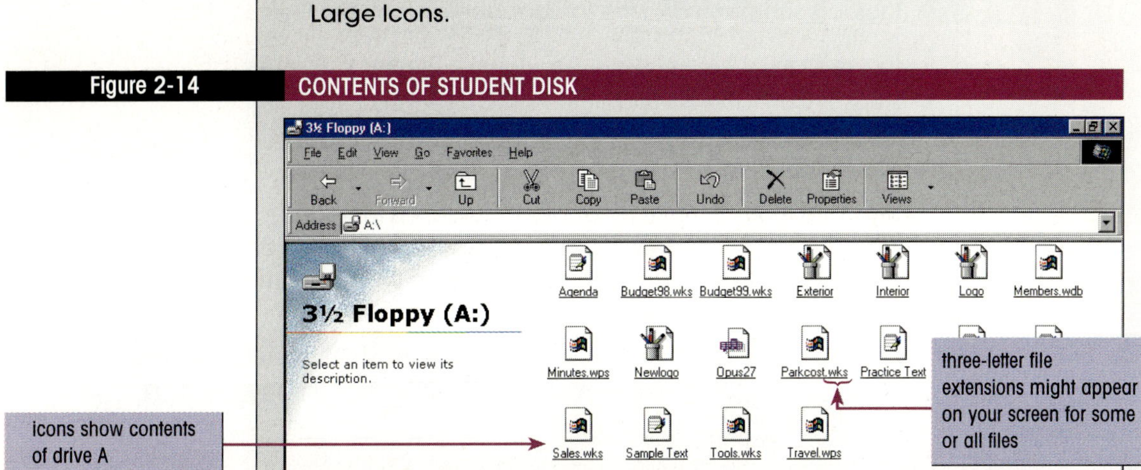

Changing My Computer View Options

Windows 98 offers several different options that control how toolbars, icons, and buttons appear in the My Computer window. You can choose to hide or display these options, depending on the task you are performing. To make the My Computer window on your computer look the same as it does in the figures in this book, you need to ensure four things: that only the Address and Standard toolbars are visible and Text Labels is enabled, that Web view is disabled, that Large Icons view is enabled, and that file extensions are hidden.

Controlling the Toolbar Display

The My Computer window, in addition to featuring a Standard toolbar, allows you to display the same toolbars that can appear on the Windows 98 taskbar, such as the Address toolbar or the Links toolbar. These toolbars make it easy to access the Web from the My Computer window. In this tutorial, however, you need to see only the Address and Standard toolbars. You can hide one or all of the My Computer toolbars, and you can determine how they are displayed, with or without text labels. Displaying the toolbars without text labels takes up less room on your screen, but it is not as easy to identify the button's function.

To display only the Address and Standard toolbars and to hide text labels:

1. Click **View**, point to **Toolbars**, and then examine the Toolbars submenu. The Standard Buttons, Address Bar, and Text Labels options should be preceded by a check mark. The Links option should not be checked.
2. If the Standard Buttons option ***is not checked***, click it.
3. If necessary, reopen the Toolbars submenu, and then repeat Step 2 with the Address Bar and Text Labels options.
4. Open the Toolbars submenu once again, and if the Links option ***is checked***, click it to disable it.

5. Click **View** and then point to **Toolbars** one last time and verify that your Toolbars submenu and the toolbar display look like Figure 2-15.

TROUBLE? If the checkmarks are distributed differently than in Figure 2-15, repeat Steps 1–5 until the correct options are checked.

TROUBLE? If your toolbars are not displayed as shown in Figure 2-15 (for example, both the Standard and Address toolbars might be on the same line, or the Standard toolbar might be above the Address toolbar), you can easily rearrange them. To move a toolbar, drag the vertical bar at the far left of the toolbar. By dragging that vertical bar, you can drag the toolbar left, right, up, or down.

Figure 2-15 CHECKING VIEW OPTIONS

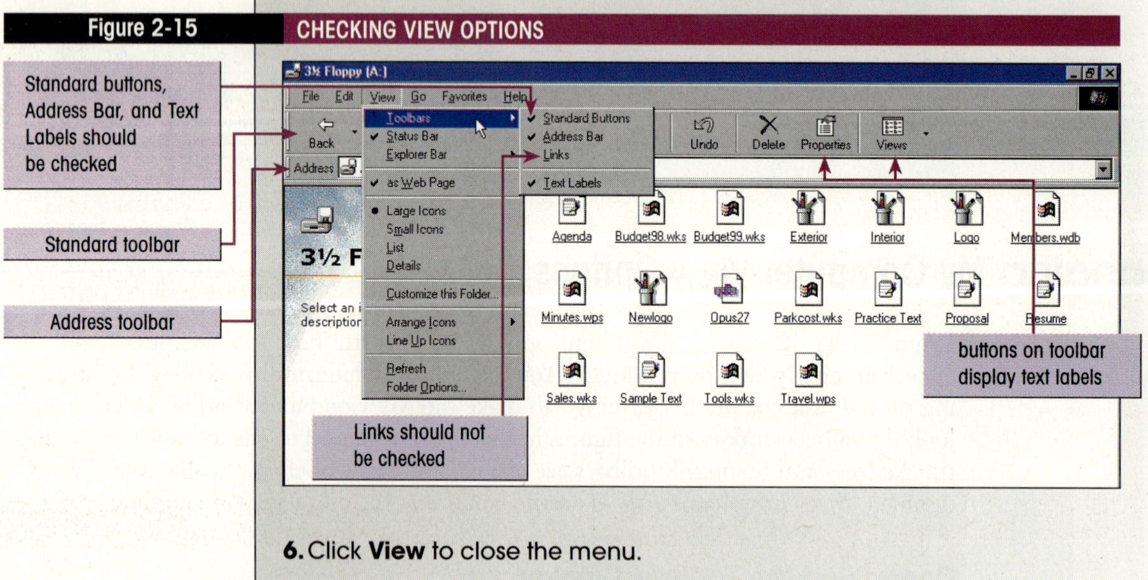

6. Click **View** to close the menu.

Web View

The My Computer window also can be viewed in **Web view**, which allows you to display and customize the My Computer window as a document you would see on the Web. Web view is automatically enabled when you switch to Web style; in its default appearance Web view shows information about the open folder or selected file, along with a decorated background. There are many advantages to Web view, including the ability to place information, graphics, and Web content in a folder window. Shannon says you'll find this feature useful once you've started your distance education courses. For now, however, you don't need to customize Web view, so you'll disable it.

To disable Web view:

1. Click **View**.

2. If the option "as Web Page" is preceded by a check mark, click **as Web Page** to disable Web view.

3. Click **View** again and ensure that as Web Page is not checked.

TROUBLE? If as Web Page is checked, repeat Steps 1 and 2.

4. Click **View** again to close the View menu.

Changing the Icon Display

Windows 98 provides four ways to view the contents of a disk—large icons, small icons, list, or details. The default view, Large Icons view, displays a large icon and title for each file. The icon provides a visual cue to the type and contents of the file, as Figure 2-16 illustrates.

Figure 2-16 TYPICAL ICONS AS THEY APPEAR IN MY COMPUTER

FILE AND FOLDER ICONS	
	Text documents that you can open using the Notepad accessory are represented by notepad icons.
	Graphic image documents that you can open using the Paint accessory are represented by drawing instruments.
	Word-processed documents that you can open using the WordPad accessory are represented by a formatted notepad icon, unless your computer designates a different word-processing program to open files created with WordPad.
	Word-processed documents that you can open using a program such as Microsoft Word are represented by formatted document icons.
	Files created by programs that Windows does not recognize are represented by the Windows logo.
	A folder icon represents folders.
	Certain folders created by Windows 98 have a special icon design related to the folder's purpose.
PROGRAM ICONS	
	Icons for programs usually depict an object related to the function of the program. For example, an icon that looks like a calculator represents the Calculator accessory.
	Non-windows programs are represented by the icon of a blank window.

Large Icons view helps you quickly identify a file and its type, but what if you want more information about a set of files? Details view shows more information than the large icon, small icon, and list views. Details view shows the file icon, the filename, the file size, the application you used to create the file, and the date/time the file was created or last modified.

To view a detailed list of files:

1. Click **View** and then click **Details** to display details for the files on your disk, as shown in Figure 2-17. Your files might be in a different order.
2. Look at the file sizes. Do you see that Exterior and Interior are the largest files?
3. Look at the dates and times the files were modified. Which is the oldest file?

Figure 2-17 DETAILS VIEW

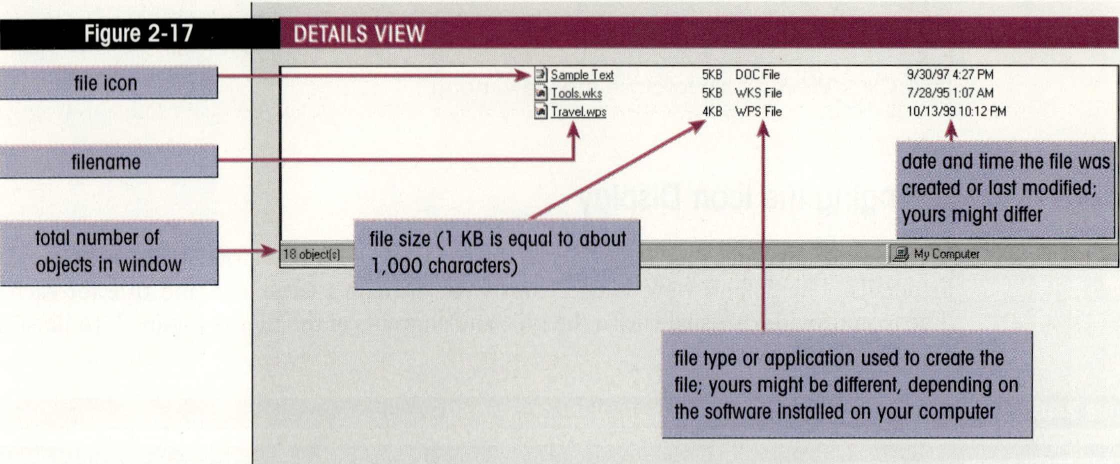

Now that you have looked at the file details, switch back to Large Icon view.

To switch to Large Icon view:

1. Click **View** and then click **Large Icons** to return to the large icon display.

Hiding File Extensions

You have the option to show or hide file extensions for file types that Windows recognizes. Showing them takes up more room but gives more information about the file. In this tutorial, however, you don't need to see file extensions, so you'll hide them. They might already be hidden on your computer.

To hide file extensions:

1. Click **View** and then click **Folder Options**. Note this is the same dialog box you saw when switching to Web style. It is accessible from the Start menu and the My Computer window.
2. Click the **View** tab.
3. Make sure the **Hide file extensions for known file types** check box is checked. If it is not, click it to insert a check mark.
4. Click the **OK** button.

The only file extensions that now appear are those whose file type Windows doesn't recognize.

Folders and Directories

A list of related files located in the same place is referred to as a **directory**. The main directory of a disk is sometimes called the **root directory**, or the **top-level directory**. The root directory is created when you format a disk, and it is designated by a letter—usually A for your floppy disk and C for your hard disk. All of the files on your Student Disk are currently in the root directory of your floppy disk.

If too many files are stored in a directory, the directory list becomes very long and difficult to manage. You can divide a directory into **folders**, into which you group similar files. The directory of files for each folder then becomes much shorter and easier to manage. A folder within a folder is called a **subfolder**. Now, you'll create a folder called Practice to hold your documents.

To create a Practice folder:

1. Click **File**, and then point to **New** to display the submenu.
2. Click **Folder**. A folder icon with the label "New Folder" appears.
3. Type **Practice** as the name of the folder.

   TROUBLE? If nothing happens when you type the folder name, it's possible that the folder name is no longer selected. Right-click the Practice folder, click Rename, and then repeat Step 3.

4. Press the **Enter** key.

When you first create a folder, it doesn't contain any files. In the next set of steps, you will move a file from the root directory to the Practice folder.

Moving and Copying a File

You can move a file from one directory to another, or from one disk to another. When you move a file, it is copied to the new location you specify, and then the version in the old location is erased. The move feature is handy for organizing or reorganizing the files on your disk by moving them into appropriate folders. The easiest way to move a file is to hold down the right mouse button and drag the file from the old location to the new location. A menu appears and you select Move Here.

REFERENCE WINDOW **RW**

Moving a File

- Locate the file in the My Compuuter window.
- Hold down the right mouse button while you drag the file icon to its new folder or disk location.
- Click Move Here.

Suppose you want to move the Minutes file from the root directory to the Practice folder. Depending on your computer's settings, this file appears either as Minutes or Minutes.wps. In the following steps, the file is referred to as Minutes.

To move the Minutes file to the Practice folder:

1. Point to the **Minutes** icon.
2. Press and hold the right mouse button while you drag the Minutes icon to the Practice folder. See Figure 2-18.

TROUBLE? If you release the mouse button by mistake before dragging the Minutes icon to the Practice folder, the Minutes shortcut menu opens. Press Esc and then repeat Steps 1 and 2.

Figure 2-18 MOVING A FILE

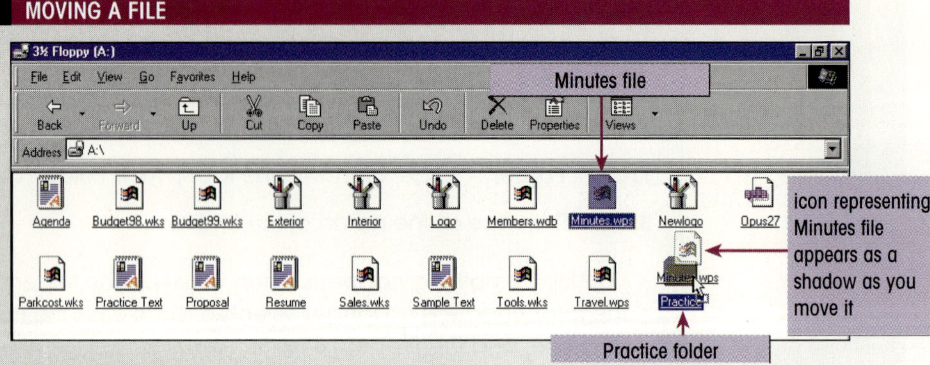

3. Release the right mouse button. A menu appears.

4. Click **Move Here**. The Minutes icon disappears from the window showing the files in the root directory.

Anything you do to an icon in the My Computer window is actually done to the file represented by that icon. If you move an icon, the file is moved; if you delete an icon, the file is deleted.

You can also copy a file from one folder to another, or from one disk to another. When you copy a file, you create an exact duplicate of an existing file in whatever disk or folder you specify. To copy a file from one folder to another on your floppy disk, you use the same procedure as for moving a file, except that you select Copy Here from the menu.

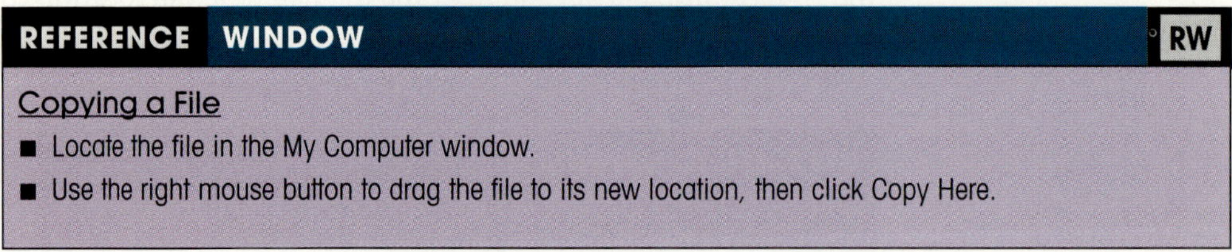
REFERENCE WINDOW RW

Copying a File

- Locate the file in the My Computer window.
- Use the right mouse button to drag the file to its new location, then click Copy Here.

Try copying the Resume file into the Practice folder.

To copy the Resume file into the Practice folder:

1. Using the right mouse button, drag the Resume file into the Practice folder.

2. Click **Copy Here**. Notice this time the file icon does not disappear, because you didn't actually move it, you only copied it.

After you move or copy a file, it is a good idea to make sure it was moved to the correct location. You can easily verify that a file is in its new folder by displaying the folder contents.

To verify that the Minutes file was moved and the Resume file was copied to the Practice folder:

1. Click the **Practice** folder icon. The Practice window appears, and it contains two files—Minutes, which you moved, and Resume, which you copied.

   TROUBLE? If you are using Classic style, click Settings, click the Practice folder icon and then press Enter to open the Practice window.

Navigating Explorer Windows

The title bar of the open window on your computer, "Practice," identifies the name of the folder you just opened. Before you opened the Practice folder, you were viewing the contents of your floppy disk, so the window's title bar, 3½ Floppy (A:) (or possibly just A:/, depending on how your computer is set up), identified the drive containing your disk, drive A. Before you opened that window you were viewing the My Computer window. Windows that show the objects on your computer are called **Explorer windows** because they allow you to explore the contents of your computer's devices and folders.

You've seen that to navigate through the devices and folders on your computer, you open My Computer and then click the icons representing the objects you want to explore. But what if you want to move back to a previous Explorer window? The Standard toolbar, which stays the same regardless of which Explorer window is open, includes buttons that help you navigate through your Explorer windows. Figure 2-19 summarizes the navigation buttons on the Standard toolbar.

Figure 2-19 NAVIGATIONAL BUTTONS

BUTTON	ICON	DESCRIPTION
Back	⇦	Returns you to the Explorer window you were most recently viewing. This button is active only when you have viewed more than one Explorer window in the current session.
Forward	⇨	Reverses the effect of the Back button.
Up		Moves you up one level on the hierarchy of your computer's objects; for example, moves you from a folder Explorer window to the drive containing the folder.

Try returning to the 3½ Floppy (A:) window using the Back button.

To navigate Explorer windows:

1. Click the **Back** button ⇦ to return to the 3½ Floppy (A:) window.
2. Click the **Forward** button ⇨ to reverse the effect of the Back button and return to the Practice window.
3. Click the **Up** button to move up one level. You again return to the 3½ Floppy (A:) window because the Practice folder is contained within the 3½ Floppy (A:) drive.

Deleting a File

You delete a file or folder by deleting its icon. However, be careful when you delete a folder, because you also delete all the files it contains! When you delete a file from a *hard drive* on your computer, the filename is deleted from the directory but the file contents are held in the Recycle Bin. The **Recycle Bin** is an area on your hard drive that holds deleted files until you remove them permanently; an icon on the desktop allows you easy access to the Recycle Bin. If you change your mind and want to retrieve a file deleted from your hard drive, you can recover it by using the Recycle Bin.

When you delete a file from a *floppy disk*, it does not go into the Recycle Bin. Instead, it is deleted as soon as its icon disappears.

Try deleting the file named Agenda from your Student Disk. Because this file is on the floppy disk and not on the hard disk, it will not go into the Recycle Bin, and if you change your mind you won't be able to recover it.

To delete the file Agenda:

1. Right-click the icon for the file Agenda.
2. Click **Delete**.
3. If a message appears asking, "Are you sure you want to delete Agenda?", click **Yes**. The file is deleted and the Agenda icon no longer appears.

Renaming a File

Sometimes you decide to give a file a different name to clarify the file's contents. You can easily rename a file by using the Rename option on the file's shortcut menu or by using the file's label. The same rules apply for renaming a file as applied for naming a file, and you are limited in the number and type of characters you can use.

When you rename a file when file extensions are showing, make sure to include the extension in the new name. If you don't, Windows warns you it might not be able to identify the file type with the new name. Since you set up View options to hide file extensions, this should not be an issue unless you are trying to rename a file whose type Windows doesn't recognize.

Practice using this feature by renaming the Logo file to give it a more descriptive filename.

To rename Logo:

1. Right-click the **Logo** icon.
2. Click **Rename**. After a moment, a box appears around the label.
3. Type **Corporate Logo Draft** as the new filename.
4. Press the **Enter** key. The file now appears with the new name.
5. Click the **Up** button to move up one level to the My Computer window.

You can also edit an existing filename when you use the Rename command. Click to place the cursor at the location you want to edit, and then use the text-editing skills you learned with WordPad to edit the filename.

Copying an Entire Floppy Disk

You can have trouble accessing the data on your floppy disk if the disk is damaged, is exposed to magnetic fields, or picks up a computer virus. To avoid losing all your data, it is a good idea to make a copy of your floppy disk.

If you wanted to make a copy of an audio cassette, your cassette player would need two cassette drives. You might wonder, therefore, how your computer can make a copy of your disk if you have only one disk drive. Figure 2-20 illustrates how the computer uses only one disk drive to make a copy of a disk.

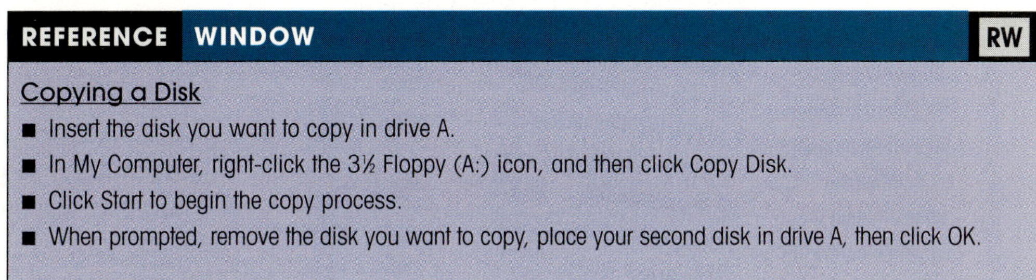

REFERENCE WINDOW RW

Copying a Disk

- Insert the disk you want to copy in drive A.
- In My Computer, right-click the 3½ Floppy (A:) icon, and then click Copy Disk.
- Click Start to begin the copy process.
- When prompted, remove the disk you want to copy, place your second disk in drive A, then click OK.

Figure 2-20 USING ONE DISK DRIVE TO COPY A DISK

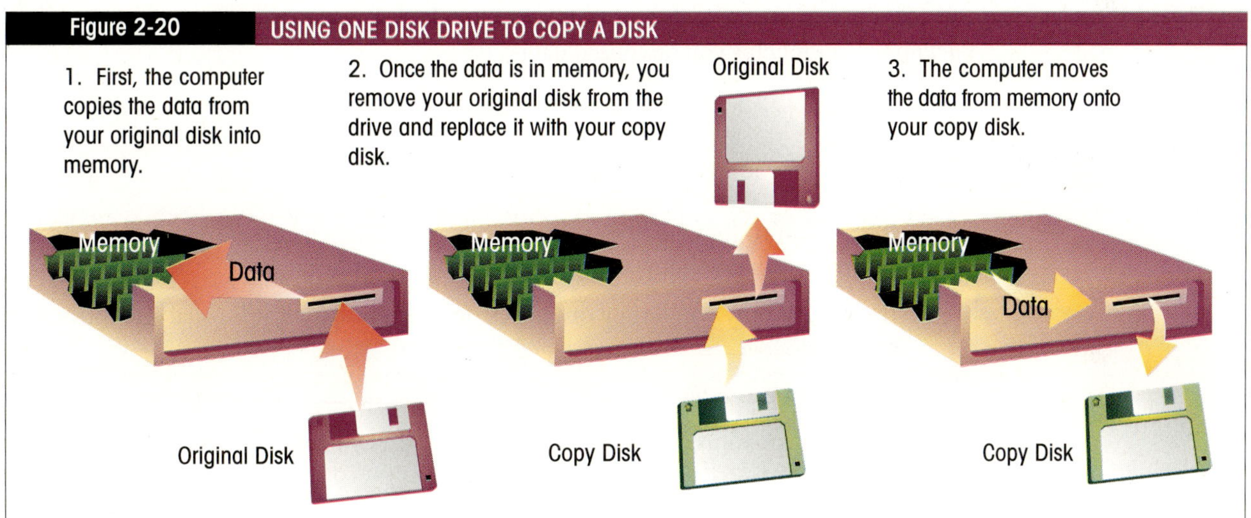

If you have an extra floppy disk, you can make a copy of your Student Disk now. If you change the files on your disk, make sure you copy the disk regularly to keep it updated.

To copy your Student Disk:

1. Write your name and "Windows 98 Disk 1 Student Disk Copy" on the label of your second disk. Make sure the disk is blank and formatted.

   TROUBLE? If you aren't sure the disk is blank, place it in the disk drive and open the 3½ Floppy (A:) window to view its contents. If the disk contains files you need, get a different disk. If it contains files you don't need, you could format the disk now, using the steps you learned at the beginning of this tutorial.

2. Make sure your Student Disk is in drive A and the My Computer window is open.

3. Right-click the **3½ Floppy (A:)** icon, and then click **Copy Disk**. The Copy Disk dialog box opens.
4. Click the **Start** button to begin the copy process.
5. When the message "Insert the disk you want to copy to (destination disk)..." appears, remove your Student Disk and insert your Windows 98 Disk 1 Student Disk Copy in drive A.
6. Click the **OK** button. When the copy is complete, you will see the message "Copy completed successfully." Click the **Close** button.
7. Close the My Computer window.
8. Remove your disk from the drive.

As you finish copying your disk, Shannon emphasizes the importance of making copies of your files frequently, so you won't risk losing important documents for your distance learning course. If your original Student Disk were damaged, you could use the copy you just made to access the files.

Keeping copies of your files is so important that Windows 98 includes with it a program called **Backup** that automates the process of duplicating and storing data. In the Projects at the end of the tutorial you'll have an opportunity to explore the difference between what you just did in copying a disk and the way in which a program such as the Windows 98 Backup program helps you safeguard data.

Quick Check

1. If you want to find out about the storage devices and printers connected to your computer, what window can you open?
2. If you have only one floppy disk drive on your computer, it is usually identified by the letter ____________.
3. The letter C is typically used for the ____________ drive of a computer.
4. What information does Details view supply about a list of folders and files?
5. The main directory of a disk is referred to as the ____________ directory.
6. True or False: You can divide a directory into folders.
7. If you have one floppy disk drive, but you have two disks, can you copy the files on one floppy disk to the other?

TUTORIAL ASSIGNMENT

1. **Opening, Editing, and Printing a Document** In this tutorial you learned how to create a document using WordPad. You also learned how to save, open, and print a document. Practice these skills by opening the document called Resume in the Practice folder of your Student Disk. This document is a resume for Jamie Woods. Make the changes shown in Figure 2-21, and then save the document in the Pratice folder with the name "Resume 2" using the Save As command. After you save your revisions, preview and then print the document. Close WordPad.

Figure 2-21

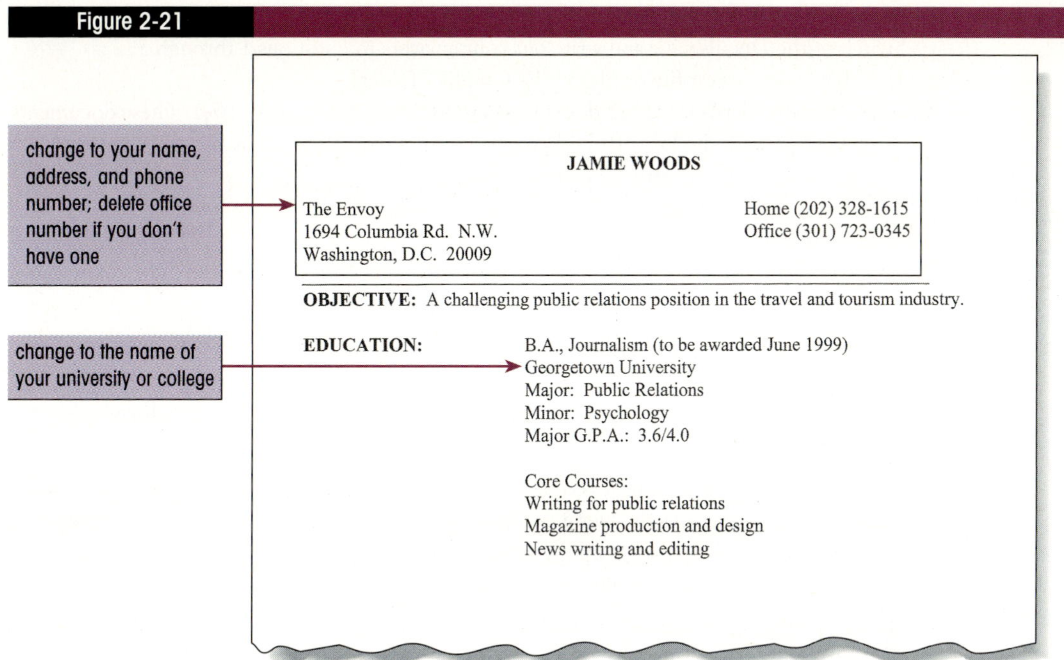

2. **Creating, Saving, and Printing a Letter** Use WordPad to write a one-page letter to a relative or a friend. Save the document in the Practice folder on your Student Disk with the name "Letter." Use the Print Preview feature to look at the format of your finished letter, then print it, and be sure to sign it. Close WordPad.

3. **Managing Files and Folders** Using the copy of the disk you made at the end of the tutorial, complete parts a through f below to practice your file management skills.
   a. Create a folder called Spreadsheets on your Student Disk.
   b. Move the files Parkcost, Budget98, Budget99, and Sales into the Spreadsheets folder.
   c. Create a folder called Park Project.
   d. Move the files Proposal, Members, Tools, Corporate Logo Draft, and Newlogo into the Park Project folder.
   e. Delete the file called Travel.
   f. Switch to the Details view and write out your answers to questions 1 through 5:
      1. What is the largest file or files in the Park Project folder?
      2. What is the newest file or files in the Spreadsheets folder?
      3. How many files (don't include folders) are in the root directory of your Student Disk?
      4. How are the Opus and Exterior icons different? Judging from the appearance of the icons, what would you guess these two files contain?
      5. Which file in the root directory has the most recent date?

4. **More Practice with Files and Folders** For this assignment, you need a third blank disk. Complete parts a through g below to practice your file management skills.
   a. Write "Windows 98 Tutorial 2 Assignment 4" on the label of the blank disk, and then format the disk if necessary.
   b. Create a new Student Disk, using the Assignment 4 disk. Refer to the section "Creating Your Student Disk" in Session 2.2.
   c. Create three folders on the Assignment 4 Student Disk you just created: Documents, Budgets, and Graphics.
   d. Move the files Interior, Exterior, Logo, and Newlogo to the Graphics folder.
   e. Move the files Travel, Members, and Minutes to the Documents folder.

f. Move Budget98 and Budget99 to the Budgets folder.
g. Switch to the Details view and write out your answers to questions 1 through 5:
   1. What is the largest file or files in the Graphics folder?
   2. How many word-processed documents are in the root directory? *Hint*: These documents will appear with the WordPad, Microsoft Word, or some other word-processing icon, depending on what software you have installed.
   3. What is the newest file or files in the root directory (don't include folders)?
   4. How many files in all folders are 5 KB in size?
   5. How many files in the root directory are WKS files? *Hint*: Look in the Type column to identify WKS files.
   6. Do all the files in the Graphics folder have the same icon? What type are they?

5. **Finding a File** The Help system includes a topic that discusses how to find files on a disk without looking through all the folders. Start Windows Help, then locate this topic, and answer questions a through c:
   a. To display the Find dialog box, you must click the ______________ button, then point to ______________ from the menu, and finally click ______________ from the submenu.
   b. Do you need to type in the entire filename to find the file?
   c. How do you perform a case-sensitive search?

6. **Help with Files and Folders** In Tutorial 2 you learned how to work with Windows 98 files and folders. What additional information on this topic does Windows 98 Help provide? Use the Start button to access Help. Use the Index tab to locate topics related to files and folders. Find at least two tips or procedures for working with files and folders that were not covered in the tutorial. Write out the tip in your own words and include the title of the Help screen that contains the information.

Explore

7. **Formatting Text** You can use a word processor such as WordPad to **format** text, that is, to give it a specific look and feel by using bold, italics, and different fonts, and by applying other features. Using WordPad, type the title and words to one of your favorite songs and then save the document on your Student Disk (make sure you use your original Student Disk) with the name Song.
   a. Select the title, and then click the Center, Bold, and Italic buttons on the toolbar.
   b. Click the Font list arrow and select a different font. Repeat this step several times with different fonts until you locate a font that matches the song.
   c. Experiment with formatting options until you find a look you like for your document. Save and print the final version.

PROJECTS

1. Formatting a floppy disk removes all the data on a disk. Answer the following questions using full sentences:
   a. What other method did you learn in this tutorial to remove data from a disk?
   b. If you wanted to remove all data from a disk, which method would you use? Why?
   c. What method would you use if you wanted to remove only one file? Why?

2. A friend who is new to computers is trying to learn how to enter text into WordPad. She has just finished typing her first paragraph when she notices a mistake in the first sentence. She can't remember how to fix a mistake, so she asks you for help. Write the set of steps she should try.

3. Computer users usually develop habits about how they access their files and programs. Take a minute to practice methods of opening a file, and then evaluate which method you would be likely to use and why.
   a. Using WordPad, create a document containing the words to a favorite poem, and save it on your Student Disk with the name Poem.
   b. Close WordPad and return to the desktop.
   c. Open the document using a *document-centric* approach.
   d. After a successful completion of part c, close the program and reopen the same document using another approach.
   e. Write the steps you used to complete parts c and d of this assignment. Then write a paragraph discussing which approach is most convenient when you are starting from the desktop, and indicate what habits you would develop if you owned your own computer and used it regularly.

Explore

4. The My Computer window gives you access to the objects on your computer. In this tutorial you used My Computer to access your floppy drive so you could view the contents of your Student Disk. The My Computer window gives you access to other objects too. Open My Computer and write a list of the objects you see, including folders. Then click each icon and write a two-sentence description of the contents of each window that opens.

Explore

5. In this tutorial you learned how to copy a disk to protect yourself in the event of data loss. If you had your own computer with an 80 MB hard drive that was being used to capacity, it would take many 1.44 MB floppy disks to copy the contents of the entire hard drive. Is copying a reasonable method to use for protecting the data on your hard disk? Why, or why not?
   a. As mentioned at the end of the tutorial, Windows 98 also includes an accessory called Backup that helps you safeguard your data. Backup doesn't just copy the data—it organizes it so that it takes up much less space than if you simply copied it. This program might not be installed on your computer, but if it is, try starting it (click the Start button, point to Programs, point to Accessories, point to System Tools, and then click Backup) and opening the Help files to learn what you can about how it functions. If it is not installed, skip part a.
   b. Look up the topic of backups in a computer concepts textbook or in computer trade magazines. You could also interview experienced computer owners to find out which method they use to protect their data. When you have finished researching the concept of the backup, write a single-page essay that explains the difference between copying and backing up files, and evaluates which method is preferable for backing up large amounts of data, and why.

LAB ASSIGNMENTS

Using Files In this Lab you manipulate a simulated computer to view what happens in memory and on disk when you create, save, open, revise, and delete files. Understanding what goes on "inside the box" will help you quickly grasp how to perform basic file operations with most application software. See the Read This Before You Begin page for instructions on starting the Using Files Course Lab.

1. Click the Steps button to learn how to use the simulated computer to view the contents of memory and disk when you perform basic file operations. As you proceed through the Steps, answer all of the Quick Check questions that appear. After you complete the Steps, you will see a Quick Check Summary Report. Follow the instructions on the screen to print this report.

2. Click the Explore button and use the simulated computer to perform the following tasks:
   a. Create a document containing your name and the city in which you were born. Save this document as NAME.
   b. Create another document containing two of your favorite foods. Save this document as FOODS.
   c. Create another file containing your two favorite classes. Call this file CLASSES.
   d. Open the FOOD file and add another one of your favorite foods. Save this file without changing its name.
   e. Open the NAME file. Change this document so it contains your name and the name of your school. Save this as a new document called SCHOOL.
   f. Write down how many files are on the simulated disk and the exact contents of each file.
   g. Delete all the files.
3. In Explore, use the simulated computer to perform the following tasks.
   a. Create a file called MUSIC that contains the name of your favorite CD.
   b. Create another document that contains eight numbers and call this file LOTTERY.
   c. You didn't win the lottery this week. Revise the contents of the LOTTERY file, but save the revision as LOTTERY2.
   d. Revise the MUSIC file so it also contains the name of your favorite musician or composer, and save this file as MUSIC2.
   e. Delete the MUSIC file.
   f. Write down how many files are on the simulated disk and the exact contents of each file.

QUICK CHECK ANSWERS

Session 2.1

1. file
2. Formatting
3. True
4. insertion point
5. Word wrap
6. Move the I-beam pointer to the left of the first word you want to select, then drag the I-beam pointer over the text to the end of the last word you want to select.
7. file extension

Session 2.2

1. My Computer
2. A
3. hard
4. file name, size, type, and date modified
5. root or top-level
6. True
7. yes

LEVEL I

New Perspectives on

MICROSOFT® WORD® 2000

Read This Before You Begin

To the Student

Data Disks

To complete the Level I tutorials, Review Assignments, and Case Problems, you need 1 Data Disk. Your instructor will either provide you with this Data Disk or ask you to make your own.

If you are making your own Data Disk, you will need 1 blank, formatted high-density disk. You will need to copy a set of folders from a file server or standalone computer or the Web onto your disks. Your instructor will tell you which computer, drive letter, and folders contain the files you need. You could also download the files by going to www.course.com, clicking Data Disk Files, and following the instructions on the screen.

The following shows you which folders go on your disk, so that you will have enough disk space to complete all the tutorials, Review Assignments, and Case Problems:

Data Disk 1

Write this on the disk label:

Data Disk 1: Word 2000 Tutorials 1-4

Put these folders on the disk:

Tutorial.01,Tutorial.02, Tutorial.03, Tutorial.04

When you begin each tutorial, be sure you are using the correct Data Disk. Refer to the "File Finder" Chart at the back of this text for more detailed information on which files are used in which tutorials. See the inside front cover of this book for more information on Student Disk files, or ask your instructor or technical support person for assistance.

Course Labs

The Word Level I tutorials feature an interactive Course Lab to help you understand word processing concepts. There are Lab Assignments at the end of Tutorial 1 that relate to this Lab.

To start a Lab, click the **Start** button on the Windows taskbar, point to **Programs**, point to **Course Labs**, point to **New Perspectives Course Labs**, and click the name of the Lab you want to use.

Using Your Own Computer

If you are going to work through this book using your own computer, you need:

- **Computer System** Microsoft Windows 95, 98, NT, or higher must be installed on your computer. This book assumes a typical installation of Microsoft Word.
- **Data Disk** You will not be able to complete the tutorials or exercises in this book using your own computer until you have your Data Disk.
- **Course Labs** See your instructor or technical support person to obtain the Course Lab software for use on your own computer.

Visit Our World Wide Web Site

Additional materials designed especially for you are available on the World Wide Web. Go to http://www.course.com.

To the Instructor

The Data Files and Course Labs are available on the Instructor's Resource Kit for this title. Follow the instructions in the Help file on the CD-ROM to install the programs to your network or standalone computer. For information on creating Data Disks or the Course Labs, see the "To the Student" section above.

You are granted a license to copy the Data Files and Course Labs to any computer or computer network used by students who have purchased this book.

OBJECTIVES

In this tutorial you will:

- Start and exit Word
- Identify the components of the Word window
- Choose commands using the toolbars and menus
- Create and edit a document
- Enter the date with AutoComplete
- Correct spelling errors with AutoCorrect
- Scroll through a document
- Save, preview, and print a document
- Record properties for a document
- Use the Word Help system to get help

LAB

CREATING A DOCUMENT

Writing a Business Letter for Crossroads

CASE

Crossroads

Karen Liu is executive director of Crossroads, a small, nonprofit organization in Tacoma, Washington. Crossroads distributes business clothing to low-income clients who are returning to the job market or starting new careers. To make potential clients in the community more aware of their services, Crossroads reserves an exhibit booth each year at a local job fair sponsored by the Tacoma Chamber of Commerce. Crossroads needs to find out the date and location of this year's fair, as well as some other logistical information, before reserving a booth. Karen asks you to write a letter requesting this information from the Tacoma Chamber of Commerce.

In this tutorial you will create Karen's letter using Microsoft Word 2000, a popular word-processing program. Before you begin typing the letter, you will learn to start the Word program, identify and use the elements of the Word screen, and adjust some Word settings. Next you will create a new Word document, type the text of the Crossroads letter, save the letter, and then print the letter for Karen. In the process of entering the text, you'll learn several ways of correcting typing errors. You'll also find out how to use the Word Help system, which allows you to quickly find answers to your questions about the program.

SESSION 1.1

In this session you will learn how to start Word, how to identify and use the parts of the Word screen, and how to adjust some Word settings. With the skills you learn in this session, you'll be prepared to use Word to create a variety of documents, such as letters, reports, and memos.

Four Steps to a Professional Document

Word helps you produce quality work in minimal time. Not only can you type a document in Word, you can quickly make revisions and corrections, adjust margins and spacing, create columns and tables, and add graphics to your documents. The most efficient way to produce a document is to follow these four steps: (1) planning and creating, (2) editing, (3) formatting, and (4) printing.

In the long run, *planning* saves time and effort. First, you should determine what you want to say. State your purpose clearly and include enough information to achieve that purpose without overwhelming or boring your reader. Be sure to *organize* your ideas logically. Also, decide how you want your document to look. In this case, your letter to the Tacoma Chamber of Commerce will take the form of a standard business letter. Karen has given you a handwritten note with all her questions for the Tacoma Chamber of Commerce, as shown in Figure 1-1.

Figure 1-1 **KAREN'S QUESTIONS ABOUT THE JOB FAIR**

Please write the Tacoma Chamber of Commerce and find out the following:

What are the location and dates for this year's job fair?

Is a map of the exhibit area available? What size booths are available and how can we reserve a booth?

Who do we contact about what physical facilities are available at each booth?

Send the letter to the Chamber's president. The address is 210 Shoreline Vista, Suite 1103, Tacoma WA 98402.

After you've planned your document, you can go ahead and *create* it using Word. The next step, *editing*, consists of reading the document you've created, then correcting your errors, and, finally, adding or deleting text to make the document easy to read.

Once your document is error-free, you can *format* it to make it visually appealing. Formatting features, such as white space (blank areas of a page), line spacing, boldface, and italics can help make your document easier to read. *Printing* is the final phase in creating an effective document. In this tutorial, you will preview your document before you spend time and resources to print it.

Starting Word

Before you can apply these four steps to produce a letter in Word, you need to start Word and learn about the general organization of the Word screen. You'll do that now.

To start Microsoft Word:

1. Make sure Windows is running on your computer and the Windows desktop appears on your screen.
2. Click the **Start** button on the taskbar to display the Start menu, and then point to **Programs** to display the Programs menu.
3. Point to **Microsoft Word** on the Programs menu. See Figure 1-2.

Figure 1-2 STARTING MICROSOFT WORD

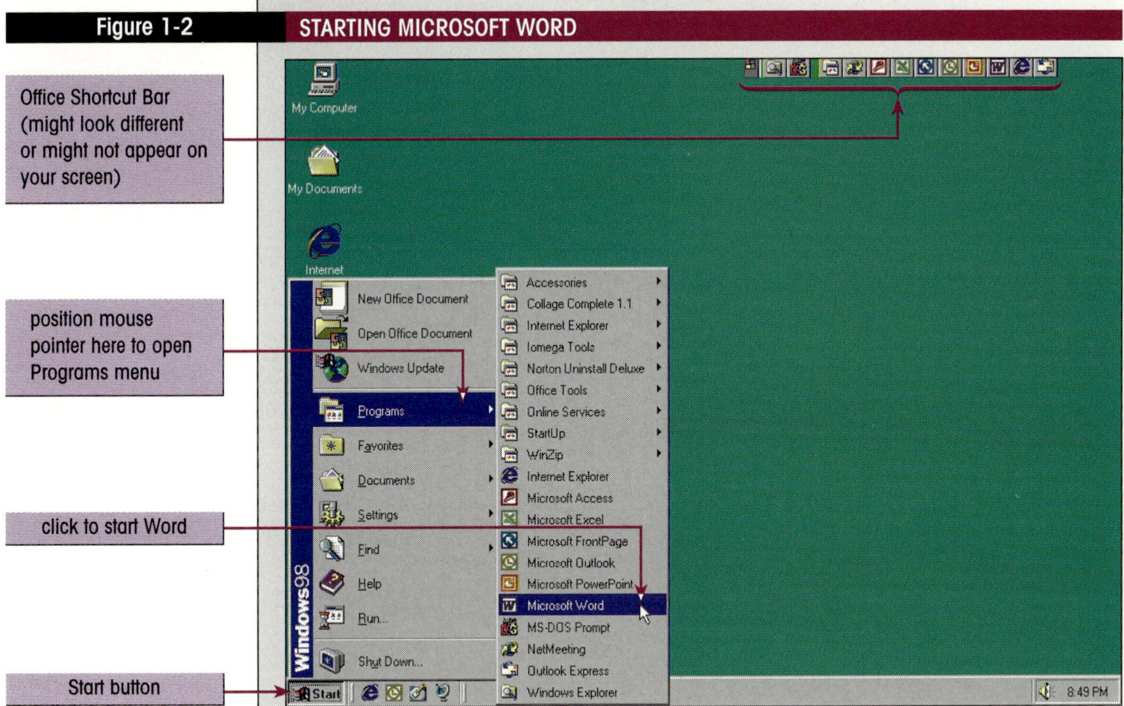

TROUBLE? Don't worry if your screen differs slightly from Figure 1-2. Although the figures in this book were created while running Windows 98 in its default settings, these operating systems share the same basic user interface. Microsoft Word should run equally well using Windows 95, Windows 98 in Web style, Windows NT, or Windows 2000.

TROUBLE? If you don't see the Microsoft Word option on the Programs menu, ask your instructor or technical support person for help.

TROUBLE? If the Office Shortcut Bar appears on your screen, your system is set up to display it. Because the Office Shortcut Bar is not required to complete these tutorials, it has been omitted from the remaining figures in this text. You can close it or simply ignore it.

4. Click **Microsoft Word**. After a short pause, the Microsoft Word copyright information appears in a message box and remains on the screen until the Word program window, containing a blank Word document, is displayed. See Figure 1-3.

Figure 1-3 MAXIMIZED WORD SCREEN

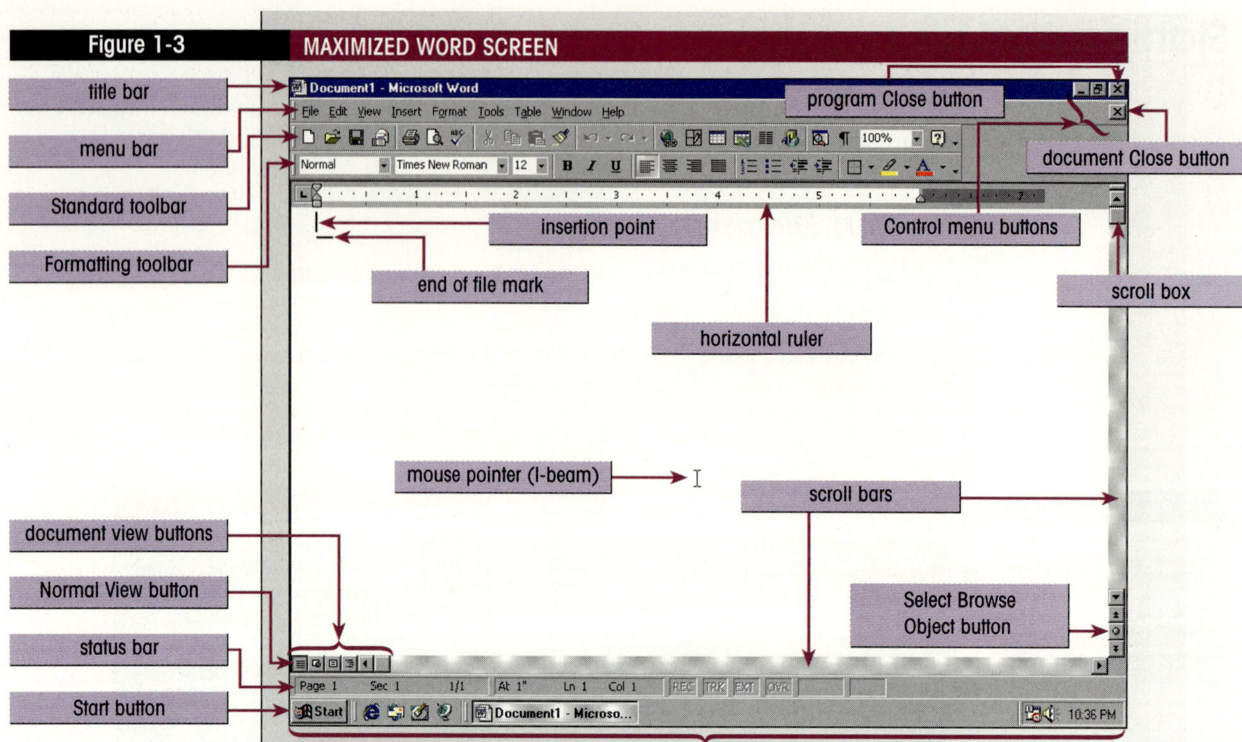

TROUBLE? Depending on how your system is set up, the Office Assistant might open when you start Word. For now, click Help on the menu bar, and then click Hide the Office Assistant. You'll learn more about the Office Assistant later in this tutorial. If you've just installed Microsoft Word, you'll need to click the Start Using Microsoft Word button, which the Office Assistant displays, before closing the Office Assistant window.

5. If the Word window does not fill the entire screen, click the **Maximize** button in the upper-right corner of the Word window. Your screen should now resemble Figure 1-3.

TROUBLE? If your screen looks slightly different from Figure 1-3 (for example, if you see the paragraph mark character ¶ on your screen, the Standard and Formatting toolbars appear on one row, or an additional toolbar is displayed), just continue with the steps. You will learn how to make some adjustments to the Word screen shortly.

Word is now running and ready to use.

Viewing the Word Screen

The Word screen is made up of a number of elements, each of which is described in Figure 1-4. You are already familiar with some of these elements, such as the menu bar, title bar, and status bar, because they are common to all Windows screens.

If at any time you would like to check the name of a Word toolbar button, just position the mouse pointer over the button without clicking. A **ScreenTip**, a small yellow box with the name of the button, will appear.

Figure 1-4 DESCRIPTION OF WORD SCREEN ELEMENTS

SCREEN ELEMENT	DESCRIPTION
Control menu buttons	Size and close the Word window and the document
Document Close button	Closes the open document when only one document is open
Document view buttons	Switch the document between four different views: normal view, Web layout view, print layout view, and outline view
Document window	Area where you enter text and graphics
End-of-file mark	Indicates the end of the document
Formatting toolbar	Contains buttons to activate common font and paragraph formatting commands
Horizontal ruler	Adjusts margins, tabs, and column widths; vertical ruler appears in print layout view
Insertion point	Indicates location where characters will be inserted or deleted
Menu bar	Contains lists or menus of all the Word commands. When you first display a menu, you see a short list of the most frequently used commands. To see the full list of commands in the menu, you can either click the menu and then wait a few seconds for the remaining commands to appear or click the menu and then click or point to the downward-facing double-arrow at the bottom of the menu.
Mouse pointer	Changes shape depending on its location on the screen (i.e., I-beam pointer in text area; arrow in nontext areas)
Program Close button	Closes the current document if more than one document is open. Closes Word if one or no document is open.
Scroll bars	Shifts text vertically and horizontally on the screen so you can see different parts of the document
Scroll box	Helps you move quickly to other pages of your document
Select Browse Object button	Displays buttons that allow you to move quickly through the document
Standard toolbar	Contains buttons to activate frequently used commands
Start button	Starts a program, opens a document, provides quick access to Windows Help
Status bar	Provides information regarding the location of the insertion point
Taskbar	Shows programs that are running and allows you to switch quickly from one program to another
Title bar	Identifies the current application (i.e., Microsoft Word); shows the filename of the current document

Keep in mind that the commands on the menu bars initially display the commands that are used most frequently on your particular computer. When you leave the menu displayed for a few seconds or point to the double-arrow, a more complete list of commands appears. Throughout these tutorials, point to the double-arrow if you do not see the command you need.

Checking the Screen Before You Begin Each Tutorial

Word provides a set of standard settings, called **default settings**, that are appropriate for most documents. However, the setup of your Word document might have different default settings from those shown in the figures. This often happens when you share a computer and another user changes the appearance of the Word screen. The rest of this section explains what your screen should look like and how to make it match those in the tutorials.

Setting the Document View to Normal

You can view your document in one of four ways—normal, Web layout, print layout, or outline. **Web layout view** and **outline view** are designed for special situations that you don't need to worry about now. You will, however, learn more about **print layout view**—which allows you to see a page's design and format—in later tutorials. You will use **normal view,** which allows you to see more of the document, for this tutorial. Depending on the document view selected by the last person who used Word, you might need to change the document back to normal view.

To make sure the document window is in normal view:

1. Click the **Normal View** button to the left of the horizontal scroll bar. See Figure 1-5. If your document window was not in normal view, it changes to normal view now. The Normal View button looks pressed in to indicate that it is selected.

Figure 1-5 CHANGING TO NORMAL VIEW

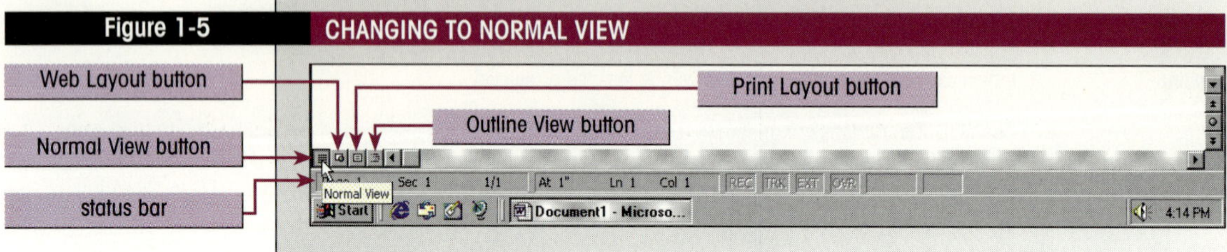

Displaying the Toolbars and Ruler

These tutorials frequently use the Standard toolbar and the Formatting toolbar to help you work more efficiently. Each time you start Word, check to make sure both toolbars appear on your screen, with the Standard toolbar on top of the Formatting toolbar. Depending on the settings specified by the last person to use your computer, you may not see both toolbars, or your toolbars may appear all on one row, rather than one on top of another. You also may see additional toolbars, such as the Drawing toolbar.

If either toolbar is missing, or if other toolbars are displayed, perform the next steps.

To display or hide a toolbar:

1. Position the pointer over any visible toolbar and click the right mouse button. A shortcut menu appears. The menu lists all available toolbars and displays a check mark next to those currently displayed.

2. If the Standard or Formatting toolbar is not visible, click its name on the shortcut menu to place a check mark next to it. If any toolbars besides the Formatting and Standard toolbars have check marks, click each one to remove the check mark and hide the toolbar. Only the Standard and Formatting toolbars should be visible, as shown in Figure 1-6.

Figure 1-6 TWO TOOLBARS ON ONE ROW

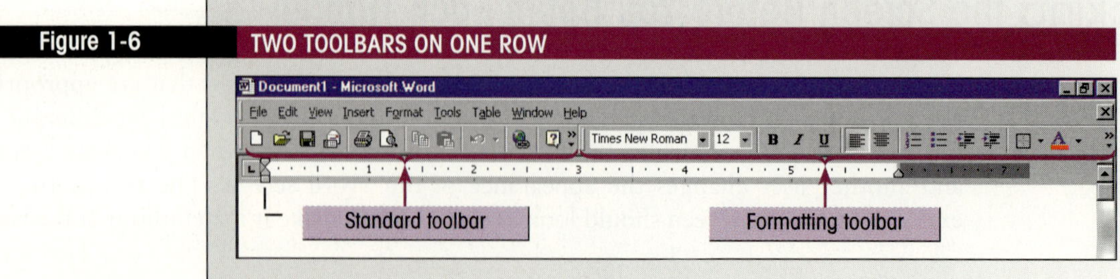

If the toolbars appear on one row, as in Figure 1-6, perform the next steps to move the Formatting toolbar below the Standard toolbar.

To move the Formatting toolbar:

1. Click **Tools** on the menu bar, and then click **Customize**. The Customize dialog box opens.

   TROUBLE? If you don't see the Customize command on the Tools menu, point to the double-arrow, as explained earlier in this tutorial, to display the full list of commands.

2. Click the **Options** tab, and then click the **Standard and Formatting toolbars share one row** check box to remove the check.

3. Click **Close**. The Customize dialog box closes. The toolbars on your screen should now match those in Figure 1-3.

As you complete these tutorials, the ruler also should be visible to help you place items precisely.

To display the ruler:

1. Click **View** on the menu bar, and then point to the double-arrow at the bottom of the menu to display the hidden menu commands.

2. If "Ruler" does not have a check mark next to it, then click **Ruler**.

Setting the Font and Font Size

A **font** is a set of characters that has a certain design, shape, and appearance. Each font has a name, such as Courier, Times New Roman, or Arial. The **font size** is the actual height of a character, measured in points, where one point equals 1/72 of an inch in height. You'll learn more about fonts and font sizes later, but for now simply keep in mind that most of the documents you create will use the Times New Roman font in a font size of 12 points. Word usually uses a default (or predefined) setting of Times New Roman 12 point in new documents, but someone else might have changed the setting after Word was installed on your computer. You can see your computer's current settings in the Font list box, and the Font Size list box, in the Formatting toolbar, as shown in Figure 1-7.

Figure 1-7 DEFAULT FONT AND FONT SIZE SETTINGS

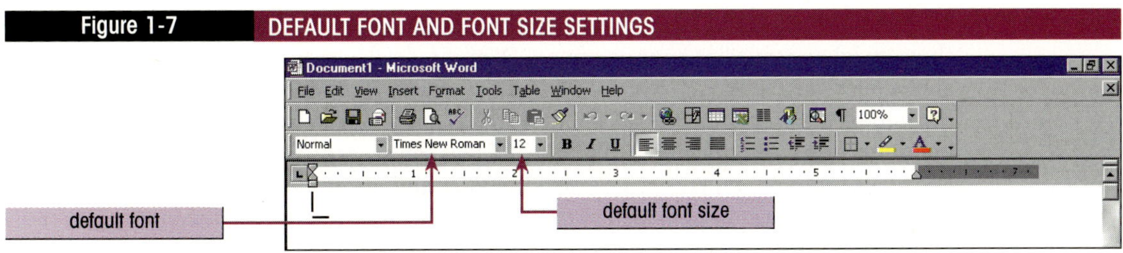

If your font setting is not Times New Roman 12 point, you should change the default setting now. You'll use the menu bar to choose the desired commands.

To change the default font and font size:

1. Click **Format** on the menu bar, and then click **Font** to open the Font dialog box. If necessary, click the Font tab. See Figure 1-8.

Figure 1-8 FONT DIALOG BOX

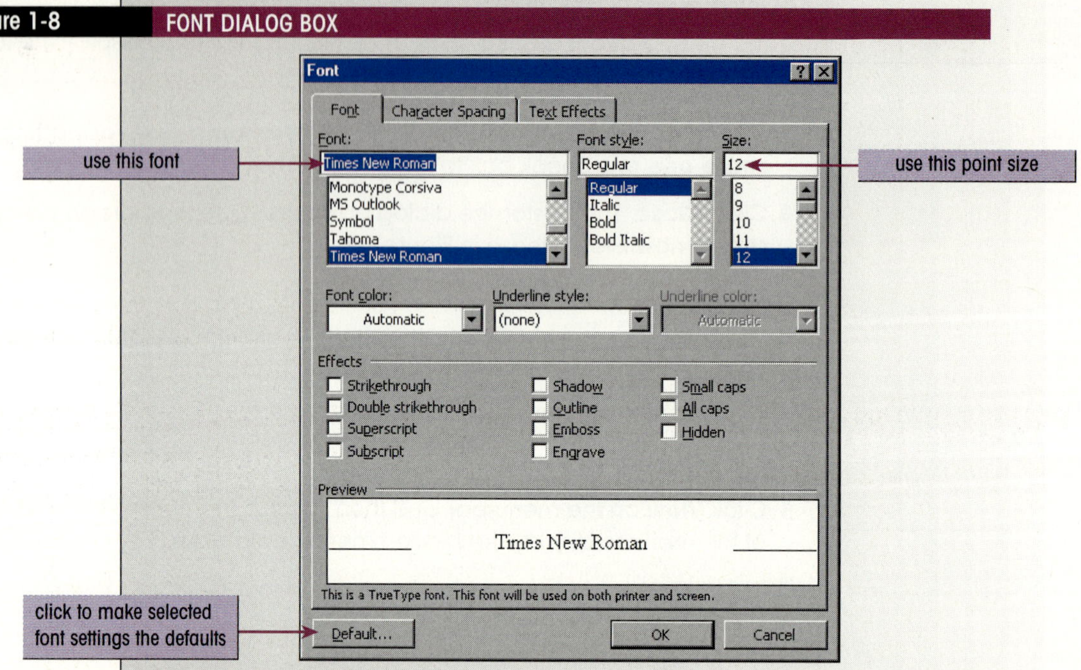

2. In the Font text box, click **Times New Roman**.

3. In the Size list box, click **12** to change the font to 12 point.

4. Click the **Default** button to make Times New Roman and 12 point the default settings. Word displays a message asking you to verify that you want to make 12-point Times New Roman the default font.

5. Click the **Yes** button.

Displaying Nonprinting Characters

Nonprinting characters are symbols that can be displayed on the screen but that do not show up when you print your document. You can display them when you are working on the appearance, or **format**, of your document. For example, one nonprinting character marks the end of a paragraph (¶), and another marks the space between words (•). It's sometimes helpful to display nonprinting characters so you can see whether you've typed an extra space, ended a paragraph, typed spaces instead of tabs, and so on. Generally, in these tutorials, you will display nonprinting characters only when you are formatting a document. You'll display them now, though, so you can use them as guides when typing your first letter.

To display nonprinting characters:

1. Click the Show/Hide ¶ button ¶ on the Standard toolbar. A paragraph mark (¶) appears at the top of the document window. See Figure 1-9.

Figure 1-9 NONPRINTING CHARACTERS ACTIVATED

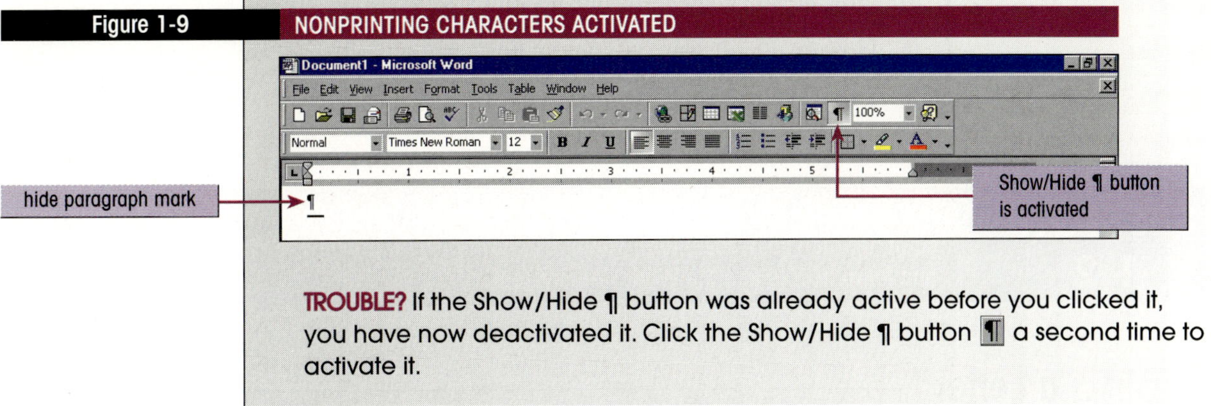

TROUBLE? If the Show/Hide ¶ button was already active before you clicked it, you have now deactivated it. Click the Show/Hide ¶ button ¶ a second time to activate it.

To make sure your screen always matches the figures in these tutorials, remember to complete the checklist in Figure 1-10 each time you sit down at the computer.

Figure 1-10 WORD SCREEN SESSION CHECKLIST

SCREEN ELEMENT	SETTING	CHECK
Document view	Normal view	❑
Word window	Maximized	❑
Standard toolbar	Displayed, below the menu bar	❑
Formatting toolbar	Displayed, below the Standard toolbar	❑
Other toolbars	Hidden	❑
Nonprinting characters	Hidden	❑
Font	Times New Roman	❑
Point size	12 point	❑
Ruler	Displayed	❑

Now that you have planned a document, opened the Word program, identified screen elements, and adjusted settings, you are ready to create a new document. In the next session, you will create Karen's letter to the Tacoma Chamber of Commerce.

Session 1.1 QUICK CHECK

1. In your own words, list and describe the steps in creating a document.
2. How do you start Word from the Windows desktop?
3. Define each of the following in your own words:
   a. nonprinting characters
   b. document view buttons
   c. font size
   d. default settings

4. How do you change the default font size?
5. How do you display or hide the Formatting toolbar?
6. How do you change the document view to normal view?

SESSION 1.2

In this session you will create a one-page document using Word. You'll correct errors and scroll through your document. You'll also name, save, preview, and print the document, and learn how to use the Word Help system.

Typing a Letter

You're ready to type Karen's letter to the Tacoma Chamber of Commerce. Figure 1-11 shows the completed letter printed on the company letterhead. You'll begin by opening a new blank page (in case you accidentally typed something in the current page). Then you'll move the insertion point to about 2½ inches from the top margin of the paper to allow space for the Crossroads letterhead.

Figure 1-11 JOB FAIR LETTER

1414 East Bellingham S.W.
Suite 318
Tacoma, WA 98402

February 21, 2001

Deborah Brown, President
Tacoma Chamber of Commerce
210 Shoreline Vista, Suite 1103
Tacoma, WA 98402

Dear Deborah:

Recently, you contacted our staff about the Chamber's decision to sponsor a job fair again this year. We are interested in participating as we have done in the past.

Please send us information about the dates and location for this year's fair. If a map of the exhibit area is available, we would appreciate receiving a copy of it. Also, please send us the name and address of someone we can contact regarding the on-site physical facilities. Specifically, we need to know what size the exhibit booths are and how we can reserve one.

Thank you for your help in this matter. We look forward to participating in the job fair and hope to hear from you soon.

Sincerely yours,

Karen Liu
Executive Director

To open a new document:

1. If you took a break after the last session, make sure the Word program is running, that nonprinting characters are displayed, and that the font settings in the Formatting toolbar are set to 12-point Times New Roman. Also verify that the toolbars and the ruler are properly displayed.

2. Click the **New Blank Document** button on the Standard toolbar to open a fresh document.

   If you have the taskbar displayed at the bottom of your screen, you see an additional button for the new document. If you wanted to switch back to Document1, you could simply click its button on the taskbar. Notice that the new document has only one set of Control menu buttons. When two or more documents are open, you click the Close button in the upper-right corner of the title bar to close that document. When only one document is open, you can click the Close Window button in the upper-right corner of the menu bar to close the document and leave Word open, or you can click the Close button in the upper-right corner of the title bar to close the document and exit Word.

3. Press the **Enter** key eight times. Each time you press the Enter key, a nonprinting paragraph mark appears. In the status bar (at the bottom of the document window), you should see the setting "At 2.5"," indicating that the insertion point is approximately 2½ inches from the top of the page. Another setting in the status bar should read "Ln 9," indicating the insertion point is in line 9 of the document. Note that your settings may be slightly different. See Figure 1-12.

Figure 1-12 DOCUMENT WINDOW AFTER INSERTING BLANK LINES

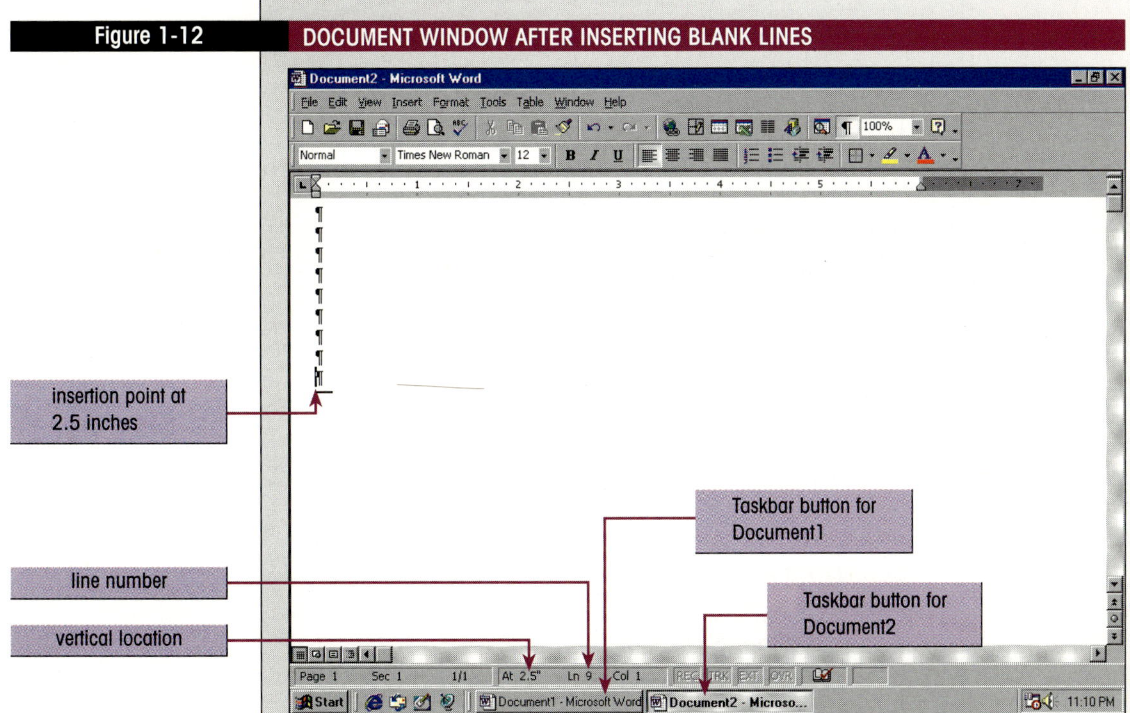

TROUBLE? If the paragraph mark doesn't appear each time you press the Enter key, the nonprinting characters might be hidden. To show the nonprinting characters, click the Show/Hide ¶ button on the Standard toolbar, as described earlier in this tutorial.

TROUBLE? If you pressed the Enter key too many times, press the Backspace key to delete each extra line and paragraph mark. If you're on line 9 but the "At" number is not 2.5", don't worry. Different monitors produce slightly different measurements when you press the Enter key.

Using AutoCompleteTips

Now you're ready to type the date. You'll take advantage of Word's **AutoComplete** feature, which automatically types dates and other regularly used words and text for you.

To insert the date using an AutoComplete tip:

1. Type **Febr** (the first four letters of February). An AutoComplete tip appears above the line, as shown in Figure 1-13. If you wanted to type something other than February, you would simply continue typing to complete the word. In this case, though, you want to accept the AutoComplete tip, so you will press the Enter key in the next step.

Figure 1-13 AUTOCOMPLETE TIP

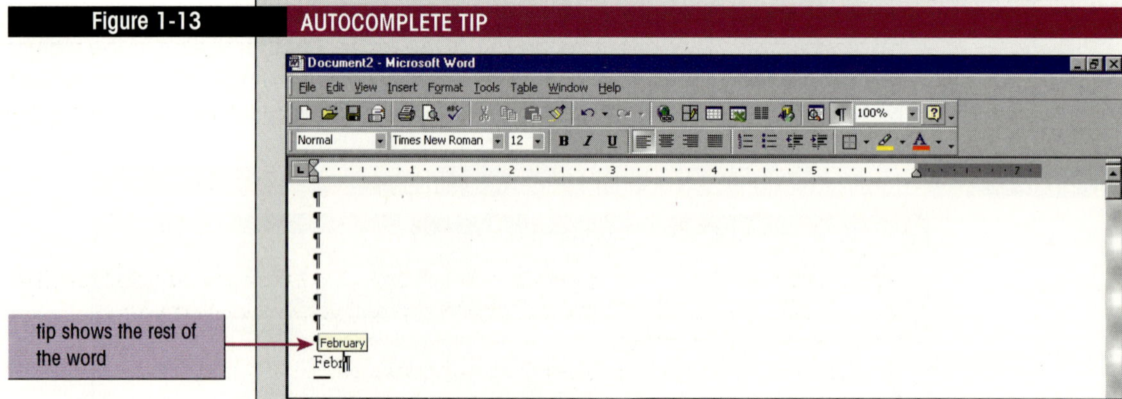

TROUBLE? If the AutoComplete tip doesn't appear, this feature may not be active. Click Tools on the menu bar, click AutoCorrect, click the AutoText tab, click the Show AutoComplete tip for AutoText and dates check box to insert a check, and then click OK.

2. Press the **Enter** key to insert the rest of the word "February."

3. Press the **spacebar** and then type **21, 2001** to complete the date. See Figure 1-14.

TROUBLE? If February happens to be the current month, you will see an AutoComplete tip displaying the current date after you press the spacebar. To accept that AutoComplete tip, press Enter. Otherwise, simply type the rest of the date as instructed in Step 3.

Figure 1-14 DATE ENTERED IN THE DOCUMENT

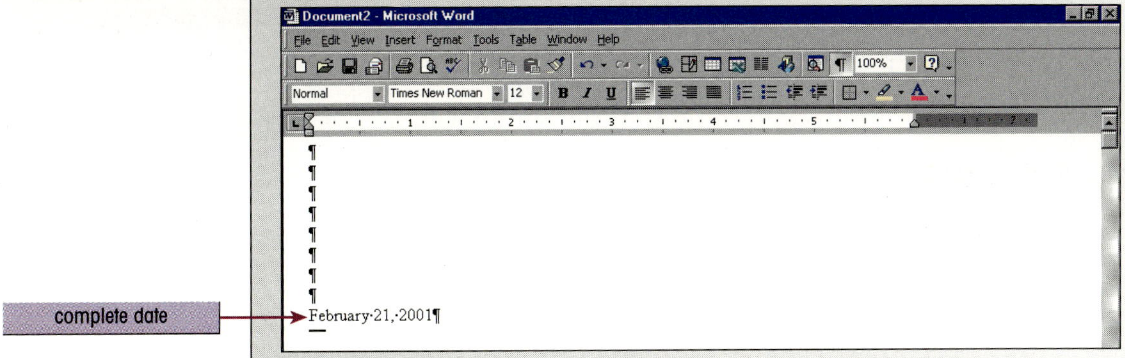

4. Press the **Enter** key four times to insert three blank lines between the date and the inside address. The status bar now should display "Ln13."

Next, you'll enter the inside address shown on Karen's note.

Entering Text

You'll enter the inside address by typing it. If you type a wrong character, simply press the Backspace key to delete the mistake and then retype it.

To type the inside address:

1. Type **Deborah Brown, President** and then press the **Enter** key. As you type, the nonprinting character (•) appears between words to indicate a space.

TROUBLE? If a wavy red or green line appears beneath a word, check to make sure you typed the text correctly. If you did not, use the Backspace key to remove the error, and then retype the text correctly.

2. Type the following text, pressing the **Enter** key after each line to enter the inside address:

Tacoma Chamber of Commerce
210 Shoreline Vista, Suite 1103
Tacoma, WA 98402

3. Press the **Enter** key again to add a blank line between the inside address and the salutation.

4. Type **Dear Deborah:** and press the **Enter** key twice to double space between the salutation and the body of the letter. When you press the Enter key the first time, the Office Assistant might appear, asking if you would like help writing your letter. Depending on the settings on your computer, you might see a different Office Assistant than the one shown in Figure 1-15.

Figure 1-15 OFFICE ASSISTANT

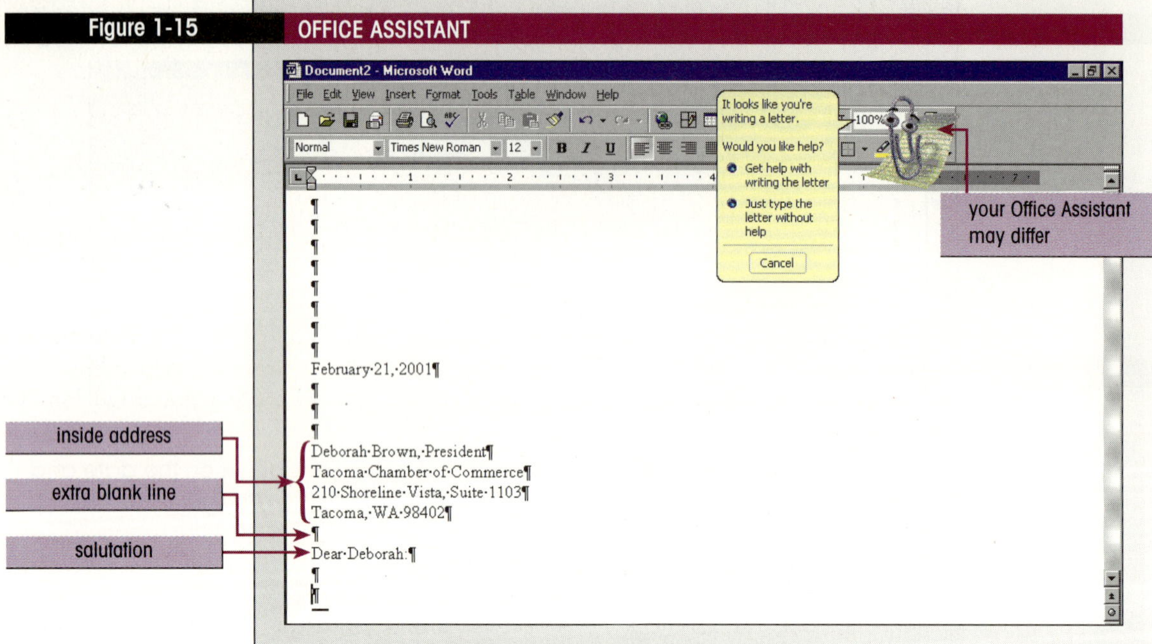

The Office Assistant is an interactive feature that sometimes appears to offer help on routine tasks. In this case, you could click the "Get help with writing the letter" button and have the Office Assistant lead you through a series of dialog boxes designed to set up the basic elements of your letter. You'll learn more about the Office Assistant later in this tutorial. For now, though, you'll close the Office Assistant and continue writing your letter.

5. Click the **Just type the letter without help** button to close the Office Assistant.

TROUBLE? If the Office Assistant remains open, right-click the Office Assistant, and then click Hide to close it.

You have completed the date, the inside address, and the salutation of Karen's letter, using a standard business letter format. You're ready to complete the letter. Before you do, however, you should save what you have typed so far.

Saving a Document for the First Time

The letter on which you are working is stored only in the computer's memory, not on a disk. If you were to exit Word, turn off your computer, or experience an accidental power failure, the part of Karen's letter that you just typed would be lost. You should get in the habit of frequently saving your document to a disk.

The first time you save a document, you need to name it. The name you use is usually referred to as the **filename**. To make it easy for you to keep track of the various documents stored on your computer, or 3½-inch disk, or Zip disk, it's important to use names that accurately describe their contents. For example, if you use a generic name such as "Letter" for this particular document, you won't be able to differentiate it from other letters in the future. Instead, you should use a more descriptive name, such as Tacoma Job Fair Letter.

REFERENCE WINDOW RW

Saving a Document for the First Time

- Click the Save button on the Standard toolbar (or click File on the menu bar, and then click Save).
- If necessary, change the folder and drive information.
- In the File name text box, type the filename.
- Click the Save button (or press the Enter key).

After you name your document, Word automatically appends the .doc filename extension to identify the file as a Microsoft Word document. However, depending on how Windows is set up on your computer, you might not actually see the .doc extension. These tutorials assume that filename extensions are hidden.

To save the document:

1. Place your Data Disk in the appropriate disk drive.

TROUBLE? If you don't have a Data Disk, you need to get one before you can proceed. Your instructor or technical support person will either give you one or ask you to make your own by following the instructions on the "Read This Before You Begin" page at the beginning of this tutorial. See your instructor or technical support person for more information.

2. Click the **Save** button on the Standard toolbar. The Save As dialog box opens. See Figure 1-16. Note that Word suggests using the first few characters of the letter ("February 21") as the filename. You will replace the suggested filename with something more descriptive.

Figure 1-16 SAVE AS DIALOG BOX

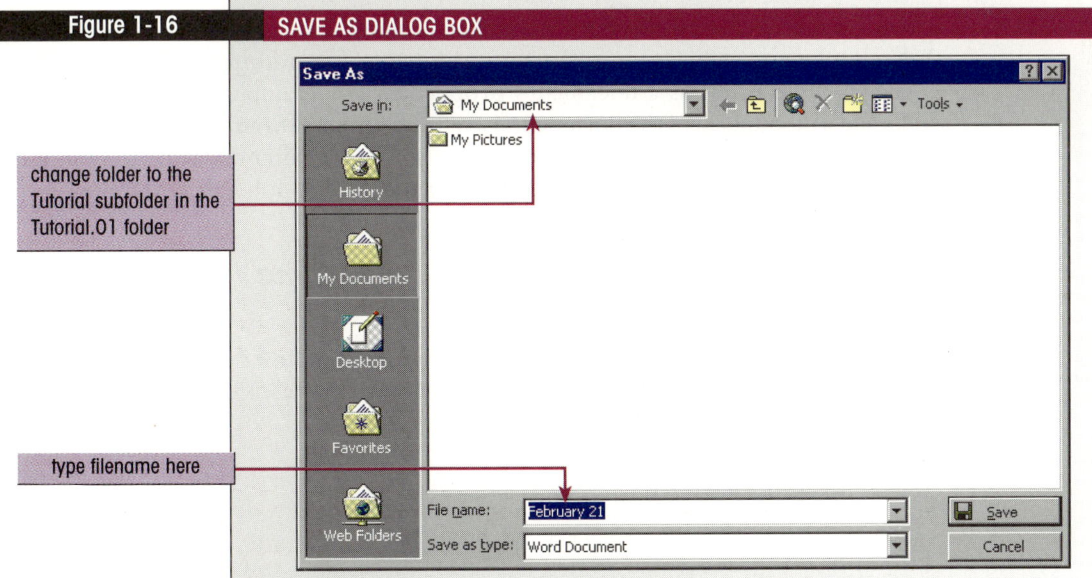

3. Type **Tacoma Job Fair Letter** in the File name text box.

4. Click the **Save in** list arrow, click the drive containing your Data Disk, double-click the **Tutorial.01** folder, then double-click the **Tutorial** folder. The Tutorial folder is now open and ready for you to save the document. See Figure 1-17.

Figure 1-17 SAVE AS DIALOG BOX WITH TUTORIAL FOLDER OPEN

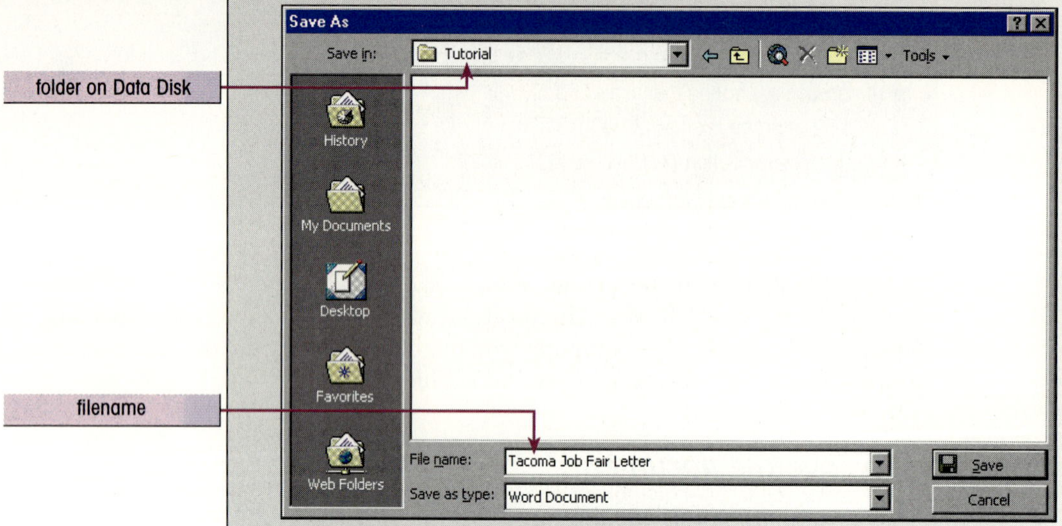

TROUBLE? If Word automatically adds the .doc extension to your filename, then your computer is configured to show filename extensions. Just continue with the tutorial.

5. Click the **Save** button in the Save As dialog box. The dialog box closes, and you return to the document window. The name of your file appears in the title bar.

Adding Properties to a Document

After you save a document, you should record some descriptive information in a special dialog box known as the document's **properties page**. The information that you record here is known, collectively, as a document's **properties**. For example, you might include your name and a description of the document. Later, you or one of your co-workers can review the document's properties for a quick summary of its purpose, without having to skim the entire document. You'll look at the properties page for the Tacoma Job Fair Letter next.

To view the properties page for the Tacoma Job Fair Letter document:

1. Click **File** on the menu bar, click **Properties**, and then, if necessary, click the **Summary** tab. The Tacoma Job Fair Letter Properties dialog box opens, as shown in Figure 1-18.

Figure 1-18 PROPERTIES PAGE FOR THE ACTIVE DOCUMENT

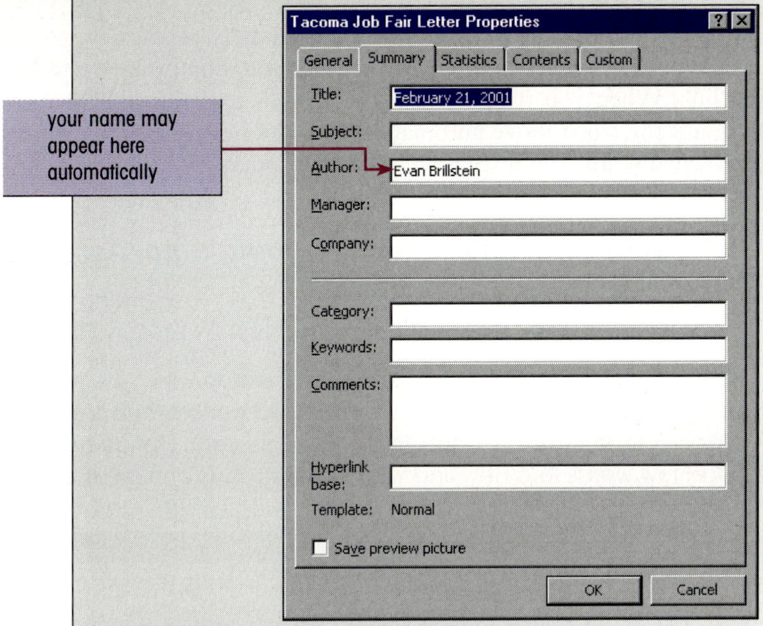

TROUBLE? If you don't see the Properties command on the File menu, point to the double-arrow to display the hidden menu commands.

This dialog box takes its name from the active document (in this case, "Tacoma Job Fair Letter"). Depending on how your computer is set up, the Author text box already may contain your name or the name of the registered owner of your copy of Word. In addition, the Title text box may contain the document's first line of text, "February 21, 2001." Because you already have assigned a descriptive name to this file ("Tacoma Job Fair Letter"), there's no reason to include a title here. You can delete this title and then enter relevant information in the appropriate text boxes. The Comments text box is a good place to record useful notes about the document, such as its purpose.

To edit the contents of the properties page:

1. Verify that the text in the Title text box is highlighted, and then press the **Delete** key.
2. Press the **Tab** key twice. The insertion point moves to the Author text box.
3. If necessary, type your name in the Author text box.
4. Click the Comments text box, and then type **A letter requesting information on the job fair.**
5. Click **OK**. The Tacoma Job Fair Letter dialog box closes, and the document's new properties are saved.

It's good practice to add information to a document's properties page right after you save the document for the first time. You will find such information useful once you have accumulated a number of Word documents and want to organize them. You can use the properties to find documents quickly. As you will see in the Review Assignments at the end of this tutorial, you can view a document's properties page without actually opening the document.

Word Wrap

Now that you have saved your document and its properties, you're ready to complete Karen's letter. As you type the body of the letter, do not press the Enter key at the end of each line. When you type a word that extends into the right margin, both the insertion point and the word move automatically to the next line. This automatic line breaking is called **word wrap**. You'll see how word wrap works as you type the body of Karen's letter.

To observe word wrap while typing a paragraph:

1. Make sure the insertion point is at Ln 20 Col 1 (according to the settings in the status bar). If it's not, move it to that location by pressing the arrow keys.
2. Type the following sentence slowly and watch when the insertion point jumps to the next line: **Recently, you contacted our staff about the Chamber's decision to sponsor a job fair again this year.** Notice how Word moves the last few words to a new line when the previous one is full. See Figure 1-19.

Figure 1-19 WORD WRAPPING TEXT

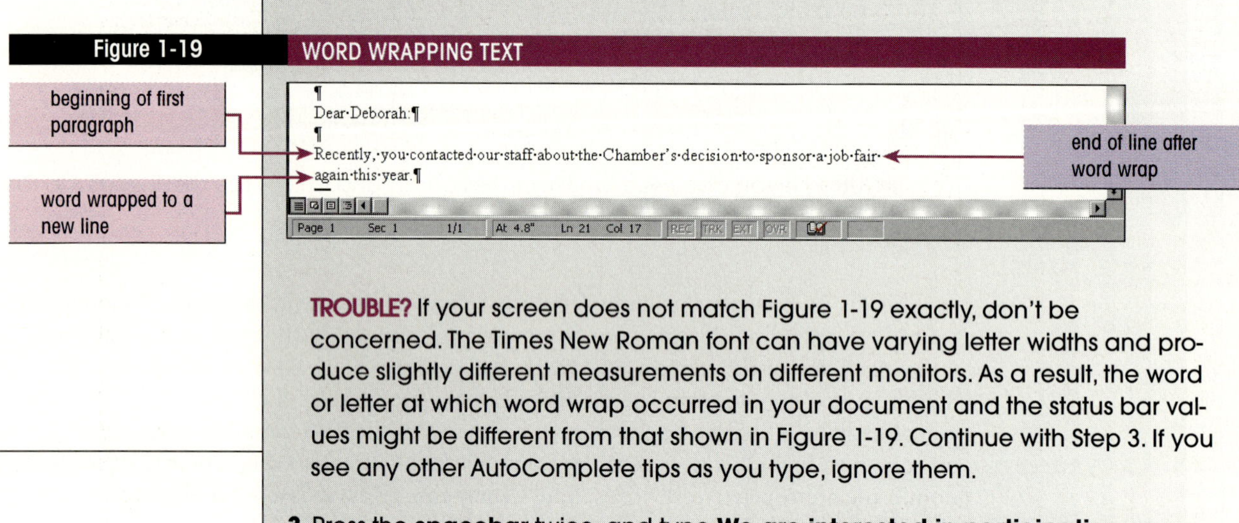

TROUBLE? If your screen does not match Figure 1-19 exactly, don't be concerned. The Times New Roman font can have varying letter widths and produce slightly different measurements on different monitors. As a result, the word or letter at which word wrap occurred in your document and the status bar values might be different from that shown in Figure 1-19. Continue with Step 3. If you see any other AutoComplete tips as you type, ignore them.

3. Press the **spacebar** twice, and type **We are interested in participating as we have done in the past.** This completes the first paragraph of the letter.
4. Press the **Enter** key to end the first paragraph, and then press the **Enter** key again to double space between the first and second paragraphs.

Scrolling a Document

After you finish the last set of steps, the insertion point will be at or near the bottom of your document window. It might seem that no room is left in the document window to type the rest of Karen's letter. However, as you continue to add text at the end of your document, the text that you typed earlier will **scroll** (or shift up) and disappear from the top of the document window. You'll see how scrolling works as you enter the final text of Karen's letter.

To observe scrolling while you're entering text:

1. Make sure the insertion point is at the bottom of the screen, to the left of the second paragraph mark in the body of the letter.

TROUBLE? If you are using a very large monitor, your insertion point may still be some distance from the bottom of the screen. In that case, you may not be able to perform the scrolling steps that follow. Simply read the steps to familiarize yourself with the process of scrolling. You'll scroll longer documents later.

2. Type the second paragraph, as shown in Figure 1-20, and then press the **Enter** key twice to insert a blank line. Notice that as you type the paragraph, the top of the letter scrolls off the top of the document window. Don't worry if you make a mistake in your typing. You'll learn a number of ways to correct errors in the next section.

TROUBLE? If you have difficulty reading the text in Figure 1-20, refer back to Figure 1-11.

Figure 1-20 TOP OF THE LETTER SCROLLED OFF THE SCREEN

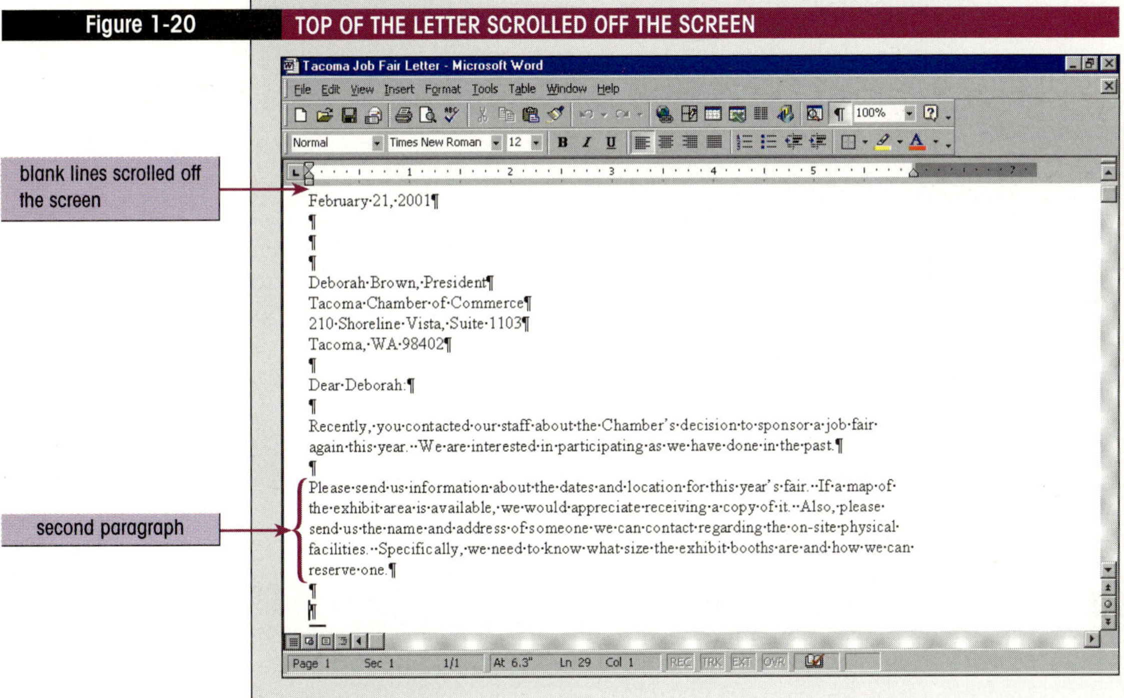

Correcting Errors

Have you made any typing mistakes yet? If so, don't worry. The advantage of using a word processor is that you can correct mistakes quickly and efficiently. Word provides several ways to correct errors when you're entering text.

If you discover a typing error as soon as you make it, you can press the Backspace key to erase the characters and spaces to the left of the insertion point one at a time. Backspacing will erase both printing and nonprinting characters. After you erase the error, you can type the correct characters.

Word also provides a feature, called **AutoCorrect**, that checks for errors in your document as you type and automatically corrects common typing errors, such as "adn" for "and." If the spelling of a particular word differs from its spelling in the Word electronic dictionary, or if a word isn't in the dictionary at all (for example, a person's name), a wavy *red* line appears beneath the word. A wavy red line also appears if you type duplicate words (such as "the the"). If you accidentally type an extra space between words or make a grammatical error (such as typing "He walk to the store." instead of "He walks to the store."), a wavy *green* line appears beneath the error. You'll see how AutoCorrect works when you intentionally make typing errors.

To correct common typing errors:

1. Carefully and slowly type the following sentence exactly as it is shown, including the spelling errors and the extra space between the last two words: **Word corects teh commen typing misTakes you make.** Press the **Enter** key when you are finished typing. Notice that as you press the spacebar after the word "commen," a wavy red line appears beneath it, indicating that the word might be misspelled. Notice also that when you pressed the spacebar after the words "corects," "teh," and "misTakes," Word automatically corrected the spelling. After you pressed the Enter key, a wavy green line appeared under the last two words, alerting you to the extra space. See Figure 1-21.

Figure 1-21 DOCUMENT WINDOW SHOWING TYPING ERRORS

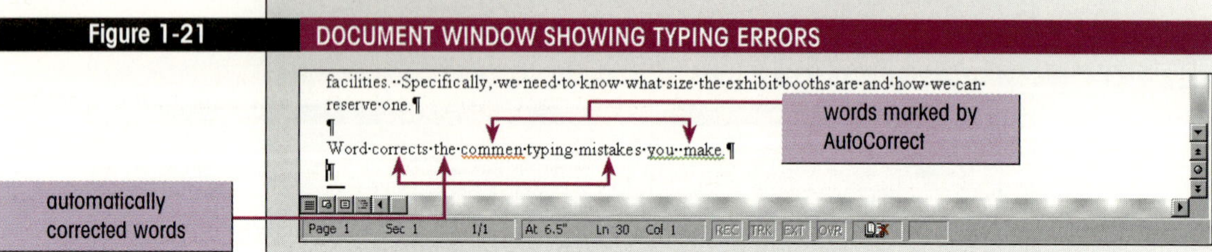

TROUBLE? If red and green wavy lines do not appear beneath mistakes, Word is probably not set to automatically check spelling and grammar as you type. Click Tools on the menu bar, and then click Options to open the Options dialog box. Click the Spelling & Grammar tab. Make sure there are check marks in the Check spelling as you type and the Check grammar as you type check boxes, and click OK. If Word does not automatically correct the incorrect spelling of "the," click Tools on the menu bar, click AutoCorrect, and make sure that all five boxes at the top of the AutoCorrect tab have check marks. Then scroll down the AutoCorrect list to make sure that there is an entry that changes "teh" to "the," and click OK.

2. Position the I-Beam pointer over the word "commen" and click the right mouse button. A list box appears with suggested spellings. See Figure 1-22.

Figure 1-22 LIST BOX SHOWING AUTOCORRECT SUGGESTED SPELLINGS

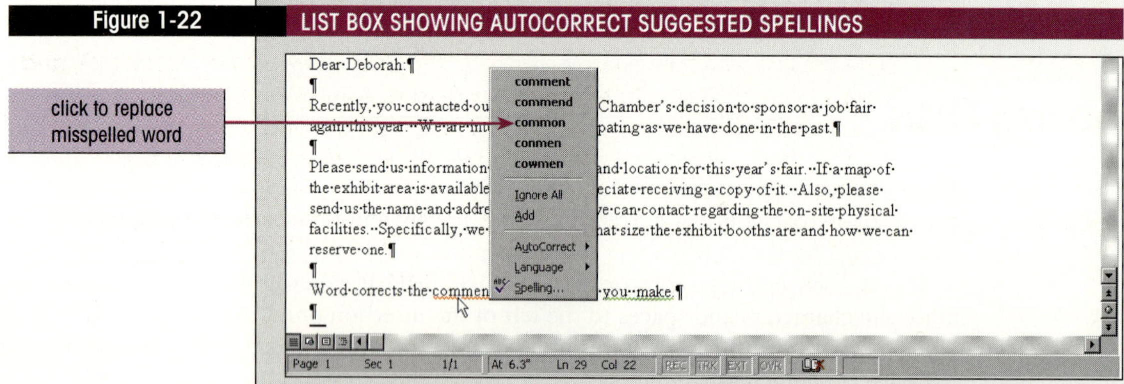

TROUBLE? If the list box doesn't appear, repeat Step 2, making sure you click the right mouse button, not the left one.

3. Click **common** in the list box. The list box disappears, and the correct spelling appears in your document. Notice that the wavy red line disappears after you correct the error.

4. Click to the right of the letter "u" in the word "you." Press the **Delete** key to delete the extra space.

You can see how quick and easy it is to correct common typing errors with AutoCorrect. Remember, however, that there is no substitute for your own eyes. You should thoroughly proofread each document you create, keeping in mind that AutoCorrect will not catch words that are spelled correctly, but used improperly (such as "your" for "you're"). Proofread your document now, and use AutoCorrect or the Backspace or Delete keys to correct any mistakes.

Before you continue typing Karen's letter, you'll need to delete your practice sentence.

To delete the practice sentence:

1. Click between the period and the paragraph mark at the end of the sentence.

2. Press and hold the **Backspace** key until the entire sentence is deleted. Then press the **Delete** key to delete the extra paragraph mark.

3. Make sure the insertion point is in line 29. There should be one nonprinting paragraph mark between the second paragraph and the paragraph you will type next.

Finishing the Letter

You're ready to complete the rest of the letter. As you type, you can use any of the techniques you learned in the previous section to correct mistakes.

To complete the letter:

1. Type the final paragraph of the body of the letter, as shown in Figure 1-23, and then press the **Enter** key twice. Accept or ignore AutoComplete tips as necessary. Unless you have a very large monitor, the date and, possibly, part of the inside address scroll off the top of the document window completely.

Figure 1-23 FINAL PARAGRAPH

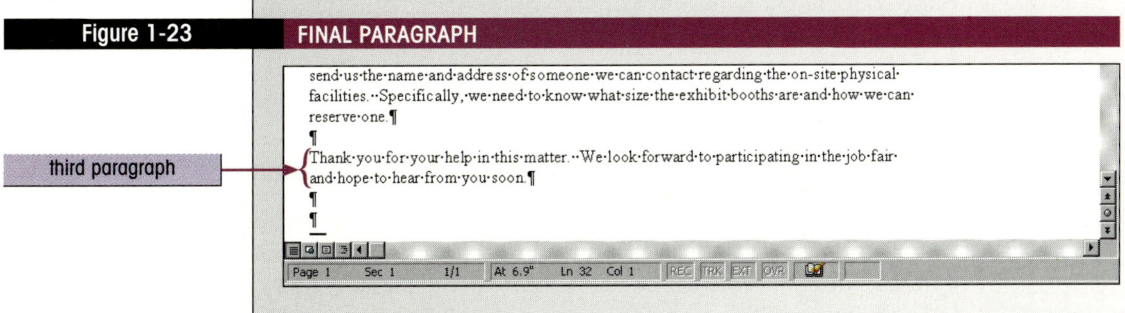

2. Type **Sincerely yours,** (including the comma) to enter the complimentary close.
3. Press the **Enter** key four times to allow space for your signature.
4. Type your name. See Figure 1-24.

Figure 1-24 COMPLIMENTARY CLOSING OF LETTER

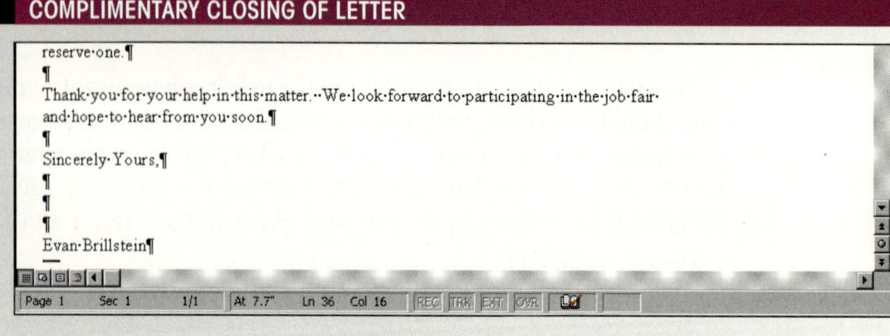

In the last set of steps, you watched the text at the top of your document move off your screen. You can scroll this hidden text back into view so you can read the beginning of the letter. When you do, the text at the bottom of the screen will scroll out of view.

To scroll the text using the scroll bar:

1. Position the mouse pointer on the up arrow at the top of the vertical scroll bar. Press and hold the mouse button to scroll the text. When the text stops scrolling, you have reached the top of the document and can see the beginning of the letter. Note that scrolling does not change the location of the insertion point in the document.

If you wanted to view the end of the letter, you would use the down arrow at the bottom of the vertical scroll bar. Because you have completed the letter, you'll save the document.

Saving a Completed Document

Although you saved the letter earlier, the text that you typed since then exists only in the computer's memory. That means you need to save your document again. It's especially important to save your document before printing. Then, if you experience problems that cause your computer to stop working while you are printing, you will still have on your disk a copy of the document containing your most recent additions and changes.

To save the completed letter:

1. Make sure your Data Disk is still in the appropriate disk drive.
2. Click the **Save** button on the Standard toolbar. Because you named and saved this file earlier, you can save the document without being prompted for information. Word saves your letter with the same name and to the same location you specified earlier.

Previewing and Printing a Document

The current document window displays the text, but you cannot see an entire page without scrolling. To see how the page will look when printed, you need to use the Print Preview window.

To preview the document:

1. Click the **Print Preview** button on the Standard toolbar. The Print Preview window opens and displays a full-page version of your letter, as shown in Figure 1-25. This shows how the letter will fit on the printed page.

Figure 1-25 PRINT PREVIEW VIEW OF THE LETTER

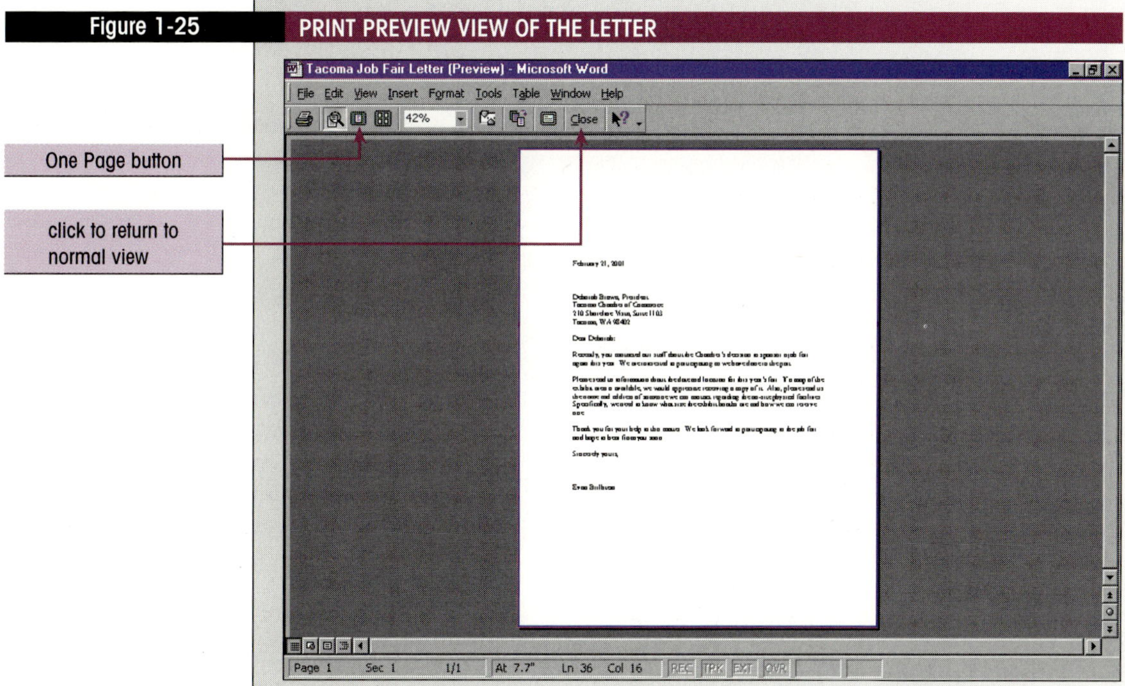

TROUBLE? If your letter in the Print Preview window is smaller and off to the left rather than centered in the window, click the One Page button on the Print Preview toolbar.

TROUBLE? If you see rulers above and to the left of the document, your rulers are displayed. You can hide the rulers in Print Preview by clicking the View Rulers button on the Print Preview toolbar.

2. Click the **Close** button on the Print Preview toolbar to return to normal view.

Note that you should always preview a document before printing. That way, you can correct problems without wasting paper on an imperfect document. It's especially important to preview documents if your computer is connected to a network so that you don't keep a shared printer tied up with unnecessary printing. In this case, the text looks well-spaced and the letterhead will fit at the top of the page. You're ready to print the letter.

When printing a document, you have two choices. You can use the Print command on the File menu, which opens the Print dialog box in which you can adjust some printer settings. Also, you can use the Print button on the Standard toolbar, which simply prints the document using default settings, without displaying a dialog box. In each session of these tutorials, the first time you print from a shared computer, you should check the settings in the Print dialog box and make sure the number of copies is set to one. After that, you can use the Print button.

To print a document:

1. Make sure your printer is turned on and contains paper.
2. Click **File** on the menu bar, and then click **Print**. The Print dialog box opens. See Figure 1-26.

Figure 1-26 PRINT DIALOG BOX

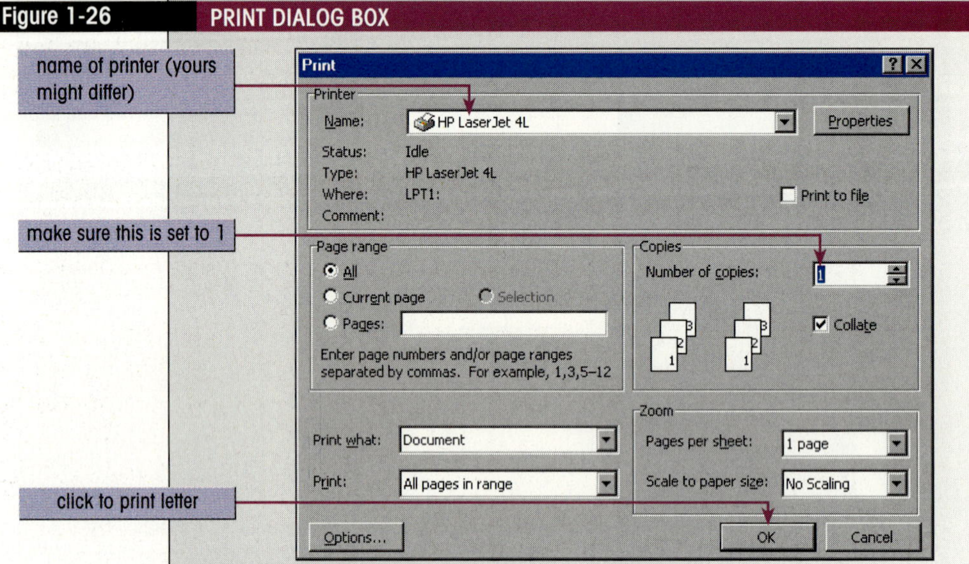

3. Verify that your settings match those in Figure 1-26. In particular, make sure the number of copies is set to 1. Also make sure the Printer section of the dialog box shows the correct printer. If you're not sure what the correct printer is, check with your instructor or technical support person.

   TROUBLE? If the Print dialog box shows the wrong printer, click the Printer Name list arrow, and then select the correct printer from the list of available printers.

4. Click the **OK** button to print Karen's letter. A printer icon appears at the far right of the taskbar to indicate that your document is being sent to the printer.

Your printed letter should look similar to Figure 1-11 but without the Crossroads letterhead. The word wraps, or line breaks, might not appear in the same places on your letter because the size and spacing of characters vary slightly from one printer to the next.

Karen also needs an envelope to mail her letter in. Printing an envelope is easy in Word. You'll have a chance to try it in the Review Assignments at the end of this tutorial. If you wanted to find out how to print an envelope yourself, you could use the Word Help system.

Getting Help

The Word Help system provides quick access to information about commands, features, and screen elements.

The **What's This?** command on the Help menu provides context-sensitive Help information. When you choose this command, the pointer changes to the Help pointer ?, which you can then use to click any object or option on the screen, including menu commands, to see a description of the item.

You've already encountered another form of help, the animated Office Assistant. The **Office Assistant** is an interactive guide to finding information on Microsoft Word. As you learned earlier in this tutorial, the Office Assistant sometimes opens automatically to help you with routine tasks. You also can ask the Office Assistant a direction question, and it will search the Help system to find an answer in plain English. The Office Assistant is a context-sensitive tool, which means that it is designed to offer information related to your current task. If you simply want to look up some information in Word's Help system, as you would in an Encyclopedia, you can use the Index and Contents tabs. You will learn how to use the Office Assistant as well as to display the Index and Contents tabs in the following steps.

REFERENCE WINDOW RW

Getting Help from the Office Assistant

- Click the Microsoft Word Help button on the Standard toolbar (or click Help on the menu bar and then click Microsoft Word Help).
- Type your question, and then click the Search button.
- Click a topic from the list of topics displayed.
- Read the information in the Microsoft Word Help window. For more information, click the relevant underlined text.
- To display the Index or Contents tab, click the Show button in the Microsoft Word Help window. Click the Hide button to hide these tabs.
- To close the Microsoft Word Help window, click its Close button.
- To hide the Office Assistant, click Help on the menu bar, and then click Hide the Office Assistant.

You'll use the Office Assistant now to learn how to print an envelope.

To use the Office Assistant to learn how to print an envelope:

1. Click the **Microsoft Word Help** button on the Standard toolbar. The Office Assistant opens, offering help on topics related to the task you most recently performed (if any), and asking what you'd like to do. The Office Assistant shown in Figure 1-27 takes the form of an animated paperclip, but your Office Assistant may differ.

Figure 1-27 OFFICE ASSISTANT

your options might be in a different order

Office Assistant suggests topics related to printing because you just printed a document

type your question here

your Office Assistant might display a light bulb indicating a tip is available

you may see a different animated figure

Tacoma Job Fair Letter - Microsoft Word

What would you like to do?

Prevent a document from flowing onto an additional printed page

Edit text in print preview

Print a document

Troubleshoot printing

Print property information or other document information

Type your question here, and then click Search.

Options Search

2. Type **How do I print an envelope?** and then click the **Search** button. The Office Assistant window shows topics related to envelopes.

TROUBLE? If you do not see a space to type a question, click the Help with something else option button, and then continue with Step 2.

3. Click **Create and print envelopes.** The Microsoft Word Help window opens next to or on top of the Word window, with even more specific topics related to printing envelopes.

4. Click **Create and print an envelope.** The Microsoft Word Help window displays the precise steps involved in printing an envelope. See Figure 1-28. To scroll through the steps, drag the vertical scroll bar. Note that within a Help window, you can click on underlined text to display more information.

Figure 1-28 STEPS FOR PRINTING AN ENVELOPE

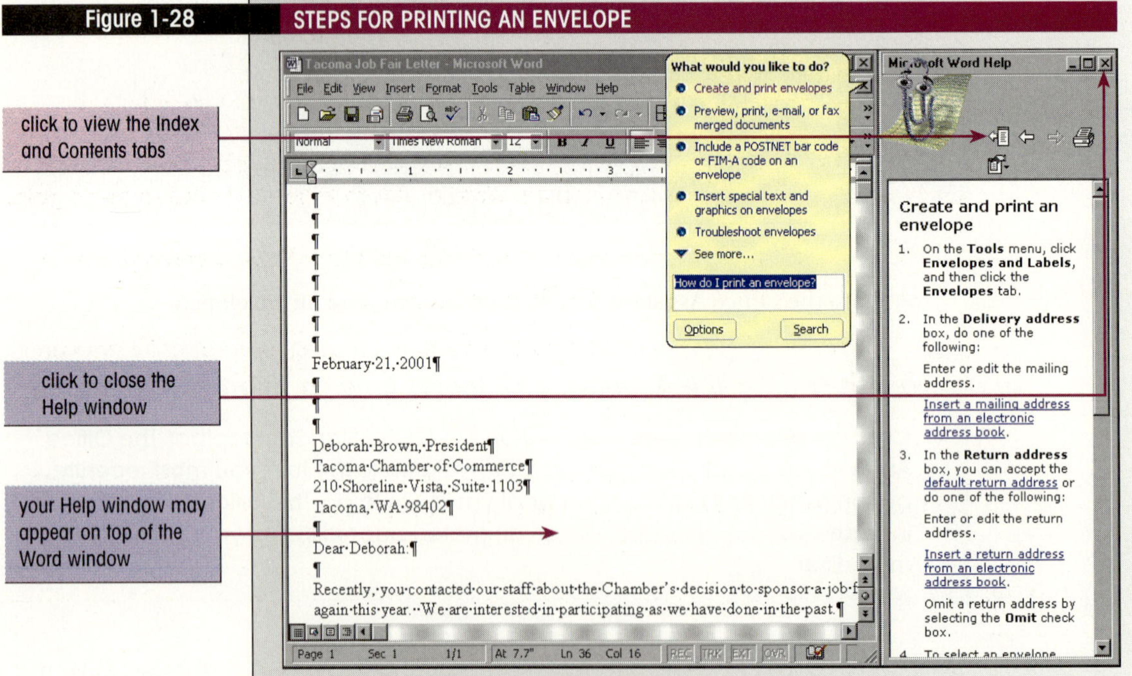

TROUBLE? If your Help window doesn't exactly match the one in Figure 1-28, just continue with these steps. You will learn how to display and hide additional tabs of the Help Window shortly.

5. Click the **Show** button. Additional Help window tabs appear, as in Figure 1-29. The most useful of these are the Contents tab (where you can search by general topics) and the Index tab (where you can look up a specific entry). You will have a chance to practice using these tabs in the Review Assignments at the end of this tutorial.

Figure 1-29 ADDITIONAL HELP TABS

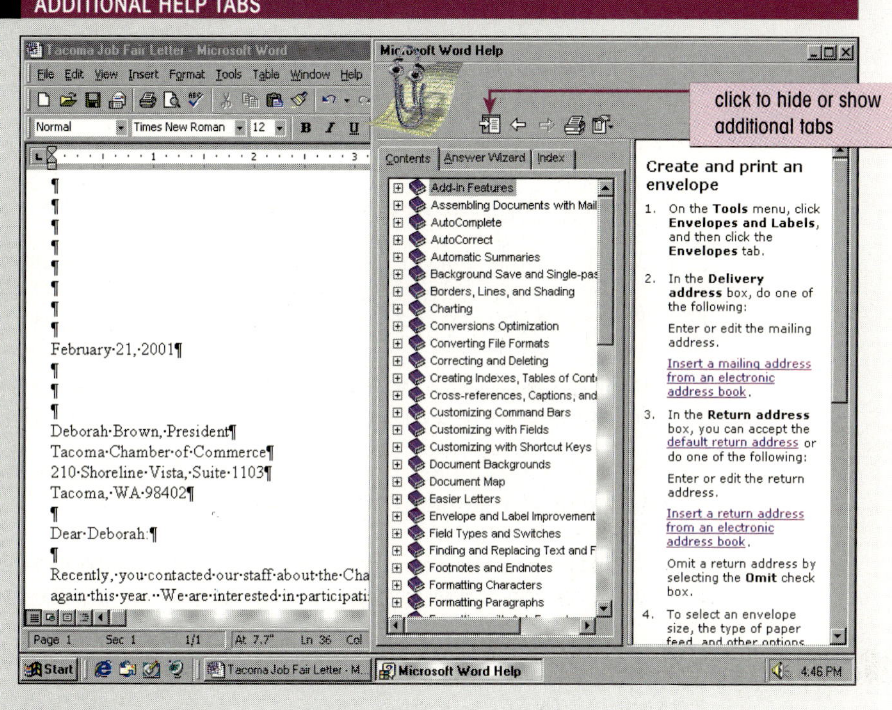

6. Click the **Hide** button to return the Help window to its original size.

7. Click the **Close** button on the Microsoft Word Help window. The Microsoft Word Help window closes, and the Word program window fills the screen again.

8. Click **Help** on the menu bar, and then click **Hide the Office Assistant**. The animated Office Assistant disappears.

TROUBLE? If the Office Assistant asks if you want to hide it permanently, choose the "No just hide me" option.

Some Help windows have different formats than those you've just seen. However, they all provide the information you need to complete any task in Word.

Exiting Word

You have now finished typing and printing the letter to the Tacoma Chamber of Commerce, and you are ready to **exit**, or quit, Word. When you exit Word, you close both the document and the program window.

REFERENCE WINDOW RW

Exiting Word

- Click the Close button for each open document (or click File on the menu bar, and then click Exit).
- If you're prompted to save changes to the document, click the Yes button; then, if necessary, type a document name and click the Save button.

Because you've completed the first draft of Karen's letter, you can close the document window and exit Word now.

To close documents and exit Word:

1. Click the **Close** button in the title bar to close the letter.

   TROUBLE? If you see a dialog box with the message "Do you want to save the changes you made to Tacoma Job Fair Letter?," you have made changes to the document since the last time you saved it. Click the Yes button to save the current version and close it.

2. Click the **Close Window** button on the right side of the menu bar to close the blank Document1.

   TROUBLE? If you see a dialog box with the message "Do you want to save the changes you made to Document1?," click the No button.

3. Click the **Close** button in the upper-right corner of the Word window. Word closes, and you return to the Windows desktop.

You give the letter for the Tacoma Chamber of Commerce to Karen for her to review. Now that you have created and saved your letter, you are ready to learn about editing and formatting a document in the next tutorial.

Session 1.2 QUICK CHECK

1. Explain how to save a document for the first time.
2. What is the advantage of recording information about a document in its Properties dialog box?
3. Explain how word wrap works in a Word document.
4. What is the Office Assistant, and how do you use it?
5. In your own words, define each of the following:
   a. scrolling
   b. AutoComplete
   c. AutoCorrect
   d. print preview
6. Describe two methods for exiting Word.

REVIEW ASSIGNMENTS

Karen received a response from the Tacoma Chamber of Commerce containing the information she requested about the job fair, and Crossroads has firmed up its plans to participate as an exhibitor. Karen must now staff the booth with Crossroads employees for each day of the five-day fair. She sends a memo to employees asking them to commit to two dates. Create the memo shown in Figure 1-30 by completing the following:

1. If necessary, start Word and make sure your Data Disk is in the appropriate disk drive, and then check your screen to make sure your settings match those in the tutorials.
2. If the Office Assistant is open, hide it by using the appropriate command on the Help menu.
3. Click the New Blank Document button on the Standard toolbar to display a new document.
4. Press the Enter key six times to insert approximately 2 inches of space before the memo headings.
5. Press the Caps Lock key, and then type "MEMORANDUM" (without the quotation marks) in capital letters.
6. Press the Enter key twice, type "TO:" (without the quotation marks), press the Caps Lock key to turn off capitalization, press the Tab key three times, and then type "Crossroads Staff Members" (without the quotation marks).
7. Press the Enter key twice, type "FROM:" (without the quotation marks), press the Tab key twice, and then type your name. Throughout the rest of this exercise, use the Caps Lock Key as necessary to turn capitalization on and off.

Explore

8. Press the Enter key twice, type "DATE:" (without the quotation marks), press the Tab key three times. Insert today's date from your computer clock by clicking Insert on the menu bar, clicking Date and Time, clicking the date format that corresponds to June 16, 2001, and then clicking OK.
9. Continue typing the rest of the memo exactly as shown in Figure 1-30, including any misspellings and extra words. Notice how Word automatically corrects some misspellings. (You will have a chance to practice correcting the remaining errors later.) Press the Tab key twice after "SUBJECT:" to align the memo heading evenly. Include two blank lines between the Subject line and the body of the memo.

Figure 1-30 SAMPLE MEMO

MEMORANDUM

TO: Crossroads Staff Members

FROM: Karen Liu

DATE: June 16, 2001

SUBJECT: Dates for 2001 Job Fair

The the 2001 Job Fair sponsored by the Tacoma Chamber of Commerce will be held October 20-25, 2001,from 11:00 a.m. to 5:00 p.m.. This fiar provvides us with an oportunity to inform Tacoma residents about our services. Previously, we have each spent two days helping at the exhibet. Please let me know which days you would prefer this year. I would like this information by tomorrow.

Thanks for your help.

10. Save your work as **Job Fair Reminder Memo** in the Review folder for Tutorial 1.
11. Click File on the menu bar, and then click Properties. Delete the existing title for the document, verify that your name appears in the Author text box, and type a brief description of the document in the Comments text box. Click OK to close the document's properties page.
12. Correct the misspelled words, indicated by the wavy red lines. If the correct version of a word does not appear in the list box, press the Escape key to close the list, and then make the correction yourself. To ignore an AutoCorrect suggestion, click Ignore All. Then correct any grammatical or other errors indicated by wavy green lines. Use the Backspace key to delete any extra words or spaces.
13. Scroll to the beginning of the memo. Click at the beginning of the first line and insert room for the letterhead by pressing the Enter key until MEMORANDUM is at line 12.
14. Save your most recent changes.

Explore

15. Use the What's This? feature to learn about the Word Count command on the Tools menu. Click Help on the menu bar, and then click What's This? Click Tools on the menu bar, click Word Count, and then read the text box. When you are finished, click the text box to close it.
16. Preview and print the memo.
17. Use the Office Assistant to open a Microsoft Word Help menu with the steps necessary for printing an address on an envelope.

Explore

18. With the Help window open on one side of the screen, and the Word window open on the other, follow the instructions for printing an envelope. (Check with your instructor or technical support person to make sure you can print envelopes. If not, print on an 8½ x 11-inch sheet of paper.) To place the Help and Word windows side by side, right-click the taskbar and then click Tile Windows Vertically. When you are done, right-click the taskbar and then click Undo Tile.

Explore

19. With the Help window open, click the Show button, if necessary, to display the additional Help tabs. Click the Index tab, type "Help" (without the quotation marks) and then click the Search button. View the topics related to Word's Help system in the Choose a topic list box. Click any topic in the right-hand window to read more about it. Next, click the Contents tab, review the main topics on that tab, and then click any plus sign to display subtopics. Click a subtopic to display additional topics in the right-hand window, then click one of those topics to display even more information. Continue to explore the Contents and Index tabs. When you are finished, close the Microsoft Word Help window. Hide the Office Assistant.
20. Close the document without saving your most recent changes.
21. Click the Open button on the Standard toolbar.

Explore

22. Verify that the Review folder for Tutorial 1 is displayed in the Look in list box, right-click the Job Fair Reminder Memo, and then click Properties in the shortcut menu. Review the document's properties page. You can use this technique to find out about the contents of a document quickly, without opening the document. Click OK to close the document's properties page, and then click Cancel to close the Open dialog box.
23. Close any open documents.

CASE PROBLEMS

Case 1. Letter to Confirm a Conference Date As catering director for the Madison Convention and Visitors Bureau, you are responsible for managing food service at the convention center. The Southern Wisconsin chapter of the National Purchasing Management Association has requested a written confirmation of a daily breakfast buffet during its annual convention scheduled for July 6-10, 2001.

Create the letter using the skills you learned in the tutorial. Remember to include today's date, the inside address, the salutation, the date of the reservation, the complimentary close, and your name and title. If the instructions show quotation marks around text you type, do not include the quotation marks in your letter. To complete the letter, do the following:

1. If necessary, start Word, make sure your Data Disk is in the appropriate disk drive, and check your screen to make sure your settings match those in the tutorials.
2. Open a new, blank document and press the Enter key until the insertion point is positioned about 2 inches from the top of the page. (Remember that you can see the exact position of the insertion point, in inches, in the status bar.)

Explore

3. Begin typing today's date. If an AutoComplete tip appears to finish the month, press Enter to accept it. Press the spacebar. If another AutoComplete tip appears with the rest of the date, press Enter to accept it. Otherwise, continue typing the date.
4. Press the Enter key six times after the date, and, using the proper business letter format, type the inside address: "Charles Quade, 222 Sydney Street, Whitewater, WI 57332."
5. Double space after the inside address (that is, press the Enter key twice), type the salutation "Dear Mr. Quade:," and then double space again. If the Office Assistant opens, click Cancel to close it.
6. Write one paragraph confirming the daily breakfast buffets for July 6-10, 2001.
7. Double space and type the complimentary close "Sincerely," (include the comma).

8. Press the Enter key four times to leave room for the signature, and then type your name and title.
9. Save the letter as **Confirmation Letter** in the Cases folder for Tutorial 1.
10. Use the document's properties page to record your name and a brief summary of the document.
11. Reread your letter carefully, and correct any errors.
12. Save any new changes.
13. Preview and print the letter.
14. Close the document.

Case 2. Letter to Request Information about a "Climbing High" Franchise You are the manager of the UpTown Sports Mall and are interested in obtaining a franchise for "Climbing High," an indoor rock-climbing venture marketed by Ultimate Sports, Inc. After reading an advertisement for the franchise, you decide to write for more information.

Create the letter by doing the following:

1. If necessary, start Word, make sure your Data Disk is in the appropriate disk drive, and check your screen to make sure your settings match those in the tutorials.
2. Open a new blank document, and press the Enter key until the insertion point is positioned about 2 inches from the top of the page. (Remember that you can see the exact position of the insertion point, in inches, in the status bar.)
3. Use AutoComplete (as described in Step 3 of the previous case project) to type today's date at the insertion point.
4. Press the Enter key six times after the date, and, using the proper business letter format, type the inside address: "Ultimate Sports, Inc., 2124 Martin Luther King Jr. Avenue, Rockton, CO 80911."
5. Insert a blank line after the inside address, type the salutation "Dear Franchise Manager:," and then insert another blank line.
6. Type the first paragraph as follows: "I'd like some information about the Climbing High indoor rock-climbing franchise. As manager of UpTown Sports Mall, a large sporting goods store, I've had success with similar programs, including both bungee jumping and snowboarding franchises."(Do not include the quotation marks.)
7. Save your work as **Rock Climbing Request Letter** in the Cases folder for Tutorial 1.
8. Use the document's properties page to record your name and a brief summary of the document.

Explore

9. Insert one blank line, and type the following: "Please answer the following questions:". Then press the Enter key, and type these questions on separate lines: "How much does your franchise cost?" "Does the price include the cost for installing the 30-foot simulated rock wall illustrated in your advertisement?" "Does the price include the cost for purchasing the ropes and harnesses?" Open the Office Assistant, type the question, "How can I add bullets to lists?," click the Search button, and then click the "Add bullets to lists" topic. In the Microsoft Word Help window, click the "Add bullets or numbering" subtopic, and then follow the instructions to insert a bullet in front of each question in the document. Close the Office Assistant and the Microsoft Word Help window when you are finished.

10. Correct any typing errors indicated by wavy lines. (*Hint:* Because "UpTown" is spelled correctly, click Ignore All on the shortcut menu to remove the wavy red line under the word "UpTown" and prevent Word from marking the word as a misspelling.)
11. Insert another blank line at the end of the letter, and type the complimentary close "Sincerely," (include the comma).
12. Press the Enter key four times to leave room for the signature, and type your full name and title. Then press the Enter key and type "UpTown Sports Mall." Notice that UpTown is not marked as a spelling error this time.
13. Save the letter with changes.
14. Preview the letter using the Print Preview button.
15. Print the letter.
16. Close the document.

Case 3. Memo of Congratulations Judy Davidoff is owner, founder, and president of Blossoms Unlimited, a chain of garden stores. She was recently honored by the Southern Council of Organic Gardeners for her series of free public seminars on organic vegetable gardening. Also, she was named businesswoman of the year by the Georgia Women's Business Network. Do the following:

1. If necessary, start Word, make sure your Data Disk is in the appropriate disk drive, and check your screen to make sure your settings match those in the tutorials.
2. Write a brief memo congratulating Judy on receiving these awards. Remember to use the four-part planning process. You should plan the content, organization, and style of the memo, and use a standard memo format similar to the one shown in Figure 1-30.
3. Save the document as **Awards Memo** in the Cases folder for Tutorial 1.
4. Use the document's properties page to record your name and a brief summary of the document.
5. Preview and print the memo.
6. Close the document.

Explore

Case 4. Writing a Personal Letter with the Letter Template Word provides templates—that is, models with predefined formatting—to help you create documents quickly and effectively. For example, the Letter template helps you create letters with professional-looking letterheads and with various letter formats. Do the following:

1. If necessary, start Word, make sure your Data Disk is in the appropriate disk drive, and check your screen to make sure your settings match those in the tutorials.
2. Click File on the menu bar, and then click New. The New dialog box opens.
3. Click the Letters & Faxes tab, click Elegant Letter, and then click the OK button. A letter template opens, as shown in Figure 1-31, containing generic, placeholder text that you can replace with your own information.

Figure 1-31 ELEGANT LETTER TEMPLATE

placeholder text

4. Click the line "CLICK HERE AND TYPE COMPANY NAME" (at the top of the document), and type the name of your school or company.
5. Click the line "Click here and type recipient's address," and type a real or fictitious name and address.
6. Delete the placeholder text in the body of the letter, and replace it with a sentence or two explaining that you're using the Word letter template to create this letter.
7. At the end of the letter, replace the placeholder text with your name and job title.
8. At the bottom of the page, replace the placeholder text with your address, phone number, and fax number. (Use fictious information if you prefer.)
9. Save the letter as **My Template Letter** (in the Cases folder for Tutorial 1), and then print it.
10. Use the document's properties page to record your name and a brief summary of the document.
11. Close the document.

LAB ASSIGNMENTS

The New Perspectives Labs are designed to help you master some of the key computer concepts and skills presented in each chapter of the text. If you are using your school's lab computers, your instructor or technical support person should have installed the Labs software for you. If you want to use the Labs on your home computer, ask your instructor for the appropriate software. See the Read This Before You Begin page for more information on installing and starting the Lab.

Each Lab has two parts: Steps and Explore. Use Steps first to learn and review concepts. Read the information on each page and do the numbered steps. As you work through the Lab, you will be asked to answer Quick Check questions about what you have learned. At the end of the Lab, you will see a Summary Report of your answers to the Quick Checks. If your instructor wants you to turn in this Summary Report, click the Print button on the Summary Report screen.

When you have completed the Steps, you can click the Explore button to complete the Lab Assignments. You also can use Explore to practice the skills you learned and to explore concepts on your own.

Word Processing Word-processing software is the most popular computerized productivity tool. In this Lab, you will learn how word-processing software works. When you have completed this Lab, you should be able to apply the general concepts you learned to any word-processing package you use at home, at work, or in your school lab.

1. Click the Steps button to learn how word-processing software works. As you proceed through the Steps, answer all of the Quick Check questions that appear. After you complete the Steps, you will see a Quick Check Summary Report. Follow the instructions on the screen to print this report.
2. Click the Explore button to begin. Click File, then click Open to display the Open dialog box. Click the file **Timber.tex**, then press the Enter key to open the letter to Northern Timber Company. Make the following modifications to the letter, then print it. You do not need to save the letter.
   a. In the first and last lines of the letter, change "Jason Kidder" to your name.
   b. Change the date to today's date.
   c. The second paragraph begins "Your proposal did not include…". Move this paragraph so it is the last paragraph in the text of the letter.
   d. Change the cost of a permanent bridge to $20,000.
   e. Spell check the letter.
3. In Explore, open the file **Stars.tex**. Make the following modifications to the document, then print it. You do not need to save the document.
   a. Center and boldface the title.
   b. Change the title font to size-16 Arial.
   c. Boldface the DATE, SHOWER, and LOCATION.
   d. Move the January 2-3 line to the top of the list.
   e. Double space the entire document.
4. In Explore, compose a one-page double-spaced letter to your parents or to a friend. Make sure you date the letter and check your spelling. Print the letter and sign it. You do not need to save your letter.

INTERNET ASSIGNMENTS

The purpose of the Internet Assignments is to challenge you to find information on the Internet that you can use to create effective documents. The actual assignments are updated and maintained on the Course Technology Web site. Log on to the Internet and use your Web browser to go to the Student Online Companion to accompany this text at **www.course.com/NewPerspectives/office2000**. Click the Word link, and then click the link for Tutorial 1.

Quick Check Answers

Session 1.1

1. (1) Plan the content, purpose, organization, and look of your document. (2) Create and then edit the document. (3) Format the document to make it visually appealing. (4) Preview and then print the document.
2. Click the Start button, point to Programs, and then click Microsoft Word.
3. **a.** symbols you can display on-screen but that don't print
   b. buttons to the left of the horizontal status bar that switch the document to normal view, Web layout view, print layout view, or outline view
   c. actual height of a character measured in points
   d. standard settings
4. Click Format on the menu bar, click Font, select the font size in the Size list box, click the Default button, and then click Yes.
5. Right-click a toolbar, and then click Formatting on the shortcut menu.
6. Click the Normal View button.

Session 1.2

1. Click the Save button on the Standard toolbar, switch to the drive and folder where you want to save the document, enter a filename in the File name text box, and then click the Save button.
2. Anyone can determine the document's purpose without having to open the document and skim it.
3. When you type a word that extends into the right margin, Word moves that word and the insertion point to the next line.
4. An interactive guide to finding information about Word; click the Microsoft Word Help button on the Standard toolbar, type your question and click Search, click the help topic you want to read.
5. **a.** as you type, text shifts out of view
   b. typing dates and other regularly used words and text for you
   c. checks for spelling and grammar errors as you type and fixes common typing errors automatically
   d. shows how the document will look when printed
6. Click the Close button in the upper-right corner of the screen; click File on the menu bar and then click Exit.

OBJECTIVES

In this tutorial you will:

- Open, rename, and save a previously saved document
- Check spelling and grammar
- Move the insertion point around the document
- Select and delete text
- Reverse edits using the Undo and Redo commands
- Move text within the document
- Find and replace text
- Change margins, line spacing, alignment, and paragraph indents
- Copy formatting with the Format Painter
- Emphasize points with bullets, numbering, boldface, underlining, and italics
- Change fonts and adjust font sizes

EDITING AND FORMATTING A DOCUMENT

Preparing an Annuity Plan Description for Right-Hand Solutions

CASE

Right-Hand Solutions

Reginald Thomson is a contract specialist for Right-Hand Solutions, a company that provides small businesses with financial and administrative services. Right-Hand Solutions contracts with independent insurance companies to prepare insurance plans and investment opportunities for these small businesses. Brandi Paxman, vice president of administrative services, asked Reginald to plan and write a document that describes the tax-deferred annuity plan for their clients' employee handbooks. Now that Brandi has commented on and corrected the draft, Reginald asks you to make the necessary changes and print the document.

In this tutorial, you will edit the annuity plan description according to Brandi's comments. You will open a draft of the annuity plan, resave it, and delete a phrase. You will check the plan's grammar and spelling, and then move text using two different methods. Also, you will find and replace one version of the company name with another.

Next, you will change the overall look of the document by changing margins and line spacing, indenting and justifying paragraphs, and copying formatting from one paragraph to another. You'll create a bulleted list to emphasize the types of financial needs the annuity plan will cover and a numbered list for the conditions under which employees can receive funds. Then you'll make the title more prominent by centering it, changing its font, and enlarging it. You'll italicize the questions within the plan to set them off from the rest of the text and underline an added note about how to get further information to give it emphasis. Finally, you will print a copy of the plan.

SESSION 2.1

In In this session you will learn how to use the Spelling and Grammar checker to correct any errors in your document. Then you will edit Reginald's document by deleting words and moving text. Finally, you'll find and replace text throughout the document.

Opening the Document

Brandi's editing marks and notes on the first draft are shown in Figure 2-1. You'll begin by opening the first draft of the description, which has the filename Annuity.

Figure 2-1 DRAFT OF ANNUITY PLAN SHOWING BRANDI'S EDITS (PAGE 1)

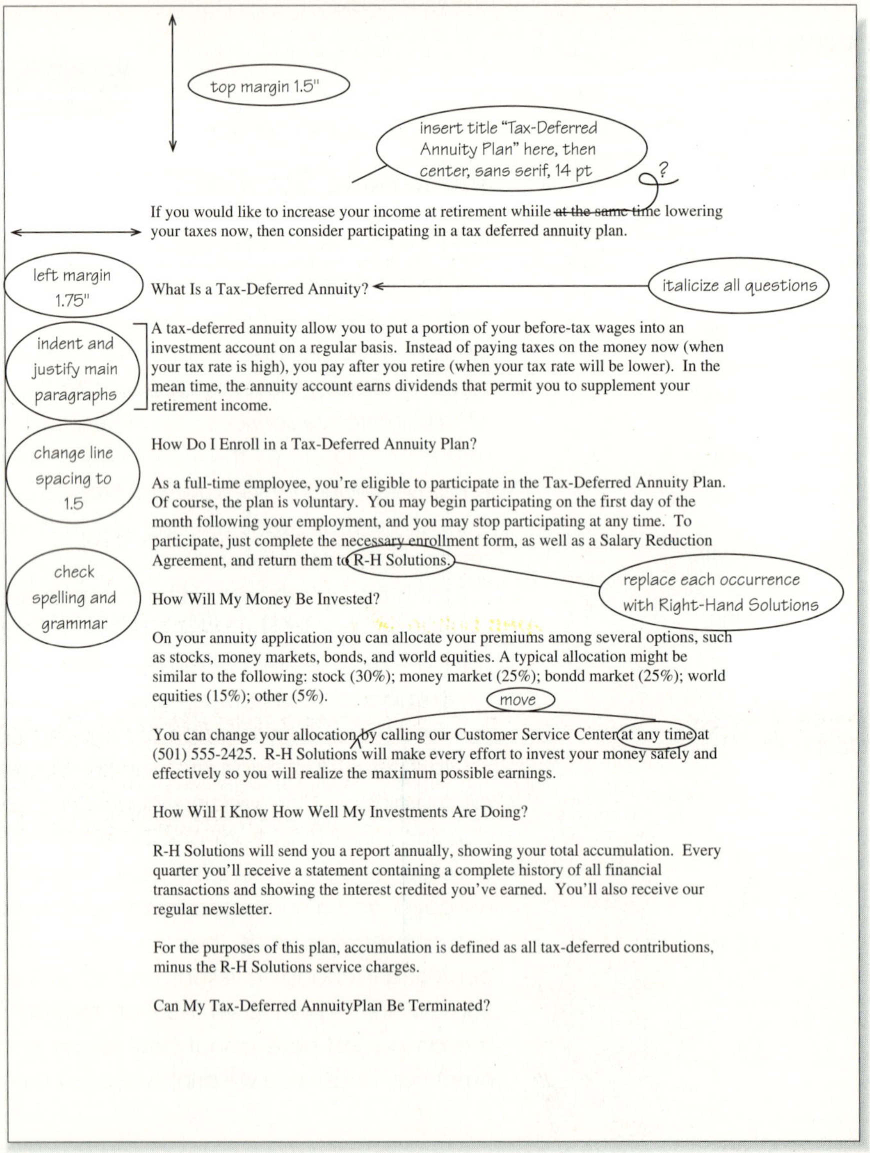

top margin 1.5"

insert title "Tax-Deferred Annuity Plan" here, then center, sans serif, 14 pt

If you would like to increase your income at retirement whiile ~~at the same time~~ lowering your taxes now, then consider participating in a tax deferred annuity plan.

left margin 1.75"

What Is a Tax-Deferred Annuity?

italicize all questions

indent and justify main paragraphs

A tax-deferred annuity allow you to put a portion of your before-tax wages into an investment account on a regular basis. Instead of paying taxes on the money now (when your tax rate is high), you pay after you retire (when your tax rate will be lower). In the mean time, the annuity account earns dividends that permit you to supplement your retirement income.

change line spacing to 1.5

How Do I Enroll in a Tax-Deferred Annuity Plan?

As a full-time employee, you're eligible to participate in the Tax-Deferred Annuity Plan. Of course, the plan is voluntary. You may begin participating on the first day of the month following your employment, and you may stop participating at any time. To participate, just complete the ~~necessary~~ enrollment form, as well as a Salary Reduction Agreement, and return them to R-H Solutions.

check spelling and grammar

replace each occurrence with Right-Hand Solutions

How Will My Money Be Invested?

On your annuity application you can allocate your premiums among several options, such as stocks, money markets, bonds, and world equities. A typical allocation might be similar to the following: stock (30%); money market (25%); bondd market (25%); world equities (15%); other (5%).

move

You can change your allocation by calling our Customer Service Center at any time at (501) 555-2425. R-H Solutions will make every effort to invest your money safely and effectively so you will realize the maximum possible earnings.

How Will I Know How Well My Investments Are Doing?

R-H Solutions will send you a report annually, showing your total accumulation. Every quarter you'll receive a statement containing a complete history of all financial transactions and showing the interest credited you've earned. You'll also receive our regular newsletter.

For the purposes of this plan, accumulation is defined as all tax-deferred contributions, minus the R-H Solutions service charges.

Can My Tax-Deferred AnnuityPlan Be Terminated?

Figure 2-1 DRAFT OF ANNUITY PLAN SHOWING BRANDI'S EDITS (PAGE 2)

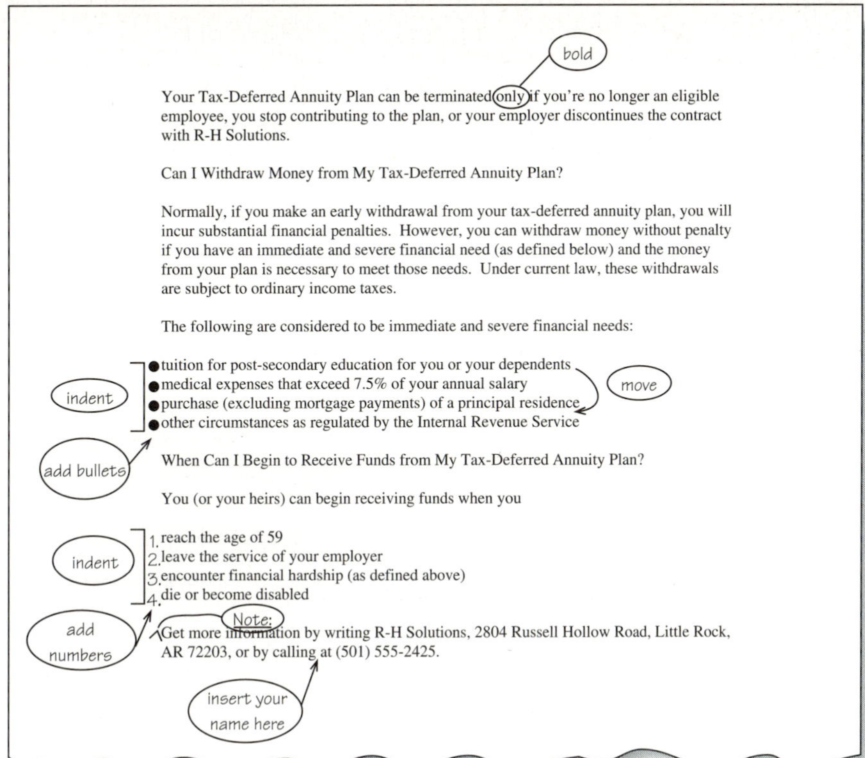

Your Tax-Deferred Annuity Plan can be terminated only if you're no longer an eligible employee, you stop contributing to the plan, or your employer discontinues the contract with R-H Solutions.

Can I Withdraw Money from My Tax-Deferred Annuity Plan?

Normally, if you make an early withdrawal from your tax-deferred annuity plan, you will incur substantial financial penalties. However, you can withdraw money without penalty if you have an immediate and severe financial need (as defined below) and the money from your plan is necessary to meet those needs. Under current law, these withdrawals are subject to ordinary income taxes.

The following are considered to be immediate and severe financial needs:

tuition for post-secondary education for you or your dependents
medical expenses that exceed 7.5% of your annual salary
purchase (excluding mortgage payments) of a principal residence
other circumstances as regulated by the Internal Revenue Service

When Can I Begin to Receive Funds from My Tax-Deferred Annuity Plan?

You (or your heirs) can begin receiving funds when you

reach the age of 59
leave the service of your employer
encounter financial hardship (as defined above)
die or become disabled

Get more information by writing R-H Solutions, 2804 Russell Hollow Road, Little Rock, AR 72203, or by calling at (501) 555-2425.

To open the document:

1. Place your Data Disk into the appropriate disk drive.
2. Start Word as usual.
3. Click the **Open button** on the Standard toolbar to display the Open dialog box, shown in Figure 2-2.

Figure 2-2 THE OPEN DIALOG BOX

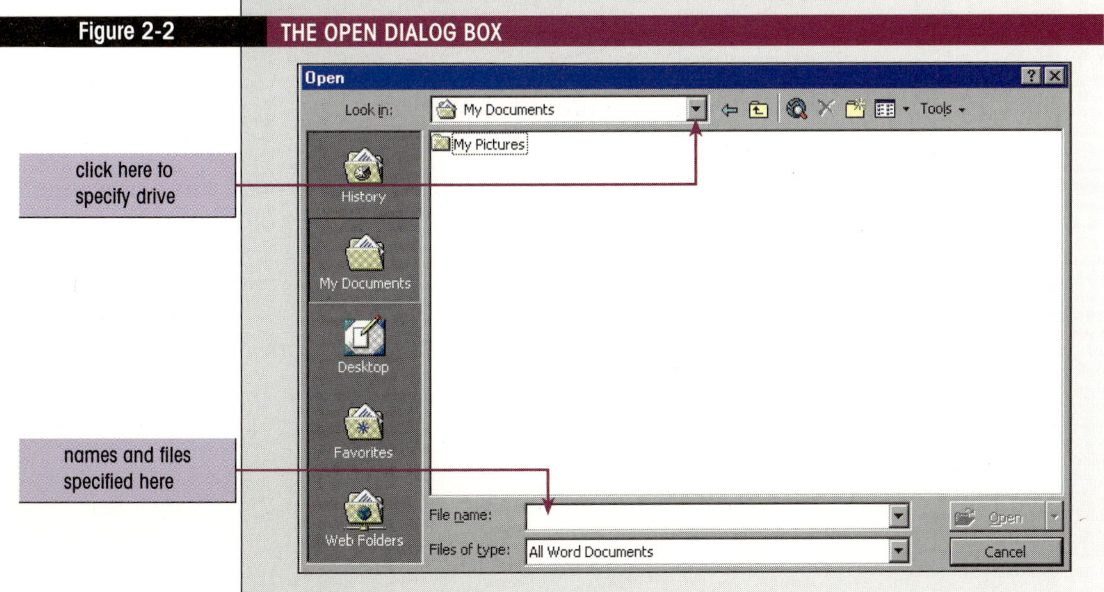

4. Click the **Look in** list arrow. The list of drives and files appears.

5. Click the drive that contains your Data Disk.

6. Double-click the **Tutorial.02** folder, then double-click the **Tutorial** folder.

7. Click **Annuity** to select the file, if necessary.

   TROUBLE? If you see "Annuity.doc" in the folder, Windows might be configured to display filename extensions. Click Annuity.doc and continue with Step 8. If you can't find the file with or without the filename extension, make sure you're looking in the Tutorial subfolder within the Tutorial.02 folder on the drive that contains your Data Disk, and check to make sure the Files of type text box displays All Word Documents or All Files. If you still can't locate the file, ask your instructor or technical support person for help.

8. Click the **Open** button. The document opens, with the insertion point at the beginning of the document. See Figure 2-3.

Figure 2-3 THE OPEN DOCUMENT

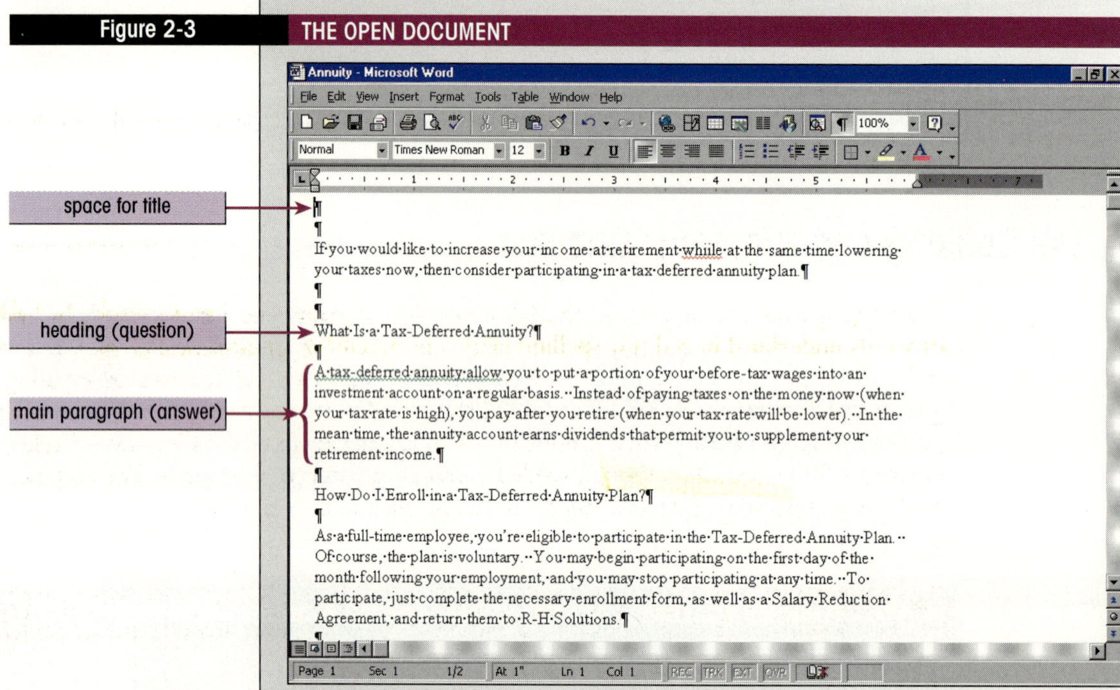

9. Check that your screen matches Figure 2-3. For this tutorial, display the nonprinting characters so that the formatting elements (tabs, paragraph marks, and so forth) are visible and easier to change.

Now that you've opened the document, you can save it with a new name.

Renaming the Document

To avoid altering the original file, Annuity, you will save the document using the filename RHS Annuity Plan. Saving the document with another filename creates a copy of the file and leaves the original file unchanged in case you want to work through the tutorial again.

To save the document with a new name:

1. Click **File** on the menu bar, and then click **Save As**. The Save As dialog box opens with the current filename highlighted in the File name text box. You could type an entirely new filename, or you could edit the current one. In the next step, practice editing a filename.
2. Click to the left of "Annuity" in the File name text box, type **RHS**, and then press the **spacebar**. Press the → key to move the insertion point to the right of the letter "y" in "Annuity," press the **spacebar**, and then type **Plan**. The filename changes to RHS Annuity Plan.
3. Click the **Save** button to save the document with the new filename.

Now you're ready to begin working with the document. First, you will check it for spelling and grammatical errors.

Using the Spelling and Grammar Checker

When typing a document, you can check for spelling and grammatical errors simply by looking for words underlined in red (for spelling errors) or green (for grammatical errors). But when you're working on a document that someone else typed, it's a good idea to start by using the Spelling and Grammar checker. This feature checks a document word by word for a variety of spelling and grammatical errors. Among other things, the Spelling and Grammar checker can sometimes find words that, though spelled correctly, are not used properly. For example, the word "their" instead of the word "there" or "form" instead of "from."

REFERENCE WINDOW **RW**

Checking a Document for Spelling and Grammatical Errors

- Click at the beginning of the document, then click the Spelling and Grammar button on the Standard toolbar.
- In the Spelling and Grammar dialog box, review any errors highlighted in color. Grammatical errors appear in green; spelling errors appear in red. Review the possible corrections in the Suggestions list box.
- To accept a suggested correction, click it in the Suggestions list box. Then click Change to make the correction and continue searching the document for errors.
- Click Ignore to skip this instance of the highlighted text and continue searching the document for errors.
- Click Ignore All to skip all instances of the highlighted text and continue searching the document for errors. Click Ignore Rule to skip all instances of a particular grammatical error.
- To type your correction directly in the document, click outside the Spelling and Grammar dialog box, make the desired correction, and then click Resume in the Spelling and Grammar dialog box.

You'll see how the Spelling and Grammar checker works as you check the annuity plan document for mistakes.

To check the annuity plan document for spelling and grammatical errors:

1. Verify that the insertion point is located at the beginning of the document, to the left of the first paragraph mark.
2. Click the **Spelling and Grammar** button on the Standard toolbar. The Spelling and Grammar dialog box opens with the word "whiile" highlighted in red. The word "while" is suggested as a possible replacement. The line immediately under the title bar indicates the type of problem, in this case, "Not in Dictionary." See Figure 2-4.

Figure 2-4 SPELLING AND GRAMMAR DIALOG BOX

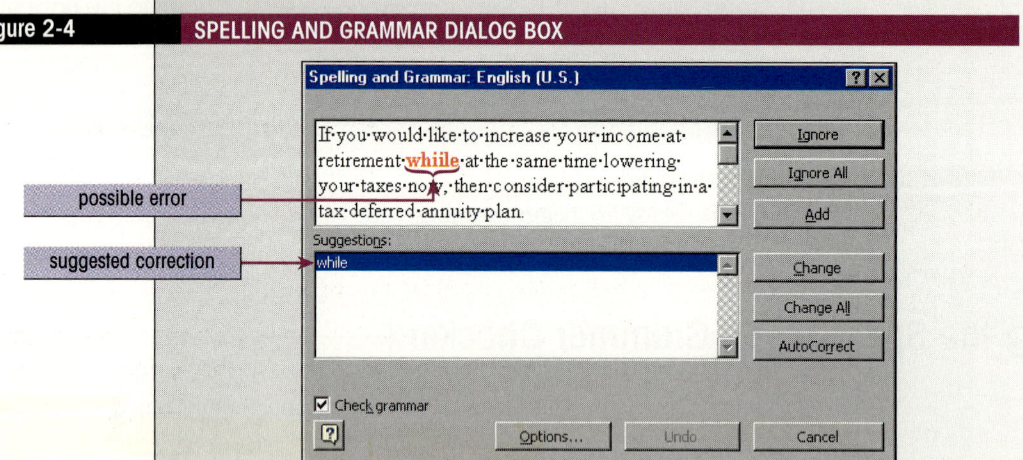

3. Verify that "while" is highlighted in the Suggestions list box, and then click **Change**. "While" is inserted into the document. Next, the grammatical error "A tax-deferred annuity allow" is highlighted in green, with two possible corrections listed in the Suggestions box. The dialog box indicates that the problem concerns subject-verb agreement.

   TROUBLE? If you see the word "bondd" selected instead of "a tax-deferred annuity allow," your computer is not set up to check grammar. Click the Check grammar check box to insert a check, and then click Cancel to close the Spelling and Grammar dialog box. Next, click at the beginning of the document, and then repeat Step 2.

4. Click **A tax-deferred annuity allows** in the Suggestions box, if necessary, and then click **Change**. The misspelled word "bondd" is highlighted in red, with two possible replacements listed in the Suggestions list box.
5. Click **bond**, if necessary, to highlight it, and then click **Change**.
6. Click the **Ignore Rule** button to prevent the Spelling and Grammar checker from stopping at each of the remaining seven bullets in the document. You see a message indicating that the spelling and grammar check is complete. The Spelling and Grammar checker next selects the word "tuition," with the capitalized version

of the same word, "Tuition," listed in the Suggestions box. You do not want to accept the change because the highlighted word is the beginning of a bulleted list, not a sentence, and doesn't have to be capitalized.

7. Click **OK**. You return to the annuity plan document.

Although the Spelling and Grammar checker is a useful tool, remember that there is no substitute for careful proofreading. Always take the time to read through your document to check for errors the Spelling and Grammar checker might have missed. Keep in mind that Spelling and Grammar checker probably won't catch *all* instances of words that are spelled correctly but used improperly. And of course, the Spelling and Grammar checker cannot pinpoint phrases that are simply confusing or inaccurate. To produce a professional document, you must read it carefully several times, and, if necessary, ask a co-worker to read it, too.

To proofread the annuity plan document:

1. Scroll to the beginning of the document and begin proofreading.

   The first error is a missing hyphen in the phrase "tax deferred annuity plan" at the end of the first paragraph.

2. Click after the "x" in "tax," type **-** (a hyphen), and then press the **Delete** key to remove the space. Now the phrase is hyphenated correctly.

   The next error is the word "mean time" in the paragraph below the "What Is a Tax-Deferred Annuity?" heading. You need to delete the space.

3. Click after the letter "n" in "mean" and then press the **Delete** key.

4. Continue proofreading the document.

Once you are certain the document is free from errors, you are ready to make some more editing changes. To make all of Brandi's editing changes, you'll need to learn how to quickly move the insertion point to any location in the document.

Moving the Insertion Point Around a Document

The arrow keys on your keyboard, ↑, ↓, →, and ←, allow you to move the insertion point one character at a time to the left or right, or one line at a time up or down. If you want to move more than one character or one line at a time, you can point and click in other parts of a line or the document. You also can press a combination of keys to move the insertion point. As you become more experienced with Word, you'll decide which method you prefer.

To see how quickly you can move through the document, you'll use keystrokes to move the insertion point to the beginning of the second page and to the end of the document.

To move the insertion point with keystrokes:

1. Press the **Ctrl** key and hold it down while you press the **Home** key. The insertion point moves to the beginning of the document.

2. Press the **Page Down** key to move the insertion point down to the next screen.

3. Press the **Page Down** key again to move the insertion point down to the next screen.

4. Notice that the status bar indicates the location of the insertion point.

5. Press the ↓ or ↑ key to move the insertion point to the paragraph that begins "Your Tax-deferred Annuity Plan can be terminated...." The insertion point is now at the beginning of page 2. Notice the **automatic page break**, a dotted line that Word inserts automatically to mark the beginning of the new page. See Figure 2-5. As you insert and delete text or change formatting in a document, the location of the automatic page breaks in your document continually adjusts to account for the edits.

Figure 2-5 AUTOMATIC PAGE BREAK

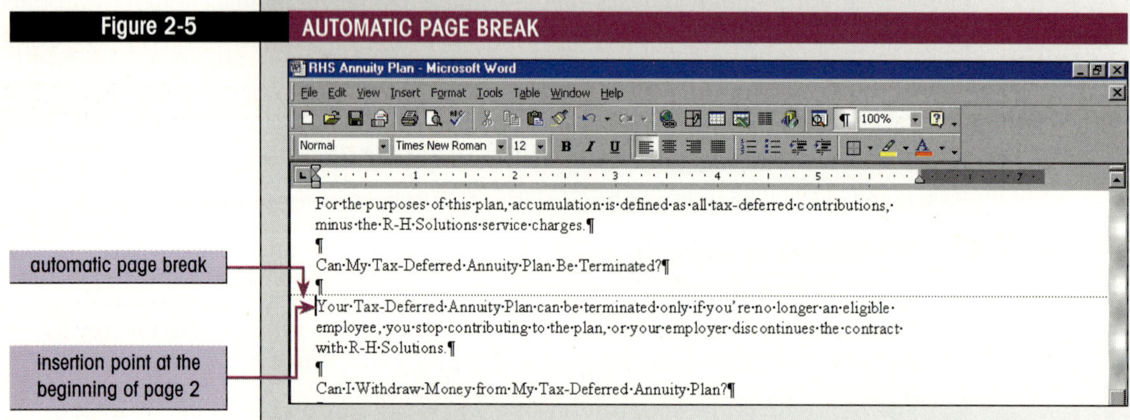

6. Press **Ctrl+End**. (That is, press and hold down the **Ctrl** key while you press the **End** key.) The insertion point moves to the end of the document.

7. Use the ← key to move the insertion point immediately before the phrase "at (501) 555-2425," and then type your name and a space.

8. Move the insertion point back to the beginning of the document.

Figure 2-6 summarizes the keystrokes you can use to move the insertion point around the document.

Figure 2-6 KEYSTROKES FOR MOVING THE INSERTION POINT

PRESS	TO MOVE INSERTION POINT
← or →	Left or right one character at a time
↑ or ↓	Up or down one line at a time
Ctrl+← or Ctrl+→	Left or right one word at a time
Ctrl+↑ or Ctrl+↓	Up or down one paragraph at a time
Home or End	To the beginning or to the end of the current line
Ctrl+Home or Ctrl+End	To the beginning or to the end of the document
PageUp or PageDown	To the previous screen or to the next screen
Alt+Ctrl+PageUp or Alt+Ctrl+PageDown	To the top or to the bottom of the document window

Using Select, Then Do

One of the most powerful editing features in Word is the "select, then do" feature. It allows you to select (or highlight) a block of text and then do something to that text, such as deleting, moving, or formatting it. You can select text using either the mouse or the keyboard; however, the mouse is usually the easier and more efficient way. With the mouse, you can quickly select a line or paragraph by clicking the **selection bar**, which is the blank space in the left margin area of the document window. Also, you can select text using various combinations of keys. Figure 2-7 summarizes methods for selecting text with the mouse and the keyboard. The notation "Ctrl+Shift" indicates that you should press and hold two keys (the Ctrl key and the Shift key) at the same time.

Figure 2-7 METHODS FOR SELECTING TEXT WITH THE MOUSE AND KEYBOARD

TO SELECT	MOUSE	KEYBOARD	MOUSE AND KEYBOARD
A word	Double-click the word.	Move the insertion point to the beginning of the next word, hold down Ctrl+Shift, and then press → once.	
A line	Click in the selection bar next to the line.	Move the insertion point to the beginning of the line, hold down Ctrl+Shift, and then press → until the line is selected.	
A sentence			Press and hold down the Ctrl key, and click within the sentence.
Multiple lines	Click and drag in the selection bar next to the lines.	Move the insertion point to the beginning of the first line, hold down Ctrl+Shift, and then press → until all the lines are selected.	
A paragraph	Double-click in the selection bar next to the paragraph, or triple-click within the paragraph.	Move the insertion point to the beginning of the paragraph, hold down Ctrl+Shift, and then press ↓.	
Multiple paragraphs	Click and drag in the selection bar next to the paragraphs, or triple-click within the first paragraph and drag.	Move the insertion point to the beginning of the first paragraph, hold down Ctrl+Shift, and then press ↓ until all the paragraphs are selected.	
Entire document	Triple-click in the selection bar.	Press Ctrl+A.	Press and hold down the Ctrl key and click in the selection bar.
A block of text			Click at the beginning of the block, press and hold down the Shift key, and then click at the end of the block.

Deleting Text

Brandi wants you to delete the phrase "at the same time" in the first paragraph of the document. You'll use the "select, then do" feature to delete the phrase now.

To select and delete a phrase from the text:

1. Click and drag over the phrase **at the same time** located in the first line of the first paragraph. The phrase and the space following it are highlighted, as shown in Figure 2-8. Notice that dragging the pointer over the second and successive words automatically selects the entire words and the spaces following them. This makes it much easier to select words and phrases than selecting them one character at a time.

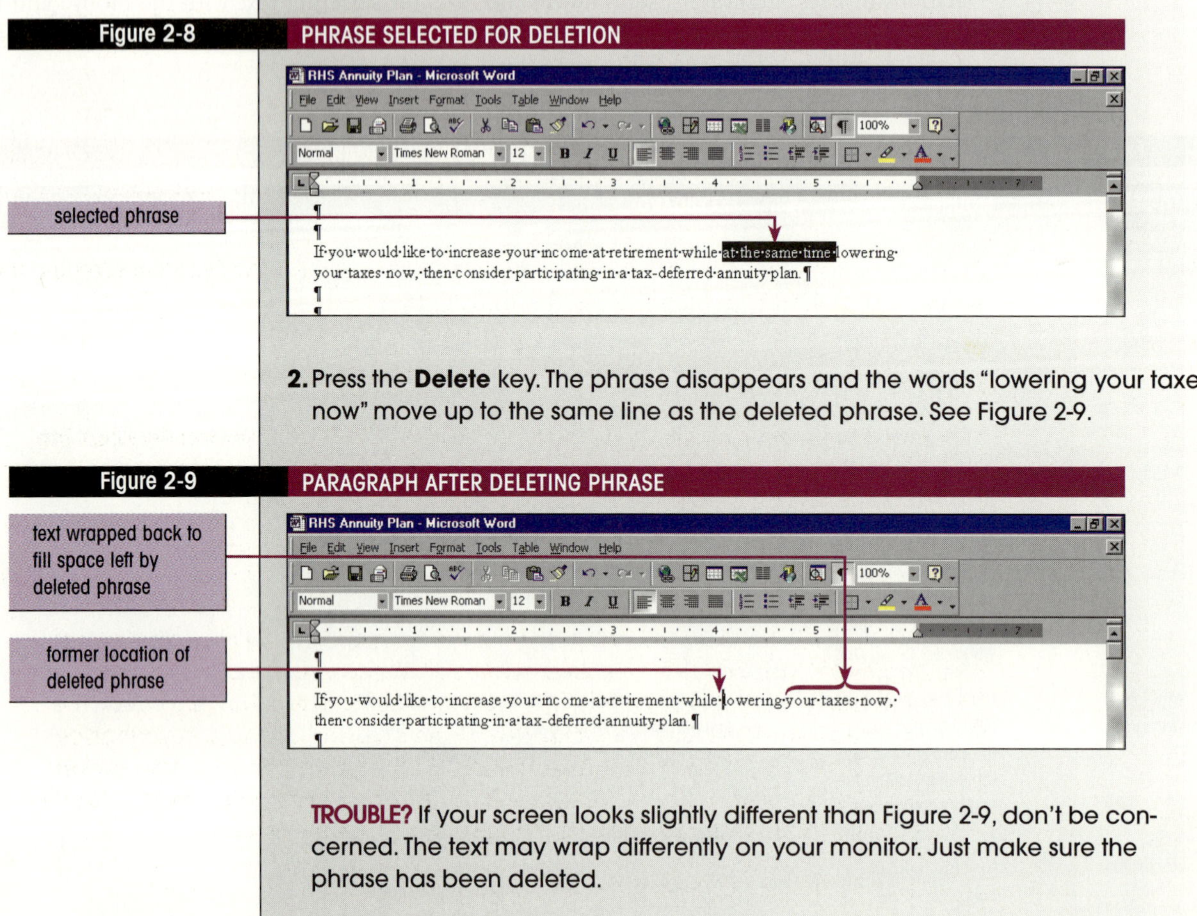

2. Press the **Delete** key. The phrase disappears and the words "lowering your taxes now" move up to the same line as the deleted phrase. See Figure 2-9.

TROUBLE? If your screen looks slightly different than Figure 2-9, don't be concerned. The text may wrap differently on your monitor. Just make sure the phrase has been deleted.

After rereading the paragraph, Reginald decides the phrase shouldn't have been deleted after all. He checks with Brandi, and she agrees. You could retype the text, but there's an easier way to restore the phrase.

Using the Undo and Redo Commands

To undo (or reverse) the very last thing you did, simply click the **Undo button** on the Standard toolbar. If you want to reinstate your original change, the **Redo button** reverses the action of the Undo button (or redoes the undo). To undo anything more than your last action, you can click the Undo list arrow on the Standard toolbar. This list shows your most recent actions. Undo reverses the action only at its original location. You can't delete a word or phrase and then undo it at a different location.

REFERENCE WINDOW RW

Using Undo and Redo

- Click the Undo button on the Standard toolbar to reverse your last action. Or click Edit on the menu bar, and then click Undo. Note that the exact command you see on the Edit menu will reflect your most recent action, such as "Undo Typing."
- To reverse several previous actions, click the Undo list arrow on the Standard toolbar. Click an action on the list to reverse all actions up to and including the one you click.
- To display a ScreenTip reminder of your last action, place the mouse pointer over the Undo button.
- To undo your previous actions one-by-one, in the reverse order in which you performed them, click the Undo button once for every action you want to reverse.
- If you undo an action by mistake, click the Redo button on the Standard toolbar (or click Edit on the menu bar, and then click Redo) to reverse the undo.

You decide to undo the deletion to see how the sentence reads. Rather than retyping the phrase, you will reverse the edit using the Undo button.

To undo the deletion:

1. Place the mouse pointer over the Undo button on the Standard toolbar. The label "Undo Clear" appears in a ScreenTip, indicating that your most recent action involved deleting (or clearing) text.
2. Click the **Undo** button. The phrase "at the same time" reappears in your document and is highlighted.

   TROUBLE? If the phrase doesn't reappear and something else changes in your document, you probably made another edit or change to the document (such as pressing the Backspace key) between the deletion and the undo. Click the Undo button on the Standard toolbar until the phrase reappears in your document. If a list of possible changes appears under the Undo button, you clicked the list arrow next to the Undo button rather than the Undo button itself. Click the Undo button to restore the deleted phrase and close the list box.

3. Click within the paragraph to deselect the phrase.

   As you read the sentence, you decide that it reads better without the phrase. Instead of deleting it again, you'll redo the undo. As you place the pointer over the Redo button, notice that its ScreenTip indicates the action you want to redo.

4. Place the mouse pointer over the Redo button on the Standard toolbar and observe the "Redo Clear" label.
5. Click the **Redo** button. The phrase "at the same time" disappears from your document again.
6. Click the **Save** button on the Standard toolbar to save your changes to the document.

You have edited the document by deleting the text that Brandi marked for deletion. Now, you are ready to make the rest of the edits she suggested.

Moving Text Within a Document

One of the most important uses of "select, then do" is moving text. For example, Brandi wants to reorder the four points Reginald made in the section "Can I Withdraw Money from My Tax-Deferred Annuity Plan?" on page 2 of his draft. You could reorder the list by deleting the sentence and then retyping it at the new location, but a much more efficient approach is to select and then move the sentence. Word provides several ways to move text: drag and drop, cut and paste, and copy and paste.

Dragging and Dropping Text

One way to move text within a document is called drag and drop. With **drag and drop**, you select the text you want to move, press and hold down the mouse button while you drag the selected text to a new location, and then release the mouse button.

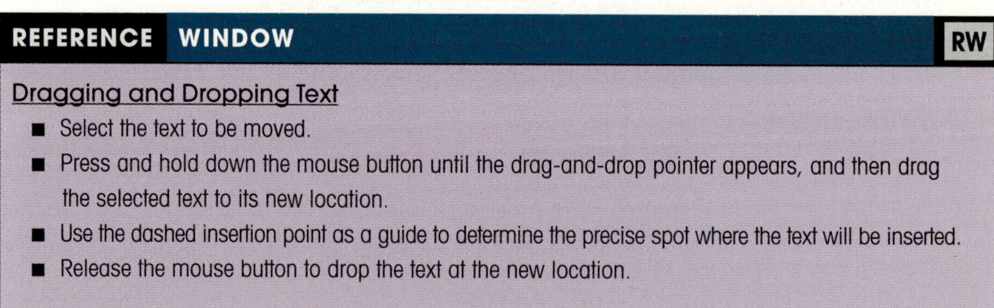

REFERENCE WINDOW RW

Dragging and Dropping Text

- Select the text to be moved.
- Press and hold down the mouse button until the drag-and-drop pointer appears, and then drag the selected text to its new location.
- Use the dashed insertion point as a guide to determine the precise spot where the text will be inserted.
- Release the mouse button to drop the text at the new location.

Brandi requested a change in the order of the items in the bulleted list on page 2 of the document, so you'll use the drag-and-drop method to reorder the items. At the same time, you'll practice using the selection bar to highlight a line of text.

To move text using drag and drop:

1. Scroll through the document until you see "tuition for post-secondary education...," the first item in the list of "immediate and severe financial needs:" that begins in the middle of page 2.

2. Click in the selection bar to the left of the line beginning "tuition..." to select that line of text, including the return character. See Figure 2-10.

Figure 2-10 SELECTED TEXT TO DRAG AND DROP

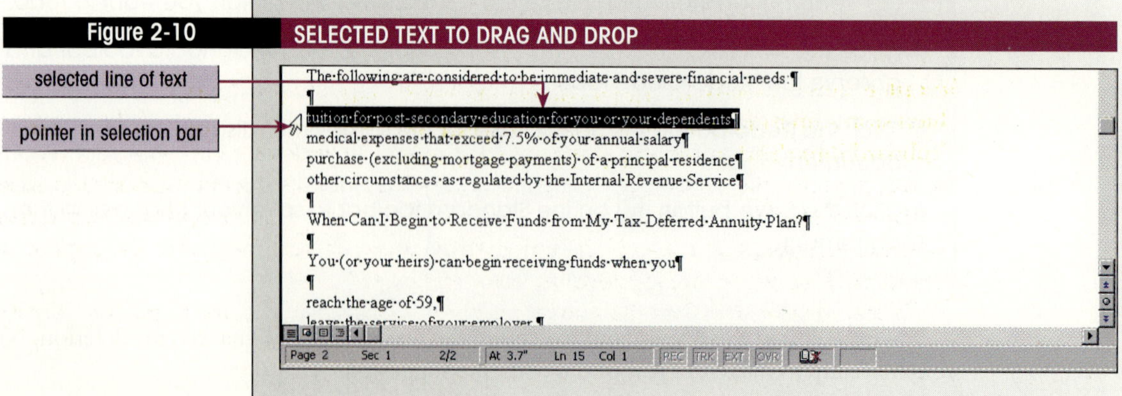

3. Position the pointer over the selected text. The pointer changes from a right-facing arrow to a left-facing arrow.

4. Press and hold down the mouse button until the drag-and-drop pointer, which has a dashed insertion point, an arrow, and a small square called a move box, appears.

5. Drag the selected text down three lines until the dashed insertion point appears to the left of the word "other." Make sure you use the dashed insertion point to guide the text to its new location rather than the mouse pointer or the move box; the dashed insertion point marks the precise location of the drop. See Figure 2-11.

Figure 2-11 MOVING TEXT WITH DRAG-AND-DROP POINTER

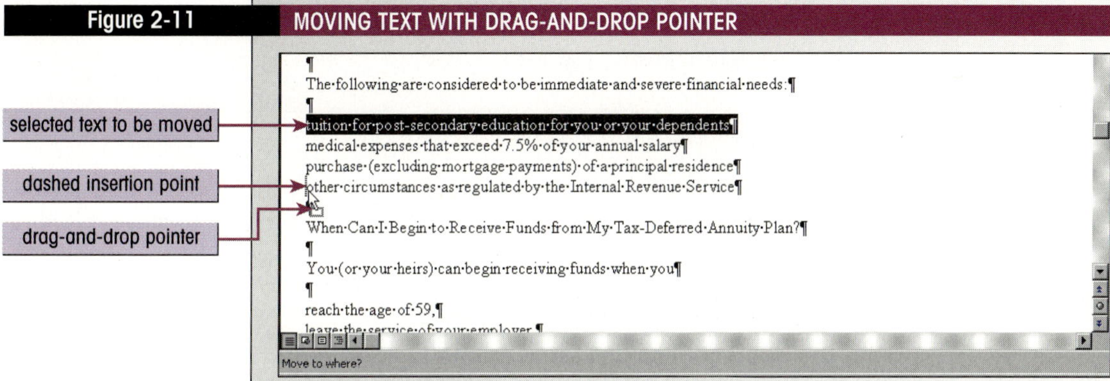

6. Release the mouse button. The selected text moves to its new location, as the third item in the list.

TROUBLE? If the selected text moves to the wrong location, click the Undo button on the Standard toolbar, and then repeat Steps 3 through 6, making sure you hold the mouse button until the dashed insertion point appears in front of the word "other."

7. Deselect the highlighted text by clicking anywhere in the document window.

Dragging and dropping works well if you're moving text a short distance in a document; however, Word provides another method, called cut and paste, that works well for moving text either a short distance or beyond the current screen.

Cutting or Copying and Pasting Text

To **cut** means to remove text from the document and place it on the **Office Clipboard**, which stores up to 12 items at a time. To **paste** means to transfer a copy of the text from the Clipboard into the document at the insertion point. To perform a cut-and-paste action, you select the text you want to move, cut (or remove) it from the document, and then paste (or restore) it into the document in a new location. If you don't want to remove the text from its original location, you can copy it (rather than cutting it) and then paste the copy in a new location. This procedure is known as "copy and paste."

If you cut or copy more than one item, the Clipboard toolbar opens, making it easier for you to select which items you want to paste into the document.

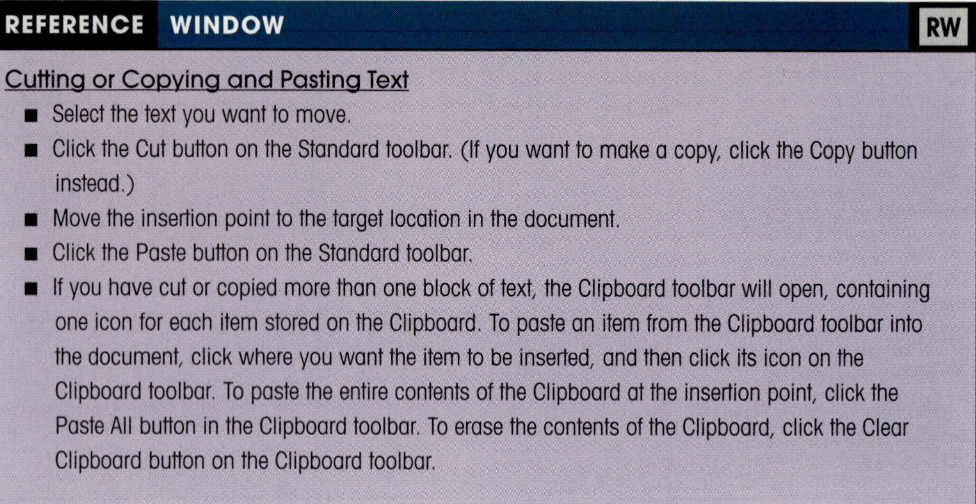

REFERENCE WINDOW RW

Cutting or Copying and Pasting Text

- Select the text you want to move.
- Click the Cut button on the Standard toolbar. (If you want to make a copy, click the Copy button instead.)
- Move the insertion point to the target location in the document.
- Click the Paste button on the Standard toolbar.
- If you have cut or copied more than one block of text, the Clipboard toolbar will open, containing one icon for each item stored on the Clipboard. To paste an item from the Clipboard toolbar into the document, click where you want the item to be inserted, and then click its icon on the Clipboard toolbar. To paste the entire contents of the Clipboard at the insertion point, click the Paste All button in the Clipboard toolbar. To erase the contents of the Clipboard, click the Clear Clipboard button on the Clipboard toolbar.

Brandi suggested moving the phrase "at any time" (in the paragraph beginning "You can change your allocation…") to a new location. You'll use cut and paste to move this phrase.

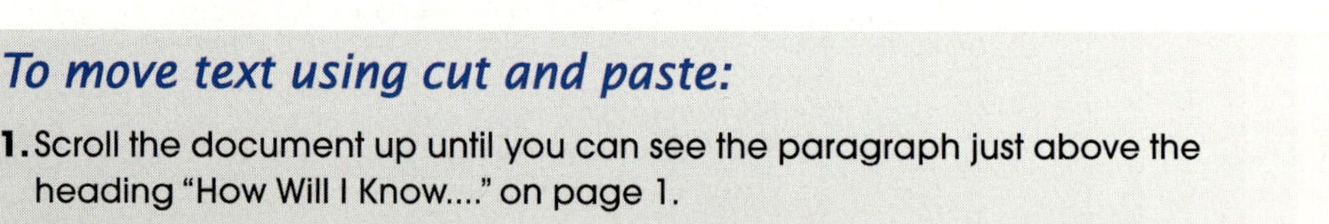

To move text using cut and paste:

1. Scroll the document up until you can see the paragraph just above the heading "How Will I Know...." on page 1.
2. Click and drag the mouse to highlight the complete phrase **at any time**. See Figure 2-12.

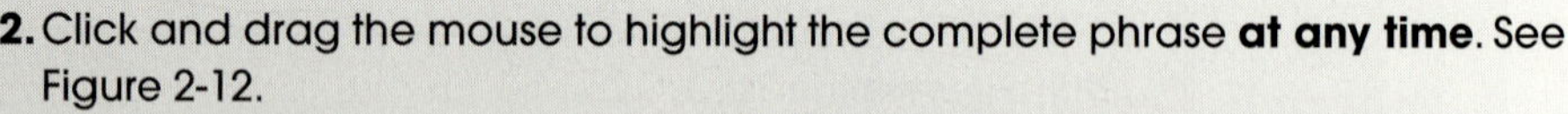

Figure 2-12 TEXT TO MOVE USING CUT AND PASTE

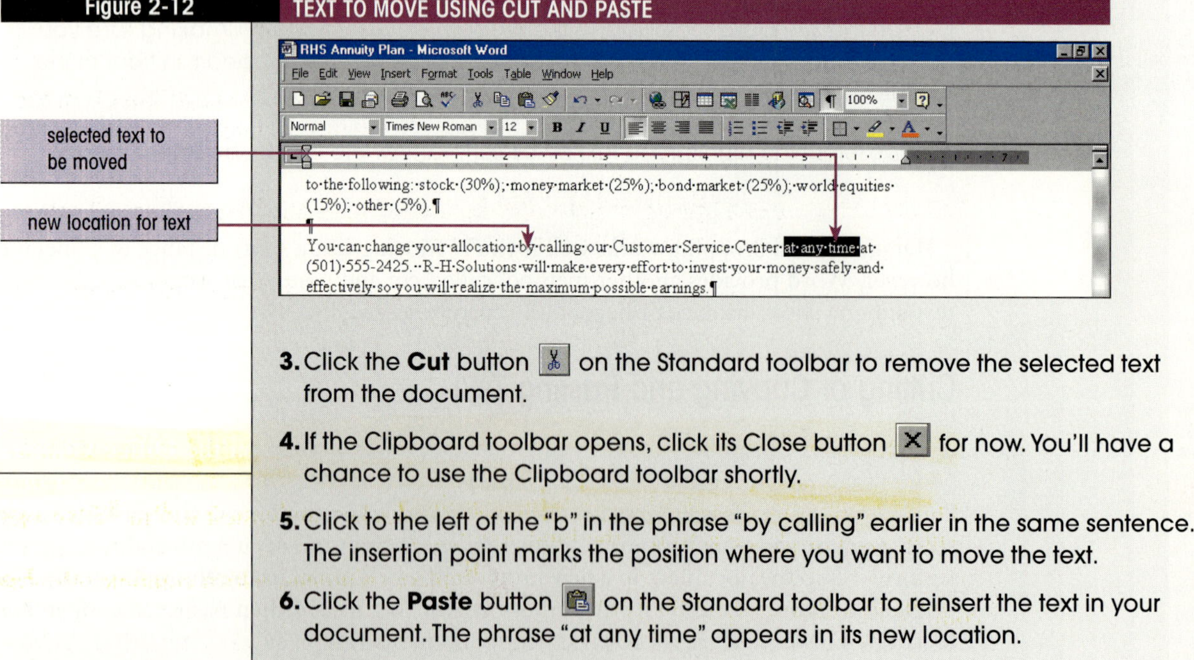

3. Click the **Cut** button on the Standard toolbar to remove the selected text from the document.
4. If the Clipboard toolbar opens, click its Close button for now. You'll have a chance to use the Clipboard toolbar shortly.
5. Click to the left of the "b" in the phrase "by calling" earlier in the same sentence. The insertion point marks the position where you want to move the text.
6. Click the **Paste** button on the Standard toolbar to reinsert the text in your document. The phrase "at any time" appears in its new location.

The copy and paste feature works much the same way as cut and paste. You can try using this technique now, as you copy the phrase "Tax-Deferred Annuity Plan" from the middle of the document and then paste it at the top of the document.

1. Scroll the document up until you can see the heading "How Do I Enroll in a Tax-Deferred Annuity Plan?" on page 1.
2. In the headings, click and drag the mouse to highlight the complete phrase "Tax-Deferred Annuity Plan."
3. Click the **Copy** button on the Standard toolbar. The Clipboard toolbar opens, containing icons for each item currently stored on the Clipboard, as shown in Figure 2-13. The "W" on the icons indicates that the copied items contain Word text. Note that your Clipboard toolbar might contain more than two icons, depending on whether you (or another user) cut or copy text before completing this tutorial. You also may see icons for other Office programs, such as Excel.

Figure 2-13 CLIPBOARD TOOLBAR WITH CUT AND COPIED ITEMS

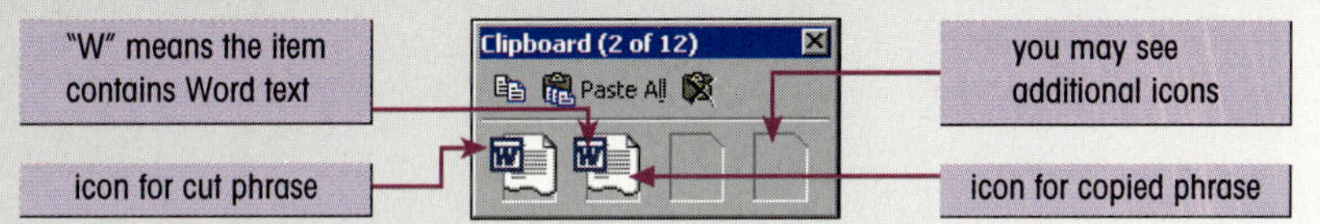

TROUBLE? If the Office Assistant opens, hide it and continue with Step 4.

4. Place the mouse pointer over each of the icons, one at a time, until the ScreenTip "at any time" appears, indicating that this is the icon for the text you cut in the previous set of steps.
5. Place the mouse pointer over each of the icons, one at a time, until the ScreenTip "Tax-Deferred Annuity Plan" appears, indicating that this is the icon for the text you just copied.
6. Scroll up and click at the beginning of the document to move the insertion point there.
7. Click the **Tax-Deferred Annuity Plan** icon in the Clipboard toolbar. The phrase is inserted at the top of the document. Now that you are finished using the Clipboard toolbar, you will delete its contents.
8. Click the **Clear Clipboard** button button on the Clipboard toolbar. All of the icons disappear from the Clipboard toolbar.
9. Click the **Close** button on the Clipboard toolbar. The Clipboard toolbar disappears.

Finding and Replacing Text

When you're working with a longer document, the quickest and easiest way to locate a particular word or phrase is to use the Find command. If you want to replace characters or a phrase with something else, you can use the Replace command, which combines the Find command with a substitution feature. The Replace command searches through a document and substitutes the text you're searching for with the replacement text you specify. As Word performs the search, it stops and highlights each occurrence of the search text and lets you determine whether to substitute the replacement text by clicking the Replace button.

If you want to substitute every occurrence of the search text with the replacement text, you can click the Replace All button. When using the Replace All button with single words, keep in mind that the search text might be found within other words. To prevent Word from making incorrect substitutions in such cases, it's a good idea to select the "Find whole words only" check box along with the Replace All button. For example, suppose you want to replace the word "figure" with illustration. Unless you select the "Find whole words only" check box, Word would replace "configure" with "conillustration."

As you search through a document, you can search from the current location of the insertion point down to the end of the document, from the insertion point up to the beginning of the document, or throughout the document.

REFERENCE WINDOW RW

Finding and Replacing Text

- Click the Select Browse Object button on the vertical scroll bar, and then click the Find button on the Select Browse Object menu. (You also can click Edit on the menu bar, and then click either Find or Replace.)
- To find text, click the Find tab; or, to find and replace text, click the Replace tab.
- Click the More button to expand the dialog box to display additional options (including the "Find whole words only" option). If you see the Less button, the additional options are already displayed.
- In the Search list box, select Down if you want to search from the insertion point to the end of the document, select Up if you want to search from the insertion point to the beginning of the document, or select All to search the entire document.
- Type the characters you want to find in the Find what text box.
- If you are replacing text, type the replacement text in the Replace with text box.
- Click the Find Next button.
- Click the Replace button to substitute the found text with the replacement text and find the next occurrence.
- Click the Find whole words only check box, and then click the Replace All button to substitute all occurrences of the found text with the replacement text.

Brandi wants the shortened version of the company name, "R-H Solutions," to be spelled out as "Right-Hand Solutions" every time it appears in the text.

To replace "R-H Solutions" with "Right-Hand Solutions:"

1. Click the **Select Browse Object** button near the bottom of the vertical scroll bar.
2. Click the **Find** button on the Select Browse Object menu. The Find and Replace dialog box appears.
3. Click the **Replace** tab.
4. If necessary, click the **More** button to display the additional search options.
5. If necessary, click the **Search** list arrow, and then click **All**.
6. Click the **Find what** text box, type **R-H Solutions**, press the **Tab** key, and then type **Right-Hand Solutions** in the Replace with text box. Note that because the search text is made up of more than one word, the "Find whole words only" option is unnecessary and is therefore unavailable. See Figure 2-14.

Figure 2-14 FIND AND REPLACE DIALOG BOX

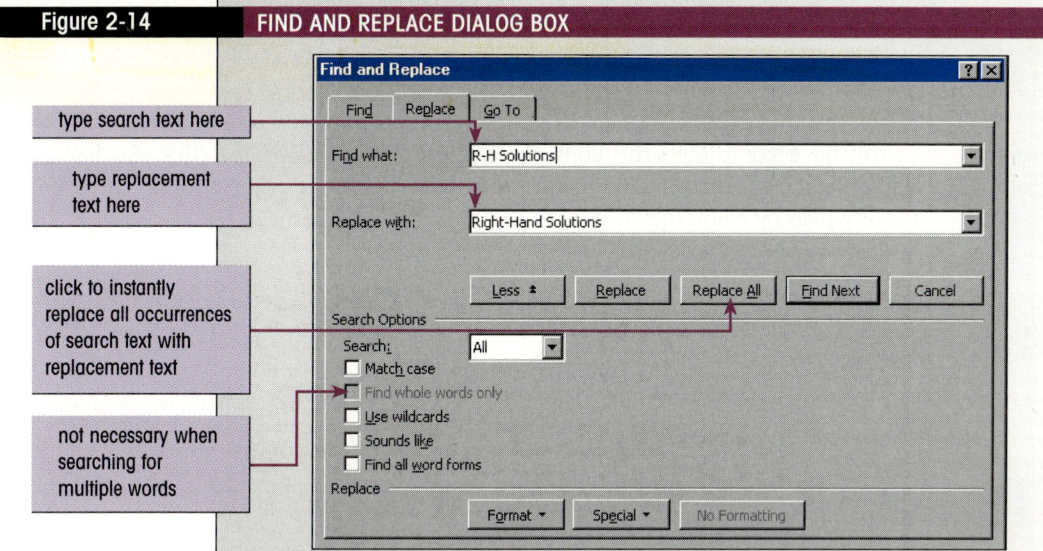

TROUBLE? If you already see the text "R-H Solutions" and "Right-Hand Solutions" in your Find and Replace dialog box, someone already performed these steps on your computer. Simply continue with Step 7.

7. Click the **Replace All** button to replace all occurrences of the search text with the replacement text. When Word finishes making the replacements, you see a dialog box telling you that six replacements were made.

8. Click **OK** to close the dialog box, and then click the **Close** button in the Find and Replace dialog box to return to the document. The full company name has been inserted into the document, as shown in Figure 2-15.

Figure 2-15 THE NAME "RIGHT-HAND SOLUTIONS" INSERTED INTO THE DOCUMENT

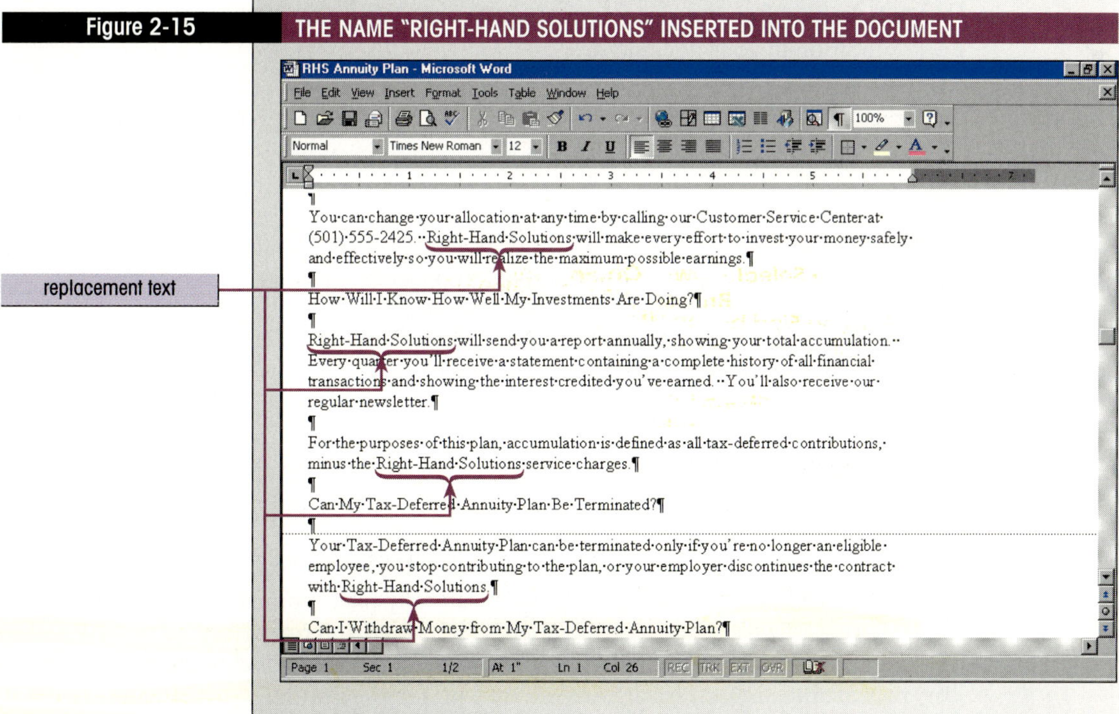

9. Click the **Save** button on the Standard toolbar to save your changes to the document.

You can also search for and replace formatting, such as bold, and special characters, such as paragraph marks, in the Find and Replace dialog box. Click in the Find what text box or the Replace with text box, enter any text if necessary, click the Format button, click Font to open the Font dialog box, and then select the formatting you want to find or replace. Complete the search or replace as usual.

You have completed the content changes Brandi suggested, but she has some other changes that will improve the plan's appearance. In the next session, you'll enhance the annuity plan by changing the width, spacing, and alignment of text.

Session 2.1 Quick Check

1. Explain how to open a document and save a copy of it with a new name.
2. Which key(s) do you press to move the insertion point to the following places:
   - a. down one line
   - b. end of the document
   - c. to the next screen
3. Describe the "select, then do" feature.
4. Define the following terms in your own words:
   - a. selection bar
   - b. Redo button
   - c. drag and drop
5. Explain how to select a single word. Explain how to select a complete paragraph.
6. Describe a situation in which you would use the Undo button and then the Redo button.
7. True or False: You can use the Redo command to restore deleted text at a new location in your document.
8. What is the difference between cut and paste, and copy and paste?
9. List the steps involved in finding and replacing text in a document.

SESSION 2.2

In this session you will make the formatting changes Brandi suggested. You'll use a variety of formatting commands to change the margins, line spacing, text alignment, and paragraph indents. Also, you'll learn how to use the Format Painter, how to create bulleted and numbered lists, and how to change fonts, font sizes, and emphasis.

Changing the Margins

In general, it's best to begin formatting by making the changes that affect the document's overall appearance. Then you can make changes that affect only selected text. In this case, you need to adjust the margin settings of the annuity plan summary.

Word uses default margins of 1.25 inches for the left and right margins and 1 inch for the top and bottom margins. The numbers on the ruler (displayed below the Formatting toolbar) indicate the distance in inches from the left margin, not from the left edge of the paper. Unless you specify otherwise, changes you make to the margins will affect the entire document, not just the current paragraph or page.

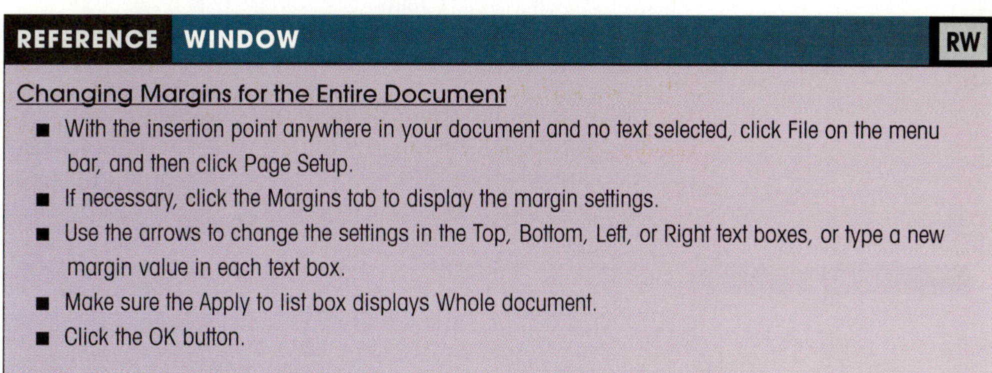

REFERENCE WINDOW RW

Changing Margins for the Entire Document

- With the insertion point anywhere in your document and no text selected, click File on the menu bar, and then click Page Setup.
- If necessary, click the Margins tab to display the margin settings.
- Use the arrows to change the settings in the Top, Bottom, Left, or Right text boxes, or type a new margin value in each text box.
- Make sure the Apply to list box displays Whole document.
- Click the OK button.

You need to change the top margin to 1.5 inches and the left margin to 1.75 inches, as Brandi requested. The left margin needs to be wider than usual to allow space for making holes so that the document can be inserted in a three-ring binder. In the next set of steps, you'll change the margins with the Page Setup command. You also can change margins in print layout view; you'll practice that method in the Review Assignments.

To change the margins in the annuity plan document:

1. If you took a break after the last lesson, make sure Word is running, the RHS Annuity Plan document is open, and nonprinting characters are displayed.
2. Click once anywhere in the document to make sure no text is selected.
3. Click **File** on the menu bar, and then click **Page Setup** to open the Page Setup dialog box.
4. If necessary, click the **Margins** tab to display the margin settings. The Top margin setting is selected. See Figure 2-16.

Figure 2-16 PAGE SETUP DIALOG BOX

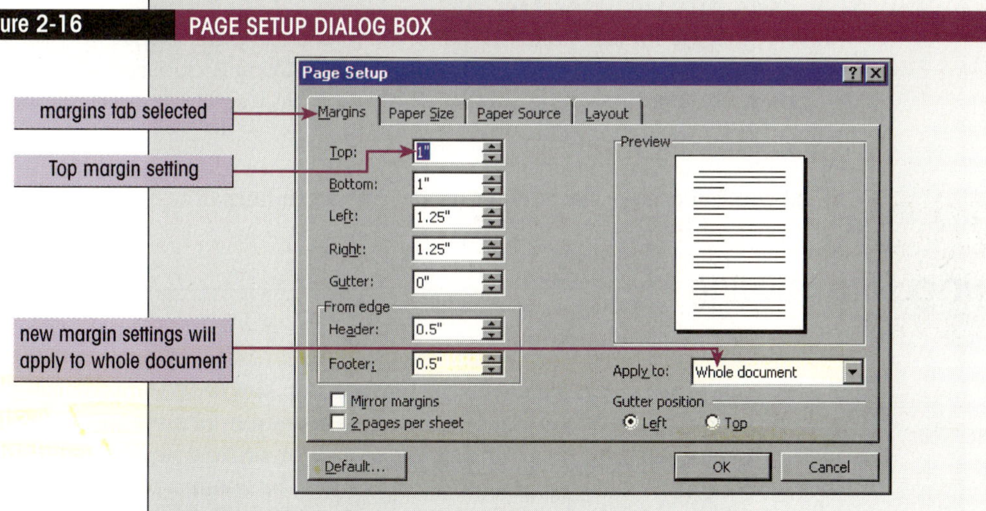

5. Type **1.5** to change the Top margin setting. (You do not have to type the inches symbol.)
6. Press the **Tab** key twice to move to the Left text box and select the current margin setting. Notice how the text area in the Preview box moves down to reflect the larger top margin.

7. Type **1.75** and then press the **Tab** key. Watch the Preview box to see how the margin increases.

8. Make sure the **Whole document** option is selected in the Apply to list box, and then click the **OK** button to return to your document. Notice that the right margin on the ruler has changed to reflect the larger margins and the reduced page area that results. See Figure 2-17.

Figure 2-17 RULER AFTER SETTING LEFT MARGIN TO 1.75 INCHES

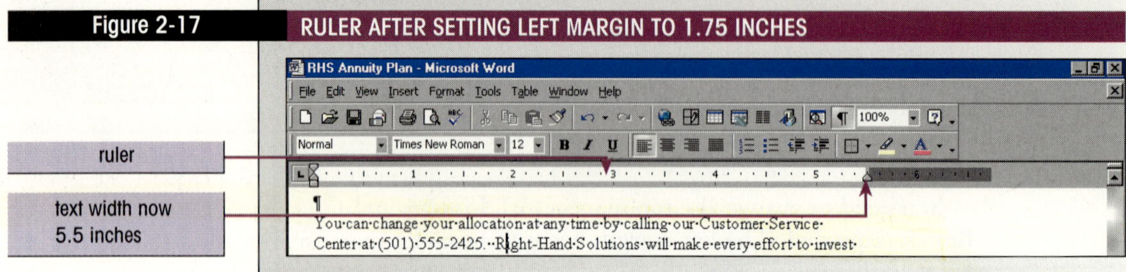

TROUBLE? If a double dotted line and the words "Section Break" appear in your document, text was selected in the document and Whole document wasn't specified in the Apply to list box. If this occurs, click the Undo button on the Standard toolbar and then repeat Steps 1 through 8, making sure you select the Whole document option in the Apply to list box.

Now that you've made numerous changes to your document, it's a good idea to save it with a new name. That way, if the file you are working on somehow becomes corrupted, you can at least return to the earlier draft, rather than having to start all over again.

To save the document with a new name:

1. Click **File** on the menu bar, then click **Save As**.

2. Verify that the Tutorial subfolder within the Tutorial.02 folder appears in the Save in list box, change the filename to **RHS Annuity Plan Copy 2**, and then click the **Save** button. The document is saved with the new margin settings and a new name.

Next you will change the amount of space between lines of text.

Changing Line Spacing

The line spacing in a document determines the amount of vertical space between lines of text. You have a choice of three basic types of line spacing: **single spacing** (which allows for the largest character in a particular line as well as a small amount of extra space); **1.5 line spacing** (which allows for one and one-half times the space of single spacing); and **double spacing** (which allows for twice the space of single spacing). The annuity plan document is currently single-spaced because Word uses single spacing by default. Before changing the line-spacing setting, you should select the text you want to change. You can change line spacing by using the Paragraph command on the Format menu, or by using your keyboard.

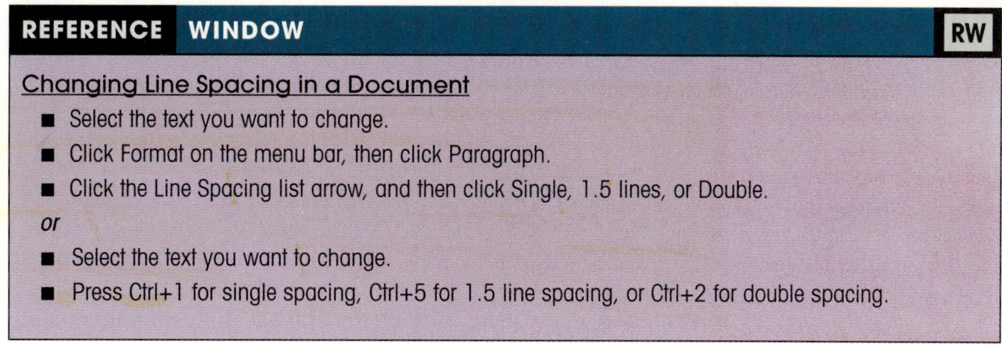

REFERENCE WINDOW RW

Changing Line Spacing in a Document

- Select the text you want to change.
- Click Format on the menu bar, then click Paragraph.
- Click the Line Spacing list arrow, and then click Single, 1.5 lines, or Double.

or

- Select the text you want to change.
- Press Ctrl+1 for single spacing, Ctrl+5 for 1.5 line spacing, or Ctrl+2 for double spacing.

Brandi has asked you to change the line spacing for the entire annuity plan document to 1.5 line spacing. You will begin by selecting the entire document.

To change the document's line spacing:

1. Triple-click in the selection bar to select the entire document.
2. Click **Format** on the menu bar, and then click **Paragraph** to open the Paragraph dialog box.
3. If necessary, click the **Indents and Spacing** tab.
4. Click the **Line spacing** list arrow, and then click **1.5 lines**. The Preview box shows the results of the new line spacing. See Figure 2-18.

Figure 2-18 CHANGING THE DOCUMENT'S LINE SPACING

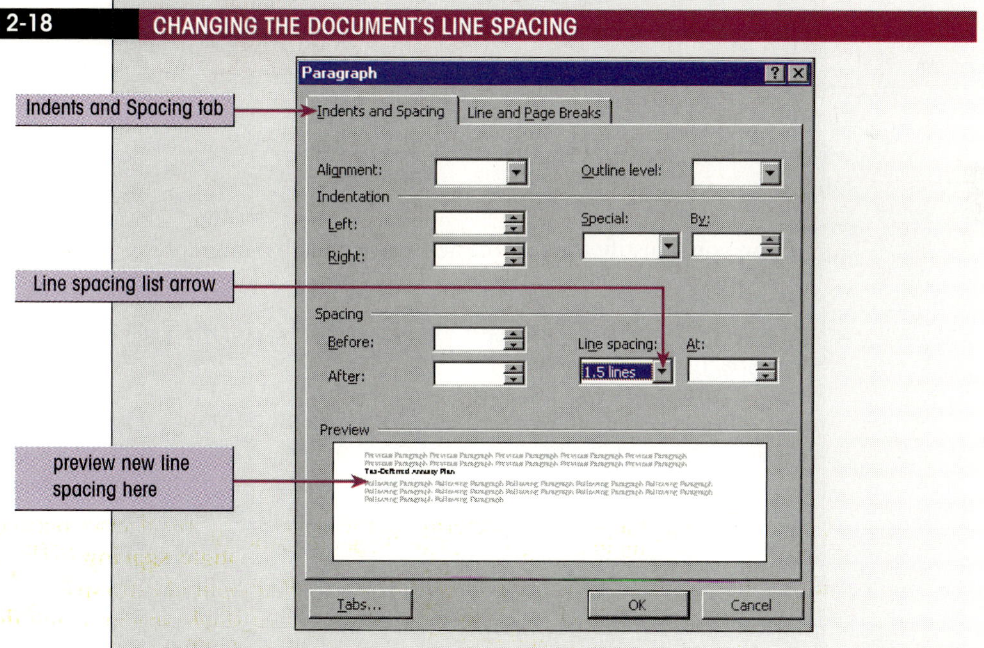

5. Click the **OK** button, and then click anywhere in the document to deselect it. Notice the additional space between every line of text in the document.

Now, you are ready to make formatting changes that affect individual paragraphs.

Aligning Text

Word defines a **paragraph** as any text that ends with a paragraph mark symbol (¶). The alignment of a paragraph or document refers to how the text lines up horizontally between the margins. By default, text is aligned along the left margin but is **ragged**, or uneven, along the right margin. This is called **left alignment**. With **right alignment**, the text is aligned along the right margin and is ragged along the left margin. With **center alignment**, text is centered between the left and right margins. With **justified alignment**, full lines of text are spaced between or aligned along both the left and the right margins. The paragraph you are reading now is justified. The easiest way to apply alignment settings is by clicking buttons on the Formatting toolbar.

Brandi indicated that the title of the annuity plan description should be centered and that the main paragraphs should be justified. First, you'll center the title.

To center-align the title:

1. Click anywhere in the title "Tax-Deferred Annuity Plan" at the beginning of the document.
2. Click the **Center** button on the Formatting toolbar. The text centers between the left and right margins. See Figure 2-19.

Figure 2-19 TITLE CENTERED

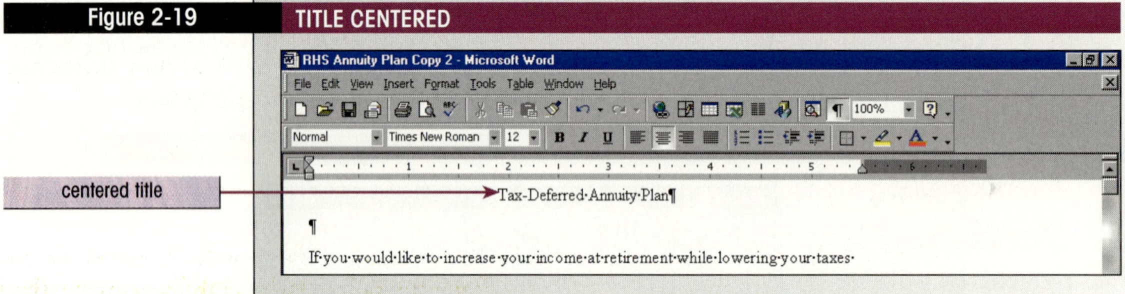

Now, you'll justify the text in the first two main paragraphs.

To justify the first two paragraphs using the Formatting toolbar:

1. Click anywhere in the first paragraph, which begins "If you would like to increase...," and click the **Justify** button on the Formatting toolbar. The justification would be easier to see if the paragraph had more lines of text. You'll see the effects more clearly after you justify the second paragraph in the document.
2. Move the insertion point to the second main paragraph, which begins "A tax-deferred annuity allows... ."
3. Click again. The text is evenly spaced between the left and right margins. See Figure 2-20.

Figure 2-20 TEXT JUSTIFIED USING THE FORMATTING TOOLBAR

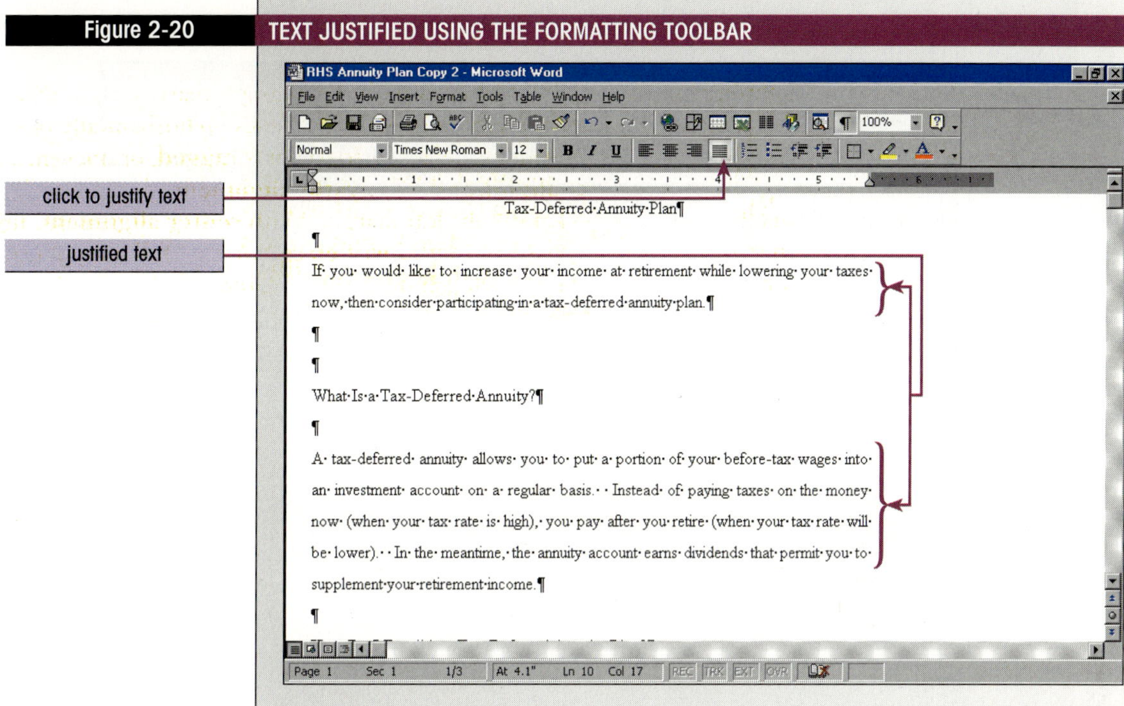

You'll justify the other paragraphs later. Now that you've learned how to change the paragraph alignment, you can turn your attention to indenting a paragraph.

Indenting a Paragraph

When you become a more experienced Word user, you might want to use some special forms of paragraph formatting, such as a **hanging indent** (where all lines except the first line of the paragraph are indented from the left margin) or a **right indent** (where all lines of the paragraph are indented from the right margin). You can select these types of indents on the Indents and Spacing tab of the Paragraph dialog box.

In this document, though, you'll need to indent only the main paragraphs 0.5 inches from the left margin. This left indent is a simple kind of paragraph indent, which requires only a quick click on the Formatting toolbar's Increase Indent button. According to Brandi's notes, you need to indent all of the main paragraphs, starting with the second paragraph.

To indent a paragraph using the Increase Indent button:

1. Make sure the insertion point is still located anywhere within the second paragraph, which begins "A tax-deferred annuity allows… ."
2. Click the **Increase Indent** button on the Formatting toolbar twice. (Don't click the Decrease Indent button by mistake.) The entire paragraph moves right 0.5 inches each time you click the Increase Indent button. The paragraph is indented 1 inch, 0.5 inches more than Brandi wants.
3. Click the **Decrease Indent** button on the Formatting toolbar to move the paragraph left 0.5 inches. The paragraph is now indented 0.5 inches from the left margin, as shown in Figure 2-21.

Figure 2-21 INDENTED PARAGRAPH

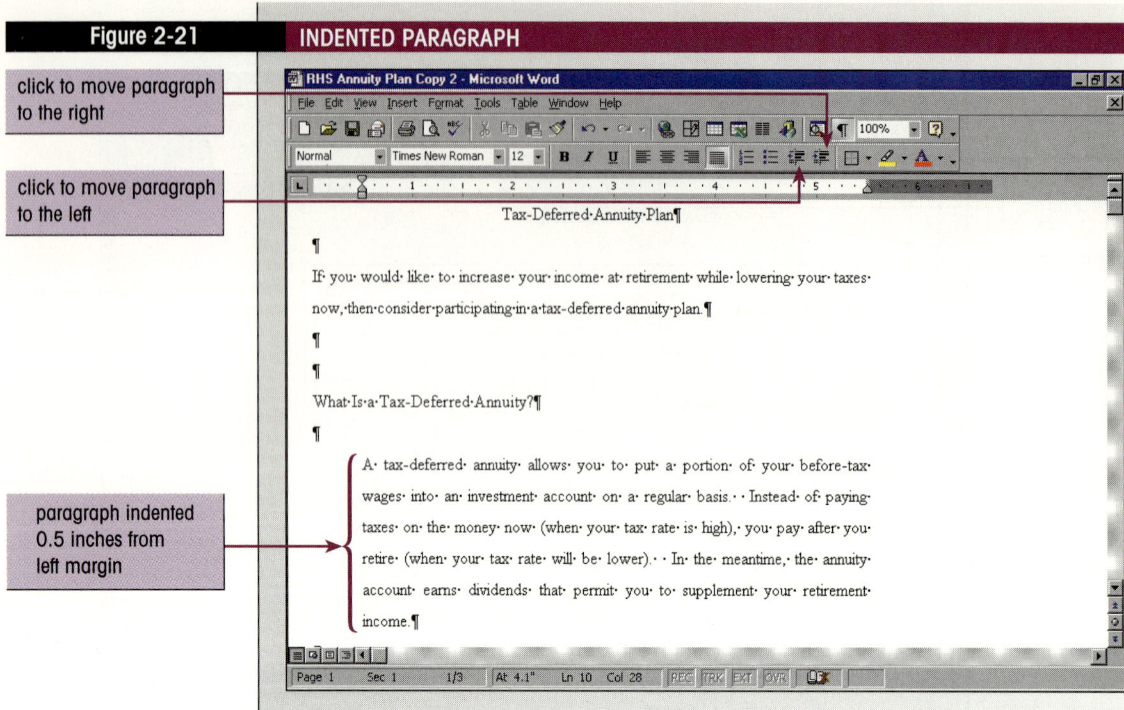

You could continue to indent, and then justify, each paragraph individually, but there's an easier way—the Format Painter command. The Format Painter allows you to copy both the indentation and alignment changes to all the other main paragraphs in the document.

Using Format Painter

The **Format Painter** makes it easy to copy all the formatting features of one paragraph to one or more other paragraphs. You'll use the Format Painter now to copy the formatting of the second paragraph to other main paragraphs. Begin by highlighting the paragraph whose format you want to copy. (Note that you can't simply move the insertion point to that paragraph.)

To copy paragraph formatting with the Format Painter:

1. Double-click in the selection bar to select the second paragraph, which is indented and justified and begins "A tax-deferred annuity... ."
2. Double-click the **Format Painter** button on the Standard toolbar. The Format Painter button will stay pressed until you click the button again. When you move the pointer over text, the pointer changes to to indicate that the format of the selected paragraph can be painted (or copied) onto another paragraph.
3. Scroll down, and then click anywhere in the third paragraph, which begins "As a full-time employee... ." The format of the third paragraph shifts to match the format of the selected paragraph. See Figure 2-22. As you can see, both paragraphs are now indented and justified. The pointer remains as the Format Painter pointer.

Figure 2-22 FORMATS COPIED WITH FORMAT PAINTER

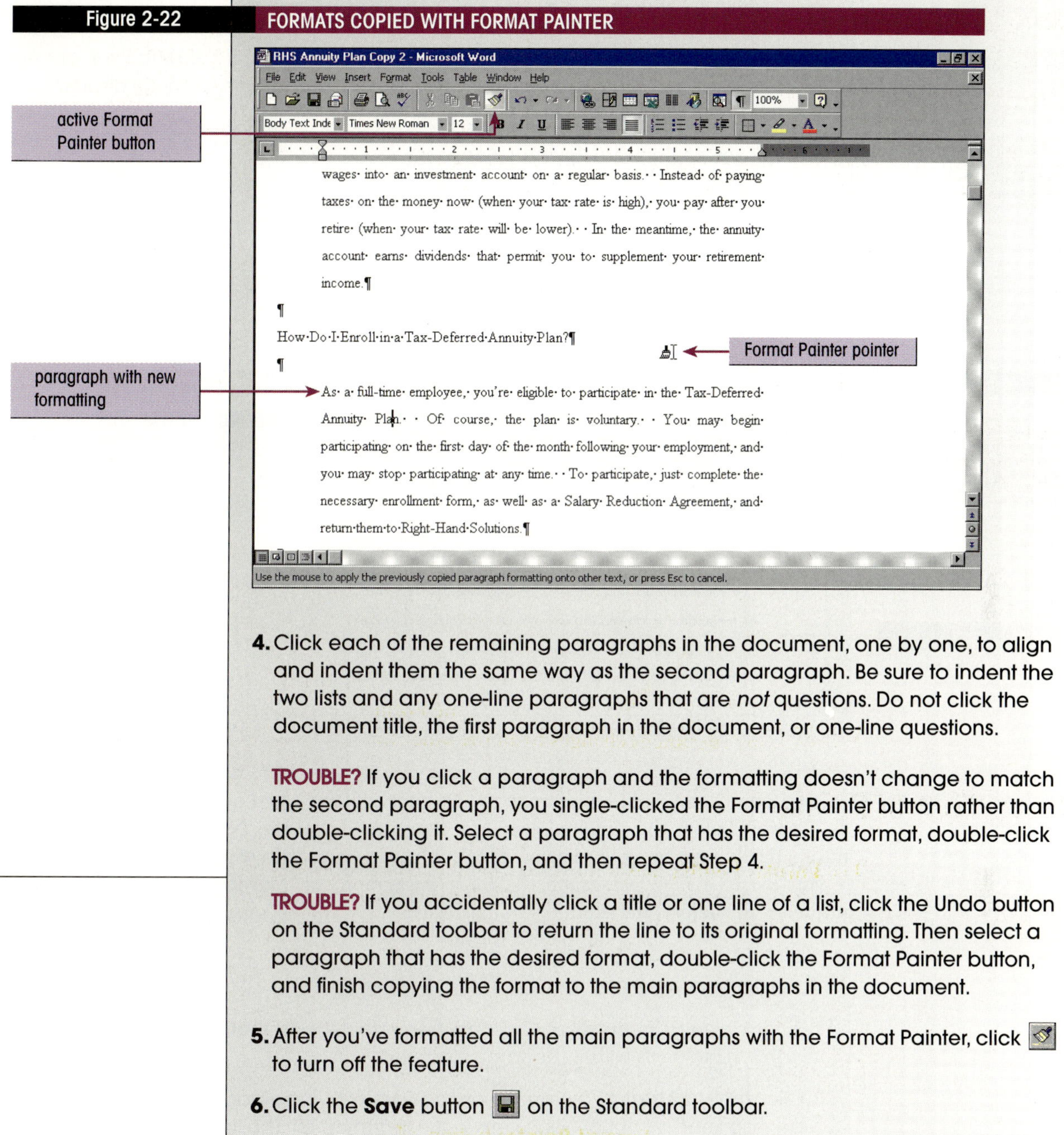

4. Click each of the remaining paragraphs in the document, one by one, to align and indent them the same way as the second paragraph. Be sure to indent the two lists and any one-line paragraphs that are *not* questions. Do not click the document title, the first paragraph in the document, or one-line questions.

   TROUBLE? If you click a paragraph and the formatting doesn't change to match the second paragraph, you single-clicked the Format Painter button rather than double-clicking it. Select a paragraph that has the desired format, double-click the Format Painter button, and then repeat Step 4.

   TROUBLE? If you accidentally click a title or one line of a list, click the Undo button on the Standard toolbar to return the line to its original formatting. Then select a paragraph that has the desired format, double-click the Format Painter button, and finish copying the format to the main paragraphs in the document.

5. After you've formatted all the main paragraphs with the Format Painter, click to turn off the feature.

6. Click the **Save** button on the Standard toolbar.

All the main paragraphs in the document are formatted with the correct indentation and alignment. Your next job is to make the lists easier to read by adding bullets and numbers.

Adding **Bullets and Numbers**

You can emphasize a list of items by adding a heavy dot, known as a **bullet**, before each item in the list. For consecutive items, you can use numbers instead of bullets. Brandi requested that you add bullets to the list of financial needs on page 3 to make them stand out.

To apply bullets to a list of items:

1. Scroll the document until you see the list of financial needs below the sentence "The following are considered to be immediate and severe financial needs."
2. Select the four items that appear in the middle of page 3 (from "medical expenses" to "Internal Revenue Service").
3. Click the **Bullets** button on the Formatting toolbar to activate the Bullets feature. A rounded bullet, a special character, appears in front of each item, and each line indents to make room for the bullet.
4. Click anywhere within the document window to deselect the text. Figure 2-23 shows the indented bulleted list.

Figure 2-23 INDENTED BULLETED LIST

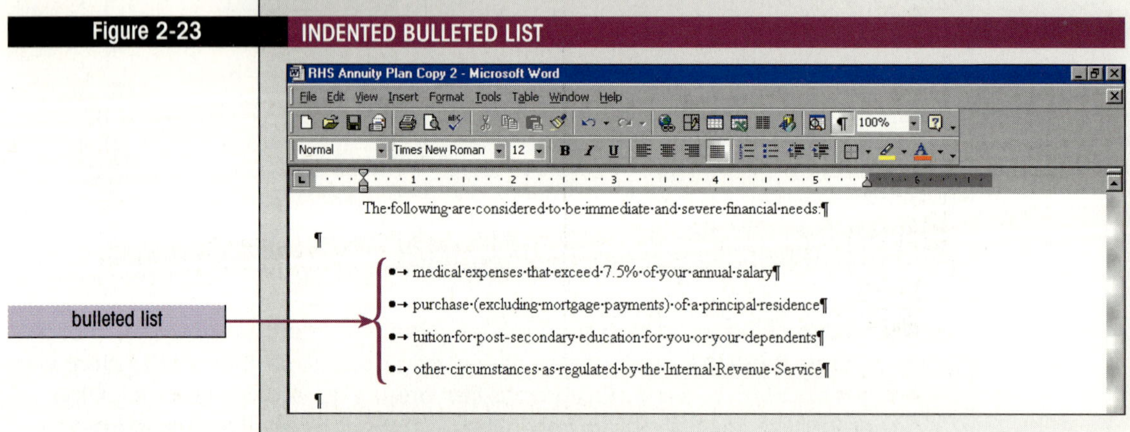

Next you need to add numbers to the list that explains when benefits can be received, in the section below the bulleted list. For this, you'll use the Numbering button, which automatically numbers the selected paragraphs with consecutive numbers and aligns them. If you insert a new paragraph, delete a paragraph, or reorder the paragraphs, Word automatically adjusts the numbers to make sure they remain consecutive.

To apply numbers to the list of items:

1. Scroll down to the next section, and then select the list that begins "reach the age..." and ends with "...become disabled."
2. Click the **Numbering** button on the Formatting toolbar. Consecutive numbers appear in front of each item in the indented list. The list is indented, similar to the bulleted list above.
3. Click anywhere in the document to deselect the text. Figure 2-24 shows the indented and numbered list.

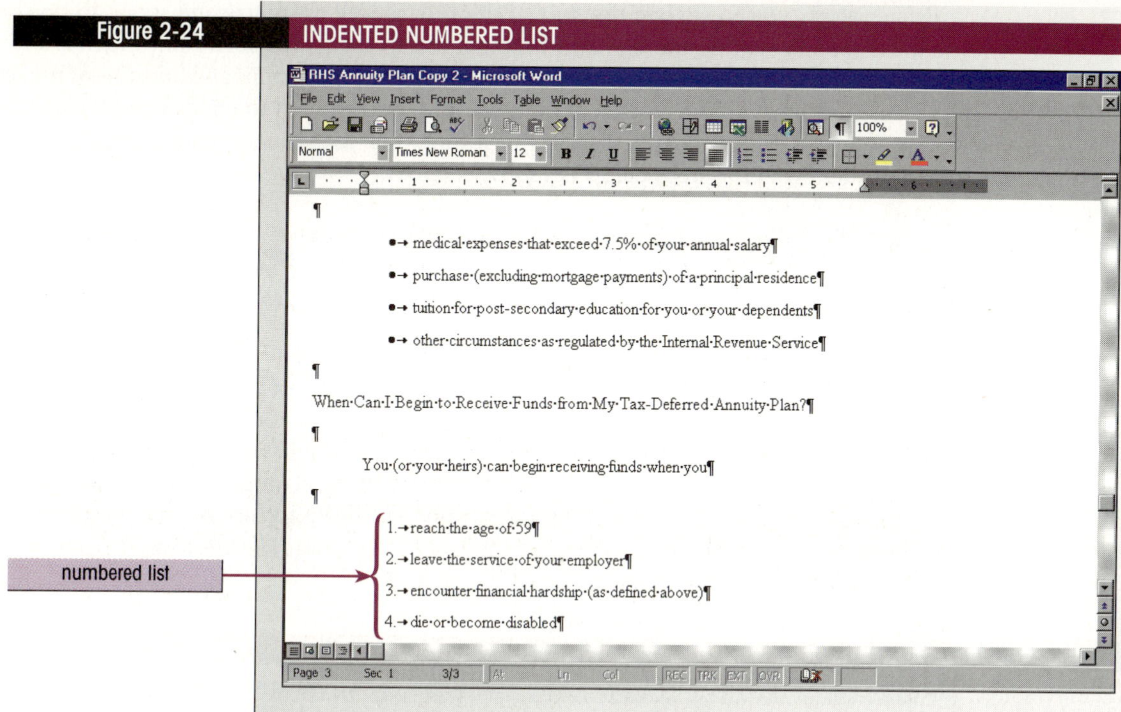

Figure 2-24 INDENTED NUMBERED LIST

The text of the document is now properly aligned and indented. The bullets and numbers make the lists easy to read and give readers visual clues about the type of information they contain. Next, you need to adjust the formatting of individual words.

Changing the Font and Font Size

All of Brandi's remaining changes concern changing fonts, adjusting font sizes, and emphasizing text with font styles. The first step is to change the font of the title from 12-point Times New Roman to 14-point Arial. This will make the title stand out from the rest of the text.

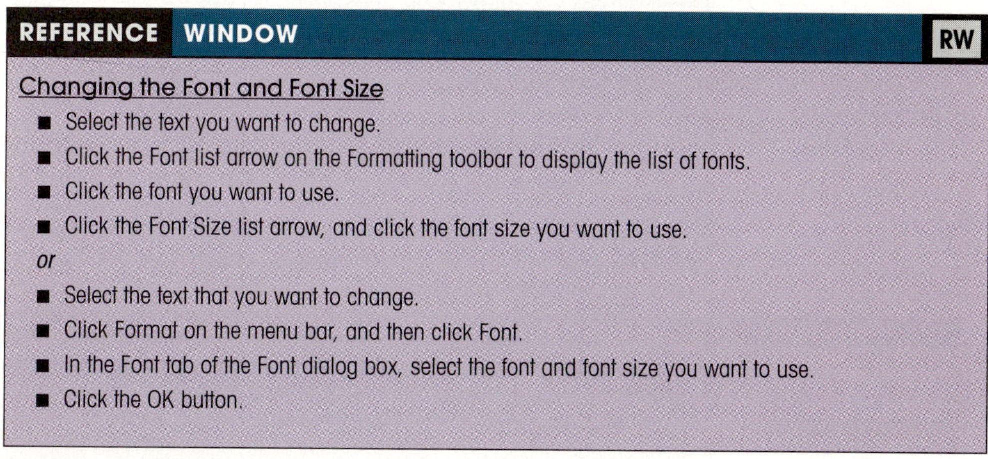
REFERENCE WINDOW RW

Changing the Font and Font Size
- Select the text you want to change.
- Click the Font list arrow on the Formatting toolbar to display the list of fonts.
- Click the font you want to use.
- Click the Font Size list arrow, and click the font size you want to use.

or
- Select the text that you want to change.
- Click Format on the menu bar, and then click Font.
- In the Font tab of the Font dialog box, select the font and font size you want to use.
- Click the OK button.

Brandi wants you to change the font of the title as well as its size and style. To do this, you'll use the Formatting toolbar. Brandi wants you to use a **sans serif** font, which is a font that does not have the small horizontal lines (called serifs) at the tops and bottoms of the letters. Sans serif fonts are often used in titles so they contrast with the body text. Times New Roman is a serif font, and Arial is a sans serif font. The text you are reading now is a serif font, and the text in the steps below is a sans serif font.

To change the attributes of the title using the Font command:

1. Press **Ctrl+Home** to move to the beginning of the document, and then select the title.
2. Click the **Font** list arrow on the Formatting toolbar. A list of available fonts appears in alphabetical order, with the name of the current font highlighted in the font list and in the Font text box. See Figure 2-25. (Your list of fonts might be different from those shown.) Fonts that have been used recently might appear above a double line. Note that each name in the list is formatted with that font. For example, "Arial" appears in the Arial font, and "Times New Roman" appears in the Times New Roman font.

Figure 2-25 FONT LIST

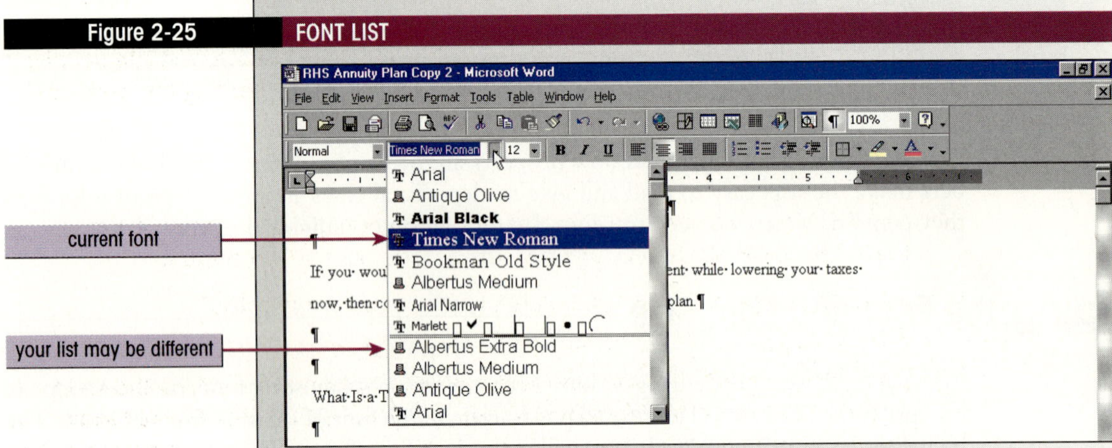

3. If necessary, scroll the list box until Arial appears, and then click **Arial** to select it as the new font. As you click, watch the font in the title change to reflect the new font.

   TROUBLE? If Arial doesn't appear in the font list, use another sans serif font.

4. Click the **Font Size** list arrow on the Formatting toolbar, and then click **14** in the size list. As you click, watch the title's font increase from 12 to 14 point.
5. Click the **Save** button on the Standard toolbar to save your changes, and then click within the title to deselect it. See Figure 2-26.

Figure 2-26 TITLE FONT AND FONT SIZE CHANGED

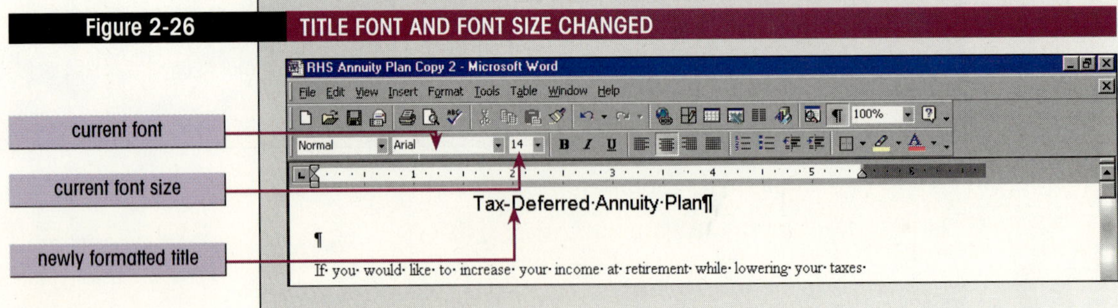

TROUBLE? If your font and font size settings don't match those in Figure 2-26, you may not have selected the title. Select the title, view the font and font size settings displayed on the Formatting toolbar, and then make the necessary changes. Because of differences in fonts and monitors, the characters in your document might look different from the figure.

Emphasizing Text with Boldface, Underlining, and Italics

You can emphasize words in your document with boldface, underlining, or italics. These styles help you make specific thoughts, ideas, words, or phrases stand out. Brandi marked a few words on the document draft (shown in Figure 2-1) that need this kind of special emphasis. You add boldface, underlining, or italics by using the relevant buttons on the Formatting toolbar. Note that these buttons are toggle buttons, which means you can click them once to format the selected text, and then click again to remove the formatting from the selected text.

Bolding Text

Brandi wants to make sure that clients' employees see that the tax-deferred annuity plan can be terminated only under certain conditions. You will do this by bolding the word "only."

To change the font style to boldface:

1. Scroll down so you can view the first line of the paragraph beneath the question "Can My Tax-Deferred Annuity Plan Be Terminated?" on page 2.
2. Select the word "only" (immediately after the word "terminated").
3. Click the **Bold** button on the Formatting toolbar, and then click anywhere in the document to deselect the text. The word appears in bold, as shown in Figure 2-27. After reviewing this change, you wonder if the word would look better without boldface. As you will see in the next step, you can easily remove the boldface by selecting the text and clicking the Bold button again to turn off boldfacing.

Figure 2-27 WORD IN BOLDFACE

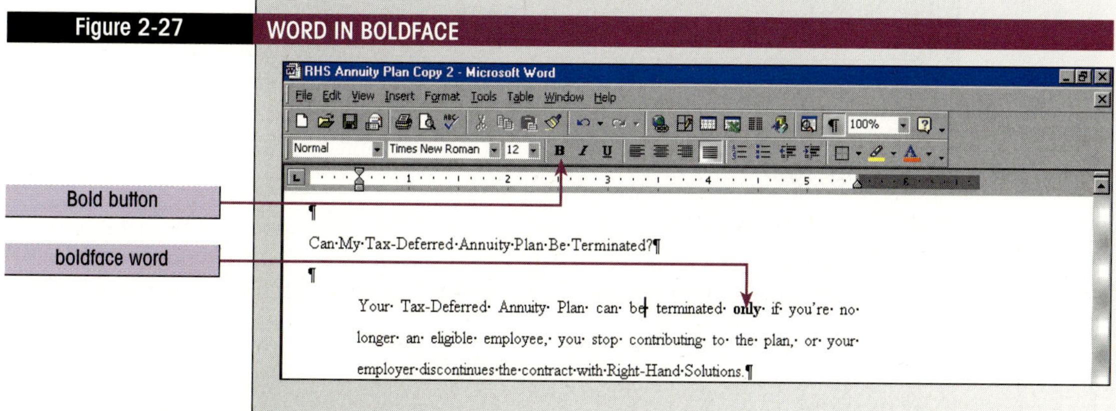

4. Double-click the word **only** to select it, then click **B**. The word now appears without boldface. You decide you prefer to emphasize the word with boldface after all.

5. Verify that the word "only" is still selected, and then click **B**. The word appears in boldface again.

Underlining Text

The Underline command works in the same way as the Bold command. Brandi's edits indicate that the word "Note" should be inserted and underlined at the beginning of the final paragraph. You'll make both of these changes at once using the Underline command.

To underline text:

1. Press **Ctrl+End** to move the insertion point to the end of the document. Then move the insertion point to the left of the word "Get" in the first line of the final paragraph.

2. Click the **Underline** button **U** on the Formatting toolbar to turn on underlining. Notice that the Underline button remains pressed. Now, whatever text you type will be underlined on your screen and in your printed document.

3. Type **Note:** and then click **U** to turn off underlining. Notice that the Underline button is no longer pressed, and "Note:" is underlined.

4. Press the **spacebar** twice. See Figure 2-28.

Figure 2-28 WORD TYPED WITH UNDERLINE

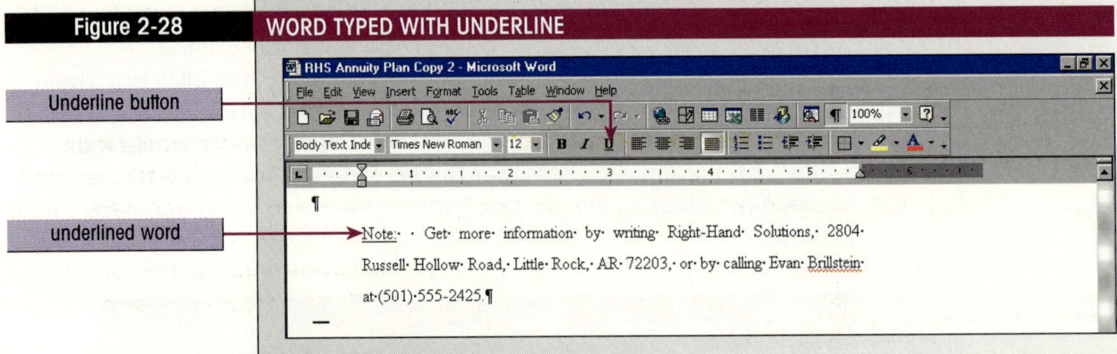

Italicizing Text

Next, you'll make the annuity plan conform with the other documents that Right-Hand Solutions produces by changing each question (heading) in the document to italics. This makes the document easier to read by clearly separating the sections. You'll begin with the first heading.

To italicize the question headings:

1. Press **Ctrl+Home** to return to the beginning of the document, and then select the text of the first heading, "What Is a Tax-Deferred Annuity?," by triple-clicking the text.
2. Click the **Italic** button on the Formatting toolbar. The heading changes from regular to italic text.
3. Repeat Steps 1 and 2 to italicize the next heading. Now try a shorter way to italicize the text by repeating the formatting you just applied.
4. Select the next heading, and then press the **F4** key. Repeat for each of the remaining four questions (headings) in the document. The italicized headings stand out from the rest of the text and help give the document a visual structure.

Saving and Printing

You have made all the editing and formatting changes that Brandi requested for the annuity plan description. When a document is complete, it's a good idea to save it with a name that indicates that it is final. After saving the document, you can preview and print it. It's especially useful to preview a document before printing when you made a number of formatting changes because the Print Preview window makes it easy to spot text that is not aligned correctly.

To save, preview, and print the document:

1. Click **File** on the menu bar, and then click **Save As**. Save the file as **RHS Annuity Plan Final Copy** in the Tutorial subfolder, within the Tutorial.02 folder.
2. Move the insertion point to the beginning of the document.
3. Click the **Print Preview** button on the Standard toolbar, and examine the first page of the document. Use the vertical scroll bar to display the second and third pages. (If you notice any headings as the last line of a page or other formatting errors, click the Close button on the Print Preview toolbar, correct the errors in normal view, and then return to the Print Preview window. To move a heading to the next page with its paragraph, click at the beginning of the heading and press **Ctrl+Enter** to insert a manual page break.)
4. Click the **Print** button on the Print Preview toolbar. After a pause, the document prints.
5. Click the **Close** button on the Print Preview toolbar, and then click the **Close** button on the program window to close your document and exit Word.

You now have a hardcopy of the final annuity plan description, as shown in Figure 2-29.

Figure 2-29 FINAL VERSION OF RHS ANNUITY PLAN

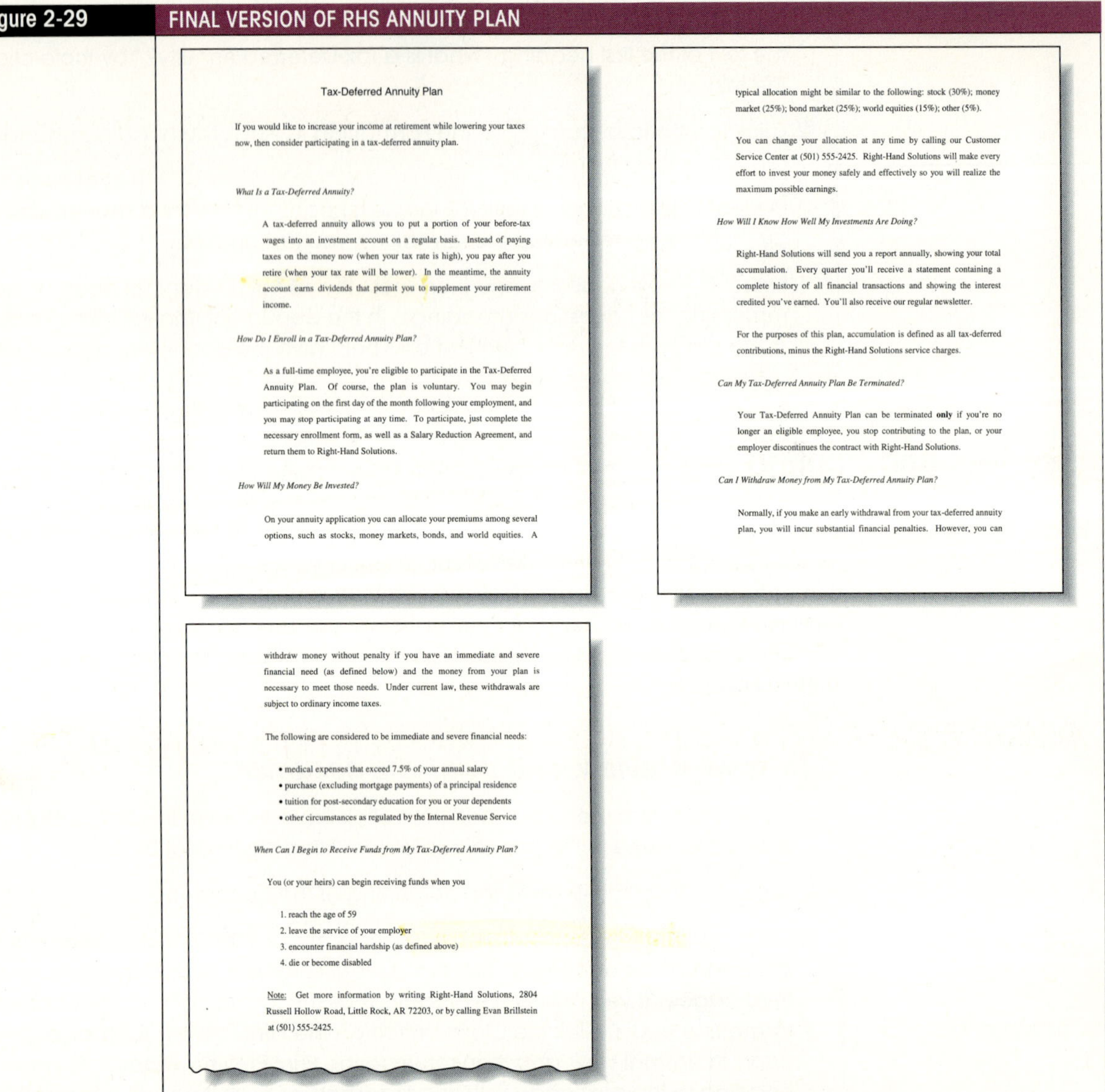

Tax-Deferred Annuity Plan

If you would like to increase your income at retirement while lowering your taxes now, then consider participating in a tax-deferred annuity plan.

What Is a Tax-Deferred Annuity?

A tax-deferred annuity allows you to put a portion of your before-tax wages into an investment account on a regular basis. Instead of paying taxes on the money now (when your tax rate is high), you pay after you retire (when your tax rate will be lower). In the meantime, the annuity account earns dividends that permit you to supplement your retirement income.

How Do I Enroll in a Tax-Deferred Annuity Plan?

As a full-time employee, you're eligible to participate in the Tax-Deferred Annuity Plan. Of course, the plan is voluntary. You may begin participating on the first day of the month following your employment, and you may stop participating at any time. To participate, just complete the necessary enrollment form, as well as a Salary Reduction Agreement, and return them to Right-Hand Solutions.

How Will My Money Be Invested?

On your annuity application you can allocate your premiums among several options, such as stocks, money markets, bonds, and world equities. A typical allocation might be similar to the following: stock (30%); money market (25%); bond market (25%); world equities (15%); other (5%).

You can change your allocation at any time by calling our Customer Service Center at (501) 555-2425. Right-Hand Solutions will make every effort to invest your money safely and effectively so you will realize the maximum possible earnings.

How Will I Know How Well My Investments Are Doing?

Right-Hand Solutions will send you a report annually, showing your total accumulation. Every quarter you'll receive a statement containing a complete history of all financial transactions and showing the interest credited you've earned. You'll also receive our regular newsletter.

For the purposes of this plan, accumulation is defined as all tax-deferred contributions, minus the Right-Hand Solutions service charges.

Can My Tax-Deferred Annuity Plan Be Terminated?

Your Tax-Deferred Annuity Plan can be terminated **only** if you're no longer an eligible employee, you stop contributing to the plan, or your employer discontinues the contract with Right-Hand Solutions.

Can I Withdraw Money from My Tax-Deferred Annuity Plan?

Normally, if you make an early withdrawal from your tax-deferred annuity plan, you will incur substantial financial penalties. However, you can withdraw money without penalty if you have an immediate and severe financial need (as defined below) and the money from your plan is necessary to meet those needs. Under current law, these withdrawals are subject to ordinary income taxes.

The following are considered to be immediate and severe financial needs:

- medical expenses that exceed 7.5% of your annual salary
- purchase (excluding mortgage payments) of a principal residence
- tuition for post-secondary education for you or your dependents
- other circumstances as regulated by the Internal Revenue Service

When Can I Begin to Receive Funds from My Tax-Deferred Annuity Plan?

You (or your heirs) can begin receiving funds when you

1. reach the age of 59
2. leave the service of your employer
3. encounter financial hardship (as defined above)
4. die or become disabled

Note: Get more information by writing Right-Hand Solutions, 2804 Russell Hollow Road, Little Rock, AR 72203, or by calling Evan Brillstein at (501) 555-2425.

In this tutorial, you have helped Reginald plan, edit, and format the annuity plan that will appear in the employee handbooks of Right-Hand Solutions' clients. Now that you have fine-tuned the content, adjusted the text appearance and alignment, and added a bulleted list and a numbered list, the plan is visually appealing and easy to read.

You give the hardcopy to Reginald, who makes two photocopies—one for Brandi and one for the copy center, which copies and distributes the document to all clients of Right-Hand Solutions.

Session 2.2 QUICK CHECK

1. What are Word's default margins for the left and right margins? For the top and bottom margins?
2. Describe the four types of text alignment.
3. Explain how to indent a paragraph 1 inch or more from the left margin.
4. Describe a situation in which you would use the Format Painter.
5. Explain how to add underlining to a word as you type it.
6. Explain how to transform a series of short paragraphs into a numbered list.

7. Explain how to format a title in 14-point Arial.
8. Describe the steps involved in changing the line spacing in a document.

REVIEW ASSIGNMENTS

Now that you have completed the description of the annuity plan, Brandi explains that she also wants to include a sample quarterly statement and a sample contract change notice in the client's employee handbooks to show employees how easy the statements are to read. You'll open and format this document now.

1. If necessary, start Word, make sure your Data Disk is in the appropriate disk drive, and check your screen to make sure your settings match those in the tutorial.
2. Open the file **RHSQuart** from the Review folder for Tutorial 2 on your Data Disk, and save the document as **RHS Quarterly Report**.
3. Use the Spelling and Grammar checker to correct any spelling or grammatical errors. If the Suggestions list box does not include the correct replacement, click outside the Spelling and Grammar dialog box, type the correction yourself, click Resume in the Spelling and Grammar dialog box, and continue checking the document. After you finish using the Spelling and Grammar checker, proofread the document carefully to check for any additional errors, especially words that are spelled correctly but used improperly. Pay special attention to the second main paragraph of the letter.
4. Make all edits and formatting changes marked on Figure 2-30. To substitute "Right-Hand Solutions" for "We" in the first paragraph, copy the company name from the top of the letter (without the paragraph mark) and paste it into the first paragraph as marked. (Copy and paste this text *before* you format it in Arial 14 point.)

Figure 2-30

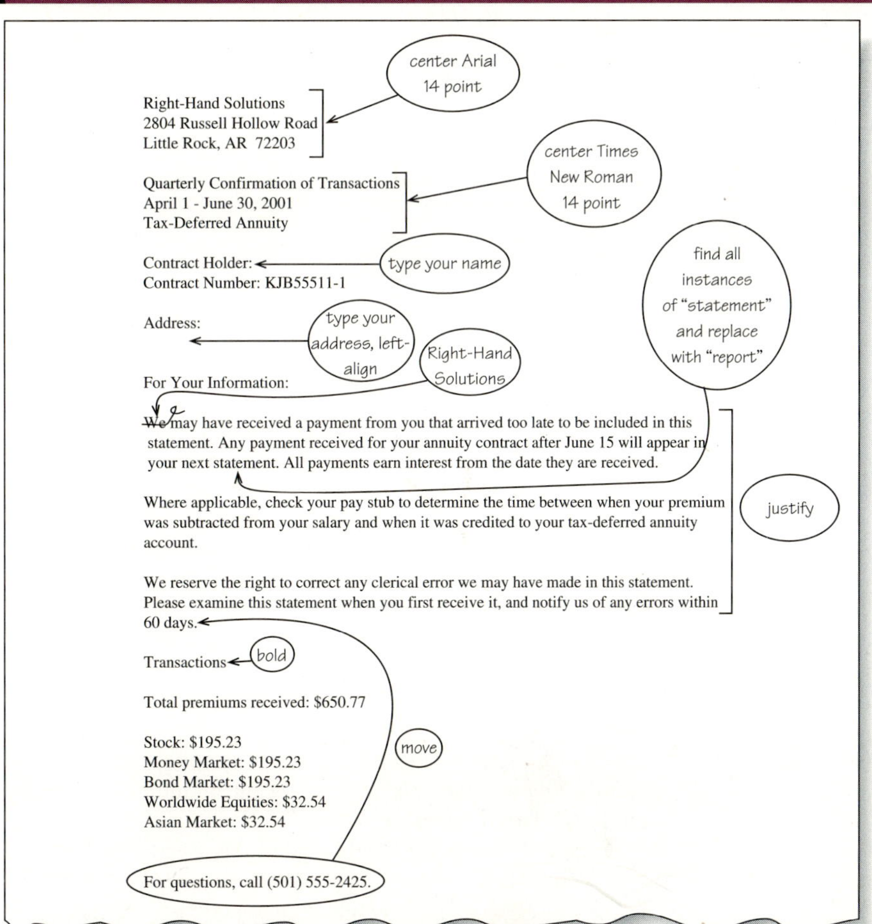
Right-Hand Solutions
2804 Russell Hollow Road
Little Rock, AR 72203

Quarterly Confirmation of Transactions
April 1 - June 30, 2001
Tax-Deferred Annuity

Contract Holder:
Contract Number: KJB55511-1

Address:

For Your Information:

We may have received a payment from you that arrived too late to be included in this statement. Any payment received for your annuity contract after June 15 will appear in your next statement. All payments earn interest from the date they are received.

Where applicable, check your pay stub to determine the time between when your premium was subtracted from your salary and when it was credited to your tax-deferred annuity account.

We reserve the right to correct any clerical error we may have made in this statement. Please examine this statement when you first receive it, and notify us of any errors within 60 days.

Transactions

Total premiums received: $650.77

Stock: $195.23
Money Market: $195.23
Bond Market: $195.23
Worldwide Equities: $32.54
Asian Market: $32.54

For questions, call (501) 555-2425.

5. Save the document, preview it, and then print it.
6. Close th document.
7. Open the file **RHSPort** from the Review folder for Tutorial 2 on your Data Disk, and save the file as **RHS Portfolio Changes**.

Explore

8. Make all the edits and formatting changes marked on Figure 2-31. However, instead of using the Formatting toolbar to change Current Allocation Accounts to underline 14 point, click Format on the menu bar, and then click Font to open the Font dialog box. Click the appropriate selections in the Underline style and Size list boxes. Notice that you should only replace "Right-Hand Solutions" with "RHS" in the list of Allocation Accounts. To skip an instance of "Right-Hand Solutions" without changing it, click the Find Next button in the Find and Replace dialog box.

Figure 2-31

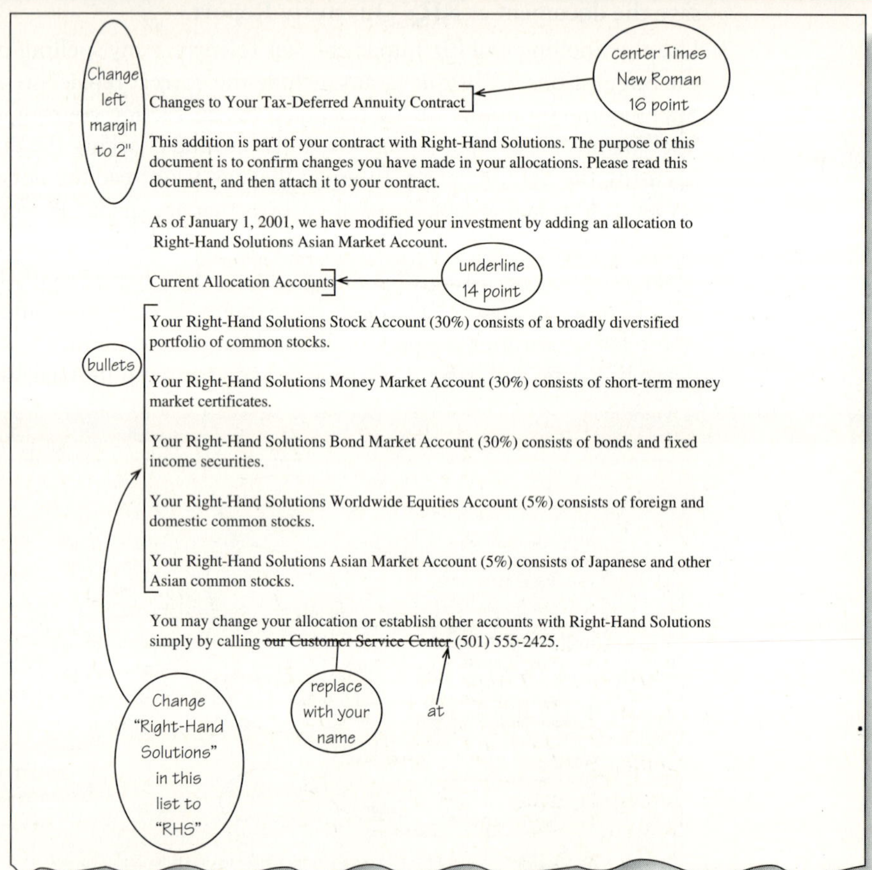

Explore

9. Change the right margin using the ruler in print layout view:
   a. Click the Print Layout View button, and then select the entire document.
   b. Position the pointer on the ruler at the right margin, above the Right Indent marker (a small, gray triangle).
   c. Press and hold down the mouse button. A dotted line appears in the document window, indicating the current right margin. Drag the margin left to the 5-inch mark on the ruler, and then release the mouse button.
   d. Click the Normal View button to return to normal view.
   e. Save the document.

Explore

10. Change the line spacing of individual paragraphs within the document.
    a. Select the first two paragraphs in the document, immediately under the heading "Changes to Your Tax-Deferred Annuity Contract."
    b. Press Ctrl+5 to change the line spacing of the selected paragraphs to 1.5 line spacing.
    c. Save the document.

11. Cut and paste text using the Clipboard:
    a. Select the second sentence in the document ("The purpose of this document is to confirm…"), and then click the Cut button on the Standard toolbar to remove the sentence from the document. If the Clipboard toolbar appears, leave it open while you continue with the next step.
    b. Select the last sentence in the document ("You may change your allocation…"), and then click the Cut button on the Standard toolbar to remove the sentence from the document. If the Clipboard toolbar did not open at the end of the previous step, it should be open now.
    c. Move the insertion point to the beginning of the first sentence, to the left of the "T" in "This addition is part of your contract… ." Move the pointer over the icons on the Clipboard toolbar, until you find one labeled "The purpose of this document is to confirm… ." Click that icon to insert the sentence (which was originally the second sentence in the document) at the insertion point. Insert an extra space, if necessary.
    d. Repeat the previous step to insert the sentence beginning, "You may change your allocation or establish other…" at the end of the second paragraph.
    e. Click the Clear Clipboard button on the Clipboard toolbar to erase the contents of the Clipboard, and then click the Close button to close the Clipboard toolbar.
12. Click the Print Preview button on the Standard toolbar to check your work.

Explore

13. Use the Print command on the File menu to open the Print dialog box. Print two copies of the document by changing the Number of copies setting in the Print dialog box.

Explore

14. You can find out the number of words in your documents by using the Word Count command on the Tools menu. Use this command to determine the number of words in the document, and then write that number in the upper-right corner of one of the printouts.
15. Save and close the document.

CASE PROBLEMS

Case 1. Store-It-All Katie Strainchamps manages Store-It-All, a storage facility in Huntsville, Alabama. She has written the draft of a tenant-information sheet outlining Store-It-All's policies for new customers. She asks you to edit and format the document for her.

1. If necessary, start Word, make sure your Data Disk is in the appropriate disk drive, and check your screen to make sure your settings match those in the tutorials.
2. Open the file **Store** from the Tutorial 2 Cases folder on your Data Disk, and save it as **Store-It-All Policies**.
3. Use the Spelling and Grammar checker to correct any errors in the document. Then proofread the document to check for errors the Spelling and Grammar checker missed. Pay particular attention to the paragraph under "Rental Payments" and the company name throughout the document.
4. Delete the word "basic" from the first sentence of the first full paragraph. (Remember to use the Undo and Redo buttons as you work to correct any editing mistakes.)
5. Delete the second sentence in the second paragraph, which begins "You renew your contract… ."
6. Insert the bolded sentence "A bill will not be sent to you." before the first sentence under the heading "Rental Payments."
7. Under the heading "Insurance," delete the sentence in parentheses and the extra paragraph mark.
8. Change all of the margins (top, bottom, left, and right) to 1.75 inches.
9. For each paragraph following a heading, set the alignment to justify. (*Hint:* Format the first paragraph and then use the Format Painter to format each successive paragraph.)
10. Find the phrase "not negotiable" using the Find command and italicize it.
11. Indent the four-item list under the heading "Delinquent Accounts" 0.5-inch and add bullets.
12. Change both lines of the title to 14-point Arial (or another sans serif font of your choice).
13. Center and bold both lines of the title.
14. Underline all of the headings.

15. Insert two blank lines at the end of the document, and then type the following, making sure to replace "*your name*" with your first and last name: Direct all questions to *your name* in the main office.
16. Save, preview, and print the rental information sheet, and close the document.

Case 2. UpTime Matt Patterson is UpTime's marketing director for the Northeast region. The company provides productivity training for large companies across the country. Matt wants to provide interested clients with a one-page summary of UpTime's productivity training.

1. If necessary, start Word, make sure your Data Disk is in the appropriate disk drive, and check your screen to make sure your settings match those in the tutorials.
2. Open the file **UpTime** from the Tutorial 2 Cases folder on your Data Disk, and save it as **UpTime Training Summary**.
3. Change the title at the beginning of the document to a 16-point serif font other than Times New Roman. Be sure to pick a font that looks professional and is easy to read. (Remember to use the Undo and Redo buttons as you work to correct any editing mistakes.)
4. Center and bold the title.
5. Delete the word "general" from the second sentence of the first paragraph after the document title.
6. Convert the list of training components following the first paragraph to an indented, numbered list.
7. Under the heading "Personal Productivity Training Seminar," delete the third sentence from the first paragraph.
8. Under the heading "Personal Productivity Training Seminar," delete the phrase "at the seminar" from the first sentence in the second paragraph.
9. In the first paragraph under the heading "Management Productivity Training," move the first sentence (beginning with "UpTime provides management training…") to the end of the paragraph.
10. Switch the order of the first and second paragraphs under the "Field Services Technology and Training" heading.
11. Search for the text "your name," and replace it with your first and last name.
12. Change the top margin to 1.5 inches.
13. Change the left margin to 1.75 inches.
14. Bold each of the headings.
15. Italicize both occurrences of the word "free" in the second paragraph under the "Field Services Technology and Training" heading.
16. Save and preview the document.
17. Print the document, and then close the file.

Case 3. Ridge Top Thomas McGee is vice president of sales and marketing at Ridge Top, an outdoor and sporting-gear store in Conshohocken, Pennsylvania. Each year, Thomas and his staff mail a description of new products to Ridge Top's regular customers. Ralph has asked you to edit and format the first few pages of this year's new products' description.

1. If necessary, start Word, make sure your Data Disk is in the appropriate disk drive, and check your screen to make sure your settings match those in the tutorials.
2. Open the file **Ridge** from the Tutorial 2 Cases folder on your Data Disk, and save it as **Ridge Top Guide**.
3. Use the Spelling and Grammar checker to correct any errors in the document. Because of the nature of this document, it contains some words that the Word dictionary on your computer may not recognize. It also contains headings that the Spelling and Grammar checker may consider sentence fragments. As you use the Spelling and Grammar checker, use the Ignore All button, if necessary, to skip over brand names. Use the Ignore Rule button to skip over sentence fragments.

4. Delete the phrase "a great deal" from the first sentence of the paragraph below the heading "Snuggle Up to These Prices." (Remember to use the Undo and Redo buttons to correct any editing mistakes as you work.)
5. Reverse the order of the first two paragraphs under the heading, "You'll Eat Up the Prices of This Camp Cooking Gear!"
6. Cut the last sentence of the first full paragraph ("Prices are good through...") from the document. Then move the insertion point to the end of the document, press the Enter key twice, and insert the cut sentence as a new paragraph. Format it in 12-point Arial, and italicize it.
7. Format the Ridge Top tip items as a numbered list.

Explore

8. Reorder the items under the "Ridge Top Tips!" heading by moving the fourth product idea and the following paragraph to the top of the list.
9. Search for the text "your name," and replace with your first and last name.

Explore

10. Experiment with two special paragraph alignment options: first line and hanging. First, select everything from the heading "Ridge Top Guarantees Warmth at Cool Prices" through the paragraph just before the heading "Ridge Top Tips." Next, click Format on the menu bar, click Paragraph, click Indents and Spacing tab, click the Help button in the upper-right corner of the dialog box, click the Special list arrow, and review the information on the special alignment options. Experiment with both the First line and the Hanging options. When you are finished, return the document to its original format by choosing the none option.
11. Justify all the paragraphs in the document. (*Hint:* To select all paragraphs in the document at one time, click Edit on the menu bar, and then click Select All.)
12. Replace all occurrences of "RidgeTop" with "Ridge Top."
13. Apply a 12-point, bold, sans serif font to each of the headings. Be sure to pick a font that looks professional and is easy to read. (*Hint:* Use the Format Painter.)
14. Change the title's font to the same font you used for the headings, except set the size to 16 point.
15. Bold both lines of the title.
16. Underline the names and prices for all of the brandname products in the Trekker's Guide. Make sure you don't underline spaces or periods. (*Hint:* Use the Words only underline style option in the Font dialog box.)
17. Save and preview the document. Print the document, and then close the file.

Case 4. Restaurant Review Your student newspaper has asked you to review four restaurants in your area.

1. If necessary, start Word, make sure your Data Disk is in the appropriate disk drive, and check your screen to make sure your settings match those in the tutorials.
2. Write a brief summary (one to two paragraphs) for each restaurant and provide a rating for each one. Correct any spelling or grammatical errors.
3. Add a title and subtitle to your review. The subtitle should include your name.
4. Save the document as **Restaurant Review** in the Tutorial 2 Cases folder on your Data Disk, and print it.
5. Rearrange the order in which you discuss the restaurants to alphabetical order. (Remember to use the Undo and Redo buttons as you work to correct any editing mistakes.)
6. Change the top margin to 2 inches.
7. Change the left margin to 1.75 inches.
8. Center and bold the title and subtitle.
9. Change the paragraph alignment to justify.
10. Italicize the title of each restaurant.
11. Save the edited document as **Edited Restaurant Review**.
12. Print the document.
13. Save and close your document.

INTERNET ASSIGNMENTS

The purpose of the Internet Assignments is to challenge you to find information on the Internet that you can use to create effective documents. The actual assignments are updated and maintained on the Course Technology Web site. Log on to the Internet and use your Web browser to go to the Student Online Companion to accompany this text at **www.course.com/NewPerspectives/office2000**. Click the Word link, and then click the link for Tutorial 2.

QUICK CHECK ANSWERS

Session 2.1

1. Click the Open button on the Standard toolbar, or click File, click Open, and double-click the file. Click File, click Save As, select the location, type the new filename, and then click OK.
2. (a) ↓; (b) Ctrl+End; (c) Page Down
3. The process of first selecting the text to be modified, and then performing the operations such as moving, formatting, or deleting.
4. (a) The blank space in the left margin area of the document window, which allows you to easily select entire lines or large blocks of text. (b) The button on the Standard toolbar that redoes an action you previously reversed using the Undo button. (c) The process of moving text by first selecting the text, then pressing and holding the mouse button while moving the text to its new location in the document, and finally releasing the mouse button.
5. To select a single word, double-click the word, or click at the beginning of the word, and drag the pointer to the end of the word. To select a complete paragraph, triple-click in the selection bar next to the paragraph, or click at the beginning of the paragraph and drag the pointer to the end of the paragraph.
6. You might use the Undo button to remove the bold formatting you had just applied to a word. You could then use the Redo button to restore the bold formatting to the word.
7. False
8. Cut and paste removes the selected material from its original location and inserts it in a new location. Copy and paste makes a copy of the selected material and inserts the copy in a new location; the original material remains in its original location.
9. Click the Select Browse Object button, click the Find button, click the Replace tab, type the search text in the Find what text box, type the replacement text in the Replace with text box, click Find Next or click Replace all.

Session 2.2

1. The default top and bottom margins are 1 inch. The default left and right margins are 1.25 inches.
2. Align-left: each line flush left, ragged right.
   Align-right: each line flush right, ragged left.
   Center: each line centered, ragged right and left.
   Justify: each line flush left and flush right.
3. Click in the paragraph you want to indent, and then click the Increase Indent button on the Formatting toolbar once for each half-inch you want to indent.
4. You might use the Format Painter to copy the formatting of a heading with bold italic to the other headings in the document.
5. Click the Underline button on the Formatting toolbar, type the word, and then click the Underline button again to turn off underlining.
6. Select the paragraphs, and then click the Numbering button on the Formatting toolbar.
7. Select the title, click the Font list arrow, and click Arial in the list of fonts. Then click the Font Size list arrow, and click 14.
8. Select the text you want to change, click Format on the menu bar, click Paragraph, click the Line Spacing list arrow, and then click Single, 1.5, or Double. Or, select the text, and then press Ctrl+1 for single spacing, Ctrl+5 for 1.5 line spacing, or Ctrl+2 for double spacing.

OBJECTIVES

In this tutorial you will:

- Set tab stops
- Divide a document into sections
- Change the vertical alignment of a section
- Center a page between the top and bottom margins
- Create a header with page numbers
- Create a table
- Sort the rows in a table
- Modify a table's structure
- Total a column of numbers with AutoSum
- Format a table

CREATING A MULTIPLE-PAGE REPORT

Writing a Recommendation Report for AgriTechnology

CASE

AgriTechnology

Brittany Jones works for AgriTechnology, a biotechnology company that develops genetically engineered food products. Recently, AgriTechnology began shipping the EverRipe tomato to supermarkets. The EverRipe tomato is genetically engineered to stay ripe and fresh nearly twice as long as other varieties. Because of its longer shelf life and vine-ripened taste, the new tomato is popular with supermarkets, and demand for it has been high. Unfortunately, the EverRipe tomato also is more susceptible to bruising than standard varieties. Nearly 20 percent of the first year's crop was unmarketable because of damage sustained during shipping and handling. AgriTechnology's vice president, Ramon Espinoza, appointed Brittany to head a task force to determine how to increase the profitability of the EverRipe. The task force is ready to present the results of their study in the form of a report with an accompanying table. Brittany asks you to help prepare the report.

In this tutorial, you will format the report's title page so that it has a different layout from the rest of the report. The title page will contain only the title and subtitle and will not have page numbers like the rest of the report. You also will add a table to the AgriTechnology report that summarizes the task force's recommendations.

SESSION 3.1

In this session you will review the task force's recommendation report. Then you will learn how to set tab stops, divide a document into sections, center a page between the top and bottom margins, create a header, and create a table.

Planning the Document

As head of the task force, Brittany divided the responsibility for the report among the members of the group. Each person gathered information about one aspect of the problem and wrote the appropriate section of the report. Now, Brittany must compile all the findings into a coherent and unified report. In addition, she also must follow the company's style guidelines for the content, organization, style, and format.

The report content includes the results of the study—obtained from interviews with other employees and visits to the packaging and distribution plant, trucking company, and so forth—and recommendations for action.

Because Brittany knows some executives will not have time to read the entire report, she organized the report so it begins with an executive summary. The body of the report provides an in-depth statement of the problem and recommendations for solving that problem. At the end of the report, she summarizes the cost of the improvements.

The report's style follows established standards of business writing, and emphasizes clarity, simplicity, and directness.

In accordance with AgriTechnology's style guide, Brittany's report will begin with a title page, with the text centered between the top and bottom margins. Every page except the title page will include a line of text at the top, giving a descriptive name for the report, as well as the page number. The text and headings will be formatted to match all AgriTechnology's reports, and will follow company guidelines for layout and text style.

At the end of the report, there will be a table that summarizes the costs of the proposed changes.

Opening the Report

Brittany already has combined the individual sections into one document. She also has begun formatting the report by changing the font size of headings, adding elements such as bold and italics, and by indenting paragraphs. You'll open the document and perform the remaining formatting tasks on page 1, as indicated in Figure 3-1.

Figure 3-1 INITIAL DRAFT OF TASK FORCE'S REPORT WITH EDITS (PAGE 1)

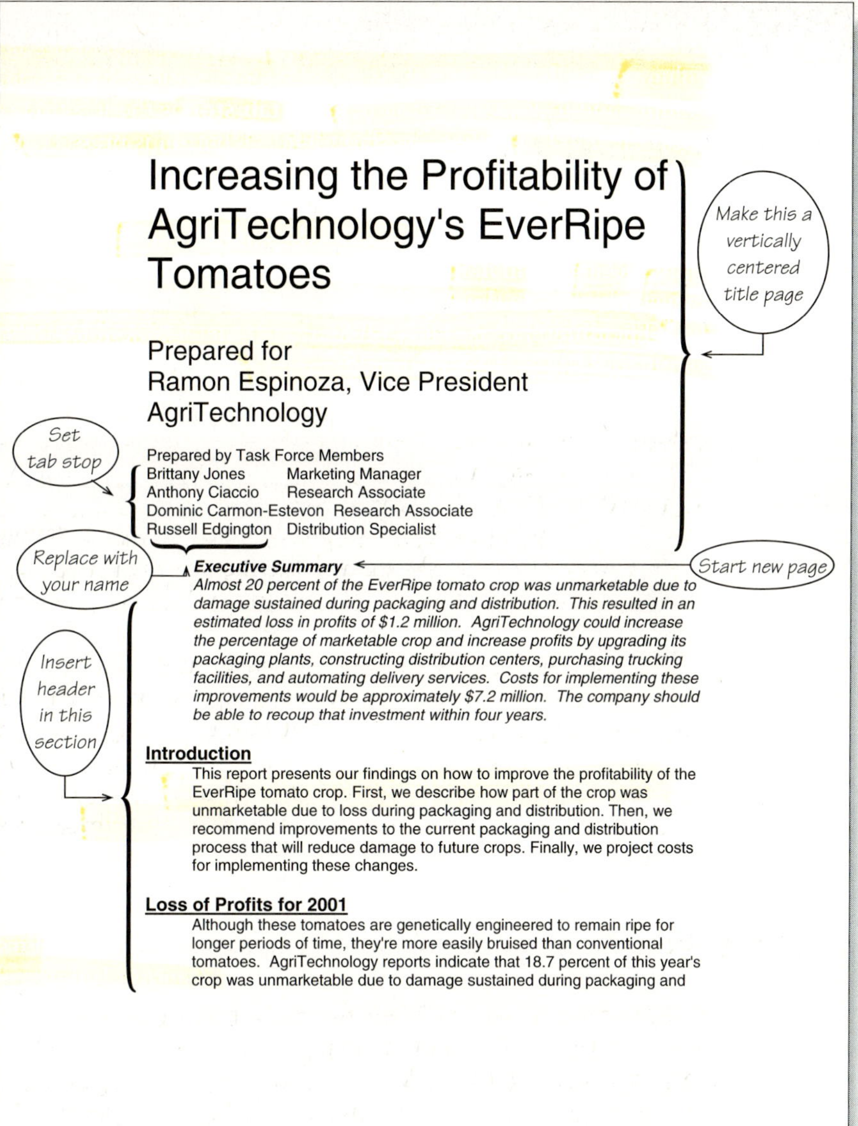

To open the document:

1. Start Word, and place your Data Disk in the appropriate drive. Make sure your screen matches the figures in this tutorial. In particular, be sure to display the nonprinting characters.
2. Open the file **EverRipe** from the **Tutorial** folder in the **Tutorial.03** folder on your Data Disk.
3. To avoid altering the original file, save the document as **EverRipe Report** in the same folder.
4. In the first page, replace the name "Russell Edgington" with your name.

Setting Tab Stops

Tabs are useful for indenting paragraphs and for vertically aligning text or numerical data in columns. A **tab** adds space between the margin and text in a column or between text in one column and text in another column. A **tab stop** is the location where text moves when you press the Tab key. When the Show/Hide ¶ button is pressed, the nonprinting tab character → appears wherever you press the Tab key. A tab character is just like any other character you type; you can delete it by pressing the Backspace key or the Delete key.

Word provides several **tab-stop alignment styles**. The five major styles are left, center, right, decimal, and bar, as shown in Figure 3-2. The first three tab-stop styles position text in a similar way to the Align Left, Center, and Align Right buttons on the Formatting toolbar. The difference is that with a tab, you determine line by line precisely where the left, center, or right alignment should occur.

Figure 3-2 TAB STOP ALIGNMENT STYLES

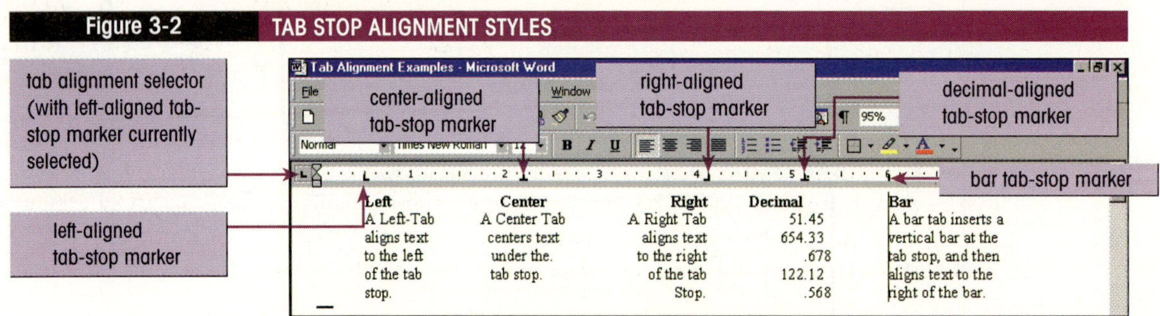

The default tab stops on the ruler are **Left tabs**, which position the left edge of text at the tab stop and extend the text to the right. **Center tabs** position text so that it's centered evenly on both sides of the tab stop. **Right tabs** position the right edge of text at the tab stop and extend the text to the left. **Decimal tabs** position numbers so that their decimal points are aligned at the tab stop. **Bar tabs** insert a vertical bar at the tab stop and then align text to the right of the bar. In addition, you also can use a **First Line Indent tab**, which indents the first line of a paragraph, and the **Hanging Indent tab**, which indents every line of a paragraph *except* the first line.

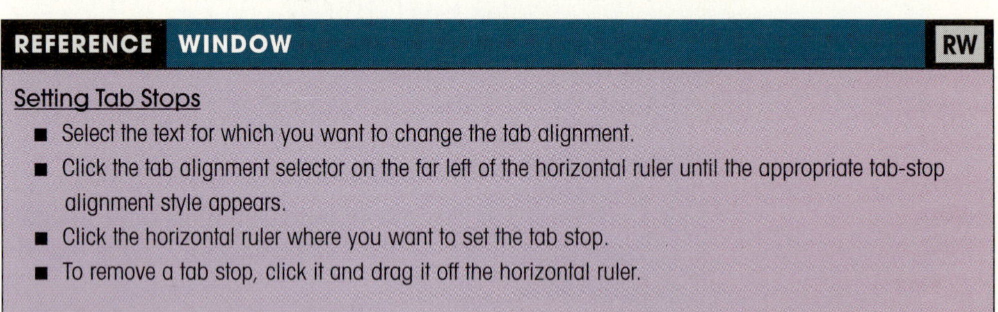

REFERENCE WINDOW RW

Setting Tab Stops

- Select the text for which you want to change the tab alignment.
- Click the tab alignment selector on the far left of the horizontal ruler until the appropriate tab-stop alignment style appears.
- Click the horizontal ruler where you want to set the tab stop.
- To remove a tab stop, click it and drag it off the horizontal ruler.

The Word default tab-stop settings are every one-half inch, as indicated by the small gray ticks at the bottom of the ruler shown in Figure 3-3. You set a new tab stop by selecting a tab-stop alignment style (from the tab alignment selector at the left end of the horizontal ruler) and then clicking on the horizontal ruler to insert the tab stop. You can remove a tab stop from the ruler by clicking it and dragging the tab stop off the ruler.

Figure 3-3 RULER WITH TAB STOPS

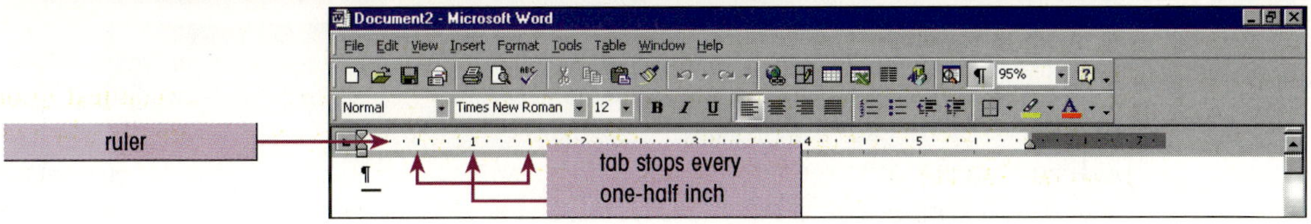

ruler

tab stops every one-half inch

You should never try to align columns of text by adding extra spaces with the spacebar. Although the text might seem precisely aligned in the document window, it might not be aligned when you print the document. Furthermore, if you edit the text, the extra spaces might disturb the alignment. However, if you edit text aligned with tabs, the alignment remains intact. If you want to align a lot of text in many columns, it is better to use a table, as described later in this tutorial.

To align columns using tabs, you can type some text, and press the Tab key. The insertion point will then move to the next tab stop to the right, where you can type more text. You can continue in this way until you have typed the first row of each column. Then you can press the Enter key, and begin typing the next row of each column.

However, sometimes you'll find that text in a column stretches beyond the next default tab stop, and as a result the columns will fail to line up evenly. In this situation, you need to set new tab stops on the horizontal ruler. For example, even though the list of task force members in the EverRipe report contains tab stops, the columns do not line up evenly. To fix this formatting problem, you need to move the tab stop farther to the right.

To add a new tab stop on the ruler:

1. Make sure the current tab-stop alignment style is left tab, as shown in Figure 3-3. If it doesn't appear at that location, click the tab alignment selector one or more times until it appears.
2. Select the list of task force members and their titles on page 1. (Do not select the heading "Prepared by Task Force Members.")
3. Click the tick mark on the ruler that occurs at 3.0 inches. Word automatically inserts a left tab stop at that location and removes the tick marks to its left. The second column of text shifts to the new tab stop.

4. Deselect the highlighted text and then move the insertion point anywhere in the list of names and titles. See Figure 3-4.

Figure 3-4 LEFT TAB STOP ON RULER

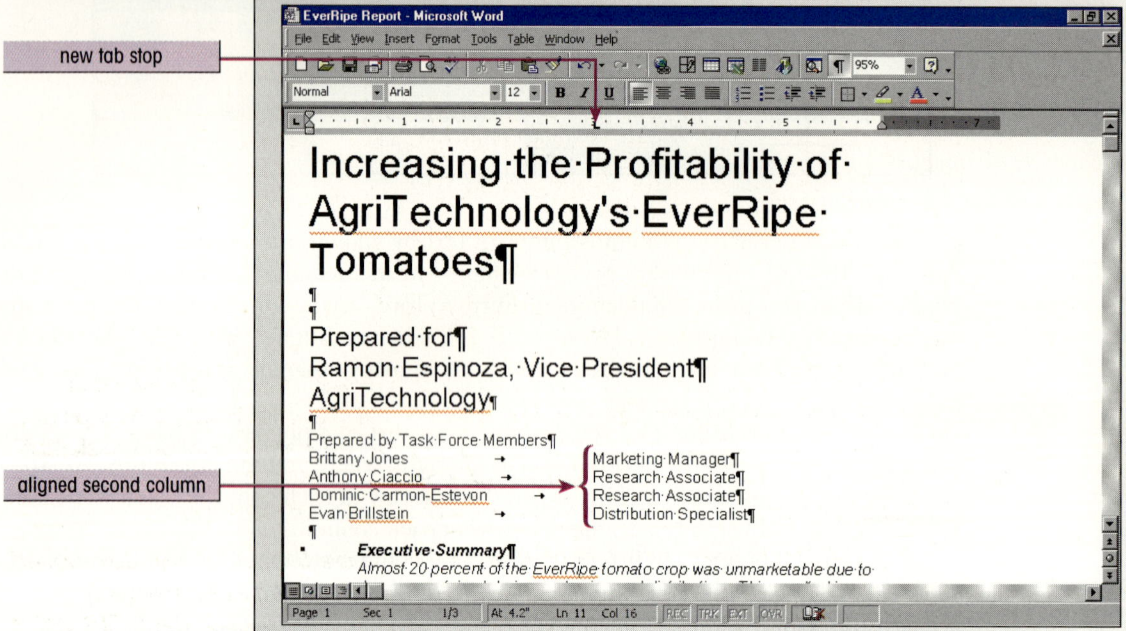

5. Click the **Save** button on the Standard toolbar to save your work.

The two columns of information are now aligned, as Brittany requested. Notice that Word changed the tab stops only for the selected paragraphs, not for all the paragraphs in the document. You set the other tabs the same way. Next, you need to change the layout of the title page.

Formatting the Document in Sections

According to the company guidelines, the title page of the report should be centered between the top and bottom margins of the page. In order to format the title page differently from the rest of the report, you need to divide the document into sections. A **section** is a unit or part of a document that can have its own page orientation, margins, headers, footers, and vertical alignment. Each section, in other words, is like a mini-document within a document.

To divide a document into sections, you insert a **section break** (a dotted line with the words "End of Section") that marks the point at which one section ends and another begins. Sections can start on a new page or continue on the same page. You can insert a section break with the Break command on the Insert menu.

To insert a section break after the title:

1. Position the insertion point immediately to the left of the "E" in the heading "Executive Summary." You want the text above this heading to be on a separate title page and the executive summary to begin the second page of the report.
2. Click **Insert** on the menu bar, and then click **Break** to open the Break dialog box. See Figure 3-5.

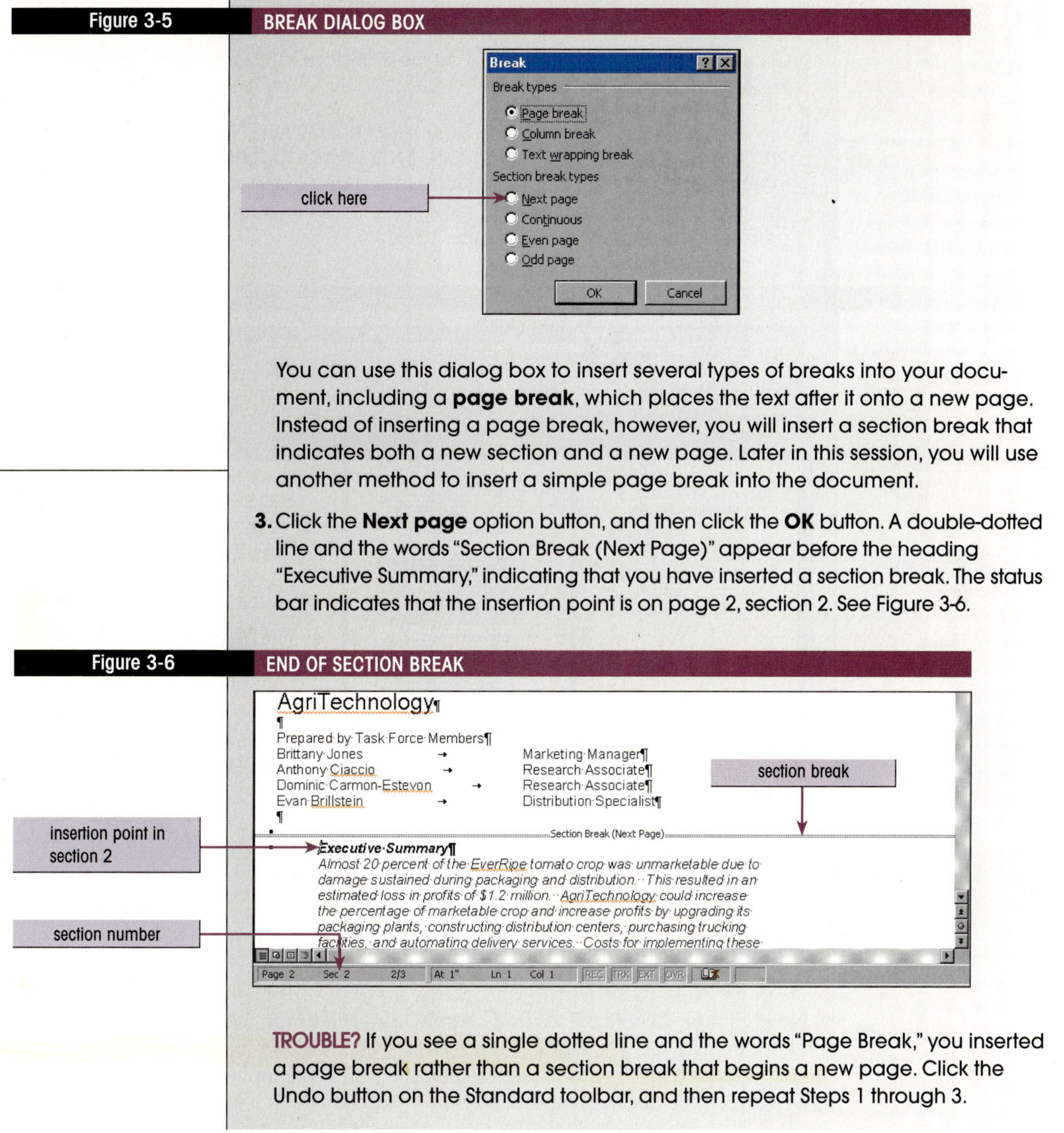

Figure 3-5 BREAK DIALOG BOX

You can use this dialog box to insert several types of breaks into your document, including a **page break**, which places the text after it onto a new page. Instead of inserting a page break, however, you will insert a section break that indicates both a new section and a new page. Later in this session, you will use another method to insert a simple page break into the document.

3. Click the **Next page** option button, and then click the **OK** button. A double-dotted line and the words "Section Break (Next Page)" appear before the heading "Executive Summary," indicating that you have inserted a section break. The status bar indicates that the insertion point is on page 2, section 2. See Figure 3-6.

Figure 3-6 END OF SECTION BREAK

TROUBLE? If you see a single dotted line and the words "Page Break," you inserted a page break rather than a section break that begins a new page. Click the Undo button on the Standard toolbar, and then repeat Steps 1 through 3.

Now that the title page is a separate section and page from the rest of the report, you can make changes affecting only that section, leaving the rest of the document unchanged.

Changing the Vertical Alignment of a Section

You're ready to center the text of page one vertically on the page. But first, you will switch to the Print Preview window, so you can more easily observe your changes to page one.

To see the document in Print Preview:

1. Click the **Print Preview** button on the Standard toolbar to open the Print Preview window.

2. Click the **Multiple Pages** button on the Print Preview toolbar, and then click and drag across the top three pages in the list box to select "1 x 3 Pages." The three pages of the report are reduced in size and appear side-by-side. See Figure 3-7. Although you cannot read the text on the pages, you can see the general layout.

Figure 3-7 PRINT PREVIEW OF REPORT

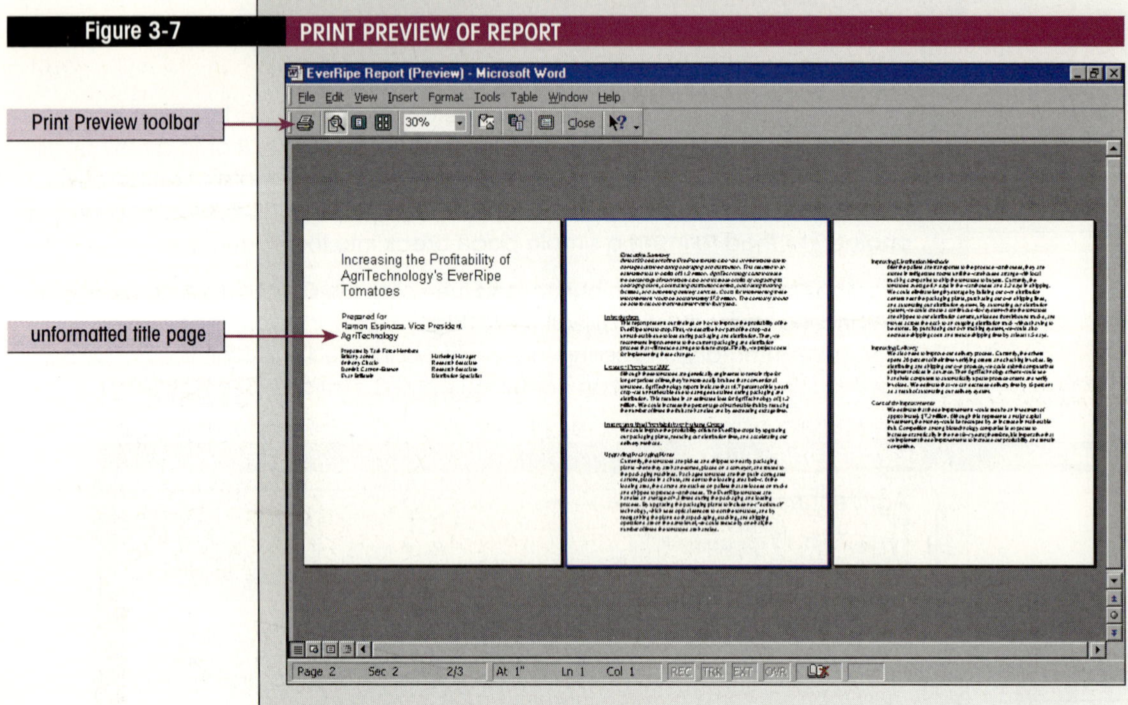

TROUBLE? If you see the vertical and horizontal rulers, you can click the View Ruler button on the Print Preview toolbar to hide the rulers.

Now, you can change the vertical alignment to center the lines of text between the top and bottom margins. The **vertical alignment** specifies how a page of text is positioned on the page between the top and bottom margins—flush at the top, flush at the bottom, or centered between the top and bottom margins.

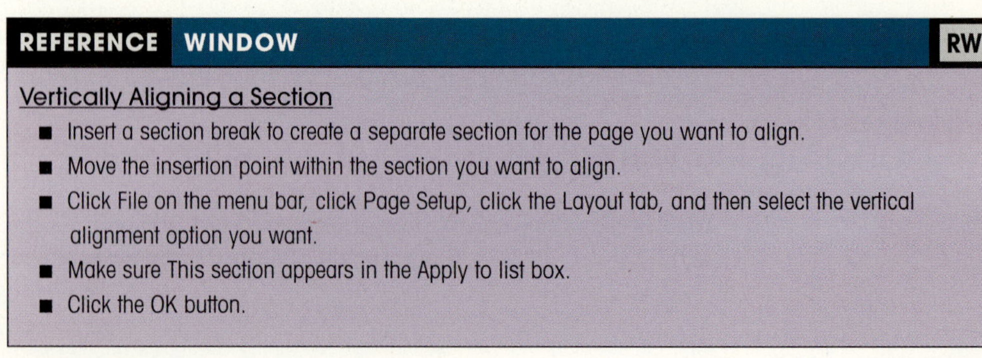

REFERENCE WINDOW RW

Vertically Aligning a Section

- Insert a section break to create a separate section for the page you want to align.
- Move the insertion point within the section you want to align.
- Click File on the menu bar, click Page Setup, click the Layout tab, and then select the vertical alignment option you want.
- Make sure This section appears in the Apply to list box.
- Click the OK button.

You'll center the title page text from within the Print Preview window.

To change the vertical alignment of the title page:

1. If the **Magnifier** button is selected, click it once to deselect it.
2. Click the leftmost page in the Print Preview window to make sure the current page is page 1 (the title page). The status bar in the Print Preview window indicates the current page.
3. Click **File** on the menu bar, and then click **Page Setup**. The Page Setup dialog box opens.
4. Click the **Layout** tab. In the Apply to list box, click **This section** (if it is not already selected) so that the layout change affects only the first section, not both sections, of your document.
5. Click the **Vertical alignment** list arrow, and then click **Center** to center the pages of the current section—in this case, just page 1—vertically between the top and bottom margins.
6. Click the **OK** button to return to the Print Preview window. The text of the title page is centered vertically, as shown in Figure 3-8.

Figure 3-8 TITLE PAGE VERTICALLY CENTERED

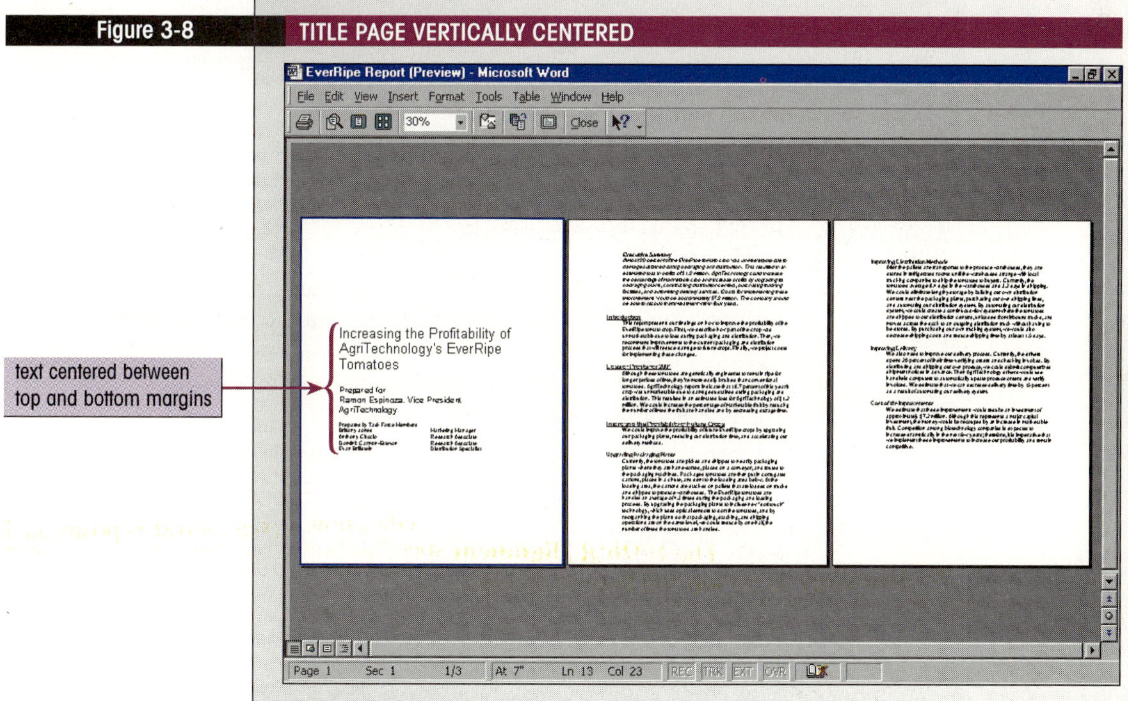

7. Click the **Close** button on the Print Preview toolbar to return to normal view.

You have successfully centered the title page text. Next you turn your attention to placing a descriptive name for the report and the page number at the top of every page.

Adding Headers

The AgriTechnology report guidelines require a short report title and the page number to be printed at the top of every page except the title page. Text that is printed at the top of every page is called a **header**. For example, the page number, tutorial number, and tutorial name printed at the top of the page you are reading is a header. Similarly, a **footer** is text that is printed at the bottom of every page. (You'll have a chance to work with footers in the Review Assignments at the end of this tutorial.)

When you insert a header or footer into a document, you switch to Header and Footer view. The Header and Footer toolbar is displayed, and the insertion point moves to the top of the document, where the header will appear. The main text is dimmed, indicating that it cannot be edited until you return to normal or print layout view.

REFERENCE WINDOW RW

Inserting a Header or Footer

- Click View on the menu bar, and then click Header and Footer.
- Type the text for the header. The header will appear in all subsequent pages.
- To insert a footer, click the Switch Between Header and Footer button on the Header and Footer toolbar.
- To create different headers for odd and even pages, click the Page Setup button on the Header and Footer toolbar, click the Layout tab, and then select the Different odd and even check box. To create a different header or footer for the first page of the document or section, select the Different first page check box. Click OK.
- Click the Close button on the Header and Footer toolbar.

You'll create a header for the main body of the report (section 2) that prints "EverRipe Recommendation Report" at the left margin and the page number at the right margin.

To insert a header for section 2:

1. Make sure the insertion point is positioned after the heading "Executive Summary" on page 2 so that the insertion point is in section 2 and not in section 1.
2. Click **View** on the menu bar, and then click **Header and Footer**. The screen changes to Header and Footer view, and the Header and Footer toolbar appears in the document window. The header area appears in the top margin of your document surrounded by a dashed line and displays the words "Header -Section 2-." See Figure 3-9. (If the Header and Footer toolbar covers the header area, drag the toolbar below the header area, similar to its position in Figure 3-9.)

Figure 3-9 CREATING A HEADER

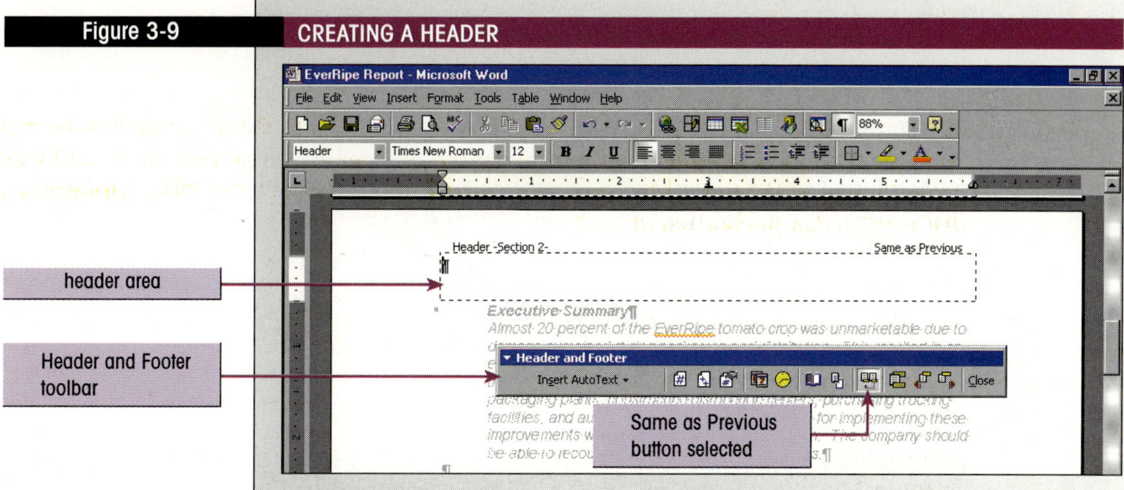

TROUBLE? If the header area displays "Header -Section 1-," click the Show Next button on the Header and Footer toolbar until the header area displays "Header -Section 2-."

TROUBLE? If the main text of the document doesn't appear on the screen, click the Show/Hide Document Text button on the Header and Footer toolbar, and continue with Step 3.

3. Click the **Same as Previous** button on the Header and Footer toolbar so that the button is *not* selected. When Same as Previous is selected, Word automatically inserts the same header text as the previous section. You deselected it to ensure that the text of the current header will apply only to the current section (section 2), not to the previous section (section 1) also.

4. Type **EverRipe Recommendation Report**. The title is automatically aligned on the left. See Figure 3-10.

Figure 3-10 TEXT OF HEADER

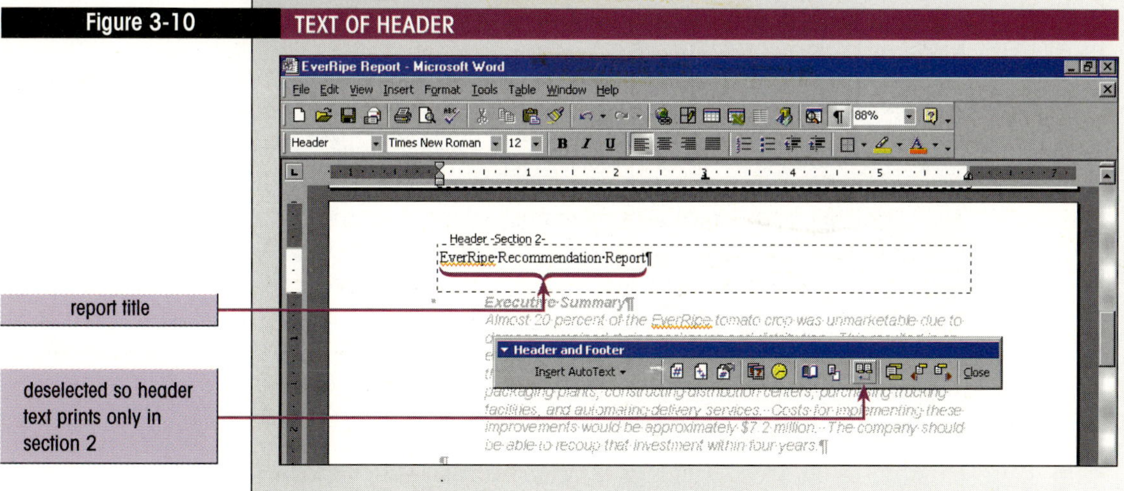

5. Press the **Tab** key twice to move the insertion point to the right margin of the header area. (Notice that by default the header contains a center and right-align tab stop.)

6. Type the word **Page** and press the **spacebar** once.

7. Click the **Insert Page Number** button on the Header and Footer toolbar. The page number "2" appears at the right-aligned tab.

   The page number in the header looks like you simply typed the number 2, but you actually inserted a special instruction telling Word to insert the correct page number on each page. Now consecutive page numbers will print on each page of the header within this section.

8. Click the **Close** button on the Header and Footer toolbar to return to normal view, and then save your changes.

Notice that you can't see the header in normal view. To see exactly how the header will appear on the printed page, you will switch to print layout view, which lets you read the headers and footers as well as see the margins.

To view the header and margins in print layout view:

1. Click the **Print Layout View** button. You can now see the header and the page margins. Next, you'll use the browse buttons to examine each page. Begin by using the Select Browse Object button to select the feature, or object, you want to browse for. In this case, you will browse by page.

2. Click the **Select Browse Object** button below the vertical scroll bar and click the **Browse by Page** button. The insertion point moves to the top of the third page. Now that you've selected the browse object (page), you can use the Next and Previous buttons to move quickly from one page to the next.

3. Click the **Previous Page** button (just above the Select Browse Object button) twice to move to page 1.

4. Click the **Next Page** button (just below the Select Browse Object button) to move to the top of page 2.

5. Click again to move to the top of page 3. Notice that the header appears only on pages 2 and 3. The header does not appear on the title page because the title page is in a different section of the document. Also notice that the correct page numbers appear on pages 2 and 3. See Figure 3-11.

Figure 3-11 HEADER IN PRINT LAYOUT VIEW

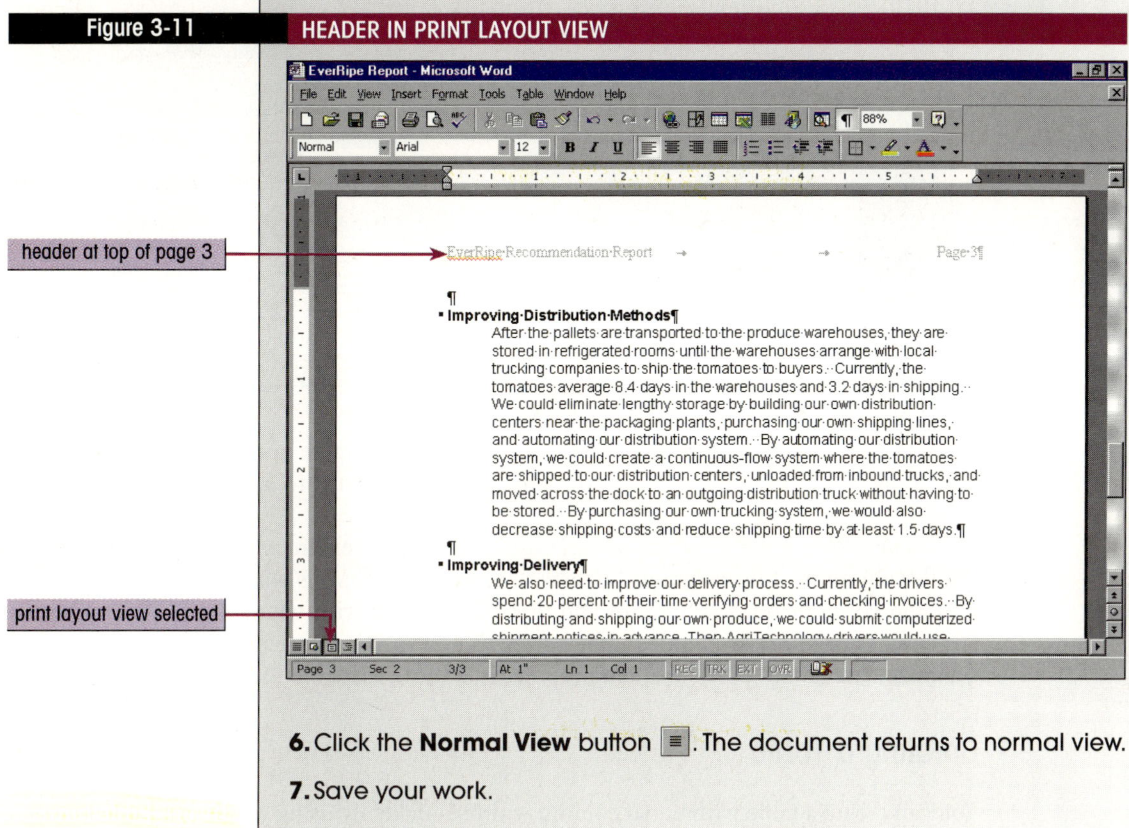

6. Click the **Normal View** button. The document returns to normal view.

7. Save your work.

The recommendation report now has the required header. You have formatted Brittany's recommendation report so that the results are professional-looking, clearly presented, and easy to read. Next you will add a table that summarizes the costs and benefits of the task force's recommendations.

Inserting Tables

You can quickly organize data and arrange text in an easy-to-read table format. A **table** is information arranged in horizontal rows and vertical columns. As shown in Figure 3-12, table rows are commonly referred to by number (row 1 at the top, row 2 below row 1, and so forth), while columns are commonly referred to by letter (column A on the far left, column B to the right of column A, and so forth). However, you do not see row and column numbers on the screen. The area where a row and column intersect is called a **cell**. Each cell is identified by a column and row label. For example, the cell in the upper-left corner of a table is cell A1 (column A, row 1), the cell to the right of that is cell B1, the cell below cell A1 is A2, and so forth. The table's structure is shown by **gridlines**, which are light gray lines that define the rows and columns. By default, gridlines do not appear on the printed page. You can emphasize specific parts of a table on the printed page by adding a **border** (a line the prints along the side of a table cell). When you move the pointer over a table that is displayed in print layout view, the Table move handle and the Table resize handle appear. To quickly select the entire table, click the **Table move handle**. Then you can drag the Table move handle to move the table to a new location. To change the size of the entire table, drag the **Table resize handle**.

Figure 3-12 ELEMENTS OF A WORD TABLE

With the Word Table feature you can create a blank table and then insert information into it (as you'll do next), or you can convert existing text into a table (as you'll do in the Review Assignments).

You may be wondering why you can't use tabs to align text in columns. Tabs work well for smaller amounts of information, such as two or three columns with three or four rows, but tabs and columns become tedious and difficult to work with when you need to organize a larger amount of more complex information. The Word Table feature allows you to quickly organize data and to place text and graphics in a more readable format.

Creating a Table

You can create a table with equal column widths quickly by using the Insert Table button on the Standard toolbar. (You will use this technique to create the table Brittany requested.) You also can create a table by dragging the Draw Table pointer to draw the table structure you want. (You'll practice this method in the Case Problems.) However you create a table, you can modify it by using commands on the Table menu or the buttons on the Tables and Borders toolbar.

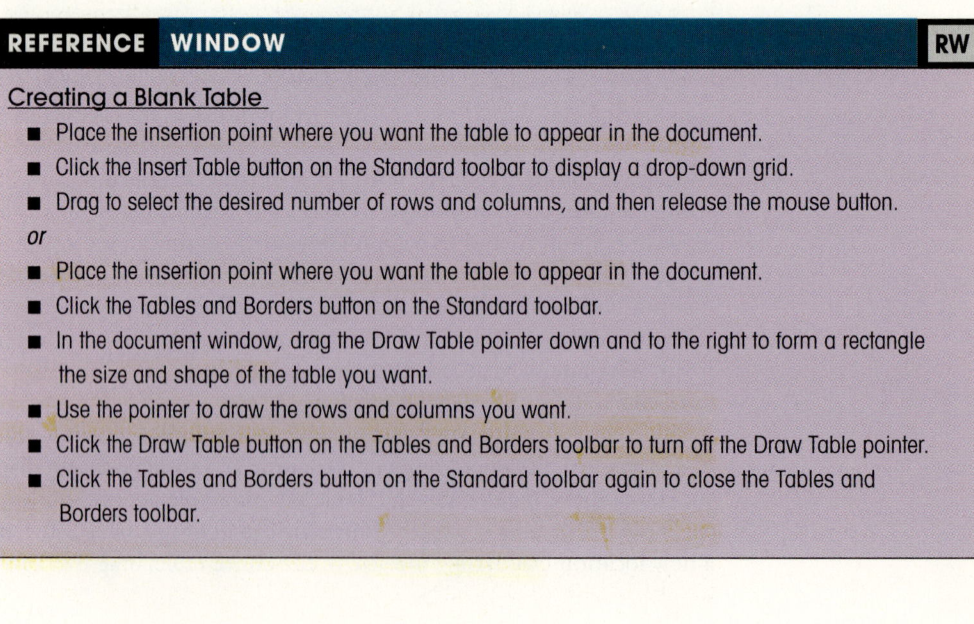

REFERENCE WINDOW RW

Creating a Blank Table

- Place the insertion point where you want the table to appear in the document.
- Click the Insert Table button on the Standard toolbar to display a drop-down grid.
- Drag to select the desired number of rows and columns, and then release the mouse button.

or

- Place the insertion point where you want the table to appear in the document.
- Click the Tables and Borders button on the Standard toolbar.
- In the document window, drag the Draw Table pointer down and to the right to form a rectangle the size and shape of the table you want.
- Use the pointer to draw the rows and columns you want.
- Click the Draw Table button on the Tables and Borders toolbar to turn off the Draw Table pointer.
- Click the Tables and Borders button on the Standard toolbar again to close the Tables and Borders toolbar.

Brittany wants you to create a table that summarizes information in the EverRipe report. Figure 3-13 shows a sketch of what Brittany wants the table to look like. The table will allow AgriTechnology's executives to see at a glance the cost and benefit of each improvement.

Figure 3-13 SKETCH OF EVERRIPE TABLE

Projected Improvement	Benefit	Percent of Total Cost	Initial Cost
Upgrade packaging plants	Reduce by one-half the number of times tomatoes are handled	21%	$1,000,000
Administrative improvements	Facilitate transition to new system	.2%	$200,000
Improve distribution methods	Decrease shipping costs and reduce shipping time by 1.5 days	51%	$3,700,000
Automate delivery paperwork	Decrease delivery time by 15%	35%	$2,500,000

Before you begin creating the table, you insert a page break so that the table will appear on a separate page.

To insert a page break:

1. Press **Ctrl+End** to position the insertion point at the end of the last paragraph in the report.
2. Press **Ctrl+Enter**. A dotted line with the words "Page Break" appears in the document window. (Note that you also could add a page break using the Break dialog box you used earlier to insert a section break.)

   TROUBLE? If you do not see the words "Page Break," check to make sure the document is displayed in normal view.

The insertion point is now at the beginning of a new page, where you want to insert the table. You'll use the Insert Table button to create the table.

To create a blank table using the Insert Table button:

1. Click the **Insert Table** button on the Standard toolbar. A drop-down grid resembling a miniature table appears below the Insert Table button. The grid initially has four rows and five columns. You can drag the pointer to extend the grid to as many rows and columns as you need. In this case, you need five rows and four columns.

2. Position the pointer in the upper-left cell of the grid, and then click and drag the pointer down and across the grid until you highlight five rows and four columns. As you drag the pointer across the grid, Word indicates the size of the table (rows by columns) at the bottom of the grid. See Figure 3-14.

Figure 3-14 SELECTING ROWS AND COLUMNS

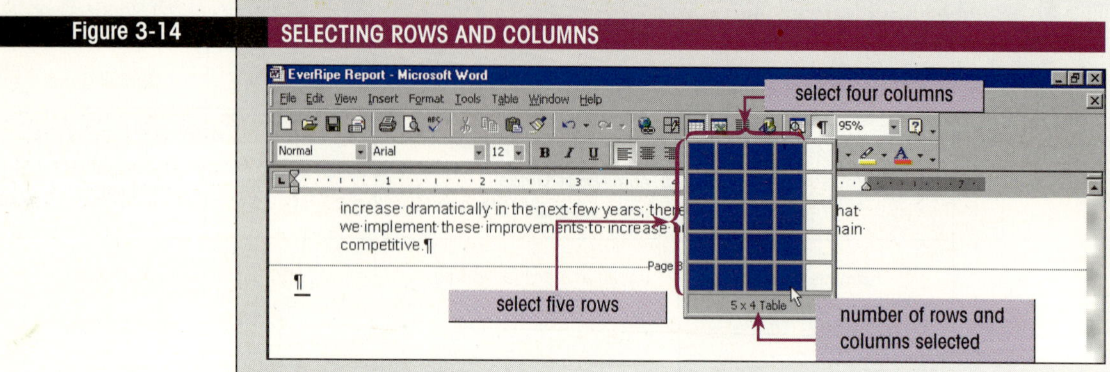

3. Release the mouse button. An empty table, five rows by four columns, appears in your document with the insertion point blinking in the upper-left corner (cell A1). See Figure 3-15.

Figure 3-15 EMPTY TABLE INSERTED INTO DOCUMENT

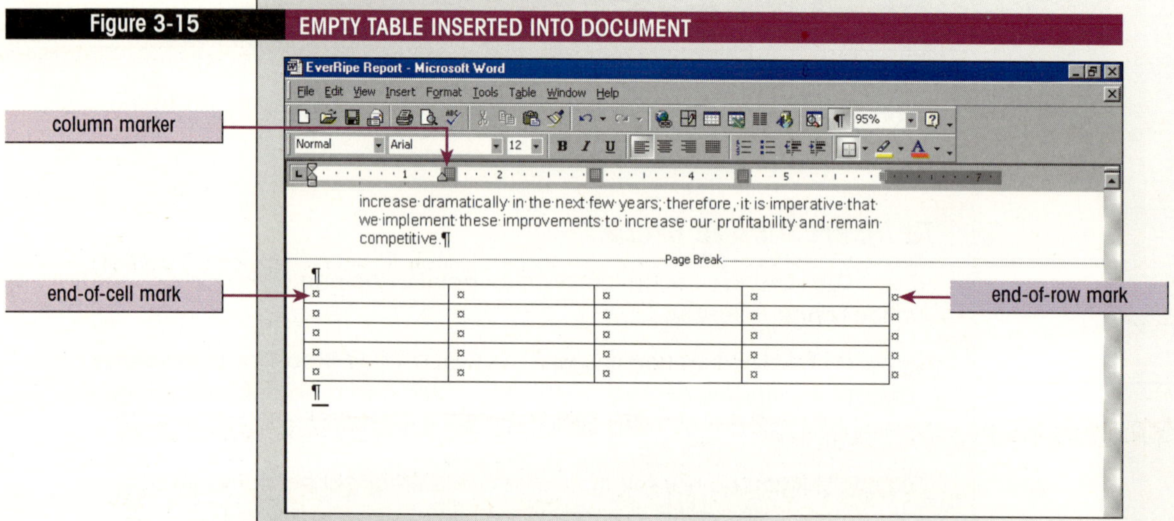

The table is outlined with borders, and the four columns are of equal width. The column widths are indicated by column markers on the ruler. Each cell contains an end-of-cell mark, and each row contains an end-of-row mark.

TROUBLE? If you don't see the end-of-cell and end-of-row marks, you need to show nonprinting characters. Click the Show/Hide ¶ button on the Standard toolbar to show nonprinting characters.

TROUBLE? If you see the Tables and Borders toolbar displayed along with the new blank table, simply continue with this tutorial. You will learn how to use the Tables and Borders toolbar in the next session.

Entering Text in a Table

You can enter text in a table by moving the insertion point to a cell and typing. If the text takes up more than one line in the cell, Word automatically wraps the text to the next line and increases the height of that cell and all the cells in that row. To move the insertion point to another cell in the table, you can either click in that cell or use the Tab key. Figure 3-16 summarizes the keystrokes for moving within a table.

Figure 3-16 KEYSTROKES FOR MOVING AROUND A TABLE

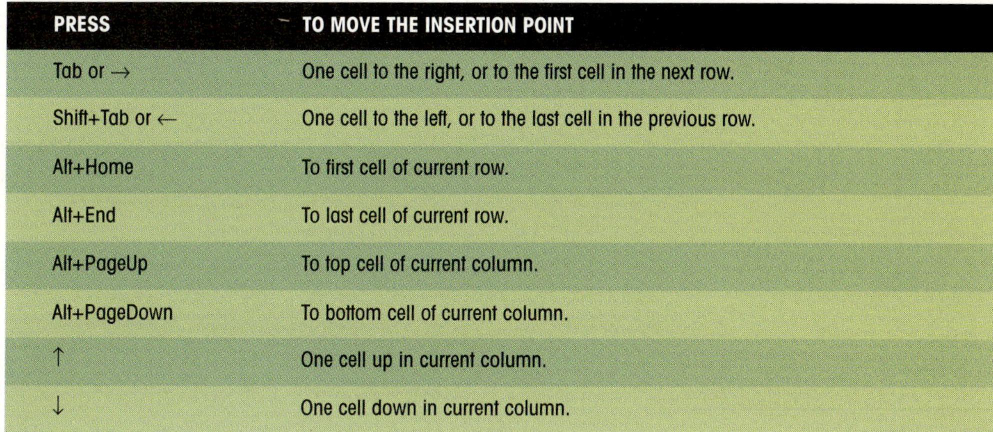

PRESS	TO MOVE THE INSERTION POINT
Tab or →	One cell to the right, or to the first cell in the next row.
Shift+Tab or ←	One cell to the left, or to the last cell in the previous row.
Alt+Home	To first cell of current row.
Alt+End	To last cell of current row.
Alt+PageUp	To top cell of current column.
Alt+PageDown	To bottom cell of current column.
↑	One cell up in current column.
↓	One cell down in current column.

Now, you are ready to insert information into the table.

To insert data into the table:

1. Verify that the insertion point is located in cell **A1** (in the upper-left corner).
2. Type **Projected Improvement**.
3. Press the **Tab** key to move to cell B1. See Figure 3-17.

Figure 3-17 ADDING TEXT TO THE TABLE

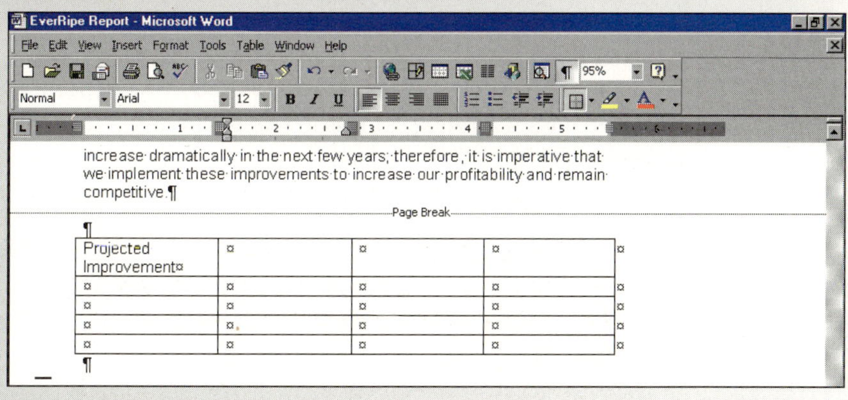

TROUBLE? If Word created a new paragraph in cell A1 rather than moving the insertion point to cell B1, you accidentally pressed the Enter key instead of the Tab key. Press the Backspace key to remove the paragraph mark, and then press the Tab key to move to cell B1.

4. Type **Benefit**, and then press the **Tab** key to move to cell C1.
5. Type **Percent of Total Cost**, and then press the **Tab** key to move to cell D1.
6. Type **Initial Cost**, and then press the **Tab** key to move the insertion point from cell D1 to cell A2. Notice that when you press the Tab key in the last column of the table, the insertion point moves to the first column in the next row.

   You have entered the **heading row**, the row that identifies the information in each column.

7. Type the remaining information for the table, as shown in Figure 3-18, pressing the **Tab** key to move from cell to cell. Don't worry if the text in your table doesn't wrap the same way as shown here. You'll change the column widths in the next session.

Figure 3-18 TABLE WITH COMPLETED INFORMATION

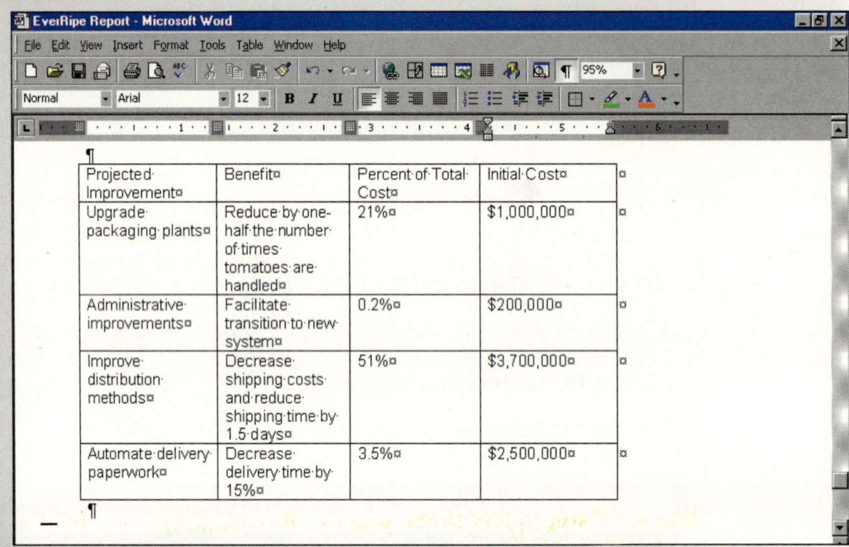

Projected Improvement	Benefit	Percent of Total Cost	Initial Cost
Upgrade packaging plants	Reduce by one-half the number of times tomatoes are handled	21%	$1,000,000
Administrative improvements	Facilitate transition to new system	0.2%	$200,000
Improve distribution methods	Decrease shipping costs and reduce shipping time by 1.5 days	51%	$3,700,000
Automate delivery paperwork	Decrease delivery time by 15%	3.5%	$2,500,000

TROUBLE? If a new row (row 6) appeared in your table, you pressed the Tab key when the insertion point was in cell D5, the last cell in the table. Click the Undo button on the Standard toolbar to remove row 6 from the table.

You've now completed a substantial amount of work on the report document, so you decide to save the document with a new name. That way, if for some reason the current document becomes corrupted, you still will have a previous version.

8. Save the document as **EverRipe Report Copy 2** in the **Tutorial** folder of the **Tutorial.03** folder.

Keep in mind that many document-editing features, such as the Backspace key, the copy-and-paste feature, the Undo button, and the AutoCorrect feature, work the same way in a table. Just like in a paragraph, you must select text within a table in order to edit it. You will edit and format this table in the next session.

Session 3.1 QUICK CHECK

1. Define the following in your own words:
   a. tab stop
   b. cell
   c. table
   d. decimal-aligned tab stop
   e. section (of a document)
2. Explain how to center the title page vertically between the top and bottom margins.
3. What is the difference between a header and a footer?
4. Describe how to insert a blank table consisting of four columns and six rows.
5. How do you move the insertion point from one row to the next in a table?
6. How do you insert the page number in a header?
7. Explain how to insert a new tab stop.
8. Describe a situation in which you would want to divide a document into sections.
9. Describe a situation in which it would be better to use a table rather than tab stops.
10. Explain how to select an entire table.

SESSION 3.2

In this session you will learn how to make changes to the table you just created. First you will rearrange the existing rows, and then you will learn how to add and delete rows. Next you will use the AutoSum feature to total a column of numbers, and then format the table to improve its appearance. You also will learn how to merge and split cells as well as how to rotate text within a cell.

Sorting Rows in a Table

The term **sort** refers to the process of rearranging information in alphabetical, numerical, or chronological order. When you sort a table, you arrange the rows based on the contents of one of the columns. For example, you could sort the table you just created based on the contents of the Projected Improvement column—either in ascending alphabetical order (from A to Z) or in descending alphabetical order (from Z to A). Alternatively, you could sort the table based on the contents of the Initial Cost column—either in descending numerical order (highest to lowest) or in ascending numerical order (lowest to highest). When you sort table data, Word usually does not sort the heading row along with the other information, but instead leaves the heading row at the top of the table.

The easiest way to sort a table is to use the Sort buttons on the **Tables and Borders toolbar**. You'll display the Tables and Borders toolbar in the following steps. As you will see, it contains a number of useful buttons that simplify the process of working with tables.

1. If you took a break after the last session, make sure Word is running and that the EverRipe Report Copy 2 document is open. Check that the nonprinting characters are displayed and that the document is displayed in normal view.
2. Right-click the **Standard toolbar**, and then click **Tables and Borders** in the shortcut menu. The Tables and Borders toolbar appears.
3. If necessary, drag the Tables and Borders toolbar down and to the right, so that it doesn't block your view of the EverRipe table. See Figure 3-19.

Figure 3-19 TABLE AND BORDERS TOOLBAR

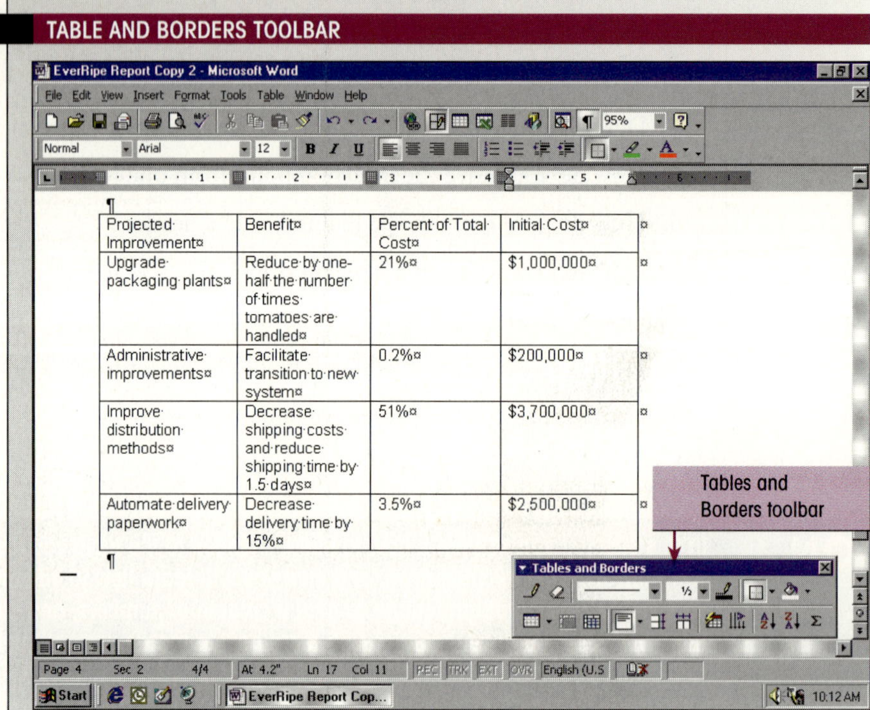

Brittany would like you to sort the table in ascending numerical order, based on the contents of the Initial Cost column. You start by positioning the insertion point in that column.

To sort the information in the table:

1. Click cell **D2** (which contains the value $1,000,000). The insertion point is now located in the Initial Cost column.
2. Click the **Sort Ascending** button on the Tables and Borders toolbar. Rows 2 through 5 now are arranged numerically from the lowest to the highest according to the numbers in the Initial Cost column. See Figure 3-20.

Figure 3-20 TABLE AFTER BEING SORTED

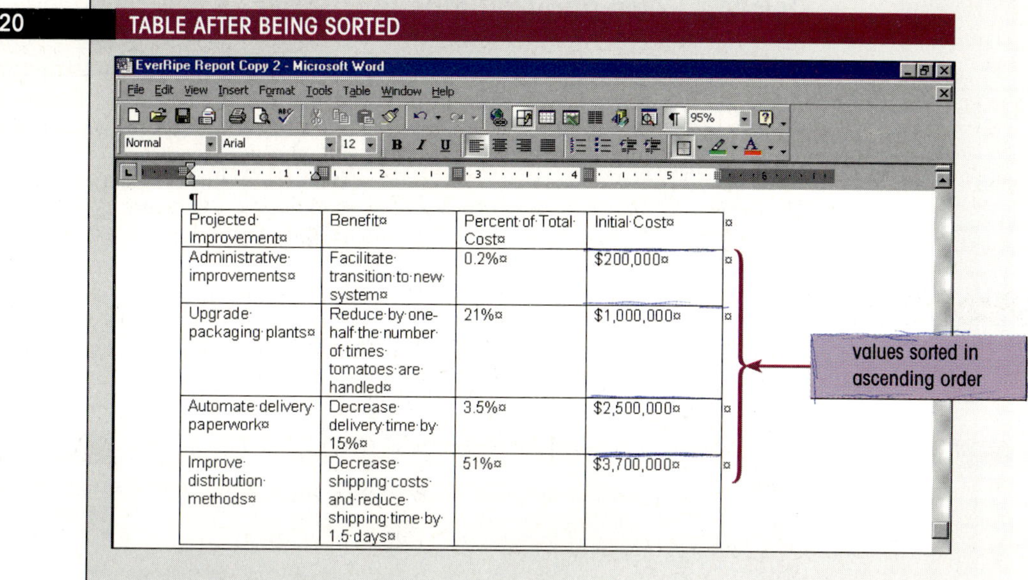

Projected Improvement	Benefit	Percent of Total Cost	Initial Cost
Administrative improvements	Facilitate transition to new system	0.2%	$200,000
Upgrade packaging plants	Reduce by one-half the number of times tomatoes are handled	21%	$1,000,000
Automate delivery paperwork	Decrease delivery time by 15%	3.5%	$2,500,000
Improve distribution methods	Decrease shipping costs and reduce shipping time by 1.5 days	51%	$3,700,000

TROUBLE? If the sort was unsuccessful, immediately click the Undo button on the Standard toolbar, and then repeat Steps 1 and 2 to retry the sort.

Brittany stops by and asks you to delete the "Administrative improvements" row because it represents such a small percentage of the total cost. She also would like you to insert a new row to display the total of the Initial Cost column. You'll need to modify the structure of the table in order to complete these tasks.

Modifying an Existing Table Structure

Often, after you create a table, you'll need to delete extra rows and columns or insert additional ones. Figure 3-21 summarizes ways to insert or delete rows and columns in a table.

Figure 3-21 WAYS TO INSERT OR DELETE TABLE ROWS AND COLUMNS

TO	DO THIS
Insert a row within a table	Select the row below where you want the row added, click Table on the menu bar, point to Insert, and then click Rows Above.
	Select the row below where you want the row added, and then click the Insert Rows button on the Standard toolbar.
Insert a row at the end of a table	Position the insertion point in the rightmost cell of the bottom row, and then press the Tab key.
Insert a column within a table	Select the column to the right of where you want the column added, click Table on the menu bar, point to Insert, and then click Columns to the Right.
	Select the column to the right of where you want the column added, and then click the Insert Columns button on the Standard toolbar.
Insert a column at the end of a table	Select the end-of-row markers to the right of the table, click Table on the menu bar, point to Insert, and then click Columns to the Left.
	Select the end-of-row markers to the right of the table, and then click the Insert Columns button on the Standard toolbar.
Delete a row	Select the row or rows to be deleted, click Table on the menu bar, point to Delete, and then click Rows.
Delete a column	Select the column or columns to be deleted, click Table on the menu bar, point to Delete, and then click Columns.

Deleting Rows and Columns in a Table

With Word, you can delete either the contents of the cells or the structure of the cells. To delete the contents of the cells in a selected row, you press the Delete key. However, to delete both the contents and structure of a selected row or column from the table entirely, you must use one of the methods described in Figure 3-21.

To delete a row using the Table menu:

1. Click the selection bar next to row 2 to select the Administrative improvements row.
2. Click **Table** on the menu bar, point to **Delete**, and then click **Rows**. The selected row is deleted from the table structure. See Figure 3-22.

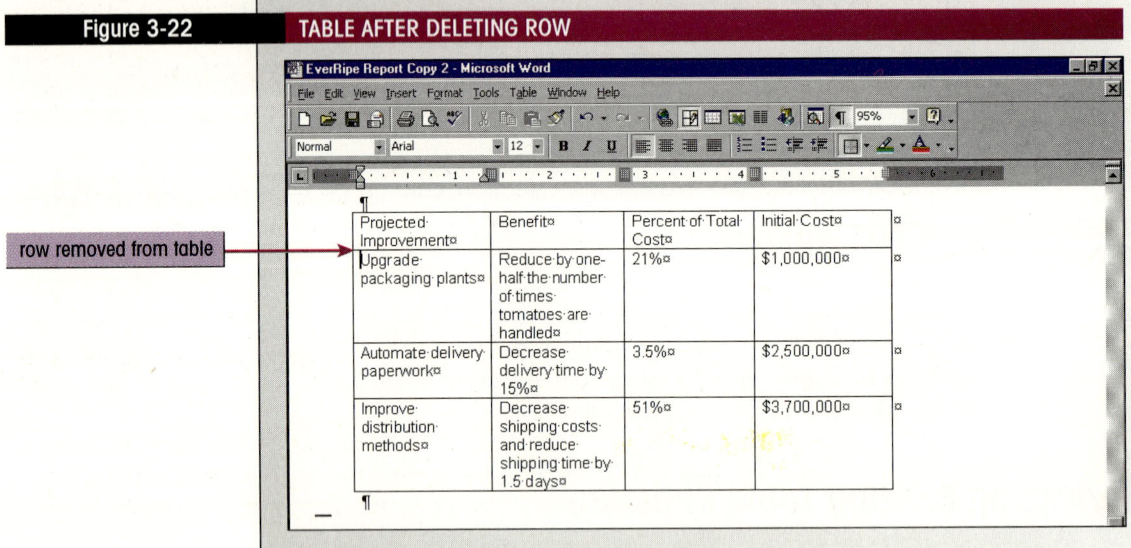

Projected Improvement	Benefit	Percent of Total Cost	Initial Cost
Upgrade packaging plants	Reduce by one-half the number of times tomatoes are handled	21%	$1,000,000
Automate delivery paperwork	Decrease delivery time by 15%	3.5%	$2,500,000
Improve distribution methods	Decrease shipping costs and reduce shipping time by 1.5 days	51%	$3,700,000

Figure 3-22 TABLE AFTER DELETING ROW

Inserting Additional Rows in a Table

You can insert additional rows within the table or at the end of a table. You now need to insert a row at the bottom of the table, so you can include the total of the Initial Cost column.

To insert a row at the bottom of the table:

1. Click cell **D4**, the last cell of the last row in the table, which contains the number "$3,700,000."
2. Press the **Tab** key. A blank row is added to the bottom of the table.

   TROUBLE? If a blank row is not added to the bottom of the table, click the Undo button on the Standard toolbar. Check to make sure the insertion point is in the last cell of the last row, and then press the Tab key.

3. Type **Total** in cell A5.

You are nearly ready to insert the total of the Initial Cost column in cell D5. First, you need to make it clear that the "Total" heading only applies to the Initial Cost column. You can do that by combining cell A5 with cells at the bottom of the Benefit and Percent of Total Cost columns.

Merging Cells

In addition to adding and deleting rows and columns, you also can change the structure of a table by changing the structure of individual cells. Specifically, you can combine, or **merge**, cells. You also can **split** one cell into multiple rows or columns.

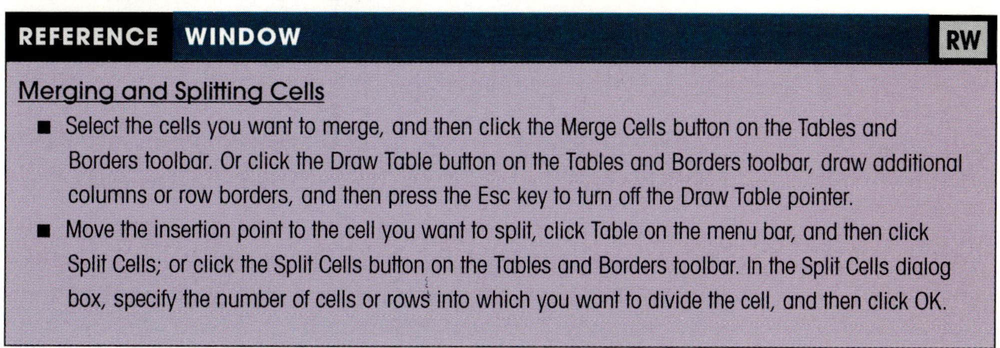

REFERENCE WINDOW RW

Merging and Splitting Cells

- Select the cells you want to merge, and then click the Merge Cells button on the Tables and Borders toolbar. Or click the Draw Table button on the Tables and Borders toolbar, draw additional columns or row borders, and then press the Esc key to turn off the Draw Table pointer.
- Move the insertion point to the cell you want to split, click Table on the menu bar, and then click Split Cells; or click the Split Cells button on the Tables and Borders toolbar. In the Split Cells dialog box, specify the number of cells or rows into which you want to divide the cell, and then click OK.

You decide to merge cells A5, B5, and C5 to avoid the impression that you intend to insert totals at the bottom of the Benefit column or the Percent of Total Cost column.

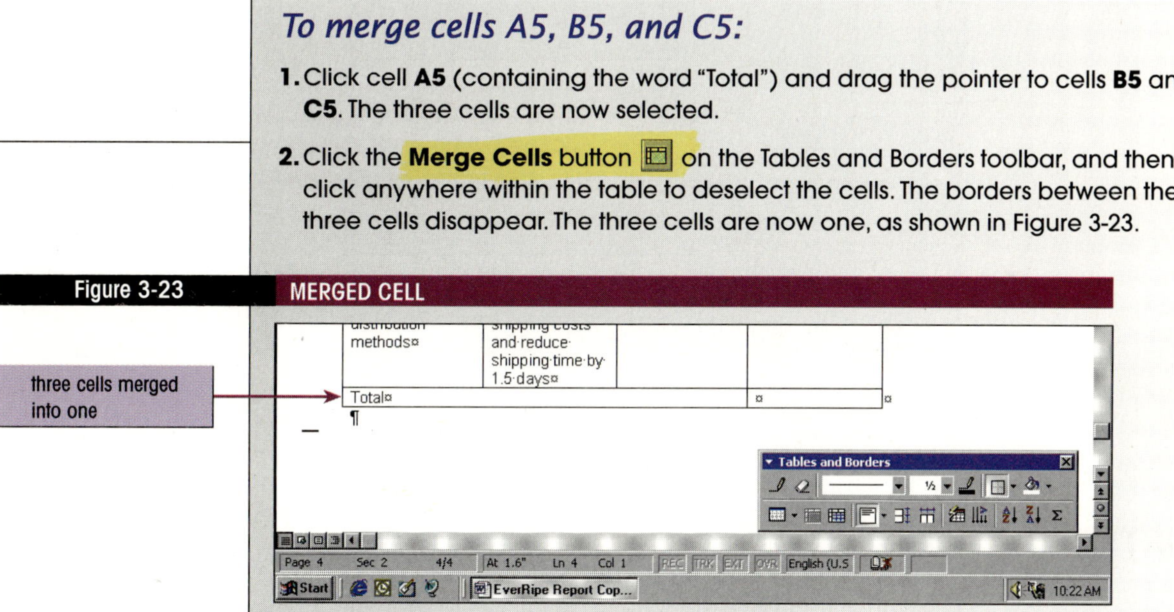

To merge cells A5, B5, and C5:

1. Click cell **A5** (containing the word "Total") and drag the pointer to cells **B5** and **C5**. The three cells are now selected.
2. Click the **Merge Cells** button on the Tables and Borders toolbar, and then click anywhere within the table to deselect the cells. The borders between the three cells disappear. The three cells are now one, as shown in Figure 3-23.

Figure 3-23 MERGED CELL

Eventually you need to format the text "Total" so that it is aligned next to the Initial Cost column. You will do that later in this tutorial, when you align the percentage values in column C.

Now you are ready to calculate the total of the Initial Cost column.

Using AutoSum to Total a Table Column

Rather than calculating column totals by hand and entering them, you can have Word compute the totals of numeric columns in a table. The **AutoSum** feature automatically totals a column of numbers. Note that if you edit any number in the column, you need to click the cell containing the formula, and then press the F9 key to recalculate the total.

To total the values in the Initial Cost column:

1. Click the bottom cell in the Initial Cost column.
2. Click the **AutoSum** button Σ on the Tables and Borders toolbar. The total of the column appears in the cell formatted with a dollar sign and two decimal places. Although you see a number ($7,200,000.00), the cell contains a formula that calculates the total of all the numbers in the column. You can change the way the total looks by formatting the formula. In this case, you want to remove the decimal point and the two zeros.
3. Click the total to select it. The total becomes highlighted in gray.
4. Click **Table** on the menu bar, and then click **Formula**. The Formula dialog box opens.
5. Click the **Number format** list arrow, and select the only format with a dollar sign. You'll remove the part of the formula that specifies how to format negative numbers as well as the decimal codes.
6. In the Number format text box, click to the right of the format and press the **Backspace** key until only $#, ##0 remains, as shown in Figure 3-24.

Figure 3-24 FORMULA DIALOG BOX AFTER ADJUSTING NUMBER FORMAT

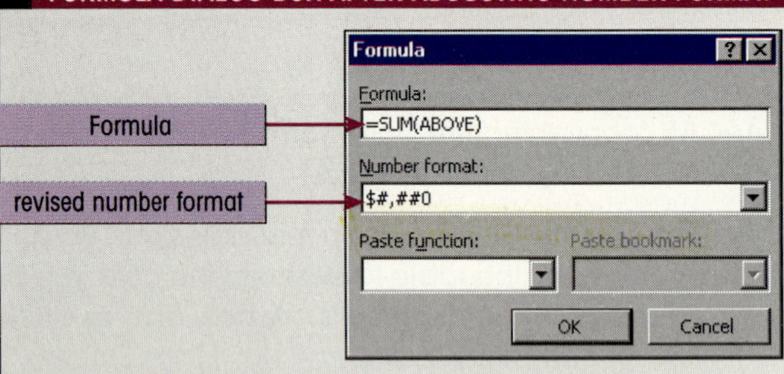

7. Click **OK**. The Initial Cost total is now formatted like the numbers above it.

You have finished creating the table, entering data, and modifying the table's structure. Now, you can concentrate on improving the table's appearance.

Formatting Tables

Word provides a variety of ways to enhance the appearance of the tables you create: You can alter the width of the columns and the height of the rows, or change the alignment of text within the cells or the alignment of the table between the left and right margins. You also can change the appearance of the table borders, add a shaded background, and rotate the text within cells.

Changing Column Width and Row Height

Sometimes, you'll want to adjust the column widths in a table to make the text easier to read. If you want to specify an exact width for a column, you should use the Table Properties command on the Table menu. However, it's usually easiest to drag the column's right border to a new position. Note that when adjusting columns and rows, you should switch to print layout view so that the vertical ruler is displayed.

The Percent of Total Cost column (column C) is too wide for the information it contains and should be narrowed. The values in the Initial Cost column look crowded and would be easier to read if the column were wider. You'll change these widths by dragging the column borders, using the ruler as a guide. Keep in mind that to change the width of a column, you need to drag the column's rightmost border.

To change the width of columns by dragging the borders:

1. Switch to print layout view.
2. Position the insertion point anywhere in the EverRipe table (without selecting any text or cells) and then move the pointer over the table without clicking. Notice that in print layout view, the Table move handle and the Table resize handle appear whenever you move the pointer over the table. You will learn more about these two handles in the Review Assignments at the end of this tutorial.
3. Move the pointer over the border between columns C and D (in other words, over the right border of column C, the Percent of Total Cost column). The pointer changes to ↔.
4. Press and hold down the **Alt** key and the mouse button. The column widths are displayed in the ruler, as shown in Figure 3-25.

Figure 3-25 COLUMN WIDTHS DISPLAYED IN RULER

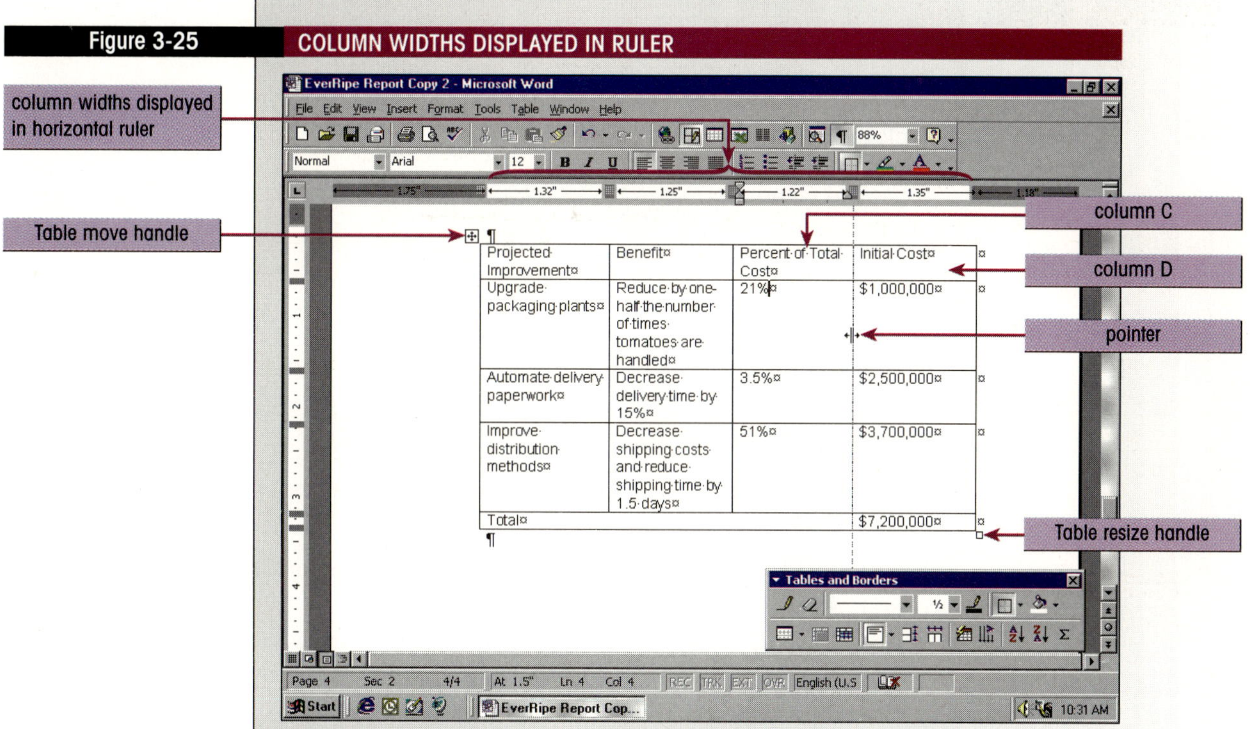

5. While holding down the **Alt** key, drag the pointer to the left until column C (the Percent of Total Cost column) is about **0.75** inches wide, and then release the mouse button. Notice that column C decreases in width and the width of column D (the Initial Cost column) increases. However, the overall width of the table does not change. See Figure 3-26.

Figure 3-26 TABLE AFTER DECREASING THE WIDTH OF COLUMN C

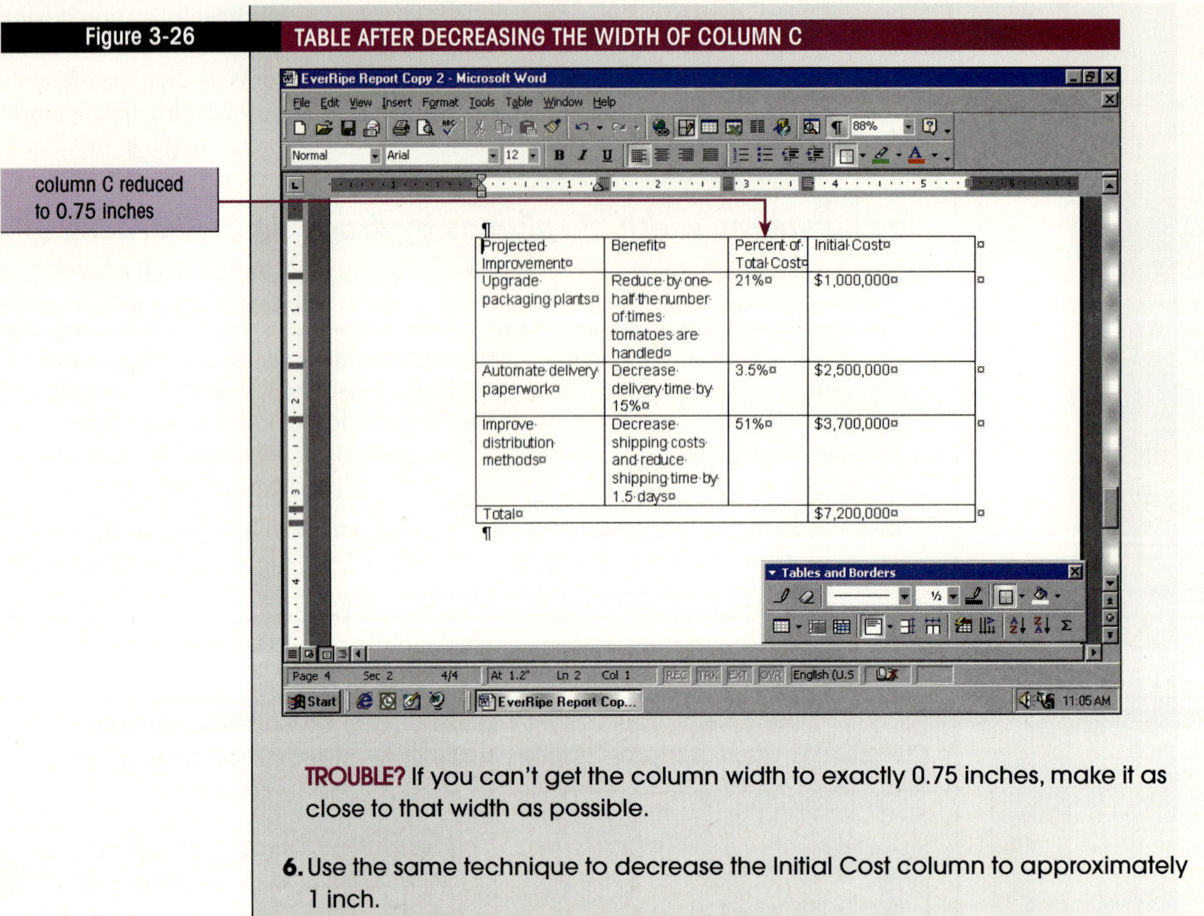

TROUBLE? If you can't get the column width to exactly 0.75 inches, make it as close to that width as possible.

6. Use the same technique to decrease the Initial Cost column to approximately 1 inch.

You also can change the height of rows by dragging a border. You'll make row 1 (the header row) taller so it is more prominent.

To change the height of row 1:

1. Position the pointer over the bottom border of the header row. The pointer changes to ╪.
2. Press and hold down the **Alt** key and the mouse button. The row heights are displayed in the vertical ruler.
3. While holding down the **Alt** key, drag the pointer down until row 1 is about 1 inch high, and then release the mouse button. Notice that the height of the other rows in the table is not affected by this change.

The EverRipe table now looks much better with its new column width and row height. Next you'll align the text to make the table even more attractive.

Aligning Text Within Cells

Aligning the text within the cells of a table makes the information easier to read. For example, aligning a column of numbers or percentages along the right margin helps the reader to quickly compare the values. At the same time, centering a row of headings makes a table more visually appealing. You can align text within the active cell the same way you do other text—with the alignment buttons on the Formatting toolbar. However, the alignment buttons on the Tables and Borders toolbar provide more options.

The percentage and dollar amounts in columns C and D would be much easier to read if you were to align the numbers on the right side of the cells. In the process of right-aligning the numbers, you can also right-align the word "Total" in the merged cell at the bottom of columns A, B, and C. The table also would look better with the headings centered. You'll begin by selecting and formatting all of columns C and D.

To right-align the numerical data and center the headings:

1. Move the pointer to the top of column C until the pointer changes to ⬇, and then click the top of the column to select the entire column (including the merged cell at the bottom of the column.)
2. Drag the pointer to the right to select column D as well. Now that you've selected the columns, you can align the text within them.
3. Click the **Align Right** button on the Formatting toolbar. The numbers line up along the right edges of the cells. In addition, the word "Total" in the merged cell aligns next to the bottom cell in the Initial Cost column.

   TROUBLE? If more than just the numbers, column headings, and Total cell are right-aligned within the table, you may have selected the wrong block of cells. Click the Undo button on the Standard toolbar, and then repeat Steps 1 through 3.

   Notice that in the process of formatting Columns C and D, you right-aligned two of the headings ("Percent of Total Cost" and "Initial Cost"). You will reformat those headings in the next step, when you center the text in row 1 both horizontally and vertically in each cell.
4. Click the selection bar next to row 1. All of row 1 is selected.
5. Click the **Align** list arrow on the Tables and Borders toolbar to display a palette of nine alignment options.
6. Click the **Align Center** button in the middle of the palette. The text becomes centered both horizontally and vertically in the row.
7. Click anywhere in the table to deselect the row. See Figure 3-27.

Figure 3-27 TABLE WITH NEWLY ALIGNED TEXT

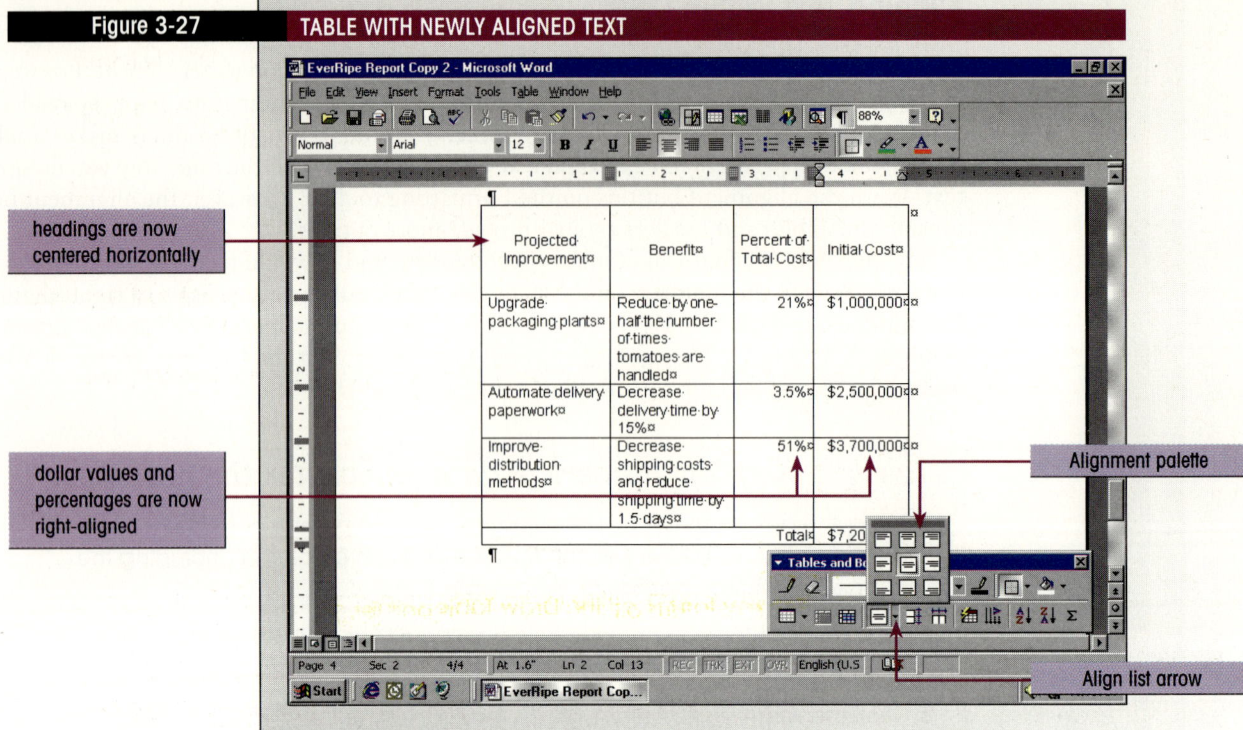

TROUBLE? If more than just the heading row is centered, click the Undo button on the Standard toolbar, and then repeat Steps 4 through 7.

8. Save the document with the current changes.

The tables look better with the headings centered and the numbers right-aligned. You now decide to make the table more attractive and easier to read by changing the table's borders and rules.

Changing Borders

It's important to keep in mind the distinction between gridlines and borders. Gridlines are light gray lines that indicate the structure of the table on the screen and that do not show up on the printed page. Borders are darker lines overlaying the gridlines, which do appear on the printed page. When you create a table using the Insert Table button, Word automatically applies a thin black border, so you can't actually see the underlying gridlines.

After you have created a table, you can add new borders, erase existing borders, or modify existing borders by changing their line weights and line styles. **Line weight** refers to the thickness of the border. You can use any combination of these formats you like.

To modify the table's existing borders:

1. Verify that the insertion point is located within the table.
2. Click the **Line Weight** list arrow on the Tables and Borders toolbar, and then click **2¼ pt**.

   TROUBLE? If the Office Assistant opens, click the Cancel button to close it. Then continue with Step 3.

3. Move the Draw Table pointer to the upper-left corner of the table, and then click the top of each cell in row 1. The top border becomes a thicker line.

4. Repeat Step 3 to draw a thicker line below the header row, above the Totals row, and at the bottom of the table. If you make a mistake, click the Undo button on the Standard toolbar to reverse it.

   Now you'll use a similar method to remove borders (without removing the underlying gridlines) between rows of the table.

5. Click the **Line Style** list arrow on the Tables and Borders toolbar, and then click **No Border**.

6. Click the bottom of each cell in row 2. Only the light gray gridline remains between the first two rows of data.

   TROUBLE? If you don't see the light gray gridline, click Table on the menu bar and then click Show Gridlines.

7. Repeat Step 6 to remove the horizontal line below row 3.

8. Press the **Esc** key to turn off the Draw Table pointer. See Figure 3-28.

Figure 3-28 TABLE AFTER CHANGING LINE WEIGHTS AND STYLES

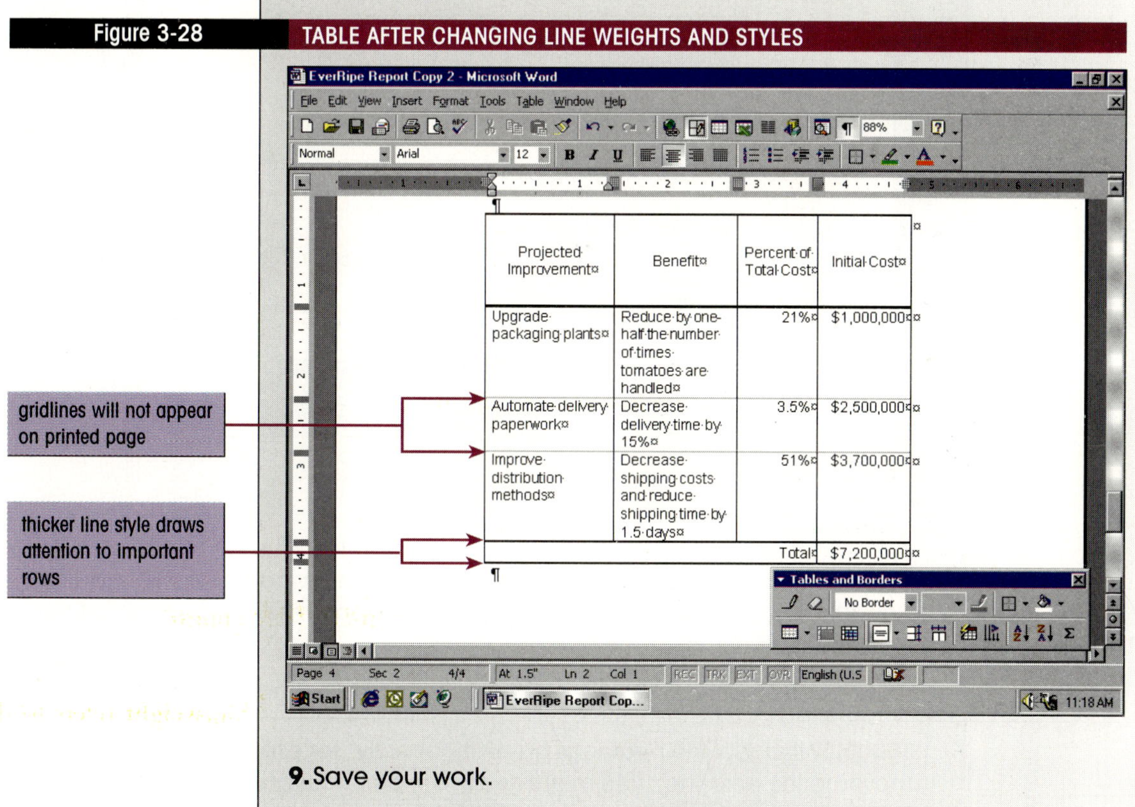

9. Save your work.

Changing the borders has made the table more attractive. You finish formatting the table by adding shading to the cells containing the headings.

Adding Shading

With the Borders and Shading dialog box, adding **shading** (a gray or colored background) to text is a simple task. Shading is especially useful in tables when you want to emphasize headings, totals, or other important items. In most cases, when you add shading to a table, you also need to bold format the shaded text to make it easier to read.

You now will add a light gray shading to the heading row and format the headings in bold.

To add shading to the heading row and change the headings to bold:

1. Click the selection bar to the left of row 1 to select the heading row of the table.
2. Click the **Shading Color** list arrow on the Tables and Borders toolbar. A palette of shading options opens.
3. Point to the fifth gray square from the left, in the top row. The ScreenTip "Gray-15%" appears. See Figure 3-29.

Figure 3-29 SHADING OPTIONS

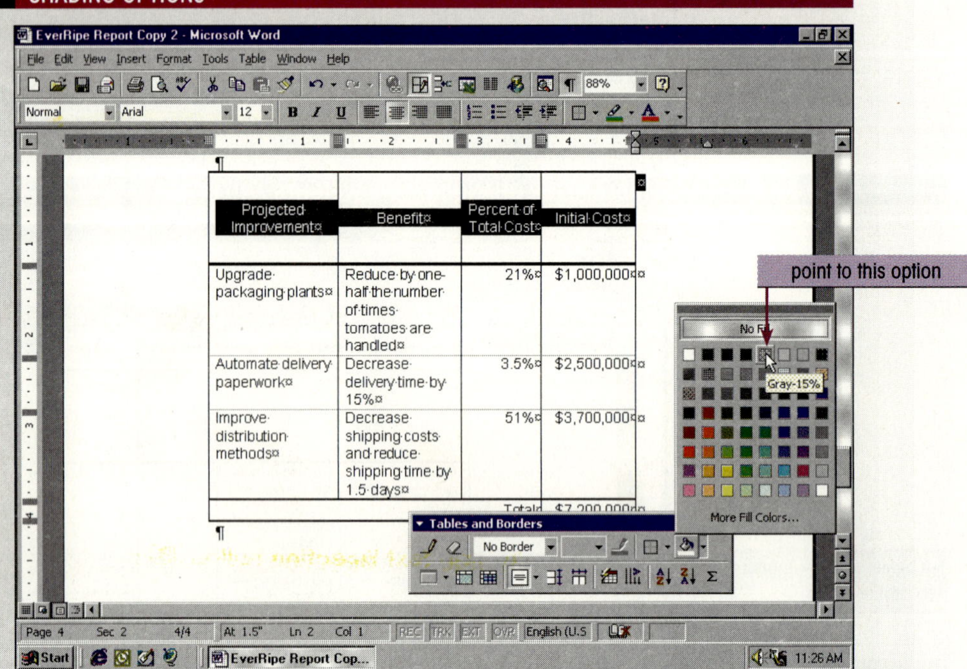

4. Click the **Gray-15%** square. A light gray background appears in the heading row. Now you need to format the text in bold to make the headings stand out from the shading.
5. Click the **Bold** button **B** on the Formatting toolbar to make the headings bold.

   TROUBLE? If any of the headings break incorrectly (for example, if the "t" in "Cost" moves to the next line), you might need to widen columns to accommodate the bold letters. Drag the column borders as necessary to adjust the column widths so that all the column headings are displayed correctly.

6. Click in the selection bar next to the last row to select the Total row.
7. Click **B**. The Total row now appears in bold.
8. Click anywhere outside the Total row to deselect it. Your table should look like Figure 3-30.

Figure 3-30 FORMATTED HEADING AND TOTAL ROWS

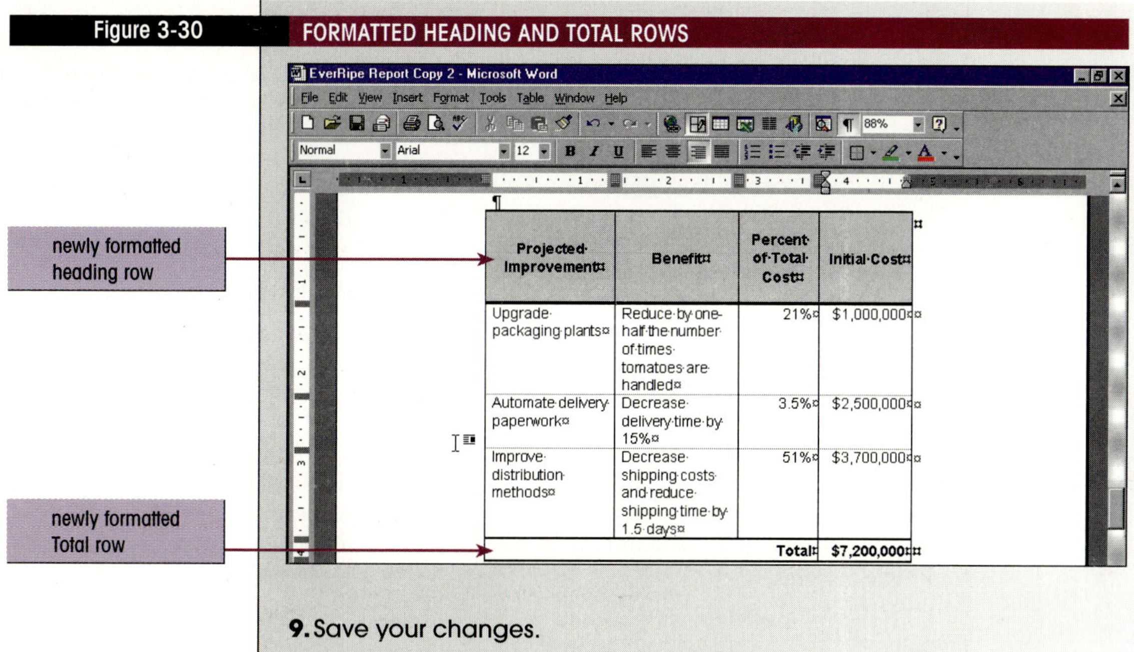

9. Save your changes.

Rotating Text in a Cell

Brittany stops by to take a look at the table so far. She mentions that it is possible to rotate text within the cells of a table. You decide to try rotating the headings to a vertical position to see how they look.

To rotate the headings vertically:

1. Select the heading row.

2. Click the **Change Text Direction** button in the Tables and Borders toolbar, and then click anywhere in the table to deselect the heading row. The table headings are now formatted vertically in their cells, as shown in Figure 3-31.

Figure 3-31 ROTATED TEXT

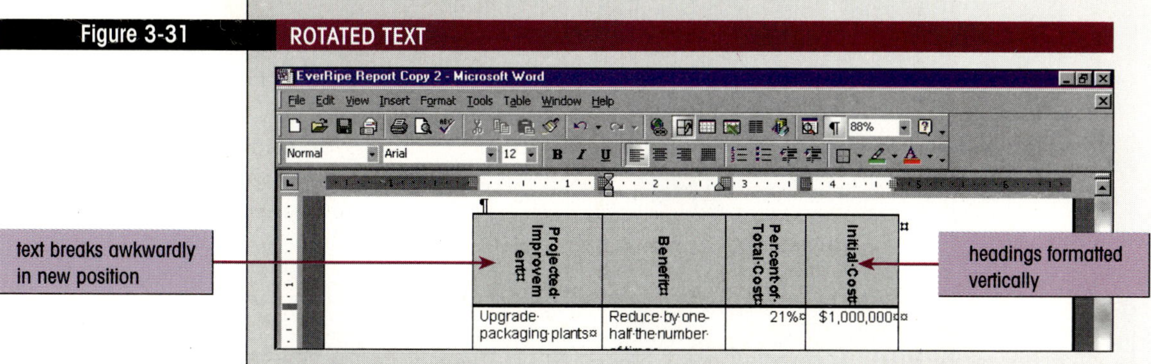

Notice that the "Project Improvement" heading now breaks awkwardly. You could widen the first row to improve its appearance. But after reviewing the rotated headings, you decide you like them better formatted horizontally. You'll return them to their original position by using the Change Text Direction button again.

3. Select the heading row, and then click again. The headings are still formatted vertically, but now the text flows from bottom to top.

4. Click again. The headings are now formatted horizontally. Because you are finished with the Tables and Borders toolbar, you will close it.

5. Click the **Close** button on the Tables and Borders toolbar to close the toolbar.

You will finish formatting your table by centering it on the page.

Centering a Table

If a table doesn't fill the entire page width, you can center it between the left and right margins. The Center button on the Formatting toolbar centers only text within each selected cell. It does not center the entire table across the page. To center a table across the page (between the left and right margins), you use the Table Properties command.

The EverRipe table will stand out more and look better if it is centered between the left and right margins.

To center the table across the page:

1. Click anywhere in the table, click **Table** on the menu bar, and then click **Table Properties**. The Table Properties dialog box opens.

2. Click the **Table** tab if necessary.

3. In the Alignment section click the **Center** option. See Figure 3-32.

Figure 3-32 TABLE TAB OF THE TABLE PROPERTIES DIALOG BOX

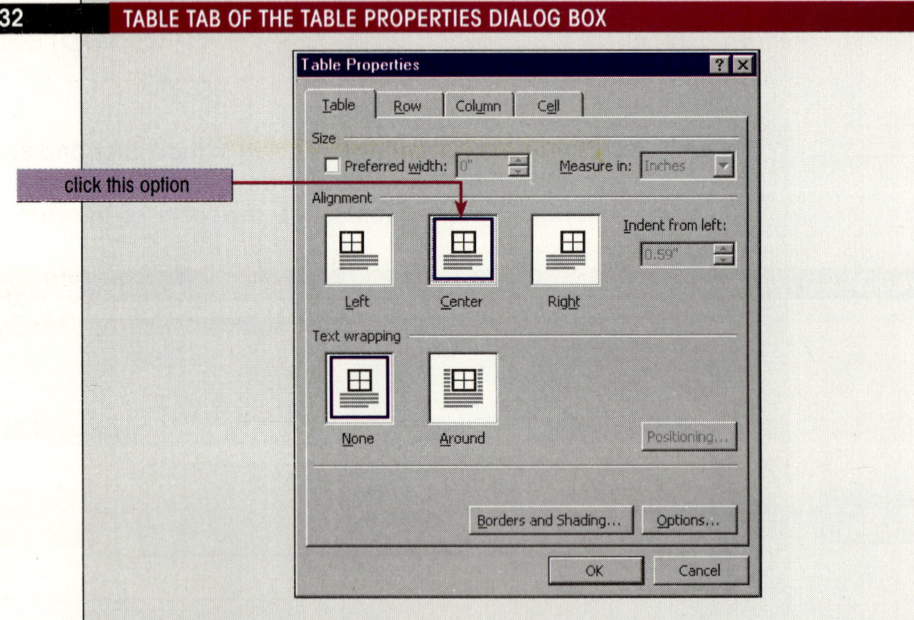

4. Click the **OK** button. The table centers between the left and right margins.

5. Save the document as **EverRipe Report Final Copy**.

Now that you're finished with the EverRipe table, you want to print a copy of the full report for Brittany. You'll preview the report first to make sure the table fits on the fourth page.

To preview the table:

1. Click the **Print Preview** button on the Standard toolbar to open the Print Preview window.
2. Scroll to view all the pages of the report.
3. Click the **Print** button on the Print Preview toolbar to print the report, then close the document and exit Word.

You now have a hardcopy of the EverRipe report including the table, which summarizes the report text. Your four-page finished report should look like Figure 3-33.

Figure 3-33 FINISHED EVERRIPE REPORT

Increasing the Profitability of AgriTechnology's EverRipe Tomatoes

Prepared for
Ramon Espinoza, Vice President
AgriTechnology

Prepared by Task Force Members

Brittany Jones	Marketing Manager
Anthony Ciaccio	Research Associate
Dominic Carmon-Estevon	Research Associate
Evan Brillstein	Distribution Specialist

EverRipe Recommendation Report Page 2

Executive Summary
Almost 20 percent of the EverRipe tomato crop was unmarketable due to damage sustained during packaging and distribution. This resulted in an estimated loss in profits of $1.2 million. AgriTechnology could increase the percentage of marketable crop and increase profits by upgrading its packaging plants, constructing distribution centers, purchasing trucking facilities, and automating delivery services. Costs for implementing these improvements would be approximately $7.2 million. The company should be able to recoup that investment within four years.

Introduction
This report presents our findings on how to improve the profitability of the EverRipe tomato crop. First, we describe how part of the crop was unmarketable due to loss during packaging and distribution. Then, we recommend improvements to the current packaging and distribution process that will reduce damage to future crops. Finally, we project costs for implementing these changes.

Loss of Profits for 2001
Although these tomatoes are genetically engineered to remain ripe for longer periods of time, they're more easily bruised than conventional tomatoes. AgriTechnology reports indicate that 18.7 percent of this year's crop was unmarketable due to damage sustained during packaging and distribution. This resulted in an estimated loss for AgriTechnology of $1.2 million. We could increase the percentage of marketable fruit by reducing the number of times the fruit are handled and by decreasing storage time.

Improving the Profitability of Future Crops
We could improve the profitability of future EverRipe crops by upgrading our packaging plants, reducing our distribution time, and accelerating our delivery methods.

Upgrading Packaging Plants
Currently, the tomatoes are picked and shipped to nearby packaging plants where they are hand-sorted, placed on a conveyor, and routed to the packaging machines. Packaged tomatoes are then put in corrugated cartons, placed in a chute, and sent to the loading area below. At the loading area, the cartons are stacked on pallets that are loaded on trucks and shipped to produce warehouses. The EverRipe tomatoes are handled an average of 4.3 times during the packaging and loading process. By upgrading the packaging plants to include new "soft touch" technology, which uses optical sensors to sort the tomatoes, and by reorganizing the plants so that packaging, stacking, and shipping operations are on the same level, we could reduce by one-half, the number of times the tomatoes are handled.

EverRipe Recommendation Report Page 3

Improving Distribution Methods
After the pallets are transported to the produce warehouses, they are stored in refrigerated rooms until the warehouses arrange with local trucking companies to ship the tomatoes to buyers. Currently, the tomatoes average 8.4 days in the warehouses and 3.2 days in shipping. We could eliminate lengthy storage by building our own distribution centers near the packaging plants, purchasing our own shipping lines, and automating our distribution system. By automating our distribution system, we could create a continuous-flow system where the tomatoes are shipped to our distribution centers, unloaded from inbound trucks, and moved across the dock to an outgoing distribution truck without having to be stored. By purchasing our own trucking system, we would also decrease shipping costs and reduce shipping time by at least 1.5 days.

Improving Delivery
We also need to improve our delivery process. Currently, the drivers spend 20 percent of their time verifying orders and checking invoices. By distributing and shipping our own produce, we could submit computerized shipment notices in advance. Then AgriTechnology drivers would use handheld computers to automatically update produce orders and verify invoices. We estimate that we can decrease delivery time by 15 percent as a result of automating our delivery system.

Cost of the Improvements
We estimate that these improvements would require an investment of approximately $7.2 million. Although this represents a major capital investment, the money would be recouped by an increase in marketable fruit. Competition among biotechnology companies is expected to increase dramatically in the next few years; therefore, it is imperative that we implement these improvements to increase our profitability and remain competitive.

EverRipe Recommendation Report Page 4

Projected Improvement	Benefit	Percent of Total Cost	Initial Cost
Upgrade packaging plants	Reduce by one-half the number of times tomatoes are handled.	21%	$1,000,000
Automate delivery paperwork	Decrease delivery time by 15%.	35%	$2,500,000
Improve distribution methods	Decrease shipping costs and reduce shipping time by 1.5 days.	51%	$3,700,000
		Total	**$7,200,000**

In this tutorial, you have planned and formatted Brittany's recommendation report and added a table to summarize the report recommendations. As a result, the report information is readily available to readers who want to skim for the most important points, as well as to those who want more detailed information.

Session 3.2 QUICK CHECK

1. How do you adjust the width of the columns in a table?
2. Why would you usually right-align numbers in a table?
3. Define the following terms in your own words:
   a. merge
   b. rotate
   c. border
   d. shading
4. Explain how to add a row to the bottom of a table.
5. Explain how to total a column of numbers in a table.
6. In what order would the following numbers appear in a table if you sorted them in ascending numerical order: 25, 10, 75, 45?
7. How do you center a table between the left and right margins?

REVIEW ASSIGNMENTS

AgriTechnology adopted the recommendations the task force made in the EverRipe report. It is now two years later and the task force is issuing a report on the progress of the new packaging, distribution, and delivery policies. You'll format this report now.

1. If necessary, start Word and make sure your Data Disk is in the appropriate disk drive, and check your screen to make sure your settings match those in the tutorial. Display nonprinting characters as necessary.
2. Open the file **StatRep** from the Review folder for Tutorial 3 on your Data Disk, and then save it as **AgTech Status Report**.
3. Select the list of task force members and their titles, and then insert a left tab stop 2.5 inches from the left margin.
4. Click after the "t" in "Distribution Specialist," press the Enter key, and then type your name. Press the Tab key to move the insertion point to the tab stop, and then type a title for yourself.
5. Divide the document into two sections. Insert a section break so that the executive summary begins on a new page.
6. *Explore* Vertically align the first section of the document using the Justified alignment option in the Page Setup dialog box, and view the results in Print Preview.

Explore

7. Add a footer to section 2. Click View on the menu bar, and then click Header and Footer. Use the Word online Help system to learn the functions of the buttons on the Header and Footer toolbar. Then, on the Header and Footer toolbar, click the Switch Between Header and Footer button to move to the footer area of section 2. Click the Same as Previous button to deselect it. Using the same techniques you used to create a header in the tutorial, create a footer for section 2 that reads "EverRipe Status Report" at the left margin. Insert the current date at the right margin. (*Hint:* Use the Insert Date button on the Header and Footer toolbar to insert the date.) Use the Formatting toolbar to format the footer and date in 9-point bold Arial.

Explore

8. Create a header for section 2 that aligns your name at the left margin and centers the page number preceded by the word "Page." Don't forget to deselect the Same as Previous button. (*Hint:* To center the page number, use the second tab stop.) Click Close on the Header and Footer toolbar.

9. Save, preview, and print the document; then close it.

Open the file **ZonReq** from the Review folder for Tutorial 3 on your Data Disk, save the document as **Zoning Request**, and then complete the following:

10. On the first page, replace "Your Name" with your first and last name.

11. Under the heading "Benefits to the Community," select the three lines of text containing tabs. Insert a left tab stop 3 inches from the left margin.

12. Divide the document into two sections. Begin the second section with the introduction on a new page.

13. Use the Ctrl+Enter key combination to insert a page break before the line "The new jobs would be divided as follows:".

14. Vertically align the first section of the document using the Center alignment option in the Page Setup dialog box.

15. Create a header for section 2 that prints "Zoning Request" at the left margin and has a right-aligned page number preceded by the word "Page." (*Hint*: Deselect the Same as Previous button on the Header and Footer toolbar.)

16. On the Header and Footer toolbar, click the Switch Between Header and Footer button to move to the footer area of section 2. Using the same techniques you used to create a header in the tutorial, create a footer for section 2 that aligns your name at the left margin and the date on the right margin.

17. Click the Close button on the Header and Footer toolbar, then review the new headers and footers in print layout view.

Explore

18. Modify the page number in the header so that it indicates the total number of pages in the document. Click View on the menu bar, click Header and Footer, click to the right of the page number, press the spacebar, type "of" (without the quotation marks), press the spacebar, and then click the Insert Number of Pages button on the Header and Footer toolbar.

19. Save the document.

20. Insert a page break at the end of the document.

21. Insert a table consisting of four rows and three columns.

22. Type the headings "Project," "Cost," and "Jobs Added" in row 1.

23. In row 2, type "Expand Packaging Plant," "$1,200,000," and "175" in the appropriate cells.

24. In row 3, type "Miscellaneous Items," "$200,000," and "2" in the appropriate cells.
25. In row 4, type "Build Distribution Center," "$1,300,000," and "125" in the appropriate cells.
26. Sort the table in ascending numerical order, by the Jobs Added column.
27. Select the entire Project column, click Table on the menu bar, point to Insert, and then click Columns to the Right to insert a new column between the Project column and the Cost column. Type the heading "Priority" in the new cell B1, press the down arrow, type 3, press the down arrow, type 2, press the down arrow, and then type 1.
28. Add a new row to the bottom of the table. Type "Total" in the new cell A5, at the bottom of the Project column.
29. Merge the "Total" cell with the cell to its right. Align the word "Total" on the right of the newly merged cell.
30. Use the AutoSum button on the Tables and Borders toolbar to total the Cost and Jobs Added columns. Click the Cost total to select it, and then format it without decimal points using the Formula command on the Table menu. Notice that the Total of the Cost column is $2,700,000, and the total of the Jobs Added column is 302.
31. Delete the Miscellaneous Items row.

Explore

32. Update both AutoSum formulas to reflect the deleted row. To update a formula, select the cell containing the formula, and then press the F9 key. The totals are updated to include only the rows currently in the table. The total of the Cost column should now be $2,500,000. The total of the Jobs Added column should now be 300.
33. Center the table on the page.
34. Drag the right border of column C (the Cost column) to the left until the column is about 0.8 inches wide. Drag the right border of column D (the Jobs Added column) to the left until the column is about 0.9 inches wide.

Explore

35. Switch to print layout view, if necessary, and then use the Table move handle to select the entire table, and then format the text as 14-point Times New Roman.

Explore

36. Try adjusting the column widths to accommodate the newly formatted text by double-clicking the borders between columns. First click anywhere within the table to deselect any selected text or cells. Double-click the border between columns A and B. The width of column A adjusts automatically to accommodate the longest entry. Adjust the widths of the other columns by clicking on their right borders.
37. Right-align the numbers in the table. The "Total" label should also be right-aligned.
38. Format the heading row by adding a light gray shading. Format the headings in bold as well.
39. Use the Line Weight list arrow on the Tables and Borders toolbar to add a 2¼-point border around the outside of the table. Also, change the border above the Total row to 2¼ point. Instead of clicking the borders you want to change, try drawing with the pointer. If you don't drag the pointer far enough, the Office Assistant may appear to offer some advice. Read the information it provides and click OK. To turn off the Draw Tables pointer, press the Esc key.
40. Increase the height of the heading row to approximately 0.8 inches. Center the headings vertically and horizontally using the Align Center option on the Tables and Borders toolbar.
41. Save, preview, print, and close the document.

Word will convert text separated by commas, paragraph marks, or tabs into a table. To try this feature, open the file **Members** from the Review folder for Tutorial 3 on your Data Disk, and save it as **Zoning Board Members**. Then complete the following:

42. Select the list of zoning board members (including the heading), click Table on the menu bar, and point to Convert, and then click Text to Table. In the Convert Text to Table dialog box, make sure the settings indicate that the table should have two columns and that the text is separated by commas. Then click the OK button. Word converts the list of task force members into a table.
43. Click cell B5, in the lower-right corner of the table, and then press the Tab key. Type your own name in the new cell A6, press the Tab key, and then type "Ward 2" in cell B6.
44. Format the table appropriately using the techniques you learned in the tutorial. Be sure to adjust the column widths to close up any extra space.

Explore

45. Place the pointer over the Table resize handle, just outside the lower-right corner of the table. Drag the double-arrow pointer to increase the size of the height and width of each cell. Notice that all the parts of the table increase proportionally. Click the Undo button to return the table to its original format.
46. Save the document; then preview and print it.

CASE PROBLEMS

Case 1. Ocean Breeze Bookstore Annual Report As manager of Ocean Breeze Bookstore in San Diego, California, you must submit an annual report to the Board of Directors.

1. If necessary, start Word, make sure your Data Disk is in the appropriate drive, and check your screen to make sure your settings match those in the tutorials.
2. Open the file **OceanRep** from the Cases folder for Tutorial 3 on your Data Disk, and save it as **Ocean Breeze Report**.
3. Divide the document into two sections. Begin section 2 with the introduction on a new page.
4. Format the title ("Annual Report") and the subtitle ("Ocean Breeze Bookstore") using the font and font size of your choice. Vertically align the first section using the alignment option of your choice.

Explore

5. Move the insertion point to section 2. Create a header for the entire document that aligns "Ocean Breeze Annual Report" on the left margin, your name in the center, and the current date on the right margin. Click the Show Previous button on the Header and Footer toolbar to view the header text for section 1.
6. Select the list of members under the heading "Board of Directors." Insert a left tab stop 4.5 inches from the left margin.
7. Preview and save the document.
8. Insert a page break at the end of the document.
9. Insert a table consisting of four rows and three columns.
10. Insert the headings "Name," "Title," and "Duties." Fill in the rows with the relevant information about the store personnel, which you will find listed in the report. Add new rows as needed.

11. Adjust the table column widths so the information is presented attractively.
12. Increase the height of the heading row, center the column headings horizontally and vertically, and then bold them.

Explore

13. Use Help to learn how to insert a row within a table. Insert a row in the middle of the table, and add your name to the list of store managers. Readjust the column widths as needed.
14. Format the heading row with a light gray shading of your choice.
15. Change the outside border of the table to 2¼-point line weight.
16. Save, preview, print, and close the document.

Case 2. Ultimate Travel's "Europe on a Budget" Report As director of Ultimate Travel's "Europe on a Budget" tour, you need to write a report summarizing this year's tour.

1. If necessary, start Word, make sure your Data Disk is in the appropriate drive, and check your screen to make sure your settings match those in the tutorials.
2. Open the file **Europe** from the Cases folder for Tutorial 3 on your Data Disk, and save it as **Europe Tour Report**.
3. Replace "Your Name" in the first page with your first and last name.
4. Divide the document into two sections. Begin the second section on a new page, with the summary that starts "This report summarizes and evaluates…."
5. Vertically align the first section using the Center alignment option.
6. Create a header for section 2 that contains the centered text "Ultimate Travel." (*Hint:* To center text in the header, use the second tab stop. Deselect the Same as Previous button before you begin.)
7. On the Header and Footer toolbar, click the Switch Between Header and Footer button to move to the footer area of the document. Using the same techniques you used to create a header in the tutorial, create a footer for section 2 that aligns "Evaluation Report" on the left margin and the date on the right margin. (*Hint*: Deselect the Same as Previous button first.)
8. In the table, bold the text in column A (the left column), and then rotate it so that text is formatted vertically, from bottom to top.
9. Adjust the row and column widths as necessary.
10. Delete the blank row 2.
11. Format column A with a light gray shading.
12. Change the border around column A to 2¼-point line weight.
13. Save, preview, print, and close the document.

Case 3. Classical CD Sales at The Master's Touch Austin Cornelius is the purchasing agent for The Master's Touch, a music store in Little Rock, Arkansas. Each month, Austin publishes a list of the classical CDs that are on sale at The Master's Touch. He has asked you to create a table showing this month's list of sale items.

1. Open the file **Classics** from the Cases folder for Tutorial 3 on your Data Disk, and save it as **Classical Music CDs**.

Explore

2. Highlight the list of CDs—Chopin Nocturnes through The Nine Symphonies—separated by commas, and convert it into a table. (*Hint:* Click Table on the menu bar, point to Convert, and then click Text to Table. In the dialog box, select Commas as the Separate text at option. Make sure the Number of columns is set to 5.)

Explore

3. Insert an additional row for headings by selecting the top row of the table, and then clicking the Insert Rows button in the Standard toolbar.
4. Type the following headings (in a sans serif boldface font) in this order: "Title," "Artist," "Label," "Number of CDs in Set," and "Price."
5. Insert a row below "The Best of Chopin," and then type the following in the cells: "Beethoven Piano Sonatas," "Alfred Brendel," "Vox," "2," "18.95."
6. Open the Tables and Borders toolbar if necessary, and then sort the rows in the table in ascending alphabetical order by title.
7. Center the numbers in the "Number of CDs in Set" column.

Explore

8. Split cells to allow for two columns of pricing information. Select the cells containing prices (cells E2 through E10), and then click the Split Cells button on the Tables and Borders toolbar. In the Split Cells dialog box, deselect the "Merge cells before split" check box. (If you keep this option selected, Word moves all the prices into one cell before splitting each of the cells into two.) Verify that the Number of columns setting is 2, so that Word will divide each cell into two cells (or columns). Click OK.

Explore

9. Click the Line Weight list arrow on the Tables and Borders toolbar, click 1½ pt, and then use the Draw Table pointer to draw a horizontal line in cell E1 directly below the word "Price." Next, use the Split Cells button again to divide the new, empty cell below the "Price" cell into two. In the new, empty cell on the left (directly above the column of prices), type "CD Club Members." In the new, blank cell on the right (directly above the blank column), type "Non-Members." For each title, enter a Non-Members' price that is $1.00 more than the CD Club Members price.
10. Adjust column widths as necessary.
11. Add 2¼-point horizontal borders to make the table easier to read.
12. Save your document; then preview, print, and close it.

Case 4. Computer Training at Pottery Row, Inc. Joseph Keats is the director of the Human Resources department at Pottery Row, Inc., a mail-order firm specializing in home furnishings. He has contracted with Bright Star Learning systems for a series of in-house training seminars on intermediate and advanced word processing skills. He asks you to create an informational flier for posting on bulletin boards around the office. Among other things, the flier should include Bright Star Learning Systems' corporate logo (an orange, five-pointed star). You begin by drawing a sketch, similar to the one shown in Figure 3-34. You decide to take advantage of the Word table features to structure the information in the flier.

Figure 3-34 SKETCH FOR BRIGHT STAR FLIER

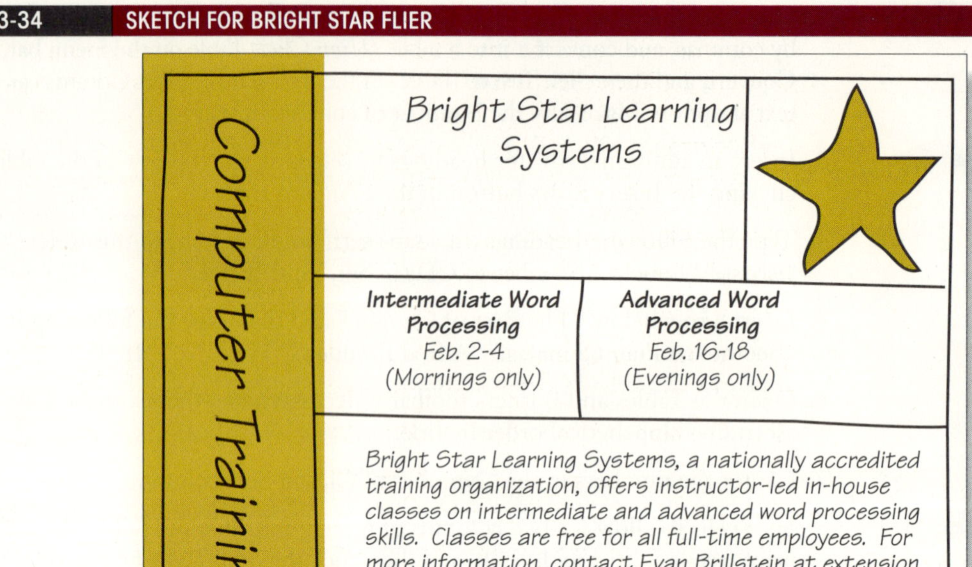

1. Open a new, blank document and save it as **Bright Star Training** in the Cases folder for Tutorial 3.
2. If necessary, switch to print layout view and display the Tables and Borders toolbar.
3. ***Explore*** Click the Draw Table button on the Tables and Borders toolbar, if necessary, to select the button and change the pointer to a pencil shape. Click in the upper-left corner of the document (near the paragraph mark), and drag down and to the right to draw a rectangle about 6 inches wide and 3.5 inches high.
4. ***Explore*** Continue to use the Draw Table pointer to draw the columns and rows shown in Figure 3-34. For example, to draw the column border for the "Computer Training" column, click at the top of the rectangle, where you want the column to begin, and drag down to the bottom of the rectangle. Use the same technique to draw rows. If you make a mistake, use the Undo button. To delete a border, click the Eraser button in the Tables and Borders toolbar, click the border you want to erase, and then click the Eraser button again to turn it off. Keep in mind that you can also merge cells, if necessary. Don't expect to draw the table perfectly the first time. You may have to practice a while until you become comfortable with the Draw Table pointer, but once you can use it well, you will find it a helpful tool for creating complex tables.
5. In the left column, type the text "Computer Training," rotate the text to position it vertically in the table, and format the text in 26-point Times New Roman, so that it fills the height of the column. If the text does not fit in one row, drag the table border down until it does. (*Hint:* You will probably have to adjust and readjust the row and column borders throughout this project, until all the elements of the table are positioned properly.)
6. Type the remaining text, as shown in Figure 3-34. Replace the name "Evan Brillstein" with your own name. Use bold and italic as necessary to draw attention to key elements. Use the font styles, font sizes, and alignment options you think appropriate.

Explore

7. Click the Drawing button on the Standard toolbar to display the Drawing toolbar. Now you can insert the Bright Star corporate logo in the upper-right cell, using one of the tools on the Drawing toolbar. Click the AutoShapes button on the Drawing toolbar, point to Stars and Banners, and then click the 5-Point Star. Move the cross-hair pointer over the upper-right cell, then click and drag to draw a star that fits roughly within the cell borders. After you draw the star, it remains selected, as indicated by the square boxes, called selection handles, that surround it. Click the lower-right selection handle, and drag up or down to adjust the size of the star so that it fits within the cell borders more precisely. With the star still selected, click the Fill Color list arrow on the Drawing toolbar, and then click a gold color in the color palette.
8. Use the Shading Color button on the Tables and Borders toolbar to add the same color background to the "Computer Training" column.
9. Adjust column widths and row heights so that the table is attractive and easy-to-read.

Explore

10. Now that you have organized the information using the Word table tools, you can remove the borders so that the printed flier doesn't look like a table. Click the Table move handle to select the entire table, click Table on the menu bar, click Table Properties, click the Table tab, click the Borders and Shading button, and then click the Borders tab, click the None option, click the OK button, and then click the OK button again. The borders are removed from the flier, leaving only the underlying gridlines, which will not appear on the printed page.
11. Save your work, preview the flier, make any necessary adjustments, print it, and then close the document.

INTERNET ASSIGNMENTS

The purpose of the Internet Assignments is to challenge you to find information on the Internet that you can use to create effective documents. The actual assignments are updated and maintained on the Course Technology Web site. Log on to the Internet and use your Web browser to go to the Student Online Companion to accompany this text at **www.course.com/NewPerspectives/office2000**. Click the Word link, and then click the link for Tutorial 3.

QUICK CHECK ANSWERS

Session 3.1

1. **a.** The location where text moves when you press the Tab key.

   b. The intersection of a row and a column in a table.

   c. Information arranged in horizontal rows and vertical columns.

   d. A tab stop that aligns numerical data on the decimal point.

   e. A unit or part of a document that can have its own page orientation, margins, headers, footers, and vertical alignment.
2. Insert a section break, move the insertion point within the section you want to align, click File, click Page Setup, click the Layout tab, select Center in the Vertical alignment list box, make sure This section is selected in the Apply to list box, and then click OK.

3. A header appears at the top of a page, whereas a footer appears at the bottom of a page.
4. Move the insertion point to the location where you want the table to appear. Click the Insert Table button on the Standard toolbar. In the grid, click and drag to select four columns and six rows, and then release the mouse button
5. If the insertion point is in the rightmost cell in a row, press the Tab key. Otherwise, press the ↓ key.
6. Click View on the menu bar, click Header and Footer, verify that the insertion point is located in the Header area, press Tab to move the insertion point to where you want the page number to appear, and then click the Insert Page Number button on the Header and Footer toolbar.
7. Select the text whose tab alignment you want to change, click the tab alignment selector on the far left of the horizontal ruler until the appropriate tab stop alignment style appears, and then click in the horizontal ruler where you want to set the new tab stop.
8. You might want to divide a document into sections if you wanted to center part of the document between the top and bottom margins.
9. It's better to use a table rather than tab stops when you need to organize a lot of complicated information.
10. Click the Table move handle.

Session 3.2

1. Drag the right border of each column to a new position.
2. Right-aligning numbers in a table makes the numbers easier to read.
3. **a.** Combine two or more cells into one.

   b. Move text in a cell so that it is formatted vertically rather than horizontally.

   c. The outline of a row, cell, column, or table.

   d. A gray or colored background used to highlight parts of a table.
4. Click the rightmost cell in the bottom row of the table, and then press the Tab key.
5. Click the cell where you want the total to appear, click the AutoSum button on the Tables and Borders toolbar, click the total to select it, click Table on the menu bar, click Formula, select the number format you want, and then click OK.
6. 10, 25, 45, 75
7. Click anywhere in the table, click Table on the menu bar, click Table Properties, click the Table tab, click Center, and then click OK.

OBJECTIVES

In this tutorial you will:

- Identify desktop-publishing features
- Create a title with WordArt
- Create newspaper-style columns
- Insert clip art
- Wrap text around a graphic
- Incorporate drop caps
- Use symbols and special typographic characters
- Add a page border

DESKTOP PUBLISHING A NEWSLETTER

Creating a Newsletter for FastFad Manufacturing Company

CASE

FastFad Manufacturing Company

Gerrit Polansky works for FastFad Manufacturing Company, which designs and manufactures plastic figures (action figures, vehicles, and other toys) for promotional sales and giveaways in the fast-food and cereal industries. Gerrit keeps FastFad's sales staff informed about new products by producing and distributing a monthly newsletter that briefly describes these new items and gives ideas for marketing them. Recently, FastFad added MiniMovers—small plastic cars, trucks, and other vehicles—to its line of plastic toys. Gerrit needs to get the information about these products to the sales staff quickly so that the company can market the toys to FastFad's clients while the toys are still popular. He has asked you to help him create the newsletter.

The newsletter must be eye-catching because the quantity of printed product material sales reps get makes it difficult for them to focus on any one product. Gerrit also wants you to create a newsletter that is neat, organized, and professional-looking. He would like it to contain headings (so the sales reps can scan it quickly for the major points) as well as graphics that will give the newsletter a memorable "look." He wants you to include a picture that will reinforce the newsletter content and distinguish the product.

In this tutorial, you'll plan the layout of the newsletter, keeping in mind the audience (the sales representatives). Then you'll get acquainted with the desktop-publishing features and elements you'll need to use to create the newsletter. Also, you'll learn how desktop publishing differs from other word-processing tasks. You'll format the title using an eye-catching design and divide the document into newspaper-style columns to make it easier for the sales reps to read. To add interest and focus to the text, you'll include a piece of predesigned art. You'll then fine-tune the newsletter layout, give it a more professional appearance with typographic characters, and put a border around the page to give the newsletter a finished look.

SESSION 4.1

In this session you will see how Gerrit planned his newsletter and learn about desktop-publishing features and elements. Then you will create the newsletter title using WordArt, modify the title's appearance, and format the text of the newsletter into newspaper-style columns.

Planning the Document

The newsletter will provide a brief overview of the new FastFad products, followed by a short explanation of what the MiniMovers are and why children will like them. Like most newsletters, it will be written in an informal style that conveys information quickly. The newsletter title will be eye-catching and will help readers quickly identify the document. Newsletter text will be split into two columns to make it easier to read, and headings will help readers scan the information quickly. A picture will add interest and illustrate the newsletter content. Drop caps and other desktop-publishing elements will help draw readers' attention to certain information and make the newsletter design attractive and professional.

Elements of Desktop Publishing

Desktop publishing is the production of commercial-quality printed material using a desktop computer system from which you can enter and edit text, create graphics, compose or lay out pages, and print documents. The following elements are commonly associated with desktop publishing:

- **High-quality printing.** A laser printer or high-resolution inkjet printer produces final output.
- **Multiple fonts.** Two or three font types and sizes provide visual interest, guide the reader through the text, and convey the tone of the document.
- **Graphics.** Graphics, such as horizontal or vertical lines (called **rules**), boxes, electronic art, and digitized photographs help illustrate a concept or product, draw a reader's attention to the document, and make the text visually appealing.
- **Typographic characters.** Typographic characters such as typographic long dashes, called **em dashes** (—), in place of double hyphens (--), separate dependent clauses; typographic medium-width dashes, called en dashes (–), are used in place of hyphens (-) as minus signs and in ranges of numbers; and typographic bullets (•) signal items in a list.
- **Columns and other formatting features.** Columns of text, **pull quotes** (small portions of text pulled out of the main text and enlarged), page borders, and other special formatting features that you don't frequently see in letters and other documents distinguish desktop-published documents.

You'll incorporate many of these desktop-publishing elements into the FastFad newsletter for Gerrit.

Word's Desktop-Publishing Features

Successful desktop publishing requires that you first know what elements professionals use to desktop publish a document. Figure 4-1 defines some of the desktop-publishing features included in Word. Gerrit wants you to use these features to produce the final newsletter shown in Figure 4-2. The newsletter includes some of the typical desktop-publishing elements that you can add to a document using Word.

Figure 4-1 WORD DESKTOP PUBLISHING FEATURES

ELEMENT	DESCRIPTION
Columns	Two or more vertical blocks of text that fit on one page
WordArt	Text modified with special effects, such as rotated, curved, bent, shadowed, or shaded letters
Clip art	Prepared graphic images that are ready to be inserted into a document
Drop cap	Oversized first letter of word beginning a paragraph that extends vertically into two or more lines of the paragraph
Typographical symbols	Special characters that are not part of the standard keyboard, such as em dashes (—), copyright symbols (©), or curly quotation marks (")

Figure 4-2 FASTFAD NEWSLETTER

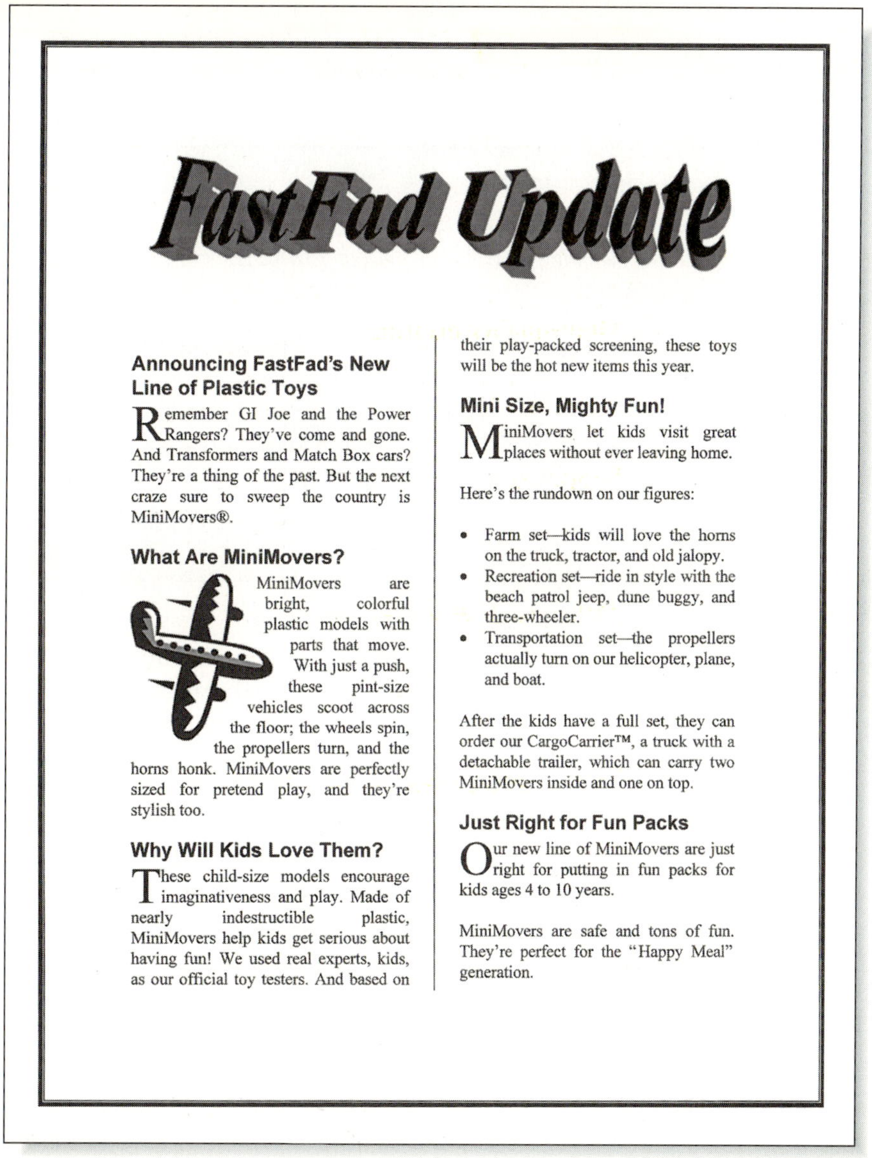

FastFad Update

Announcing FastFad's New Line of Plastic Toys

Remember GI Joe and the Power Rangers? They've come and gone. And Transformers and Match Box cars? They're a thing of the past. But the next craze sure to sweep the country is MiniMovers®.

What Are MiniMovers?

MiniMovers are bright, colorful plastic models with parts that move. With just a push, these pint-size vehicles scoot across the floor; the wheels spin, the propellers turn, and the horns honk. MiniMovers are perfectly sized for pretend play, and they're stylish too.

Why Will Kids Love Them?

These child-size models encourage imaginativeness and play. Made of nearly indestructible plastic, MiniMovers help kids get serious about having fun! We used real experts, kids, as our official toy testers. And based on their play-packed screening, these toys will be the hot new items this year.

Mini Size, Mighty Fun!

MiniMovers let kids visit great places without ever leaving home.

Here's the rundown on our figures:

- Farm set—kids will love the horns on the truck, tractor, and old jalopy.
- Recreation set—ride in style with the beach patrol jeep, dune buggy, and three-wheeler.
- Transportation set—the propellers actually turn on our helicopter, plane, and boat.

After the kids have a full set, they can order our CargoCarrier™, a truck with a detachable trailer, which can carry two MiniMovers inside and one on top.

Just Right for Fun Packs

Our new line of MiniMovers are just right for putting in fun packs for kids ages 4 to 10 years.

MiniMovers are safe and tons of fun. They're perfect for the "Happy Meal" generation.

Your first step is to create the newsletter's title.

Using WordArt to Create the Newsletter Title

Gerrit wants the title of the newsletter, "FastFad Update," to be eye-catching and dramatic, as shown in Figure 4-2. **WordArt**, available in Word as well as other Microsoft Office programs, provides great flexibility in designing text with special effects that expresses the image or mood you want to convey in your printed documents. With WordArt, you can apply color and shading, as well as alter the shape and size of the text. You can easily "wrap" the document text around WordArt shapes.

You begin creating a WordArt image by choosing a text design. Then you type in the text you want to enhance and format it.

When you create a WordArt image, Word switches to print layout view because WordArt images are not visible in normal view. Print layout view is the most appropriate view to use when you are desktop publishing with Word because it shows you exactly how the text and graphics fit on the page. The vertical ruler that appears in print layout view helps you position graphical elements more precisely.

REFERENCE WINDOW RW

Creating Special Text Effects Using WordArt

- Click the Drawing button on the Standard toolbar to display the Drawing toolbar.
- Click the Insert WordArt button on the Drawing toolbar.
- Click the style of text you want to insert, and then click the OK button.
- Type the text you want in the Edit WordArt Text dialog box.
- Click the Font and Size list arrows to select the font and font size you want.
- If you want, click the Bold or Italic button, or both.
- Click the OK button.
- With the WordArt selected, drag any handle to reshape and resize it. To keep the text in the same proportions as the original, press and hold down the Shift key while you drag a handle.

To begin, you'll open the file that contains the unformatted text of the newsletter, often called **copy**, and then you'll use WordArt to create the newsletter title.

To create the title of the newsletter using WordArt:

1. Start Word and insert your Data Disk in the appropriate drive. Make sure your screen matches the figures in this tutorial, and display the nonprinting characters so you can see more accurately where to insert text and graphics.
2. Open the file **MiniInfo** from the Tutorial folder for Tutorial 4 on your Data Disk, and then save it as **FastFad Newsletter** in the same folder.

3. With the insertion point at the beginning of the document, click the **Drawing** button on the Standard toolbar to display the Drawing toolbar, which appears at the bottom of the screen, if it is not already displayed.

   TROUBLE? If the Drawing toolbar is not positioned at the bottom of the document window, drag it there by its title bar. If you do not see the Drawing toolbar anywhere, right-click the Standard toolbar, and then click Drawing on the shortcut menu.

4. Click the **Insert WordArt** button on the Drawing toolbar. The WordArt Gallery dialog box opens, displaying the 30 WordArt styles available.

5. Click the WordArt style in the bottom row, the fourth column from the left, as shown in Figure 4-3.

Figure 4-3 WORDART GALLERY STYLES

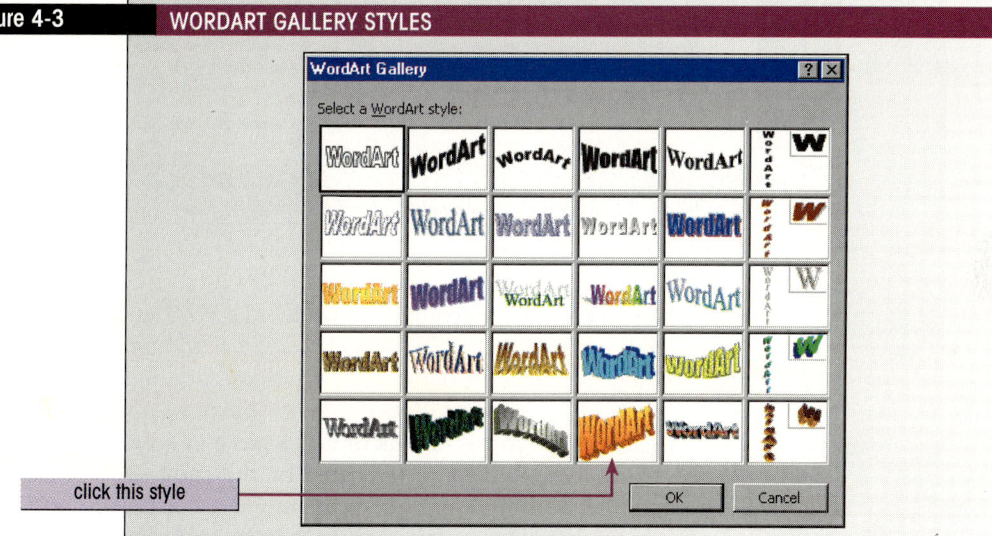

6. Click the **OK** button. The Edit WordArt Text dialog box opens, displaying the default text "Your Text Here," which you will replace with the newsletter title.

7. Type **FastFad Update**. Make sure you make "FastFad" one word with no space.

8. Click the **OK** button.

   The WordArt image appears over the existing text at the top of the newsletter, the WordArt toolbar appears on the screen, and the document changes to print layout view. See Figure 4-4. Don't be concerned that the image partially covers the newsletter text or if it's below the first paragraph. You'll fix that later. Note that the position of the WordArt object relative to the text is indicated by a small anchor symbol in the left margin. If you want to add text before the WordArt object, you need to type the text before the anchor symbol. If you want to add a section break to the document after the WordArt, you need to insert a section break after the anchor symbol.

Figure 4-4 WORDART TITLE INSERTED INTO DOCUMENT

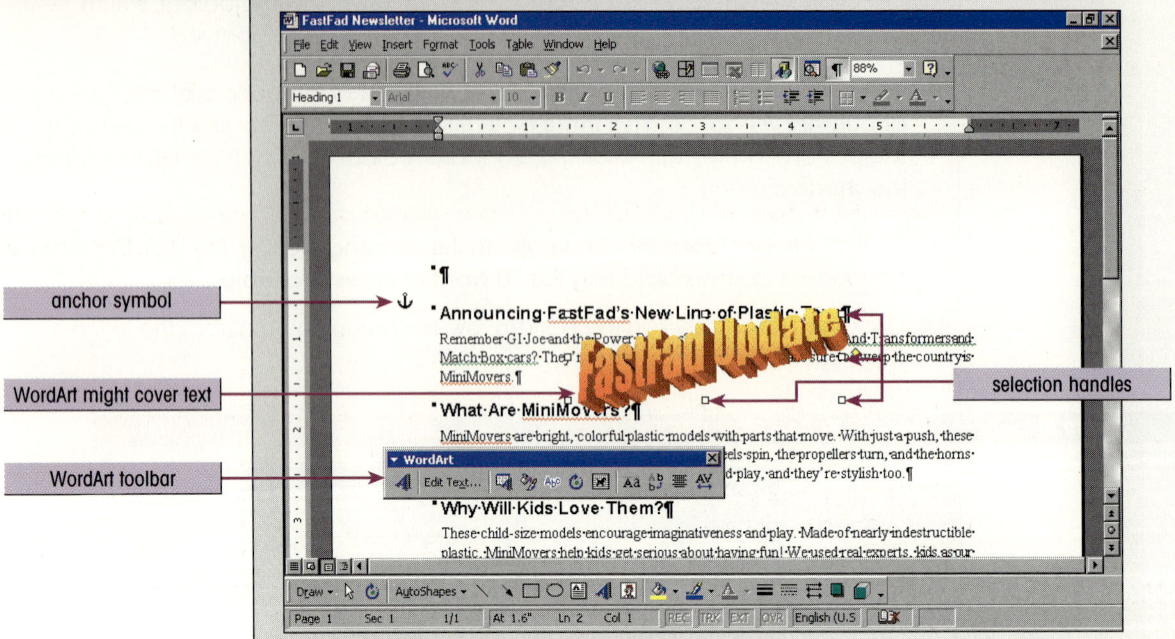

The WordArt image you have created is considered a Word drawing **object**. This means that you can modify its appearance (color, shape, size, alignment, and so forth) using the buttons on the Drawing toolbar or the WordArt toolbar. Although the object looks like text, Word does not treat it like text. The object is not visible in normal view, and Word will not spell check it as it does regular text. Think of it as a piece of art rather than as text.

The WordArt object is selected, as indicated by the eight small squares, called **resize handles**, surrounding it, and the small yellow diamond called an **adjustment handle**. The resize and adjustment handles let you change the size and shape of the selected object. Before you change the size of the object, you'll first alter its font size and formatting. The default font for this WordArt style is Impact (a sans serif font), but Gerrit wants you to change it to Times New Roman (a serif font) to provide contrast to the sans serif headings in the newsletter.

To change the font and formatting of the WordArt object:

1. Verify that the WordArt object is selected, as indicated by the selection handles.
2. Click the **Edit Text** button on the WordArt toolbar. The Edit WordArt Text dialog box opens.
3. Click the **Font** list arrow, scroll to and then click **Times New Roman**. The text in the preview box changes to Times New Roman.

   TROUBLE? If you do not have Times New Roman available, choose another serif font.

4. Click the **Size** list arrow, scroll to and then click **40**, click the **Bold** button, and then click the **Italic** button. The text in the preview box enlarges to 40-point bold, italic.

5. Click the **OK** button. The newsletter title changes to 40-point, bold, italic Times New Roman.

The default shape of the WordArt style you selected is an upward-slanting shape called Cascade Up. Gerrit wants something a little more symmetrical. In WordArt, you can change the object to any of the WordArt shapes.

To change the shape of the WordArt object:

1. Click the **WordArt Shape** button on the WordArt toolbar. The palette of shapes appears, with the Cascade Up shape selected.

2. Click the **Deflate** shape (fourth row down, second column from the left), as shown in Figure 4-5.

Figure 4-5 WORDART SHAPES

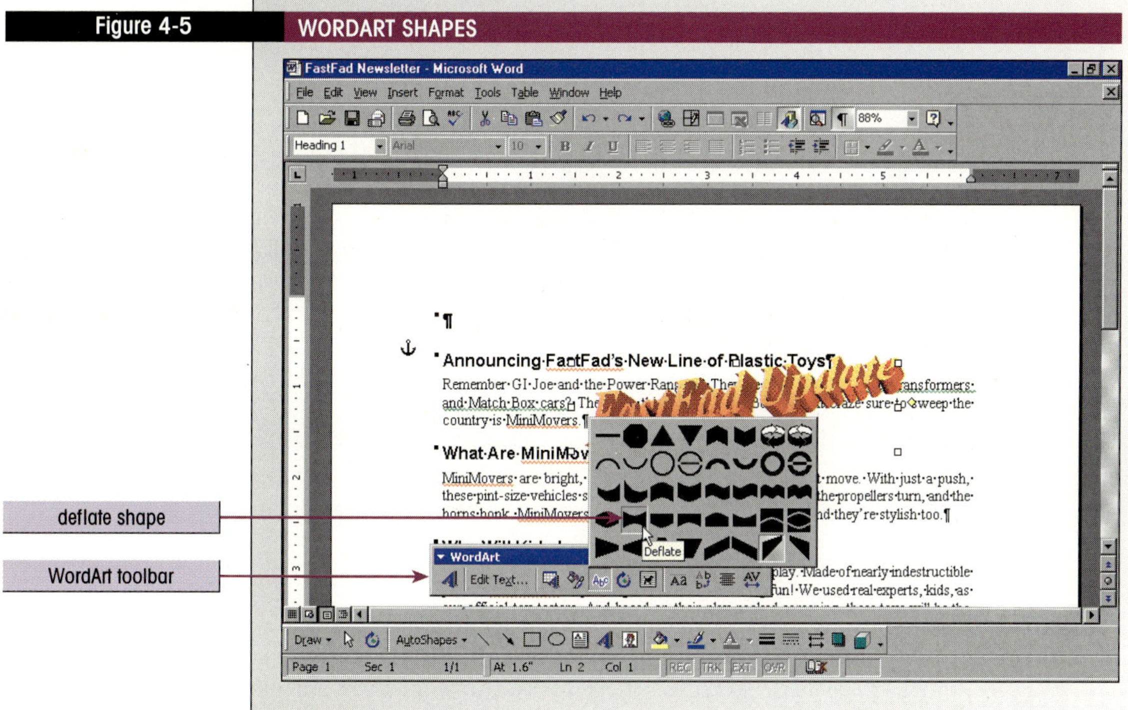

The newsletter title changes to the new WordArt shape.

Editing a WordArt Object

Now that the newsletter title is the font and shape you want, you'll move the title to the top of the newsletter and wrap the newsletter text below the WordArt object. **Text wrapping** is often used in newsletters to prevent text and graphic objects from overlapping, to add interest, and to prevent excessive open areas, called **white space**, from appearing on the page. You can wrap text around objects many different ways in Word. For example, you can have the text wrap above and below the object, through it, or wrap the text to follow the shape of the object, even if the graphic has an irregular shape. The Text Wrapping button on the WordArt or Picture toolbar provides some basic choices, whereas the Layout tab of the Format Picture dialog box provides more advanced options. Because you want a simple wrap, you'll use the Text Wrapping button on the WordArt toolbar.

To insert space between the WordArt object and the newsletter text:

1. With the WordArt object selected, click the **Text Wrapping** button on the WordArt toolbar. A menu of text-wrapping options opens. See Figure 4-6.

Figure 4-6 TEXT WRAPPING OPTIONS

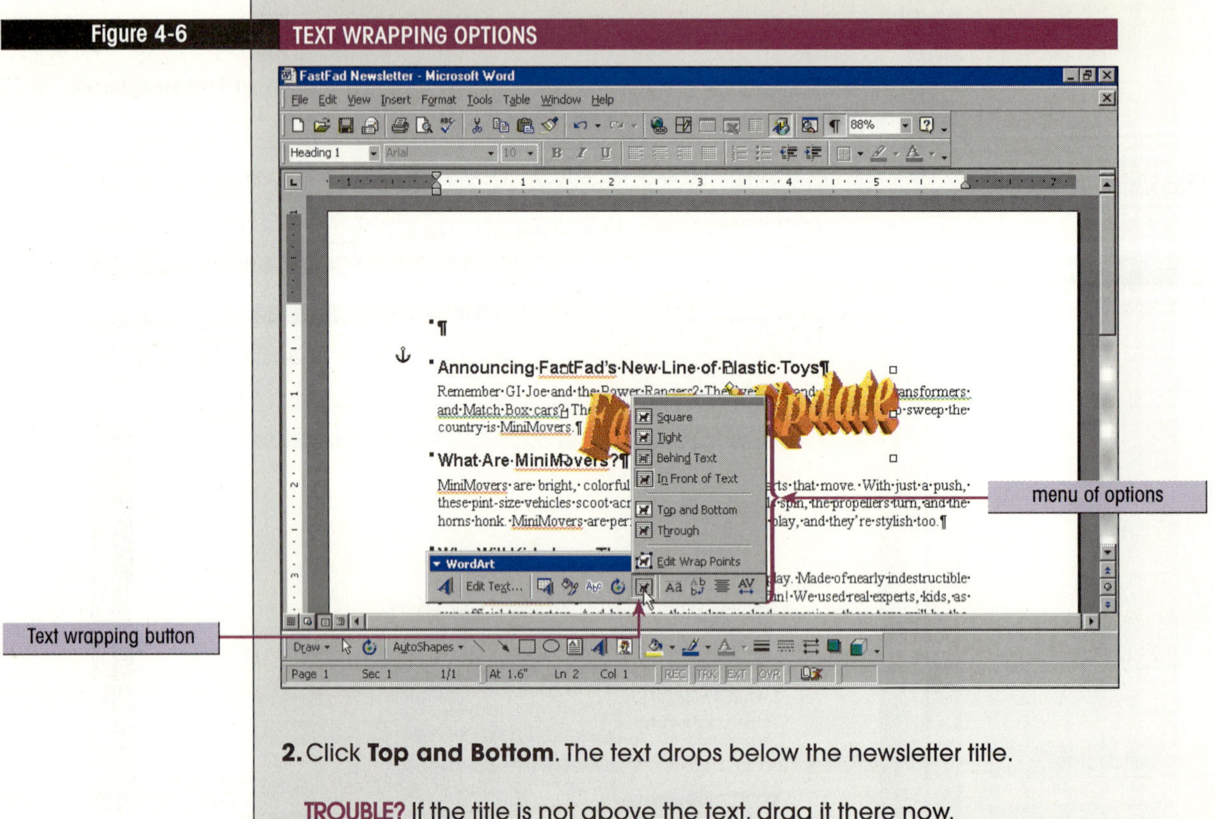

2. Click **Top and Bottom**. The text drops below the newsletter title.

   TROUBLE? If the title is not above the text, drag it there now.

Next, you'll position the title and widen it proportionally so it fits neatly within the newsletter margins. You can widen any WordArt object by dragging one of its resize handles. To keep the object the same proportion as the original, you hold down the Shift key as you drag the resize handle. This prevents "stretching" the object more in one direction than the other. After you stretch the WordArt, you'll rotate it slightly so it looks more balanced. Then you'll check the position of its anchor to make sure it is located in a separate paragraph from the text of the newsletter.

To position, enlarge, and rotate the WordArt object:

1. Drag the WordArt object to the left until the lower-left corner of the first "F" in the word "FastFad" is aligned with the left margin and then release the mouse button. Because you can see only the text outline (not the text itself) as you drag the object, you might need to repeat the procedure. Use the left edge of the text or the left margin in the ruler as a guide.
2. With the WordArt object still selected, position the pointer over its lower-right resize handle. The pointer changes to ↘.
3. Press and hold the **Shift** key while you drag the resize handle to the right margin, using the horizontal ruler as a guide. See Figure 4-7. As you drag the handle, the pointer changes to +. If necessary, repeat the procedure to make the rightmost edge of the "e" in the word "Update" line up with the right margin. Note that in the process of resizing, the anchor symbol might have moved. You'll fix that later. Now, you'll lower the right side of the WordArt object.

Figure 4-7 RESIZING THE WORDART OBJECT

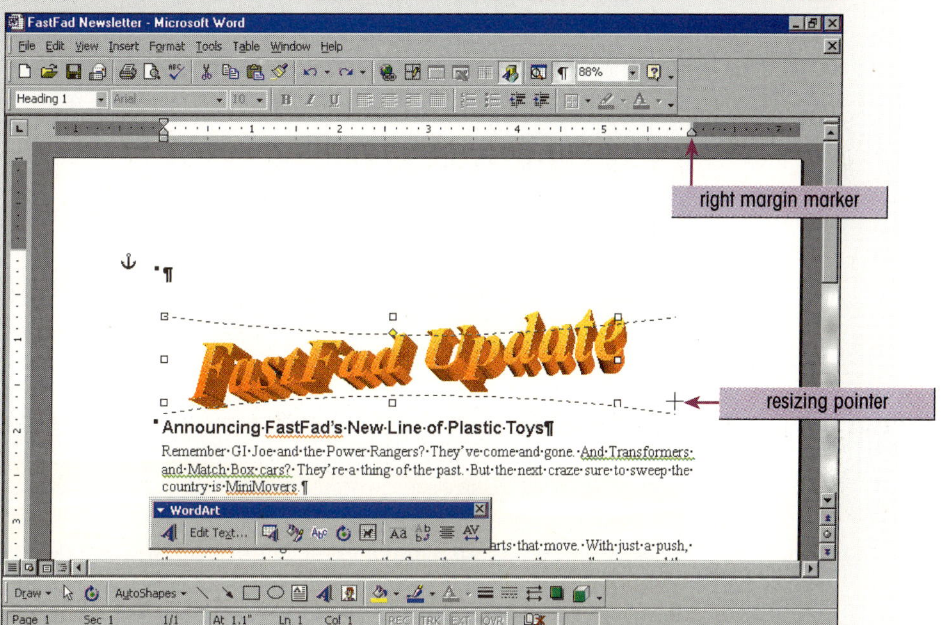

4. With the WordArt object still selected, click the **Free Rotate** button on the WordArt toolbar. Round, green rotation handles surround the object.
5. Move the pointer anywhere on the document except over the WordArt text. The pointer changes to .
6. Position the pointer over the green circle on the lower-right corner of the object, and then drag the rotation handle clockwise about a half inch, or until the title text appears to be horizontal. See Figure 4-8.

Figure 4-8 ROTATING THE WORDART OBJECT

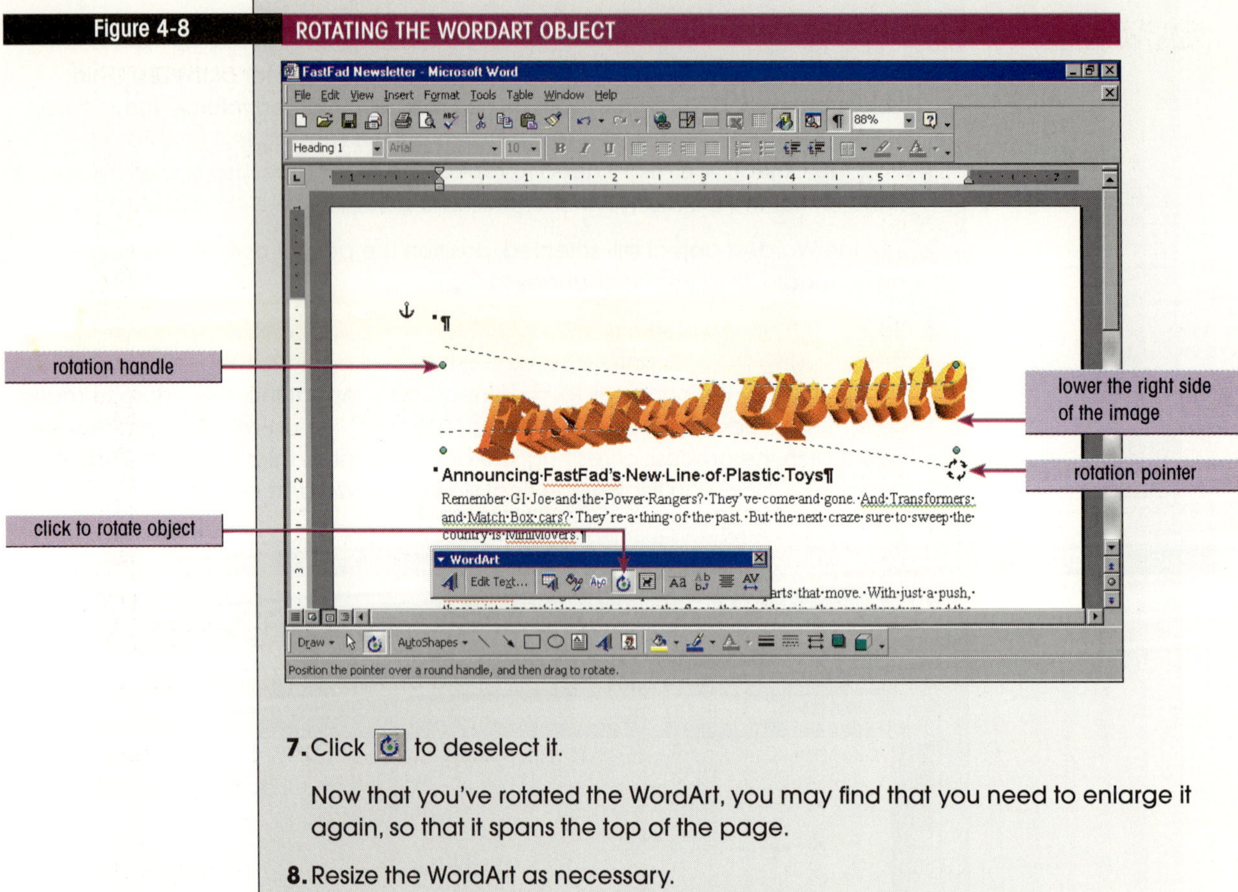

7. Click [rotate button] to deselect it.

Now that you've rotated the WordArt, you may find that you need to enlarge it again, so that it spans the top of the page.

8. Resize the WordArt as necessary.

Anchoring the WordArt

Now that you have sized and rotated the WordArt, you need to make sure it is properly positioned within the document as a whole—a process known as anchoring. The process draws its name from the **anchor** symbol in the left margin, which indicates the position of the WordArt relative to the text. To ensure that changes to the text (such as section breaks) do not affect the WordArt, you need to anchor the WordArt to a blank paragraph before the text. That is, you should make sure the anchor symbol is located to the left of, or just above, the paragraph symbol. Also, make sure that the paragraph mark is positioned below the WordArt image on the screen. Depending on exactly how you sized and rotated your WordArt, the anchor and paragraph symbols may or may not be in the proper position now. For instance, in Figure 4-8, the anchor is located just above the paragraph symbol, just as it should be. However, the paragraph symbol itself is located above the WordArt rather than below. It's up to you to decide if your WordArt is anchored properly.

To anchor the FastFad WordArt:

1. Drag the WordArt image up or down as necessary, until the anchor symbol and the paragraph symbol are positioned similarly to Figure 4-9.

Figure 4-9 PROPERLY ANCHORED WORDART

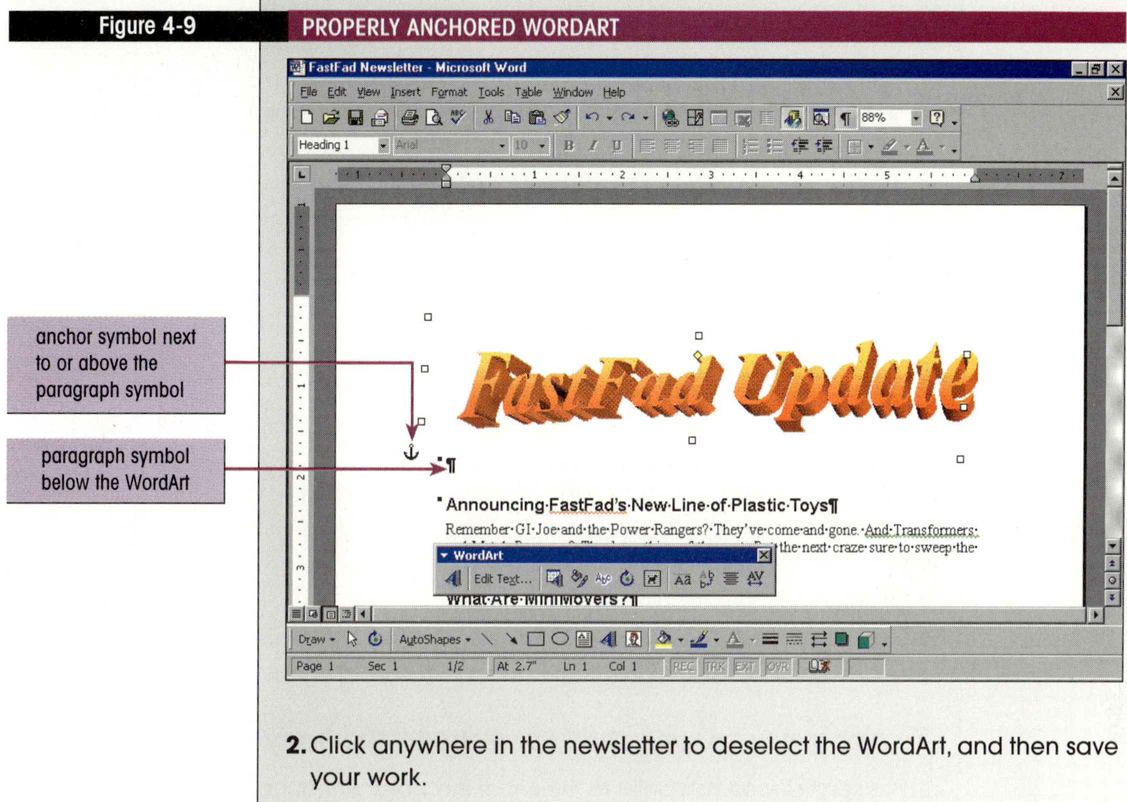

2. Click anywhere in the newsletter to deselect the WordArt, and then save your work.

Your WordArt is now finished. The formatted WordArt title will draw the sales reps' attention to the newsletter as they review this document.

Formatting Text into Newspaper-Style Columns

Because newsletters are meant for quick reading, they usually are laid out in newspaper-style columns. In **newspaper-style columns**, a page is divided into two or more vertical blocks, or columns. Text flows down one column, continues at the top of the next column, flows down that column, and so forth. Newspaper-style columns are easier to read because the columns tend to be narrow and the type size is a bit smaller than the text in a letter. This enables the eye to see more text in one glance than when text is set in longer line lengths and in a larger font size.

If you want some of your text to be in columns and other text to be in full line lengths, you must insert section breaks into your document and apply the column format only to those sections you want in columns. You could select the text and use the Columns button on the Standard toolbar to automatically insert the needed section breaks and divide the text into columns. But because Gerrit wants you to divide the text below the title into two columns and add a vertical line between them, you'll use the Columns command on the Format menu. This lets you do both actions and insert a section break in the location you specify. Without the section break, the line between the columns would extend up through the title.

REFERENCE WINDOW 

Formatting Text Into Newspaper-Style Columns

- Select the text you want to divide into columns, or don't select any text if you want the entire document divided into columns.
- Click the Columns button on the Standard toolbar, and highlight the number of columns you want to divide the text into.

or

- Move the insertion point to the location where you want the columns to begin.
- Click Format on the menu bar, and then click Columns to open the Columns dialog box.
- Select the column style you want in the Presets section.
- Deselect the Line between check box if you do *not* want a vertical line between columns.
- If necessary, click the Equal column width check box to deselect it, and then set the width of each column in the Width and spacing section.
- Click the Apply to list arrow, and select This point forward if you want Word to insert a section break. Otherwise, select the Whole document option.
- If you want a vertical rule between the columns, click the Line between check box and click the OK button.

To apply newspaper-style columns to the body of the newsletter:

1. Position the insertion point to the left of the word "Announcing" just below the title.
2. Click **Format** on the menu bar, and then click **Columns**. The Columns dialog box opens.
3. In the Presets section, click the **Two** icon.
4. If necessary, click the **Line between** check box to select it. The text in the Preview box changes to a two-column format with a vertical rule between the columns.

   You want these changes to affect only the text after the title, so you'll need to insert a section break and apply the column formatting to the text after the insertion point.
5. Click the **Apply to** list arrow, and then click **This point forward** to have Word automatically insert a section break at the insertion point. See Figure 4-10.

Figure 4-10 COMPLETED COLUMNS DIALOG BOX

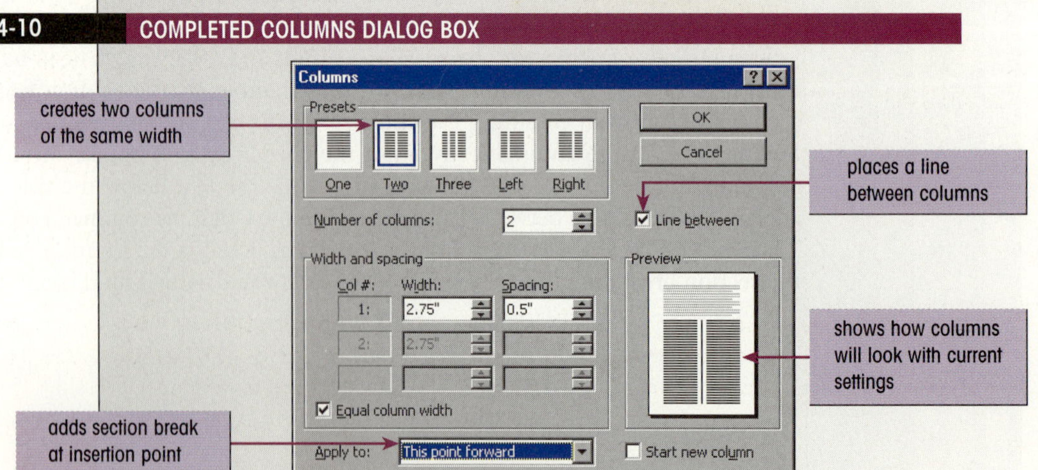

6. Click the **OK** button to return to the document window. A section break appears, and the insertion point is now positioned in section 2. The text in section 2 is formatted in two columns.

TROUBLE? If the WordArt moves below the section break, drag it above the section break, and then click anywhere in the newsletter text to deselect the WordArt object.

Viewing the Whole Page

As you create a desktop-published document, you should periodically look at the whole page to get a sense of the overall layout. You can view the page in Print Preview as you've done before, or you can use the Zoom list arrow on the Standard toolbar to enlarge or reduce the percentage of the page you see onscreen.

To zoom out and view the whole page:

1. Click the **Zoom** list arrow on the Standard toolbar, and then click **Whole Page**. Word displays the entire page of the newsletter so you can see how the two-column format looks on the page. See Figure 4-11.

Figure 4-11 WHOLE PAGE VIEW SHOWING THE TWO COLUMNS

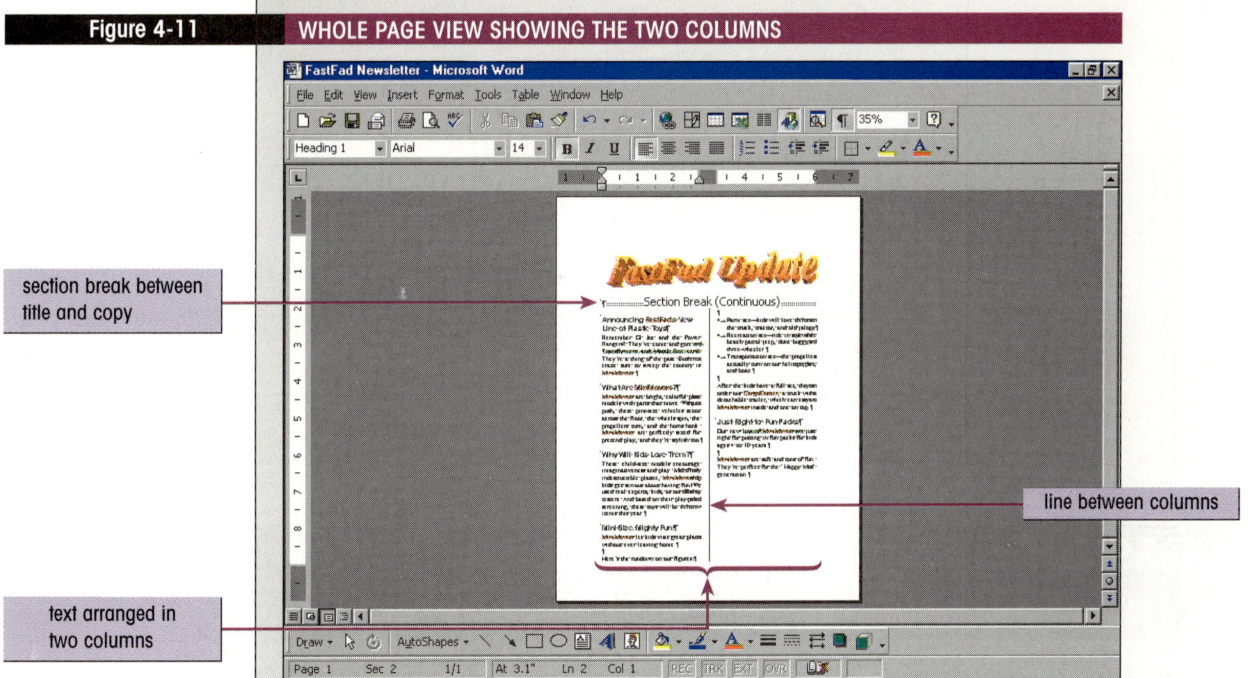

TROUBLE? Your columns may break at a slightly different line from those shown in the figure. This is not a problem; just continue with the tutorial.

The newsletter title is centered on the page, and the copy is in a two-column format. The text fills the left column but not the right column. You'll fix this later, after you add a graphic and format some of the text.

2. Click the **Zoom** list arrow again, and then click **Page Width**. Now you can read the text again. Finally, you should save the document with a new name.

3. Save the document as **FastFad Newsletter Copy 2** in the Tutorial folder for Tutorial 4.

You have set up an eye-catching title for the FastFad newsletter and formatted the text in newspaper-style columns to make it easier to read. Next, you will insert a graphic that illustrates the newsletter content. After you add clip art, you'll add more graphic interest by formatting some of the text. Then you'll finish the newsletter by making the columns equal in length and adding a border to the page.

Session 4.1 QUICK CHECK

1. Describe four elements commonly associated with desktop publishing.
2. In your own words, define the following terms:
   a. desktop publishing
   b. drawing object
   c. copy
   d. anchor
3. True or False: When using Word's desktop-publishing features, you should display your document in normal view.
4. True or False: Word treats WordArt the same way as any other document text.
5. How do you change the size of a WordArt object after you have inserted it into a Word document?
6. What is the purpose of the WordArt Shape button on the WordArt toolbar?
7. True or False: To format part of a document in newspaper-style columns, you need to insert a section break.
8. True or False: When you first format a document into newspaper-style columns, the columns will not necessarily be of equal length.

SESSION 4.2

In this session you will insert, resize, and crop clip art, and change the way the text wraps around the clip art. Then you'll create drop caps, insert typographic symbols, balance columns, place a border around the newsletter, and print the newsletter.

Inserting Clip Art

Graphics, which can include artwork, photographs, charts, tables, designs, or even designed text such as WordArt, add variety to documents and are especially appropriate for newsletters. Word allows you to draw pictures in your document, using the buttons on the Drawing toolbar. To produce professional-looking graphics, though, it's best to use one of two methods. In the first method, you begin by drawing a picture in a special graphics program or by scanning an existing image, such as a photograph. You can then save the graphic (often in a picture format known as a bitmapped graphic) and insert it into your document using the Picture command on the Insert menu. (You will have a chance to practice adding a bitmapped graphic to a document in Case Projects at the end of this tutorial.)

In the second method, you simply choose from a collection of pre-made, copyright-free images included along with Word. To add visual appeal to the FastFad newsletter, you will insert a piece of clip art now. Gerrit wants you to use a graphic that reflects the newsletter content.

REFERENCE WINDOW RW

Working With Clip Art

- Move the insertion point to the location in your document where you want the graphic image to appear.
- Click the Insert Clip Art button on the Drawing toolbar, or click Insert on the menu bar, point to Picture, and then click Clip Art to open the Insert ClipArt window.
- If necessary, click the Pictures tab.
- Click the category that best represents the type of art you need.
- Click the image you want to use.
- Click the Insert Clip icon.
- If you plan to use a particular clip art regularly, click the Add to Favorites or other category icon, verify that Favorites is selected in the list box, and then click OK. Click the Add to Favorites or other category icon again to hide the list box.
- To search for a particular image, type a description of the image you want in the Search for clips text box, and then press the Enter key.
- To re-display all the categories of clip art, click the All Categories button in the toolbar at the top of the Insert ClipArt window.
- To delete a graphic from a document, select it, and then press the Delete key.

To insert the clip-art image of an airplane into the newsletter:

1. If you took a break after the last session, make sure Word is running, the FastFad Newsletter is open, the document is in print layout view, and the nonprinting characters are displayed. Verify that the Drawing toolbar is displayed also.
2. Position the insertion point to the left of the word "MiniMovers" in the second paragraph of the newsletter just below the heading "What are MiniMovers?"
3. Click the **Insert Clip Art** button on the Drawing toolbar. The Insert ClipArt window opens.

4. If necessary, click the **Pictures** tab.

5. Click the **All Categories** button to make sure all the clip art categories are displayed.

6. Scroll down and click the Transportation category. The Pictures tab now displays a variety of transportation-related images.

   TROUBLE? If you click the wrong category by mistake, click the All Categories button at the top of the Insert ClipArt window to redisplay all categories, and then click the Transportation category.

7. Scroll down, and click the airplane image. A menu of options opens, as shown in Figure 4-12.

Figure 4-12 PICTURES TAB OF THE INSERT CLIPART WINDOW

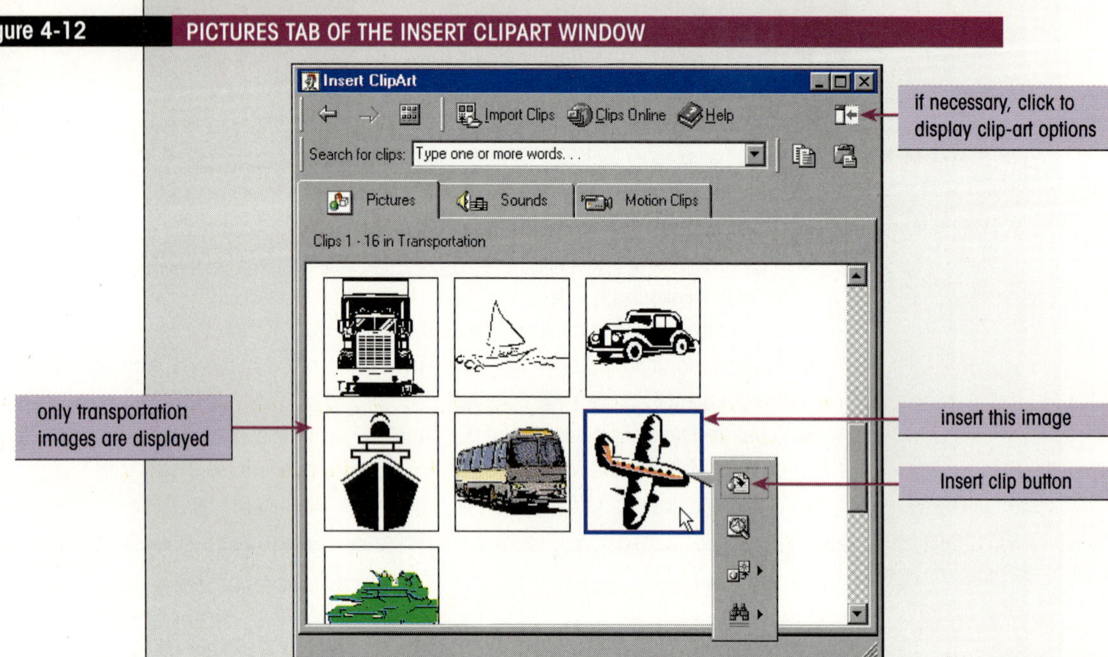

   TROUBLE? If your Insert ClipArt window is narrower than the one shown in Figure 4-12, click the Change to Full Window button at the top of the Insert ClipArt window, and then repeat Step 7.

8. Click the **Insert clip** button to insert the airplane in the newsletter at the insertion point.

9. Click the **Close** button to close the Insert ClipArt window.

10. Save the document. The airplane clip art fills the left column. The text below the heading moves down to make room for the image.

11. Click the airplane image to select it. Like the WordArt object you worked with earlier, the clip-art image is a graphic object with resize handles that you can use to change its size. The Picture toolbar appears whenever the clip-art object is selected. See Figure 4-13.

Figure 4-13 THE NEWSLETTER WITH THE CLIP ART OBJECT INSERTED

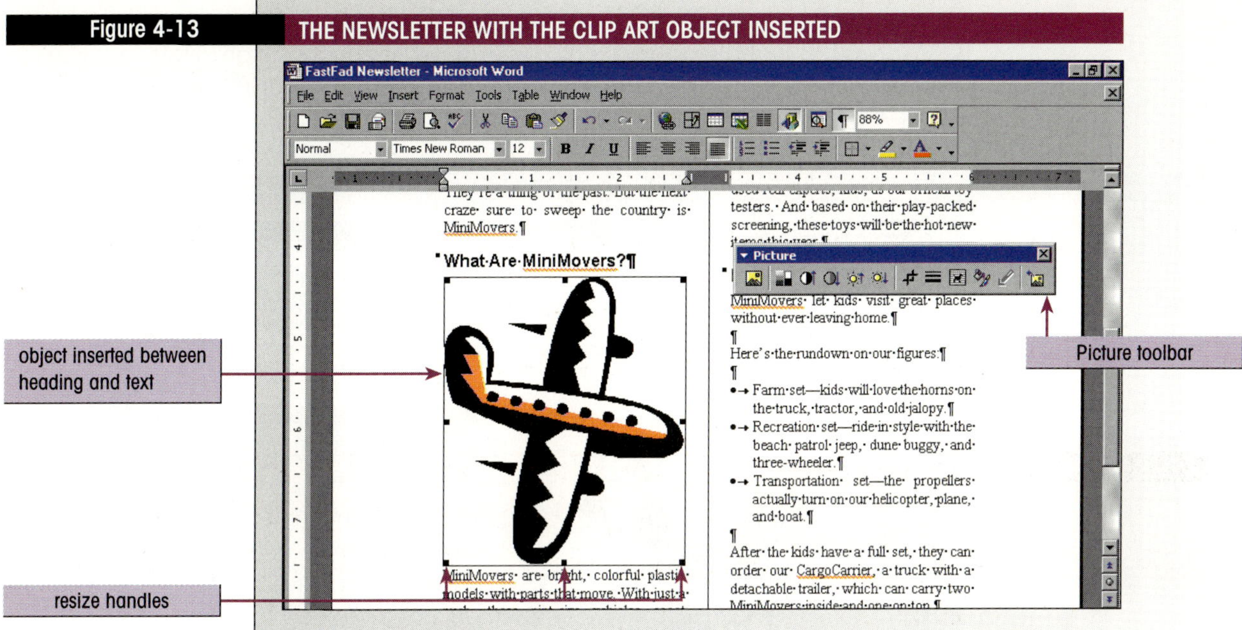

Gerrit would like the image to be smaller so it doesn't distract attention from the text.

Resizing a Graphic

Often, you need to change the size of a graphic so that it fits into your document better. This is called **scaling** the image. You can resize a graphic by either dragging its resize handles or, for more precise control, by using the Format Picture dialog box.

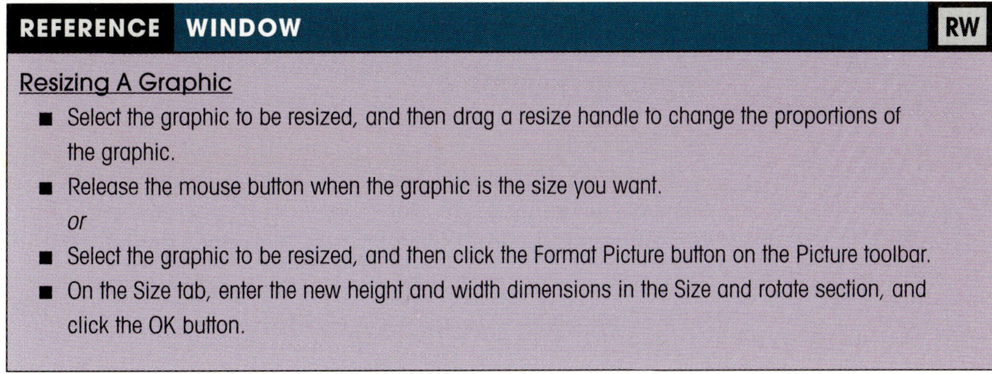

REFERENCE WINDOW RW

Resizing A Graphic

- Select the graphic to be resized, and then drag a resize handle to change the proportions of the graphic.
- Release the mouse button when the graphic is the size you want.

or

- Select the graphic to be resized, and then click the Format Picture button on the Picture toolbar.
- On the Size tab, enter the new height and width dimensions in the Size and rotate section, and click the OK button.

For Gerrit's newsletter, the dragging technique will work fine.

To resize the clip-art graphic:

1. Make sure the clip-art graphic is selected, and scroll down so you can see the lower-right resize handle of the object.

2. Drag the lower-right resize handle up and to the left until the dotted outline forms a rectangle about 1.5 inches wide by 1.75 inches high. (Note that you don't have to hold down the Shift key, as you do with WordArt, to resize the picture proportionally.) See Figure 4-14.

Figure 4-14 RESIZING THE AIRPLANE GRAPHIC

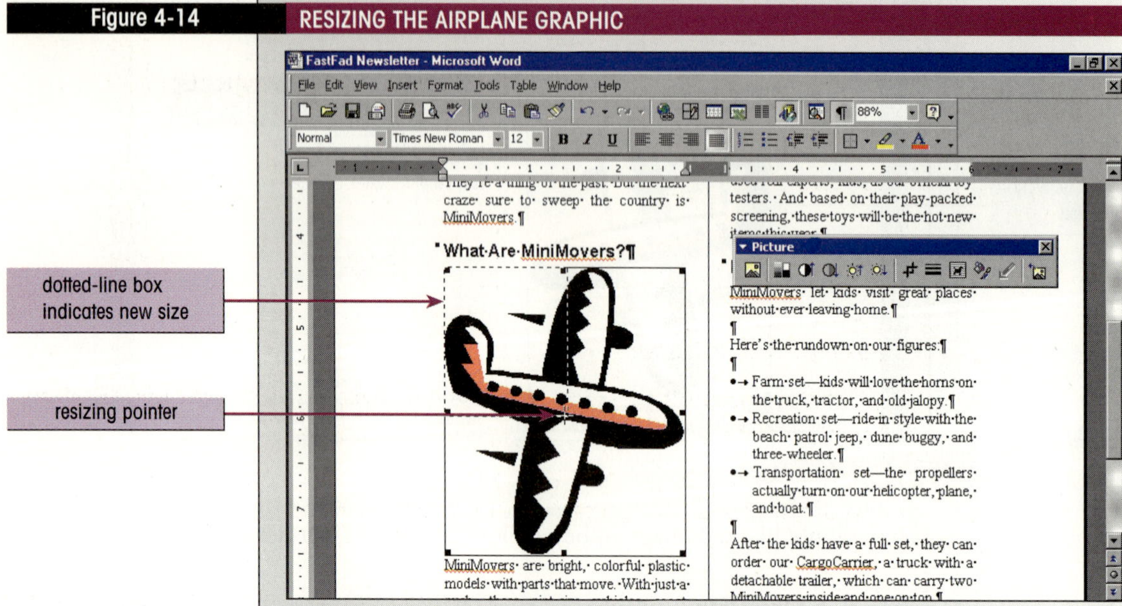

3. Release the mouse button. The airplane image is now about half as wide as the first column.

Gerrit wonders if the airplane image would look better if you cut off the back end and showed only the front half.

Cropping a Graphic

You can **crop** the graphic—that is, cut off one or more of its edges—using either the Crop button on the Picture toolbar or the Format Picture dialog box. Once you crop a graphic, the part you cropped is hidden from view. It remains a part of the graphic image, though, so you can change your mind and restore a cropped graphic to its original form.

To crop the airplane graphic:

1. If necessary, click the clip art to select it. The resize handles appear.
2. Click the **Crop** button on the Picture toolbar.
3. Position the pointer directly over the middle resize handle on the left side of the picture. The pointer changes to .
4. Press and hold down the mouse button, and drag the handle to the right so that only the wings and the nose of the plane are visible. See Figure 4-15.

Figure 4-15 CROPPING THE AIRPLANE GRAPHIC

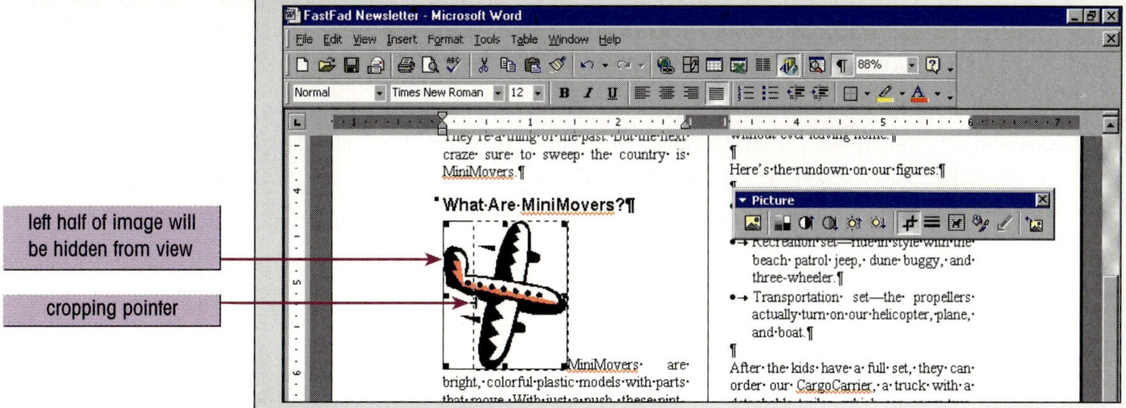

left half of image will be hidden from view

cropping pointer

5. Release the mouse button.

Gerrit decides he prefers to display the whole airplane, so he asks you to return to the original image.

6. Click the **Undo** button on the Standard toolbar. The cropping action is reversed, and the full image of the airplane reappears.

Now Gerrit wants you to make the text to wrap to the right of the graphic, making the airplane look as if it's flying into the text.

Wrapping Text Around a Graphic

For the airplane to look as though it flies into the newsletter text, you need to make the text wrap around the image. Earlier, you used text wrapping to position the WordArt title above the columns of text. Now you'll try a more advanced text-wrapping option to make the text follow the shape of the plane. You'll use the Format Picture dialog box to do this because it gives you more control over how the text flows around the picture.

To wrap text around the airplane graphic:

1. Verify that the airplane graphic is selected.

2. Click the **Format Picture** button on the Picture toolbar. The Format Picture dialog box opens.

3. Click the **Layout** tab. This tab contains a number of text-wrapping options, but to fine-tune the way text flows around the graphic, you need a more advanced set of options. You want the text to flow around the graphic, but only on the right side of the plane.

4. Click the **Advanced** button. The Advanced Layout dialog box opens.

5. Click the **Text Wrapping** tab, if necessary.

6. In the Wrapping style section, click the **Tight** icon, the second icon from the left.

7. In the Wrap text section, click the **Right only** option button. This option ensures that all text will flow to the right of the graphic. If you had used the options in the Layout tab (which you saw in Step 4), some of the text would have flowed into the white space to the left of the airplane, making the text difficult to read.

8. In the Distance from text section, click the **Right** up arrow once to display 0.2". Don't worry about the Left setting because the text will wrap only around the right side.

9. Click the **OK** button. You return to the Format Picture dialog box.

10. Click the **OK** button. The Format Picture dialog box closes.

11. Scroll down, if necessary, to view the picture. The text wraps to the right of the airplane, following its shape.

12. Click anywhere in the text to deselect the graphic, and then save the newsletter. Your screen should look similar to Figure 4-16.

Figure 4-16 TEXT WRAPPED AROUND GRAPHIC

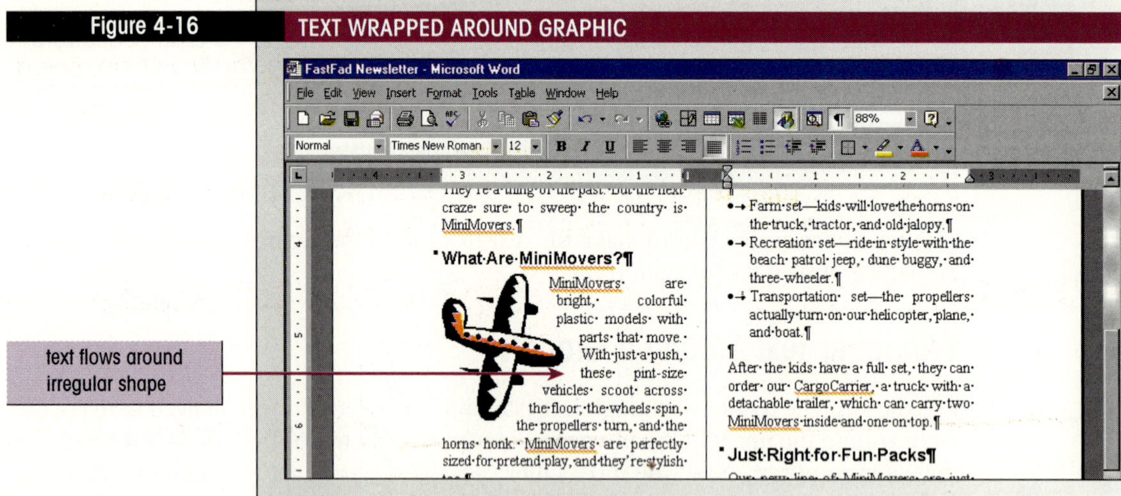

The image of the airplane draws the reader's attention to the beginning of the newsletter, but the rest of the text looks plain. Gerrit suggests adding a drop cap at the beginning of each section.

Inserting Drop Caps

A **drop cap** is a large, uppercase (capital) letter that highlights the beginning of the text of a newsletter, chapter, or some other document section. The drop cap usually extends from the top of the first line of the paragraph down two or three succeeding lines of the paragraph. The text of the paragraph wraps around the drop cap. Word allows you to create a drop cap for the first letter of the first word of a paragraph.

You will create a drop cap for the first paragraph following each heading in the newsletter (except for the first heading, where the clip-art image is located). The drop cap will extend two lines into the paragraph.

REFERENCE WINDOW RW

Inserting Drop Caps

- Click in the paragraph for which you want to create a drop cap.
- Click Format on the menu bar, and then click Drop Cap to open the Drop Cap dialog box.
- In the Position section, click the icon for the type of drop cap you want: Dropped or In Margin.
- Click the Font list arrow, and select the font you want for the drop cap.
- Set the appropriate number in the Lines to drop text box. This setting indicates the number of lines the drop cap will extend vertically into the text.
- If necessary, enter a new value for the Distance from text option, and click the OK button.

To insert drop caps in the newsletter:

1. Click in the paragraph following the first heading that starts with the word "Remember."
2. Click **Format** on the menu bar, and then click **Drop Cap**. The Drop Cap dialog box opens.
3. In the Position section, click the **Dropped** icon.
4. Click the **Lines to** drop down arrow once to display 2. You don't need to change the default distance from the text. See Figure 4-17.

Figure 4-17 DROP CAP DIALOG BOX

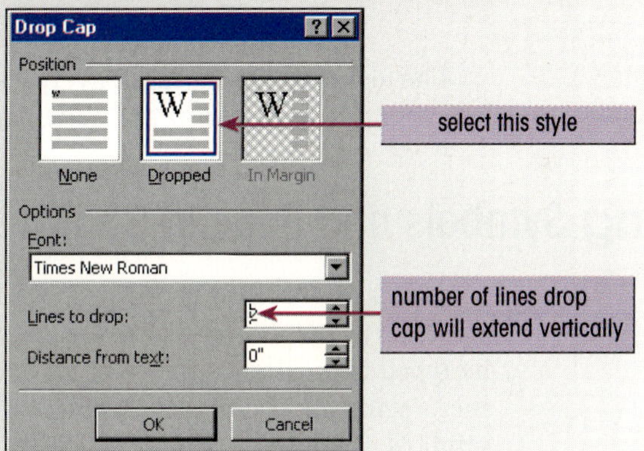

5. Click the **OK** button to close the dialog box, then click anywhere in the newsletter to deselect the new drop cap. Word formats the first character of the paragraph as a drop cap.
6. Click anywhere in the newsletter text to deselect the drop cap. See Figure 4-18.

Figure 4-18 DROP CAP BEGINS THE PARAGRAPH

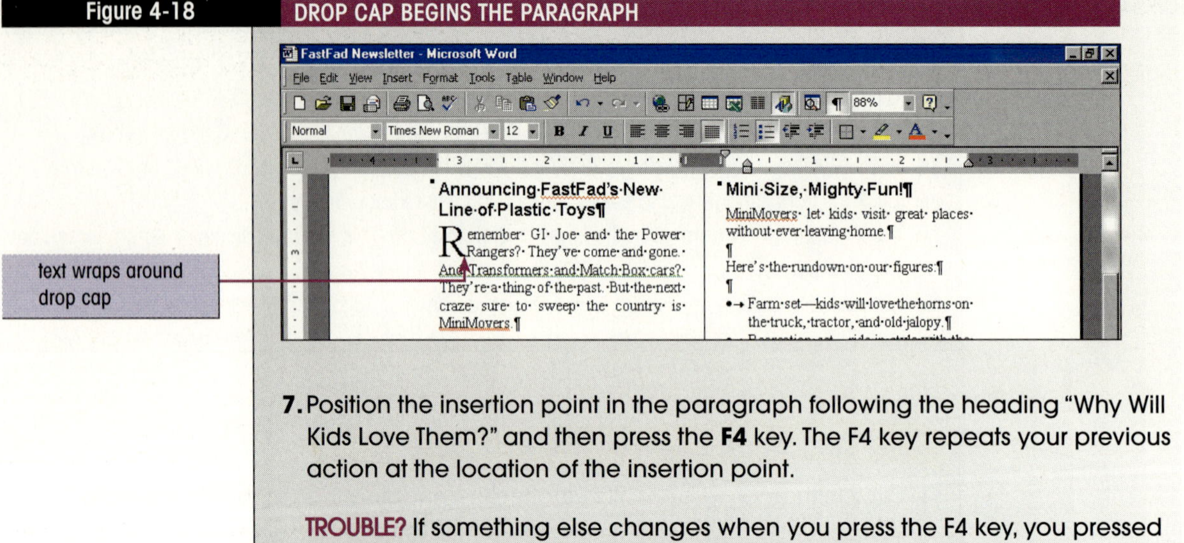

7. Position the insertion point in the paragraph following the heading "Why Will Kids Love Them?" and then press the **F4** key. The F4 key repeats your previous action at the location of the insertion point.

   TROUBLE? If something else changes when you press the F4 key, you pressed another key or performed another action after Step 6. Click the Undo button on the Standard toolbar, position the insertion point in the next paragraph to which you want to add a drop cap, and then repeat Steps 2 though 6 for the paragraph specified in Step 7.

8. Repeat Step 7 for the text under the remaining two headings. Don't use a drop cap in the paragraph with the airplane image because it would make the paragraph difficult to read. If necessary, use the horizontal scroll bar to bring the second column into view.

The newsletter looks more lively with the drop caps. Next, you turn your attention to the issue of inserting a registered trademark symbol beside the trademark names.

Inserting Symbols and Special Characters

Gerrit used standard word-processing characters rather than **typographic characters** (special symbols and punctuation marks) when he typed the newsletter copy. For example, he typed two dashes in place of an em dash. Word's AutoCorrect feature converts some of these standard characters (such as the dashes) into more polished-looking typographic symbols as you type. Figure 4-19 lists some of the characters that AutoCorrect automatically converts to symbols. In some cases, you need to press the spacebar before Word will convert the characters to the appropriate symbol.

Figure 4-19 COMMON TYPOGRAPHICAL SYMBOLS

TO INSERT THIS SYMBOL OR CHARACTER	TYPE	WORD CONVERTS IT TO
em dash	word--word	word—word
smiley	:)	☺
copyright symbol	(c)	©
registered trademark symbol	(r)	®
trademark symbol	(tm)	™
ordinal numbers	1st, 2nd, 3rd, etc.	1ST, 2ND, 3RD, etc.
fractions	1/2, 1/4	½, ¼
arrows	--> or <--	→ or ←

To insert typographic characters into a document after you've finished typing it, you also can use the Symbol command on the Insert menu.

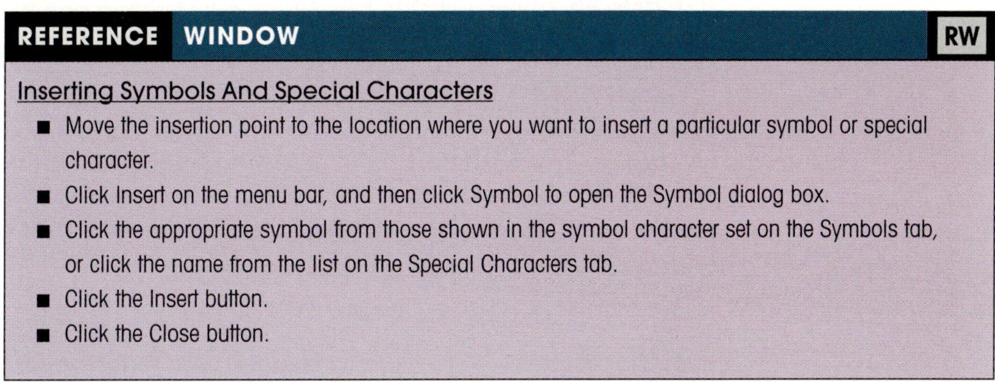

REFERENCE WINDOW RW

Inserting Symbols And Special Characters

- Move the insertion point to the location where you want to insert a particular symbol or special character.
- Click Insert on the menu bar, and then click Symbol to open the Symbol dialog box.
- Click the appropriate symbol from those shown in the symbol character set on the Symbols tab, or click the name from the list on the Special Characters tab.
- Click the Insert button.
- Click the Close button.

To make the newsletter look professionally formatted, you'll insert two special characters now—a registered trademark symbol and a trademark symbol—at the appropriate places.

FastFad protects the names of its products by registering the names as trademarks. You'll indicate that in the newsletter by inserting the registered trademark symbol (®) at the first occurrence of the trademark name "MiniMovers" and a trademark symbol (™) for the first occurrence of "CargoCarrier."

To insert the registered trademark symbol:

1. Position the insertion point at the end of the word "MiniMovers" in the first paragraph, just before the period.
2. Click **Insert** on the menu bar, and then click **Symbol** to open the Symbol dialog box.
3. If necessary, click the **Special Characters** tab. See Figure 4-20.

Figure 4-20 SPECIAL CHARACTERS TAB IN SYMBOL DIALOG BOX

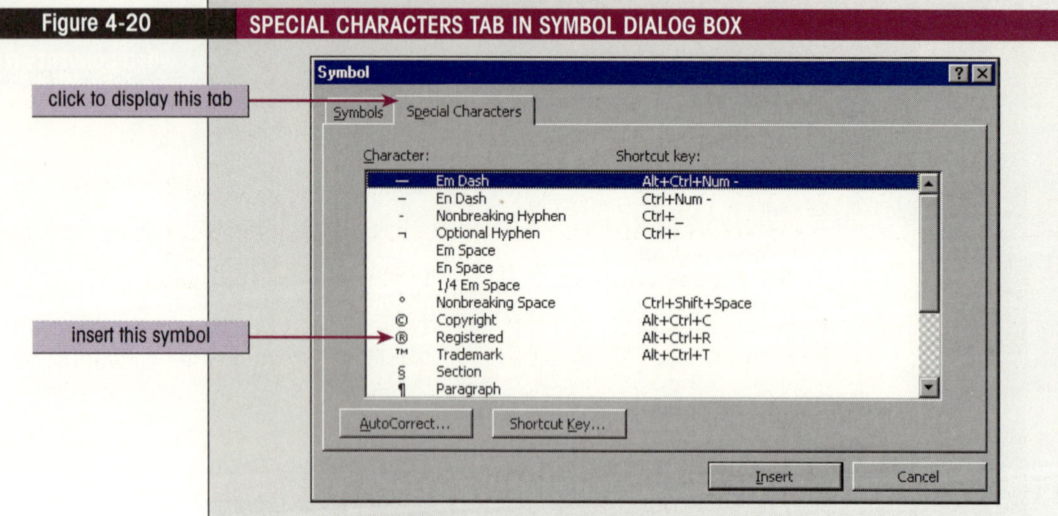

4. Click **Registered** to select it, and then click the **Insert** button. The dialog box stays open so you can insert additional symbols and characters in this location.
5. Click the **Close** button to close the Symbol dialog box. Word has inserted ® immediately after the word "MiniMovers."

If you have to insert symbols repeatedly, or if you want to insert them quickly as you type, it's often easier to use the Word AutoCorrect feature to insert them. You'll use AutoCorrect now to insert the trademark symbol (™) after the first occurrence of CargoCarrier. First, you'll look in the AutoCorrect settings to make sure the correct entry is there.

To enter a symbol using AutoCorrect:

1. Click **Tools** on the menu bar, and then click **AutoCorrect**. The AutoCorrect tab of the AutoCorrect dialog box opens. In the Replace column on the left side of the dialog box, you see (tm), which means that any occurrence of (tm) in the document will change to the trademark symbol. Now that you know the symbol is there, you'll try entering it in the document.
2. Click the **Cancel** button.
3. Position the insertion point just after the word "CargoCarrier" in the second column, in the paragraph above the heading "Just Right for Fun Packs."
4. Type **(tm)**. Word converts your typed characters into the trademark symbol.

The trademark symbols ensure that everyone who reads the newsletter is aware that these names are protected. Next, you decide to adjust the columns of text so they are approximately the same lengths.

Balancing the Columns

You could shift text from one column to another by adding blank paragraphs to move the text into the next column or by deleting blank paragraphs to shorten the text so it will fit into one column. The problem with this approach is that any edits you make could throw off the balance. Instead, Word can automatically balance the columns, or make them of equal length.

To balance the columns:

1. Position the insertion point at the end of the text in the right column, just after the period following the word "generation." Next, you need to change the zoom to Whole Page so you can see the full effect of the change.
2. Click the **Zoom** list arrow on the Standard toolbar, and then click **Whole Page**.
3. Click **Insert** on the menu bar, and then click **Break**. The Break dialog box opens.
4. Below "section break types," click the **Continuous** option button.
5. Click the **OK** button. Word inserts a continuous section break at the end of the text, which, along with the first section break you inserted earlier, defines the area in which it should balance the columns. As shown in Figure 4-21, Word balances the text between the two section breaks.

Figure 4-21 NEWSLETTER WITH BALANCED COLUMNS

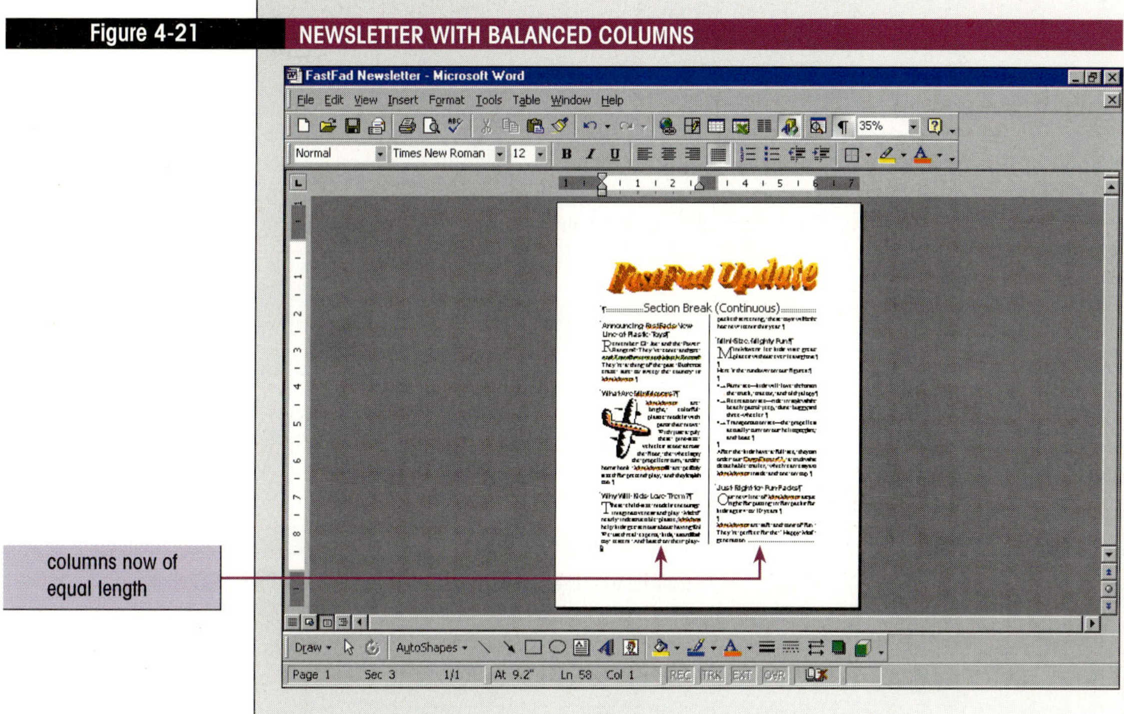

Drawing a Border Around the Page

Gerrit wants to give the newsletter a little more pizzazz. He suggests adding a border around the newsletter.

To draw a border around the newsletter:

1. Make sure the document is in print layout view and that the zoom setting is set to Whole Page so that you can see the entire newsletter.
2. Click **Format** on the menu bar, and then click **Borders and Shading**. The Borders and Shading dialog box opens.
3. Click the **Page Border** tab. You can use the Setting options, on the left side, to specify the type of border you want. In this case, you want a simple box.

4. In the Setting section, click the **Box** option. Now that you have selected the type of border you want, you can choose the style of line that will be used to create the border.

5. In the Style list box, scroll down and select the ninth style down from the top (the thick line with the thin line underneath), and then verify that the Apply to list option is set to Whole document. See Figure 4-22.

Figure 4-22 BORDERS AND SHADING DIALOG BOX

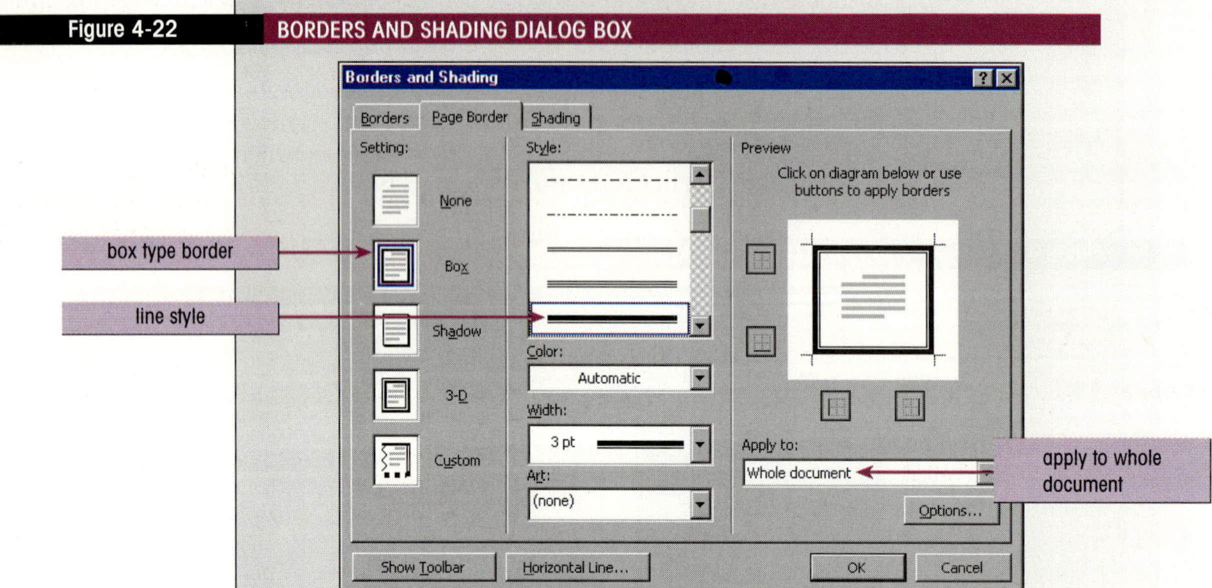

6. Click **OK**. The newsletter is now surrounded by an attractive border, as shown in Figure 4-23.

Figure 4-23 FINISHED NEWSLETTER

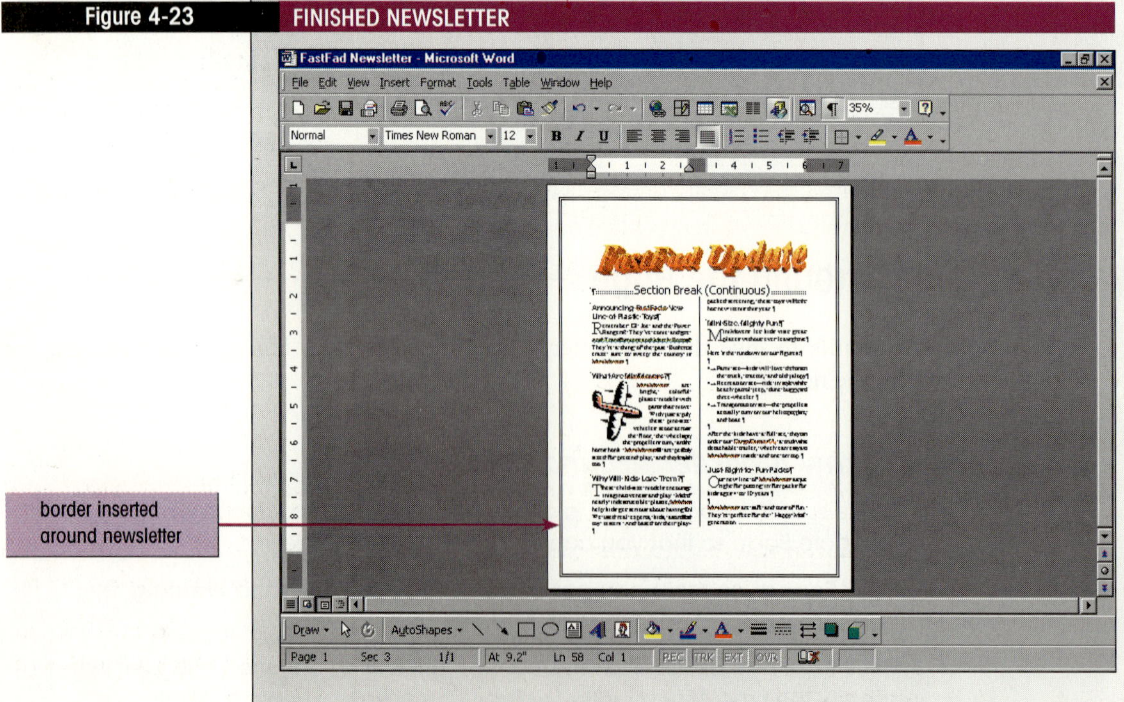

7. Save the completed newsletter as **FastFind Newsletter Final Copy** in the Tutorial folder for Tutorial 4.

8. Create a footer that centers "Prepared by *your name*" at the bottom of the document. Be sure to replace *your name* with your first and last name. Format the footer in a small font to make it as unobtrusive as possible.

9. Preview the newsletter and then print it. Unless you have a color printer, the orange and yellow letters of the title and the airplane will print in black and white.

10. If necessary, click the **Close** button on the Print Preview toolbar to return to print layout view, then close the newsletter and exit Word.

You give the printed newsletter to Gerrit, along with a copy on disk. He thinks it looks great and thanks you for your help. He'll print it later on a high-quality color printer (to get the best resolution for printing multiple copies) and distribute the newsletter to FastFad's sales staff.

Session 4.2 Quick Check

1. Define the following in your own words:

   a. drop cap
   b. scaling
   c. clip art
   d. balance

2. Explain how to insert a clip-art graphic in Word.

3. Describe a situation in which you would want to scale a graphic. Describe a situation in which you would want to crop a graphic.

4. True or False: When inserting a drop cap, you can specify the number of lines you want the drop cap to extend into the document vertically.

5. Describe two different methods for inserting the registered trademark symbol in a document.

6. Besides the Symbol command on the Insert menu, what is another way of entering typographic symbols?

7. Describe the process for drawing a border around the page.

REVIEW ASSIGNMENTS

Gerrit's FastFad newsletter was a success; the sales representatives all seemed to have good product knowledge, and the sales for MiniMovers were brisk. Now the sales reps want a product information sheet (similar to the newsletter) about another product, FastFad Action Pros, that they can print and send directly to their clients. You'll create that newsletter now.

1. If necessary, start Word and make sure your Data Disk is in the appropriate disk drive. Check your screen to make sure your settings match those in the tutorial and that the nonprinting characters and Drawing toolbar are displayed.

2. Open the file **FigSpecs** from the Review folder for Tutorial 4 on your Data Disk, and then save it as **Action Pros**.
3. In the second-to-last line of the document, replace "our toll free-number" with your name.
4. Click the Insert WordArt button on the Drawing toolbar.
5. Choose the WordArt style in the fourth row down, second column from the left.
6. Type "FastFad Pros" in the Edit WordArt Text dialog box, and then click OK.
7. Drag the WordArt above the first heading so that the anchor symbol is positioned to the left of the first paragraph symbol and so that the paragraph symbol is positioned below the WordArt on the screen.
8. Use the WordArt Shape button on the WordArt toolbar to apply the Inflate shape (fourth row down, leftmost column).
9. Click the Edit Text button on the WordArt toolbar and change the font to 32-point Times New Roman bold.
10. Use the Text Wrapping button on the WordArt toolbar to apply the Top and Bottom wrapping style.
11. Drag the lower-right and then the lower-left resize handles to enlarge the image to span the entire width between the left and right margins. Be sure to hold down the Shift key while you drag. Size the WordArt to make it approximately two-inches tall.
12. Save the document.
13. Position the insertion point to the left of the first word in the first heading, and then format the text into two columns using the Columns dialog box. Insert a section break so that the columns appear from this point forward. Do not insert a line between columns.
14. View the whole newsletter in print layout view, using the Whole Page zoom setting.
15. Return to Page Width zoom, and then position the insertion point at the beginning of the first paragraph, right before the phrase "FastFad Action Pros are the latest…".
16. Use the Insert Clip Art button on the Drawing toolbar to insert the baseball player clip-art image from the Sports & Leisure category.
17. Select and resize the sports image so it fits in the left half of the first column.
18. Click the Crop button on the Picture toolbar, and then try cropping the image horizontally and vertically by dragging the appropriate selection handles.
19. Use the Undo button to uncrop the image.
20. Select the picture, click the Format Picture button on the Picture toolbar, click the Layout tab, and then click the Advanced button. Set the Wrapping style to Tight, and wrap the text around the right side of the image.
21. Format a drop cap for the first paragraph following the "Five Sets of Figures" heading, using the default settings for the Dropped position.
22. Insert the trademark symbol after the first occurrence of "FastFad Action Pros."

Explore

23. As you might have noticed, Word automatically justifies text in newspaper columns, but you can easily change that alignment. Select both columns of text by clicking before the first word of text ("Product"), pressing and holding down the Shift key, and then clicking after the last word of text in the second column ("business"). Use the Align Left button on the Formatting toolbar to change the columns' text alignment to left alignment.

24. Make the columns of equal length by balancing the columns. Position the insertion point at the end of the document, click Insert on the menu bar, and then click Break. Below Section break types, click the Continuous option button, and then click the OK button.

Explore

25. A pull quote is a phrase or quotation taken from the text that summarizes a key point. To insert a pull quote, click the Text Box button on the Drawing toolbar, and then drag the pointer below the two columns to draw a text box that spans the page width and fills the space between the columns and the bottom margin. Use the Enter key to center the insertion point vertically in the text box. Type "FastFad: Playing is our business." Now format the text in the text box as 18-point Times New Roman italic, bold, and then use the Center button to center the text horizontally in the box.

Explore

26. You can use the Replace command to replace standard word-processing characters with typographic characters. To replace every occurrence of -- (two dashes) with — (an em dash), position the insertion point at the beginning of the first paragraph of text. Click Edit on the menu bar, and then click Replace. In the Find what text box, type "--" (two hyphens), and then press the Tab key to move the insertion point to the Replace with text box. Click the More button to display additional options and then click the Special button at the bottom of the dialog box. Click Em Dash in the list to display the special code Word has for em dashes in the Replace with text box. Click the Replace All button. When the operation is complete, click the OK button, and then click the Close button.

27. Add a border to the page using the Page Border command and the line style of your choice.

28. Look at the newsletter in print layout view, using the Whole Page zoom setting.

29. Preview, save, and print the document.

CASE PROBLEMS

Case 1. City of Madison, Wisconsin Claudia Mora is the manager of information systems for the city of Madison. She and her staff, along with the city manager, have just decided to convert all city computers from the Windows 3.1 operating system to Windows 98 and to standardize applications software on Microsoft Office 2000. Claudia writes a monthly newsletter on computer operations and training, so this month she decides to devote the newsletter to the conversion to Windows 98 and Microsoft Office 2000.

1. If necessary, start Word, make sure your Data Disk is in the appropriate drive, and check your screen to make sure your settings match those in the tutorial.

2. Open the file **CityComp** from the Cases folder for Tutorial 4 on your Data Disk, and then save the file as **Computer**.

Explore

3. If the text you want to format as WordArt has already been typed, you can cut it from the document and paste it into the WordArt dialog box. You can try this technique now. Cut the text of the newsletter title, "Computer News." Click the Insert WordArt button on the Drawing toolbar, and then choose the WordArt style in the third row down, second column from the left. Paste the text (using the Ctrl+V shortcut keys) into the Edit WordArt Text dialog box, and then click OK.

4. Drag the WordArt to the top of the newsletter, so that the anchor symbol is positioned to the left of the first paragraph symbol, and set the wrapping style to Top and Bottom.

5. In the Edit WordArt Text dialog box, set the font to 32-point Arial bold, then use the WordArt Shape button on the Drawing toolbar to apply the Arch Up (Curve) shape.

Explore

6. Experiment with changing the shape of the WordArt object by dragging the yellow adjustment handle.
7. Resize the WordArt object so that it spans the width of the page from left margin to right margin and so that its maximum height is about 1 inch. (*Hint:* Use the resize handles while watching the horizontal and vertical rulers in print layout view to adjust the object to the appropriate size.)
8. Center and italicize the subtitle of the newsletter, "Newsletter from the Madison Information Management Office."
9. Replace "INSERT YOUR NAME HERE" with your name, then center and italicize it.
10. Insert a continuous section break before the subtitle. (*Hint:* The section break may appear above the WordArt title, depending on where the anchor is positioned, but this is not a problem.)

Explore

11. To emphasize the subtitle paragraph with the city name, insert a border around all four sides and shade the paragraph using the Borders and Shading command. (*Hint:* In the Borders and Shading dialog box, click the Shading tab, select a light, see-through color from the Fill grid, such as Gray-15%, and then click OK.)
12. Move the insertion point to the beginning of the heading "The Big Switch." Then format the body of the newsletter into two newspaper-style columns; set the format of the columns so that no vertical rule appears between the columns. Use the This point forward option in the Apply to list box to make the columns a separate section.
13. Position the insertion point at the beginning of the first paragraph under the heading "Training on MS Office 2000," and insert the clip-art image from the Business category that shows a person using a laptop computer in front of a group.

Explore

14. Resize the picture so that it is 35 percent of its original size. Instead of dragging the resize handles as you did in the tutorial, use the Size tab in the Format Picture dialog box to scale the image. Adjust the Height and Width settings to 35 percent in the Scale section, and make sure the Lock aspect ratio check box is selected.

Explore

15. Click the Text Wrapping button on the Picture toolbar and select the Tight option.
16. Replace any double hyphens with typographic em dashes.
17. Make sure the newsletter fits on one page; if necessary, decrease the height of the WordArt title until the newsletter fits on one page.
18. Insert a border around the newsletter.
19. If necessary, balance the columns.
20. Save and print the newsletter, and then close it.

Case 2. Morning Star Movers Martin Lott is the executive secretary to Whitney Kremer, director of personnel for Morning Star Movers (MSM), a national moving company with headquarters in Minneapolis, Minnesota. Whitney assigned you the task of preparing the monthly newsletter News and Views, which provides news about MSM employees. You decide to update the layout and to use the desktop-publishing capabilities of Word to design the newsletter. You will use text assembled by other MSM employees for the body of the newsletter.

1. If necessary, start Word, make sure your Data Disk is in the appropriate drive, and check your screen to make sure your settings match those in the tutorial.

2. Open the file **MSM_NEWS** from the Cases folder for Tutorial 4 on your Data Disk, and then save it as **MSM Newsletter**.
3. Use the Find and Replace command to replace all instances of the name "Katrina" with your first name. Then replace all instances of "Pollei" with your last name.
4. Create a "News and Views" WordArt title for the newsletter, and set the font to 24-point Arial bold. Use the WordArt style in the third row, fourth column from the left, and set the shape of the text to Wave 2 (third row, sixth column from the left).
5. Drag the WordArt title to the top of the newsletter so that the anchor symbol is positioned to the left of the first paragraph symbol, and set the wrapping style to Top and Bottom.
6. Resize the WordArt proportionally so that the title spans the width of the page from left margin to right margin and so that the height of the title is about 1 inch. (*Hint:* Use the resize handles while watching the horizontal and vertical rulers in print layout view to adjust the object to the appropriate size.)
7. Format the body of the newsletter into two newspaper-style columns, and place a vertical rule between the columns.

Explore

8. You can change the structure of a newsletter by reformatting it with additional columns. Change the number of columns from two to three using the same technique you used in the previous step (that is, the Columns command on the Format menu). Make sure that the Equal column width check box is selected.

Explore

9. You can insert your own bitmapped graphics, stored on a disk, just as easily as you can insert clip art. Position the insertion point at the beginning of the paragraph below the heading "MSM Chess Team Takes Third." Click Insert on the menu bar, point to Picture, and then click From File. Look in the Cases folder for Tutorial 4 on your Data Disk, select the file named **Knight**, and then click the Insert button.

Explore

10. You can easily delete a graphic by selecting it, and then pressing the Delete key. To practice this technique, click the Knight graphic to select it, and then press the Delete key. To reinsert the graphic, click the Undo button.

Explore

11. Scale the height and the width of the picture to 60 percent of its original size. (*Hint:* To scale the size, use the Format Picture button on the Picture toolbar, and then set the Scale values on the Size tab, making sure the Lock aspect ratio check box is selected.)

Explore

12. Use the Picture tab in the Format Picture dialog box, and change the values in the Crop from text boxes. Crop 0.3, 0.4, 0.2, and 0.4 inches from the left, right, top, and bottom of the picture, respectively.
13. Wrap the text around the clip art.
14. Format drop caps in the first paragraph after each heading except the "MSM Chess Team Takes Third" heading. Use the default settings for number of lines, but change the font of the drop cap to Arial.
15. View the entire page. If necessary, decrease the height of the WordArt title or change the page margins until the entire newsletter fits onto one page and until each column starts with a heading.
16. Add a border around the entire page of the newsletter using the Page Border command.
17. Save the newsletter, and then preview and print it. Close the document.

Case 3. Lake Mendota Wellness Clinic The Lake Mendota Wellness Clinic, located in Vicksburg, Mississippi, is a private company that contracts with small and large businesses to promote health and fitness among their employees. Mary Anne Logan, an exercise physiologist, is director of health and fitness at the clinic. As part of her job, she writes a newsletter for the employees of the companies with which the clinic contracts. She's asked you to transform her document into a polished, desktop-published newsletter.

1. If necessary, start Word, make sure your Data Disk is in the appropriate drive, and check your screen to make sure your settings match those in the tutorials.
2. Open the file **Wellness** from the Cases folder for Tutorial 4 on your Data Disk, and then save it as **Wellness Newsletter**.
3. In the third line, replace "YOUR NAME HERE" with your first and last names.
4. At the beginning of the newsletter, create a WordArt title "Feeling Good." Choose any WordArt style that you feel would be appropriate to the newsletter content, and set the font to 24-point, italic Times New Roman.
5. Set the shape of the text to any option that looks appropriate to the subject matter.
6. Move the title to the top of the document, so the anchor symbol is positioned to the left of the first paragraph symbol.
7. ***Explore*** Add a shadow to the WordArt title (or adjust the existing one) by clicking the Shadow button on the Drawing toolbar and selecting a Shadow option. Then use the Shadow Settings option on the Shadow button to open the Shadow Settings toolbar. Click the Shadow Color button on the Shadow Settings toolbar, select a good color for the shadow, then close the Shadow Settings toolbar. For the purpose of this exercise, choose a shadow style that is behind the text, not in front of it.
8. ***Explore*** Rotate the WordArt 90 degrees. (*Hint:* In the Format WordArt dialog box, click the Size tab and set the Rotation option to 90 degrees.)
9. ***Explore*** Resize the WordArt graphic box so that the WordArt object spans the height of the page from the top margin to the bottom margin and the width of the object is about 1 inch. (*Hint:* Use the resize handles while watching the horizontal and vertical rulers in print layout view to adjust the object to the appropriate size.)
10. Drag the WordArt object to the right edge of the page.
11. Use the Advanced wrapping options to change the Wrapping style to Square and Left only.
12. At the top of the page, italicize the subtitles, the line that contains the issue volume and number of the newsletter, and the line that contains your name.
13. Format the body of the newsletter as a separate section, in two newspaper-style columns with a vertical rule between the columns. (*Hint:* The columns' widths will be uneven because the WordArt title takes up part of the second column space.)
14. To the right of each of the words "NordicTrack" and "HealthRider," insert a registered trademark symbol (®), and then change the font size of the symbol to 8 points. (*Hint:* Highlight the symbol and change the font size.)
15. Balance the columns.
16. Save the newsletter, and then preview and print it. Close the document.

Case 4. New Home Newsletter You've just moved to a new part of the country and decide to send out a newsletter to friends and family describing your new home. In the one-page newsletter, you'll include articles about you and your family or friends, your new job, your new abode, and future plans. You'll desktop publish the copy into a professional-looking newsletter.

1. If necessary, start Word, make sure your Data Disk is in the appropriate drive, and check your screen to make sure your settings match those in the tutorials.
2. Write two articles to include in the newsletter; save each article in a separate file.
3. Plan the general layout of your newsletter.
4. Create a title ("New Home News") for your newsletter with WordArt.
5. Save the document as **New Home** in the Cases folder for Tutorial 4.
6. Insert the current date and your name as editor below the title.

Explore

7. Insert the articles you wrote into your newsletter. Position the insertion point where you want the first article to appear, click Insert on the menu bar, click File, select the article you want to insert, and then click the Insert button. Repeat to insert the second article.
8. Format your newsletter with multiple columns.
9. Insert at least one clip-art picture into your newsletter, and wrap text around it.
10. Format at least two drop caps in the newsletter.

Explore

11. Create a border around the page and then add shading to the entire document using the Shading and Borders command on the Format menu. (*Hint:* Click CTRL+A to select the entire document, open the Borders and Shading dialog box, select a page border, click the Shading tab, select a light, see-through color from the Fill grid, such as Gray-15%, and then click OK.)
12. Save and print the newsletter, and then close the document.

INTERNET ASSIGNMENTS

The purpose of the Internet Assignments is to challenge you to find information on the Internet that you can use to create effective documents. The actual assignments are updated and maintained on the Course Technology Web site. Log on to the Internet and use your Web browser to go to the Student Online Companion to accompany this text at **www.course.com/NewPerspectives/office2000**. Click the Word link, and then click the link for Tutorial 4.

QUICK CHECK ANSWERS

Session 4.1

1. (list 4) The printing is high-quality; the document uses multiple fonts; the document incorporates graphics; the document uses typographic characters; the document uses columns and other special formatting features.
2. (a) Using a desktop computer system to producing commercial-quality printed material. With desktop publishing you can enter and edit text, create graphics, lay out pages, and print documents. (b) An image whose appearance you can change using the Drawing toolbar or WordArt toolbar (c) The unformatted text of a newsletter (d) A symbol that appears in the left margin, which shows a WordArt object's position in relation to the text
3. False
4. False
5. To resize a WordArt object, select the object and drag its resize handles. To resize the WordArt object proportionally, press and hold the Shift key as you drag a resize handle.
6. The WordArt Shape button allows you to change the basic shape of a WordArt object.
7. True
8. True

Session 4.2

1. (a) a large, uppercase letter that highlights the beginning of the text of a newsletter, chapter, or some other document section; (b) resizing an image to better fit a document; (c) existing, copyright-free artwork that you can insert into your document; (d) to make columns of equal length
2. Position the insertion point at the location where you want to insert the image, click the Insert Clip Art button on the Drawing toolbar, click the Pictures tab in the Insert ClipArt window, click the category that best represents the type of art you need, click the image you want to use, click the Insert clip button.
3. You might scale a graphic to better fit the width of a column of text. You might crop a graphic to emphasize or draw attention to a particular part of the image or to eliminate unnecessary borders.
4. True
5. Click where you want to insert the symbol in the document, click Insert on the menu bar, click Symbol, click the Special Characters tab in the Symbol dialog box, click Registered Trademark in the list, click the Insert button, and then click the Close button. Type (tm).
6. Using the AutoCorrect feature, which lets you type certain characters and then changes those characters into the corresponding symbol
7. Click Format on the menu bar, click Borders and Shading, click the Page Border tab in the Borders and Shading dialog box, select the border type you want in the Setting section, choose a line style from the Style list box, make sure Whole document appears in the Apply to list box, and then click OK.

LEVEL II

New Perspectives on

MICROSOFT® WORD 2000

Read This Before You Begin

To the Student

Data Disks

To complete the Level II tutorials, Review Assignments, and Case Problems in this book, you need three Data Disks. Your instructor will either provide you with Data Disks or ask you to make your own.

If you are making your own Data Disks, you will need three blank, formatted high-density disks. You will need to copy a set of folders from a file server or standalone computer or the Web onto your disks. Your instructor will tell you which computer, drive letter, and folders contain the files you need. You could also download the files by going to www.course.com, clicking Data Disk Files, and following the instructions on the screen.

The following list shows you which folders go on each of your disks, so that you will have enough disk space to complete all the tutorials, Review Assignments, and Case Problems:

Data Disk 1

Write this on the disk label:
Data Disk 1: Level II Tutorial 5

Put these folders on the disk:
Tutorial.05

Data Disk 2

Write this on the disk label:
Data Disk 2: Level II Tutorial 6

Put these folders on the disk:
Tutorial.06

Data Disk 3

Write this on the disk label:
Data Disk 3: Level II Tutorial 7

These folders need to be put on the hard drive:
Tutorial.07

When you begin each tutorial, be sure you are using the correct Data Disk. See the inside front or inside back cover of this book for more information on Data Disk files, or ask your instructor or technical support person for assistance.

Course Lab

The Level II tutorials in this book feature one interactive Course Lab to help you understand Internet World Wide Web concepts. There are Lab Assignments at the end of Tutorial 7 that relate to this Lab.

To start a Lab, click the **Start** button on the Windows taskbar, point to **Programs**, point to **Course Labs**, point to **New Perspectives Applications**, and click The Internet World Wide Web.

Using Your Own Computer

If you are going to work through this book using your own computer, you need:

- **Computer System** Microsoft Word 2000 and Windows 95 or higher must be installed on your computer. This book assumes a complete installation of Word 2000.
- **Data Disks** You will not be able to complete the tutorials or exercises in this book using your own computer until you have Data Disks.
- **Course Lab** See your instructor or technical support person to obtain the Course Lab software for use on your own computer.

Visit Our World Wide Web Site

Additional materials designed especially for you are available on the World Wide Web. Go to http://www.course.com.

To the Instructor

The Data Files and Course Lab are available on the Instructor's Resource Kit for this title. Follow the instructions in the Help file on the CD-ROM to install the programs to your network or standalone computer. For information on creating Data Disks or the Course Lab, see the "To the Student" section above. Please note, students need to install the data files for Tutorial 7 onto their hard drives due to the complexity of the tutorial.

You are granted a license to copy the Data Files and Course Lab to any computer or computer network used by students who have purchased this book.

CREATING STYLES, OUTLINES, TABLES, AND TABLES OF CONTENTS

Writing a Business Plan for EstimaTech

OBJECTIVES

In this tutorial you will:

- Use the Thesaurus
- Create a new folder
- Use fonts appropriately to add interest to a document
- Create and modify styles
- Attach a template to a document and create a new one
- Create and modify an outline
- Hyphenate the document
- Add footnotes and endnotes
- Insert text with Click and Type
- Apply text highlighting
- Adjust Character and Paragraph spacing
- Create a table of contents and browse by headings

CASE

EstimaTech

Chiu Lee Hwang and Robert Camberlango, recent college graduates majoring in computer science, earned their college tuition by working summers and vacations for a company that specializes in historically accurate renovations of older homes. Their employer asked them to use their computer skills to help him estimate the cost of restoring or renovating buildings and homes. They developed a computer program for the task that lets them easily create well-formatted documents they can present to potential customers. It has worked so well that Chiu Lee and Robert have decided to develop it commercially and call it EstimaQuote. They hope to sell the product to contractors, subcontractors, and individuals, as well as to agencies and foundations.

To bring the product to market, Chiu Lee and Robert must secure a $475,000 loan from Commercial Financial Bank of New England for the start-up of EstimaTech, the company that will let them fine-tune the product for commercial use and let them market the software. To obtain the necessary financing, Chiu Lee and Robert are writing a business plan—a report that details all aspects of starting a new business, including market, operations, financial information, and personnel. They have written a draft of the plan and asked you to help them complete it.

SESSION 5.1

In this session, you'll see how Chiu Lee and Robert planned their report. Then you'll open the report and use the Microsoft Word Thesaurus to edit the report. You'll learn about using fonts and then modify, create, and apply styles to format the report.

Planning the Document

A thorough business plan informs prospective investors about the purpose, organization, goals, and projected profits of the proposed business. It also analyzes the target industry, including available market research. A business plan should convince readers that the venture is viable, well-thought-out, and worthy of funding. Chapter 2 of the EstimaTech business plan analyzes the industry and discusses the market research on potential customers for the new cost-estimating software.

Chiu Lee and Robert want to follow a standard business plan organization. The industry analysis begins by explaining how they performed the market research, followed by a summary of the results. They also want to include a table of contents for the chapter. Chiu Lee and Robert use facts and statistics in their business plan to convince potential investors that the company would be profitable and that the cost-estimating software would fill an existing need in the marketplace. They write in a formal business style.

Chiu Lee and Robert have begun to format the document but want you to check the fonts, headers, and styles and make sure the formatting is consistent. They also need you to create a table of contents. You'll start by creating a new folder in which to store your version of the document.

Creating a New Folder

Chiu Lee and Robert have written a draft of Chapter 2 of their business plan. You'll begin by opening a draft of Chapter 2. Robert wants you to create a new folder for this chapter. You'll create the folder and then save the document in the new folder, using a different filename.

To open the document and save it in a new folder:

1. Start Word, if necessary, make sure your Data Disk is in the appropriate drive, and check the screen. For this tutorial, make sure that the ruler appears below the Formatting toolbar and that the nonprinting characters are displayed.
2. Open the file **Industry** from the Tutorial subfolder in the Tutorial.05 folder on your Data Disk.
3. Click **File** on the menu bar, and then click **Save As** to display the Save As dialog box. You'll now create a new folder called Chapter 2 within the Tutorial folder.
4. Click the **Create New Folder** button located near the top of the Save As dialog box. The New Folder dialog box opens, as shown in Figure 5-1.

Figure 5-1 NEW FOLDER DIALOG BOX

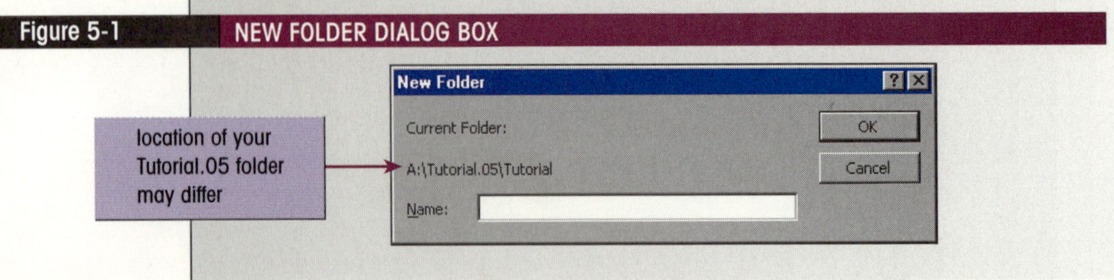

5. Type **Chapter 2**, the name of the new folder, and then click the **OK** button. The new folder now appears in the Save in list box, at the top of the Save As dialog box.
6. Save the document in the new Chapter 2 folder using the filename **Industry Analysis**.

Now, the **Industry Analysis** document is in the Chapter 2 folder. Before you begin formatting this document, read through it carefully to check for word usage.

Using the Thesaurus

Under the heading "Size of the Market" on page 2, the word "restore" occurs twice, and Robert has asked you to find another word that has the same meaning for the second occurrence. You can do this easily using the Thesaurus. The **Thesaurus** is a Word feature that contains a list of words and their synonyms. Similar to a thesaurus reference book, the Word Thesaurus lets you look up a specific word and then find its synonyms and related words. After you have found an appropriate replacement word, you can immediately substitute the word you looked up with its synonym. The Thesaurus is a good editing tool to help make your word choices varied and exact.

REFERENCE WINDOW

Using the Thesaurus

- Move the insertion point anywhere within the word that you want to replace with a synonym.
- Click Tools on the menu bar, point to Language, and then click Thesaurus.
- In the Meanings list box, click the word that most closely defines the selected word.
- In the Replace with Synonym list box, scroll to find a good replacement word.
- Click the replacement word, and then click the Replace button.

You'll use the Thesaurus to find a synonym for the word "restore" in the "Size of Market" paragraph.

To find a synonym for "restore" using the Thesaurus:

1. Below the heading "Size of Market," click the second occurrence of the word "restore". If necessary, you can use the Find command on the Edit menu to find the first occurrence and then click the Find Next button to go to the second occurrence.
2. Click **Tools** on the menu bar, point to **Language**, and then click **Thesaurus**. The Thesaurus: English (U.S.) dialog box opens. The word "restore" appears in the Looked Up list box. Two words, each representing a related definition, appear in the Meanings list box, and several synonyms of the selected meaning "reinstate" appear in the Replace with Synonym list box.

   The meaning of "restore" closest to your meaning is "refurbish."

3. Click **refurbish (v.)** in the Meanings list box. The synonyms for "refurbish" appear in the Replace with Synonyms list box on the right. Your Thesaurus dialog box should look similar to Figure 5-2, although your list of synonyms may differ. Robert feels that "renovate" is the best synonym.

Figure 5-2 THESAURUS DIALOG BOX WITH SYNONYMS FOR "RESTORE"

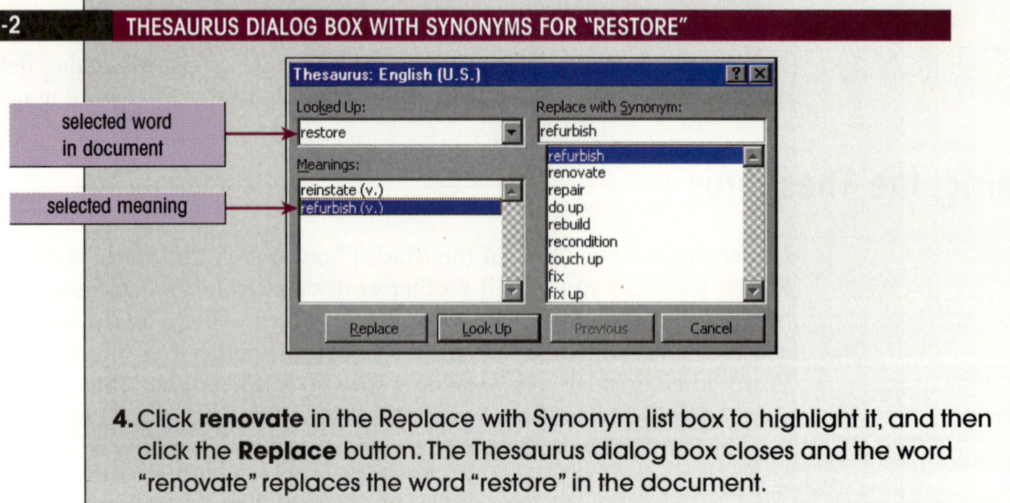

4. Click **renovate** in the Replace with Synonym list box to highlight it, and then click the **Replace** button. The Thesaurus dialog box closes and the word "renovate" replaces the word "restore" in the document.

As you can see, the Thesaurus helps you increase your word power as you write. Now that you know that the text of the chapter is finished, you work on its appearance. To create a professional-looking document, you need to understand how to use fonts effectively, as the following section explains.

Choosing Fonts

Although the Word default font is Times New Roman, this is not the best font for many documents. In fact, Times New Roman was specifically designed for narrow-column newspaper text. For books, manuals, and other documents that have wider columns, a wider font is easier to read. Here are some general principles that might help you decide which fonts to use in your documents:

- Use a serif font as the main text of your documents. A **serif** is a small embellishment at the tips of the lines of a character, as shown in Figure 5-3.

Figure 5-3 SERIF AND SANS SERIF FONTS

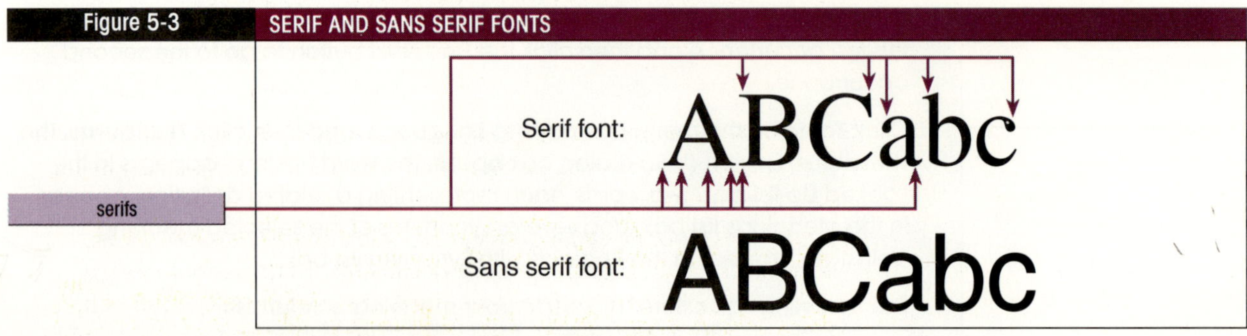

- Common serif fonts include Baskerville Old Face, Book Antiqua, Century Schoolbook (also called New Century Schoolbook), Courier, Garamond, Goudy Old Style, Rockwell, and Times New Roman, some of which are shown in Figure 5-4. Because serif fonts are easy to read, they are appropriate not only for the main text but also for titles and headings.

Figure 5-4 SAMPLE SERIF FONTS

Century Schoolbook

Courier

Garamond

Times New Roman

- "Sans" is French for "without"; thus, a **sans serif font** is a font without the embellishments. Generally, you should avoid sans serif fonts except in titles, headings, headers and footers, captions, and other special parts of the document. Examples of common sans serif fonts include Arial, Arial Narrow, Century Gothic, Eras Light, Eurostile, Franklin Gothic Book, and Lucida Sans, some of which are shown in Figure 5-5. Studies have shown that large blocks of text in sans serif font are harder to read than serif fonts. However, sans serif fonts in titles and headings are attractive and legible.

Figure 5-5 SAMPLE SANS SERIF FONTS

Arial

Arial Narrow

Century Gothic

Franklin Gothic Book

- Avoid all-uppercase sans serif text, which is difficult to read. All-uppercase serif font is easier to read, but mixed uppercase and lowercase text in any font is better still.
- Avoid unusual or fancy fonts except for use in certificates, invitations, advertisements, and other specialty documents. Examples of fonts that might be appropriate in these specialty documents include Brush Script, Braggadocio, French Script, Lucida Blackletter, Monotype Corsiva, and Stencil, as shown in Figure 5-6.

Figure 5-6 SAMPLE SPECIALTY FONTS

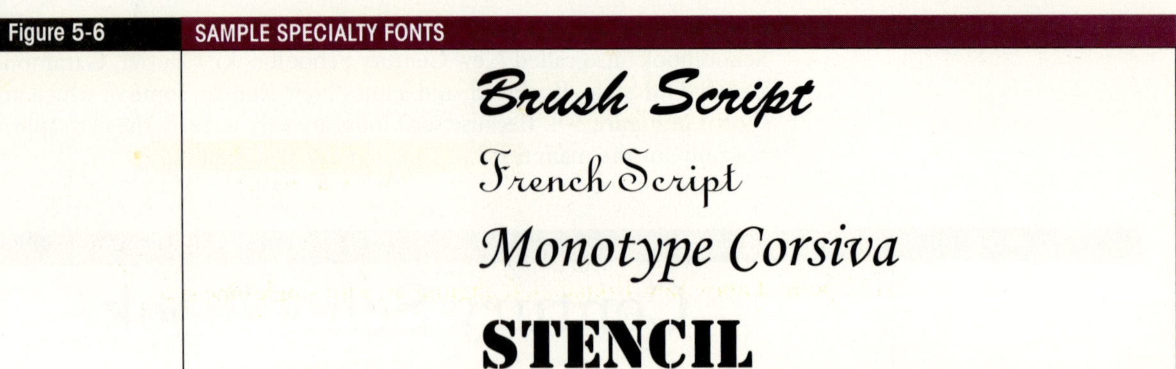

- Avoid excessive changes in fonts and font attributes. Typically, the text of a document should include only one or two fonts—one for the main paragraphs and another one for the titles and headings. Excessive use of boldface and italics makes documents cluttered and sloppy and detracts attention from the content.
- You can add special effects to most fonts by adjusting the formatting settings in the Font dialog box. (To open this dialog box, click Format on the menu bar, and then click Font.) Among other things, you can format a font as small caps (a reduced version of regular capital letters), superscript (slightly above the main line), subscript (slightly below the main line), outline (only the outline of the letters), or with shadows. Figure 5-7 shows samples of common font effects. Take care not to overuse these effects, or your document will end up looking cluttered and unprofessional.

Figure 5-7 COMMON FONT EFFECTS

SMALL CAPS

Super^{script}

Sub$_{\text{script}}$

Outline

Shadow

Robert wants you to choose some appropriate fonts and apply them to the business plan. As you'll see, the most efficient way to apply fonts is to use the Style list arrow in the Formatting toolbar.

Using Styles

As you know, it's often helpful to use the Format Painter to copy formatting from one paragraph to another. However, when you're working on a long document, you'll find it easier to use the sets of predefined formats known as **styles**. Every Word document opens with a set of styles that includes: Normal (the default style for paragraphs in a Word document), Heading 1, Heading 2, and Heading 3. Word's default Normal style is defined as 12 point Times New Roman, left alignment, with single-line spacing.

All available styles are listed in the Style list on the Formatting toolbar, as shown in Figure 5-8. To apply a style, you select the text you want to format, and then select the desired style in the style list. The Style list includes both character and paragraph styles. A **paragraph style** is a style that you apply to complete paragraphs, including one-line paragraphs such as titles and headings. (To apply a paragraph style to a particular paragraph, you must first select the paragraph or simply move the insertion point to any location within the paragraph.) A **character style** is a style that you apply to a single character or to a selection of characters, such as a phrase, sentence, or paragraph. (To apply a character style, you must first select the character or range of characters you want to format.) It might help you understand the difference between the two types of styles if you keep in mind that character styles generally affect font-related options, such as font styles and font sizes. Paragraph styles can include font options, but also have other options generally associated with page formatting, such as line spacing and margins.

Character styles are indicated in the style list by an "a" in the gray box to the right of the style name (for example, the Page Number style in Figure 5-8). Paragraph styles are indicated by a paragraph icon in the gray box (for example, the Heading 1 style in Figure 5-8). The font size of a particular style also appears in the gray box. For example, the Footer style is 12 point. All styles in the list appear with the formatting characteristics applied so you can see what they look like before choosing one. The style of the current paragraph (the paragraph where the insertion point is located) appears in the Style list box on the Formatting toolbar.

Figure 5-8 DEFAULT STYLES IN THE STYLE LIST BOX

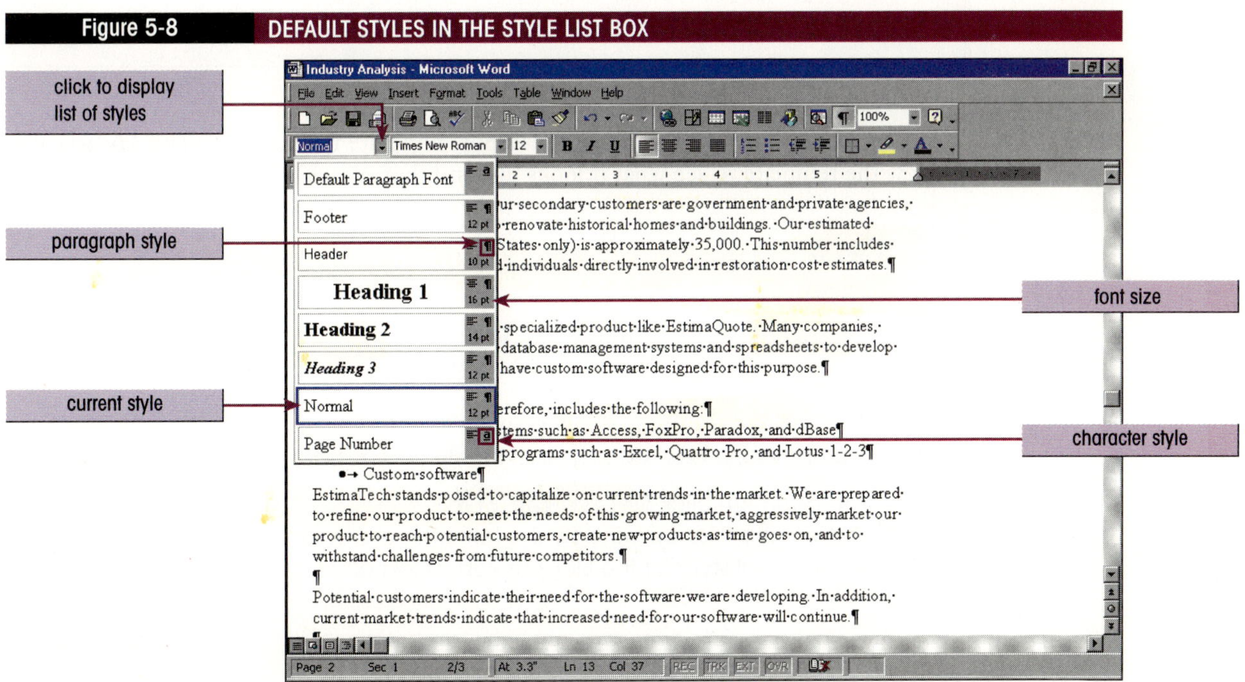

Using a Word Template

A **template** is a set of predefined styles designed for a specific type of document. For example, Word provides templates for formatting reports, brochures, memos, letters, or resumes. The Word default template, the Normal template, contains the Normal paragraph style described earlier. You can change the available styles by attaching a different template to a document. Also, you can use a Word template as the basis for a completely new document.

Another Word feature, related to templates, is known as a theme. A **theme** is a unified design for a document that can include background colors, horizontal and vertical lines, and graphics. Themes are designed for documents you plan to present online. Because elements of a theme can be distracting, you should use templates rather than themes for professional documents, especially those you'll print on a black and white printer.

Attaching a template requires two steps. First, you attach the template to the document. Then you apply the template's styles to the various parts of the document. You'll begin by attaching a new template to Robert's document. Notice that the process of attaching a predefined Word template is different from attaching a template you create yourself. In this section, you'll learn how to attach a Word template. Later in this chapter, you'll learn how to attach a newly created template. You'll have a chance to use a template as the basis for a brand-new document in the review assignments at the end of this chapter.

REFERENCE WINDOW RW

Attaching a Word Template to a Document

- Click Format on the menu bar, click Theme, and then click the Style Gallery button to open the Style Gallery dialog box.
- In the Template list box, click the template you want to preview.
- In the Preview box, click the Document option button to see how the template's Normal styles look when applied to your document, or click the Example option button to see a sample file that uses all the template styles.
- Click the OK button to attach the template to your document.

Robert would like to use the Elegant Report template for his document. He asks you to preview the template to see what it looks like and then attach it to the draft of Chapter 2.

To preview and attach the Elegant Report template to your document:

1. Click **Format** on the menu bar, and then click **Theme**. The Theme dialog box opens.

2. Click the **Style Gallery** button. The Style Gallery dialog box opens, with the first page of the document displayed in the Preview window.

3. Scroll to and then click **Elegant Report** in the Template list box to select the template. In the Preview window, the text of your document changes to reflect the new Normal style for the Elegant Report template. See Figure 5-9.

Figure 5-9 STYLE GALLERY WITH PREVIEW OF ELEGANT REPORT TEMPLATE

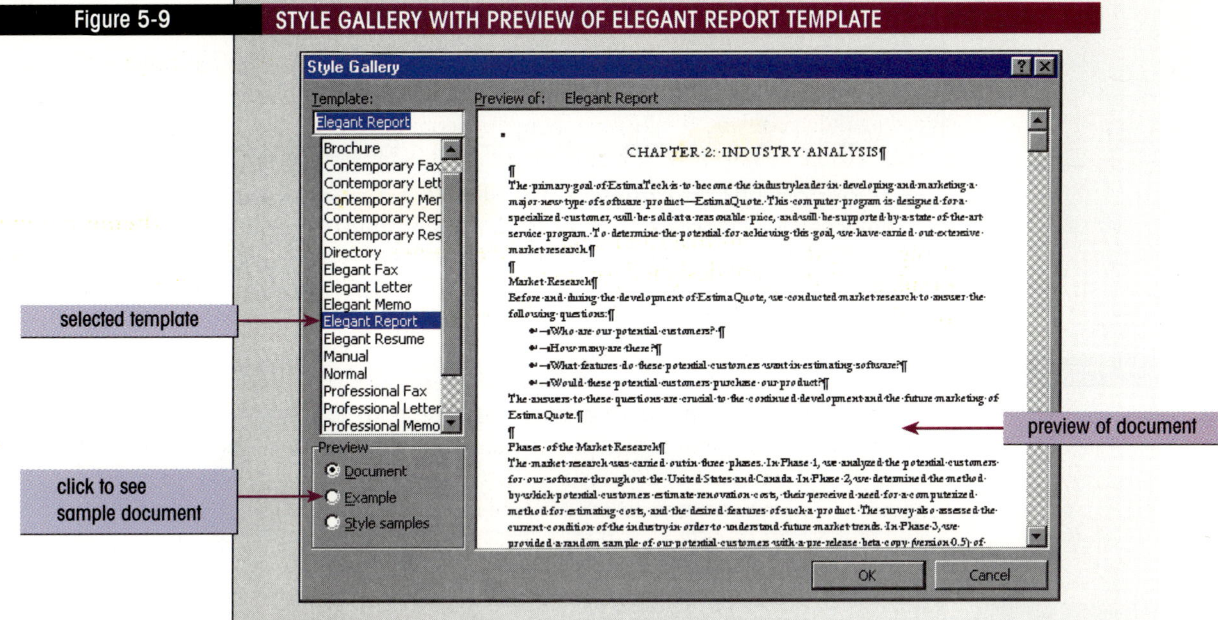

TROUBLE? If you see a message asking if you would like to install the Elegant Report template, insert the Office 2000 CD into your CD-ROM drive, and then click Yes. If the Office 2000 CD is not available to you, choose another template.

4. In the Preview box, click the **Example** option button to see a sample document that uses all the Elegant Report template styles. Scroll through the sample document to preview all the styles that are available in this template.

5. Click the **OK** button to attach the template to the report and return to the document window. The template's Normal style (11-point Garamond) is applied to the entire document except for the title, which is formatted in 12 point Garamond. You'll see the various styles of the Elegant Report template when you apply them in the next section.

6. Click the **Style list arrow** on the Formatting toolbar. Scroll through the style list to verify that the styles of the Elegant Report template are now available in this document, and then click the **Style list arrow** again to close the style list.

Now that the Elegant Report template is attached to the report, you can begin applying its styles to the document.

Applying Styles

The best way to apply a template's styles to a document is to move the insertion point to (or highlight) individual parts of the document and then select the appropriate style from the Style list on the Formatting toolbar. For example, to format the chapter title, you could highlight "Chapter 2: Industry Analysis" at the top of the first page and then select the Heading 1 style from the Style list.

You'll apply the Elegant Report template styles now, beginning with the chapter title.

To apply styles to the chapter:

1. Click anywhere within the chapter title ("Chapter 2: Industry Analysis") near the top of the first page.
2. Click the **Style list** arrow on the Formatting toolbar to open the Style list.
3. Scroll down the list, and then click **Heading 1**. Word applies the style to the selected text. Notice that the font of the Heading 1 style is 9-point Garamond bold. Note that this style also changes the title to all capital letters and centers the title on the page, with horizontal lines above and below. See Figure 5-10.

Figure 5-10 TITLE FORMATTED WITH HEADING 1 STYLE

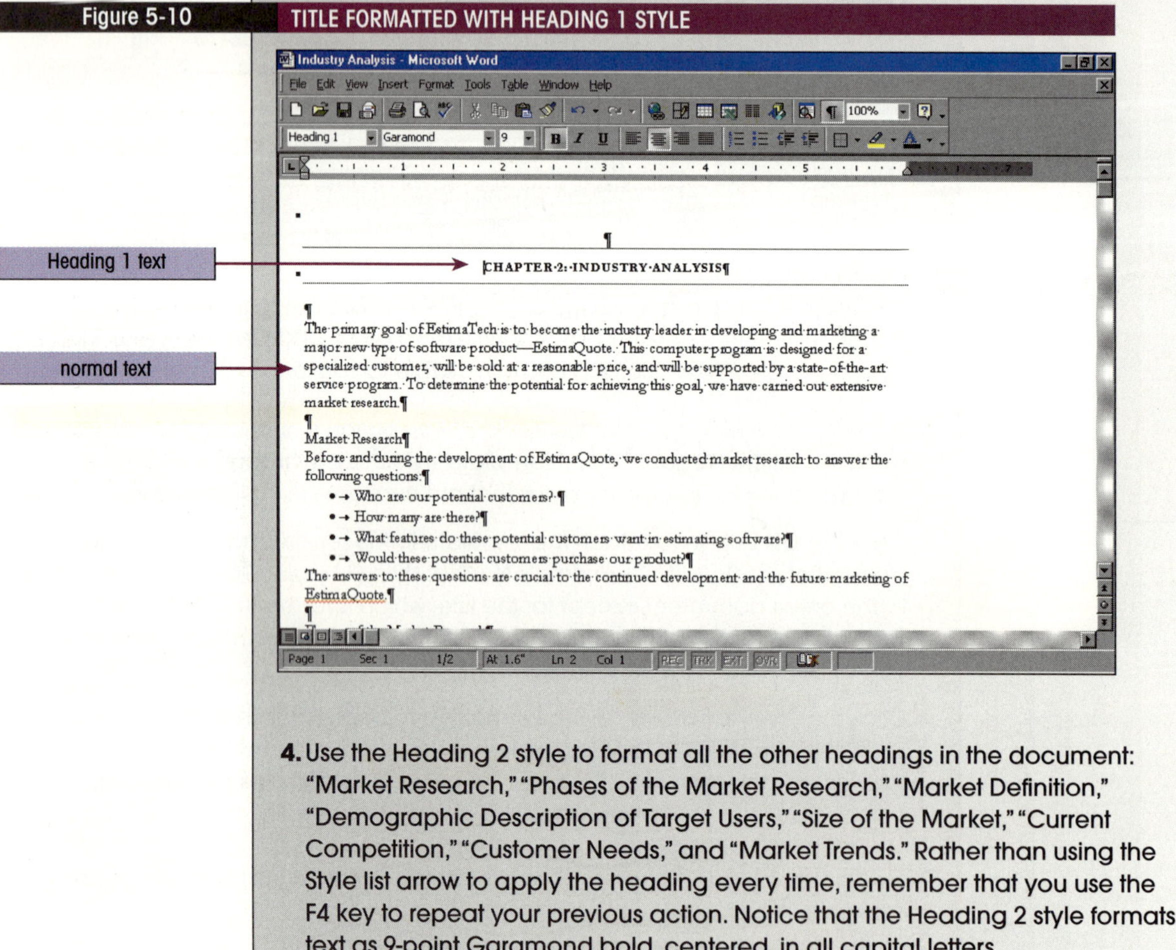

4. Use the Heading 2 style to format all the other headings in the document: "Market Research," "Phases of the Market Research," "Market Definition," "Demographic Description of Target Users," "Size of the Market," "Current Competition," "Customer Needs," and "Market Trends." Rather than using the Style list arrow to apply the heading every time, remember that you use the F4 key to repeat your previous action. Notice that the Heading 2 style formats text as 9-point Garamond bold, centered, in all capital letters.

The newly formatted headings are attractive and make the chapter easier to read by breaking it up into distinct sections. Robert suggests that the headings within the chapter would look better in a larger point size.

Modifying a Predefined Style

Now that you have applied the heading styles, you're ready to modify them. Robert asks that you change the font size of the headings from 9-point to 10-point. To do this, you need to change the style definition, which specifies the particular font, size, and format for that style. Once you change the style definition, all the headings with that style applied to them will automatically be reformatted with the new, modified style. (You don't have to go back and reapply any of the styles with new definitions.) This automatic updating capability makes styles one of the most flexible and helpful Word tools.

To change the Heading 2 style to 10-point:

1. Make sure the insertion point is located within one of the headings formatted with the Heading 2 style. Click **Format** on the menu bar, and then click **Style**. The Style dialog box opens.
2. Verify that **Heading 2** is selected in the Style list box. (It should be selected because the insertion point was located in text formatted with that style when you opened the Style dialog box.)
3. Click the **Modify** button. The Modify Style dialog box opens.
4. Click the **Format** button, and then click **Font**. The Font dialog box opens, as shown in Figure 5-11. The name of the current font, Garamond, is highlighted in the Font text box, and the font size, 9, appears in the Size text box. The Font style is set to bold.

Figure 5-11 FONT DIALOG BOX

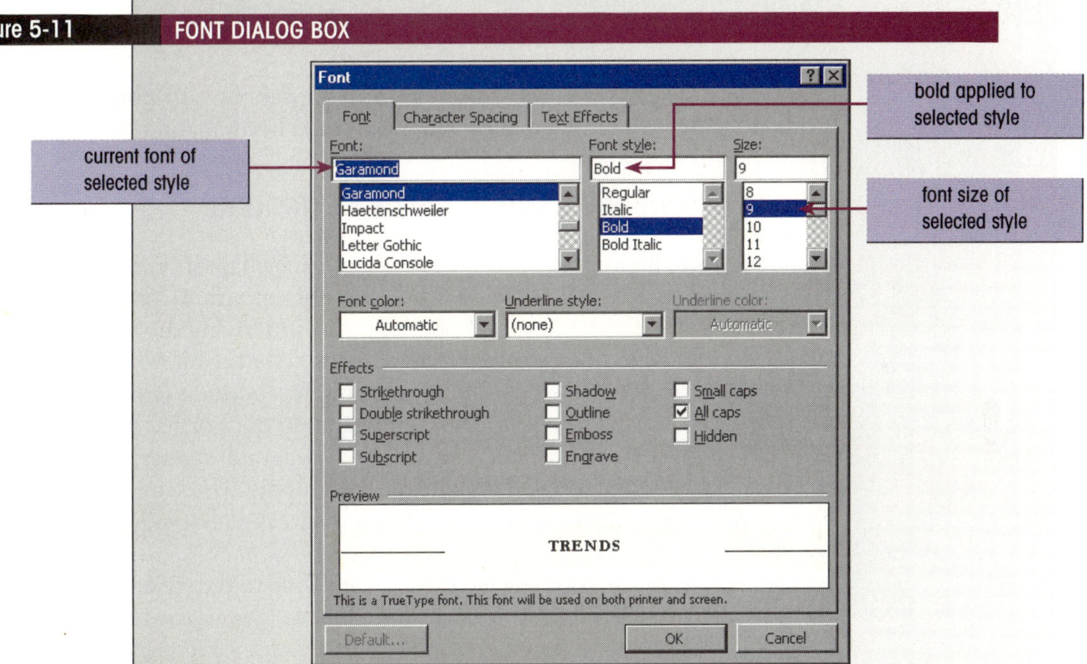

5. In the Size list box, click **10**. The new font size now appears highlighted in the Size text box.
6. Click the **OK** button. You return to the Modify Style dialog box.
7. Click the **OK** button. You return to the Style dialog box.
8. Click **Apply**. You return to the document.
9. Scroll through the document to view the new style definition applied to the document headings. Click one of the headings, and then observe the new font size (10) on the Formatting toolbar, as shown in Figure 5-12.

Figure 5-12 NEW FONT DEFINITION APPLIED TO DOCUMENT

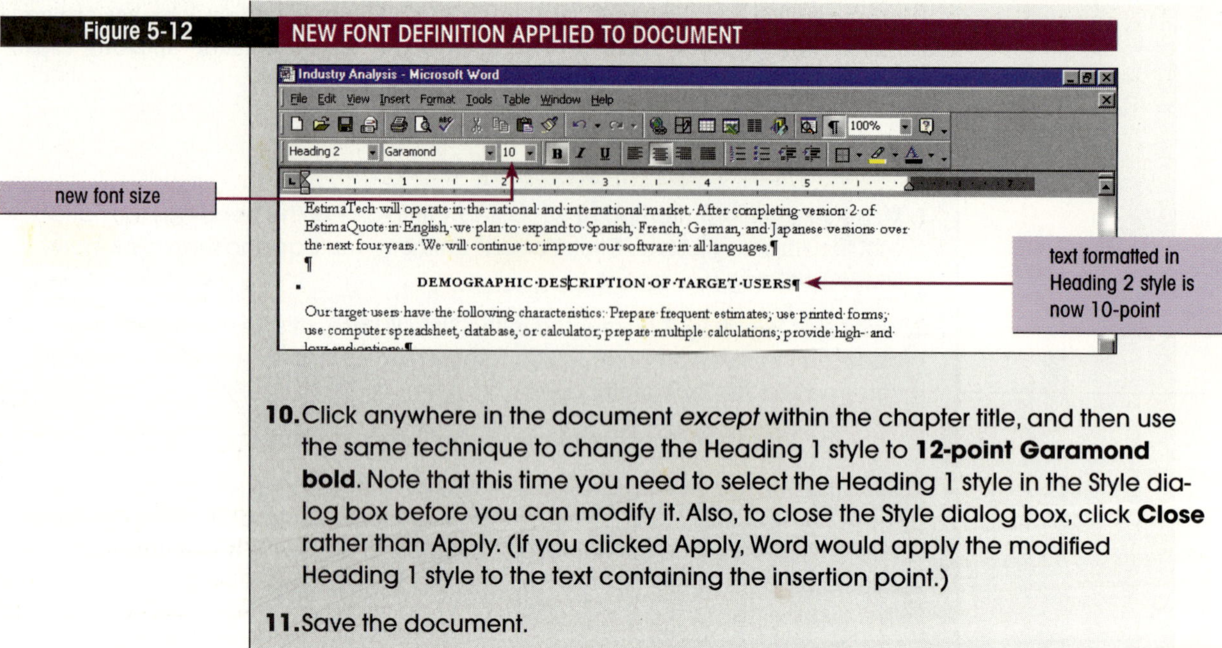

10. Click anywhere in the document *except* within the chapter title, and then use the same technique to change the Heading 1 style to **12-point Garamond bold**. Note that this time you need to select the Heading 1 style in the Style dialog box before you can modify it. Also, to close the Style dialog box, click **Close** rather than Apply. (If you clicked Apply, Word would apply the modified Heading 1 style to the text containing the insertion point.)

11. Save the document.

The Heading 2 style in the document now appears in a 10-point font size, whereas the Heading 1 style is in 12-point. This emphasizes the headings and makes them easier to read.

Defining New Styles with the Style Command

To add interest and improve the appearance of each chapter in their business plan, Robert asks you to define a new style for the introductory (first) paragraph of each chapter. **Defining**, or creating, a new style is similar to modifying an existing style. To define a new style, you assign it a name and give it a new style definition. You can define a style by example by formatting document text, selecting it, and then typing the new style name in the style list box, or by using the Style command on the Format menu. If you use the latter method, you must specify whether the style is a paragraph style or a character style. As mentioned earlier, a paragraph style is one that you apply to complete paragraphs, including short paragraphs such as titles and headings, whereas a character style is one you apply to a single character or to a range of characters.

Word automatically adds any new styles you define to the style list (in the Style list box) of your current document, but it doesn't attach a new style to the template unless you specify that it should. Word provides two ways to define a new style: using an existing paragraph as an example and using the Style command on the Format menu.

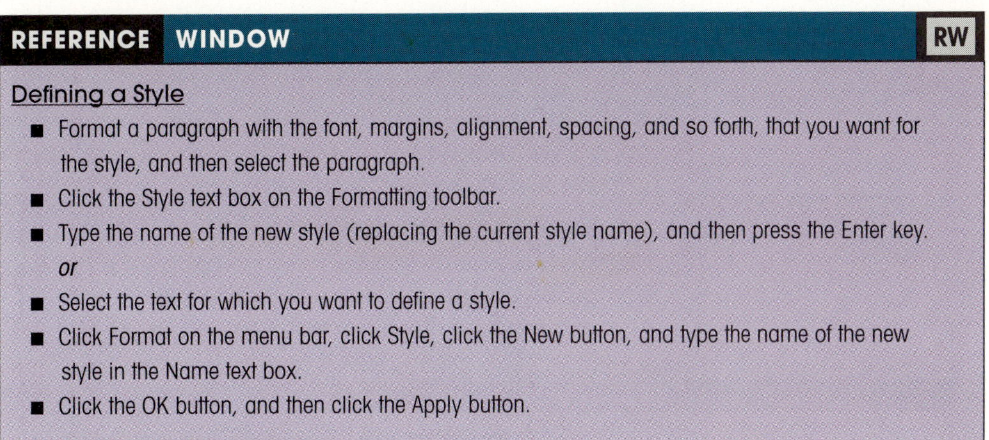

REFERENCE WINDOW RW

Defining a Style

- Format a paragraph with the font, margins, alignment, spacing, and so forth, that you want for the style, and then select the paragraph.
- Click the Style text box on the Formatting toolbar.
- Type the name of the new style (replacing the current style name), and then press the Enter key.

or

- Select the text for which you want to define a style.
- Click Format on the menu bar, click Style, click the New button, and type the name of the new style in the Name text box.
- Click the OK button, and then click the Apply button.

Now, Robert wants you to define a new style to apply to the first paragraph of each chapter in their business plan. He wants the first paragraph to present the major topic and set the direction for the entire chapter. Therefore, he would like the first paragraph to be indented and justified and to appear in Arial font. You'll now define a style, called First Paragraph, that contains these formatting features.

To define the new style:

1. Move the insertion point anywhere within the first paragraph of the document, below the chapter title. You'll now define the style.
2. Click **Format** on the menu bar, and then click **Style**. The Style dialog box opens. See Figure 5-13.

Figure 5-13 STYLE DIALOG BOX

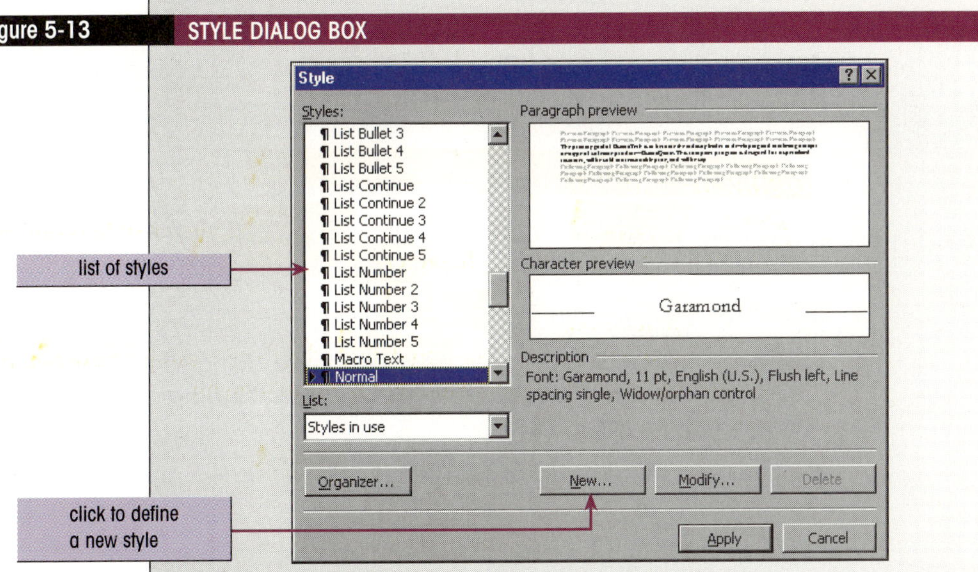

3. Click the **New** button. This tells Word that you want to define a new style. The New Style dialog box opens. The default name Style1 is highlighted and ready to be replaced with your style name.

4. Type **First Paragraph**, the name of your new style. Now, you need to make sure that your new style is a paragraph style, based on the settings of the Normal style.

5. Verify that "Paragraph" appears in the Style type list box and that "Normal" appears in the Based on text box. Now you need to specify the style you want to follow your new style by default.

6. Click the **Style for following paragraph** list arrow, scroll down, and then click **Normal**. This setting specifies that if you apply the First Paragraph style to a paragraph and then press the Enter key at the end of the paragraph, the new paragraph will have the Normal style. See Figure 5-14.

Figure 5-14 NEW STYLE DIALOG BOX

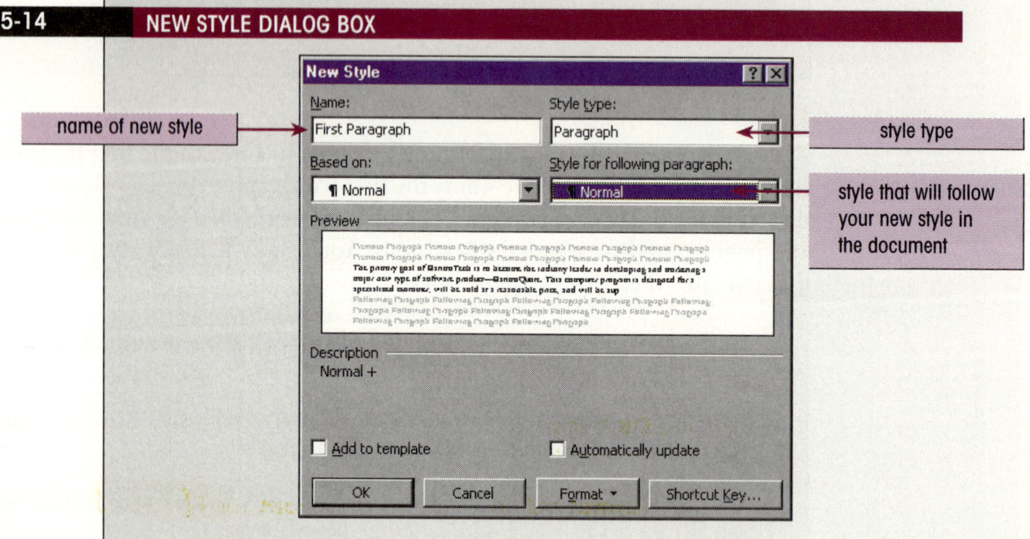

You have specified the name and type of the new style as well as the style that should apply to any paragraph after it when you press the Enter key in your document. Now you're ready to specify the format of the new style.

To specify the format of the new style:

1. Click the **Format** button, and then click **Paragraph**. The Paragraph dialog box opens. If necessary, click the **Indents and Spacing** tab.

2. Change the Alignment to **Justified**.

3. Change the Spacing Before to **12 pt** and the Spacing After to **6 pt**. These settings will add white space above and below the paragraph so it stands out from the text surrounding it.

4. In the Indentation section, change Left to **0.5"**. See Figure 5-15.

Figure 5-15 PARAGRAPH DIALOG BOX

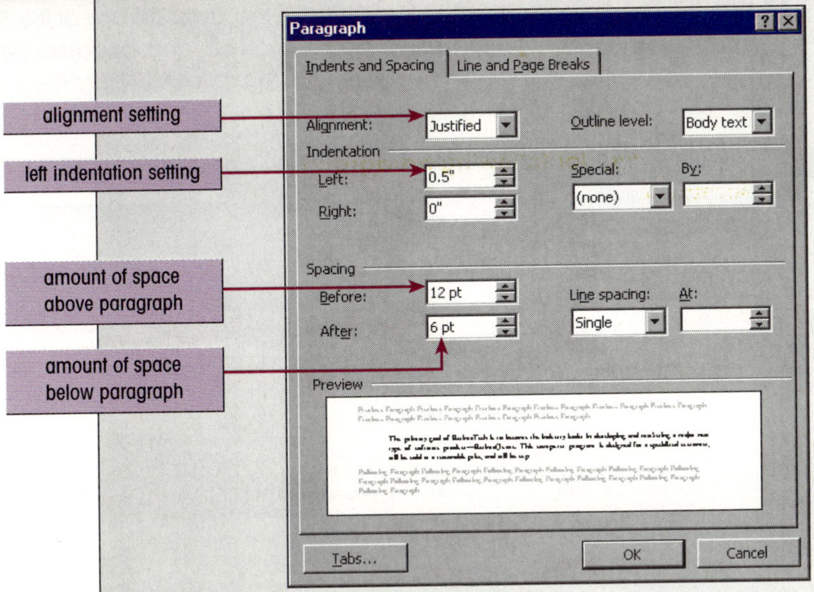

This completes the paragraph formatting. Next, you'll change the font of the style from Garamond to Arial.

5. Click the **OK** button. The Paragraph dialog box closes, and you return to the New Style dialog box.

6. Click the **Format** button, and then click **Font**. The Font dialog box opens.

7. Change the font to Arial. Leave the font style as Regular and the font size as 11-point.

8. Click the **OK** button. The Font dialog box closes. Now, you'll add a border around the paragraph.

9. Click the **Format** button, and then click **Border**. The Borders and Shading dialog box opens. If necessary, click the **Borders** tab.

10. In the Setting section of the dialog box, click the **Box** icon to place a box border around the paragraph, and then click the **OK** button.

11. Look over the New Style dialog box, especially the Description, to make sure you have defined the style as you would like it. At this point, you could click the **Add to template** check box to add this new style to the Elegant Report template. However, because you may want to use the Elegant Report template later for some other purpose besides Robert's business plan, you won't add the new style to the template now. Instead, you'll simply apply the new style; in the process, Word will add it to the style list for the current document. In the next section, you'll learn how to save the current document as a completely new template, which you can use to create new chapters of the business plan.

12. Click the **OK** button to close the New Style dialog box.

13. With the First Paragraph style highlighted in the Styles list box of the Style dialog box, click the **Apply** button. The dialog box closes and, because the insertion point was in the first paragraph at the time you clicked Apply, the new paragraph style is applied to it. See Figure 5-16.

Figure 5-16 NEWLY DEFINED STYLE

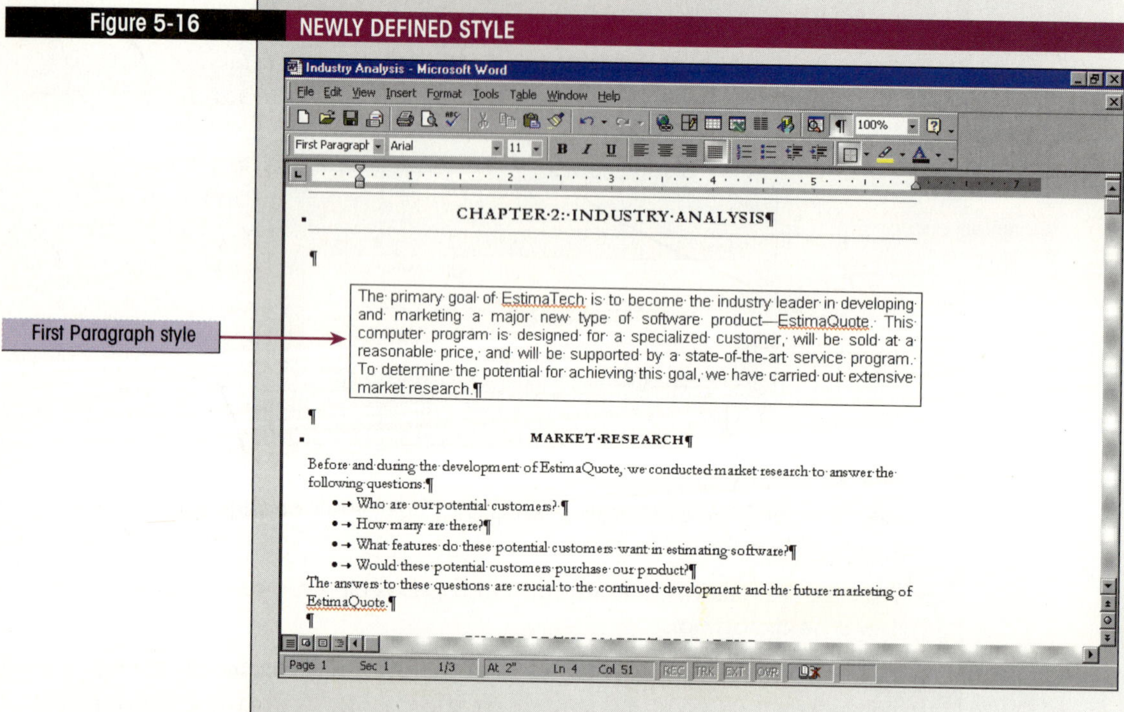

You have defined and applied the new paragraph style called First Paragraph. In the next section, you'll learn how to use this document's styles to create other documents.

Creating a New Template

Now that the document contains all the styles needed for future chapters, you'll save it as a new template. By default, Word will offer to save your new template in the Template folder. Any templates saved to this folder can be accessed later by the New command on the File menu. For this tutorial, however, you'll choose to save your template in the same folder as the rest of your data files.

REFERENCE WINDOW RW

Creating and Using a New Template

- Create a new document containing all the styles you want to include in your template, save it as a Word document, and then delete all text from the document.
- Click File on the menu bar, click Save As, click the Save As type list arrow, and then click Document Template.
- Verify that the Templates folder is displayed in the Save in list box. If you save your template to this folder, it will appear as one of the options in the New dialog box. If you prefer, you can save the template in a different location, such as your Data Disk.
- Type a descriptive name for the template in the filename text box, click Save, and then close the template.
- To begin creating a document based on a template stored in the Template folder, click File on the menu bar, click New, click the icon for your template in the General tab, and then click OK. Begin typing the text of your new document, applying styles as necessary. Save the new document as a Word document.
- To begin creating a document based on a template saved in any location, open a blank document, click Tools on the menu bar, click Templates and Add-ins, and then click the Attach button to open the Attach Template dialog box. Use the Look in list box to locate and select your template, and then click the Open button to return to the Templates and Add-ins dialog box. Click the Automatically update document styles check box to select it, and then click the OK button to return to the current document. Verify that the template styles are available in the Styles list box.

You're ready to save the styles in the **Industry Analysis** document as a new template. You'll save the template to the Chapter 2 folder that you created earlier, so that you can easily give it to Robert.

To save the styles of the current document as a new template:

1. Save the Industry Analysis document to preserve all the work you've done so far. *Be absolutely certain you have saved the document before proceeding to the next step.*
2. Press **Ctrl+A**, and then press **Delete.** The text of the document is selected and then deleted, but the styles are still available from the Style list box.
3. Click **File** on the menu bar, click **Save As**, click the **Save As type** list arrow and then click **Document Template**.
4. Verify that the Templates folder is displayed in the Save in list box. Because you want your new template handy, so you can pass it on to Robert easily, you'll save it to a different location.
5. Use the **Save in list** arrow to switch to the Chapter 2 file on your Data Disk, where you originally saved the Industry Analysis document.
6. Change the filename to **Business Plan Template,** click Save, and then close the template.

The new template is now saved and ready for whenever Robert wants to begin creating a new chapter of the business plan. He asks you to show him exactly how to begin using the new template. You explain that the process of attaching the template, which you just created, is different from attaching a predefined Word template. Earlier in this tutorial, you attached a predefined Word template with the Theme command on the Format menu. To attach a newly created template to an existing document, you use the Templates and Add-ins command on the Tools menu. You'll try attaching the template you just created to a new document now.

To attach the new template to a new document:

1. Open a new, blank document.
2. Click **Tools** on the menu bar, click **Templates and Add-ins**, and then click the **Attach** button. The Attach Template dialog box opens.
3. Use the Look in list box to locate and select your template, and then click the **Open** button to return to the Templates and Add-ins dialog box.
4. Click the **Automatically update document styles** check box to select it. Note that if you did not select this option, the template styles would not be available in the Styles list box. See Figure 5-17.

Figure 5-17 TEMPLATES AND ADD-INS DIALOG BOX

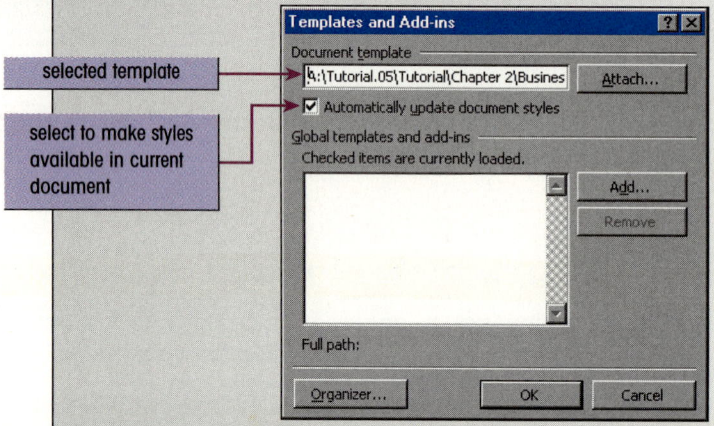

5. Click the **OK** button to return to the current document.
6. Click the **Styles** list arrow and verify that the template styles are available. Note that the styles list includes the First Paragraph style, which you created in the previous section.

   You could begin typing the new document now and apply the styles to the document text as you worked. Instead, you'll simply close the document.
7. Close the document without saving any changes.

The template you have just created will make it easy for Robert and Chiu Lee to create new chapters. You'll give them a copy on a disk after you have completed the rest of the Chapter 2 document.

Session 5.1 Quick Check

1. Explain how to create a new folder.
2. What is the Thesaurus?
3. List at least two synonyms that the Thesaurus provides for the word "restore."
4. Define serif and sans serif fonts. When would you use each of these types of fonts? Give two examples of each.
5. Explain how to attach a Word template to a document.
6. Explain how to create a new template and attach it to a document.
7. How do you modify a predefined style?
8. Describe one method for defining a new style.

You have improved the EstimaTech business plan chapter by modifying the word choice and writing style, by selecting proper fonts, and by using styles to give the plan a consistent look. Next, you'll change the business plan's organization using Outline view.

SESSION 5.2

In this session, you'll learn how to rearrange the document using outline view. You'll also learn how to improve the appearance of the right margin by hyphenating the document. Finally, you'll add a footnote to the document that will help readers locate additional information.

Creating and Editing an Outline

Chiu Lee and Robert created an outline of their business plan with the Word Outline feature. An **outline** is a list of the basic points of a document and the order in which they are presented. You can create an outline before typing any other text of a document, or you can view and edit the outline of an existing document. To construct an outline when you first create a document, you open a blank document and change to Outline view. Word then automatically applies heading styles (Heading 1, Heading 2, and so forth) to the outline paragraphs that you type. To create an outline as you type the text of a document in Normal view or Print layout view, you must apply heading styles (Heading 1, Heading 2, and so forth) to all the headings in your document. Chiu Lee and Robert used this latter method as they wrote their business plan. You'll change to Outline view to modify and reorganize the outline.

In Outline view, you can see and edit as many as nine levels of headings in a document. As with any outline, the broadest or most general topic is the first-level heading (in Heading 1 style), and the remaining topics become increasingly narrow or more specific with second-level headings (in Heading 2 style) and in subsequent headings (in Heading 3 style, and so on).

After reviewing the organization of the business plan, you realize that the topic "Current Competition" should appear after the topic "Market Trends." Also, the topic "Size of the Market" should appear before "Demographic Description of Target Users." Because you have applied the predefined heading styles to the headings, you can easily reorder the text in Outline view. As you reorder the headings, the text below the headings will move as well. Notice that in Outline view, the Outline toolbar replaces the ruler.

REFERENCE WINDOW RW

Creating and Editing Outlines

- Click the Outline View button.
- Click the appropriate Show Heading button to show only the desired number of headings in your document.
- Enter new heading text or edit existing headings.
- Click the Move Up button or the Move Down button to reorder text.
- Click the Promote button or the Demote button to increase or decrease the levels of headings.
- Click the All button to display the entire document again.
- Click the Normal View button.

Now you're ready to reorganize the order of topics in outline view.

To use Outline view:

1. If you took a break after the last session, make sure Word is running.
2. Open the **Industry Analysis** document in the Chapter 2 folder of the Tutorial sub-folder in the Tutorial.05 folder. Display nonprinting characters, and switch to Print Layout view.
3. Make sure the insertion point is at the beginning of the document, and then click the **Outline View** button. The Outline toolbar replaces the horizontal ruler.

   TROUBLE? Depending on how your machine is set up, your Outline toolbar may be in a different location.

4. Click the **Show Heading 3** button 3 on the Outline toolbar to display three levels of headings. In outline terminology, text formatted in the Heading 1 style is considered a level-1 head, text formatted in the Heading 2 style is considered a level-2 heading, and so on. Although the document has only two levels of headings now, you'll add a third level soon. Notice that the headings are displayed in the outline without the rest of the document text. The plus sign next to each line of text indicates that the text is a heading, rather than part of the main text of the document. See Figure 5-18.

Figure 5-18 DOCUMENT IN OUTLINE VIEW

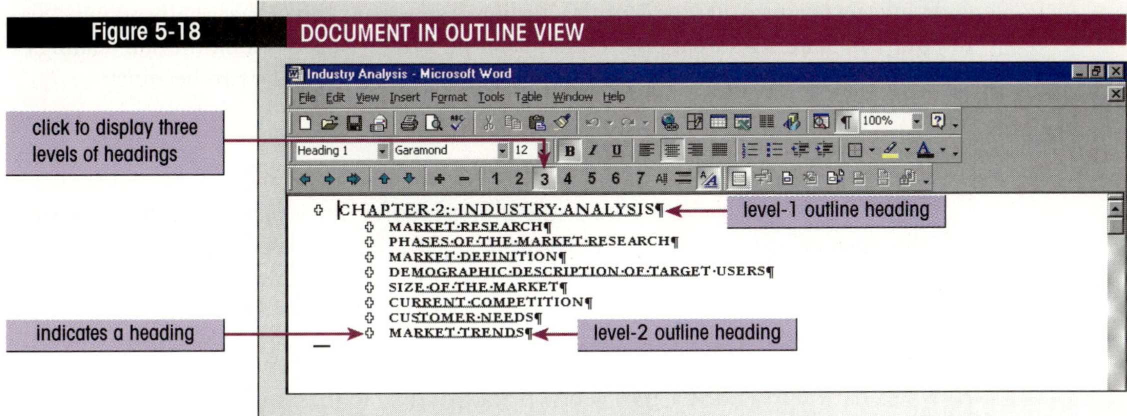

Now that you see only the headings of the business plan, you can change the organization by reordering some headings and by changing the level of others.

Moving Headings Up and Down in an Outline

You can rearrange the order of topics in an outline by moving the headings up and down. When you move a heading in outline view, any text below that heading (indicated by the underline) moves with it. First, you'll move the section "Current Competition" (and its accompanying text) to follow the section "Market Trends." As you work in outline view, keep in mind that the Undo button will reverse any mistakes, just as in Normal view.

To move headings in outline view:

1. Place the insertion point anywhere in the heading "Current Competition," and then click the **Move Down** button on the Outline toolbar. The heading and the text below it move down one line to follow the heading "Customer Needs," which does not move.

2. Click again to move the "Current Competition" heading to the end of the chapter, after "Market Trends."

   Next, you can move the heading "Size of the Market" up, to position it before "Demographic Description of Target Users."

3. Place the insertion point anywhere in the heading "Size of the Market," and then click the **Move Up** button on the Outline toolbar. The heading (and the text below it) move up one line to just below "Market Definition."

Now that the topics of the outline are in a better order, you realize that some level-2 headings (text in Heading 2 style) should be level-3 headings (in Heading 3 style).

Promoting and Demoting Headings in an Outline

You can easily change the levels of headings in outline view. To **promote** a heading means to increase the level of a heading—for example, to change an item from a level-3 heading to a level-2 heading. To **demote** a heading means to decrease the level—for example, to change a level-1 heading to a level-2 heading.

While reviewing Chapter 2 of the business plan, you realize that the headings "Size of the Market" and "Demographic Description of Target Users" should be subheadings that follow the heading "Market Definition." You'll now demote these two headings.

To demote headings:

1. While still in Outline view, make sure the insertion point is in the heading "Size of the Market" and then click the **Demote** button on the Outline toolbar. (Take care not to click the Demote to Body Text button by mistake, which would make the heading part of the main text of the document, rather than a heading.) The heading moves right and becomes a level-3 heading with the Heading 3 style.

   TROUBLE? If the heading now has a square next to it, rather than a plus sign, you clicked the Demote to Body Text button by mistake. Click the Undo button, and then repeat Step 1.

2. Place the insertion point anywhere in the heading "Demographic Description of Target Users," and then click . Again, the heading moves right and becomes a level-3 heading. See Figure 5-19.

Figure 5-19 PROMOTING AND DEMOTING HEADINGS

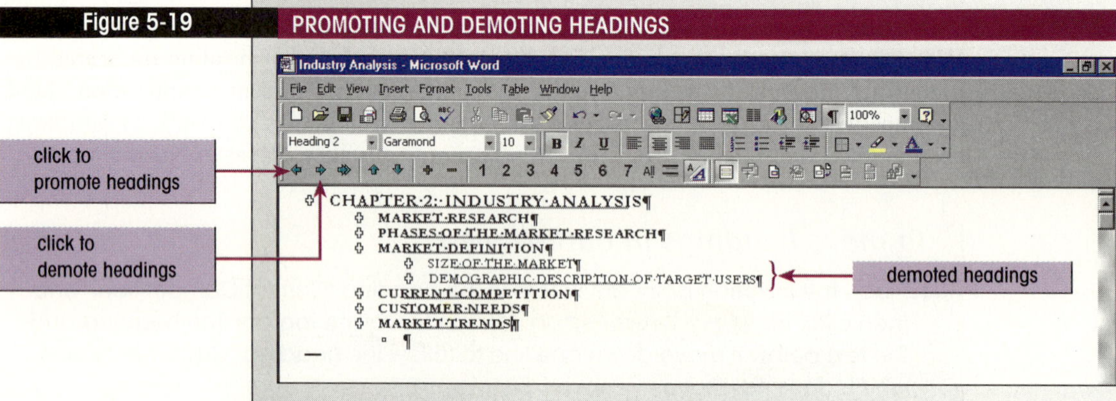

3. Click the **Normal View** button to return to normal view, and then scroll down to view the entire document. The headings you demoted in Outline view are formatted in Heading 3 style. As a result of moving headings in the outline, entire sections of the document have been rearranged. Because you have made so many changes to the document, you'll now save it with a different name. That way, if one file becomes corrupted, you'll have a backup.

4. Save the document as **Industry Analysis Copy 2**.

Notice that promoting a heading in outline view is just as easy as demoting. You simply place the insertion point in the desired heading and click the Promote button.

Printing the Outline

Word makes it easy to print whatever you see on the screen in outline view. Robert asks you to print the outline of Chapter 2, so he can refer to it in his conversation with the bank personnel. Before you do so, you'll turn off the formatting of the headings, to make them easier to read.

To print the outline:

1. Click the **Outline View** button.
2. Click the **Show Formatting** button on the Outline toolbar to deselect it. Word converts the outline to the Normal style. In the closely spaced lines of the outline, a simpler style like this is much easier to read.
3. Click the **Print** button on the Standard toolbar to print the outline. See Figure 5-20.

Figure 5-20 THE PRINTED OUTLINE

Chapter 2: Industry Analysis
- Market Research
- Phases of the Market Research
- Market Definition
  - Size of the Market
  - Demographic Description of Target Users
- Customer Needs
- Market Trends
- Current Competition

4. Click again to show the formatting of the outline text.
5. Switch to Normal view.

You have reorganized Chapter 2 of the business plan and printed the outline. Now you're ready to address some other concerns. First, Robert has noticed that the right edges of most of the paragraphs in the document are rather uneven. You'll correct this problem in the next section.

Hyphenating a Document

One potential problem with left-aligned text is excessive raggedness along the right margin. You can solve the problem of raggedness by justifying the text, but that introduces another problem: Word inserts extra white space between words to stretch the lines of text to align along the right margin. Sometimes, this causes unsightly **rivers**, that is, blank areas running through the text of a page, as shown in Figure 5-21.

Figure 5-21 **RIVERS WITHIN A JUSTIFIED COLUMN OF TEXT**

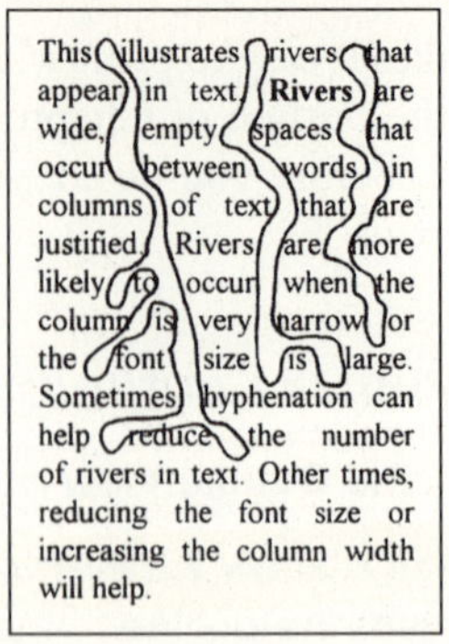

This illustrates rivers that appear in text. **Rivers** are wide, empty spaces that occur between words in columns of text that are justified. Rivers are more likely to occur when the column is very narrow or the font size is large. Sometimes hyphenation can help reduce the number of rivers in text. Other times, reducing the font size or increasing the column width will help.

Hyphenating the text can sometimes reduce the raggedness in left-aligned text or reduce the rivers in justified text. The Hyphenation feature allows you to hyphenate a document either automatically—in which case, Word decides the exact point at which to divide a word—or manually, in which case you can accept, reject, or change the suggested hyphenation.

To hyphenate a document, you need to specify a width for the **hyphenation zone**, which is the distance from the right margin within which words will be hyphenated. A smaller hyphenation zone results in more words being hyphenated but creates a less-ragged right margin. A larger hyphenation zone results in fewer hyphenated words but a more ragged right margin. In justified text, increasing the number of hyphenated words reduces the amount of white space inserted between words. Notice that to decrease the total number of hyphenated words, you can increase the size of the hyphenation zone. You also can specify the number of successive lines that can end with hyphenated words. Too many lines in a row ending in a hyphen can be distracting and difficult to read.

Robert asks you to hyphenate the business plan to eliminate as much raggedness as possible. This means you need to decrease the hyphenation zone.

To set the hyphenation zone and to hyphenate the newsletter:

1. With the insertion point anywhere in the document, click **Tools** on the menu bar, point to **Language**, and then click **Hyphenation**. The Hyphenation dialog box opens.
2. Decrease the Hyphenation zone to **0.1"**.
3. Change the Limit consecutive hyphens setting to **3**. This prevents Word from hyphenating words at the end of more than three lines in a row.
4. Click the **Automatically hyphenate document** check box. See Figure 5-22.

Figure 5-22 **HYPHENATION DIALOG BOX**

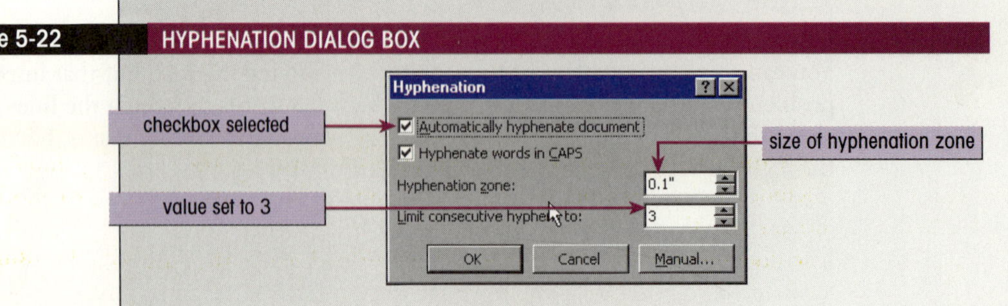

5. Click the **OK** button. Word hyphenates words in the document as needed. For example, scroll the document so that the heading "Phases of Market Research" is at the top of the document window. You can now see several hyphenated words as shown in Figure 5-23.

   TROUBLE? If you see a message asking if you would like to install the hyphenation feature, insert the Office 2000 CD into the CD-ROM drive, and then click Yes.

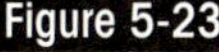

Figure 5-23 DOCUMENT WITH AUTOMATIC HYPHENATION

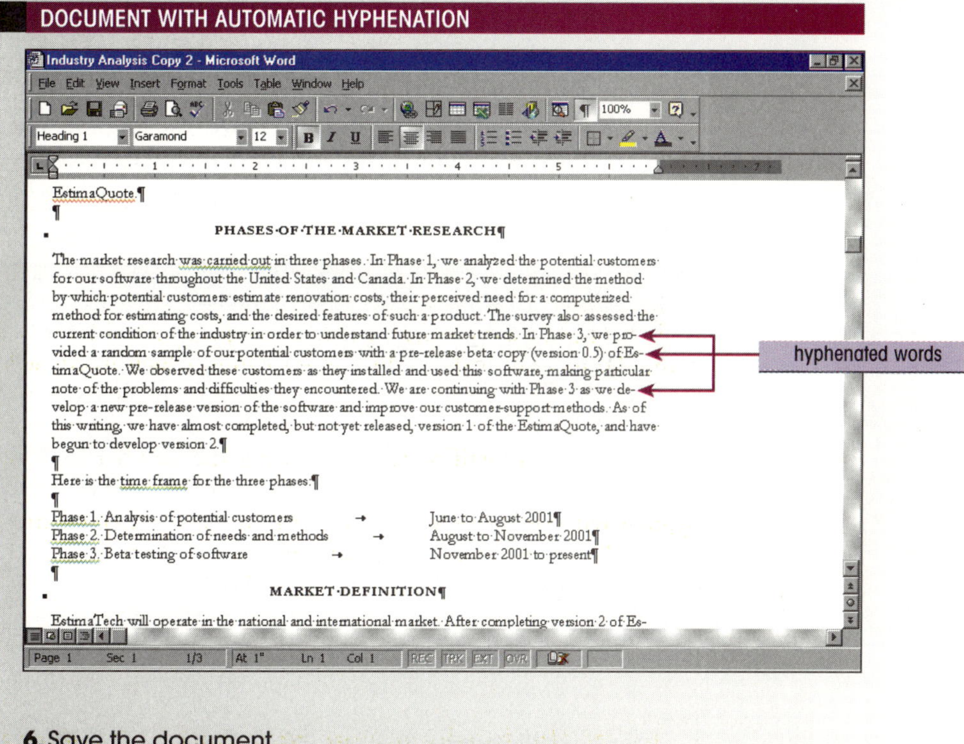

6. Save the document.

You should look through your document to make sure you like how Word has hyphenated it. If you don't like its hyphenations, you can click the Undo button, repeat the preceding steps, and then click the Manual button instead. Then Word will stop at each word before it is hyphenated to let you accept or reject the suggested hyphenation. In this case, Robert is satisfied with the automatic hyphenation.

Adding Footnotes and Endnotes

As you read through the chapter, you realize that under the heading "Customer Needs," the text refers to the results of a survey. Robert wants to include the survey results in an appendix at the end of the business plan and wants a cross-reference to this fact in a footnote.

A **footnote** is a line of text that appears at the bottom of the printed page and often includes an explanation, the name of a source, or a cross-reference to another place in the document. When all notes for a document are gathered together and printed at the end of the document, instead of at the bottom of each page, they are called **endnotes**. Usually, a document will contain footnotes or endnotes, but not both. You can insert footnotes and endnotes into a Word document quickly and easily with the Footnote command on the Insert menu.

The Footnote feature provides several benefits over simply typing notes at the bottom of a page or at the end of a document:

- Word numbers footnotes or endnotes automatically. If you add a note anywhere in the document, delete a note, or move a note, Word automatically renumbers all the remaining footnotes or endnotes consecutively.
- Word automatically formats the footnote text at the bottom of the page or the endnote text at the end of the document.
- You can edit a footnote or endnote at any time. To modify the text, select Footnotes from the View menu and then use the same editing commands you use in the document window. (You'll have a chance to practice editing a footnote in the case problems at the end of this chapter.)
- If you add or delete text that moves the footnote reference onto a different page, the footnote also will move to that page. The reference in the text and the footnote at the bottom of the page will always be on the same page.

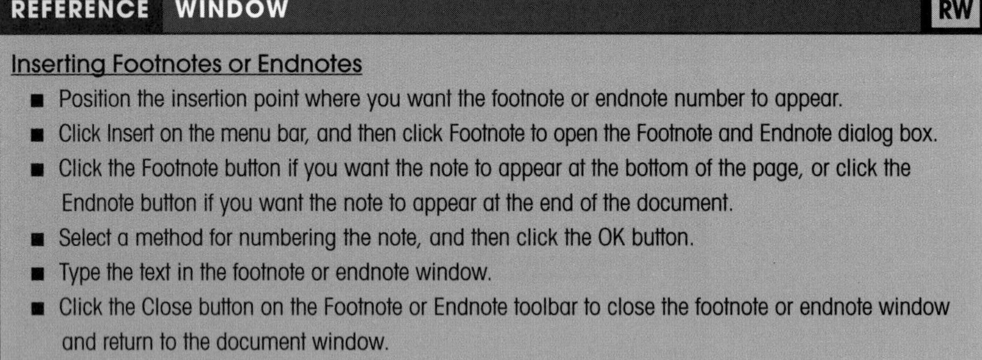

REFERENCE WINDOW RW

Inserting Footnotes or Endnotes

- Position the insertion point where you want the footnote or endnote number to appear.
- Click Insert on the menu bar, and then click Footnote to open the Footnote and Endnote dialog box.
- Click the Footnote button if you want the note to appear at the bottom of the page, or click the Endnote button if you want the note to appear at the end of the document.
- Select a method for numbering the note, and then click the OK button.
- Type the text in the footnote or endnote window.
- Click the Close button on the Footnote or Endnote toolbar to close the footnote or endnote window and return to the document window.

Now, you'll insert a footnote in the business plan that refersthe reader to the survey information in the appendix.

To insert a footnote:

1. Switch to normal view if necessary, scroll down until you can see the heading "Customer Needs," and then position the insertion point after the period at the end of the first sentence, which ends "such as EstimaQuote." This is where you will add the first footnote number.
2. Click **Insert** on the menu bar, and then click **Footnote**. The Footnote and Endnote dialog box opens.
3. Make sure the Footnote option button is selected, make sure the AutoNumber option button is selected, and then click the **OK** button. The footnote number appears in the text and the insertion point moves to a blank footnote window at the bottom of the page. See Figure 5-24.

Figure 5-24 CREATING A FOOTNOTE

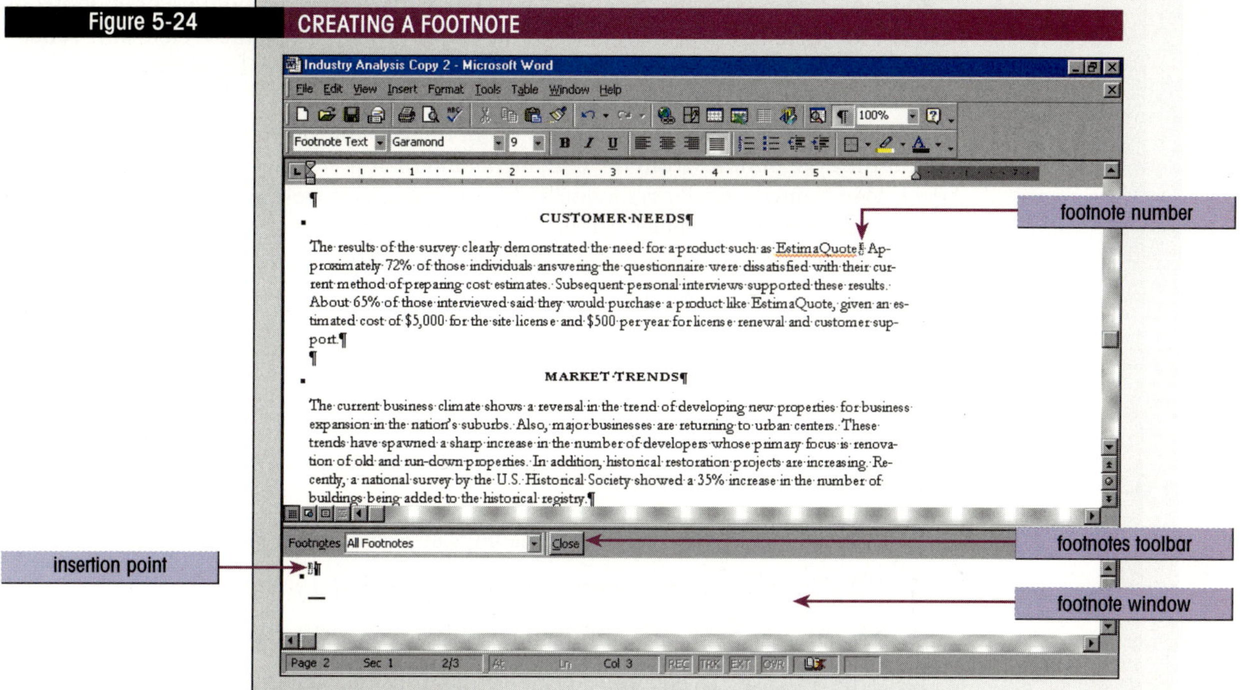

4. Without pressing the spacebar or the Tab key at the beginning of the line, type the following text: **See Appendix 1, "Survey of Potential EstimaQuote Customers."** (Include the period and quotation marks.) Don't press the Enter key at the end of the note.

TROUBLE? If you made a typing mistake, you can use any Word editing feature to edit the footnote.

5. Click the **Close** button on the Footnote toolbar to return to the main document window.

6. Switch to print layout view, and scroll to the bottom of page 2 to view the footnote. See Figure 5-25.

Figure 5-25 FOOTNOTE AT BOTTOM OF PAGE IN PRINT LAYOUT VIEW

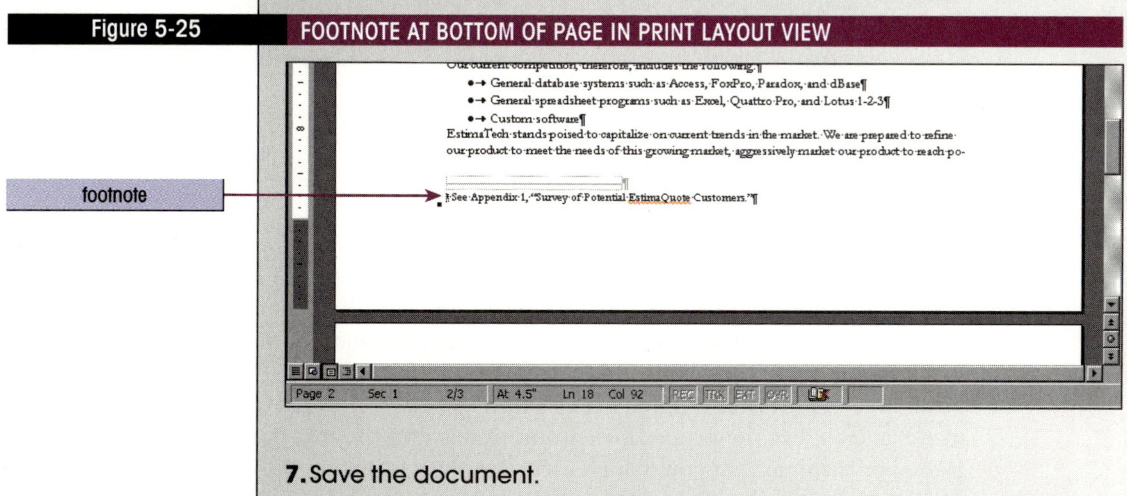

7. Save the document.

You can delete a note just as easily as you added it. To delete a footnote or endnote, highlight the footnote or endnote number in the document and press the Delete key. When you delete the number, Word automatically deletes the text of the footnote or endnote and renumbers the remaining notes consecutively.

You can move a footnote or endnote using the cut-and-paste method. Simply highlight and cut the note number from the document, and then paste it anywhere in your document. Again, Word automatically renumbers the notes consecutively and places the footnote on the same page as its reference number. You can edit the text of an endnote or footnote by clicking in the footnote or endnote while in print layout view. Finally, note that you can display the text of the footnote in a ScreenTip, by placing the pointer over the footnote number in the document. This feature is especially useful when you are sharing documents in electronic form only, rather than distributing printouts.

Session 5.2 Quick Check

1. Why would you want to move headings up and down in an outline?
2. What happens when you promote a heading? When you demote a heading?
3. Explain how to promote or demote a heading in a Word outline.
4. True or False: To take full advantage of outline view, you should apply the Word predefined heading styles in normal or print layout view first.
5. What does the term *river* mean in relation to justified text.
6. What is the hyphenation zone? If you increase its size, how will the number of hyphenated words be affected?
7. What are the advantages of using the Footnote feature to insert footnotes into a document?
8. What is the difference between a footnote and an endnote?

SESSION 5.3

In this session, you'll learn how to position the insertion point with Click and Type and how to insert the current date. You'll also learn how to highlight text with colors and adjust character and paragraph spacing. Finally, you'll create a table of contents and browse through the document by quickly jumping from one heading to another.

Positioning the Insertion Point with Click and Type

Your next task is to create a cover page at the beginning of the document. To draw attention to the text of the new cover page, you want it to appear in the middle of a separate page. You could position the insertion point at the beginning of a blank page by pressing the Enter key multiple times until you have inserted the appropriate number of paragraph marks. But it is much easier to use the Word **Click and Type** feature, which allows you to double-click a blank area of a page and immediately begin typing. Word inserts the necessary paragraph marks and applies the proper formatting to position the text in that particular area of the page. For example, you could double-click in the center of a page and then type a centered title; or you could double-click the lower-right margin and type a right-aligned date.

Keep in mind that Click and Type only works in print layout view. As you move the pointer over a blank area of a page, the pointer changes shape to reflect the alignment that will be applied to text inserted in that particular area of the page. For example, when you move the pointer over the center of the page, the pointer indicates that text inserted there will be formatted with center alignment. Table 5-1 describes some useful Click and Type pointers.

Table 5-1 CLICK AND TYPE POINTERS

POINTER	DESCRIPTION
I≡	Aligns text on the left side of the page.
≡I	Aligns text on the right side of the page.
I (centered)	Centers text on the page.
▤I	Formats text to flow around the right side of a graphic.

To create the new cover page for the document, you'll first verify that the Click and Type feature is turned on. Then, you'll insert a new page, double-click the center of the blank page, and begin typing the centered text.

To create a title page using Click and Type:

1. Verify that the **Industry Analysis Copy 2** document is open, that nonprinting characters are displayed, and that the document is displayed in print layout view.
2. Click **Tools** on the menu bar, click **Options**. The Options dialog box opens.
3. Click the Edit tab, verify that the **Enable click and type** check box is selected, and then click the **OK** button.
4. Press **Ctrl+Home** to move the insertion point to the blank paragraph at the beginning of the document.
5. Format the blank paragraph using the Normal style. Note that if you plan to insert a page *before* a heading in a document, it's a good idea to keep a blank paragraph (formatted with the Normal style) between the heading and the new page. Otherwise, you may have difficulties using styles you want on the new page.
6. Press **Ctrl+Enter**. Word inserts a page break at the beginning of the chapter.
7. Press the ↑ key to move the insertion point to the top of the new page.
8. Move the pointer over the center of the page, about 4 inches down from the top margin. (Use the vertical ruler on the left side of the screen as a guide.) The pointer changes to I.
9. Double-click the mouse. Word inserts the appropriate number of paragraph mark breaks and applies formatting to position the insertion point where you double-clicked. See Figure 5-26.

Figure 5-26 INSERTION POINT POSITIONED WITH CLICK AND TYPE

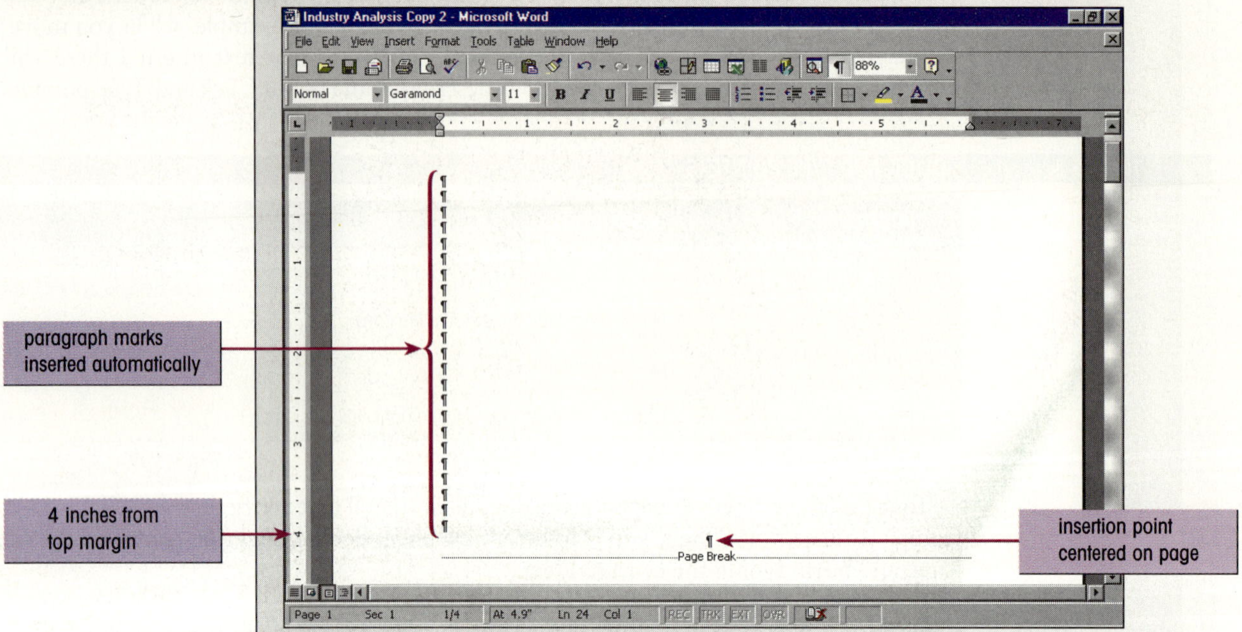

10. Now, type the title page text as follows, making sure to replace "Evan Brillstein" with your name:

Chapter 2
Prepared by Evan Brillstein
Draft

11. Format the cover page text in **18-point Times New Roman, bold**. (Because the cover page will not be included in the final document, its font doesn't have to match the rest of the document.)

Next, you need to add the current date to the cover page.

Inserting the Current Date

You could begin typing the date and have Word finish it for you using AutoComplete. But you decide to use the Insert Date and Time command on the Insert menu instead, to take advantage of its many options. You can use this command to insert both the current date and time into a document.

To insert the date into the title page:

1. Click at the end of your name, and then press **Enter** to move the insertion point to a new line.

2. Click **Insert** on the menu bar, and then click **Date and Time**. The Date and Time dialog box opens, as shown in Figure 5-27. The Available formats list box contains the current date and time in a variety of formats. Notice the Update automatically checkbox, which you could click if you wanted Word to update the date and time each time you open the document. In this case, however, you simply want to insert today's date without having it updated automatically when you reopen the document.

Figure 5-27 DATE AND TIME DIALOG BOX

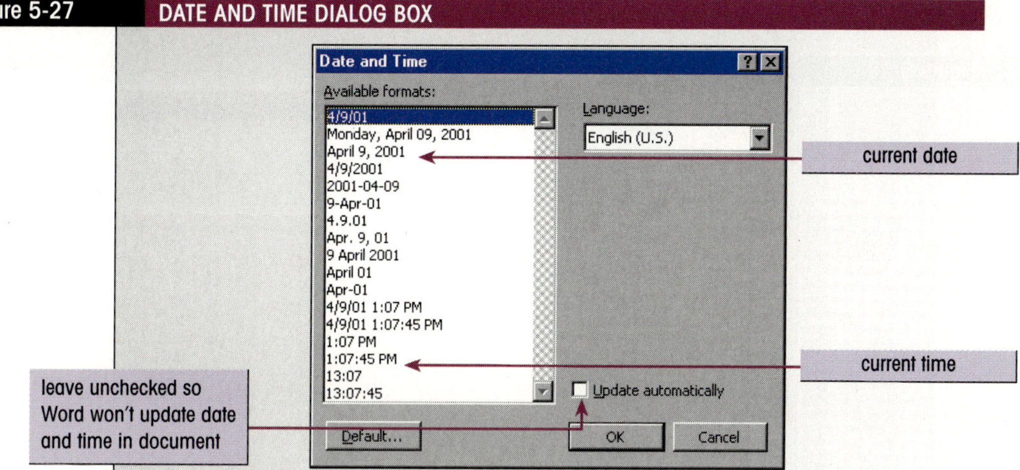

3. In the Available formats list box, click the format that provides both the day of the week, and the date—for example, Monday, April 9, 2001.

4. Click **OK**. Word inserts the date into the title page.

5. Verify that the date is formatted in 18-point Times New Roman, bold, to match the rest of the title page text.

Robert is happy to have the day of the week included in the date because it will remind him that the final draft of the chapter is due exactly a week later. He plans to remove the cover page text in the final document. To make sure he remembers to do so, you offer to highlight it with a special color.

Highlighting Text with Color

The **Highlight** button on the Formatting toolbar serves the same function as a highlighting pen; you use it to add a shading of bright color over portions of a document. You'll find it useful when you need to draw attention to specific text. If you want, you can click the Highlight list arrow to select a highlighting color from the palette of options. But most people prefer yellow (which is selected by default) because its light shade makes it easy to read the text.

You'll use the yellow highlighting now to draw attention to the cover page text.

To highlight the title page text:

1. Select all the text on the cover page.

2. Place the pointer over the **Highlight** button in the Formatting toolbar and observe the screentip, which indicates the selected highlighting color (for example, "Highlight (Yellow)"). Notice that the selected highlighting color also is displayed in the Highlight button itself.

3. If yellow is the selected color, click to highlight the text. If yellow is *not* the

selected color, click the **Highlight list** arrow and then click the yellow square (top row, left-most square) in the color palette. The title page text is now highlighted in yellow. The highlighting will remind Robert to remove the cover page when the document is final. See Figure 5-28.

Figure 5-28 HIGHLIGHTED TEXT

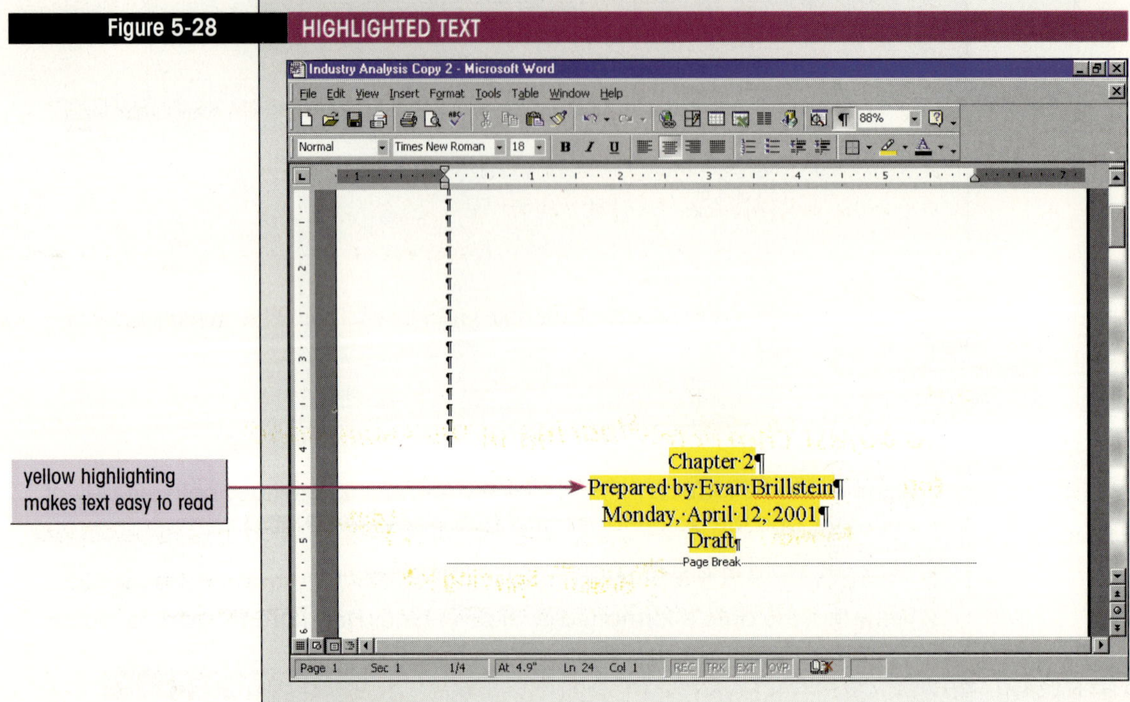

Finally, you decide the cover page text would be easier to read if you adjusted the spacing between the characters. Specifically, you want to add space between the characters. While you're at it, you'll also adjust some paragraph spacing within the chapter.

Changing Character and Paragraph Spacing

As you know, you can quickly change the spacing between lines of a document to make it single-spaced, 1.5-spaced, or double-spaced. (If you prefer, you can choose even more precise line-spacing options by using the Paragraph command on the Format menu.)

To add polish to a document, you can also adjust the spacing between characters or between individual paragraphs. Adjusting **Character spacing** is useful when you want to emphasize titles, whereas adjusting **paragraph spacing** allows you to fine-tune the appearance of specially formatted elements, such as a bulleted list.

Adjusting Spacing between Characters

Word offers a number of ways to adjust the spacing between characters. In some situations, you might want to use **kerning**, the process of adjusting the spacing between specific combinations of characters to improve their appearance. In most documents, however, it's easiest to select a group of characters and then uniformly expand or condense the spacing between them. Notice that space between characters is measured in points, with one point equal to 1/72 of an inch.

REFERENCE WINDOW RW

Expanding or Condensing Spacing between Characters

- Select the text where you want to adjust character spacing.
- Click Format on the menu bar, click Font, and then click the Character Spacing tab.
- Click the Spacing list arrow, and then click Expanded or Condensed. If you like, you can increase or decrease the exact amount of spacing that will be applied to each character by adjusting the settings in the By text box.
- To switch from expanded or condensed spacing back to regular spacing, click the Spacing list arrow and then click Normal.
- Observe the newly formatted characters in the Preview box.
- Click OK to apply the new character spacing.

In this case, you want to expand the spacing between the characters in the cover page. You'll do that now.

To adjust character spacing in the cover page:

1. Select the four lines of the cover page.
2. Click **Format** on the menu bar, and then click **Font**. The Font dialog box opens.
3. If necessary, click the **Character Spacing** tab. This tab, shown in Figure 5-29, offers a number of ways to adjust the spacing between characters.

Figure 5-29 CHARACTER SPACING TAB IN THE FONT DIALOG BOX

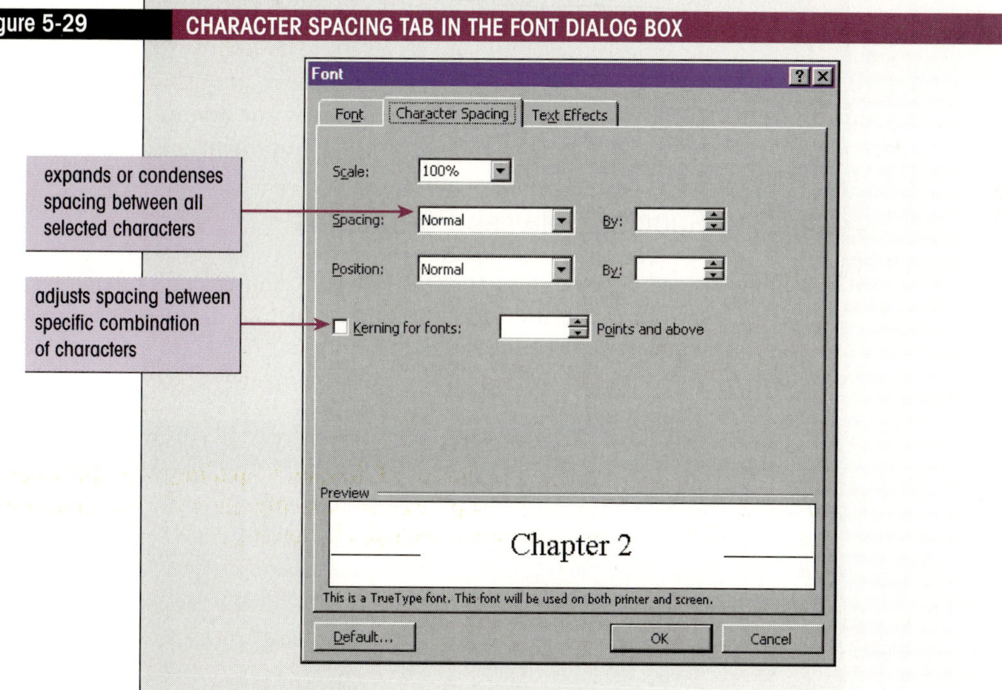

4. Click the **Spacing** list arrow, and then click **Expanded**.
5. Change the number of points between characters (in the top By text box) to **1.5**.

6. Observe the expanded spacing (applied to the first line of the selected text) in the Preview box.

7. Click **OK,** and then click anywhere in the cover page to deselect the text. The new character spacing is applied to the text of the cover page. See Figure 5-30.

Figure 5-30 EXPANDED CHARACTER SPACING IN TITLE PAGE

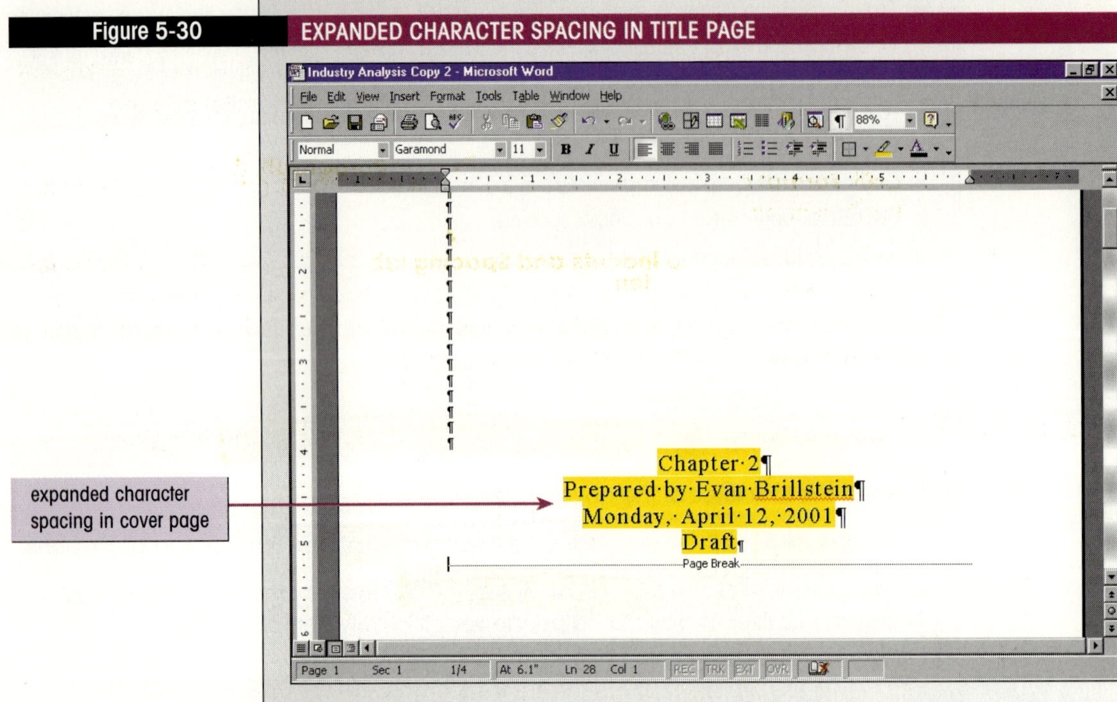

Now that the cover page is finished, you turn your attention to adjusting the spacing before and after the bulleted list on page 2 of the document.

Adjusting Spacing between Paragraphs

In a single-spaced document, such as the draft of Chapter 2, it's often a good idea to insert extra spacing before specially formatted items, such as a bulleted list. As with character spacing, paragraph spacing is measured in points.

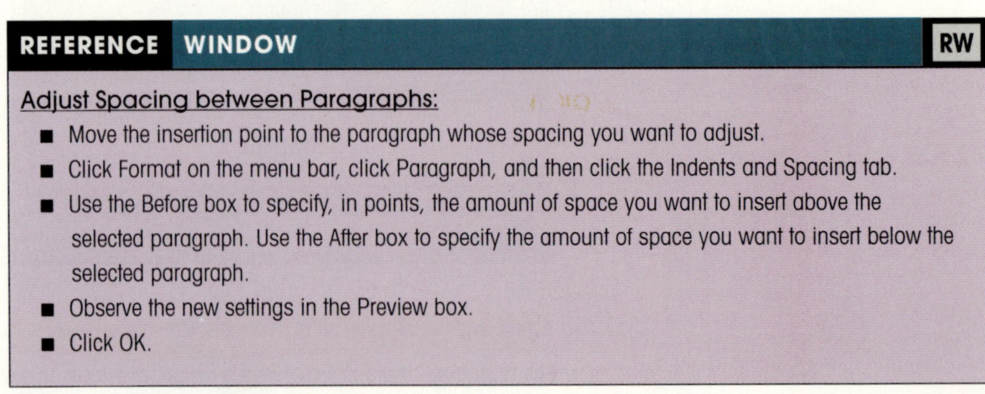

REFERENCE WINDOW RW

Adjust Spacing between Paragraphs:

- Move the insertion point to the paragraph whose spacing you want to adjust.
- Click Format on the menu bar, click Paragraph, and then click the Indents and Spacing tab.
- Use the Before box to specify, in points, the amount of space you want to insert above the selected paragraph. Use the After box to specify the amount of space you want to insert below the selected paragraph.
- Observe the new settings in the Preview box.
- Click OK.

Robert has asked you to insert extra space before and after the bulleted list on Page 2, under the heading "Market Research."

To change the paragraph spacing before and after the bulleted list:

1. Scroll to the second page of the document, and then click at the beginning of the first bullet ("Who are our potential customers?") under the heading "Market Research." Now you can insert extra space between this bullet and the introductory sentence before it.
2. Click **Format** on the menu bar, and then click **Paragraph**. The Paragraph dialog box opens.
3. If necessary, click the **Indents and Spacing** tab. See Figure 5-31. As mentioned earlier, you can use the Line spacing settings to choose precise line-spacing options. You'll use the Before box now to specify, in points, the amount of space you want to insert above the selected paragraph.

Figure 5-31 INDENTS AND SPACING TAB IN THE PARAGRAPH DIALOG BOX

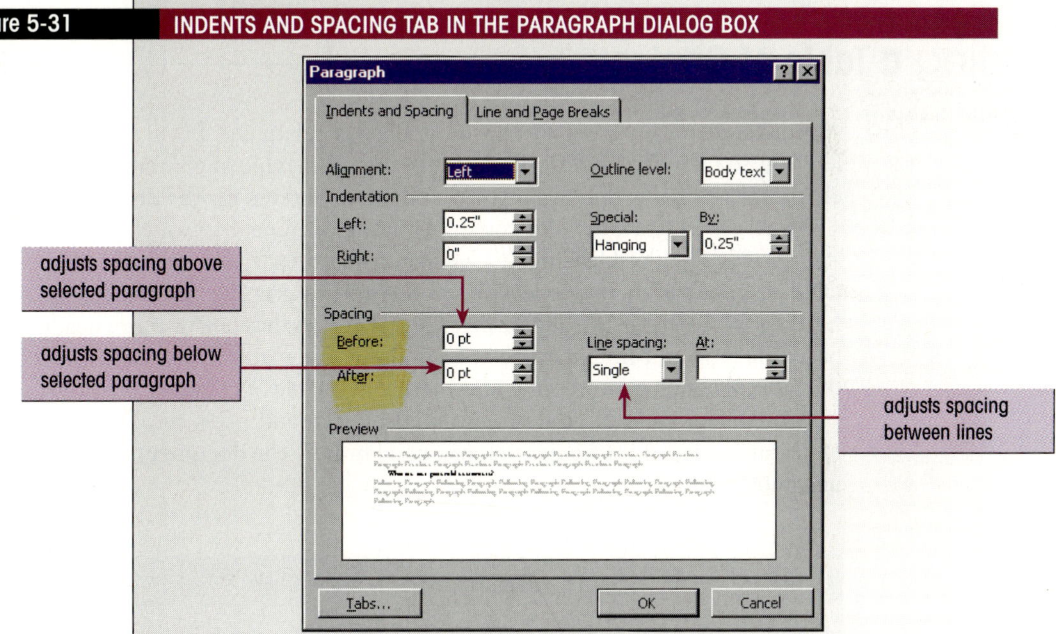

4. Click the up arrow in the Before text box to change the setting to **6 pt**.
5. Observe the effects of this new setting in the Preview box.
6. Click **OK**. The first bullet is now positioned six points (roughly 1⁄12 of an inch) below the previous paragraph.
7. Click at the beginning of the last bullet, which begins "Would these potential customers...."
8. Insert 6 points of space after the last bullet. The newly formatted bulleted list, with space inserted above and below, is shown in Figure 5-32.

Figure 5-32 NEW PARAGRAPH SPACING BEFORE AND AFTER THE BULLETED LIST

space inserted before the list

space inserted after the list

MARKET RESEARCH

Before and during the development of EstimaQuote, we conducted market research to answer the following questions:

- Who are our potential customers?
- How many are there?
- What features do these potential customers want in estimating software?
- Would these potential customers purchase our product?

The answers to these questions are crucial to the continued development and the future marketing of EstimaQuote.

The additional space draws attention to the bulleted list and makes it easier to read.

Now, Robert wants you create a table of contents, which should usually be one of the last tasks you perform in creating a document.

Creating a Table of Contents

Although this chapter of the business plan is relatively short, the entire business plan is lengthy, so Chiu Lee and Robert want to include a table of contents at the beginning of each chapter. Eventually, they will create a table of contents for the entire business plan.

Word can create a table of contents for any document to which you have applied heading styles in the form of Heading 1, Heading 2, Heading 3, and so forth. Word quickly creates a table of contents in the style you choose and inserts the relevant page numbers for each heading. Note that if you add or delete text later, so that one or more headings move to a new page, the table of contents will not be updated automatically. However, you can easily update the table of contents by clicking anywhere in the table of contents and pressing the F9 key.

To delete a table of contents, simply select it and press the Delete key. To modify the appearance of a table of contents, you need modify the document styles and then re-create a new table of contents.

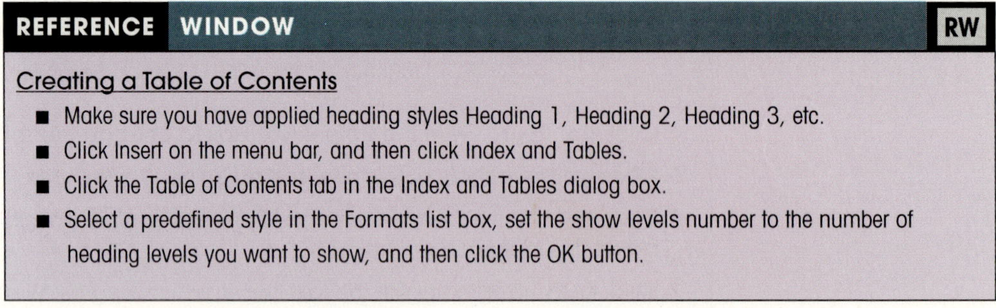

REFERENCE WINDOW RW

Creating a Table of Contents

- Make sure you have applied heading styles Heading 1, Heading 2, Heading 3, etc.
- Click Insert on the menu bar, and then click Index and Tables.
- Click the Table of Contents tab in the Index and Tables dialog box.
- Select a predefined style in the Formats list box, set the show levels number to the number of heading levels you want to show, and then click the OK button.

Now, you're ready to create a table of contents for Chapter 2 of the EstimaTech business plan, inserting it just below the title of the chapter.

To insert the table of contents for Chapter 2:

1. Move the insertion point to the blank line immediately below the chapter title on page 2.
2. Switch to normal view. First you need to type the heading for the table of contents.
3. Click the **Bold** button **B** on the Formatting toolbar, type **Contents**, click **B** again to turn off bold formatting, and then press **Enter** three times. The insertion point is now located where you want to insert the table of contents.
4. Click **Insert** on the menu bar, and then click **Index and Tables**. The Index and Tables dialog box opens.
5. If necessary, click the **Table of Contents** tab. Word provides a variety of formats for the Table of Contents page. In this case, you'll accept the From template setting in the Formats list box, which indicates that you want to format the table of contents using the Normal style from the current template.
6. Make sure **From template** is selected in the Formats list box. The Print Preview box shows a sample of the format. See Figure 5-33.

Figure 5-33 INDEX AND TABLES DIALOG BOX

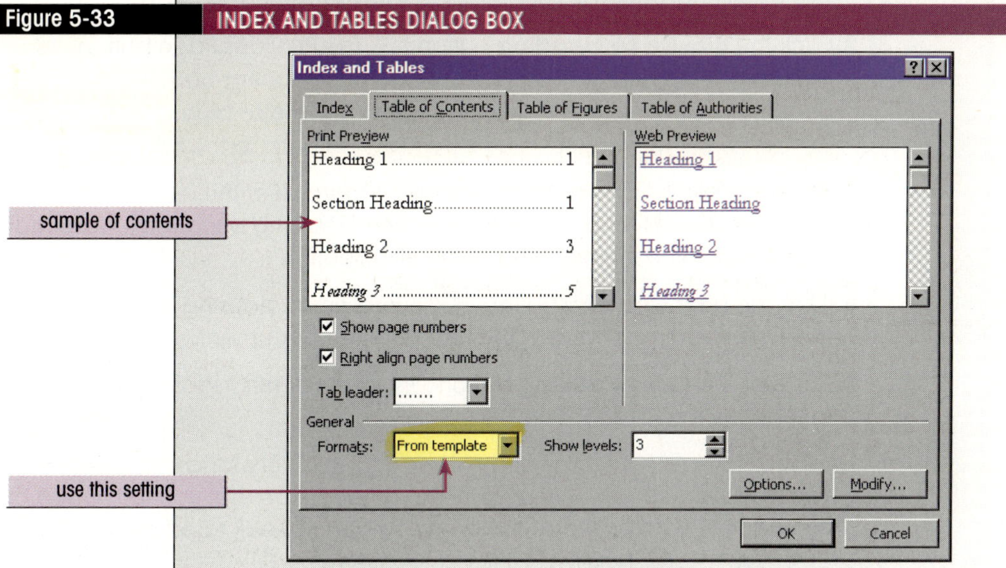

7. Click the **OK** button. Word searches for any text formatted with styles Heading 1, Heading 2, Heading 3, and so on, and then assembles that text and its corresponding page number in a table of contents. The table of contents appears below the "Contents" heading. When selected, the text is grayed to indicate that Word created the list and considers the text a single object.
8. Save the completed document.

With the table of contents at the beginning of the chapter, you're almost ready to print the document. Before you print, however, it's a good idea to review the document on-screen first. In the next section, you'll browse through the document by heading.

Browsing by Heading

Now that you have finished working on Chapter 2 of the business plan, you can print it for Robert and Chiu Lee. Before you print the business plan, however, you should browse through it to double-check its appearance and organization. Word provides various ways for you to move through a document quickly, a process known as **browsing.** For example, you could browse by headings (that is, move from one heading to another) or browse by page (that is, move from one page to another). The particular element by which you choose to browse (for example, headings or pages) is known as the **browse object.** Right now, you'll browse through the chapter by heading.

To browse by heading:

1. Click the **Select Browse Object** button located near the bottom of the vertical scroll bar. A palette of browse objects opens. To review these options, place the pointer over each object, and read its description in the gray box at the bottom of the palette. Note that if you don't see the browse object you need here, you can click the Go To button in the lower-left corner of the palette to display a dialog box with additional options.
2. Click the **Browse by Heading** button. The Previous Page button and Next Page button are now called the Previous Heading button and the Next Heading button, respectively. Note that they are also blue. When you click one of these buttons, Word will move the insertion point to the next heading.
3. Move the insertion point to the first full paragraph of the document, below the table of contents, and then click the **Next Heading** button. Word moves the insertion point to the heading, "Market Research."
4. Click the **Next Heading** button several times, pausing after each click to read the heading and view the format of the document.
5. Click the **Previous Heading** button several times, again pausing each time to read the heading.

   As you can imagine, browsing by heading in a very long document can allow you to move through a lot of material quickly. Now that you're finished browsing by heading, you'll change the browsing object back to pages.
6. Click , and then click the **Browse by Page** button. The Previous and Next buttons are black again, indicating that your browse object is now set back to Page.
7. Save the document as **Industry Analysis Final Copy**.
8. Preview, and then print the chapter. If Word displays a message about updating the table of contents, then click the **OK** button in the message dialog box. Your completed document should look like Figure 5-34. Notice that the yellow highlighting on the cover page appears as a gray background on a black and white print-out.

Figure 5-34 THE COMPLETED DOCUMENT (PAGES 1 AND 2)

Chapter 2
Prepared by Evan Brillstein
Monday, April 12, 2001
Draft

ESTIMATECH BUSINESS PLAN INDUSTRY ANALYSIS PAGE 2

CHAPTER 2: INDUSTRY ANALYSIS

Contents

The primary goal of EstimaTech is to become the industry leader in developing and marketing a major new type of software product—EstimaQuote. This computer program is designed for a specialized customer, will be sold at a reasonable price, and will be supported by a state-of-the-art service program. To determine the potential for achieving this goal, we have carried out extensive market research.

MARKET RESEARCH

Before and during the development of EstimaQuote, we conducted market research to answer the following questions:

- Who are our potential customers?
- How many are there?
- What features do these potential customers want in estimating software?
- Would these potential customers purchase our product?

The answers to these questions are crucial to the continued development and the future marketing of EstimaQuote.

PHASES OF THE MARKET RESEARCH

The market research was carried out in three phases. In Phase 1, we analyzed the potential customers for our software throughout the United States and Canada. In Phase 2, we determined the method by which potential customers estimate renovation costs, their perceived need for a computerized

Figure 5-34 THE COMPLETED DOCUMENT (PAGES 3 AND 4)

ESTIMATECH BUSINESS PLAN INDUSTRY ANALYSIS PAGE 3

method for estimating costs, and the desired features of such a product. The survey also assessed the current condition of the industry in order to understand future market trends. In Phase 3, we provided a random sample of our potential customers with a pre-release beta copy (version 0.5) of EstimaQuote. We observed these customers as they installed and used this software, making particular note of the problems and difficulties they encountered. We are continuing with Phase 3 as we develop a new pre-release version of the software and improve our customer-support methods. As of this writing, we have almost completed, but not yet released, version 1 of the EstimaQuote, and have begun to develop version 2.

Here is the time frame for the three phases:

Phase 1. Analysis of potential customers	June to August 2001
Phase 2. Determination of needs and methods	August to November 2001
Phase 3. Beta testing of software	November 2001 to present

MARKET DEFINITION

EstimaTech will operate in the national and international market. After completing version 2 of EstimaQuote in English, we plan to expand to Spanish, French, German, and Japanese versions over the next four years. We will continue to improve our software in all languages.

SIZE OF THE MARKET

Our primary customers include large- and medium-sized contracting companies that restore existing buildings. Our secondary customers are government and private agencies, and wealthy individuals who renovate historical homes and buildings. Our estimated market size (for the United States only) is approximately 35,000. This number includes only those organizations and individuals directly involved in restoration cost estimates.

DEMOGRAPHIC DESCRIPTION OF TARGET USERS

Our target users have the following characteristics: Prepare frequent estimates; use printed forms; use computer spreadsheet, database, or calculator; prepare multiple calculations; provide high- and low-end options

Our target users desire a software program that can: Provide a tabular view of data; calculate costs based on overall building requirements; perform a one-step calculation of high and low prices; update costs of materials and labor; interface with project management software

CUSTOMER NEEDS

The results of the survey clearly demonstrated the need for a product such as EstimaQuote.[1] Approximately 72% of those individuals answering the questionnaire were dissatisfied with their current method of preparing cost estimates. Subsequent personal interviews supported these results. About 65% of those interviewed said they would purchase a product like EstimaQuote, given an estimated cost of $5,000 for the site license and $500 per year for license renewal and customer support.

[1] See Appendix 1, "Survey of Potential EstimaQuote Customers."

ESTIMATECH BUSINESS PLAN INDUSTRY ANALYSIS PAGE 4

MARKET TRENDS

The current business climate shows a reversal in the trend of developing new properties for business expansion in the nation's suburbs. Also, major businesses are returning to urban centers. These trends have spawned a sharp increase in the number of developers whose primary focus is renovation of old and run-down properties. In addition, historical restoration projects are increasing. Recently, a national survey by the U.S. Historical Society showed a 35% increase in the number of buildings being added to the historical registry.

CURRENT COMPETITION

No company currently has a specialized product like EstimaQuote. Many companies, however, use computerized database management systems and spreadsheets to develop estimates. Some companies have custom software designed for this purpose.

Our current competition, therefore, includes the following:

- General database systems such as Access, FoxPro, Paradox, and dBase
- General spreadsheet programs such as Excel, Quattro Pro, and Lotus 1-2-3
- Custom software

EstimaTech stands poised to capitalize on current trends in the market. We are prepared to refine our product to meet the needs of this growing market, aggressively market our product to reach potential customers, create new products as time goes on, and to withstand challenges from future competitors.

Potential customers indicate their need for the software we are developing. In addition, current market trends indicate that increased need for our software will continue.

Page breaks in your document might be at different locations, depending on the fonts you use. Don't be concerned about this. Simply scroll through your document and add return characters as necessary so that the lines of text are well-grouped.

9. Close the Preview window, close the document, and then exit Word.

You now have a hardcopy of the final Chapter 2 of the business plan, which you take to Robert and Chiu Lee.

Session 5.3 QUICK CHECK

1. Explain how to position the insertion point in the middle of a blank page without pressing Enter to insert paragraph marks.
2. True or False: If you use the Date and Time dialog box to insert the current date in your document, Word will automatically revise the date each time you open the document.
3. Describe a situation in which you might want to highlight text in a document, and then explain how to do so.
4. What is the difference between character spacing and paragraph spacing?
5. True or False: It is only possible to adjust the spacing before the selected paragraph.
6. Explain the steps required to create a table of contents in Word.
7. How do you browse by heading through a document?

In this tutorial, you have edited the business plan content with the Thesaurus and improved its appearance using fonts and styles. You reorganized the document in Outline view, hyphenated the document, and added a footnote. Also, you created a highlighted cover page, adjusted character and paragraph spacing, and added a table of contents. Chiu Lee and Robert plan to revise the chapter in the coming week. You also gave them a copy of the new document template, which they will use as they write additional chapters.

REVIEW ASSIGNMENTS

Chiu Lee and Robert have received the startup funding they wanted and are almost ready to begin marketing their software. They have written a summary of their customer training and support policies and have asked you to help edit and format the document.

1. Start Word, if necessary, and make sure that nonprinting characters and the ruler are displayed.
2. Open the file Training from the Review folder for Tutorial 5 on your Data Disk.
3. Open the Save As dialog box, and create a new folder called Policies (within the Review folder).

4. Save the file Training in the new folder as Training Courses.
5. Use the Thesaurus to replace "periodic" (in the first line of the first paragraph under the heading "Training") with a simpler word.
6. Attach the Word Contemporary Report template to the document. If this template is not available, choose another, and then use appropriate headings in the following step.
7. Apply the Chapter Label style to the first line of the document, "Training and Technical Support." Apply the Heading 1 style to all of the headings in the body of the document: "Training," "Introduction," "Technical Support," "Using Technical Support," "Average Wait Times," and "Frequently Asked Questions." Do not apply a style to the company address and phone number at the top of the document.

Explore

8. Create a new style by example for the company address and phone number at the top of the document. First, format the text as 12-point Arial bold, and then center it on the page. Change the character spacing to expanded, with 1.5 points between each character. Once the text is formatted properly, click Format on the menu bar, click Style, click the New button, name the new style "Company Information," review the style description, click OK, and then click Apply. (Do not save the new style to the template.) Click anywhere in the document outside the first six lines, and verify that the new style is available in the Style list box on the Formatting toolbar.
9. Modify the Chapter Label heading so that it formats text with center alignment, using the small caps font effect, in 20-point Times New Roman. (Look for the alignment setting on the Indents and Spacing tab of the Paragraph dialog box. Look for the font settings on the Font tab of the Font dialog box.)
10. Under the heading "Using Technical Support," select the list of technical support options (beginning "Call our telephone support….and ending with "…and then press Enter"), and then apply the List Bullet style. Under the heading "Average Wait Times," apply the List Bullet style to the list of waiting times for the four technical support plans (Bronze through Platinum). Modify the List Bullet Style by changing its paragraph spacing to 6 points before and 0 points after. (Do not save the modified style to the template.)
11. Using Outline view, reorganize the document so the Introduction section is the first section of the document.
12. Demote the headings "Using Technical Support," "Average Wait Times," and "Frequently Asked Questions" to make them level-2 headings, and then switch to Normal view to review your changes.
13. Below the heading, "Technical Support," after the period at the end of the second sentence, insert the following footnote: "As the needs and resources of your company change, you can change your technical support plan. Changes can be made only at the expiration of the current contract period."

Explore

14. Hyphenate the document with a hyphenation zone of 0.1", using manual hyphenation. Don't hyphenate words so that only two letters appear alone on a line.

15. Create a cover page for the document. Use Click and Type to insert your name, and the word "Draft" in the center of the page. Insert the current date and time, using the format of your choice.
16. Highlight the word "Draft" to call attention to it.
17. Save and preview your document.
18. Insert a table of contents immediately following the company address and phone numbers. In the Formats list box, specify the Distinctive format for your table of contents. (If the Distinctive format is not available, choose another.) Be sure to include the necessary number of heading levels.

Explore

19. A table of contents provides a quick way to move the insertion point to a document heading. Try clicking a heading in the table of contents, and watch the insertion point jump to that heading in the document.

Explore

20. Click at the top of the document, click the Select Browse Object button, click the Go To button, and then use the Go To dialog box to move the insertion point to the footnote.
21. Save the document, and then print it. If you are asked if you want to update the table of contents, click cancel.
22. Use the Training Courses document to create a new template called "Policy Template." Save the new template in the Policies folder.
23. Open a blank document, and attach the Policy Template to it. Verify that the template headings are available in the document, save the new document as "New Policy," and then close the document.

Explore

24. To experiment with using a Word template as the basis for a brand-new document, click File on the menu bar, and then click New. Click the tabs in the New dialog box to review the various templates provided with Word. Some tabs include icons for wizards, which guide you through the steps involved in creating complicated documents such as Web pages. Click the General tab. Note that if you create a new template, and save it in the Templates folder, it will appear as an option on this tab. Click the Reports tab, click the Contemporary Report icon, and then click OK. A document opens with placeholder text for all the elements of a report. For example, in the upper-right corner you see "Type Address Here." A place-holder company name, "blue sky associates," appears at the top of the first page formatted in the Company Name style. Review the remaining styles in the templates. To use this template, you could delete the placeholder text with text you type, and then save the document with a new name. When you're finished, close the document without saving changes. Open and examine two other templates.
25. Close any open documents.

CASE PROBLEMS

Case 1. Mountainland Nursery Raynal Stubbs is the sales manager of Mountainland Nursery in Steamboat Springs, Colorado. Twice each year, he provides sales representatives with guidelines for helping customers with their planting needs. Raynal has asked you to help him prepare this year's list of spring-blooming perennials.

1. Start Word, if necessary, open the file Flowers from the Cases folder for Tutorial 5 on your Data Disk, and save it as Mountainland Flowers.

2. Using outline view, promote the section "Guidelines for Helping Customers" to a first-level heading. (*Hint:* Show all text by clicking the Show All Headings button, so you can see the sentence to promote.)
3. Reorder the document so the introduction section is the first section of the document.
4. Make "Guidelines for Helping Customers" the last section in the document.
5. Print the outline, without showing the formatting of the headings.
6. Change the font of the Title style and the Heading 1 style to a sans serif font.
7. Change the font of the Normal style to a serif font other than Times New Roman.
8. Click at the end of the telephone number, at the top of the document press Enter twice, type "Draft Prepared by," and then type your name. Highlight the new line, using the color of your choice.
9. Format the four lines containing the nursery's name, address, and phone number using one of the font effects (such as small caps) available in the Font dialog box. Adjust the character spacing as necessary to make the text easy to read.
10. In the last item of the bulleted list, change "patrons" to one of its synonyms in the Thesaurus.
11. In the first sentence under the heading "Suggested Spring Blooming Perennials," after the word "perennials," insert a footnote reference. Type the following text for the footnote: "Information taken from Andrea Macula's *Gardening in the West*, published by Gladstone Press, Flagstaff, Arizona." Be sure to italicize the book title.
12. Hyphenate the document using automatic hyphenation.
13. Move the insertion point to the paragraph above the table, and change the paragraph spacing after the paragraph to 12-point.

Explore

14. Insert a table of contents for the document above the introduction, using the Formal style. Because the document is so short, there's no need for page numbers, so you can deselect the Show page numbers checkbox.

Explore

15. Change the heading "Guidelines for Helping Customers" to "Guidelines for Assisting Customers." Now that you've changed the heading, you need to update the table of contents, as follows: right-click the table of contents, and then click Update Field in the shortcut menu.
16. Save your changes. Preview the document for problems, fix any formatting problems, and print the document.

Explore

17. Word's AutoCorrect feature allows you to preserve formatted text and then insert it into documents later simply by typing a few characters. To see how this works, select the nursery's name, address, and phone number at the top of the document, as well as the blank paragraph below the phone number. Click Tools on the menu bar, click AutoCorrect, click the AutoCorrect tab, type "mf address" (without the quotes) in the Replace text box, verify that the Formatted text option button is selected, click the Add button, and then click OK. To try out the new Autocorrect entry, close the Mountainland Flowers document, open a blank document, type mf address, and press the spacebar. Verify that the formatted text is inserted into the document, and then delete your AutoCorrect entry as follows: Click Tools, click AutoCorrect, scroll down and select the mn address entry in the list box, click Delete, and click OK.

Case 2. Menus for Classic Catering Clarissa Ruffolo and Tom Jenkins own Classic Catering, an upscale catering service that specializes in home entertaining for people who like to socialize but don't have time to cook. Tom has prepared a brochure with the company's latest menu choices, which he formatted using the Word default heading styles. However, he is not happy with the brochure's appearance and has asked for your help.

1. Start Word, if necessary, and check your screen, making sure that nonprinting characters are displayed.
2. Open the file Catering from the Cases folder for Tutorial 5 on your Data Disk, and save it as Classic Catering.
3. **Explore** Notice that the headings in the document are formatted using the Word default Heading 1 and Heading 2 styles. Now, use the Templates and Add-Ins command on the Tools menu to attach the template named Menu Template, which is stored in the Cases folder for Tutorial 5, to the current document. Remember to select the Automatically update document styles checkbox. Verify that the document's styles are updated to reflect the template's styles.
4. Apply the Bulleted List style to all the bulleted lists in the document.
5. In outline view, promote the headings "Lunch," "Dinner," and "Our Famous Desserts," to level-1 headings.
6. Move the "Our Famous Desserts" heading up, to make it the first heading in the document, above "Bagel Brunch."
7. Print the outline, with only the headings displayed.
8. In the first sentence under the heading "Our Famous Desserts," use the Thesaurus to find a synonym for "delectable."
9. **Explore** Switch to print layout view, insert a new first page, move the insertion point up to the new page, select the Company Name style, then use Click and Type to insert "Classic Catering" (without the quotes) about 3 inches down, in the center of the document. Notice how the Click and Type Feature automatically applies the selected style.
10. Press [Enter], select the Company Address style, and then type the following:

    2567 Eton Ridge
    Madison, Wisconsin 53708
    Prepared by Your Name

    Be sure to replace "Your Name" with your first and last name. Then, insert the current date below your name, in the format of your choice.
11. Highlight your name in yellow.
12. Save, preview, and print the document.

Case 3. The Business of Basketball As part of the requirements for your advanced writing class, your writing group has written a term paper on "The Business of Basketball." Your assignment is to edit the preliminary outline.

1. Start Word, if necessary, and check your screen, making sure that nonprinting characters are displayed. Open the file Business from the Cases folder for Tutorial 5 on your Data Disk.

2. Within the Cases folder for Tutorial 5, create a new folder called "Writing Project," and then save the document in the new folder as "Business of Basketball."
3. Using outline view, reorder the headings so that "Team Philosophy" follows "Management Style."
4. Demote the section "Marketing" to make it a second-level heading.
5. Print the completed outline of the document, with the Show Formatting feature turned off.
6. Use the Thesaurus to find a synonym to replace "lucrative" in the first sentence under the heading "Introduction."
7. Scroll to the table in the document, and then at the end of the table title, add the footnote with the text, "Data taken from *Financial World*, May 25, 2001, page 29." Scroll up and place the pointer over the footnote number, in the main document. Observe the text of the footnote displayed in a screen tip.
8. Change the Heading 1 style to a sans serif font.
9. Create a new paragraph style called Abstract. For this style, specify 12-point Arial, with single-line spacing. Add a box border around the paragraph. Apply the style to the paragraph under the heading "Abstract."
10. Add your name to the list of authors on the first page.
11. Below the class name, insert the current date, and on another line, the word "Draft". Highlight the date and the word "Draft" in yellow.
12. Insert a section break following the word "Draft" on the title page, so that the Table of Contents begins a new page.
13. Create a table of contents for the report to appear on its own page following the title page. Use the Formal style.
14. If the heading "Abstract" is on a separate page from the boxed paragraph below it, insert a hard page break above the heading "Abstract." Do the same for the table title, if necessary. (*Hint:* To insert a hard page break, move the insertion point to the desired location, and press Ctrl + Enter.)
15. Save the changes to your report; then preview and print it. Close the file.

Case 4. Report on Median Family Income Arlene Littlefield is an economic analyst for a consulting firm that helps minority businesses market their products. She is preparing a short report on the median family income of American families, from 1980 to 1991, based upon the ethnicity of the head of household. She has obtained a government report that contains two tables of data, which she gives to you as unformatted Word tables and asks you to help her analyze the information and write her report.

1. Start Word, if necessary, making sure that nonprinting characters are displayed. Open the file Income from the Cases folder for Tutorial 5 on your Data Disk, and print the document. Analyze the two tables. On scratch paper (or in a Word document window), jot down your observations, ideas, and conclusions about the data in the two tables. As you analyze the data, you might be interested in noting that the average family income for all families in the United States in 1950, 1960, and 1970 was \$3,319, \$5,630, and \$9,867 in current dollars and \$18,757, \$25,850, and \$34,636 in constant dollars. (Data for minorities during those time periods is scarce or unavailable.)

2. Plan a logical order of topics for your talk, with headings and subheadings. Your headings might be the following: "Introduction" (which explains the purpose of your report), "Income Increases During the 1980s" (with subheadings "Income Increase for Whites," "Income Increases for Blacks," and "Income Increases for Hispanics"), "Comparison of Incomes Based on Ethnicity," "Are Minorities Catching Up with Whites in Income?," and "Economic Progress during the 1980s: Did We Get Richer?," "Economic Progress in the U.S." You might want to use some of these sample headings or none of them. Organize your outline in a logical manner. Make sure your final heading is "Summary" or "Conclusion."

Explore

3. Open a new Word document, and type a title for your talk.

Explore

4. In addition to creating an outline using document headings, you can create a numbered list in outline format, using the Numbering button on the Formatting toolbar. To experiment with this feature now, move the insertion point to a new line, click the Numbering button on the Formatting toolbar, and type your first heading. Press Enter, and type the next heading. To demote a level-1 heading to a level-2 heading, click the Increase Indent button on the Formatting toolbar. To demote a level-2 heading to a level-3 heading, click the Increase Indent button again. Use the Decrease Indent to promote headings. You can promote and demote headings as you type or after you've typed all the headings. After you type the last item in the outline, press Enter twice.

Explore

5. Now that you have created your outline, you can format it using the Word default heading styles. Select your outline numbered list, click Format on the menu bar, click Bullets and Numbering, and then click the Outline Numbered tab, which offers two rows of formatting styles. Click the second style from the right, in the bottom row (which uses the form I. Heading 1, A. Heading 2), and then click OK.

6. Switch to outline view, and print two versions of your outline, using two different organizations.

7. Switch to print layout view, and write your report. One or two paragraphs under each heading is sufficient.

8. At the appropriate places in your document, copy the tables from the document Income into your document.

9. Format your tables to be attractive and readable. Make sure they are single-spaced and each table appears in its entirety on one page rather than spanning two pages.

10. At the end of each table title, insert a footnote with the citation for the table: U.S. Department of Commerce, Bureau of the Census, Current Population Reports, Series P-60, *Money Income of Families and Persons*, nos. 105 and 107. Use this same citation for both tables.
11. Change the fonts of the Normal and heading styles as desired.
12. Hyphenate your document as desired.

Explore

13. Edit the footnotes by adding "*in the United States*" after the word "Persons." The final footnote should read: "U.S. Department of Commerce, Bureau of the Census, Current Population Reports, Series P-60, *Money Income of Families and Persons in the United States*, nos. 105 and 107."
14. Create a table of contents at the appropriate location in your document.
15. Save your report as Median Family Income in the Cases folder for Tutorial 5 and then preview and print it. Close the documents.

INTERNET ASSIGNMENTS

The purpose of the Internet Assignments is to challenge you to find information on the Internet that you can use to create effective documents. The actual assignments are updated and maintained on the Course Technology Web site. Log on to the Internet and use your Web browser to go to the Student Online Companion to accompany this text at **www.course.com/NewPerspectives/office2000**. Click the Word link, and then click the link for Tutorial 5.

QUICK CHECK ANSWERS

Session 5.1

1. In the Save As dialog box, click the New Folder button, type the name of the folder, and then click OK.
2. The Thesaurus is a feature you can use to find synonyms for words in a document.
3. The following are synonyms for "restore" included in Word's Thesaurus: refurbish, renovate, repair, do up, rebuild, recondition, touch up, fix, fix up, reinstate, reestablish, bring back, and return.
4. A serif font is a font in which each character has a small embellishment (called a serif) at its tips. A sans serif font is a font in which the characters do not have serifs. Serif fonts are useful for the main text of a document because they are easy to read. Sans serif fonts are best for headings and titles. Two examples of serif fonts are Times New Roman and Garamond. Two examples of sans serif fonts include Arial and Century Gothic.
5. Click Format on the menu bar, click Theme, and then click the Style Gallery button. In the Template list box, click the template you want to preview. In the Preview box, click the Document option button to see how the template's Normal styles look when applied to your document, or click the Example option button to see a sample file that uses all the template styles. Click the OK button to attach the template to your document.

6. First, create a new document containing all the styles you want to include in your template, save it as a Word document, and delete all text from the document. Then save the file as a Document Template. Verify that the Templates folder is displayed in the Save in list box. If you save your template to this folder, it will appear as one of the options in the New dialog box. If you prefer, you can save the template in a different location, such as your data disk. To use a template saved in the Template folder, use the New command on the File menu. To attach a template saved in a different location, click Tools on the menu bar, click Templates and Add-ins, and then click the Attach button to open the Attach Template dialog box. Use the Look in list box to locate and select your template, and then click the Open button to return to the Templates and Add-ins dialog box. Click the Automatically update document styles check box to select it, and then click the OK button to return to the current document.
7. Click Format on the menu bar, and then click Style. Select the style you want to modify in the Style list box, and then click the Modify button. Use the options available from the Format button to specify new settings for the style.
8. Format a paragraph with the font, margins, alignment, spacing, and so forth that you want for the style, and then select the paragraph. Click the Style text box on the Formatting toolbar. Type the name of the new style (replacing the current style name), and then press the Enter key. Or, select the text for which you want to define a style. Click Format on the menu bar, click Style, click the New button, and type the name of the new style in the Name text box. Finally, click the OK button, and then click the Apply button.

Session 5.2

1. By moving the headings in an outline, you can reorganize the document text.
2. When you promote a heading, it becomes a higher-level heading in the outline. For example, you could promote a level-2 heading to a level-1 heading. When you demote a heading, it becomes a lower-level heading. For example, you could demote a level-1 heading to a level-2 or level-3 heading.
3. To promote a heading, click that heading in outline view, and then click the Promote button on the Outline toolbar. To demote a heading, click that heading and then click the Demote button.
4. True
5. A river is a blank area running through the text of a page.
6. The hyphenation zone is the distance from the right margin within which words will be hyphenated. Increasing its size reduces the number of hyphenated words.
7. The advantages of using the Footnote feature are:
   - Word numbers footnotes or endnotes automatically. If you add a note anywhere in the document, delete a note, or move a note, Word automatically renumbers all the remaining footnotes or endnotes consecutively.
   - Word automatically formats the footnote text at the bottom of the page or the endnote text at the end of the document.
   - You can edit a footnote or endnote at any time. To modify the text, select Footnotes from the View menu and then use the same editing commands you use in the document window.
   - If you add or delete text that moves the footnote reference onto a different page, the footnote will also move to that page. The reference in the text and the footnote at the bottom of the page will always be on the same page.

8. A footnote appears at the bottom of a page, whereas an endnote appears at the end of a document.

Session 5.3

1. Double-click a blank area of a page using the Click and Type pointer.
2. False
3. It is sometimes helpful to highlight text that you'll want to delete from a document later. To highlight text, first select it and then click the Highlight button on the Formatting toolbar.
4. Character spacing affects the positioning of individual characters, whereas paragraph spacing affects the spacing between paragraphs.
5. False
6. Make sure you have applied heading styles Heading 1, Heading 2, Heading 3, and so forth. Click Insert on the menu bar, and then click Index and Tables. Click the Table of Contents tab in the Index and Tables dialog box. Select a predefined style in the Formats list box, set the show-levels number to the number of heading levels you want to show, and then click the OK button.
7. Click the Select Browse Object button, click the Browse by Heading button, and then click the Previous Heading or Next Heading buttons.

OBJECTIVES

In this tutorial you will:

- Create, edit, and format a mail merge main document
- Create, edit, and format a mail merge data source
- Sort records in a data source
- Merge files to create personalized form letters
- Create, format, and print mailing labels
- Create a telephone list from a data source

CREATING FORM LETTERS AND MAILING LABELS

Writing a Sales Letter for The Pet Shoppe

CASE

The Pet Shoppe

Alicia Robles is vice-president of sales for The Pet Shoppe, a chain of 15 superstores based in Colorado Springs, Colorado. The Pet Shoppe, which has customers throughout the state, sells a wide variety of pets, pet food, supplies, and services. As part of her job, Alicia sends information about The Pet Shoppe's products and services to customers who request to be on the company's mailing list. Alicia needs to send the same information to many customers, but because of the large number of Pet Shoppe customers, she and her staff don't have the time to write personalized letters. Instead, she can create a **form letter** that contains the content she wants to send all customers and then add personal information for each customer, such as the name, address, type of pet, and so on, in specific places. To do this manually would be very time-consuming. Fortunately, Microsoft Word provides a time-saving method that simplifies Alicia's job. By using Word's Mail Merge feature, Alicia can produce multiple copies of the same letter yet personalize each copy with customer-specific information in about the same amount of time it takes to personalize just one letter. She also could use this feature to create such documents as catalogs, directories, and contracts.

The Pet Shoppe is celebrating its 10th anniversary. As a promotional tool, Alicia wants to send out a form letter to all customers on the mailing list telling them about the chain's 10th Anniversary Celebration and offering them a discount if they purchase a product or service anytime during the store's anniversary month. Alicia has already written the letter she wants to send, but she needs to add the personal information for each customer. She asks you to create the form letters and the mailing labels for the envelopes.

In this tutorial, you'll help Alicia create a form letter and mailing labels using Word's Mail Merge feature. First, you'll open the letter that will serve as the main document. Next, you'll create a data source document that contains the name and address of each customer who will receive the customized letter.

Then, you'll have Word merge the main document with the data source, which creates the customized letters, and sorts them in ZIP code order. You'll also send a special version of the letter offering special savings on surplus inventory to customers in a particular ZIP code. Finally, you'll use the data source document to create mailing labels Alicia can put on the envelopes and to create a telephone list so Alicia can have the sales representatives follow up the mailing with a phone call to each customer.

SESSION 6.1

In this session, you'll see how Alicia planned her letter. Then you'll open the form letter and create a document containing the specific customer information that will be inserted into the form letter using Word's Mail Merge feature.

Planning the Form Letter

Alicia hopes to generate increased sales for The Pet Shoppe chain by announcing a 10-percent discount on the purchase of any product or service as part of the company's 10th Anniversary Celebration. Alicia's sales letter will inform current customers about The Pet Shoppe's 10th Anniversary Celebration and offer them a special discount on products and services during November. Her letter is organized to capture the reader's attention. First, she cites a few examples of the need The Pet Shoppe fills, and then she briefly describes The Pet Shoppe's services and products. Finally, she offers a discount to encourage readers to visit their local stores.

Alicia writes in a persuasive, informal style. She illustrates the need and quality of The Pet Shoppe's services by including personal experiences of current customers. Alicia wants to send a professional-looking, personalized letter to each customer on The Pet Shoppe's mailing list. She uses a standard business-letter format and plans to print the letters on stationery preprinted with the company letterhead.

The Merge Process

Alicia asks you to use Word's Mail Merge feature to create the form letters. In general, a **merge** combines information from two separate documents to create many final documents, each of which contains customized information. In Word, the two separate documents are called a main document and a data source.

A **main document** is a document (such as a letter or a contract) that, in addition to text, contains areas of placeholder text (called **merge fields**) to mark where variable information (such as a name or an address) will be inserted. Alicia's main document is a letter that looks like Figure 6–1, except that merge fields will replace the red text to mark the locations of the customer's name, address, and other information.

Figure 6-1 ALICIA'S FORM LETTER

The Pet Shoppe

121 Stilltoe Avenue ■ Colorado Springs, CO 80901
Phone: (719) 555-5555 ■ Fax: (719) 555-5556

[Date]

[FirstName] [LastName]
[Address1]
[City,] CO [PostalCode]

Dear [FirstName]:

Ten years ago, Stephen Mueller was unable to find suitable grooming facilities for his dog, Rusty. Maria Fuentes drove 100 miles to buy food for her cat, Sneakers. And Carole Cochran only dreamed of owning an armadillo lizard. Today, Stephen, Maria, and Carole are among The Pet Shoppe's loyal customers.

Established in 1988, The Pet Shoppe chain provides a complete line of high quality yet affordable pet supplies and services for customers throughout Colorado. We're committed to helping you meet the needs of your [PetKind] in a caring manner.

We invite you and your pet to join us in our 10th Anniversary Celebration. Just bring this letter to The Pet Shoppe in the [Branch] anytime during the month of November and you'll receive a 10% discount on the purchase of any product or service. And remember to register [PetName] for our month-long "Purrfect Pet" drawing. We'll be giving away over $1,000 worth of prizes and services each week.

We look forward to seeing you at The Pet Shoppe.

Sincerely yours,

Alicia Robles
Vice President, Sales

A **data source** is a document that contains information, such as customers' names and addresses that will be merged into the main document. Alicia's data source is a name and address list of The Pet Shoppe customers.

Inserting information from a data source into a main document produces a final document, called a **merged document**. Figure 6–2 illustrates how the data source and main document combine to form a merged document.

Figure 6-2 MERGING A MAIN DOCUMENT WITH A DATA SOURCE TO CREATE A MERGED DOCUMENT

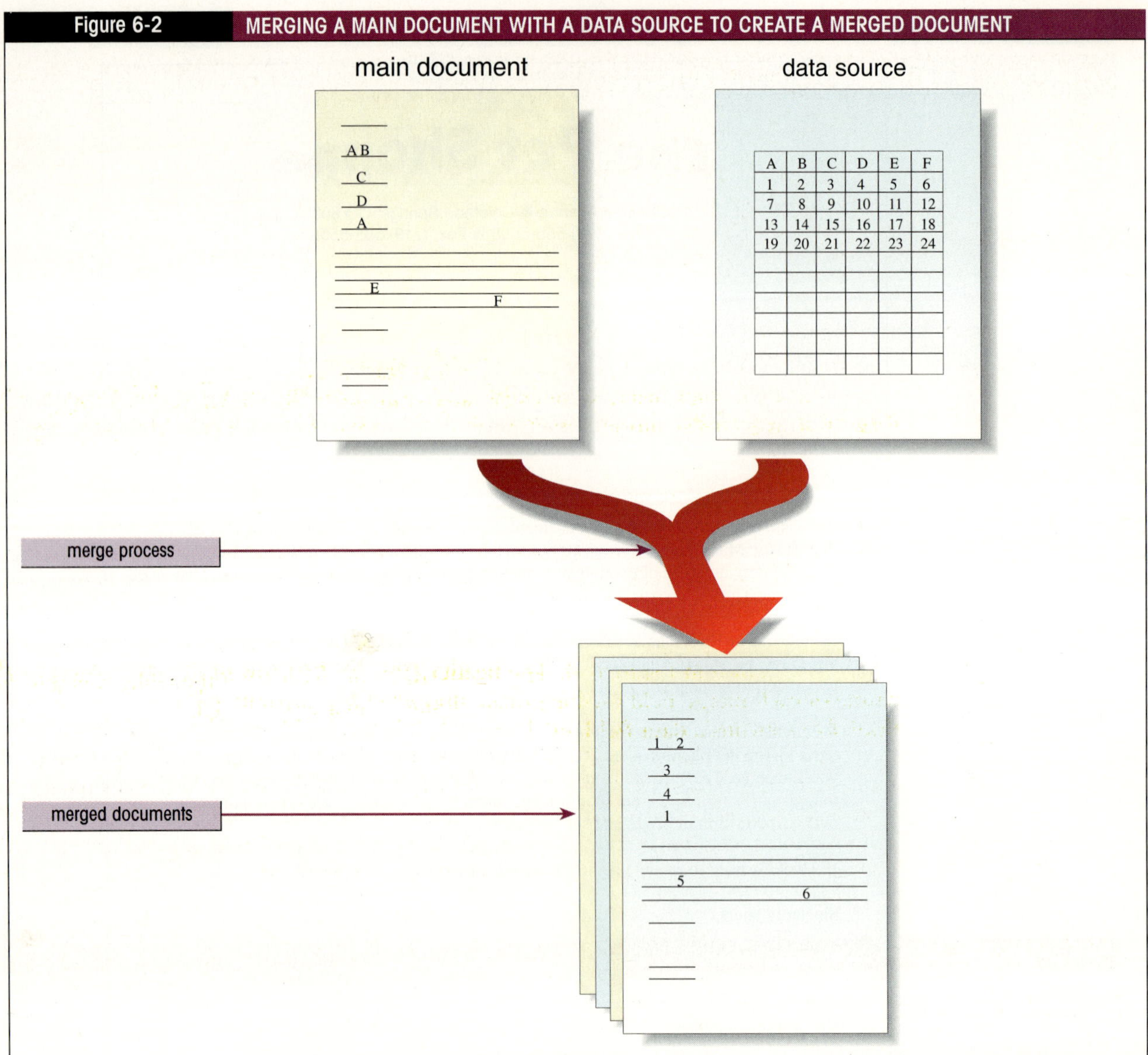

Mail Merge Fields

During a mail merge, the **merge fields** (the placeholders for text that changes in the main document) instruct Word to retrieve specific information from the data source. For example, one merge field in the main document might retrieve a name from the data source, whereas another merge field might retrieve an address. For each complete set of data (in this instance, a name and address) in the data source, Word will create a new, separate page in the merged document. Thus, if Alicia has five sets of customer names and addresses in her data source, the merge will produce five versions of the main document, each one containing a different customer name and address in the appropriate places.

In addition to merge fields, a main document also can contain **Word fields**, which retrieve information from sources other than the data source. For example, a Word field might insert the current date into a main document, prompt you to input text from the keyboard, or print information only if certain, specified conditions are met. Figure 6–3 lists some of the most common Word and merge fields.

Figure 6-3 COMMON FIELDS USED IN MAIL MERGE

WORD FIELDS	ACTION
DATE	Inserts current date
FILLIN	Displays a prompt during merge; response is inserted into the merged document
IF	Prints information only if a specified condition is met
MERGEFIELD	Extracts information from the data source document and inserts it into the merged document

You can distinguish merge fields from the other text of the main document because each merge field name is enclosed by pairs of angled brackets like this: << >>. You don't type the merge field into your main document; instead, you use the Insert Merge Field command to place the merge fields into your main document, and Word automatically inserts the brackets.

Data Fields and Records

Data for a mail merge can come from many sources, including a Microsoft Word document, a Microsoft Excel workbook, or a Microsoft Access database. In the Review Assignments, you will learn how to use a Microsoft Excel workbook as a data source. For Alicia's mail merge, you will use a Word table in which information is organized into data fields and records, as shown in Figure 6–4. The **header row**, the first row of the table, contains the name of each merge field used in a main document in a separate cell. Every other cell of the table contains a **data field**, or the specific information that replaces the merge field in the main document. As shown in Figure 6–4, one data field might be the first name of a customer, another data field the customer's address, another data field the customer's city, and so forth. Each row of data fields in the table makes up a complete record, or all the information about one individual or object. For proper functioning of a mail merge, every record in the data source must have the same set of merge fields.

Figure 6-4 WORD TABLE USED AS A DATA SOURCE

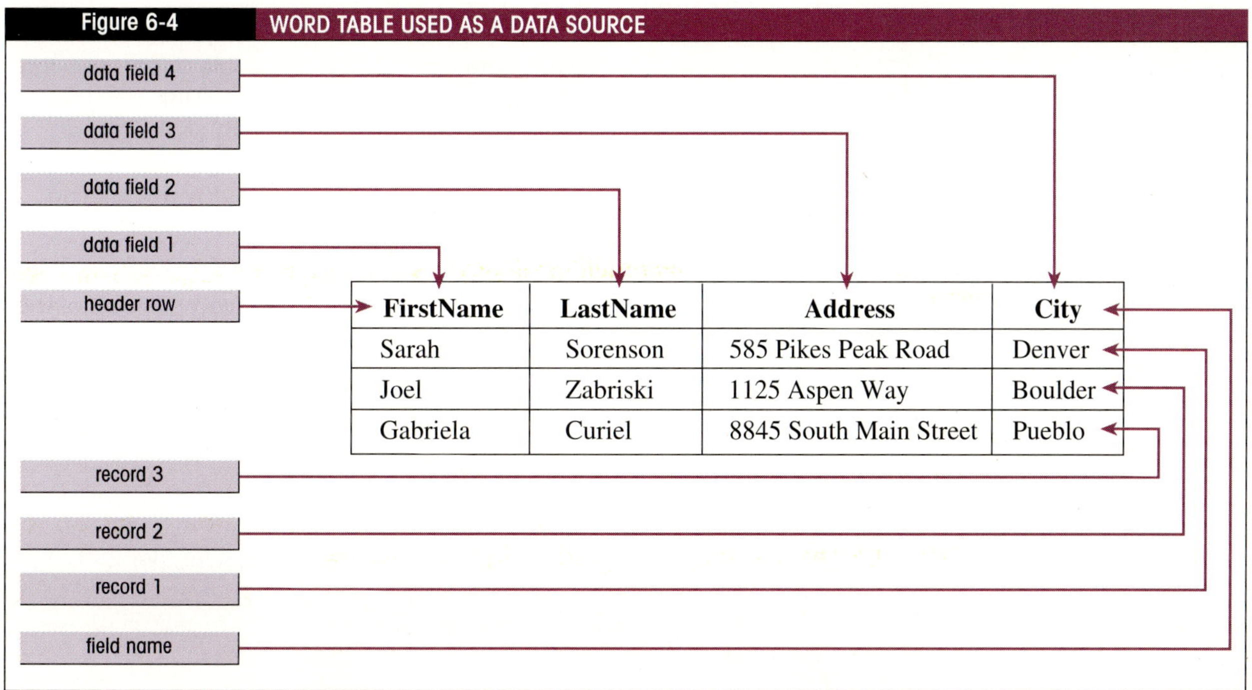

Data sources are not limited to records about customers. You could create data sources with inventory records, records of suppliers, or records of equipment. After you understand how to manage and manipulate the records in a data source, you'll be able to use them for many applications.

Creating a Main Document

The main document contains the text that will appear in all the letters, as well as the merge fields that tell Word where to insert the information from the data source. In the first step of the merge process, you must indicate which document you intend to use as the main document. You can either create a new document or use an existing document as the main document.

Alicia has already written the letter she wants to send out to all Pet Shoppe customers, so you don't need to create a new document. Instead, you'll modify an existing document to create the main document.

REFERENCE WINDOW 

<u>Creating a Main Document</u>

- Click Tools on the menu bar, and then click Mail Merge to display the Mail Merge Helper dialog box.
- Click the Create button in the Main document section of the dialog box, and then click the type of main document that you want to create (such as Form Letters).
- Click the Active Window button to use the active, open document as the main document. Click the New Main Document button if you want to open a new, blank document as the main document.
- Click the Edit button on the Mail Merge Helper dialog box. If necessary, click the appropriate filename.
- Edit (or create) the text of the main document; add merge fields into the main document by clicking the Insert Merge Field button on the Mail Merge toolbar.

To start Word and create the main document:

1. Start Word as usual and insert your Data Disk in the appropriate drive, open the **PetShopp** file from the Tutorial folder for Tutorial 6 on your Data Disk, and then save the document on the disk as **Pet Shoppe Form Letter**. This is the text of the letter that Alicia wrote to send to Pet Shoppe customers and will become the main document of your form letter. You don't have to display nonprinting characters for this tutorial.
2. Click **Tools** on the menu bar, and then click **Mail Merge**. The Mail Merge Helper dialog box opens. See Figure 6-5. The Mail Merge Helper dialog box contains a checklist to help you create merged documents.

Figure 6-5 MAIL MERGE HELPER DIALOG BOX

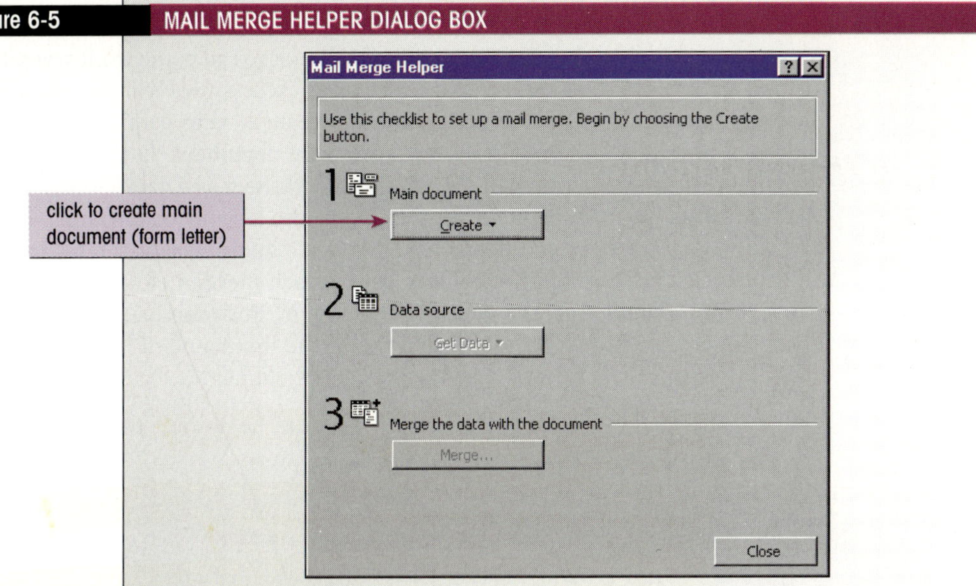

3. Click the **Create** button in the Main document section. A list of main document types appears.

4. Click **Form Letters**. A message dialog box opens, prompting you to select the document you want to use as the main document. You'll use the document in the active window (the letter you just opened) as the main document.

5. Click the **Active Window** button. The Main document section of the dialog box shows the type of merge (Form Letters) and the name of the main document (the active document Pet Shoppe Form Letter). See Figure 6-6.

Figure 6-6 MAIL MERGE HELP DIALOG BOX AFTER SELECTING A MAIN DOCUMENT

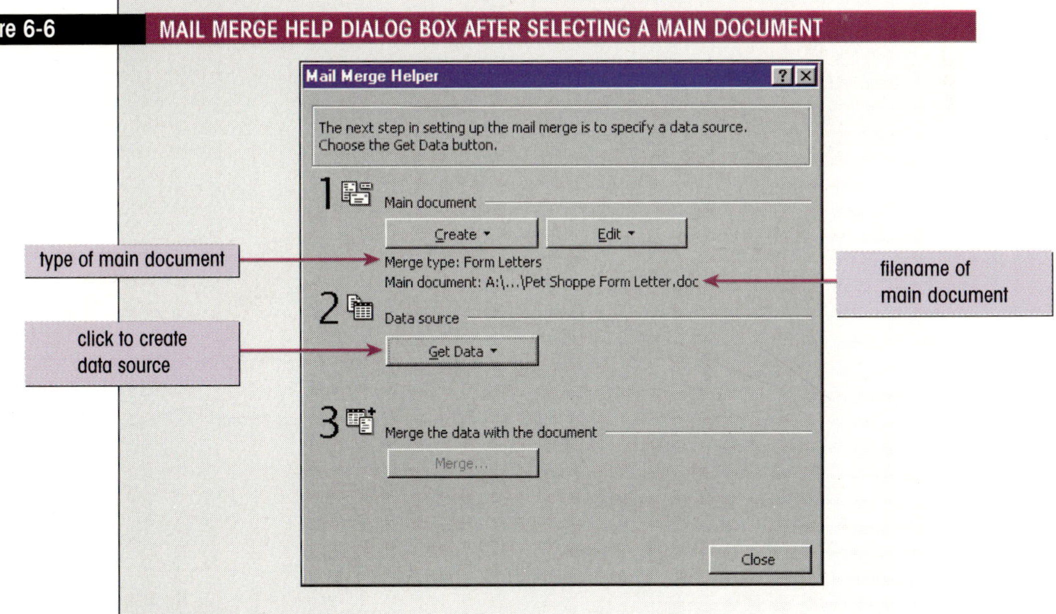

You'll add the merge instructions to the main document later, after you create the data source.

Creating a Data Source

As mentioned earlier, the data source for a mail merge can come from several different kinds of files, such as a Word file, an Excel file, or an Access file. You can use a file that already contains names and addresses, or you can create a new data source, enter names and addresses into it, and then merge it with the main document. In the Review Assignments at the end of this tutorial, you will use an Excel worksheet as a data source.

In this case, you will create a Word table to use as your data source. The table's header row will contain the merge field names. Just as a column label in a table indicates what kind of information is stored in the column below, each merge field name indicates the type of information contained in the data fields below it. For example, you'll use the field name FirstName to label the data field that contains the first name of Pet Shoppe customers. You must follow several conventions when choosing field names:

- Each field name in the header row must be unique; that is, you can't have two fields with the same name.
- Names of data fields can contain underscores, but not spaces.
- Names of data fields must begin with a letter.
- Names of data fields can be as long as 40 characters (including numbers and letters).

In a mail merge, you link the data source document to the main document so that Word will know in which file to find the information you want inserted into the main document.

You need to create a data source that contains all the information about The Pet Shoppe's customers. Alicia has given you a list of the type of information you'll merge into the letter and the field names you should use, as Figure 6-7 shows.

Figure 6-7 FIELD NAMES FOR THE RECORDS IN THE DATA SOURCE

Data Field Name	Description
FirstName	Customer's first name
LastName	Customer's last name
Address1	Customer's street address
City	Customer's city (in Colorado)
PostalCode	Customer's zip code
HomePhone	Customer's phone number
Branch	Location of The Pet Shoppe branch
PetKind	The kind of pet owned by the customer
PetName	The name of the customer's pet

REFERENCE WINDOW RW

Creating a Data Source

- Click Tools on the menu bar, click Mail Merge to open the Mail Merge Helper dialog box, and then select the main document.
- In the Data source section of the Mail Merge Helper dialog box, click the Get Data button, and then click Create Data Source. The Create Data Source dialog box opens.
- Add or delete field names in the Field names in header row list, and then click the OK button. The Save As dialog box opens.
- In the Save As dialog box, save the new data source file to your disk. A message dialog box opens, asking you what document you want to edit: the data source or the main document.
- Click the Edit Data Source button. The Data Form dialog box opens.
- Enter the information into the data fields for each record of the data source, and then click the OK button.

Attaching the Data Source and Creating the Header Row

The first step in creating a data source document is to specify the field names in the data source and then attach the data source to the main document. In this context, **attach** means to associate or link the data source to the main document so that Word knows where to find the specific information (data fields) that replace the merge fields in the main document. Although the order of field names in the data source doesn't affect their placement in the main document, you'll want to arrange them logically. This way, you can enter information quickly and efficiently. For example, you probably want first and last name fields adjacent, or city, state, and ZIP code fields adjacent.

Just as you did with the main document, you can either open an existing data source document and attach it to the main document, or you can create a new data source document and attach it to the main document. Alicia doesn't have an existing data source document, so you'll create a new one, and attach it to the file listed in the Main document section of the dialog box.

To attach the data source to the main document:

1. Click the **Get Data** button in the Data source section of the Mail Merge Helper dialog box. The Get Data list box opens. See Figure 6-8.

Figure 6-8 MAIL MERGE HELPER DIALOG BOX WITH GET DATA LIST BOX

Mail Merge Helper

The next step in setting up the mail merge is to specify a data source. Choose the Get Data button.

1 Main document

Create ▾ Edit ▾

Merge type: Form Letters
Main document: A:\...\Pet Shoppe Form Letter.doc

2 Data source

Get Data ▾

Create Data Source...
Open Data Source...
Use Address Book...
Header Options...

3

Close

click to create new data source

data source you create will be attached to this main document

2. Click **Create Data Source** in the Get Data list box. The Create Data Source dialog box opens. See Figure 6-9. The Field names in the header row list box provide a list of commonly used field names, which you can add to and remove from as needed. Alicia determined the field names for the data fields based on the information cards that customers complete to join the mailing list. You'll use these field names to create the header row of the table in the data source.

Figure 6-9 CREATE DATA SOURCE DIALOG BOX

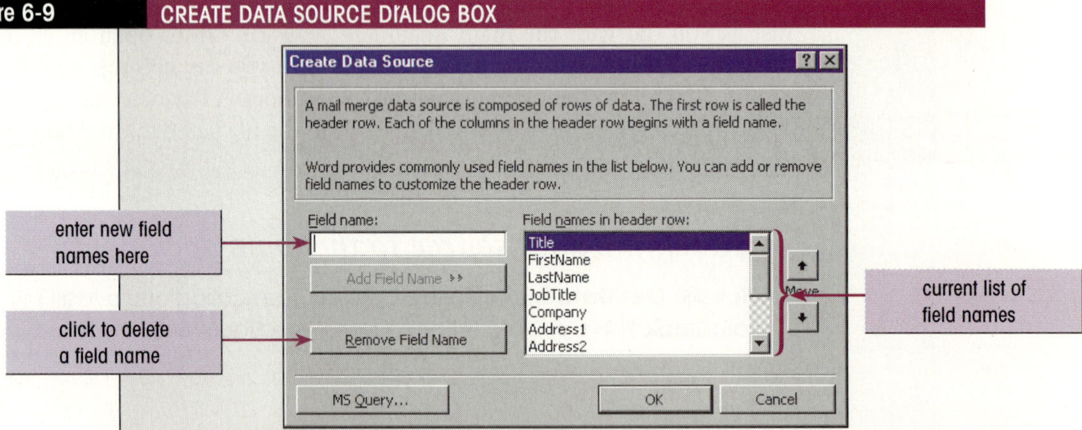

3. Scroll through the list of field names in the Field names in header row list box. The form letter will include some of these field names—FirstName, LastName, Address1, City, PostalCode, and HomePhone. However, you will need to create field names for the store branch, the type of pet, and the name of the pet.

4. In the Field name text box, type **Branch**, and then click the **Add Field Name** button to add "Branch" to the list of field names in the Field names in header row list box. This tells Word that one data field in each record will contain the name of The Pet Shoppe store nearest the customer.

5. Repeat Step 4 to add the field names **PetKind** and **PetName** to the Field names in the header row list box. Now, each customer record will contain fields with the kind of pet the customer owns and the name of that pet.

TROUBLE? If the Add Field Name button is dimmed, you might have entered "PetKind" or "PetName" as two separate words. Word won't accept field names that contain spaces. Delete the space between the words, and then click the Add Field Name button.

Some of the field names in the Field names in header row list box aren't applicable to The Pet Shoppe, so you'll remove those field names.

6. Scroll to the top of the Field names in header row list, click **Title** and click the **Remove Field Name** button. The field name "Title" disappears from the list.

7. Repeat Step 6 to remove the following field names: JobTitle, Company, Address2, State, Country, and WorkPhone. See Figure 6-10. Check the Field names in the header row list carefully to make sure it contains the following: FirstName, LastName, Address1, City, PostalCode, HomePhone, Branch, PetKind, and PetName.

Figure 6-10 COMPLETED CREATE DATA SOURCE DIALOG BOX

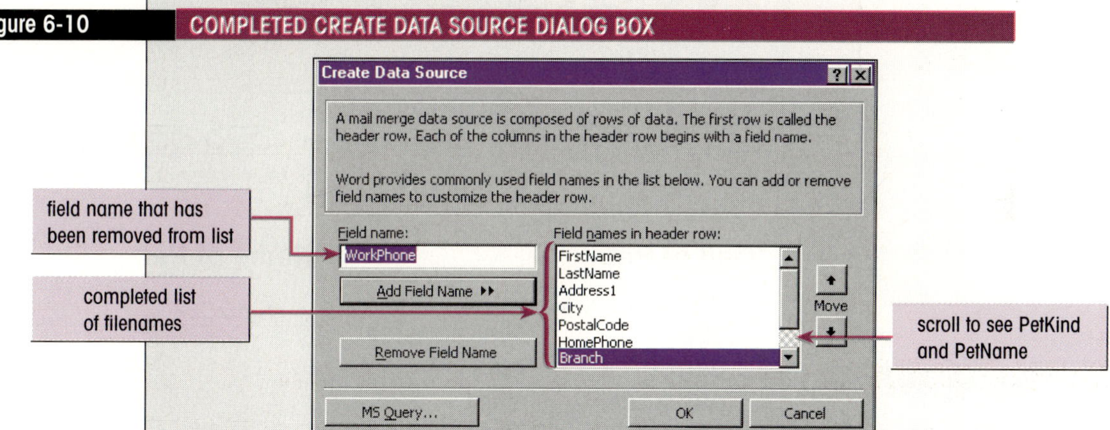

TROUBLE? If your list of field names doesn't match the list in Figure 6-10 exactly, you need to edit the list. Remove any extra or incorrect field names and add the correct ones.

8. Click the **OK** button in the Create Data Source dialog box to accept the field name list. The Save As dialog box opens, allowing you to save the data source document and attach it to the letter.

9. Make sure the Tutorial subfolder within the Tutorial.06 folder is selected, type **Pet Shoppe Data** in the File name text box, and then click the **Save** button. The data source document Pet Shoppe Data is now attached to the main document Pet Shoppe Form Letter. Word now displays a message dialog box, noting that the data source you just created contains no records.

At this point you could edit either the data source or the main document. First, you'll edit the data source by entering the data for each customer record; in the next session, you'll edit the main document by adding the merge fields to it.

Entering Data into a Data Source

The Pet Shoppe staff uses customer information cards to collect data from their customers, as shown in Figure 6-11. The data source will contain a field for each piece of information on the card. You'll add the information for three customers (the first three records) into the data source document.

Figure 6-11 CUSTOMER INFORMATION TO BE USED AS A DATA RECORD

The Pet Shoppe

First Name Sarah Last Name Sorenson

Address 585 Pikes Peak Road

City Denver, Colorado

ZIP 80207 Home Phone 303-555-8976

Store Branch High Prairie Mall

Kind of Pet:

- ☒ dog
- ☐ cat
- ☐ parrot
- ☐ parakeet
- ☐ turtle
- ☐ pigeon
- ☐ armadillo
- ☐ Gila monster
- ☐ fish
- ☐ lizard
- ☐ Other ____________

Name of Pet: Rascal

Word provides two methods for adding records to the data source: entering data directly into a data source table, just as you would enter information into any other Word table, or using the Data Form dialog box, in which you can enter, edit, or delete records. You'll use the data form to enter information about three of The Pet Shoppe's customers into the data source.

To enter data into a record using the data form:

1. In the message dialog box, click the **Edit Data Source** button. The Data Form dialog box opens with blank text boxes beside each field name of the data source. See Figure 6-12.

Figure 6-12 DATA FORM DIALOG BOX

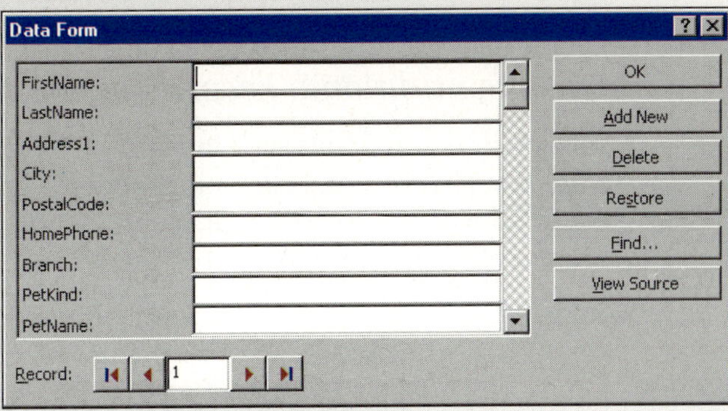

2. With the insertion point in the FirstName text box, type **Sarah** to enter the first name of the first customer. Make sure you do not press the spacebar after you finish typing any entry in the Data Form dialog box. If you do so, you'll add the necessary spaces in the text of the main document, not in the data source.

3. Press the **Enter** key to move the insertion point to the LastName field. You could also click in that text box, or you could press the Tab key to move the insertion point to the next field text box. You would press Shift + Tab to move to the previous text box.

4. Type **Sorenson**, and then press the **Enter** key to move the insertion point to the next field.

5. Type **585 Pikes Peak Road**, and then press the **Enter** key to move the insertion point to the next field.

6. Type **Denver**, and then press the Enter key to move the insertion point to the next field.

7. Type **80207**, and then press the Enter key to move to the next field.

8. Type **303-555-8076** and press **Enter**, type **High Prairie Mall** and press **Enter**, and then type **dog** and press **Enter**. You have inserted the customer's home phone number, the branch location of The Pet Shoppe, and the kind of pet the customer owns. The insertion point is now in the text box of the last field, PetName.

9. Type **Rascal**, but do not press the Enter key yet. Your Data Form dialog box should match Figure 6-13.

Figure 6-13 DATA FORM DIALOG BOX WITH COMPLETED RECORD 1

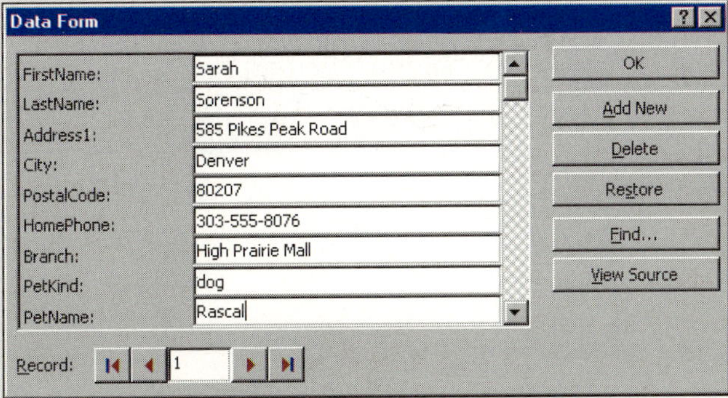

You have completed the information for the first record of the data source document. Now, you're ready to enter the information for the remaining two records.

To create additional records in the data source:

1. With the insertion point still at the end of the last field of the first record, press the **Enter** key. This creates a new, blank record. Notice that the Record text box at the bottom of the data form displays "2," indicating that you're editing the second record.

2. Enter the information for the second record, as shown in Figure 6-14.

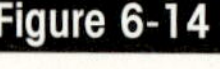

Figure 6-14 COMPLETED RECORD 2

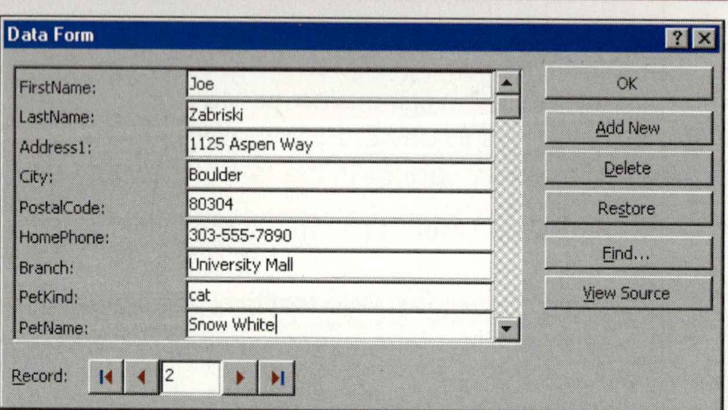

3. After entering data into the last field, click the **Add New** button to open another blank record. Notice that you can press the Enter key or click the Add New button to create a blank record.

4. Enter the information for the third record, as shown in Figure 6-15, but do not press the Enter key after the last field. If you were to press Enter or click the Add New button, you would add a blank record as the fourth record.

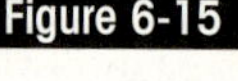

Figure 6-15 COMPLETED RECORD 3

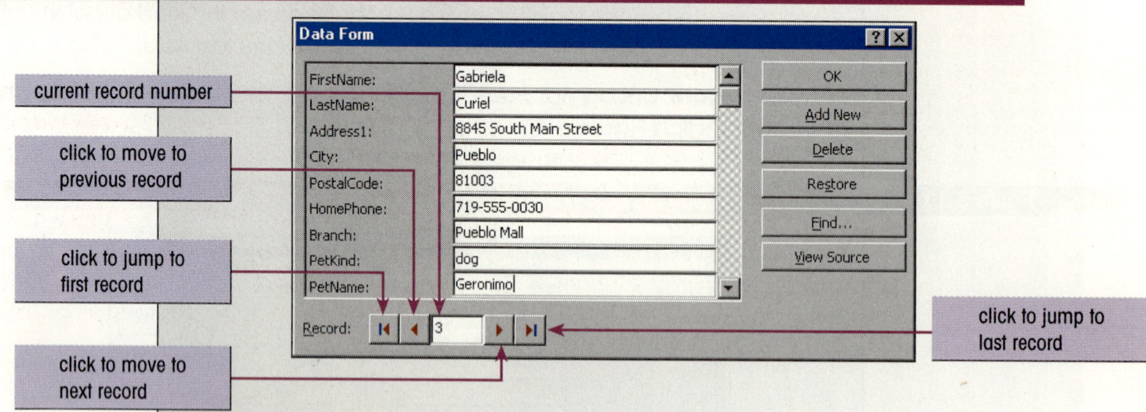

TROUBLE? If a new, blank record opens, you pressed the Enter key at the end of the third record or you clicked the Add New button in the Data Form dialog box. Click the Delete button in the Data Form dialog box to remove the unneeded fourth record.

You have entered the records for three customers. Next, you need to proofread each record to make sure you typed the information correctly. Any misspelled names or other typos will print in the final letters and reflect poorly on The Pet Shoppe. You can move among individual records within the data source by using the Record arrow buttons. You'll begin by proofreading the first data record.

To move to the first record within the data source:

1. Click the **First Record** button at the bottom of the Data Form dialog box to move to the first record. The record number changes to 1, and the first record appears in the data form with the data you entered.
2. Proofread the data by comparing your information with Figure 6-13. Make any necessary corrections by selecting the text and retyping it.
3. Click the **Next Record** button at the bottom of the Data Form dialog box to move to the next record. The record number changes to 2, and the information for the second data record appears. Compare your record with Figure 6-14.
4. Click to review the third record. Compare your record with Figure 6-15. Make corrections where necessary.

You have entered and edited the three records using the data form. Also, you can add and edit records in the data source while viewing the records as a Word table.

Krishan, a Pet Shoppe employee, created a Word table with the other records you need to add to the data source. You'll view the data source as a table and add those records.

To view the data source as a table and add new records to the data form:

1. Click the **View Source** button in the **Data Form** dialog box. The data source table appears in the document window, and the Database toolbar appears above the document window. See Figure 6-16. Depending on your monitor, you may find the contents of the cells difficult to read because they wrap onto one or more lines or break between words. Don't worry about this. You won't be printing the table, but instead will only be merging the information it contains with the main document. Once the data is merged, it will be formatted properly in the main document. However, note that you could edit, format, or print the data source table just as you would any other Word table.

Figure 6-16 DATA SOURCE TABLE

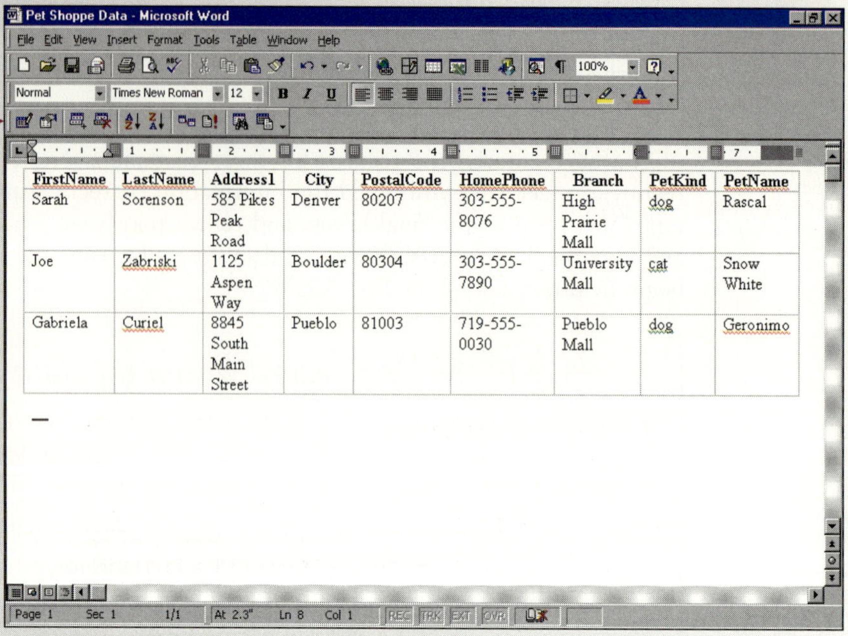

Pet Shoppe Data - Microsoft Word

database toolbar

FirstName	LastName	Address1	City	PostalCode	HomePhone	Branch	PetKind	PetName
Sarah	Sorenson	585 Pikes Peak Road	Denver	80207	303-555-8076	High Prairie Mall	dog	Rascal
Joe	Zabriski	1125 Aspen Way	Boulder	80304	303-555-7890	University Mall	cat	Snow White
Gabriela	Curiel	8845 South Main Street	Pueblo	81003	719-555-0030	Pueblo Mall	dog	Geronimo

TROUBLE? If your data source table does not show the gridlines shown in Figure 6–16, display them by clicking Table on the menu bar and then clicking Show Gridlines.

2. Move the insertion point to the end of the document, to the blank line below the table. Now, you can insert the file containing additional customer information.
3. Click **Insert** on the menu bar, and then click **File**. The Insert File dialog box opens.
4. Make sure the Tutorial folder for Tutorial 6 on your Data Disk is selected, click the filename **ShopDat**, and then click the **Insert** button. Word automatically adds the 11 records in the ShopDat data source table to the three records of the Pet Shoppe Data source table.
5. Scroll up to view all 14 records in the data source table. On most computers, the column borders are not aligned properly. You'll fix that in the next step. (Even if your column borders are properly aligned, you should complete Step 6.)
6. Click **Table** on the menu bar, point to **Select**, click **Table** to select the entire table. Then click **Table** on the menu bar, click **Table AutoFormat**, select **(none)** in the list of formats, click the **OK** button, and then click anywhere in the table to deselect it. The header row is no longer formatted in boldface. All the columns in the table should now be aligned.

   Now that you've entered and edited records using the data form and inserted additional customer records, you should save the data source document.
7. Save the document. Word saves the file using the current filename, Pet Shoppe Data.

Alicia's data source eventually will contain hundreds of records for all The Pet Shoppe customers. The current data source, however, contains only the records Alicia wants to work with now.

You have opened the main document for the form letter and created the data source that will supply the customer-specific information for Alicia's mailings. In the next session, you'll insert merge fields into the main document and merge the main document with the data source. Then, you'll sort the data source by ZIP code and repeat the merge using the sorted data with the main document.

Session 6.1 QUICK CHECK

1. Define the following in your own words:
   a. form letter
   b. main document
   c. data source
   d. merge field
   e. record
   f. data field
2. Which of the following are valid field names?
   a. Number of Years on the Job
   b. PayGrade
   c. 3rdQuarterProfits
   d. StudentIdentificationNumber
   e. ThePetShoppeCompanyEmployeeSocialSecurityNumber
   f. Birth Date
3. All the information about one individual or object in a data source is called a _______________.
4. True or False: For a mail merge to work properly, every record in the data source must have the same set of fields.
5. Suppose you want to insert information for a field named "Gender" into the data source. How would you do it?
6. What is the purpose of the data form?
7. How do you move to individual records within the data source?

SESSION 6.2

In this session, you'll return to the form letter main document and insert merge fields into it. Then you'll create the merged document. You'll also sort the data source and merge it with the main document. Finally, you'll filter the data source, edit the main document, and merge the two.

Editing a Main Document

You opened Alicia's sales letter earlier but didn't enter any of the merge instructions. Now that the data source contains all the records you need to use, you're ready to edit the sales letter.

Alicia wants the date to print below the company letterhead. Instead of just typing today's date, you'll insert a date field. By entering the date field, you won't have to modify the main document each time you send it; the date field will automatically insert the current date when you print the document.

To insert the date field:

1. If you took a break after the last session, make sure Word is running and the Pet Shoppe Form Letter and Pet Shoppe Data are open. The Pet Shoppe Data document should be displayed on the screen.

2. Click the **Mail Merge Main Document** button on the Database toolbar to switch from the data source document to the main document, Pet Shoppe Form Letter. You should now be viewing Alicia's form letter. Notice that the Mail Merge toolbar appears below the Formatting toolbar. See Figure 6-17.

Figure 6-17 MAIN DOCUMENT BEFORE INSERTING MERGE FIELDS

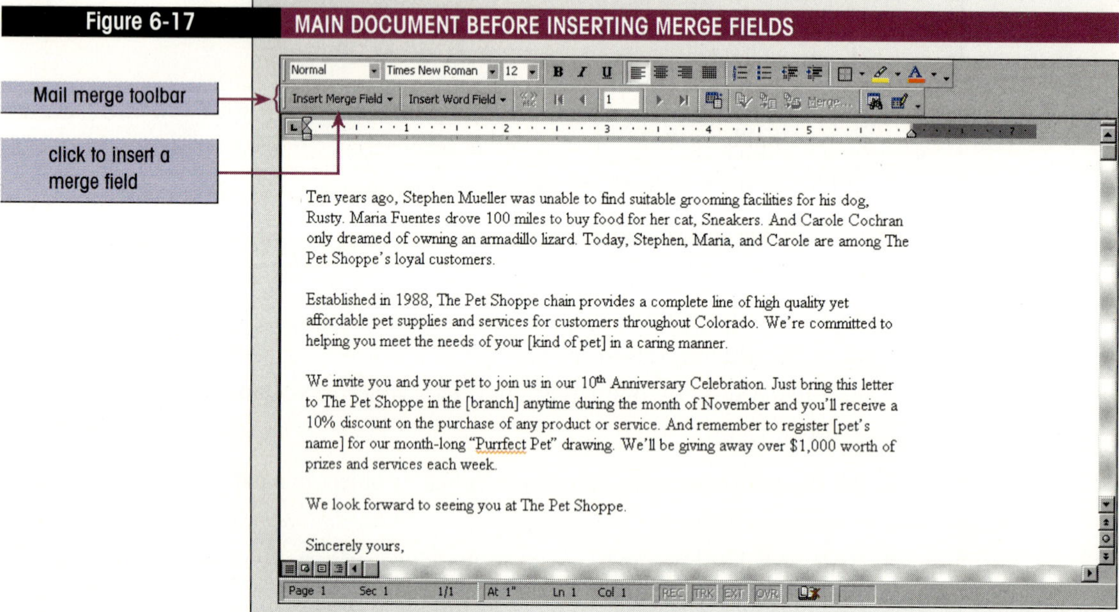

TROUBLE? If the main document, Pet Shoppe Form Letter, is already in the document window, your document window should match Figure 6-17. Continue with Step 3.

3. Make sure the insertion point is at the beginning of the form letter, on the first blank line, and then press the **Enter** key five times to position the insertion point approximately two inches from the top margin, leaving enough space for the company letterhead that is preprinted on the company stationery. Here, you'll insert the date.

   Now, rather than typing today's date, you'll insert a Word date field, so that no matter when you print the document, the current date will appear.

4. Click **Insert** on the menu bar, and then click **Date and Time**. The Date and Time dialog box opens. You have used this dialog box before to insert the current date. Now, you will use the Update automatically check box to tell Word to revise the date every time you use the document.

5. Click the month-day-year format from the list of available formats, and then click the **Update automatically** check box to select it. See Figure 6-18.

Figure 6-18 DATE AND TIME DIALOG BOX

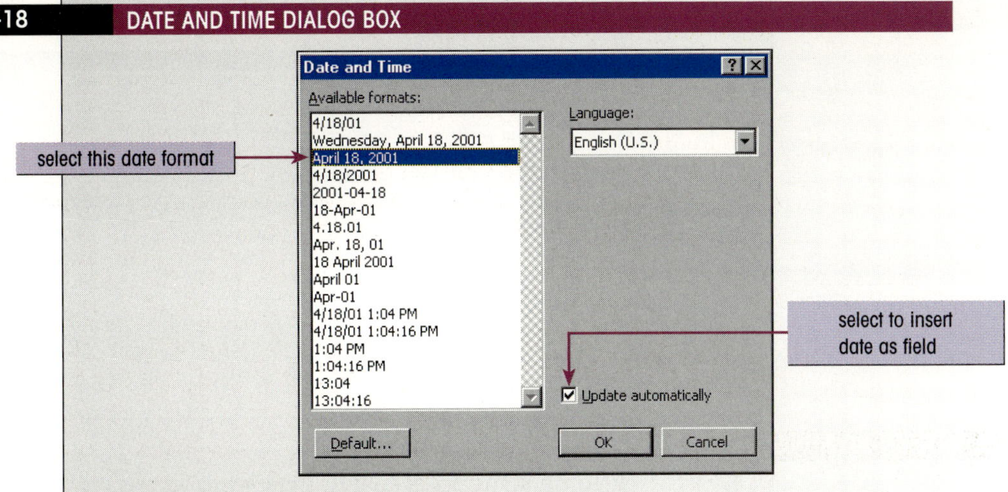

TROUBLE? The date that shows in your dialog box will differ from the one shown in Figure 6-18. Just click the format that lists the month, the day, and then the year.

6. Click the **OK** button. The current date appears in the document. Now, whenever you or Alicia print the merged document letter for Pet Shoppe's customers, the current date will print.

TROUBLE? If you see TIME \@ "MMMM d, yyyy"} instead of the date, then your system is set to view field codes. To view the date, click Tools on the menu bar, click Options, click the View tab, click the Field codes check box in the Show section of the View tab to deselect that option, and then click the OK button.

You're now ready to insert the merge fields for the inside address of the form letter.

Inserting Merge Fields

The sales letter is a standard business letter, so you'll place the customer's name and address below the date. You'll use merge fields for the customer's first name, last name, address, city, and ZIP code to create the inside address of the form letter. As you insert these merge fields into the main document, you must enter proper spacing and punctuation around the fields so that the information in the merged document will be formatted correctly.

To insert a merge field:

1. Press the **Enter** key six times to leave the standard number of blank lines between the date and the first line of the inside address.

2. Click the **Insert Merge Field** button on the Mail Merge toolbar. A list appears with all the field names that you created earlier in the data source. See Figure 6-19.

Figure 6-19 INSERT MERGE FIELD LIST

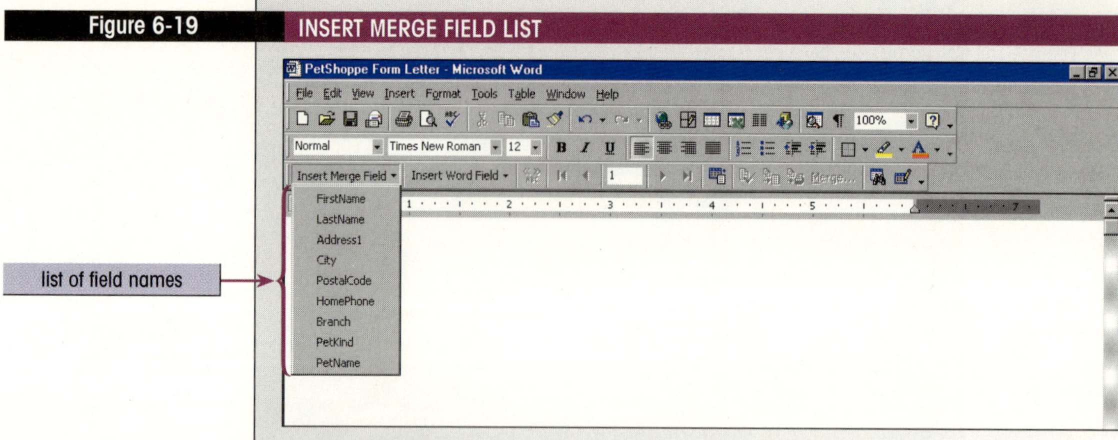

3. Click **FirstName** in the list of field names. Word inserts the merge code for the field name, FirstName, in the form letter at the location of the insertion point.

   Word places angled brackets << >>, also called chevrons, around the merge field to distinguish it from normal text.

   TROUBLE? If you make a mistake and insert the wrong merge field, select the entire merge field, including the chevrons, press the Delete key, and then insert the correct merge field.

Later, when you merge the main document with the data source, Word will retrieve the first name from the data source and insert it into the letter at that location. Now, you're ready to insert the merge fields for the rest of the inside address. You'll add the spacing and punctuation to the main document as well.

To insert the remaining merge fields for the inside address:

1. Press the **spacebar** to insert a space after the FirstName field, click the **Insert Merge Field** button on the Mail Merge toolbar, and then click **LastName** in the Insert Merge Field list. Word inserts the LastName merge field into the form letter.
2. Press the **Enter** key to move the insertion point to the next line, click the **Insert Merge Field** button, and then click **Address1** in the Insert Merge Field list. Word inserts the Address1 merge field into the form letter.
3. Press the **Enter** key to move the insertion point to the next line, click the **Insert Merge Field** button, and then click **City** in the Insert Merge Field list. Word inserts the City merge field into the form letter.
4. Type **,** (a comma), press the **spacebar** to insert a space after the comma, and then type **CO** to insert the abbreviation for the state of Colorado. If The Pet Shoppe had customers outside Colorado, you would need to use the State field name in the data source and, here, in the main document form letter. Because all of the customers live in Colorado, you can make the state name part of the main document, where it will be the same for every letter.
5. Press the **spacebar** to insert a space after the state abbreviation, click the **Insert Merge Field** button, and then click **PostalCode** in the list of fields. Word inserts the PostalCode merge field into the form letter. See Figure 6-20.

Figure 6-20 FORM LETTER WITH MERGE FIELDS

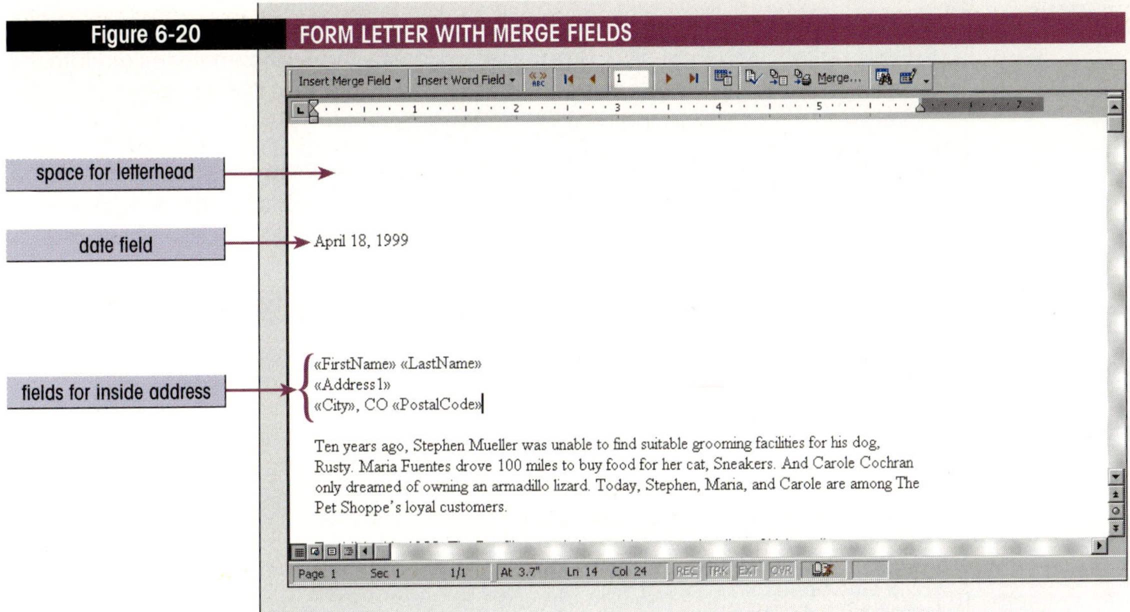

The inside address is set up to match the form for a standard business letter. You can now add the salutation of the letter, which will contain each customer's first name.

To insert the merge field for the salutation:

1. Press the **Enter** key twice to leave a line between the inside address and the salutation, and then type **Dear** and press the **spacebar**.
2. Click the **Insert Merge Field** button on the Mail Merge toolbar, and then click **FirstName**. Word inserts the FirstName merge field into the form letter.
3. Type **:** (a colon). This completes the salutation.

   TROUBLE? If the Office Assistant asks if you want help writing the letter, click Simply type the letter without help.

Alicia wants each customer to know that The Pet Shoppe values its customers and remembers them and their pets. You'll personalize the letter even further by including the kind of pet each customer owns and the pet's name.

To finish personalizing the letter:

1. Select the placeholder **(kind of pet)** (including the brackets) in the second paragraph of the form letter. You'll replace this phrase with a merge field.
2. Click the **Insert Merge Field** button on the Mail Merge toolbar, and then click **PetKind**. Word replaces your placeholder with the PetKind merge field into the form letter. If necessary, press the **spacebar** to make sure there is a space between the field and the next word, "in."

3. Select **(branch)** in the third paragraph of the form letter, click the **Insert Merge Field** button, and then click **Branch**. Word inserts the Branch merge field into the form letter. Press the **spacebar** if necessary to make sure there is a space between the field and the next word, "anytime."

4. Similarly, replace **(pet's name)** in the third sentence of the third paragraph of the form letter with the **PetName** field, and make sure there is a space between the merge field and the next word, "for." Your document should look like Figure 6-21.

Figure 6-21 FORM LETTER AFTER INSERTING MERGE FIELDS

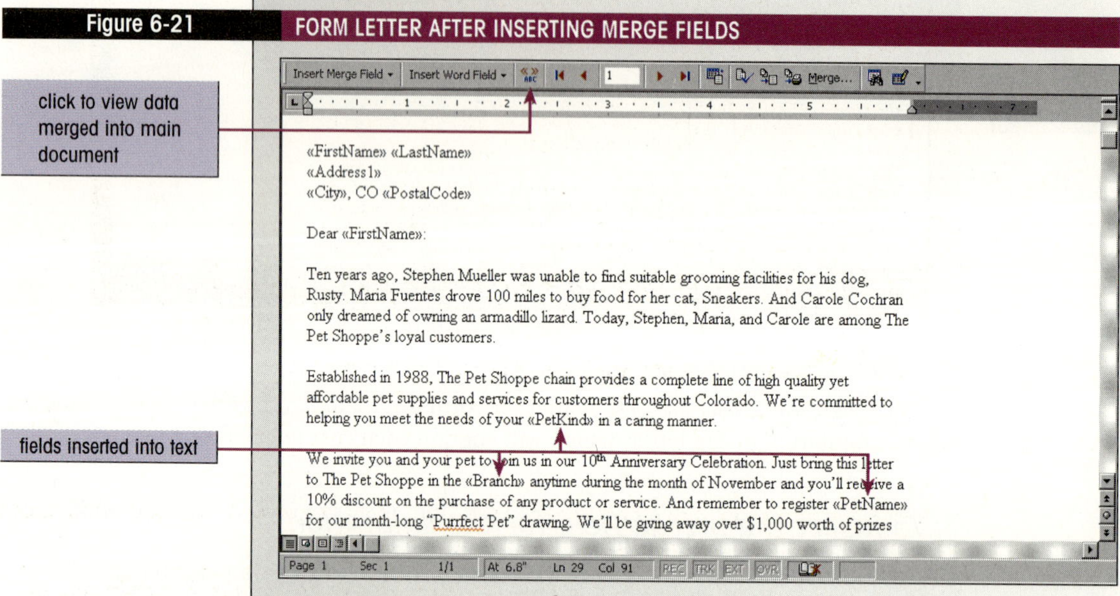

5. Carefully check your document to make sure all the field names and spacing are correct.

TROUBLE? If you see errors, use the Word editing commands to delete the error, and then insert the correct merge field or spacing.

You can use the View Merged Data button on the Mail Merge toolbar to see how the letter will look when the merge fields are replaced by actual data.

6. Click the **View Merged Data** button on the Mail Merge toolbar. The data for the first record replaces the merge fields in the form letter. See Figure 6-22. Scroll to the top of the document so you can see the inside address and salutation. Carefully check the letter to make sure the text and format are correct. In particular, check to make sure that the spaces before and after the merged data are correct because it is easy to omit spaces or add extraneous spaces around merge fields.

Figure 6-22 FORM LETTER WITH MERGED DATA

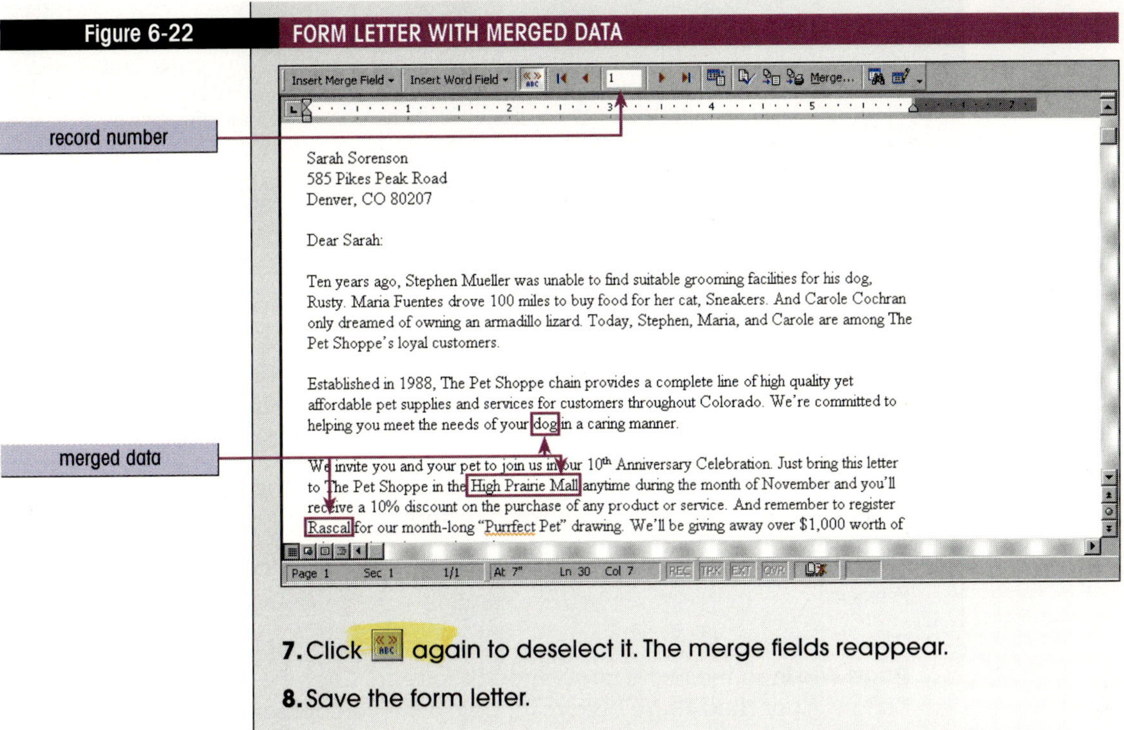

7. Click again to deselect it. The merge fields reappear.

8. Save the form letter.

The form letter (main document) of the mail merge is complete. As you saw while creating the main document, merge fields are easy to use and flexible:

- You can use merge fields anywhere in the main document. For example, in Alicia's form letter, you inserted fields for the inside address and you placed fields within the body of the letter.
- You can use the same merge field more than once. For example, Alicia's form letter uses the FirstName field in the inside address and in the salutation.
- You don't have to use all the fields from the data source in your main document. For example, Alicia's form letter doesn't use the HomePhone field.

Merging the Main Document and Data Source

Now that you've created the form letter (main document) and the list of customer information (data source), you're ready to merge the two files and create personalized letters to send to The Pet Shoppe's customers. Because the data source consists of 14 records, you'll create a merged document with 14 pages, one letter per page.

You could merge the data source and main document directly to the printer using the Merge to Printer button on the Mail Merge toolbar, which is often quicker and doesn't require disk space. However, Alicia wants to keep a copy of the merged document on disk for her records. So you'll merge the data source and main document to a new document on disk.

REFERENCE WINDOW RW

Merging a Main Document and Data Source to a New Document

- Make sure the mail merge main document is in the document window with the Mail Merge toolbar above it.
- Click the Merge to New Document button on the Mail Merge toolbar.

To merge to a new document:

1. Click the **Merge to New Document** button on the Mail Merge toolbar. Word creates a new document called Form Letters1, which contains 14 pages, one for each record in the data source. The Mail Merge toolbar closes.
2. Save the merged document in the Tutorial subfolder within the Tutorial.06 folder, using the filename **Pet Shoppe Form Letters1**.
3. Click the **Print Preview** button on the Standard toolbar to switch to Print Preview.
4. Click the **Zoom Control** list arrow on the Print Preview toolbar, and then click **Page Width** so the text is large enough to read. Click the **Previous Page** button or **Next Page** button below the vertical scroll bar to move to the beginning of each letter. Notice that each letter is addressed to a different customer and the branch location, kind of pet, and pet name are different in each letter.

   TROUBLE? If the Next and Previous Page buttons are blue and don't display the beginning of each letter, click the Select Browse Object button and click the Browse by Page button.

5. Click the **Close** button on the Print Preview toolbar to return to the Normal view.
6. Press **Ctrl + End** to move the insertion point to the end of the document. Notice on the status bar that you're viewing page 14, the final letter in the merged document.
7. Click **File** on the menu bar, and then click **Print** to open the Print dialog box.
8. Click the **Current page** option button in the **Page** range section of the dialog box so Word will print only the current page (the last letter) of the merged document, and then click the **OK** button to print the document. Figure 6-23 shows what the letter will look like when Alicia prints it on company letterhead.

Figure 6-23 LAST PAGE OF MERGED DOCUMENT

The Pet Shoppe

121 Stilltoe Avenue ■ Colorado Springs, CO 80901
Phone: (719) 555-5555 ■ Fax: (719) 555-5556

September 25, 2001

Amelia Gutierrez
623 Heather Drive
Lamar, CO 81052

Dear Amelia:

Ten years ago, Stephen Mueller was unable to find suitable grooming facilities for his dog, Rusty. Maria Fuentes drove 100 miles to buy food for her cat, Sneakers. And Carole Cochran only dreamed of owning an armadillo lizard. Today, Stephen, Maria, and Carole are among The Pet Shoppe's loyal customers.

Established in 1988, The Pet Shoppe chain provides a complete line of high quality yet affordable pet supplies and services for customers throughout Colorado. We're committed to helping you meet the needs of your dog in a caring manner.

We invite you and your pet to join us in our 10th Anniversary Celebration. Just bring this letter to The Pet Shoppe in the Olde West Shopping Center anytime during the month of November and you'll receive a 10% discount on the purchase of any product or service. And remember to register Nieve for our month-long "Purrfect Pet" drawing. We'll be giving away over $1,000 worth of prizes and services each week.

We look forward to seeing you at The Pet Shoppe.

Sincerely yours,

Alicia Robles
Vice President, Sales

You have completed the mail merge and generated a merged document. Alicia stops by to see how the letters are coming.

Sorting Records

As Alicia looks through the letters to Pet Shoppe customers in the merged document, she notices one problem—the letters are not grouped by ZIP codes. Currently, the letters are in the order in which customers were added to the data source file. She plans to use bulk mailing rates to send her letters, and the U.S. Postal Service requires bulk mailings to be separated into groups according to ZIP code. She asks you to sort the data file by ZIP code (the PostalCode field) and perform another merge, this time merging the main document with the sorted data source.

You can sort information in a data source table just as you sort information in any other table. Recall that to sort means to rearrange a list or a document in alphabetical, numerical, or chronological order. You can sort information in ascending order (A to Z, lowest to highest, or earliest to latest) or in descending order (Z to A, highest to lowest, or latest to earliest) using the Sort Ascending button or the Sort Descending button on the Database toolbar.

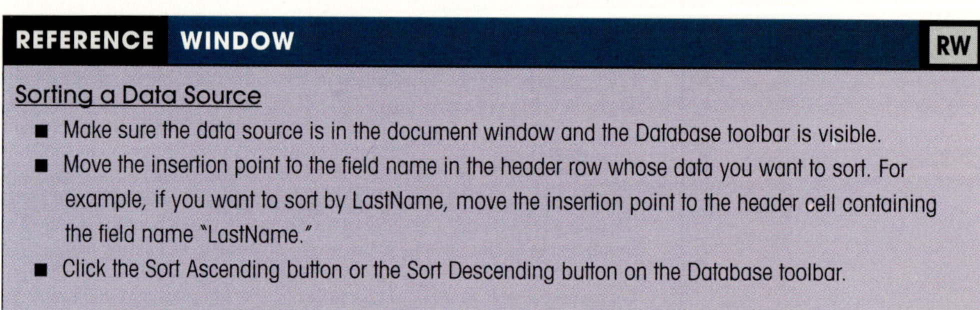
REFERENCE WINDOW RW

Sorting a Data Source

- Make sure the data source is in the document window and the Database toolbar is visible.
- Move the insertion point to the field name in the header row whose data you want to sort. For example, if you want to sort by LastName, move the insertion point to the header cell containing the field name "LastName."
- Click the Sort Ascending button or the Sort Descending button on the Database toolbar.

You'll sort the records in ascending order of the PostalCode field in Pet Shoppe Data.

To sort the data source file by ZIP code:

1. With the merged file still in the document window, click **File** on the menu bar, and then click **Close** to close the file. If you're prompted to save your changes, click **Yes**.
2. Click the **Edit Data Source** button on the Mail Merge toolbar to open the Data Form dialog box, and then click the **View Source** button. The data source table appears in the document window.
3. Position the insertion point in the PostalCode cell in the header row of the data table. The exact location of the insertion point in the cell doesn't matter.
4. Click the **Sort Ascending** button on the Database toolbar. Word sorts the rows of the data table from lowest ZIP code number to highest. See Figure 6-24.

Figure 6-24 DATA SOURCE TABLE AFTER SORTING BY POSTALCODE

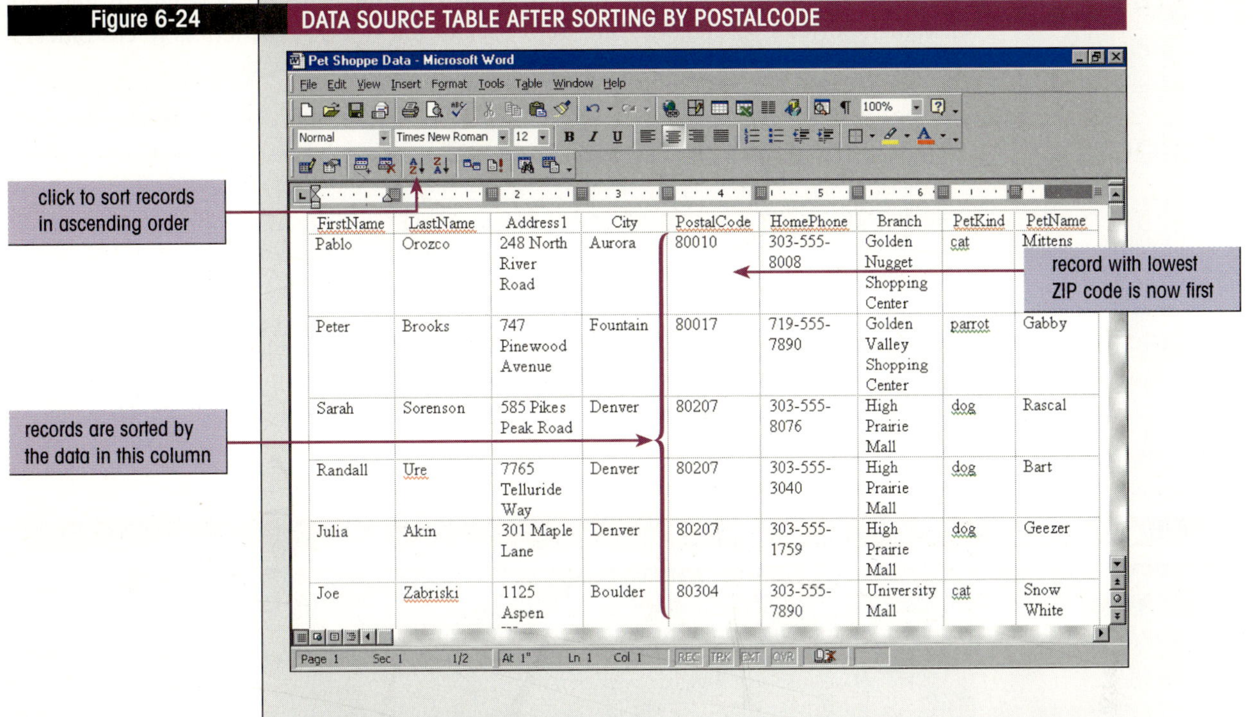

FirstName	LastName	Address1	City	PostalCode	HomePhone	Branch	PetKind	PetName
Pablo	Orozco	248 North River Road	Aurora	80010	303-555-8008	Golden Nugget Shopping Center	cat	Mittens
Peter	Brooks	747 Pinewood Avenue	Fountain	80017	719-555-7890	Golden Valley Shopping Center	parrot	Gabby
Sarah	Sorenson	585 Pikes Peak Road	Denver	80207	303-555-8076	High Prairie Mall	dog	Rascal
Randall	Ure	7765 Telluride Way	Denver	80207	303-555-3040	High Prairie Mall	dog	Bart
Julia	Akin	301 Maple Lane	Denver	80207	303-555-1759	High Prairie Mall	dog	Geezer
Joe	Zabriski	1125 Aspen	Boulder	80304	303-555-7890	University Mall	cat	Snow White

Now, when you merge the data source with the form letter, the letters will appear in the merged document in order of the ZIP codes.

5. Click the **Mail Merge Main Document** button on the Database toolbar to switch to the Pet Shoppe Form Letter.

6. Click the **Merge to New Document** button on the Mail Merge toolbar. Word generates the new merged document with 14 letters, one letter per page, as before, but this time the first letter is to Pablo Orozco, who has the lowest ZIP code (80010). See Figure 6-25.

Figure 6-25 LETTER OF CUSTOMER WITH LOWEST ZIP CODE

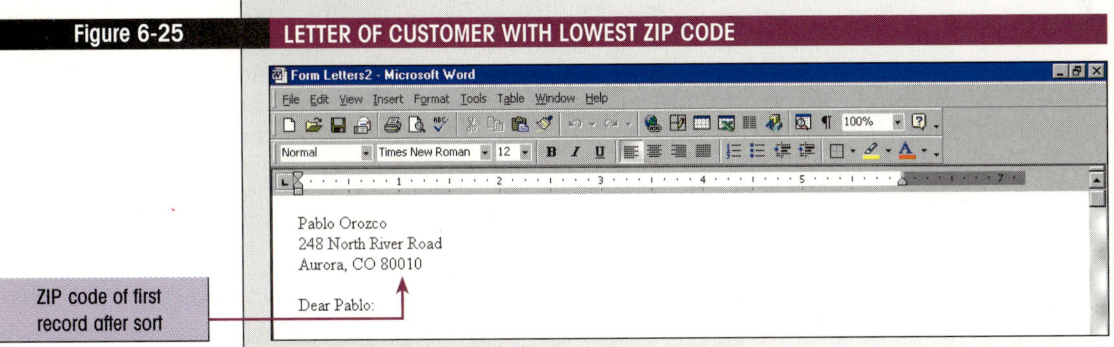

7. Scroll through the letters in the new merged document to see that they are in order of ZIP code.

8. Save the new merged document in the Tutorial subfolder within the Tutorial.06 folder, using the filename **Pet Shoppe Form Letters2**.

9. Close the document.

As Alicia requested, you've created a merged document with the letters to Pet Shoppe customers sorted by ZIP code. She stops back to tell you that the letters to customers who frequent one branch of The Pet Shoppe need additional information.

Selecting Records to Merge

The Pet Shoppe is going to offer additional savings on certain surplus items at the High Prairie Mall in Denver. Alicia wants to modify the form letter slightly and then merge it with only those records of customers of The Pet Shoppe in the High Prairie Mall.

You can select specific records from the data source, or **filter** records, to merge with the main document by specifying values for one or more fields with a filtering operation. A **filtering operator** is a mathematical or logical expression (such as Equal to, Not Equal to, or Less than) that you use to include certain records and exclude others. Figure 6–26 shows the filtering operators available for a mail merge.

Figure 6-26 FILTERING OPERATORS AVAILABLE IN WORD

OPERATOR	RETRIEVES A RECORD IF DATA FIELD
Equal to	Matches value of Compare to text box
Not Equal to	Does not match value of Compare to text box
Less than	Is less than the value of Compare to text box
Greater than	Is greater than the value of Compare to text box
Less than or Equal	Is less than or equal to the value of the Compare to text box
Greater than or Equal	Is greater than or equal to the value of the Compare to text box
Is Blank	Is blank or empty
Is Not Blank	Contains any value

A complete expression is called a **query**. An example of a query is "PostalCode Greater than 80010," which tells Word to filter the records in a data source by the PostalCode field and select any records that include a ZIP code that is higher than 80010. In the following steps, you'll set the Branch field so that it is equal to "High Prairie Mall." That way, Word will select only records of customers who shop at the High Prairie Mall branch of The Pet Shoppe and filter out all other records. But first, you'll modify the form letter.

To edit the form letter:

1. In the Pet Shoppe Form Letter, position the insertion point to the right of the phrase "10% discount on the purchase of any product or service" in the third paragraph of the form letter, just before the period.
2. Press the **spacebar**, and type **and a 25% discount on the purchase of selected items**. See Figure 6–27.

Figure 6-27 FORM LETTER WITH INSERTED TEXT

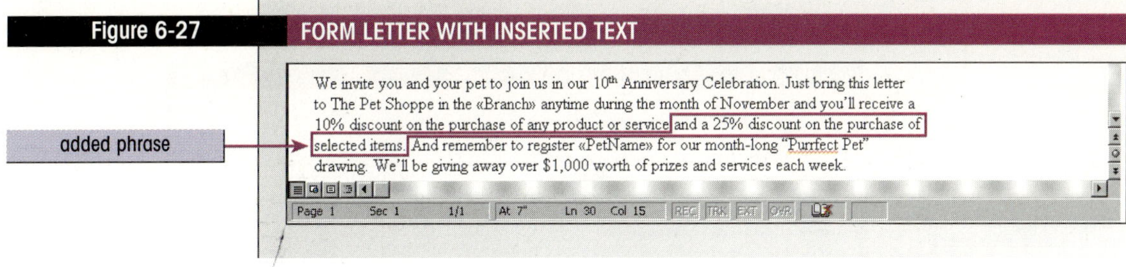
We invite you and your pet to join us in our 10th Anniversary Celebration. Just bring this letter to The Pet Shoppe in the «Branch» anytime during the month of November and you'll receive a 10% discount on the purchase of any product or service and a 25% discount on the purchase of selected items. And remember to register «PetName» for our month-long "Purrfect Pet" drawing. We'll be giving away over $1,000 worth of prizes and services each week.

Alicia wants to send this version of the letter only to customers of the High Prairie Mall store. You'll use the Equal to filtering operator to select only those records for High Prairie Mall, and then you'll merge the revised form letter with the records in the data source that match the query.

To filter records for a merge:

1. Make sure the main document appears in the document window, and then click the **Mail Merge Helper** button on the Mail Merge toolbar. The Mail Merge Helper dialog box opens.
2. Click the **Query Options** button on the dialog box. The Query Options dialog box opens. If necessary, click the **Filter Records** tab. See Figure 6-28. This is where you'll specify the query using a filtering operator.

Figure 6-28 QUERY OPTIONS DIALOG BOX

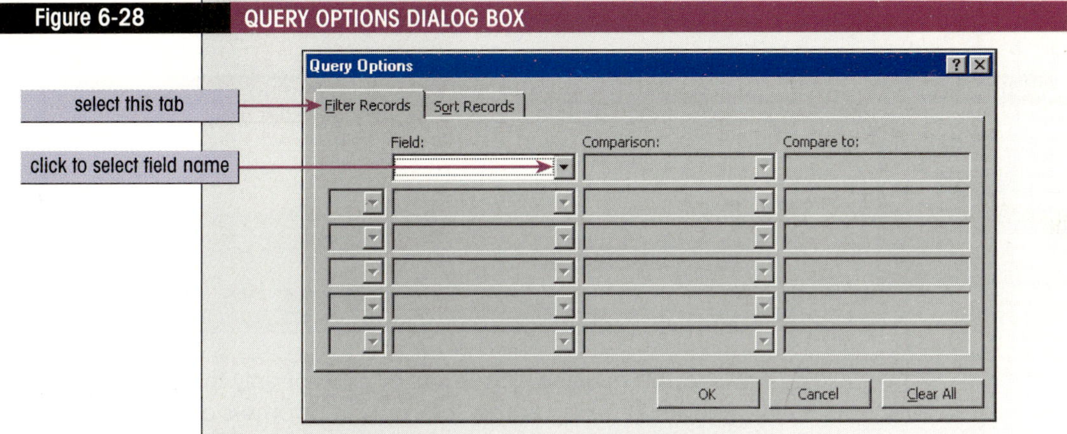

3. Click the **Field** list arrow, and then scroll through the list of field names and click **Branch**. Word fills in the Field text box with Branch.
4. If necessary, click the **Comparison** list arrow, and then click **Equal to**. This selects the filtering (comparison) operator, which tells Word that you want the value of the Branch field to be equal to something.

   Next, you'll specify what you want the Branch field to equal.
5. Position the insertion point in the Compare to text box, and type **High Prairie Mall**. Be careful to spell it exactly as shown. If any character or space differs, Word will fail to find any records that match. The completed Query Options dialog box should look like Figure 6-29. This is the only condition that Alicia needs to select customers who shop at High Prairie Mall.

Figure 6-29 COMPLETED QUERY IN QUERY OPTIONS DIALOG BOX

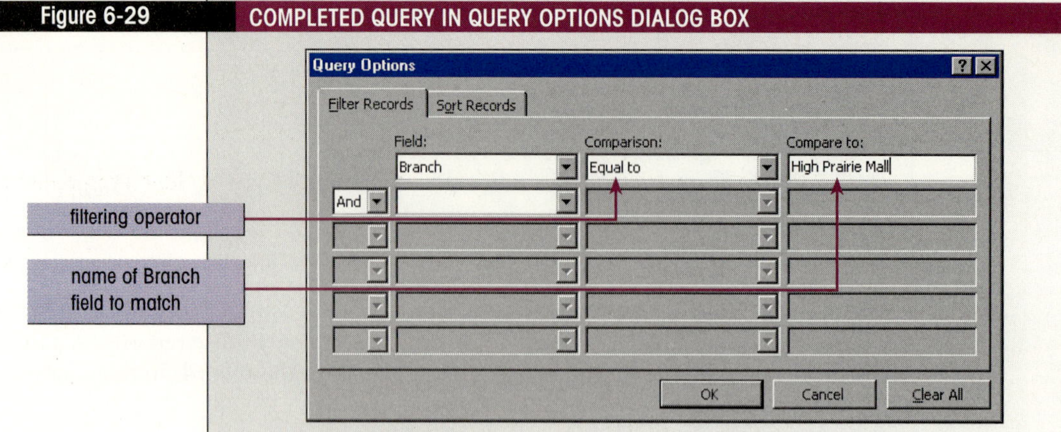

6. Click the **OK** button to accept the query options and return to the Merge dialog box. Notice that, among other things, the phrase "Query Options have been set" appears at the bottom of the dialog box.

7. Click the **Merge** button in the Mail Merge Helper dialog box to display the Merge dialog box. Make sure the Merge to text box displays **New Document**, and then click the **Merge** button. Word performs the merge and creates a new document that merges the modified form letter with all the records that match the query. Notice that the document is only three pages because only three records list High Prairie Mall in the Branch field. Scroll through the merged document to see the three letters. See Figure 6-30.

Figure 6-30 SECOND PAGE OF MERGE DOCUMENT AFTER FILTERING RECORDS

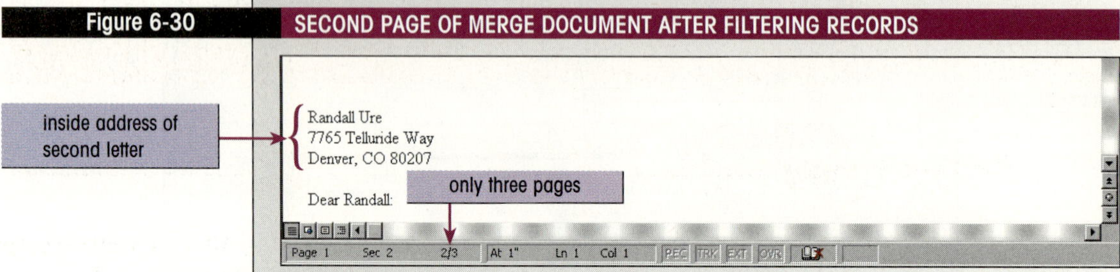

As you can see, this merged document consists of only three letters, those to Julia Akin, Randall Ure, and Sarah Sorenson—customers of The Pet Shoppe in the High Prairie Mall.

8. Save the document in the Tutorial subfolder within the Tutorial.06 folder using the name **Pet Shoppe Form Letters 3**, and close the document.

9. Close the Pet Shoppe Form Letter document without saving your revisions, and then save and close the data source file, Pet Shoppe Data.

You give the completed file to Alicia, who will print the letters on letterhead.

You now have created merged documents for a sorted data source file, filtered records in a data source, and an edited main document. In the next session, you'll create mailing labels and a phone list for Alicia to use when she has the sales reps make follow-up phone calls.

Session 6.2 Quick Check

1. What is the purpose of a date merge in a main document?
2. How do you insert a merge field into a main document?
3. How can you distinguish the merge field from the rest of the text in a main document?
4. Define the following in your own words:
   a. merged document
   b. sort
   c. query
   d. filtering operator
5. Suppose one of the data fields contains the ZIP code of your customers. How would you select only those customers with a certain ZIP code?
6. How can you preview how the main document will look when the merge fields are replaced by actual data?
7. If your main document is a form letter and you have 23 records in your data source, how many letters will the merged document create?
8. Do you have to print every letter in a merged form-letter document?

SESSION 6.3

In this session, you'll create and print mailing labels for the form-letter envelopes and create a telephone list, both using the mail merge feature.

Creating Mailing Labels

Now that you've created and printed the personalized sales letters, Alicia is ready to prepare envelopes in which to mail the letters. She could print the names and addresses directly onto envelopes, or she could create mailing labels to attach to the envelopes. The latter method is easier because 14 labels come on each sheet, and the envelopes don't have to go through the printer one by one. Alicia asks you to create the mailing labels.

She has purchased Avery® Laser Printer labels, product number 5162™ Address. These labels, which are available in most office-supply stores, come in 8½ × 11-inch sheets designed to feed through a laser printer. Each label measures 4 × 1.33 inches, and each sheet has seven rows of labels with two labels in each row, for a total of 14 labels per sheet, as shown in Figure 6–31. Word supports most of the Avery label formats.

Figure 6-31 LAYOUT OF A SHEET OF AVERY 5162 LABELS

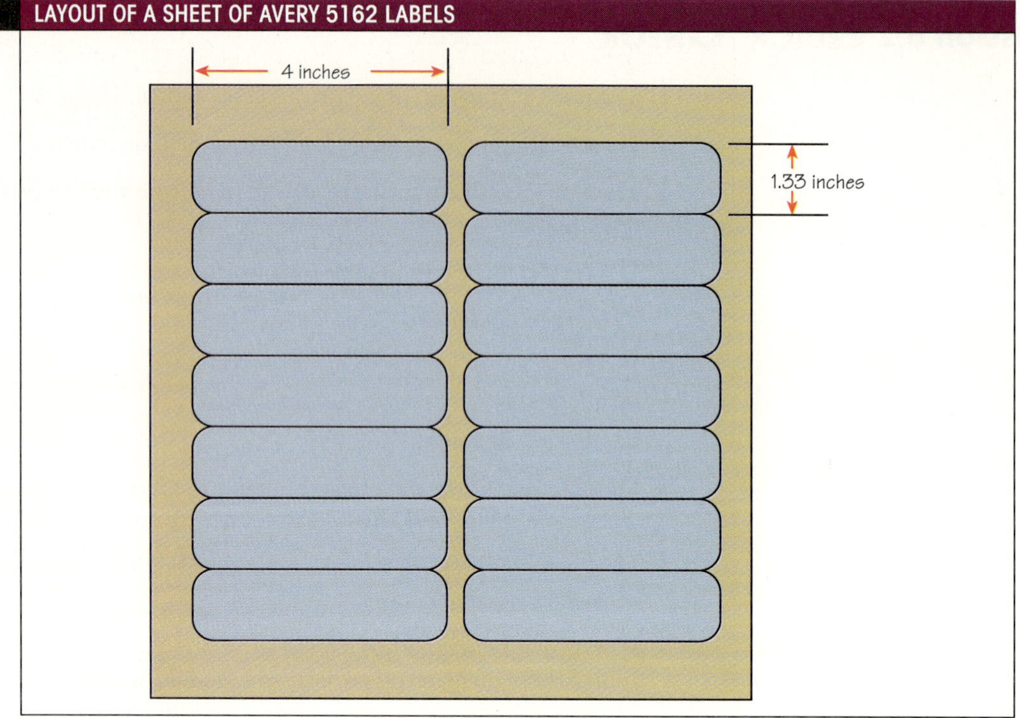

You can use the same data source file (Pet Shoppe Data) as you did earlier, but you'll have to create a new main document. The main document will be of type Mailing Labels instead of type Form Letters.

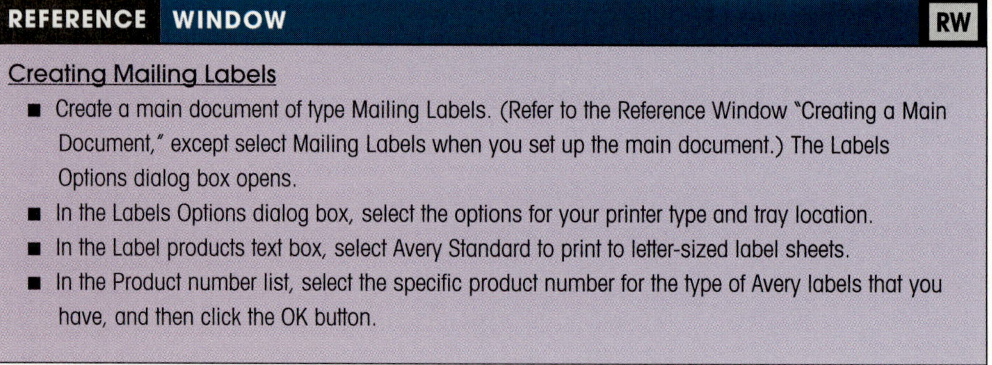
REFERENCE WINDOW RW

Creating Mailing Labels

- Create a main document of type Mailing Labels. (Refer to the Reference Window "Creating a Main Document," except select Mailing Labels when you set up the main document.) The Labels Options dialog box opens.
- In the Labels Options dialog box, select the options for your printer type and tray location.
- In the Label products text box, select Avery Standard to print to letter-sized label sheets.
- In the Product number list, select the specific product number for the type of Avery labels that you have, and then click the OK button.

You'll begin creating the mailing labels by specifying the main document and data source.

To specify the main document and data source for creating mailing labels:

1. If you took a break after the last session, make sure Word is running and that your Data Disk is in the appropriate drive.

2. If a blank document doesn't already appear on your screen, click the **New Blank Document** button on the Standard toolbar to open a new, blank document.
3. Click **Tools** on the menu bar, and then click **Mail Merge** to open the Mail Merge Helper dialog box.
4. Click the **Create** button in the Main document section of the dialog box, and then click **Mailing Labels**. Word displays a message asking if you want to use the current document or a new one.
5. Click the **Active Window** button so that the current blank document window is the mailing label main document.
6. Click the **Get Data** button on the Mail Merge Helper dialog box, and then click **Open Data Source**. You'll use an existing data source—the table you created earlier that contains Pet Shoppe customer information. The Open Data Source dialog box opens.
7. Make sure the Tutorial subfolder within the Tutorial.06 folder is selected, click the filename **Pet Shoppe Data** (if necessary), and then click the **Open** button. Word displays a message advising that you need to set up your main document.
8. Click the **Set Up Main Document** button on the message dialog box. The Label Options dialog box opens.

You've specified the main document, which is the blank document in the document window, and the data source, which is the file Pet Shoppe Data. Now, you're ready to select the type of labels and create the merged document of labels.

To create the mailing labels:

1. In the Printer information section of the dialog box, select the type of printer you'll use—dot matrix or laser and ink-jet. If you use a laser or ink-jet printer, you might also have the option of specifying the printer tray that will contain the mailing-label sheets. For example, if you have an HP LaserJet 4000 printer, the printer type is a laser printer and the tray is tray 1. For other printers, the tray might be the upper tray. You should select the options that are appropriate for your printer.

   TROUBLE? If you're not sure which options to choose for your printer, consult your instructor or technical support person.

2. Make sure **Avery standard** displays in the Label products text box. Even if you don't have Avery labels, you can print the merged document in the format of an Avery label sheet on an $8\frac{1}{2} \times 11$-inch letter-sized sheet of paper.
3. Scroll down the Product number list box and click **5162 - Address**. Your dialog box should look like Figure 6-32, except your printer specifications might be different.

Figure 6-32 LABEL OPTIONS DIALOG BOX

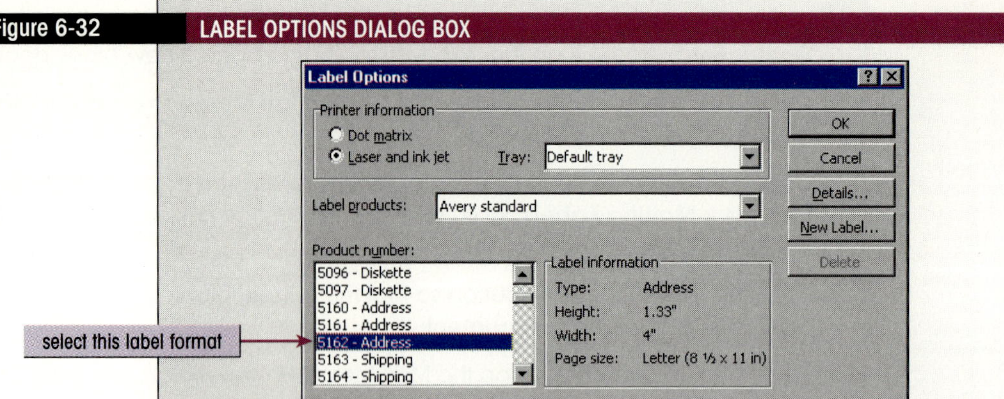

4. Click the **OK** button. Word opens the Create Labels dialog box, which contains an area in which you can insert the merge fields in a sample label.

5. Click the **Insert Merge Field** button on the dialog box and click **FirstName** to insert the field, press the **spacebar** to insert a space between the first and last names, click the **Insert Merge Field** button, and then click **LastName** to insert the field.

6. Press the **Enter** key to move to the next line; use the same method as in Step 5 to insert the **Address1** field, press the **Enter** key, insert the **City** field, type **,** (a comma), press the **spacebar**, type **CO** (the abbreviation for Colorado), press the **spacebar**, and insert the **PostalCode** field. The completed Create Labels dialog box should look like Figure 6-33.

Figure 6-33 CREATE LABELS DIALOG BOX

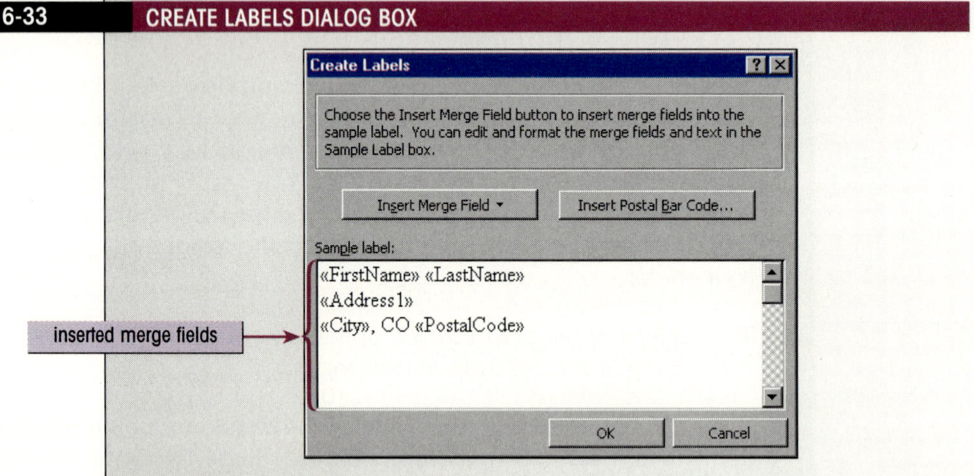

7. Click the **OK** button. The Mail Merge Helper dialog box is still open, and you're ready to merge the data source into the mailing-labels document.

8. Click the **Merge** button in the Merge the data with the document section. The Merge dialog box opens.

9. Make sure that the Merge to option is set to **New Document** and that the Records to be merged option is set to **All**, and then click the **Merge** button. Word creates a new merged document formatted for the Avery 5162 - Address mailing-label sheets. See Figure 6-34.

Figure 6-34 MERGED DOCUMENT WITH MAILING LABELS

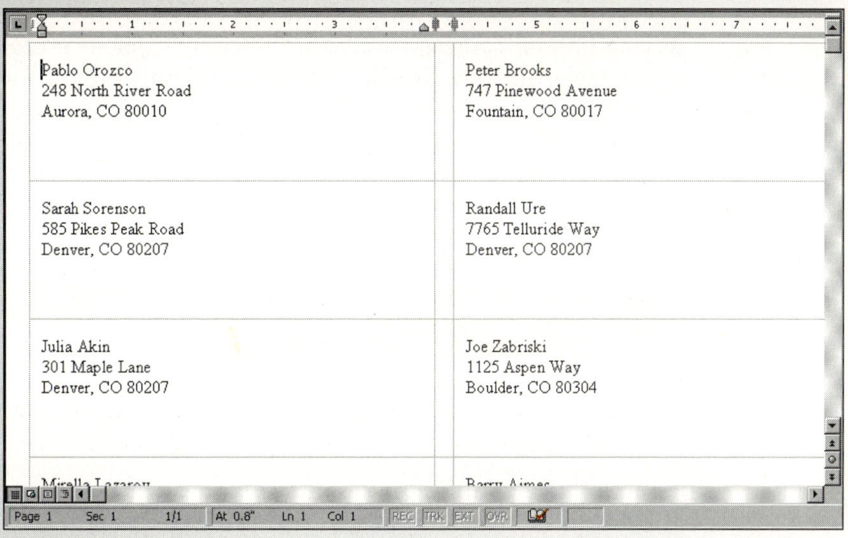

Pablo Orozco 248 North River Road Aurora, CO 80010	Peter Brooks 747 Pinewood Avenue Fountain, CO 80017
Sarah Sorenson 585 Pikes Peak Road Denver, CO 80207	Randall Ure 7765 Telluride Way Denver, CO 80207
Julia Akin 301 Maple Lane Denver, CO 80207	Joe Zabriski 1125 Aspen Way Boulder, CO 80304

Page 1 Sec 1 1/1 At 0.8" Ln 1 Col 1 REC TRK EXT OVR

The labels are all set up. All you need to do is save the document and print the labels. For now, you'll just print the labels on an 8½ × 11-inch sheet of paper so you can see what they look like. Later, Alicia will print them again on the sheet of labels.

To save and print the labels:

1. Save the merged document to the Tutorial subfolder within the Tutorial.06 folder using the filename **Pet Shoppe Labels**.
2. Scroll through the document to preview the labels.
3. Print the merged document of labels just as you would print any other document.

   TROUBLE? If you want to print on a sheet of labels, consult your instructor or technical support person about how to feed the sheet into the printer. If you're using a shared printer, you may need to make special arrangements so other users' documents aren't accidentally printed on your label sheets.

4. Close the merged document.
5. Save the main document to the Tutorial subfolder within the Tutorial.06 folder using the filename **Pet Shoppe Labels Form**, and then close the document.
6. If necessary, close the data source file, but do not exit Word.

If Alicia wanted you to print envelopes instead of mailing labels, you would have created a new main document similar to the one for creating mailing labels, except you would choose Envelopes as the type of main document rather than Mailing Labels.

Creating a Telephone List

As your final task, Alicia wants you to create a telephone list for all the customers in the data source table. She asked some of the sales personnel to call customers and remind them of The Pet Shoppe's anniversary sale; the sales reps will call all the customers on the phone list you create.

You'll begin by setting up a mail merge as before, except this time you'll use a Catalog type of main document rather than a Form Letter. Even though you aren't actually creating a catalog, you'll use the Catalog type because in Form Letter, Word automatically inserts a section break, which forces a page break, after each merged record. In a Catalog type of main document, all the entries (records) in the telephone list will print on one page rather than each record printing on its own page.

To prepare for creating the telephone list:

1. Click the **New Blank Document** button on the Standard toolbar to open a new, blank document window.
2. Click **Tools** on the menu bar, and then click **Mail Merge**. The Mail Merge Helper dialog box opens.
3. Click the **Create** button in the Main document section of the dialog box. A list of main document types appears.
4. Click **Catalog**.
5. Click the **Active Window** button.
6. Click the **Get Data** button, and then click **Open Data Source** and open **Pet Shoppe Data** from the Tutorial folder for Tutorial 6 on your Data Disk.
7. Click the **Edit Main Document** button in the message dialog box.

You're ready to create the main document for the telephone list and merge the main document with the data source. The format of the telephone list is the customer's name (last name first) at the left margin of the page and the phone number at the right margin. You'll set up the main document so that the phone number is preceded by a dot leader. A **dot leader** is a dotted line that extends from the last letter of text on the left margin to the beginning of text aligned at a tab stop.

To create the main document:

1. With the insertion point in a blank document window, insert the **LastName** merge field, type **,** (a comma), press the **spacebar**, and insert the **FirstName** merge field.

   Now, you'll set a tab stop at the right margin (position 6 inches) with a dot leader.

2. Click **Format** on the menu bar, and then click **Tabs** to open the Tabs dialog box.
3. Type **6** in the Tab stop position text box, click the **Right** option button in the Alignment section, and then click **2 ....** in the Leader section to create a dot leader. See Figure 6-35.

Figure 6-35 TABS DIALOG BOX

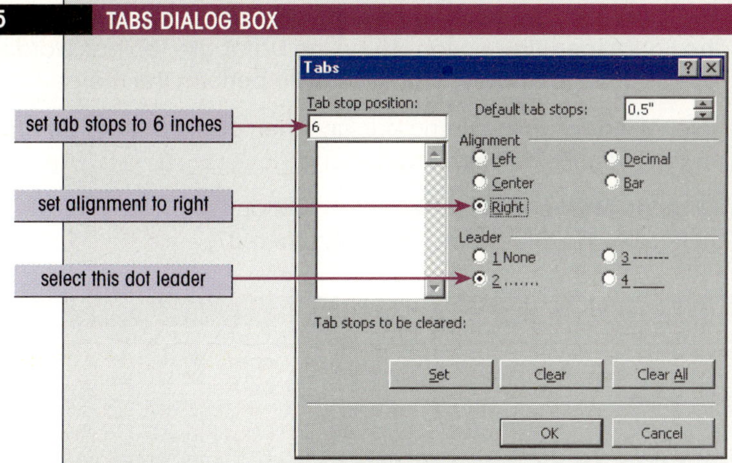

4. Click the **OK** button. Word clears the current tab stops and inserts a right-aligned tab stop at position 6 inches, the right margin of the page.

5. Press the **Tab** key to move the insertion point to the new tab stop. A dot leader appears in the document from the end of the FirstName field to the tab stop.

6. Insert the **HomePhone** merge field at the location of the insertion point, and then press the **Enter** key. You must insert a hard return here so that each name and telephone number will appear on a separate line. Notice that the dot leader shortened to accommodate the inserted text. The completed main document looks like Figure 6-36.

Figure 6-36 COMPLETED MAIN DOCUMENT FOR TELEPHONE LIST

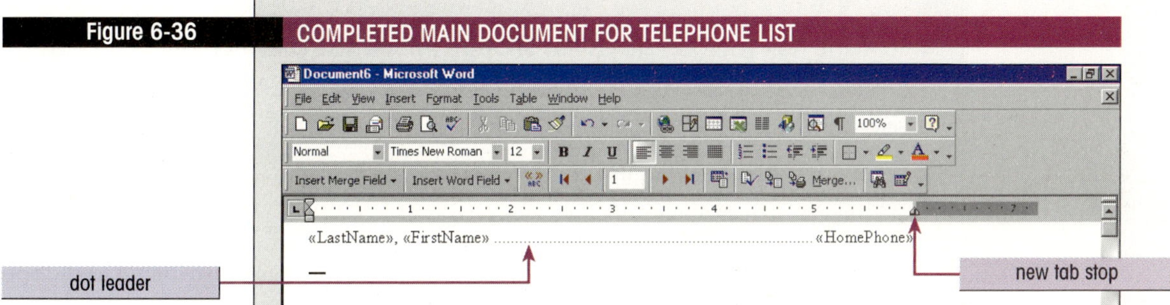

7. Save the document to the Tutorial subfolder within the Tutorial.06 folder using the filename **Pet Shoppe Phone Form**.

You're almost ready to merge this file with the data source, except that you want the name and phone numbers list to be alphabetized by the customers' last names. First, you'll sort the data source, and then you'll merge the files.

To sort the data source by last name and merge the files:

1. Click the **Edit Data Source** button on the Mail Merge toolbar, and then click the **View Source** button to display the data table.

2. Move the insertion point to the LastName cell in the header row, and then click the **Sort Ascending** button on the Database toolbar. Word sorts the records by customer last name. You're ready to perform the merge.

3. Click **Window** on the menu bar, and then click **Pet Shoppe Phone Form** to switch to the Pet Shoppe Phone Form.

4. Click the **Merge to New Document** button on the Mail Merge toolbar. Word generates the telephone list. See Figure 6-37.

Figure 6-37 MERGED DOCUMENT OF TELEPHONE LIST

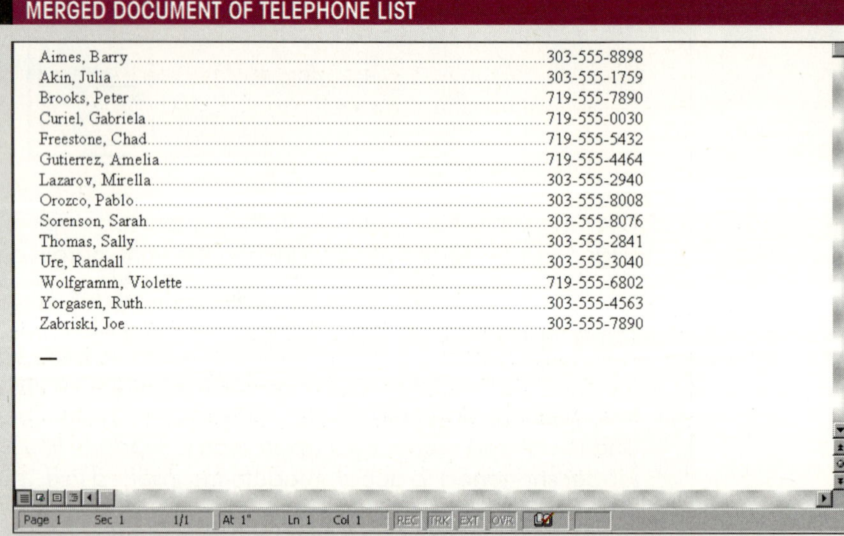

Aimes, Barry 303-555-8898
Akin, Julia 303-555-1759
Brooks, Peter 719-555-7890
Curiel, Gabriela 719-555-0030
Freestone, Chad 719-555-5432
Gutierrez, Amelia 719-555-4464
Lazarov, Mirella 303-555-2940
Orozco, Pablo 303-555-8008
Sorenson, Sarah 303-555-8076
Thomas, Sally 303-555-2841
Ure, Randall 303-555-3040
Wolfgramm, Violette 719-555-6802
Yorgasen, Ruth 303-555-4563
Zabriski, Joe 303-555-7890

5. Save the new merged file as **Pet Shoppe Phone List**, and then print and close the file.

6. Save, and close the Pet Shoppe Phone form.

7. Exit Word without saving the sorted data source file.

You have created the telephone list. Alicia will have it copied and distributed to the appropriate sales personnel. She thinks that The Pet Shoppe's 10th Anniversary Celebration will be a great success.

In this tutorial, you've created a form letter and merged it with a data source to create a personalized mailing to Pet Shoppe customers. You've also created mailing labels and a telephone list to help in their marketing efforts. Alicia thanks you for your help and prepares the letters for mailing to Pet Shoppe's customers.

Session 6.3 QUICK CHECK

1. Which of the following are not types of main documents:
   - **a.** mailing labels
   - **b.** merge fields
   - **c.** envelopes
   - **d.** telephone list
   - **e.** form letters

2. True or False: To create mailing labels, you can use the same data source file you used for a form letter.
3. Describe the general process for creating and printing an address list that will print directly to envelopes.
4. True or False: Word automatically inserts an end of section break, which forces a page break, after each merged record in a Catalog type of main document.
5. What is a dot leader? (The telephone list you created in this tutorial used a dot leader.)
6. How do you display a data table?
7. How do you sort a data source using the LastName field so that all the customers are arranged in reverse alphabetical order (Z to A)?

REVIEW ASSIGNMENTS

The Pet Shoppe's 10th Anniversary Celebration was a great success, and Alicia was pleased with how convenient it was to send out form letters with the Word Mail Merge feature. She decides to use it to remind customers about the pet vaccines that the shop offers, using the services of a visiting veterinarian. She asks you to help her with a mailing.

1. If necessary, start Word and make sure your Data Disk is in the appropriate drive. Open the file **Vaccines** from the Review folder in the Tutorial.06 folder on your Data Disk, and then save it on your Data Disk as **Pet Shoppe Vaccines**.
2. In mail merge, create a form letter main document using the Pet Shoppe Vaccines file.
3. Create a data source document, using the filename Pet Vaccine Data, with the following eight field names: FirstName, LastName, Address1, City, PostalCode, Branch, PetKind, and PetName.
4. Create records using the following information:
   - Delbert Greenwood, 2483 Teluride Drive, Boulder, 80307, University Mall, dog, Barkley
   - Ariel Cornell, 471 S. Mountain View, Cortez, 81321, Cortez, dog, Charity
   - Edna Peacemaker, 372 Wildwood Ave., Greeley, 80631, Rocky Mountain Mall, cat, Tawny
   - Silvester Polansky, 988 Heather Circle #32, Denver, 80204, High Prairie Mall, cat, Simon.
5. Sort the data source by postal code from the lowest to the highest postal code.
6. Save your changes to the data source document Pet Vaccine Data.
7. Switch to the main document, and replace the text of the field names in brackets with actual merge fields. Remember to use a Word date field to replace "[Date]".
8. Save the changes to the main document, and then view the document as it will appear when it is merged. Check for any mistakes in the records you've added.

Explore

9. Print only those records for customers who own a dog.

10. Close all documents, saving changes as needed.

As you learned in the tutorial, you can use many types of files as your data source. For example, right now Alicia needs to send out a memo to her own employees regarding their payroll deductions. The data you'll need for this mail merge is stored in a Microsoft Excel worksheet named "Payroll Data," which contains the following field names: FirstName, LastName, Address1, WorkPhone, and Exemptions. To learn how to merge this alternate data source with a Word document, first open the file **Payroll** from the Review folder in the Tutorial.06 folder on your Data Disk, and then save it as **Pet Shoppe Payroll Memo**. Complete the following:

11. Create a form letter main document using Pet Shoppe Payroll Memo file.

Explore

12. Now, you can select an Excel worksheet as your data source. To select this data source, click Get Data in the Mail Merge Helper, and then click Open Data Source. Use the Look in arrow to select the Review folder for Tutorial 6. Click the Files of type list arrow, select MS Excel Worksheets, click the Payroll Data file, and then click Open. The Microsoft Excel dialog box opens. Verify that "Entire Spreadsheet" is selected in the Named or cell range text box, and then click OK. You see a message box indicating that the main document does not contain any merge fields. Click Edit Main Document. In the next step, you will edit the main document to insert the necessary merge fields. The Insert Merge Field button automatically displays the field names contained in the Excel file.

    Edit the main document by doing the following:

13. Move the cursor to the right of "TO:," press the Tab key and insert the FirstName field (for the employee's first name), press the spacebar, and then insert the LastName field (for the employee's last name). Select the name fields, and turn off bold formatting.
14. To the right of "DATE:" in the memo, press the Tab key and insert the Word date field. Select the Word date field and toggle off the Bold button.
15. In the body of the memo, immediately before the word "exemption(s)," insert the Exemptions field followed by a space.
16. Save the main document with the changes, and then view the memo as it will appear when merged and check each record for any mistakes.
17. Merge to a new document. Scroll through the new document to verify that names and exemptions have been inserted into the memos correctly, and then save the new document as Pet Shoppe Payroll Memo 2.

Explore

18. Print only the memo for Minh Lien.
19. Close all documents, saving any changes. If Word asks if you want to save changes to a template, click No.
20. Create a new main document of the Envelopes type.

Explore

21. Select the Microsoft Excel worksheet "Payroll Data" as the data source, following the directions in Step 12, except that you will need to click Set Up Main Document, rather than Edit Main Document.

Explore

22. In the Envelope Options dialog box, select the Size 10 envelope in the Envelope size list box, and then click OK. (The steps that follow assume you will be printing the envelope text on a piece of paper rather than on an actual envelope. If you plan to print to an envelope, use the Envelope size list box to select the appropriate envelope size.)

Explore

23. In the Envelope Address dialog box, use the Insert Merge Field button to insert the FirstName, LastName, and Address1 fields into the Envelope Address dialog box, and then click OK. Click Close to close the Mail Merge Helper dialog box.
24. Save the envelopes main document as **Payroll Envelope Form**.
25. Merge the envelopes main document and data source Payroll Data, and then save the merged document as **Payroll Envelopes**. If Word asks you which return address to use, use the default return address, or substitute your own.
26. Print the last employee address on an 8½ × 11-inch sheet of paper, and then close all documents.
27. Open a new, blank document window and create a main document for generating a one-page telephone list. Use Payroll Data as the data source.
28. Create an employee telephone list by inserting the LastName and FirstName fields, separated by a comma and space, at the left margin. Insert the WorkPhone field at the right margin with a dot leader.
29. Format the main document so that each telephone number appears on a separate line, save the main document as **Employee Phone List Form**, and then sort the data source alphabetically by last name in ascending order.
30. Generate the telephone list, and save the new merged document as **Employee Phone List**.
31. Print the telephone list, and then close all documents, saving changes as needed.

CASE PROBLEMS

Case 1. Amber Christensen for Mayor Amber Christensen is preparing to run for the office of mayor of Joplin, Missouri. Amber's campaign staff is creating a data file of prospective supporters of her campaign, and asks you to help.

1. If necessary, start Word and make sure your Data Disk is in the appropriate drive. Open the file **Campaign** from the Cases folder in the Tutorial.06 folder on your Data Disk, and then save it as **Campaign Form Letter**.
2. Create a form letter main document using the Campaign Form Letter file.

Explore

3. Create a data source document with the following field names: LastName, FirstName, NickName, WorkField, Title, Company, Address1, and Phone. After you have added and removed the necessary fields, use the Move arrows in the Create Data Source dialog box to arrange the field names in the order given in this step. (To move a field name, select it in the Field names in header row list box, and then click the up or down arrow as necessary to move it up or down in the list.)
4. Save the data source document as **Supporters Data**.
5. Enter the following four records into the data source. (Don't include the commas in the records.)
   - Montoya, Andrea, Andrea, community, Chief Medical Officer, Joplin Medical Center, 1577 Lancelot Drive, 552-7740
   - Zabriski, David, Dave, business, President, Zabriski Appraisal Services, 633 Wentworth, 552-1095

- Kinikini, Leilani, Lani, business, Business Manager, Astor and Bradford Architects, 4424 Bedford, 552-9850
- Norman, Theodore, Tad, education, Principal, Joplin High School, 844 Tiger Way, 552-0180

Edit the Campaign Form Letter as follows:

6. At the beginning of the document, insert the Word date field, and then leave five blank lines between the date and the inside address.
7. Insert merge fields for the inside address. Include fields for each person's first and last name, title, company, and address. All the inside addresses should include the city (Joplin), the abbreviation for the state (MO), and the ZIP code (64801).
8. Insert a blank line below the fields for the inside address, and create the salutation of the letter. Use the field name NickName in the salutation. Make sure there is a blank line between the salutation and the body of the letter.
9. In the third paragraph, replace "[Nickname]" with the actual field name.
10. Save the edited main document.
11. Merge the files to create a set of letters to prospective contributors.
12. Save the merged letters document as **Campaign Letters**.
13. Print the first two letters.

Explore

14. Create a main document to print envelopes for the letters, and save the document as **Campaign Envelope Form**.
15. Merge the envelopes main document with the Supporters Data data source, and save the merged document as **Campaign Envelopes**.
16. Print the first page of the envelope file on an $8^1/_2 \times 11$-inch sheet of paper.
17. Sort the data source in descending order by phone numbers.

Explore

18. Create a telephone list of prospective contributors. Use a dot leader to separate the name on the left from the phone number on the right.
19. Save the main document for the telephone list as **Campaign Phone Form**.
20. Save the merged document of the telephone list as **Campaign Phone List**.
21. Print the telephone list on a sheet of paper.
22. Close the documents.

Case 2. Jeri's Gems Jeri Moak owns a small jewelry store in Dubuque, Iowa. Frequently, she notifies her regular customers (who live in nearby communities in Iowa, Wisconsin, and Illinois) of upcoming sales. She decides to prepare personalized form letters to mail to all her regular customers one month before their birthdays. She'll mail the letters in manila envelopes along with a two-page color catalog and a gift certificate. She asks you to help her perform a mail merge using Word.

1. If necessary, start Word and make sure your Data Disk is in the appropriate drive. Open the file **Gems** from the Cases folder in the Tutorial.06 folder of your Data Disk, and then save it as **Gems Form Letter**.
2. Create a form letter main document using the Gems Form Letter document.
3. Create a data source document with the following field names: FirstName, LastName, Address1, City, State, PostalCode, BirthDay, BirthMonth, BirthStone.

4. Save the data source document as **Gems Data**.
5. Enter the following five records into the data source. (Don't include the commas in the records.) Enter months by numbers (1, 2, 3), not names (January, February, March), so you can sort in chronological order.

   Kayleen, Mitchell, 882 River Way, Dubuque, IA, 52001, 23, 1, garnet
   Tammy, Minervini, 8244 Westbrook Way, Platteville, WI, 52143, 31, 8, sapphire
   Susan, Gardner, 804 Derby Road, Dubuque, IA, 52001, 14, 6, pearl
   Garth, Poduska, 77 Catskill Circle, Rockford, IL, 51345, 7, 1, garnet
   Oscar, Pike, 402 Waverly Avenue, Waterloo, IA, 53400, 22, 8, sapphire
6. At the beginning of the main document, Gems Form Letter, insert the date field and data fields for the inside address and salutation, in a proper business-letter format. Remember to include the state field in the inside address. Use the customer's first name in the salutation.
7. In the body of the letter, insert the fields BirthMonth, BirthDay, and BirthStone at the locations indicated by the bracketed words. Put a slash (/) between the BirthDay and BirthMonth.
8. Sort the data source alphabetically by the customer's last name.
9. Save the main document using its current filename.

Explore

10. Using Query Options, select those records for customers whose birthdays are in January, and then merge the main document with the data source.
11. Save the merged document as **Gems Letters**.
12. Print the letters that result from the merge.
13. Create a main document for generating mailing labels on sheets of Avery 5162 – Address Labels, using the Gems Data file as your data source.
14. Save the main document as **Gems Labels Form**.
15. Merge the main document and the data source to a new file.
16. Print the labels on an 8½ × 11-inch sheet of paper, and save the labels as **Gems Labels**.
17. Create a catalog main document for generating a list of customers, using the Gems Data file as your data source. Use the following example to format your merge fields, putting a blank line after the last line, and using bold formatting for the first line:

    Name: Garth Poduska
    Address: 77 Catskill Circle, Rockford, IL 51345
    Birth date: 1/7
    Birthstone: garnet
18. Save the main document as **Gems Customer List Form**.

Explore

19. Sort the data source in ascending order by birth month, then by birth day. (*Hint:* Click the Query Options button on the Mail Merge Helper dialog box, use the Sort Records tab, set the Sort by text box to BirthMonth and the Then by text box to BirthDay.)
20. Merge the customer list form with the data source.
21. Save the merged document as **Gems Customer List**.
22. Print the list.
23. Close the files.

Case 3. Liberty Auto Sales Tom Reynolds is the customer relations manager for Liberty Auto Sales in Cadillac, Michigan. After a customer purchases a new car, Tom sends out a Sales Satisfaction Survey accompanied by a personalized letter. He would like you to help him use the Word Mail Merge feature to perform this task.

1. If necessary, start Word and make sure your Data Disk is in the appropriate drive. Open the file **AutoSale** from the Cases folder in the Tutorial.06 folder on your Data Disk, and then save it as **Auto Sale Form Letter**.
2. Create a main document using the Auto Sale Form Letter file.
3. Create a data source with the following field names: FirstName, LastName, Address1, City, PostalCode, CarMake, CarModel, SalesRep.
4. Save the data source document as **Auto Sale Data**.
5. Enter the following five records into the data source. (Don't include the commas in the records.)
   - Donald, Meyers, 344 Spartan Avenue, Detroit, 48235, Honda, Civic, Bruce
   - Arlene, Snow, 46 North Alberta Road, Ecorse, 48229, Toyota, Camry, Lillie
   - Lance, Nakagawa, 4211 Livonia Drive, Kentwood, 49508, Honda, Accord, Martin
   - Peter, Siskel, 92 Waterford Place, Walker, 49504, Toyota, Corolla, Bruce
   - Marilee, Peterson, 8211 University Drive, Detroit, 48238, Honda, Civic, Lillie
6. Edit the main document to include the following in the letter, using a proper letter format: date, inside address, and salutation. (*Hint:* You'll need to add the state as text.)
7. Edit the body of the form letter to replace words in brackets with their corresponding merge field names.
8. Save the form letter. If Word asks if you want to save changes to a template, click No.
9. Sort the data source alphabetically by the last name.

Explore

10. Use the Query Option dialog box to select only those records whose sales representative was Lillie.
11. Merge the form letter with the data source.
12. Save the merged document as **Auto Letters**.
13. Print letters in the merged document.

Explore

14. Create a main document for printing envelopes for the letters that you printed.
15. Save the new main document as **Auto Envelopes Form**.
16. Merge the main document with the data to generate a file for printing envelopes.
17. Save the merged document as **Auto Envelopes**.
18. Print the envelopes in the file on 8½×11-inch sheets of paper.
19. Close all the files, saving any changes as needed.

Case 4. Graduation Announcements Mailing List Suppose that, upon your graduation from college, you want to send announcements to your friends and family telling them about this special event in your life. You can do this easily with Word's Mail Merge feature. Do the following:

1. If necessary, start Word and make sure your Data Disk is in the appropriate drive.
2. Open a new, blank document and use it to create a main document form letter.
3. Create a data source containing the names and addresses of at least five people. You can use real or fictitious names and addresses. Be sure to include addresses in at least two different states.

4. Save the data source document as **Graduation Guest Data** in the Cases folder in the Tutorial.06 folder on your Data Disk.
5. Write a brief form letter telling your friends and relatives about your graduation. Include the following in the letter:
   a. Word field for the current date
   b. merge fields for the inside address and salutation of the letter
   c. at least one merge field within the body of the letter
   d. information to your friends and family about the time, date, and location of the graduation exercises
6. Save the main document as **Graduation Form Letter**.
7. Sort the data source in ascending order by last name.
8. Merge the main document and data source.
9. Save the merged document as **Graduation Merge**.
10. Print the first two letters of the merged document.
11. Create a labels main document. You can use any printer label type you like, as long as each name and address fits on one label and all the labels fit on one page.
12. Save the labels main document as **Graduation Labels Form**.
13. Merge the files, and save the merged document of labels as **Graduation Labels**.
14. Print the labels on a plain sheet of paper.

INTERNET ASSIGNMENTS

The purpose of the Internet Assignments is to challenge you to find information on the Internet that you can use to create effective documents. The actual assignments are updated and maintained on the Course Technology Web site. Log on to the Internet and use your Web browser to go to the Student Online Companion to accompany this text at **www.course.com/NewPerspectives/office2000**. Click the Word link, and then click the link for Tutorial 6.

QUICK CHECK ANSWERS

Session 6.1

1. **a.** A form letter is a document containing general information to be sent to many recipients, to which you can add personalized data for each recipient, such as name, address, and so on.
   b. A **main document** is a document (such as a letter or a contract) that, in addition to text, contains placeholder text to mark where variable information from the data source (such as a name or an address) will be inserted.
   c. A **data source** is a document (often in the form of a table) that contains information, such as customers' names and addresses, that can be merged with the main document.
   d. A merge field is placeholder text in a main document. When the main document and the data source are merged, merge fields are replaced by specific information from each record in the data source.
   e. A record is a collection of information about one individual or object in a data source. For example, a record might include the first name, last name, address and phone numbers for a customer.
   f. A **data field** is one specific piece of information a record. For example, a record might include a first name data field, a last name data field, and a phone number address field. Each row of data fields in a data source make up a complete record.

2. PayGrade and StudentIdentificationNumber are valid field names. Options a and f are invalid because they contain spaces. Option e is invalid because it is longer than 40 characters.
3. record
4. True
5. Type "Gender" in the Field name text box of the Create Data Source dialog box, and then click the Add Field Name button.
6. The data form simplifies the process of entering, editing, and deleting data records.
7. To move among records in the data source, open the data form, and then use the Record arrow buttons in the lower-left corner of the data form to move forward or backward to the record you want.

Session 6.2

1. Using a data field in a main document ensures that the current date will be inserted every time the document is printed.
2. To insert a merge field into a main document, click the Insert Merge Field button on the Mail Merge toolbar, and then click a field name.
3. Within the main document, a merge field is indicated by chevrons.
4. **a.** A merged document is a document containing the text of the main document, combined with the data from the data source.
   b. When you sort a list or a document, you rearrange its contents in alphabetical, numerical, or chronological order.
   c. A query is the process by which you can select specific records from a data source.
   d. A filtering operator is a mathematical or logical expression used to include or exclude certain records.
5. Open the Mail Merge Helper, click the Query Options button, click the Field list arrow and select the ZIP code field, verify that "Equal to" appears in the Comparison text box, type the desired ZIP code in the Compare to text box, and then click OK.
6. To preview the merged document, create a main document and a data source, verify that the main document is displayed in the document window, and then click the View Merged Data button on the Mail Merge toolbar.
7. 23
8. No, you do not have to print every letter in a merged form letter document.

Session 6.3

1. Merge fields (b) and telephone list (d) are not types of main documents.
2. True
3. Create main document of type Envelopes, specify the main document and the data source, select the type of printer, create a sample envelope with merge fields in the Create Envelopes dialog box, and then create a new merge document and print.
4. True
5. A dot leader is a dotted line extending from text on the left margin to text at the tab stop.
6. To display a data table, click the Edit Data Source button on the Mail Merge toolbar, and then click View Source.
7. Display the data table, move the insertion point to the LastName field, and then click the Sort Descending button on the Database toolbar.

OBJECTIVES

In this tutorial you will:

- Embed and modify an Excel worksheet
- Link an Excel chart
- Modify and update the linked chart
- Modify a document for online viewing
- Explore Web Layout view and the Document Map
- Save a Word document as a Web page
- Format a Web document
- View a Web document in a Web browser

LAB

INTEGRATING WORD WITH OTHER PROGRAMS AND WITH THE WORLD WIDE WEB

Writing a Proposal to Open a New Branch of Family Style, Inc.

CASE

Family Style, Inc.

Nalani Tui is one of the founders and owners of Family Style, Inc., a retail company with six outlets in the central and southern regions of Indiana. When she and her partners founded Family Style in 1988, their concept was simple. They would buy high-quality used home merchandise—clothing, sports equipment, appliances, furniture, televisions, personal computers, and so forth—and resell it at a profit, but still for far less than consumers would pay for similar, new merchandise.

The concept was immediately popular. Customers who have items for sale can receive immediate cash, and customers who want to buy items can purchase them at very low prices. Family Style is successful because the outlets readily attract sellers and buyers and because the management has kept administrative, marketing, and overhead expenses low.

Nalani thinks that Family Style is ready to expand to cities in northern Indiana. She is preparing a written proposal for the other owners and investors of Family Style on the advantages and disadvantages of opening new outlet stores. The proposal will include an overview of the company's current financial picture, the rationale for expanding, possible sites for new outlets, and Nalani's recommendations for the first new branch site and manager. She wants you to help organize this information in the proposal document.

Nalani needs to make her proposal available to three different groups of people:

- Current owners and stockholders of the company, who live in different parts of the country
- The Family Style management team, who work in the Bloomington office
- Potential investors in the company, who could reside anywhere

Nalani can simply mail a printed copy of her proposal to the current owners and stockholders. For the company's management team, she can make the proposal available through the company's network. To reach a worldwide audience of potential investors, she can post her proposal on the company's World Wide Web site.

In this tutorial, you'll combine the text that Nalani has already written in Word with a worksheet file and a chart that other Family Style employees prepared using different software. Then, you'll prepare the document for online viewing on the company's network. Your modifications will enable online viewers to easily navigate the document and view additional, more detailed information. Finally, you'll save the document in a special format that is readable by Web browsers such as Internet Explorer or Netscape Navigator, and you'll enhance the Web document's appearance.

SESSION 7.1

In this session, you'll see how Nalani planned the proposal. Then you'll embed a worksheet file that was created in Microsoft Excel and modify it from within Word. Next, you'll insert a link to an Excel chart. You'll modify the chart from Excel and learn how to update it in Word to see the effects of your modifications.

Planning the Document

Nalani has written the text of the proposal in Word. She has asked you to add two other components to her proposal: a worksheet and a chart, both from Excel. Together, the text, data, and chart will show the company's current financial state and the possible sites for new retail outlets. The proposal also presents Nalani's recommendations for a new site and branch manager. Nalani gives you two files to combine with the Word document: a Microsoft Excel spreadsheet of financial data created by one of the store managers and an Excel chart created by the Accounting department. Figure 7-1 shows how Nalani wants to combine these elements into a complete proposal.

The proposal begins with an executive summary; then it reviews the company objectives, explains the current situation and future expansion ideas, suggests some location options, and gives a final recommendation.

Your immediate task is to place the Excel worksheet and chart into the Word proposal document.

Figure 7-1 PROPOSAL NALANI ENVISIONS

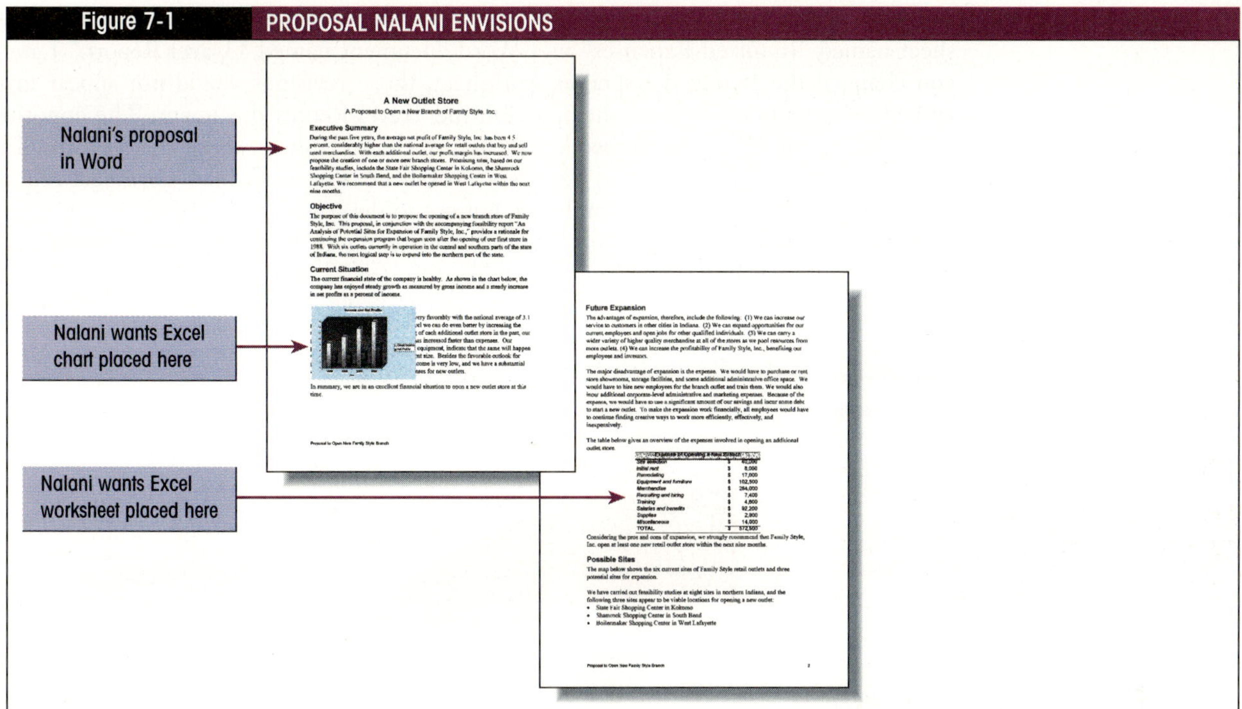

Integrating Objects from Other Programs

Every software program is designed to accomplish a set of specific tasks. As you've seen with Microsoft Word, you can use a word-processing program to create, edit, and format documents such as letters, reports, newsletters, and proposals. A **spreadsheet program**, on the other hand, allows you to organize, calculate, and analyze numerical data. A spreadsheet created in Microsoft Excel is known as a **worksheet.** For example, one of Family Style's managers used a Microsoft Excel worksheet to prepare a breakdown of expenses involved in opening a new branch. The Accounting department created an Excel chart that provides a visual representation of income and profit data.

Both the worksheet and the chart are Excel objects. An **object** is an item such as a graphic image, clip art, a WordArt image, a chart, or a section of text, that you can modify and move from one document to another. Nalani asks you to place the worksheet and chart objects into her proposal, but she also wants to be able to modify the Excel objects after they are inserted into the document. A technology called **object linking and embedding**, or **OLE** (pronounced "oh-lay"), allows you to integrate information created in one program into a document created in another and then to modify the object using the tools originally used to create it.

The program used to create the original version of the object is called the **source program** (in this case, Excel). The program into which the object is integrated is called the **destination program** (in this case, Word). Similarly, the original file is called the **source file** and the file into which you insert the object is called the **destination file**.

The next two sections describe two options for transferring data between source files and destination files: embedding and linking.

Embedding

Embedding is a technique that allows you to insert a copy of an existing object into a destination document and edit the object by double-clicking it to bring up the tools of the source program. Because the embedded object is a copy, any changes you make to it are not reflected in the original source file, and vice versa. For instance, you could embed a worksheet named "Itemized Expenses" in a Word document named "Travel Report." Later, if you changed the Itemized Expenses worksheet, those revisions would not appear in the embedded version of the worksheet, within the Travel Report document. The opposite is also true. If you edited the embedded version of the worksheet, those changes would not show up in the original Itemized Expenses worksheet. The embedded worksheet retains a connection to the source program, Excel, but not to the source worksheet.

Figure 7-2 illustrates how you can use embedding to place the Excel worksheet in Nalani's Word proposal.

Figure 7-2 EMBEDDING AN EXCEL WORKSHEET IN A WORD DOCUMENT

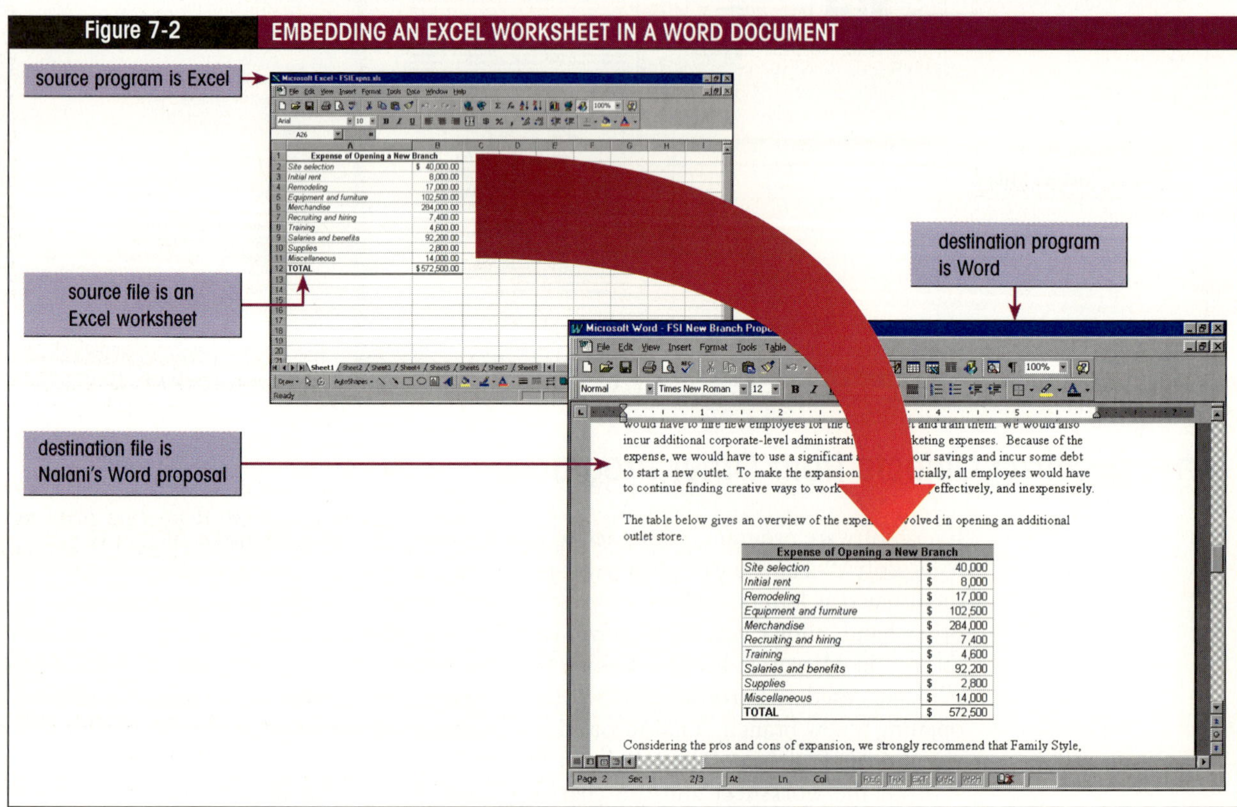

Once an object is embedded, you can edit it using the source program's editing tools. You simply double-click the embedded Excel chart, and the Excel menus and toolbars appear without your having to leave Word. Excel must be installed on the computer you are using if you want to edit the Excel worksheet while you are still in Word.

Linking

Linking is similar to embedding, except that the linked object maintains a two-way connection between the source file and destination file. If you want to edit the linked object, you can open the source program from within the destination program and make changes that will also appear in the original source file. Likewise, if you edit the original file in the source program, the changes will appear in the linked object. The linked object you see in the destination document is not a copy; it is only a representation of the original object in the source file. As a result, a document that contains a linked object usually takes up less space on a disk than a document containing an embedded version of the same object. Figure 7-3 illustrates how you can use linking to place the Excel chart into Nalani's Word document proposal.

Figure 7-3 LINKING AN EXCEL CHART TO A WORD DOCUMENT

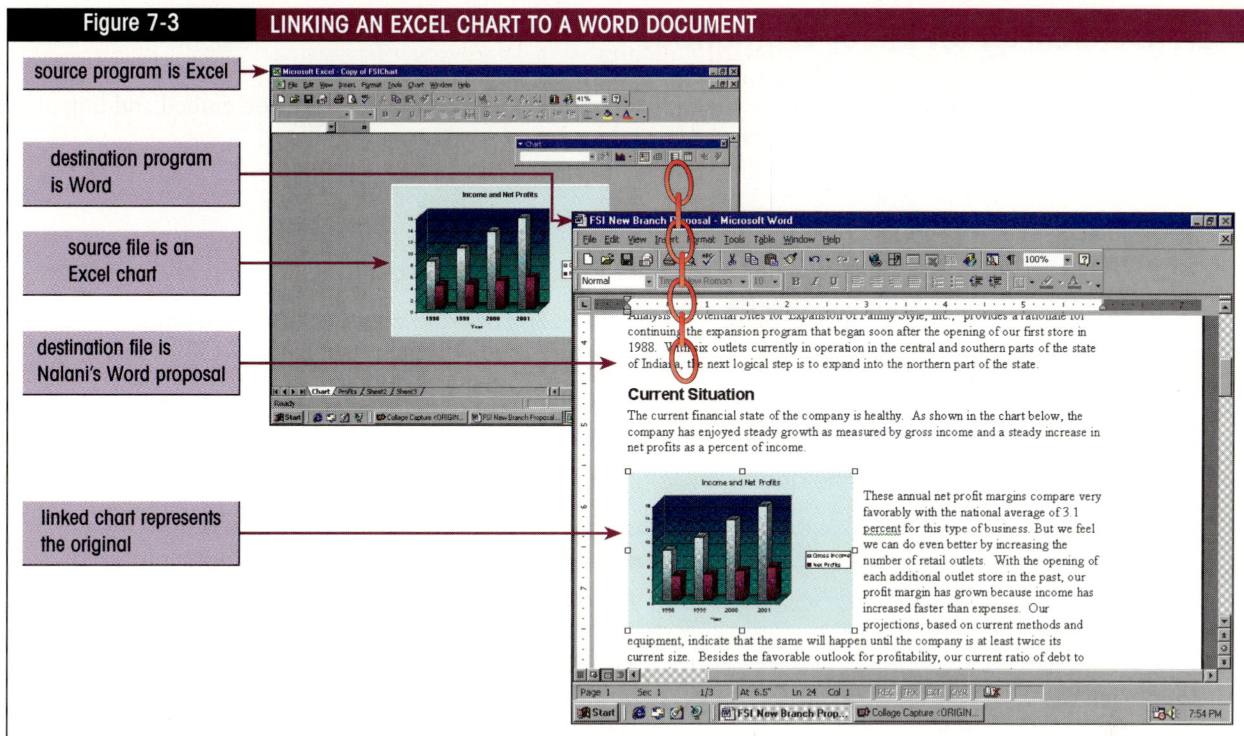

Keep in mind that not all software programs allow you to embed or link objects. Only those programs that support OLE let you embed or link objects from one program to another. Office 2000 programs such as Word, Excel, and PowerPoint, are OLE-enabled programs and fully support object linking and embedding.

Choosing between Embedding and Linking

If you need to make changes to an object after inserting it in a Word document, and you know that you have the source program installed on your computer, then you can use either embedding or linking. Of these two options, embedding is best when you know the information in the source file is not likely to change often. For example, if you want to integrate an Excel worksheet into your Word document, you should embed the worksheet so you can access Excel commands occasionally to modify formatting or data. The original Excel worksheet (the source file) remains unchanged, and you could even delete it from your disk without affecting the copy embedded in your Word document.

Link a file whenever you have data that is likely to change over time. For example, suppose you created a Word document called "Refinancing Options" into which you want to insert an Excel worksheet containing the latest interest rates for home mortgages. Suppose also that your assistant updates the Excel worksheet daily to make sure it contains the latest information. By linking the worksheet to the Refinancing Options document, you can be certain that the mortgage rates will be updated every time your assistant updates the Excel worksheet. The advantage to linking is that the data in both the Excel worksheet and the Word document can reflect the latest revisions. The disadvantages to linking are that you must have access to both Excel and the linked file on your computer.

Keep in mind that files containing embedded and linked objects can be very large. Because of this (and because of the many Web page files you will create later in this tutorial) you will need to copy the Tutorial.07 folder to your computer's hard drive before proceeding with the steps in the next section.

Embedding an Excel Worksheet

Nalani prepared the new branch proposal using Word. Before you embed and link objects, you'll first open Nalani's Word document (the destination file).

To open the destination file:

1. Verify that you have copied the Tutorial.07 folder to your computer's hard drive.
2. Start Word. For this tutorial, you don't need to display the nonprinting characters.
3. Open the file **FSIProp** from the Tutorial folder for Tutorial 7, and then save it as **FSI New Branch Proposal** in the same folder.
4. Read the document to get an idea of its content.

   Because this tutorial will use many files, you'll want to make efficient use of your available disk space. You'll turn off the Word Fast Save feature to save disk space.
5. Click **Tools** on the menu bar, click **Options**, click the **Save** tab, if necessary remove the check mark from the Allow fast saves check box and click the **OK** button.

The proposal begins with an Executive Summary that quickly summarizes the main points of the document. Notice that in the "Current Situation" section, there is the placeholder "[insert chart]" where you'll insert the Excel chart that illustrates the company's growth in income and profits. In the "Future Expansion" section, there is the placeholder "[insert spreadsheet]" where you'll insert the worksheet outlining the expenses involved in opening a new retail outlet. Under Possible Sites, there is a map, originally created in Microsoft Paint (a graphics program included with Microsoft Windows), that has been inserted into the document via linking. At the end of the proposal, Nalani has also inserted a photograph of Virgil Jackson, the proposed manager for the new location.

You'll start by embedding the Excel worksheet into the "Future Expansion" section of the proposal, in place of the "[insert spreadsheet]" placeholder. By embedding the worksheet, you can maintain a one-way connection between Excel and the worksheet in Word. You'll use the Object command on the Insert menu to embed the existing Excel worksheet in the proposal.

REFERENCE WINDOW 

Embedding An Existing File

- Move the insertion point to the location in your document where you want the embedded file to appear.
- Click Insert on the menu bar, and then click Object to open the Object dialog box.
- Click the Create from File tab.
- Click the Browse button, select the file you want to embed, click Insert, and then click the OK button.

Once the expense worksheet is embedded in the proposal document, you'll be able to modify its contents and appearance using Excel commands from within Word, as long as Excel is installed on your computer.

To embed the Excel worksheet:

1. Scroll until you see the bracketed phrase "(insert spreadsheet)" a few lines above the "Possible Sites" heading.
2. Select the entire line, and then delete the placeholder (insert spreadsheet) and the line on which it was located. The insertion point should appear on the blank line between the two paragraphs. This is where you want to embed the Excel worksheet.

   TROUBLE? If the insertion point is not on a blank line, or if two blank lines appear between the paragraphs, edit the proposal so that only one blank line appears between the paragraphs and that the insertion point blinks on that line.
3. Click **Insert** on the menu bar, and then click **Object** to open the Object dialog box, which has two tabs—Create New and Create from File.
4. Click the **Create from File** tab. You'll use the Browse feature to find the Excel worksheet file on your Data Disk.
5. Click the **Browse** button. The Browse dialog box opens.
6. Select the **FSIExpns** file in the Tutorial folder for Tutorial 7.
7. Click the **Insert** button. The Browse dialog box closes and the filename FSIExpns.xls appears in the File name text box in the Object dialog box. See Figure 7-4. Make sure the Link to file check box is not selected. You don't want to link the worksheet—only embed it.

Figure 7-4 OBJECT DIALOG BOX

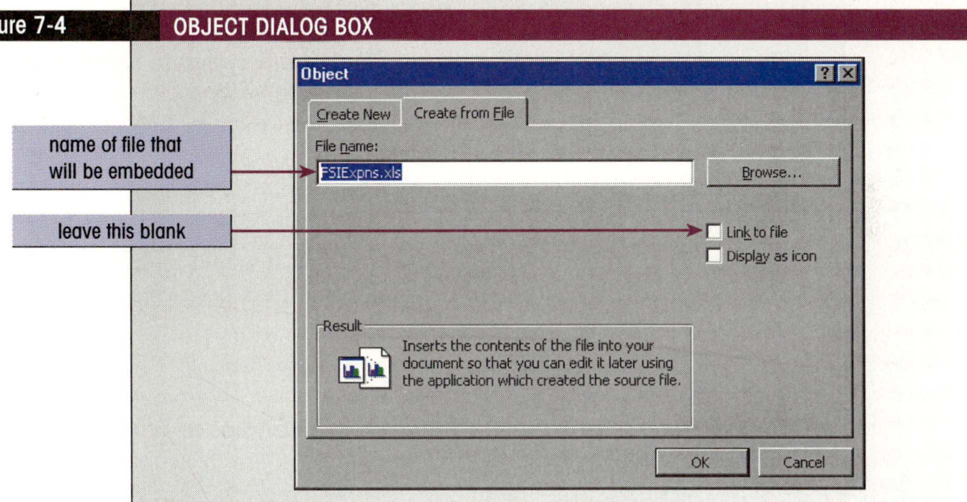

8. Click the **OK** button. The Excel worksheet appears in the document. See Figure 7-5.

Figure 7-5 DOCUMENT WITH EMBEDDED EXCEL WORKSHEET

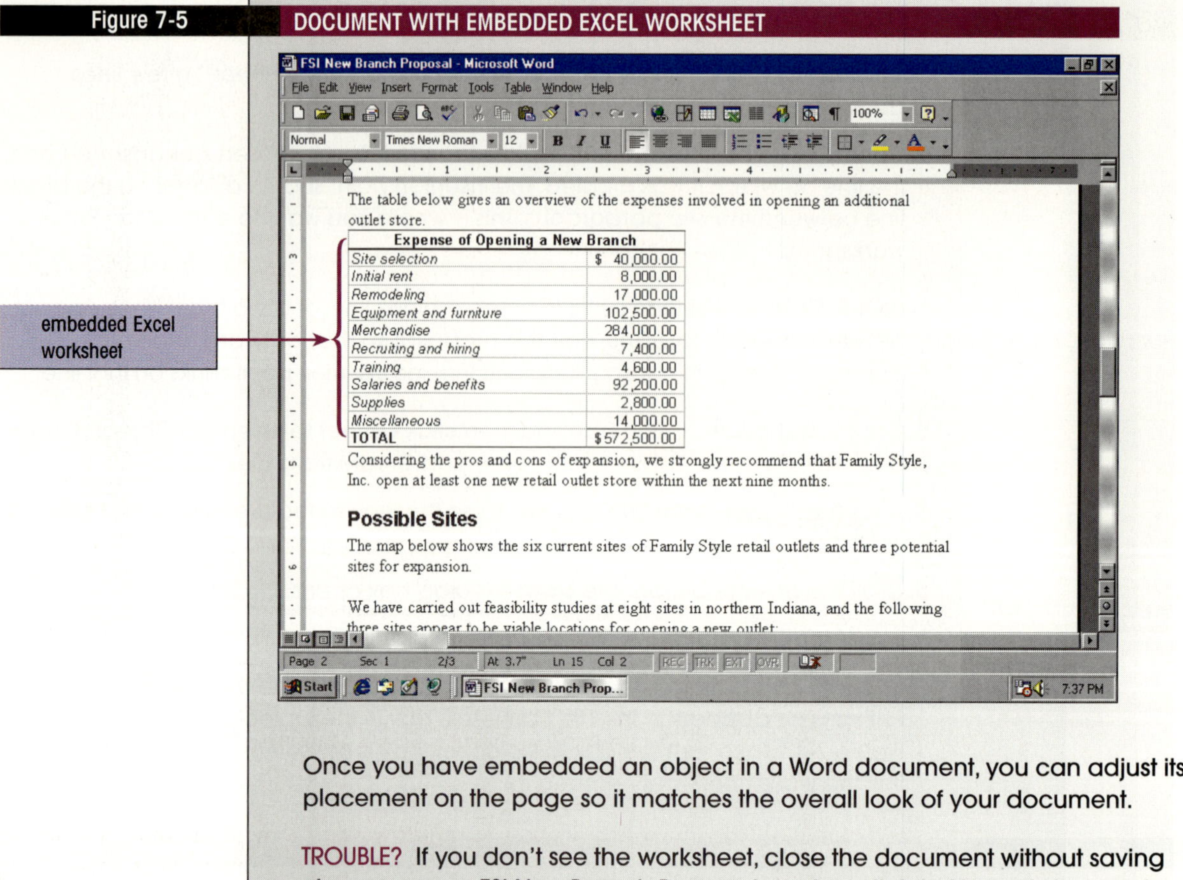

The table below gives an overview of the expenses involved in opening an additional outlet store.

Expense of Opening a New Branch	
Site selection	$ 40,000.00
Initial rent	8,000.00
Remodeling	17,000.00
Equipment and furniture	102,500.00
Merchandise	284,000.00
Recruiting and hiring	7,400.00
Training	4,600.00
Salaries and benefits	92,200.00
Supplies	2,800.00
Miscellaneous	14,000.00
TOTAL	$572,500.00

Considering the pros and cons of expansion, we strongly recommend that Family Style, Inc. open at least one new retail outlet store within the next nine months.

Possible Sites

The map below shows the six current sites of Family Style retail outlets and three potential sites for expansion.

We have carried out feasibility studies at eight sites in northern Indiana, and the following three sites appear to be viable locations for opening a new outlet:

Once you have embedded an object in a Word document, you can adjust its placement on the page so it matches the overall look of your document.

TROUBLE? If you don't see the worksheet, close the document without saving changes, open FSI New Branch Proposal again, switch to Normal view, and begin again with Step 1.

Centering the Embedded Worksheet

You have embedded the worksheet in the proposal. It would look better, however, if it were centered between the left and right margins rather than positioned at the left margin.

To center the worksheet:

1. Click the worksheet to select it. Black resize handles appear around the outside of the worksheet.
2. Click the **Center** button on the Formatting toolbar. The Excel worksheet is centered horizontally in Nalani's proposal document. See Figure 7-6.

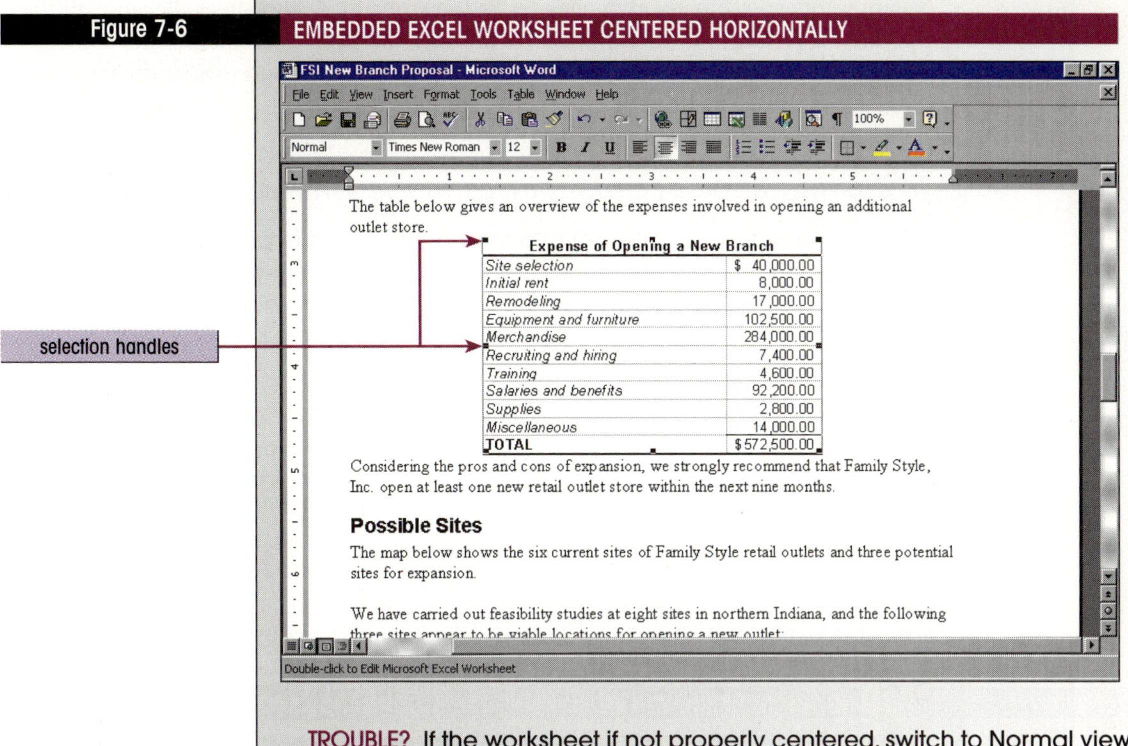

Figure 7-6 EMBEDDED EXCEL WORKSHEET CENTERED HORIZONTALLY

TROUBLE? If the worksheet if not properly centered, switch to Normal view.

Once you have embedded an object, you might want to change the information it contains. It would be inconvenient to go back to the original Excel spreadsheet, make changes, and then embed it in your document again. Because the spreadsheet object is embedded, you can make changes to the object from within Word, which you'll do in the next section.

Modifying the Embedded Worksheet

Because the worksheet is embedded, and as long as the source program (Excel) is installed on your computer, you can edit the worksheet by double-clicking it and using Excel commands and tools. After you modify the worksheet, you can click anywhere else in the Word document to deselect the worksheet and re-display the usual Word editing commands and tools. Any changes that you make in the embedded worksheet will affect only the copy in Word and will not affect the original FSIExpns file.

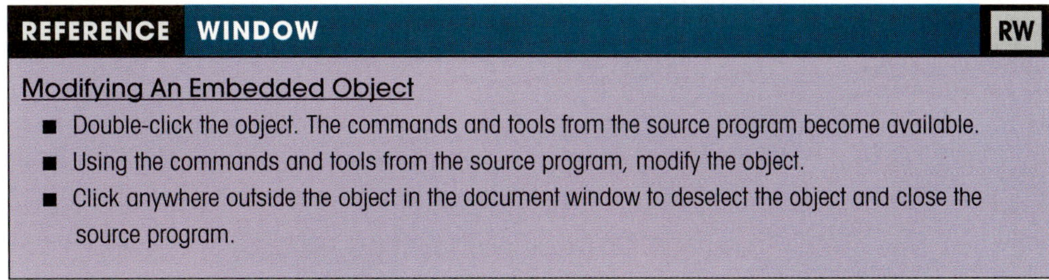

REFERENCE WINDOW RW

Modifying An Embedded Object

- Double-click the object. The commands and tools from the source program become available.
- Using the commands and tools from the source program, modify the object.
- Click anywhere outside the object in the document window to deselect the object and close the source program.

Nalani wants you to make two changes to the embedded worksheet. Because all the cost figures are large and are all rounded to the nearest $100 increment, she wants you to remove the decimal points and trailing zeroes. She also asks you to format the table heading to make it more prominent.

To eliminate the decimal places in the embedded worksheet:

1. Double-click the worksheet. After a moment, the menu bar and toolbars display Excel commands and tools, although the title bar retains the title of the Word program and document. See Figure 7-7. Depending on how your computer is set up, the Excel toolbars may appear one on top of the other, as in Figure 7-7, or they may appear side by side on one row.

   Notice that an Excel worksheet is arranged in rows and columns, just like a Word table. The intersection between a particular row and column is called a **cell** and takes its name from its column letter and the row number. For example, the intersection of column B and row 2 is known as "cell B2."

   TROUBLE? If the Excel commands and toolbar don't appear or a message tells you it can't find the source program, ask your instructor or technical support person for assistance. Excel might not be installed on your computer.

Figure 7-7 EDITING THE WORKSHEET IN WORD USING EXCEL COMMANDS AND TOOLS

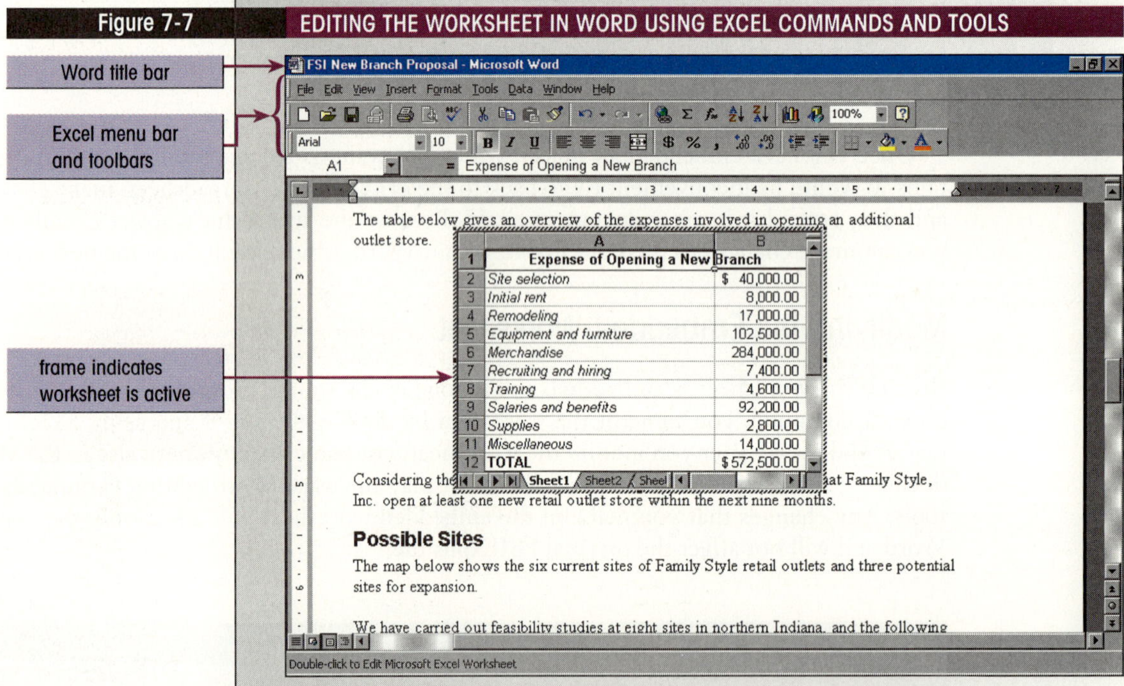

2. Click cell **B2**, which currently contains the figure $40,000.00, hold down the mouse button, and drag downward to highlight all the cells from B2 through B12. The column of cost figures should be highlighted.

3. Click the **Decrease Decimal** button on the Excel Formatting toolbar twice. The numbers in the worksheet change to whole dollar amounts.

TROUBLE? If you don't see the Decrease Decimal button on your screen, click Format on the menu bar, then click Cells. The Format Cells dialog box opens. Click the Number tab, if necessary, click Number in the Category list box, change the setting in the Decimal places box to 0, and then click the OK button.

Now you'll use the Excel tools to format the heading row of the worksheet with a shade of gray, to make it more prominent.

To add shading to the heading row of the embedded worksheet:

1. Click cell **A1** and drag to the right to cell B1 to select the worksheet heading in cells A1 and B1, "Expense of Opening a New Branch."
2. Click the Fill Color list arrow on the Excel Formatting toolbar, and on the fill color palette click the Gray - 25% color tile (4th row down, far right column). The heading row is now shaded with the gray color you selected.

   TROUBLE? If you don't see the Fill Color list arrow on your screen, click Format on the menu bar, and then click Cells. The Format Cells dialog box opens. Click the Patterns tab. In the palette of colors click the gray square in the fourth row down (on the far right side) and then click the OK button.

3. Click anywhere on the proposal document outside the embedded worksheet. The Excel commands and toolbars are replaced by the Word commands and toolbars, and the embedded worksheet displays the newly formatted figures and heading row. See Figure 7-8.

Figure 7-8 EDITED AND FORMATTED WORKSHEET EMBEDDED IN THE PROPOSAL

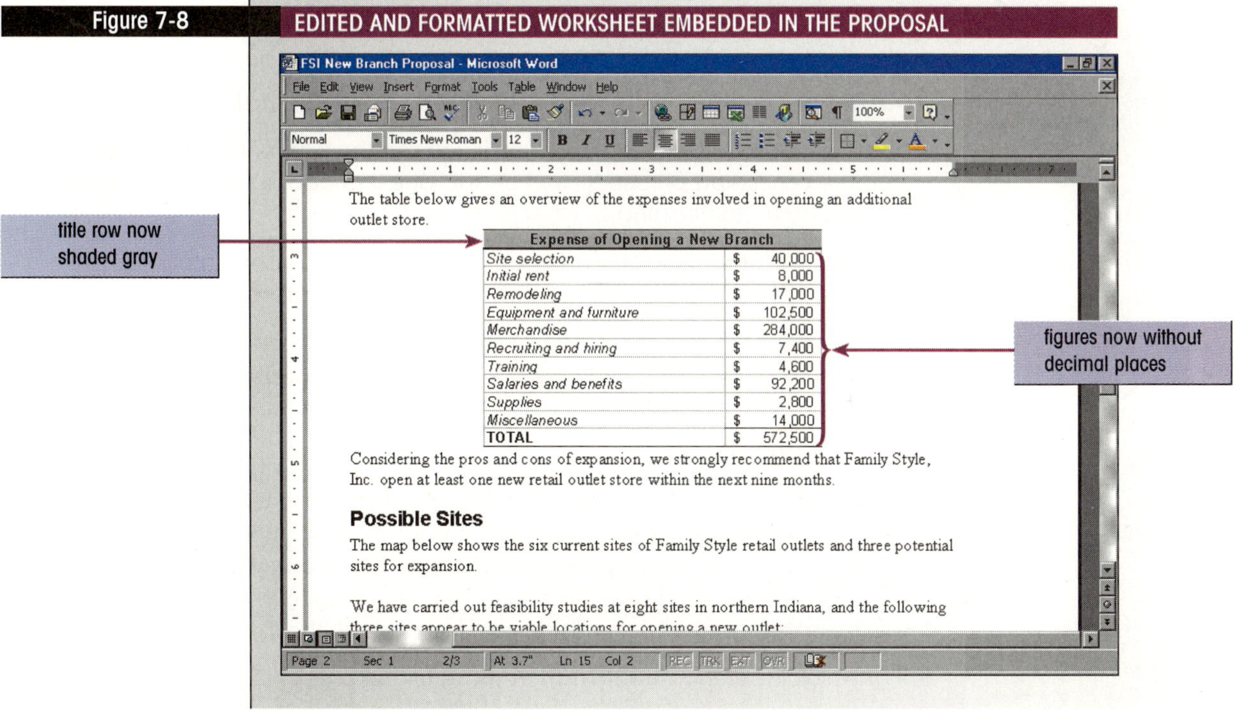

The original Excel worksheet, FSIExps, remains in its original form on your disk, with the two decimal places and the unshaded heading row. You have only modified the embedded copy in Nalani's proposal.

Linking an Excel Chart

Nalani wants you to incorporate the financial chart that shows the increase in gross income and net profit of Family Styles for the previous four years because she thinks this information will help convince others to open a new outlet. However, the Accounting department is currently auditing the sales and profit figures and might have to modify the chart they have given her. Because the source document might change over time, and Nalani wants her proposal to display the most current information at the time it is printed or viewed online, she recommends that you link the chart to the proposal.

REFERENCE WINDOW RW

Linking an Object

- Move the insertion point to the location in your document where you want the file to appear.
- Click Insert on the menu bar, and then click Object to open the Object dialog box.
- Click the Create from File tab on the dialog box.
- Click the Browse button, select the file you want to link, and then click the OK button.
- Click the Link to File check box, and then click the OK button.

You'll link your proposal document to the FSIChart file on your Data Disk. Because you'll make changes to the chart after you link it, you'll make a copy of the chart as you link it. Leave the original file on your Data Disk unchanged in case you want to repeat the tutorial steps later.

To link an Excel chart to the proposal document:

1. Scroll up to the middle of page 1, until you see the "Current Situation" heading and the bracketed phrase "(insert chart)" one line above the second paragraph under the heading.
2. Delete the placeholder "(insert chart)". Make sure the insertion point is positioned on the second blank line between the two paragraphs.
3. Click **Insert** on the menu bar, and then click **Object** to open the Object dialog box. You used this same dialog box earlier to embed the Excel worksheet in the proposal. This time, you'll use it to link to a file.
4. Click the **Create from File** tab.
5. Click the **Browse** button to open the Browse dialog box, and then, if necessary, use the Look in list arrow to open the Tutorial folder within the Tutorial.07 folder. The Browse dialog box displays a list of files in the Tutorial folder for Tutorial 7. Because you want to leave the original file unchanged in your Tutorial folder, you'll make a copy of it now. That way you can use the file again if necessary.
6. Right-click the filename **FSIChart**. A shortcut menu opens.

7. Click **Copy**, and then press **Ctrl** + **V**. A new file, Copy of FSI Chart, appears in the file list.

8. Make sure the filename Copy of FSIChart is selected, and click the **Insert** button. The chart name appears in the File name text box. Now, you need to specify that you want the chart file to be linked, not embedded, in the proposal document.

9. Click the **Link to file** check box to select it. See Figure 7-9.

Figure 7-9 COMPLETED CREATE FROM FILE TAB IN THE OBJECT DIALOG BOX

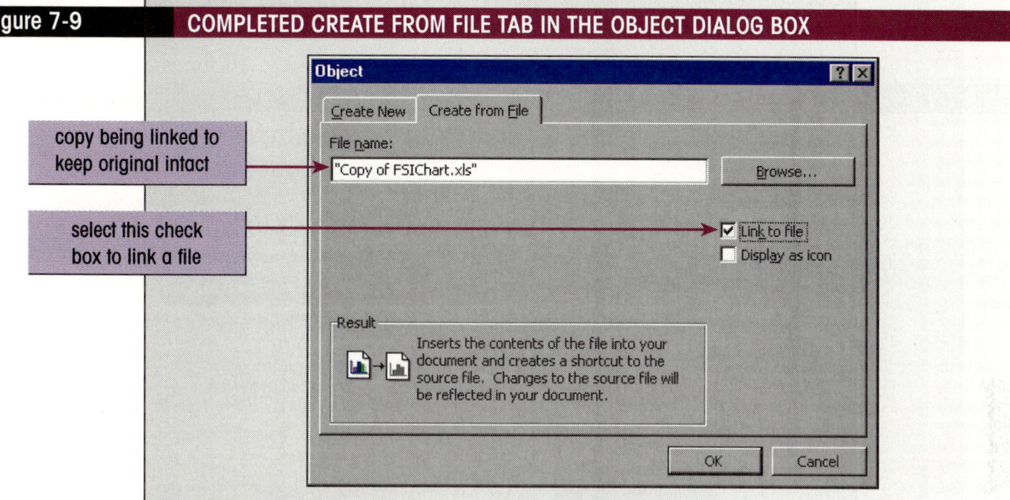

10. Click the OK button. After a moment, the chart image appears in the proposal, displaying income and profit numbers for the last four years.

The figure is far too large for the document, but you can change its size easily.

To resize the chart and wrap text around it:

1. Click the chart. Black resize handles appear around its border.

2. Click **Format** on the menu bar, and then click **Object**.

3. Click the **Size** tab, and in the Scale section, use the **Height** down arrow to decrease the Height and Width settings to 30%. Both the height and width of the selected object will be reduced by 30%, because the Lock aspect option is selected. (If it is not selected, select it now.) Click the **OK** button.

4. Scroll up, if necessary, to display the chart. After a pause, the chart appears in the Word document in a smaller size. Next, you'll wrap text around the chart.

   TROUBLE? If the chart is no longer located below the first paragraph after the heading "Current Situation," just continue with the steps. You will have a chance to adjust its position later.

   TROUBLE? Don't be concerned if it takes a few moments for the chart to appear. Some computers need extra time to display graphics on screen. You may notice similar delays through this tutorial. You also may observe that the colors of your graphics change slightly after you have scrolled through the document.

5. Click the chart to select it, if necessary, click **Format** on the menu bar, and then click **Object**.

6. Click the **Layout** tab, and then click the **Advanced** button. The Advanced Layout dialog box opens.

7. Click the **Tight** icon, click the **Right only** option button, click the **OK** button, and then click the **OK** button again. The document text now wraps to the right of the chart.

8. If necessary, drag the chart to the left margin, so that it is positioned after the first paragraph under the "Current Situation" heading. See Figure 7-10.

Figure 7-10 LINKED EXCEL CHART IN WORD PROPOSAL

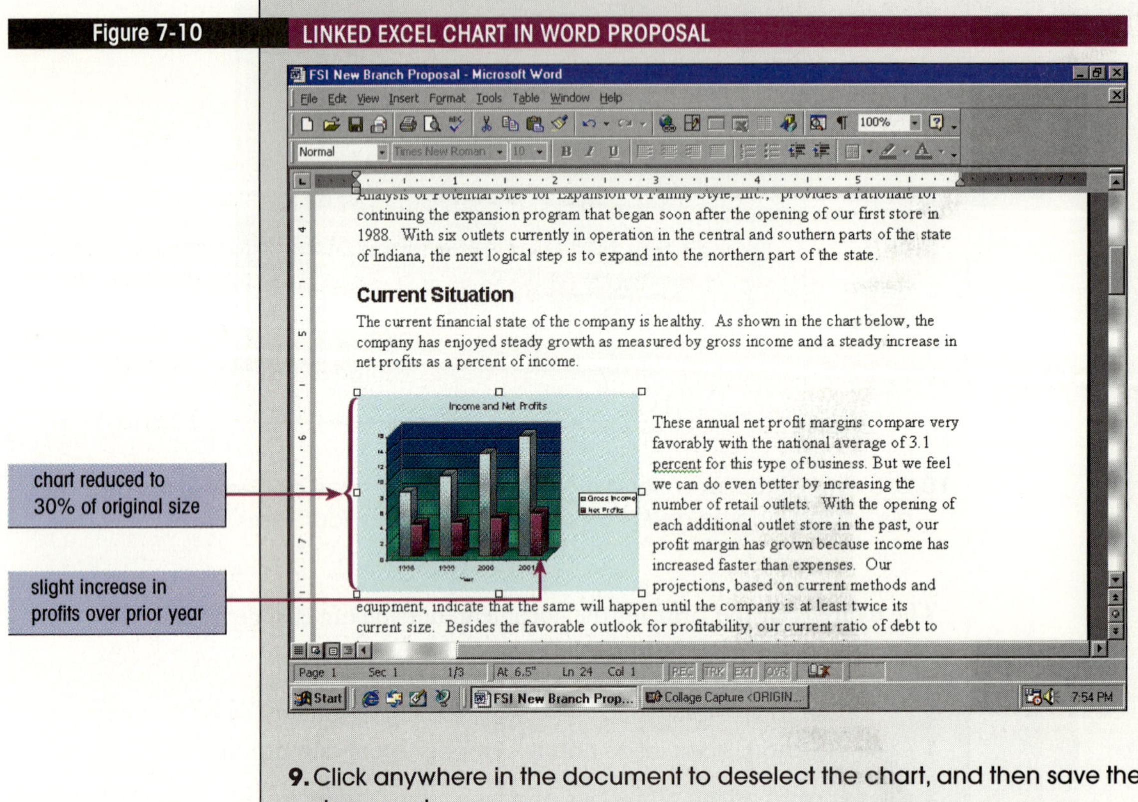

9. Click anywhere in the document to deselect the chart, and then save the document.

Because you have linked the file, you have not inserted a copy of the file in the proposal but merely a visual reference to the original. The size of the proposal file on disk has not increased significantly as a result of the link. If you double-clicked the chart, Excel would start and display the original source file. Instead of seeing the Word title bar at the top of the screen, you would see the Excel title bar. Because Nalani wants to leave Accounting's chart intact, she will not modify it now. However, when Accounting updates the figures, the changes will be reflected in the linked chart in the proposal. You'll see how this works in the next section.

Modifying the Linked Chart

The advantage of linking a file over embedding it is that the destination file is updated whenever you modify the source file. Furthermore, you can update the source file either from within the source program or from within the destination program. In the following steps, you'll simulate what would happen if the Accounting department modified the file in

Excel. You'll open the chart in Excel, the source program, change some figures, and then view the updated information in the Word proposal.

To modify the chart in the source program:

1. Click the **Start** button on the taskbar, point to **Programs**, and then click **Microsoft Excel**. The Excel program window opens.

   TROUBLE? You must have the Microsoft Excel 2000 program installed to complete this section. If you do not see Microsoft Excel on your Programs menu, see your instructor or technical support person.

   TROUBLE? If the Office Assistant opens asking if you want help, click the Start Using Excel button.

2. Click the **Open** button on the Standard toolbar to display the Open dialog box.
3. Use the Look in list arrow to open the Tutorial folder for Tutorial 7.
4. Double-click **Copy of FSIChart**. The chart showing Family Style's income and profits opens. The profit figure for 2001 is somewhat higher than for 2000, indicating a modest growth in profit. See Figure 7-11.

Figure 7-11 CHART IN SOURCE PROGRAM, EXCEL

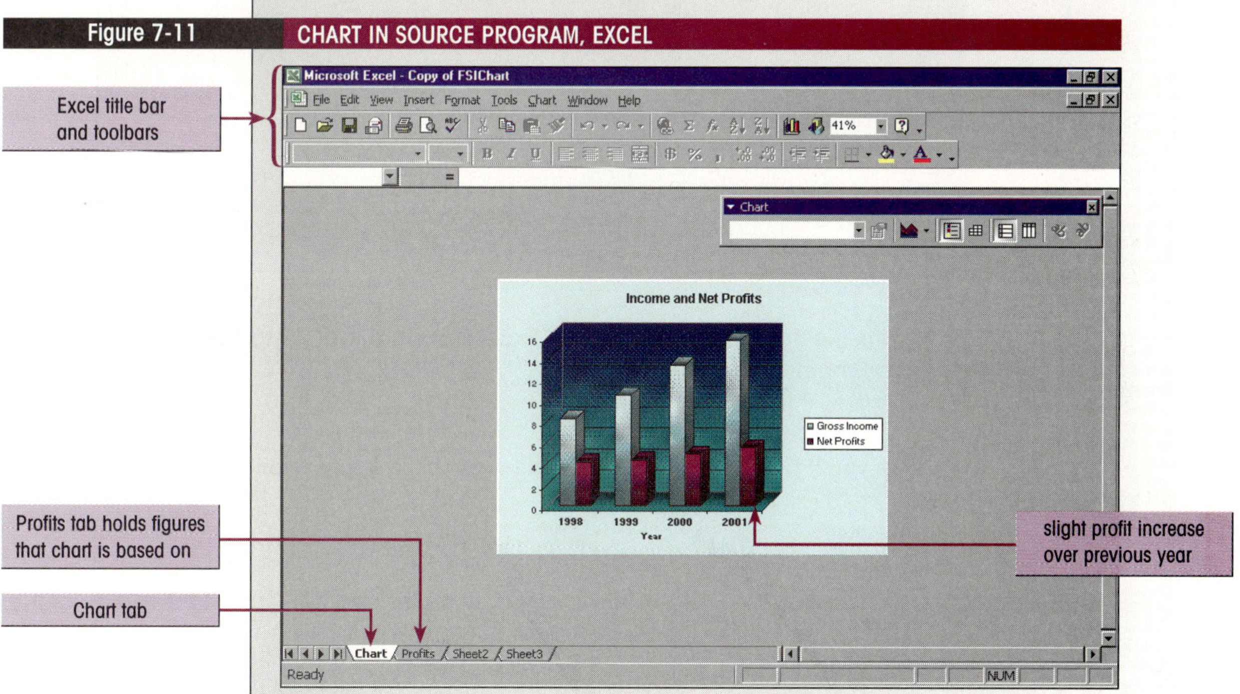

At the bottom of the window are four tabs. The Chart tab contains the chart, and the Profits tab contains the figures from which the chart was created. Any changes you make to the figures on the Profits tab will automatically be reflected in the chart. Now, assume Accounting has audited its figures and has found that the profit as a percent of sales is actually higher than their original figure. You'll enter the new figure next.

5. Click the **Profits** tab. The worksheet containing the profits information appears. You'll change the Net profit figure for 2001. Click cell **E4**, which currently contains the value "5.5".

6. Type **7.5**, and press the **Enter** key. Now you'll look at the chart in Excel and see the effect of the change.

7. Click the Chart tab, and see that the Net Profits bar for 2001 is now higher, reflecting the new figure you entered. See Figure 7-12.

Figure 7-12 EXCEL CHART REFLECTING HIGHER PROFIT MARGIN

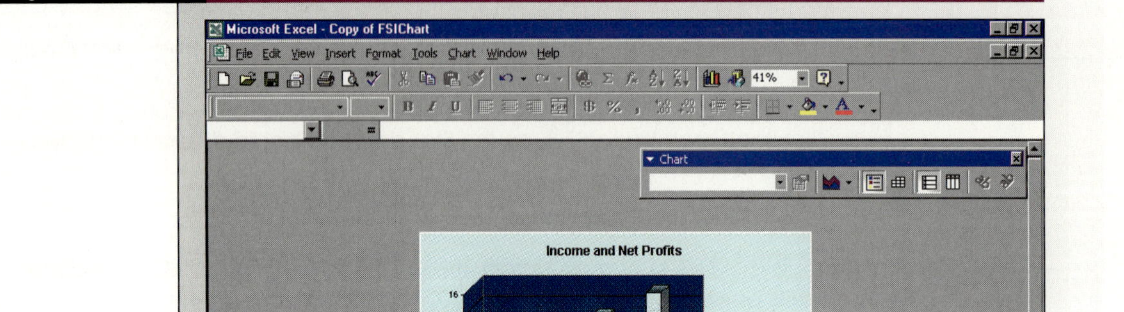

8. Click the **Save** button on the Excel Standard toolbar to save the Chart worksheet.

Now, you'll return to the proposal and view the linked version.

To view the linked chart in the proposal:

1. Close Excel. The Word program window redisplays, with the linked version of the chart displayed in the FSI New Branch Proposal file.

You notice that the linked version of the chart still has the 2001 Net Profits bar that represents the older figure. Why doesn't it reflect the change you made in the source program? You must perform one more step to make sure the changes are carried to the linked version: updating the link.

Updating the Link

When you **update** a link, you ensure that the linked object in the destination file reflects the latest version of the source file. If you modify a linked object in the source program and the Word document to which it's linked is closed, Word will automatically update the link the next time you open the document. (Alternatively, it might ask if you want to update the link.) But if you modify a linked object in the source program and the Word document is still open, you'll have to tell Word to update the link.

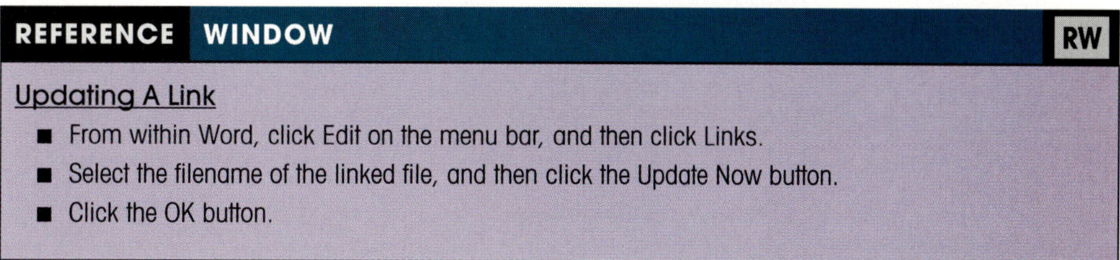

REFERENCE WINDOW RW

Updating A Link

- From within Word, click Edit on the menu bar, and then click Links.
- Select the filename of the linked file, and then click the Update Now button.
- Click the OK button.

Once the linked chart is updated, it will reflect the change you made in Excel.

To update a linked file:

1. Make sure Microsoft Word appears in the title bar and that you still see the linked chart in the document window. You should be looking at the original version of the chart, not the one with the higher profits bar.
2. Click anywhere in the Microsoft Word window to activate it if necessary.
3. Click **Edit** on the menu bar, and then click **Links** to open the Links dialog box. See Figure 7-13. Two linked files are listed, Copy of FSI Chart and Indiana.bmp, the graphic image of the state of Indiana, although the file names are probably truncated.

Figure 7-13 LINKS DIALOG BOX

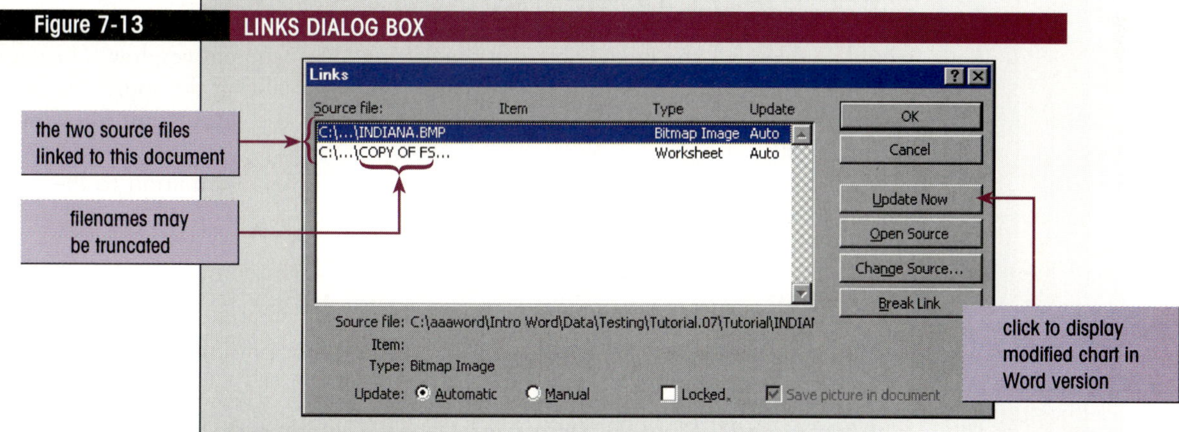

4. Click **COPY OF FS...**, and then click the **Update Now** button. Word momentarily switches back to the document window, retrieves the latest version of the linked file, and then returns to the Links dialog box.
5. Click the **Close** button in the Links dialog box to close it.

6. If necessary, deselect the chart. The updated version of the chart appears in Word; the maroon bar representing Net Profits for 2001 reflects the higher number (7.5) you entered in Excel. See Figure 7-14.

Figure 7-14 LINKED COPY OF CHART REFLECTING HIGHER NET PROFITS FIGURE

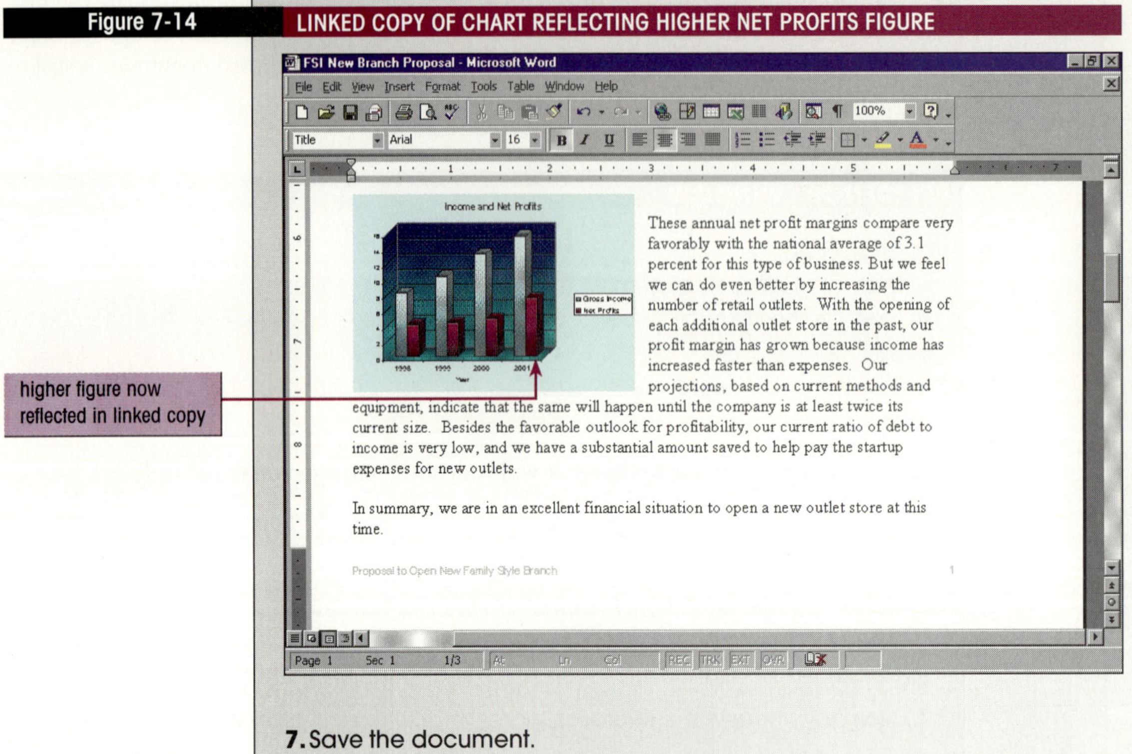

7. Save the document.

Now, you can be assured that any updates that Accounting makes to the chart will be reflected whenever the proposal is opened.

Keep in mind that although you just edited the source file by opening it in the source program (Excel), you could just as easily edit the source file in the destination program. You would double-click the linked object in the destination document window. The source program would start, and the source file would open. After editing the source file, you would simply close the source program. The linked object in the destination file would update automatically.

Your document is finished. You are ready to print it for distribution to the owners and stockholders of Family Style.

To print and then close the document:

1. Preview the document. If necessary, change the bottom margin to 1.5" so that the map falls on the third page.

2. Print the document. Your three-page document should look similar to Figure 7-15, although the exact layout of the text and graphics may differ.

Figure 7-15 PRINTED DOCUMENT READY FOR DISTRIBUTION TO OWNERS AND STOCKHOLDERS

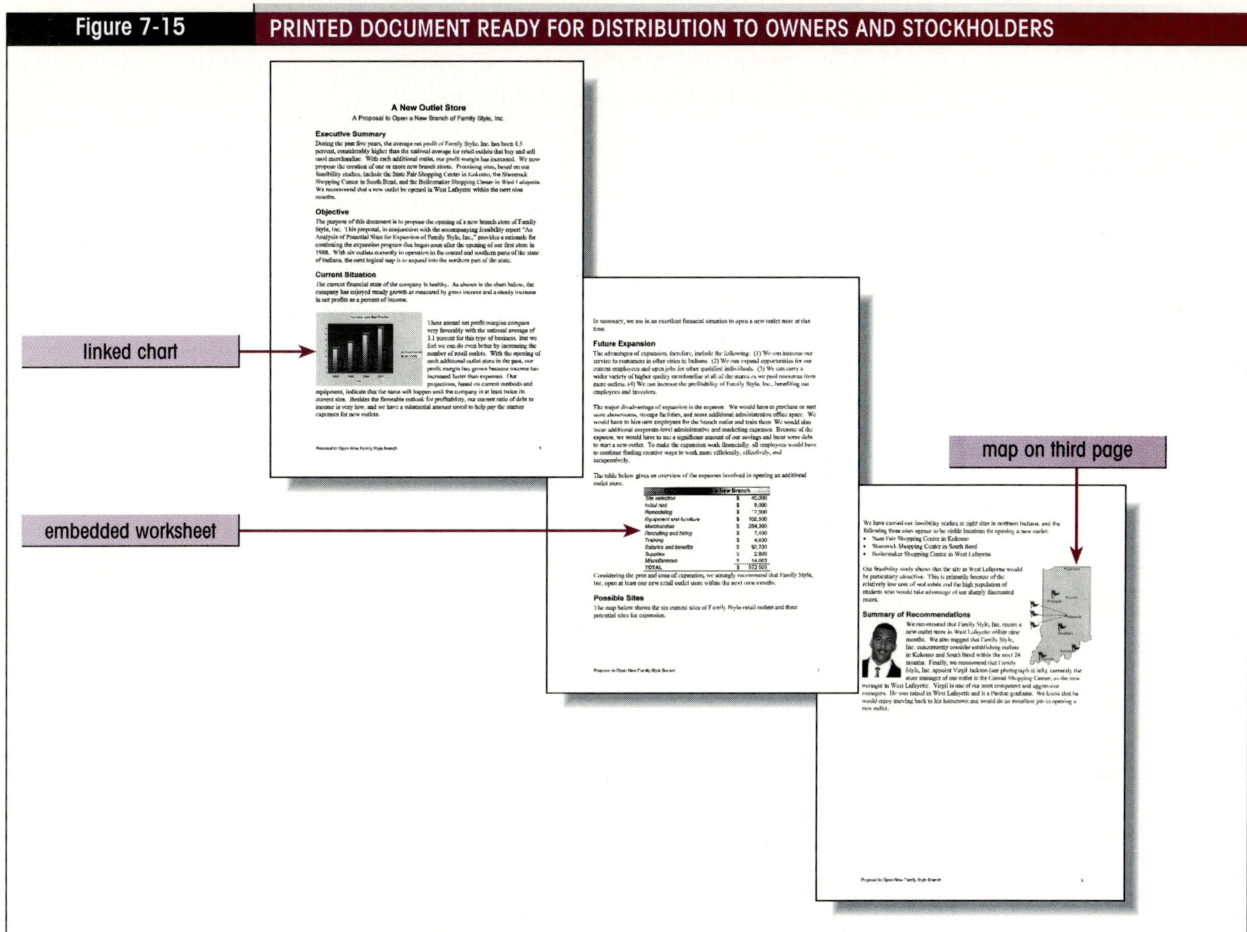

3. Close the FSI New Branch Proposal document. If you did not save changes to it earlier, do so now. You will not save the document with a new name at this point because doing so might interfere with the link between the proposal and the Excel chart.

You give the completed proposal to Nalani, who is pleased with your work. She distributes the proposal to the owners and stockholders who are considering the proposed expansion. Now, she wants you to focus on the task of distributing the document electronically, which you'll do in the next session.

Session 7.1 Quick Check

1. Define the following in your own words:
   a. source file
   b. object
   c. source program
   d. destination file
2. What is the difference between embedding and linking?
3. In what situations would you choose linking over embedding?
4. What does OLE stand for? What is an OLE-enabled program?
5. How do you embed an Excel worksheet into a Word document? How do you link an Excel chart to a Word document?
6. Explain how to create a copy of a file from within the Browse dialog box.
7. How do you modify an embedded object from the destination program?
8. True or False: When you modify an embedded object, your changes are also made to the source file.

You've learned how to combine information created in different source programs into a single document. The OLE technology that makes this integration of information possible allows users of ordinary word-processing programs to create highly informative, interesting, and well-illustrated documents. In the next session, you'll create the electronic document that Nalani will distribute to company employees.

SESSION 7.2

In this session, you'll modify the proposal so that it is better suited to online viewing by Family Style management, who will access it over the company's network. You'll begin by creating hyperlinks that allow users to navigate through the document more easily and to access additional information. Then, you'll see how the document looks in Web Layout view. Finally, you'll modify the document's appearance to make it more interesting for online viewers.

Creating and Navigating Hyperlinks

In addition to printing the proposal for company owners and investors, Nalani wants to place her proposal in a shared folder on the company's network so that other company employees will be able to read it. She wants you to modify the document so people can read it **online**, which means they will read it on the computer screen rather than on a printed page. Because people can't efficiently "flip through pages" when they read online, you should add navigational aids to the online document.

One such navigational aid is a **hyperlink** (short for "hypertext link" and also called a "hot link" or just "link"), which is a word, phrase, or graphic image that users click to "jump to" (or display) another location, called the **target**. Text hyperlinks are usually underlined and appear in a different color from the rest of the document. The target of a hyperlink can be a location within the document, a different document, or a page on the World Wide Web. Figure 7-16 shows a hyperlink pointing to a different document, a resume.

Figure 7-16 EXAMPLE OF HYPERLINK POINTING TO A TARGET (IN THIS CASE, A DIFFERENT DOCUMENT)

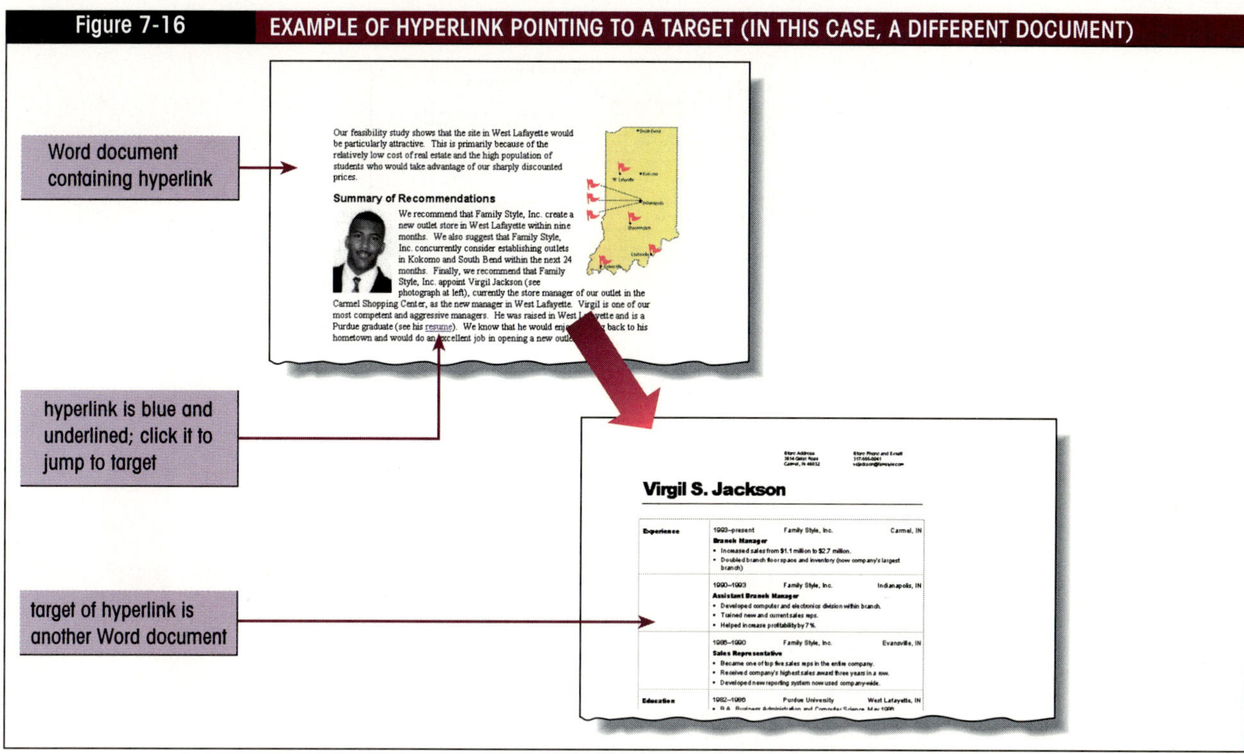

All Office 2000 programs support hyperlinking. If you have many Office 2000 documents that are related to each other, you can create a useful hyperlink system that allows users to retrieve and view related material. Nalani wants you to add two hyperlinks to the proposal document—one that targets a location within the proposal and one that targets a different document.

Inserting a Hyperlink to a Bookmark in the Same Document

Nalani wants users to be able to jump directly to the proposal's conclusions without having to scroll through topics sequentially. You can add a hyperlink at the beginning of the proposal that users can click to jump to the summary of recommendations at the end of the document. Creating a hyperlink to a location in the same document requires two steps. First, you insert an electronic marker called a bookmark at the location you want Word to target. Second, you enter the text that you want users to click and format it as a hyperlink. Figure 7-17 illustrates this process.

Figure 7-17 HYPERLINK THAT TARGETS A BOOKMARK

hyperlink

when user clicks hyperlink, Word jumps to target bookmark

you'll place bookmark here

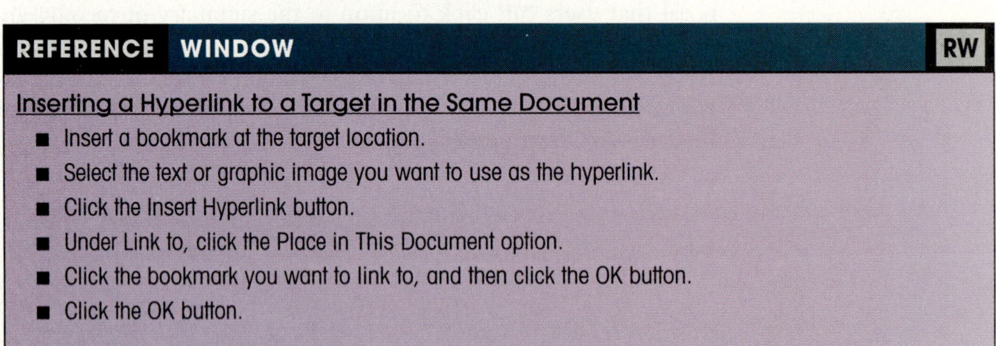

REFERENCE WINDOW RW

Inserting a Hyperlink to a Target in the Same Document

- Insert a bookmark at the target location.
- Select the text or graphic image you want to use as the hyperlink.
- Click the Insert Hyperlink button.
- Under Link to, click the Place in This Document option.
- Click the bookmark you want to link to, and then click the OK button.
- Click the OK button.

First, you'll open the document you saved at the end of the previous session. Then you'll insert the hyperlink to the Summary of Recommendations just below the Executive Summary.

To insert a hyperlink to a location within the same document:

1. If you took a break after the last session, make sure Word is running, and then open the **FSI New Branch Proposal** document.
2. Move the insertion point to the beginning of the heading "Summary of Recommendations," near the end of the document. This is where you'll insert a bookmark required for the hypertext link.
3. Click **Insert** on the menu bar, and then click **Bookmark**. The Bookmark dialog box opens. You can now type the bookmark name, which must be one word, without spaces.
4. Type **Recommendations**, and click the **Add** button. Although you can't see it, a bookmark has been inserted before the heading. This bookmark will be the target of the hyperlink. In other words, when you click the hyperlink (which you will create next), the insertion point will jump to this bookmark.
5. Move the insertion point to the end of the "Executive Summary" paragraph, near the beginning of the document. The insertion point should immediately follow the phrase, "within the next nine months."
6. Press the **Enter** key twice to insert two new blank lines into your document, and type **Go to Summary of Recommendations**. Now, you'll create the hyperlink in this line of text.
7. Select the phrase **Summary of Recommendations** that you just typed, and then click the **Insert Hyperlink** button on the Standard toolbar. The Insert Hyperlink dialog box opens.
8. Under Link to, click the **Place in this Document** option, if necessary. The right side of the dialog box now displays a list of headings and bookmarks in the document. See Figure 7-18.

Figure 7-18 INSERT HYPERLINK DIALOG BOX

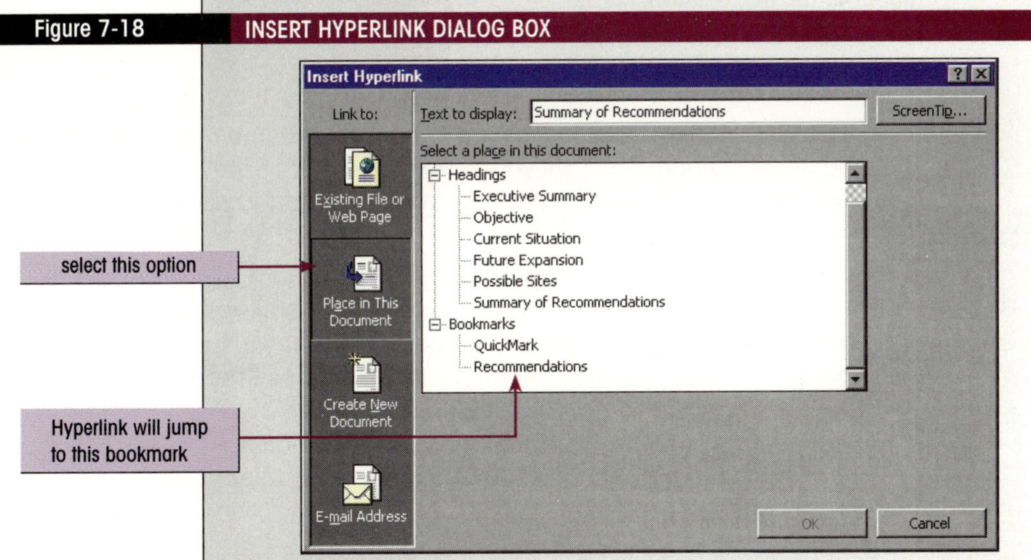

TROUBLE? If you only see three items in the right side of the dialog box, click the plus signs next to "Headings" and "Bookmarks".

9. Click **Recommendations**, and then click the **OK** button. Word formats the hyperlink as underlined blue text. The hyperlink now targets the Recommendations bookmark. See Figure 7-19.

TROUBLE? If you formatted the wrong text as a hyperlink (such as the words "Go to"), click the Undo button and begin again with Step 7.

Figure 7-19 DOCUMENT WINDOW WITH HYPERLINK

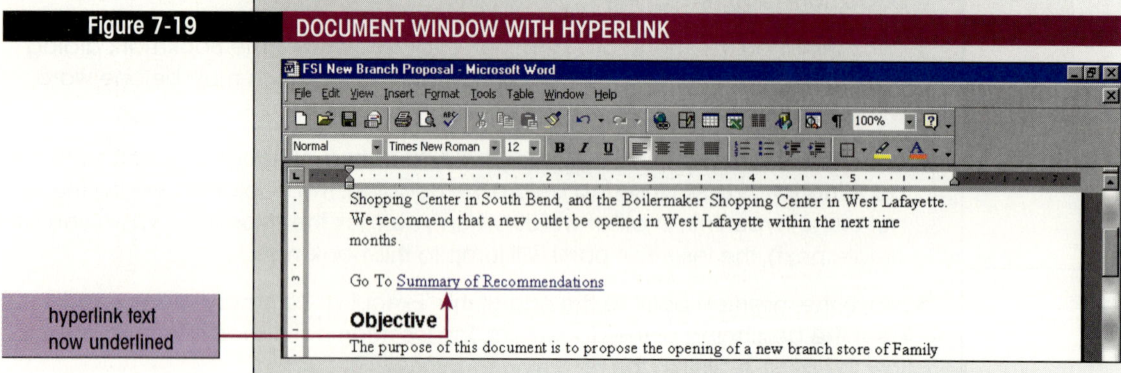

Your proposal now features a hyperlink that points to the proposal summary of recommendations.

Navigating Hyperlinks and the Web Toolbar

Now that you have inserted a hyperlink into the document, you should test it to make sure that it targets the correct location. When you click a hyperlink in a document, Word automatically displays the **Web toolbar**, a toolbar with buttons that let you access and navigate your document and the World Wide Web, a global information-sharing system you'll learn about in the next session.

To test the hyperlink in your document:

1. Move the insertion point to the blue underlined text (the hyperlink). Notice that the pointer changes to . If you leave the pointer on the hyperlink for a moment, Word displays a ScreenTip (yellow rectangle) with the name of the bookmark.

2. Click the hyperlink. The insertion point jumps to the Recommendations bookmark, and the "Summary of Recommendations" section appears. The Web toolbar appears above the document. See Figure 7-20. You'll use one of the Web toolbar buttons to return to the beginning of the document.

Figure 7-20 HYPERLINK DESTINATION AND WEB TOOLBAR

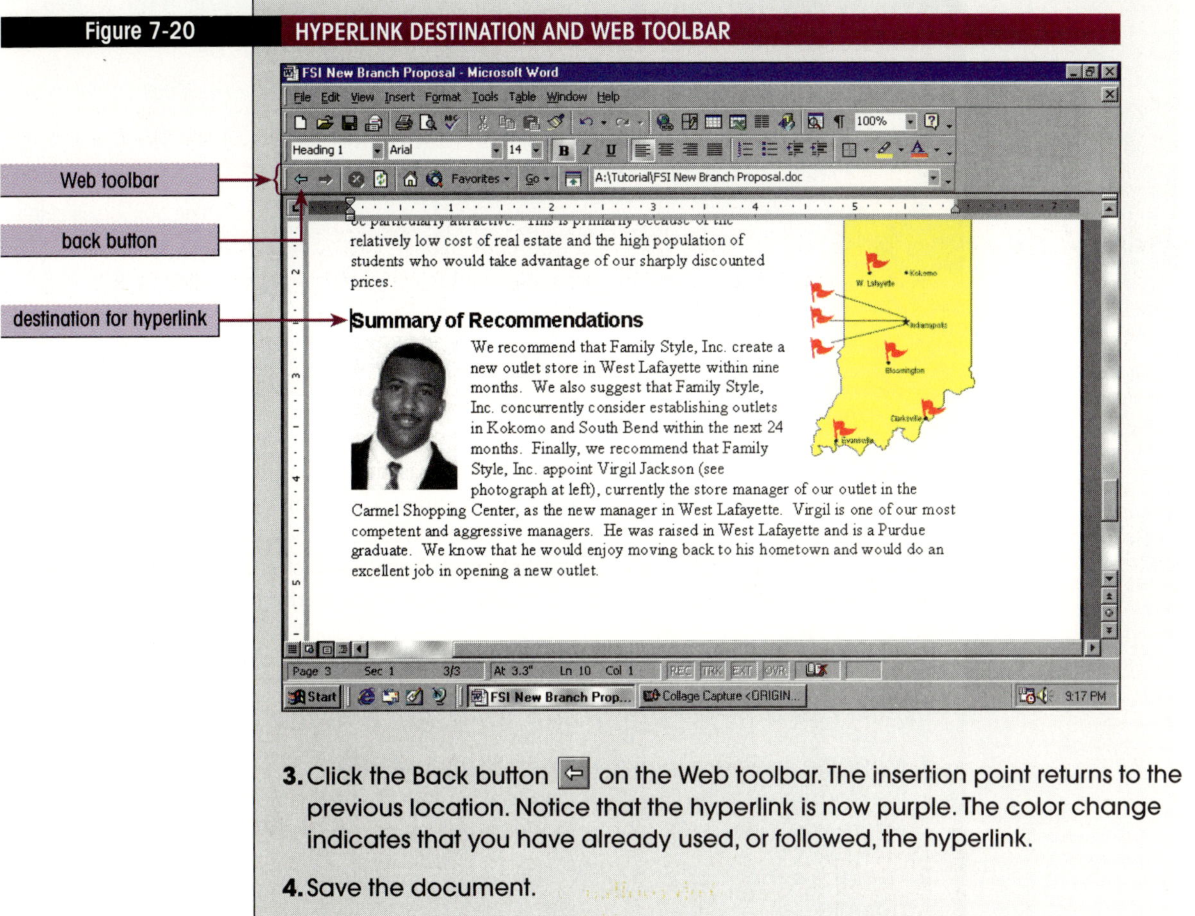

3. Click the Back button on the Web toolbar. The insertion point returns to the previous location. Notice that the hyperlink is now purple. The color change indicates that you have already used, or followed, the hyperlink.

4. Save the document.

The fact that the hyperlink changes color after you use it doesn't have much importance in this document. However, hyperlinks can also point to other documents, including Web documents on the World Wide Web. In that environment, it's helpful to know which links you've already tried. If you were to close and then reopen the document, the hyperlink would be blue again until you clicked it.

Creating Hyperlinks to Other Documents

The greatest power of hyperlinks lies not in jumping to another location within the same document, but in jumping to other documents. These documents can be located on the World Wide Web, on your computer's hard drive, or on your company's network server. When you add a hyperlink to another document, you don't necessarily target a bookmark as you do for hyperlinks pointing to a location within the same document. Instead, you target either a Web document address, called a **URL**, or a path and filename of a file on your computer or network.

REFERENCE WINDOW RW

Creating a Hyperlink to Another Document

- Move the insertion point to the desired location for the hyperlink.
- Click the Insert Hyperlink button.
- Under Link to, click the Existing File or Web Page option.
- To target a specific file, click the File button, and then use the Link to File dialog box to select the file you want to link to.
- To target a Web page, open your browser, connect to the Internet, and then click the Web Page button to go to the Web page you want to link to.
- Click the OK button.

Nalani's proposal recommends Virgil Jackson as the manager for the new Family Style branch. She has a Word file containing his résumé, VJResume.doc, and she would like to make it available to interested Family Style employees so they can evaluate his skills. You can add a hyperlink that targets Virgil's resume. Because this hyperlink will take users to a different document, you don't need to insert a bookmark as the target. Instead, you use the name of the target document.

To create a hyperlink to another document:

1. Move the insertion point to the next-to-the-last sentence of the last paragraph of the document, after the period following the phrase "a Purdue graduate." This is where you'll insert text, some of which will become the hyperlink.
2. Press the **spacebar**, and type **(See his resume.)** making sure to include the parentheses.
3. Select the word "resume" in the text you just typed. See Figure 7-21.

Figure 7-21 SELECTED WORD IN NEW TEXT

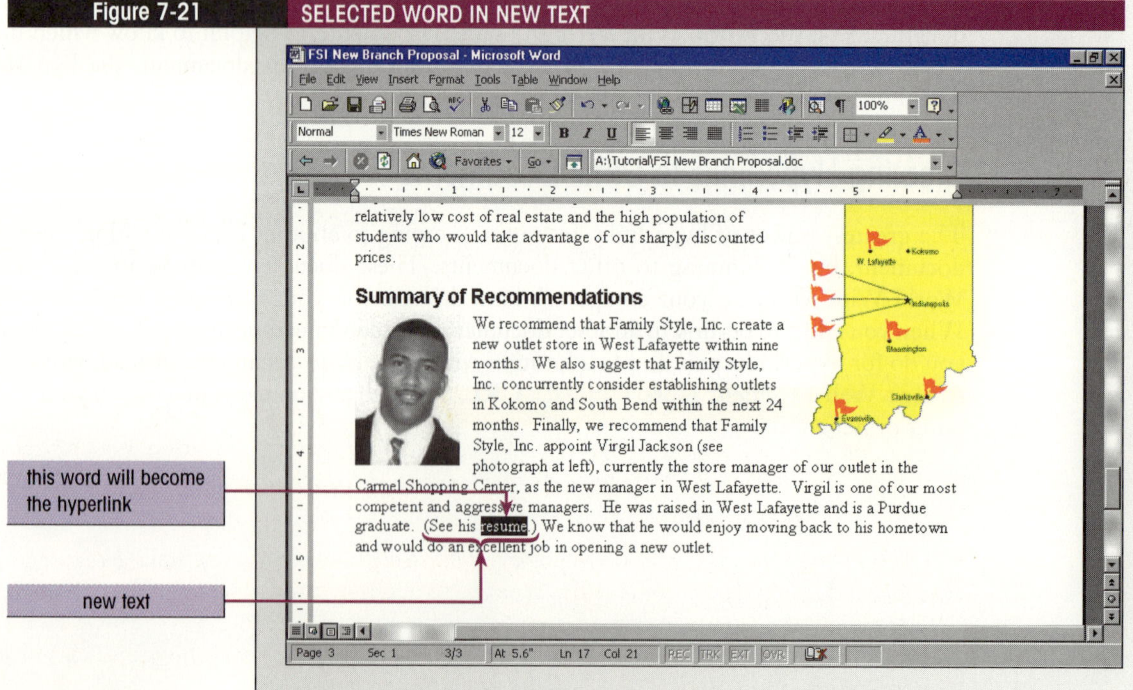

4. Click the **Insert Hyperlink** button on the Standard toolbar. The Insert Hyperlink dialog box opens.
5. Under Link to, click the **Existing File or Web Page** option. The right side of the dialog box displays options related to selecting a file or a Web page.
6. Click the **File** button. The Link to File dialog box opens.
7. Select the file **VJResume** in the Tutorial folder for Tutorial 7, and then click the **OK** button.
8. Click the **OK** button. The word "resume" now appears as a hyperlink. It looks the same as the first hyperlink you created, even though the target is another file, not a location within the same document.

When your documents include hyperlinks to other documents, you need to pay special attention to where you store those target documents. If you move a target document to a different location, any hyperlinks to it contained in other documents may not function properly. In this case, you created a hyperlink in the proposal document that links to the résumé document. Both documents are stored in the Tutorial subfolder within the Tutorial.07 folder, which is most likely located on a hard disk. To ensure that the hyperlink in the proposal document will continue to function, you must keep the two documents in the same folder.

Now, you're ready to test the hyperlink you just created.

To use a hyperlink to jump to another file:

1. Move the pointer to the hyperlink "resume." Again, the pointer changes to .
2. Click the hyperlink. Word opens the file VJResume.
3. Read through the resume, and then click the **Back** button on the Web toolbar to return to the Proposal document. Notice that the hyperlink color is now purple, indicating that you have used the hyperlink.
4. Save the proposal.

Viewing a Document in Web Layout View

Because the version of the proposal you are working on now is intended for an online audience, Nalani suggests that you place it in Web Layout view. **Web Layout view** offers several advantages for online viewers:

- Text appears larger in Web Layout view.
- Text wraps to the window, not to the printed page.
- Documents can be displayed with different background effects.
- Page setup elements, such as footers, headers, and breaks, are not displayed. Because users don't view the document as printed pages, these page elements aren't necessary.

Web Layout view is useful when you need to format a document for online viewing. Text wrapping doesn't always survive the conversion from a Word document to a Web page, which means that graphics will often shift position when you save a document as a Web page. Web Layout view prepares you for this by showing you what the graphics will look like in their new positions.

But keep in mind that, despite its name, Web Layout view does not show you exactly how a document will look when saved as a Web page. Some of the features that are visible in Web Page view (such the animation you will add in the next section) will disappear when you save the document as a Web page. (You will learn more about saving a document as a Web page later in this tutorial.)

If you switch to Web Layout view and then save the document in that view, it will open that way automatically. Within Web Layout view, you might want to use the Document Map, a list of the headings in your document that you can use as a navigational aid. If you want to move immediately to a certain section of your document, you click its heading in the Document Map. For this reason, the Document Map is an especially useful tool for online viewers, who might not want to scroll through an entire document. They can simply jump to the sections they are interested in.

To display a document in Web Layout view:

1. Click the **Web Layout View** button (next to the Normal View button, just above the status bar). Notice that the text now wraps to the width of the right window pane—not to the printed page boundaries.

2. Click the **Document Map** button on the Standard toolbar. The document appears on the right, with the Document Map on the left. The text and graphics shift position again to accommodate the Document Map. See Figure 7-22.

   TROUBLE? If you don't see the Document Map button, click View, and then click Document Map.

Figure 7-22 WEB LAYOUT VIEW AND DOCUMENT MAP

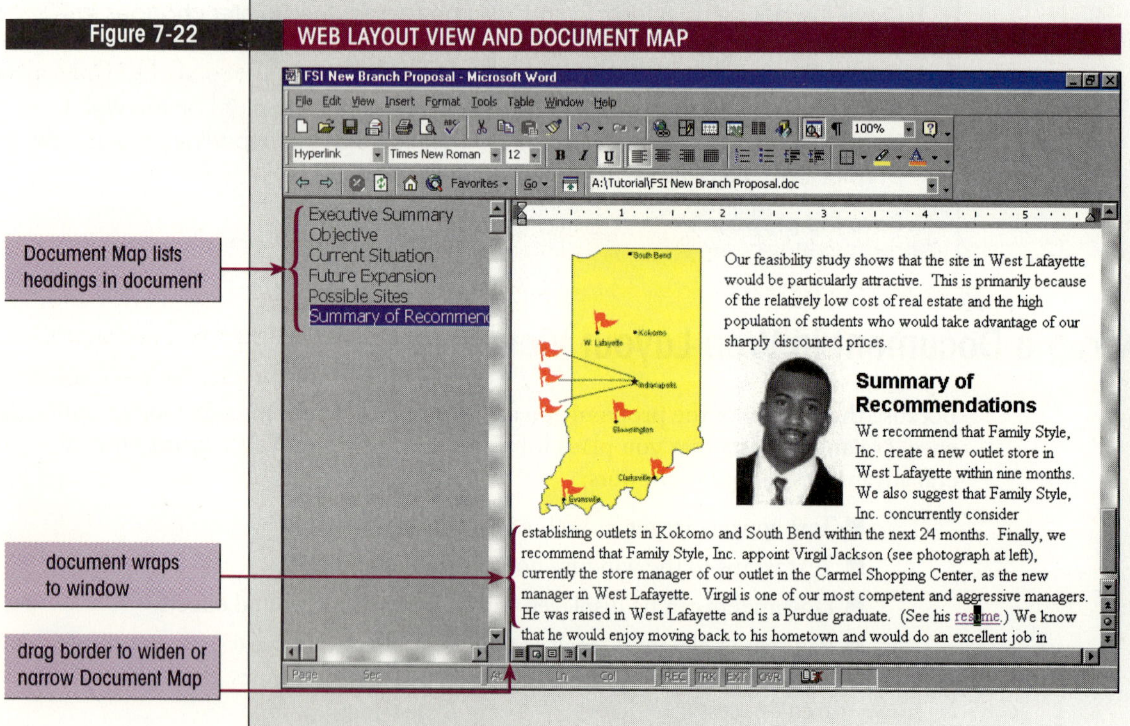

3. Click the **Future Expansion** heading in the Document Map. You jump to that heading.

4. Click the **Executive Summary** heading in the Document Map. You jump back to the beginning of the document.

5. Click [icon] to close the Document Map.

Although the Document Map is especially useful in Web Layout view, you can display it in any view. You can also change the width of the Document Map by dragging its right border to the left or to the right. Now that you have inserted a hyperlink, and have seen how to navigate the document with the document map, you'll improve its appearance for online viewing.

Improving the Appearance of an Online Document

Nalani suggests you use two features to make the online version of the proposal more visually interesting for online viewers—animated text and a textured background. Keep in mind that some features that are visible in Web Layout view are not visible when you convert the document to a Web page. (You will learn more about converting a document to a Web page in the next session.)

Animating Text

Animated text is text that "comes alive," like a cartoon animation, because the text blinks, sparkles, shimmers, or displays a moving border. Word offers several animation formats. Nalani suggests you try animating the subtitle of the proposal, "A Proposal to Open a New Branch of Family Style, Inc.," with a moving border.

To animate the subtitle of the proposal:

1. Scroll to the beginning of the document.

2. Select the subtitle text **A Proposal to Open a New Branch of Family Style, Inc.**

3. Click **Format** on the menu bar, click **Font**, and then click the **Text Effects** tab.

4. Click **Marching Black Ants**. Notice the Preview box displays the sample text with a moving black border. See Figure 7-23.

Figure 7-23 PREVIEWING ANIMATED TEXT

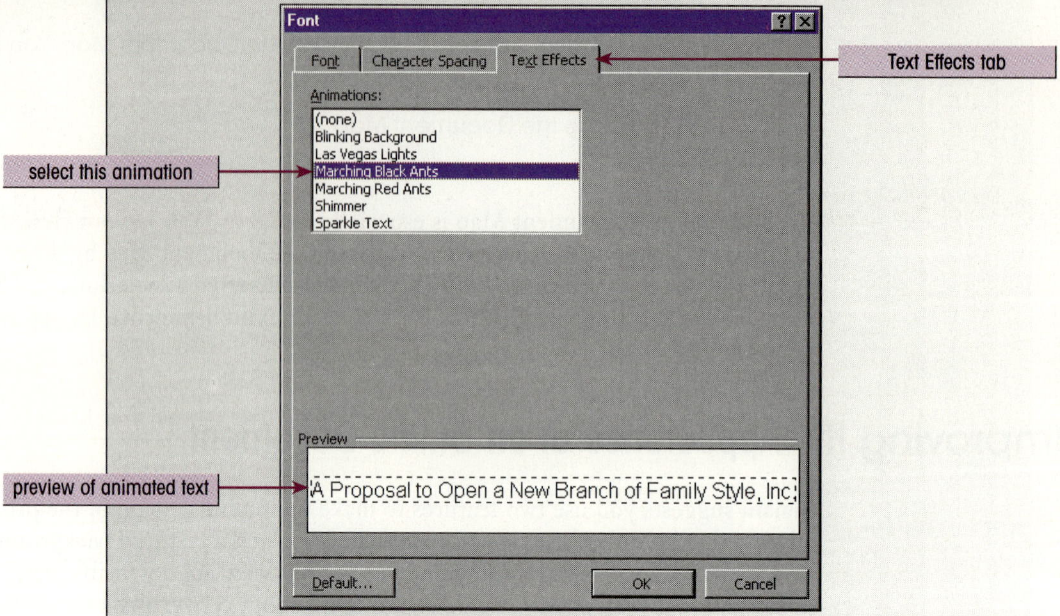

5. **Click the OK button, and then click anywhere outside the subtitle to deselect it.** The subtitle now has a moving border.

Animation draws an online viewer's eyes immediately to the animated text, so use this feature only for your most important words or phrases. Overusing animated text makes your document difficult to view. Also, keep in mind that animation effects don't appear in printed documents.

Applying a Textured Background

You can make an online document more visually appealing by applying background effects. As with animated text, backgrounds do not appear in printed documents. You can apply one of the following background effects:

- Solid color
- Gradient—a color or combination of colors that fades from one side of the screen to the other
- Texture—choose from a collection of textures
- Pattern—choose from a collection of interesting patterns; you designate the colors in the pattern
- Picture—a graphic image

In choosing a background color or texture, make sure your text is still readable. In poorly designed online documents, the background might be so dark or the pattern so obtrusive that the text is illegible. In addition, a background that contains a complicated background pattern will increase the file size and take longer to appear on a user's screen. Nalani suggests you use a parchment texture to give the background a professional, but not distracting, appearance.

To apply a texture to a document:

1. Click **Format** on the menu bar, point to **Background**, click **Fill Effects**, and then click the **Texture** tab. A selection of textures appears.
2. Click the third box on the left in the top row. The name of this texture, "Parchment," appears below the texture options. See Figure 7-24.

Figure 7-24 SELECTING A TEXTURED BACKGROUND

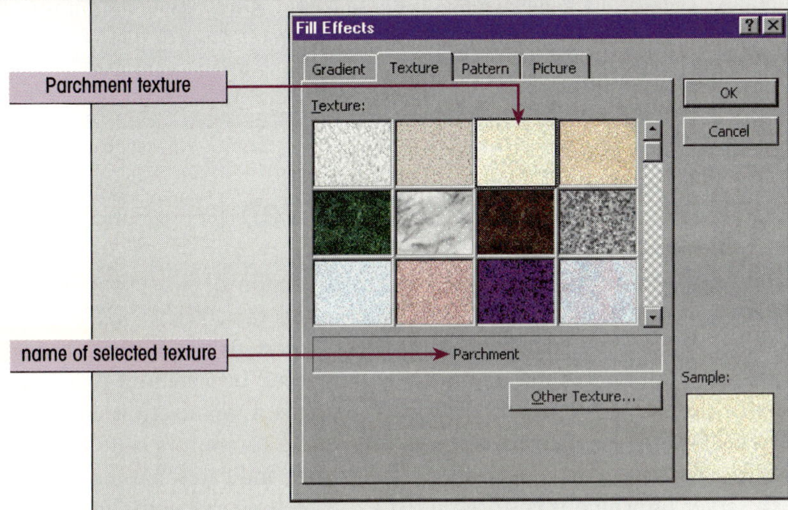

3. Click the **OK** button. The texture fills the background of your document.
4. Save the document in Web Layout view, and close it.
5. Close the VJResume document, which opened earlier when you clicked the hyperlink in the proposal document.

The background texture is light in color and attractive and leaves the black text easy to read. Nalani agrees that the Parchment background enhances the look of the online document.

Session 7.2 Quick Check

1. What is a hyperlink?
2. True or False: A hyperlink can only take a user to a location within the current document.
3. Explain how to create a bookmark.
4. Which name is an invalid bookmark name? a) Recommendations, b) Executive Summary, c) README
5. What does a change in the color of a hyperlink indicate?
6. True or False: Web Layout view shows you exactly what your document will look like when saved as a Web page.
7. What is the purpose of the Document Map?

You have finished preparing the proposal document for online viewing. Nalani places the document and its linked files in a shared folder on the company network and e-mails her colleagues that it is available for viewing. Any employee who opens it in Word has the immediate benefit of easy viewing in Web Layout view. The hyperlink you added, as well as the Document Map, make it easy to navigate, and your visual enhancements make it a pleasure to view.

SESSION 7.3

In this session, you'll convert Nalani's proposal into a Web page for placement on the World Wide Web and then format the Web page to make it easier to read in a Web browser. Finally, you'll insert and edit hyperlinks that link the proposal and résumé documents, and then preview your Web page in a browser.

Publishing Documents on the World Wide Web

Nalani now wants you to prepare the final version of her proposal, which she will make available on the World Wide Web (also called the "Web" or "WWW"). The Web is a global information-sharing system, which is part of the **Internet**, a worldwide network made up of millions of interconnected computers. Information is stored on the Web in the form of electronic documents, called **Web pages**. Organizations and individuals make their Web pages available by storing them on special computers called Web servers. Each Web page is assigned a Web address (or **URL**) which indicates, among other things, the specific Web server on which it is stored. URLs can be long and complicated or fairly simple. One example of a simple URL is: *http://www.course.com*. To access a Web page, you need to open a special program called a **browser**, such as Netscape Navigator or Microsoft Internet Explorer. Once you open your browser, you need to enter the page's URL. The browser then retrieves the page and displays it on your computer screen.

A collection of interrelated Web pages is known as a **Web site**. Most companies and many private computer users operate their own Web sites. Keep in mind that Web sites may not be designed for public access on the World Wide Web. Increasingly, companies use Web sites to make information available to their own employees, within the company's private network.

Most Web sites include a **home page**, a Web page that contains general information about the site. Home pages are like "home base"—a starting point for online viewers. They usually contain hyperlinks targeting other documents or Web pages that online viewers can click to locate the information they need. Nalani wants to include a hyperlink on the Family Style home page that targets her proposal. Potential investors can click that hyperlink to view the proposal.

The hyperlinks the document already contains will remain intact after the conversion to HTML. You also may want to create additional hyperlinks, such as one to the company's home page. You can add these links before or after you convert the document.

Saving a Word Document as a Web Page

Web browsers only read documents formatted in **HTML** (HyperText Markup Language), a special programming language that tells a Web browser how the page should look on the screen. So to distribute a Word document on the World Wide Web, you have to convert it to HTML by saving the document as a Web page. The HTML codes in a file tell the browser exactly how to format the text. Fortunately, you don't have to learn the Hypertext Markup Language to create HTML documents; Word does this work for you when you save the document as a Web page. When you save the document as a Web page, Word creates the necessary HTML codes (called markings, or tags) for the desired format. This process is transparent to you, which means you won't actually see the HTML tags in your new Web pages.

The relatively small size of Web pages makes them easy to share on the Internet. For example, a Word document containing a moderate amount of formatting and a few graphics, might be 500 kilobytes in size. The same document saved as a Web page might be only 20 kilobytes in size, along with about 50 kilobytes of graphics files. To help keep your Web-page file small, Word automatically puts any graphics it might contain into a separate folder. This folder also contains other small files that your Web browser needs in order to display the Web page correctly. By default, this folder has the same name as your Web page, plus an underscore and the word "files." For instance, a Web page saved as "Finance Summary" would be accompanied by a folder named "Finance Summary_files."

Although saving a Word document as a Web page is easy, it's not foolproof, particularly when it comes to formatting. Some Word formatting features (such as special borders, or certain font effects) will not "translate" into HTML. This means that when you save your document as a Web page, document formatting might be lost, or it will look different. Also, keep in mind that the formatting that does translate into HTML might not look as nice on screen as it does on the printed page. So after translating the document to a Web page, you might want to adjust the formatting to make it more suitable for online viewing. At the same time, you might want to add some special formatting features that are not always available in printed documents, such as color and animation. (In some cases, the original document might contain special features, such as animation, that don't survive the translation to HTML. In that case, you may need to reapply the feature once the document has been saved as a Web page.) As a general rule, once you save a document as a Web page, you'll probably want to modify it to make it more attractive for users of the World Wide Web. At the very least, you will probably need to reposition graphics.

Keep in mind that to create really sophisticated Web pages, you'll probably want to use a dedicated HTML editor, such as Microsoft Front Page. You can also use a Word Web Page Wizard, as explained in the case projects at the end of this tutorial, to create a Web page from scratch. But to share an existing Word document as a Web page, you must convert it to HTML.

REFERENCE WINDOW RW

Converting a Word Document to a Web Page

- Click File on the menu bar, and then click Save as Web Page.
- If desired, give the file a new filename. Word will automatically add the file extension .html at the end of the document, although this extension probably won't be visible in the Save As dialog box.
- Click the Save button.
- If Word warns you that the document has formatting not supported by Web browsers, click the Continue button.

To prepare Nalani's proposal for viewing on the Web, you'll begin by saving the current document as an HTML file.

To save a document as a Web page:

1. If you took a break after the last session, make sure Word is running. Close any Internet-related programs, such as e-mail editors or browsers.
2. Open the **FSI New Branch Proposal** document.

3. Click **File** on the menu bar, and then click **Save as Web Page**. The Save As dialog box, with which you are already familiar, opens. The only difference between this dialog box and the one you used earlier to save the proposal document with a new name, is that the Save as type text box indicates that the document will be saved as a Web page.

4. Change the filename so it reads **FSI New Branch Proposal Web Page**.

5. Click the **Save** button. Word displays a warning message indicating that animated text and text wrapping around pictures are not supported by Web browsers. These features will appear differently in the Web page. See Figure 7-25.

Figure 7-25 WARNING MESSAGE

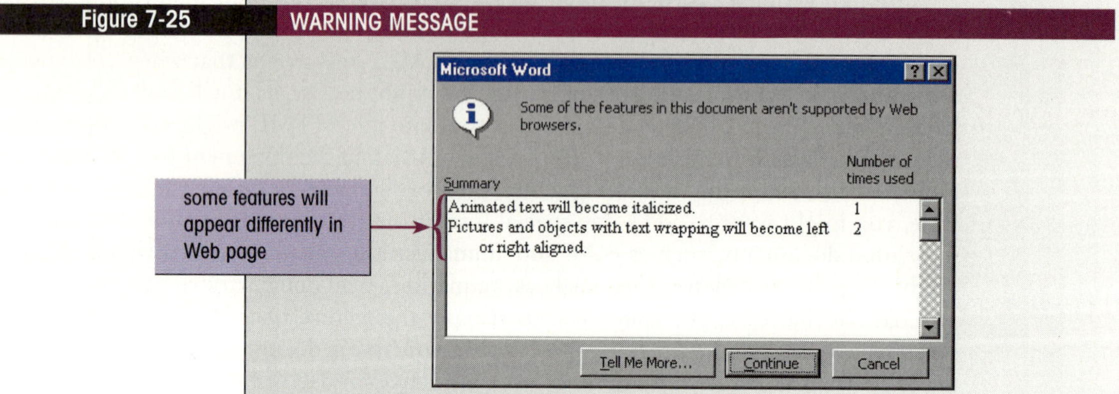

6. Click **Continue**. After a pause, the document is converted into a Web page.

TROUBLE? If you think that Word is taking a long time to convert and save the file in HTML format, don't worry. Depending upon the speed of your system, it could take several minutes.

7. If the Web toolbar doesn't appear automatically below the formatting toolbar, click **View** on the menu bar, point to **Toolbars**, and click **Web**. Your document should now look similar to Figure 7-26.

TROUBLE? If you see a dialog box saying that the dimensions after resizing are too small or too large, click the OK button.

Figure 7-26 DOCUMENT FORMATTED AS A WEB PAGE

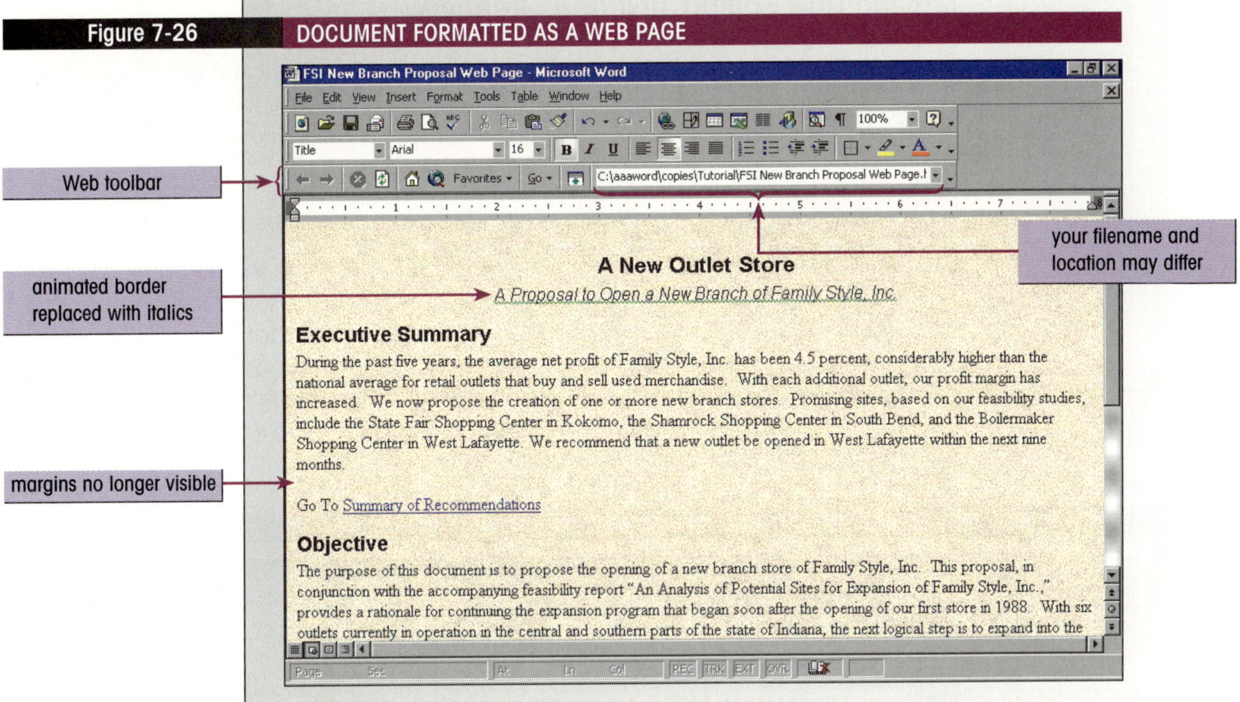

As you look through the document, you'll notice two differences between the Web page and the original document:

- The margin settings are no longer the same. In fact, Web pages don't have margin settings. The lines of text wrap so that the text fits within the width of the browser (or in this case, the document window), whatever size it might be.
- The graphic images (that is, the map and the photograph) may have shifted position.
- The animated border around the subtitle no longer appears. Instead, the subtitle is italicized.

You might notice other differences as well. One of the major differences, in fact, is not apparent by viewing the document: The file size has decreased from about 500 KB to only about 19 KB (plus about 65–70 KB of graphics files). This reduced size is a tremendous advantage for Web pages that must be transferred electronically over long distances and often through slow modems. The smaller file size allows them to display more quickly in Web browsers.

Formatting a Web Page

You're now ready to format the Web page to give it the look and feel of a typical Web page and to correct some of the problems that occur when you convert a file from a normal Word document to a Web page. You'll begin by correcting the text formatting.

Moving and Editing Text and Graphics

You can edit and format a Web page the same way you would edit and format a normal Word document. Now, you'll change the text wrapping around the last two graphic images to adjust for changes that occurred in the document when you saved it as a Web page.

To change the text wrapping around graphics:

1. Scroll so you can see the map of Indiana. It might have shifted on the page and increased in size, so that it is now positioned to the left of the photograph, as in Figure 7-27. (Your map could have shifted somewhat differently, so that it is positioned below the bulleted list, or elsewhere on the page. Your map may also have decreased in size.) You could adjust the position of the map by adjusting settings in the Format Picture dialog box. But it's often easier simply to drag the graphic to the correct location.

Figure 7-27 MAP AND PHOTOGRAPH IN WRONG POSITION

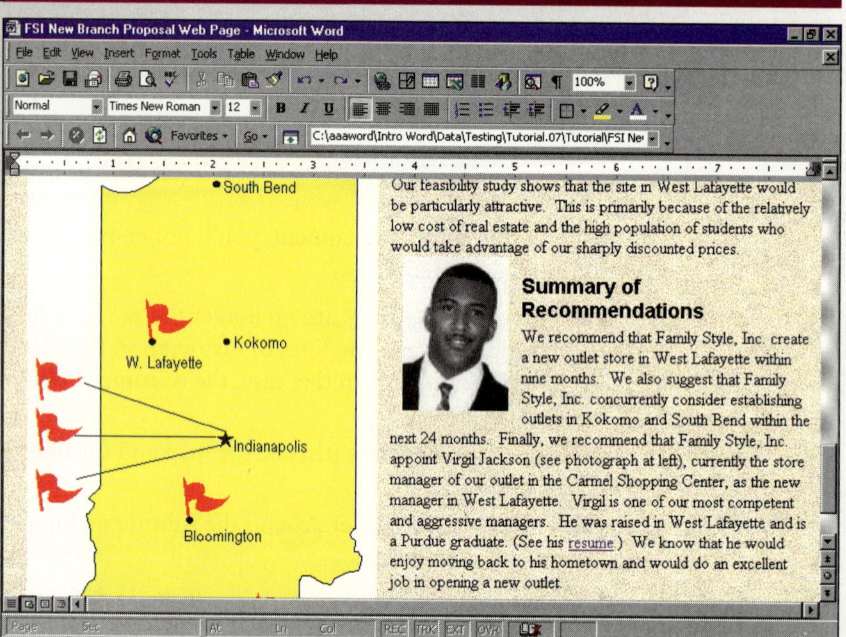

2. If necessary, click the map to select it, and then drag it up so that it is positioned under the sentence that begins "The map below shows the six current....".
3. Click **Format** on the menu bar, click **Picture**, click the **Size** tab, verify that the Lock aspect ratio check box is selected, change the Height setting to 50% and click the **OK** button.
4. Verify that the sentence that begins "We have carried out..." and the bulleted list wrap to the right of the map. The top of the map should be just slightly above the top of the "W" in "We." If the text does not wrap correctly, adjust the position or size of the map. Next, you need to adjust the position of the photograph, which you will do by adding more space between before the "Summary of Recommendations" heading.

5. Click to the left of the "S" in the heading "Summary of Recommendations," and then press **Enter** three times. The heading moves down below the map, and the photograph moves along with it.

6. If necessary, drag the photograph down to position it below the "Summary of Recommendations" heading. The text wraps to the right of the photograph.

7. To verify that the map and the photograph are positioned correctly, click **View** on the menu bar, and then click **Full Screen**. The map and the photograph should now be positioned as in Figure 7-28.

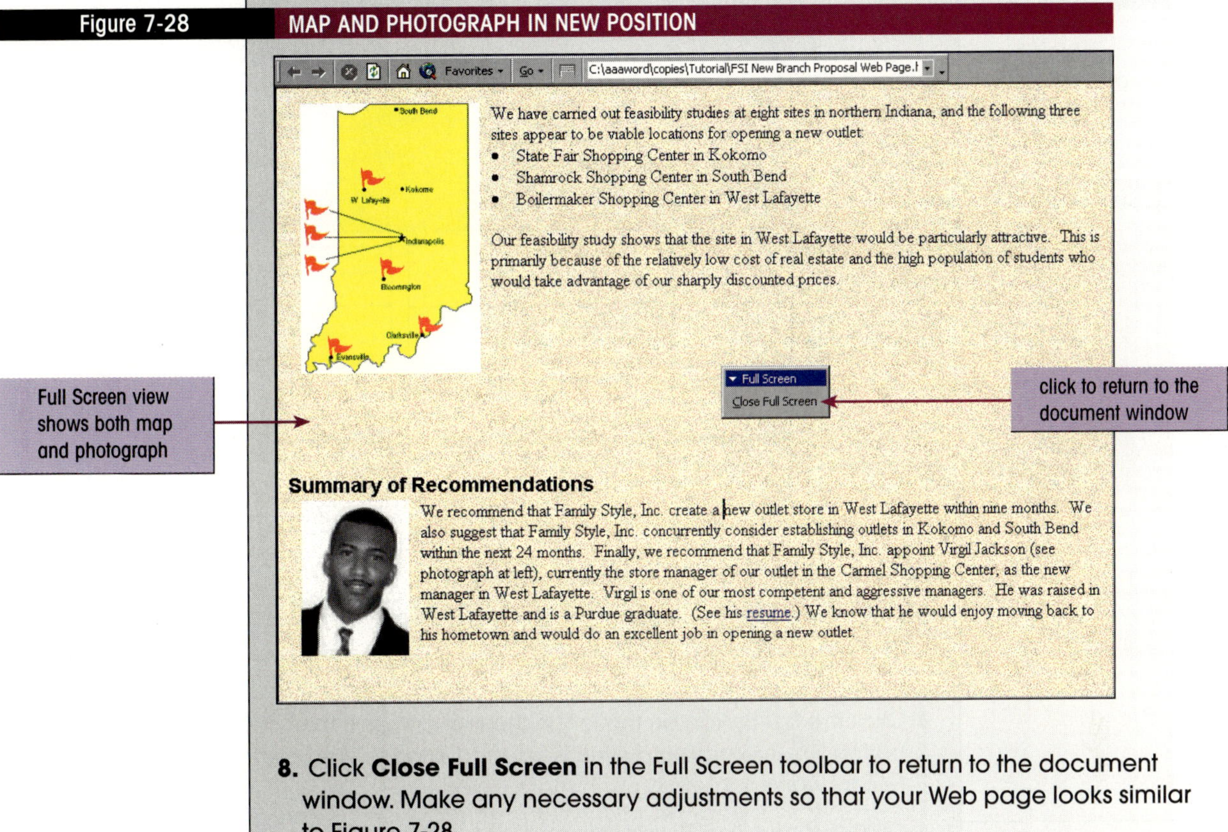

Figure 7-28 MAP AND PHOTOGRAPH IN NEW POSITION

8. Click **Close Full Screen** in the Full Screen toolbar to return to the document window. Make any necessary adjustments so that your Web page looks similar to Figure 7-28.

Now that you've corrected the placement of the text and graphics in Nalani's proposal, you'll add some rules (horizontal lines) to the online document.

Inserting Horizontal Lines

Many Web pages have horizontal lines that separate sections of a document to make it easier to read and navigate. You'll add a horizontal line below the subtitle of the proposal Web page and at the end of the Web page.

To insert horizontal lines into the Web page:

1. Move the insertion point to the left of the "E" in "Executive Summary" near the beginning of the document.
2. Click **Format** on the menu bar, click **Borders and Shading**, click the **Borders** tab in the Borders and Shading dialog box, and then click the **Horizontal Line** button. The Horizontal Line dialog box opens, where you can select from a number of horizontal lines. See Figure 7-29.

Figure 7-29 HORIZONTAL LINE DIALOG BOX

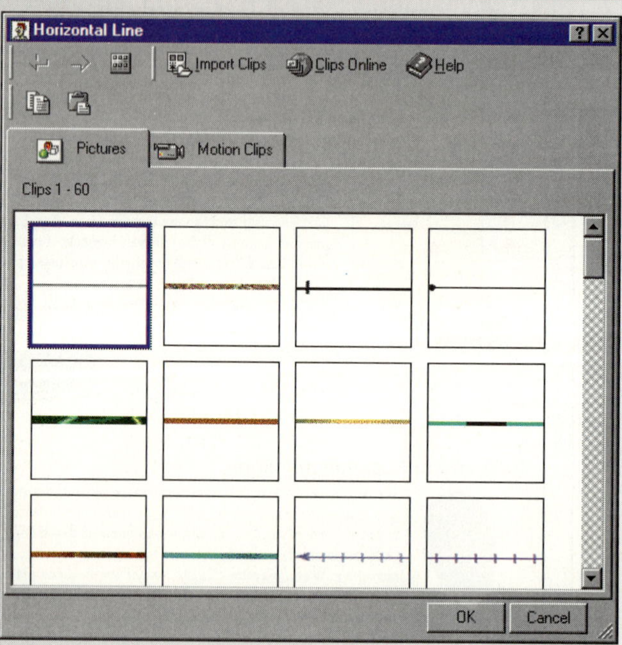

3. Click the first option on the left, in the top row, and then click the **Insert clip** button. A simple gray line is inserted into the Web page, below the subtitle. Nalani wants something with more color.
4. Click the gray line to select it, and then press the **Delete** key. The line is removed from the page.
5. Repeat Steps 2 through 4, but select the horizontal line with shades of blue and green (third row down, second from left). Your Web page should look similar to Figure 7-30.

Figure 7-30 WEB PAGE AFTER INSERTING HORIZONTAL LINE

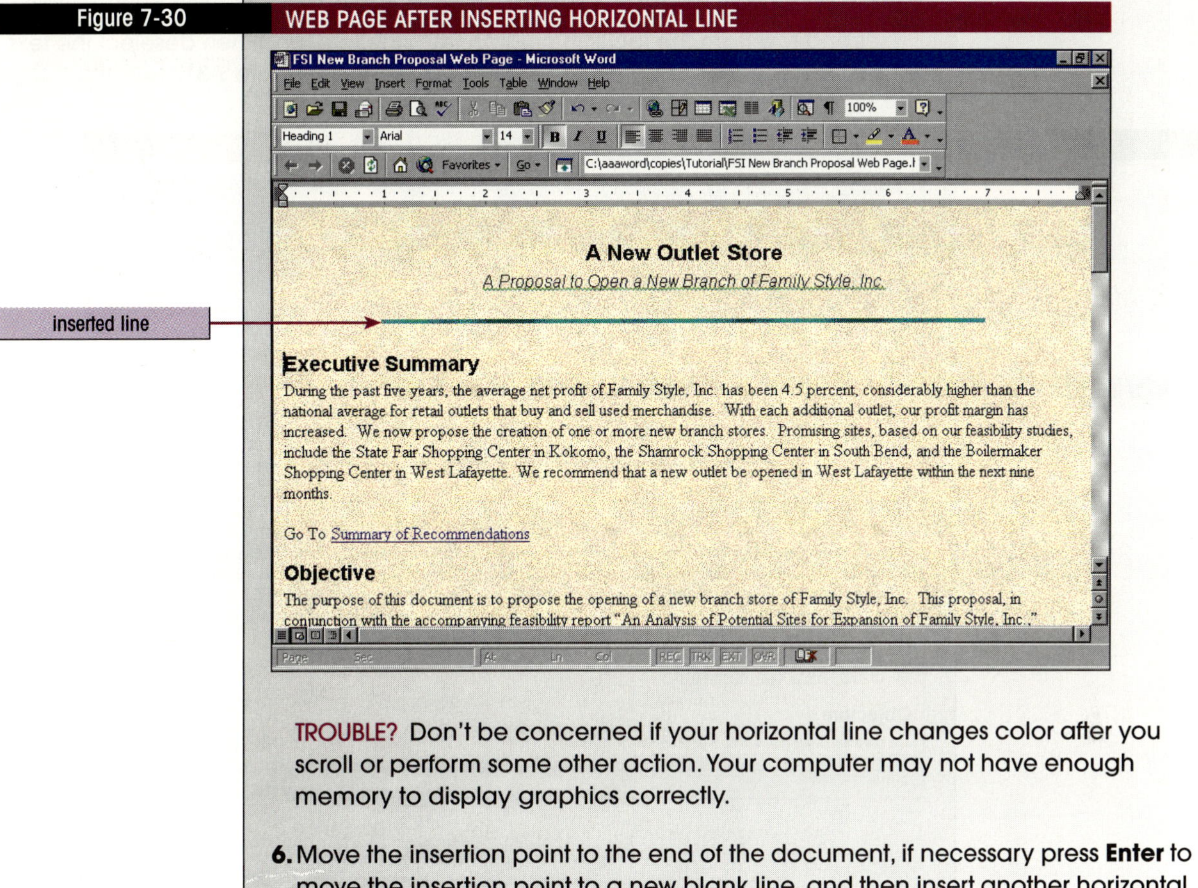

TROUBLE? Don't be concerned if your horizontal line changes color after you scroll or perform some other action. Your computer may not have enough memory to display graphics correctly.

6. Move the insertion point to the end of the document, if necessary press **Enter** to move the insertion point to a new blank line, and then insert another horizontal blue line.

7. Scroll back to the top of the document.

Now that you've given shape to the document with horizontal lines, you decide to improve the appearance of the document's text.

Modifying Text Size and Color

Web pages use colored text to enhance the appearance of the page and to call attention to important information. You also can adjust font sizes on a Web page just as you would on a printed document. To improve the proposal's readability and appearance, Nalani wants you to increase the font size of the title text and to change its color to teal, to match the horizontal lines.

To change the size and color of text:

1. Select the title **A New Outlet Store** at the beginning of the Web page.

2. Use the **Font Size** list arrow on the Formatting toolbar to change the font size from 16-point to 24-point.

3. Click the **Font Color** list arrow on the Formatting toolbar, click the teal tile (second row from the top, fifth column from the left), and then deselect the text. The title matches the color of the horizontal line. See Figure 7-31.

Figure 7-31 TITLE WITH FONT CHANGES

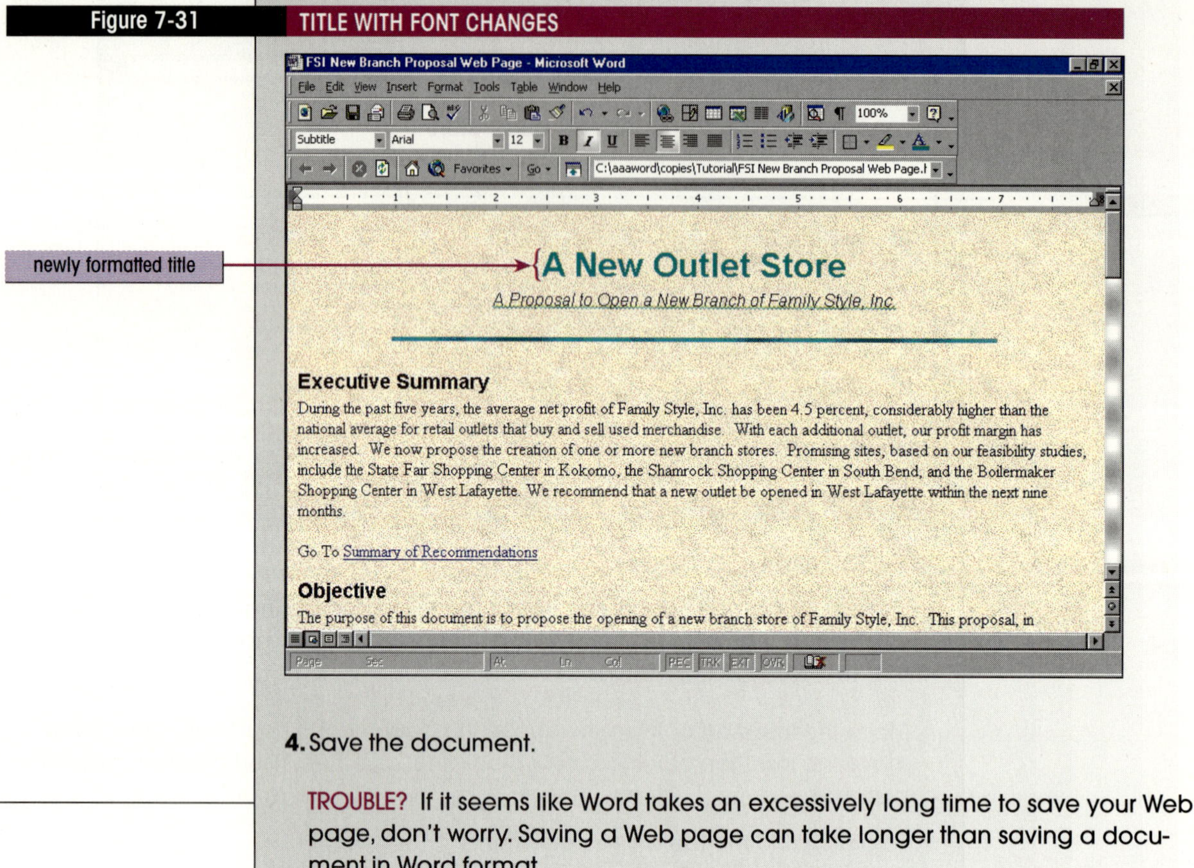

4. Save the document.

TROUBLE? If it seems like Word takes an excessively long time to save your Web page, don't worry. Saving a Web page can take longer than saving a document in Word format.

You've now formatted Nalani's proposal document so that it will be visually appealing on screen. Next, you'll create some additional hypertext links and edit one of the existing links.

Creating and Editing Hyperlinks in a Web Page

As you looked through the HTML version of the proposal, you probably noticed that the blue underlined hyperlink text is still present. Most likely, any Web browser could successfully display the target of the first hyperlink (that is, the Summary of Recommendations at the end of the page), but, depending on the browser, it might not be able to display the Virgil Jackson resume (VJResume.doc) unless you save it as a Web page, too. In the following steps, you will convert the resume to a Web page, create a new link from the resume back to the proposal, and then modify the hyperlink in the proposal so that browsers can easily jump between the two documents.

To convert the resume to a Web page:

1. Open the file **VJResume** from the Tutorial folder for Tutorial 7, and save it (in the same folder) as a Web page using the filename **VJResume Web Page**. While you have the Open dialog box displayed, notice that Word has created a new folder, named "FSI New Branch Proposal Web Page_files," in which to store the files related to the proposal Web page. Note that you should never save any other documents to this folder.

Now, you'll make some minor formatting changes so that the résumé Web page has the same look as the proposal Web page. You'll use the procedures you learned earlier.

To format the VJResume Web Page:

1. Apply the Parchment background texture to the Web page.
2. Select the text **Virgil S. Jackson** at the top of the page, and format it in teal.
3. Click the **Spelling and Grammar** button on the Standard toolbar, click the **Ignore All** button to remove any red or green underlinings, and click the **OK** button.
4. If necessary, switch back to Web Page layout.
5. Change the font color of "Experience," to teal. Note that the headings "Education" and "Interest" change color as well.
6. Move the insertion point to the end of the document and insert the same horizontal line you used in the proposal.
7. Save the document.

The resume and the proposal now have a similar appearance.

Inserting a Hyperlink to a Web Page

Users who read Virgil's resume will most likely want to return to the proposal, so you decide to insert a hyperlink that targets the proposal. You insert hyperlinks into Web pages in the same way you do Word documents.

To insert a hyperlink:

1. Make sure the insertion point is below the horizontal line at the end of the document, and then type **Return to FSI New Branch Proposal**.
2. Select the text "FSI New Branch Proposal" in the phrase you just typed, click the **Insert Hyperlink** button on the Standard toolbar, under Link to click **Existing File or Web Page**, click the **File** button, locate and select **FSI New Branch Proposal Web Page**, and click the **OK** button twice. Word inserts the hyperlink to the proposal.
3. Save, and close the resume document. You return to the proposal.

The resume now contains a hyperlink that takes users back to the proposal.

Editing a Hyperlink

Recall that the proposal itself still contains the hyperlink that targets the resume in its Word document format. You need to edit the hyperlink so that it targets the resume with its new Web page name. Rather than deleting the hyperlink and reinserting a new one, you can edit the existing hyperlink and indicate the new target path. You want to target the file named VJResume Web page.

To edit a hyperlink:

1. Scroll to the end of the proposal, and right-click the resume hyperlink. Word displays a shortcut menu.

   TROUBLE? If the original resume document opens, you clicked the link with the left mouse button by mistake. Close the document, and repeat Step 1.

2. Point to **Hyperlink**, and then click **Edit Hyperlink**. The Edit Hyperlink dialog box opens.
3. Verify that the Existing File or Web Page option is selected under "Link to".
4. Click the **File** button, and the Link to File dialog box opens.
5. Delete the filename "VJResume" from the Filename text box.
6. Click the **Files of type** list arrow, and select **All Files**.
7. Select **VJResume Web Page** in the Tutorial folder for Tutorial 7, and then click the OK button. You return to the Edit Hyperlink dialog box. Note that you could type the correct filename in the Type the file or Web page name text box, but if you made even a small typing error, the link would not work. Selecting the correct file using the File button is a less error-prone method.
8. Click **OK**. You return to the proposal Web page.
9. Save the document.

The edited hyperlink in the proposal Web page correctly targets the resume Web page. You're now ready to view the finished Web pages in a Web browser and to test the hyperlinks.

Viewing the Web Page in a Web Browser

While you're editing a Web page in Word, the document window shows how the document will look when viewed from a Web browser. But it's always a good idea to view your Web pages with a Web browser to see exactly how they will look and to test the hyperlinks. Before attempting to display your document in a browser, however, make sure you save any changes first. Also, if your browser is open at the time you make and save changes, you might need to update or reload the document in your browser to display the latest updates to the HTML file.

To view the Web pages in a Web browser:

1. Click **File** on the menu bar, and then click **Web Page Preview**. Word opens your default Web browser and displays the FSI New Branch Proposal in its document window. See Figure 7-32. Your browser might be Netscape Navigator or some other browser, but the view of the FSI New Branch Proposal should be similar. Maximize the browser window, if necessary.

Figure 7-32 VIEWING THE WEB PAGE IN INTERNET EXPLORER

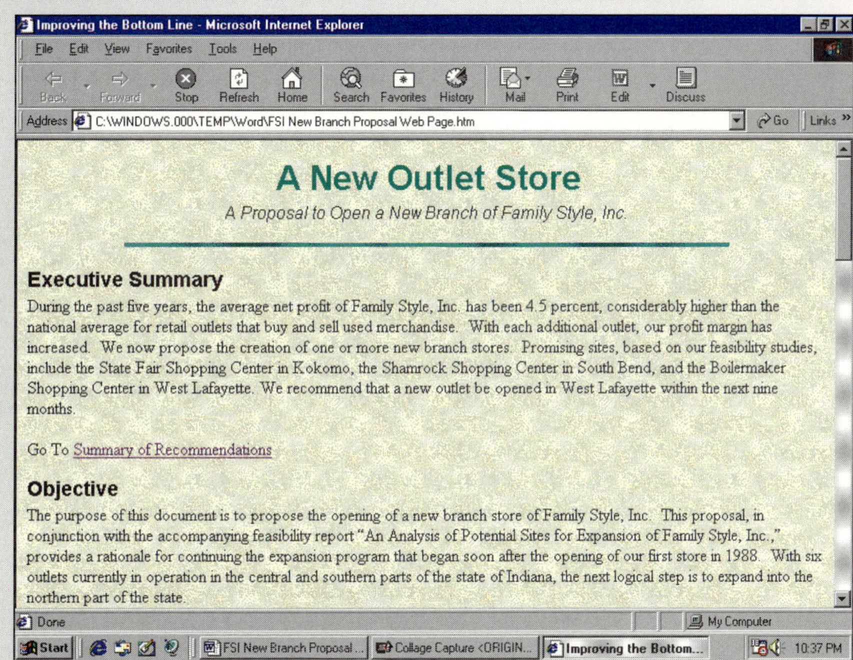

TROUBLE? If a message appears informing you that you have to save the document first, click the Yes button to save the document and display it in the Web browser.

TROUBLE? If you see a message informing you that Internet Explorer is not your default browser and asking you if you want to make it your browser, click the No button.

2. Scroll through the document so you can see how it looks in the browser.
3. Move the insertion point to the beginning of the document, and click the Summary of Recommendations hyperlink. The heading "Summary of Recommendations" is displayed in the browser window.
4. Click the resume hyperlink in the last paragraph of the document. The browser opens the Resume Web page. See Figure 7-33.

Figure 7-33 BROWSER SHOWING RESUME DOCUMENT

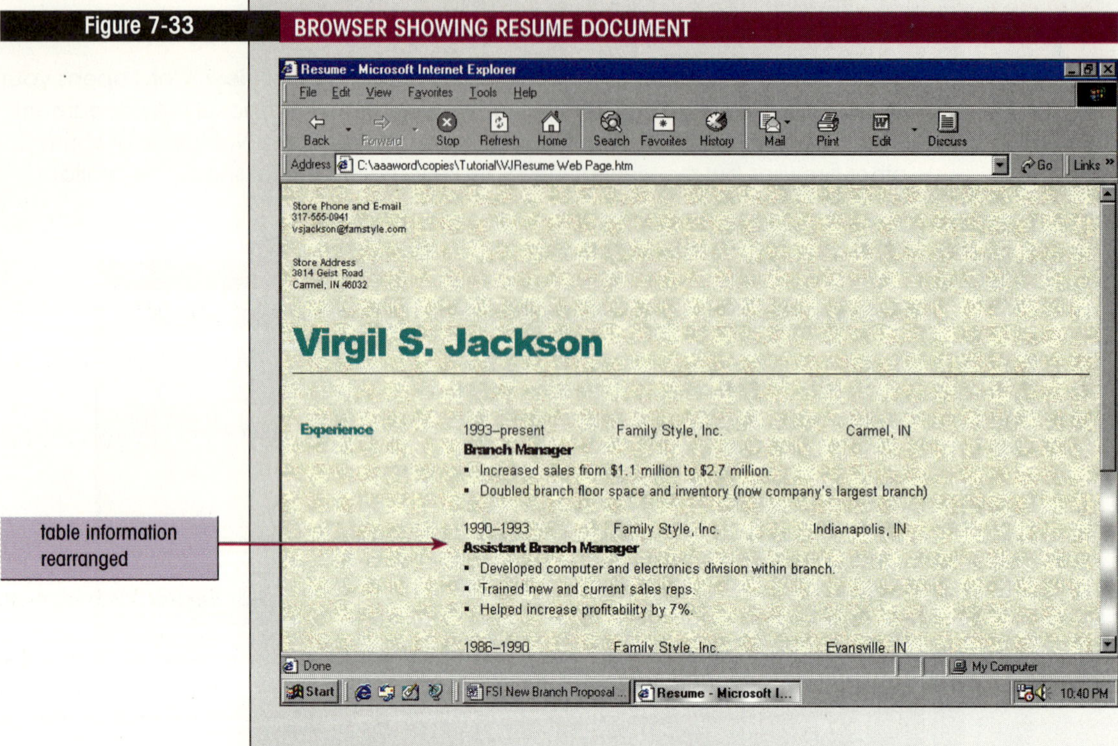

5. Scroll through the document to view it. Notice that when you view the resume in the browser, the table format disappears. But in this case, the format is still acceptable.

6. Click the **Return to FSI New Branch Proposal** hyperlink. The Browser now returns to the proposal Web page.

TROUBLE? If any of these hyperlinks don't work properly, edit them so they link to the proper document.

7. Close the browser window. You return to the proposal document in the Word window.

8. Scroll to the bottom of the Web page and insert the text **Prepared by** followed by your first and last name.

9. Print the document, and save and close the proposal. The printed Web page looks similar, but not identical, to the printed Word document.

You have now finished preparing two Web pages, the proposal and the resume, for online viewing.

Session 7.3 QUICK CHECK

1. Define the following terms:
   a. Web browser
   b. Web site
   c. HTML
   d. Web page
2. Name two types of formatting that cannot be translated into HTML.
3. True or False: After you convert a Word document to a Web page, you need to re-create all hypertext links.
4. Explain how to insert a horizontal line into a Web page. What is the purpose of such a line?
5. List the various tasks you should perform after converting a Word document into a Web page.
6. Describe the steps necessary to preview a Web page in your default Web browser.

You show your documents to Nalani, who tests them and sends them to the company's Internet service provider (ISP), which manages the Family Style Web site. The ISP will make the documents available on the World Wide Web by storing them on its Web server. At that point, anyone with Internet access and a Web browser can view the documents. Nalani hopes that posting the proposal on the World Wide Web will attract new investors for the Family Style expansion.

REVIEW ASSIGNMENTS

Marina Leavitt is the director of sales for Family Style, Inc. She is preparing a quarterly sales report to give to each of the company's sales representatives. The main purpose of the short report is to show sales, income, and expenses over the last three months, but it will also include new policies for purchasing used merchandise. Marina has written the body of the report in Word and wants you to embed a spreadsheet of sales figures in the report and then modify one of the figures. She also asks you to link a Paint graphics file showing the quarterly profits for each branch outlet, and then modify the file. Finally, she requests that you save the report as a Web page for publication on the World Wide Web, and create appropriate hyperlinks to related documents, including a URL for a Web page that contains additional information on Family Style procedures.

1. Make sure that Word is running, open the file **Salesrep** from the Review folder for Tutorial 7 on your Data Disk, and save it as **Family Style Sales Report**.
2. Below the subheading "2nd Quarter 2001 Sales Report," insert the text "Prepared by" and then type your first and last name. Center this new text below the subheading.
3. Delete the "[insert worksheet here]" placeholder, and in its place, insert a linked copy of the worksheet 2QSales from the Review folder for Tutorial 7 on your Data Disk. So that you can repeat the review assignments later, be sure to create a duplicate of the worksheet from within the Browse dialog box, and name the duplicate "Copy of 2Qsales." Remember to select the Link to file check box in order to link the worksheet to the Word document.

4. Center the worksheet using the Center button on the Formatting toolbar.
5. Save, and close the Word document.
6. Open Excel and modify the Copy of 2QSales worksheet by changing the June sales figure to 1.42.
7. Click the Save button on the Excel Standard toolbar, and then close Excel.
8. Open the Family Style Sales Report document, and verify that the change you made in Step 6 appears in the linked copy of the worksheet.

Explore

9. Double-click the worksheet within the Word document, and then use the Excel tools to format the column titles (April, May, and June) with a bright yellow fill and format the type in bold. Format the Expenses and Sales cells with boldface type only. Close the Excel window, and click Yes when asked if you want to save your changes to the Copy of 2Qsales.xls workbook. Verify that your changes to the worksheet appear in the Word document.
10. Locate and delete the line containing the phrase "[embed figure here],"and in its place insert the graphic file Brnchsls from the Review folder for Tutorial 7 on your Data Disk.
11. Click the graphic to select it, and verify that the Picture toolbar is displayed. Click the Format Object button on the Picture toolbar, and use the Size tab to reduce the graphic's height to 70% of its original size. (Make sure the Lock aspect ratio is selected so that the picture's proportions remain constant.) Click the Text Wrapping button on the Picture toolbar, and select the Tight option. The text wraps around the graphic.
12. Verify that the top of the graphic is level with the sentence beginning "The figure shows…." If it is not, drag the figure to position it properly.
13. Click outside the graphic to deselect it.

Explore

14. Change the color of the star at Indianapolis to red as follows: Double-click the graphic to display the tools of the Paint program. If necessary, scroll to display the Indianapolis star. Click the Magnifier button on the Paint toolbar, and then click the Indianapolis star to zoom in on it. Click the Fill with Color button on the Paint toolbar, click the red tile in the color palette in the bottom-left corner of the Paint window, and then click the Indianapolis star. The star fills with the bright red color. Click outside the graphic to return to the Word tools and menus.
15. Save the Word document.
16. Create a bookmark at the beginning of the document's title. At the end of the document, insert a hyperlink to that bookmark that reads "Return to Sales Report." Save the document.
17. View the document in Web Layout view.
18. Format the background with the Parchment texture.
19. Format the subtitle with the Las Vegas Lights animation. Remove any Spelling and Grammar markings, and save the document.
20. Save the report as Web page under the name Family Style Sales Report Web Page.
21. Review the information regarding the document features that are not supported by Web browsers and click Continue.

Explore

22. In the tutorials, you repositioned a graphic by dragging it. Now you can try using the Format Picture dialog box to position the map so the text wraps to its left. Click the map graphic to select it, click the Format Picture button on the Picture toolbar, click the Layout tab, click the Advanced button, click the Picture Position tab, click the Alignment option button in the Horizontal section (if necessary) to select it, and then click the Alignment list arrow and click Right. Click the OK button twice. Make sure the text "The figure shows…" is placed so the map is to its right.
23. Add or delete return characters to improve the layout of the document.
24. Enlarge the title, bold format the subtitle, and apply the color blue to the title, subtitle, and the "New Policies" heading.
25. Insert a horizontal separator line below the subtitle and another line at the end of the document. Save the document, and leave it open.
26. Open the file FSIAds in the Review folder for Tutorial 7 of your Data Disk, and save it as a Web page with the name FSIAds Web Page.
27. Format the FSIAds Web Page with the Parchment texture, enlarge the "Family Styles Inc." title, and color the title blue. Enlarge the "Advertising Summary" subhead. Put a horizontal line under Q1 2001, and delete the extra return character above the line. Put another horizontal line at the end of the document. Save the document.
28. In the sales report document, locate the text in the first paragraph that reads "advertising efforts in the first quarter," and format it as a hyperlink that jumps to the FSIAds Web page. Test the hyperlink.
29. At the end of the FSIAds Web page, insert the text "Return to Sales Report," and enlarge it. Format this new text as a hyperlink that jumps to the Family Style Sales Report Web page, and test the link.

Explore

30. Now, create the hyperlink to the URL for a related Family Style Web page. Scroll to the bottom of the Family Style Sales Report Web page document, press the Enter key twice to add two new blank lines, and then type "Click to see more information on Family Style purchasing procedures for new merchandise." Highlight the line you just typed. Open the Insert Hyperlink dialog box, click the Existing File or Web Page option under Link to, click the Type the file or Web page name text box, and then type the following URL: *http://www.course.com/cti/NewPerspectives/office2000/famstyle.html*
31. Click the OK button. Save the document, and then use the Web Page Preview command to view it in your Web browser. Test the hyperlinks you added, including the one at the bottom of the document. (*Hint:* To test the hyperlink at the bottom of the document, your computer must have access to the Internet.)

Explore

32. Right-click the Start button, click Explore, and then use the Windows Explorer to display the contents of the Family Style Sales Report Web Page_files folder (which you'll find within the Review folder for Tutorial 7 on your data disk). How many files does this folder contain? What is their total size? What size is the Family Style Sales Report Web Page file, in the Review folder?
33. Close the Windows Explorer.

Explore

34. Save the Family Style Sales Report Web Page as a Word document, using the name "Family Style Sales Report Word Document." Remember to select "Word Document" as the file type in the Save As dialog box. Do you notice any changes to the document now that it is a Word document again, rather than a Web page?
35. Save, and close your documents.

Explore

36. Use your e-mail program to send the Family Style Sales Report Word Document file to a fellow student. In most e-mail programs, you need to create a new message, and then attach the file to the message. Ask the recipient of the file to open it, display it in Web Layout view, and test the various links. Can he or she access the source file for the Excel workbook? Why or why not? Do the other links in the document work? Why or why not?
37. Close all open files.

CASE PROBLEMS

Case 1. Office Location for Vista Insurance Company Steven Woodhouse works for the Vista Insurance Company, a new, rapidly growing company. Emma Knightly, vice president of operations for the company, has proposed that Vista open a new downtown office and has assigned Steven the responsibility of finding a good location. Steven has contacted local real estate agencies through the World Wide Web, and he has located an available office building that seems satisfactory. He has downloaded an image of the office building and asks you to prepare a memo to Emma describing the office site. He'd like you to include the image in the memo. When you've finished, he requests that you e-mail the memo to Emma for online viewing. Emma won't be viewing the memo in her browser; she'll just open it directly in Word.

1. If necessary, start Word. Open the file **NewOffic** from the Cases folder for Tutorial 7 and then save it to the same folder as **New Office Memo**.
2. In the From: section of the memo heading, replace "Steve Woodhouse" with your name.
3. At the end of the third paragraph, delete the bracketed phrase "[insert chart]," and embed the chart called Rent from the Cases folder for Tutorial 7.
4. Double-click the chart to display the Excel tools. Click the chart title, click after the "e" in "Average," press the spacebar, and then type "monthly" so that the title reads "Average monthly rent ($)."
5. Reduce the size of the chart to 30% of its original size, and center it between the left and right margins.
6. Link a copy of the Logo file (located in the Cases folder for Tutorial 7) to the top-left margin of the document. (Be sure to make a copy of the file from within the Browse dialog box before you link it.)
7. Save and close the Word document, open the Paint program from the Start menu, and then open the Copy of Logo file. Change the red bar at the bottom of the logo to a light turquoise, save the file, and exit Paint.
8. Reopen the New Office Memo document, and make sure the color change was automatically made to the linked version of the logo.
9. Animate the "Interoffice Memorandum" heading with Las Vegas Lights.

Explore

10. Format the document with a solid tan background. (*Hint:* Click Format on the menu bar, point to Background, then click the Tan tile on the color palette.) Preview the New Office Memo document in Web Layout view. Notice how Word switched automatically to Web Layout view when you added the tan background.

11. In the second paragraph, just after the sentence that ends with "...downtown business district," insert text that reads "See Recent Downtown Developments" for a listing of recent renovations in the area." Make "Recent Downtown Developments" a hyperlink, targeting a copy of the Devel file in the Cases folder for Tutorial 7 on your Data Disk. Be sure to make a copy of the Devel file in the Link to File dialog box, and then link the copy to the New Office Memo document.

12. Open your copy of the Devel file by clicking the hyperlink to it, insert a hyperlink at the end that takes users back to the New Office Memo, add a tan background, and save the file.

13. Return to the memo and save it. Test all the links in the two documents one last time, and then close the copy of the Devel file.

14. Print the New Office Memo document while it is displayed in Web Layout view. Close the document.

Explore

15. Use your e-mail program to send the New Office Memo document to a fellow student. (If you prefer, send the file to yourself.) In most e-mail programs, you need to create a new message, and then attach the file to the message. Ask the recipient of the file to open it, display it in Web Layout view, and test the various links. Can he or she access the source file for the logo? Why or why not? Do the other links in the document work? Why or why not?

Case 2. Pacific Views Brochure Leah Bakula is a sales representative for Pacific Views, a company that offers guided tours to many of the popular tourist sites in the western United States. She is preparing a flyer describing upcoming tours to selected western National Parks. She asks you to help finish the project and then convert it to a Web page so she can post it on the company's home page and make it available to prospective tourists.

1. If necessary, start Word. Open the file **Natbroch** from the Cases folder for Tutorial 7 and then save it as **National Parks Tours** in the same folder.

2. Position the photograph of the arch against the left margin, wrap text around it, and enlarge it so that the entire second paragraph wraps to the right of the photo.

Explore

3. In the tutorial you learned how to link and embed objects using the Object command on the insert menu. If you prefer, you can also link or embed an object by copying it to the Clipboard, and then pasting it into the destination file using the Paste Special command on the Edit menu. To experiment using Paste Special now, move the insertion point to the last line of the document, start Excel and open the worksheet PacTours from the Cases folder for Tutorial 7. Click cell A1, and then drag down and to the right to cell E7. The worksheet data should now be selected. Click the Copy button on the Excel toolbar, click the Microsoft Word button on the taskbar, click Edit on the menu bar, and then click Paste Special. The Paste Special dialog box allows you to paste objects from the Clipboard in a variety of formats, including HTML, unformatted text and formatted text. To embed the worksheet data as a worksheet, you could select the Microsoft Excel Worksheet Object option. To simply embed a worksheet, you can select the Paste option button. To link a worksheet, you can select the Paste link option button. In this case, you will experiment with pasting the worksheet data as formatted text. Click the Formatted Text (RTF) option in the As list box, verify that the Paste option button is selected, and then click OK. The worksheet is inserted into the document as a Word table.

4. Format the new table as necessary to make it attractive and easy to read.

Explore

5. Design a logo of your own at the top of the document. Open the Paint program from the Start menu. Click Image in the menu bar, click Attributes, and change the Width settings to 200 and the height setting to 50. Use the text tool to draw a text box the same size as the image, and then create a logo using the words "Pacific Tours." Format the text in the style and size of your choice, using the Text toolbar, which you can display, if necessary, by selecting it on the View menu. Use the Rectangle tool to draw a rectangle the same size as the image, and then use the Fill tool to fill the rectangle with a blue color. You may need to click inside some of the letters to fill them with the blue color, too. (*Hint:* Use the Undo command on the Edit menu to reverse any mistakes. Use the Magnifier tool to zoom in on the image, if necessary, to make it easier to edit.) Save the logo as a 256-color bitmap file named **Tours Logo** in the Cases folder for Tutorial 7. (Click Yes if you see a Paint Warning dialog box.) Link a copy of the logo at the top of the National Parks Tours flyer. After saving the flyer, double-click the logo and edit it any way you want to improve its appearance.
6. At the bottom of the document type "Prepared by:" followed by your fist and last name.

Explore

7. Preview the document. Because this document does not fill the entire page, it would look better formatted horizontally on the page, in landscape orientation. Click File, click Page Setup, click the Paper Size tab, in the Orientation section click the Landscape option button, and then click OK. Review the newly formatted document in the preview window. Note that landscape orientation is also useful for tables containing many columns, or large, embedded Excel worksheets, save your changes, print the document, and then close the Preview window.
8. Save the flyer as a Web page with the name **National Parks Tours Web Page**. Adjust the placement of text and graphics as necessary. Give it an appropriate background color or pattern, and add one or two lines. Adjust the size and color of the text headings so they go well with the background.
9. Place a hyperlink at the bottom of the document that reads "Click here to see a photo of last year's tour!," and have the hyperlink display a copy of the file PacPhoto in the Cases folder for Tutorial 7 on your Data Disk. Be sure to make a copy of the PacPhoto file in the Link to File dialog box and then link the copy to the National Parks Tours document.
10. Place a hyperlink at the bottom of the PacPhoto page that takes the user back to the flyer.
11. Save both files, view them in a browser, and test the links. Print the files from your browser.

Case 3. Maple Tree Sports Sales Report Nicholas Paulsen is vice president of marketing for Maple Tree Sports, a national sporting goods distributor headquartered in Birmingham, Alabama. Because of the enormous volume of sales in California, Nicholas has decided to reorganize the sales regions. To lessen the load on the western region, he has decided to enlarge the southeast region to include Texas. He will explain this change in a report to all regional sales representatives. He asks you to create an integrated document that includes an Excel chart and a Paint image file of a map. He wants you to prepare the file for online viewing because he plans to post it on his company's network. Then he wants you to save and format the file for posting on the Web.

1. If necessary, start Word. Open the file **MapleRep** from the Cases folder for Tutorial 7, and save it to the same file as **Maple Sales Org**.
2. Between the first and second paragraphs, embed the Excel chart Maple, and reduce it to 30% of its original size.
3. Center the chart between the left and right margins.

Explore

4. Double-click the chart to display the Excel tools, click any bar, and select the fill color of your choice using the Fill Color button on the Formatting toolbar. Then, click the background and choose a contrasting color.
5. At the end of the document, link a copy of the Paint image file Salesreg, naming the copy Sales Regions Map. Center the map between the left and right margins with no text wrapping.
6. Edit the linked Paint image from within Word: Fill the state of Texas with the blue color that matches the other southern states. Save the image, and close Paint.
7. Save, preview, and print the document.
8. Switch to Web Layout view, and apply an appropriate background. Animate text with an animation of your choice. Save the Word document.
9. Save the report as a Web page. Adjust the placement of text and graphics. Change the font sizes and colors to make the on-screen document more visually appealing. Print the file from within your browser.
10. Create another Word document containing additional information that readers of this report might want to see. It might contain text, a chart, or graphics; avoid using Word tables. (If you are using floppy disks to save your files, be aware that graphics files can be quite large. You might want to use only text.) Save it as a Web page, and format it so it is compatible with the report. Create hyperlinks to move the user back and forth between the two documents. Save and preview the documents in a browser, and then test the links. Print the file from your browser.

Case 4. Educational Expenses Your local community education program is hosting a seminar for adults who want to return to college. The program coordinator has asked you to create a Web page providing information about the current cost of going to college. You will create the Web page using Word's Web Page Wizard, which leads you through the steps of creating a Web site:

1. Open a new Word document, and then, in several paragraphs, explain the various types of expenses that a student faces.

Explore

2. Use Microsoft Graph to create a chart detailing three major expenses, as follows: Click Insert on the menu bar, point to Picture, and then click Chart. In the Datasheet window, replace the row labels "East," "West," and "North" with your three major expenses. Replace the existing numbers with expense data for four quarters, and then click your report document to embed the completed chart.
3. Save the report as a Web page using the name **School Expenses**.

Explore

4. Notice that the New Blank Document button in the Standard toolbar has been replaced with a New Web Page button. Click the New Web Page button, and begin creating a new Web page.
5. At the top of the document add the title "Additional Data," and then link a picture or diagram that would enhance your report's content. For example, if you have access to a scanner, you could scan a picture of a campus building or your own picture. You can use Paint to modify the map of the United States in the graphics file SalesReg, showing the location of selected educational institutions.

Explore

6. If you have access to the World Wide Web, use a search engine to find relevant information about college costs and incorporate the information into the Additional Data document. Credit the source with a footnote, or create a hyperlink to the Web address in your report.
7. Save the new Web page as **Additional Information.**

8. Format both Web pages attractively, using the techniques you learned in the tutorial. Remember to make the pages look similar.

Explore

9. Close all open documents. Now you can use the Web Page Wizard to create a sophisticated Web site containing the two pages. Click File on the menu bar, and then click New. In the New dialog box, click the Web Pages tab, and double-click the Web Page Wizard icon. The first Web Page Wizard dialog box opens.
10. Read the dialog box, and then click Next. Type an appropriate title for your Web site, such as "School Expense Information." In the Web site location text box, verify that the file path in the Web site location text box indicates a folder within the Cases folder for Tutorial 7. Word assigns a default name, such as "New Web" to this folder.
11. Click Next, and read the information in the next dialog box.
12. Verify that the Vertical frame option is selected, and then click Next.
13. In the Current pages in Web site list box, select Personal Web Page, and then click the Remove Page button. Repeat for Blank Page 2, and Blank Page 1. Click the Add Existing File button, and select the School Expenses Web page. Repeat to select the Additional Information page, and then click Next.
14. Review the information regarding organizing links, and then click Next.
15. Click the Browse Themes button, select a formatting scheme (called a "theme") in the Choose a Theme list box, preview your scheme in the Sample of theme window, and then click OK. If a theme is not installed on your computer, click Install. (You may need to insert the Office 2000 installation CD in order to install a theme.) Click OK, and then click Next.
16. Click Finish. After a pause, Word creates your Web site, including a home page with links to the pages you created earlier. If the Frames toolbar opens, close it. Click a link in the left pane to display the relevant page on the right. Note that Word has assigned the filename "default" to the home page. All the files related to the Web site are stored in a new folder whose name is the same as the Web Site name you specified earlier.
17. Preview the new home page in your Web browser. Print the page once with the School Expenses link selected and once with the Additional Data link selected.
18. Close your browser, and then close the home page in Word.

LAB ASSIGNMENTS

The Internet: World Wide Web

These Lab Assignments are designed to accompany the interactive Course Lab called Internet World Wide Web. To start the Lab, click the Start button on the taskbar, point to Programs, point to Course Labs, point to New Perspectives Applications, and click Internet World Wide Web. If you do not see Course Labs on your Programs menu, see your instructor or technical support person.

The Internet: World Wide Web One of the most popular services on the Internet is the World Wide Web. This Lab is a Web simulator that teaches you how to use Web browser software to find information. You can use this Lab whether or not your school provides you with Internet access.

1. Click the Steps button to learn how to use Web browser software. As you proceed through the steps, answer all of the Quick Check questions that appear. After you complete the steps, you'll see a Quick Check summary report. Follow the instructions on the screen to print this report.

2. Click the Explore button. Use the Web browser to locate a weather map of the Caribbean Virgin Islands. What is its URL?
3. Enter the URL http://www.atour.com. A SCUBA diver named Wadson Lachouffe has been searching for the fabled treasure of Greybeard the pirate. A link from the Adventure Travel Web site leads to Wadson's Web page called "Hidden Treasure." Locate the Hidden Treasure page, and answer the following questions:
   a. What was the name of Greybeard's ship?
   b. What was Greybeard's favorite food?
   c. What does Wadson think happened to Greybeard's ship?
4. In the steps, you found a graphic of Jupiter from the photo archives of the Jet Propulsion Laboratory. In the Explore section of the Lab, you can also find a graphic of Saturn. Suppose one of your friends wants a picture of Saturn for an astronomy report. Make a list of the blue underlined links your friend must click to find the Saturn graphic. Assume that your friend begins at the Web Trainer home page.
5. Jump back to the Adventure Travel Web site. Write a one-page description of the information at the site, including the number of pages the site contains, and diagram the links it contains.
6. Chris Thomson, a student at UVI, has his own Web page. In Explore, look at the information Chris included on his page. Suppose you could create your own Web page. What would you include? Use word-processing software to design your own Web page. Make sure to indicate the graphics and links you would use.

INTERNET ASSIGNMENTS

The purpose of the Internet Assignments is to challenge you to find information on the Internet that you can use to create effective documents. The actual assignments are updated and maintained on the Course Technology Web site. Log on to the Internet and use your Web browser to go to the Student Online Companion to accompany this text at **www.course.com/NewPerspectives/office2000**. Click the Word link, and then click the link for Tutorial 7.

QUICK CHECK ANSWERS

Session 7.1

1. **a.** A source file is the file containing the original object.
   b. An object is an item such as a graphic image, clip art, a WordArt image, a chart, or a section of text that you can modify and move from one document to another.
   c. The source program is the program in which an object was originally created.
   d. A destination file is the file into which you want to insert an object.
2. With embedding, you place an object into a document and retain the ability to use the tools of the source program. With linking, you place a representation of an object into a document. With embedding, there is no connection maintained between the source file and the destination file; with linking there is.
3. Linking is the best choice for data that might change over time.

4. "OLE" is short for "object linking and embedding". An OLE-enabled program is one whose objects can be integrated into other documents using OLE technology.
5. To embed an existing worksheet, click Insert on the menu bar, click Object, click the Create from File tab, select the file, click Insert, and then click OK without selecting the Link to file check box. To link an Excel chart, follow the same procedure but select the Link to file check box.
6. To copy a file, right-click it, click Copy, and then press Ctrl+V.
7. To modify an embedded object from within the destination program, double-click the object and then use the tools and menus of the source program.
8. False

Session 7.2

1. A hyperlink is a word, phrase, or graphic image that you can click to move to another location.
2. False
3. Click where you want to insert the bookmark, click Insert on the menu bar, click Bookmark, type the bookmark name, and then click Add.
4. "Executive Summary" (b) is an invalid bookmark name because it has a space.
5. A change in the color of hyperlink text indicates that the link has been used, or followed.
6. False
7. The Document Map is a navigational aid that you can use to move quickly from one heading to the next in a document.

Session 7.3

1. **a.** A program used to download and display Web pages.
   b. A Web site is a collection of inter-related Web pages.
   c. "HTML" is short for "Hypertext Markup Language," a special programming language that tells a Web browser how a Web page should look on the screen.
   d. A Web page is an electronic document. Organizations and individuals make their Web pages available on the World Wide Web by storing them on special computers called Web servers.
2. Text wrapping around graphics and animated text cannot be translated into HTML.
3. False
4. Click Format on the menu bar, click Borders and Shading, click the Borders tab, click the Horizontal Line button, and then click the Insert clip button. A horizontal line separates sections of a document to make it easier to read and navigate.
5. After converting a Word document to a Web page, you should adjust the formatting to make it more suitable for online viewing and possibly add some special formatting features that are not always available in printed documents, such as color and animation. In some cases, the original document might already contain special features such as animation that don't survive the translation to HTML. In that case, you may need to reapply the feature once the document has been saved as a Web page. At the very least, you will probably need to reposition graphics.
6. To preview a Web page in the default Web browser, click File on the menu bar, and then click Web Page Preview.

LEVEL III

New Perspectives on

MICROSOFT® WORD 2000

Read This Before You Begin

To the Student

Data Disks

To complete the Level III Tutorials, Review Assignments, and Case Problems in this book, you need three Data Disks. Your instructor will either provide you with Data Disks or ask you to make your own.

If you are making your own Data Disks, you will need three blank, formatted high-density disks. You will need to copy a set of folders from a file server or standalone computer or the Web onto your disks. Your instructor will tell you which computer, drive letter, and folders contain the files you need. You could also download the files by going to www.course.com, clicking Data Disk Files, and following the instructions on the screen.

The following list shows you which folders go on each of your disks, so that you will have enough disk space to complete all the Tutorials, Review Assignments, and Case Problems:

Data Disk 1

Write this on the disk label:
Data Disk 1: Level III Tutorial 8

Put this folder on the disk:
Tutorial.08

Data Disk 2

Write this on the disk label:
Data Disk 2: Level III Tutorial 9

Put this folder on the disk:
Tutorial.09

Data Disk 3

Write this on the disk label:
Data Disk 3: Level III Tutorial 10

Put this folder on the disk:
Tutorial.10

When you begin each tutorial, be sure you are using the correct Data Disk. See the inside front or inside back cover of this book for more information on Data Disk files, or ask your instructor or technical support person for assistance.

Using Your Own Computer

If you are going to work through this book using your own computer, you need:

- **Computer System** Microsoft Word 2000 and Windows 95 or higher must be installed on your computer. This book assumes a complete installation of Word 2000.
- **Data Disks** You will not be able to complete the tutorials or exercises in this book using your own computer until you have Data Disks.
- **Course Lab** See your instructor or technical support person to obtain the Course Lab software for use on your own computer.

Visit Our World Wide Web Site

Additional materials designed especially for you are available on the World Wide Web. Go to http://www.course.com.

To the Instructor

The Data files are available on the Instructor's Resource Kit for this title. Follow the instructions in the Help file on the CD-ROM to install the programs to your network or standalone computer. For information on creating Data Disks, see the "To the Student" section above.

You are granted a license to copy the Data Files to any computer or computer network used by students who have purchased this book.

OBJECTIVES

In this tutorial you will:

- Create a template
- Define and modify styles within the template
- Apply borders and shading to a paragraph
- Create, insert, and print AutoText entries
- Customize the toolbars
- Automate parts of a document using field codes
- Record, edit, and run macros
- Record and use an AutoNew macro
- Open a new document based on a customized template
- Create and modify a chart using data from an Excel worksheet

CUSTOMIZING WORD AND AUTOMATING YOUR WORK

Automating a Product Proposal Memo at Creekside Wood Crafts

CASE

Creekside Wood Crafts

Darrell Brousseau is the assistant product manager for Creekside Wood Crafts, a wholesale mail-order crafts company that specializes in high-quality, finely tooled, unfinished, unassembled wood furniture. Founded three years ago in Columbia, South Carolina, the company now has about 15 employees, most of whom have several job titles and responsibilities. For example, Darrell is not only the assistant product manager, but he also helps employees resolve computer hardware and software problems as the computer resource specialist. In addition, he is a member of the product development group, which recently came up with an idea for a new product line: wood furniture kits.

Margaret Fox, vice president of product development, mentioned to Darrell that some product proposal memos are incomplete. Also, every memo presents the information in different formats, which makes it difficult for the executive board to evaluate new items. Because the product development group often presents new, additional merchandise to the Creekside Wood Crafts catalog, Darrell decides to automate the product proposal memos so employees can write them more efficiently while using a consistent layout and organization.

You'll help Darrell develop the automated memo system and use it to complete the product proposal memo for wood furniture kits on behalf of the product development group. Darrell will then distribute the template to all Creekside Wood Crafts employees. This will help ensure that all proposals include the required information and have a consistent look and feel.

In this tutorial, you'll create and test a template that the employees of Creekside Wood Crafts will use to write product proposal memos. As you know, a **template** is a blueprint for the text, graphics, and format of a document. First, you'll format the template and insert a graphic (the company logo) into the template. You'll also add AutoText entries to the template. Next, you'll modify the toolbars and add field codes to the template to automate much of the work of creating product proposal memos. Then, you'll record macros, including an AutoNew macro, and attach them to the template. Finally, you'll use the template to create a product proposal memo on the wood furniture kits and then print the memo as a fax with a cover sheet.

SESSION 8.1

In this session, you'll set up a template, add graphics to it, and create new styles and change existing styles within the template. You'll also apply a border and shading to a paragraph. Finally, you'll create AutoText entries so you can quickly insert common phrases into a document.

Planning the Memo

The product proposal memo and its template will follow Creekside Wood Crafts specifications for content, organization, style, and presentation.

Each product proposal memo must contain the following five sections:

- **Executive Summary**. A brief description of the proposed product and reasons it might be successful.
- **Product Description**. A detailed description of the product, including dimensions (size), proposed wholesale (discount) price, suggested retail price, and, usually, a drawing of the product.
- **Rationale**. An explanation of why the product is being proposed and reasons it might be successful.
- **Competition**. A description of the same or similar products sold by competing mail-order crafts stores.
- **Projected Earnings**. A chart showing projected income and profit for five years after product introduction.

Each product proposal memo will begin with the "Date," "To," and "From" headings, along with a "Product" heading for the name of the new item. Because every product proposal memo at Creekside Wood Crafts must contain this information, Darrell will set up a template that includes **boilerplate text**—one or more pages of text (and possibly graphics) that you can use over and over again. The boilerplate text will ensure that every product proposal contains all sections and the proper headings.

Company policy requires memos to be clear, direct, and succinct so company officers can read them and make decisions quickly. Each memo will include the company logo and an appealing layout to help maintain the company image among the employees and foster a positive image outside the company.

Understanding DocumentTemplates

When you build a document template, you create a blueprint that anyone can follow to produce new documents. The template you'll create for Darrell will ensure that all product proposal memos include the same type of information in the same order with the same format. You already know how to use a template to apply styles to text. The template you'll create in this tutorial will contain a number of additional features.

A template can contain a variety of helpful features designed to streamline the process of creating a document. The following list describes some common template elements:

- **Boilerplate** text and graphics that you want to appear in every document created by the template.
- **Styles** that provide preset formats for the common elements.
- **AutoText**, which helps users quickly and accurately insert common words and phrases.
- **Custom toolbars, menus, and shortcut keys** that contain the most frequently used commands.
- **Fields** that insert information automatically.
- **Macros**, which automate a series of keystrokes or mouse operations.

You'll include most of these features in the template you prepare for Darrell. Figure 8–1 shows some of the template features that are visible in the printed document.

Figure 8-1 FEATURES OF CREEKSIDE PRODUCT MEMO TEMPLATE

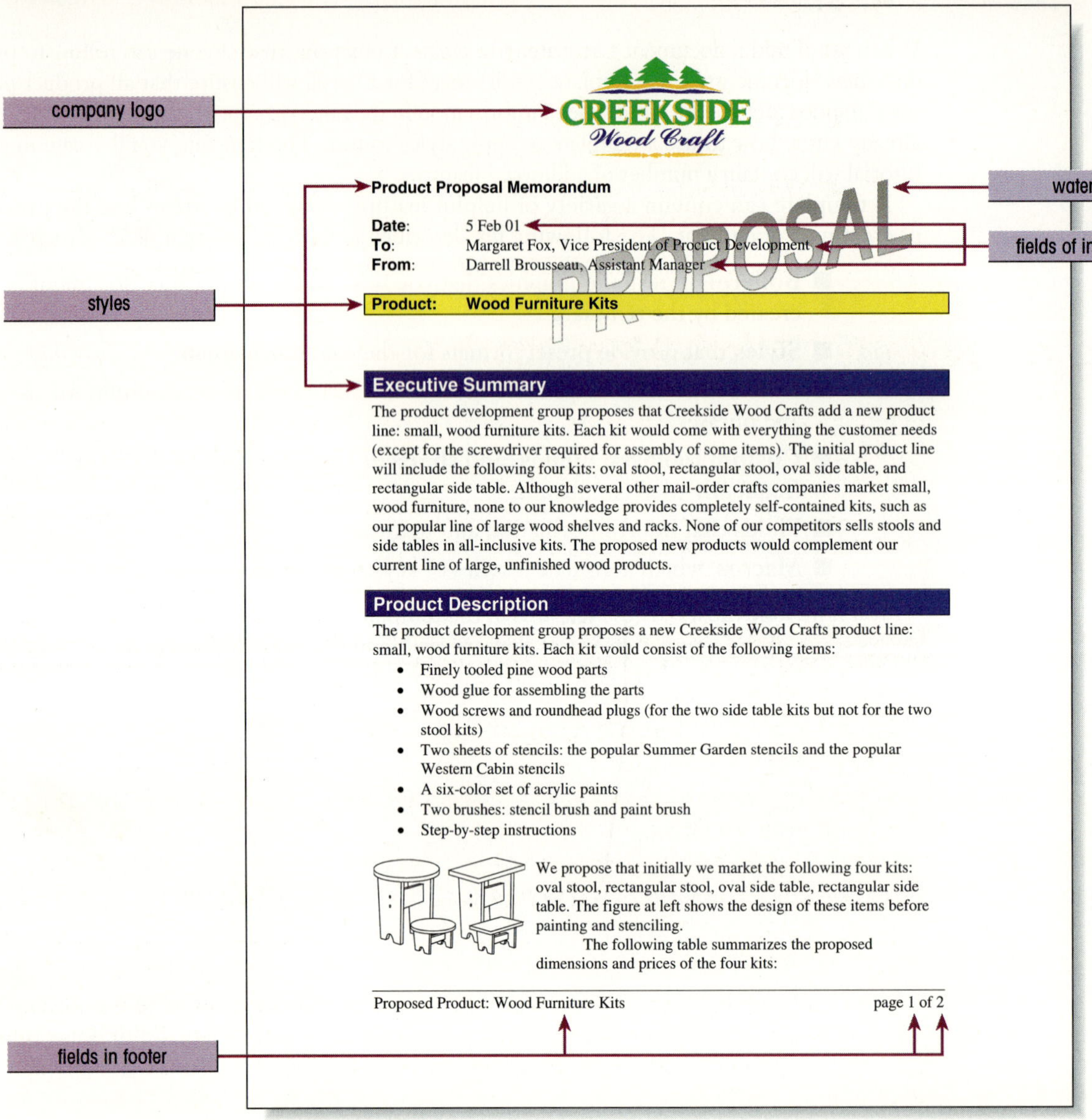

company logo

CREEKSIDE
Wood Craft

watermark

Product Proposal Memorandum

fields of information

Date: 5 Feb 01
To: Margaret Fox, Vice President of Procuct Development
From: Darrell Brousseau, Assistant Manager

PROPOSAL

styles

Product: Wood Furniture Kits

Executive Summary

The product development group proposes that Creekside Wood Crafts add a new product line: small, wood furniture kits. Each kit would come with everything the customer needs (except for the screwdriver required for assembly of some items). The initial product line will include the following four kits: oval stool, rectangular stool, oval side table, and rectangular side table. Although several other mail-order crafts companies market small, wood furniture, none to our knowledge provides completely self-contained kits, such as our popular line of large wood shelves and racks. None of our competitors sells stools and side tables in all-inclusive kits. The proposed new products would complement our current line of large, unfinished wood products.

Product Description

The product development group proposes a new Creekside Wood Crafts product line: small, wood furniture kits. Each kit would consist of the following items:

- Finely tooled pine wood parts
- Wood glue for assembling the parts
- Wood screws and roundhead plugs (for the two side table kits but not for the two stool kits)
- Two sheets of stencils: the popular Summer Garden stencils and the popular Western Cabin stencils
- A six-color set of acrylic paints
- Two brushes: stencil brush and paint brush
- Step-by-step instructions

We propose that initially we market the following four kits: oval stool, rectangular stool, oval side table, rectangular side table. The figure at left shows the design of these items before painting and stenciling.

The following table summarizes the proposed dimensions and prices of the four kits:

Proposed Product: Wood Furniture Kits page 1 of 2

fields in footer

As you can see in Figure 8-1, the template will provide the styles, company logo, "proposal" watermark, and information fields required for each product proposal memo. To transform a blank template into a completed memo, users need only add the text and graphics specific to their particular product proposal. The template also will contain some additional tools, such as macros and special toolbars, designed to simplify the process of creating a memo.

Advantages of Templates

You can define templates for many kinds of frequently used documents: memos, invoices, fax cover sheets, reports, contracts, or any document for which you want to automate much of the work and have a consistent look and feel. Using a template to create a document has the following advantages:

- **Consistency**. All documents based on the template will have the same format.
- **Accuracy**. Including boilerplate text or graphics in a template helps prevent a user from introducing typos and other errors into the document.
- **Efficiency**. Customized toolbars, menus, shortcut keys, AutoText, and macros help simplify and automate the process of creating a document.

You'll begin creating the template by adding boilerplate graphics and text.

Creating the Product Proposal Template

As you know, to create a template, you save a new or existing document just as you would any other Word document, except that you change the type to Document Template. Word adds the filename extension ".dot" (for "document template") to distinguish the template from regular documents with the filename extension ".doc." After you save the template, you can copy or move it just as you would other files.

REFERENCE WINDOW RW

Creating a Document Template

- Enter boilerplate text and graphics, format the document, create and modify styles, or make other changes to the document.
- Customize the toolbars, menus, and shortcut keys, record macros, create AutoText entries, and make other modifications to Word.
- Click File on the menu bar, click Save As, type the filename in the File name text box, click the Save as type list arrow, click Document Template, and then click the Save button.

Darrell already has typed some of the boilerplate text and made some of the formatting changes he wants in the template. You'll save his document as a template file, and then insert the Creekside Wood Crafts logo, create and modify styles, and customize the template in other ways.

To create the document template:

1. Start Word as usual, insert your Data Disk into the appropriate drive, and open the **ProdMemo** file from the Tutorial folder in the Tutorial.08 folder on your Data Disk.
2. Click **File** on the menu bar, click **Save As** to open the Save As dialog box, type **Creekside Product Memo** in the File name text box, click the **Save as type** list arrow, and then click **Document Template (*.dot)**.

   Notice that the default Templates folder on your computer's hard disk automatically opens in the Save in list box. You need to switch it back to your Data Disk.
3. Change the Save in list box to the Tutorial subfolder within the Tutorial.08 folder on your Data Disk, and then click the **Save** button in the Save As dialog box. Creekside Product Memo becomes a template that you can use when you start a new document.

The Creekside Product Memo template looks similar to the **Normal template** (also called the **global template**), which is the template you usually use when you start a new document, with a few exceptions. Darrell makes sure the Normal style is 12-point Times New Roman and then modifies the Heading-1 style to 14-point, bold Arial with Space Before set to 12 points, Space After set to 3 points, and the text flow set to Keep with next. (This way, if a heading appears at the bottom of the page, it's not separated from the paragraph that follows it.) Another difference is that the product memo template will contain boilerplate text and graphics, whereas the Normal template is blank. Darrell also set some tab stops to align the memo-heading entries. You'll continue to add features to the template that will help automate the creation of product proposal memos.

Inserting Graphics into a Template

Next, you will insert the Creekside Wood Crafts logo at the beginning of the product memo template. The company's logo is a TIFF file (with the filename extension .tif), which you can import into the template just as you would into a normal document.

To insert the Creekside Wood Crafts logo into the template:

1. If necessary, switch to Print Layout View, and make sure the nonprinting characters are displayed and the insertion point is at the beginning of the document.
2. Click **Insert** on the menu bar, point to **Picture**, and then click **From File**. The Insert Picture dialog box opens.
3. Use the **Look in** list arrow to open the Tutorial subfolder for Tutorial 8 on your Data Disk, and then double-click **CrkLogo**. The Creekside Wood Craft logo appears at the top of the template.

   You'll resize the logo, make sure no text can wrap on either side of the logo, and center the logo. When you resize the logo, you'll want to maintain the **aspect ratio**, which is the relative height and width of the picture. If the aspect ratio changes, the picture becomes too wide for its height or too tall for its width. You'll also change the size relative to the original picture size, not relative to the current picture size, which might be different from the original picture size.
4. Click the logo to select it, and click the **Center** button on the Formatting toolbar. The picture becomes centered between the left and right margins. The Picture toolbar is now displayed.

   TROUBLE? If the Picture toolbar does not appear, right-click any toolbar and then click Picture.
5. Click the **Format Picture** button on the Picture toolbar to open the Format Picture dialog box, click the **Size** tab, make sure the **Lock aspect ratio** and **Relative** to original picture size check boxes are selected, change the **Height** (in the Scale section) to **80%**, and press the **Tab** key to select the **Width** option, which automatically changes to 80% to maintain the aspect ratio. See Figure 8-2.

Figure 8-2 FORMAT PICTURE DIALOG BOX

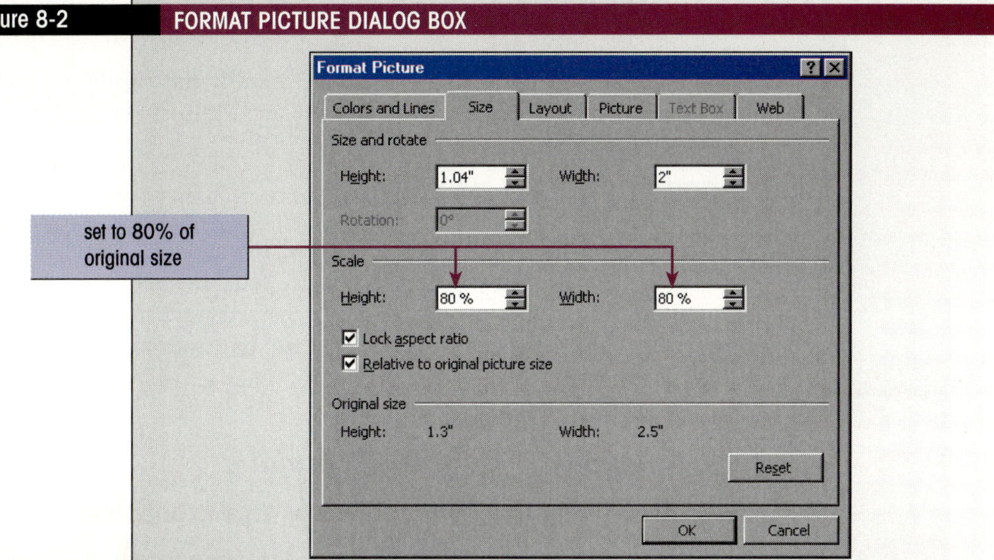

TROUBLE? If the Width value doesn't automatically change to 80%, change it to 80% now.

6. Click the **Layout** tab, and make sure the **In line with text** icon is selected. This keeps text from appearing either to the left or to the right of the logo but does allow text above and below it. In the template, however, you won't type any text above the logo.

7. Click the **OK** button, and deselect the picture by clicking anywhere else in the document window. See Figure 8-3.

Figure 8-3 LOGO SIZED AND POSITIONED

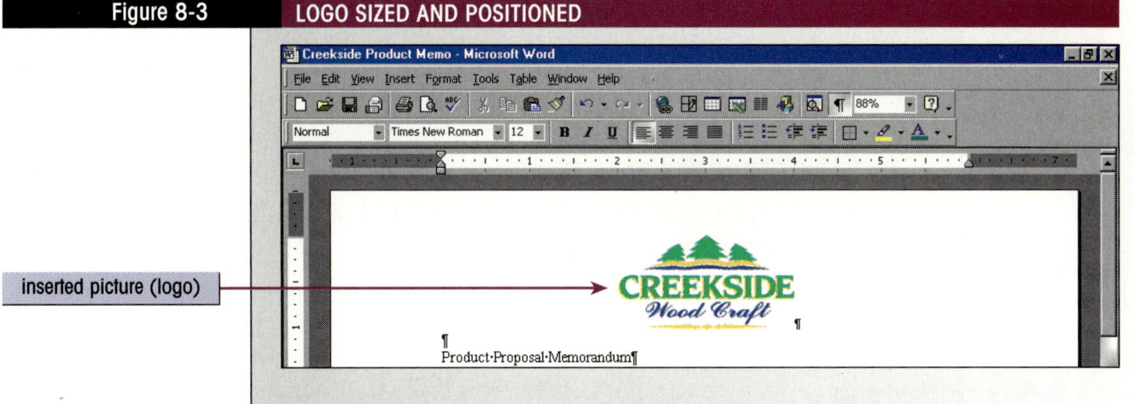

8. Save the template by clicking the **Save** button on the Standard toolbar.

Now, any document based on this template will contain the company logo.

Creating and Modifying Styles in a Template

Darrell wants you to create a new style and further modify the Heading-1 style in the product memo template. These will both be available in any document created from the template.

Defining and Applying a New Style

Currently, the memo headings "Product Proposal Memorandum," "Date," "To," and "From" are 12-point Times New Roman—the Normal style. You'll define a new character style called "Memo Heading" to format this text. Recall that a character style includes only character-level formats, such as font type and size, italic, or small caps. In this case, the character-level formats will be 12-point, bold Arial.

To define the new style in the template:

1. Click **Format** on the menu bar, and then click **Style** to open the Style dialog box.
2. Click the **New** button in the Style dialog box to open the New Style dialog box.
3. Type **Memo Heading** in the Name text box, click the **Style type** list arrow, and then click **Character**. The Based on list box changes to Default Paragraph Font, and the Style for following paragraph list box becomes blank.
4. Click the **Format** button, click **Font** to open the Font dialog box, and then, if necessary, click the **Font** tab.
5. Change the Font to **Arial**, the Font style to **Bold**, and the Font size to **12**.
6. Click the **OK** button to accept the new font, style, and size; click the **OK** button in the New Style dialog box; and then click the **Close** button in the Style dialog box.

You'll use the Memo Heading style to format the text of the memo heading.

To apply the new style:

1. Select the phrase "Product Proposal Memorandum" located just below the logo.
2. Click the **Style** list arrow on the Formatting toolbar, and then click **Memo Heading**. The memo title changes to the Memo Heading style: 12-point, bold Arial.
3. Select the word "Date" (but not the colon after it), and then repeat Step 2 (or use the (F4) key) to apply the Memo Heading style. Note that if the Memo Heading were a paragraph style, the colon also would change to the 12-point, bold Arial because paragraph styles affect all text in the paragraph.
4. Apply the Memo Heading style to the words "To," and "From," but not the colons following each word, and then deselect any selected text. See Figure 8-4.

Figure 8-4 TEXT FORMATTED WITH MEMO HEADING STYLE

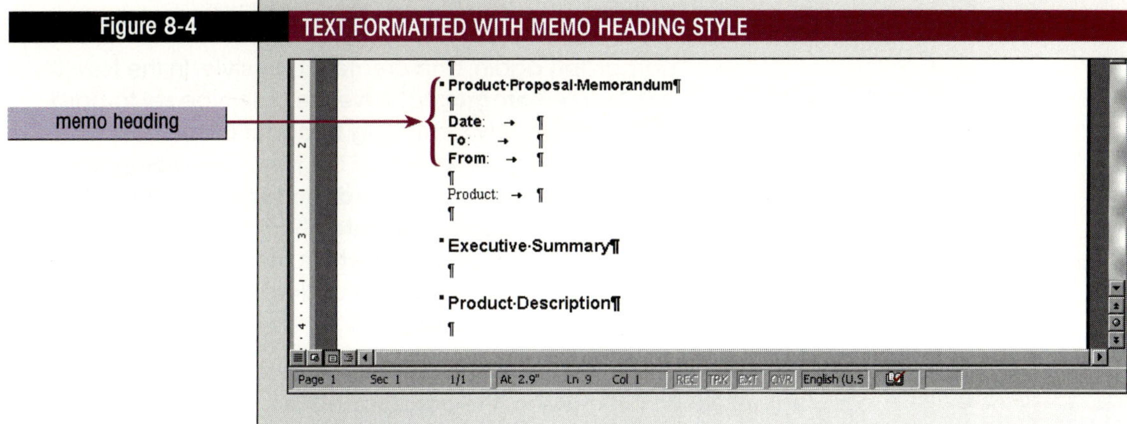

The text with this style applied, as well as the style itself, will be available whenever a Creekside Wood Crafts employee uses the template.

Applying Borders and Shading with a Style

You'll now create another style, called Key Paragraph. This is a paragraph style that emphasizes a particular paragraph, such as the product name in the memorandum heading. This time, you'll create the style by example.

To create a new style by example:

1. Click to the left of "Product:" located in the memo heading to select the entire paragraph.
2. Change the font of the selected paragraph to bold Arial. Now, you're ready to apply borders and shading to the paragraph.
3. Click **Format** on the menu bar, click **Borders and Shading** to open the Borders and Shading dialog box, and, if necessary, click the **Borders** tab.
4. Click the **Box** icon in the Setting section of the dialog box. This places a box (or a border) around the paragraph.
5. Click the **Shading** tab, and then click the **Yellow** tile located on the seventh row down, third column from the left, on the grid of color tiles. This creates a yellow shaded background for the paragraph. Note that you can use the procedure outlined in Steps 3 through 5 to shade any paragraph.
6. Click the **OK** button on the Borders and Shading dialog box to return to the document, and then deselect the paragraph. See Figure 8-5.

Figure 8-5 PARAGRAPH FORMATTED WITH KEY PARAGRAPH STYLE

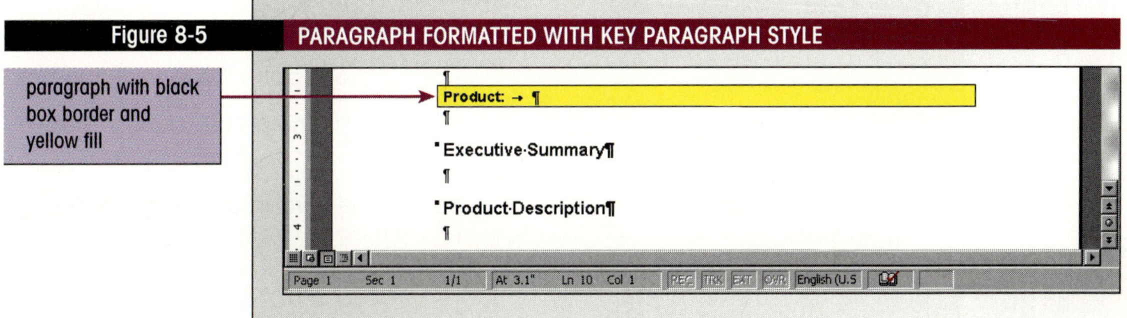

Now you're ready to create a style based on the formatting of this paragraph.

7. Select the "Product:" paragraph again, and create a new style. In the New Style dialog box, name the style **Key Paragraph**. Leave the Style type set to paragraph. You don't need to change any formatting because all the new formatting features appear in the Description section of the New Style dialog box. Within the New Style dialog box, make sure the **Add to template** check box is unchecked, and check the **Automatically update** checkbox to select it. This tells Word that if you change any paragraph to which the Key Paragraph style has been applied, the style will be automatically updated so that the change appears in all paragraphs with that style applied.
8. Click the **OK** button on the New Style dialog box, click the **Close** button on the Style dialog box, and then deselect the paragraph.
9. Click the **Style** list arrow on the Formatting toolbar to verify that the Key Paragraph style appears on the list. See Figure 8-6. Close the list without applying a style by clicking anywhere in the document window.

Figure 8-6 STYLE LIST

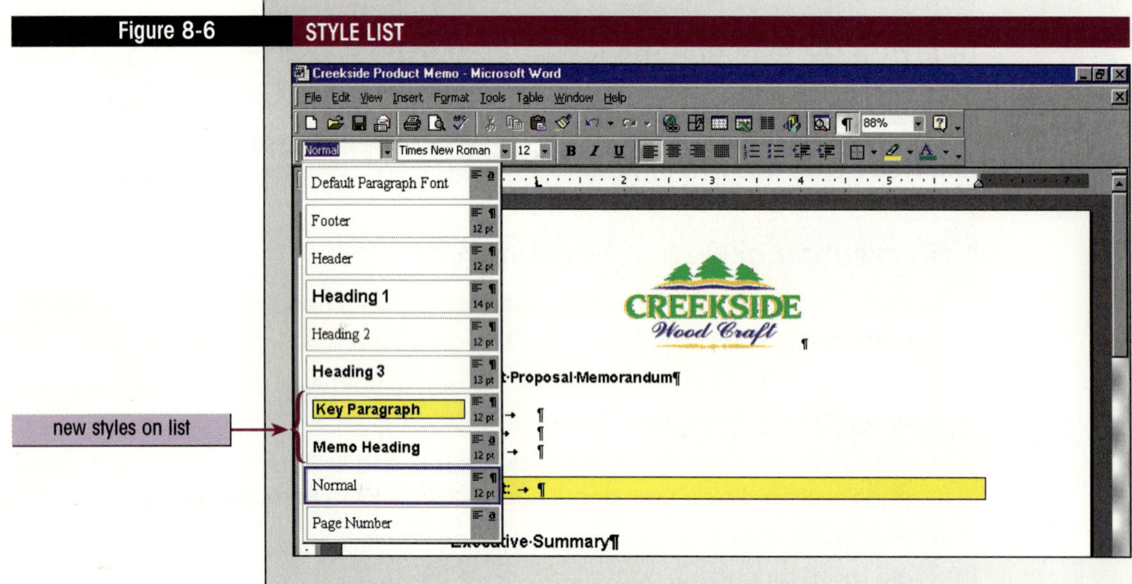

Modifying an Existing Style

Darrell has already modified the Heading-1 style, but he wants you to add borders and shading to it. You decide to place a box border around the heading, fill the box with blue, and make the text white so it stands out.

To modify the Heading-1 style:

1. Click **Format** on the menu bar, and then click **Style** to open the Style dialog box.
2. Click **Heading 1** in the Styles list box, and then click the **Modify** button. The Modify Style dialog box opens.
3. Click the **Format** button, and then click **Border**. The Borders and Shading dialog box opens.

4. Change the border setting to **Box** and the shading to **Blue** (fifth row down, sixth column from the left).
5. Click the **OK** button to close the Borders and Shading dialog box. You return to the Modify Style dialog box. Next, you'll change the font color to white so that the heading appears as white text on a blue background.
6. Click the **Format** button, click **Font** to open the Font dialog box, change the **Font color** from Automatic to white, and then click the **OK** button. You return to the Modify Style dialog box.
7. Click the **OK** button in the Modify Style dialog box, and then click the **Close** button in the Style dialog box. Word applies the new formatting to any existing Heading-1 text, so all the headings change to white text on a blue background. See Figure 8-7.

Figure 8-7 DOCUMENT WINDOW WITH NEW HEADING-1 STYLE

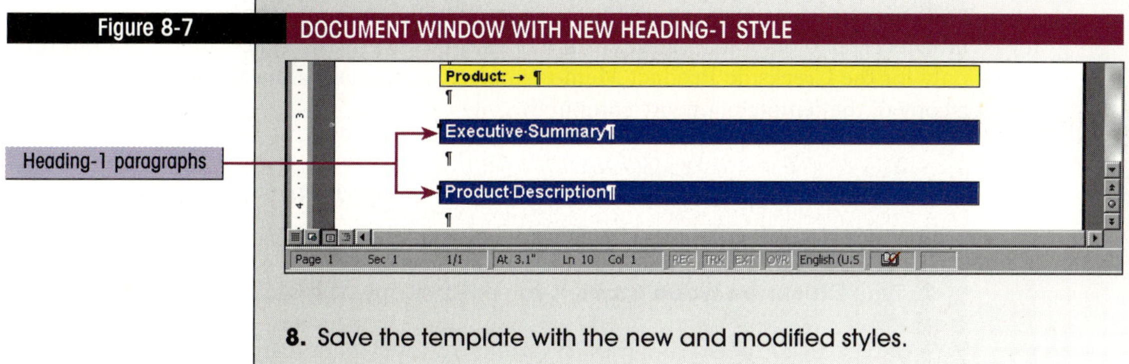

8. Save the template with the new and modified styles.

You're ready to begin to automate the template by creating AutoText entries.

Automating Word with AutoText

AutoText enables you to insert frequently used text (such as a phrase or blocks of text) or graphics (such as a drawing or scanned photograph) into your documents, quickly and efficiently, with just a few keystrokes or mouse clicks. For example, you might make your signature block for a letter ("Sincerely," four blank lines, and your name and title) an AutoText entry, so you could insert the text in an instant; or, you might create an AutoText entry with a company name and a sized logo.

Two advantages of AutoText are its speed and its accuracy. After you create an error-free AutoText entry, you can insert it into your document accurately every time using only a few keystrokes or mouse clicks. This is especially valuable for difficult-to-type text such as phone numbers, serial numbers, e-mail addresses, or other words and numbers not in the Word dictionary. Furthermore, Word provides a useful set of default AutoText entries for inserting common phrases, such as "Sincerely Yours," "CONFIDENTIAL," and "Dear Sir or Madam".

Creating AutoText Entries

In the product memo template, you'll create AutoText entries for the company name, "Creekside Wood Crafts," and the names and titles of two Creekside employees. (Later, Darrell will add AutoText entries for all the other employees who frequently write product proposal memos.)

REFERENCE WINDOW RW

Creating an AutoText Entry

- If necessary, type text or insert graphics into your document.
- Select the text or graphics you want as an AutoText entry.
- Click Insert on the menu bar, point to AutoText, and then click AutoText. (Clicking New adds the entry to the default template, usually Normal.dot, and not necessarily to the template you're creating.)
- Click the Look in list arrow, and select the template to which you want to attach the AutoText.
- Type a new name for the AutoText entry.
- Click the Add button.

Now you are ready to create your own AutoText entry. In most cases, you will probably want to create AutoText entries for the Normal template, so that they can be used in all documents created on your computer. In this case, however, you will create the AutoText entry only for the Creekside Product Memo template, so that it will be available to any user with a copy of the template, on any computer.

To create an AutoText entry for the company name:

1. Move the insertion point to the blank line below the "Executive Summary" heading.
2. Type **Creekside Wood Crafts**. If you misspell any words, correct the spelling now.

   TROUBLE? If AutoCorrect marks "Creekside" as a misspelled word, right-click the word, and then click Ignore All. The template will now accept Creekside as correctly spelled.

3. Select the phrase "Creekside Wood Crafts," but don't select the end-of-paragraph symbol. Remember that any text you select, including typos and spaces, will be included in the AutoText entry.
4. Click **Insert** on the menu bar, point to **AutoText**, and then click **AutoText** to open the AutoCorrect dialog box with the AutoText tab selected. Click the **Look in** list arrow, and click **Creekside Product Memo (template)**. This ensures that the AutoText is attached to the indicated template and not to the Normal template.

   Next, you'll type a new name for the AutoText entry. Usually, you'll want to select a short abbreviation so you can insert the AutoText entry into your document by typing only a few letters.

5. If necessary, highlight the suggested AutoText name (or click in the Enter AutoText entries here text box), and then type **cr** as the abbreviation for "Creekside Wood Crafts." See Figure 8-8.

Figure 8-8 AUTOTEXT TAB OF AUTOCORRECT DIALOG BOX

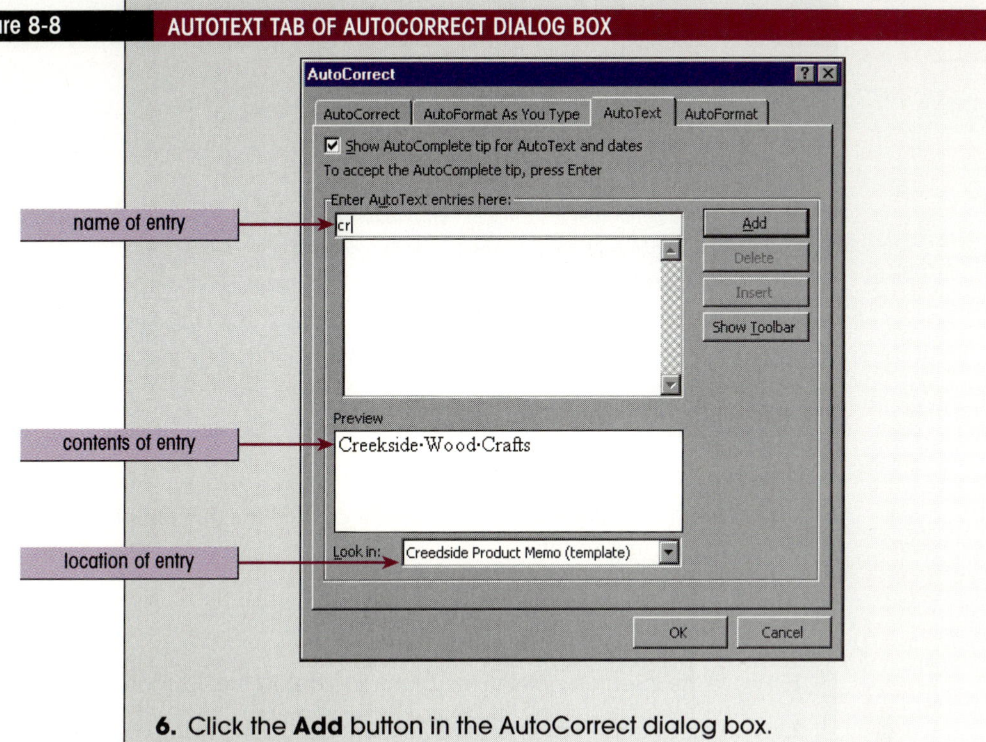

6. Click the **Add** button in the AutoCorrect dialog box.

Now, Creekside employees can use AutoText to insert the company name into a product proposal memo. After you create AutoText entries for two employees, you'll test the entries to see how easy they are to use.

To create additional AutoText entries:

1. Type **Darrell Brousseau, Assistant Product Manager** to replace the company name. Don't worry that Word marks "Brousseau" as misspelled, but correct any other typing errors.
2. Select the phrase you just typed, but not the end-of-paragraph symbol.
3. Click **Insert** on the menu bar, point to **AutoText**, click **AutoText**, type the abbreviation **db**, and click the **Add** button. Notice that you didn't have to change the Look in list box because you've already set the default template to Creekside Product Menu.
4. Repeat Steps 1 through 3 for **Margaret Fox, Vice President of Product Development**, using the abbreviation **mf**.
5. Delete the employee name and title so it doesn't become boilerplate in the template, and then save the template.

You can add as many AutoText entries to a template as you like, but for now you'll work with just these three entries.

Inserting an AutoText Entry into a Document

When you use AutoText to insert text into a document, the insertion point should be located exactly where you want the AutoText entry to appear.

REFERENCE WINDOW RW

Inserting AutoText into a Document
- Move the insertion point where you want to insert the entry.
- Type the name (or abbreviation) of the AutoText entry.
- Press the F3 key.

Or, if you don't remember the AutoText entry abbreviation:
- Move the insertion point where you want to insert the entry.
- Click Insert on the menu bar, point to AutoText, and then click AutoText.
- Click the AutoText tab in the AutoCorrect dialog box, and then click a name (or abbreviation) in the list of AutoText entries.
- Click the Insert button.

You'll test the three AutoText entries you created for this template. Because this is a test, the location isn't important.

To insert an AutoText entry:

1. Leave the insertion point in the blank line below the "Executive Summary" heading.
2. Type **cr**, and then press the **F3** key. The company name appears.

   This is the simplest way to insert an AutoText entry. But if you don't remember the abbreviation, you can use the menus to insert the entry.
3. Delete the company name from the current line.
4. Click **Insert** on the menu bar, point to **AutoText**, and then click **AutoText** to open the AutoCorrect dialog box.
5. Double-click **db** in the list of AutoText entries. Darrell Brousseau's name and title appear in the document. Both methods of inserting AutoText are simpler than typing the full entry each time.
6. Test the AutoText entry for Margaret Fox.
7. Delete any text you inserted with AutoText, so it doesn't become boilerplate in the template.

As you can see, AutoText entries are easy to create and to use.

Printing a List of the AutoText Items

If you create many AutoText entries or if you use Word's many default entries, you might find it difficult to remember all of them. You also might want to let others know what entries are available for a particular template. In either case, you can print a list of all the AutoText entries.

REFERENCE WINDOW RW

Printing a List of the AutoText Entries

- Click File on the menu bar, and then click Print.
- Click the Print what list arrow, and then click AutoText entries.
- Click the OK button.

You'll print the AutoText entries you just created so Darrell can tell what abbreviations you've used when he adds entries for other employees.

To print AutoText entries:

1. Click **File** on the menu bar, and then click **Print** to open the Print dialog box.
2. Click the **Print what** list arrow, and then click **AutoText** entries.
3. Click the **OK** button. Word prints a list of AutoText entries for the Creekside Product Memo template. Your printout also lists the default entries in the global template.
4. Save the current version of the template.

The AutoText entries are available for any document created from the product memo template.

Customizing **AutoCorrect**

A feature closely related to AutoText is AutoCorrect. As you recall, AutoCorrect checks your document for errors as you type and automatically corrects common typing errors, such as letter transposition ("adn" to "and"), a lowercase first letter in a sentence, and two initial capital letters ("CReekside" to "Creekside").

Sometimes, however, AutoCorrect makes unwanted corrections. For example, many Creekside product proposal memos refer to one of Creekside's competitors, Creative Crafts, Incorporated. The company officially calls itself CCinc (pronounced "C-sink"), so Darrell wants you to make "CCinc" an exception in AutoCorrect. An **exception** is a word or phrase that AutoCorrect doesn't automatically modify. When you create an exception, it applies to all templates, not just the Normal template.

To create an exception in AutoCorrect:

1. Click **Tools** on the menu bar, click **AutoCorrect**, and then, if necessary, click the **AutoCorrect** tab.
2. Make sure the five check boxes are checked. Now, you're ready to create an exception.
3. Click the **Exceptions** button on the AutoCorrect dialog box to open AutoCorrect Exceptions dialog box, and then click the **INitial CAps** tab. Here, you'll type the name you want as an exception to the initial capitalization rule of AutoCorrect.

4. Type **CCinc** in the **Don't correct** text box, and then click the **Add** button.

   You can use the First Letter tab to add abbreviations that you don't necessarily want followed by a capitalized word.

5. Click the **OK** button in the AutoCorrect Exceptions dialog box, and then click the **OK** button on the AutoCorrect dialog box.

6. Save the template.

Now, when you type CCinc, AutoCorrect won't change the name to "Ccinc." Note that this AutoCorrect exception applies to all documents created or edited with your installation of Word; it doesn't become part of the Creekside Product Memo template or the Normal template. Therefore, all Creekside employees will have to make the same AutoCorrect exception on their computers.

So far, the template contains boilerplate text and graphics, modified styles, and AutoText entries. Next, you'll add a watermark, customize the toolbars, and insert fields.

Session 8.1 Quick Check

1. What is a template? List three types of documents for which you might create a template.
2. What is boilerplate? How are templates and boilerplates related?
3. List five features a template might contain.
4. List three advantages of using templates.
5. In general, how do you create and save a template?
6. In general, how do you define the Heading-1 style as white characters on a blue background?
7. What are the advantages of AutoText?
8. What is an AutoCorrect exception?

SESSION 8.2

In this session, you'll add a watermark to the Creekside Product Memo template and customize the toolbars in the template. Also, you'll automate the template by inserting fields within the template.

Creating a Watermark

A **watermark** is text or graphics that appear behind or in front of existing text in a document. Usually, the text or graphic appears in a lighter shade in the background of each printed page. You add a watermark to a header or footer so that it will appear on every page in the document (or on every page on which the header or footer appears). Placing the watermark in a header or footer also ensures that it will appear behind the document text.

REFERENCE WINDOW RW

Creating a Watermark

- Click View on the menu bar, and click Header and Footer.
- Insert and position a graphic (clip art, drawing, WordArt, picture, etc.) anywhere on a document page.
- If you inserted a graphic, select it, click Format on the menu bar, click Picture, click the Picture tab if necessary, click the Color list arrow, click Watermark, and then click OK.
- To prevent your watermark from obscuring the main text, you may want to change its color to gray or some other light shade.
- Click the Close button on the Header and Footer toolbar.

Darrell wants you to add a light background watermark containing the word "PROPOSAL" to the product memo template.

To add a watermark to the template:

1. If you took a break after the last session, make sure Word is running, the Creekside Product Memo template is open, Word is in Print Layout View, and nonprinting characters are displayed.
2. Click **View** on the menu bar, and then click **Header and Footer**. The Header and Footer toolbar appears on the screen, a Header text box opens at the top of the page, and the main text of the document becomes dimmed. Next, you will insert a WordArt image with the word "PROPOSAL" in 48-point, bold, Arial font.
3. Click **Insert** on the menu bar, point to **Picture**, and click **WordArt**. The WordArt Gallery dialog box opens with a selection of WordArt styles.
4. Click the style in the top row, second column from the left (the one in which the text angles upward), and then click the **OK** button. The WordArt Gallery dialog box closes and the Edit WordArt Text dialog box opens.
5. Type **PROPOSAL**, set the font to **Arial**, set the font size to **48** points, click the **Bold** button **B**, and click the **OK** button.

You'll position the image and change the WordArt font color and fill so that the WordArt is lighter and more attractive. You'll use a gradient fill effect. A **gradient** is a type of fill in which one color blends into another.

To position the image and change the fill:

1. Position the pointer over one of the letters in the WordArt, and then drag the WordArt to the approximate position shown in Figure 8-9. You might want to move the Header and Footer toolbar or the WordArt toolbar to see the document better.

   TROUBLE? If the WordArt disappears, you probably clicked outside its borders. Click View on the menu bar, click Headers and Footers, and then repeat Step 1.

Figure 8-9 DOCUMENT WITH WATERMARK

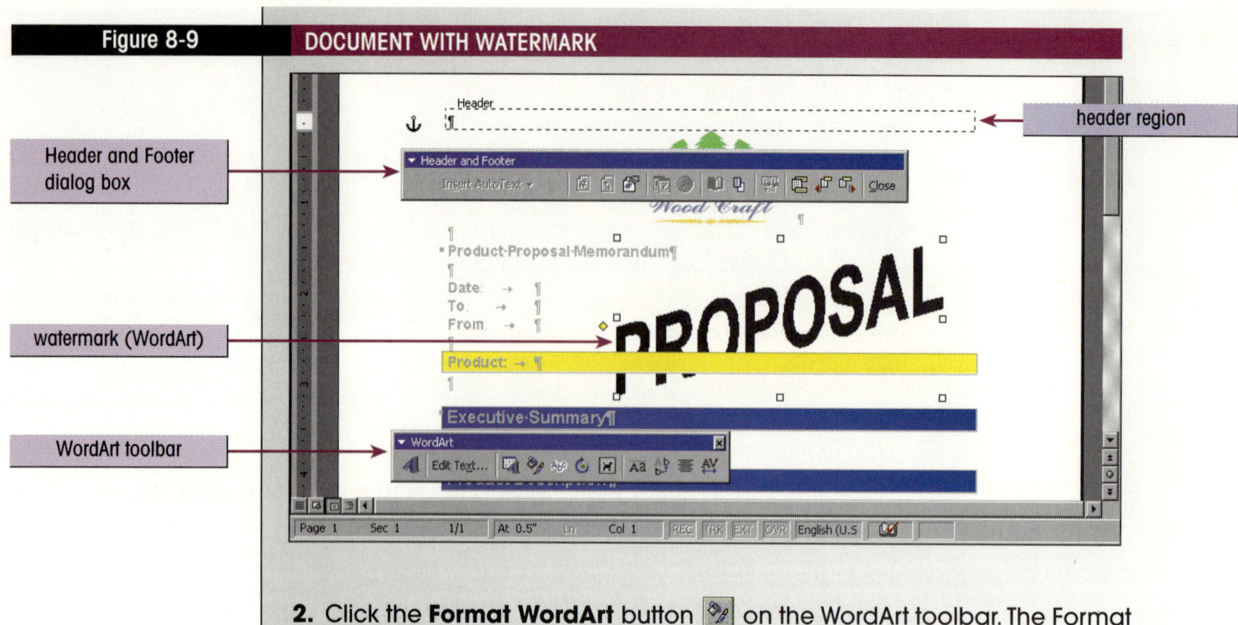

2. Click the **Format WordArt** button on the WordArt toolbar. The Format WordArt dialog box opens.

3. Click the **Colors and Lines** tab, click the **Color** list arrow in the Fill section, click **Fill Effects** to open the Fill Effects dialog box, if necessary click the Gradient tab, click the **One color** option button, click the **Color 1** list arrow, click the **Gray-40%** tile (located in the rightmost column, middle row), and if necessary, click the **Horizontal** option button in the Shading styles section. Accept the default shading variant. See Figure 8-10.

Figure 8-10 FILL EFFECTS DIALOG BOX

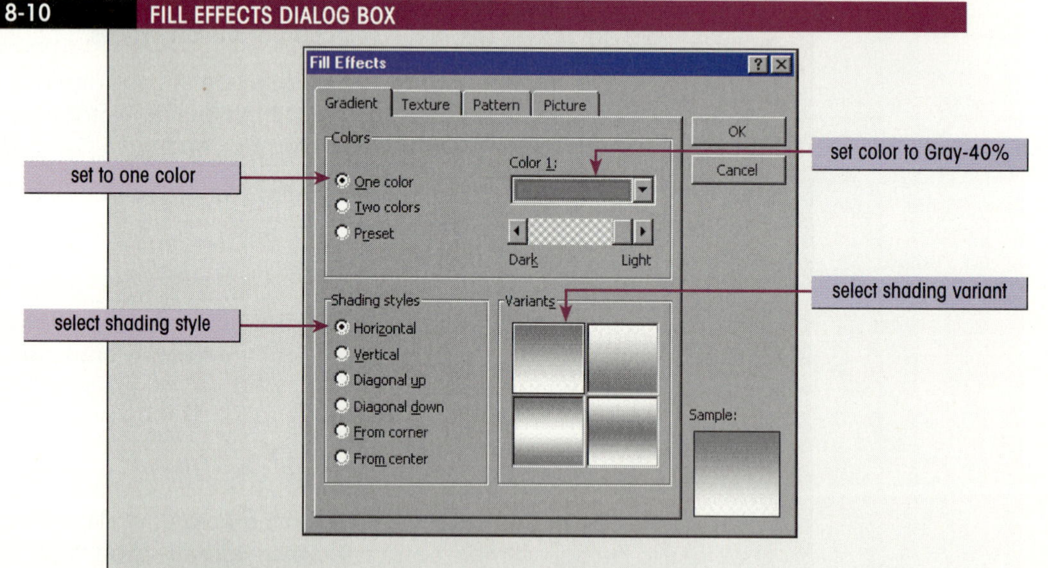

4. Click the **OK** button in the Fill Effects dialog box. You return to the Format WordArt dialog box.

5. In the Line section, change the Color to the same Gray-40%, click the **Layout** tab and click the **Behind text** icon, and then click the **OK** button.

6. Click the **Close** button on the Header and Footer toolbar. See Figure 8-11.

Figure 8-11 DOCUMENT WITH COMPLETED WATERMARK

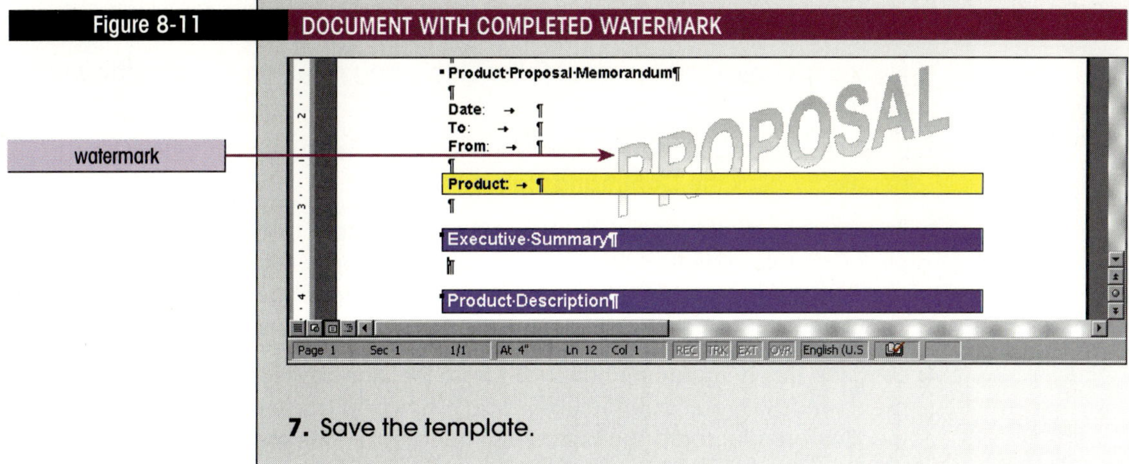

7. Save the template.

Every page of a proposal created from the product memo template will contain this background watermark. To edit the watermark, click View on the menu bar, click Header and Footer to open the Header and Footer toolbar, scroll to the watermark, and click the watermark to open the WordArt toolbar. Then you could edit the WordArt image using items on the toolbar.

Customizing the Toolbars

Word allows you to customize every part of a template, including the toolbars, menus, and shortcut keys.

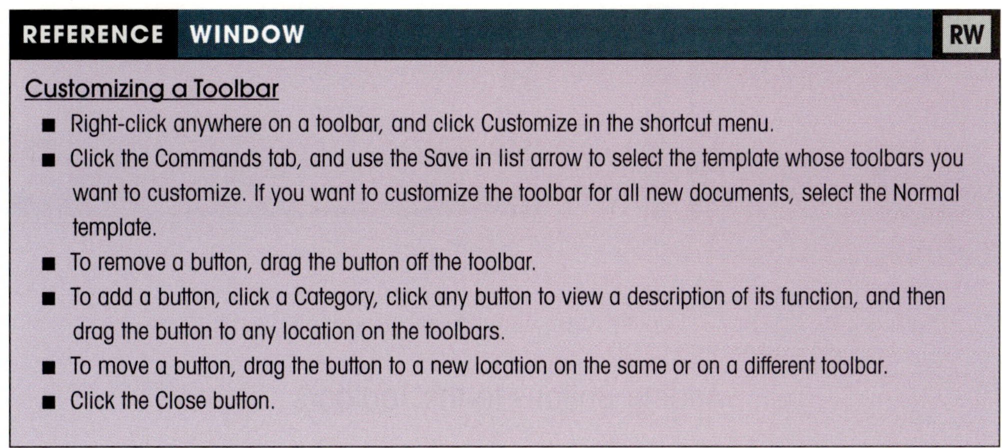

REFERENCE WINDOW RW

Customizing a Toolbar

- Right-click anywhere on a toolbar, and click Customize in the shortcut menu.
- Click the Commands tab, and use the Save in list arrow to select the template whose toolbars you want to customize. If you want to customize the toolbar for all new documents, select the Normal template.
- To remove a button, drag the button off the toolbar.
- To add a button, click a Category, click any button to view a description of its function, and then drag the button to any location on the toolbars.
- To move a button, drag the button to a new location on the same or on a different toolbar.
- Click the Close button.

Darrell wants you to customize the Standard and the Formatting toolbars in the template to meet the special needs of Creekside employees who create product proposal memos.

Removing Buttons from the Toolbars

Darrell has asked you to remove the Insert Hyperlink button from the Standard toolbar and the Highlight buttons from the Formatting toolbar because he doesn't want employees using these features when creating product proposal memos.

To remove buttons from the toolbars:

1. Right-click anywhere on any toolbar, including a button, to open the shortcut menu.
2. Click **Customize** on the shortcut menu to open the Customize dialog box. If necessary, click the **Commands** tab.
3. If necessary, click the **Save** in list arrow at the bottom of the dialog box, and click Creekside Product Memo. (You probably won't be able to see the entire name of the template.) This ensures that the changes you make to the toolbars affect only the current template, not the Normal template.
4. Drag the **Insert Hyperlink** button from the Standard toolbar into the document window. (You could actually drag the button anywhere except to another location on a toolbar.) The button disappears from the toolbar.
5. Drag the **Highlight** button from the Formatting toolbar. See Figure 8-12.

Figure 8-12 CUSTOMIZING THE TOOLBARS

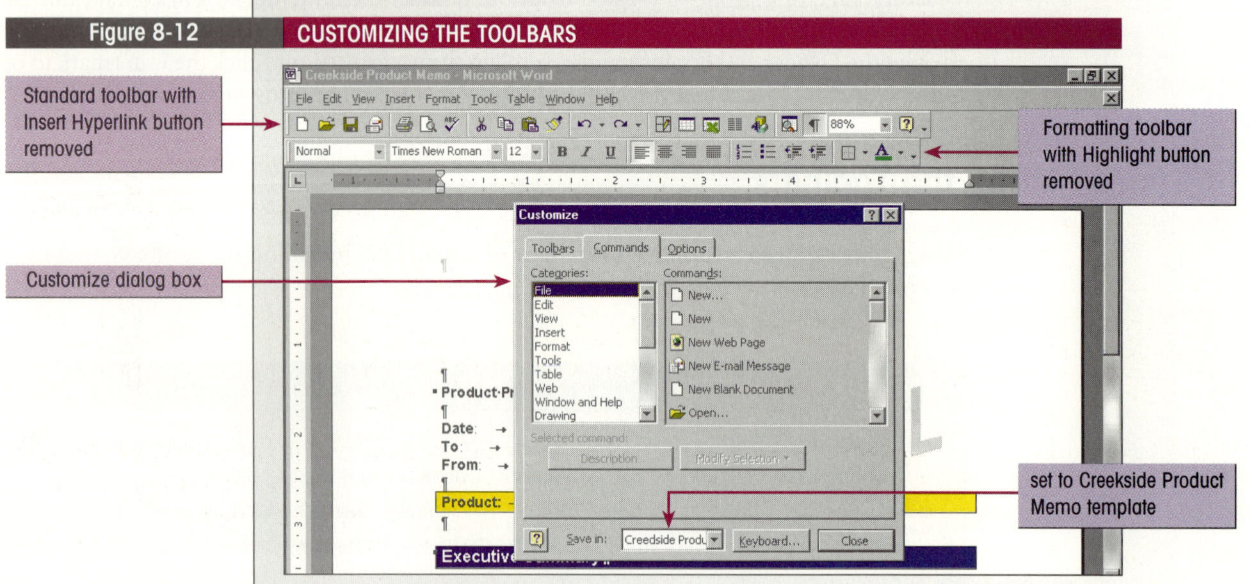

The buttons you removed are no longer visible on the screen.

Adding Buttons to the Toolbars

With the Customize dialog box still open, you're ready to add new buttons to the toolbars. As you can see, the dialog box displays a list of categories and the buttons available for the current category. Darrell wants you to add the View Field Codes button to the Standard toolbar, which will be useful later, when you add field codes to the template. Then, he wants you to create an AutoText button for the company name and add it to the Formatting toolbar.

To add buttons to the toolbar:

1. Make sure the Save in list box is still set to the Creekside Product Memo template.
2. Click **View** in the **Categories** list. The View commands, including the View Field Codes command you want to add, appear.

   Notice the Description button. When you click it, a brief description of the selected name in the Commands list box appears.
3. Click the **View Field Codes** button {a}, and then click the Description button. See Figure 8-13.

Figure 8-13 ADDING THE VIEW FIELD CODES BUTTON TO THE STANDARD TOOLBAR

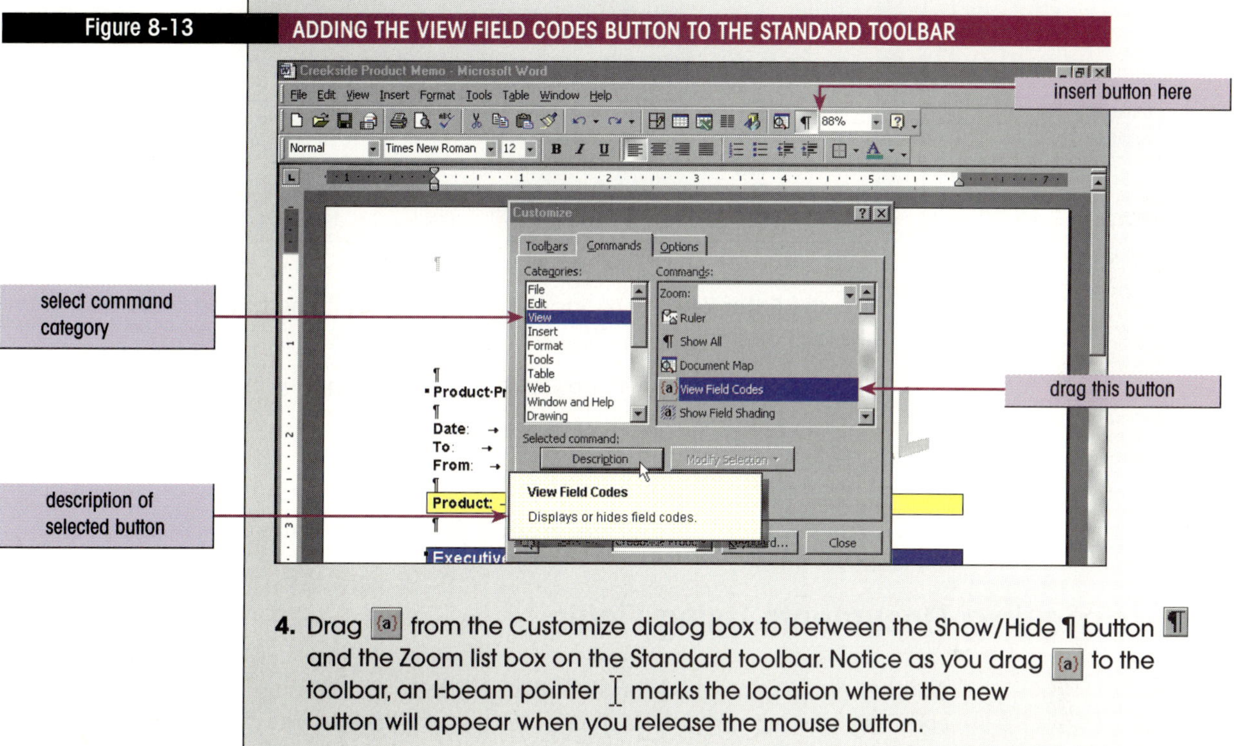

4. Drag {a} from the Customize dialog box to between the Show/Hide ¶ button ¶ and the Zoom list box on the Standard toolbar. Notice as you drag {a} to the toolbar, an I-beam pointer marks the location where the new button will appear when you release the mouse button.

Next, you'll add an AutoText button for the company name to the Formatting toolbar.

To add an AutoText button to the toolbar:

1. Verify that the Commands tab of the Customize dialog box is displayed, and then click **AutoText** near the end of the Categories list. The AutoText entries you created earlier replace the command names. You want to create a toolbar button for the "cr" entry (for "Creekside Wood Crafts").
2. Drag **cr** to the immediate right of the **Border** button on the Formatting toolbar, right-click the **cr** AutoText button to display a shortcut menu, and then if necessary, click **Text Only (Always)** to select it.

   TROUBLE? If you release the mouse button and the cr AutoText button doesn't appear on the toolbar, you might have positioned the button too far to the right of the Borders button. Make sure the I-beam pointer appears on the toolbar before you release the mouse button.

   Next, you'll change the button name from "cr" (lowercase) to "CR" (uppercase).

3. Right-click the **cr** button to display the shortcut menu, select **cr** in the **Name** text box on the shortcut menu, and then type **CR** in the Name text box. See Figure 8-14.

Figure 8-14 RENAMING AN AUTOTEXT BUTTON

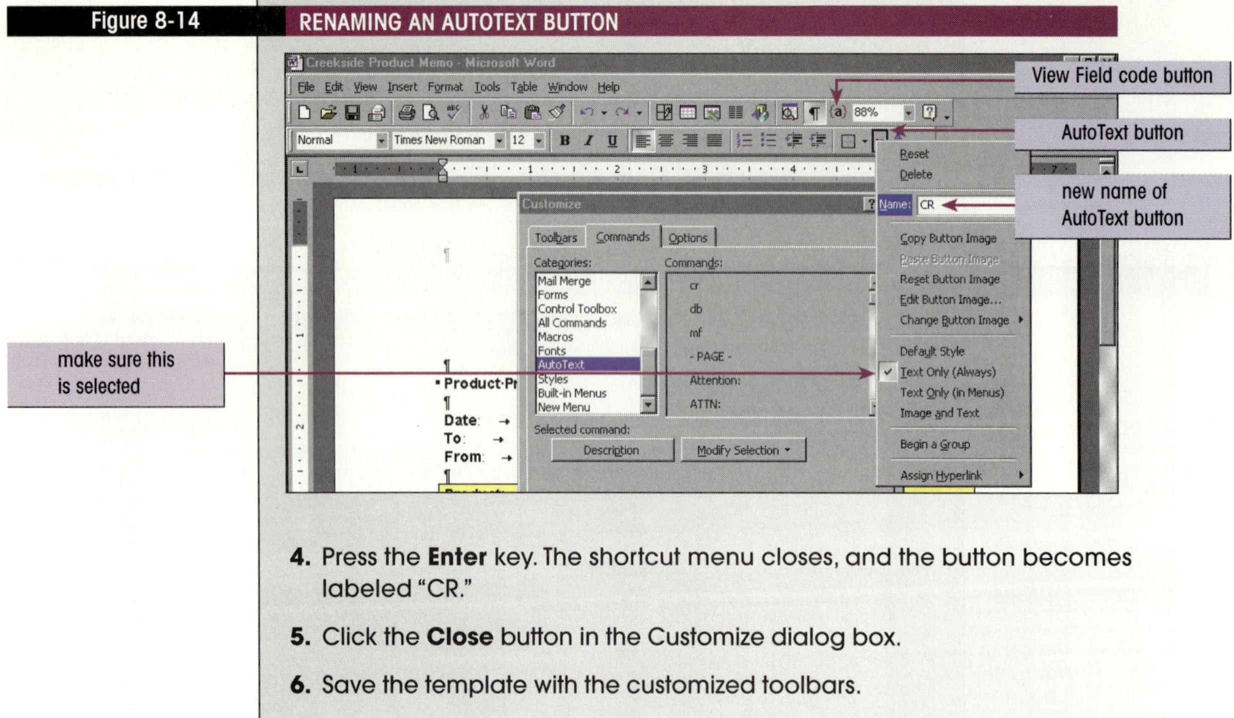

4. Press the **Enter** key. The shortcut menu closes, and the button becomes labeled "CR."
5. Click the **Close** button in the Customize dialog box.
6. Save the template with the customized toolbars.

With these customized toolbars, creating product proposal memos is faster.

Automating Documents Using Fields

Another powerful method for automating a document is using fields. A **field** is a special code that instructs Word to insert information, such as the current date, filename, or author's name, into a document. You already know how to use fields to create a mail merge. Figure 8-15 lists the fields that you'll include in the product memo template.

Figure 8-15 FIELDS FOR CREEKSIDE PRODUCT MEMO TEMPLATE

FIELD	CODE (EXAMPLE)	ACTION
Author	{AUTHOR}	Inserts document's author name from Summary tab of Properties dialog box
Date	{DATE\@"MMMM d, yyyy"	Inserts current date/time according to date-time picture
Fill-in	{FILLIN "Your name?"*MERGEFORMAT}	Inserts information filled in by user
NumPages	{NUMPAGES}	Inserts total number of pages in document
Page	{PAGE}	Inserts current page number
Ref	{REF BookmarkName}	Inserts contents of specified bookmark

When you insert a field into a document, the corresponding code includes the name of the field and optional instructions and switches enclosed in braces ({ }, also called French brackets or curly brackets) that mark the beginning and end of the code. An **instruction** is a word or phrase that specifies what the field should do—such as display a prompt (a phrase that tells the user how to proceed). A **switch** is a command following *,\#,\@, or \! that turns on or off certain features of the field. Among other things, a switch can specify how the result of the field is formatted. Figure 8-16 shows a field code that contains a field name, instructions, and a switch. The field name, FILLIN, specifies that this field asks the user to supply ("fill-in") some information. The instruction is a prompt ("Product Name:") that tells the user what to type. The switch ("* MERGEFORMAT") specifies that the field's result (the user fill-in information) should retain any formatting applied to the field even if the user fills in new information.

Figure 8-16 COMPONENTS OF A FIELD CODE

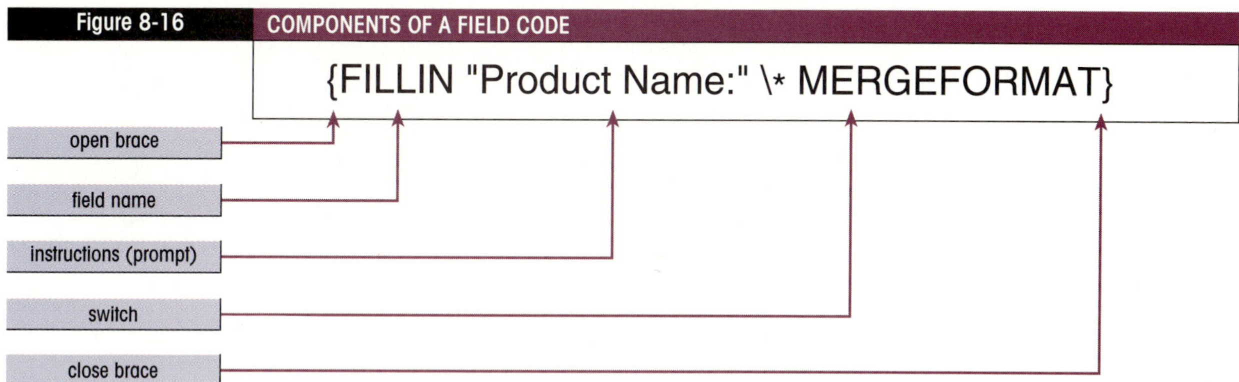

Whereas all field codes must include braces and a field name, not all field codes include instructions and switches. The Field dialog box shows which elements each field code must contain.

Inserting and Editing the Date Field

You're already familiar with the Date field, which inserts the current date and time, or specified parts of the date and time in the format you select, such as the full name for the current month ("February") without the day, year, or any part of the time. Creekside Wood Crafts uses the Date field in the title of its monthly report template.

You can designate the exact format of the date and time by changing the date-time picture field switch. The **date-time picture** is a pattern of abbreviations and punctuation that follows the switch code \@ and that specifies the content and format of the date and time. Figure 8–17 shows the date-time picture options.

You could use the characters in this table to create a date-time picture in any date and time format. For example, the full Date code for the date format "Friday, February 5, 2001" would be: DATE \@ "dddd, MMMM d, yyyy"}. For product proposal memos, the company uses the "5 Feb 01" date format.

REFERENCE WINDOW RW

Inserting and Editing Fields

- Move the insertion point where you want to insert the field.
- Click insert on the menu bar, and then click Field.
- Click a field category.
- Click the field you want to insert.
- If necessary, click the Options button and change all desired switches.
- Either click the OK button and then edit the field code (that is, modify the field code's instructions or switches) from within the document, or edit the field code in the dialog box and then click the OK button.

Figure 8-17 DATE-TIME PICTURE OPTIONS

CHARACTER	PURPOSE	EXAMPLE
M	Month in numeric format	2 (for Feb)
MM	Month in numeric format with leading zero	02
MMM	Month as three-letter abbreviation	Feb
MMMM	Month as full name	February
d	Day in numeric format	5 (for 5th day of month)
dd	Day in numeric format with leading zero	05
ddd	Day of week as three-letter abbreviation	Mon
dddd	Day of week as full name	Monday
yy	Year in two-digit format	01
yyyy	Year in four-digit format	2001

You'll insert the Date field into the template with the Field command (not with the Date command) so you can modify the date-time picture.

To insert the Date field using the Insert Field command:

1. Move the insertion point to the right of the tab mark on the "Date" line near the beginning of the memo.
2. Click **Insert** on the menu bar, and then click **Field**. The Field dialog box opens.
3. Click **Date and Time** in the Categories list, and then click **Date** in the Field names list. See Figure 8-18.

Figure 8-18 FIELD DIALOG BOX

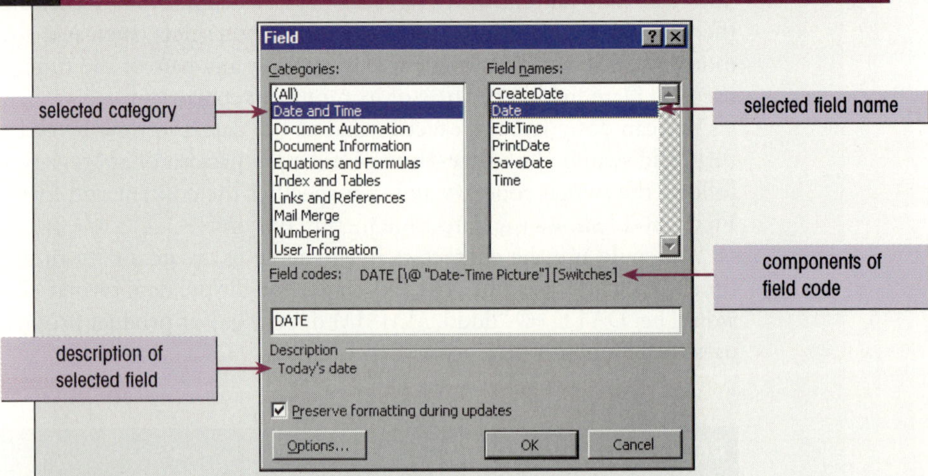

4. Click the **OK** button in the dialog box to insert the Date code in the document.

5. If you see today's date (that is, the result of the field code) but not the date code itself, click the **View Field Codes** button on the customized Standard toolbar. Notice that the View Field Codes button is a toggle switch; it alternates between showing the results of the fields and showing the field codes. You can also toggle between the results and the codes by pressing (Alt)+F9.

Currently, the format switch in the Date field code is "* MERGEFORMAT," which tells Word to retain the current formatting even if the result changes. For example, if you were to change the current field result to bold, Word would retain the bold characters even if the date changed. Because the Creekside employees always use the regular font for the date, you'll edit the field code to remove the MERGEFORMAT switch and insert the date-time picture switch using the usual Word editing commands. You need to change the format so that it displays dates similar to "5 Feb 01"—Creekside's standard date format.

To edit the Date field code:

1. Click the **View Field Codes** button on the customized Standard toolbar so you can see the field results—today's date in the format "2/5/01."
2. Click again to view the field code.
3. Select * MERGEFORMAT in the Date field code. Because you're editing a field code, the background for the code is gray and the selected text is white on a darker gray background. See Figure 8-19.

Figure 8-19 FIELD CODE IN DOCUMENT TEMPLATE

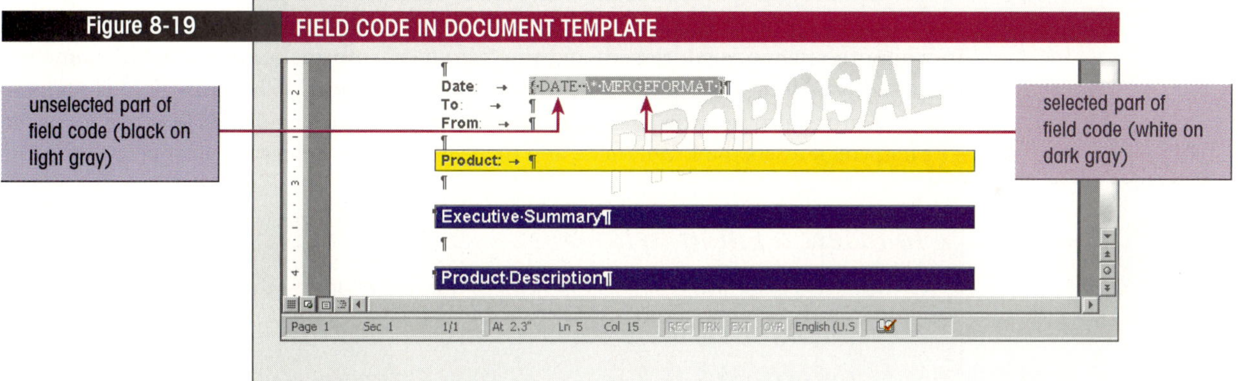

TROUBLE? If the field code is not shaded, click Tools on the menu bar, click Options, click the View tab, click the Field shading list arrow in the Show section, click When selected, and then click the OK button.

4. Type **\@ "d MMM yy"** (including the quotation marks). Be sure to type the letter "M" in uppercase. The complete field code is: DATE \@ "d MMM yy"}.

TROUBLE? If the quotation marks on your screen are curly rather than straight, don't worry. Word accepts either the typographic ("curly") or the straight quotation marks in field codes.

5. Click on the customized Standard toolbar to see the result of the edited field code.

At this point, the date still appears in the format "2/5/01." Before it will appear in the new format, you need to update the field.

Updating a Field

The date format hasn't changed even though you changed the format switch. This is because you simply changed the text of the field code in the document, not the underlying field itself. For the change to take effect in the field, you must update it.

To update the Date field:

1. If necessary, click the date (the result of the field code) to select it. The date appears in light gray.
2. Press the **F9** key. The date changes from the "2/5/01" format to the "5 Feb 01" format (but with today's date).
3. Click the **View Field Codes** button {a} on the customized Standard toolbar to view the field code. As you can see, the field code retains your editing.

Every product proposal memo will contain the current date in the desired format.

Inserting and Editing the Fill-in Field

When Creekside employees begin a new document using the product memo template, you want Word to prompt them to fill in the "To" information (that is, the name of the person to whom the memo is addressed) and the "Product" information (that is, the name of the proposed product). That is the purpose of the **Fill-in field**. When this field is updated, it causes Word to prompt you to "fill in" specific information.

First, you'll insert the Fill-in field, and then you'll edit it to provide an appropriate prompt.

To insert a Fill-in field:

1. Move the insertion point to the right of the tab mark on the "To" line.
2. Click **Insert** on the menu bar, and then click **Field**. The Field dialog box opens.
3. Click the **Mail Merge** category, and then click **Fill-in** in the Field names list box. The Field dialog box displays information about the Fill-in field.
4. Click the **OK** button. A blank dialog box labeled "Microsoft Word" appears. You'll edit the Fill-in field code so this dialog box will display a prompt for users to enter information.
5. Click the **OK** button without entering any text. Creekside employees will fill in the requested information in the text box when they create memos.
6. If necessary, click the **View Field Codes** button {a} on the customized Standard toolbar to view the field code.

The Fill-in field code appears in your template. This field code has a switch, but no prompt information. You'll insert the prompt so Creekside employees will know what information to enter.

To insert a prompt into the Fill-in field:

1. Click in the middle of the two spaces between "FILLIN" and "*" in the Fill-in field code.
2. Type **"Who should receive this memo?"** (including the quotation marks).
3. Press the **F9** key to update the field. The Microsoft Word dialog box opens with the prompt you just typed. See Figure 8-20.

Figure 8-20 UPDATING THE FILL-IN FIELD

Microsoft Word

prompt

Who should receive this memo?

OK

Cancel

text box for user "fill-in" information

4. As a test, type **Executive Board**, and then click the **OK** button.
5. Click the **View Field Codes** button on the customized Standard toolbar to look at the result of the Fill-in field. As you can see, the memo is addressed to "Executive Board."
6. Click again to display the field codes.

When the Creekside employees use this template to create new product proposals, it will prompt them to insert the person or group to whom their memo is addressed. Now, you'll use the Fill-in field to create a prompt for the proposed product name.

To insert and edit another Fill-in field:

1. Move the insertion point to the right of the tab mark on the "**Product**" line.
2. Insert a Fill-in field. When the Microsoft Word dialog box opens, click the **OK** button.
3. Insert the prompt **"What is the proposed product name?"** (including the quotation marks) in the Fill-in field code at the appropriate location.
4. Press the **F9** key to update the field, type **Furniture Stencils** as a test, and then click the **OK** button.
5. Deselect the field, and then view the results of the fields. See Figure 8-21.

Figure 8-21 RESULTS FOR FIELD CODES

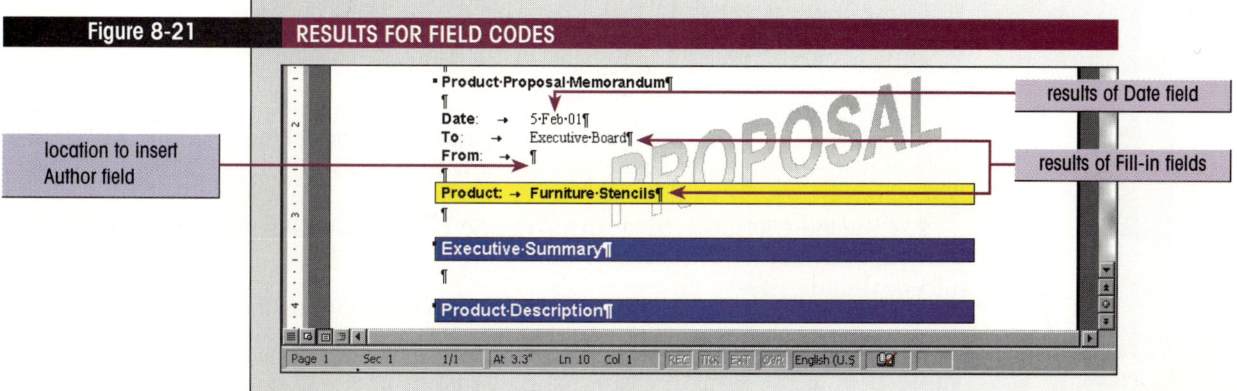

6. Return to the Field Codes View.

You're ready to insert the Author field.

Inserting the Author Field

You could simply type Darrell Brousseau's name next to the "From" heading, but then the template would be automated only for Darrell and not for other Creekside employees, or you could use a Fill-in field. The best approach, however, is to add a field that inserts the name of the document's author. The **Author field**, as it's called, gets the author's name from the Summary tab of the Properties dialog box. Word lists the registered owner of the Word application in the Author text box of the Summary tab, unless someone types in another name.

You'll make sure the author for this template is set to "Darrell Brousseau, Assistant Product Manager," and then you'll insert the Author field in the memo.

To view the author name and insert the Author field:

1. Click **File** on the menu bar, and then click **Properties** to open the Properties dialog box.
2. If necessary, click the **Summary** tab to display a summary of the document. See Figure 8-22.

Figure 8-22 PROPERTIES DIALOG BOX

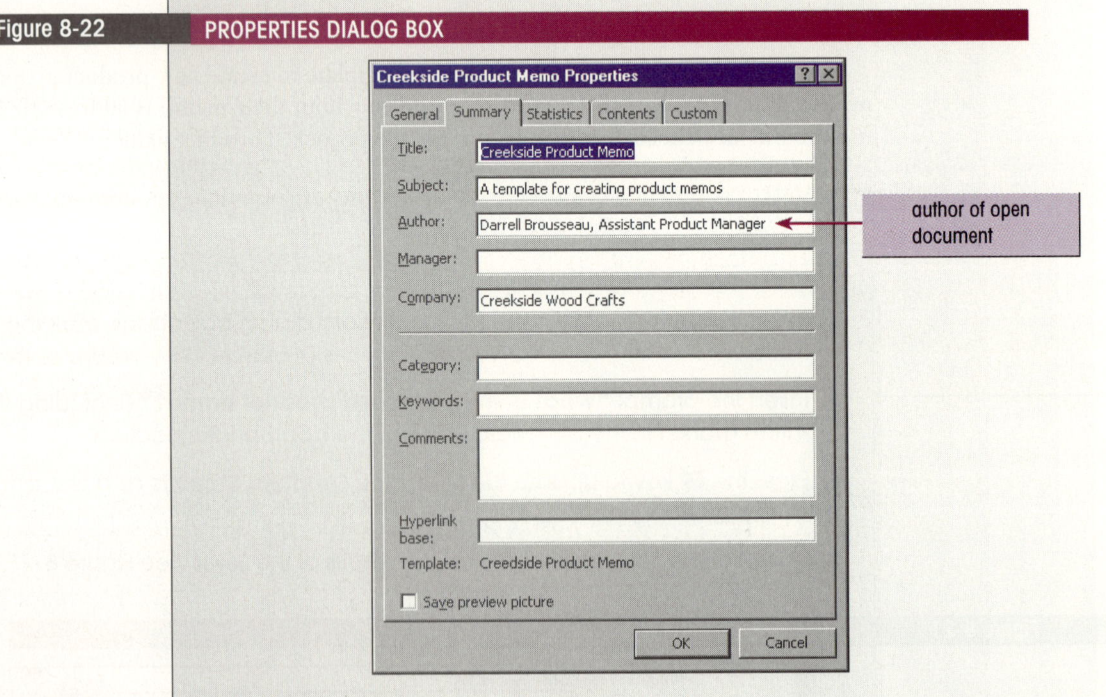

TROUBLE? If the Author isn't "Darrell Brousseau, Assistant Product Manager," delete the current author's name, and type the correct one.

3. Click the **OK** button to close the dialog box. Now, you're ready to insert the Author field.
4. Move the insertion point to the right of the tab mark on the "From" line.
5. Click **Insert** on the menu bar, and then click **Field** to open the Field dialog box.

6. Click **Document Information** in the Categories list, and then make sure **Author** is selected in the Field names list.
7. Click the **OK** button. The Author field is inserted into your template.
8. If necessary, click the **View Field Codes** button {a} on the customized Standard toolbar to view the field code. See Figure 8-23.

Figure 8-23 DOCUMENT TEMPLATE WITH FIELD CODE

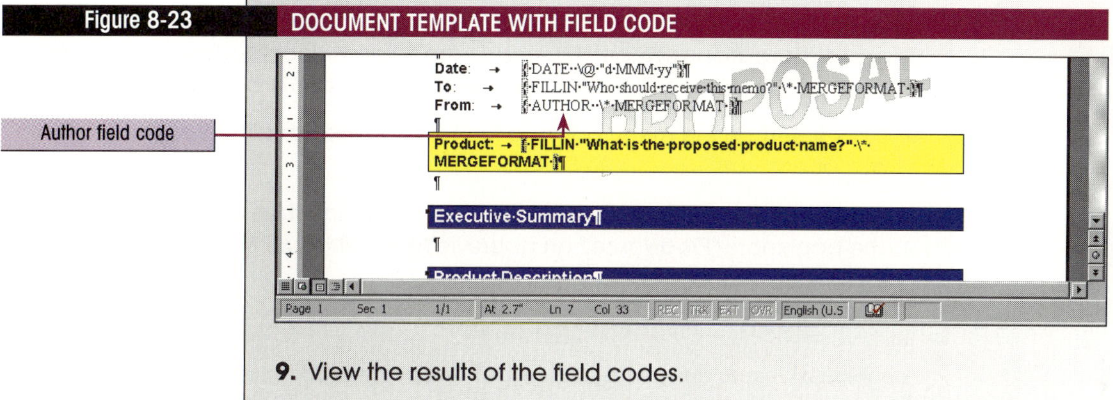

9. View the results of the field codes.

As you can see, the Author field inserts the document author's name. Whenever an employee uses this template, that employee's name will appear to the right of the "From" heading.

Inserting a Reference Field

Darrell wants the template to include a footer with specific information about the document. In particular, he wants the proposed product name and the page number to be printed at the bottom of every page. You'll use fields to insert both items in the footer. The employees who use the template will never need to edit the footer; all the information will appear automatically.

How can the proposed product name appear automatically in the footer? Recall that the template will prompt the Creekside employees to type the proposed product name in a Fill-in field. You can mark that Fill-in field as a Bookmark (text, graphics, tables, or a location that you select and assign a name) and then use a **Ref field** to cross-reference (or insert into another part of the document) the information contained in that bookmark. In the product memo template, the Ref field will duplicate the text of the Fill-in field in the footer.

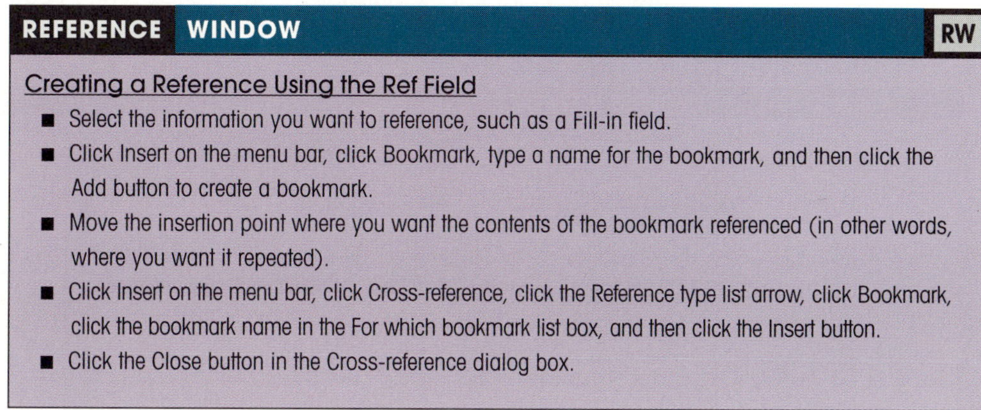

REFERENCE WINDOW RW

Creating a Reference Using the Ref Field

- Select the information you want to reference, such as a Fill-in field.
- Click Insert on the menu bar, click Bookmark, type a name for the bookmark, and then click the Add button to create a bookmark.
- Move the insertion point where you want the contents of the bookmark referenced (in other words, where you want it repeated).
- Click Insert on the menu bar, click Cross-reference, click the Reference type list arrow, click Bookmark, click the bookmark name in the For which bookmark list box, and then click the Insert button.
- Click the Close button in the Cross-reference dialog box.

You'll mark the product name Fill-in field as a bookmark, create a footer, and then insert the Ref field to insert the product name.

To mark the Fill-in field as a bookmark:

1. Make sure the document is not in Field Codes View. In this case, it's easier to work with the field results.
2. Select **Furniture Stencils**, the text of the product name Fill-in field, but not the end-of-paragraph symbol. Make sure the field is selected (dark gray or black) and not just shaded (light gray or blue); the text should be white.
3. Click **Insert** on the menu bar, and then click **Bookmark**. The Bookmark dialog box opens.
4. Type **ProdName** as the name of the bookmark, and then click the **Add** button. The bookmark "ProdName," an abbreviation of "Product Name," is added to the list of bookmarks.

A bookmark name must be a single word that begins with a letter and can be as many as 40 letters or numbers; it can't contain any spaces or symbols, such as a hyphen, slash, or asterisk. With the product name Fill-in field bookmarked, you're ready to create a footer and insert the Ref field.

To create a footer and insert the Ref field:

1. Click **View** on the menu bar, and then click **Header and Footer**. The Header and Footer toolbar opens with a blank Header text box.
2. Click the **Switch Between Header and Footer** button on the Header and Footer toolbar to display the blank Footer text box. Darrell asks you to draw a horizontal line above the footer to separate it from the body text.
3. Click the **All Borders** list arrow on the Formatting toolbar to open the Borders toolbar, and then click the **Top Border** button to insert a horizontal line across the top of the Footer text box. Now, you can type the text of the footer and insert the Ref field.
4. Type **Proposed Product:** (including the colon), and press the **spacebar**.
5. Click **Insert** on the menu bar, and then click **Cross-reference** to open the Cross-reference dialog box. Change the **Reference type** to **Bookmark**, and make sure **ProdName** is selected in the **For which bookmark** list. See Figure 8-24.

Figure 8-24 CROSS-REFERENCE DIALOG BOX

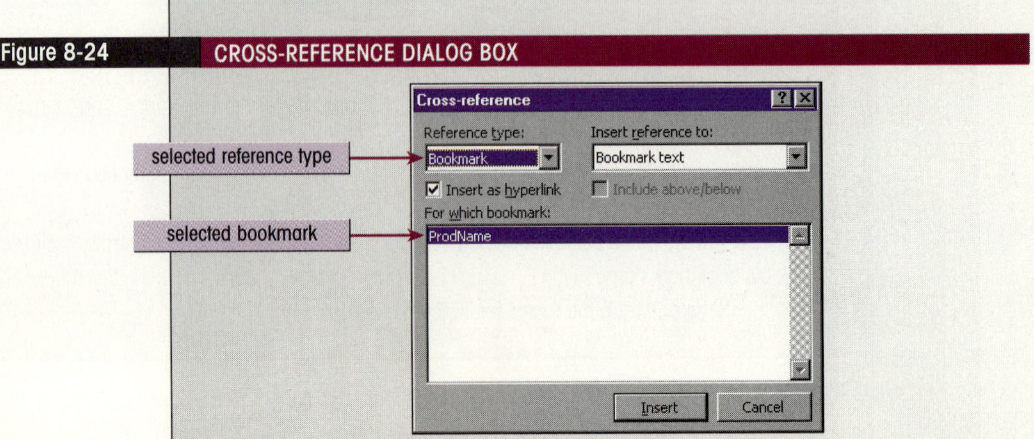

6. Click the **Insert** button, and then click the **Close** button in the Cross-reference dialog box. The phrase "Furniture Stencils" appears in the footer.
7. Turn on the Field Codes View to verify that REF field refers to the ProdName bookmark, and then display the results of the field code again.

Whatever an employee enters in the Product line at the top of the product proposal memo will now appear in the footer.

Inserting the Page Number and Number of Pages Fields

Darrell also wants the footer to show the current page number and the total number of pages in the product proposal memo, in the double-number format "page *x* of *y*," where *x* is the current page and *y* is the total number of pages. You can use the Page field and the NumPages field to insert the page number and the total number of pages, respectively.

To insert the fields for the page number and the number of pages:

1. Press the **Tab** key twice to move the insertion point from the end of the Ref field to the right margin of the footer.
2. Type **page**, press the **spacebar**, and then click the **Insert Page Number** button on the Header and Footer toolbar. This button is a quick way to insert the Page field into a document. The page number "1" appears at the location of the Page field.
3. Press the **spacebar**, type **of**, and then press the **spacebar** again. Next, you'll insert the NumPages field, which inserts the total number of pages in the document.
4. Click the **Insert Number of Pages** button on the Header and Footer toolbar. Note that you could have opened the Field dialog box, clicked Document Information in the Categories list, clicked NumPages in the Field names list, and then clicked the OK button. This Header and Footer toolbar button, however, is a quicker way to insert the field for the total number of pages in the document.

   The completed footer now contains the "page *x* of *y* " information. See Figure 8-25.

Figure 8-25 FOOTER WITH FIELDS

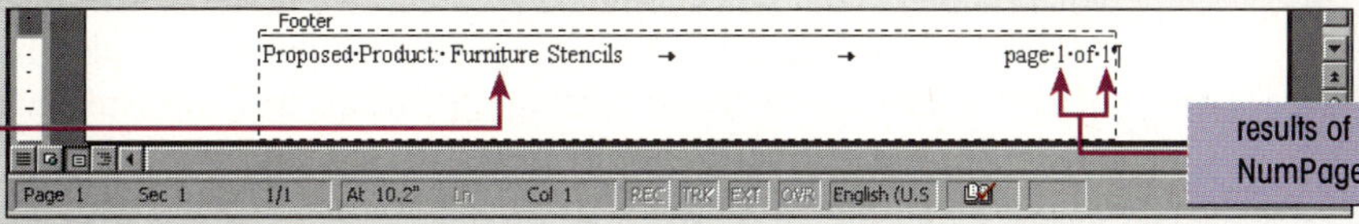

5. Switch to the Field Codes View to verify that you have indeed inserted the Page field and the NumPages field, and then turn off Field Codes View.
6. Click the **Close** button on the Header and Footer toolbar.
7. Save the current version of the template.

When Darrell and other employees use the Creekside Product Memo template to create new proposals, the footers automatically contain the proposed product name, the page number, and the total number of pages in the memo.

You have inserted fields into the template to help automate the task of creating a product proposal memo. Next, you'll record macros to further automate the template, and then you'll create a product proposal memo based on the template.

Session 8.2 Quick Check

1. What is a watermark?
2. How do you add and remove buttons from a toolbar?
3. What is a field? Name and describe three fields.
4. What would the Date field look like if today were February 3, 2001, and you wanted the date to appear in the format "05 February 01"?
5. How do you update a field?
6. In general, how do you change the prompt of a Fill-in field?
7. What is a Ref field, and why would you use it?
8. To set up page numbering in the form "Page 2 of 5," what two fields do you use?

SESSION 8.3

In this session, you'll record three macros for the Creekside Product Memo template, start a new document based on the template you created, and then write a specific product proposal using all the features of the template.

Automating Word with Macros

Darrell knows that every Creekside employee who creates a product proposal memo will have to perform at least two routine tasks: resizing drawings of the new product and creating a table of financial projections about the proposed product. Such tasks are prime candidates for macros. A **macro**, in its simplest form, is a recording of keystrokes and mouse operations that you can play back at any time by pressing a key combination or by performing one to four mouse operations. You can record a macro to perform almost any word-processing procedure that you repeat routinely.

Recording a macro to run frequently executed commands has several advantages. Combining a number of keystrokes and mouse operations into a macro saves time and helps you complete your work faster. If you record a macro accurately without typos or other mistakes, the keystrokes and mouse operations will always play back error-free. A macro that inserts text or performs formatting operations will consistently insert the same text and perform the same formatting operations.

Before you record a macro, you need to do the following:

- Name the macro. A macro name must begin with a letter and can contain a maximum of 80 letters and numbers; the name can't contain spaces, periods, or other punctuation. The macro name should summarize its function. For example, if you record a macro to resize a picture, you could name the macro "ResizePicture."

- Describe the macro (optional). You should always provide a detailed description of a macro to help you recall its exact function. This is especially important if a macro performs a complex series of operations that can't be summarized in the macro name. For example, a simple macro name, such as "MakeTable," doesn't describe the number of columns in the table, what kind of information the table will contain, the heading text, or the table format. You could include that type of information in the description.
- Attach the macro to a template. Unless you specify otherwise, every macro you create is attached to the global template, Normal.dot, and is available in every Word document, regardless of what template you used to create them. If you attach a macro to only the template you're editing, the macro is available only in documents created from that template. For example, you'll record two macros and attach them to the product memo template so they'll be available only in product proposal memos.
- Assign the macro to a toolbar button, menu, or keyboard shortcut (optional). A macro is easier to run if you assign it to a toolbar button, menu, or keyboard shortcut. For example, you can run a macro with one mouse click or a combination of keystrokes if you assign it to a toolbar button or to a shortcut key, and two mouse clicks if you assign it to a menu. Otherwise, it will require four mouse clicks to run.

You'll record two macros to help Creekside employees automate writing product proposal memos.

Recording a Macro

Recording a macro is just like recording your voice on a cassette tape: You turn on the tape recorder, speak into the microphone, and then turn off the tape recorder when you're finished. When you play back the cassette recording, you hear exactly what you recorded. Similarly, to record a macro, you turn on the macro recorder, perform keystrokes and mouse operations, and then turn off the macro recorder. When you play back the macro, Word performs the same sequence of keystrokes and mouse clicks. You can't use the mouse within the document window while you record a macro, but you can use the mouse to perform toolbar or menu commands.

REFERENCE WINDOW RW

Recording a Macro

- Double-click the REC button on the status bar, or click Tools on the menu bar, point to Macro, and then click Record New Macro.
- Type a macro name in the Macro name text box.
- If necessary, click the Store macro in list arrow, and then select the desired active template.
- Type a description of the macro in the Description text box.
- Click the Toolbars or Keyboard icon to assign the macro to one of these items, specify the specific toolbar, menu, or shortcut keys for the macro, and then click the Close button.
- Perform the keystrokes and mouse operations you want to record.
- Click the Stop Recording button on the Stop toolbar.

Recording a Macro to Resize a Picture

The first macro you'll record is one that will resize a picture within the product proposal memo. (You could also have the macro position the picture on the page and set the text wrapping, but a problem in the initial release of Word 2000 doesn't allow recording of these features in macros.)

The task of resizing a picture would usually require a total of six or more keystrokes or mouse clicks. Once these steps are recorded as a macro and assigned to a toolbar button, the tasks require only one mouse click.

Before you begin recording the macro, you need to insert a sample picture into the template so the macro has something to resize.

To insert the sample picture:

1. If you took a break after the last session, make sure Word is running, the Creekside Product Memo template is open, Word is in Print Layout View, and nonprinting characters are displayed.
2. Move the insertion point to the blank line below the "Product Description" heading, the location where Creekside employees will usually run the macro.
3. Click **Insert** on the menu bar, point to **Picture**, click **From File**, if necessary click the **Look in** list arrow, and click **Tutorial** within the Tutorial.08 folder.
4. Double-click the picture file **WoodFurn** to insert the picture into the template.
5. Click the picture to make sure it's selected.

Before you record the tasks as a macro, you'll name the macro "ResizePicture," attach the macro to the product memo template, add a description of the macro, and assign the macro to a toolbar button.

To prepare to record the ResizePicture macro:

1. Double-click the **REC** button (even though it's dimmed) on the status bar at the bottom of the document window. The Record Macro dialog box opens.

   Notice that Word suggests a macro name ("Macro1"); however, you should always use a name that describes the function of the macro.
2. Type **ResizePicture** in the Macro name text box to specify the macro name. Recall that macro names can't contain spaces, so make sure you type this name without a space between "Resize" and "Picture."

   TROUBLE? If you type the macro name incorrectly, edit it now so that it becomes the one-word macro name "ResizePicture."
3. Click the **Store macro in** list arrow, and then click **Documents Based On Creekside Product Memo** to attach the macro to only this template.
4. Select the text in the Description text box, and then type **Resizes a picture of a proposed Creekside product**. The Record Macro dialog box now looks like Figure 8-26.

Figure 8-26 RECORD MACRO DIALOG BOX

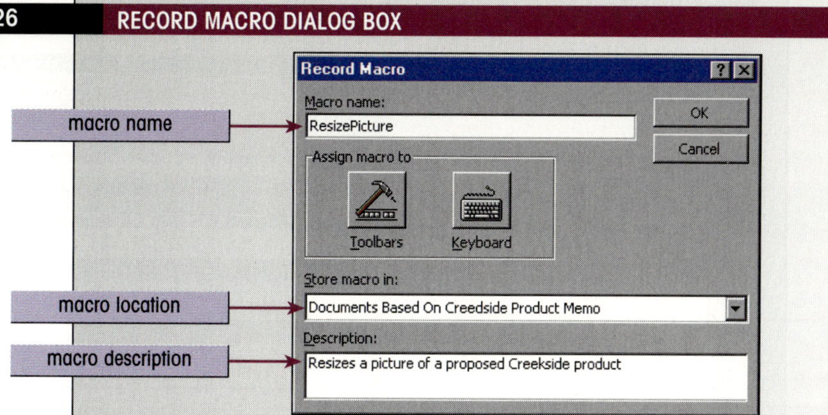

Next, you'll assign the macro to the Formatting toolbar.

5. Click the **Toolbars** icon in the Record Macro dialog box to open the Customize dialog box, which is similar to the Customize dialog box you used earlier.

6. Drag **TemplateProjects.NewMacros.ResizePicture** onto the Formatting toolbar, immediately to the right of the CR button. The macro name is long and awkward, so you'll change the name to an icon.

   TROUBLE? If part of the Formatting toolbar wraps to a new line, don't worry; you'll reduce the size of the macro button next so the toolbar will fit on one line.

7. Right-click the macro toolbar button, click **Default Style** on the shortcut menu to convert the macro button to an icon, right-click the macro button again, point to **Change Button Image** on the shortcut menu, and click the **Pencil Image** button.

   TROUBLE? If your macro button shows both the text name and the image, right-click the button and then click Default Style to show only the image on the button.

   The macro button is now assigned this pencil image, which might remind users that the macro edits a picture.

8. Click the **Close** button to close the Customize dialog box. You're ready to record the commands of the macro.

The Stop toolbar opens, the REC button on the status bar becomes highlighted, and the pointer changes to . From this point, Word will record every keystroke and mouse operation until you stop the recording. Be careful as you record the macro; if you make a mistake, you might have to stop recording and start over.

To record the ResizePicture macro:

1. Click the **Format Picture** button on the Picture toolbar. The Format Picture dialog box opens. You'll resize the picture to 50% of its original size.

2. Click the **Size** tab on the Format Picture dialog box, make sure the **Lock aspect ratio** and the **Relative to original picture size** check boxes are selected, and then change the Height value in the Scale section to **50%**.

3. Click the **OK** button. The picture reduces to 50% of its original size. See Figure 8-27.

Figure 8-27 RECORDING THE RESIZEPICTURE MACRO

Stop Recording button

resized picture

macro pointer

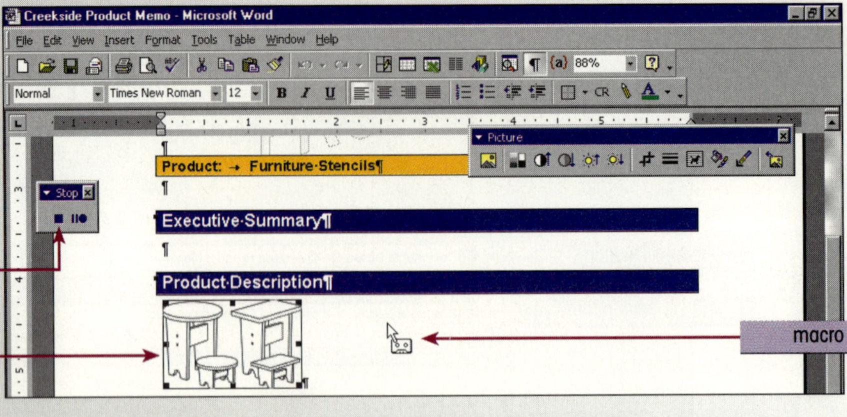

4. Click the **Stop Recording** button on the Stop toolbar to end the recording. Because you don't want this picture as a boilerplate graphic in the template, you'll delete it.

5. If necessary, click the picture to select it, and then press the **Delete** key. The picture disappears from the document window.

   TROUBLE? If you made a mistake while recording the macro, return to the section "Recording a Macro to Resize a Picture," and repeat all the steps to this point. Click the Yes button when Word prompts you to replace the existing macro.

The ResizePicture macro you just recorded will format a drawing of any proposed product. You'll test this macro after you record the second macro.

Recording a Macro to Create a Table

The second macro will be a recording of the steps to create a table for the financial projections for the proposed product. As with the first macro, you'll specify a name, attach the macro to the product memo template, add a description of the macro, and then assign the macro to a toolbar button. This time, you'll use the Macro command on the Tools menu to begin recording the macro.

To record the ProductTable macro:

1. With the insertion point still on the blank line below the "Product Description" heading, click **Tools** on the menu bar, point to **Macro**, and click **Record New Macro** to open the Record Macro dialog box.

2. Type **ProductTable** as one word in the Macro name text box, type the description as **Inserts a table with headings**, make sure the macro gets recorded in the Creekside Product Memo template (and not in the global template), place the macro on the toolbar to the right of the ResizePicture macro icon, and change the new macro button to an image of a pair of shoe prints.

3. Click the **Close** button on the Customize dialog box.

   You're ready to record the commands for the macro. Darrell wants this macro to insert a table with two rows and four columns and to insert the heading for each column.

4. Click the **Insert Table** button on the Standard toolbar, drag the pointer to select a 2 × 4 table (2 rows by 4 columns), and then release the mouse button. Word inserts a 2 × 4 table into the document.

5. With the insertion point in the upper-left cell, press **Ctrl + B** to turn on bold formatting, type **Product**, press the **Tab** key to move to the top row of the second column, press **Ctrl + B**, type **Dimensions**, press the **Tab** key, press **Ctrl + B**, type **Discount Price**, press the **Tab** key, press **Ctrl + B**, and then type **Retail Price**. The table's structure, format, and headings are complete. See Figure 8-28.

Figure 8-28 RECORDING THE PRODUCTTABLE MACRO

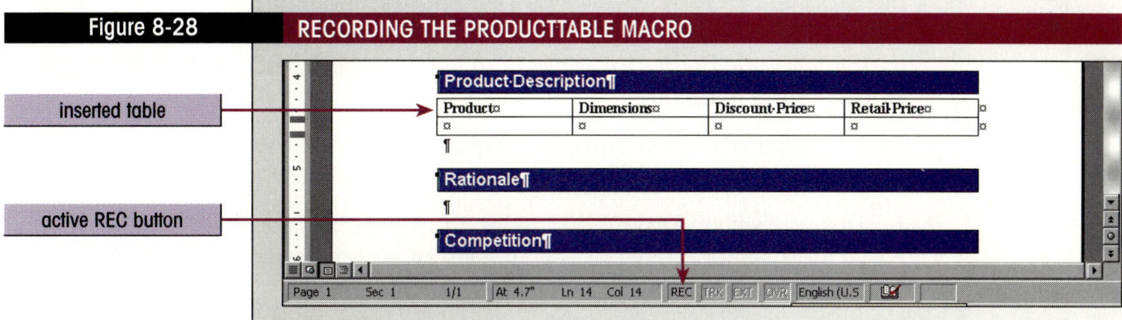

6. Click the **Stop Recording** button on the Stop toolbar to end the recording. Because you don't want this table as boilerplate in the template, you'll delete it.

7. Click **Table** on the menu bar, point to **Delete**, and click **Table**. The entire table disappears from the document.

Now, Darrell or other Creekside employees can run the ProductTable macro to insert a table at the location of the insertion point. Why did Darrell choose to record a macro that creates the table, rather than to create a boilerplate table within the template? Boilerplate text remains at a fixed location within a template, whereas a macro can be run anywhere within a template. So if Darrell needs two or more tables in a product proposal memo, he can run the macro two or more times, and each time the macro will set up a table structure, format, and headings.

You've finished recording the ProductTable macro, but you realize that the table heading "Product" should be "Proposed Product." Rather than record the macro again, you'll edit the existing ProductTable macro.

Editing a Macro

You can edit a macro just as you would any other document. In a macro "document," however, every line of text is actually a macro command. You don't need to understand all the macro commands in a macro document to make minor changes. For instance, it's easy to make changes of typed text in the macro. Advanced editing, which includes adding programming features to the macros, is beyond the scope of this text.

To edit the macro:

1. Click **Tools** on the menu bar, point to **Macro**, and then click **Macros**. The Macros dialog box opens, displaying a list of all the macros available in this template.

   TROUBLE? If you don't see the ProductTable macro, change the Macros in the list to "Creekside Product Memo (Template)."

   You can use this dialog box to delete a macro by clicking the macro name and then clicking the Delete button. You can click the Organizer button to open the Organizer dialog box, click a macro name, and then click the Rename button to rename a macro or click the Copy button to copy a macro from one template to another, for example, from the Creekside Product Memo template to the Normal template.

2. Click **ProductTable**, and then click the **Edit** button in the Macros dialog box. Microsoft Visual Basic opens, with the macro commands in the document window.

3. Find the line with the command **Selection.TypeText Text:="Product"**, and move the insertion point between the first quotation mark and the "P" in "Product." See Figure 8-29.

Figure 8-29 MICROSOFT VISUAL BASIC WINDOW

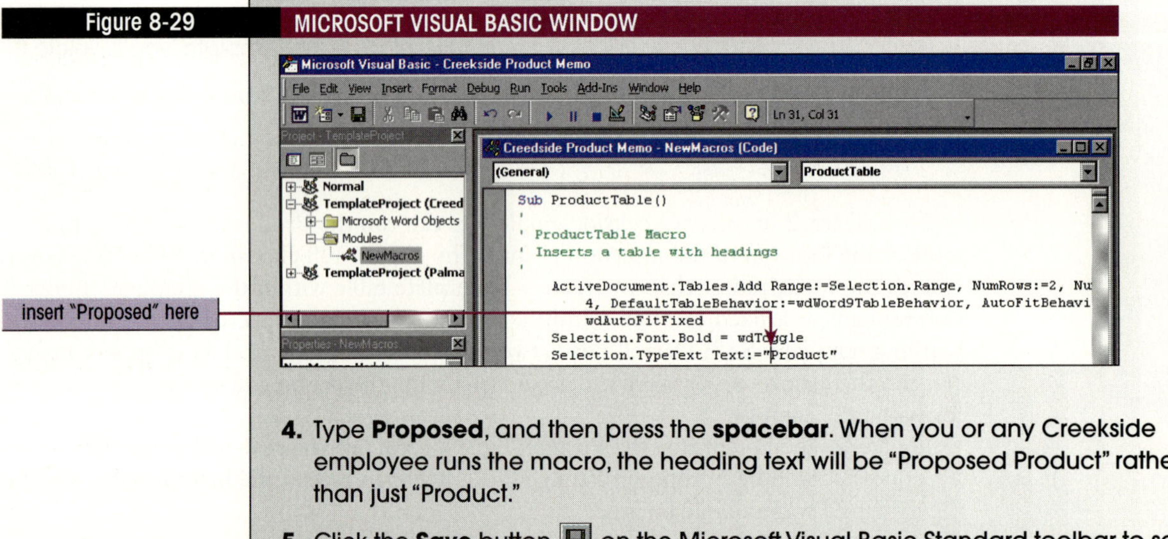

4. Type **Proposed**, and then press the **spacebar**. When you or any Creekside employee runs the macro, the heading text will be "Proposed Product" rather than just "Product."

5. Click the **Save** button on the Microsoft Visual Basic Standard toolbar to save the revised macro.

6. Click **File** on the menu bar, and then click **Close and Return to Microsoft Word**. Microsoft Visual Basic closes, and the Word window reappears.

As you have seen, Word makes it easy to edit a macro.

Recording an AutoMacro

Darrell suggests that you add an AutoMacro to the template. An **AutoMacro** is a macro that runs automatically when Word performs certain basic operations, such as starting Word, creating a new document, opening an existing document, closing a document, and exiting Word. Figure 8–30 lists the AutoMacros and their purposes.

Figure 8-30 DESCRIPTIONS OF AUTOMACROS

AUTOMACRO NAME	PURPOSE
AutoExec	Runs each time you start Word
AutoNew	Runs when you open a blank document
AutoOpen	Runs each time you open an existing document
AutoClose	Runs each time you close a document
AutoExit	Runs each time you exit Word

Darrell asks you to record an AutoNew macro, which runs whenever a new document is created from a template, to move the insertion point below the "Executive Summary" heading—the location employees would usually begin writing.

To create the AutoNew macro:

1. Move the insertion point to the beginning of the document, double-click the **REC** button on the status bar to open the Record Macro dialog box, and then type **AutoNew** into the Macro name text box. This special macro name tells Word to run the macro when you begin a new document.
2. Click **Documents Based On Creekside Product Memo** in the Store macro in list box so the macro will run only if a new document is opened from the product proposal template.
3. Change the description to **Place insertion point below Executive Summary**. You won't assign this macro to a toolbar or the keyboard because it runs automatically when the new document is opened.
4. Click the **OK** button. You're now ready to record the commands of the AutoNew macro.
5. Click **Edit** on the menu bar, click **Find** to open the Find dialog box, type **Executive Summary** in the **Find what** text box, and click the **Find Next** button. Word finds and highlights the heading "Executive Summary."
6. Click the **Cancel** button on the Find dialog box, and then press the ↓ key to deselect the text and move the insertion point below the heading. This completes the operations for the AutoNew macro.
7. Click the **Stop Recording** button ■ on the Stop toolbar to end the macro recording.

The AutoNew macro is now ready to run whenever a Creekside employee starts a new document from the product memo template.

Saving the Completed Template in the Templates Folder

The product memo template contains boilerplate text and graphics, styles, AutoText, customized toolbars, fields, and macros. You'll save the completed template both to a disk and to the Templates folder on your computer so you can test the template.

To save the completed template in the Templates folder:

1. Make sure that only one blank line still appears below the "Product Description" heading, and then save the completed template.

   The final version of the template is now saved to your Data Disk. If you want to be able to open the template from within the New dialog box, you need to copy it to the Templates folder. You can determine the exact location of this folder by checking the File Locations tab in the Options dialog box.

2. Click **Tools** on the menu bar, click **Options** to open the Options dialog box, click the **File Locations** tab if necessary, and then click **User templates** in the File types list. See Figure 8-31.

Figure 8-31 FILE LOCATIONS TAB OF OPTIONS DIALOG BOX

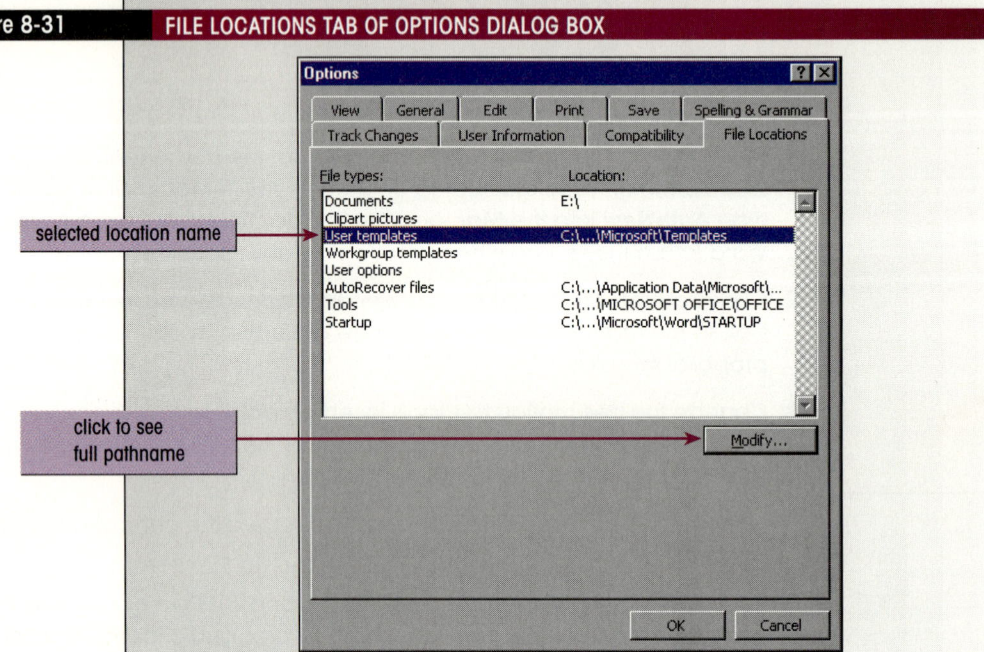

3. Carefully write down the complete path to the User templates shown on your screen.

   TROUBLE? If your pathname appears with ellipses (. . .) because the pathname is too long, click the Modify button shown in Figure 8-31. The complete pathname appears in the Folder name text box, at the bottom of the Modify Location dialog box. Carefully write down the complete path, for example, C:\WINDOWS\Application Data\Microsoft\Templates or C:\Program Files\Microsoft Office\Templates, and then click the Cancel button in the Modify Location dialog box.

4. Click the **OK** button in the Options dialog box.
5. Click **File** on the menu bar, and then click **Save As** to open the Save As dialog box.
6. Change the **Save in** list box to the folder that contains the templates (follow the path you wrote down in Step 3, such as C:\WINDOWS\Application Data\Microsoft\Templates).
7. Click the **Save** button in the Save As dialog box to save the template in the Memos folder.
8. Close the template.

With the template saved to both your Data Disk and the Templates folder, you're now ready to start a new document using the Creekside Product Memo template.

Starting a New Document from the Template

Darrell wants you to test the new template by writing a product proposal memo for small wood-furniture kits.

To start a new document from the product memo template:

1. Click **File** on the menu bar, and then click **New** to open the New dialog box. Note that to open a document based on a template other than Normal, you have to use the New command on the File menu, not the New button on the Standard toolbar.
2. Double-click the **Creekside Product Memo** icon. When Word opens the template, the fields are updated automatically, and the Fill-in fields display a prompt.
3. At the "Who should receive this memo?" prompt, type **Margaret Fox, Vice President of Product Development** to replace the highlighted text, and then click the **OK** button. Margaret is Darrell's supervisor and the person to whom he wants to send the memo.
4. At the "What is the proposed product name?" prompt, type **Wood Furniture Kits** to replace the highlighted text, and then click the **OK** button. With the Fill-in fields completed, the AutoNew macro places the insertion point below the "Executive Summary" heading.
5. If necessary, click the **View Field Codes** button {a} on the customized Standard toolbar to see the field results, and then scroll down to view the footer.

As you can see, the proposed product name and the page numbers appear in the footer. As you add pages to your memo, you'll see that the NumPages field is not updated automatically. Instead of manually updating the Ref field and NumPages field before you print the document, you can tell Word to do this.

To set Word to update fields upon printing:

1. Click **Tools** on the menu bar, and then click **Options**. The options dialog box opens.
2. Click the **Print** tab in the Options dialog box.
3. If necessary, click the **Update fields** check box in the Printing Options section to select it.
4. Click the **OK** button.

Darrell will instruct all the Creekside employees to set this option on their computers so that the fields, including those in the footer, will update properly when they create a product proposal memo.

Importing Text into the Memo

Creekside employees usually will type their memos directly into a document based on the product memo template. However, Darrell wrote the text of his new product proposal memo while you were creating the template. You'll delete all the duplicated headings and import his file into the current document.

To insert the text of Darrell's memo:

1. Delete all the text of the memo (that is, the memo headings) from the blank line beneath the "Executive Summary" heading to the end of the document.
2. If necessary, press the **Enter** key to add a blank line below the "Executive Summary" heading. Whenever you press the Enter key, Word inserts a hard return, which marks the end of a paragraph. If the nonprinting characters are visible, the location of the hard return is marked by the end-of-paragraph symbol ¶. (If necessary, display nonprinting characters.) See Figure 8-32.

Figure 8-32 DOCUMENT READY FOR IMPORTING TEXT

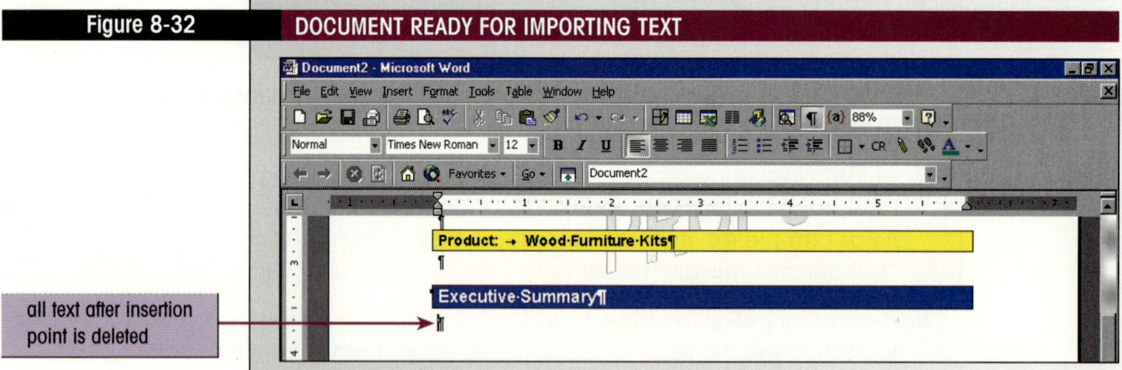

3. With the insertion point on the blank line at the end of the document, click **Insert** on the menu bar, and then click **File**. The Insert File dialog box opens.
4. Select the file **NewProd** in the Tutorial subfolder with the Tutorial.08 folder on your Data Disk, and then click the **Insert** button.

   Darrell's text is inserted into the product proposal memo. As you scroll through the text, you decide to apply the Memo Heading style to the phrase "Projected Income and Profit," near the end of the document.
5. Select the phrase "Projected Income and Profit," near the end of the document, but not the colon after the phrase.
6. Click the Style list arrow on the Formatting toolbar, and then click the style **Memo Heading**. The formatting changes to 12-point, bold Arial.

As you can see, the template styles are available in the new proposal memo document created from the template.

Inserting Text with AutoText

As you read through the beginning of the memo, you decide to make some minor revisions to the first two paragraphs. You'll use the AutoText feature to make the changes.

To insert text with AutoText:

1. Delete the word "we" in the first line of the first paragraph below the "Executive Summary" heading. You want to insert "Creekside Wood Crafts" in its place.
2. Click the **CR** button on the customized Formatting toolbar to insert "Creekside Wood Crafts" in the document, and if necessary, press the **spacebar** to insert a space between the company name and the next word.
3. Move the insertion point to the right of the word "new" in "new product line" in the first line of the first paragraph below the "Product Description" heading.
4. Press the **spacebar** to add a space after "new," type **cr**, and then press the **F3** key. The AutoText entry "cr" expands to the full company name.

In other product proposal memos, the employees also will want to insert their own names and titles or the names and titles of other company employees. Darrell will create AutoText entries for the remaining names and titles so the employees can quickly enter any name in a memo.

Darrell notices that in the Competition section, the company CCinc was excluded, so he asks you to insert it and to change the commas that separate the company names from the rest of the sentence to em dashes. Recall that an em dash is a hyphen (—) that has the width of a capital M.

To insert CCinc and em dashes:

1. Move the insertion point immediately to the left of the "L" in "L & P Industries" in the Competition section, press the **Backspace** key twice to delete the space and the comma. Now, you're ready to insert an em dash and the new company name.
2. Press the hyphen key twice to insert "--" into the document, type **CCinc**, (including the comma), and then press the **spacebar**. Notice that the double hyphens switch to a single em dash. This is one of the automatic features of AutoCorrect. Also notice that AutoCorrect did not convert "CCinc" to "Ccinc" because you made it an AutoCorrect exception.
3. In the next line, move the insertion point between the word "Works" and the comma that immediately follows it, press the **Delete** key twice to delete the space and the comma, and then type a double hyphen. See Figure 8-33.

Figure 8-33 USING AUTOCORRECT (AUTOFORMAT) TO INSERT SPECIAL CHARACTERS

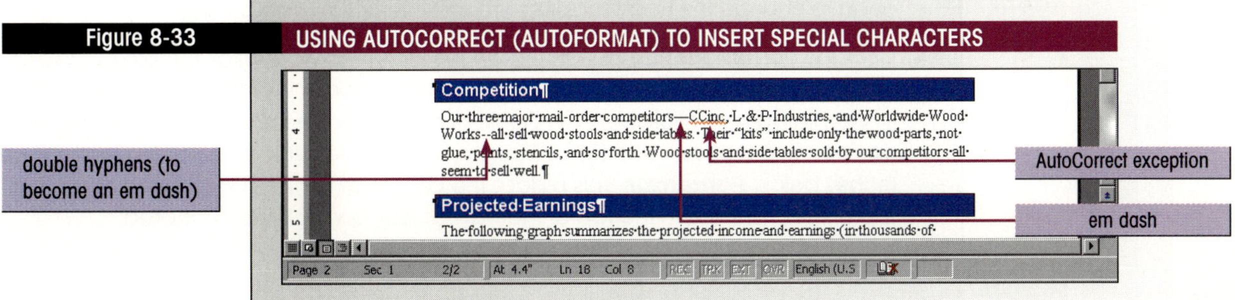

As you can see, the double hyphen doesn't convert to an em dash unless you press the spacebar after the word that follows.

4. Move the insertion point to the right of the word after the double hyphen, that is, following "all," and press the **spacebar**. The double hyphen converts to an em dash.
5. Delete the extra space before the word "all."

The product proposal memo is complete except for three things. First, you'll insert a picture of the proposed products and run the ResizePicture macro. Next, you will create a table summarizing the four kits using the macros that you created earlier. Finally, you'll insert a chart with projected income and Profit using data from an Excel worksheet.

Running **Macros**

You'll begin by inserting a picture, created by the company's design department, of two stools and two end tables. Then, you will run the ResizePicture macro. Because you assigned the macro to a customized toolbar, you can use the toolbar button to run your macro.

REFERENCE WINDOW RW

Running a Macro

- Click the toolbar button, select the menu command, or press the shortcut keys to which the macro was assigned.

Or

- Click Tools on the menu bar, point to Macro, and then click Macros.
- Click the name of the macro you want to run.
- Click the Run button.

To insert the picture and run the ResizePicture macro:

1. Move the insertion point before the first word in the paragraph that begins "We propose that initially...," after the bulleted list below the "Product Description" heading.
2. Insert the picture file **WoodFurn** in the Tutorial subfolder within the Tutorial.08 folder on your Data Disk to insert the drawing of the proposed products. The picture spans half the page.
3. Click the picture to select it, click the **ResizePicture** macro button on the customized Formatting toolbar. The picture is resized to 50% of its original size. Now, you need to change the text wrapping around the picture and change its position.
4. Click the **Format Picture** button on the Picture toolbar, click the **Layout** tab on the Format Picture dialog box, click the **Square** icon in the Wrapping style section of the dialog box, click the **Advanced button**, change the Horizontal **Absolute position** to **0** inches to the left of **Margin**, and set the Vertical Absolute position to **0** inches below **Paragraph**. This places the picture at the left margin and aligns the top of the picture with the top of the paragraph to which it is anchored.

5. Click the **OK** button twice, click anywhere in the document outside the picture, and turn off nonprinting characters. The picture is now sized and positioned as desired. See Figure 8-34.

Figure 8-34 DOCUMENT AFTER INSERTING PICTURE AND RUNNING MACRO

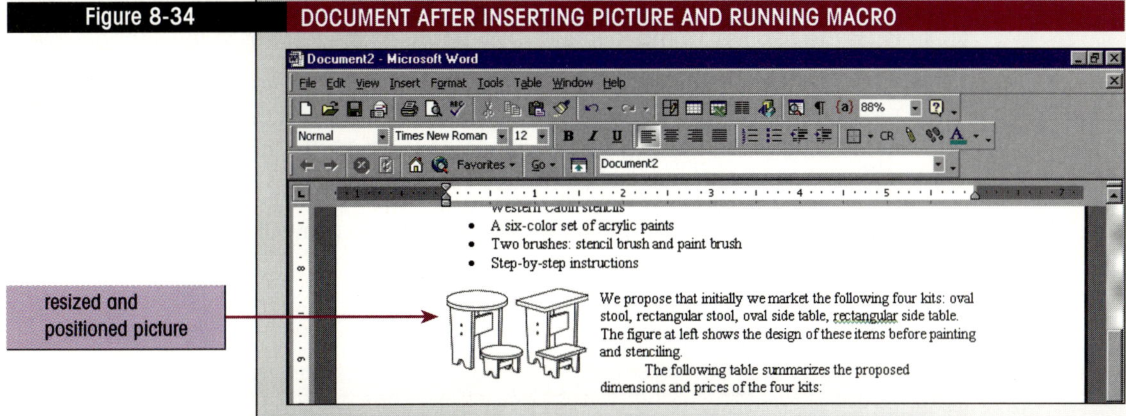

TROUBLE? If the picture disappears, look for it in the upper-left corner of the first page, make sure it is selected, and repeat steps 4 and 5.

Now, you'll run the ProductTable macro to create a table of information about the proposed product.

To run the ProductTable macro:

1. Move the insertion point to the right of the colon at the end of the phrase "prices of the four kits" in the paragraph below the current one.
2. Press the **Enter** key twice to insert two hard returns, leaving a blank line between the paragraph and the table, and then remove the tab automatically inserted into the paragraph.
3. Click the **ProductTable** macro button on the customized Formatting toolbar. The table is inserted into your document.

   TROUBLE? If this macro doesn't work properly, repeat the steps in the section "Recording a Macro to Create a Table," paying careful attention to each operation you perform. If you still have problems, ask your instructor or technical support person for help.

The table contains the heading row and one blank row in which to enter data. You'll enter all the data for the table.

To insert the data into the table:

1. Press the **Tab** key to move the insertion point to the first cell in the second row (cell A2).
2. Type **Oval stool**, press the **Tab** key, type **9.5 × 12.5 × 8 in**, press the **Tab** key, type **12.95**, press the **Tab** key, and then type **22.00**. This completes the data for the first row.
3. Press the **Tab** key to create a new blank row, and move the insertion point to cell A3.
4. Continue typing data until your table looks like Figure 8-35.

Figure 8-35 COMPLETED TABLE BEFORE FORMATTING

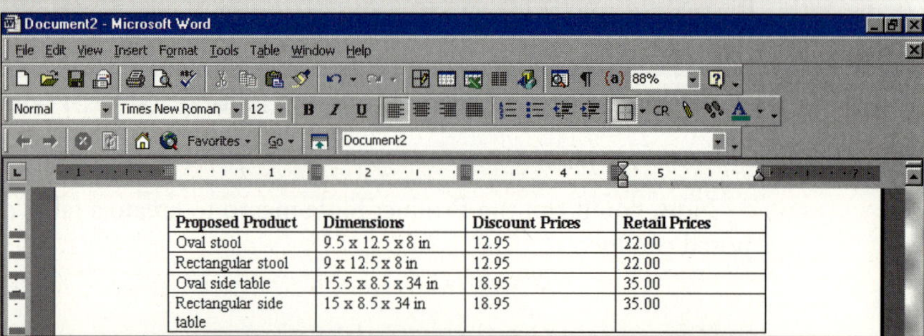

Proposed Product	Dimensions	Discount Prices	Retail Prices
Oval stool	9.5 x 12.5 x 8 in	12.95	22.00
Rectangular stool	9 x 12.5 x 8 in	12.95	22.00
Oval side table	15.5 x 8.5 x 34 in	18.95	35.00
Rectangular side table	15 x 8.5 x 34 in	18.95	35.00

5. Select the cells **B2** through **B5** (the Dimensions column), and then click the **Center** button on the Formatting toolbar to center the data.
6. Select cells **C2** through **D5** (the Discount Price and the Retail Price columns), and then click the **Right align** button on the Formatting toolbar.
7. Increase the width of the first column so that the information in each cell fits on one line, and decrease the widths of the last two columns so that the headings barely fit on one line.
8. Save the document as **Product Proposal Memo** in the Tutorial subfolder with the Tutorial.08 folder on your Data Disk. Notice that Word automatically saves the new file as a Word document, rather than as a Word template.

Your next task is to insert a chart with projected income and profit for the first five years after introducing the proposed product.

Creating a Chart

Now Darrell wants you to create a chart that shows the income and profits projected for the proposed product line. You'll use Microsoft Graph 2000 to create the chart. Rather than typing the data you need for the chart, you will import the data from an Excel worksheet.

To create a Microsoft Graph chart using data from an Excel worksheet:

1. Move the insertion point to the line below the phrase "Projected Income and Profit."

2. Click **Insert** on the menu bar, point to **Picture** and then click **Chart**. A sample graph appears at the end of your document, the Microsoft Graph 2000 commands become available on the menu and bar and toolbars, and a datasheet window appears. See Figure 8-36. A **datasheet** is a grid of cells, similar to an Excel worksheet, in which you can add data and labels. In our case, you could insert the data by hand, but instead you'll import the data from an Excel worksheet.

Figure 8-36 CREATING A CHART

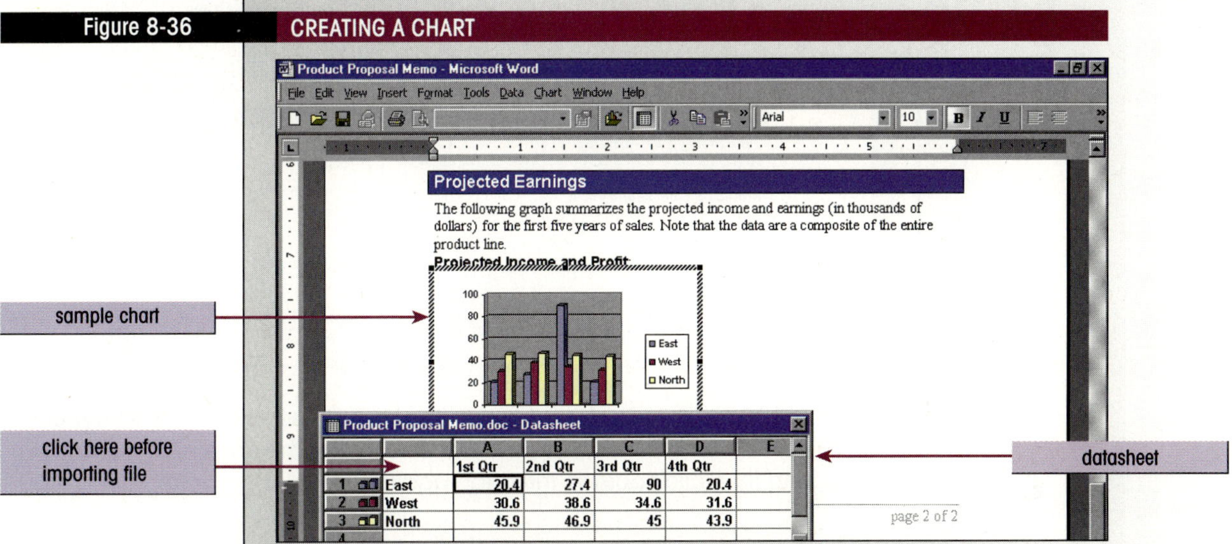

TROUBLE? If the Microsoft Graph window opens separately from Word, maximize the window, move the chart window so it doesn't cover the datasheet, and continue to the next step. If your data sheet opens in a position different from that shown in Figure 8-36, simply continue with Step 3.

3. Click ✚ in the upper-left cell of the data sheet, as indicated in Figure 8-36, click **Edit** on the menu bar, click **Import File**, select the file **IncProf** from the Tutorial subfolder with the Tutorial.08 folder, and click the **Open** button. The Import Data Options dialog box opens.

4. Make sure **Sheet1** is selected, make sure the **Entire sheet** option button is selected, and then deselect the **Overwrite existing cells** check box. Deselecting this latter option will ensure that the data from the Excel worksheet are positioned properly in the datasheet.
5. Click the **OK** button on the Import Data Options dialog box. The new data appear in the datasheet. Now you want to delete row 3 of the datasheet because this row is left over from the sample chart.
6. Click the button labeled **3** to the left of "North" to select the entire row 3, and then press the **Delete** key. The entire row disappears. This completes the chart.
7. Click anywhere in the text of the Word document window to deselect the chart object, click the chart to select it again, and then click the **Center** button to center the chart between the margins. Deselect the chart. See Figure 8-37.

Figure 8-37 DOCUMENT WITH COMPLETED CHART

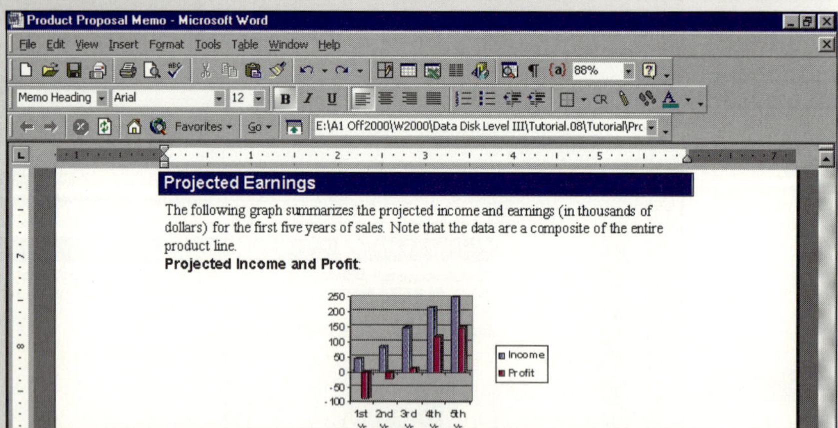

If your chart does not center properly, simply continue with Step 8. If your chart does not match the one in Figure 8-37, double-click the chart, edit the data sheet, and then click outside the chart again.

8. Make sure your own name appears to the right of **From:** near the beginning of the document.
9. Save, preview, and print the document. Click the **OK** button in the Fill-in field prompts to accept the current information and print the memo. See Figure 8-38.

Figure 8-38 COMPLETED MEMO (PAGES 1 AND 2)

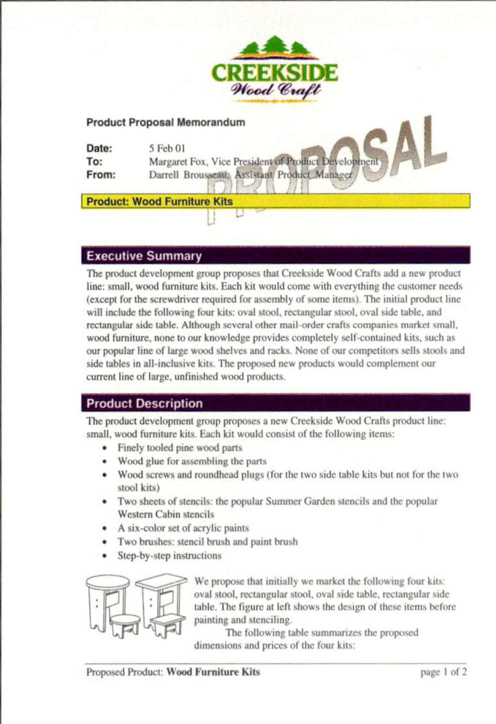

CREEKSIDE Wood Craft

Product Proposal Memorandum

Date: 5 Feb 01
To: Margaret Fox, Vice President of Product Development
From: Darrell Brousseau, Assistant Product Manager

PROPOSAL

Product: Wood Furniture Kits

Executive Summary

The product development group proposes that Creekside Wood Crafts add a new product line: small, wood furniture kits. Each kit would come with everything the customer needs (except for the screwdriver required for assembly of some items). The initial product line will include the following four kits: oval stool, rectangular stool, oval side table, and rectangular side table. Although several other mail-order crafts companies market small, wood furniture, none to our knowledge provides completely self-contained kits, such as our popular line of large wood shelves and racks. None of our competitors sells stools and side tables in all-inclusive kits. The proposed new products would complement our current line of large, unfinished wood products.

Product Description

The product development group proposes a new Creekside Wood Crafts product line: small, wood furniture kits. Each kit would consist of the following items:

- Finely tooled pine wood parts
- Wood glue for assembling the parts
- Wood screws and roundhead plugs (for the two side table kits but not for the two stool kits)
- Two sheets of stencils: the popular Summer Garden stencils and the popular Western Cabin stencils
- A six-color set of acrylic paints
- Two brushes: stencil brush and paint brush
- Step-by-step instructions

We propose that initially we market the following four kits: oval stool, rectangular stool, oval side table, rectangular side table. The figure at left shows the design of these items before painting and stenciling.

The following table summarizes the proposed dimensions and prices of the four kits:

Proposed Product: **Wood Furniture Kits** page 1 of 2

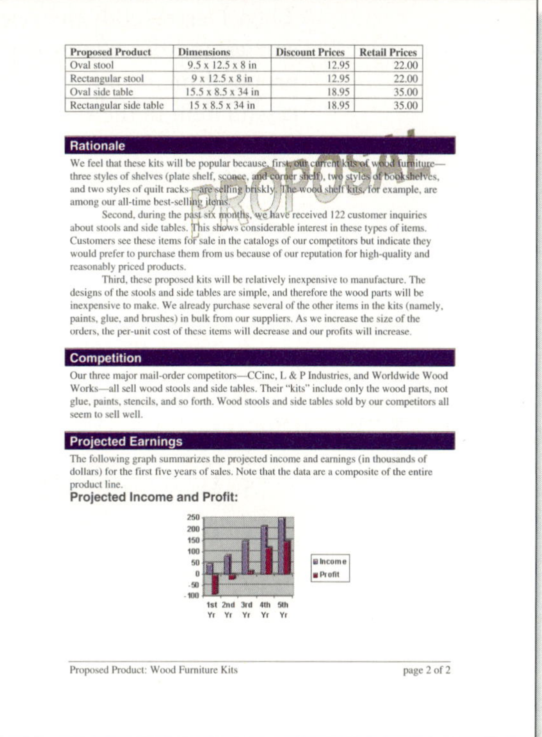

Proposed Product	Dimensions	Discount Prices	Retail Prices
Oval stool	9.5 x 12.5 x 8 in	12.95	22.00
Rectangular stool	9 x 12.5 x 8 in	12.95	22.00
Oval side table	15.5 x 8.5 x 34 in	18.95	35.00
Rectangular side table	15 x 8.5 x 34 in	18.95	35.00

PROPOSAL

Rationale

We feel that these kits will be popular because, first, our current kits of wood furniture—three styles of shelves (plate shelf, sconce, and corner shelf), two styles of bookshelves, and two styles of quilt racks—are selling briskly. The wood shelf kits, for example, are among our all-time best-selling items.

Second, during the past six months, we have received 122 customer inquiries about stools and side tables. This shows considerable interest in these types of items. Customers see these items for sale in the catalogs of our competitors but indicate they would prefer to purchase them from us because of our reputation for high-quality and reasonably priced products.

Third, these proposed kits will be relatively inexpensive to manufacture. The designs of the stools and side tables are simple, and therefore the wood parts will be inexpensive to make. We already purchase several of the other items in the kits (namely, paints, glue, and brushes) in bulk from our suppliers. As we increase the size of the orders, the per-unit cost of these items will decrease and our profits will increase.

Competition

Our three major mail-order competitors—CCinc, L & P Industries, and Worldwide Wood Works—all sell wood stools and side tables. Their "kits" include only the wood parts, not glue, paints, stencils, and so forth. Wood stools and side tables sold by our competitors all seem to sell well.

Projected Earnings

The following graph summarizes the projected income and earnings (in thousands of dollars) for the first five years of sales. Note that the data are a composite of the entire product line.

Projected Income and Profit:

Proposed Product: Wood Furniture Kits page 2 of 2

Your printed Product Proposal Memo should look like Figure 8-38, except that your name or the name set as Author in the Summary tab will appear in place of Darrell's name.

As a courtesy, you should delete any templates or AutoCorrect exceptions you add when you're working on someone else's computer. You'll remove the Creekside Product Memo template because you have a copy on your Data Disk and Darrell will be updating the template by adding AutoText entries for the remaining names of titles of employees.

To delete a template from the Word Template folder and delete the AutoCorrect exception:

1. Close the document, click **File** on the menu bar, and then click **New** to open the New dialog box.
2. Right-click the **Creekside Product Memo** icon, click **Delete** on the shortcut menu, and then click the **Yes** button to verify that you want to delete the template. Word moves the template to the Recycle Bin.
3. Click the **Cancel** button on the New dialog box, and then close the Product Proposal Memo document.
4. Click the **New** button on the Standard toolbar to open a new document so that Tools on the menu bar becomes active. Click **Tools** on the menu bar, click **AutoCorrect**, and, if necessary, click the **AutoCorrect** tab.
5. Click the **Exceptions** button, if necessary click the **INitial CAps** tab, click **CCinc** in the Don't correct list, and click the **Delete** button.
6. Click the **OK** button on the AutoCorrect Exceptions dialog box, and click the OK button on the AutoCorrect dialog box.
7. Exit Word without saving the current (blank) document.

Darrell is pleased with the product memo template you created. He sends the wood furniture kits proposal to Margaret Fox, his supervisor, who approves the format of the memo. Then Darrell adds the remaining employee names and titles to the template as AutoText entries and distributes copies of the template to any employee who might write product proposal memos. Eventually, Darrell's proposed product is approved and becomes a successful item in the company product list.

Session 8.3 QUICK CHECK

1. What is a macro?
2. What are three advantages to using a macro?
3. In general, how do you record a macro?
4. Why would you need to edit a macro? How would you do it?
5. What are AutoMacros? Give three examples.
6. Why does a template need an AutoNew macro?
7. In general, how do you open a new document based on a template other than Normal?
8. How do you run a macro named MyMacro if it's not assigned to a toolbar, menu, or shortcut key?
9. In general terms, how do you create chart using data from an Excel worksheet?

REVIEW ASSIGNMENTS

Megan Smith, director of customer relations for Creekside Wood Crafts, responds to any customer letters that don't deal with active orders. Most of the letters are complaints about a missing part or product quality or suggestions for a new product line. Megan asks you to create a template to automate writing the letters of response.

1. If necessary, start Word, and make sure your Data Disk is in the appropriate disk drive. Open the file **CrLetter** from the Review subfolder within the Tutorial.08 Review folder on your Data Disk, and then save it as a Word template (in the same folder) as **Creekside Letter**.
2. Insert the Creekside logo (CrkLogo) (from the Tutorial subfolder within the Tutorial.08 folder on your Data Disk) at the beginning of the document. Set the height to 1.6 inches and the width to 3.08 inches, and center the logo between the left and right margins.
3. Below the logo, center the Creekside Wood Crafts address, phone numbers, and e-mail address.
4. Redefine the Normal style as 12-point Arial.
5. Add a watermark to the template. Select the WordArt style in the third row from the top and the far right row, type the company name with a hard return after each word, use 44-point Arial italic, and then change the Fill Effects to one color and make the gradient lighter. In the Layout tab of the Format WordArt dialog box, click the Behind text icon. Position the watermark so it is centered approximately between the top and bottom margins and between the left and right margins.

Explore

6. Delete "[Date]" from the document, and insert the Date field formatted to the style "05 February 2001." (*Hint*: Press [Alt] + F9 to toggle between the field results and the field codes.)
7. Delete "[Inside Address]", and insert a Fill-in field. Make "Type the name of the addressee" the prompt for the field.
8. On a new blank line below the first Fill-in field, insert a second Fill-in field with the prompt, "Type the street address, press Enter, and type the city, state, and zip code."
9. Format the salutation ("Dear...") so that it automatically inserts the name of the addressee (for example, "Dear Sandra Gomez:") without requiring Jennifer to retype the name of the addressee. Remember to include a space after "Dear" and a colon after the name.
10. Make the second paragraph of the body of the letter an AutoText entry called "MissingPart," attached only to this document template, not to the Normal template. Then delete the paragraph and the blank line after it.
11. Make the new second paragraph an AutoText entry called "ProductQuality". Attach the paragraph only to this template. Then delete the paragraph and the blank line after it.
12. Make the new second paragraph an AutoText entry called "NewProduct". Also attach the paragraph only to this template. Then delete the paragraph and the blank line after it.
13. Print a list of the AutoText entries.

Explore

14. Assign the shortcut keys Alt + M, Alt + P, and Alt + N to the AutoText entries MissingPart, ProductQuality, and NewProduct respectively. (*Hint*: To customize the keyboard, click Tools on the menu bar, click Customize, click the Keyboard button, click AutoText in the Categories list, click the desired AutoText entry, click the Press new shortcut key text box, and then press the desired shortcut keys. Repeat for other AutoText entries.)

Explore

15. Make sure two blank lines appear in the body of the letter between the remaining two paragraphs. Move the insertion point to the second blank line between the two paragraphs in the body of the letter, and insert a bookmark with the name "CustomerParagraph." You'll use this bookmark when you create an AutoNew macro for this template.

Explore

16. For this template, create an AutoNew macro that moves the insertion point automatically to the "CustomerParagraph" bookmark.
17. At the end of the letter, below the signature block, insert the paragraph: "P.S. Creekside Wood Crafts is continually adding new products to its product line. The chart below shows the number of products available for each of the past five years." Below that paragraph, insert a chart. Erase all the data from the datasheet, and then add column labels (that will appear along the x-axis of the chart) "1996," "1997," "1998," "1999," and "2000." Add the row label "# of products" and then enter (in the appropriate cells) the number of products for the years 1996-2000, as follows: 16, 21, 34, 88, 102. Deselect the chart.

Explore

18. Double-click the chart to select it and display the datasheet. Click the legend with the label # of products, and press the Delete key to delete the legend.

Explore

19. Add the axis title "Number or Products" to the left of the chart, and rotate the title so it is vertical rather than horizontal. (*Hint*: Click Chart on the menu bar, click Chart Options on the Title tab, type the axis title in the Value (Z) axis text box, and click the OK button. Right-click the axis title, click Format Axis Title, click the Alignment tab, and set the Orientation to 90 degrees.)
20. Save the completed template. Make sure your system is set to update fields automatically upon printing.
21. Copy the Creekside Letter template into the Templates folder on your computer. Close the template, and open a new document based on the Creekside Letter template.
22. Address the letter to Pamela Hamblin, 138 New Flag Blvd., Biloxi, MS 39531.

23. Use the shortcut keys to insert the paragraph about suggestions for a new product line in the body of the letter.
24. Change the name "Megan Smith" to your name, save the letter to your Data Disk as **Creekside Customer Letter**, and then print the letter. Delete the Creekside Letter template from the Templates folder.
25. **Explore** Open the Creekside Letter template (if it's not still open) and delete the AutoNew macro. (*Hint*: Display the Macros dialog box, select the macro, and click the Delete button.) Note: The purpose of this step is to demonstrate deleting macros; just close the template without saving the changes.
26. Delete the Creekside Letter template from the Templates folder.

CASE PROBLEMS

Case 1. Vermillion Cliffs Music Catherine Parisi owns Vermillion Cliffs Music, a store in Santa Fe, New Mexico, which sells hard-to-find musical instruments—from harps and hammer dulcimers to slide dobros and didgeridoos. Catherine wants to give each customer a brochure that has information about Vermillion Cliffs Music and, more specifically, about the instrument they just purchased and the manufacturer. She has started to create a template for her brochure but asks you to complete it and to produce the first brochure using the finished template.

1. If necessary, start Word and make sure your Data Disk is in the appropriate drive. Open the file **MuStore** in the Cases subfolder within the Tutorial.08 folder on your Data Disk, and then save it as a template in the same folder on your Data Disk with the filename **Vermillion Cliffs Brochure**.
2. **Explore** Change the Normal style to 12-point Arial, if necessary set the "Style for the Following Paragraph" to Normal in the Modify Style dialog box, and then set the text alignment to justified and indent the first line 0.5". (*Hint:* In the Modify Style dialog box, click the Format button, click Paragraph, then click the Indents and Spacing tab. In the Indentation section, select First line from the Special list box, and then select Justified from the Alignment list box.)
3. **Explore** Define a new paragraph style named "Brochure Heading 1" that is 20-point Mistral (if Mistral isn't available, use any font of your choice except Arial or Times New Roman), teal in color, left-aligned, no first-line indent, single-spaced, with the following paragraph style Normal.
4. **Explore** Create a new paragraph style named "Brochure Title" that is 24-point Arial MT Light in dark blue with center alignment, single spacing, and the following paragraph style set to Normal.
5. Apply the Brochure Heading-1 style to the four headings: "Unique Musical Instruments," "Classes and Demonstrations," "About Your New [instrument]," and "Caring for your New [instrument]."
6. At the beginning (blank) line of the document, type "Vermillion Cliffs Music and Your New [instrument]" on the new line, and then apply the Brochure Title style.
7. Customize the toolbars by removing the Font and Font Size list boxes from the Formatting toolbar, and adding the View Field Codes button in their place. Save the changes in only this template.
8. Create an AutoText entry for the store name, Vermillion Cliffs Music, that has a custom text button on the Formatting toolbar just to the right of the View Field Codes button. Use "fMM" for the text button name, and save the button in only this template.

9. Create an AutoText entry for the phone number "505-555-7090" that has a custom button on the Formatting toolbar immediately to the right of the one you just created. Use "PH" for the text button name, and save the button in only this template.
10. Delete the word "[instrument]" (including the brackets) from the title, and insert a Fill-in field in its place. Type "Name of instrument purchased" as the prompt.
11. Delete the word "[instrument]" (including the brackets) from the heading "About Your New [instrument]," and insert a Ref field in its place. (*Hint*: Remember to create a bookmark first; use "InstrumentName" as the bookmark name.) Apply the Brochure Heading-1 style to the new field.
12. Copy the field you just created to replace the word "[instrument]" in the "Caring for Your New [instrument]" heading.
13. Use the AutoText button you created for the store name to insert the store name in the footer, on the first line aligned on the left margin. Use the AutoText button for the phone number to insert the phone number on the second line below the store name.
14. Insert a Date field in the footer below the e-mail address that will show the date the document was last printed in the format "February 2001."
15. Insert any clip-art image related to music from the Clipart Gallery on your computer in a blank line below the last paragraph in the main body of the brochure. With the picture selected, record a macro called "ResizePicture" with the description "Resizes picture of instrument" that will be available in only this template. Assign the macro to a toolbar, place the button to the right of the PH button, and change the button image to the music note. Record the macro so it sets the height scale to 60%.
16. Delete the clip-art picture from the template.
17. Add a watermark to the template. Select the WordArt style in row 3 and column 5, type the company name, use 60-point Footlight MT Light, set the Horizontal and Vertical positions so the watermark is approximately centered on the page, and change the Fill Effects to one color using Gray-25%.
18. Create an AutoNew macro for this template only that moves the insertion point below the "About Your New [instrument]" heading when you open a new document based on this template.
19. Save your changes to the template, and make sure your computer is set to update fields upon printing.
20. Copy the Vermillion Cliffs Brochure template into the Templates folder on your computer.
21. Close the template, and open a new document using the Brochure template.
22. Type "Hammer Dulcimer" as the name of the instrument, and then save the document as **Hammer Dulcimer Brochure** in the Cases folder on your Data Disk.
23. Type the following text into the brochure under the heading "About Your New Hammer Dulcimer"; use the AutoText entries you created whenever possible: "Your hammer dulcimer was handcrafted at Mahogany Music in Seattle, a company with which Fire Mountain Music has worked since the early 1980s. The primary wood in your dulcimer is Honduras mahogany, the best choice because it combines strength and musical tone. The trim, bridges, and binding are constructed from a variety of high-quality cosmetic woods, including cherry, maple, and American black walnut."
24. Insert a blank line after the paragraph you just typed, then type the following paragraph under the heading "Caring for Your New Hammer Dulcimer." Again use AutoText whenever possible: "Well-built hammer dulcimers like yours need very little care. The greatest concern is humidity; watch for too much, too little, or a big change too quickly. Vermillion Cliffs Music recommends you monitor the humidity level in your home or studio—a humidity level between 40% and 60% is okay for your dulcimer. If you find your location is too dry or too moist, use a vaporizer or dehumidifier as needed.

Vermillion Cliffs Music suggests that you dust your dulcimer with a dry cloth and avoid any oils or polishes."

"With this minimal care, your hammer dulcimer from Vermillion Cliffs Music will allow you to produce beautiful music for a lifetime. If you have any questions about the care of your dulcimer, please call Vermillion Cliffs Music at 505-555-7090."

"This information was prepared by [*insert your name*]."

25. In the blank line below the paragraph you just typed, insert a music-related clip-art image, and then run the Resize Picture macro you recorded earlier.
26. Below the figure, add the paragraph, "The following chart shows the relationship between the humidity and the time (in months) recommended between servicing. The longer the time, the better. For best results keep the humidity near 50%." Below that paragraph, insert a chart that compares the humidity and time between servicing. Begin by erasing all the cells of the datasheet. Below the cells labeled A, B, C, and D (above the top data row), type "15%", "40%", "50%", "60%", and "85%," respectively. In the cell to the right of the cell labeled "1," type the label "Time (in days)." In cells A1 through E1, type the data "8", "14", "26", "12", and "4," respectively.
27. Save the brochure, and then print a copy.
28. Delete the Vermillion Cliffs Brochure template from the Templates folder.

Case 2. Falcon Custom Hot Tubs Jim Faulconer owns a contracting business that specializes in the design and installation of residential hot tubs and accompanying decks and gazebos in LaCrosse, Wisconsin. Jim wants to send every client a memo that outlines the tasks their company will perform, a tentative schedule, and a list of the workers assigned to each task. Jim wrote most of the text but asks you to create a template to generate these memos and then write a memo for a new contract.

1. If necessary, start Word and make sure your Data Disk is in the appropriate drive. Open the file **FalcMemo** in the Cases subfolder within the Tutorial.08 folder on your Data Disk, and then save it as a template (in the same folder) with the filename **Falcon Memo**.
2. Insert the graphic Falcon (the company logo) from the Cases folder for Tutorial 8 on your Data Disk into the blank line at the beginning of the memo, reduce the size to 50%, and center the picture between the left and right margins.
3. Below the logo, type the company address (on two lines): 1478 Lake Superior Drive, LaCrosse, WI 54601; and type the phone number and Web address on a third and fourth line: 608-555-5632, www.falcontubs.com. Make sure there's a blank line between the Web address and the first line of the memo heading.
4. Change the font of the Normal style to 12-point Arial.

Explore

5. Create a new paragraph style named "Memo Address" as bold, 14-point Times New Roman with centered alignment.
6. Apply the Memo Address style to the entire company address including the phone number and Web address.
7. Define a new character style named "Memo Heading 1" that is bold, italic, blue, 12-point Times New Roman.
8. Apply the Memo Heading-1 style to the words "To," "From," "Re," and "Date," but not to the colons.
9. Define a new paragraph style named "Memo Heading 2" that is blue, bold, double-spaced, 12-point Times New Roman.
10. Apply the Memo Heading-2 style to the phrases "Your choices, "Your schedule," and "Your crew."

11. Create an AutoText entry for each name and title in the "Your crew" section; use each person's initials as the abbreviation for the entry. For example, use "gc" for "George Crandall, Decking."
12. Delete the list of names and titles from the template.

Explore

13. Insert the View Field Codes command after the Document Map command on the View menu in this template. (*Hint*: Click Tools on the menu bar, click Customize, click the Commands tab, and then drag the command to the correct location.)
14. After the word "To" at the beginning of the memo, insert a space, and then insert a Fill-in field that has "Who is the customer?" as a prompt. After the word "Re," insert a space, and then insert a Fill-in field that has "What is the job?" as a prompt.
15. After the word "From," insert a space, and then insert the Author field; if your name isn't listed as the author of the template, then change the document Summary.
16. After the word "Date," insert a space, insert the Date field, and format it so the current date appears in the format "February 18, 2001" (including the comma).
17. Delete the word "[Brand]" (including the brackets) from the second paragraph, and insert a Fill-in field that has "What is the brand of the tub?" as a prompt. Delete the words "[Decks and Gazebo]" (including the brackets), and insert a Fill-in field that has "Describe the decking and gazebo selected." as a prompt.
18. Insert a field that will display the page number and the total number of pages in the document in the form "Page *x* of *y*" in the footer.
19. Record a macro for this template that inserts a table with seven columns and two rows. Name the macro "JobTable." AutoFormat the table with the Grid-1 style, move the insertion point to cell B1, and type the following column headings in boldface, making sure to press Tab to move the insertion point from one column to the next: "Decking," "Install tub," "Decking around tub," "Electrical," "Gazebo," and "Hook-up." Then move the insertion point to cell A2, and type "Est. Time" in boldface. Adjust column widths so the headings fit on one line.

Explore

20. Add the JobTable macro to the menu bar, to the right of Table. (*Hint*: Drag the macro name from the Customize dialog box to the appropriate position on the menu.)

Explore

21. Record an AutoNew macro that moves the insertion point to the beginning of page 2 when you open a new document based on this template. (*Hint*: Use the Go To command.)
22. Delete the table and the results of all the fields, and then save the completed template.
23. Copy the Falcon memo template to the Templates folder, and then close the template.
24. Open a new document based on the Falcon Memo template.
25. Fill in the memo using the customer name "Tom Russell" and the job "Your hot tub and deck installation"; use "Williams Sunriser" as the brand of the tub and "a 10'×10' cedar deck addition and a Garden gazebo" as the decking and gazebo description.
26. Move the insertion point to the second blank line in the section "Your schedule," run the JobTable macro, and then beginning in cell B2, type the following information: "one week," "one day," "two days," "one to two days," "one day," and "one-half day."
27. In the section "Your crew," use the AutoText abbreviations (gc, bs, rp, jc) you assigned earlier to insert the necessary names and titles. Insert each name on its own own line.
28. Save the memo in the Cases folder on your Data Disk as Falcon-Russell Memo. Preview the memo, make sure the table isn't split onto two pages and your computer is set to update fields upon printing, and then print the memo.
29. Close the memo and delete the Falcon Memo template from the Templates folder.

Case 3. QualiTemps Employee Services QualiTemps Employee Services, located in Sacramento, California, provides temporary employees to area businesses. Connie Parker runs the resources department, which publishes descriptions of the temporary positions available at local companies. Connie wants a template that she or others in her department can use to prepare these job descriptions so they are consistent and more professional-looking. She asks you to create a template for her and to prepare the first job description.

1. If necessary, start Word and make sure your Data Disk is in the appropriate drive. Open the file **QualTmps** from the Cases subfolder within the Tutorial.08 folder on your Data Disk, and then save it as a template (in the same folder) using the filename **QualiTemps Job Form**.
2. Insert the picture **QTLogo** (the company logo) from the Cases folder for Tutorial 8 on your Data Disk into the blank line at the top of the template. Center the logo between the left and right margins.
3. Define a new paragraph style named "Address"; use 14-point Desdemona (or the font of your choice), center the paragraph, and draw a ¾-point box border around the paragraph.
4. Apply the Address style to the QualiTemps company name, address, and phone number at the top of the document. Inside the border, add one blank line above the company name and one below the phone number.
5. Delete any blank lines between the company logo and address box you just created.
6. Define a new character style named "Form Heading 1" that is 14-point Arial Black with a single underline.
7. Apply the new style to each heading ("Company Name," "Company Phone," "Job Number," "Job Category," and so forth) but not to the colons.
8. Change the font of the Normal style to 12-point Times New Roman.
9. Customize the toolbar for this template by replacing the Font list and Font Sizes boxes on the Formatting toolbar with the View Field Codes button.
10. After the space following the "Job Number:" heading, insert a Fill-in field that uses "What is the number for the job?" as the prompt.

Explore

11. Copy the Fill-in field you just created, and insert it after the space following each heading. (*Hint*: Copy the field just one time; you can use the Paste command repeatedly.)

Explore

12. Change the prompts for the Fill-in fields to the following:

Job Category	What is the job category?
Company Name	What is the company name?
Company Address	What is the company street, city, state, and ZIP code?
Company Phone	What is the company phone number, including the area code?
Job Description	Enter the description from the company's request form.
Qualifications	Enter the qualifications from the company's request form.
Start Date	When does the job begin?
End Date	When does the job end?
Salary	What is the hourly rate for the job?

13. Create a bookmark for the Company Name using the name "CompanyName" and a bookmark for the Company Phone using the name "CompanyPhone."

Explore

14. In the third blank line after the Salary line, record a macro attached to only this template named "Interview" that has the description "Types and formats text about a required interview." Assign the macro to a button on the Formatting toolbar using the telephone image for the button." Record the macro with the following steps:
    - Insert the following text with the indicated fields: "Interview required! Call [field that will insert the Company Name] at [field that will insert the Company Phone]." Make sure you use proper spacing around both fields and end them with a period. Do not include the quotation marks.
    - Change the left and right indentations to 0.5" each. (*Hint*: Before changing the margins, press Ctrl + Shift + ↑ to select all the text you just typed.)
    - Add a ¾-point border and light green shading.
    - Move the insertion point to the blank line below the new text.
15. Delete the results of the macro in the template.
16. Save the completed template, and then make sure your computer is set to update fields upon printing.
17. Copy the QualiTemps Job Form template to the Templates folder on your computer, and then close the template.
18. Open a new document based on the QualiTemps Job Form template.
19. Complete the form for the new job opening.

Job Number	01-1315
Job Category	Office Assistant
Company Name	Sierra Mortgage Company
Company Address	1807 C Street, Sacramento, CA 95866
Company Phone	916-555-2371
Job Description	Answer incoming calls (about 300 per day); create files for new loan applicants; distribute the daily update from the central office; copy documents for loan officers as needed; perform other miscellaneous office tasks.
Qualifications	At least one year of office experience; college degree preferred; cleanliness, timeliness, and a cheerful attitude.
Start Date	March 16, 2001
End Date	May 29, 2001
Salary	$9.60 per hour

20. In the third blank line after the Salary line, run the Interview macro you created.
21. Save the document as "QualiTemps 01-1315," preview, and then print it.
22. Close the document and delete the template from the Other Documents folder in the Templates folder on your computer.

Case 4. Permian Basin Home Health Care Permian Basin Home Health Care employs more than 30 doctors, nurses, and home health aides at two locations in Odessa, Texas. Owners Julia and Gregorio Salazar have always relied on employee newsletters to keep their employees informed about events in both locations. They want to improve the appearance of the newsletter and reduce the amount of time it takes to produce the newsletter each quarter. They asked you to design a newsletter and create the newsletter template.

1. If necessary, start Word and make sure your Data Disk is in the appropriate drive. Open a new, blank document, and save the document as a Word template with the filename **Permian Basin Newsletter** in the Cases subfolder within the Tutorial.08 folder on your Data Disk.

2. Insert a graphic of your choice that relates to medicine into the blank line at the top of the template. You can use a clip-art image already on your computer or create your own image. Resize and align the graphic as needed.
3. Below or next to the graphic, type the following: "Permian Basin Home Health Care, 8147 Midland Drive, Odessa, TX 79761, 915-555-4917." Arrange the information on the page attractively.
4. Below the phone number and graphic, type the title "Employee Newsletter," and format the title to create an attractive, professional design.
5. Type each of the following headings on its own line, and skip a line between each heading: "From the Desk of the Director," "Last Quarter at Permian Basin Home Health Care," "Next Quarter's Meetings and Scheduled Training," and "Employee of the Quarter."
6. Create at least three new styles that are appropriate for the text you just typed, and then assign the styles to the text you typed in Steps 3, 4, and 5.
7. Customize the toolbar for only this template by removing the Insert Hyperlink buttons from the Standard toolbar and adding the View Field Codes button.

Explore

8. Customize the keyboard for only this template by creating a shortcut key for each style you created. (*Hint*: Click Tools, click Customize, and then click the Keyboard button. Make sure you don't use any key combinations that are already assigned. If a key combination is assigned already, you'll see a message indicating its current purpose immediately below the Press new shortcut key text box.)
9. Type a colon (:) and a space after the heading "Employee of the Quarter," and then insert a field that will prompt the user to enter the name of the employee. Make sure the entire line is formatted with the same style.
10. Create a bookmark for the employee name.

Explore

11. After the Employee Newsletter title (but before the "From the Desk of the Director" heading), type "Congratulations to" followed by a space, and then insert a field that will automatically enter the name of the Employee of the Quarter; include an exclamation point after the field. Type a space, "See page" followed by a space, and then insert a field that will insert the page number of the employee bookmark you created earlier, followed by a period. (*Hint*: Use the PageRef field in the Links and References category; use Help to learn how to format the field.)
12. Type "Quarter" in an appropriate section near the top of the document, and then type a space and insert a field that will prompt the user to enter the number of the quarter and the year, separated by a comma (for example, Quarter 3, 2001).
13. Apply the styles you created earlier to the text you entered in Steps 11 and 12.

Explore

14. Create a watermark using the same graphic you inserted at the top of the newsletter. (*Hint*: Insert and position the graphic, click Format on the menu bar, click Picture, and then click Watermark in the Color list box.)
15. Record a macro for this template only that will insert a table with two columns and four rows, AutoFormat it to the Classic 1 style, center it on the page (if possible), insert the column headings "Date" and "Time," center the title "Monthly Meetings" above the table, and move the insertion point to the blank line below the table.
16. Record another macro for this template only that does the following: inserts a table with three columns and four rows, AutoFormats it to the Classic 1 style; centers it on the page (if possible), inserts the column headings "Date," "Time," and "Topic;" centers the title "Monthly Training" above the table; and moves the insertion point to the blank line below the table.
17. Record an AutoNew macro for this template only that moves the insertion point to the blank line below the heading "From the Desk of the Director."

18. Delete any field entries and macro results, and then save the completed template.
19. Copy the Permian Basin Newsletter template into the Templates folder on your computer, and close the template.
20. Open a new document based on the Permian Basin Newsletter template.
21. Insert appropriate information into the Fill-in fields and run both macros, leaving one blank line between the tables below the heading "Next Quarter's Meetings and Scheduled Training." Fill in the two tables with (fictitious) information.

Explore

22. Insert a page break before the "Employee of the Quarter" heading, if necessary, to move that section to page 2 of the newsletter.
23. At an appropriate place in the document, insert a chart that shows the gross income and net profit over the previous three months. Insert text before the chart to explain the chart's purpose. The chart should include data for the months of April, May, and June. The gross income (in millions of dollars) for those three months was 21.7, 28.4, and 26.8, respectively. The net profit (in millions of dollars) for those three months was 3.4, 3.6, and 3.9, respectively.
24. Save the file as **Permian Basin Sample Newsletter**, and make sure your computer is set to update fields automatically upon printing.
25. Preview and print a copy of the sample newsletter, and then close the file.
26. Delete the Permian Basin Newsletter template from the Templates folder.

QUICK CHECK ANSWERS

Session 8.1

1. Blueprint for the text, graphics, and format that ensures all documents follow a specified pattern. Memos, invoices, contracts.
2. Text and graphics that are used repeatedly. Templates can contain boilerplate text or graphics that automatically appear in every document based on the template
3. Styles; AutoText; custom toolbars, menus, and shortcut keys; fields; macros.
4. consistency, accuracy, efficiency.
5. Create a normal Word document, customize or modify toolbars, menus, and shortcut keys, add fields, create macros, and save as a document template.
6. Open the Style dialog box, select the style to change, click Modify, click Format, click Border, change the shading to blue, and then change the font color.
7. Allows you to insert frequently used text or graphics into a document with speed and accuracy.
8. A word or phrase that AutoCorrect doesn't automatically modify.

Session 8.2

1. Text or graphics, usually in a lighter shade, that usually appears behind existing text on each page of a document.
2. Right-click anywhere on a toolbar, click Customize, click the Command tab, click a category, drag a button from the dialog box to a toolbar or drag buttons off the toolbar.
3. Special code to insert information into a document. Author: inserts name of document's author; Date: inserts current date and/or time; Ref: inserts text marked with a specified bookmark. Fillin: prompts user to fill-in specified information; Page: inserts current page number; NumPages: inserts number of pages in document.

4. dd MMMM yy
5. Select the field and press the F9 key, or right-click the field and click Update Field.
6. After you insert the Fill-in field, click between the two spaces after the field name, and type the desired prompt in quotation marks.
7. A field that refers or references some other object in the document (often a bookmark) and repeats that text at the location of the REF field.
8. Page and NumPages

Session 8.3

1. A recording of keystroke or mouse operations that you can perform by pressing fewer key combinations or mouse operations
2. speed, accuracy, consistency
3. Double-click the REC button on the status bar, give the macro a name and a description, optionally assign it to a keyboard or toolbar, record the keystrokes and mouse operations, and click the Stop Record button.
4. If you've typed the wrong text or performed the wrong keyboard or mouse operations. Click the name of the macro in the Macro dialog box, click Edit, change the macro, click Save, and return to the document.
5. Macros that run automatically with certain Word events. AutoExec runs when you open Word; AutoNew runs when you open a blank document; AutoOpen runs when you open an existing document.
6. To automatically perform some operation when you open a new document based on that template.
7. Click File, click New, and double-click the desired template icon.
8. Click Tools, point to Macros, click Macros, click MyMacro, click Run.
9. Insert the chart as an object newly created by the program Microsoft Graph 2000, click in the upper-left corner of the datasheet, click Edit, click Import File, and import the Excel worksheet.

OBJECTIVES

In this tutorial you will:

- Design and create an on-screen form in landscape orientation
- Set borders, shade cells, and move gridlines in a form table
- Rotate fonts and create reverse type in a form table
- Insert form fields for text, drop-down lists, and check boxes
- Create regular, date, and number text form fields
- Perform automatic calculations in an on-screen form
- Record macros to perform special functions in an on-screen form
- Protect, save, fill in, and fax an on-screen form

CREATING ON-SCREEN FORMS USING ADVANCED TABLE TECHNIQUES

Developing an Order Form for the Sun Valley Ticket Office

CASE

Sun Valley Summer Music Festival

The Sun Valley Summer Music Festival is held each summer in Sun Valley, Idaho, as well as in the nearby town of Ketchum, both of which are located at the edge of the Sawtooth National Forest. The festival provides educational and performance opportunities for high school students from the intermountain west (Idaho, western Washington, eastern Montana, Utah, and Nevada). Sponsored by a consortium of western colleges and universities, the festival provides master classes by well-known musicians, private instruction by university music faculty, seminars by professors and professional musicians, and performances by youth ensembles and the Sun Valley Youth Orchestra, as well as by the Gem State Symphony Orchestra and other professional musicians.

As marketing manager, Richard Vanderkloot is responsible for promoting the ticket sales for the festival. In addition, he manages the Sun Valley Ticket Office, which takes ticket orders for the various concerts and recitals held throughout the summer. Recently, he decided that the manual method of filling out customer order forms, using pen and paper, is inefficient. Richard asks you to create an on-screen (computerized) order form based on his design, that all the ticket agents can use when taking orders from both telephone and walk-in customers. Agents will fill in an order form for each ticket order, print a copy of the order form for the customer, and save the form data for the ticket office records.

In this tutorial, you'll create and then test an on-screen order form template that the Sun Valley Ticket Office ticket agents will use to process ticket purchases for its Summer Music Festival. First, you'll modify the order form table by inserting rows, drawing borders, shading cells, merging and splitting cells, creating reverse type and other effects, and moving gridlines. Next, you'll create form fields to accept certain types of information and add help messages and status-bar prompts. Finally, you'll automate the form field with macros and calculation form fields; you'll test the template by filling in an order form; and then you'll print, fax, and save only the data for the order form.

SESSION 9.1

In this session you'll create a table for an on-screen order form. You'll modify the form table by inserting new rows, setting borders, shading cells, merging cells, splitting cells, creating reverse type and other text effects, and moving gridlines.

Planning the Document

The Sun Valley on-screen form will consist of text and a Word table formatted to be attractive and easy to read, both on-screen for the ticket agent and printed for the customer. The order-form table will contain the Sun Valley Ticket Office's address, phone number, fax number, and e-mail address, as well as information (such as taxes and handling fees) to help process the order. Ticket agents will enter the specific information for each order, including:

- **Event information**: name, date, time, and location of event
- **Customer information**: name, address, and phone number
- **Order information**: date and time of order, number of tickets, price per ticket, ticket cost, sales tax, handling fee, and total cost
- **Credit card information**: account type, card number, expiration date, and name on card (if different from customer name)

The customer ticket order form will be in a table form, with specific sections (or blocks of cells) containing the information required to process the order. Some cells will contain titles and headings; others will have space in which the ticket agents will enter information; and some cells will include both text and space for entering information.

The text of the order form will consist primarily of names, titles, and headings. Only the Help text and the Festival regulations will be complete sentences. The order form must be eye-catching and readable. It must be easy to use by ticket agents, easy to read by customers, and portray a positive image for the Sun Valley Summer Music Festival.

Creating and Using On-Screen Forms

An **on-screen form** is a Word template that contains spaces for you to insert information. A well-designed form makes it easy to enter information accurately and efficiently. In addition to the usual template elements (text, graphics, styles, AutoText, customized toolbars, menus, shortcut keys, fields, and macros), the on-screen form template can contain form fields. A **form field** stores a certain type of information, such as a name or a price, to which you can assign a specific format. For example, you can insert a form field that accepts only numbers (not letters) and formats them as a currency. In this instance, Word would not accept the text "twenty-three and a half," but you could type "23.5" into the field, and the number would automatically change to "$23.50"—with the dollar sign ($) and final zero added.

Moreover, form fields provide other types of controls to help you fill out a form quickly and correctly. You can insert form fields that provide drop-down lists, check boxes, and numeric calculations. Also, you can set a prompt for each field that appears in the status bar, and you can include additional help that appears when the F1 (Help) key is pressed.

When someone opens a new document based on the on-screen form template, the insertion point automatically selects the first form field. After the person enters the requested information and presses the Tab key, the insertion point moves to the second field in the form. The person types the required information and presses the Tab key again. This continues until the form is completely filled out. A properly designed on-screen form allows only the filled-in information to be modified.

Notice that throughout this tutorial the term *on-screen forms* refers to Word documents that contain form fields. However, these forms are called "online forms" or simply "Word forms" in the Microsoft Word Help Topics. The use of "online" has been avoided because in recent years "online" has come to mean connected to the Internet or to an Internet service provider, such as Microsoft Network, America Online, or CompuServe. If you use the Microsoft Word Help Topics to get additional information about on-screen forms, be sure to look under "online forms," not "on-screen forms."

Designing an On-Screen Form

Figure 9–1 shows Richard's design for the on-screen ticket order form.

Figure 9-1 TABLE STRUCTURE OF ORDER FORM

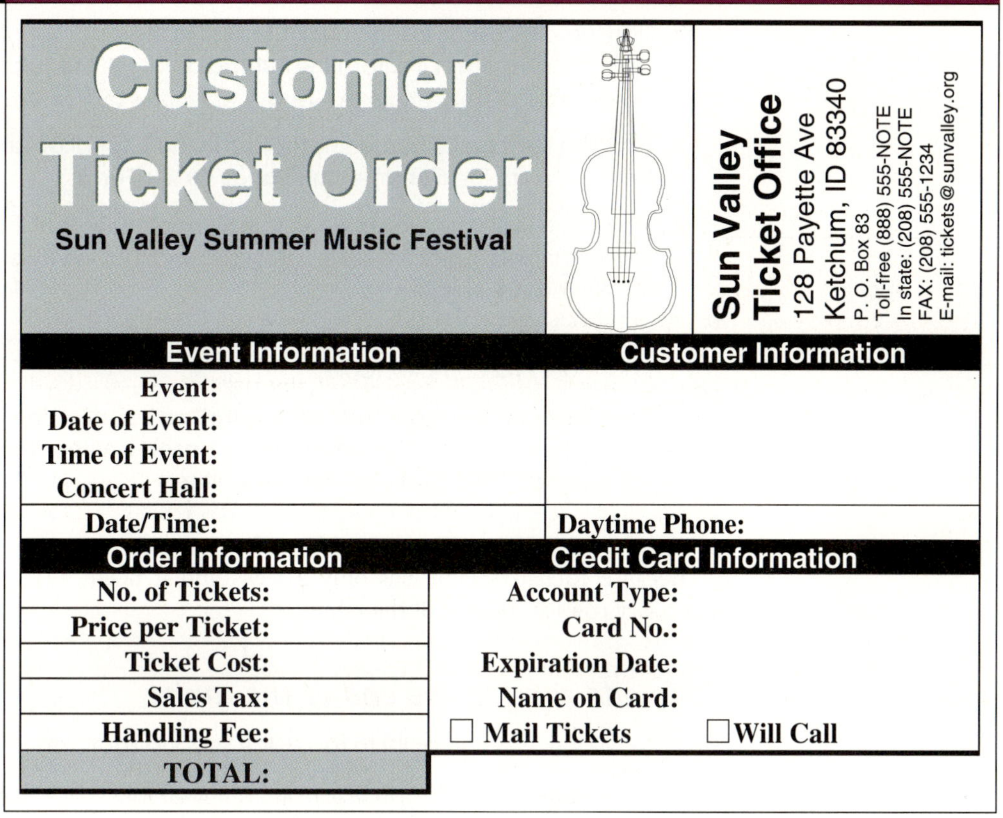

Customer Ticket Order
Sun Valley Summer Music Festival

Sun Valley
Ticket Office
128 Payette Ave
Ketchum, ID 83340
P. O. Box 83
Toll-free (888) 555-NOTE
In state: (208) 555-NOTE
FAX: (208) 555-1234
E-mail: tickets@sunvalley.org

Event Information	Customer Information
Event: Date of Event: Time of Event: Concert Hall:	
Date/Time:	Daytime Phone:

Order Information	Credit Card Information
No. of Tickets:	Account Type:
Price per Ticket:	Card No.:
Ticket Cost:	Expiration Date:
Sales Tax:	Name on Card:
Handling Fee:	☐ Mail Tickets ☐ Will Call
TOTAL:	

Richard designed the order-form template with the following features:

- The key text, graphics, and form fields with ordering information appear in a table with the festival's regulations in a column next to the table.
- The table includes three fonts (Times New Roman, Arial, and Braggadocio), two font styles (normal and bold), two font colors (black and white), and rotated text.
- The table design includes border lines of different thicknesses (¾-point and 2 ¾-points), cells of different shading (none, 20%, and 100%), and cells with different types of contents (text, graphics, and form fields, or a combination of these).
- The table structure has cells of different heights and widths.

When designing an on-screen form, you don't need all of these features. In fact, you don't even need to use a table. You can insert form fields into regular text, tables, or frames. This gives you the flexibility to design nearly any type of on-screen form. For example, you might create a business contract with fields for such entries as payment terms and contract length.

Modifying the Form Table

Richard already started the table for the on-screen form. You'll open his document, save it as a template, and then modify the table to match Figure 9–1.

To open the document and save it as a template:

1. Start Word as usual, insert your Data Disk in the appropriate drive, and then open the **OrdrForm** file from the **Tutorial** folder in the Tutorial.09 folder on your Data Disk.
2. Save the file as a Document Template in the Tutorial.09 Tutorial folder on your Data Disk with the filename **Sun Valley Order Form**.
3. Make sure that your Word screen is in **Normal View**, that the default Normal style is defined as 12-point Times New Roman, and that the Ruler and nonprinting characters are visible.

   You'll turn off automatic definition of styles, which can sometimes cause problems in formatting a complex table.
4. Click **Tools** on the menu bar, click **AutoCorrect**, click the **AutoFormat As You Type** tab, make sure the **Define styles based on your formatting** check box is not selected, and then click the **OK** button.

Because Richard's table has only 2 rows and it needs 11, you'll begin by adding the necessary rows at the end of the table.

To add rows to the end of the table:

1. Move the insertion point to row 2, the second (bottom) row in the table.
2. Click **Table** on the menu bar, point to **Insert**, and click **Rows Below**. Word inserts one additional row into the table. With three rows in the table, you need eight more.
3. Move the insertion point to the blank line below the table, again click **Table**, point to **Insert**, and click **Rows Above**. The Insert Rows dialog box opens, asking how many rows to add to the table.
4. Type **8**, and then click the **OK** button.
5. Deselect the new rows, and move the insertion point to cell A11. Recall that each table cell is labeled by a column letter (A, B, C, and so forth) and row number (1, 2, 3, and so forth). Therefore, cell A11 is in the last row (row 11) of the first column (column A).

Now that your table has the proper dimensions, you'll change the lines around some cells.

Drawing and Erasing Rules

When you create a table, ½-point borders usually appear along all the gridlines. A **border** is a box that frames tables and table cells; it consists of four rules. A **rule** is a horizontal or vertical line drawn along one or more edges (gridlines) of a cell or group of cells.

You'll modify the table by drawing borders of different weights (thicknesses) and by erasing some rules. This will help to distinguish sections of the order form. You'll begin by erasing the borders of cells A6 to C10.

To erase the borders of a group of cells in the table:

1. Select rows 6 through 10 in the table. Make sure the bottom row (11) is not selected.
2. Click the **Border** list arrow on the Formatting toolbar to display a palette of border styles. See Figure 9-2.

Figure 9-2 REMOVING BORDERS

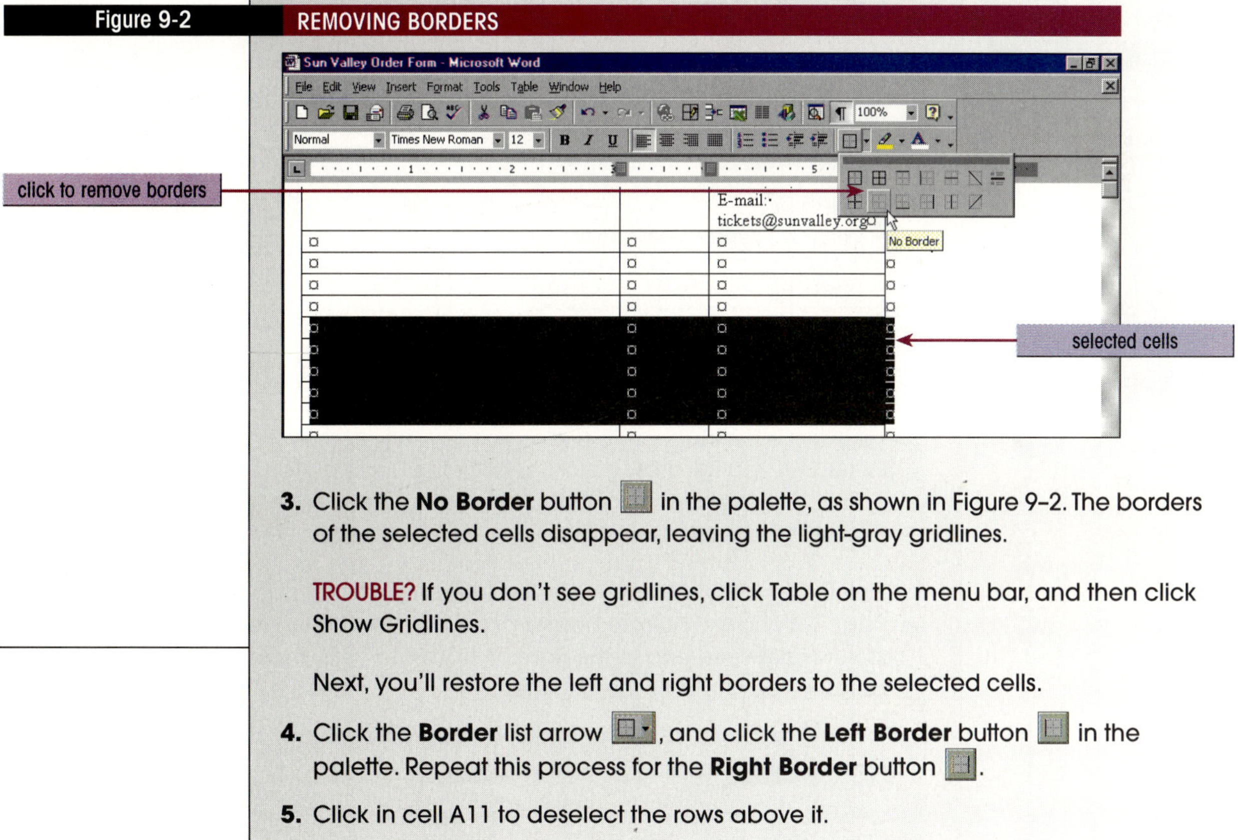

3. Click the **No Border** button in the palette, as shown in Figure 9-2. The borders of the selected cells disappear, leaving the light-gray gridlines.

   TROUBLE? If you don't see gridlines, click Table on the menu bar, and then click Show Gridlines.

   Next, you'll restore the left and right borders to the selected cells.

4. Click the **Border** list arrow, and click the **Left Border** button in the palette. Repeat this process for the **Right Border** button.
5. Click in cell A11 to deselect the rows above it.

You've used the Border buttons to remove and draw rules around selected cells. Now, you'll use the Tables and Borders toolbar to draw other rules.

To draw rules:

1. Click the **Tables and Borders** button on the Standard toolbar to display the Tables and Borders toolbar. The document window switches to Print Layout View.

TROUBLE? If a dialog box appears asking if you want to switch to Print Layout View, click the Yes button and then continue with Step 2.

2. Click the **Line Weight** list arrow on the Tables and Borders toolbar, and then click **2 ¼ pt**. Now, when you click any Border buttons or draw any rules with the **Draw Table** pointer, the rule will be 2 ¼ points thick rather than the default ½ point.

   Notice that when you move the pointer into the document, it appears as .

   TROUBLE? If the pointer doesn't change to , click the Draw Table button on the Tables and Borders toolbar.

3. If necessary, scroll up so you can see the top of the table, and then drag along the top rule of the table, above the entire row 1.
4. In three separate operations, drag along the bottom of cell A11, along the right border of cell A11, and then along the bottom of cells B10 and C10. Your table should look like Figure 9-3.

Figure 9-3 DRAWING RULES

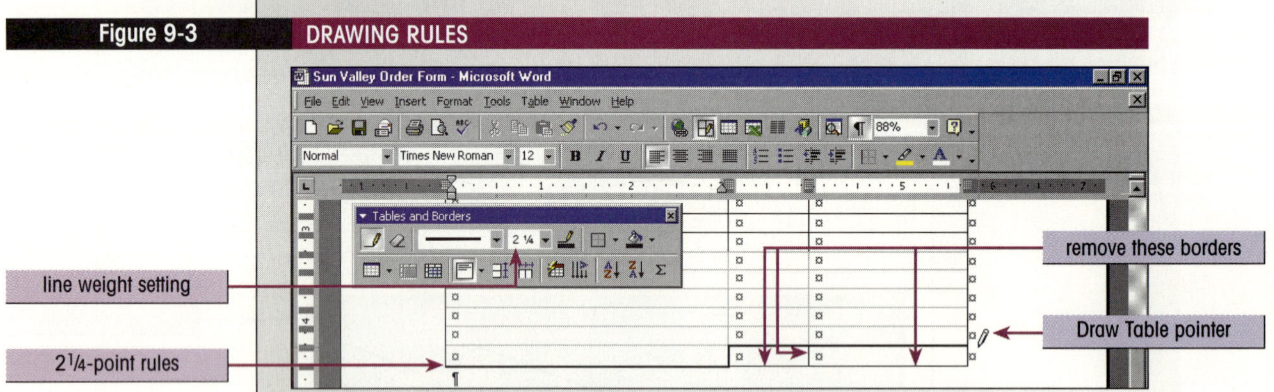

TROUBLE? If you misdraw a border, click the Undo button on the Standard toolbar until the new border disappears, and then repeat the necessary steps to draw the borders correctly.

5. Click the **Line Style** list arrow on the Tables and Borders toolbar, click **No Border**, drag along the bottom border of cells B11 and C11, and then along the vertical rules between and to the right of those two cells. Those rules disappear from the table, leaving only the gridlines.
6. Click again to close the Tables and Borders toolbar, and then switch to **Normal View**.
7. Save the document.

As you continue to modify the table, you'll draw or erase other rules.

Changing Fonts, Font Sizes, and Font Effects

As you can see, the text in the top row of the table is unsightly and hard-to-read. Richard wants you to make the form more attractive, readable, and professional-looking by changing its orientation, fonts, sizes, effects, and styles.

To change the font of the existing text within the table:

1. Select row 1 in the table. Recall that you can select a row by clicking ↗ in the margin to the left of the row.
2. Click the **Font** list arrow on the Formatting toolbar, click **Arial** to change the font of the selected text to Arial, and then deselect the row.
3. Select the phrase **Customer Ticket Order** in cell A1, click **Format** on the menu bar, and then click **Font** to open the Font dialog box. See Figure 9-4.

Figure 9-4 FONT DIALOG BOX

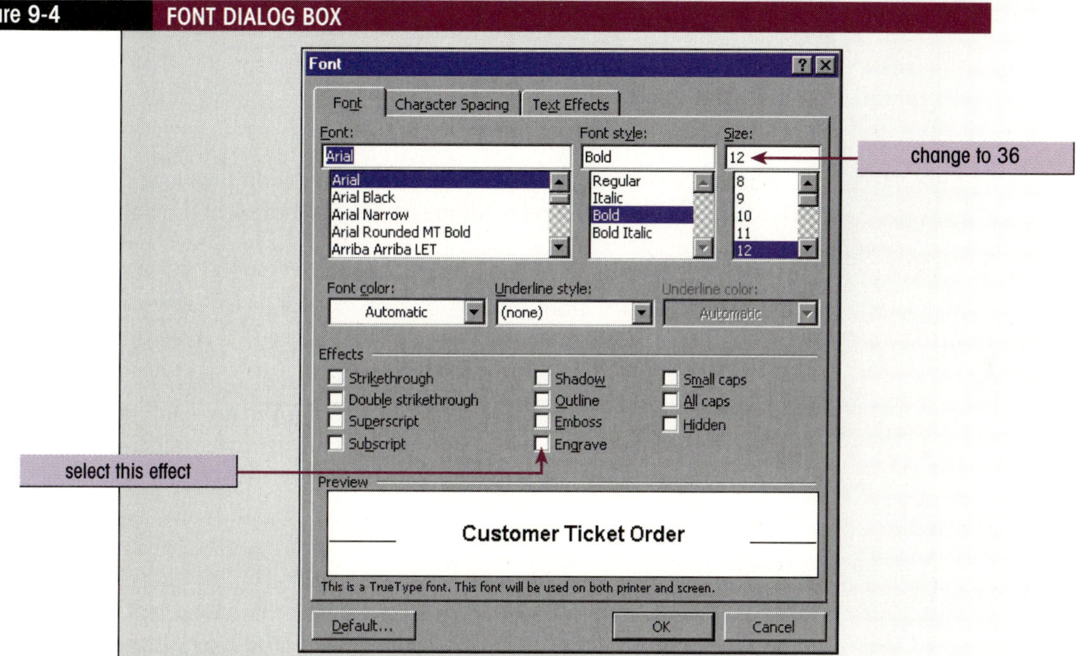

You'll use this dialog box to change the font size to 36 points and the font effects to Engrave. Also, you could use this dialog box to change the underline style by clicking the Underline list arrow and selecting from among the 17 underline styles.

4. Click **36** points in the Size list, click the **Engrave** check box in the Effects section, and then click the **OK** button. The Engrave effect sets the letters in white with a gray-shaded edge. Later, you'll fill the cell with a gray background to make these letters stand out.
5. Select the last lines in cell C1 (beginning with "P. O. Box 83" and ending with the e-mail address), and then change the font size to **8** points.
6. Select the phrase "Sun Valley Ticket Office" in cell C1, change the font to **16-point Arial bold**, and then deselect the text. See Figure 9-5.

Figure 9-5 TEXT IN TABLE AFTER FONT CHANGES

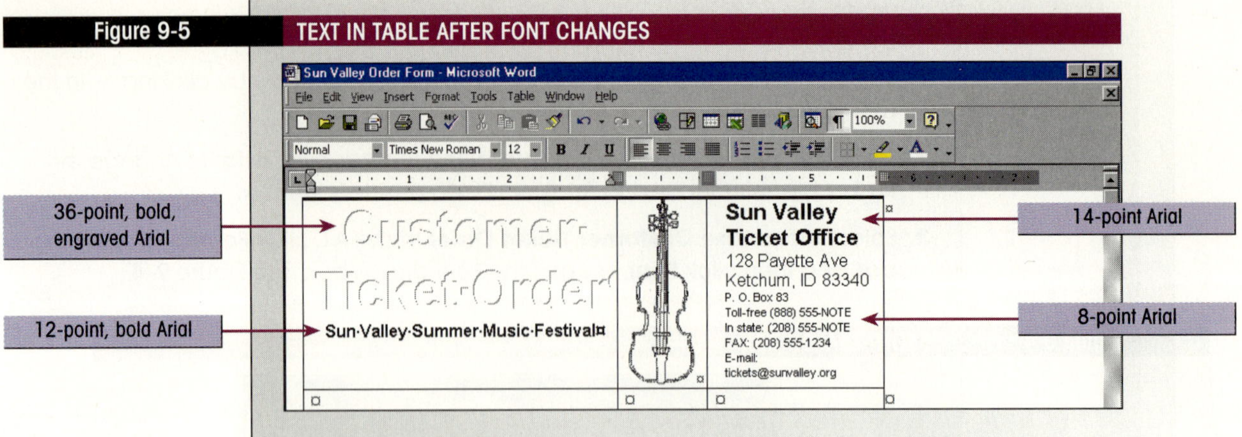

Later, as you enter text in other cells, you'll make additional font and font style changes. Next, you'll rotate the text in the cell with the name and address of the Sun Valley Ticket Office.

Rotating Text in a Table

Richard wants you to rotate the text in cell C1 not only to add emphasis to the text, but also to better fit the text into the cell, which is narrower than it is tall. In general, rotating text in tables allows you to fit wide labels (that is, text with many characters) into narrow columns. For example, if a table has many columns of two- or three-digit numbers, you could rotate the text of each label to keep the columns narrow.

To rotate text in the table:

1. Click anywhere in cell C1, click **Format** on the menu bar, and then click **Text Direction**. The Text Direction - Table Cell dialog box opens. See Figure 9-6.

Figure 9-6 TEXT DIRECTION - TABLE CELL DIALOG BOX

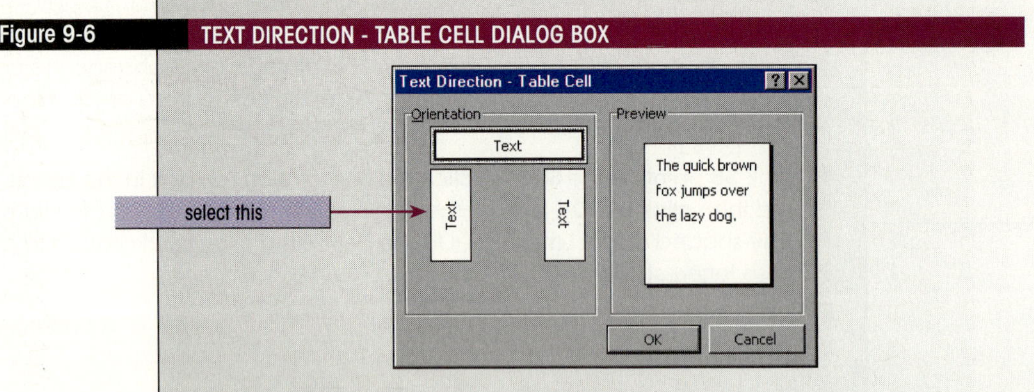

2. In the Orientation section of the dialog box, click the lower-left icon, with "Text" written from bottom to top. The Preview box shows you an example of the selected text orientation.

3. Click the **OK** button. The dialog box closes, and the text in the table rotates. The window switches to Print Layout View so you can see the rotated text. In Normal View, the text appears unrotated.

   TROUBLE? If a dialog box appears asking if you want to switch to Print Layout View, click the Yes button and then continue with Step 4.

4. Save the form template.

Shading Cells

Richard wants you to shade some cells so they stand out more. **Shading** is a gray or colored background that fills table cells and on which you can print text. You decide to shade the upper-left cell, which contains the text "Customer Ticket Order Form," and the lower-left cell, which will contain the total amount of the order, with a 20% gray scale.

To shade cells:

1. Click in cell A1, and then open the Tables and Borders toolbar.
2. Click the **Shading Color** list arrow on the Tables and Borders toolbar to open the color palette, and then click the **Gray-20%** tile in the top row, sixth row from the left. Cell A1 becomes shaded.
3. Click in cell A11, and then press the **F4** key to repeat your previous action. See Figure 9-7.

Figure 9-7 TABLE AFTER FORMATTING ROWS 1 AND 11

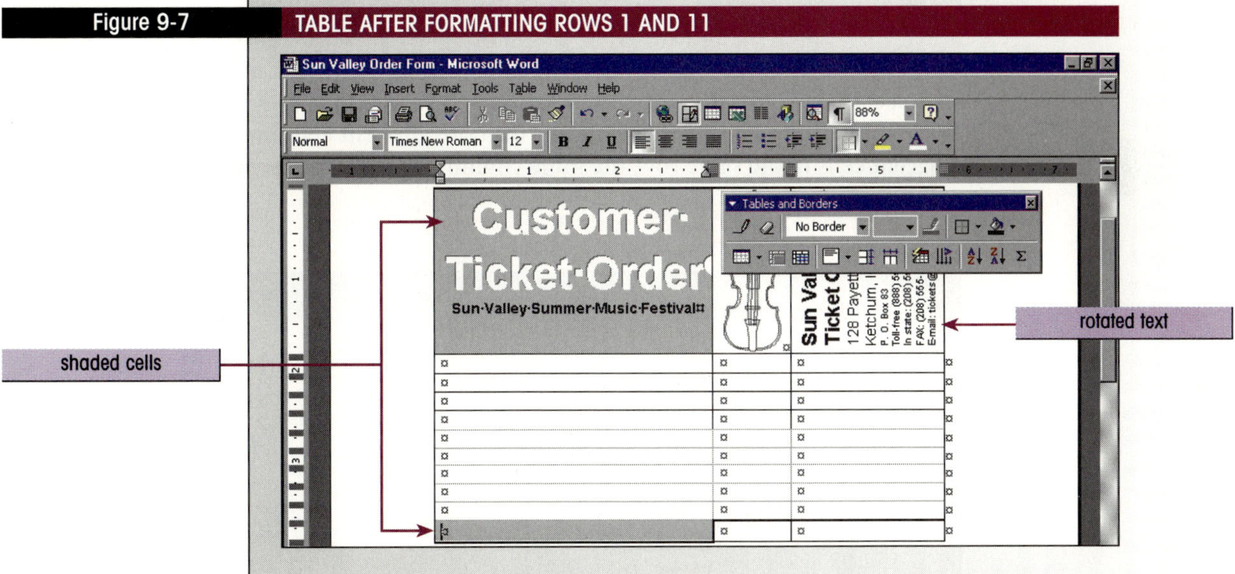

If you look back to Figure 9–1, you'll see that Richard designed some cells to be black. You'll shade those later, after you enter the text.

Merging Cells

Richard typed only the title text before he turned over his order-form file to you; he left the section headings for you to type.

To enter headings into the table:

1. Click in cell A2 (the second row of the first column).
2. Type **Event Information**, and then press the **Tab** key to move the insertion point to cell B2 (the next cell in the same row).
3. Type **Customer Information**. As you can see, the text doesn't fit on one line within this cell. You'll fix this problem after you type the other headings.
4. Click in cell A5, type **Order Information**, press the **Tab** key to move to cell B5, and then type **Credit Card Information**. Like the text in cell B2, the text in cell B5 doesn't fit on one line. See Figure 9-8.

Figure 9-8 TABLE AFTER TYPING NEW TEXT

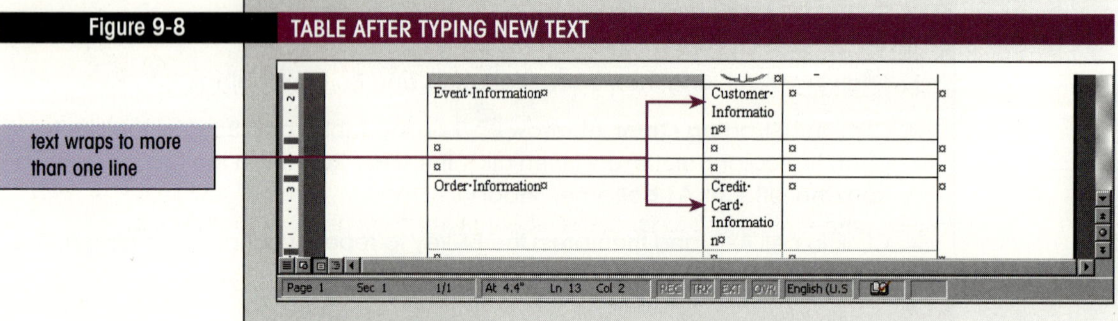

As you can see, the two headings in column B don't fit well in the cells. You can merge some cells in column B to the cells in column C so that the headings span the width of both cells. To **merge** cells means to join two or more adjacent cells into one cell. You can merge adjacent cells in the same row, the same column, or the same rectangular block of rows and columns.

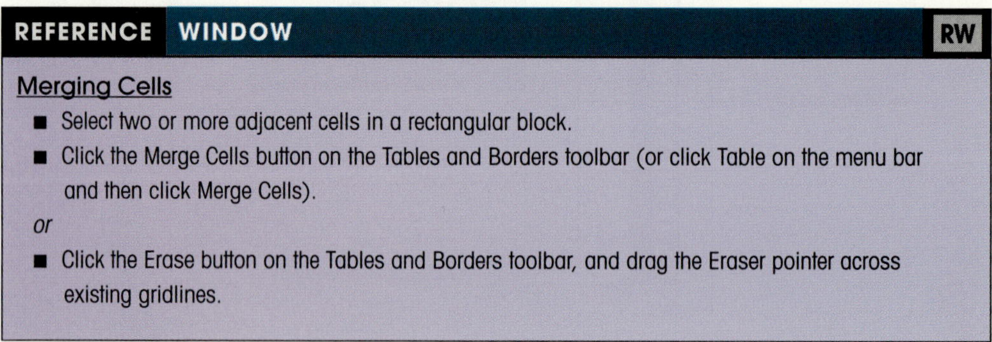

REFERENCE WINDOW RW

Merging Cells

- Select two or more adjacent cells in a rectangular block.
- Click the Merge Cells button on the Tables and Borders toolbar (or click Table on the menu bar and then click Merge Cells).

or

- Click the Erase button on the Tables and Borders toolbar, and drag the Eraser pointer across existing gridlines.

You'll merge cells to keep each heading on a single line.

To merge cells in a table

1. Select cells B2 and C2, that is, the cell containing "Customer Information" and the cell to its right.
2. Click the **Merge Cells** button on the Tables and Borders toolbar. The two cells combine and the row now contains only two columns—A and B.
3. Select cells B3 and C3, and click to combine the cells.
4. Use the F4 key to merge cells B4 and C4, and then cells B5 and C5. Deselect any selected cells. See Figure 9-9.

Figure 9-9 TABLE AFTER MERGING CELLS

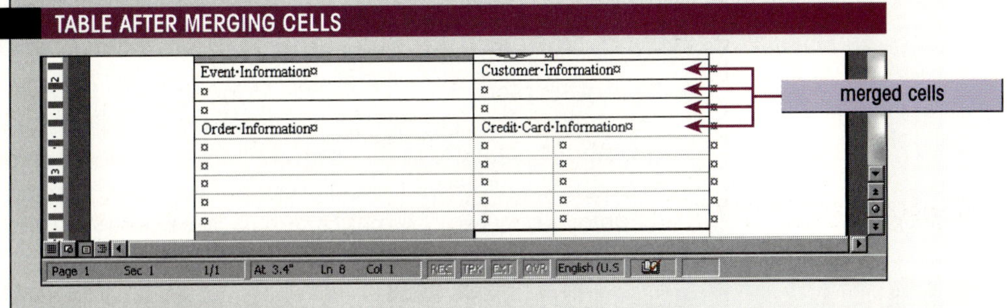

As you can see, a common reason for merging cells is to create cells that span more than one column in which to enter titles, labels, or large amounts of information.

Splitting Cells

Just as you can merge cells, you also can split them. To **split** cells means to divide one cell into two or more cells. You can split cells vertically to increase the number of columns in a row or horizontally to increase the number of rows in a column. Alternatively, you can do both to increase the number of rows and columns. Each cell is still labeled by its column letter and row number, but the same column might not be aligned vertically in different rows or the same row might not be horizontally aligned in different columns.

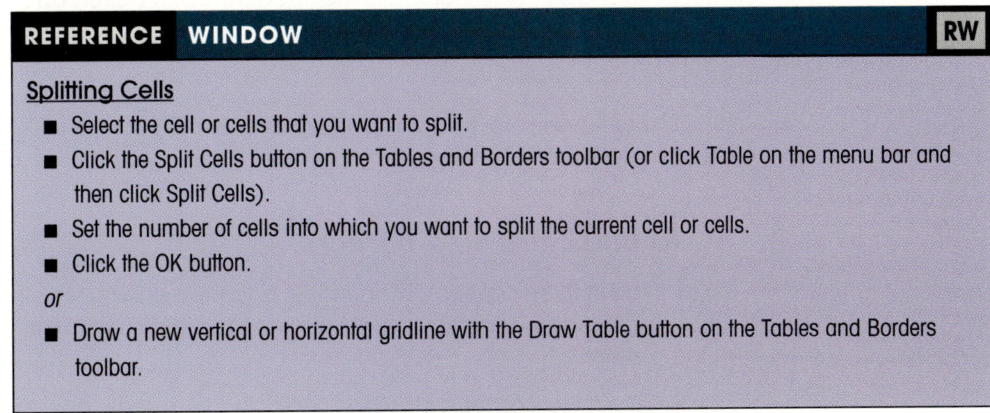

REFERENCE WINDOW RW

Splitting Cells

- Select the cell or cells that you want to split.
- Click the Split Cells button on the Tables and Borders toolbar (or click Table on the menu bar and then click Split Cells).
- Set the number of cells into which you want to split the current cell or cells.
- Click the OK button.

or

- Draw a new vertical or horizontal gridline with the Draw Table button on the Tables and Borders toolbar.

Richard wants you to convert the Event Information column into two columns so you can insert labels into the left column and data into the right column.

To split a cell into several cells on the same row:

1. Select cells A3 and A4, below the "Event Information" heading. You want to split each cell into two.
2. Click the **Split Cells** button on the Tables and Borders toolbar to open the Split Cells dialog box. The default number of columns is 2, which you'll accept. You'll also keep the default value of two rows, which is the current number of rows.
3. Click the **OK** button, and then deselect the cells. The cells split in two—cells A3 and B3 and cells A4 and B4.

   Sometimes, when you split cells that contain borders, Word draws a rule along an edge of the new cell that you don't want. That's what happened in the order form. You'll remove the vertical border on the right of cells A3 and A4 later.
4. Repeat this procedure to split cells A6 through A11, the cells below the "Order Information" heading into two columns, with the same six rows, and then deselect any selected cells. Notice that rows 6 through 11 now contain four columns (A through D), while rows 3 and 4 contain only three columns (A through C), and row 2 contains only two columns (A and B). See Figure 9-10.

Figure 9-10 TABLE AFTER SPLITTING CELLS

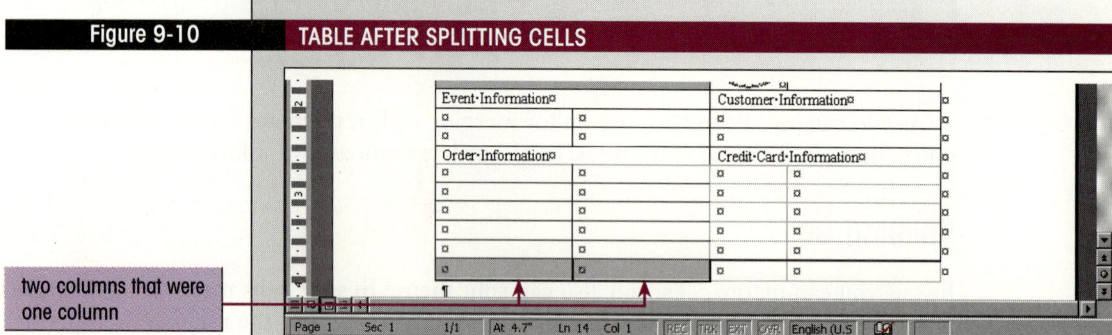

TROUBLE? If your table doesn't match the table in Figure 9-10, merge or split cells as necessary to make it match.

TROUBLE? If splitting cells removed the Gray-20% color from cells A11 and B11, or changed the fill color, use the Shading Color button on the Tables and Borders toolbar to recolor the cells.

The table structure for the order form is essentially complete. You'll finish drawing borders to complete the table design.

To finish drawing borders:

1. Select the plain straight line style, and then draw a ¾-point vertical line from the right of the Gray-20% cell A1 down to the thick rule in the lower-right corner of cell B11.
2. Select **No Border** for the Line Style, and then draw a vertical rule to separate cells A3 and A4 from B3 and B4, as shown in Figure 9-11. This erases the border, leaving only the gridline.

3. Erase the borders (but not the gridlines) to the right of cells A6 to A11. Make sure your table matches Figure 9-11.

Figure 9-11 TABLE AFTER DRAWING AND ERASING BORDERS

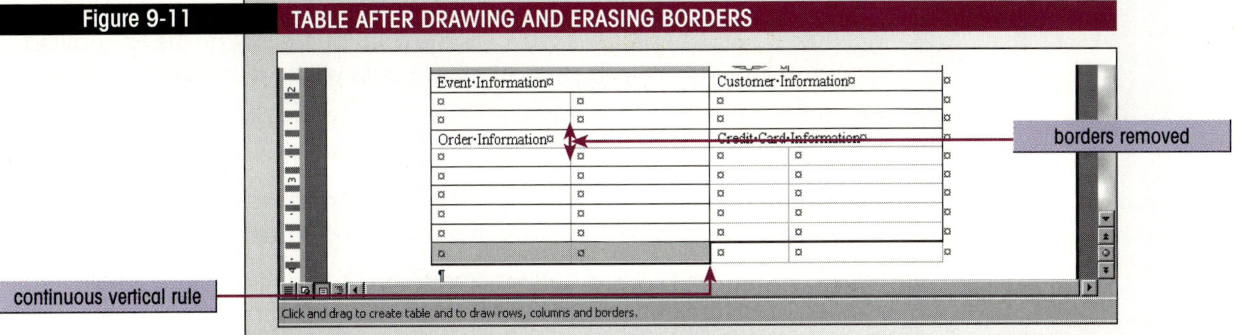

4. Close the Tables and Borders toolbar, switch to Normal View, and then save the order form template.

Your table structure now matches Richard's design, although you still need to format some labels and move some gridlines.

Aligning Text in Cells

To make the order-form design more attractive, you decide to change the text alignment in table cells. For example, you'll center the section headings and right-align cells that will contain prices. Recall that to change the alignment of text in table cells, you select the cells, and then click the Align Left, Center, Align Right, or Justify button on the Formatting toolbar.

To center text in cells:

1. Move the insertion point to cell A2, which contains the phrase "Event Information." You want to center this text.
2. Click the **Center** button on the Formatting toolbar to center the text in the cell.
3. Press the **Tab** key to select the contents of cell B2—the text "Customer Information"—and then click to center the text.

   As you will see in the next step, you can center text in two or more cells at one time.
4. Select the entire row 5 (which contains the text "Order Information" and "Credit Card Information), click to center the text in both cells, and then deselect the row.

You have aligned existing text in several cells. You also can set the alignment before you type the text.

To right-align text in cells:

1. Select cells A3 and A4—the two leftmost blank cells below the heading "Event Information."

2. Click the **Align Right** button on the Formatting toolbar. The end-of-cell markers move to the right edge of the cells, indicating that any text you enter will be right-aligned.
3. With cells A3 and A4 still selected, click the **Bold** button on the Formatting toolbar so that the text you enter into these cells will be in boldface as well.
4. Select cells A6 through B11 (the two columns below the heading "Order Information"), and then click to right-align the cells.
5. Select cells A6 through A11 (just the first column), and then click . Again, any text typed in these cells also will be in boldface when you type it.
6. Set cells C6 through C9, just below "Credit Card Information," for right-aligned and boldface text. (You might want to compare your table with Figure 9-1 to see why you're performing these operations.)

Now that you have aligned and formatted the cells, you're ready to enter some text.

To enter text into formatted cells:

1. Move the insertion point to cell A3, just below the heading "Event Information," type **Event:** (including the colon), and then press the **Enter** key to add a second line to cell A3. Don't move to cell A4 because you want several lines of text in this cell.
2. Type **Date of Event:**, press the **Enter** key, type **Time of Event:**, press the **Enter** key, and then type **Concert Hall:** to enter the remaining labels for cell A3.
3. Move the insertion point to cell A4, and then type **Date/Time:**, which is the label for the date and time of the current order.
4. Type the text shown in Figure 9-12 into cells A6 through A11. Make sure you enter each line of text into a separate cell, and type "TOTAL" in all uppercase letters.

Figure 9-12 TABLE WITH ALIGNED AND BOLDFACE TEXT

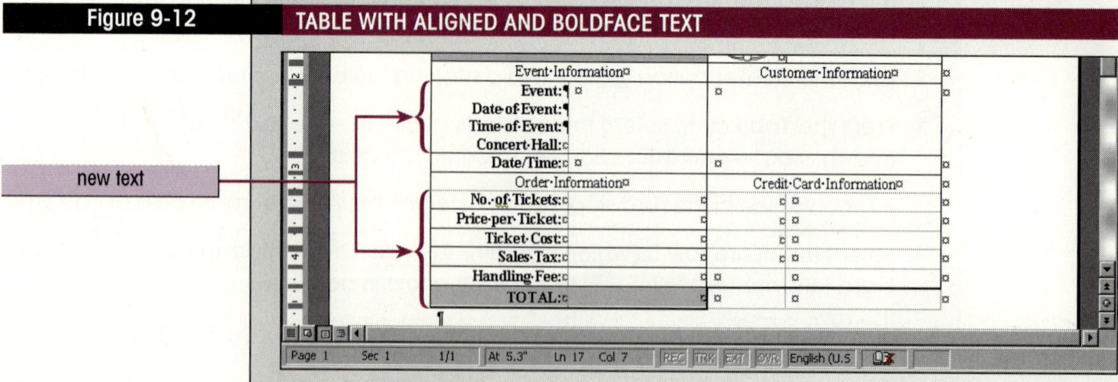

TROUBLE? If your table doesn't look like the one in Figure 9-12, carefully edit, format, or align text until it is correct.

5. Save the order form.

Now, you have entered most of the necessary labels. However, the "Information" headings don't stand out or clearly distinguish each section.

Formatting Text as Reverse Type

One way to make some of the section headings stand out from the rest of the order form is to set them in reverse type. **Reverse type** (also called **dropout** or **surprinted** type) is white text on a black background, the opposite of the usual black text on a white background. Reverse type is effective for making a line of text or a title attract the reader's eye; however, large amounts of reverse type can be difficult to read.

REFERENCE WINDOW RW

Creating Reverse (White on Black) Type

- Select the table cell or the paragraph you want to set in reverse type.
- If necessary, display the Tables and Borders toolbar, and then click the Shading Color list arrow, and then click the Black tile.
- Click the Font Color list arrow on the Formatting toolbar, and then click the White tile.
- Click the OK button.

You'll change the section headings to reverse type.

To create reverse type:

1. Select cells A2 and B2, which contain the headings "Event Information" and "Customer Information."
2. Open the Tables and Borders toolbar, click the **Shading Color** list arrow, and then click the Black tile (fourth row down, first column on the left). The cells become black—which you can't see because the cells are selected. When you select text on a white background, the background changes to black. On the other hand, selected text on a black background changes to white.
3. With row 2 still selected, click the Font Color list arrow on the Formatting toolbar, and then click the **White tile** (bottom row, right-most column) to change the text color to white.
4. Change the font to bold Arial. The text is reverse bold Arial, although it still appears black on white because the row is selected.
5. Repeat Steps 1 through 4 to change the headings in row 5 ("Order Information" and "Credit Card Information") to 12-point, bold Arial in reverse type. Deselect the row. See Figure 9-13.

Figure 9-13 TABLE AFTER CREATING REVERSE TYPE

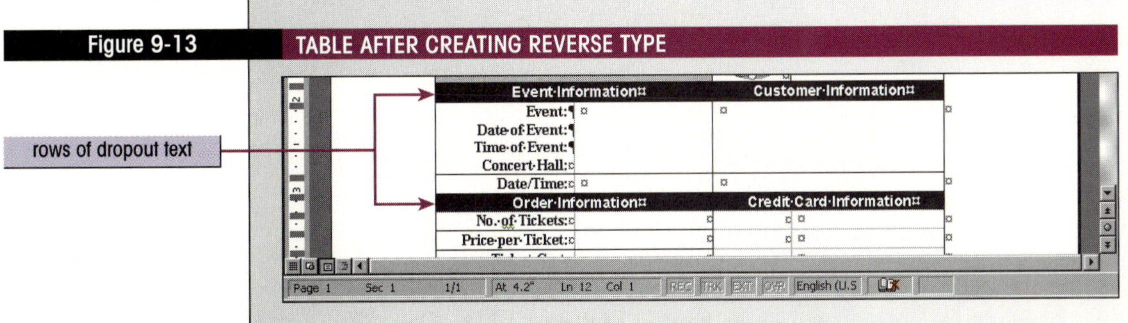

6. Close the Tables and Borders toolbar, and then save the order-form template.

You're ready to insert the last group of labels. Before you do this, you'll need to make some cells wider and others narrower.

Moving Gridlines

You can change the width of an individual cell or a group of cells without changing the entire column width. You select the cell or cells and drag the gridlines (the cell boundaries) to a new location.

The Event Information and Order Information sections have extra white space left of the right-aligned text. You'll decrease the width of the cells that will contain the event and order information, which will increase the width of the cells that will contain credit card information.

To change the width of cells by moving gridlines:

1. Switch to Normal View, and then select cells A3 and A4, the cells whose widths you want to decrease.
2. Press and hold the **Alt** key. If you keep this key pressed while dragging the gridlines, you can see the precise width of the selected column on the Ruler.
3. Move the pointer to the gridline between columns A and B (the right side of the selected rectangle) until it becomes +||+, and then drag the gridline left until the column A width is about 1.11 inches. See Figure 9-14.

Figure 9-14 MOVING A GRIDLINE

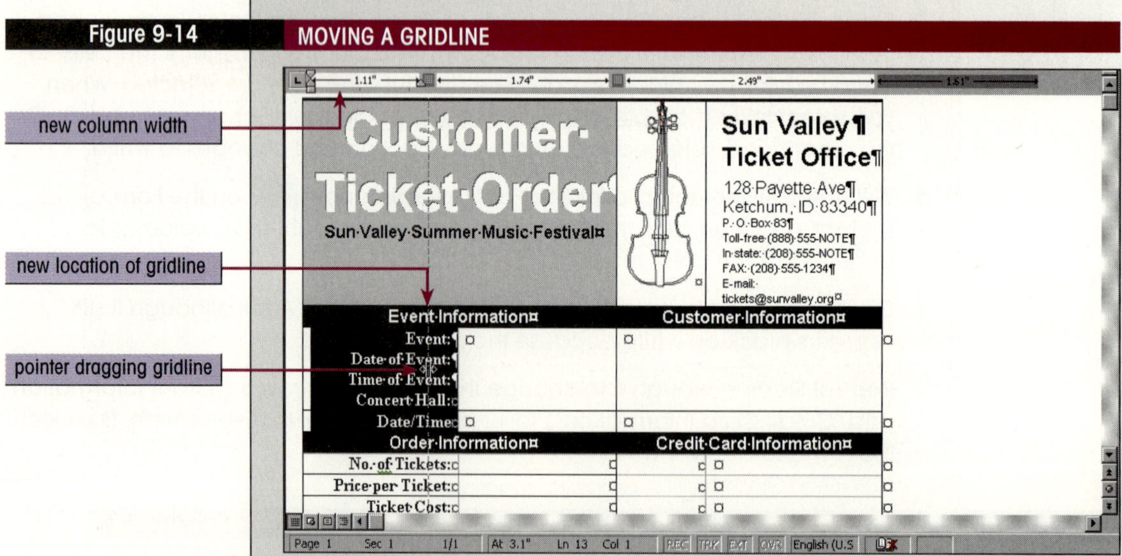

TROUBLE? If you try to drag the gridline, but it doesn't seem to "stick" to the pointer when you hold down the mouse button, try again. If you still have problems, try moving the pointer very slightly to the left of the gridline before you press the mouse button.

4. Release the **Alt** key and the mouse button.

5. Select cells A5 through B11 (the entire Order Information section including the title, labels, and total), move the pointer to the gridline between columns B and C (that is, the rightmost edge of the selected cells), and then hold down the **Alt** key while you drag the gridline left until the width of column B is **0.73** inch.
6. Release the **Alt** key and the mouse button.

   TROUBLE? If the border on the far right of the table also moves to the left, undo the operation and repeat Steps 5 and 6, being careful to select only the desired cells.

You're ready to complete the main text of the table.

To insert text into the table:

1. Move the insertion point to cell C4, just above the "Credit Card Information" heading, press **Ctrl + B** to turn on boldface, type **Daytime Phone:** (including the colon), press **Ctrl + B** to turn off boldface, and then press the **spacebar** to insert a space after the text.
2. Move the insertion point to cell C6, just below the word "Card" in "Credit Card Information," type **Account Type:** (including the colon), move to cell C7, type **Card No.:**, move to cell C8, type **Expiration Date:**, move to cell C9, and then type **Name on Card:** to enter the credit card information labels.
3. Move the insertion point to cell C10, turn on boldface, type **Mail Tickets**, move to cell D10, turn on boldface, and type **Will Call**. See Figure 9-15.

Figure 9-15 TABLE WITH COMPLETED TEXT AND BORDERS

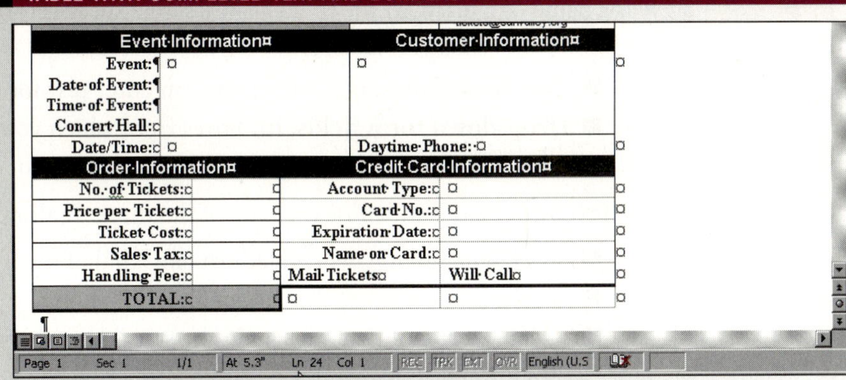

Event·Information		Customer·Information	
Event:¶ Date·of·Event:¶ Time·of·Event:¶ Concert·Hall:			
Date/Time:		Daytime·Phone:	
Order·Information		Credit·Card·Information	
No.·of·Tickets:		Account·Type:	
Price·per·Ticket:		Card·No.:	
Ticket·Cost:		Expiration·Date:	
Sales·Tax:		Name·on·Card:	
Handling·Fee:		Mail·Tickets	Will·Call
TOTAL:			

   TROUBLE? If your table doesn't look like Figure 9-15, fix any problems with text, format, alignment, borders, or column widths now.

4. Save the current version of the order form.

You have completed the table structure and inserted all the boilerplate text—that is, the text that won't vary—in the order-form template. Next, you'll add form fields to the order-form table.

Session 9.1 Quick Check

1. What is an on-screen form?
2. What is a form field?
3. In a table, what is a border? How does it differ from a gridline?
4. How do you rotate text in a table cell?
5. What does it mean to merge cells in a table?
6. What does it mean to split cells in a table?
7. How do you shade a cell with 20% gray?
8. What is reverse type?

SESSION 9.2

In this session you'll create and format regular text form fields, date text form fields, and number text form fields. Within these form fields, you'll create prompts and help messages and use the number format setting. In addition, you'll create and format drop-down form fields and check box form fields.

Using Form Fields

You have formatted the order form table to make it look attractive and easy-to-read, but you still need to insert the most important elements of an on-screen form—form fields. The form fields will help you and the Sun Valley employees enter information into the order form quickly and efficiently. Recall that a form field stores a certain type of information, such as a name or a price, to which you can assign a specific format.

Word supports three general types of form fields:

- **Text form fields**, into which you can enter text for the form
- **Drop-down form fields**, list boxes from which you can select an item
- **Check box form fields**, which you can check or uncheck

The text form field is the most versatile of the three. It allows you to:

- Specify the input type: regular text (any kind of text), numbers only, or dates only.
- Set the maximum number of input
- Create a prompt that appears in the status bar when the insertion point moves into the text field.
- Compose a help message that appears in a dialog box when the user presses the F1 (Help) key.
- Perform calculations based on values in other cells in the table.

For example, if you wanted a Sun Valley employee to enter an area code, you would specify numbers only as the input type and set the maximum number of characters to three.

Inserting Regular Text Form Fields

The first text form field you'll add to the order form is one to prompt Sun Valley employees to enter the name of the event for which someone wants to purchase tickets. When you insert the form field for the Event entry, you'll specify many options. First, you'll indicate a maximum of

20 characters of regular text to keep the event name to one line of text. You'll specify Title Text format to capitalize the first letter of each word and lowercase the other letters even if the ticket agent doesn't type the event name that way. Also, you'll set the field's default text to "Gem State Orchestra," which is the most common event. Ticket agents will type the event name only if it is not the Gem State Orchestra. Finally, you'll enter a status-bar prompt and additional text in the Help dialog box, which opens when a ticket agent presses the F1 key.

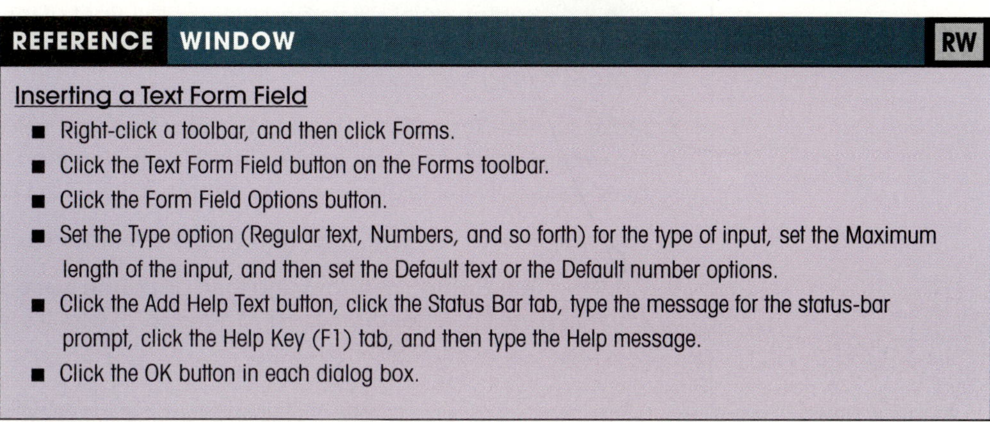

REFERENCE WINDOW RW

Inserting a Text Form Field

- Right-click a toolbar, and then click Forms.
- Click the Text Form Field button on the Forms toolbar.
- Click the Form Field Options button.
- Set the Type option (Regular text, Numbers, and so forth) for the type of input, set the Maximum length of the input, and then set the Default text or the Default number options.
- Click the Add Help Text button, click the Status Bar tab, type the message for the status-bar prompt, click the Help Key (F1) tab, and then type the Help message.
- Click the OK button in each dialog box.

To insert a text form field and set the text options:

1. If you took a break after the last session, make sure Word is running, the Sun Valley Order Form template is open in Normal View, and nonprinting characters are displayed.
2. Move the insertion point to cell B3, to the right of the "Event" cell and below "Event Information."

   You could insert the text form field using the Form Field command on the Insert menu, but it's easier to use the Forms toolbar.
3. Right-click any toolbar to display the shortcut menu, and then click **Forms**. The Forms toolbar opens.
4. If necessary, double-click the title bar of the floating Forms toolbar so it becomes a row of buttons below the Formatting toolbar. Now, you're ready to insert the text form field.
5. Make sure the insertion point is still in cell B3, and then click the **Text Form Field** button abl on the Forms toolbar. Word inserts a text form field with the default options. See Figure 9-16.

Figure 9-16 ON-SCREEN FORM WITH TEXT FORM FIELD

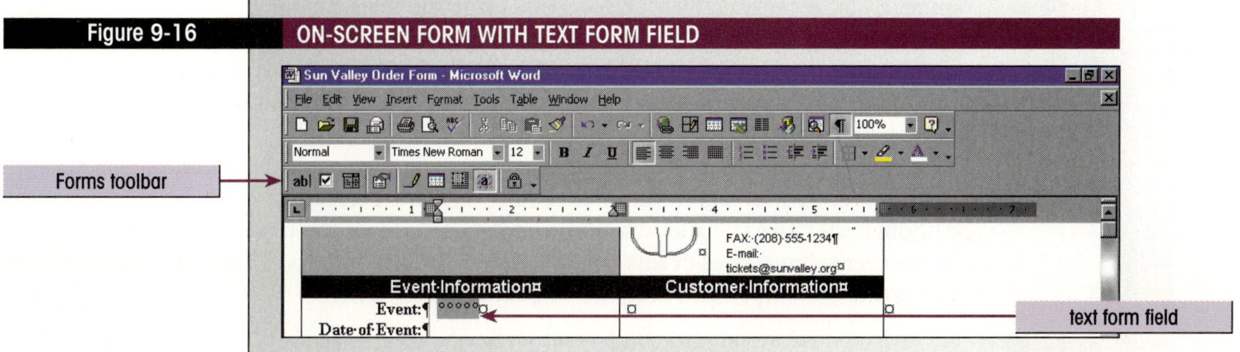

TROUBLE? If the form field doesn't appear in a gray box, click the Form Field Shading button on the Forms toolbar.

TROUBLE? If you see {FORMTEXT}, the name of the field code, press Alt + F9 to switch from Field Code View to Results View.

Next, you'll change the options of the text form field.

6. With the insertion point still immediately to the right of the form field, click the **Form Field Options** button on the Forms toolbar. The Text Form Field Options dialog box opens.
7. Make sure the **Type** list box is set to **Regular text** (the default), double-click the **Maximum** length text box to select its contents, and then type **20**. Next, you need to specify the text you want to appear in the Event field as the default entry.
8. Click the Default text box, and then type **Gem State Orchestra**.
9. Click the **Text format** list arrow, and then click **Title case** so that Word will capitalize the first letter of any text, regardless of how it's typed. Leave the dialog box open. See Figure 9-17.

Figure 9-17 TEXT FORM FIELD OPTIONS DIALOG BOX

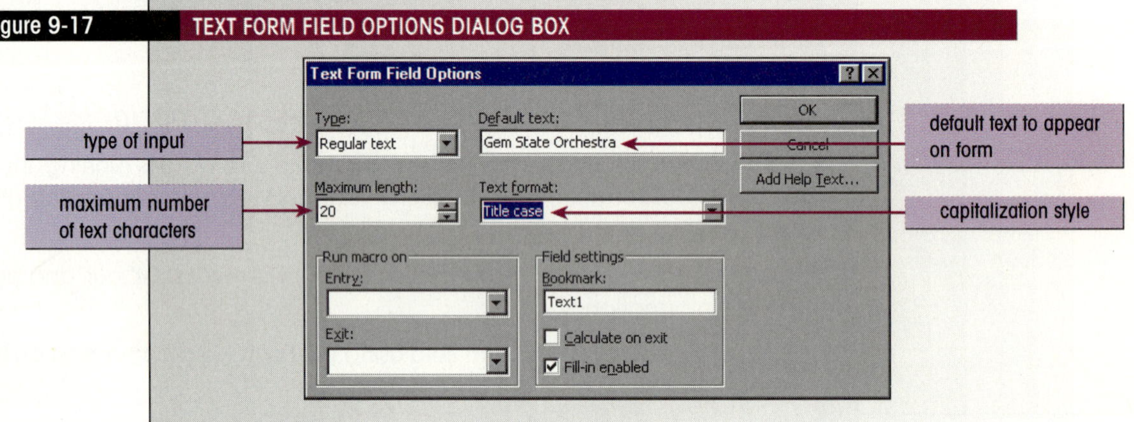

You have completed all the options for the text form field except for specifying the Help information.

Creating Prompts and Help Messages

Form fields enable users to complete an on-screen form quickly by moving them to the location into which they can type the required information. Usually, the person knows what information to enter. However, someone using the form for the first time might need some instructions for every field, and both new and experienced people sometimes need clarification of what to enter into less-obvious fields. To assist in answering these questions, you can create prompts that appear in the status bar, as well as Help dialog boxes that contain even more information.

When the Sun Valley ticket agents open a new on-screen order form, the insertion point will appear in the text form field you're currently creating (that is, the Event field). Although the "Event" label should be enough to inform the ticket agents to type the name of the event, sometimes events have special codes or numbers. Therefore, Richard suggests you create a prompt and a Help message for this form field.

To add a prompt and a help message to the text form field:

1. Click the **Add Help Text** button in the Text Form Field Options dialog box. The Form Field Help Text dialog box opens.
2. If necessary, click the Status Bar tab, and then click the **Type your own** option button. The insertion point moves to the text box.
3. Type **Enter name of performing group** (don't type a period). This text will appear in the status bar whenever the insertion point is in the Events field.

   You'll also create a Help dialog box with more information about what to type into the field.
4. Click the **Help Key (F1)** tab on the dialog box, click the **Type your own** option button, and then type **For the event, type the name (maximum of 20 characters) of the group presenting the concert. The most common performing groups are the Gem State Orchestra, Boise Quartet, and Sun Valley Youth Orchestra.** (Be sure to type the periods at the end of the sentences.)
5. Click the **OK** button in the Form Field Help Text dialog box, and then click the **OK** button in the Text Form Field Options dialog box. You return to the Sun Valley Order Form, where you can see that the default text "Gem State Orchestra" appears in the field. See Figure 9-18.

Figure 9-18 ON-SCREEN FORM AFTER CHANGING FIELD OPTIONS

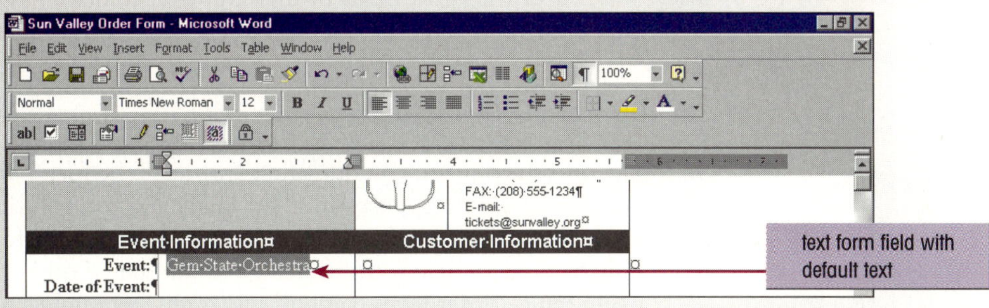

You have inserted the first form field. Now, you'll insert one under "Customer Information" and another to the right of "Name on Card."

To insert two more regular text form fields:

1. Move the insertion point to cell C3, below the "Customer Information" heading.
2. Click the **Text Form Field** button ab| on the Forms toolbar to insert the form field, and then double-click the gray-shaded field. Notice that when you double-click a form field, the Text Form Field Options dialog box opens, just as if you had clicked the Form Field Options button on the Forms toolbar.

   You'll leave all the defaults, including Unlimited as the Maximum length, because the ticket agents might have to type several long lines of text to fill in the customer's complete name and address.

3. Click the **Add Help Text** button, click the **Status Bar** tab, click the **Type your own** option button, and then type **Enter name and address of customer who will receive tickets** into the text box.
4. Click the **Help Key (F1)** tab, click in the **Type your own** text box, and then type **If the name of the person who will receive the tickets is different from the person placing the order, enter the name and address of the person to whom the tickets will be sent. You'll enter the name of the person placing the order below**. (Remember to include the periods at the end of the sentences.)
5. If necessary, correct any typing errors in the text you just typed, click the **OK** button to close the Form Field Help Text dialog box, and then click the **OK** button to close the Text Form Field Options dialog box. Notice that the text field doesn't show any text entered because you didn't type any default text.
6. Repeat Steps 1 through 5 to insert a regular text form field in cell D9, to the right of the cell labeled "Name on Card." Leave Unlimited set as the Maximum length, with no default text. Use the text **Insert name on credit card if different from customer name; otherwise, leave blank** as the status-bar prompt, but don't create a Help dialog box for this field.
7. Save the order-form template.

You have inserted the first three form fields into the order form template. Before you insert the rest of the form fields in the template, Richard suggests you test these three to verify that they work.

Testing the Form Fields

To test an on-screen form, you must first "protect" the form. To **protect** an on-screen form means to permit only responses to form fields and to prohibit any changes to the text or structure of the on-screen form. In a protected on-screen form, the insertion point will move only from form field to form field, and not to any other locations.

The Sun Valley order form contains just three form fields, which the insertion point will move among when you protect the form. The insertion point won't move into any other location.

To protect the form and test the form fields:

1. Click the **Protect Form** button on the Forms toolbar.

   Because you can't edit the form now, the entire Formatting toolbar and many buttons on the Standard and Forms toolbars become inactive (dimmed). Word doesn't check spelling in protected forms, so the red wavy lines disappear from beneath any words that might be misspelled. Furthermore, nothing happens if you click anywhere in the document window, except within a form field.
2. Press the **Tab** key until the Event field is selected. The default event name "Gem State Orchestra" is then selected (white text on a dark background), and the prompt appears in the status bar below the horizontal scroll bar.
3. Press the **F1** key to test the Help on this form field. The Help dialog box opens. See Figure 9-19.

Figure 9-19 PROTECTED ON-SCREEN FORM

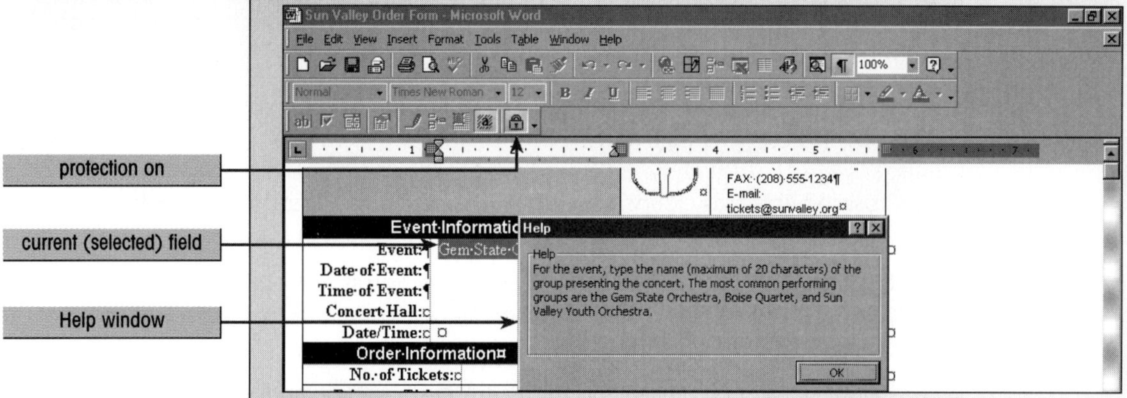

protection on

current (selected) field

Help window

4. Read the message in the Help dialog box, and then click the **OK** button.

   If you were filling in a form, you would type the name of the event or accept the default event (Gem State Orchestra). Because you're testing the fields, you'll move to the next form field without entering any text.

5. Press the **Tab** key to move the insertion point to the Customer Information form field, and then read the status-bar prompt.

6. Press the **F1** key to open the Help dialog box, read the Help text, and then click the **OK** button. If you were actually taking a customer order, you would type a name and address here. You can enter multiple lines of text into one text form field.

7. Press the **Tab** key to move the insertion point to the Name on Card form field, read the prompt, and then press the **F1** key. This form field has no Help dialog box, so nothing happens.

8. Click [protect button] again to turn off protection so you can continue to edit the form. Notice that the toolbars become active and the red wavy lines reappear beneath words that are not in the Word dictionary.

You'll fill out an order using the finished template later.

Inserting **Date Text Form Fields**

You can customize text form fields so they accept only certain types of information. With the Type option set to Date, the text form field will accept only a date or time. If you enter information that Word doesn't recognize as a date or time and then press the Tab key to move to the next field, Word displays the error message, "A valid date or time is required," and returns the insertion point to the field. This helps to ensure that everyone enters the proper information in a field.

Richard wants you to insert a form field for the "Date of Event." You'll use a text form field set to accept information in a date or time format only.

To insert a date text form field:

1. Move the insertion point to cell B3, to the right of the Event form field, which displays "Gem State Orchestra."

   TROUBLE? If the form field is selected and you can't see the blinking insertion point, press the → key.

2. Press the **Enter** key to insert a blank line below the Event form field in the same cell. Notice that you can insert more than one field in a cell.
3. Click the **Text Form Field** button abl on the Forms toolbar to insert a new form field, and then double-click the form field to open the Text Form Field Options dialog box.
4. Click the **Type** list arrow, and then click **Date**. When the ticket agents use this form, they'll be forced to type a date or time. Of course, Word can't verify that the entered date or time is correct, but at least it will check that the information is in the proper format.
5. Click the **Date format** list box, and then type **d MMM yy** (which is the date-time picture for a date in the format "23 Jan 01.") Word will convert the date to this specified style, regardless of how a ticket agent enters it. See Figure 9-20.

Figure 9-20 TEXT FORM FIELD OPTION DIALOG BOX

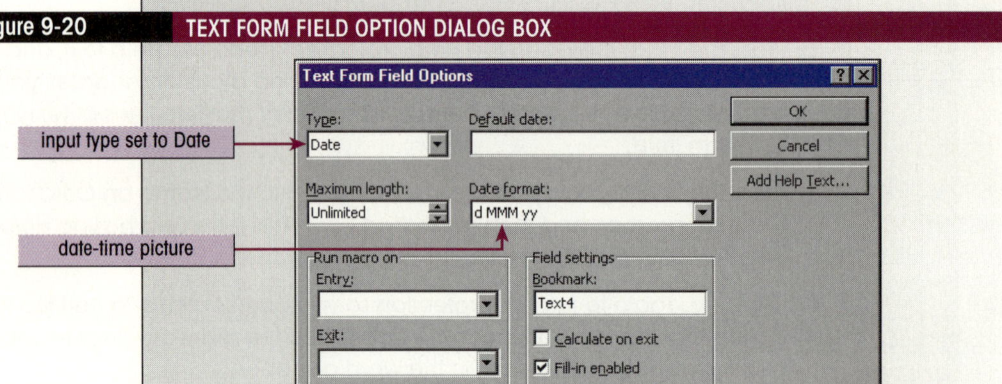

Preset date-time picture options are available in the Date format list box, but you can also enter your own. For additional information about date-time pictures, refer to Tutorial 8 or check the Microsoft Word Help Topics.

Now, you're ready to type the prompt for this field.

6. In the Text Form Field Options dialog box, click the **Add Help Text** button, if necessary click the **Status Bar** tab, click the **Type your own** option button, and then type **Enter date of event in the style 23 Jan 01** (no period).
7. Click the **OK** button in each dialog box to return to your order form.

You have inserted the Date of Event form field. The next form field, for the Time of Event, also requires a date-time picture.

To insert another date text form field:

1. Press the → key to deselect the Date of Event form field and move the insertion point to the right of the field, and then press the **Enter** key to add a line in this cell.
2. Insert a text form field, open the Text Form Field Options dialog box, and then click **Date** in the Type list box. Recall that the date type refers to the date and time, not just to the date.
3. Click the **Default date** text box, and type **7:30 PM**, the start time for most events.
4. Click the **Date** format list box, and then type (or select) the date-time picture **h:mm am/pm** to specify a time in the style "7:30 PM." If a ticket agent types "19:30," for example, Word will convert the format to "7:30 PM."
5. Type **Enter time of event in the style 7:30 PM** for the status-bar prompt.
6. Click the **OK** button in each dialog box to return to the order form.

The only remaining form field to insert in this cell is the one for the Concert Hall, which will specify the location of the event. You'll do this later. Instead, you'll insert a date text form field for the credit card expiration date now.

To insert another date text form field:

1. Move the insertion point to cell D8, to the right of the cell labeled "Expiration Date."
2. Insert a text form field, open the Text Form Field Options dialog box, click **Date** in the Type list box, leave the Default date text box blank, and then type **MM/yy** in the Date format list box so Word will ensure that the date is formatted like "01/01."
3. Type **Enter credit card expiration date in the style 01/01** for the status-bar prompt. Don't specify a Help message.
4. Click the **OK** button in each dialog box to return to the order form.
5. Save the order-form template.

You have specified all form fields that represent a date or time. Next, you'll insert a Word field—not a form field—that inserts the date of the order.

Inserting a Date and Time Field

The "Date/Time" label on the order form is for the date and time when a ticket agent fills out the form. Rather than have the ticket agents enter the current date every time they fill out the order form, you can use the Word date field to insert the current date and time.

What is the difference between a *date text form field* and a *date field*? The date text form field allows you to insert any date—past, present, or future—into a form. The date field, on the other hand, always inserts the current date, as specified by your computer's clock, on which a document is opened and printed.

To insert the date field for the date and time:

1. Move the insertion point to cell B4, to the right of the cell labeled "Date/Time."
2. Click **Insert** on the menu bar, and then click **Date and Time** to open the Date and Time dialog box.
3. Make sure the **Update** automatically check box is selected because you want to insert a date field, not just today's date.
4. Select the date style **1/23/01 10:48 AM** in the Available formats list (your date and time will be different).
5. Click the **OK** button to close the Date and Time dialog box. The current date and time appear in the cell, although this field will change every time an agent opens a new order form based on this template.

When the ticket agents fill in new forms, their current date and time will appear in this cell automatically.

Inserting Number Text Form Fields

So far, you have inserted text form fields with regular text and a date. You also can insert text form fields with numbers in a certain format. The number text form field uses a numeric picture, which is similar to the date-time picture in date text form fields. A **numeric picture** is a pattern of digits and symbols that specifies the content and format of the number. Figure 9–21 shows the most commonly used numeric picture symbols.

Figure 9-21 NUMERIC PICTURE SYMBOLS FOR NUMBER FORM FIELDS

SYMBOL	PURPOSE	EXAMPLE
0 (zero)	Displays a digit in place of the zero in the field result. If the result doesn't include a digit in that place, the field displays a zero.	Numeric picture "00.0" displays "05.0" Numeric picture "0" displays an integer of any number of digits.
#	Displays a digit in place of the # only if the result requires it. If the result doesn't include a digit in that place, the field displays a space.	Numeric picture "$##.00" displays "$ 5.00"
. (decimal point)	Determines the decimal point position.	See examples above.
, (comma)	Separates a series of three digits.	Numeric picture "$#,###,###" displays "$3,450,000"
- (hyphen)	Includes a minus sign if the number is negative or a space if the number is positive.	Numeric picture "-0" displays an integer as " 5" or "-5"
; (semicolon)	Separates the positive and negative numeric picture.	Numeric picture "$##0.00;-$##0.00" displays "$ 55.50" if positive, "-$ 55.50" if negative
(parentheses around negative)	Puts parentheses around a negative result.	Numeric picture "$##0.00;($##0.00)" displays "$ 55.50" if positive, "($ 55.50)" if negative
$, %, etc.	Displays a special character in the results.	Numeric picture "0.0%" displays "5.0%"

You'll insert several text form fields that accept only numbers into the order-form template.

To insert number text form fields:

1. Move the insertion point to cell B6, to the right of the cell labeled "No. of Tickets."
2. Insert a text form field, and then open the Text Form Field Options dialog box.
3. Click the **Type** list arrow, and then click **Number**.
4. Type **3** in the **Maximum length** text box. This ensures that the field doesn't accept a number with more than three digits. In other words, the largest acceptable number is 999. You must set the maximum length to the largest possible number that could occupy that field. Richard mentioned that on rare occasions an organization (school or company) will order more than 100 tickets, but no concert hall holds more than 500 people. Therefore, you need to include three digits.
5. Type **2** in the **Default number** text box because that is the most common number of tickets per order, and then type **0** in the Number format list box to display the value as an integer.
6. Type **Enter number of tickets ordered** for the status-bar prompt, and then click the **OK** button in each dialog box to return to the order form. The default text "2" appears in the cell.
7. Move the insertion point to cell B7, to the right of the cell labeled "Price per Ticket."
8. Insert a text form field, open the Text Form Field Options dialog box, click **Number** in the Type list box, type **12** (the most common ticket price) in the Default number text box, and then click **$#,##0.00;($#,##0.00)** in the Number format list box. Leave Unlimited as the Maximum length. This converts any number a ticket agent enters in this field to a currency format.
9. Type **Enter price per ticket** for the status-bar prompt, and then click the **OK** button in each dialog box to return to the order form. See Figure 9-22.

Figure 9-22 ON-SCREEN FORM WITH NUMBER FORM FIELDS

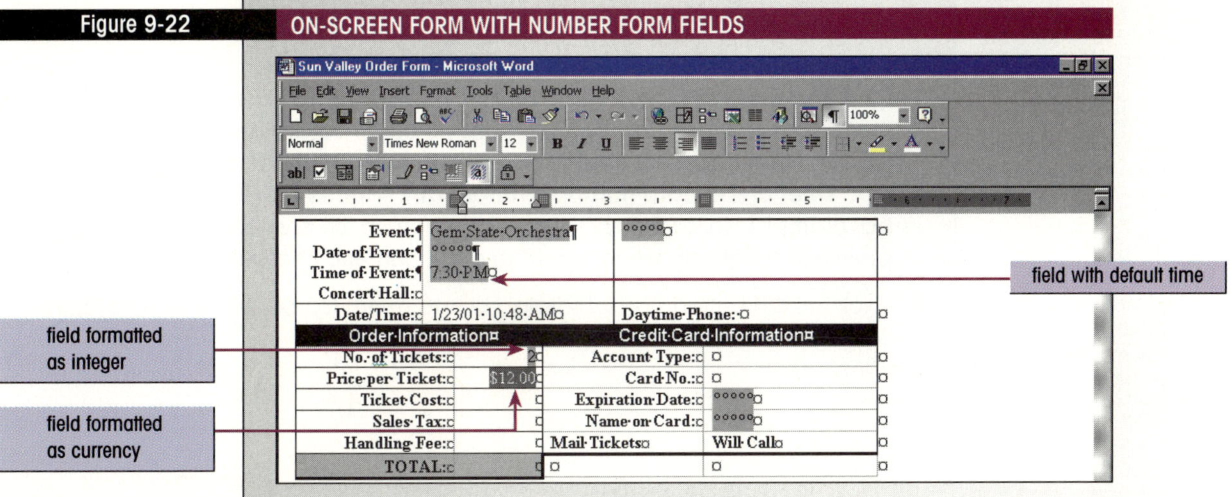

Notice that the default value for each number form field you inserted so far appears in the number format you specified—integer or currency. Next, you'll insert two number form fields in which ticket agents will enter a customer's phone number. Because most customers will live within the state, you'll insert one form field with the state's area code as the default, and one for the rest of the phone number.

To insert the number text form fields:

1. Move the insertion point to cell C4, which contains the text "Daytime Phone," and then move the insertion point to the right of the space after the colon. Here, you'll insert one form field for the area code and another for the rest of the telephone number.
2. Type **(** (an open parenthesis), and then insert a text form field and open the Text Form Field Options dialog box. Click **Number** in the Type list box, type **208** (the Idaho area code) in the Default number text box, type **3** (the number of digits in an area code) in the Maximum length text box, type **0** (a zero) in the Number format list box to ensure the number is an integer, and then type **Enter 3-digit area code** for the status-bar prompt.
3. Click the **OK** button in each dialog box to return to the order form, press the → key to deselect the field and position the insertion point to its right, type **)** (a close parenthesis), and then press the **spacebar**.

   You're ready to insert the text form field for the rest of the telephone number.
4. Insert a text form field, and open the Text Form Field Options dialog box. Leave the Type list box set to Regular text so the ticket agents can type a phone number that includes a hyphen (for example "555-1234"), which is not considered a numeric character.
5. Type **8** in the Maximum length text box to leave enough space for ticket agents to enter the seven-digit phone number and the hyphen, leave the Default text box and the Text format list box blank, and then type **Enter daytime telephone number with a hyphen** for the status-bar prompt.
6. Click the **OK** button in each dialog box to return to the order form, move to cell D7, which is to the right of the cell labeled "Card No.," insert a text form field, and then open the Text Form Field Options dialog box.
7. Click **Number** in the Type list box, leave the Default number box blank, type **20** in the Maximum length text box because no credit card has more than 20 digits, type **0** in the Number format list box to ensure the number is an integer, and then type **Enter credit card number without any spaces or hyphens** for the status bar prompt. Disallowing spaces and hyphens in the credit card number will prevent a ticket agent from entering a nonnumeric character.
8. Click the **OK** button in each dialog box to return to your order-form template. See Figure 9-23.

Figure 9-23 ON-SCREEN FORM AFTER INSERTING OTHER FIELDS

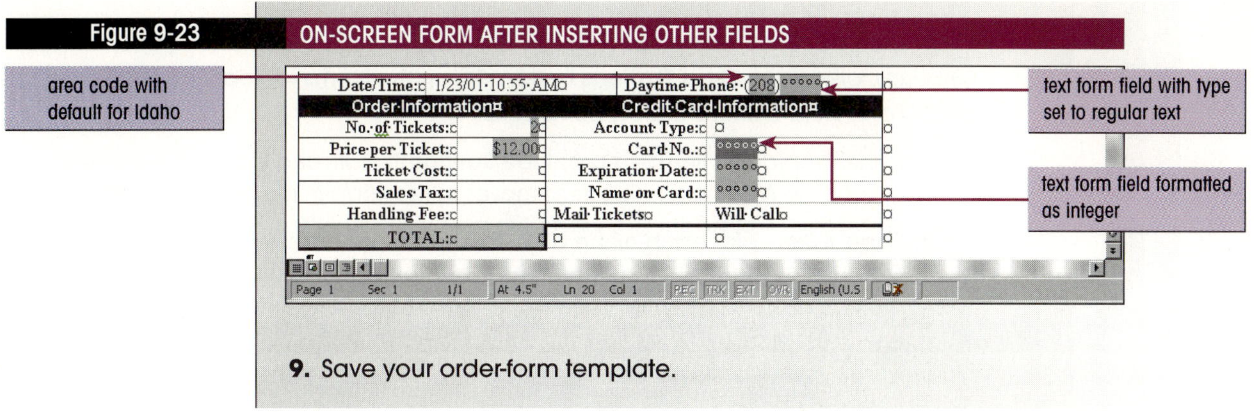

9. Save your order-form template.

You've inserted all the text form fields that accept only numeric input in your order form template. Later, you'll insert other form fields that perform calculations.

Inserting Drop-Down Form Fields

The form fields you inserted so far will allow the Sun Valley ticket agents to enter any event name, date, time, and so forth. But not all information in a form requires such flexibility. When the required information is limited to a short list of entries, you can use up a drop-down form field, which is a list box that contains the possible entries.

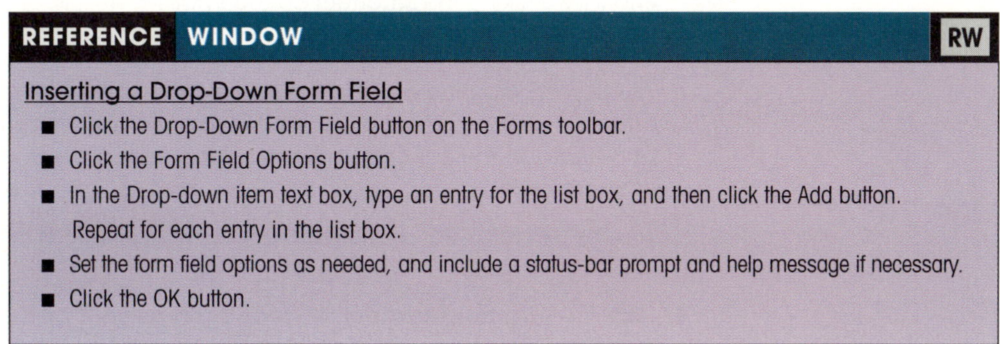
REFERENCE WINDOW RW

Inserting a Drop-Down Form Field

- Click the Drop-Down Form Field button on the Forms toolbar.
- Click the Form Field Options button.
- In the Drop-down item text box, type an entry for the list box, and then click the Add button. Repeat for each entry in the list box.
- Set the form field options as needed, and include a status-bar prompt and help message if necessary.
- Click the OK button.

All Sun Valley Summer Music Festival events are held at Sawtooth Hall, Sacagawea Hall, Coeur d'Alene Hall, or Shoshone Hall. Rather than requiring that ticket agents type these names repeatedly, Richard suggests you create a drop-down form field. By selecting from a list, ticket agents can complete the form faster and ensure that the hall names are always spelled correctly.

To insert a drop-down form field:

1. Move the insertion point to the end of cell B3, to the right of the Time of Event field (which contains the time "7:30 PM"), and then press the **Enter** key to create a new blank line at the bottom of the cell.

2. Click the **Drop-Down Form Field** button on the Forms toolbar, and then click the **Form Field Options** button on the Forms toolbar. The Drop-Down Form Field Options dialog box opens.
3. In the Drop-down item text box, type **Sawtooth Hall**, and then press the **Enter** key or click the **Add** button. The item moves to the Items in the drop-down list box.
4. Repeat Step 3 for each of the other three concert halls: **Sacagawea Hall**, **Coeur d'Alene Hall**, and **Shoshone Hall**. See Figure 9-24.

Figure 9-24 DROP-DOWN FORM FIELD OPTIONS DIALOG BOX

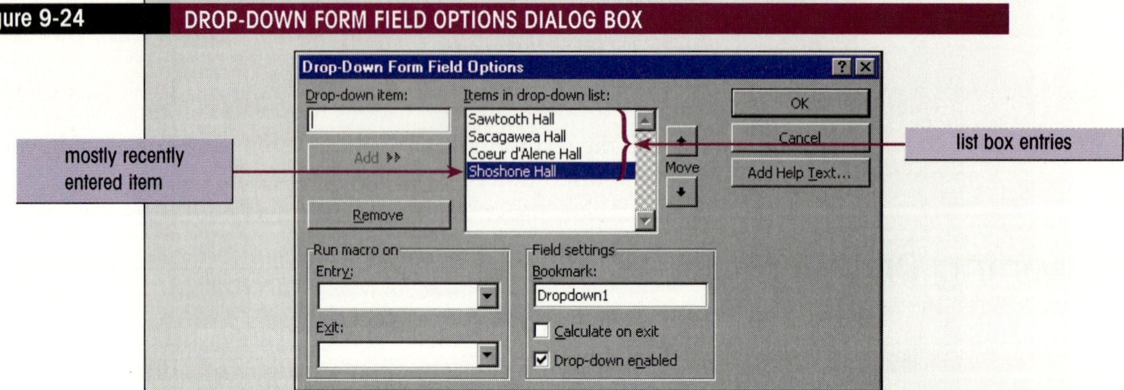

TROUBLE? If your dialog box doesn't match Figure 9-24, correct any typing errors by clicking the incorrect concert hall name, clicking the Remove button, making the correction, and then clicking the Add button.

You can change the order of the list by clicking the entry you want to move and then clicking the appropriate Move arrow. You decide to leave the list as is because the concert halls are arranged in order from most to least frequently used.

You set the status-bar prompt for drop-down form fields the same way you do for text form fields.

5. Click the **Add Help Text** button, click the **Type your own** option button, and then type **Select concert hall in which performance will be held** for the status-bar prompt.
6. Click the **OK** button in each dialog box to return to the order form. Sawtooth Hall appears in the cell.

You have inserted a drop-down form field that lists the concert halls. You decide to insert another one for the credit card account type. The Sun Valley Ticket Office accepts VISA, MasterCard, American Express, and Discover.

To insert another drop-down form field:

1. Move the insertion point to cell D6, to the right of the cell labeled "Account Type" in the Credit Card Information section.

2. Insert a drop-down form field, and then open the Drop-Down Form Field Options dialog box.
3. Type **VISA** in the Drop-down item text box, and then press **Enter** to enter the first item in the Items in drop-down list box.
4. Repeat Step 3 to add **MasterCard**, **American Express**, and **Discover** to the Items in the drop-down list box.
5. Type **Select credit card account type** for the status-bar prompt.
6. Click the **OK** button in each dialog box to return to your order form. See Figure 9-25.

Figure 9-25 ON-SCREEN FORM WITH DROP-DOWN FORM FIELD

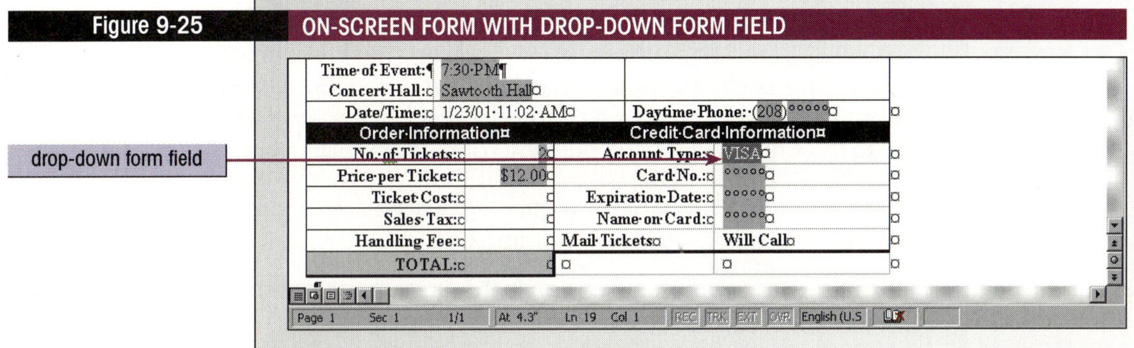

7. Save your order-form template.

   If you ever want to modify a form field (sometimes called a form control), click the form field to select it and click the Form Fields Options button on the Form toolbar.Then make any change you desire to the field options, such as adding another item to a drop-down list or modifying the text format.

Next, you need to insert some check box form fields.

Inserting Check Box Form Fields

A **check box** is a box that you can click to toggle on or off. Inserting check box form fields is similar to inserting other form fields. If you want users to select any number of options in a list, you can include each option as boilerplate text in the template and then place a check box form field before each item in the list. Unlike a drop-down form field, you can select more than one entry in a list. You might include check box form fields in an on-screen survey form for questions such as, "Which of the following items do you plan to purchase in the next six months?"

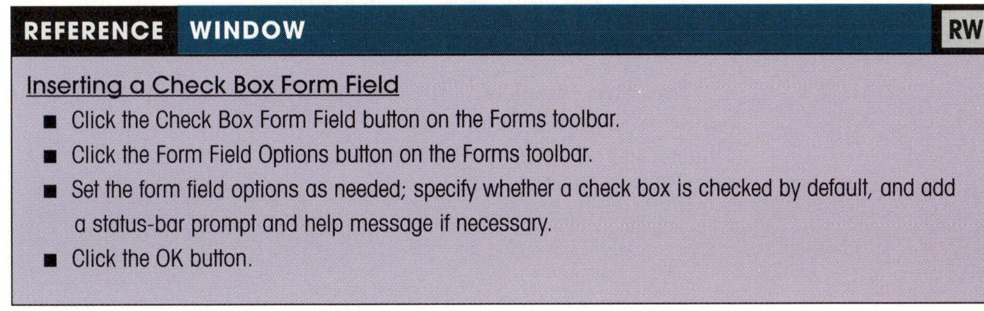

REFERENCE WINDOW RW

Inserting a Check Box Form Field

- Click the Check Box Form Field button on the Forms toolbar.
- Click the Form Field Options button on the Forms toolbar.
- Set the form field options as needed; specify whether a check box is checked by default, and add a status-bar prompt and help message if necessary.
- Click the OK button.

If a customer orders tickets more than one week before an event, the Sun Valley Ticket Office mails the tickets to the customer. But if the customer places the order less than one week before an event, the customer must pick up the tickets in person at the Will Call booth. The ticket order form will indicate whether the tickets are to be mailed or placed in Will Call. For this reason, you'll add two check box form fields to the order form.

To insert two check box form fields:

1. Move the insertion point immediately to the left of the phrase "Mail Tickets" in cell C10.
2. Click the **Check Box Form Field** button on the Forms toolbar to insert a check box.

   TROUBLE? If the Check Box Form Field button is not included on your Forms toolbar, right-click the toolbar, click the Command tab, click Forms in the Categories list box, scroll the Commands list box to display the Check Box button, drag the Check box button onto the Forms toolbar, and then click Close.

3. Click the **Form Field Options** button on the Forms toolbar to open the Check Box Form Field Options dialog box.
4. Click the **Checked** option button in the Default value section of the dialog box so this box will be checked when a ticket agent starts a new form.
5. Type **Press spacebar or click with mouse (toggle)** as the status-bar prompt.
6. Click the **OK** button in each dialog box to return to the order form.
7. Press the → key to deselect the form field, and place the insertion point between the form field and the phrase "Mail Tickets," and then press the **space-bar** to insert a space at that location.
8. Repeat Steps 1 through 7 to create a check box to the left of "Will Call," but keep the Default value section set to Not checked. Type the same entry for the status-bar prompt. See Figure 9-26.

Figure 9-26 ON-SCREEN FORM WITH CHECK BOX FORM FIELDS

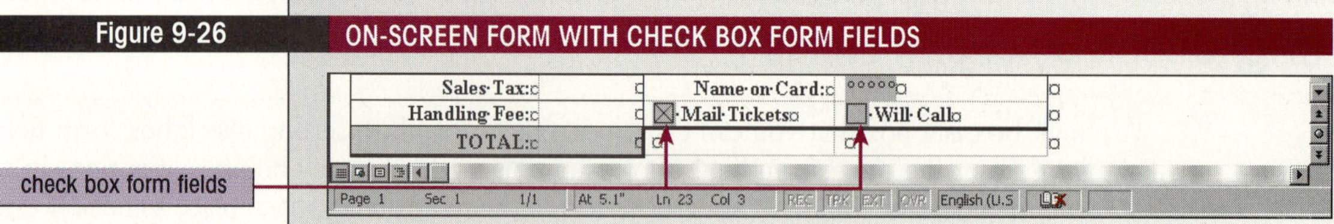

   TROUBLE? If your order form doesn't match Figure 9-26, make any necessary changes.

9. Save the current version of the order-form template.

You have completed all the form fields in which the ticket agents will enter or select information. Next, you'll insert form fields that perform calculations, record macros, and format the text outside the table.

Session 9.2 Quick Check

1. Describe each of the following types of text form fields:
   a. regular text form field
   b. number form field
   c. date form field
2. What are the two types of Help text, and how do they differ?
3. Give the date-time picture required to give the following date text form field results:
   a. 03 Feb 99
   b. 3 February 1999
   c. 8:50 PM
   d. 19:30 (*Hint*: Look in the Microsoft Word Help Topics Index for "Time instructions.")
4. What is a numeric picture? What numeric picture would you use if you want the result of a numeric form field to have the style "3.50%"?
5. Why would you use a drop-down form field?
6. How do you create a list of items for a drop-down form field?
7. Why would you use a check box form field?
8. How do you set the default value of a check box form field to checked?

SESSION 9.3

In this session you'll automate the on-screen form by inserting form fields that perform calculations and attaching macros that help users enter information in the most logical order. You'll change the page orientation of the document and set the document in columns. Finally, you'll protect and save the on-screen form, use the template to prepare a sample order, fax a filled-in form, and save only the data for an order.

Performing Automatic Calculations

The order-form template already contains the fields into which a ticket agent can enter the number of tickets and the price per ticket in the Order Information section. The ticket agent could multiply these two numbers to calculate the ticket cost, multiply this value by the tax rate (6¼%, or 0.0625) to determine the sales tax, calculate the handling fee ($1.50 per ticket), and then sum all these numbers to determine a total amount for the order.

But why have the ticket agent perform these routine calculations? Not only is it time-consuming, but it also increases the chance for mathematical errors. You can have Word perform the calculations by inserting a calculation text form field.

REFERENCE WINDOW 

Performing Calculations with Form Fields

- Move to the cell in which you want to display the calculation results.
- Insert a text form field, and then open the Text Form Field Options dialog box.
- Click the Type list arrow, and then click Calculation.
- Type an expression (or formula) in the Expression text box. For example, the expression "=B6+B7" yields the sum of the values in cells B6 and B7.
- Set the number format and other options as needed.
- Click the OK button.

To insert the form field that calculates the cost of the tickets:

1. If you took a break after the last session, make sure Word is running, the Sun Valley Order Form template is open in Normal View, and that the Forms toolbar and nonprinting characters are displayed.
2. Move the insertion point to cell B8, to the right of the cell labeled "Ticket Cost," click the **Text Form Field** button abl on the Forms toolbar to insert a text form field, and then open the Text Form Field Options dialog box.
3. Click the **Type** list arrow, and then click **Calculation**. The dialog box displays the Expression text box in which you can type a formula for the calculation you want to perform. Here, you want the contents of cell B6 (number of tickets ordered) to be multiplied by the contents of cell B7 (the price per ticket).
4. Click to the right of the equal sign in the **Expression** text box, and then type **b6*b7** to calculate the cost for the number of tickets ordered. (Notice that in most computer programs, an asterisk (*) is used as a multiplication sign.)
5. Click the **Number format** list arrow, and then click **$#,##0.00;($#,##0.00)** to set the number format as a dollar amount. See Figure 9-27.

Figure 9-27 TEXT FORM FIELD OPTIONS DIALOG BOX

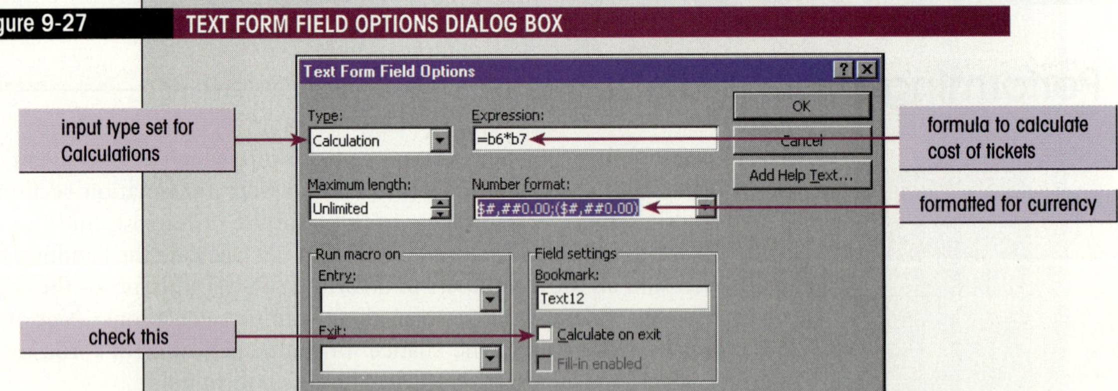

6. Click the **Calculate on exit** check box, and click the **OK** button. The Calculate on exit check box ensures that Word carries out the calculation when the user exits this field. If the check box isn't selected, Word won't carry out the calculation until the field is updated.

The field appears with the number "$24.00," the product of the "No. of Tickets" default value 2, and the Price per Ticket default value "$12.00." You didn't type a status bar prompt or a Help message because the calculation information is inserted automatically.

You're ready to insert the form fields that calculate the sales tax, handling fee, and total costs.

To insert the rest of the form fields:

1. Move the insertion point to cell B9, to the right of the cell labeled "Sales Tax," and then repeat Steps 2 through 6 in the previous set of steps, except type **b8*0.0625** after the equal sign in the Expression text box. This formula calculates the sales tax, which is the ticket cost multiplied by 6.25%. Be sure to check the **Calculate on exit** check box and to choose the **$#,##0.00;($#,##0.00)** number format.

   Now, you can insert the form field that calculates the handling fee.

2. Move to cell B10, to the right of the cell labeled "Handling Fee," and then repeat the procedure to insert a calculation field, except type **b6*1.5** after the equal sign in the Expression text box to calculate the handling fee, which is the number of tickets multiplied by $1.50.

   Finally, you'll insert the form field that calculates the total amount of the order.

3. Move to cell B11, to the right of the cell labeled "TOTAL," and then repeat the procedure to insert a calculation field, except type **b8+b9+b10** after the equal sign in the Expression text box to calculate the total order amount, which is the sum of the ticket cost (cell B8), the sales tax (cell B9), and the handling fee (cell B10).

4. Save the order-form template. Your order-form template should look like Figure 9-28.

   TROUBLE? If the results of your calculation fields wrap to more than one line, adjust column widths as necessary.

Figure 9-28 ON-SCREEN FORM WITH CALCULATION FIELDS

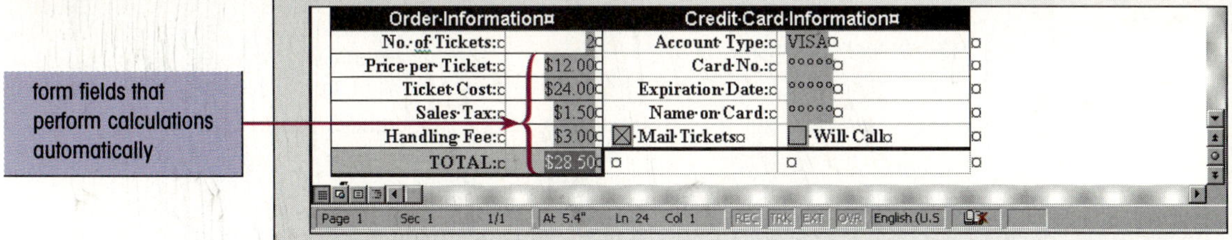

Order Information		Credit Card Information	
No. of Tickets:	2	Account Type:	VISA
Price per Ticket:	$12.00	Card No.:	ooooo
Ticket Cost:	$24.00	Expiration Date:	ooooo
Sales Tax:	$1.50	Name on Card:	ooooo
Handling Fee:	$3.00	☒ Mail Tickets	☐ Will Call
TOTAL:	$28.50		

Page 1 Sec 1 1/1 At 5.4" Ln 24 Col 1 REC TRK EXT OVR English (U.S

form fields that perform calculations automatically

TROUBLE? If your form is different—for example, a label is misspelled, text is not aligned properly, or a border is out of place or missing—make the corrections now. You can change the form field options for a field by double-clicking the field to open the Form Field Options dialog box.

The order form contains all the form fields that perform calculations. When a ticket agent enters the number of tickets and price per ticket, the calculation text form fields will compute the ticket cost, sales tax, handling fee, and total amount.

Recording a Macro to Change Field Order

When you fill out a form, it's easiest to enter similar information as a group. For example, enter all the event information before entering any of the customer information; enter all the order information before entering any of the credit card information. In an on-screen form, press the Tab key to move from one field to the next. Where is the "next" field? Word selects the next field just like you read a book. When you read, your eyes scan from left to right until they reach the end of a line (row), and then they move down to the left edge of the next line. Similarly, when you press the Tab key from within a form field, the insertion point moves to the next field in the same cell if there is another field in that same cell, to the next field on that same row, or to the first (leftmost) field on the next row.

When ticket agents fill out the Sun Valley ticket order form, they'll want to enter the number of tickets and then the price per ticket. But right now, when a ticket agent enters the number of tickets and presses the Tab key, the insertion point moves to the Account Type field in the Credit Card Information section. The agent must press the Tab key again to move the insertion point to the Price per Ticket field, as shown in Figure 9-29.

Figure 9-29 MOVEMENT OF INSERTION POINT UPON PRESSING TAB KEY

Order Information		Credit Card Information	
No. of Tickets:		Account Type:	
Price per Ticket:		Card No.:	
Ticket Cost:		Expiration Date:	

Macros can solve this problem. You can create a macro to run whenever the insertion point enters or exits a particular field. For example, you can record a macro so that after a ticket agent enters the number of tickets and presses the Tab key, the insertion point moves to the Price per Ticket field.

How do you record a macro to move the insertion point from the No. of Tickets field to the Price per Ticket field? First, you assign a bookmark to the Price per Ticket field. Second, you record a macro to move the insertion point to that bookmark. And third, you assign the macro to the No. of Tickets field. You'll create the macro now.

REFERENCE WINDOW 

Recording a Macro to Change the Form Field Order

- Specify a bookmark name for the desired field.
- Double-click the REC button on the status bar, type the name of the macro, specify that the macro should be available only to the current template document, and then click the OK button.
- Click Edit on the menu bar, click Go To, click Bookmark, and then click the bookmark name for the target field.
- Click the Go To button, and then click the Close button.
- Click the Stop Recording button on the Stop toolbar.
- Double-click the form field that you want to precede the target field.
- Click the Exit list arrow in the Text Form Field Option dialog box, and then click the name of the macro that moves to the target field.
- Click the OK button.

To record the macro to change the field order:

1. Double-click the **Price per Ticket** form field in cell B7. The Text Form Field Options dialog box opens.

2. In the Field Settings section of the dialog box, double-click the **Bookmark** text box to highlight its contents (if the text box is blank, just click in it), type **PricePerTicket** (all one word, without spaces), and then click the **OK** button.

   Next, you'll record the macro that moves the insertion point to the PricePerTicket bookmark.

3. Double-click the **REC** button on the status bar to open the Record Macro dialog box, type **MoveToPricePerTicket** in the Macro name text box, click the **Store macro in** list arrow, click **Documents Based On Sun Valley Order Form**, select the text in the **Description** text box, type **Go to Price per Ticket field**, and then click the **OK** button. Word will record each of your actions.

4. Click **Edit** on the menu bar, click **Go To**, click **Bookmark** in the Go to what list, click the **Enter bookmark name** list arrow, click **PricePerTicket** in the list of bookmarks, click the **Go To** button, and then click the **Close** button.

   (You might wonder why you used the GoTo command to move the insertion point to the bookmark, rather than using the Bookmark command on the Edit menu. The Bookmark command allows you to edit the document. You need to avoid any command related to editing the macro, because later in this tutorial you will protect the form to prevent users from changing it inadvertently. Once you protect the form, all editing commands become unavailable. Thus, if you use the Bookmark command now, the macro would not work later after you protect the document.)

5. Click the **Stop Recording** button ■ on the Stop toolbar. You have recorded the entire macro. Now, you need to tell Word to execute this macro whenever the Tab key is pressed in the No. of Tickets field.

6. Open the Text Form Field Options dialog box for the No. of Tickets text form field in cell B6.

7. Click the **Exit** list arrow in the Run macro on section of the dialog box, and then click **MoveToPricePerTicket**. See Figure 9-30.

Figure 9-30 TEXT FORM FIELD OPTIONS DIALOG BOX

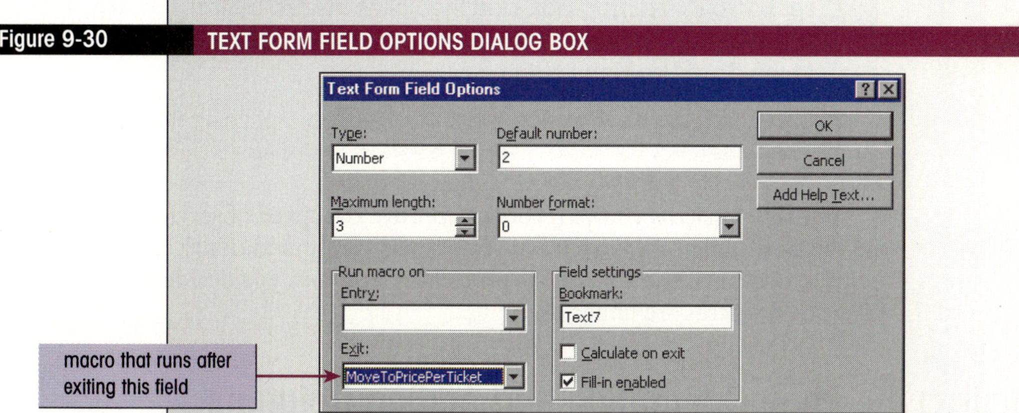

8. Click the **OK** button to return to the document window, and then save the order-form template.

Now, whenever a Sun Valley ticket agent presses the Tab key after entering the number of tickets being ordered, the insertion point will move to the Price per Ticket field, not to the Account Type field.

You need to create two more macros. One macro will move the insertion point from the Price per Ticket field to the Account Type field, and the other will position the insertion point from the Account Type field to the Card Number field. All the other fields appear in a logical sequence within the form.

To record the other two macros:

1. Double-click the **Account Type** form field in cell D6 to open the Drop-Down Form Field Options dialog box, type **AccountType** in the Bookmark text box, and then click the **OK** button.
2. Double-click the **Card No.** form field in cell D7 to open the Text Form Field Options dialog box, type **CardNum** in the Bookmark text box, and then click the **OK** button.
3. Record a macro named **MoveToCardNum** that uses the **Go To** command to move the insertion point from the Account Type field to the bookmark CardNum. Remember to make the macro available only to this template.

   TROUBLE? If you need help, refer to Steps 3 through 5 in the previous set of steps.
4. Record a macro named **MoveToAccountType** that uses the **Go To** command to move the insertion point from the Price per Ticket field to the bookmark AccountType. Remember to make the macro available only to this template.

   TROUBLE? If you need help, refer to Steps 3 through 8 in the previous set of steps.
5. Open the Text Form Field Options dialog box for the **Price per Ticket** form field, click the **MoveToAccountType** macro in the **Exit** list box in the **Run macro on** section of the dialog box, and then click the **OK** button. This way, when you press the Tab key after entering the price per ticket, the insertion point will move to the Account Type form field.
6. Open the Drop-Down Form Field Options dialog box for the Account Type form field, click the **MoveToCardNum** macro in the **Exit** list box in the **Run macro on** section of the dialog box, and then click the **OK** button. This way, when you press the Tab key after entering the account type, the insertion point will move to the Card No. form field.
7. Save the order-form template.

The three macros you've recorded improve the speed of service and accuracy of records at the Sun Valley Ticket Office. You could create additional macros, such as AutoText entries, that further automate the procedure. For now, you decide that AutoText entries and additional macros are unnecessary.

Changing the Page Orientation and Adding Columns

Richard wants you to change the page orientation for the order-form template from portrait, in which the page is taller than it is wide (8.5" × 11.0"), to landscape, in which the page is wider than it is tall (11.0" × 8.5"). The purpose for changing the page orientation of the order form is primarily to add visual appeal. In other circumstances, changing the page orientation might be more functional. For example, if your table or diagram is very wide, you might want to print the document in landscape orientation.

To change the page orientation of the order-form template:

1. Click **File** on the menu bar, click **Page Setup**, and then, if necessary, click the **Paper Size** tab.
2. Click the **Landscape** option button in the Orientation section. Notice that the Preview box changes. See Figure 9-31.

Figure 9-31 PAGE SETUP DIALOG BOX

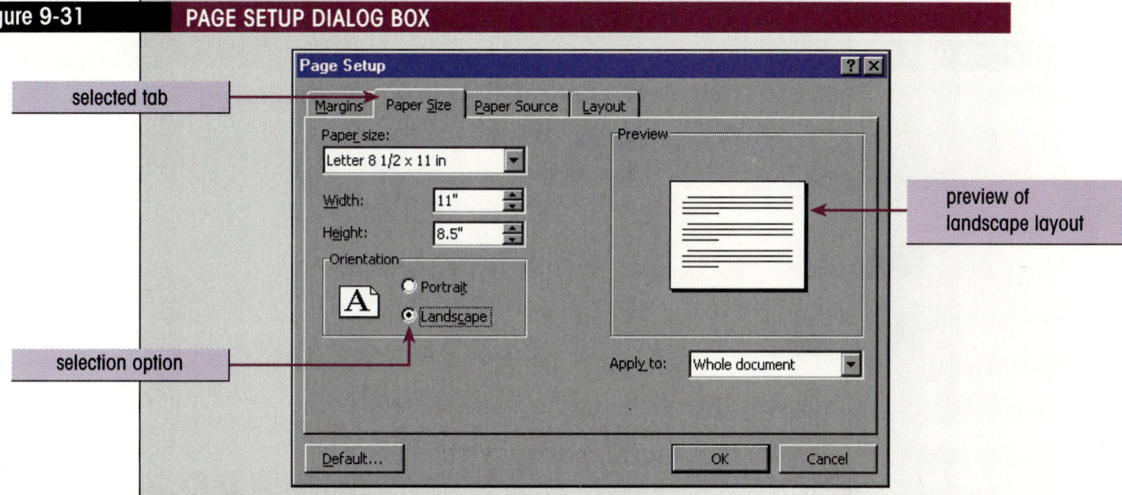

3. Click the **OK** button. The document becomes wider than it is tall. You can see this better in Print Layout View.
4. Switch to Print Layout View, click the **Zoom** list arrow on the Standard toolbar, and then click **Page Width**.

Now that you've changed the page orientation to landscape, the document appears on two pages. This occurs because the page height is now 8.5 inches instead of the usual 11 inches. You fix this problem by moving the text from below the table to the right of the table. The easiest way to do this is to divide the document into columns. Richard suggests setting the document in three columns, with the table in the first column, and the text to the right of the table in the second and third columns. You'll set the first column to 5.5 inches—the width of the table—and then split the remaining space for the other two columns.

To format the document into three columns:

1. Click **Format** on the menu bar, and then click **Columns** to open the Columns dialog box.

   TROUBLE? If your document splits into three even columns, you probably clicked the Columns button on the Standard toolbar instead of using the Columns command on the Format menu. Click the Undo button on the Standard toolbar, and then repeat Step 1.

2. In the Presets section, click the **Three columns** icon. This formats the document for three, evenly spaced columns, but you want one column to be wider than the other two.

3. Click the **Equal column width** check box to deselect it, so you can set the columns to unequal widths.

4. Change the width of column 1 to **5.5"**, and then press the **Tab** key to move to the Spacing box. Notice that Word divides the remaining space evenly between columns 2 and 3. You want to make sure that the column format applies to the entire document.

5. Click the **Apply to** list arrow, and then click **Whole document**. See Figure 9-32.

Figure 9-32 COLUMN DIALOG BOX

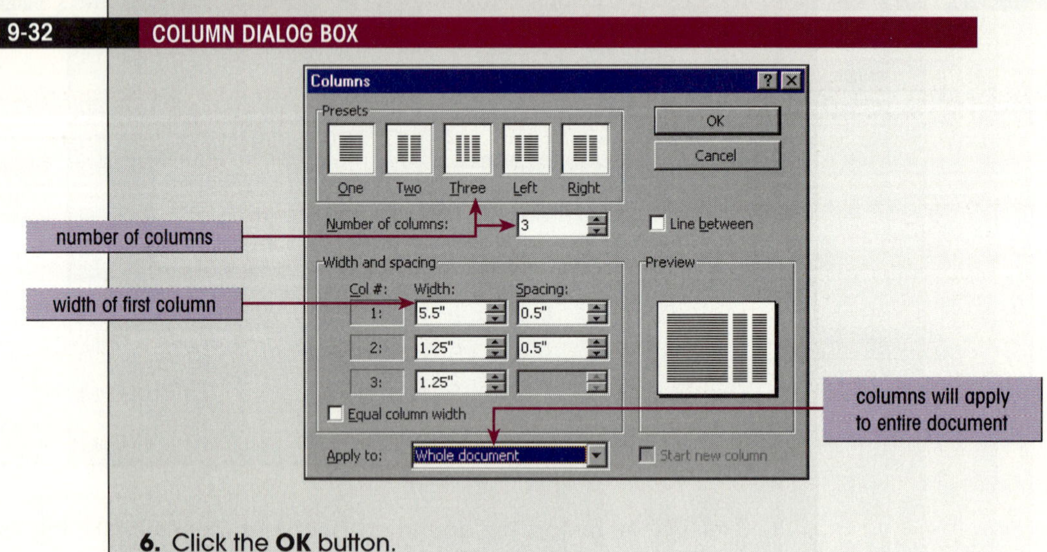

6. Click the **OK** button.

The text of the document wraps into three columns. You want to force all the text located below the table into the second and third columns. However, because the text currently appears in only the first (and possibly second) column, you decide to change the document to two columns, with one column for the table and one column for the text.

To change the column structure and force the text into the second column:

1. Open the Columns dialog box again, set the **Number of columns** to **2**, deselect the **Equal column widths** checkbox, set the width of the first column to **5.5"**, make sure the **Spacing** text box is set to **0.5**, apply the settings to the **Whole document**, and then click the **OK** button. Now your document has only two columns.

   Next, you'll force the text below the table into the second column by adding a column break before the text.

2. Move the insertion point to the left of "All performances..." at the beginning of the paragraph below the table.

3. Click **Insert** on the menu bar, click **Break** to open the Break dialog box, click the **Column break** option button in the Insert section of the dialog box, and then click the **OK** button. The column break forces all the text to the right of the table.

   Richard asks you to add a statement about lost or stolen items below the bulleted list.

4. If you can't read the text, change the Zoom value on the Standard toolbar to **100%**.

5. Move the insertion point to the end of the last bulleted item in the second column, and press the **Enter** key twice to leave a blank line and start a new paragraph.

6. Type **The Sun Valley Summer Music Festival cannot be held responsible for lost or stolen items.** (Be sure to include the period.) See Figure 9-33.

Figure 9-33 ON-SCREEN FORM AFTER APPLYING COLUMNS AND INSERTED TEXT

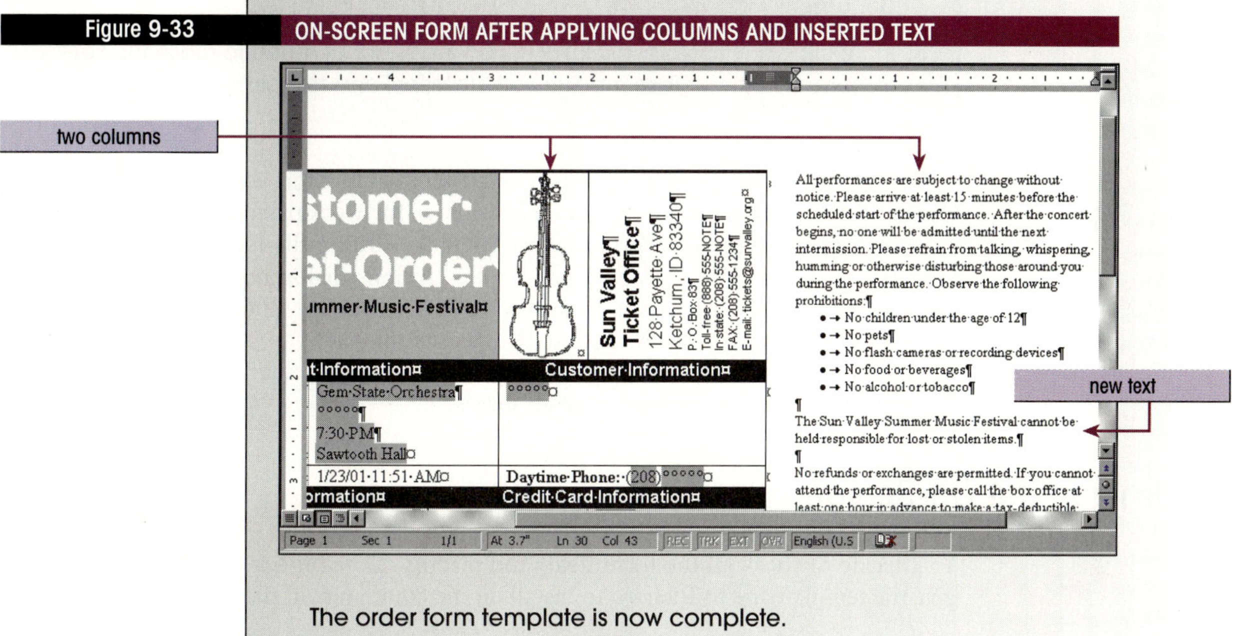

The order form template is now complete.

Protecting and Saving the On-Screen Form

With the table formatted, all the form fields in place, the macros recorded, and the text in columns, you're ready to save the Sun Valley order form template. Before the ticket agents can use the template to create new ticket orders, you'll have to protect the form as you did when you tested the first few form fields you inserted. Then, you or Richard will have to save the file to the Templates folder on the computer system in the Sun Valley Ticket Office.

To protect and save the on-screen form:

1. Click the **Protect Form** button on the Forms toolbar.
2. Save the template.

With the template protected and saved, you'll copy it to the Templates folder on your computer so you can open a new document based on the template.

3. If you don't know in which folder document template files are stored, click **Tools** on the menu bar, click **Options**, click the **File Locations** tab, write down the location of the folder for User Templates, which might be, for example, "C:\Program Files\Microsoft Office\Templates" or "C:\Windows\Application Data\Microsoft\Templates," and then click the **Close** button to close the dialog box. If necessary, click **User templates** in the File Types text box, and then click the **Modify** button to see the entire pathname.
4. Click **File** on the menu bar, then click **Save As**, change the Save in list box to the location of the Templates folder that you wrote down in Step 3, and then click the **Save** button.

   Before you continue, you'll close the Forms toolbar to regain the space in the document window.
5. Right-click any toolbar, click **Forms** on the shortcut menu to close the Forms toolbar, and then close the Sun Valley Order Form template.

Besides saving template files to the default template folder, you also can change the file location of the templates or set a template folder for workgroup templates (template files available to your entire workgroup). To change an existing file location or to set a new file location, go to the File Locations tab of the Options dialog box, as described in Step 3 above, click the file type whose location you want to change, and click the Modify button. You then can change or set the path to the desired folder.

Having protected and saved the file into the Templates folder, you'll use the Sun Valley order-form template to fill out an order form.

Filling in the On-Screen Form

You decide to check all the form fields and macros in the on-screen order form before you give the template file to Richard to install on the computers in the Sun Valley Ticket Office.

REFERENCE WINDOW RW

Filling in On-Screen Forms

- Click File on the menu bar, and then click New.
- If applicable, click the tab that corresponds to the Templates folder where the template is saved.
- Click the icon of the document template you want (for example, the Sun Valley Order Form icon), and then click the OK button.
- Read the status-bar prompt for directions, and then type the requested information into the first field of the form. If you need additional help, press the F1 key.
- Press the Tab key to move to the next field, or press Shift + Tab to move to the previous field. If you don't want to change the information in a field, press the Tab key to go to the next field.
- Save and print, fax, or route the completed form.

You'll begin a new order form and fill in a customer's ticket order from earlier in the day.

To open a new order form and fill in some of the information:

1. Click **File** on the menu bar, and then click **New** to open the New dialog box. (Recall that you only use the New button on the Standard toolbar to start a document based on the Normal template.)
2. If necessary, click the **General** tab in the New dialog box to see the general templates available on your computer.
3. Double-click the **Sun Valley Order Form** icon. Word opens a new document window with the blank order form. The Event form field is selected, and is waiting for you to type the name of the event or press the Tab key to accept the default name "Gem State Orchestra."
4. Switch to Normal view (if necessary) so that you can see as much of the document as possible, make sure the Zoom value is 75% or higher, press the **F1** key to get help on what you should enter into this field, read the Help dialog box, click the **OK** button to close it, and then type **S.V. Youth Orchestra**.

   TROUBLE? If you tried to type the full name, "Sun Valley Youth Orchestra," you found that you can't type past "Sun Valley Youth Orc," the maximum 20 characters allowed in this field. If you type "S. V." with a space between the two initials, you won't be able to complete the word "Orchestra." Edit the text so that the name fits in the 20 characters.

5. Press the **Tab** key to move to the next field. The Date of Event field becomes highlighted, and a status-bar prompt appears.

   TROUBLE? If you moved past the Time of Event field, you pressed the Tab key more than once. Press Shift + Tab to return to the previous field. You can press Shift + Tab to move to a previous cell, unless a cell has an exit macro that sends the insertion point to a different location.

6. Type **16 Jul 01** to insert the date of the performance, and then press the **Tab** key to go to the next field.
7. Because this event begins at 7:30 PM, press the **Tab** key to accept the default time. The Concert Hall field list arrow appears.
8. Click the list arrow to display a list of concert halls, click **Shoshone Hall**, and then press the **Tab** key.

You have completed the first section of the Sun Valley order form. Now, you'll test the customer information sections.

To complete the order form:

1. Make sure the Customer Information field is selected. If necessary, press the **Tab** key to move forward, or press **Shift + Tab** to move backward to that field.
2. Type **Ardell Adamson**, press **Enter**, type **2255 East Texas Ave.**, press the **Enter** key, and type **Boise, ID 83708** to enter all three lines of the name and address into the same field.

TROUBLE? If you accidentally press the Tab key before you finish typing the name and address, click the Customer Information field at the location you stopped typing.

3. Press the **Tab** key to move to the area code field, and then press the **Tab** key again to move to the phone number field. This accepts the default area code, which is **208**.
4. Type **555-8008**, the customer's daytime telephone number, and then press the **Tab** key. The new field prompts you to enter the number of tickets in this order.
5. Type **4**, then press the **Tab** key to move to the next field. If your macro worked properly, you should be in the Price per Ticket field.

   TROUBLE? If your macro did not work properly—for example, if it gave you an error message or if the current field is not prompting you for the price per ticket—close this document without saving it, open the Sun Valley Ticket Form template in the Tutorial.09 Tutorial folder on your Data Disk, open the Forms toolbar, unprotect the file by clicking the Protect button, and then carefully work through all the sections again, beginning with the section "Recording a Macro to Change Field Order."

6. Type **14.5** (Word changes it to currency format—$14.50—although you could type it yourself), press the **Tab** key to move to the Account Type field in the Credit Card Information section of the form, click the list arrow, click **American Express**, and then press the **Tab** key.
7. Type the credit card number **378700000011111** without any hyphens or spaces, press the **Tab** key, type the expiration date **12/01**, and then press the **Tab** key again.
8. Press the **Tab** key again to leave the Name on Card field blank because the American Express cardholder is the same as the customer (Ardell Adamson).
9. Press the **spacebar** to uncheck the Mail Tickets check box, press the **Tab** key, and then press the **spacebar** to check the Will Call check box. This completes the form. See Figure 9-34.

Figure 9-34 COMPLETED ON-SCREEN FORM

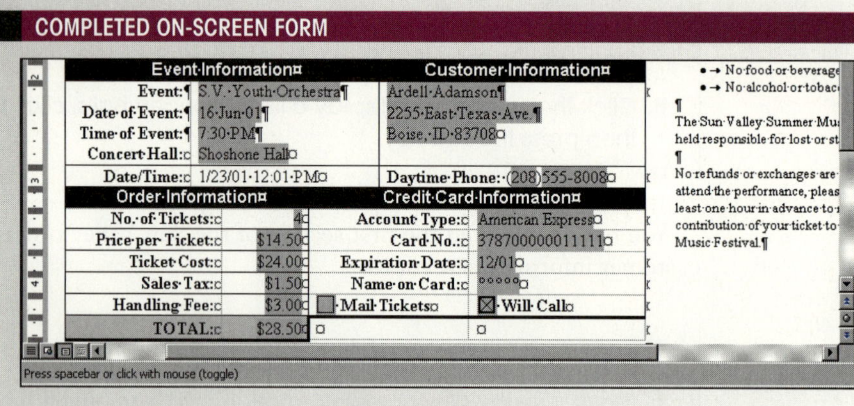

TROUBLE? If the information in your form is not the same as in Figure 9-34, you should fix it now. Remember that to move forward from one field to the next, you press the Tab key; to move backward, you press Shift + Tab. (The Shift + Tab key combination won't work, however, if you try to go backward from a field that has a macro to send you forward.)

Even though you have filled out the form completely, the calculation fields have not been updated. The only way to update them in a protected form is to specify that you want fields updated when you print the form.

To update fields when you print a form:

1. Click **Tools** on the menu bar, and then click **Options** to open the Options dialog box.
2. Click the **Print** tab.
3. In the Printing options section, if necessary, click the **Update fields** check box to select that option.
4. Click the **OK** button. Now whenever you print a completed order form, Word will update the fields. You only have to set this option once, not each time you want to print an order form.
5. Click the **Print** button on the Standard toolbar to print the order form. See Figure 9-35.

Figure 9-35 FINAL FILLED-OUT FORM

Customer Ticket Order
Sun Valley Summer Music Festival

Sun Valley Ticket Office
128 Payette Ave
Ketchum, ID 83340
P. O. Box 83
Toll-free (888) 555-NOTE
In state: (208) 555-NOTE
FAX: (208) 555-1234
E-mail: tickets@sunvalley.org

Event Information		Customer Information
Event:	S.V. Youth Orchestra	Ardell Adamson
Date of Event:	16 Jun 01	2255 East Texas Ave.
Time of Event:	7:30 PM	Boise, ID 83708
Concert Hall:	Shoshone Hall	
Date/Time:	1/23/01 12:06 PM	Daytime Phone: (208) 555-8008

Order Information		Credit Card Information	
No. of Tickets:	4	Account Type:	American Express
Price per Ticket:	$14.50	Card No.:	378700000011111
Ticket Cost:	$58.00	Expiration Date:	12/01
Sales Tax:	$3.62	Name on Card:	
Handling Fee:	$6.00	☐ Mail Tickets	☒ Will Call
TOTAL:	$67.62		

All performances are subject to change without notice. Please arrive at least 15 minutes before the scheduled start of the performance. After the concert begins, no one will be admitted until the next intermission. Please refrain from talking, whispering, humming or otherwise disturbing those around you during the performance. Observe the following prohibitions:

- No children under the age of 12
- No pets
- No flash cameras or recording devices
- No food or beverages
- No alcohol or tobacco

The Sun Valley Summer Music Festival cannot be held responsible for lost or stolen items.

No refunds or exchanges are permitted. If you cannot attend the performance, please call the box office at least one hour in advance to make a tax-deductible contribution of your ticket to the Sun Valley Summer Music Festival.

You'll save the filled-in order form as a normal document because you need to fax it to the customer. Later, you'll save only the fill-in data, which takes up less disk space.

6. Save the document as **Adamson Order** in the Tutorial folder for Tutorial 9 on your Data Disk.

Ticket agents will mail or fax a printed form to customers who order tickets for the Sun Valley Summer Music Festival.

Faxing or Routing an Order Form

With the Fax Wizard, you can send an electronic facsimile (fax) of a document just as easily as you can print it. As long as you have a fax program, such as Microsoft Fax, installed on your computer and a modem, you can send a fax right from your computer. Or you can print a cover sheet and the document, and then fax it from a separate fax machine.

If you want to share a document with a group of people who have access to e-mail that supports attachments, then you might want to route the document. To **route** a document means to send an e-mail message attachment to a group of people, one person at a time. After each person reads the document, he or she sends it along to the next recipient on the routing slip (a list of recipients). Using a class trip as an example, a ticket agent might route the order form to Richard for approval, then to the special groups coordinator who will arrange a backstage tour, then to the advertising director who calls to see if the group wants to order special T-shirts, and so on.

REFERENCE WINDOW RW

Routing a Document

- Log on to the Internet, and then return to your Word document.
- Click File on the menu bar, point to Send To, and then click Routing Recipient.
- Click the Address button, and then select or enter the names and e-mail addresses for all recipients.
- Click the Route button, or click the OK button, and then click File on the menu bar, point to Send To, and then click Next Routing Recipient.

For now, you don't need to route a document. Instead, Ardell Adamson requested that you fax her a copy of the order form so she has a permanent record of her order. You'll create and send the fax using the Fax Wizard.

To create and send a fax:

1. Click **File** on the menu bar, point to **Send To**, and then click **Fax Recipient**. The Fax Wizard dialog box opens. Read the information on the dialog box.

   TROUBLE? If you don't see the Fax Wizard icon, consult your instructor or technical support person.

2. Click the **Next** button to go to the next Fax Wizard dialog box, where you can select the document you want to fax. The default document name is **Adamson Order.doc**, which is the document you want to fax.

3. Make sure the **With a cover sheet** option button is selected so that the Wizard will create a cover sheet for your fax, and then click the **Next** button. Now, you can select the fax program you want to use. In this example, you'll print the document to the default Windows printer.

   TROUBLE? If you would like to send a fax, you must have a fax program and know a fax number to which you can send the form. If you have questions, consult your instructor or technical support person.

4. Now, you could select the Microsoft Fax option button (if you have Microsoft Fax installed on your computer), or you could select a different fax program. In this case, however, you should simply click the **I want to print my document so I can send it from a separate fax machine** option button, and then click the **Next** button. Now, you'll type the name and fax numbers of the recipients.

5. With the insertion point in the first Name text box, type **Ardell Adamson**, press the **Tab** key, type **1-208-555-8088**, and then click the **Next** button.

6. Make sure the Professional option button is selected for the cover sheet style, click the **Next** button, and fill in the information as shown, except type your name instead of Richard Vanderkloot as shown in Figure 9-36.

Figure 9-36 FAX WIZARD DIALOG BOX WITH INFORMATION FOR FAX FORM

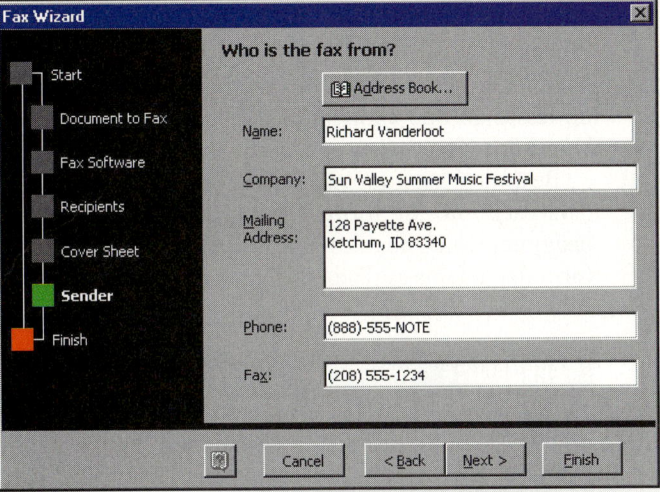

7. Click the **Next** button, read the information in the final Fax Wizard dialog box, and click the **Finish** button.

8. Click in each of the five "(Click here . . .)" regions of the document, and type the information as shown in Figure 9-37. Save the cover letter as **Adamson Fax** to the Tutorial folder for Tutorial 9. Print the cover letter, and then close it.

Figure 9-37 DOCUMENT WINDOW WITH FAX COVER SHEET

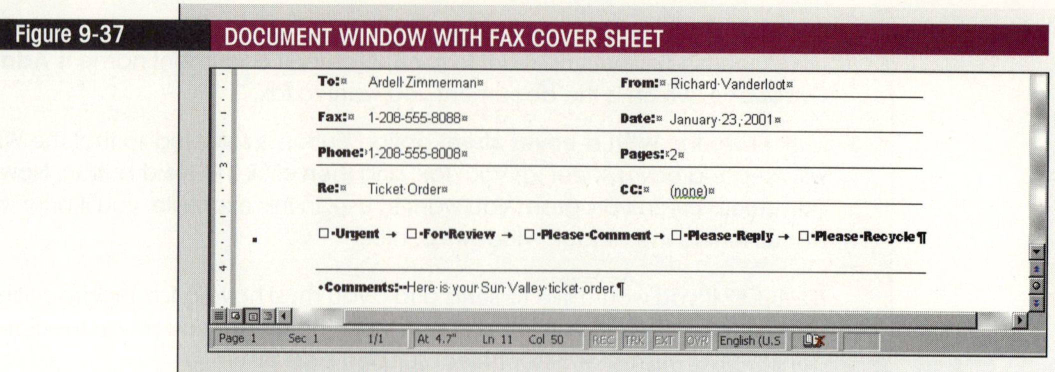

Richard wants to reduce the amount of paper files in the Sun Valley Ticket Office, so instead of keeping a copy of the printed form, you'll save only the information.

Saving Only the Data from a Form

You can save the entire on-screen form as a Word document, as you did earlier, or you can save the information contained in an on-screen form as a text file. When you save an on-screen form as a Word document, you save the complete document, including the table, graphics, fields, and information. The advantage of this method is that any time you want to view or print the completed form, you can open the document just as you would any other Word document.

When you save the information contained in an on-screen form as a text file, you save only the data entered into or calculated by the fields, not the table, graphics, fields, or anything else in the document. Word saves the data in a text file, with the filename extension ".txt." The advantage of this method is that you save disk space. A file with only data takes up less than one kilobyte of disk space, whereas a complete document saved as a normal Word document takes up about 32 kilobytes.

Be aware that after you save a form as a text file with only the data, you can't retrieve the data back into the form. You can, however, open the data into a spreadsheet or database program, which enables you to analyze the data you have collected. If you want to save all form documents as data only, you can specify this option in the Options dialog box.

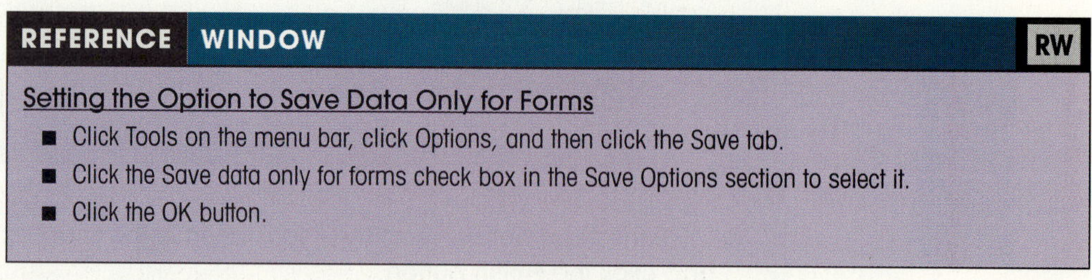
REFERENCE WINDOW RW

Setting the Option to Save Data Only for Forms

- Click Tools on the menu bar, click Options, and then click the Save tab.
- Click the Save data only for forms check box in the Save Options section to select it.
- Click the OK button.

You'll set all forms to save as data only.

To set the Save data only for forms option:

1. Make sure Adamson Order is still in the document window, click **Tools** on the menu bar, click **Options**, and then click the **Save** tab. Notice the Save data only for forms check box in the Save options section of the dialog box. When this check box is selected, you save filled-in forms with only the data, not as complete Word documents with the form table.
2. If necessary, click the **Save data only for forms** check box to select it. Now, whenever you save a new completed form, only the data will be saved to your disk.
3. Click the **OK** button.

With the Save data only for forms option set, you can save the form that you just completed for Ardell Adamson.

To save the completed form:

1. Click the **Save** button on the Standard toolbar. Because you haven't yet saved this document as data only, the Save As dialog box opens.
2. Make sure the Save in list box is set to the Tutorial folder for Tutorial 9 on your Data Disk, leave the default file name Adamson Order in the File name text box, leave Text Only as the default file type, and then click the **Save** button. Word saves the file with the filename extension ".txt." because it is a text file.
3. When you are prompted that you'll lose formatting by saving as data only, click the **Yes** button to continue. The document is saved as "data only," that is, only the information you entered into the form is saved, not the form itself.

   The only way you can save the entire form as a normal Word document is to deselect the Save data only for forms check box on the Save tab in the Options dialog box. You'll do that now.
4. Click **Tools** on the menu bar, click **Options**, click the **Save** tab, click the **Save data only for forms** check box to deselect it, and then click the **OK** button.
5. Click **Tools** on the menu bar, click **AutoCorrect**, click the **AutoFormat As You Type** tab, click the **Define styles based on your formatting** check box to select it, and then click the **OK** button.
6. Close any open documents. Click the **No** button if you're prompted to save changes to the document.
7. Delete the **Sun Valley Order Form** template from the Templates folder on your computer.

   You'll turn back on automatic definition of styles; but remember to turn off this feature when you're formatting complex tables because it may cause problems.
8. Exit Word.

Richard is pleased with the form you created. He's sure it will help speed up the order-taking process as well as improve the accuracy of the records kept at the Sun Valley Ticket Office.

Session 9.3 QUICK CHECK

1. What is a calculation form field?
2. In a calculation form field, what is an expression?
3. In general, how would you tell Word to calculate the sum of the values in two cells of a table in an on-screen form?
4. When you're filling out an on-screen form, what key or keys do you press to move from one field to the next? To move from one field to a previous field?
5. In general, how would you change the order in which the insertion point moves from one field to another in a form?
6. Why do you protect a form template before you save it?
7. What are the two ways in which you can save a completed form? Name one advantage and one disadvantage of each.
8. How do you save only the data in a form rather than the entire form as a normal Word document?

REVIEW ASSIGNMENTS

Briana Schow is director of admissions for the Sun Valley Summer Music Festival. Her responsibilities include processing applications from student participants, scheduling auditions, sending acceptance letters, and collecting tuition and fees. She decides to streamline the invoice process by creating an on-screen form that the admissions department can use to record information about each student and about tuition and fees payment, and to print a copy of the form as an invoice.

1. If necessary, start Word and make sure your Data Disk is in the appropriate drive. Open the file **SVAdm** from the Review folder in the Tutorial.09 folder on your Data Disk, and then save it on your Data Disk as a template with the filename **Sun Valley Admissions Form**.

Explore

2. Modify the table to match the one in Figure 9–38, but without the specific information about the student Miriam Scheraga and the three check boxes. (*Hint*: You'll use: ¾-point and 2 ¼-point borders; 20% and 100% shading; 12-point Times New Roman; 12- and 14-point Arial; black and white font colors; bold, shadow, and small cap text; and thick and double underlines.)

Figure 9-38

OFFICE OF ADMISSIONS
542 West Sawtooth Ave.
Ketchum, Idaho 83340
Voice: (208) 555-1234
FAX: (208) 555-9876

Sun Valley Summer Music Festival
Student Information

Student Information				
Last: Scheraga	First: Miriam	☐Male	☒Female	Age: 17
Guardian name: Greta Scheraga		Phone: (702) 555-0841		
Street: 51992 Silver Road		FAX: (702) 555-5201		
City: Winnemucca		State: NV	ZIP: 89304	

Festival Participation	
Start Date:	08 Jun 2001
Weeks of participation:	5
Instrument:	Cello

Tuition and Fees		
Tuition:	$900.00	
Housing:	$710.00	
Meal card:	$670.00	
Deposit (nonrefundable):	100.00	
TOTAL:	$2,3800.00	
Amount Prepaid:	$200.00	
Amount Due:	$2,1800.00	← Pay this amount

Please remit amount due prior to first day of festival.
Make checks payable to the Sun Valley Music Festival.
Mail to address given above.

Check here to print: ☐

As you add form fields to cells, make sure you add a space between the labels and the form fields as necessary. Refer to Figure 9-38 as needed.

3. In the cell labeled "Last," insert a regular text form field for the student's last name. Set the maximum length to 25, the text format to First Capital, and the bookmark name to "LastName" (one word).
4. In the First, Guardian name, Street, and City cells and to the cell to the right of Instrument, insert regular text form fields with Unlimited maximum lengths. Set the text formats to First Capital, but leave the bookmarks set to the default names.
5. In the Male and Female cells and next to "Check here to print" (below the table), insert check box form fields with the default set to Not Checked.
6. In the State cell, insert a regular text form field with a maximum length set to 2 and the text format set to Uppercase.
7. In the Age and ZIP cells and to the right of the Weeks of participation cell, insert a number text form field for integers only, set with a maximum length of 2 for Age, 5 for ZIP, and 1 for Weeks of participation.
8. In the Phone cell, insert two text form fields (one for the area code and one for the rest of the telephone number), each with the appropriate settings for the type of characters and the maximum length. Do the same for the FAX cell.
9. To the right of the Start Date cell, insert a date text form field in the format "08 June 2001."

Explore

10. The Festival tuition is $180 per week. In the cell to the right of the Tuition cell, insert a calculation text form field that uses the "Weeks of participation" field to calculate the total tuition in the currency format "$900.00."
11. The cost per week is $142 for housing and $134 for a meal card. In the cells to the right of the Housing and Meal card cells, insert and format the appropriate calculation text form fields.
12. In the cell to the right of the Deposit (nonrefundable) cell, type "100.00"—the required deposit. Add a Thick underline below this value.
13. Insert a form field to calculate and format the "TOTAL" amount in currency format.

Explore

14. Insert a number text form field to accept input on the amount prepaid. Format the number appropriately.
15. Insert a form field to calculate and format the Amount Due. Add a double-underline below the field.

16. Change the page orientation to portrait.
17. Format the text below the table into 2 columns, insert a column break above the last line of text. Change the column format to Right.
18. Record a macro (for this template only) named "MoveToLastName" that moves the insertion point from the Amount Prepaid field to the last name field. This macro will prevent a user from going to the "Check here to print" field by pressing the Tab key.

Explore

19. Record a macro (for this template only) named "PrintForm" that prints two copies of the form. Set the Check here to print check box form field so that when the insertion point enters that field (that is, when the user checks the box), Word prints two copies of the form. (*Hint*: Make sure fields are set to be updated upon printing and your computer is not set to Save data only for forms in the Options dialog box.)
20. Protect and save the form. Copy the protected form into the Templates folder on your computer.
21. Start a new document based on the Sun Valley Admissions Form template, and complete it as shown in Figure 9–38, but use your own name and guardian rather than Miriam Scheraga's. Click the Check here to print check box to print two copies of the form. Save the form as a normal Word document, using the filename Sun Valley Filled-in Form.
22. Delete the Sun Valley Admissions Form template from the Templates folder on your computer.

CASE PROBLEMS

1. Sparkling Housecleaning Cindy Porter manages Sparkling Housecleaning, a full-service cleaning company for homes, apartments, and offices in Mobile, Alabama. She is responsible for assigning cleaning jobs to each of her 25 staff members. She wants you to create a form she can fill out and give to employees as they leave to complete a job. The form will outline the parameters of each job, including special instructions.

1. If necessary, start Word, and make sure your Data Disk is in the appropriate drive. Open the file **Cleaning** from the Cases folder in the Tutorial.09 folder on your Data Disk, and save it as a template in the same folder with the filename **Sparkling Form**.
2. Format the company name in cell A1 in 20-point, bold, outline, all-caps Arial. Change the three lines of the address and phone numbers to 14-point, bold, all caps, Times New Roman. Center all four lines.
3. Change the words "PHONE" and "FAX" to 14-point, bold, Times New Roman.
4. Insert a new, blank row below row 1. Using 12-point, bold, Times New Roman, type "Customer Information" in cell A2 and "Cleaning Information" in cell B2. Center the text in both cells.
5. Insert two new rows below row 3 (just above the text "# Level 1 cleanings"). Merge all the cells in row 4, type "Billing Information" in 14-point, bold, Times New Roman, and center the text. Make sure there are only 2 cells in row 5. In cell A5, type "Cleanings since last payment (on)" in the merged cell. Type "Amount Due" in the new cell B5. Adjust the left border of cell B5 to align it with the left border of cell C6.

Explore

6. Split cells B6, B7, and B8 each into five cells. Type "@" in cells C6, C7, and C8. Type "=" (an equal sign) in cells E6, E7, and E8. Reduce the column widths until "@" and "=" just fit, and columns D and F are about even. Don't change column G. (*Hint*: Select cells B6 through F8 before changing the column widths to ensure that column G doesn't change.) If the width of column G changes, drag its borders back to their original positions.
7. Type "Subtotal:" in cell G6 (directly under "Amount Due"), type "Less coupons/discounts:" in cell G7, and type "Total Due:" in cell G8.

Explore

8. Format rows 2, 4, and 5 with light yellow shading. (*Hint*: Use the Borders and Shading Color command on the Tables and Borders toolbar.) Change the font color in rows 2, 4, and 5 to Blue. Add a 3-point Blue outside border around the table and then remove the vertical borders to the right of cells A6 through A8, B6 through B8, C6 through C8, D6 through D8, and E6 through E8.

9. In cell A3, insert regular text form fields with a maximum length of 40 after the space to the right of the Name, Address, and City labels. Add text form fields with a maximum length of 2, formatted as Uppercase, after the State label. After the ZIP label, insert a number text form field with a maximum length of 5 formatted as integers. After the space to the right of the Home and Work phone labels, insert regular text form fields with maximum lengths of 8.
10. In cell B3, after the space to the right of Job Number label, insert a number text form field with a maximum length of 5. After the Key is for which door label, insert a regular text form field with a maximum length of 35. After the Cleaning level label, insert a drop-down form field with the three items: "Level 1," "Level 2," and "Level 3." After the Okay to leave bill on kitchen table? label, type "Yes," insert a space, and insert a check box form field that is checked by default. After the Special instructions label, insert a regular text form field of unlimited length. Adjust the column widths as necessary to keep the labels and their corresponding form fields on one line.
11. In cell A5 after the word "on" and before the right parenthesis, insert a date text form field formatted as 3/10/01. Make sure no spaces appear between the field and the closing parenthesis. Add "Last payment date can be found in the Invoices folder under customer's last name" for the status-bar prompt.
12. In cells B6, B7, and B8, insert number text form fields with a maximum length of 2 formatted as integers. In cells D6, D7, and D8, insert number text form fields formatted as currency with default values of 75, 145, and 210, respectively. Add "Enter a new value here only if customer receives a special rate" as the status bar prompt. In cells F6, F7, and F8, insert calculation text form fields formatted as currency that display the total amount for each cleaning level. (*Hint*: Multiply the number of cleanings by the cost at each level.) Right-align these nine cells.
13. In cell G6 after the Subtotal label, insert a space and then enter a calculation text form field formatted as currency that adds the values in cells F6, F7, and F8. After the Less discounts/coupons label, enter a space and then enter a number text form field formatted as currency with a default value of 0. Add "Enter amount of coupons or discounts the customer receives as positive number" for the status bar prompt. After the Total Due label, enter a space and then insert a form field that calculates the Subtotal value minus the Coupons and discounts value. Adjust the column widths as necessary to make the currency values fit on one line.
14. Create the following three macros for this template only:
    - "MoveToLevel3Cleanings" moves the insertion point from cell D7 (the Level 2 cleaning cost) to cell B8 (the number of Level 3 cleanings). Use the bookmark name "Level3Cleanings."
    - "MoveToCouponsDiscounts" moves the insertion point from cell D8 (the Level 3 cleaning cost) to cell G7 (the Coupons and discounts value). Use the bookmark name "CouponsDiscounts."
    - "MoveToName" moves the insertion point from cell G7 (the coupons and discounts value) to the field after the Name label in cell A3. Use the bookmark name "Name."
15. Insert two columns below the form table. In column 2, type "Printed: " and insert a current date field in the format 3/10/01.
16. Protect and save the form, and then print a copy of the form. Close the form.

Explore

17. Open a new document based on the Sparkling Form template, but without placing the document template in the Template folder. (*Hint*: Use Windows Explorer to locate the template file on your Data Disk, and then double-click the filename.)
18. Complete the form with the following information: [*your name*]; 1004 Church Street, Mobile, AL 36601; home phone 555-9610; work phone 555-3205; job number 20015; key location Side door (left of garage door); cleaning Level 2; Okay to leave bill: Yes; special instructions: Dog (Bruno) is friendly; be sure not to let him out; Last payment (cell A5): 1/16/01; # Level 1 cleanings: 2; # Level 2: 0; # Level 3: 1; and Coupons and discounts: $35.
19. Make sure your system is set up to update fields upon printing, and print a copy of the filled-in form. If the totals are wrong, print the form again so Word updates the calculations properly.

20. Save only the data in your Cases folder in the Tutorial.09 folder on your Data Disk with the filename **Sparkling Data**.

Explore 21. Open the Sparkling Data text file from within Word, print the document, and then close the file without saving any changes.

2. *Alaskan PhotoMart* Alaskan PhotoMart is a small exhibit hall in Anchorage, Alaska, where photographers can rent booths in which to display and sell their work. As a service to its photographers, Alaskan PhotoMart processes the sales transactions with customers. Josie McAuley, the owner, asks you to complete an on-screen form that she can use to create the monthly invoices she sends to the photographers.

1. If necessary, start Word, and make sure your Data Disk is in the appropriate drive. Open the **Alaskan** file from the Cases folder in the Tutorial.09 folder on your Data Disk, and save it as a template with the filename **Alaskan PhotoMart Invoice** in the same folder.
2. With the insertion point in cell A2, insert a new row between the two current rows, and insert five new rows at the bottom of the form.
3. Merge cells A4 and B4, and cells A8 and B8.
4. Change the column widths in rows 1, 2, 5, 6, and 7 so that columns A and B are even. Be sure not to change the width of any other column. (*Hint:* Use the Distribute Columns Evenly button on the Tables and Borders toolbar.)

Explore 5. Type "Date:" in 10-point Times New Roman in the second blank line after Leased Booth in cell B1, and center the label. Type "Photographer #:" in 10-point Times New Roman in the blank line at the bottom of cell B1 and leave the text left-aligned. Press Ctrl + Tab to move to the tab at the right edge of the cell, and type "Invoice #:" in 12-point Times New Roman.

6. Type "Photographer Information" in cell A2 and type "Booth Information" in cell B2 using 12-point Times New Roman. Center both headings.
7. In cell B3, type each of the following labels on its own line: "Booth #:"; "Booth Size:"; "Booth Location:"; and "Lease Length:" in 12-point Times New Roman.
8. Type "This Month's Billing" in cell A4 and center the text.
9. Type "Booth Cost Per Month:" in cell A5, "Tax:" in cell A6, "Total Due:" in cell A7, and then right-align each label.
10. Type "Please submit payment by. Thank you." (include both periods) in cell A8, and center the text. You'll insert a form field to complete the first sentence.
11. In cells A1 and B1, add Light Turquoise shading.
12. In cells A2, B2, and A4, add Blue shading and change the font color to White.
13. Add a 2 ¼-point Blue outside border to the table.
14. Insert form fields in cell B1. After the Date label, insert a text form field that displays the current date in the format 3/9/01. After the Photographer # label, insert a number text form field with a maximum length of 5 and an integer format. Add "Enter five-digit number from original booth space contract" for the status-bar prompt. Add "Original contract is located in the Photographer files under photographer's last name." as the Help message. After the Invoice # label, insert a number text form field with a maximum length of 6 and an integer format. Add "Enter the next available invoice number" for the status-bar prompt.
15. In cell A3, insert a regular text form field after each label. Set a maximum length of 40 for the name and the street form fields, 30 for the city form field, and 2 with an Uppercase format for the state form field. Set the ZIP code form field to number with a maximum length of 5 in integer format. Set the area code form field to Number with a maximum length of 3 in integer format. Set the phone number and fax form fields to regular text with a maximum length of 8. Adjust the form fields as necessary to keep the labels and their corresponding form fields on one line.
16. In cell B3, insert a number text form field after the Booth # label with a maximum length of 4 in integer format. After the Booth Size label, insert a drop-down form field with the following items: "5 × 8"; "10 × 10"; "10 × 15"; "15 × 20"; and "20 × 20." After the Booth Location label, insert a drop-down form field with the following items: "Area A"; "Area B"; "Area C." After the Lease Length label, insert a number text form field with a maximum length of 2 in integer format, press the spacebar, and type "months."

17. In cell B5 (to the right of the Booth Cost Per Month label), insert a number text form field in currency format. Add "Use the Booth Cost Table posted on the bulletin board" as the status-bar prompt. In cell B6 (to the right of the Tax label) insert a form field that will calculate 7.25% tax in currency format. In cell B7 (to the right of the Total Due label), insert a form field that will add the Booth Cost Per Month and the tax in currency format.
18. After the word "by" in cell A8, insert a space and then a Date text form field in the format "March 9, 2001." Enter "Add three weeks to the current date; if due date falls on a legal holiday, use the next business day" for the status-bar prompt.
19. Change the orientation to landscape, protect, save, and close the form, and set your computer to update fields upon printing.

Explore

20. Open a new document based on the Alaskan PhotoMart Invoice template, but without placing the document template in the Template folder. (*Hint*: Use Windows Explorer to locate the template file on your Data Disk, and then double-click the filename.)
21. Fill in the following information:

Photographer #: 32904	Invoice #: 985003
Name: [*your name*]	Street: 8831 North Ridge Lane
City: Seward	State: AK
ZIP: 99664	Area Code: 907
Phone: 555-3175	Fax: 555-3916
Booth #: 2005	Booth Size: 10 × 15
Booth Location: Area B	Lease Length: 12
Booth Cost Per Month: 650	Base the payment date (the last field) on the current date

Explore

22. Use the FaxWizard to print an appropriate cover letter and invoice to the default Windows printer, or route a copy of the completed form to your instructor.
23. Save the data only with the filename **PhotoMart Sample Data** in the Cases folder in the Tutorial.09 folder on your Data Disk, and then close the file.

3. Thousand Lakes Apparel Gilbert Kastendo owns Thousand Lakes Apparel franchise in Stillwater, Minnesota. Thousand Lakes Apparel sells casual clothing for women. A small percentage of the clothing the store receives from manufacturers arrives with minor defects. In most cases, the store management is only made aware of the defect when a customer returns the item. Once an item has been labeled "defective,' the store sells it at a significant markdown. Gilbert asks you to create an on-screen form that will print tags indicating the location and type of defect and the reduced price. He asks you to test the form with sample information.

1. If necessary, start Word, and make sure your Data Disk is in the appropriate drive. Open the **Apparel** file from the Cases folder in the Tutorial.09 folder on your Data Disk, and save it in the same folder as a template with the filename Apparel Mark-Down Form.

Explore

2. Insert 11 rows after row 1. Divide rows 5, 6, and 7 into two columns of equal width, and do the same with rows 9, 10, and 11. (*Hint*: In each row, merge the cells and then split the cells into two columns.)
3. Merge the cells in rows 2, 3, 4, 8, and 12 into one cell per row.
4. Type "Defect noticed in store? Customer return?" in row 2. Type "Defect Location:" in row 3. Type "Defect Type" in row 4 and center it. (Don't center the labels in rows 2 and 3.)
5. Type "Seams:" in cell A5, "Colors:" in cell B5, "Fabric Construction:" in cell A6. "Shrinkage:" in cell B6, "Buttons & Zippers:" in cell A7, "Other:" in cell B7. Make sure all labels are left-aligned.
6. Type "Price" in row 8, and center it. Type "Regular Price" in cell A9, "Discount Amount" in cell A10, and "Discounted Price" in cell A11. Right-align the labels in cells A9, A10, and A11. Type "Sorry, no returns on discounted merchandise." in row 12, and center the sentence.
7. In cell A1, change "Thousand Lakes Apparel" to 16-point bold, italic, engraved. Change the address and phone number (including the city, state, and ZIP) to 14-point, and "Store Number" to 12-point. In cell A2 change "Defect I.D. Tag" to 14-point. Change all other cells in the table to 12-point. (*Hint*: Change the Normal style.)
8. Change all the borders to ¾-point blue. (*Hint*: Use the Borders and Shading dialog box.)

9. In cell A1 after the Store Number label, insert a Number text form field with a maximum length of 5 in integer format. In cell B1, insert two blank lines after the Defect I.D. Tag label and insert a field that displays the current date and time in the form "3/11/01 3:39 PM" in 12-point Times New Roman.

Explore

10. In cell C1 after the Vendor Number label, insert a space and then insert a number text form field with a maximum length of 5 in integer format. Copy the Vendor Number form field. Paste it after the Vendor Style Number label, but change the maximum length to 3. Paste the form field after the Department Number label, but change the maximum length to 4. Paste the form field after the SKU Number label, but change the maximum length to 10. Change all the fonts in this cell to 10-point.

Explore

11. Format the four form fields you created in Step 10 so that the data entered in them will be underlined with a Thick line. (*Hint*: Use the Font dialog box.)
12. After the question "Defect noticed in store?" in row 2, insert a check box form field. After the question "Customer return?", insert another check box form field, with the default value set to checked.
13. In row 3, after the Defect Location: label, insert a regular text form field of unlimited length.

Explore

14. In cell A4 after the Seams label, insert a drop-down form field with the items: "Okay"; "Open"; "Twisting"; and "Uneven". Copy this new form field, and paste it after each of the following four labels: Colors, Fabric Construction, Shrinkage, and Buttons & Zippers. Change the items in the Color form field to "Okay"; "Fading/Bleeding"; "Oil Spots"; and "Poor Screen". Change the items in the Fabric Construction form field to "Okay"; "Embroidery"; "Holes"; "Stitching"; and "Tearing". Change the items in the Shrinkage form field to "Okay"; "Excessive"; and "Uneven". Change the items in the Buttons & Zippers form field to "Okay"; "Buttons missing"; and "Zipper broken". (*Hint*: Use the Remove button to delete the original items.) Make sure Okay is the first item in each list.
15. In cell B7 (after the Other label), insert a regular text form field of unlimited length.
16. In cell B9, enter a number text form field formatted as currency. In cell B10, insert a form field that will calculate 25% of the value in cell B9. In cell B11, insert a form field that will subtract the value in cell B10 from the value in cell B9. Format all these cells in currency format.

Explore

17. Rotate the text in rows 4 and 8 to vertical orientation. Center the text both vertically and horizontally using the Align Center button on the Tables and Borders toolbar. Copy the text in row 4 and paste it in the cell 12 times to fill the cell; do the same for row 8. Add a 10%-Gray shading to cell A1 and rows 4, 8, and 12. In row 4, set the row height to one inch. (*Hint*: Use the Table Properties dialog box.)
18. Below the table, type "Prepared by [*your name*]" including your own name.
19. Protect and save the form, and then print a copy of it.
20. Close the form and then copy the Apparel Mark-Down Form template in the Templates folder on your computer. Open a new document based on the template.
21. Fill out the template using the following information:

Store Number: 50021	Defect Location: bottom hem, left side
Vendor Number: 47743	Defect type: Okay, but Fabric Construction is Tearing
Vendor Style Number: 602	
Department Number: 1267	Other: leave blank
Sku Number: 5062201196	Regular Price: 28.95
Defect noticed in store? Yes (checked)	Customer return? No (not checked)

22. Set your computer to update fields upon printing, print a copy of the completed form, and save only the data in the Cases folder for Tutorial 9 on your Data Disk, using the filename Apparel Sample.
23. Close the files, and delete the Apparel Mark-Down Form template from the Templates folder.

4. Family Video Paul Naegle manages Family Video, a video store in the Henderson/Las Vegas area of Nevada. Paul will special-order any video for a customer. He regularly orders tapes of current movies as well as old classics from many distributors, a few of whom are sometimes slow to send their tapes. Gary asks you to create a form letter using form fields that he can send to distributors whose orders are overdue. Once you've created the form, Family Video employees will be able to write a standard letter by tabbing from one field to the next.

1. If necessary, start Word, and make sure your Data Disk is in the appropriate drive. Open a new, blank document.
2. Using 12-point Times New Roman, create the form letter shown in Figure 9-39, leaving spaces for fields where indicated.

Figure 9-39

Family Video
1204 17th Avenue, Suite 9A
Las Vegas, NV 89125
[field—current date]
[three blank lines]
[field—name of distributor]
[field—address of distributor]
[field—city], [field—state] [field—zip]

Dear [field—distributor],

On [field—order date] we ordered [field--# copies] copies of the film [field—name of film, underlined], and have not received the order or any notice of a delay. Please check your records to ensure that you shipped the order. Our order number is [field—order #]. We prepaid a total of [field—order total] for this order.

If you are not able to expedite the order, please refund our money. If you are able to fill the order, we expect you to credit our account with [field—5% of order total], the shipping charge, as per your contract with us.

If you need additional information, please contact our manager, Gary Siebenaller. Thank you.

Sincerely,
[four blank lines]
[field—name of letter writer]

3. Format the store's name and address with the fonts, effects, and alignments of your choice. Format the body text of the letter into two columns.

Explore

4. Insert and format the appropriate form fields for the information indicated in Figure 9-39. Use at least one drop-down form field with at least three items. Add a status-bar prompt for at least two form fields and a Help message for at least one form field. Make sure you insert and delete commas, spaces, and blank lines where appropriate. (*Hint*: The shipping cost is 5% of the total.To calculate the shipping cost, create a formula that multiplies 0.05 times the order total, where the order total is represented by a bookmark which you assign to the order total field.)
5. Protect the form, save it as a template with the filename Family Video Letter in the Cases folder in the Tutorial.09 folder on your Data Disk, and print a copy.
6. Close the Family Video Letter template and then copy it to the Template folder on your computer, open a new document based on the template, and fill in the fields you created with appropriate (but fictitious) information, using your own name as the letter writer.

Explore

7. Use the FaxWizard to print the letter to the default Windows printer; don't send a cover letter. If you prefer, route a copy of the completed form to your instructor.
8. Save only the form data as Family Video Sample in the Cases folder in the Tutorial.09 folder on your Data Disk.
9. Close the files, and delete the Family Video Letter template from the Templates folder.

QUICK CHECK ANSWERS

Session 9.1

1. Word template that people use to fill in information at the computer.
2. An element in a document that stores a certain type of information, such as a name or a price, to which you can assign a specific format.
3. Outside lines (rules) of a cell or group of cells. Borders appear when you print the table, whereas gridlines appear only on the screen.
4. Click Format on the menu bar, click Text Direction, click an orientation icon, and click OK.
5. Join two or more adjacent cells into one cell.
6. Divide one cell into two adjacent cells or divide one column or row of cells into two or more columns or rows of cells.
7. Click the Shading Color list arrow on the Tables and Borders toolbar, and click Gray-20%.
8. White text on a black background.

Session 9.2

1. **a.** Accepts both letters and numbers.
   b Accepts only numbers.
   c. Accepts information only in a valid date/time format.
2. A status-bar prompt appears on the status bar when the insertion point enters the form field; a Help message appears when you press F1 with the insertion point in the form field.
3. **a.** dd MMM yy **c.** h:mm am/pm
   b. d MMMM yyyy **d.** H:mm
4. Digits and symbols that specify the content and format of numbers in form field. 0.00%
5. To enable users to select only from certain options.
6. Click the Drop-Down Form Field option on the Forms toolbar, and enter a list of items in the Drop-Down Item text box.
7. Allows user to check a box with a single mouse click or a press of the spacebar.
8. Set default value to Not Checked in the Check Box Form Field Options dialog box.

Session 9.3

1. Form field that performs simple calculations automatically.
2. Formula that Word uses to perform mathematical calculations.
3. Insert a text form field in the cell where you want the results, set the type to Calculations, enter a summation expression in the Expressions text box.
4. Tab, Shift + Tab
5. Assign a bookmark to the second (target) field, create a macro to move the insertion point to that bookmark, attach the macro to the first field.
6. To prevent the form from being changed by anyone else and so the insertion point moves from one field to the next when a new document is created using that template.
7. You can save a form as as a normal Word document, or you can save data only as a text file. The advantage of saving as a normal Word document is that you can open and view the form like any other document; the disadvantage is that you must save the complete document, which takes a lot of disk space. The advantage of saving data only as a text file is that the data takes up less disk space than a normal Word document; the disadvantage is that you can't reinsert the data back into the form.
8. Click Tools on the menu bar, click Options, click the Save tab, and click the Save data only in forms check box.

OBJECTIVES

In this tutorial you will:

- Create a master document and insert subdocuments
- Split, merge, and remove subdocuments
- Number headings automatically
- Create a cross-reference to a figure caption
- Track revisions and insert comments
- Set different numbering styles for different sections
- Set up odd and even pages and footers
- Create a 3-D graphic
- Mark main index entries, subentries, and cross-references

MANAGING LONG DOCUMENTS

Creating a Customer Information Manual for Market Web Technology

CASE

Market Web Technology

Tasha Robinson is director of documentation services at Market Web Technology, a nationwide Internet service provider (ISP) headquartered in Des Moines, Iowa. Market Web leases space on the Internet, supplies browsers and other software for navigating the Internet, and helps businesses set up home pages on the World Wide Web (WWW). Tasha and the members of her department are creating a customer information manual for Market Web's customers.

Tasha organized her employees into two WET teams (consisting of a Writer, technical Editor, and software Tester) to help her create the first two chapters of the manual. Team 1, composed of Judi Badgett, Justin Masie, and Elona Weidner, will create a chapter that explains what the Internet is and why Market Web's customers would want to use it. Team 2, composed of Austin Probst, Christian Koncke, and Pei-Lin Wong, will create a chapter that explains how to use Market Web's services and software. (Later, these teams will work on chapters about how to select and purchase computer systems for the Internet, install and use the Market Web's Internet software, get technical support, determine Market Web's Internet fees, and so forth.) Teams 1 and 2 have given Tasha an initial draft of their chapters, which she wants to use to develop a consistent format for the manual, mark revisions, insert cross-references, and create an index. Tasha asks you to help her prepare the manual.

In this tutorial you'll assist Tasha to create a master document so she can work with the multichapter manual more efficiently. First, you'll create the master document and subdocuments. Then, you'll use the Heading Numbering feature, insert a figure and caption, create a cross-reference to the figure, track revisions, and add comments to the text. Finally, you'll set up the manual to print with odd and even pages, create odd and even footers, compile a table of contents and index, and create a three-dimensional (3-D) logo for the manual.

SESSION 10.1

In this session you'll see how Tasha planned the manual. You'll then create a master document by inserting existing document files into the master document. Finally, you'll split, merge, and remove subdocuments.

Planning a Document

The manual will follow Market Web Technology's specifications for content, organization, style, and presentation. The complete manual will contain chapters that explain many aspects of the Internet and the World Wide Web (WWW) and that outline the services Market Web Technology provides.

WET teams will use a consistent organization and format. Each chapter will contain a main heading (the chapter title) and subheadings that label the various topics included in the chapter. The completed manual will include front matter (title page, preface, and table of contents), several chapters, and an index.

The teams will write in a user-friendly style—that is, personal and informal, yet straightforward. They will avoid jargon and will clearly define any technical terms. The chapters will have a uniform and attractive look and follow standard desktop-publishing principles. The manual will be set up to print on both sides of the paper, and therefore will require a different format and footer for the text on each side.

Working with Master Documents

When you work with a long document, such as Tasha's multichapter manual or a very long thesis or term paper, it can be time-consuming and difficult to manipulate many pages in a single file. But if you split the file into several shorter documents, it becomes difficult to ensure consistent formatting and accurate numbering. The Master Document feature combines the benefits of splitting documents into separate small, manageable files with the advantages of working with a single, long document. A **master document** is a long document divided into several smaller, individual files, called **subdocuments**, as shown in Figure 10-1.

Figure 10-1 **MASTER DOCUMENT AND SUBDOCUMENTS**

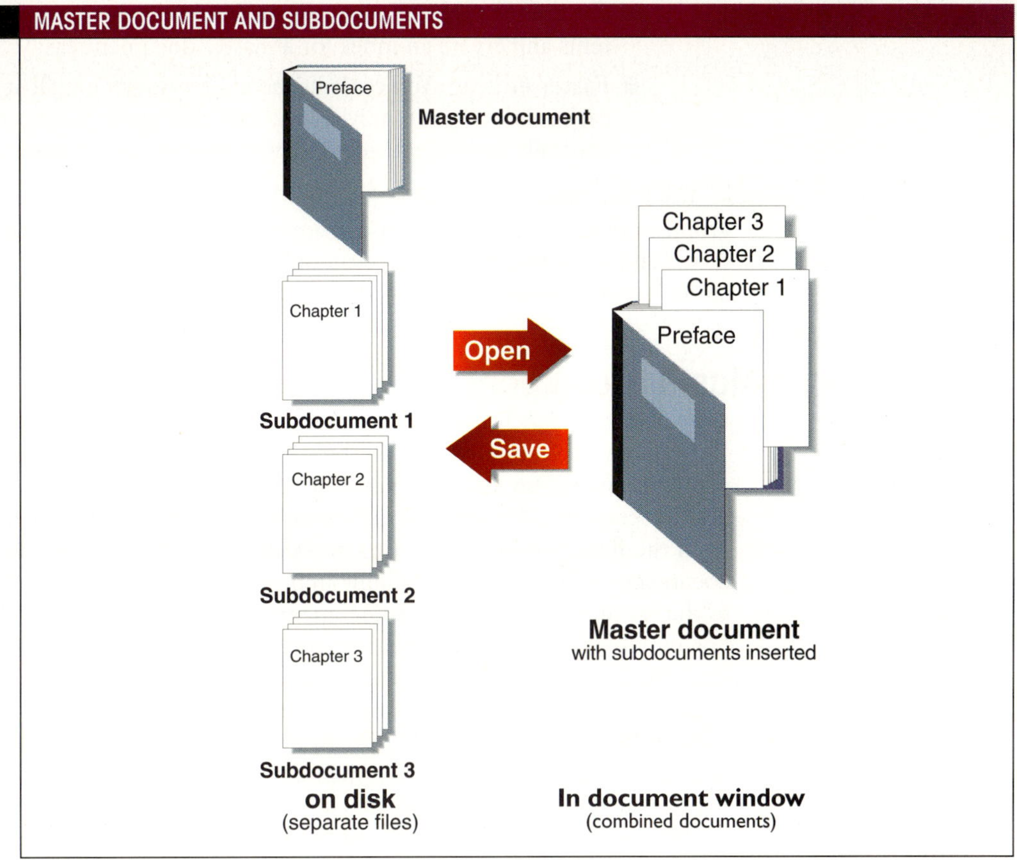

A master document is especially valuable for a document that is several chapters long. By working on each chapter individually, you avoid the extra time required to open, save, and edit a very large document. Similarly, when several people work on different parts of the same document simultaneously, you can quickly organize their individual files into the final long document by creating a master document. A master document is also helpful when you write a document that contains many graphics, which require a large amount of computer memory and disk space. You can divide the graphics among the various subdocuments to reduce the amount of time you spend opening, saving, and editing.

Although you could work with and print smaller documents individually, combining them into a master document has several advantages:

- **Consistent formatting elements.** You set up styles, headers, footers, and other formatting elements in only the master document; all the subdocuments use those same formatting elements.
- **Accurate numbering.** You can number the entire master document, including all subdocuments, with consecutive page numbers, chapter numbers, and figure numbers. If you rearrange, delete, or add material, Word automatically updates all the numbers to reflect your changes.
- **Accurate cross-referencing.** You can refer to figures or tables in other subdocuments and have Word update the fields in the master document if you alter the document.

- **Complete table of contents and index.** You can compile a table of contents and create an index for a master document easily.
- **Faster editing.** You can edit the master document all at once, or you can edit each subdocument individually. Any changes in the master document automatically take effect and are saved into the subdocument files, and vice versa.

You'll use these features as you set up the master document and subdocuments for workgroup members. A **workgroup** is a team of colleagues who have access to the same network server and work together on a common project. The two WET teams form a workgroup under Tasha's direction.

Creating a Master Document

You can create a master document by converting an existing document into a master document and subdocuments. Alternatively, you can insert separate files into a master document as subdocuments. You also can use a combination of these two methods.

In the first method, converting an existing document into a master document and subdocuments, you attach Word's built-in heading styles (Heading 1, Heading 2, and so forth) to the text and then divide the document into subdocuments at a heading level you select. For example, if you divide a master document into subdocuments at the Heading 1 style, each Heading 1 and its accompanying text would be saved as a subdocument.

In the second method, creating a master document from existing documents, you insert existing files as subdocuments into an open Word document. Word converts the inserted files into subdocuments and the open document file into the master document. Unlike in the first method, the subdocuments don't need to begin with a built-in heading.

You can use both methods to create and manage a master document. For example, you can divide your original document into a master document and subdocuments and then insert separate files as subdocuments into the master document.

After you create a master document, you can open, edit, and print the subdocuments individually; or you can open, edit, and print the entire master document as a single unit. When you save a master document, Word saves the file for each subdocument. The master document file contains only the filenames of its subdocuments, but not their text and objects (such as graphics).

Inserting subdocuments into a master document is different from importing files into a document. Imported files become part of the document in which they're inserted, whereas the files of subdocuments remain separate from the document in which they're inserted (the master document).

Opening a Master Document

You can convert any document into a master document. To create a master document, you must first switch to Master Document View. Once in Master Document View, you can insert, create, or remove subdocuments as well as view and reorganize the document just as you can in Outline View.

Tasha has already written the title page and preface of the manual for Market Web Technology using the company's standard styles. You'll open her existing file and convert it into a master document.

To convert an existing file into a master document:

1. Start Word as usual and insert your Data Disk in the appropriate drive, and then open the **WebMan** file from the Tutorial folder for Tutorial 10 on your Data Disk.
2. Click **Tools** on the menu bar, click **Options**, click the **User Information** tab, write down the name exactly as shown in the Name text box, and then click the Cancel button.
3. Click **File** on the menu bar, click **Properties**, click the **Summary** tab, type the User Information name as the Author, and then click the **OK** button. This ensures that the same person "owns" the master document and the Word file. Whenever you create a master document from someone else's file, make sure the Author name matches the User Information name.
4. Save the file as **Market Web Manual** in the same folder.
5. To avoid cluttering the screen with grammar marks, click **Tools** on the menu bar, click **Options**, click the **Spelling & Grammar** tab, click the **Check grammar as you type** check box to deselect it and turn off grammar checking, and then click the **OK** button.
6. Click the **Show/Hide ¶** button on the Standard toolbar if necessary to display nonprinting characters.
7. Click the **Outline View** button on the View toolbar. The document switches to Outline View, and the Outlining toolbar opens.
8. If necessary, click the **Master Document View** button on the Outlining toolbar to make sure it's selected (pressed down). Notice that the Outlining toolbar contains a set of buttons for managing master documents. See Figure 10-2.

Figure 10-2 WORD IN MASTER DOCUMENT VIEW

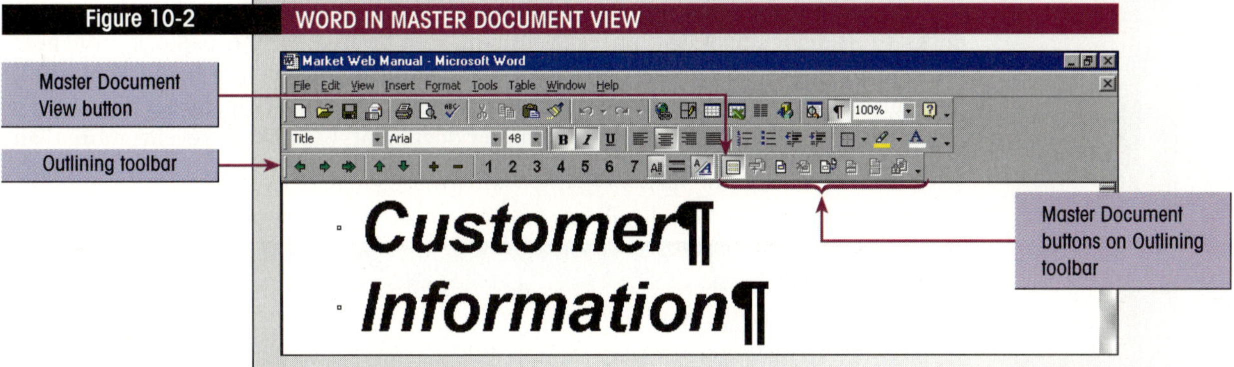

Even though the Master Document View button is selected, the Market Web manual won't be a true master document until you insert a subdocument. Before you do this, however, Tasha asks you to make backup copies of the files in case a problem arises and you have to revert to the originals.

To make a backup copy of the subdocuments:

1. Click the **Open** button on the Standard toolbar, and then make sure the Tutorial folder for Tutorial 10 is displayed in the Look in list box.
2. Right-click the **Team1** filename, and then click **Copy** on the shortcut menu.

3. Press **Ctrl + V** to paste a copy of the Team1 file into the Tutorial.10 Tutorial folder. The file Copy of Team1 appears in the Open dialog box.

4. Right-click the filename **Copy of Team1**, click **Rename** on the shortcut menu, type **The Internet**, and then press the **Enter** key to change the name of the file.

   TROUBLE? If an error message appears indicating that you're trying to change the filename extension, click the No button, and use the filename "The Internet.doc" (with the .doc filename extension). If you cannot successfully rename the files from within the Open dialog box, open Windows Explorer, display the files in the Tutorial folder for Tutorial 10, and repeat Step 4.

5. Repeat Steps 2 through 4 to create a copy of the Team2 file with the filename **Market Web Technology**.

   TROUBLE? If an error message appears indicating that you're trying to change the filename extension, click the No button, and use the filename "Market Web Technology.doc" (with the .doc filename extension).

6. Click the **Cancel** button in the Open dialog box to return to the manual.

Now you can insert the subdocuments into the master document, which contains the title page and preface.

Inserting Subdocuments

When you insert a subdocument, it opens at the location of the insertion point. Word always draws a box around the inserted subdocument, marks it with a Subdocument icon, and places End of Section breaks both before and after it. Sometimes, Word automatically locks the subdocument so you can't edit it, as indicated by the padlock icon near the Subdocument icon. If you try to edit a subdocument, but all the menu commands are unavailable, check to see if the subdocument is locked. (The Lock feature is important when more than one person is working on a master document, because it prevents more than one person at a time from editing a subdocument.)

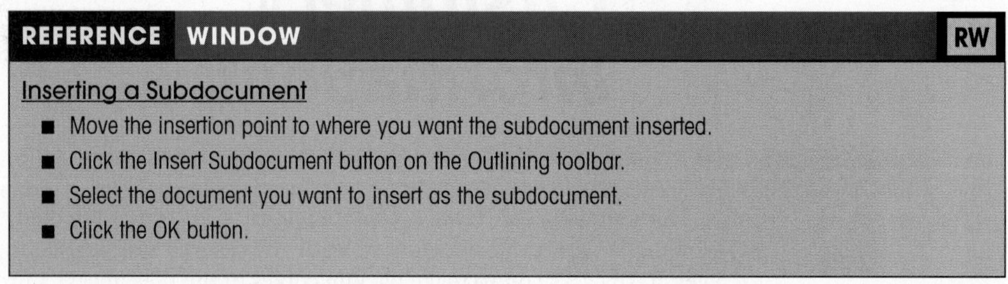

REFERENCE WINDOW RW

Inserting a Subdocument

- Move the insertion point to where you want the subdocument inserted.
- Click the Insert Subdocument button on the Outlining toolbar.
- Select the document you want to insert as the subdocument.
- Click the OK button.

Tasha asks you first to insert the document The Internet (created by Team 1) and then insert the document Market Web Technology (created by Team 2). This should put the chapters in the correct order.

To insert subdocuments into the master document:

1. Move the insertion point to the blank line below "March 2001" at the end of page 2, above "Bibliography." This is where you want to insert the subdocument.
2. Click the **Import Subdocument** button on the Outlining toolbar. The Insert Subdocument dialog box, which is similar to the Open dialog box, opens.
3. Double-click **The Internet** (which is located in the Tutorial folder for Tutorial 10). The file is inserted as a subdocument at the location of the insertion point. Scroll up so you can see the beginning of the subdocument. See Figure 10-3.

Figure 10-3 SUBDOCUMENT INSERTED INTO MASTER DOCUMENT

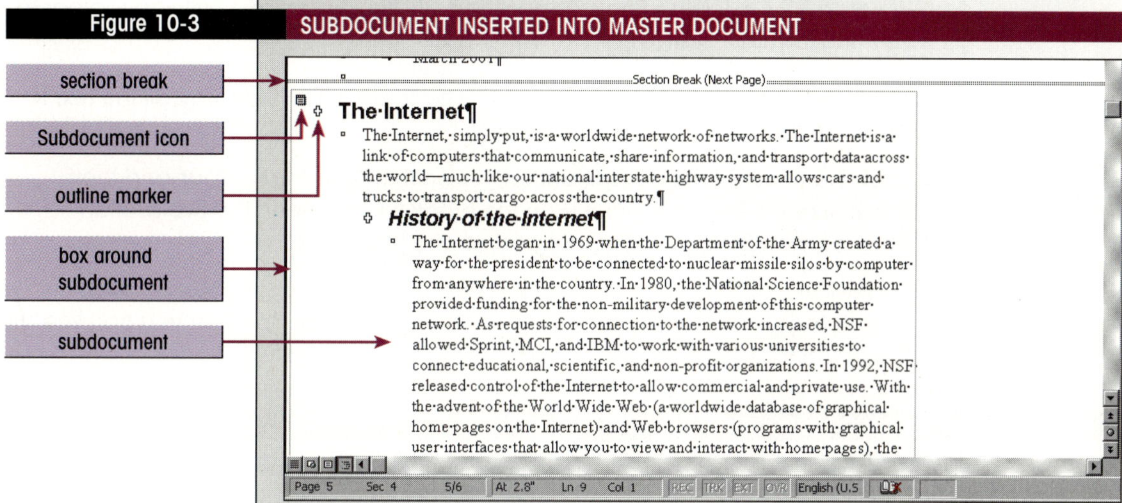

TROUBLE? If a dialog box opens with the message "Style 'Heading 1' exists in both the subdocument you're adding (The Internet) and the master document. Would you like to rename the style in the subdocument?", click the No to All button to use the Heading-1 style defined in the master document, not in the subdocument.

To ensure that you can edit this subdocument, check that it isn't locked.

4. Look for a Lock icon near the Subdocument icon at the beginning of the subdocument; if you see , move the insertion point within the subdocument, and then click the **Lock Document** button on the Outlining toolbar to unlock the subdocument.

Just like in an outline, you can select the amount of text you want to view—all of it or only a certain number of heading levels. At this point, you want to see only the first three levels of headings.

5. Click the **Show Heading 3** button on the Outlining toolbar so you can view all the headings in the manual but not the main text. The gray line below each heading indicates that text follows the heading. See Figure 10-4.

Figure 10-4 MASTER DOCUMENT SHOWING ONLY HEADINGS

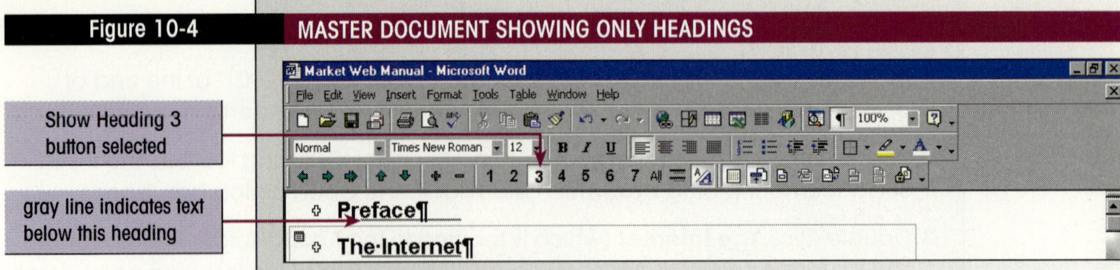

TROUBLE? If your document doesn't show the same formatting as the document in Figure 10-4, click the **Show Formatting** button on the Outlining toolbar to view the formatting styles of the visible text.

Now, you'll insert the document created by Team 2. You'll display all the text to verify the location of the insertion point.

6. Click the **Show All Headings** button on the Outlining toolbar, and then make sure the insertion point is on the blank line between the two section breaks below the subdocument and above "Bibliography."

7. Repeat Steps 2 through 5 to insert the second subdocument, **Market Web Technology**, and display only three levels of headings. Scroll so you can see all the headings of the second subdocument. See Figure 10-5.

Figure 10-5 SECOND SUBDOCUMENT IN MASTER DOCUMENT

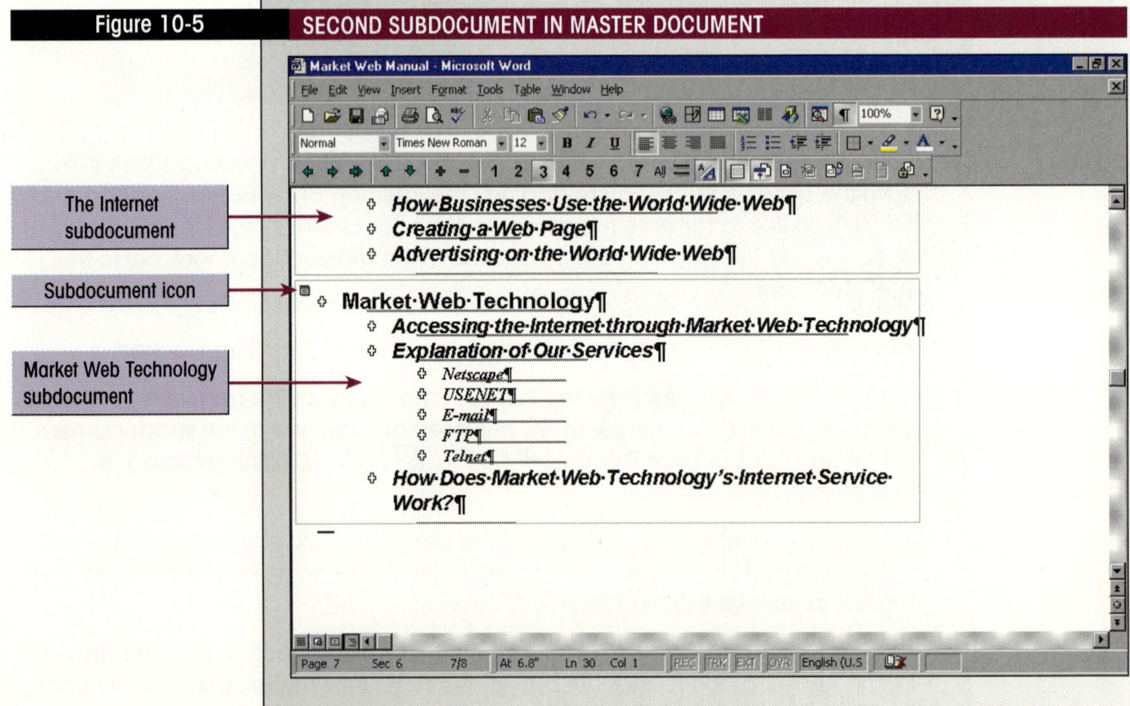

The master document Market Web Manual now contains two subdocuments. Even though you can manipulate the subdocuments in the master document, the text of these subdocuments is stored in the files The Internet and Market Web Technology, and not in the Market Web Manual file, even after you save the master document.

Saving the Master Document

After you insert subdocuments, you should save the master document. You can save the master document in the same way you would save any other file.

To save the master document:

1. Click the **Save** button on the Standard toolbar. Market Web Manual is now saved as a master document with two subdocuments.

The names and locations of the two subdocument files, The Internet and Market Web Technology, are recorded in the master document. The subdocuments will appear in the master document as long as the files aren't renamed or moved.

Splitting and Merging Subdocuments

When you use a master document to produce a long document, it's easy to reorganize subdocuments and their associated files as you work. For example, if one subdocument becomes too long and unwieldy, or if you want two people to work on the same subdocument, you can split the subdocument. To **split** a subdocument means to divide one subdocument into two subdocument files. When you save the master document, Word creates a new file using the subdocument's first heading as the filename. Word saves the new file in the same folder as the master document.

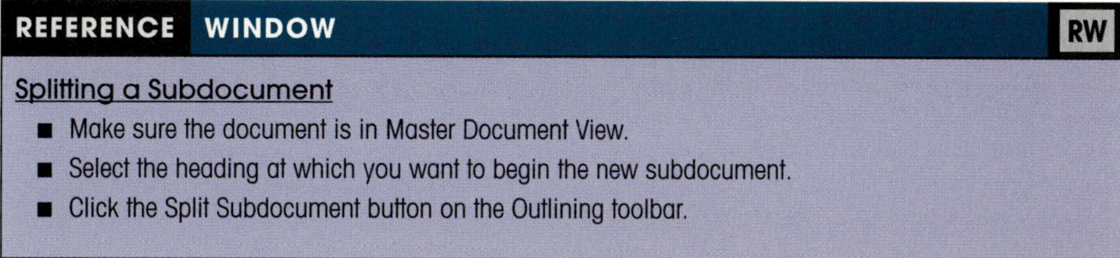
REFERENCE WINDOW RW

Splitting a Subdocument

- Make sure the document is in Master Document View.
- Select the heading at which you want to begin the new subdocument.
- Click the Split Subdocument button on the Outlining toolbar.

Tasha wants to organize a third team to work on the section of the manual that discusses the WWW, so she asks you to create a separate chapter for this material. Right now, this information is part of Team 1's Internet chapter; you'll need to split the Internet document into two subdocuments.

To split the subdocument:

1. Click anywhere within "The World Wide Web" heading in the middle of the first subdocument.

   As you can see in the Style list box on the Formatting toolbar, this heading is tagged with the Heading-2 style. Because subdocuments are set up to begin with the Heading-1 style, you need to change this heading level.

2. Click the **Promote** button on the Outlining toolbar. The heading changes from level 2 to level 1. Next, you must select the heading where you want to split the subdocument.

3. Click the outline marker (the plus sign) to the left of the "The World Wide Web" heading so that this heading and all its subheadings are selected.

4. Click the **Split Subdocument** button on the Outlining toolbar, and then deselect the text. Word draws a box around the new subdocument and inserts section breaks. See Figure 10-6.

Figure 10-6 ONE SUBDOCUMENT SPLIT INTO TWO

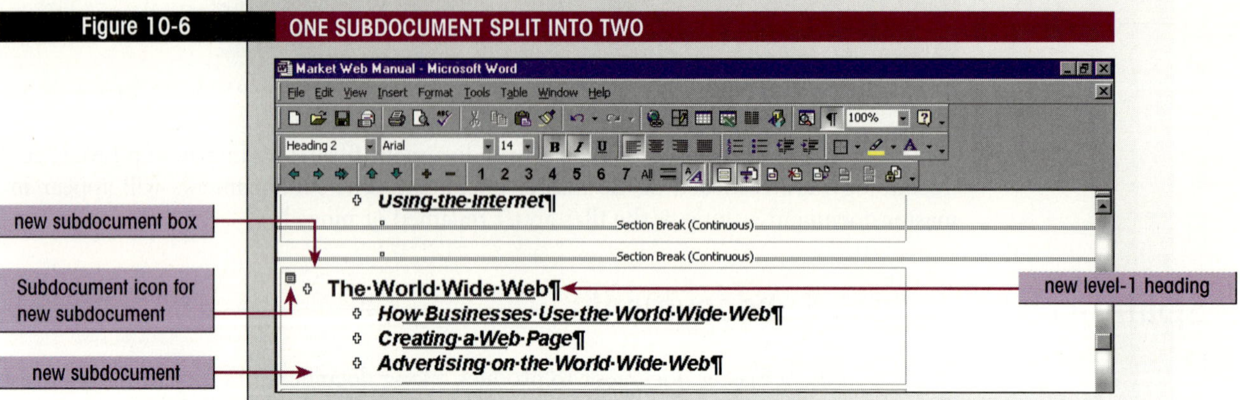

5. Save the manual with the new subdocument. Word creates a new file named The World Wide Web. Note that this filename is the same as the subdocument's first heading. The subdocument is saved in the same folder as the master document.

6. Click the **Open** button on the Standard toolbar. Verify that the Tutorial folder for Tutorial 10 contains a new file—The World Wide Web.

   TROUBLE? If you don't see the new file, click the Cancel button in the Open dialog box, make sure the heading "The World Wide Web" appears at the top of the subdocument box, and then repeat Steps 4 and 5.

7. Click the **Cancel** button in the Open dialog box to return to the master document, which consists of the title page and preface and contains three subdocuments.

Sometimes, you want to do the opposite of splitting a subdocument; that is, you want to merge two subdocuments. To **merge** subdocuments means to combine the files and text of two adjacent subdocuments into one. This is helpful, for example, if the current subdocuments are short and the same person is writing or editing them. When you merge subdocuments, Word inserts the text of the second subdocument into the first one, so that when you save the master document, the first subdocument file contains the text of both subdocuments. The second subdocument file remains on your disk but is no longer used by the master document. You could delete this file without affecting your master document.

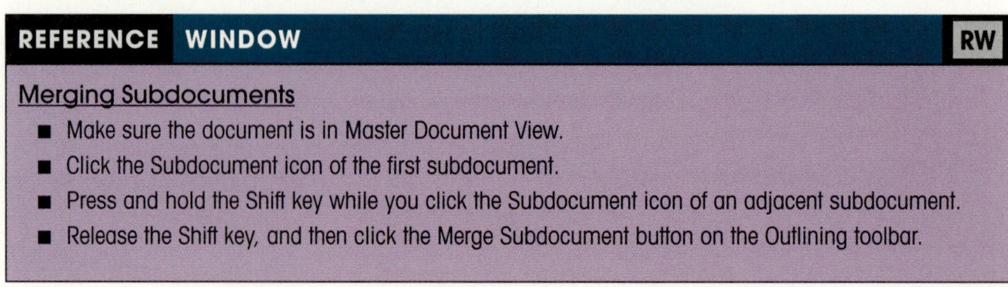

REFERENCE WINDOW RW

Merging Subdocuments

- Make sure the document is in Master Document View.
- Click the Subdocument icon of the first subdocument.
- Press and hold the Shift key while you click the Subdocument icon of an adjacent subdocument.
- Release the Shift key, and then click the Merge Subdocument button on the Outlining toolbar.

Tasha had planned to organize a new team to complete the WWW section, but she determined that she doesn't have the resources right now. Instead, she asks you to merge The World Wide Web subdocument with the Market Web Technology subdocument.

To merge two subdocuments into one:

1. Click the **Subdocument** icon for The World Wide Web subdocument. The entire second subdocument becomes selected.

   TROUBLE? If you click the Subdocument icon but the entire subdocument isn't selected, move the pointer to the center of the icon and try again.

2. Press and hold the **Shift** key while you click for the Market Web Technology subdocument (you might need to scroll), and then release the Shift key. With both subdocuments selected, you can merge them.
3. Click the **Merge Subdocument** button on the Outlining toolbar. The two subdocuments become one.
4. Deselect the text. See Figure 10-7.

Figure 10-7 TWO SUBDOCUMENTS MERGED INTO ONE

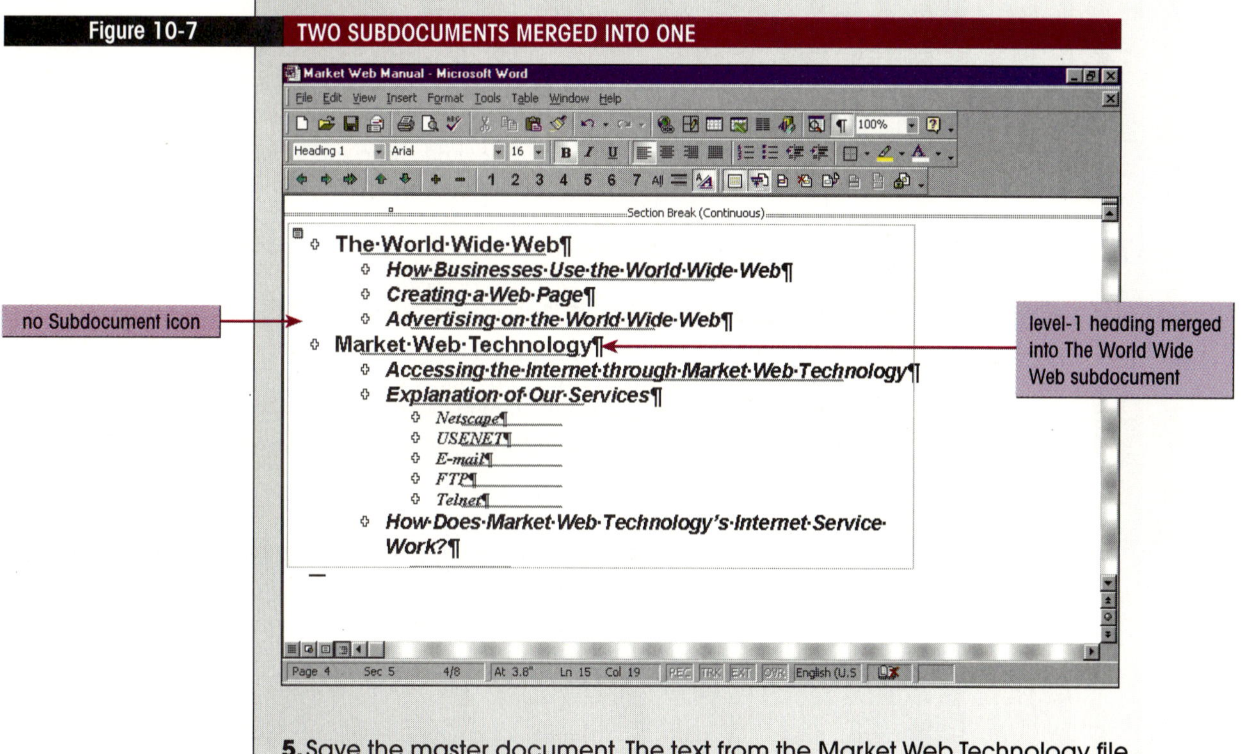

5. Save the master document. The text from the Market Web Technology file merges into The World Wide Web file; the master document no longer uses the Market Web Technology file.

You have moved a section of one subdocument into another by splitting and merging subdocuments. In addition to splitting and merging, you can create subdocuments from text in the master document.

Creating a Subdocument

Not only can you create a new subdocument from an existing one, you also can create a subdocument from text in the master document.

Tasha decides to add more information to the preface, which is part of the master document. She could do this right in the master document, but she asks you to make the preface a separate subdocument so she can edit it while you're working with the other files in the master document.

To create a new subdocument from text in the master document:

1. Scroll to the beginning of the outline, and then click the "Preface" outline marker to select it.
2. Click the **Create Subdocument** button on the Outlining toolbar. Word draws a box around the preface and marks it as a subdocument.
3. Save the master document. Word creates a file for the new subdocument (Preface) in the Tutorial folder for Tutorial 10.

Use the Open dialog box to verify that Word created a new file named **Preface** in the Tutorial folder for Tutorial 10.

The master document now has a title page and three subdocuments.

Removing a Subdocument

Sometimes, as you work on a master document, you'll want to remove a subdocument. To remove a subdocument means to incorporate the text of a subdocument into the master document. This decreases the number of subdocuments but increases the size of the master document. The removed subdocument stays on your disk, but the master document no longer uses it. You could delete this unused subdocument file without affecting the master document.

REFERENCE WINDOW RW

Removing a Subdocument

- Click the Subdocument icon of the subdocument you want to move into the master document.
- Click the Remove Subdocument button on the Outlining toolbar.

After reading the preface, Tasha decides that she doesn't want to make any changes to it. She asks you to remove the subdocument with the preface text and return it to the master document.

To remove the Preface subdocument:

1. Click the **Subdocument** icon for the Preface to select all the text in that subdocument.
2. Click the **Remove Subdocument** button on the Outlining toolbar. The "Preface" heading and its accompanying text become part of the master document.

   Your master document now consists of the title page, preface, and bibliography, and includes The Internet and The World Wide Web subdocuments. Your Data Disk has two additional files, Market Web Technology and Preface, which are no longer part of the master document.
3. Deselect the preface text.
4. Switch to Normal View and scroll through the document, noting the location of page breaks.

As you recall, a **page break** is a location in your document where one page ends and another one begins. In Normal View, page breaks are marked by a horizontal dotted line that extends across the document window. If the page break is part of a section break, the section break marks the page break.

Controlling Text Flow and Page Breaks

As you scroll through the document, you might notice some problems with the location of page breaks. Don't worry if your document is different; subtle differences in printer drivers can cause page breaks to appear at different locations. Here's what you might observe:

- A page break appears just before the last word of the third paragraph below "Types of Internet Connections." See Figure 10-8.

Figure 10-8 DOCUMENT WITH MISPLACED PAGE BREAK

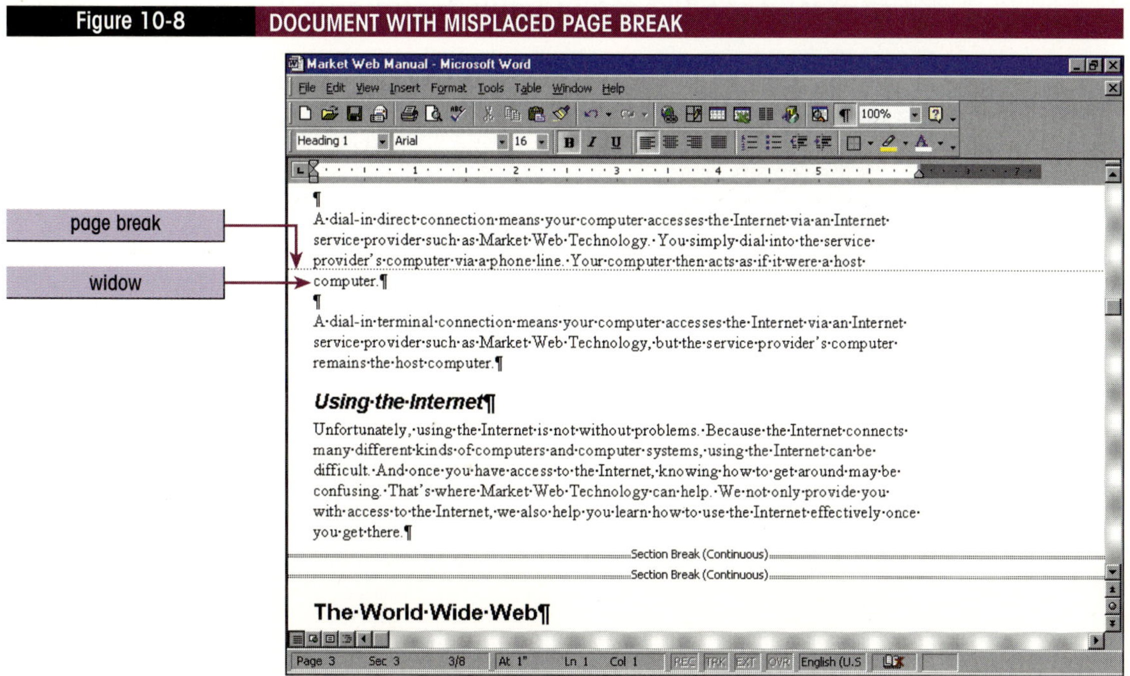

The single word "computer" is an example of a **widow**, which is the last line of a paragraph appearing alone at the top of a page. A widow looks strange and can be hard to read when isolated on the page.

- A page break appears after the first line just below the "Creating a Web Page" heading at the bottom of page 4. See Figure 10-9.

Figure 10-9 DOCUMENT WITH MISPLACED PAGE BREAK

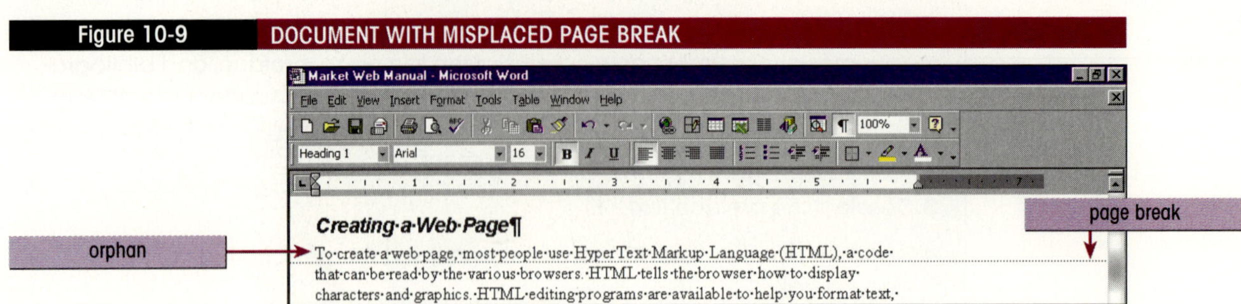

This page break creates the related problem of an **orphan**, which is the first line of a paragraph appearing alone at the bottom of a page. If you omitted this orphan, you would then have a heading isolated at the bottom of the page.

You could manually insert hard page breaks to solve these specific problems, but you would probably create more problems than you solve. For example, if you insert a hard page break (by pressing Ctrl + Enter) just above the heading near the bottom of page 4, the heading would appear at the top of page 5, as it should. But if then you added more text to the paragraph above the heading that spilled over to page 5, the heading would shift to page 6, leaving most of page 5 blank. You would soon find yourself continually inserting and deleting hard page breaks to fix widows, orphans, and isolated headings as you edit your document.

In Word, these problems have a much simpler solution: the automatic control page breaks commands. You can apply commands to any named style so Word fixes problems such as widows, orphans, and isolated headings for you.

To control page breaks in your document:

1. Click **Format** on the menu bar, click **Style** to open the Style dialog box, and then click **Heading 1** in the Styles list. You'll edit Heading 1 so all level-1 headings stay on the same page as the first paragraph below them.
2. Click the **Modify** button to open the Modify Style dialog box, click the **Format** button, and then click **Paragraph**. The Paragraph dialog box opens.
3. If necessary, click the **Line and Page Breaks** tab, which contains various options you can use to control breaks in your document. See Figure 10-10.

Figure 10-10 PARAGRAPH DIALOG BOX

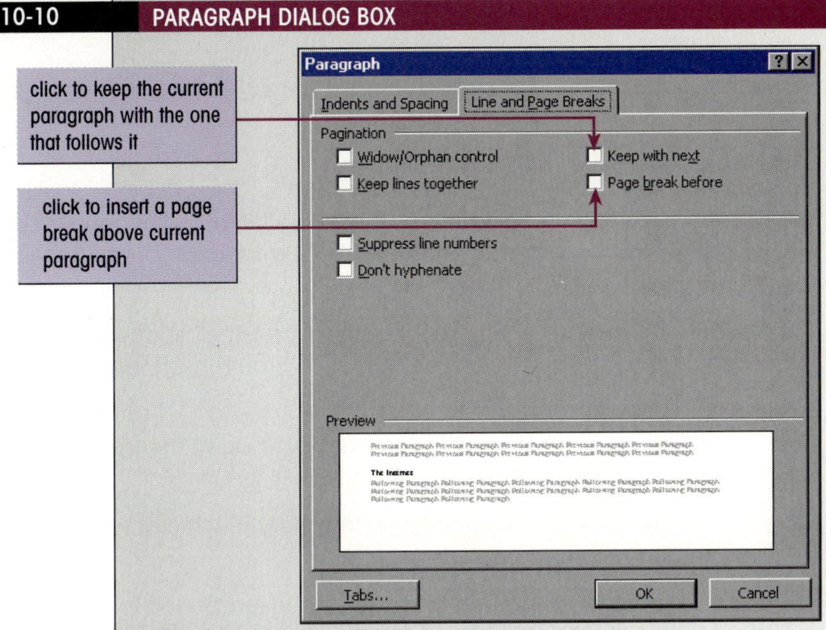

4. Click the **Keep with next** check box in the Pagination section of the dialog box. This instructs Word to force all text in the Heading-1 style onto the same page as the paragraph that follows it.

5. Click the **Page break before** check box. Now, all text in the Heading-1 style, which marks the beginning of chapters, will have a page break just above it.

6. Click the **OK** button on both dialog boxes to return to the Style dialog box.

7. Using the same procedure, set the **Keep with next** (but not Page break before) pagination option for the Heading-2 and Heading-3 styles. You don't need to modify the other headings because Market Web documents, by company policy, never have more than three levels of headings.

8. Using the same procedure, select **Widow/Orphan control** (also located in the Paragraph dialog box) for the Normal style. This tells Word to prevent the first and last lines from appearing alone on a page.

9. Click the **OK** button twice to return to the Style dialog box, click the **Close** button on the Style dialog box, save the document, and then scroll through the document to view the page breaks.

From now on, regardless of how you edit the document, headings will never appear alone at the bottom of a page, and the normal text will never have widows or orphans.

As you look through your document, you notice problems where words might break at the end of a line. For example, in the first paragraph below the "Explanation of Our Services" heading, the word "e-mail" is split between two lines. Although this isn't a serious problem, readers can find it confusing to see "e-" at the end of a line. To prevent Word from breaking a hyphenated word, you need to use a hard or nonbreaking hyphen rather than the soft hyphen Tasha used. A **nonbreaking hyphen** is a hyphen that won't allow the word or phrase it connects to break between two lines. A **soft hyphen** is a hyphen that allows the words that it connects to appear on different lines. To insert a soft hyphen, you simply press the hyphen key on your keyboard.

You'll replace the soft hyphens in the word "e-mail" with nonbreaking hyphens.

To insert a nonbreaking hyphen:

1. Move the insertion point immediately to the left of the hyphen in "e-mail" located in the first paragraph below the "Explanation of Our Services" heading, on page 6.
2. Press the **Delete** key to delete the soft hyphen. The "e" becomes joined to "mail," and "email" appears on the next line. Now, you'll insert the nonbreaking hyphen.
3. Click **Insert** on the menu bar, click **Symbol** to open the Symbol dialog box, and then click the **Special Characters** tab.

   As you can see, Word supports a wide variety of special symbols, including the nonbreaking hyphen.
4. Click **Nonbreaking Hyphen** and click the **Insert** button to insert the hyphen into the document at the location of the insertion point. Although the Symbol dialog box is still open, notice the shortcut keys for the nonbreaking hyphen: Ctrl + _ (underscore). You'll insert nonbreaking hyphens in other locations by pressing Ctrl + Shift + hyphen (Shift + hyphen accesses the underscore).
5. Click the **Close** button in the dialog box. See Figure 10-11.

Figure 10-11 INSERTED HARD HYPHEN

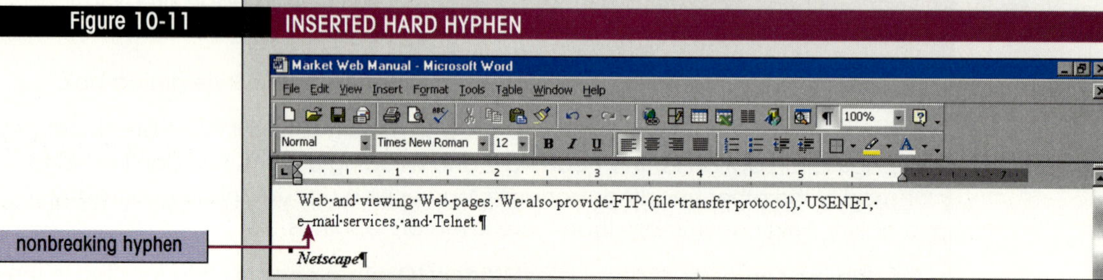

Now, you'll replace the soft hyphen with a nonbreaking hyphen in all other occurrences of "e-mail" in your document to make sure that after any revisions, the word won't be split between two lines.

6. Press **Ctrl + F** to open the Find and Replace dialog box, type **e-mail** in the Find what text box, and then click the **Find Next** button. Word finds "E-mail" in a level-3 heading. Because this is a short heading, you don't need to worry that "E" and "mail" will ever separate between two lines, so press the **Find Next** button again to find the "E-mail" at the beginning of the next paragraph, and click **Find Next** again to find "e-mail" in the middle of a paragraph.
7. Click the **Cancel** button to close the Find and Replace dialog box, delete the soft hyphen in "e-mail," and press **Ctrl + Shift + hyphen** to insert a nonbreaking hyphen.
8. Save the master document, and then close all open documents.

You have found all occurrences of "e-mail" that might become split between two lines and inserted nonbreaking hyphens.

Another important special character is the nonbreaking space. A **nonbreaking space** is a space that won't allow the words on either side to break between two lines. For example, the phrase "35 mm" (referring to 35-mm film or a 35-mm camera) might be hard to read, or at least distracting, if the "35" appeared at the end of one line and "mm" appeared at the beginning of the next line. To avoid this problem, you can insert a nonbreaking space between the "35" and the "mm." You could insert the nonbreaking space from the Special Symbols tab in the Symbols dialog box, or by pressing Ctrl + Shift + spacebar. The Market Web manual doesn't contain any words that require a nonbreaking space.

Session 10.1 Quick Check

1. Define the following terms:
   a. master document
   b. subdocument
   c. split subdocuments
   d. merge subdocuments
   e. remove subdocument
   f. widow
   g. orphan
2. What are three advantages of using a master document to manage long documents rather than working with separate, smaller documents?
3. True or False: After you insert a subdocument into a master document and save it, the master document file on the disk becomes bigger.
4. What are the two methods for creating a master document?
5. When would you split a subdocument?
6. When would you merge two subdocuments?
7. What is a nonbreaking hyphen? A nonbreaking space? Why would you use them?

You have completed setting up Market Web's customer information manual using Word's master document feature. Next, you'll use Word features to number sections and figures and then edit the manual.

SESSION 10.2

In this session you'll automatically number sections of a master document, insert a figure and caption, number the figure, and then create an automatically numbered cross-reference to the figure. Finally, you'll use revision marks and insert comments.

Adding Chapter Numbers to Headings

Tasha wants the Market Web Technology customer information manual to be well-organized and easy to use. One way to make it simple for Market Web customers to locate information is to number the sections. You'll give each subdocument a chapter number and title—for example, "Chapter 1. The Internet," "Chapter 2. The World Wide Web," and so forth. You could manually insert the text such as "Chapter 1," before each Heading 1, but what if you add, reorder, or delete a chapter? You would then need to review every heading and change the numbers, which is a time-consuming process.

Instead, you can number sections of a master document as chapters with the Heading Numbering feature, which has several advantages:

- **Automatic sequential numbering.** Word keeps the heading numbers consecutive even if you add, delete, or move a section.
- **Numbering across subdocuments.** Word formats the same-level headings of all the subdocuments in the master document with consecutive numbering.
- **Consistent style.** The subdocuments take on the number style set in the master document.

You'll modify the Heading-1 style in the master document to include automatic numbering. This way, each subdocument will be formatted with consecutive chapter numbers in the same style.

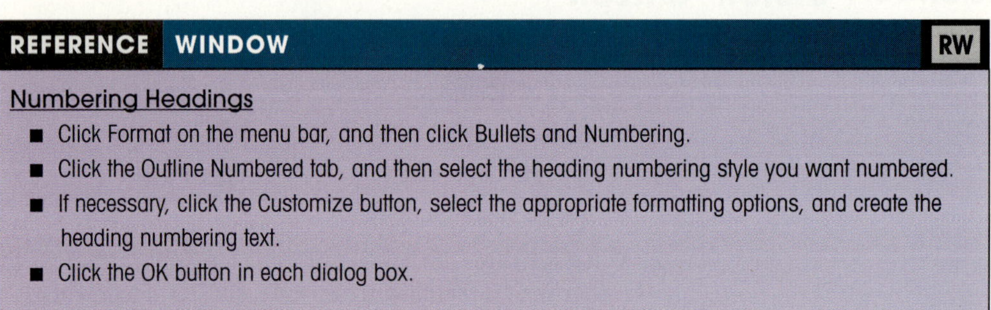

REFERENCE WINDOW RW

Numbering Headings

- Click Format on the menu bar, and then click Bullets and Numbering.
- Click the Outline Numbered tab, and then select the heading numbering style you want numbered.
- If necessary, click the Customize button, select the appropriate formatting options, and create the heading numbering text.
- Click the OK button in each dialog box.

To number headings automatically with the heading numbering feature:

1. If you took a break after the last session, make sure Word is running.
2. Open the master document Market Web Manual, switch to Outline View, verify that the Master Document View button is selected, display nonprinting characters, and make sure you can see the subdocuments located after the Preface. See Figure 10-12.

Figure 10-12 MASTER DOCUMENT BEFORE EXPANDING SUBDOCUMENTS

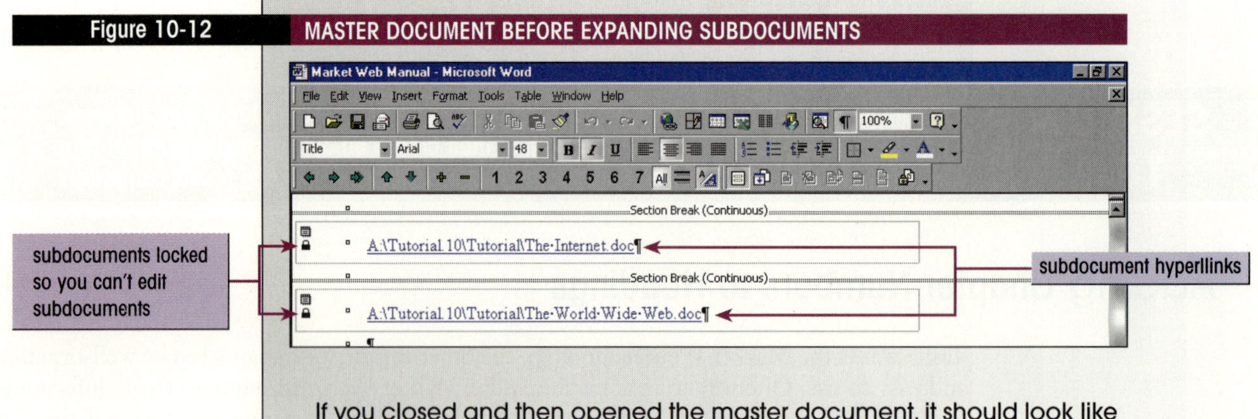

If you closed and then opened the master document, it should look like Figure 10-12, with subdocuments appearing as hyperlinks. If you click a hyperlink, Word will open that subdocument into another document window. Then you

can then work with the subdocuments separately. On the other hand, whenever you want to edit or print the entire master document, you should expand the subdocuments, which converts the hyperlink text to the full subdocument text.

3. If necessary, click the **Expand Subdocuments** button on the Outlining toolbar to expand the hyperlink files into the master document. Word replaces the hyperlinks with the text of the subdocuments.
4. Click the **Show Heading 3** button on the Outlining toolbar to view only the headings.
5. Click **Format** on the menu bar, click **Bullets and Numbering** to open the Bullets and Numbering dialog box, and then click the **Outline Numbered** tab.
6. Click the lower-right icon, which shows "Chapter" and a number. You could use this outline numbering style as is, but Market Web's standard style requires a period after the chapter number.
7. Click the **Customize** button to open the Customize Outline Numbered List dialog box.

   You want to change the default setting "Chapter 1" for Heading-1 styles to "Chapter 1." (with a period and two spaces after the number).
8. Click to the right of the number in the Number format text box, type **.** (a period), and then press the **spacebar** once. The format will automatically insert another space, so each heading will end up with two spaces after the period. Make sure all the settings match those in Figure 10-13.

Figure 10-13 CUSTOMIZE OUTLINE NUMBERED LIST DIALOG BOX

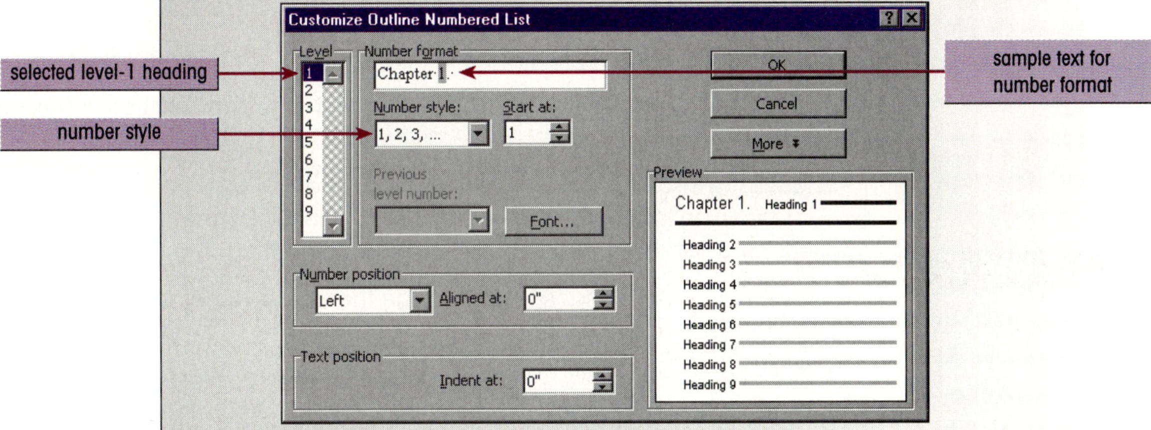

9. Click the **OK** button. All text formatted with a Heading-1 style has automatic chapter numbering. See Figure 10-14.

Figure 10-14 DOCUMENT WITH AUTOMATICALLY NUMBERED HEADINGS

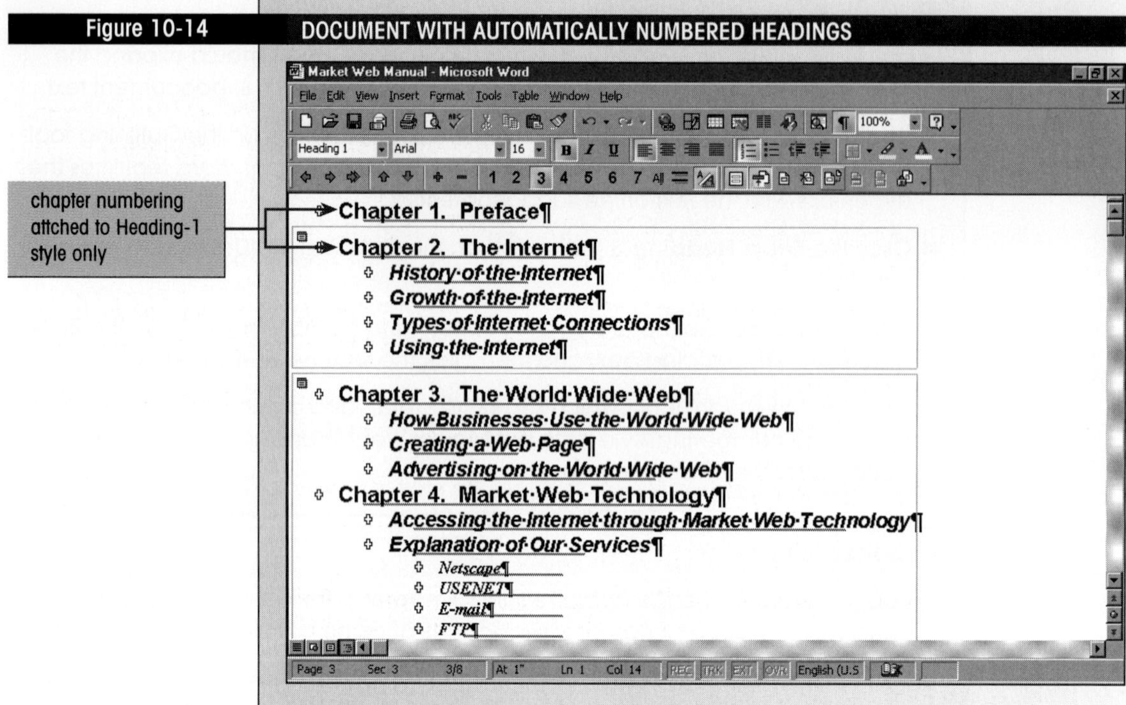

As you scroll through the manual, you see that the Preface also has a chapter number, which you don't want. You can easily solve this problem by changing "Preface" from the Heading 1 to Normal style, and then applying your own formatting.

To remove the style from and format "Preface":

1. Switch to Normal View so that you can see the normal text below the "Preface" heading.
2. Move the insertion point anywhere within the "Preface" heading, click the **Style** list arrow on the Formatting toolbar, and then click **Normal** in the Style list. The heading numbering "Chapter 1" and the formatting disappear.
3. Select the word "Preface" and change the font to 16-point, bold Arial to match the Heading 1 text.
4. Return to Outline View, and then click the **Show Heading 3** button 3 on the Outlining toolbar. As you can see, Word renumbered all the chapter headings so that the first Heading 1 is "Chapter 1. The Internet."

From now on, if Tasha adds, removes, or rearranges the level-1 headings, Word will renumber the chapter numbers consecutively.

Double-Numbering **Captions**

Tasha instructed each team to include figures that illustrate some of the key points in their chapters. For example, "Chapter 3. Market Web Technology" will have a graph that shows the company's growth (by number of customers) between 1997 and 2000.

To insert a graph showing the growth of Market Web Technology:

1. Switch to Print Layout View, and then move the insertion point to the end of the first paragraph under "Chapter 3. Market Web Technology" on page 6.
2. Click **Insert** on the menu bar, click **Object**, verify that the Create New tab is selected, click **Microsoft Graph 2000 Chart** in the Object type list, and then click the **OK** button. A sample graph and the Microsoft Graph datasheet open.
3. Click the blank, gray button in the upper-left corner of the datasheet to select the entire datasheet, and then press the **Delete** key to erase the sample data.

   TROUBLE? If only the first row or the first column is selected, you need to click the button above or to the left of the one you just clicked.

4. Click in the blank cell to the right of the gray button labeled "1," type **No. of Customers**, and press the **Tab** key to move to cell A1 (that is, the cell in column A and row 1).
5. Now, you can enter the number of Market Web customers for the past four years. Type **128**, press the **Tab** key, type **331**, press the **Tab** key, type **1089**, press the **Tab** key, and type **3121,** and then press **Enter**.
6. Click the blank cell below the gray button labeled "A," type **1997**, press the **Tab** key, type **1998**, press the **Tab** key, type **1999**, press the **Tab** key, type **2000**, and press the **Enter** key. Microsoft Graph takes the data you enter and uses it to create a bar chart, as shown in Figure 10-15.

Figure 10-15 CREATING A GRAPH

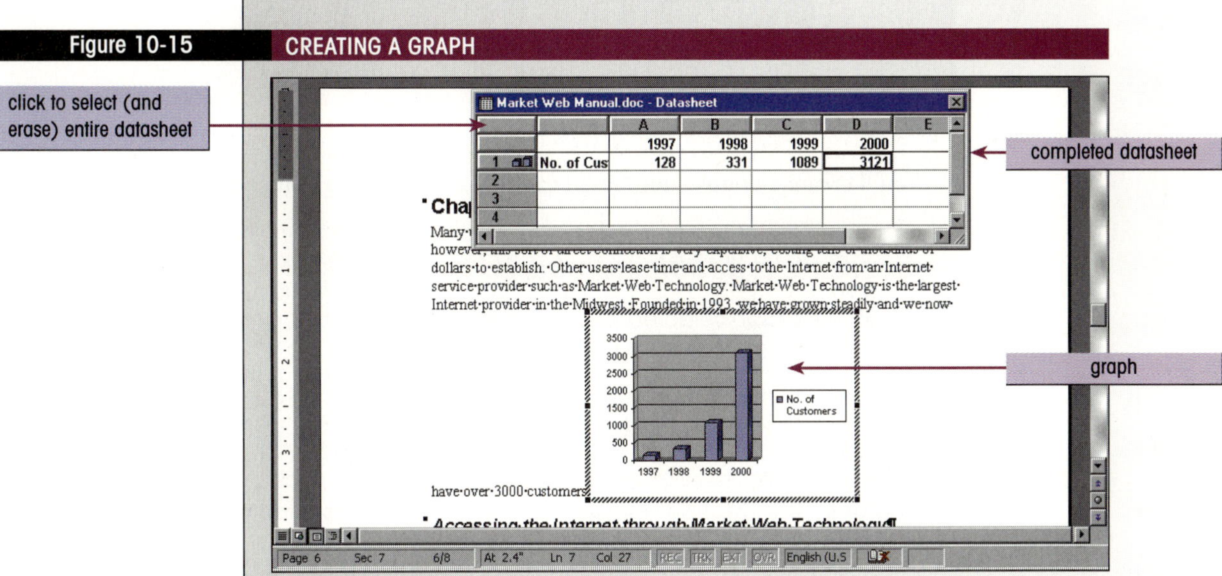

7. Click the **Close** button [X] in the upper-right corner of the datasheet to close it, and then click outside the graph to exit Microsoft Graph and deselect the graph. Now, you'll position the graph to the right of the current paragraph.
8. Right-click the graph, click **Format Object** on the shortcut menu to open the Format Object dialog box, click the **Layout** tab, click the **Square** wrapping icon, click the **Right** option button in the Horizontal alignment section of the dialog box, and then click the **OK** button.

9. Drag the chart up or down so that it's positioned to the right of the paragraph that starts "Many users . . ." rather than below it.

10. Save the manual with the new graph.

Tasha wants to include captions for each figure so the text can refer to them. She asks you to double-number the figures in the style "Figure 3.1," where the number before the period is the chapter number and the number after the period is the figure number within that chapter. Double-numbering figures by hand is time-consuming and error-prone, especially if you rearrange text, reorder chapters, add and delete figures, or haven't assigned chapter numbers yet. To make the job easier, you can use the Caption command to double-number figure captions in much the same way as you numbered the chapters. Word will update the figure captions if you insert another figure in a chapter, move a figure to another chapter, or reorder the chapters.

REFERENCE WINDOW RW

Creating Double-Numbered Captions

- Select the table or figure to which you want to apply a caption.
- Click Insert on the menu bar, and then click Caption.
- Click the Label list arrow, and then click the type of object to which you're applying the caption (for example, figure or table).
- Set other options as needed.
- Click the Numbering button, select the Include chapter number check box, and then set other options as needed.
- Click the OK button.

You'll create a double-numbered caption for the figure you just inserted.

To create a double-numbered caption:

1. With the graph selected, click **Insert** on the menu bar, and click **Caption** to open the Caption dialog box.

2. Make sure that in the Options section, the Label list box is set to **Figure** and the Position list box is set to **Below selected item**.

3. If the Caption text box doesn't display "Figure 3.1," click the **Numbering** button to open the Caption Numbering dialog box, and set the options as shown in Figure 10-16. Then click the **OK** button.

Figure 10-16 CAPTION NUMBERING DIALOG BOX

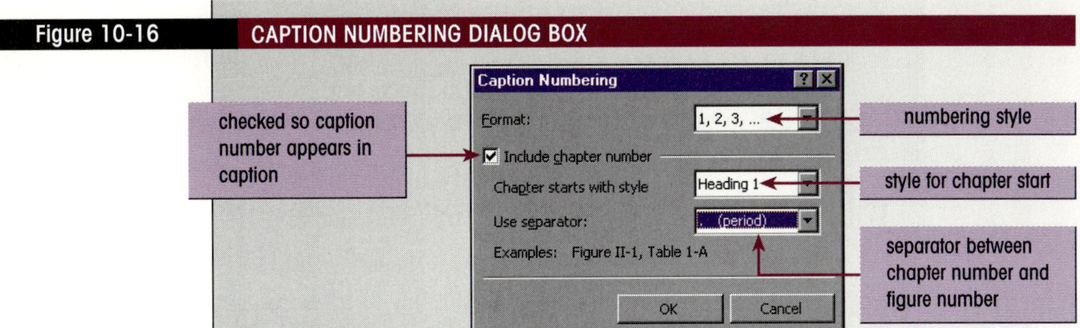

4. With the insertion point to the right of the caption number, press the **spacebar** twice, and then type **Company Growth**.

5. Click the **OK** button in the Caption dialog box to insert the double-numbered caption, which is a floating text box with a border.

TROUBLE? If the caption number is anything except 3.1, select the number by dragging the pointer I over the caption and pressing the **F9** key to update the field codes.

TROUBLE? If the text box is too narrow to display the complete caption on one line, drag the right-center resize box to the right until the text box is large enough.

The caption text box might cover text in the document because the wrapping default is set to None. Next, you'll change the wrapping setting and remove the border of the caption text box.

6. Right-click the edge of the caption text box, and then click **Format Text Box** on the shortcut menu. The Format Text Box dialog box opens.

7. Using the same procedure as above, set the Wrapping style to **Square**, and then, without closing the Format Text Box dialog box, click the **Colors and Lines** tab, and then set the line color to **No Line**, and then click the **OK** button on the dialog box. This removes the border lines from around the caption.

8. Drag the edge of the caption frame so that the text box is centered below the figure. Click outside the caption text box to deselect it. See Figure 10-17.

Figure 10-17 GRAPH WITH DOUBLE-NUMBERED CAPTION

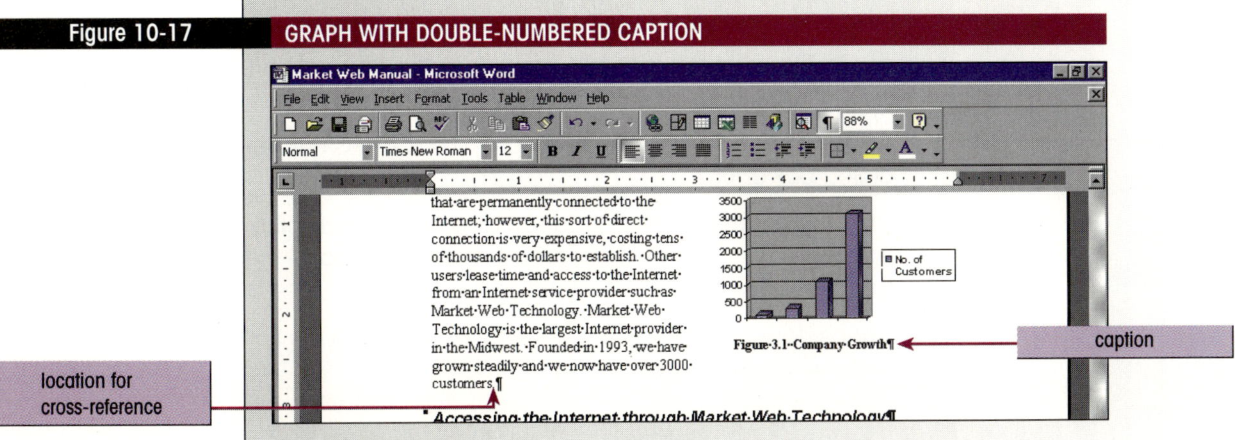

TROUBLE? If the caption isn't positioned and formatted as shown in Figure 10-17, drag it to where it should be, right-click the edge, click Format Text box on the shortcut menu, and then make any adjustments necessary. If the caption number is "3.2" rather than "3.1", select it and press the F9 key to update it.

With the graph in place, you'll add a cross-reference to it.

Creating a Cross-Reference

A **cross-reference** is a notation within a document that points the reader to another figure, table, or section. If you refer to a figure within the text—for example, "See Figure 3.1"—be sure the reference numbers change if the figure numbers change, as might happen if you add and delete figures or reorganize a document. The Cross-Reference feature updates these references just as it updates the heading numbering and figure captions.

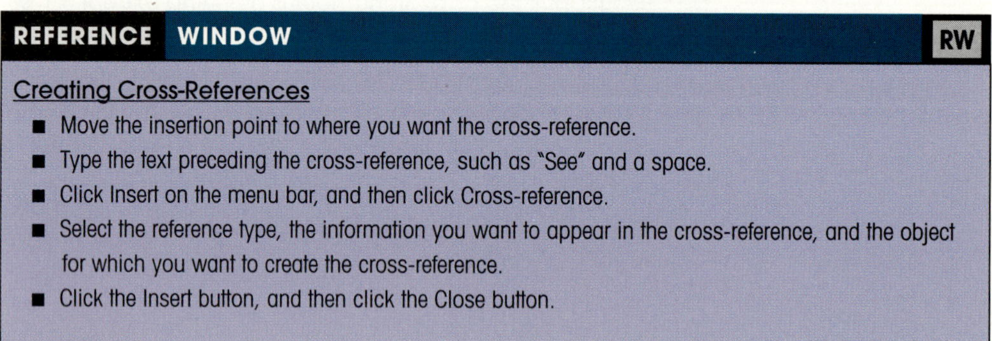

REFERENCE WINDOW RW

Creating Cross-References

- Move the insertion point to where you want the cross-reference.
- Type the text preceding the cross-reference, such as "See" and a space.
- Click Insert on the menu bar, and then click Cross-reference.
- Select the reference type, the information you want to appear in the cross-reference, and the object for which you want to create the cross-reference.
- Click the Insert button, and then click the Close button.

Tasha wants every figure in the manual referenced within the text, so you'll insert a cross-reference to the figure you created earlier.

To insert a cross-reference to a figure:

1. Move the insertion point to the end of the paragraph below the Chapter 3 heading (and next to the figure).
2. Press the **spacebar** to insert a space, type **See** and press the **spacebar** again. The cross-reference to Figure 3.1 will appear at the location of the insertion point.
3. Click **Insert** on the menu bar, and then click **Cross-reference**. The Cross-reference dialog box opens.
4. Click the **Reference type** list arrow and click **Figure**, click the **Insert as hyperlink** check box (if necessary) to deselect it, and then click **Only label and number** in the Insert reference to list box.
5. If necessary, click **Figure 3.1 Growth Company** in the For which caption list box. See Figure 10-18.

Figure 10-18 CROSS-REFERENCE DIALOG BOX

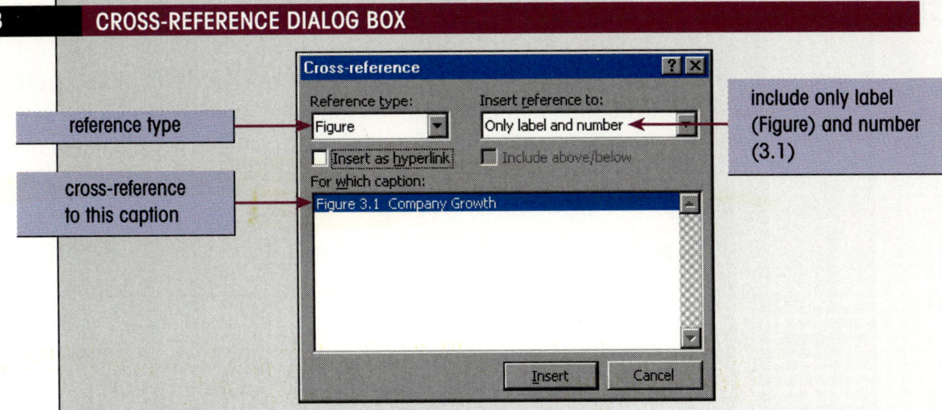

TROUBLE? If "Figure 3.1 Company Growth" doesn't appear in the For which caption list (due to a problem in some releases of Word 2000), click the Cancel button, and type "Figure 3.1," type a period, and then skip to the first paragraph after Step 6.

6. Click the **Insert** button to insert this cross-reference, click the **Close** button to close the dialog box, and then type **.** (a period) at the end of the sentence. The sentence "See Figure 3.1." appears in the manual.

TROUBLE? If the figure number changes to 3.2 (or another number), select the entire paragraph, including the figure and caption, and press the F9 key to update the field codes.

Notice that the cross-reference you created is double-numbered to match the figure caption. The power of all numbering features in Word—heading numbering, caption numbering, and cross-references—becomes evident when you edit a long document with many figures. You've finished working on the master document for now, so you'll save and close it.

To save and close the document:

1. Save the master document.
2. Click the **Close** button in the upper-right corner of the document window. Make sure you don't click the application Close button above it; you don't want to exit Word.

Next, you'll work with individual subdocuments of the Market Web Manual.

Tracking Revisions

The file you received from each team was only a draft of their chapters. Each team still needs to make final edits to their sections. Tasha wants to know exactly what additions and deletions are made to the text. You can track changes people make in a document by turning on revision marks. **Revision marks** show where text or graphics have been added, deleted, or moved. When you turn on revision marks:

- Word marks additions and deletions to text in color. Word draws a line through deleted text, underlines added text, and shows all revised text in a color, such as blue. You can set tracking to show formatting changes, such as turning boldface on or off, altering margins, and inserting page breaks, as well. Each person's edits appear in a unique color.
- Word shows or hides revision marks in the document or printout. You can display the revision marks in a document to view all the changes, or you can hide the revision marks to see how the text would look if you accepted all the revisions. In addition, you can print the document with or without the revision marks.
- Word describes the author and action of each revision as you review it. You can accept all the revisions at once, reject all the revisions at once, or review one revision at a time and decide whether to accept or reject it.

These features give you flexibility in tracking revisions that you make in your own document or that workgroup members make in a shared document.

Protecting Documents for Tracked Changes

Sometimes, you'll want to ensure that you see every change made to a document (or subdocuments), such as when many people revise a report. To do this, you **protect** the document for tracked changes, which prevents anyone from editing the document without revision marks. After you protect a document in this way, Word will track every change.

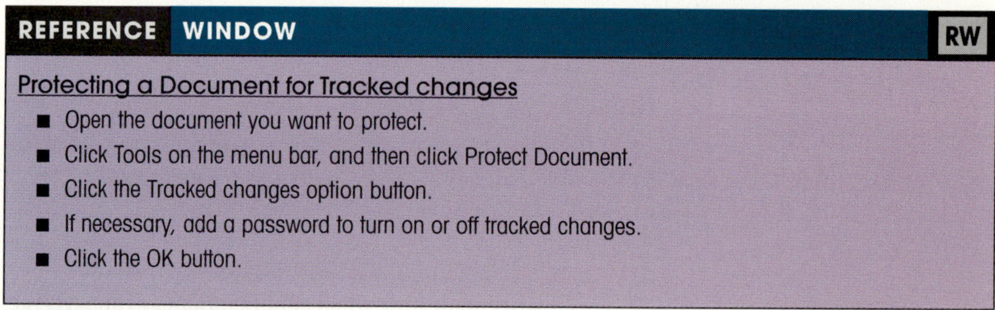

REFERENCE WINDOW RW

Protecting a Document for Tracked changes

- Open the document you want to protect.
- Click Tools on the menu bar, and then click Protect Document.
- Click the Tracked changes option button.
- If necessary, add a password to turn on or off tracked changes.
- Click the OK button.

Tasha wants to ensure that any revisions made in the chapter on the Internet are carefully tracked and reviewed.

To protect a subdocument for tracked changes:

1. Open the file **The Internet** from the Tutorial folder for Tutorial 10.
2. Click **Tools** on the menu bar, and then click **Protect Document** to open the Protect Document dialog box.

3. If necessary, click the **Tracked changes** option button to select it, and then click the **OK** button. You could add a password so that only you could unprotect the document, but you don't feel this is necessary. To remind you that all revisions will be marked, Word darkens the TRK button on the status bar.

4. Save the document.

Now that the document is protected for revisions, neither you nor anyone else can make revisions without recording them in the document file.

Editing with Revision Marks

Editing with revision marks can take some getting used to. Looking at black text with red and green wavy lines beneath some words, as well as text that is blue and possibly other colors showing several people's edits, can be distracting. With some practice, however, editing with tracked changes will become easier.

REFERENCE WINDOW RW

Marking Revisions While Editing a Document

- Click Tools on the menu bar, point to Track Changes, and click Highlight Changes to open the Highlight Changes dialog box.
- If necessary, click the Track changes while editing check box. (If the document has been protected for tracked changes, this check box will be selected and the option dimmed.)
- If necessary, click the Highlight changes on screen check box to select it.
- If you want the revisions to appear in the printed document, make sure the Highlight changes in printed document check box is selected.
- Click the OK button.

Justin Masie, the editor in WET Team 1, was planning to edit his team's chapter, "The Internet," but was called into a meeting. He has marked up a hardcopy of the chapter, and Tasha asks you to transfer his edits to the file.

To edit a document with revision marks:

1. Make sure the document The Internet is in Normal View.

   Because you have protected the document for tracking revisions, you don't need to use the Track Changes command. You're ready to make the first revision. Justin thinks the word "communicate" in the first paragraph is unnecessary.

2. Select the word **communicate** and the comma and space following it.

3. Press the **Delete** key. Normally, "communicate" would disappear, but because you are tracking changes, the word changes to red (or another color) with a line through it, and a vertical line appears in the margin so you can easily find the modified text.

4. Delete the **,** (comma), following the phrase "share information" on the same line. Again, the comma changes to red (or another color) with a horizontal line above it.

5. At the end of the first paragraph, press the **spacebar**, and then type **The Internet, in fact, is sometimes called the Information Superhighway.** (including the period). This added text appears in red (or some other color) and is also underlined. See Figure 10–19.

Figure 10-19 REVISION MARKS IN DOCUMENT

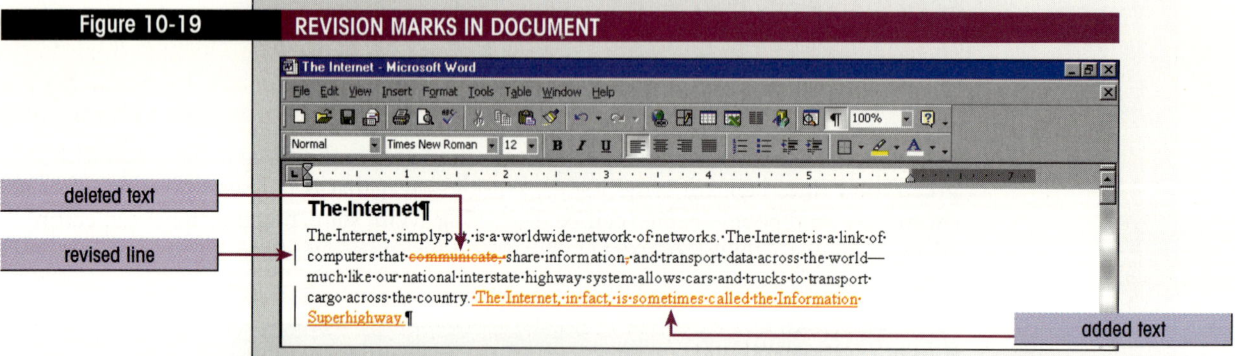

6. In the line just below the "History of the Internet" heading, select the text **the Army**, and then type **Defense** to change the phrase to "Department of Defense." It's easy to inadvertently add extra spaces or leave no spaces when editing with revision marks, so make sure an extra space doesn't follow the word "Defense."

7. After the phrase "National Science Foundation" in the same paragraph, press the **spacebar** and type **(NSF)** to insert the initials of the federal agency.

Justin has more edits, but he didn't mark them on the page you have. He'll finish editing the document after his meeting ends. For now, you'll hide the revision marks and look at the chapter as if Tasha had accepted all Justin's revisions.

To turn off revision marks:

1. Click **Tools** on the menu bar, point to **Track Changes**, and click **Highlight Changes** to open the Highlight Changes dialog box.

2. Click the **Highlight changes on screen** check box to deselect it. By turning off this option, you can see the document as it would appear if you accepted all the revisions. Notice that the Track changes while editing check box stays selected and dimmed, so that, even though the changes are no longer highlighted in the document window, they're still part of this protected document.

3. Click the **OK** button to hide the revision marks. Remember that the revision marks are still in the document; they're just not visible.

4. Read the changes you just made, and then save the document.

While Justin is still in his meeting, Elona Weidner, one of the testers, decides to work with the document and add her revisions.

Using Different Revision Colors

When two or more people edit a document, Word marks each person's edits in a unique color. How does Word know that a different person is working on a document? The answer is in the User Information tab in the Options dialog box. Word checks the name listed in the Options dialog box; if it isn't the same as the names of people who have already worked on the document, then the revisions appear in a different color. When you review revisions, Word shows who is responsible for each revision.

Tasha wants to be able to distinguish the revision marks of each member of the WET teams. Because Elona won't use the same computer or the same copy of Word that you did to make Justin's edits, her edit marks will automatically appear in a different color. However, Justin sends a message for Elona to join him in the meeting. She asks you to add her edits to The Internet. To distinguish her edits from Justin's, you'll change the User Information name.

To change the User Information name:

1. Click **Tools** on the menu bar, click **Options**, and then click the **User Information** tab in the Options dialog box.
2. Write down the name and the initials of the user listed in the Name and Initials text boxes, respectively.
3. Type **Elona Weidner** in the Name text box and **EW** in the Initials text box, and then click the **OK** button.

Now, Word "thinks" Elona is editing the document. Any changes you make will appear in a different color and be tagged with her name.

To edit the document for Elona:

1. Click **Tools** on the menu bar, point to **Track Changes**, click **Highlight Changes**, click the **Highlight changes on screen** check box so you can see all the revision marks again.
2. Click the **Options** button in the Highlight Changes dialog box to open the Track Changes dialog box, make sure By author appears in the Color list box in both the Inserted text and the Deleted text sections, and then click the **OK** button in each dialog box.

   Elona doesn't like the phrase "simply put" in the first sentence of the document.
3. Move the insertion point immediately to the right of the comma following "simply put," in the first paragraph of the document.
4. Press the **Backspace** key to delete the phrase and the two commas. Notice that the revision color is blue (or a color other than the previous highlight color).

   TROUBLE? If the revision color you see isn't blue, don't worry. Sometimes, Word selects colors in a different sequence.
5. Move the insertion point to the right of the word "president" in the second line of the second paragraph.
6. Press the **spacebar**, and then type **of the United States**. See Figure 10-20.

Figure 10-20 DOCUMENT WITH SECOND AUTHOR'S REVISIONS

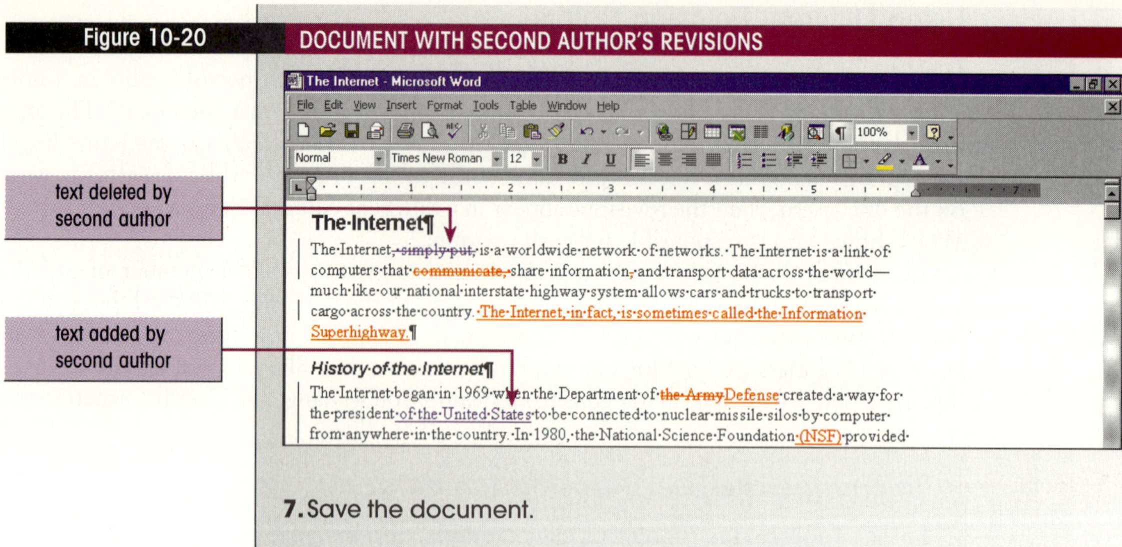

7. Save the document.

Usually, a document will undergo more extensive editing than the changes you have made for Team 1.

Accepting or Rejecting Revisions

Tasha wants to distribute the contents of these early chapters of the manual to Market Web's management. She asks you to review The Internet chapter and accept or reject the edits as appropriate.

You can accept or reject every edit at once, but usually you'll want to look at each revision separately and decide whether to accept or reject it, especially in long documents. Before you can review a document, you (or someone else) must remove the protection.

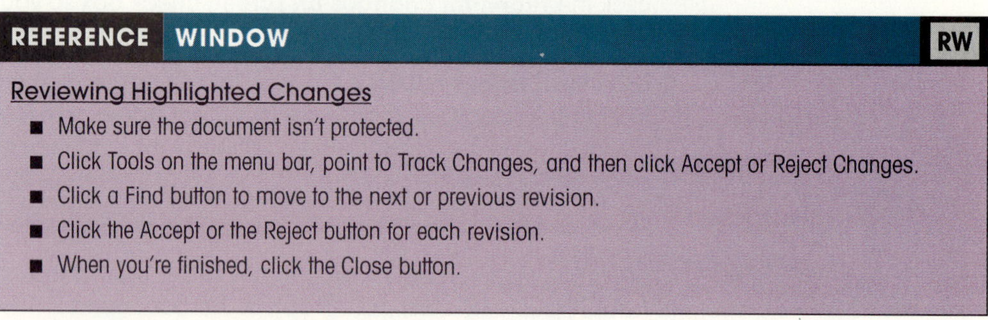
REFERENCE WINDOW RW

Reviewing Highlighted Changes

- Make sure the document isn't protected.
- Click Tools on the menu bar, point to Track Changes, and then click Accept or Reject Changes.
- Click a Find button to move to the next or previous revision.
- Click the Accept or the Reject button for each revision.
- When you're finished, click the Close button.

To review highlighted changes:

1. Click **Tools** on the menu bar, and then click **Unprotect Document** so you can accept or reject the revisions.

2. Move the insertion point to the beginning of The Internet subdocument, click **Tools** on the menu bar, point to **Track Changes**, and click **Accept or Reject Changes**. The Accept or Reject Changes dialog box opens.

3. Select the **Changes with highlighting** option box so you can find each highlighted change.

4. Click the lower **Find** button (the one with the right arrow) to find the first highlighted change. Word selects the deleted phrase "simply put" and indicates who made the revision and when. See Figure 10-21.

Figure 10-21 ACCEPT OR REJECT CHANGES DIALOG BOX

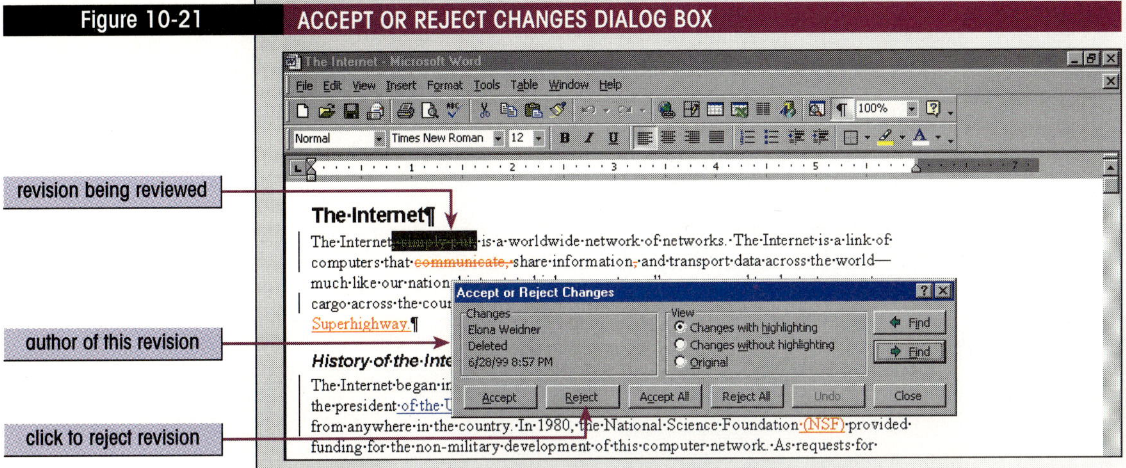

Because you think this phrase is important, you decide to reject Elona's revision.

5. Click the **Reject** button to remove Elona's revision marks and leave the original phrase intact.

   Word highlights the next revision, which includes the word "communicate." You decide that you like this edit.

6. Click the **Accept** button twice because the next change deletes the comma after "information."

   TROUBLE? If Word finds a change before the comma after "information," accept the change.

7. Click the **Accept All** button to accept all the other highlighted changes. Word displays a message asking you if you want to accept all the other changes without reviewing them. Click the **Yes** button, and then click the **Close** button in the Accept or Reject Changes dialog box.

You have rejected one edit and accepted all the others. Word removes the revision marks but keeps the accepted revisions. In this case, you reviewed the subdocument alone, but you could just as easily have reviewed it from within the master document.

Saving Multiple Versions of a Document

Tasha wants to save each version of a document because (1) she wants to be able to recover previous versions in case a later version gets excessive, unwanted changes, and (2) she wants to track who made changes because many members of the workgroup will revise the subdocuments. Fortunately, Word provides a feature for saving each version of a document or subdocument (you can't use this feature to save master documents). You'll save a new version of The Internet subdocument, while keeping the old version.

To save multiple versions of a document:

1. Click **File** on the menu bar, and then click **Versions**. The Versions in The Internet dialog box opens.
2. Click the **Save Now** button to open the Save Version dialog box.
3. Type **After reviewing changes**, and then click the **OK** button.

   Now, the file contains the saved version and the current version of The Internet. You'll edit the current version of the document after you look at the date, author, and description of the saved version.

4. Click **File** on the menu bar, and then click **Versions** to open the Versions in The Internet dialog box again. See Figure 10-22.

Figure 10-22 VERSIONS IN THE INTERNET DIALOG BOX

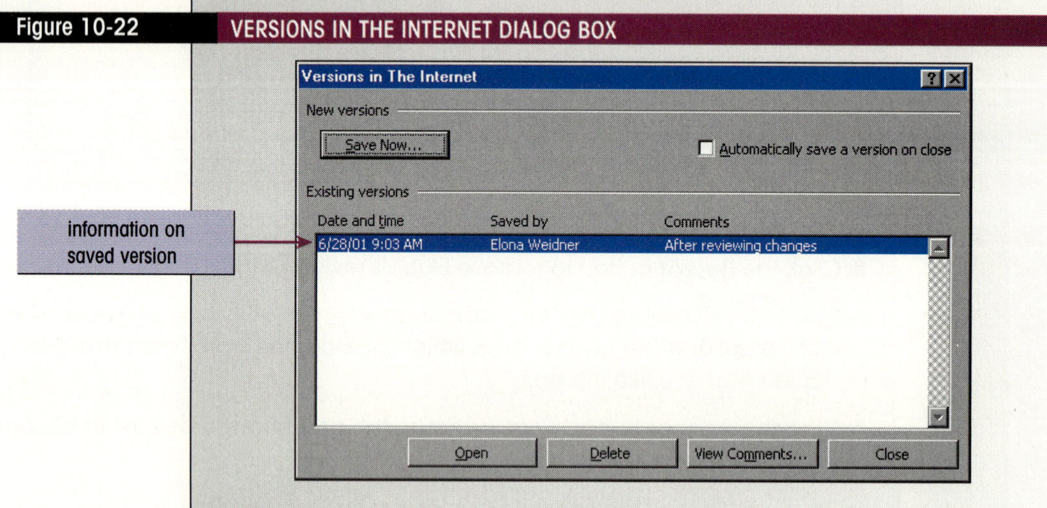

   If the disk file contained several versions, you could open any version simply by clicking the version and then clicking the Open button.

5. Click the **Close** button, and then close the document.

From now on, members of the WET team will use the Versions feature as they revise and comment on subdocuments. You also can set up Word to save versions automatically each time you close a document. If you want to do this, consult the Office Assistant for instructions. Note that if you want to edit a previous version, first you have to save it as a separate document.

Making Comments in a Document

In addition to tracking changes, Word allows you to insert **comments**, which are notes referenced with the author's initials and a number. You insert, view, and edit comments in a separate window, called the Comments pane. You can use comments, for example, to remind yourself to verify some information in a report. But comments are most powerful when more than one person is working on a document, as in a workgroup. For example, one workgroup member might write a note to explain why she made a particular revision. You can protect a document for comments, but then only comments can be added to a document and revisions cannot be made.

Because Tasha wants the WET teams to make changes as well as comments, she doesn't protect the subdocuments for comments.

Inserting Comments

Christian Koncke, the editor of Team 2, asks if you would add a note in The World Wide Web chapter for him. You'll add Christian's comment after you change the User Information name and initials to Christian Koncke and CAK so the comment will be marked with his initials.

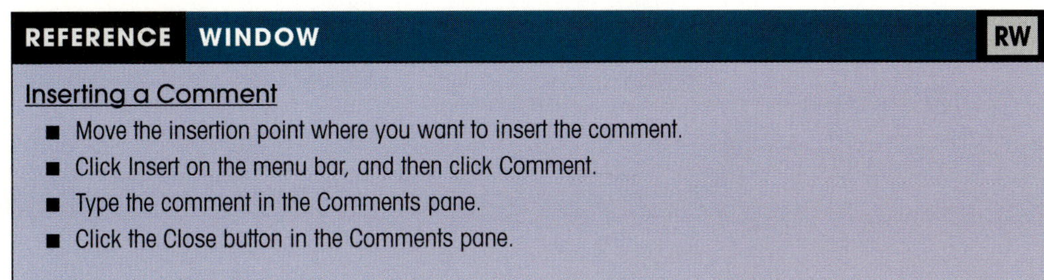

REFERENCE WINDOW RW

Inserting a Comment

- Move the insertion point where you want to insert the comment.
- Click Insert on the menu bar, and then click Comment.
- Type the comment in the Comments pane.
- Click the Close button in the Comments pane.

To insert a comment:

1. Open the subdocument **The World Wide Web** from the Tutorial folder for Tutorial 10, and make sure you're in normal view.
2. Using the same procedure as earlier, change the name and initials in the User Information tab to **Christian Koncke** and **CAK**. Now, Word will label the comment with Christian's initials.
3. Move the insertion point after the phrase "also called WWW, the Web, or W3," (but before the closed parenthesis) in the first paragraph below "The Word Wide Web." This is where you'll insert Christian's comment.
4. Click **Insert** on the menu bar, and then click **Comment**. The insertion point moves to the Comments pane, which opens at the bottom of the screen. Notice that Word has highlighted (probably in yellow) the word "W3" and inserted the comment mark "(CAK1)" to indicate the author (CAK) and comment number (1).
5. Type **I haven't heard of W3. Should we take it out?** (including the question mark). See Figure 10-23.

Figure 10-23 DOCUMENT WITH COMMENT

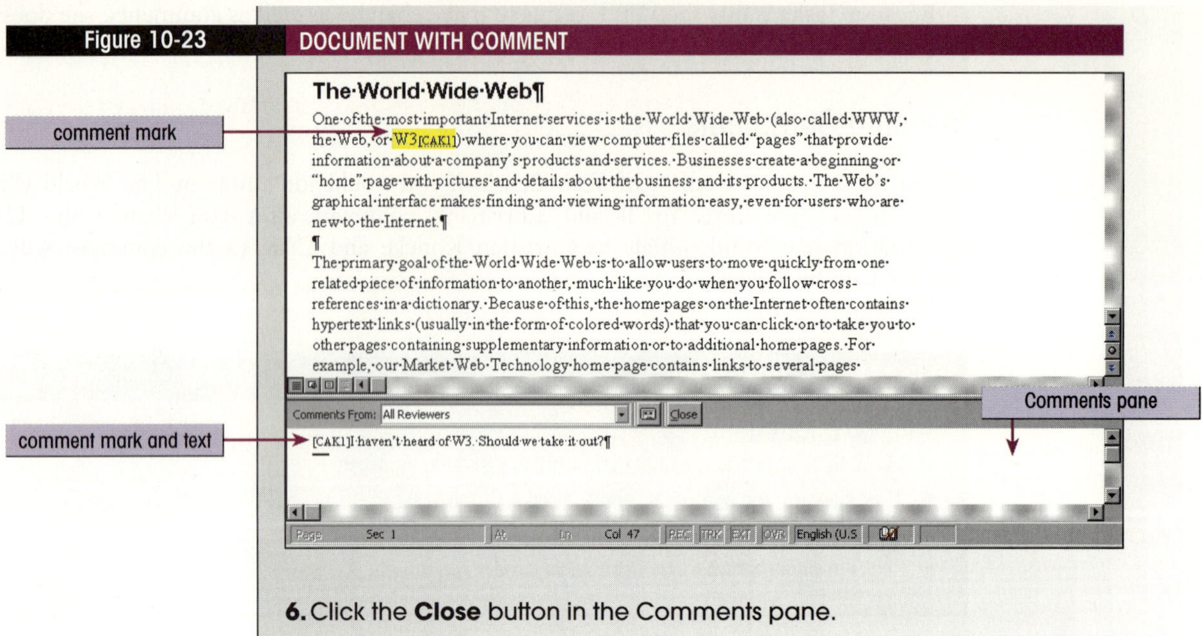

6. Click the **Close** button in the Comments pane.

Pei-Lin Wong, the tester in Team 2, sees you adding the comment for Christian and asks you to insert some comments for her. You'll need to change the User Information name and initials so that Word will use Pei-Lin's initials in the comment marks.

To add more comments to the document:

1. Using the same procedure as earlier, change the name and initials in the User Information tab to **Pei-Lin Wong** and **PLW**. Now, your system is set up as if Pei-Lin were the user.

   Pei-Lin wants you to highlight the entire phrase to which her comment refers. This will help make her note clearer.

2. Click the **Highlight Color** button on the Formatting toolbar, and drag across the phrase **"home" page** in the first paragraph in the document. The phrase turns yellow, and the insertion point appears just to the right of the word "page."

   You can highlight text whether you're going to insert a comment or not. Also, you can remove a highlight by dragging the pointer over the highlighted text. You can use the Highlight list arrow to change the highlight color.

   TROUBLE? If the highlighting in your document isn't yellow, drag across the highlighted phrase to remove the highlight, click the Highlight list arrow, and click the yellow tile. Then highlight the phrase again.

3. With the insertion point to the right of the highlighted phrase, click **Insert** on the menu bar, click **Comment**, and then type **Shouldn't the quotes be around "home page" rather than just "home"?** (including the question mark) in the Comments pane.

   Notice that the new comment mark is "(PLW2)" because Pei-Lin is the author of the comment and this is the second (albeit Pei-Lin's first) comment in the document.

4. Click in the document window, and then move the insertion point to the beginning of the same sentence, to the right of the word "Businesses."

5. Type the comment **Maybe we should also mention government agencies, professional societies, universities, and other institutions that create homepages.** (including the period).

   Notice that Word inserts this comment between the other two in the Comments pane with the comment mark "(PLW2)" and changes the other one to "(PLW3)." After a document passes through several members of a workgroup, it could have dozens of comments.

6. Close the Comments pane, and then change the User Information name and initials back to the original user.

7. Save this document as a new version, with the comment **After adding comments**.

8. Close the document.

Before you give the edited and annotated The World Wide Web file to Tasha, you decide to look at the comments.

Finding and Viewing Comments

You can see the yellow highlighting and comment marks in a document in any view (normal, online layout, print layout, outline, or master document). When you double-click a comment mark, the Comments pane opens so you can read the comments. Or you can point to the comment mark and read the comment author and message in a ScreenTip.

REFERENCE WINDOW RW

Finding and Viewing Comments

- Click Edit on the menu bar, and click Go To.
- Select Comment in the Go to what list box.
- Select a name or Any reviewer in the Enter reviewers name list box.
- Click the Next or Previous button.
- When you're finished, click the Close button.

or

- Click the Select Browse Object button on the vertical scroll bar, and then click the Browse by Comment button.
- Click the Next Comment or Previous Comment button on the vertical scroll bar.

or

- Click View on the menu bar, and then click Comments (or double-click a comment mark in the document).
- Click the Next Comment or Previous Comment button on the Reviewing toolbar.
- Read the comment in the Comments pane or the ScreenTip.
- When you're done, click the Close button in the Comments pane.

or

- Point to a comment mark in the document, and read the comment in a ScreenTip.

To find and view comments using the Reviewing toolbar:

1. Open the master document Market Web Manual, make sure all subdocuments are expanded, and switch to normal view.
2. Click **View** on the menu bar, and then click **Comments** to open the Comments pane and the Reviewing toolbar. The insertion point moves into the Comments pane. Click anywhere in the document so that the insertion point returns to the document pane.

   TROUBLE? If all the commands on the View menu are dimmed and the title bar includes the message "(Read Only)," you won't be able to make any changes to the document. The problem is that the User Information name isn't the same as the original author of the master document. Click File on the menu bar, click Properties, click the Summary tab, write down the name of the author, and then click the Cancel button. Change the User Information name to match the author name in the Properties Summary, and then close the current read-only document, and repeat Steps 1 and 2.

   You want to look at Christian Koncke's comment.

3. Click in the document window at the beginning of the document, and then click the **Next Comment** button on the Reviewing toolbar. Word moves the insertion point to the next comment mark in the document. The comment is displayed in a ScreenTip over the highlighted text. See Figure 10-24.

Figure 10-24 FINDING AND VIEWING COMMENTS

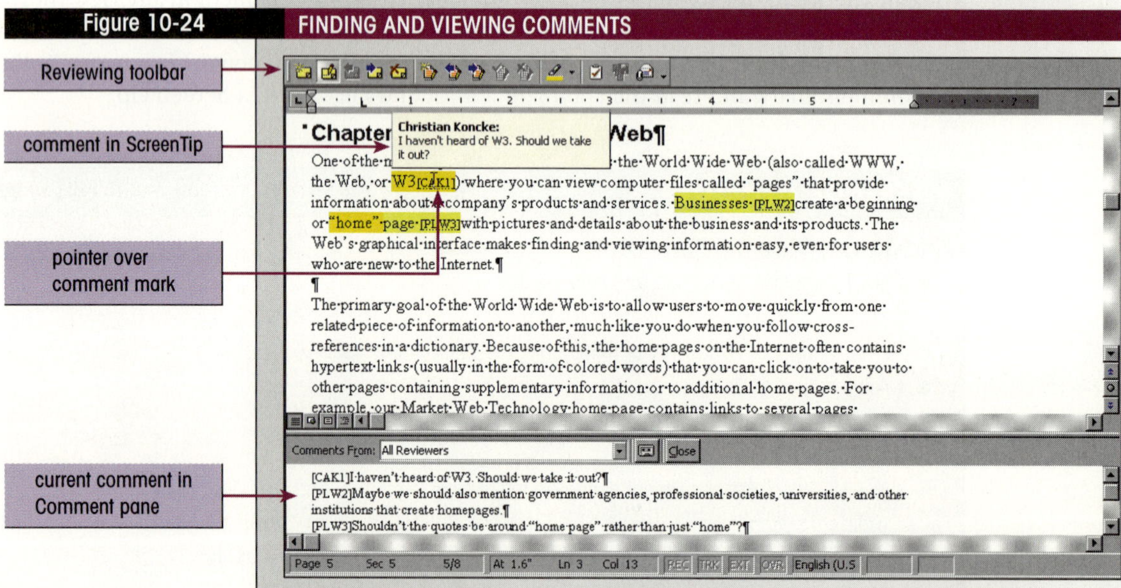

   TROUBLE? If you can't see the ScreenTip, move the mouse pointer to the comment mark in the document window.

   Notice that you can read the comment in the Comments pane or in the ScreenTip. If you wanted more space in the document window for the document, you could close the Comments pane by clicking the Edit Comments button on the Reviewing toolbar to deselect it and review the comments with the ScreenTips.

4. Click [button] as many times as necessary read both of Pei-Lin's comments.
5. Click the **Close** button in the Comments pane. The Comments pane and the Reviewing toolbar close.

   TROUBLE? If the Reviewing toolbar doesn't close, right-click it, and then click Reviewing on the shortcut menu to close the toolbar.

6. Save the master document.

You have found and viewed all the comments currently in the document.

Printing Comments

You can print all the comments in a document, which is helpful if you want to send a printed copy of a document with any related comments to someone, if you want to read all the comments at once, or if you want to keep a hardcopy of the comments on file.

You decide to print Tasha a copy of all the comments currently in the Market Web Manual so she can review them without having to be at her computer.

To print comments:

1. Click **File** on the menu bar, and then click **Print** to open the Print dialog box.
2. Click the **Print what** list arrow, and then click **Comments**.
3. Click the **OK** button in the Print dialog box to print the comments.

The workgroup has completed all the subdocuments. The teams have added all their edits and comments for this draft of the manual, and you have reviewed all of the edit marks and comments. Next, you'll format the document for printing and add a table of contents, index, and footers.

Session 10.2 QUICK CHECK

1. In general, how do you add automatic numbering to chapter titles in a master document?
2. What are three advantages of using the Heading Numbering feature?
3. What are double-numbered captions? In general, how do you create them?
4. How do you usually create a cross-reference to a double-numbered figure?
5. What are two features of using revision marks?
6. Why do you protect a document for revisions?
7. What are comments, and what are their purpose?
8. How can you tell who made a certain revision? How can you tell who made a certain comment?
9. How do you print all the comments in a document?

SESSION 10.3

In this session you'll set page numbering for all sections of the document, and create odd and even footers. You'll then create a 3-D graphic, sort and format the bibliography, and compile an index and a table of contents for the master document.

Numbering Pages with Number Formats

The master document already contains footers with page numbers in the form 1, 2, 3, and so forth. But most books, manuals, and other long documents use a different page-numbering scheme for the **front matter**, the material preceding the first page of the first chapter and which includes the title page, preface, table of contents, and so forth. The front matter is usually numbered with lowercase Roman numerals (i, ii, iii, iv), whereas the first page of the first chapter begins with page number 1 in Arabic numerals.

Tasha wants you to set up the customer information manual using this numbering method. You'll begin with the page numbers for the front matter.

To set page numbers for the front matter:

1. Make sure Word is running, the master document Market Web Manual is open, all the subdocuments are expanded, and nonprinting characters are displayed.
2. Switch to Print Layout View so you can see the page numbers in the footers.
3. Move the insertion point to the Preface title, on page 2 of the master document. This is where you want to set the page number to Roman numeral i.
4. Click **Insert** on the menu bar, click **Page Numbers** to open the Page Numbers dialog box, and then click the **Format** button to open the Page Number Format dialog box.

   TROUBLE? If all the commands on the Insert menu are dimmed and the title bar includes the message "(Read Only)," you won't be able to make any changes to the document. The problem is that the User Information name isn't the same as the original author of the master document. Click File on the menu bar, click Properties, click the Summary tab, write down the name of the author, and then click the Cancel button. Change the User Information name to match the Properties Summary name, close the current read-only document, and then repeat Steps 1 through 3.

5. Click the **Number format** list arrow, and then click **i, ii, iii, ...** so the page numbers will be lowercase Roman numerals. Don't select the Include chapter number check box.
6. Click the **Start at** option button in the Page numbering section, and then make sure i (Roman numeral one) is in the Start at text box. See Figure 10-25. (In your dialog box, the "i" will still be selected.)

Figure 10-25 PAGE NUMBER FORMAT DIALOG BOX

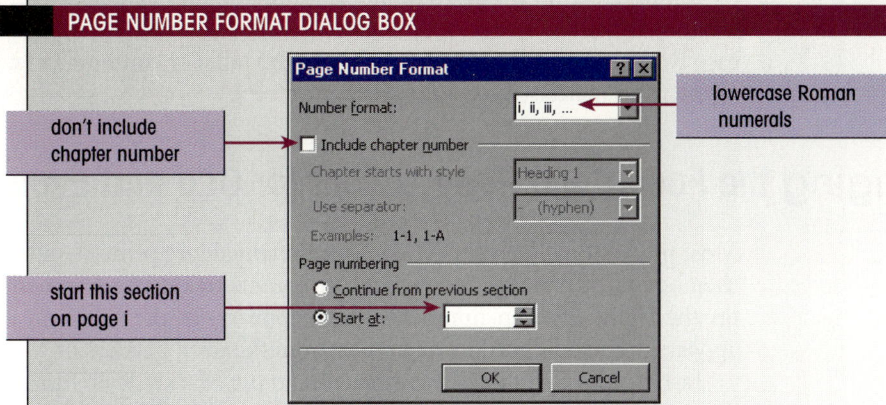

7. Click the **OK** button in both dialog boxes to return to the master document.

8. Scroll until you can see the footer on the Preface page, which shows the page number "i."

You'll now set the chapters in the manual to use Arabic numerals as the page numbers and ensure that the first page of the first chapter begins with page 1.

To set the first page of Chapter 1 to page 1:

1. Move the insertion point to "Chapter 1. The Internet."

2. Click **Insert** on the menu bar, and then click **Page Numbers** to open the Page Numbers dialog box, and then click the **Format** button to open the Page Number Format dialog box.

   TROUBLE? If the Page Number command is dimmed in the Insert menu, your subdocument is locked. To unlock it, switch to Master Document View, click the Lock Document button on the Outlining toolbar, return to Print Layout View, and then repeat Step 2.

3. Make sure the Number format list box is set to **1, 2, 3, ...** so the page numbers will be Arabic numerals. Make sure the Include chapter number check box isn't selected. Many manuals use continuous page numbering from the beginning of the first chapter to the end of the manual.

4. Click the **Start at** option button in the Page numbering section, and then make sure 1 (Arabic numeral one) appears in the Start at text box.

5. Click the **OK** button in each dialog box to return to the master document.

6. Scroll until you can see the footer on the first page of Chapter 1. As you can see, the page number is now 1. See Figure 10-26.

Figure 10-26 FOOTER WITH FIRST PAGE OF CHAPTER 1

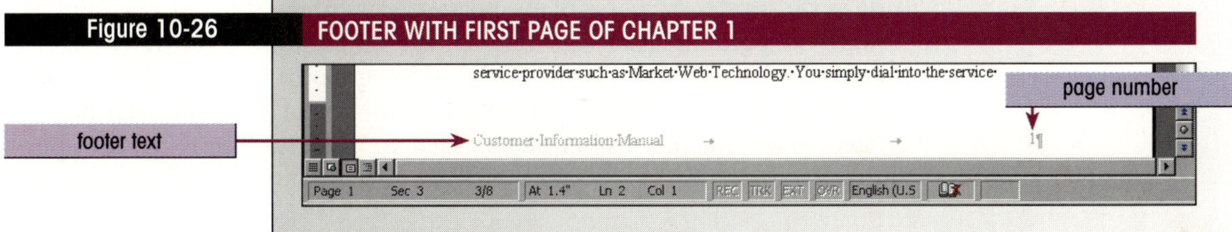

You have set up the page numbering for the master document. All the chapters will be numbered with consecutive Arabic numerals, and the front matter with consecutive lowercase Roman numerals. When you create the table of contents later, it will appear on page ii of the front matter (the page after the preface).

Changing the Footer and Page Layout for Odd and Even Pages

Most professionally produced books and manuals are printed on both sides of the paper and then bound. When you open a book or manual to any page, an odd-numbered page appears on the right, an even-numbered page appears on the left, and sometimes different text appears in the odd headers or footers from the even headers or footers.

Tasha wants to follow these standards in the Market Web manual. Specifically, she wants you to do the following, as illustrated in Figure 10-27:

Figure 10-27 PAGE SETUP FOR ODD AND EVEN PAGES

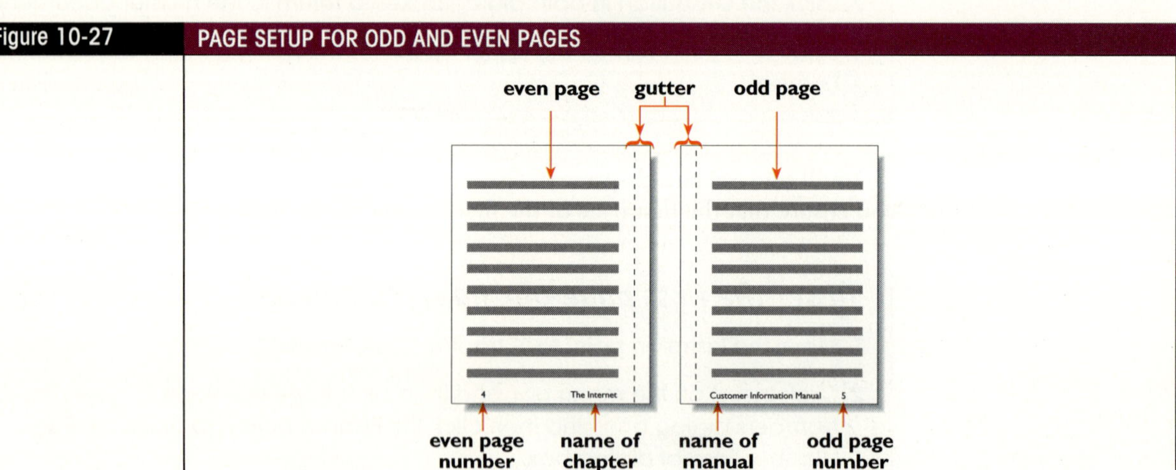

- Set the gutter to one-half inch. A **gutter** is an extra blank space on the side of each page where the pages are bound together. Word shifts the text on odd pages to the right (½-inch in this case), leaving a wider margin on the left. Word shifts the text on even pages to the left (again, ½-inch), leaving a wider margin on the right. When the even and odd pages are printed back-to-back (in a printing format called two-sided printing), the gutters line up on the same edge of the paper, providing room for the binding.
- Set up a different location for page numbers on odd and even pages. When text is set up for odd and even pages, the page numbers usually are printed near the outside edge of the page rather than near the gutter to make them easier to see in a bound copy. So, odd pages have page numbers on the right, whereas even pages have page numbers on the left.
- Set up different text for the footers on odd and even pages. Many books print the chapter titles in the header or footer of odd pages and the book title in the header or footer of even pages. Sometimes, this text is shifted toward the gutter (just as page numbers are shifted toward the outer edge). Market Web's standard style is for the odd-page footers to include the document name (such as, "Customer Information Manual") and the even-page footers to include the chapter name, (such as, "The Internet)" closer to the gutter.

First, you'll change the page setup in the master document so odd and even page footers will be different, and then you'll set the gutter so there is room to bind the manual without obscuring any text.

To change the page setup for printing odd and even pages:

1. Move the insertion point to the beginning (title page) of the master document, click **File** on the menu bar, and then click **Page Setup** to open the Page Setup dialog box.
2. Click the **Margins** tab, if necessary, and then type **0.5"** in the Gutter text box.
3. Click the **Layout** tab, and then, if necessary, click the **Different odd and even** and **Different first page** check boxes in the Headers and Footers section to select both of them.
4. Make sure "This section" appears in the Apply to list box because you want to remove the footer from the title page only.
5. Click the **OK** button. Now the footers in the front matter will be different for odd and even pages. You'll change the text and page number position in those footers after you set up odd and even pages for the rest of the document. The first pages of these sections will be the same as the other pages.
6. Move the insertion point to the beginning of the Preface, and then repeat Steps 1 through 5, but make sure the Different first page check box isn't selected, and then click **This point forward** in the Apply to list box so these options apply to the remainder of the manual.
7. Click the **OK** button. Scroll through the document to see that the text on odd pages is shifted to the right and the text on even pages is shifted to the left.

You have specified that odd and even pages are set up differently. Now, you'll type the text and set page numbering in both the odd and even footers.

To set up different footers for odd and even pages:

1. Move the insertion point to the beginning of the master document, click **View** on the menu bar, and then click **Header and Footer**. The Header and Footer toolbar opens, and the insertion point appears in the header box at the top of the page.
2. Click the **Switch Between Header and Footer** button on the Header and Footer toolbar so the insertion point moves to the footer text box, which should be blank.
3. Click the **Show Next** button on the Header and Footer toolbar until the insertion point moves to the left edge of the footer text box, which is labeled "Odd Page Footer - Section 3."
4. Make sure the footer text is "Customer Information Manual" and the page number is at the right edge of, but inside, the footer text box. If necessary, drag the right-aligned tab stop marker left until it's aligned with the right edge of the footer text box. This tab stop sometimes doesn't move when you add a gutter to an existing document.

5. Click again to move the insertion point into the footer text box labeled "Even Page Footer - Section 3."

6. Select the page number field on the right edge of the footer, and then press the **Delete** key to delete it.

Next, you'll set up the even page footers, with the page number at the left edge and the chapter title at the right edge. Rather than manually enter the chapter title in each section, you can tell Word to insert the proper text automatically.

Inserting a Style Reference into a Footer

A **style reference** is a field that inserts the text formatted with a particular style at the location of the field code. One purpose of a style reference is to easily insert the chapter title in the footer so that if Tasha changes a chapter title, the text in the footer will change accordingly.

To insert a style reference to the chapter title into the footer:

1. Move the insertion point to the left margin of the Footer box, and then click the **Insert Page Number** button on the Header and Footer toolbar. The page number 2 appears at the left margin.

2. Press the **Tab** key twice to move the insertion point to the right margin.

   TROUBLE? If the insertion point appears outside and to the right of the footer box, drag the right-aligned tab stop marker left until it's aligned with the right edge of the footer box.

3. Click **Insert** on the menu bar, and then click **Field** to open the Field dialog box. The style reference field is located in the Links and References category.

4. Click **Links and References** in the Categories list box, and then click **StyleRef** (an abbreviation of style reference) in the Field names list box. Next, you'll indicate which style should be referenced.

5. Click the **Options** button in the Field dialog box to open the Field Options dialog box, and then click the **Styles** tab to view a list of styles that you can reference.

6. Click **Heading 1** (the style for the chapter titles) in the Name list box, click the **Add to Field** button, and then click the **OK** button. The Field Codes text box shows the completed style reference field code—StyleRef "Heading 1".

7. Click the **OK** button. The chapter title "The Internet" appears in the footer.

8. Click the **Close** button on the Header and Footer toolbar to return to the document window, and then save the master document.

You'll use Print Preview to see how the footers look in the master document and make sure they're set up according to Market Web's style guidelines.

To view the odd and even footers:

1. Move the insertion point to the beginning of the document, and then click the **Print Preview** button on the Standard toolbar.
2. Click the **Multiple Pages** button on the Print Preview toolbar, and then set the number of pages to **1 x 2** so you can see odd and even pages side by side.
3. Scroll down until you see pages 4 and 5. See Figure 10-28.

Figure 10-28 PRINT PREVIEW OF PAGES 4 AND 5

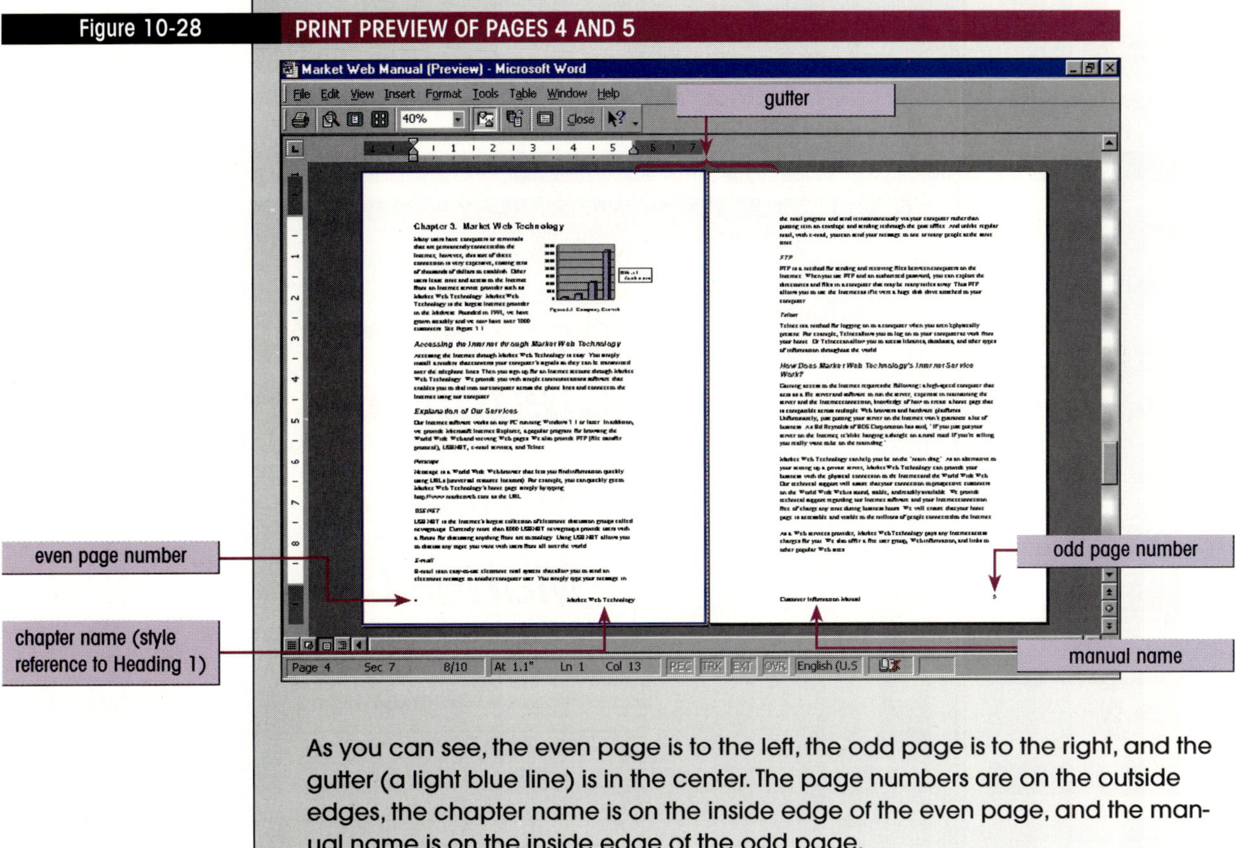

As you can see, the even page is to the left, the odd page is to the right, and the gutter (a light blue line) is in the center. The page numbers are on the outside edges, the chapter name is on the inside edge of the even page, and the manual name is on the inside edge of the odd page.

4. Click the **Close** button on the Print Preview toolbar, switch to Print Layout View, and then save the document.

The manual is set up so Tasha can print the document on both sides of the page. Next, you'll add interest to the title page of the manual by including a graphic.

Creating and Editing a 3-D Graphic

Tasha wants you to create a simple 3-D graphic for the title page of the Customer Information Manual. You'll create a text box, apply 3-D effects to the text inside the box, and then change its color and fill effect.

To insert a text box:

1. Make sure that nonprinting characters are not visible, that you're in Print Layout View, and that the insertion point is on the blank line below the title "Customer Information Manual," on the very first page of the manual.
2. Click the **Drawing** button on the Standard toolbar to display the Drawing toolbar.
3. Click the **Text Box** button on the Drawing toolbar. When you move the pointer into the document window, the pointer becomes +.
4. Drag + to draw a rectangle that has about the same size and shape as the word "Information" in the title, but located between the words "Manual" and "Market Web Technology," as shown in Figure 10-29.

Figure 10-29 CREATING A TEXT BOX

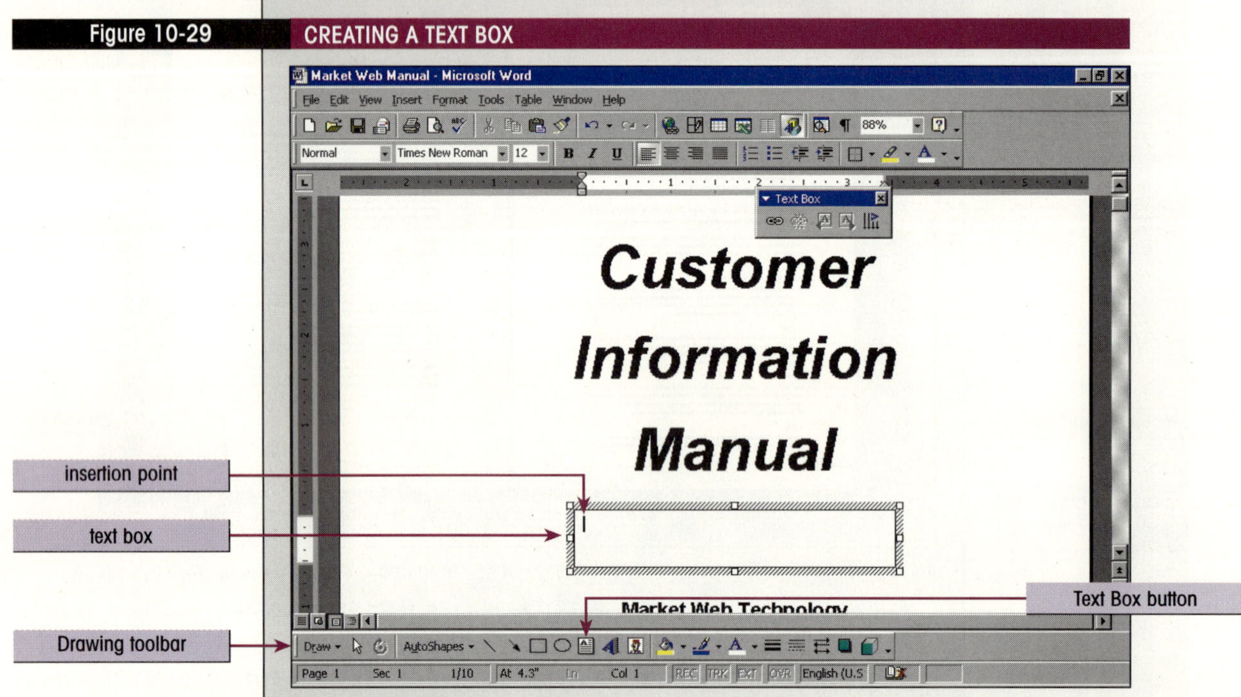

TROUBLE? If your text box is the wrong size, shape, or position, drag the resize handles to make it about the right size and shape, and drag an edge (not at a resize handle) to position the box properly.

5. With the insertion point in the text box, click the **Center** button on the Formatting toolbar so that the text in the box will be centered, type **Internet**, press the **Enter** key, and then type **E-mail FTP World Wide Web** with two spaces before and after "FTP."
6. Select all the text in the text box, and change the font to blue, 14-point, bold Arial. (Choose the color named "Blue.")
7. Select just the word "Internet" in the text box, change its font size to 20 points, and then click the edge of the text box.

You have created a text box and formatted the text. Next you'll convert the text box to a 3-D object.

To convert the text box to a 3-D object and color the box:

1. With the text box still selected, click the **3-D** button on the Drawing toolbar to display a palette of 3-D style buttons, and then click the **3-D Style 1** button in the upper-left corner of the palette.

   The text box becomes a three-dimensional, gray, shaded box. You'll modify the graphic by changing its fill color to a red and yellow gradient.

2. Click the **Fill Color** list arrow on the Drawing toolbar to display a palette of fill colors, click **Fill Effects** to open the Fill Effects dialog box, click the **Gradient** tab, click the **Two colors** option button, and change the Color 1 to **Red** and the Color 2 to **Yellow**.

3. Make sure the Horizontal option button in the Shading styles section is selected, and that the upper-left square in the Variants section is also selected, click the **OK** button, and then deselect the **3-D graphic**. See Figure 10-30.

Figure 10-30 DOCUMENT WITH 3D OBJECT

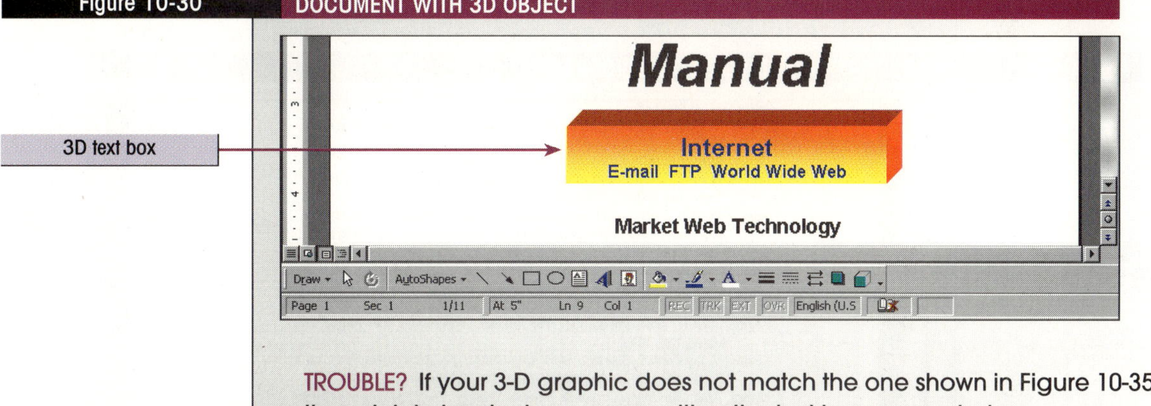

TROUBLE? If your 3-D graphic does not match the one shown in Figure 10-35, then delete hard returns or reposition the text box as needed.

4. Click the **Drawing** button on the Formatting toolbar to close the Drawing toolbar, and then save the completed manual.

Now that you have learned how to create a 3-D box, you'll sort paragraphs in a document and apply hanging indents.

Sorting and Formatting the Bibliography

Tasha typed the entries for the manual's bibliography in a random order. To make the list easier to use, she wants you to sort the bibliography alphabetically by author. She also wants you to format each entry as a hanging indented paragraph. A **hanging indent** is a paragraph format in which the first line of the paragraph is flush with the left margin but the other lines are indented. This is the standard format for bibliographic entries, making them attractive and readable.

To sort and format the bibliography:

1. Select all the entries of the bibliography. Don't select the heading "Bibliography," but rather just the authors, book titles, and other information in each entry. Now, you're ready to sort the list.
2. Click **Table** on the menu bar, and then click **Sort** to open the Sort Text dialog box.
3. Make sure **Sort by** list box is set to **Paragraphs**, the **Type** list box is set to **Text**, and the **Ascending** radio button is selected.
4. Click the **OK** button on the Sort Text dialog box. The selected text becomes sorted in alphabetical order (from A to Z) according to the first word in each entry. You'll now format the entries.
5. With the list of books still selected, click **Format** on the menu bar, click **Paragraph** to open the Paragraph dialog box, click the **Indents and Spacing** tab, click the **Special** list arrow in the Indentation section, and then click **Hanging**. This formats the paragraphs with hanging indents. If you want to alter the indentation space, you change the value in the By box.
6. Click the **OK** button, and then deselect the text. See Figure 10-31.

Figure 10-31 FORMATTED AND SORTED BIBLIOGRAPHY

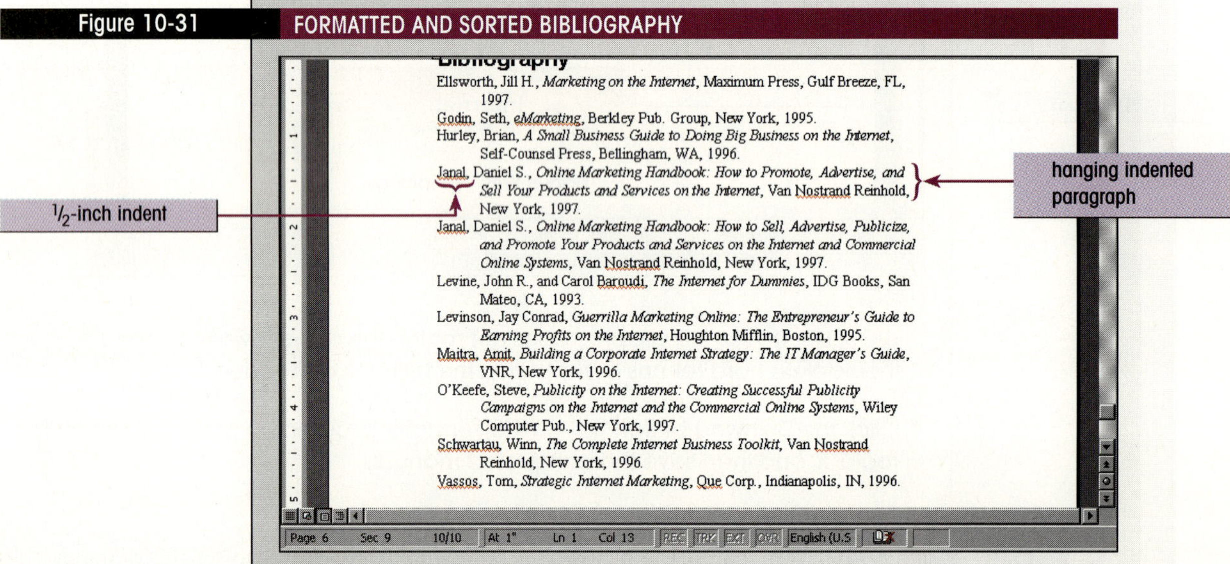

Bibliography

Ellsworth, Jill H., *Marketing on the Internet*, Maximum Press, Gulf Breeze, FL, 1997.

Godin, Seth, *eMarketing*, Berkley Pub. Group, New York, 1995.

Hurley, Brian, *A Small Business Guide to Doing Big Business on the Internet*, Self-Counsel Press, Bellingham, WA, 1996.

Janal, Daniel S., *Online Marketing Handbook: How to Promote, Advertise, and Sell Your Products and Services on the Internet*, Van Nostrand Reinhold, New York, 1997.

Janal, Daniel S., *Online Marketing Handbook: How to Sell, Advertise, Publicize, and Promote Your Products and Services on the Internet and Commercial Online Systems*, Van Nostrand Reinhold, New York, 1997.

Levine, John R., and Carol Baroudi, *The Internet for Dummies*, IDG Books, San Mateo, CA, 1993.

Levinson, Jay Conrad, *Guerrilla Marketing Online: The Entrepreneur's Guide to Earning Profits on the Internet*, Houghton Mifflin, Boston, 1995.

Maitra, Amit, *Building a Corporate Internet Strategy: The IT Manager's Guide*, VNR, New York, 1996.

O'Keefe, Steve, *Publicity on the Internet: Creating Successful Publicity Campaigns on the Internet and the Commercial Online Systems*, Wiley Computer Pub., New York, 1997.

Schwartau, Winn, *The Complete Internet Business Toolkit*, Van Nostrand Reinhold, New York, 1996.

Vassos, Tom, *Strategic Internet Marketing*, Que Corp., Indianapolis, IN, 1996.

The books are formatted and sorted as Tasha requested. As you scroll through the list of books, you can see that Ellsworth is the author of the first book and Vassos is the author of the last book in the list, and that the other authors are sorted alphabetically in between.

You can use the same method for sorting any kind of list (bulleted list, numbered list, or unformatted list) as you did for sorting the bibliographic paragraphs. You select the list to be sorted, click Table on the menu bar, click Sort, set the type of sort to Paragraph, set the other options as desired, and click the OK button.

Now that you have created the text and graphics for the manual, you're ready to complete the manual with an index and table of contents. Notice that creating these items is typically one of the last things you do when creating a long document.

Creating an Index

Tasha wants you to create an index to help readers locate specific information within the manual. An **index** is a list of words and phrases (called **entries**) accompanied by the page numbers on which they appear in a printed document. For example, if customers want information on a "Web page," they should be able to look in the index and find a list of all the pages on which the entry "Web page" appears in the manual.

Compiling an index by hand is tedious, time-consuming, and error-prone. It's also inefficient because if you insert, delete, or move text from one part of the document after you create the index, the page numbers might change. You would then have to go through the entire index again, making any necessary page changes.On the other hand, when you use the Index feature to create an index, once you set up the index, the page numbering is automatic, no matter how many times you reorganize the document.

When you create an index with Word, you must generate entries in one of four ways:

- Select a word or phrase and add it manually to the list of entries in the index. This works well if an entry occurs only a few times because you must mark every occurrence of the entry, one at a time.
- Select a word or phrase and have Word search the document for every occurrence of that entry. This is fast, efficient, and accurate. It isn't, however, foolproof. For example, sometimes a portion of the document discusses a particular topic without using the exact phrase you selected for that topic.
- Move the insertion point to the location of an entry and tell Word the entry that you want to index. This allows you to specify how the topic will appear in the index.
- Select a range of pages, assign it a bookmark, and then tell Word that an entry refers to the bookmark.

You'll use all these methods as you create the index for the customer information manual.

Marking Index Entries

Tasha asks you to index this version of the customer information manual even though it's incomplete. She's sending a sample to the Market Web managers and wants them to see all the features the manual will include. (Generally, it's more efficient to create your index after you have all the text in the final version.)

REFERENCE WINDOW RW

Marking Index Entries and Subentries

- Select the word or phrase you want to mark as an index entry.
- Click Insert on the menu bar, click Index and Tables, click the Index tab, and then click the Mark Entry button to open the Mark Index Entry dialog box.
- Make sure the Current page option button in the Options section is selected.
- If necessary, type an index entry in the Main entry text box, and then type an entry in the Subentry text box if you want.
- Click the Mark button to mark this occurrence, or click the Mark All button to mark every occurrence in the document.
- When you're finished, click the Close button.

You'll start to create the index by selecting the first occurrence of a word or phrase that you want as an index entry, and then telling Word to mark every occurrence of it throughout the document. The first entry you'll mark is "World Wide Web."

To mark every occurrence of a main index entry:

1. Scroll until you see the first paragraph below the "Preface" heading, and then select the phrase "Word Wide Web" so you don't need to retype it.

   Now, you can add this phrase to the index.

2. Click **Insert** on the menu bar, click **Index and Tables**, and then if necessary, click the **Index** tab.
3. Click the **Mark Entry** button to open the Mark Index Entry dialog box. As you can see, the phrase you selected in the document, "World Wide Web," appears in the Main entry text box.
4. If necessary, click the **Current page** option button in the Options section of the dialog box to select it. This ensures that the current page of this entry will appear in the index.
5. Click the **Mark All** button. Word searches your document for every occurrence of "World Wide Web" and marks each as an index entry.

   Instead of marking more entries, you'll return to the document to see how Word marked the phrase "World Wide Web."

6. Click the **Close** button in the dialog box to return to the document window, and then press the → key to deselect the phrase "World Wide Web" and position the insertion point to the right of the index field code. See Figure 10-32.

Figure 10-32 DOCUMENT WITH MARKED INDEX ENTRY

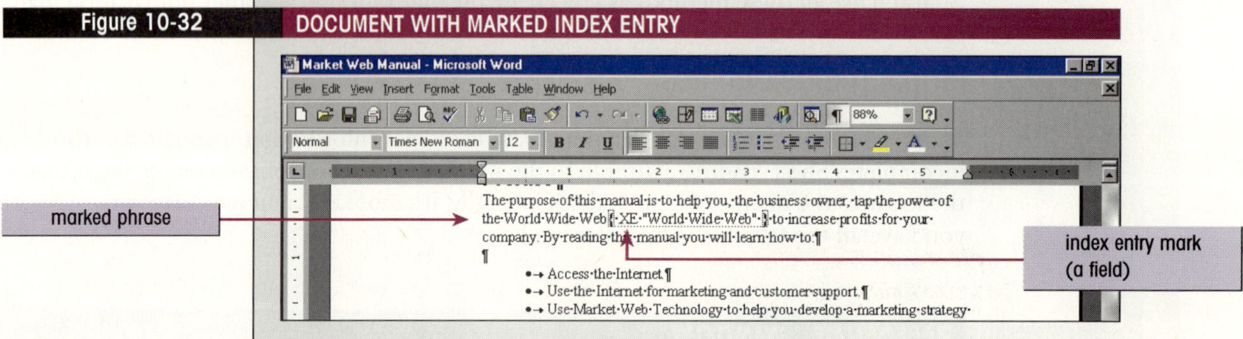

Word marked every instance of the "World Wide Web" in the manual as an index entry, as indicated by the XE field code to the right of each phrase. For example, if you scroll to the paragraph below the heading "History of the Internet," you'll see another "World Wide Web" marked with the XE field code. Because Word inserts the XE field code, you don't need to know much about it, except that "XE" stands for "index entry." If you do need to insert or modify the field, however, you can find more information in the Word online Help. You'll mark a few more index entries now.

To mark more index entries:

1. Make sure the bulleted list near the beginning of the Preface is visible.
2. Select the word "Internet" in the first bulleted item.
3. Click **Insert** on the menu bar, click **Index and Tables**, click the **Index** tab, click the **Mark Entry** button to open the Mark Index Entry dialog box, and then click the **Mark All** button. Word marks every mention of the Internet in the manual with the XE field code.

   The Mark Index Entry dialog box is one of the few dialog boxes that you can leave open while you scroll through the document and select text.
4. Click in the document window, and then select the phrase "customer support" in the second bulleted item of the Preface. You might have to drag the dialog box out of the way to see the phrase, but don't close the dialog box.
5. Click the **Mark All** button in the Mark Index Entry dialog box. Even though the button is dimmed (because the document window is active rather than the dialog box), Word immediately activates the dialog box and the button when you click the button, and marks the highlighted phrase throughout the manual.
6. Select the phrase "Information Superhighway" in the last bulleted item, and then click the **Mark All** button in the Mark Index Entry dialog box. Don't close the dialog box.

Your index contains four entries so far. If you were creating a full index for a complete document, you would continue to mark words and phrases as index entries. Instead, you'll add some subentries to the index.

Marking Subentries

A high-quality index contains not only main entries but also subentries. A **subentry** is an index item that is a division or subcategory of a main entry. For example, in Market Web's customer information manual, you want to create a main entry for "connections," which refers to "connections to the Internet." The manual, however, describes three types of connections: "direct" (also called "dedicated"), "dial-in direct," and "dial-in terminal." You'll want index entries with subentries that match those in Figure 10-33.

Figure 10-33 SUBENTRIES IN AN INDEX

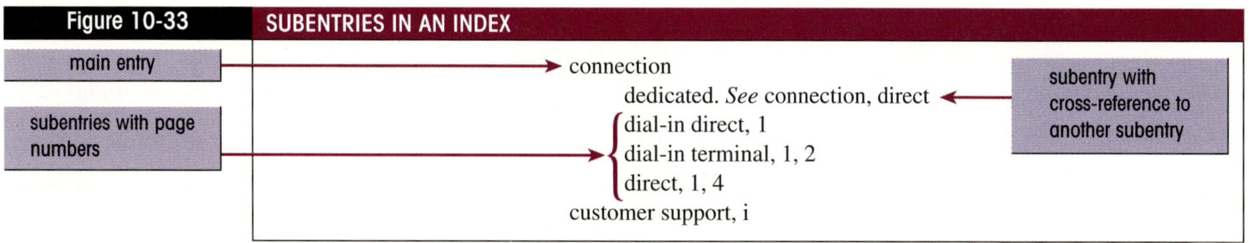

To create subentries in an index:

1. Scroll until you can see the heading "Types of Internet Connections," in Chapter 1, and then move the insertion point after the phrase "direct connection" (but before the comma) in the first paragraph.
2. Click the title bar of the Mark Index Entry dialog box to make it active without marking an index entry.
3. Type **connection** in the Main entry text box, press the **Tab** key to move to the Subentry text box, and then type **direct**. This creates a main entry for "connection," with the subentry "direct."
4. Click the **Mark** button. Word marks only this occurrence of the phrase "direct connection" as an entry with "direct" as a subentry.

   You'll mark each applicable entry of "direct connection," one at a time.
5. Move the insertion point after the phrase "direct connection" in the first line of the second paragraph below the heading "Types of Internet Connections." Make sure **connection** appears in the Main entry text box and **direct** in the Subentry text box, and then click the **Mark** button.

   You decide to search for other occurrences of "direct connection."
6. Click in the document window, press **Ctrl + F**, type **direct connection** in the Find what text box, and then click the **Find Next** button. Word locates the phrase in the context of "dial-in direction connection," which you don't want. Click the **Find Next** button again. This time the located phrase is applicable.
7. Click the **Cancel** button in the Find dialog box to close it. Don't click the Mark button because Word would mark the selected text "direct connection" as a main entry rather than an entry with a subentry.
8. Double-click the **Main entry** text box in the Mark Index Entry dialog box, type **connection**, press the **Tab** key, type **direct**, and then click the **Mark** button.
9. Find the next (and last) occurrence, if any, "direct connection," and mark it similarly.

Now that you have created the entry "connection," with the subentry "direct," you'll create the remaining subentries for "connection."

To create other subentries for an index entry:

1. Scroll until you can again see the heading "Types of Internet Connections."
2. Move the insertion point to the right of the phrase "dial-in direct connection."
3. Create a subentry for "dial-in direct" to add to the main index entry "connection."
4. Search and mark other occurrences of "dial-in direct connection."
5. Repeat Steps 1 through 4 to create a subentry for "dial-in terminal" to add to the main index entry "connection."

You have marked multiple subentries for a main index entry. Next, you'll create a cross-reference index entry.

Creating Cross-Reference Index Entries

A **cross-reference index entry** is a phrase that tells readers to look at a different index entry to find the information they seek. For example, the Market Web style is to use the term *direct connection*, rather than *dedicated connection*, even though both terms mean the same thing. You'll create a cross-reference index entry that tells readers to "*See* connection, direct" when they look up the entry "connection, dedicated."

To create a cross-reference index entry:

1. Move the insertion point to the right of the word "dedicated" in the phrase "dedicated or direct connection" in the first paragraph below the heading "Types of Internet Connections."
2. Type **connection** in the Main entry text box in the Mark Index Entry dialog box, press the **Tab** key, type **dedicated** in the Subentry text box, and then click the **Cross-reference** option button.

   The insertion point moves to the right of the word "See" in the Cross-reference text box.
3. Type **connection, direct** and then click the **Mark** button.

   Word inserts an XE field so the cross-reference will appear in the index. Now, you'll mark an index entry for "National Science Foundation" and create the cross-reference "NSF."
4. Scroll up until you see the heading "History of the Internet," and then select the phrase "National Science Foundation" in the first paragraph.
5. Click the **Mark All** button in the dialog box to mark every occurrence of the phrase.
6. In the same paragraph, select the abbreviation "NSF." Although NSF appears twice, you need to mark it as a cross-reference only once because cross-references don't contain page numbers.
7. Click the **Cross-reference** option button, type **National Science Foundation** to the right of "See," and then click the **Mark** button to add this cross-reference.

The index you're creating for the Market Web customer information manual includes two cross-references. Next, you'll add an index entry that refers to a range of pages.

Creating an Index Entry for a Page Range

In addition to main entries and subentries that list individual pages, sometimes you will want to include an index entry that refers to a range of pages, for example, the range of pages for the Market Web Technology chapter. This requires a more complicated procedure: You must select the pages of the section for which you want to mark an index entry, create a bookmark to the selected pages, and then mark that bookmark name as the page-range entry.

REFERENCE WINDOW RW

Creating a Page Range Index Entry

- Select a range of pages—for example, a section or chapter.
- Click Insert on the menu bar, and then click Bookmark.
- Type the name of the bookmark, and then click the Add button.
- Make sure the Mark Index Entry dialog box is open, and then click the Page range option button, click the Bookmark list arrow, and click the bookmark name.
- Click the Mark button.

To create an index entry with a reference to a range of pages:

1. Scroll until you see "Chapter 3. Market Web Technology."
2. In Normal View, select the entire chapter, including the chapter title.
3. Click **Insert** on the menu bar, and then click **Bookmark** to open the Bookmark dialog box.
4. Type **MarketWeb** (all one word, with no spaces) as the bookmark name, and then click the **Add** button to create a bookmark for the selected range of pages.
5. Click the **Page range** option button in the Mark Index Entry dialog box, click the **Bookmark** list arrow, and then click **MarketWeb**. See Figure 10-34.

Figure 10-34 MARK INDEX ENTRY DIALOG BOX

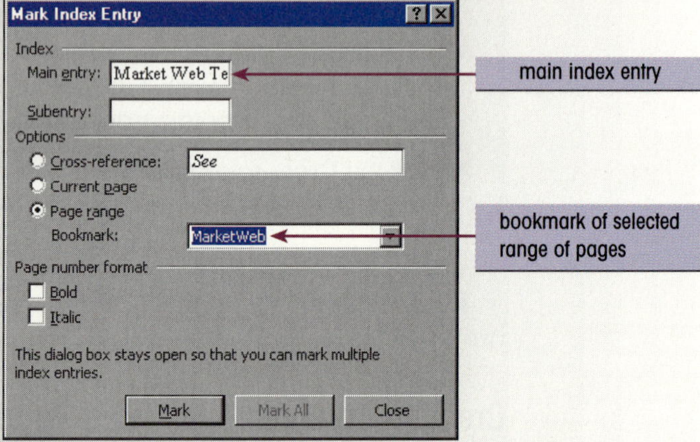

6. Click the **Mark** button to mark this index entry, and then click the **Close** button in the Mark Index Entry dialog box.
7. Save the document.

Although you have marked only a handful of words and phrases in the document, after you compile the index, Tasha can show the Market Web management the types of entries that will appear in the final index.

Compiling and Updating an Index

After you mark all the desired index entries, subentries, cross-references, and page-range references, you're ready to compile the index. To **compile** an index means to tell Word to generate the index from the marked entries at a certain location. Most often, indexes appear at the end of books, manuals, or long reports. For the entries you marked, you'll compile the index on a new page at the end of the customer information manual.

Before compiling an index, hide the nonprinting characters (which include the index codes). If you have many codes visible in a document, they might alter line breaks and even page breaks, and cause inaccurate page numbers to appear in the index.

To compile the index:

1. Move the insertion point to the end of the document, and then click the **Show/Hide** button ¶ on the Standard toolbar so nonprinting characters aren't visible. This ensures that Word compiles accurate page numbers for the index entries.

   TROUBLE? If the index codes still appear in the text, click Tools on the menu bar, click Options, click the View tab, and click the Hidden text check box in the Nonprinting characters section of the dialog box.

2. Press the **Enter** key to move the insertion point below the bibliography, type **Index**, and then press **Enter** to insert a blank line below the heading.
3. Double-click **Index** to select it, and change it to 16-point, bold Arial, the same format as the "Preface" heading. Now, you want to make sure the index begins on a new page.
4. With "Index" still selected, click **Format** on the menu bar, click **Paragraph**, click the **Line and Page Breaks** tab, click the **Keep with next** check box to select it if necessary, click the **Page break before** check box to select it, and then click the **OK** button. No matter how the final manual is reorganized, the index will always appear on its own page and the heading will never be split from the actual index.
5. Deselect the text and move the insertion point to the blank line below the heading. Make sure the blank line is formatted in Normal style, with the font set to 12-point Times New Roman. You're ready to compile the index.
6. Click **Insert** on the menu bar, click **Index and Tables**, and then click the **Index** tab, if necessary.
7. Make sure From template appears in the Formats list box to ensure that the index is formatted according to the template styles of your document, and not to another style available in the dialog box.
8. Make sure the Columns text box is set to 2 and that the Right align page numbers check box is not selected.
9. Click the **OK** button. Word compiles the index. Scroll to view the completed index. See Figure 10-35.

Figure 10-35 INDEX OF MANUAL

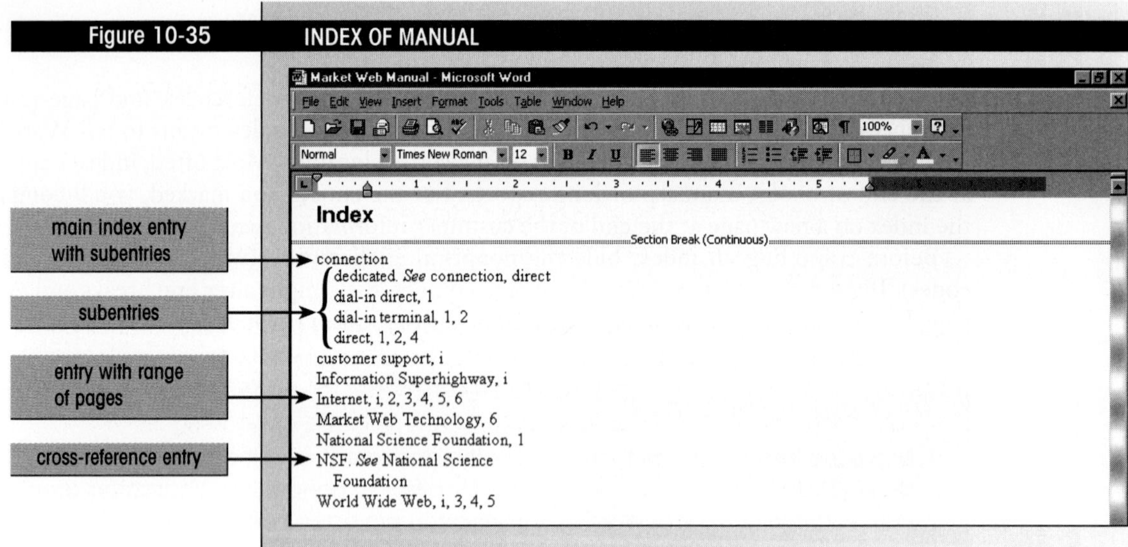

Your index is short but representative of the entries that will appear in the full index. Tasha stops by to ask you to add one more entry to the index. You'll mark the entry, and then update the index to include the new entry.

To update an index:

1. Select the phrase "user group" in the last paragraph of the last chapter, just above the bibliography. You might need to scroll up to see it.
2. Mark all occurrences of "user group" as main index entries.
3. Close the Mark Index Entry dialog box, and then if necessary, hide the nonprinting characters.
4. Click anywhere among the index entries (but not in the "Index" heading) to select the index. Because the index is a field, you update it like you do any field—by pressing the F9 key.
5. Press the **F9** key to update the index. Verify that the phrase "user group" appears in the index.

Your next task is to create the table of contents.

Creating a Table of Contents

Creating a table of contents is similar to creating an index. As you know, a **table of contents** is a listing in the front matter of all the headings in a document and the page numbers on which they appear to help readers locate specific topics or sections. A reader also can scan the table of contents in a book or manual to get a quick overview of the scope and range of topics covered.

To create a table of contents:

1. Move the insertion point to the right of "March 2001" in the last line of the preface.
2. Press the **Enter** key twice to insert two blank lines.
3. On the first new blank line, type **Contents**, change its font to 16-point, bold Arial, and then select **Keep with next** and **Page break before** in the Paragraph dialog box.
4. Move the insertion point to the blank line below this new heading, click **Insert** on the menu bar, click **Index and Tables**, click the **Table of Contents** tab, accept all the table of contents defaults, and then click the **OK** button. Word generates the table of contents based on its predefined heading styles.
5. Save the master document.

You have created and modified a 3-D graphic, which makes the title page more attractive. You also have completed the index and table of contents, which emphasize the important contents of the manual. Finally, you can print the completed manual for Tasha.

To print the completed manual:

1. Click **Tools** on the menu bar, click **Options**, click the **Print** tab, make sure the **Update fields** check box is selected in the Printing options section, and then click the **OK** button. This ensures that the fields for the index, table of contents, captions, cross-references, and so forth, will be updated when you print the manual.
2. Print the Customer Information Manual. When Word prompts you to update the table of contents, make sure the **Update page numbers only** option button is selected, and then click the **OK** button. Figure 10-36 shows the printed Customer Information Manual.
3. To turn on grammar checking, click **Tools** on the menu bar, click **Options**, click the **Spelling & Grammar** tab, click the **Check grammar as you type** check box to select it, and then click the **OK** button.
4. Close any open documents, click the **Yes** button to save the document if prompted to do so, and then exit Word.

Figure 10-36 PRINTED CUSTOMER INFORMATION MANUAL

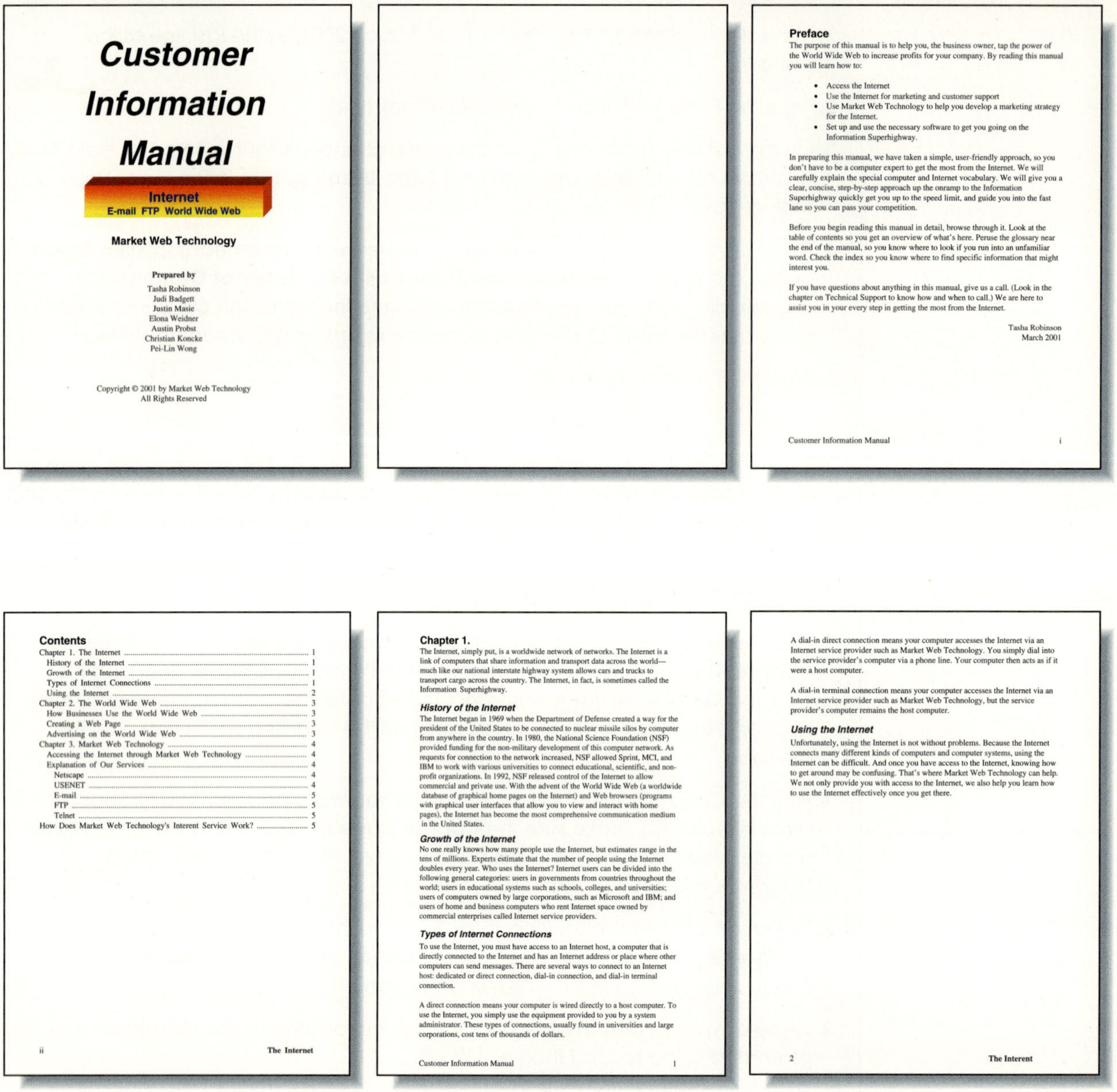

Customer Information Manual

Internet
E-mail FTP World Wide Web

Market Web Technology

Prepared by

Tasha Robinson
Judi Badgett
Justin Masie
Elona Weidner
Austin Probst
Christian Koncke
Pei-Lin Wong

Copyright © 2001 by Market Web Technology
All Rights Reserved

Preface

The purpose of this manual is to help you, the business owner, tap the power of the World Wide Web to increase profits for your company. By reading this manual you will learn how to:

- Access the Internet
- Use the Internet for marketing and customer support
- Use Market Web Technology to help you develop a marketing strategy for the Internet.
- Set up and use the necessary software to get you going on the Information Superhighway.

In preparing this manual, we have taken a simple, user-friendly approach, so you don't have to be a computer expert to get the most from the Internet. We will carefully explain the special computer and Internet vocabulary. We will give you a clear, concise, step-by-step approach up the onramp to the Information Superhighway quickly get you up to the speed limit, and guide you into the fast lane so you can pass your competition.

Before you begin reading this manual in detail, browse through it. Look at the table of contents so you get an overview of what's here. Peruse the glossary near the end of the manual, so you know where to look if you run into an unfamiliar word. Check the index so you know where to find specific information that might interest you.

If you have questions about anything in this manual, give us a call. (Look in the chapter on Technical Support to know how and when to call.) We are here to assist you in your every step in getting the most from the Internet.

Tasha Robinson
March 2001

Customer Information Manual i

Contents

ii The Internet

Chapter 1.

The Internet, simply put, is a worldwide network of networks. The Internet is a link of computers that share information and transport data across the world—much like our national interstate highway system allows cars and trucks to transport cargo across the country. The Internet, in fact, is sometimes called the Information Superhighway.

History of the Internet

The Internet began in 1969 when the Department of Defense created a way for the president of the United States to be connected to nuclear missile silos by computer from anywhere in the country. In 1980, the National Science Foundation (NSF) provided funding for the non-military development of this computer network. As requests for connection to the network increased, NSF allowed Sprint, MCI, and IBM to work with various universities to connect educational, scientific, and non-profit organizations. In 1992, NSF released control of the Internet to allow commercial and private use. With the advent of the World Wide Web (a worldwide database of graphical home pages on the Internet) and Web browsers (programs with graphical user interfaces that allow you to view and interact with home pages), the Internet has become the most comprehensive communication medium in the United States.

Growth of the Internet

No one really knows how many people use the Internet, but estimates range in the tens of millions. Experts estimate that the number of people using the Internet doubles every year. Who uses the Internet? Internet users can be divided into the following general categories: users in governments from countries throughout the world; users in educational systems such as schools, colleges, and universities; users of computers owned by large corporations, such as Microsoft and IBM; and users of home and business computers who rent Internet space owned by commercial enterprises called Internet service providers.

Types of Internet Connections

To use the Internet, you must have access to an Internet host, a computer that is directly connected to the Internet and has an Internet address or place where other computers can send messages. There are several ways to connect to an Internet host: dedicated or direct connection, dial-in connection, and dial-in terminal connection.

A direct connection means your computer is wired directly to a host computer. To use the Internet, you simply use the equipment provided to you by a system administrator. These types of connections, usually found in universities and large corporations, cost tens of thousands of dollars.

Customer Information Manual 1

A dial-in direct connection means your computer accesses the Internet via an Internet service provider such as Market Web Technology. You simply dial into the service provider's computer via a phone line. Your computer then acts as if it were a host computer.

A dial-in terminal connection means your computer accesses the Internet via an Internet service provider such as Market Web Technology, but the service provider's computer remains the host computer.

Using the Internet

Unfortunately, using the Internet is not without problems. Because the Internet connects many different kinds of computers and computer systems, using the Internet can be difficult. And once you have access to the Internet, knowing how to get around may be confusing. That's where Market Web Technology can help. We not only provide you with access to the Internet, we also help you learn how to use the Internet effectively once you get there.

2 The Interent

Figure 10-36 **PRINTED CUSTOMER INFORMATION MANUAL (CONTINUED)**

Chapter 2. The World Wide Web

One of the most important Internet services is the World Wide Web (also called WWW, the Web, or W3) where you can view computer files called "pages" that provide information about a company's products and services. Businesses create a beginning or "home" page with pictures and details about the business and its products. The Web's graphical interface makes finding and viewing information easy, even for users who are new to the Internet.

The primary goal of the World Wide Web is to allow users to move quickly from one related piece of information to another, much like you do when you follow cross-references in a dictionary. Because of this, the home pages on the Internet often contains hypertext links (usually in the form of colored words) that you can click on to take you to other pages containing supplementary information or to additional home pages. For example, our Market Web Technology home page contains links to several pages providing a guided tour of the Internet, a list of what's new at Market Web Technology, and a FAQ (Frequently Asked Questions) about our services.

How Businesses Use the World Wide Web

Businesses use the World Wide Web in many different ways. Some businesses simply create a home page with a telephone number to call for further information or to request a mail-order catalog. Other businesses create elaborate multimedia sites with sound and video. In general, companies with products that change quickly or that require regular updates benefit from marketing on the Web. Others use them to announce new products, describe changes to existing products, or to allow users to link to related companies and products. Some businesses, on the other hand, simply use their Web site for online newsletters.

Creating a Web Page

To create a web page, most people use HyperText Markup Language (HTML), a code that can be read by the various browsers. HTML tells the browser how to display characters and graphics. HTML editing programs are available to help you

Advertising on the World Wide Web

Advertising on the World Wide Web is relatively inexpensive, yet it makes information about your business available to more potential customers in the United States and around the world than any other advertising medium.

Customer Information Manual 3

Chapter 3. Market Web Technology

Many users have computers or terminals that are permanently connected to the Internet; however, this sort of direct connection is very expensive, costing tens of thousands of dollars to establish. Other users lease time and access to the Internet from an Internet service provider such as Market Web Technology. Market Web Technology is the largest Internet provider in the Midwest. Founded in 1993, we have grown steadily and we now have over 3000 customers. See a Figure 3.1.

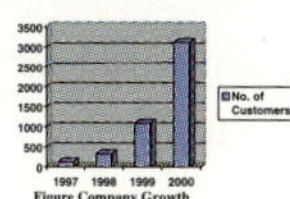

Figure Company Growth

Accessing the Internet through Market Web Technology

Accessing the Internet through Market Web Technology is easy. You simply install a modem that converts your computer's signals so they can be transmitted over the telephone lines. Then you sign up for an Internet account through Market Web Technology. We provide you with simple communications software that enables you to dial into our computer across the phone lines and connect to the Internet using our computer.

Explanation of Our Services

Our Interne software works on any PC running Windows 3.1 or later. In addition, we provide Microsoft Internet Explorer, a popular program for browsing the World Wide Weband viewing Web pages. We also provide FTP (file transfer protocol), USENET, e-mail services, and Telnet.

Netscape

Netscape is a World Wide Web browser that lets you find information quickly using URLs (universal resource locators). For example, you can quickly get to Market Web Technology's home page simply by typing http://www.marketweb.com as the URL.

USENET

USENET is the Internet's largest collection of electronic discussion groups called newsgroups. Currently more than 8000 USENET newsgroups provide users with a forum for discussing anything from art to zoology. Using USENET allows you to discuss any topic you want with users from all over the world

E-mail

E-mail is an easy-to-use electronic mail system that allow you to send an electronic message to another computer user. You simply type your message in the mail

4 **Market Web** Technology

the mail program and send it instantaneously via your computer rather than putting it in an envelope and sending it through the post office. And unlike regular mail, with e-mail, you can send your message to one or many people at the same time.

FTP

FTP is a method for sending and receiving files between computers on the Internet. When you use FTP and an authorized password, you can explore the directories and files in a computer that may be many miles away. Thus FTP allows you to use the Internet as if it were a huge disk drive attached to your computer.

Telnet

Telnet is a method for logging on to a computer when you aren't physically present. For example, Telnet allows you to log on to your computer at work from your home. Or Telnet can allow you to access libraries, databases, and other types of information throughout the world.

How Does Market Web Technology's Internet Service Work?

Gaining access to the Internet requires the following: a high-speed computer that acts as a file server and software to run the server; expertise in maintaining the server and the Internet connection; knowledge of how to create a home page that is compatible across multiple Web browsers and hardware platforms. Unfortunately, just putting your server on the Internet won't guarantee a lot of business. As Ed Reynolds of EDS Corporation has said, "If you just put your server on the Internet, it's like hanging a shingle on a rural road. If you're selling, you really want to be on the main drag."

Market Web Technology can help you be on the "main drag." As an alternative to your setting up a private server, Market Web Technology can provide your business with the physical connection to the Internet and the World Wide Web. Our technical support will assure that your connection prospective customers on the World Wide Web is sound, stable, and readily available. We provide techincal support regarding our Internet software and your Internet connection free of charge any time during business hours. We will ensure that your home page is accessible and visible to the millions of people connected to the Internet.
As a Web services provider, Market Web Technology pays any Internet access charges for you. We also offer a free user group, Web information, and links to other popular Web sites.

Custmer Information Manual 5

Bibliography

Ellsworth, Jill H., *Marketing on the Internet*, Maximum Press, Gulf Breeze, FL, 1997.
Godin, Seth, *eMarketing*, Berkley Pub. Group, New York, 1995.
Hurley, Brian, *A Small Business Guide to Doing Big Business on the Internet*, Self-Counsel Press, Bellingham, WA, 1996.
Janal, Daniel S., *Online Marketing Handbook: How to Promote, Advertise, and Sell Your Products and Services on the Internet*, Van Nostrand Reinhold, New York, 1997.
Janal, Daniel S., *Online Marketing Handbook: How to Sell, Advertise, Publicize, and Promote Your Products and Services on the Internet and Commercial Online Systems*, Van Nostrand Reinhold, New York, 1997.
Levine, John R., and Carol Baroudi, *The Internet for Dummies*, IDG Books, San Mateo, CA, 1993.
Levinson, Jay Conrad, *Guerrilla Marketing Online: The Entrepreneur's Guide to Earning Profits on the Internet*, Houghton Mifflin, Boston, 1995.
Maitra, Amit, *Building a Corporate Internet Strategy: The IT Manager's Guide*, VNR, New York, 1996.
O'Keefe, Steve, *Publicity on the Internet: Creating Successful Publicity Campaigns on the Internet and the Commercial Online Systems*, Wiley Computer Pub., New York, 1997.
Schwartau, Winn, *The Complete Internet Business Toolkit*, Van Nostrand Reinhold, New York, 1996.
Vassos, Tom, *Strategic Internet Marketing*, Que Corp., Indianapolis, IN, 1996.

6 **Market Web** Technology

Index

Customer Information Manual 7

As you can see, the manual includes one blank page. This is because you specified different odd and even pages, and then set two consecutive pages (the title page and the preface) to be numbered as page 1. You can't have two odd-numbered pages in a row (or the margins, gutter spacing, and footer text would be off), so Word inserted a blank, even-numbered page.

Tasha is pleased with your work on the manual. She will assemble the remaining chapters from the other teams into the master document and edit them. Then, she will mark many more index entries and update the index and table of contents. A professional printer will print and bind the complete Market Web customer information manual. Tasha is certain that the manual will help Market Web customers better understand the company's services and how to make the Internet work for their businesses.

Session 10.3 QUICK CHECK

1. Under what circumstances might you want to change the number format in a section of your document?
2. In general, how do you set the number format to lowercase Roman numerals?
3. What is a gutter? Why would you change the gutter value from 0"?
4. In general, how do you tell Word to insert the chapter name in a footer?
5. How do you create a 3-D graphic?
6. How do you sort a group of paragraphs?
7. What is a hanging indent?
8. In general, how do you mark a main index entry?
9. What does it mean to compile an index? How do you update an index?

REVIEW ASSIGNMENTS

Javier de Andres is a technical writer in the Documentation Services Department at Market Web Technology. His supervisor, Tasha Robinson, recently learned that more than half of Market Web Technology clients have home businesses. She asks Javier to prepare a booklet titled "How to Succeed at Your Online Home Business" to educate current clients and help them remain satisfied customers as well as to generate new clients. Javier has interviewed many current customers, researched the topic of online home businesses, and started to write the booklet. You will help him manage the current chapters, which will eventually become part of a 50-page document.

1. If necessary, start Word and make sure your Data Disk is in the appropriate drive. Open the file **OnlinBus** from the **Review** folder in the Tutorial.10 folder on your Data Disk, and save it as **Online Home Business**.
2. On the last blank line of page 1, type your name. Center it between the left and right margins.
3. Create a subdocument for each of the two sections with level-1 headings. Add automatic chapter numbers to level-1 headings in the style "Chapter 1. Starting Your Online Business." (*Hint:* Make sure the Author name matches the User Information name.)
4. Promote "Marketing Your Services or Products Online" to a level-1 heading, and then split it into its own subdocument.
5. Set up the document for two-sided printing with a 0.4-inch gutter. Turn on Widow/Orphan control for the entire document.
6. **Explore** Create headers for all pages except the title page. For even-numbered pages, place the page number at the left margin and the document title ("Online Home Business") at the right margin. For odd-numbered pages, place the page number at the right margin and the chapter title at the left margin. Draw a horizontal line below the headers. Use 10-point Arial for the font.
7. Change the page numbering so that the Introduction begins on page i (Roman numeral) and the first chapter begins on page 1 (Arabic numeral).
8. Merge Chapters 2 and 3 into one subdocument.

9. Insert comments into the document as indicated.
   a. At the end of the first paragraph in Chapter 1: "Should we mention what kind of rewards? Financial? Emotional? Intellectual?"
   b. At the end of the first sentence of the second paragraph: "Let's define or describe what we mean by an online business."
   c. At the end of the paragraph below the "Defining Your Services and Niche" heading: "Tasha, should we refer the readers to our other publications that describe home pages?"
10. Save the master document, and then close it. Open the **Equipping Your Online Home Office** subdocument.

Explore

11. Turn on tracking, and then change the revision mark color so that inserted text is violet with double-underlines and deleted text is red with a strikethrough.
12. After the last sentence of the second paragraph below the "Office Space" heading, delete the question mark, insert a comma and a space, and then type "both of which are independent of your home phone."
13. After the second sentence (which ends "when you work at home") in the next paragraph, add the sentence "Your home expenses will increase because you spend more time there."
14. Delete the last sentence of that paragraph, turn off revision tracking, and then save and close the subdocument.
15. Open the master document, and review the revisions. Reject the first two suggested revisions, accept the next one, and then accept the last one.

Explore

16. Move the insertion point to the beginning of the document, switch to Print Layout view, open the Comments pane, and then read all the comments in the document. Close the Comments pane. Print a copy of all the comments in the document. (*Hint*: Use the Next Comment button on the Reviewing toolbar.)
17. Mark index entries for every occurrence of "Internet," "business plan," "home page," "personnel," and "modem."

Explore

18. Mark every occurrence of the words "expense" and "expenses"; use "expense(s)" as the main index entry.
19. Create the index entry "equipment" that refers to the range of pages in the "Equipping Your Online Home Office" chapter.
20. Use the BookletHeading style to create and format an "Index" heading at the end of the document, and then compile the index below it.
21. Create and format a "Contents" heading with the BookletHeading style just after the title page on a separate section and page, and then compile a table of contents below the heading.

Explore

22. Draw an oval around the main title on the title page with no fill and a 1½-point orange line. Convert the oval to the 3-D-Style 2. (*Hint*: If you can't position the oval around the title, double-click the oval, click the Layout tab on the Format AutoShape dialog box, click the Advanced button, and deselect the Move object with text check box. Then, after you close the dialog box, drag the oval to the desired position.
23. Save the document, preview and print it, and then close any open files.

CASE PROBLEMS

Case 1. Author's Guide for Columbia River Press Cameron Paxman is senior editor and manager of the Professional Books Division of Columbia River Press, a Portland, Oregon-based publisher of outdoor guides for travel, hiking, backpacking, mountain biking, and windsurfing in the northwestern United States. Cameron is responsible for helping authors understand the company's policies and procedures on such issues as royalties and contracts, copyrights and credits, and manuscript preparation and processing. He and his assistants are preparing the *Columbia River Press Author's Guide*, which covers these topics, to distribute to all authors. So far, they have written the beginning text of sections that deal with the author's manuscript. You will help Cameron format and manage the guide.

1. If necessary, start Word and make sure your Data Disk is in the appropriate drive. Open the file **AuthGuid** from the **Cases** folder in the Tutorial.10 folder on your Data Disk, and save it as **Author's Guide**.
2. On the blank line under "Cameron Paxman, Senior Editor," type your name, a comma, and the title "Assistant Editor."
3. **Explore** Add a nonbreaking space between any number and the word "inch" or "inches" (for example, ½-inch) in the document.
4. Set the document to print two-sided with a ½-inch gutter.
5. Modify the GuideHeading style so that the heading always begins on a new page.
6. Change the "Note to Authors" heading style from Heading 1 to GuideHeading.
7. Modify the Normal style to 12-point Century Schoolbook, 12-point Garamond, or 13-point Times New Roman. Make sure Widow/Orphan control is turned on for all paragraphs.
8. **Explore** Add heading numbering to all levels of headings, so level-1 headings have uppercase Roman numerals, level-2 headings have uppercase letters, level-3 headings have Arabic numerals, and so forth. (*Hint:* You can make all the changes at once from the Bullets and Numbering dialog box while modifying the style.)
9. **Explore** Create headers for all pages except the cover page. For even-numbered pages, place the page number at the left margin and the Heading 1 at the right margin. For odd-numbered pages, place the page number at the right margin and the name of the guide, "Columbia River Press Author's Guide," at the left margin. Make all header text 12-point, normal Arial.
10. Create subdocuments for each of the level-1 headings and their accompanying text.
11. Promote the level-2 heading "Submitting Your Manuscript" to a level-1 heading.
12. Create a new subdocument from the new heading "II. Submitting Your Manuscript" and its accompanying text.
13. Verify that each level-1 heading begins on a new page. If necessary, change the Heading 1 style to force the headings onto a new page.
14. Save the master document, and close it. Open the **Preparing Your Manuscript** subdocument.
15. **Explore** Select the entire table in the document, and add a double-numbered caption above the table. Use "Responsibilities of Columbia River Press Team Members" for the caption text. (If you get an error message telling you there are no chapter numbers, just click the OK button. When you open the master document, the headings will be numbered again, and when you update the fields, the double numbers will be accurate.)

16. At the end of the paragraph above the table, type "The major responsibility of the team members involved in your manuscript are given in" and then insert a cross-reference to the double-numbered table.
17. Save a new version of the document with the description, "Add caption to table."
18. Set the document to track changes. Change the revision colors so inserted text appears in blue double underlines and deleted text appears in green strikethrough.
19. Edit the first paragraph of the document to change the first full sentence to "All authors have their own unique writing process."; "don't" to "do not"; the second occurrence of "process" to "method"; and "needless time and work" to "needless hours of work."
20. Turn off tracking and then save a new version of the document with the description, "Added minor text revisions"; then close the document.
21. Open the Author's Guide master document, and then review all the revisions in the document. Accept the first two revisions, reject the next two, accept the next two, and reject the last two.
22. Sort the books below the "Resources" heading alphabetically, and then format them with a hanging indent.
23. Create an index entry for all occurrences of: "author," "authors," "camera-ready copy," "proofreading," and "sexist language."
24. Mark at least three occurrences of "preparing your manuscript" or "manuscript preparation" using the main index entry "manuscript" and the subentry "preparing."
25. Mark at least one occurrence for each of the following subheadings as subentries to the "manuscript" entry: "editing," "submitting," "proofreading," and "producing."
26. Mark the entire section on "Submitting Your Manuscript with the bookmark "Submitting," and then use that bookmark for the index entry "manuscript" and subentry "submitting" with a bookmark range of pages.
27. Insert the heading "Index" at the end of the document, format it with the GuideHeading style, and then compile the index below the heading.
28. Insert the heading "Contents" below the "Note to Authors," format it with the GuideHeading style, and then compile the table of contents below it.
29. Set the page numbering so that page 1 starts on the page after the title page, and then update the index and the table of contents. Remember to hide nonprinting characters before you update the fields. Also recall that to update an index, you can click anywhere in the index and press the F9 key.
30. Save the document, preview and print it, and then close any open files.

Case 2. Seminar Workbook for Partners in Parenting Juliana Marlborough is executive director of Partners in Parenting, a nonprofit parenting support group based in Louisville, Kentucky. One of the many Partners in Parenting programs is a series of workshops designed to assist single parents in communicating effectively with their teenagers. As part of the seminar, every participant receives a copy of "Talking to Your Teens," a workbook written by the counselors at Partners in Parenting. You will help Juliana manage the revision of the workbook for the next series of workshops.

1. If necessary, start Word and make sure your Data Disk is in the appropriate drive. Open the file **TeenTalk** from the **Cases** folder in the Tutorial.10 folder on your Data Disk, and save it as **Teen Talk Workbook**.
2. On the blank line below "Partners in Parenting on page 1, type your name.
3. Modify the Title style font to 28-point, bold Arial and set the pagination option to Keep with next. Modify the Subtitle style font to 20-point, normal Arial, and set the pagination option to Keep with next.

Explore

4. In anticipation of adding chapter numbers to the Heading-1 style, define a new style based on the Normal style for the heading "Foreword" called "BookHeading," which is 14-point, bold Arial with the paragraph option set so each heading stays with the next paragraph and starts on a new page.
5. After the Foreword and just above "Why Communicating with Your Teenager Can Be Difficult," type the title "Table of Contents" with the BookHeading style, and then compile a table of contents below the heading.

Explore

6. Set the Heading-1 style so each heading starts on a new page. Then add automatic heading numbers to all the Heading-1 styles so they appear with unit numbers in the style "Unit 1. Why Communicating with Your Teenager Can Be Difficult." (*Hint*: Customize the chapter number by changing the word "Chapter" to "Unit" in the Bullets and Numbering dialog box.)
7. Set the document to print two-sided with a ½-inch gutter.

Explore

8. Create footers for all pages except the title page. Footers on even pages of the forward and table of contents appear with the page number in bold lowercase Roman numerals at the left margin, followed by a space, a bullet, and another space, and then the name "Teen Talk Workbook." Make sure the first page after the title page begins with the Roman numeral i.
9. Set up the even pages for the rest of the workbook to match the front matter even pages, but use Arabic numerals instead of Roman numerals.
10. Set up the footers for the odd pages so the text appears at the right margin with the unit name, a space, a bullet, and another space, and the Arabic numeral page number in bold.
11. Set the page numbering so the first page of Unit 1 starts on page 1.

Explore

12. Beginning with Unit 1, double-number the page numbers in the style "2-3," where 2 is the chapter number and 3 is the page number within that chapter. (*Hint*: You might have to set the numbering style in each section.)
13. Make the current document, Teen Talk Workbook, a master document, and then create a subdocument from each unit.

Explore

14. Rearrange the subdocuments so the unit on "Increasing Your Teenager's Self Esteem" becomes the last unit in the workbook. (*Hint:* Use cut and paste. You might have to adjust the section breaks after moving the text.)

Explore

15. Mark every "parent" and "parents" as a main index entry "parent(s)."
16. Mark index entries for each occurrence of "teenager," "communication," "birth order," and "gender." (*Hint*: After marking one occurrence, copy the entire XE field to the right of the other occurrences.)
17. Create an index entry for a range of pages that covers the unit "Increasing Your Teenager's Self-Esteem," using the main index entry "self-esteem."
18. Create a main index entry for "communication," with subentries for "helping," and "hindering." Find at least one place in the workbook where these entries and subentries would be appropriate, and mark the text accordingly.
19. Create an index entry cross-reference "teen. See teenager."
20. Create an "Index" heading at the end of the document with the BookHeading style, and then compile the index below the heading.
21. Add the following comments to the document:
    a. After the phrase "six simple steps" in the paragraph below the "Helping Good Communication" heading: "There are only 5 steps listed here. Are we missing a step?"

b. After the second sentence in number 5 below the "Hindering Good Communication" heading: "Rewrite this sentence to fix agreement of pronouns (his or her perspective, or your teenager's perspective)?"

22. Update the fields because the page numbers for headings and index entries might have changed since you compiled the table of contents and index.
23. Save the document, preview and print the document including the comments, and then close any open files.

Case 3. Policies and Procedures Manual for Zeke's Comedy Club Cari Kali is manager of Zeke's Comedy Club in Syracuse, New York. Cari has written most of a *Policies and Procedures Manual* that outlines the responsibilities for all the club's employees. You will help her format and organize the manual.

1. If necessary, start Word and make sure your Data Disk is in the appropriate drive. Open the file **ComClub** from the **Cases** folder in the Tutorial.10 folder on your Data Disk, and save it as **Comedy Club Manual**.
2. Create a subdocument from each section of the document that begins with a Heading-1 style.
3. **Explore** Add automatic numbering to all the headings, such that level-1 headings have the style "1. History of the Club," level-2 headings have the style "2.1. Meetings," and level-3 headings have the style "3.1.1. Pre-Show Duties."
4. Modify the level-1 headings so each begins on a new page.
5. Set the document to print two-sided with a ½-inch gutter.
6. **Explore** Create headers for all pages except the title page. For even-numbered pages, place the page number at the left margin and the document title at the right margin. For odd-numbered pages, place the page number at the right margin and Heading 1 at the left margin. Make all header text 10-point, bold Arial.
7. Number all pages consecutively, beginning with page 1 after the title page.
8. Merge the second and third subdocuments into one.
9. Insert the following comments into the document as indicated:
   a. At the end of the second paragraph below "History of the Club": "Should we mention that most of our customers are Syracuse University and Colgate College students?"
   b. At the end of the bulleted list in "Schedules" (a level-2 heading): "Should we give a more detailed description of what our employees should wear?"
10. **Explore** Protect this document to track changes, using the password "KeepOut." Save the document, and then close it.
11. Open a new, blank document. Open the User Information in the Options dialog box, carefully write down the name and initials of the person listed, and then change them to "Cari Kali" and "CK."
12. Make sure the revision colors are set to "By Author," close the blank document (do not save changes if asked), and then open the master document.
13. **Explore** Try to turn off revisions without using the password. As you can see, you must use the password to make edits without using revision marks, although you can hide the revision marks.
14. Replace every occurrence of "ZCC" with "Zeke's Comedy Club."
15. In the first sentence of the Introduction, change the phrase "This manual has been prepared" to "We have prepared this manual."
16. Below "Employee's Manual" on the title page, insert three blank lines and then the phrase "Prepared by [*your name*]" in Normal style, centered between the left and right margins.

17. Save the master document, close it, and then open the **History of the Club** subdocument.
18. Delete the last paragraph, and insert a comment at the end of the deleted paragraph that reads "I don't think this paragraph is part of the club's history."
19. Save the subdocument, and then close it.
20. *Explore* Open the master document and change the User Information name from Cari Kali back to its original name. Turn off the Track Changes feature. Make sure you use the correct password.
21. Review the revisions in the master document. Accept the three suggested revisions, but reject any others.
22. Create a 3-D graphic that surrounds the title on the title page. Use the Double Wave AutoShape in the Stars and Banners section. Change the line to 6-point Dark Blue, and then apply 3-D-Style 1. Set the Fill Color to No Fill.
23. Create a "Table of Contents" heading with the Subtitle style three lines below the Introduction text, and then compile a table of contents below the new heading.
24. Create and format an "Index" heading in the same style at the end of the document.
25. *Explore* Mark at least 10 index entries, of which at least one must include subentries and one must be a cross-reference.
26. Make sure nonprinting characters are not visible, and then compile the index.
27. Make sure Word will update fields when you print. Save the document, preview and print it, and then close any open files.

Case 4. Preparing an Instruction Booklet Your instructor will divide your class into teams of three to six students and appoint a team leader or have each team select one. Each team will collaborate to prepare an instruction booklet. You can select from any of the following topics:

- How to use Microsoft Word to prepare essays and reports
- How to find a job in a specific field (such as advertising, business management, or secretarial science)
- How to improve your grades with less study
- How to purchase a computer system (including both hardware and software)
- How to enjoy recreation and entertainment in your area

The team leader will do the following:

1. Assign each team member a chapter to write for the instruction booklet. Coordinate topics for each chapter.
2. Ask each team member to protect his or her completed document for revisions (without a password), and pass a copy of the file to another team member who should then add edits and comments, and then save a new version of the file with the description: "Edits and Comments made by *name.*" (Each team member should replace "name" with his or her first and last name.)
3. Collect the edited chapters.
4. Prepare a title page with a 3-D graphic, write a brief preface, and set up headings for the table of contents and for the index.
5. Set up the document for two-sided printing.
6. Create appropriate headers or footers for the odd and even pages. Make sure you include page numbers, the document name, and chapter names.
7. Mark index entries in the preface.
8. Insert all the chapters into the document with the title page and preface as subdocuments.

9. Review the edits from within the master document, and decide which revisions to accept and which to reject.
10. Compile the table of contents and the index.
11. Save the document, and then preview and print it.
12. Print a list of all the comments.
13. Distribute a copy of the final master document file along with all its subdocument files to each team member.

Each team member (other than the team leader) will do the following:

1. Write a chapter that is at least two (single-spaced) pages long.
2. Begin the chapter with a level-1 heading, and include one or more level-2 and level-3 headings, if appropriate.
3. Mark index entries for all appropriate words and phrases.
4. Include at least two main entries with subentries in the index; include at least two cross-references in the index.
5. Include at least one figure in the chapter. The figure can be a graph, chart, table, or picture such as clip art.
6. Create a caption with automatic double numbering for each figure in the chapter.
7. Add at least one cross-reference to a figure within the text.
8. Save the chapter to a disk, and give the disk to a team member as assigned by the team leader.
9. Edit the document from another member of the team while tracking changes. Make at least five changes to the document.
10. Include at least three comments in the document you are editing.
11. Save a new version of the edited document with the description "Edits and Comments made by *name*." (Be sure to replace "name" with your first and last name.)
12. Repeat Steps 10 through 12 for another document. Then give the file to your team leader to insert into the master document.
13. Get a copy of the final master document file along with all its subdocument files from your team leader.
14. Make sure your team leader submits a copy of the master document to your instructor.

QUICK CHECK ANSWERS

Session 10.1

1. **a.** Word document divided into several smaller, individual files, to help you organize and maintain a lengthy document.
   b. One of several small, separate files that are part of a master document
   c. Divide one subdocument into two subdocument files.
   d. Combine two adjacent subdocuments into one subdocument.
   e. Convert the text of a subdocument into the text of the master document.
   f. The last line of a paragraph appearing alone at the top of a page.
   g. The first line of a paragraph appearing alone at the bottom of a page.

2. Consistent formatting elements; accurate numbering; accurate cross-referencing; complete table of contents and index; faster editing.
3. False
4. Convert an existing document into a master document, and then divide it into subdocuments using built-in heading styles; insert existing disk files into a Word document.
5. When one subdocument gets too long, or so several people can work on it.
6. When the subdocuments are very short or when one person is writing or editing both subdocuments.
7. A hyphen that won't allow the word or phrase it connects to break between two lines. A space that won't allow the words on either side to break between two lines. When you want to keep the two words on the same line of text.

Session 10.2

1. Open the Bullets and Numbering dialog box, select the desired heading numbering style on the Outline Numbered tab, click Customize, and select the desired numbering form.
2. Automatic sequential numbering; numbering across subdocuments; consistent numbering style.
3. Table or figure numbers where the first number indicates the chapter number and the second indicates the table or figure number within that chapter. Select table or figure from the Label list box, select the Caption option on the Insert menu, set label to type of object, number the table or figure, and click the Include chapter number check box to select it.
4. Select Cross-reference on the Insert menu, and select the reference type.
5. Marks text you delete and add; marks two authors' revisions in different colors.
6. So that no one can make revisions without your knowledge.
7. Notes written from one writer or editor to another that are not part of the printed document; to allow communication within a workgroup.
8. By the color assigned to that author. By the initials of the author of the comment.
9. Before printing, select Comments from the Print what list in the Print dialog box.

Session 10.3

1. To number front matter in a different format from the rest of the document.
2. Change the Number format in the Page Numbers dialog box.
3. An extra blank space on the side of each page where the pages are bound together. To allow space for binding a document with pages printed back-to-back.
4. Insert a Style Reference field to the chapter title in the footnotes.
5. Click the Drawing button on the Standard toolbar, draw an object, click the 3-D button on the Drawing toolbar, and specify the features of the 3-D object.
6. Select the paragraphs, select Sort from the Tables menu, specify the type of sort and specify other desired features, and click OK.
7. Paragraph format in which the first line of the paragraph is flush with the left margin but the other lines are indented.
8. Insert an Index mark using the Mark Entry feature on the Index tab.
9. To tell Word to generate the index from the marked entries at a certain location. Select the index and press the F9 key.

OBJECTIVES

In this case you will:

- Use mail merge to create a form letter
- Insert, resize, and position a graphic
- Insert and format a Word date field
- Create a title using WordArt
- Format text into newspaper-style columns
- Add paragraph borders
- Change font, size, effects, colors, and underlines
- Add a watermark
- Create a style

CREATING A FORM LETTER AND A MENU FOR DELI DELIGHT

CASE

Deli Delight

Serrita Young owns Deli Delight, a popular take-out restaurant that serves breakfast and lunch to workers in Center City, California. The restaurant also provides catering services for area corporate functions. Serrita's business has done well, and she is opening a second Deli Delight in another part of the city.

Serrita wants to advertise the opening of this new restaurant to corporations located near it by sending a cover letter and new Deli Delight corporate menu to the human resources manager of these selected companies. She has written the cover letter and compiled the text of the menu. Although Serrita is a financial whiz and culinary genius, she lacks the computer skills necessary to finalize both marketing items. She asks you to use her text files to produce the form letter shown in Figure 1 and a menu similar to the one shown in Figure 2.

Figure 1 DELI DELIGHT FORM LETTER

564 Broad Street (555-1673)
1200 SW Third Avenue (555-1231)

25-May-01

«FirstName»«LastName»
«Company»
«Address1»
Center City, CA 94115

Dear «FirstName»«LastName»

Six years ago I was the new, proud owner of Deli Delight, a take-out restaurant that specializes in serving the business crowd in Center City. Today I'm pleased to announce the opening of another Deli Delight in the city. I hope this new location will increase the convenience of obtaining catered meals for corporate functions at «Company».

Enclosed please find a sample of our menu items. We do, however, have many more options available and will be pleased to put together a custom menu for you.

Do take advantage of our offer for a complimentary Breakfast Buffet order for 10. I think you and your taste buds will be pleased with our food!

Sincerely yours,

Serrita Young
President

1. If necessary, start Word and make sure your Data Disk is in the appropriate drive and nonprinting characters are displayed. Open the file **DeliLett** from the AddCases folder on your Data Disk, and then save it as **Deli Delight Promotion**.
2. Begin to create a mail merge using the Deli Delight Promotion document as the main document.
3. Create Form Letters using the Active Window as the main document.
4. Open the file **DeliData** from the AddCases folder on your Data Disk as the data source for the mail merge.
5. Switch to the Deli Delight Promotion main document so you can edit it.
6. At the top of the document, insert the Deli Delight logo (DeliLogo.tif) from the AddCases folder on your Data Disk. Center the picture and scale its height and width to 80%.

7. Type the two Deli Delight addresses and phone numbers each on their own lines: "563 Broad Street (555-1673)" on one line and "1200 SW Third Avenue (555-1231)" on the next line.
8. Format the two address lines as 14-point Brush Script MT, and then center the lines.
9. Press the Enter key twice, set the text to Align left, and then insert a Word date field in the "25-May-99" format.
10. Press the Enter key twice, and then insert the merge codes for the FirstName and LastName fields. Remember to leave a space between the codes. Press the Enter key.

Figure 2 COMPLETED DELI DELIGHT CORPORATE LETTER

Now serving Center City at two locations:
563 Broad Street (555-1673)
1200 SW Third Avenue (555-1231)

We cater breakfast, lunch, and afternoon snacks, from 7:00 A.M. to 4:30 P.M., Monday through Friday. You can order the following menu items as is, or we would be pleased to work with you to create a custom menu that fits your dining needs.

Just Coffee Your choice of three types of regular, decaffeinated, and gourmet coffee. Tea also included upon request. $1.50 per person.

Breakfast Buffet Assorted muffins, croissants, bagels and cream cheese, plus orange juice, coffee, and tea. $3.00 per person.

Breakfast Bonanza Fresh fruit, Egg McDeli's, muffins, croissants, orange juice, grapefruit juice, gourmet coffee, and teas. $4.95 per person.

Delite Lunch Garden salad, choice of pasta salad, assorted muffins, bottled water. $4.95 per person.

Lunch Munch Choice of two deli salads, plus turkey and tuna salad sandwiches, tortilla chips, and beverages. $5.95 per person.

Lotsa Lunch Variety of hearty deli sandwiches with pickles, potato salad, oversized oatmeal and chocolate chip cookies, and choice of beverages. $6.50 per person.

Just Desserts Assorted oversized cookies and brownies, guaranteed to make those afternoon meetings more lively. $2.95 per person.

*We provide cups, plates, napkins, utensils, and appropriate condiments with all orders.

Call us today to receive a complimentary Breakfast Buffet for 10!

11. Insert the merge field code for the Company field, press the Enter key, insert the merge field code for the Address1 field, and then press the Enter key.
12. Type "Center City, CA 94115," and then press the Enter key twice.
13. Type "Dear," and then insert the FirstName and LastName merge fields followed by a colon (:). Remember to add spaces and a hard return to the line as needed.
14. Replace the phrase "your company" at the end of the first paragraph with the Company merge code, and save the document.
15. Merge to a new document the Deli Delight Promotion main document with the data source.
16. Save the merged document as Deli Delight Letters to the AddCases folder on your Data Disk.
17. Print the last letter of the merged document, and then close all open files.
18. Open the file DeliMenu from the AddCases folder on your Data Disk, and save it to the disk as DeliCorporate Menu.
19. Using WordArt, create and insert the title "Deli Delight." (*Hint:* The title shown in Figure 2 uses the WordArt style in row 3, column 2 with the Bauhaus 93 font (your font might have to be different), and the fill and line colors changed to blue.) Format the WordArt and text below it as shown in Figure 2.
20. Format the menu items (from "Just Coffee" to "We provide cups, plates, ...") into newspaper-style columns. Set the normal style to 12-point Arial.
21. Add a rule, using the line style of your choice, to the top and bottom of the menu section.
22. Format the paragraph of each menu item as a hanging indent by 0.15 inch, and format the asterisk item to a hanging indent by 0.1-inch.
23. Using a style, format the titles of the menu items, "Just Coffee," "Breakfast Buffet," "Breakfast Bonanza," "Delite Lunch," "Lunch Munch," "Lotsa Lunch," and "Just Desserts," using the font, size, style, color, effects, underlines, character spacing, and so forth, of your choice. Be creative!
24. Using the font, size, style, and color of your choice, reformat the last line, "Call us today to receive a complimentary Breakfast Buffet for 10!" in an attractive manner.
25. Add a watermark to the menu, using the Deli Delight logo (Logo.tif) from the AddCases folder on your Data Disk as the watermark graphic. (*Hint:* After inserting the file, open the Format Picture dialog box, click the Picture tab, click the Color list arrow in the Image control section, and then click Watermark. Make sure the Wrapping style is set to None. Position the watermark so that it is centered behind the menu items.)
26. Save and print the menu, and then close any open documents.

OBJECTIVES

In this case you will:

- Change font and sizes
- Find and replace text, and insert special characters
- Convert text to a table, insert a column, delete a row, sort a table, center the table, and change row height
- Copy and paste text between documents
- Sort table rows
- Create and modify a bulleted list
- Format text into columns
- Move tab stops, and add a leader
- Modify and apply a style
- Insert a footer
- Run a spelling and grammar check

CREATING A SPRING SUBSCRIPTION FLYER FOR CITY PLAYHOUSE

CASE

City Playhouse

Danny Washington is the new owner and director of City Playhouse, the performing arts center (previously called Plaza Playhouse) in Greenville, South Carolina. Danny has implemented many needed renovations to the performing arts center, but now he needs to increase the center's revenues to pay for these improvements. He hopes to increase ticket sales by offering subscriptions to each season's performances. These subscriptions will offer discounts on the cost of the performances, and Danny believes that the savings will encourage more people to purchase tickets for an entire season and attend the plays.

Danny has begun to prepare a flyer to announce the subscription prices and spring season schedule of plays. However, he is too busy catering to demanding actors and therefore has asked you to complete the flyer so that it looks like the one shown in Figure 3.

Figure 3 COMPLETED CITY PLAYHOUSE SPRING FLYER

City Playhouse is pleased to announce its spring season of scheduled performances. This season, we offer an exciting variety of old favorites and recant Broadway hits:

- *A Streetcar Named Desire* (March 3–8)
- *Noises Off* (March 17–22)
- *The Heiress* (April 2–9)
- *Three Tall Women* (April 16–22)
- *Much Ado About Nothing* (May 4–11)
- *Nine Degrees of Separation* (May 19–24)
- *Nunsense* (June 3–9)
- *Phantom of the Opera* (June 20–27)

Guest performers include Tom Jones in Phantom of the Opera, Deirdre Hall in The Heiress, and Lyle Waggoner in Noises Off.

Subscription Information

Purchase tickets to all shows and receive our subscription rate. Bring a friend and save even more. Compare our subscription rates to non-subscription rates below:

Subscription	Seating Area	Non-Subscription Ticket Price	Subscription Price for One Person	Subscription Price for Two People
Popular	Balcony	$200	$180	$330
Acclaimed	Area C	$240	$210	$380
Nominated	Area B	$320	$280	$500
Award	Area A	$400	$350	$620

Group sales are also available. Seats for each subscription will be assigned on a first come basis.

How to Order

You can purchase your City Playhouse subscription with a credit card by calling (803) 555-3429, or by completing and mailing the following order form. City Playhouse accepts major credit cards—American Express, Discover, MasterCard, and Visa—and local personal checks.

✂ ....

Send your completed Order Form to:
City Playhouse
3411 Broadway
Greenville, SC 29634

Type and Number of Subscriptions ____________________

Name ____________________ Phone Number (____) ________

Address____________________

Plaza ____________ State ____ ZIP Code ______

Method of Payment (circle one): Check Credit Card: AE DS MC Visa

Credit Card Billing Address (if different from above) ____________________

Exp. Date ________

Additional 10% Discount Available for Orders Received by January 15!

1. If necessary, start Word and make sure your Data Disk is in the appropriate drive and nonprinting characters are displayed. Open the file **Flyer** from the AddCases folder on your Data Disk, and then save it as **Spring Subscription Flyer**.
2. Find and replace every instance of "Plaza Playhouse" with "City Playhouse." Make sure the Match Case option is selected.
3. Modify the Heading 1 style to 14-point Technical bold here and elsewhere in this document as requested, and apply it to the "Subscription Information" and to "How to Order" lines of text.
4. Find the list that begins with "Subscription" (around the fourth line of the document), and select that line and the next five or six lines (the last line begins with the word "Popular").
5. Convert the selected text into a table, using the predefined Grid 1 AutoFormat.
6. Format the first row of cells as 10-point Technical bold, and then center the text in that row both horizontally and vertically.
7. Add a Gray-20% fill to the first row of cells.

8. Insert a new column to the right of "Subscription Price for One Person"; label that column "Subscription Price for Two People."
9. Open the file Prices from the Cases folder on your Student Disk, and read Danny's memo.
10. Copy the contents of the second column of the table, and paste the text into the table column you just inserted in the Spring Subscription Flyer document.
11. Delete the "Basic" row from the table. Make sure that the height of the remaining rows is at least 16 points.
12. Sort the rows of the table in ascending order by ticket price. (*Hint:* You can use any of the price columns for this sort.)
13. Change the alignment of rows 2 through 5 to Center.
14. Adjust the column widths as necessary to make the table attractive and readable.
15. Make sure 1½-point border lines appear around the outside of the table.
16. Change the paragraph below the "How to Order" heading to 2 equal columns, but change the spacing between them to 0.25 inch.
17. Scroll until you see the sentence "City Playhouse is pleased to announce...." Select the words "City Playhouse" in that sentence, and change the font to 14-point Technical bold.
18. Move the paragraph beginning with "City Playhouse," the list of plays following it, and the paragraph after the list to the top of the flyer.
19. Format the list of plays as a bulleted list, and then change each bullet symbol to a right-pointing finger, as shown in Figure 3. (*Hint:* Select the bulleted list text, click Format on the menu bar, click Bullets and Numbering, click the Bulleted tab, and then click the Customize button. In the Customize Bulleted List dialog box, click the Bullet button to open the Symbol dialog box, click the Font list arrow, click Wingdings, click the right-pointing finger symbol [row 2, column 11] to select it, click the OK button to close the Symbol dialog box, and then click the OK button in the Customize Bulleted List dialog box.)
20. Increase the indent of the bulleted list so the bullets start at the ½-inch mark.
21. Change all the play names in the bulleted list to italic. In the paragraph below the bulleted list, also change the three play names to italic.
22. In the How to Order section, insert a nonbreaking hyphen and a nonbreaking space in the phone number to keep the number on one line.
23. Change the paragraph below the "How to Order" heading to one column, and then type "City Playhouse" between the words "your" and "subscription" to extend the first line to the margin.
24. In the same section, change the parentheses around the types of credit cards to em dashes. Rename any spaces before or after the em dashes.
25. Change the City Playhouse name and address in the order form to 12-point Technical bold.
26. Change the tab stops in the Method of Payment line to 2.31 inch, 3.13 inch, 4 inch, 4.38 inch, 4.75 inch, and 5.13 inch. (*Hint:* Use the Tabs dialog box to clear and then set new left-aligned tabstops, or drag the tabstops while holding down the Alt key.)
27. Add a dotted-line leader to the tabstop on the line above the order form with the scissors symbol, as shown in Figure 3. The symbol font Wingdings contains the desired symbol.
28. Change the Page Setup options for the top and bottom margins for the flyer to 0.7 inch to keep it on one page.
29. Create a footer that is centered, prints in 12-point Technical bold, and reads "Additional 10% Discount Available for Orders Received by January 15!"; add a 1 ½-point rule above the footer text.
30. Run a spelling and grammar check on the flyer, and accept those changes that concern spelling and subject-verb agreement.
31. Save and print the flyer, and then close any open documents.

OBJECTIVES

In this case you will:

- Create and use a document template
- Define and modify styles within the template
- Create and insert an AutoText entry
- Customize a toolbar with a button
- Record an AutoNew Macro
- Automate a document using field codes
- Import a Word document
- Create and modify a Microsoft Graph chart

CREATING A DOCUMENT TEMPLATE FOR ERNEST, ARTHUR, AND DELAND

CASE

Ernest, Arthur, and Deland

Alex Stedman is a newly hired associate at the CPA firm of Ernest, Arthur, and Deland. The Chicago-based company wants to increase their client base, and Alex has been asked to market the firm's services to large Midwestern corporations.

After Alex meets with representatives from these companies, he will send a follow-up letter to each person summarizing the benefits of working with Ernest, Arthur, and Deland; the company's specific needs; and Ernest, Arthur, and Deland's proposed solutions. Because the follow-up letters will be similar for each company, and because Alex wants to be sure that each follow-up letter includes all the necessary information, he decides to create a template for the follow-up letters. He asks you to help him create the template, which is shown in Figure 4. Alex then wants you to use the template to create the first follow-up letter, which is shown in Figure 5.

Figure 4 COMPLETED NEW CLIENT FOLLOW-UP LETTER TEMPLATE

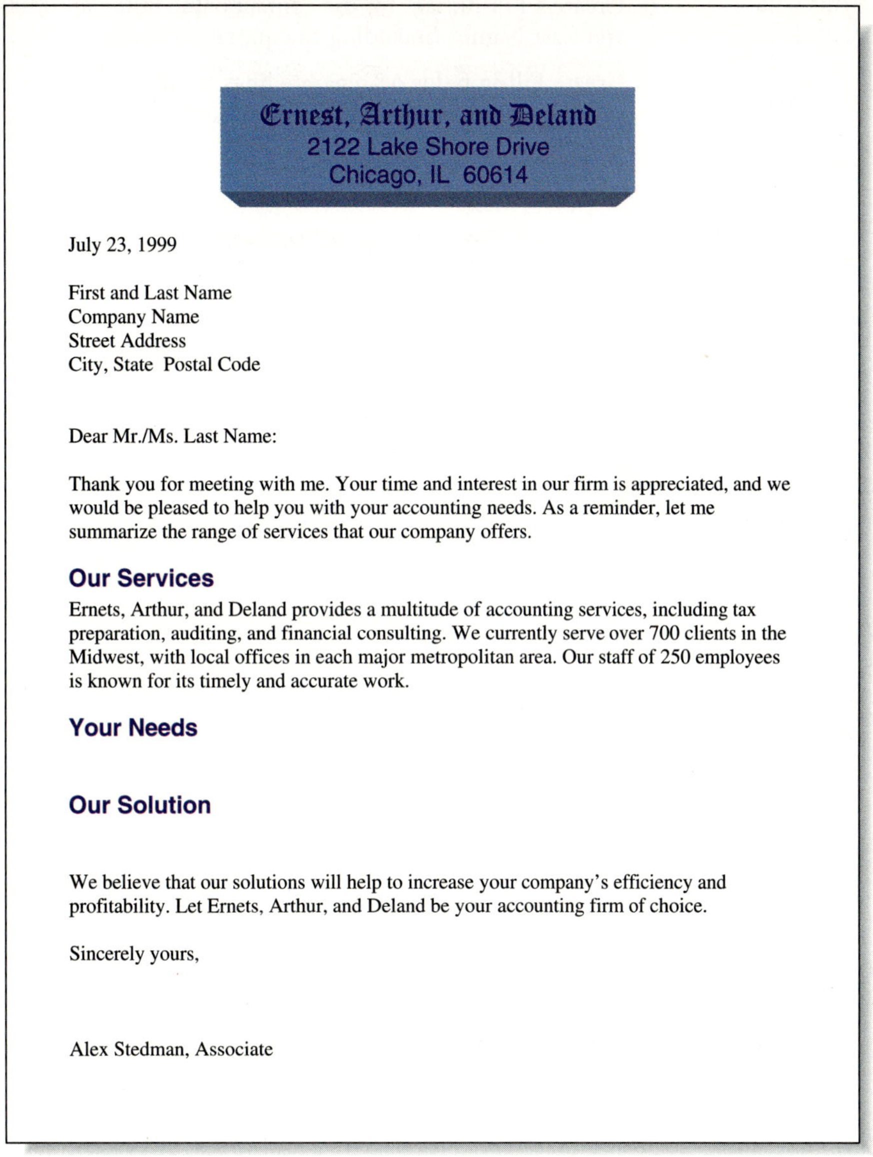

Ernest, Arthur, and Deland
2122 Lake Shore Drive
Chicago, IL 60614

July 23, 1999

First and Last Name
Company Name
Street Address
City, State Postal Code

Dear Mr./Ms. Last Name:

Thank you for meeting with me. Your time and interest in our firm is appreciated, and we would be pleased to help you with your accounting needs. As a reminder, let me summarize the range of services that our company offers.

Our Services

Ernets, Arthur, and Deland provides a multitude of accounting services, including tax preparation, auditing, and financial consulting. We currently serve over 700 clients in the Midwest, with local offices in each major metropolitan area. Our staff of 250 employees is known for its timely and accurate work.

Your Needs

Our Solution

We believe that our solutions will help to increase your company's efficiency and profitability. Let Ernets, Arthur, and Deland be your accounting firm of choice.

Sincerely yours,

Alex Stedman, Associate

1. If necessary, start Word and make sure your Data Disk is in the appropriate drive and nonprinting characters are displayed. Open the file **Template** from the AddCases folder on your Data Disk, and then save it as a template to your Data Disk with the filename **New Client Follow-up**.
2. Change the company name to 18-point, Dark Blue, Old English Text (or a similar font such as Cloister Black, Engravers, Old Eng, Marriage D, or Black letter), and change the two address lines to 14-point, Dark Blue, Arial.
3. Cut and paste the letterhead text you just formatted into a text box you create at the top of the letter. Convert the text box to a 3-D Graphic in the style of your choice. Change the fill color to Pale Blue, make sure the Wrapping style is set to "In front of text" and the horizontal alignment is set to center. Position the text box about ¾ inch from the top of the page. Insert hard returns so there are two blank lines between the text box and the main body text.
4. At the second blank paragraph marker below the textbox, insert a Word date field, using the format "MMMM d, yyyy."

5. Insert two hard returns.
6. Create a Fill-in field for the contact name in the address. Enter the text "First and Last Name" (including the quotation marks) as the Fill-in field prompt.
7. Create Fill-in fields on separate lines for the rest of the address. Enter the text "Company Name," "Address," and "City, State Postal Code" as the prompts.
8. Insert two hard returns.

Figure 5 COMPLETED FOLLOW-UP LETTER

Ernest, Arthur, and Deland
2122 Lake Shore Drive
Chicago, IL 60614

August 7, 2001

Lennie Jarvis
Pierce Pharmaceuticals
442 Main Street
Minneapolis, MN 55403

Dear Mr. Jarvis:

Thank you for meeting with me. Your time and interest in our firm is appreciated, and we would be pleased to help you with your accounting needs. As a reminder, let me summarize the range of services that our company offers.

Our Services

Ernets, Arthur, and Deland provides a multitude of accounting services, including tax preparation, auditing, and financial consulting. We currently serve over 700 clients in the Midwest, with local offices in each major metropolitan area. Our staff of 250 employees is known for its timely and accurate work.

Your Needs

During our conversation, you asked several tax-specific questions about how Pierce Pharmaceuticals can improve its tax base. You mentioned that your company also needs a new accounting information system that will automate payroll. Finally, you indicated that Pierce Pharmaceuticals would like to improve current internal audit procedures.

Our Solution

Our tax accountants will answer all your tax-specific questions as well as suggest ways to cut your taxes. The following chart shows how the average tax base of our clients has decreased each year:

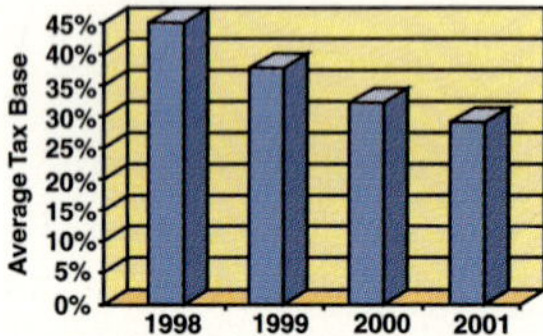

Ernets, Arthur, and Deland has already assisted several clients in planning, designing, and implementing custom accounting information systems. We also offer training classes to demonstrate the system to all appropriate employees. Further, Ernets, Arthur, and Deland routinely provides clients with an in-depth review of internal audit procedures. After we review the procedures and make recommendations, we will follow up monthly for the next year to ensure complete satisfaction.

We believe that our solutions will help to increase your company's efficiency and profitability. Let Ernets, Arthur, and Deland be your accounting firm of choice.

Sincerely yours,

Alex Stedman, Associate

9. Type "Dear," and insert a space; insert a Fill-in field with the prompt "Mr./Ms. Last Name"; then type a colon to create the salutation for the letter. Insert a hard return, if necessary, to leave a double space between the salutation and the first line of the letter.
10. Record an AutoNew macro for only this template that moves the insertion point to the blank line below the Your Needs heading. (*Hint*:Have the macro search for "Your Needs" and then move down a line.)

11. Modify the Heading-1 style to Dark Blue, bold, 13-point Arial. Apply the style to the "Our Services," "Your Needs," and "Our Solution" headings.
12. Create an AutoText entry in only this template for "Ernest, Arthur, and Deland" that uses "ead" as the abbreviation.
13. Use the AutoText entry to replace "Our company" in the Our Services section and "our company" in the Our Solution section.
14. Customize a toolbar by replacing the Insert Hyperlink button on the Standard toolbar with a button for the AutoText entry you just created that displays the pencil icon.
15. Save the New Client Follow-up template to your Student Disk, and then print it.
16. Save the New Client Follow-up template in the Templates folder on your computer, and then close the template.
17. Start a new document using the New Client Followup template.
18. At the prompts for the Fill-in fields, type "Lennie Jarvis," "Pierce Pharmaceuticals," "442 Main Street," "Minneapolis, MN 55403" (insert two spaces between the city and postal code), and "Mr. Jarvis."
19. Insert the Notes file from the AddCases folder on your Data Disk in the blank line beneath the "Your Needs" heading.
20. Move the second paragraph of the inserted file below the "Our Solution" heading.
21. Select the text "(insert chart)." (including the period) in the Our Solution section, and then insert two hard returns.
22. Create a Microsoft Graph chart on the new blank line. Clear the sample data from the datasheet, and enter the values 44%, 33%, 32%, and 29% for the years 1998, 1999, 2000, and 2001 respectively.
23. Click the series 1 Legend Key to select it, and then press the Delete key to erase it.
24. Click chart on the menu bar, click chart options, click the titles tab, and add "average tax base" as the value "z" axis.
25. Select the text box containing the value Axis title, right click it, and then click Format Axis title. Change the Alignment Orientation to 90 degrees. Deselect the chart.
26. Double-click anywhere on the chart to open the datasheet, change cell B1 (the1999 figure) to 38%, and then return to the Word document. Notice how the chart has changed to reflect the new value for 1999.
27. Use the AutoText button on the customized Standard toolbar you created earlier to change "Our company" and "Our firm" in the paragraph below the "Our Solution" heading to Ernest, Arthur, and Deland. Add "Further" (including the comma) before "Ernest, Arthur, and Deland routinely provides...."
28. Delete any extraneous hard returns, and change the top and bottom margins to 0.5 inch, and change the left and right margins to 0.95 inch. Make other adjustments as needed so the letter fits all on one page.
29. Save the completed letter as Lennie Jarvis to your Data Disk, print the letter, and then close it.
30. Delete the New Client Follow-up template from your template folder.

OBJECTIVES

In this case you will:

- Change the page orientation
- Design and create an on-screen form
- Merge and split cells and change column widths in a table
- Set borders; change font styles and colors; and shade cells in a form table
- Insert form fields for text, drop-down lists, and check boxes
- Perform automatic calculations in an on-screen form

CREATING AN ON-SCREEN FORM

CASE

Run Rampant Magazine

Lucy Wu is the Circulation Manager at *Run Rampant*, a monthly magazine that features articles written for the recreational runner, as well as reviews of the latest running wear and a calendar of running events by region. Lucy recently approved a large-scale marketing campaign that will advertise the magazine in athletic stores nationwide. She believes the campaign will increase the number of subscriptions to *Run Rampant*.

To help determine the success of the advertising campaign, Lucy wants you to create a new on-screen (computerized) subscription order form, similar to the one shown in Figure 7. This new form will help her determine whether advertising in athletic stores has resulted in new subscriptions to *Run Rampant* magazine. The form also will streamline the order-taking process.

Figure 6 SUBSCRIPTION ORDER FORM TEMPLATE

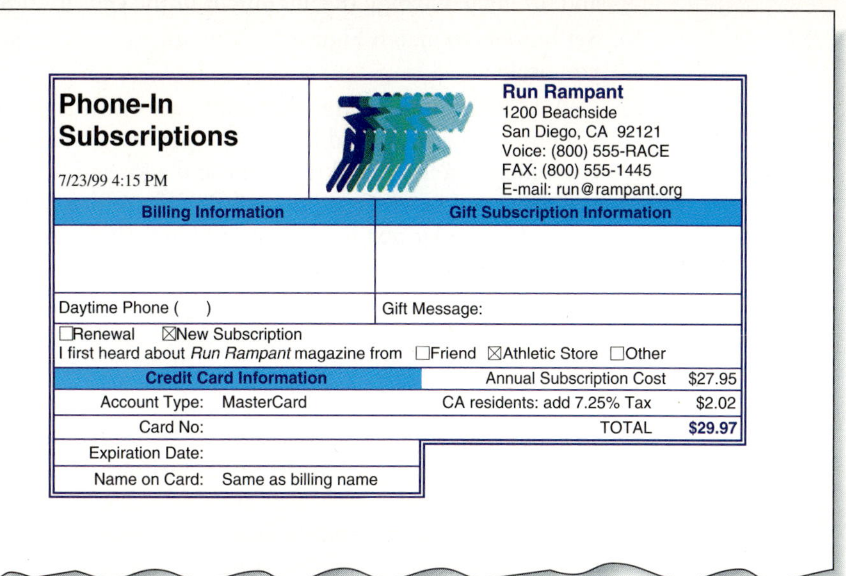

Phone-In Subscriptions 7/23/99 4:15 PM		Run Rampant 1200 Beachside San Diego, CA 92121 Voice: (800) 555-RACE FAX: (800) 555-1445 E-mail: run@rampant.org
Billing Information	Gift Subscription Information	
Daytime Phone ( )	Gift Message:	
☐Renewal ☒New Subscription I first heard about *Run Rampant* magazine from ☐Friend ☒Athletic Store ☐Other		
Credit Card Information	Annual Subscription Cost	$27.95
Account Type: MasterCard	CA residents: add 7.25% Tax	$2.02
Card No:	TOTAL	$29.97
Expiration Date:		
Name on Card: Same as billing name		

1. If necessary, start Word and make sure your Data Disk is in the appropriate drive and nonprinting characters are displayed. Open the file **Subscribe** from the AddCases folder on your Data Disk, and then save it as a template to your Data Disk with the filename **Run Rampant Subscription Form**.
2. Change the page setup from portrait orientation to landscape orientation.
3. Change the font of "Phone-In Subscriptions" in the first row of the on-screen form table to 20-point, bold Arial.
4. Move the insertion point after the phrase "Phone-In Subscriptions," press the Enter key twice, and then enter a Word date and time field in the "2/25/99 10:54 AM" format. Change the font of the field (and the blank lines above it) to 12-point, bold Arial.
5. In cell B1, insert the image file Running from the AddCases folder on your Data Disk, and then merge cell B1 with cell C1. Change the wrapping style of the picture to "In front of text."
6. Change the Running image size height to 1.05 inch and width to 1.5 inch. (*Hint:* If necessary, deselect the Lock aspect ration check box.)
7. Change the cell widths in just the first row to 2.5-inch, 1.75-inch, and 2.45-inch.
8. In what is now cell C1, change the font style of "Run Rampant" to 14-point, bold, blue Arial, and all the other text in C1 to 12-point Arial, normal.
9. Merge cell A2 with cell B2, and then merge the new cell B2 with cell C2. Do the same for rows 3 and 4. Delete any hard returns from these cells.
10. Format the "Billing Information" and "Gift Subscription Information" headings to 12-point, bold, and blue Arial. Center the text. Add a background shading of Turquoise.
11. Change the font of rows 4 through 10 to 12-point Arial.
12. Merge all the cells in row 5 as a single cell. Edit the text so that "Renewal" and "New Subscription" appear on one line, separated by four spaces.
13. Merge cell A6 with cell B6. Reformat the "Credit Card Information" cell to match the "Billing Information" and "Gift Subscription Information" cells.
14. Change the cell widths of row 6 to 3.66-inch, 2.34-inch, and 0.7-inch. Change the alignment of cells B6 and C6 to Right alignment.

15. Change the cell widths of rows 7 through 10 to 1.5-inch, 2.0-inch, 2.34-inch, and 0.7-inch. Change the alignment of the cells in these rows to right-justified.
16. Set borders to match Figure 6, although you can use any line style and weight you prefer.
17. Cell A3 will contain names and addresses of the subscriber. If the subscription is a gift, the name and address of the person ordering *Run Rampant* will be entered into cell A3, and the name and address of the person receiving the magazine will be entered into cell B3. Therefore, in cells A3 and B3, insert the necessary regular text form fields and include appropriate status bar prompts and help messages.
18. In cell A4 (Daytime Phone) replace the "with area code" text with a number text form field, and insert a regular text form field for the rest of the phone number. Insert a text form field for cell B4 (Gift Message). Include appropriate help text for all fields.
19. In cell A5, insert a check box form field with the default as unchecked before "Renewal" and a check-box form field with the default as checked before "New Subscription"; make sure there are four spaces between "Renewal" and the second check box. In the same cell, create a second line that reads "I first heard about *Run Rampant* magazine from: Friend Athletic Store Other." Insert check-box form fields with the default set to unchecked before "Friend," "Athletic Store," and "Other"; make sure there are four spaces on either side of the "Athletic Store" option. Use Figure 6 as a guide.
20. Insert a drop-down form field for the "Account Type" cell that includes VISA, MasterCard, American Express, and Discover as the list.
21. Insert a number form field with a maximum length of 16 in the cell immediately to the right of "Card No."
22. Insert a date form field in the cell immediately to the right of "Expiration Date" that uses the "09-99" format.
23. Insert a text form field in the cell immediately to the right of "Name on Card" that has "Same as billing name" as the default text.
24. Insert a number form field, in currency format, in the cell immediately to the right of "Annual Subscription Cost" that has "27.95" as the default amount.
25. In the cell immediately to the right of "Add 7.25% Tax," insert a calculation form field that will automatically multiply the subscription cost by 0.0725.
26. In the cell immediately to the right of "TOTAL," insert a calculation form field that will add the subscription cost and the sales tax. Change the "TOTAL" text to 12-point, blue, bold Arial.
27. Center vertically all the cells in the on-screen form table.
28. Change the alignment of cells B7 through B10 to Left alignment.
29. Protect your form, save and print it, and then save the Run Rampant Subscription Form template in the Templates folder on your computer.
30. Close the template, and start a new document based on the Run Rampant Subscription Form template.
31. Fill out the form as if you were ordering the magazine as a gift for a friend.Use a fictitious credit number.
32. Save the filled-in form as Test Subscription in the AddCases folder on your Data Disk, and then use the Fax Wizard to print fax and cover sheets to your default printer or route the file to your instructor.
33. Delete the Run Rampant Subscription Form template from the Templates folder on your computer.

E

F

K

L

M

Q

R

S

T

U

V

W

Z

TASK	PAGE #	RECOMMENDED METHOD
3D graphics, create	WD 10.45	Create and select object, click Drawing button, click 3D button on Drawing toolbar, select a 3D style
Action, redo	WD 2.11	Click
Action, undo	WD 2.11	Click
Author Field, insert	WD 8.30	Click Insert, click Field, click Document Information in Categories list, select Author in Field Names list, click OK
AutoMacro, create	WD 8.41	Record a macro in the normal way, but give the macro an AutoMacro name (AutoOpen, AutoClose, AutoNet, etc.), assign it to the desired template
AutoText, create	WD 8.14	Select text or graphics, click Insert, point to AutoText, click AutoText, enter name, select desired template, click Add button.
AutoText, insert	WD 8.16	Type name of AutoText entry, press F3 key
AutoText, print list of entries	WD 8.17	Click File, click Print, click Print what list arrow, click desired AutoText entry, click OK
Background, apply textured	WD 7.30	Change to Web layout view, open document, click Format, point to Background, click Fill Effects, click Texture tab, click texture, click OK
Bookmark, create	WD 7.23	Move insertion point to desired location, click Insert, click Bookmark, type bookmark name, click Add
Border, draw around page	WD 4.25	Click Format, click Borders and Shading, click Page Border tab, click Box, apply to Whole Document
Borders, draw or erase	WD 9.05	Click Tables and Borders button, specify a line weight, set Line Style to a solid or dashed line or to No Border, drag pointer along cell gridline(s)
Bullets, add to paragraphs	WD 2.25	Select paragraphs, click
Captions, create cross references	WD 10.24	Move insertion point to cross-reference location, type preceding text, click Insert, click Cross-reference, select reference type, click Insert button, and click Close button
Captions, create double-numbering	WD 10.22	Select table of figure, click Insert, click Caption, set Label type, click Numbering button, select Include Chapter Number checkbox, click OK
Catalog, create	WD 6.36	See "Telephone list, create"
Character, insert	WIN 98 2.6	Click where you want to insert the text, type the text
Character spacing, expand or condense	WD 5.34	Select text, click Format, click Font, click the Character Spacing tab, click the Spacing list arrow, click Expanded or Condensed, click OK
Check Box Form Field, insert	WD 9.31	Click Check Box Form Field button on Forms toolbar, click Form Field Options button, set options, click OK
Click and Type, enable	WD 5.31	Click Tools, click Options, click Edit tab, select the Enable click and type check box, click OK
Clip art, insert	WD 4.15	Click on Drawing toolbar, click Pictures tab, click the category you want, click the image you want, click

TASK	PAGE #	RECOMMENDED METHOD
Clipboard, erase contents of	WD 2.15	Click
Column break, insert	WD 4.25	Click Insert, click Break, click Column Break, click OK
Columns, balance	WD 4.24	Insert column break or click the end of the column, click Insert, click Break, click Continuous, click OK
Columns, format text in	WD 4.11	Select the text, click Format, click Columns, select the column style you want in the Presets section, click OK
Comments, find and view	WD 10.35	Click View, click Comments, click Edit, click Go To, select Comment, select reviewer, click Close button
Comments, insert	WD 10.33	Click Insert, click Comments, type the comment, click Close button
Comments, print	WD 10.37	Click File, click Print, click Print what list arrow, select Comments, click OK
Data source, attach	WD 6.09	Open Mail Merge Helper, click Get Data, click Create Data Source, remove and add field names as necessary, click OK, save the data source document
Data Source, create	WD 6.08	Click Tools, click Mail Merge, create or select main document, click Get Data, click Create Data Source, add or delete fields, click OK, and save source document
Data Source, filter	WD 6.29	Open main document, click on Mail Merge toolbar, click Query Options, click Filter Records tab, select field and comparison operator, type text to compare, click OK, click Close or Merge
Data Source, sort	WD 6.26	Open data source document, click in header row of desired sort column, click or on Database toolbar
Date Field, insert	WD 10.26	Click Insert, click Date and Time, select Update Automatically, select date style, click OK
Date field, insert	WD 6.18	Click Insert, click Date and Time, click a format, select the Update automatically check box, click OK
Date, insert current	WD 5.32	Click Insert, click Date and Time, click desired format, click OK
Date Text Form Fields, insert	WD 9.23	Click Text Form Field button on Forms toolbar, click Form Field Options button, click Type list arrow, select Date, click Date Format, click OK twice
Desktop, access	WIN 98 1.14	Click on the Quick Launch toolbar
Disk, copy	WIN 98 2.25	See Reference Window: Copying a Disk
Disk, format	WIN 98 2.2	Open My Computer, right-click 3½ Floppy (A:), click Format, click Start
Document, browse by heading	WD 5.40	Click , click , click or
Document, close	WD 1.30	If more than one document is open, click on title bar; if only one document is open, click on menu bar
Document, create new	WD 1.13	Click

TASK	PAGE #	RECOMMENDED METHOD
Document map, view	WD 7.28	Click
Document, open	WD 2.02	Click , select drive and folder, click the filename, click OK
Document, preview	WD 1.26	Click
Document, print	WD 1.27	Click , or click File, click Print, specify pages or number of copies, click OK
Document, save	WD 1.17	Click
Document, save with new name	WD 2.05	Click File, click Save As, select drive and folder, enter new filename, click Save
Drop cap, insert	WD 4.20	Position insertion point in paragraph, click Format, click Drop Cap, select desired features, click OK
Drop-Down Form Field, insert	WD 9.29	Click Drop-Down Form Field button on Forms toolbar, click Form Field Options button, type item in Drop Down Item text box, click OK
Embedded object, modify	WD 7.09	Double-click object, use commands and tools of source program to modify object, click outside embedded object
Envelope, print	WD 1.29	Click Tools, click Envelopes and Labels, click Envelopes tab, type delivery and return addresses, click Print
Explorer windows, navigate	WIN 98 2.23	Click , , or
Field, edit	WD 8.27	Click field to edit, if necessary press Alt+F9 to view field code, change field information or switches
Field, insert	WD 8.26	Click Insert, click Field, click desired field, click OK
Field, update	WD 8.28	Click field code, press F9 key
Field code, view	WD 8.27	Press Alt+F9
File, copy	WIN 98 2.22	See Reference Window: Copying a File
File, delete	WIN 98 2.24	Right-click the file, click Delete
File, move	WIN 98 2.21	See Reference Window: Moving a File
File, open from My Computer	WIN 98 2.9	Open My Computer, open the window containing the file; in Web style, click the file; in Classic style, click the file then press Enter
File, print	WIN 98 2.10	Click
File, rename	WIN 98 2.24	See Reference Window: Renaming a File
File, save	WIN 98 2.7	Click
File extensions, hide	WIN 98 2.20	Open My Computer click View, click Folder Options, click View tab, make sure the Hide file extensions for known file types check box is checked, click OK
File Properties, add	WD 1.19	Click File, click Properties, click Summary tab, add desired information, click OK

TASK	PAGE #	RECOMMENDED METHOD
Fill-In Field, insert	WD 8.28	Click Insert, click Field, click Mail Merge, click Fill-in, click OK
Folder, create	WIN 98 2.21	See Reference Window: Creating a New Folder
Folder, create new	WD 5.04	Click File, click Save As, click , type folder name, click OK
Font, change	WD 2.27	Select text, click Font list arrow, click new font
Font size, change	WD 2.27	Select text, click Font Size list arrow, click new font size
Font style, change	WD 2.29	Select text, click B, I, or U
Footer, change for odd/even pages	WD 10.41	Click View, click Header and Footer, click Switch Between Header and Footer, click Show Next button, select Odd Page Footer, click Show Next button, click Even Page Footer
Footer, insert	WD 3.10	Click View, click Header and Footer, click , type footer text, click Close
Footnote, add	WD 5.27	Switch to Normal view, click footnote reference location, click Insert, click Footnote, select note type and numbering method, click OK
Form Fields, perform calculations	WD 9.34	Move insertion point to results cell, insert text form field, click Options, set Type to Calculations, type expression, set format, click OK
Format Painter, use	WD 2.24	Select text with desired format, double-click , click paragraphs you want to format, click
Graph, create	WD 8.49	Click Insert, point to Picture, click Chart, fill in datasheet, click outside chart to deselect it
Graphic, crop	WD 4.18	Click graphic, click on Picture toolbar, drag resize handle
Graphic, resize	WD 4.17	Click graphic, drag resize handle
Graphic, wrap text around	WD 4.19	Select graphic, then click on Picture toolbar and select option or click on Picture toolbar, click Layout tab, click Advanced, click Text Wrapping tab, select Wrapping style option, set Distance from text, click OK twice
Header, insert	WD 3.10	Click View, click Header and Footer, type header text, click Close
Headings, number	WD 10.18	Position insertion point in heading, click Format, click Bullets and Numbering, select heading style, click Customize to modify numbering style, click OK
Help, display topic from Contents tab	WIN 98 1.28	From Help, click the Contents tab, click until you see the topic you want, click ? to display topic
Help, display topic from Index tab	WIN 98 1.28	From Help, click the Index tab, scroll to locate topic, click topic, click Display
Help, get	WD 1.28	Click ? and type a question, click Search, click topic
Help, return to previous Help topic	WIN 98 1.30	Click
Help, start	WIN 98 1.27	Click Start, click Help

TASK	PAGE #	RECOMMENDED METHOD
Horizontal line, insert	WD 7.37	Click Format, click Borders and Shading, click Borders tab, click Horizontal Line, click a line style, click Insert clip button
Hyperlink, edit	WD 7.40	Right-click hyperlink text, point to Hyperlink, click Edit Hyperlink, edit filename or select a new file, click OK
Hyperlink, use	WD 7.24	Click blue underlined hyperlink; click [button] to return to original location
Hyperlink to another document, create	WD 7.25	Select hyperlink text, click [button], click Existing File or Web Page, locate target document, click OK
Hyperlink to same document, insert	WD 7.21	Insert bookmark at target location, select hyperlink text or graphic, click [button], click Place in This Document, click bookmark name, click OK twice
Hyphenation, change	WD 5.25	Click Tools, point to Language, click Hyphenation, enter size of Hyphenation Zone, set limit for consecutive hyphens, click Automatically hyphenate document, click OK
Index, compile	WD 10.53	Move insertion point to location of index, click Insert, click Index and Tables, click Index tab, set desired options, click OK
Index, create cross reference entries	WD 10.51	Click Insert, click Index and Tables, click Index tab, click Mark Entry button, click Cross-reference radio button, type cross-reference text, click Mark button
Index, create page range references	WD 10.52	Select range of pages, click Edit, click Bookmark, type name of bookmark, click Add button, click Page Range in Mark Index Entry dialog box, click Bookmark list arrow, click bookmark name, click Mark button
Index, mark entries	WD 10.47	Select entry, click Insert, click Index and Tables, click Index tab, click Mark Entry button, select Options, click Mark button
Index, mark subentries	WD 10.47	Click Insert, click Index and Tables, click Index tab, click Mark Entry button, type main index entry, press Tab, type subentry, click Mark button
Insertion point, move	WIN 98 2.5	Click the location in the document to which you want to move
Insertion point, move with Click and Type	WD 5.30	Move pointer to location where you want to insert text, a table or a graphic; double-click
Line spacing, change	WD 2.20	Select the text you want to change, then press CTRL+1 for single spacing, CTRL+5 for 1.5 line spacing, or CTRL+2 for double spacing
Link, update	WD 7.17	Open destination file, click Edit, click Links, select filename, click Update Now, click OK
List box, change option	WIN 98 1.24	Click [button], then click option you want in list that appears
Macro, edit	WD 8.40	Click Tools, point to Macros, click Macro, click name of macro, click Edit, edit macro, click Save, click Yes, click Close
Macro, record	WD 8.35	Double-click REC on status bar, type macro name, type description, click Record button, record keystrokes, click Stop button.

TASK	PAGE #	RECOMMENDED METHOD
Macro, run	WD 8.46	Click Tools, point to Macros, click Macro, click name of macro, click Run
Mail Merge, create	WD 6.23	Create main document with merge fields, create data source, attach data source to main document, click [button] or [button]
Mailing Labels, create	WD 6.31	Click [button], click Tools, click Mail Merge, click Create, click Mailing Labels, click Active Window, click Get Data, click Open Data Source, select source file, click Set Up Main Document, select label options, click OK, insert merge fields, click OK, click Merge twice
Main Document, create	WD 6.06	Click [button], click Tools, click Mail Merge, under Main Document, click Create, click Form Letters, click Active window, under Data Source, click Get Data, and create or open Data Source, click Close, add text and merge fields
Margins, change	WD 2.18	Click File, click Page Setup, click Margins tab, enter margin values, click OK
Master Document, create subdocument from	WD 10.12	Click Outline View button, select heading, click Create Subdocument button on Outlining toolbar
Master Document, insert subdocuments in	WD 10.06	Click Insert Subdocument button on Outlining toolbar, select or type document, click OK
Master Document, merge subdocuments	WD 10.10	Click master document view, click subdocument icon of first subdocument, hold Shift key while you click the subdocument icon of second (adjacent) subdocument, click Merge Subdocument button on Outlining toolbar
Master Document, remove subdocument	WD 10.12	Click subdocument icon of desired subdocument, click Remove Subdocument button on Outlining toolbar
Master Document, save existing file as	WD 10.05	Click Outline View button, click Master Document button on Outlining toolbar, click Save button
Master Document, split subdocument	WD 10.09	Click master Document view, select heading where you want to split, click Split Subdocument button on Outlining toolbar
Menu option, select	WIN 98 1.8	Click the menu option, or, if it is a submenu, point to it
Merge fields, insert in main document	WD 6.19	Click at field location in main document, click Insert Merge Field button on the Mail Merge toolbar, click a field name
Merged data, view in main document	WD 6.22	Click [button] on the Mail Merge toolbar
My Computer, open	WIN 98 2.14	In Web style, click My Computer on the desktop; in Classic style, click My Computer on the desktop then press Enter
Nonprinting characters	WD 1.10	Click [button]
Normal view, change to	WD 1.07	Click [button]
Number Form Field, insert	WD 9.27	Insert text form field, then click Form Field Options, set the type to Number, click OK twice
Numbering, add to paragraphs	WD 2.25	Select paragraphs, click [button]

TASK	PAGE #	RECOMMENDED METHOD
NumPages field, insert	WD 8.33	Click Insert, click Field, click Numbering, click NumPages, click OK
Object, embed	WD 7.06	Click destination location, click Insert, click Object, click Create from File tab, click Browse, select file, click Insert, click OK
Object, insert with Paste Special command	WD 7.49	Copy object, click Edit, click Paste Special, select desired format in As list box, select the Paste link option button to link object to its source, click OK
Object, link	WD 7.12	Click destination location, click Insert, click Object, click Create from File tab, click Browse, select file, click Insert, click Link to File check box, click OK
Object, modify linked	WD 7.14	Double-click linked object, use source program tools to modify object, click outside linked object; or open object in source program, modify, save, open destination program, and update links
Office Assistant, close	WD 1.28	Click Help, click Hide Office Assistant
Office Assistant, open	WD 1.28	Click
On-screen Forms, fill in	WD 9.42	Click File, click New, click appropriate tab, double-click icon of document template for on-screen form
On-screen Forms, protect	WD 9.41	Click Protect Form button on Forms toolbar, click Save button, click File, click Save As, change Save In folder to templates folder, click Save, close document window
On-screen Forms, save data in	WD 9.49	Click Tools, click Options, click Save tab, click Save Data Only in Forms check box, click OK
Outline, create	WD 5.21	Click on horizontal scroll bar, enter or edit headings, click number of head levels to show
Outline, edit	WD 5.23	Click , click in line of text, click or to move line; click or to promote or demote heading
Outline numbered list, create	WD 5.49	Click , type first heading, press Enter, type next heading; to demote a heading, click ; to promote a heading, click ; press Enter twice to end list
Page, move to top of next	WD 3.12	Click
Page, move to top of previous	WD 3.12	Click
Page, view whole	WD 4.13	Click Zoom list arrow, click Whole Page
Page break, insert	WD 3.15	Position insertion point at break location, press Ctrl+Enter
Page field, insert	WD 8.33	Click Insert, click Field, click Numbering, click Page, click OK
Page number, insert	WD 3.12	Switch to header or footer, click on Header and Footer toolbar
Page numbers, change format	WD 10.38	Click Insert, click Page Numbers, click Format, change Number Format, click OK
Page orientation, change	WD 7.50	Click File, click Page Setup, click Page Size tab, click Portrait or Landscape, click OK

TASK	PAGE #	RECOMMENDED METHOD
Page setup, change for front and back printing	WD 10.40	Click File, click Page Setup, click Margins tab, set Header Footer to Different Odd/Even and Different First Page, Set Apply To to This Section, click OK
Paragraph, change indent	WD 2.23	Select paragraph, drag left or first-line indent marker on ruler; click [button] or [button]
Paragraph spacing, adjust	WD 5.36	Move the insertion point to the paragraph, click Format, click Paragraph, click Indents and Spacing tab, use Before box to specify amount of space above the selected paragraph, use After box to specify amount of space to insert below the selected paragraph, click OK
Print layout view, change to	WD 3.12	Click [button]
Program, close	WIN 98 1.12	Click [X]
Program, close inactive	WIN 98 1.15	Right-click program button then click Close
Program, start	WIN 98 1.11	See Reference Window: Starting a Program
Program, switch to another	WIN 98 1.14	Click the program button on the taskbar that contains the name of the program to which you want to switch
Reference Field, insert	WD 8.32	Select reference, click Edit, click Bookmark, type name, click Add, move to reference location, click Insert, click Cross-reference, click Bookmark in Reference Type list, set Reference To to Bookmark, click For Which Bookmark, click OK
Reference Field, insert in footer	WD 8.32	Click View, click Header and Footer, click Switch Between Header and Footer button, click Borders button, click Top Border button, click Border button to remove toolbar, type text, click Insert, click Cross-reference, click bookmark, click Insert, click Close
Reverse type, set in table	WD 9.15	Select cells, click Tables and Borders button, click Shading Color list arrow, click Black tile, click Format, click Font, click Color list arrow, click White, click OK
Reversed type, create	WD 9.15	Select text, click Format, click Borders and Shading, click Shading tab, click black tile, click OK, click Format, click Font, click Color list arrow, click White, click OK
Revision, using different colors	WD 10.29	Double-click MRK button on status bar, click Options, set desired colors and marking type, click OK
Revision marks, review	WD 10.30	Click Tools, click Revisions, click Review button, click the Accept or Reject button
Revisions, mark	WD 10.27	Double-click MRK button on status bar, click Mark Revisions While Editing checkbox
Revisions, protect a document for	WD 10.26	Click Tools, click Protect Document, click For Revisions button, click OK
Ruler, display	WD 1.09	Click View, click Ruler

TASK	PAGE #	RECOMMENDED METHOD
Section, vertically align	WD 3.07	Move insertion point into section, click File, click Page Setup, click Layout tab, click Apply to list arrow, click This section, click Vertical alignment list arrow, click desired option, click OK
Section break, create	WD 3.06	Position insertion point at break location, click Insert, click Break, click Section break types option button, click OK
Shading, insert	WD 4.30	Click Format, click Borders and Shading, click Shading tab, select Fill and Pattern options, click OK
Spelling, correct	WD 1.23	Right-click misspelled word (as indicated by red wavy underline), click correctly spelled word
Spelling and grammar, correct	WD 2.05	Click at the beginning of the document, click [icon], review any errors, accept suggestions or ignore errors as desired; to type corrections directly in the document, click outside the Spelling and Grammar dialog box, make the desired correction, and then click Resume in the Spelling and Grammar dialog box
Start menu, open	WIN 98 1.7	Click Start *or* press Ctrl-Esc
Student Disk, create	WIN 98 2.15	Click Start, point to Programs, point to NP on Microsoft Windows 98 – Level I, click Disk 1, click OK
Style, apply	WD 5.09	Select text, click Style list arrow, click style name
Style, define by example	WD 5.14	Format text as desired, select text, type new style name in the Style list box
Style, define new with style command	WD 5.14	Select text you want to format, click Format, click style, click New, type name of new style, click Format, click Paragraph or Character, specify formatting options, click OK twice, click Apply or Close
Style, modify	WD 5.12	Click in paragraph formatted with style, click Format, click Style, verify Style name is selected, click Modify, click Format, click Font or Paragraph, select new style characteristics; click OK twice, click Apply or Close
Style Reference, insert in footer	WD 10.42	Click Insert, click Field, click Links and References, click StyleRef, click Options, click Styles tab, click desired heading style, click Add to Field button, click OK, click OK
Styles, apply	WD 8.10	Move insertion point to paragraph or select text, click Format, click Style, click name of style, click Apply
Styles, create in Template	WD 8.10	Click Format, click Style, click Create, type name of style, set style type, set style features
Styles, modify	WD 8.12	Click Format, click Style, click name of style, make modifications, click OK
Symbol, insert	WD 4.22	Click Insert, click Symbol, click desired symbol, click Insert, click Close
Table cells, merge	WD 3.23	Select cells you want to merge, click [icon] on Tables and Borders toolbar

TASK	PAGE #	RECOMMENDED METHOD
Table cells, split	WD 3.23	Select cells you want to split, click [icon] on Tables and Borders toolbar, specify the number of cells or rows into which you want to divide the cell, click OK
Table column width, change	WD 3.24	Position pointer over column's right border, press and hold down ALT and mouse button, drag to adjust column width to desired measurement as indicated in horizontal ruler
Table gridlines, display	WD 3.29	Select table, click Table, click Show Gridlines
Table row, add or delete border	WD 3.28	Select line weight and style on Table and Borders toolbar, click [icon], click [icon] on cell borders; to delete, select No Border as line style
Table row, align text horizontally in	WD 3.27	Select a cell or range, click [icon], [icon], [icon], or [icon]
Table row, align text vertically in	WD 3.27	Select row, click alignment list arrow on Tables and Borders toolbar, click desired alignment
Table row, delete	WD 3.21	Select row, click Table, point to Delete, click Rows
Table row, insert at end of table	WD 3.21	Position insertion point in lower-right cell at end of table, press Tab
Table row, insert within table	WD 3.21	Select row below, then click [icon] or click Table, point to Insert, and click Rows Above
Table row height, change	WD 3.24	Position pointer over row's bottom border, press and hold down ALT and mouse button, drag to adjust row height to desired measurement as indicated in vertical ruler
Table text, rotate	WD 3.31	Select cells, click [icon] on the Tables and Borders toolbar
Table, center on page	WD 3.32	Click in table, click Table, click Table Properties, click Table tab, click Center Alignment option, click OK
Table, create	WD 3.13	Click [icon], drag pointer to select desired number of columns and rows; or click [icon] on Tables and Borders toolbar, draw desired number of columns and rows
Table, shade	WD 3.29	Select table area, click [icon] on Tables and Borders toolbar, and click a shading option
Table, sort	WD 3.19	Click within column you want to sort by, click [icon] or [icon] on Tables and Borders toolbar
Table, sum cells of	WD 3.23	Click cell where you want sum, click [icon] on Tables and Borders toolbar
Table of Contents, create	WD 5.38	Apply heading styles to document, click Insert, click Index and Tables, click Table of Contents tab, select desired format, select number of headings to include, click OK
Tables and Borders toolbar, display	WD 3.20	Click [icon]

TASK	PAGE #	RECOMMENDED METHOD
Tables, align text in	WD 9.13	Move pointer to cell, click appropriate alignment button
Tables, merge cells in	WD 9.10	Select cells, click Table, then click Merge Cells
Tables, set column width precisely	WD 9.16	Select cells, press and hold down Alt key while dragging the gridlines to precise width
Tables, shade cells in	WD 9.09	Click Borders, click Shading list arrow, select shading, click OK
Tables, split cells in	WD 9.11	Select cells, click Table, click Split Cells, set number of rows and columns, click OK
Tabs, set	WD 3.04	Select text, click tab alignment selector to display , , , or at left of ruler, click ruler to place tab; click in text and press Tab
Telephone List, create	WD 6.36	Click , click Tools, click Mail Merge, click Create, click Catalog, click Active Window, click Get Data, click Open Data Source, select source file, click Open, click Edit Main Document, insert merge fields, click
Template, create	WD 8.07	Type text, change styles, customize toolbars, etc., then click File, click Save As, change "Save as type" to Document Template, type filename, click Save
Template, create new	WD 5.19	Create a new document with styles, save as Word document, delete all text from the document, click File, click Save As, click the Save As type list arrow, click Document Template, verify that the Templates folder is displayed in the Save in list box or choose another location, click Save
Template, save	WD 8.42	Click Tools, click Options, click File Locations, click Close, click File, click Save As, enter name of templates folder, click Save button, click Close
Template, saved in any location, open	WD 5.19	Click Tools, click Templates and Add-ins, click Attach, select template, click Open, select the Automatically update document styles check box, click OK
Template, saved in Template folder, open	WD 5.19	Click File on the menu bar, click New, click the icon for your template in the General tab, and then click OK, type document text, apply styles, save as a Word document
Template, start new document with	WD 8.43	Click File, click New, click appropriate template, click OK
Template (Word predefined), attach	WD 5.10	Click Format, click Themes, click Style Gallery, click template name, click OK
Text, align	WD 2.22	Select text, click , , , or
Text, animate	WD 7.29	Select text, click Format, click Font, click Text Effects tab, click animation style, click OK
Text, copy by copy and paste	WD 2.13	Select text, click , move pointer to target location; then either click or, if Clipboard opens, click item to paste in Clipboard
Text, copy by drag and drop	WD 2.12	Select text, press and hold down Ctrl and drag pointer to target location, release mouse button and Ctrl key

TASK	PAGE #	RECOMMENDED METHOD
Text, delete	WD 2.09	Press Backspace key to delete character to left of insertion point; press the Delete key to delete character to right; press Ctrl + Backspace to delete to beginning of word; press Ctrl + Delete to delete to end of word
Text, find	WD 2.15	Click [button], click [button], type search text, click Find Next
Text, find and replace	WD 2.15	Click [button], click [button], click Replace tab, type search text, press Tab, type replacement text, click Find Next
Text Form Fields, add prompt	WD 9.21	With Text Form Field on screen, click Add Help Text button, click Status bar tab, click into Type Your Own Text box, click Help Key (F1) tab, click OK
Text Form Fields, insert	WD 9.19	Display Forms toolbar, click Text form field button, set desired options, click Add Help Text button, click Status Bar folder, click Help Key (F1) tab, and type message, click OK
Text Form Fields, protect	WD 9.22	Click Protect Form button on Forms toolbar
Text, format	WD 2.29	See "Font Style, change"
Text, highlight	WD 5.33	Select text, click [button]
Text, move by cut and paste	WD 2.13	Select text, click [button], move to target location, click [button]
Text, move by drag and drop	WD 2.12	Select text, drag pointer to target location, release mouse button
Text, rotate in table	WD 9.08	Click Format, click Text Direction, specify direction, click OK
Text, select	WIN 98 2.6	Drag the pointer over the text
Text, select a block of	WD 2.09	Click at beginning of block, press and hold down Shift and click at end of block
Text, select a paragraph of	WD 2.09	Double-click in selection bar next to paragraph
Text, select a sentence of	WD 2.09	Press Ctrl and click within sentence
Text, select entire document of	WD 2.09	Press Ctrl and click in selection bar
Text, select multiple lines of	WD 2.09	Click and drag in selection bar
Text, select multiple paragraphs of	WD 2.09	Double-click and drag in selection bar
Thesaurus, use	WD 7.05	Select word, click Tools, point to Language, click Thesaurus, click appropriate meaning and synonym, click Replace
Toolbar, display	WD 1.08	Right-click any visible toolbar, click name of desired toolbar
Toolbar button, select	WIN 98 1.24	Click the toolbar button

TASK	PAGE #	RECOMMENDED METHOD
Toolbars, add buttons to	WD 8.23	Right-click on toolbar, click Customize, click desired toolbar category, drag desired button to toolbar location, click Close
Toolbars, change location of buttons in	WD 8.21	Right-click on toolbar, click Customize, drag button to new location, click Close
Toolbars, control display	WIN 98 2.17	Click View, point to Toolbars, then select the toolbar options you want
Toolbars, remove buttons from	WD 8.22	Right-click on toolbar, click Customize, drag buttons off toolbar, click Close
ToolTip, view	WIN 98 1.7	Position the pointer over the tool
View, change	WIN 98 2.18	Click View then click the view option you want
Web page, create	WD 7.32	Create and save document, click File, click Save as Web page, click Save, click Yes, modify formatting as necessary
Web page, view in Web browser	WD 7.42	Open Web page document, click File, click Web Page Preview
Web style, switch to	WIN 98 2.12	Click Start, point to Settings, click Folder Options, click Web style, click OK
Web view, switch to	WIN 98 2.18	Open My Computer, click View then click as Web Page
Widow/orphan, turn on	WD 10.14	Click Format, click Paragraph, click Line and Page Breaks tab, click Widow/Orphan control check box, click OK
Window, maximize	WIN 98 1.20	Click
Window, minimize	WIN 98 1.18	Click
Window, move	WIN 98 1.21	Drag the title bar
Window, redisplay	WIN 98 1.20	Click the program button on the taskbar
Window, resize	WIN 98 1.21	Drag
Window, restore	WIN 98 1.20	Click
Windows 98, shut down	WIN 98 1.15	Click Start, click Shut Down, click the Shut Down option button, click OK
Windows 98, start	WIN 98 1.4	Turn on the computer
Web layout view, change to	WD 7.27	Open document, click
Word, exit	WD 1.30	Close all open documents, then click on the title bar
Word, start	WD 1.05	Click Start, point to Programs, click Microsoft Word
WordArt object, create	WD 4.04	Click , click desired WordArt style, type WordArt text, select font, size, and style, click OK

Standardized Coding Number	Certification Skill Activity	Tutorial Pages	End-of-Tutorial		
	Activity		End-of-Tutorial Pages	Exercise	Step Number
W2000.1	**Working with text**				
W2000.1.1	Use the Undo, Redo, and Repeat command	2.10–2.11 (undo, redo)	2.38 2.39 2.40 2.41	CP1 CP2 CP3 CP4	4 3 4 5
		4.22 (repeat)			
W2000.1.2	Apply font formats (Bold, Italic and Underline)	2.29–2.31	2.35, 2.36 2.38, 2.39 2.39, 2.40 2.40, 2.41 2.41	RA CP1 CP2 CP3 CP4	4, 8 6, 10, 13, 14 4, 14, 15 6, 13, 15, 16 8, 10
W2000.1.3	Use the SPELLING feature	1.22–1.24	1.33 1.35 1.36	RA CP1 CP2	12 11 10
		2.05–2.07	2.35 2.38 2.40 2.41	RA CP1 CP3 CP4	3 3 3 2
W2000.1.4	Use the THESAURUS feature	5.05–5.06	5.44 5.46 5.47 5.48	RA CP1 CP2 CP3	5 10 8 6
W2000.1.5	Use the GRAMMAR feature	2.05–2.07	2.35 2.38 2.40 2.41	RA CP1 CP3 CP4	3 3 3 2
W2000.1.6	Insert page breaks	3.06–3.07 3.15	3.34, 3.35 3.37 3.38	RA CP1 CP2	5, 13, 20 3, 8 4
W2000.1.7	Highlight text in document	2.09 (select text)	2.37–2.38 2.40	RA CP3	10, 11 10, 11
		5.33–5.34 (highlighter)	5.45 5.47 5.48	RA CP2 CP3	16 11 11
W2000.1.8	Insert and move text	1.16–1.17 (insert)	1.32–1.33 1.34 1.35–1.36 1.37	RA CP1 CP2 CP4	3–9, 13 3–8 4–6, 9, 11, 12 4–8
		2.12–2.15 (move)	2.35, 2.36 2.38, 2.39 2.39 2.40 2.41	RA CP1 CP2 CP3 CP4	4, 8 6, 15 9, 10 5, 8 5

Standardized Coding Number	Certification Skill Activity Activity	Tutorial Pages	End-of-Tutorial		
			End-of-Tutorial Pages	Exercise	Step Number
W2000.1.9	Cut, Copy, Paste, and Paste Special using the Office Clipboard	2.12–2.15	2.35, 2.36, 2.38 2.40 2.41	RA CP3 CP4	4, 8, 11 6, 8 5
		7.03–7.05	7.49	CP2	Step 3
W2000.1.10	Copy formats using the Format Painter	2.24–2.25	2.39	CP1	9
W2000.1.11	Select and change font and font size	1.09–1.10			
		2.27–2.29	2.35, 2.36 2.39 2.39 2.40, 2.41	RA CP1 CP2 CP3	4, 8 12 3 6, 13, 14
W2000.1.12	Find and replace text	2.15–2.18	2.35, 2.36 2.39 2.39 2.40	RA CP1 CP2 CP3	4, 8 10 11 12
W2000.1.13	Apply character effects (superscript, subscript, strikethrough, small caps and outline)	5.08	5.44 5.46	RA CP1	9 9
W2000.1.14	Insert date and time	1.14–1.15 (AutoCmplt)	1.32 1.34 1.35	RA CP1 CP2	8 3 3
		5.32–5.33	5.45 5.47 5.48	RA CP2 CP3	15 10 11
W2000.1.15	Insert symbols	4.22–4.24	4.28, 4.29 4.30 4.32	RA CP1 CP3	22, 26 16 14
W2000.1.16	Create and apply frequently used text with AutoCorrect		5.49	CP1	17
W2000.2	**Working with paragraphs**				
W2000.2.1	Align text in paragraphs (Center, Left, Right and Justified)	2.22–2.23	2.35, 2.36 2.39 2.39 2.40 2.41	RA CP1 CP2 CP3 CP4	4, 8 9, 13 4 11 8, 9
W2000.2.2	Add bullets and numbering	2.25–2.27	2.36 2.39 2.39 2.40	RA CP1 CP2 CP3	8 11 6 7, 8

Standardized Coding Number	Certification Skill Activity Activity	Tutorial Pages	End-of-Tutorial		
			End-of-Tutorial Pages	Exercise	Step Number
W2000.2.3	Set character, line, and paragraph spacing options	2.20–2.21 (line)	2.37	RA	10
		5.16, 5.34–5.38 (char,para)	5.44 5.46 5.48	RA CP1 CP3	8, 10 9, 13 9
W2000.2.4	Apply borders and shading to paragraphs		4.30 4.33	CP1 CP4	11 11
		5.17	5.48	CP3	9
W2000.2.5	Use indentation options (Left, Right, First Line and Hanging Indent)	2.23–2.24	2.39 2.39 2.40	CP1 CP2 CP3	11 6 10
W2000.2.6	Use TABS command (Center, Decimal, Left and Right)	3.04–3.06	3.34, 3.35 3.37 3.38	RA CP1 CP2	3, 11 6 6
W2000.2.7	Create an outline style numbered list	5.21–5.24	5.49	CP4	4, 5
W2000.2.8	Set tabs with leaders	6.36–6.37	6.41 6.42	RA CP1	28 18
W2000.3	**Working with documents**				
W2000.3.1	Print a document	1.26–1.27	1.33 1.35 1.36 1.36 1.37	RA CP1 CP2 CP3 CP4	16, 18 13 15 5 9
		2.31	2.38	RA	13
W2000.3.2	Use print preview	1.26–1.27	1.33 1.35 1.36 1.36	RA CP1 CP2 CP3	16 13 14 5
W2000.3.3	Use Web Page Preview	7.42–7.44	7.47 7.51 7.52	RA CP3 CP4	31 10 17
W2000.3.4	Navigate through a document	2.07–2.08	2.35, 2.36, 2.38 2.38–2.39 2.39, 2.40 2.40, 2.41	RA CP1 CP2 CP3	4, 8, 11 4, 5, 6, 7 5, 7, 9, 15 4, 5, 8, 16
W2000.3.5	Insert page numbers	3.11–3.12	3.3.35	RA	8, 15, 18
W2000.3.6	Set page orientation		7.50	CP2	7

Standardized Coding Number	Certification Skill Activity Activity	Tutorial Pages	End-of-Tutorial End-of-Tutorial Pages	 Exercise	 Step Number
W2000.3.7	Set margins	2.18–2.20	2.36–2.37 2.39 2.39–2.40 2.41	RA CP1 CP2 CP4	8, 9 8 12, 13 6, 7
W2000.3.8	Use GoTo to locate specific elements in a document	5.40	5.45	RA	20
W2000.3.9	Create and modify page numbers	3.11–3.12	3.35	RA	8, 15, 18
W2000.3.10	Create and modify headers and footers	3.10–3.13	3.35 3.37 3.38	RA CP1 CP2	7, 8,15–18 5 6, 7
W2000.3.11	Align text vertically	3.07–3.09 (title page) 3.27–3.28 (table cells)	3.34,3.35,3.36 3.37, 3.38 3.38	RA CP1 CP2	6, 14, 40 4, 12 5, 8
W2000.3.12	Create and use newspaper columns	4.11–4.13	4.28, 4.29 4.30 4.31 4.32 4.33	RA CP1 CP2 CP3 CP4	13, 23, 24 12, 19 7, 8 13, 15 8
W2000.3.13	Revise column structure		4.31	CP2	8
W2000.3.14	Prepare and print envelopes and labels	1.29 (envlps) 6.33–6.35	1.33 6.40–6.41 6.42 6.43 6.44 6.45	RA RA CP1 CP2 CP3 CP4	18 20–26 14–16 13–16 14–18 11–14
W2000.3.15	Apply styles	5.09–5.12	5.44 5.47 5.48 5.49	RA CP2 CP3 CP4	7, 10 4 9 5
W2000.3.16	Create sections with formatting that differs from other sections	3.06–3.09	3.34–3.35 3.37 3.38	RA CP1 CP2	5–8,12,14–16 3–5 4–7
W2000.3.17	Use click & type	5.30–5.33	5.45 5.47	RA RA	15 9
W2000.4	**Managing files**				
W2000.4.1	Use save	1.17–1.19, 1.25–1.26	1.33 1.35 1.35, 1.36 1.36 1.37	RA CP1 CP2 CP3 CP4	10 9, 12 7, 13 3 9

Standardized Coding Number	Certification Skill Activity Activity	Tutorial Pages	End-of-Tutorial		
			End-of-Tutorial Pages	Exercise	Step Number
W2000.4.2	Locate and open an existing document	2.02–2.04	2.35, 2.36 2.38 2.39 2.40	RA CP1 CP2 CP3	2, 7 2 2 2
W2000.4.3	Use Save As (different name, location or format)	2.05 7.32–7.35	2.35, 2.36 2.38 2.39 2.40 2.41 7.46, 7.47 7.50 7.51 7.51	RA CP1 CP2 CP3 CP4 RA CP2 CP3 CP4	2, 7 2 2 2 11 21, 35 6 9, 10 3, 7
W2000.4.4	Create a folder	5.04–5.05	5.43 5.49	RA CP3	3 2
W2000.4.5	Create a new document using a Wizard		5.48 7.52	RA CP4	24 9–16
W2000.4.6	Save as Web Page	7.32–7.35	7.46, 7.47 7.50 7.51 7.51, 7.52	RA CP2 CP3 CP4	21, 26 8 9, 10 3, 7
W2000.4.7	Use templates to create a new document	 5.10–5.11 5.18–5.21	1.36–1.37 5.44, 5.45 5.47	CP4 RA CP2	2–9 6, 22, 23, 24 3
W2000.4.8	Create Hyperlinks	7.20–7.27 7.40–7.42	7.46, 7.47 7.49 7.50 7.51 7.52	RA CP1 CP2 CP3 CP4	16, 28–30 11, 12 9, 10 10 14
W2000.4.9	Use the Office Assistant	1.28–1.30	1.32, 1.33–1.34 1.35	RA CP2	2, 17–19 9
W2000.4.10	Send a Word document via e-mail		7.52 7.55	RA CP1	37 15
W2000.5	**Using tables**				
W2000.5.1	Create and format tables	3.13–3.18	3.35, 3.37 3.37–3.38 3.38 3.39 3.40–3.41	RA CP1 CP2 CP3 CP4	21–25, 42–45 9–15 8–12 2–11 3–10

Standardized Coding Number	Certification Skill Activity — Activity	Tutorial Pages	End-of-Tutorial		
			End-of-Tutorial Pages	Exercise	Step Number
W2000.5.2	Add borders and shading to tables	3.28–3.31	3.36, 3.37 3.38 3.38 3.39 3.40, 3.40	RA CP1 CP2 CP3 CP4	38, 39, 44 14, 15 11, 12 11 3, 4, 8, 10
W2000.5.3	Revise tables (insert & delete rows and columns, change cell formats)	3.21–3.23, 3.27–3.28	3.35, 3.36 3.38 3.38 3.39 3.40, 3.40	RA CP1 CP2 CP3 CP4	27–29,31,35, 37, 40 12, 13 8, 10 3, 5, 7, 8 3, 4, 6, 10
W2000.5.4	Modify table structure (merge cells, change height and width)	3.23, 3.24–3.26	3.36, 3.37 3.38 3.38 3.39 3.40, 3.41	RA CP1 CP2 CP3 CP4	29, 34, 36, 40, 45 11, 12 9 8, 9, 10 4, 5, 9
W2000.5.5	Rotate text in a table	3.31	3.38 3.40	CP2 CP4	8 5
W2000.6	**Working with pictures and charts**				
W2000.6.1	Use the drawing toolbar		3.41	CP4	7
		4.05, 4.15	4.28, 4.29 4.29 4.32	RA CP1 CP3	4, 16, 25 3 7
W2000.6.2	Insert graphics into a document (WordArt, ClipArt, Images)	4.04–4.11 4.14–4.17	4.28 4.29–4.30 4.31 4.32 4.33	RA CP1 CP2 CP3 CP4	4–6, 16–17 3–7, 13, 14 4, 9 4 4, 9

Expert Standardized Coding Number	Certification Skill Activity Activity	Tutorial Pages	End-of-Tutorial Practice End-of-Tutorial Pages	Exercise	Step Number
W2000E.1	**Working with paragraphs**				
W2000E.1.1	Apply paragraph and section shading	8.11–8.12			
W2000E.1.2	Use text flow options (Windows/Orphans options and keeping lines together)	10.13–10.17	10.57 10.59	Review Assignment Case Problem 1	5 3
W2000E.1.3	Sort lists, paragraphs, tables	3.19–3.21 10.45–10.46	3.35 3.39	Review Assignment Case Problem 3	26 6
W2000E.2	**Working with documents**				
W2000E.2.1	Create and modify page borders	4.25–4.27	4.29 4.30–4.33 4.31	Review Assignment Case Problem 1 Case Problem 2 Case Problem 4	27 18 16 11
W2000E.2.2	Format first page differently than subsequent pages	3.07–3.09	3.34–3.35 3.37 3.38 10.57 10.61	Review Assignment Case Problem 1 Case Problem 2 Review Assignmen Case Problem 2	6, 14 4 5 6 8
W2000E.2.3	Use bookmarks	7.23–7.26	7.46	Review Assignment	16
W2000E.2.4	Create and edit styles	5.09–5.21	5.44 5.46 5.47 5.48 5.50	Review Assignment Case Problem 1 Case Problem 2 Case Problem 3 Case Problem 4	7, 8, 9, 10 6, 7 3, 4, 10 8, 9 11
W2000E.2.5	Create watermarks	8.18–8.21	8.54 8.56 8.62	Review Assignment Case Problem 1 Case Problem 4	5 17 14
W2000E.2.6	Use find and replace with formats, special characters and non-printing elements	2.18	4.29 4.30	Review Assignment Case Problem 1	26 16
W2000E.2.7	Balance column length (using column breaks appropriately)	4.24–4.25	4.29 4.30 4.32	Review Assignment Case Problem 1 Case Problem 3	24 19 15
W2000E.2.8	Create or revise footnotes and endnotes	5.27–5.30	5.46 5.48 5.50	Case Problem 1 Case Problem 3 Case Problem 4	11 7 10, 13
W2000E.2.9	Work with master documents and subdocuments	10.02–10.13	10.57–10.58 10.59–10.60 10.61 10.62–10.63	Review Assignment Case Problem 1 Case Problem 2 Case Problem 3	3, 4, 8, 10, 15 10–14, 21 13, 14 2, 8, 19–21

Standardized Coding Number	Certification Skill Activity Activity	Tutorial Pages	End-of-Tutorial Practice End-of-Tutorial Pages	Exercise	Step Number
W2000E.2.10	Create and modify a table of contents	5.38–5.43 10.54–10.55	5.45 5.46 5.48 5.50 10.58 10.60 10.63	Review Assignment Case Problem 1 Case Problem 3 Case Problem 4 Review Assignment Case Problem 1 Case Problem 3	18, 19 14, 15 13 14 21 29 24
W2000E.2.11	Create cross-reference	10.24–10.25			
W2000E.2.12	Create and modify an index	10.47–10.54	10.58 10.60 10.61–10.62 10.63	Review Assignment Case Problem 1 Case Problem 2 Case Problem 3	17, 18, 19, 20 23–29 15–20 25, 26, 27
W2000E.3	**Using tables**				
W2000E.3.1	Embed worksheets in a table	7.03–7.11	7.48 7.49 7.50	Case Problem 1 Case Problem 2 Case Problem 3	3 3 2
W2000E.3.2	Perform calculations in a table	3.23–3.24	3.36	Review Assignment	30, 32
W2000E.3.3	Link Excel data as a table	7.04–7.05 7.12–7.18	7.45	Review Assignment	3
W2000E.3.4	Modify worksheets in a table	7.11–7.14	7.49 7.54 7.55 7.57	Review Assignment Case Problem 1 Case Problem 2 Case Problem 3	6, 7, 8, 9, 10 4, 5 3, 4 2, 3, 4
W2000E.4	**Working with pictures and charts**				
W2000E.4.1	Add bitmapped graphics	4.14–4.16	4.31	Case Problem 2	9
W2000E.4.2	Delete and position graphics	4.08–4.11 4.17–4.19	4.28 4.30–4.31 4.31 4.32	Review Assignment Case Problem 1 Case Problem 2 Case Problem 3	7, 17 4, 7, 14 5, 6, 10, 11 6, 9, 10
W2000E.4.3	Create and modify charts	8.49–8.50	7.51 8.54–8.55 8.57	Case Problem 4 Review Assignment Case Problem 1	2 17, 18, 19 26
W2000E.4.4	Import data into charts	8.49–8.50			
W2000E.5	**Using mail merge**				
W2000E.5.1	Create main document	6.06–6.07 6.17–6.23	6.39–6.40 6.41–6.42 6.42–6.43 6.44 6.45	Review Assignment Case Problem 1 Case Problem 2 Case Problem 3 Case Problem 4	2, 11, 20 2, 14 2, 14 2, 14 2, 5, 11, 12

Standardized Coding Number	Certification Skill Activity Activity	Tutorial Pages	End-of-Tutorial Practice		
			End-of-Tutorial Pages	Exercise	Step Number
W2000E.5.2	Create data source	6.08–6.17	6.39	Review Assignment	3, 4
			6.41–6.42	Case Problem 1	3, 4, 5
			6.42–6.43	Case Problem 2	3, 4, 5
			6.44	Case Problem 3	3, 4, 5
			6.45	Case Problem 4	3, 4
W2000E.5.3	Sort records to be merged	6.26–6.31	6.39–6.41	Review Assignment	5, 29
			6.42	Case Problem 1	17
			6.43	Case Problem 2	8, 17
			6.44	Case Problem 3	9
			6.45	Case Problem 4	7
W2000E.5.4	Merge main document and data source	6.23–6.25	6.40–6.41	Review Assignment	17, 25, 30
			6.42	Case Problem 1	11, 15, 20
			6.43	Case Problem 2	10, 15, 19
			6.44	Case Problem 3	11, 16
			6.45	Case Problem 4	8, 13
W2000E.5.5	Generate labels	6.31–6.35	6.43–6.45	Case Problem 2	13, 14, 15, 16
				Case Problem 4	11, 12, 13, 14
W2000E.5.6	Merge a document using alternate data sources	6.02–6.05	6.40–6.41	Review Assignment	12, 21–25, 30
W2000E.6	**Using advanced features**				
W2000E.6.1	Insert a field	6.04	6.39–6.41	Review Assignment	7, 13–15, 23, 28
		6.15–6.17	6.42	Case Problem 1	6, 7, 8, 9
		8.25–8.34	6.43	Case Problem 2	6, 7
			6.44	Case Problem 3	7
			6.45	Case Problem 4	5
			8.54	Review Assignment	6, 7, 8
			8.57	Case Problem 1	6, 7, 8
			8.60	Case Problem 2	9, 10, 11, 12
			8.64	Case Problem 3	14–18
			8.66	Case Problem 4	9, 11, 12
W2000E.6.2	Create, apply and edit macros	8.35–8.43	8.54	Review Assignment	16
		8.46–8.47	8.56–8.57	Case Problem 1	15, 18, 25
		9.36–9.38	8.58–8.59	Case Problem 2	19, 21, 26
		9.43–9.44	8.60	Case Problem 3	15
			8.62	Case Problem 4	15, 16, 17, 21
			9.52	Review Assignment	18, 19
			9.54	Case Problem 1	14
W2000E.6.3	Copy, rename, and delete macros	8.39–8.41	8.55	Review Assignment	25
W2000E.6.4	Create and modify form	9.02–9.48	9.50–9.52	Review Assignment	1–22
			9.53–9.55	Case Problem 1	1–21
			9.55–9.56	Case Problem 2	1–23
			9.56–9.58	Case Problem 3	1–23
			9.58–9.59	Case Problem 4	1–9

Standardized Coding Number	Certification Skill Activity Activity	Tutorial Pages	End-of-Tutorial Practice		
			End-of-Tutorial Pages	Exercise	Step Number
W2000E.6.5	Create and modify a form control (e.g., add an item to a drop-down list)	9.29–9.49	9.51–9.52 9.53–9.54 9.55–9.56 9.57–9.58 9.59	Review Assignment Case Problem 1 Case Problem 2 Case Problem 3 Case Problem 4	3–11,15 9–13, 15 14–18 9, 10, 12–16 4
W2000E.6.6	Use advanced text alignment features with graphics	4.19–4.20	4.28 4.30 4.31 4.32	Review Assignment Case Problem 1 Case Problem 2 Case Problem 3	20 15 11, 13 11
W2000E.6.7	Customize toolbars	8.21–8.24	8.56 8.59–8.60 8.61	Case Problem 1 Case Problem 3 Case Problem 4	7, 8, 9, 15 10 7
W2000E.7	**Collaborating with workgroups**				
W2000E.7.1	Insert comments	10.32–10.37	10.62 10.62–10.63	Case Problem 2 Case Problem 3	21 9, 18
W2000E.7.2	Protect documents	9.41–9.42 10.26–10.27	9.52 9.54 9.56 9.58 9.59 10.62 10.64	Review Assignment Case Problem 1 Case Problem 2 Case Problem 3 Case Problem 4 Case Problem 3 Case Problem 4	19 16 19 19 5 10 2
W2000E.7.3	Create multiple versions of a document	10.31–10.32			
W2000E.7.4	Track changes to a document	10.26–10.31	10.58 10.60 10.62	Review Assignment Case Problem 1 Case Problem 3	11, 12, 13, 14 18, 19 12
W2000E.7.5	Set default file location for workgroup templates	9.42			
W2000E.7.6	Round Trip documents from HTML	7.32–7.35	7.47	Review Assignment	34

File Finder

Location in Tutorial	Name and Location of Data File	Student Saves File As...	Student Creates New File
WINDOWS 98 LEVEL I, DISK 1 & 2*			
Tutorial 2			
Session 2.1			Practice Text.doc
Session 2.2 *Note*: Students copy the contents of Disk 1 onto Disk 2 in this session.	Agenda.doc Budget98.wks Budget99.wks Exterior.bmp Interior.bmp Logo.bmp Members.wdb Minutes.wps Newlogo.bmp Opus27.mid Parkcost.wks Proposal.doc Resume.doc Sales.wks Sample Text.doc Tools.wks Travel.wps Practice Text.doc *(Saved from Session 2.1)*		
Tutorial Assignments	*Note:* Students continue to use the Student disks they used in the Tutorial. For certain Assignments, they will need a 3rd blank disk.	Resume 2.doc *(saved from Resume.doc)*	Letter.doc Song.doc
WORD, LEVEL I			
Tutorial 1			
Session 1.2			Tutorial.01\Tutorial\Tacoma Job Fair Letter.doc
Review Assignments			Tutorial.01\Review\Job Fair Reminder.doc
Case Problem 1			Tutorial.01\Cases\Confirmation Letter.doc
Case Problem 2			Tutorial.01\Cases\Rock Climbing Request Letter.doc
Case Problem 3			Tutorial.01\Cases\Awards Memo.doc
Case Problem 4			Tutorial.01\Cases\My Template Letter.doc
Tutorial 2			
Session 2.1	Tutorial.02\Tutorial\Annuity.doc	Tutorial.02\Tutorial\RHS Annuity Plan.doc	
Session 2.2	Tutorial.02\Tutorial\RHS\Annuity Plan.doc (*Saved from Session 2.1*)	Tutorial.02\Tutorial\RHS Annuity Plan Copy 2.doc Tutorial.02\Tutorial\RHS Annuity Plan Final Copy.doc	

***Note:** The "NP on Microsoft Windows 98-Level I" Make Student Disk Program must be installed to obtain the student files for the Windows 98 tutorials.*

File Finder

Location in Tutorial	Name and Location of Data File	Student Saves File As...	Student Creates New File
Review Assignments	Tutorial.02\Review\RHSQuart.doc Tutorial.02\Review\RHSPort.doc	Tutorial.02\Review\RHSQuarterly Report.doc Tutorial.02\Review\RHS Portfolio Changes	
Case Problem 1	Tutorial.02\Cases\Store.doc	Tutorial.02\Cases\Store-It-All Policies.doc	
Case Problem 2	Tutorial.02\Cases\UpTime.doc	Tutorial.02\Cases\UpTime Training Summary.doc	
Case Problem 3	Tutorial.02\Cases\Ridge	Tutorial.02\Cases\Ridge Top Guide.doc	
Case Problem 4			Tutorial.02\Cases\Restaurant Review.doc Tutorial.02\Cases\Edited Restaurant Review.doc
Tutorial 3			
Session 3.1	Tutorial.03\Tutorial\EverRipe.doc	Tutorial.03\Tutorial\EverRipe Report.doc Tutorial.03\Tutorial\EverRipe Report Copy 2.doc	
Session 3.2	Tutorial.03\Tutorial\EverRipe Report Copy 2.doc (*Saved from Session 3.1*)	Tutorial.03\Tutorial\EverRipe Report Final Copy.doc	
Review Assignments	Tutorial.03\Review\StatRep.doc Tutorial.03\Review\ZonReq.doc Tutorial.03\Review\Members.doc	Tutorial.03\Review\AgTech Status Report.doc Tutorial.03\Review\Zoning Request.doc Tutorial.03\Review\Zoning Board Members.doc	
Case Problem 1	Tutorial.03\Cases\OceanRep.doc	Tutorial.03\Cases\Ocean Breeze Report.doc	
Case Problem 2	Tutorial.03\Cases\Europe.doc	Tutorial.03\Cases\Europe Tour Report.doc	
Case Problem 3	Tutorial.03\Cases\Classics.doc	Tutorial.03\Cases\Classical Music CDs.doc	
Case Problem 4			Tutorial.03\Cases\Bright Star Training.doc
Tutorial 4			
Session 4.1	Tutorial.04\Tutorial\MiniInfo.doc	Tutorial.04\Tutorial\FastFad Newsletter.doc	
Session 4.2	Tutorial.04\Tutorial\FastFad Newsletter.doc (*Saved from Session 4.1*)	Tutorial.04\Tutorial\FastFad Newsletter Final Copy.doc	
Review Assignments	Tutorial.04\Review\FigSpecs.doc	Tutorial.04\Review\Action Pros.doc	
Case Problem 1	Tutorial.04\Cases\CityComp.doc Tutorial.04\Cases\Knight.bmp	Tutorial.04\Cases\Computer.doc	
Case Problem 2	Tutorial.04\Cases\MSM_NEWS.doc	Tutorial.04\Cases\MSM Newsletter.doc	
Case Problem 3	Tutorial.04\Cases\Wellness.doc	Tutorial.04\Cases\Wellness Newsletter.doc	
Case Problem 4			Tutorial.04\Cases\New Home.doc
WORD, LEVEL II			
Tutorial 5			
Session 5.1	Tutorial.05\Tutorial\Industry.doc	Tutorial.05\Tutorial\Chapter 2\Industry Analysis.doc	Tutorial.05\Tutorial\ Chapter 2\Business Plan Template.dot
Session 5.2	(*Continued from Session 5.1*)		Tutorial.05\Tutorial\ Chapter 2\Industry Analysis Copy 2.doc
Session 5.3	(*Continued from Session 5.2*)	Tutorial.05\Tutorial\Chapter 2\Industry Analysis Final Copy.doc	

File Finder

Location in Tutorial	Name and Location of Data File	Student Saves File As...	Student Creates New File
Review Assignment	Tutorial.05\Review\Training.doc	Tutorial.05\Review\Policies\Training Courses.doc	Tutorial.05\Review\ Policies\Policy Template.dot Tutorial.05\Review\New Policy.doc
Case Problem 1	Tutorial.05\Cases\Flowers.doc	Tutorial.05\Cases\Mountainland Flowers.doc	
Case Problem 2	Tutorial.05\Cases\Catering.doc	Tutorial.05\Cases\Classic Catering.doc	
Case Problem 3	Tutorial.05\Cases\Business.doc	Tutorial.05\Cases\Writing Project\Business of Basketball.doc	
Case Problem 4	Tutorial.05\Cases\Income.doc		Tutorial.05\Cases\Median Family Income.doc
Tutorial 6			
Session 6.1	Tutorial.06\Tutorial\PetShopp.doc Tutorial.06\Tutorial\Shopdat	Tutorial.06\Tutorial\Pet Shoppe Form Letter.doc	Tutorial.06\Tutorial\Pet Shoppe Data Tutorial.06\Tutorial\Pet Shoppe Phone List
Session 6.2	(*Continued from Session 6.1*)		Tutorial.06\Tutorial\Pet Shoppe Form Letters1 Tutorial.06\Tutorial\Pet Shoppe Form Letters2 Tutorial.06\Tutorial\Pet Shoppe Form Letters3
Session 6.3	(*Continued from Session 6.2*)		Tutorial.06\Tutorial\Pet Shoppe Labels Tutorial.06\Tutorial\Pet Shoppe Labels Form Tutorial.06\Tutorial\Pet Shoppe Phone Form
Review Assignment	Tutorial.06\Review\Vaccines.doc Tutorial.06\Review\Payroll.doc	Tutorial.06\Review\Pet Shoppe Vaccines.doc Tutorial.06\Review\Pet Shoppe Payroll Memo.doc	Tutorial.06\Review\Pet Vaccine Data Tutorial.06\Review\Pet Shoppe Payroll Memo 2 Tutorial.06\Review\Payroll Envelope Form Tutorial.06\Review\Payroll Envelopes Tutorial.06\Review\Employee Phone List Form Tutorial.06\Review\Employee Phone List
Case Problem 1	Tutorial.06\Cases\Campaign.doc	Tutorial.06\Cases\Campaign Form Letter	Tutorial.06\Cases\Supporters Data Tutorial.06\Cases\Campaign Letters Tutorial.06\Cases\Campaign Envelope Form Tutorial.06\Cases\Campaign Envelopes Tutorial.06\Cases\Campaign Phone Form Tutorial.06\Cases\Campaign Phone List

File Finder

Location in Tutorial	Name and Location of Data File	Student Saves File As...	Student Creates New File
Case Problem 2	Tutorial.06\Cases\Gems	Tutorial.06\Cases\Gems Form Letter	Tutorial.06\Cases\Gems Data Tutorial.06\Cases\Gems Letters Tutorial.06\Cases\Gems Labels Form Tutorial.06\Cases\Gems Labels Tutorial.06\Cases\Gems Customer List Form Tutorial.06\Cases\Gems Customer List
Case Problem 3	Tutorial.06\Cases\AutoSale	Tutorial.06\Cases\Auto Sale Form Letter	Tutorial.06\Cases\Auto Sale Data Tutorial.06\Cases\Auto Letters Tutorial.06\Cases\Auto Envelopes Form Tutorial.06\Cases\Auto Envelopes
Case Problem 4			Tutorial.06\Cases\Graduation Guest Data Tutorial.06\Cases\Graduation Form Letter Tutorial.06\Cases\Graduation Merge Tutorial.06\Cases\Graduation Labels Form Tutorial.06\Cases\Graduation Labels
Tutorial 7			
Session 7.1	Tutorial.07\Tutorial\FSIProp.doc Tutorial.07\Tutorial\FSIExpns.xls Tutorial.07\Tutorial\FSIChart Tutorial.07\Tutorial\Indiana.bmp	Tutorial.07\Tutorial\FSI New Branch Proposal.doc Tutorial.07\Tutorial\Copy of FSIChart.xls	
Session 7.2	*(Continued from Session 7.1)* Tutorial.07\Tutorial\VJResume.doc		Tutorial.07\Tutorial\VJResume Web Page
Session 7.3	*(Continued from Session 7.2)*		Tutorial.07\Tutorial\FSI New Branch Proposal Web Page Tutorial.07\Tutorial\VJResume Web Page
Review Assignment	Tutorial.07\Review\SalesRep.doc Tutorial.07\Review\2Qsales.xls Tutorial.07\Review\BrnchSls Tutorial.07\Review\FSIAds	Tutorial.07\Review\Family Style Sales Report.doc Tutorial.07\Review\Copy of 2Qsales.xls Tutorial.07\Review\Family Styles Sales Report Word Document.doc	Tutorial.07\Review\Family Style Sales Report Web Page Tutorial.07\Review\FSIAds Web Page
Case Problem 1	Tutorial.07\Cases\NewOffic.doc Tutorial.07\Cases\Rent.xls Tutorial.07\Cases\Logo.bmp Tutorial.07\Cases\Devel.doc	Tutorial.07\Cases\New Office Memo.doc	
Case Problem 2	Tutorial.07\Cases\NatBroh.doc Tutorial.07\Cases\PacTours.xls Tutorial.07\Cases\PacPhoto.html	Tutorial.07\Cases\National Parks Tours	Tutorial.07\Cases\Tours Logo.bmp Tutorial.07\Cases\National Parks Tours Web Page

File Finder

Location in Tutorial	Name and Location of Data File	Student Saves File As...	Student Creates New File
Case Problem 3	Tutorial.07\Cases\MapleRep Tutorial.07\Cases\Maple.xls Tutorial.07\Cases\SalesReg	Tutorial.07\Cases\Maple Sales Org Tutorial.07\Cases\Sales Regions Map	
Case Problem 4			Tutorial.07\Cases\School Expenses Web Page Tutorial.07\Cases\Additional Information Web Page
WORD LEVEL III			
Tutorial 8			
Session 8.1	Tutorial.08\Tutorial\ProdMemo.doc Tutorial.08\Tutorial\CrkLogo	Tutorial.08\Tutorial\Creekside Product Memo.dot	
Session 8.2	(Continued from Session 8.1)		
Session 8.3	(Continued from Session 8.2)	C:\...\Templates\Creekside Product Memo.dot	Tutorial.08\Tutorial\Product Proposal Memo.doc
Review Assignment	Tutorial.08\Review\CrLetter.doc Tutorial.08\Review\CrkLogo	Tutorial.08\Review\Creekside Letter.dot	Tutorial.08\Review\Creekside Customer Letter.doc
Case Problem 1	Tutorial.08\Cases\MuStore.doc	Tutorial.08\Cases\Vermillion Cliffs Brochure.dot	Tutorial.08\Cases\Hammer Dulcimer Brochure.doc
Case Problem 2	Tutorial.08\Cases\FalcMemo.doc Tutorial.08\Cases\Falcon	Tutorial.08\Cases\Falcon Memo.dot	Tutorial.08\Cases\Falcon-Russell Memo.doc
Case Problem 3	Tutorial.08\Cases\QualTmps Tutorial.08\Cases\QTLogo	Tutorial.08\Cases\QualiTemps Job Form.dot	Tutorial.08\Cases\QualiTemps 01-1315.doc
Case Problem 4		Tutorial.08\Cases\Permian Basin Newsletter.dot	Tutorial.08\Cases\Permian Basin Sample Newsletter.doc
Tutorial 9			
Session 9.1	Tutorial.09\Tutorial\OrdrForm.doc	Tutorial.09\Tutorial\Sun Valley Order Form.dot	
Session 9.2	(Continued from Session 9.1)		
Session 9.3	(Continued from Session 9.2)	Tutorial.09\Tutorial\Adamson Order.doc Tutorial.09\Tutorial\Adamson Order.txt	Tutorial.09\Tutorial\Adamson Fax.doc
Review Assignment	Tutorial.09\Review\SVAdm.doc	Tutorial.09\Review\Sun Valley Admissions Form.dot	
Case Problem 1	Tutorial.09\Cases\Cleaning.doc	Tutorial.09\Cases\Sparkling Form.dot Tutorial.09\Cases\Sparkling Data.doc	
Case Problem 2	Tutorial.09\Cases\Alaskan.doc	Tutorial.09\Cases\Alaskan PhotoMart Invoice.dot Tutorial.09\Cases\PhotoMart Sample Data.doc	
Case Problem 3	Tutorial.09\Cases\Apparel.doc	Tutorial.09\Cases\Apparel Mark-Down Form.dot Tutorial.09\Cases\Apparel Sample.doc	
Case Problem 4			Tutorial.09\Cases\Family Video Letter.dot Tutorial.09\Cases\Family Video Sample.doc

File Finder

Location in Tutorial	Name and Location of Data File	Student Saves File As...	Student Creates New File
Tutorial 10			
Session 10.1	Tutorial.10\Tutorial\WebMan.doc Tutorial.10\Tutorial\Team1.doc Tutorial.10\Tutorial\Team 2.doc	Tutorial.10\Tutorial\Market Web Manual.doc Tutorial.10\Tutorial\The Internet.doc Tutorial.10\Tutorial\Market Web Technology.doc	Tutorial.10\Tutorial\The World Wide Web.doc Tutorial.10\Tutorial\Preface.doc
Session 10.2	(Continued from Session 10.1)		
Session 10.3	(Continued from Session 10.2)		
Review Assignment	Tutorial.10\Review\Onlinebus.doc	Tutorial.10\Review\Online Home Business.doc	
Case Problem 1	Tutorial.10\Cases\AuthGuid.doc	Tutorial.10\Cases\Author's Guide.doc	
Case Problem 2	Tutorial.10\Cases\TeenTalk.doc	Tutorial.10\Cases\Teen Talk Workbook.doc	
Case Problem 3	Tutorial.10\Cases\ComClub.doc	Tutorial.10\Cases\Comedy Club Manual.doc	
Case Problem 4			Tutorial.10\Cases\Edits and Comments made by (name).doc